7. Include a *SASE* that is large enough and contains sufficient postage to return all items.

8. Address your package to the proper contact person.

9. Mail first class. Do not send your package via certified or registered mail unless requested.

10. Keep a record of the date, the song titles, and the companies to which you submit material.

For more information on submitting demos by mail, see Getting Started on page 5.

1995
Songwriter's Market

*Where & How to Market
Your Songs*

*Edited by
Cindy Laufenberg*

WRITER'S DIGEST BOOKS
Cincinnati, Ohio

Distributed in Canada by McGraw-Hill,
300 Water Street,
Whitby Ontario L1N 9B6.
Also distributed in Australia by Kirby Books,
Private Bag No. 19, P.O. Alexandria NSW
2015.

Managing Editor, Market Books Department:
Constance J. Achabal; Supervising
Editor: Mark Garvey; Production Editor:
Jamie Harding

International Standard Serial Number
0161-5971
International Standard Book Number
0-89879-676-8

Cover photo: Guildhaus Photographic

Contents

Resources

From the Editor

As a songwriter you're embarking on a noble journey, one that takes incredible perseverance and a strong belief in yourself and your songwriting ability. The road to success in the music industry is filled with many scenic views as well as, unfortunately, a few potholes. *Songwriter's Market* is here to help make your journey a little smoother by offering you up-to-date information about the inner workings of the music industry and providing you with contacts along the way.

In this new edition, we've updated Getting Started, which provides you with the nuts and bolts of the music business: how the industry is structured, how to prepare demos for submission and how to begin making valuable contacts within the industry. The Business of Songwriting now delves deeper, discussing how to protect your songs, what to look for when signing a contract and how to avoid being taken advantage of.

One of the questions most frequently asked by *Songwriter's Market* readers is, what exactly does a music publisher do? Many people still think of publishers as printers of sheet music and don't realize the vital role they play within the music industry. So, in this edition, we gathered five publishing professionals from across the country for a Publisher's Roundtable to dispel the misconceptions. They talk about the role publishers play in a songwriter's career as well as what they personally look for in the writers they sign. After reading their views, you'll find that the music publisher isn't such a mysterious creature, and can be a valuable asset to you in your musical career.

It's hard to keep up with the rapid advances in music business technology—CDs, MiniDiscs, Digital Compact Cassettes, digital transmission. Our Music Industry Trend Report provides a brief overview on trends and happenings in the music industry and how they will affect you as a songwriter.

Now on to the most important part of *Songwriter's Market* — the listings. In a business where contacts are everything, *Songwriter's Market* provides you with the names of over 2,000 markets that are actively seeking material from new writers. We've added 750 new listings that were not in last year's edition; that's 750 more possible places for you to submit your songs! Whether you're a pop songwriter or classical composer, this edition of *Songwriter's Market* contains a wealth of music publishers, record companies and producers, managers and fine arts organizations waiting to hear from you.

Be sure to refer to our Resources section as well, which lists songwriting organizations, workshops, contests and publications of interest. Songwriting organizations are some of the most valuable resources available to songwriters, offering advice and support from fellow writers as well as opportunities for meeting industry professionals. Check into local or national organizations for some valuable assistance.

While using *Songwriter's Market*, keep in mind one thing—this publication is for you. We're here to help you learn about the music industry and make contact with those in a position to help advance your career. Feedback from our readers is important, and will help make *Songwriter's Market* the most comprehensive and useful book available for songwriters. Let us know what you like about the book, what you don't, and what topics you'd like to see us cover in the future. I wish you luck on your journey through the exciting world of songwriting and look forward to hearing from you!

Cindy Laufenberg

How to Get the Most Out of Songwriter's Market

The hardest task for you, the aspiring songwriter, is deciding where and to whom to submit your music. You're reading this book in the hope of finding information on good potential markets for your work. You may be seeking a publisher who will pitch your music, a record company that will offer you a recording contract, or a chamber music group or theater company to produce and perform your music live. *Songwriter's Market* is designed to help you make those submission decisions. Read the articles, Insider Report interviews and section introductions for an overview of the industry. With careful research you can target your submissions and move toward achieving your goals.

Where do you start?

It's easiest to move from the very general to the very specific. The book is divided into Markets and Resources. The Resources section contains listings and information on organizations, workshops, contests and publications to help you learn more about the music industry and the craft of songwriting. The Markets section contains all the markets seeking new material and is the part of the book you will need to concentrate on for submissions.

Markets is further divided into sections corresponding to specific segments of the industry. This is of particular help to composers of music for the theater and concert hall, who can find prospective markets in the Play Producers & Publishers and Fine Arts sections, respectively. Composers of audiovisual (film and TV) and commercial music will also find a section of the book, Advertising, AV and Commercial Music Firms, devoted to these possibilities.

The general markets

If you don't fall into these specific areas, you will need to do a little more work to target markets. Questions you need to ask are: Who am I writing this music for? Are these songs that I have written for an act I now belong to? Am I a songwriter hoping to have my music accepted and recorded by an artist?

If you fall into the first category, writing songs for an existing group or for yourself as a solo artist, you're probably trying to advance the career of your act. If you're seeking a recording contract, the Record Companies section may be the place to start. Look also at the Record Producers section. Independent record producers are constantly on the lookout for up-and-coming artists. They may also have strong connections with record companies looking for acts, and will pass your demo on or recommend the act to a record company. And if your act doesn't yet have representation, your demo submission may be included as part of a promotional kit sent to a prospective manager listed in the Managers and Booking Agents section.

If you are a songwriter seeking to have your songs recorded by other artists, you may submit to some of these same markets, but for different reasons. The Record Producers section contains mostly independent producers who work regularly with particular artists, rather than working fulltime for one record company. Because they work closely with a limited number of clients, they may be the place to send songs written with a specific act in mind. The independent producer may be responsible for picking cuts for a recording project. The Managers and Booking Agents section may be useful for the same reason. Many personal managers are constantly seeking new song material for the acts they represent, and a good song sent at the right time can mean a valuable cut for the songwriter.

The primary market for songwriters not writing with particular artists in mind will be found in the Music Publishers section. Music publishers are the jacks-of-all-trade in the industry, having knowledge about and keeping abreast of developments in all other segments of the music business. They act as the first line of contact between the songwriter and the music industry.

If you're uncertain about which markets will have the most interest in your material, review the introductory explanations at the beginning of each section. It will aid in explaining the various functions of each segment of the music industry, and will help you narrow your list of possible submissions.

Now what?

You've identified the market categories you're thinking about sending demos to. The next step is to research each section to find the individual markets that will be most interested in your work.

Most users of *Songwriter's Market* should check three items in the listings: location of the company, the type of music they're interested in hearing, and their submission policy. Each of these items should be considered carefully when deciding which markets to submit to.

If it's important to send your work to a company close to your home for more opportunities for face-to-face contact, location should be checked first. Each section contains listings from all over the U.S. as well as the rest of the world. You may be interested in submitting to firms in the music hub cities (Nashville, Los Angeles and New York). If you're looking in the Music Publisher or Record Company sections, go first to the back of those sections for geographical listings of music publishers and record companies in or near the music hubs.

Your music isn't going to be appropriate for submission to all companies. Most music industry firms have specific music interests and needs, and you need to do your homework in this area to be sure that your submissions are being seen and heard by companies who have a genuine interest in them. To find this information turn to the Category Indexes located at the end of the Music Publishers, Record Companies, Record Producers and Managers and Booking Agents sections. Locate the category of music that best describes the material you write, and refer to the companies listed under those categories. (Keep in mind that these are general categories. Some companies may not be listed in the Category Index because they either accept all types of music or the music they are looking for doesn't fit into any of the general categories.) When you've located a listing, go to the Music subheading. It will contain, in **bold** type, a more detailed list of the styles of music a company is seeking. Pay close attention to the types of music described. For instance, if the music you write fits the category of "Rock," there can be many variations on that style. One listing under the "Rock" category may be interested in hard rock, another in country rock, and another in soft rock. These are three very different styles of music, but they all fall under the same general category. The Category Index is there to help you narrow down the listings within a certain music genre; it is up to you to narrow them down even further to fit the type of music you write. The music styles in each listing are in descending order of importance; so if your particular specialty is country music, you may want to search out those listings that list country as their first priority as your primary targets for submissions.

Finally, when you've placed the listings geographically and identified their music preferences, read the How to Contact subheading. This will give you pertinent information about what to send as part of a demo submission and how to go about sending it. Not all of the markets listed in *Songwriter's Market* accept unsolicited submissions, so it's important to read this information carefully. Most companies have carefully considered their submission policy, and packages that do not follow their directions are returned or discarded without evaluation. Follow the instructions: it will impress upon the market your seriousness about getting your work heard.

You've now identified markets you feel will have the most interest in your work. Read the complete listing carefully before proceeding. Many of the listings have individualized information important for the submitting songwriter. Then, it's time for you to begin preparing your demo submission package to get your work before the people in the industry. For further information on that process, turn to Getting Started.

Key to Symbols and Abbreviations

* *new listing in all sections*
SASE — *self-addressed stamped envelope*
SAE — *self-addressed envelope*
IRC — *International Reply Coupon, for use in countries other than your own*

(For definitions of terms and abbreviations relating specifically to the music industry, see the Glossary in the back of the book.)

Getting Started

To exist and thrive in the competitive music industry without being overwhelmed is perhaps the biggest challenge facing a songwriter in his musical career. Songwriters who not only survive but also succeed are those who have taken the time before entering the market to learn as much as they can about the inner workings of the music industry.

Newcomers to the music business can educate themselves about the industry through experience or education. Experience, while valuable, can be time-consuming and costly. Education can be just as effective, and less painful. Many sources exist to help you educate yourself about the intricacies of the industry *before* you jump in. Reading, studying and learning to use the information contained in source books such as *Songwriter's Market* expand your knowledge of the music industry and how it works, and help you market yourself and your work professionally and effectively.

Improving your craft

Unfortunately, no magic formula can guarantee success in the music business. If you want to make it in this competitive business, you have to begin by believing in yourself and your talent. As a songwriter, you must develop your own personal vision and stick with it. Why do you write songs? Is it because you want to make a lot of money, or because you love the process? Is every song you write an attempt to become famous, or a labor of love? Successful songwriters believe they have a talent that deserves to be heard, whether by two or two thousand people. Songwriting is a craft, like woodworking or painting. A lot of talent is involved, of course, but with time and practice the craft can be improved and eventually mastered.

While working on songs, learn all you can about the writing process. Realize that you're not alone, and look for support and feedback wherever you can. A great place to start is a local songwriting organization, which can offer friendly advice, support from other writers, and a place to meet collaborators. (For more information on songwriting organizations in your area, see the Organizations section on page 475.) Many organizations offer song critique sessions, which will help you identify strengths and weaknesses in your material and give you guidance to help improve your craft. Take any criticism you receive in a constructive manner, and use it to improve your writing style. The feedback you receive will help you write better songs, create connections within the industry and continue your education not only in the craft of songwriting but in the business as well.

The structure of the music business

The music business in the United States revolves around three major hubs: New York, Nashville and Los Angeles. Power is concentrated in those areas because that's where most record companies, publishers, songwriters and performers are. A lot of people trying to break into the music business, in whatever capacity, move to one of those three cities to be close to the people and companies they want to contact. From time to time a regional music scene will heat up in a non-hub city such as Austin, Chicago or Seattle. When this happens, songwriters and performers in that city experience a kind of musical Renaissance complete with better-paying gigs, a creatively charged atmosphere and intensified interest from major labels.

All this is not to say that a successful career cannot be nurtured from any city in the country, however. It can be, especially if you are a songwriter. By moving to a major music hub, you may be closer physically to the major companies, but you'll also encounter more competition than you would back home. Stay where you're comfortable; it's probably easier (and more cost-effective) to conquer the music scene where you are than it is in Los Angeles or New York. There are many smaller, independent companies located in cities across the country. Most international careers are started on a local level, and some may find a local career more satisfying, in its own way, than the constant striving to gain the attention of the major companies.

The perspective of any company, whether major or independent, begins with the buying public. Their support, in the form of money spent on records, concert tickets and other kinds of musical entertainment, keeps the music industry in business. Because of that, record companies, publishers and producers are eager to give the public what they want. In an attempt to stay one step ahead of public tastes, record companies hire people who have a knack for spotting musical talent and anticipating trends, and put them in charge of finding and developing new talent. These talent scouts are called A&R representatives. "A&R" stands for "artist and repertoire," which simply means they are responsible for discovering new talent and matching songs to particular artists. The person responsible for the recording artist's product—the record—is called the producer. It is the producer's job to develop the artist's work and come out of the studio with a good-sounding, saleable product that represents the artist in the best possible manner. His duties sometimes include choosing songs for a particular project, so record producers are also great contacts for songwriters.

Producers and A&R reps are aided in their search for talent by the music publisher. A publisher works as a songwriter's advocate who, for a percentage of the profits (typically 50% of all earnings from a particular song), attempts to find commercially profitable uses for the songs he represents. A successful publisher stays in contact with several A&R reps, trying to find out what upcoming projects are looking for new material, and whether any songs he represents will be appropriate.

When a song is recorded and subsequently released to the public, the recording artist, songwriter, record company, producer and publisher all stand to profit. Recording artists earn a negotiated royalty from their record company based on the number of records sold. Producers are usually paid either a negotiated royalty based on sales or a flat fee at the time of recording. Publishers and songwriters earn mechanical royalties (money a record company pays a publisher based on record sales) and performance royalties, which are based on radio air play.

As you can see, the people you need to make contact with are publishers, A&R reps and producers. Managers can also be added to that list—most are looking for material for the acts they represent. Getting your material to these professionals and establishing relationships with as many people in the industry as you can should be your main goal as a songwriter. The more people who hear your songs, the better your chances of getting them recorded.

Any method of getting your songs heard, published, recorded and released is the best way if it works for you. *Songwriter's Market* lists music publishers, record companies, producers and managers (as well as advertising firms, play producers and fine arts organizations) along with specifications on how to submit your material to each. If you can't find a certain person or company you're interested in, there are other sources of information you can try. The *Recording Industry Sourcebook*, an annual directory published by the Ascona Group, Inc., lists record companies, music publishers, producers and managers, as well as attorneys, publicity firms, media, manufacturers, distributors and recording studios around the United States. Trade publications such as *Billboard* or *Cash Box*, available at most local libraries and bookstores, are great sources for up-to-date information. These periodicals list new companies as well as the artists, labels, producers and publishers for each song on the charts. Album covers, CD booklets and cassette j-cards can be valuable sources of information, providing the name of the record company, publisher, producer and usually the manager of the artist or group. Use your imagination in your research and be creative—any contacts you make in the industry can only help your career as a songwriter.

Submitting your songs

When it comes to presenting your material, the tool of the music industry is a demonstration recording—a demo. Cassette tapes have been the standard in the music industry for decades because they're so convenient. Songwriters use demos to present their songs, and musicians use them to showcase their performance skills. Demos are submitted to various professionals in the industry, either by mail or in person.

Demo quality

The production quality of demos can vary widely, but even simple guitar/vocal or piano/vocal demos must sound clean, with the instrument in tune and lyrics sung clearly. Many songwriters are investing in home recording equipment such as four- or eight-track recorders, keyboards and drum machines, so they can record their demos themselves. Other writers prefer to book studio time, use hired musicians, and get professional input from an engineer or producer. Demo services are also available to record your demo for a fee. It's up to you to decide what you can afford and feel most comfortable with, and what you think best represents your song. Once a master recording is made of your song, you're ready to make cassette copies and start pitching your song to the contacts you've researched.

Some markets indicate that you may send a videocassette of your act in performance or a group performing your songs, instead of the standard cassette demo. Most of the companies listed in *Songwriter's Market* have indicated that a videocassette is not required, but have indicated the format of their VCR should you decide to send one. Be aware that television systems vary widely from country to country, so if you're sending a video to a foreign listing check with them for the system they're using. For example, a VHS format tape recorded using the U.S. system (called NTSC) will not play back on a standard British VCR (using the PAL system), even if the recording formats are the same. It is possible to transfer a video from one system to another, but the expense in both time and money may outweigh its usefulness. Systems for some countries include: NTSC—U.S., Canada and Japan; PAL—United Kingdom, Australia and Germany; and SECAM—France.

Submitting by mail

When submitting material to companies listed in this book:
● Read the listing carefully and submit exactly what a company asks for and exactly how it asks that it be submitted.
● Listen to each of your demos before sending to make sure the quality is satisfactory.
● Enclose a brief, typed cover letter to introduce yourself. Indicate what songs you are sending and why you are sending them. If you're a songwriter pitching songs to a particular artist, state that in the letter. If you're an artist/songwriter looking for a recording deal, you should say so. Have specific goals.
● Include typed lyric sheets or lead sheets if requested. Make sure your name, address and phone number appear on each sheet.

- Neatly label each tape with your name, address and phone number along with the names of the songs in the sequence in which they appear on the tape.
- If the company returns material (many do not; be sure to read each listing carefully), include a SASE for the return. Your return envelope to countries other than your own should contain a self-addressed envelope (SAE) and International Reply Coupon (IRC). Be sure the return envelope is large enough to accommodate your material, and include sufficient postage for the weight of the package.
- Wrap the package neatly and write (or type on a shipping label) the company's address and your return address so they are clearly visible. Your package is the first impression a company has of you and your songs, so neatness is very important.
- Mail first class. Stamp or write "First Class Mail" on the package and on the SASE you enclose. Don't send by registered or certified mail unless the company specifically requests it.
- Keep records of the dates, songs, and companies you submit to.

If you are writing to inquire about a company's needs or to request permission to submit (many companies ask you to do this first), your query letter should be typed, brief and pleasant. Explain the type of material you have and ask for their needs and submission policy.

To expedite a reply, you should enclose a self-addressed, stamped postcard requesting the information you are seeking. Your typed questions (see the Sample Reply Form) should be direct and easy to answer. Place the company's name and address in the upper left hand space on the front of the postcard so you'll know which company you queried. Keep a record of the queries you send for future reference.

Sample Reply Form

I would like to hear:
( ) *"Name of Song"* ( ) *"Name of Song"* ( ) *"Name of Song"*
I prefer:
( ) *cassette* ( ) *DAT* ( ) *videocassette*
( ) *Beta* ( ) *VHS*

   With:
( ) *lyric sheet* ( ) *lead sheet* ( ) *either* ( ) *both*
( ) *I am not looking for material at this time, try me later.*
( ) *I am not interested.*

_____

Name   *Title*

It's acceptable to submit your songs to more than one person at a time (this is called simultaneous submission). The one exception to this is when a publisher, artist or other industry professional asks if he may put a song of yours "on hold." This means he intends to record it, and doesn't want you to give the song to anyone else. Your song may be returned to you without ever having been recorded, even if it's been on hold for months. Or, your song may be recorded but the artist or producer decides to leave it off the album. If either of these things happens, you're free to pitch your song to other people again. (You can protect yourself from having a song on hold indefinitely. Establish a deadline for the person who asks for the hold, i.e., "You can put my song on hold for X number of months." Or modify the hold to specify that you will pitch the song to other people, but you will not sign a deal without allowing the person who has the song on hold to make you an offer.) When someone publishes your song and you sign a contract, you grant that publisher exclusive rights to your song and you may not pitch it to other publishers. You can, however, pitch it to any artists or producers interested in recording the song without publishing it themselves.

If a market doesn't respond within several weeks after you've sent your demo, don't despair. As long as your demo is in the possession of a market, there is a chance that someone is reviewing it. That opportunity ends when your demo is returned to you. If after a reasonable amount of time you still haven't received word on your submission (check the reporting time each company states in their listing), following up with a friendly letter giving detailed information about your submission is a good idea. Keep in mind that many companies do not return submissions, so don't expect a company that states "Does not return submissions" to send your materials back to you.

Submitting in person

Planning a trip to one of the major music hubs will give you insight into how the music industry functions. Whether you decide to visit New York, Nashville or Los Angeles, you should have some specific goals in mind and set up appointments to make the most of your time there. It will be difficult to get in to see some industry professionals, as many of them are extremely busy and may not feel meeting out-of-town writers is a high priority. Other people are more open to, and even encourage, face-to-face meetings. They may feel that if you take the time to travel to where they are, and you're organized enough to schedule meetings beforehand, you're more professional than many aspiring songwriters who blindly submit inappropriate songs through the mail. (For listings of companies located in the music hubs, see the Geographic Index at the end of the Music Publishers and Record Companies sections.)

You should take several cassette copies and lyric sheets of each of your songs. More than one of the companies you visit may ask that you leave a copy to review and perhaps play for other professionals in the company. There's also a good chance that the person you have an appointment with will have to cancel (expect that occasionally) but wants you to leave a copy of the songs so he can listen and contact you later. Never give someone the last or only copy of your material—if it is not returned to you, all the hard work and money that went into making that demo will be lost.

Another good place to meet industry professionals face-to-face is at seminars such as the yearly South by Southwest Music and Media Conference in Austin, New Music Seminar in New York City, or the Nashville Songwriters Association's Spring Symposium, to name a few (see the Workshops section of this book for further ideas). Many of these conferences feature demo listening sessions, where industry professionals sit down and listen to demos submitted by songwriters attending the seminars.

Many good songs have been rejected simply because they just weren't what the particular publisher or record company was looking for at the time, so don't take rejection personally. Realize that if a few people don't like your songs, it doesn't mean they're not good. However, if there seems to be a consensus about your work—for instance, the feel of a song isn't right or the lyrics need work—give the advice serious thought. Listen attentively to what the reviewers say and use their criticism constructively to improve your songs and become a better and more professional songwriter.

The Business of Songwriting

The more you know about how the music industry functions, the less likely you'll be to make a mistake dealing with contracts and agreements. Signing a contract without knowing exactly what you're agreeing to can ruin a career you've worked years to build. Becoming familiar with standard industry practices will help you learn what to look for and what to avoid.

Copyright

When you create a song and put it down in fixed form, it becomes a property you own and is automatically protected by copyright. This protection lasts for your lifetime (or the lifetime of the last surviving author, if you co-wrote the song) plus 50 years. When you prepare demos, place notification of copyright on all copies of your song—the lyric sheets, lead sheets and cassette labels. The notice is simply the word "copyright" or the symbol © followed by the year the song was created (or published) and your name: © 1995 by John L. Public.

For the best protection, register your copyright with the Library of Congress. Although a song is copyrighted whether or not it is registered, registering a song establishes a public record of your copyright and could prove useful in any future litigation involving the song. Registration also entitles you to a potentially greater settlement in a copyright infringement suit. To register your song, request government form PA from the Copyright Office. Call the 24-hour hotline at (202)707-9100 and leave your name and address on the recorder. Once you receive a form, you can photocopy it if you want to register more than one song. It is possible to register groups of songs for one fee, but you cannot add future songs to that particular collection.

Once you receive the PA form, you will be required to return it, along with a registration fee and a tape or lead sheet of your song, to the Register of Copyrights, Copyright Office, Library of Congress, Washington DC 20559. It may take as long as four months to receive your certificate of registration from the Copyright Office, but your songs are protected from the date of creation, and the date of registration will reflect the date you applied for registration. If you need additional information about registering your songs, call the Copyright Office's Public Information Office at (202)707-3000.

Don't be afraid to play your songs for people or worry about creating a song that might be similar to someone else's. It's more constructive to spend your time creating original songs, registering the copyrights and making contacts to get your music heard. True copyright infringement is rarer than most people think. First of all, a title cannot be copyrighted, nor can an idea or a chord progression. Only specific, fixed melodies and lyrics can be copyrighted. Second, a successful infringement suit would have to prove that another songwriter had access to the completed song and that he deliberately copied it, which is difficult to do and not really worthwhile unless the song is a huge hit. Song theft sometimes does happen, but not often enough for you to become paranoid. If you ever feel that one of your songs has been stolen—that someone has unlawfully infringed on your copyright—you must prove that you created the work. Copyright registration is the best proof of a date of creation. You *must* have your copyright registered in order to file a copyright infringement lawsuit. One way writers prove a work is original is to keep their rough drafts and revisions of songs, either on paper or on tape, if they record different versions of the song as they go along.

Contracts

You will encounter several types of contracts as you deal with the business end of songwriting. You may sign a legal agreement between you and a co-writer establishing percentages of the writer's royalties each of you will receive, what you will do if a third party (e.g., a recording artist) wishes to change your song and receive credit as a co-writer, and other things. As long as the issues at stake are simple, and co-writers respect each other and discuss their business philosophy in advance of writing a song, they can write up an agreement without the aid of a lawyer. In other situations—when a publisher, producer or record company wants to do business with you—you should always have any contract reviewed by a knowledgeable entertainment attorney.

Single song contracts

Probably the most common type of contract you will encounter at first will be the single song contract. A music publisher offers this type of contract when he wants to sign one or more of your songs, but he doesn't want to hire you as a staff writer. You assign your rights to a particular song to the publisher for an agreed-upon number of years (usually the life of the copyright).

Every single song contract should contain this basic information: the publisher's name, the writer's name, the song's title, the date and the purpose of the agreement. The songwriter also declares that the song is an original work and he is the creator of the work. The contract must specify the royalties the songwriter will earn from various uses of the song. These include performance, mechanical, print and synchronization royalties, as well as an agreement as to what will be paid for any uses of the song not specifically set forth in the contract.

The songwriter should receive no less than 50% of the income his song generates. That means that whatever the song earns in royalties, the publisher and songwriter should split 50/50. The songwriter's half is called the "writer's share" and the publisher's half is called the "publisher's share." If there is more than one songwriter, the songwriters split the writer's share. Sometimes songwriters will negotiate for a percentage of the publisher's share; that is, a co-publishing agreement. This is unlikely for beginning songwriters, and usually happens only if the songwriter already has a successful track record.

Other issues a contract should address include whether or not an advance will be paid to the songwriter and how much it will be; when royalties will be paid (quarterly or semiannually); who will pay for demos—the publisher, songwriter or both; how lawsuits against copyright infringement will be handled, including the cost of such lawsuits; whether the publisher has the right to sell the song to another publisher without the songwriter's consent; and whether the publisher has the right to make changes in a song, or approve of changes written by someone else, without the songwriter's consent. In addition, the songwriter should have the right to audit the publisher's books if the songwriter deems it necessary and gives the publisher reasonable notice.

Songwriters should also negotiate for a reversion clause. This calls for the rights to the song to revert to the songwriter if some provision of the contract is not met. The most common type of reversion clause covers the failure to secure a commercial release of a song within a specified period of time (usually one or two years). If nothing happens with the song, the rights will revert back to the songwriter, who can then give the song to a more active publisher if he so chooses. Some publishers will agree to this, figuring that if they don't get some action on the song in the first year, they're not likely to ever get any action on it. Other publishers are reluctant to agree to this clause. They may invest a lot of time and money in a song, re-demoing it and pitching it to a number of artists; they may be actively looking for ways to exploit the song. If a producer puts a song on hold for a while and goes into a lengthy recording project, by the time the record company (or artist or producer) decides which songs to release as singles, a year can easily go by. That's why it's so important to have a good working relationship with your publisher. You need to trust that he has your best interests in mind. If a song really is on hold you can give him more time and/or know that if your song is recorded but ultimately not released by the artist, it's not your publisher's fault and he'll work just as hard to get another artist to record the song. (For more information on music publishers, see the Publisher's Roundtable on page 15 and the Music Publishers section introduction on page 27.)

While there is no such thing as a "standard" contract, The Songwriters Guild of America (SGA) has drawn up a Popular Songwriter's Contract which it believes to be the best minimum songwriter contract available. The Guild will send a copy of the contract at no charge to any interested songwriter upon request (include a self-addressed stamped envelope). SGA will also review free of charge any contract offered to its members, checking it for fairness and completeness.

The following list, taken from a Songwriters Guild of America publication entitled "10 Basic Points Your Contract Should Include" points out the basic features of an acceptable songwriting contract:

1. Work for Hire. When you receive a contract covering just one composition, you should make sure the phrases "employment for hire" and "exclusive writer agreement" are not included. Also, there should be no options for future songs.

2. Performing Rights Affiliation. If you previously signed publishing contracts, you should be affiliated with either ASCAP, BMI or SESAC. All performance royalties must be received directly by you from your performing rights organization and this should be written into your contract.

3. Reversion Clause. The contract should include a provision that if the publisher does not secure a release of a commercial sound recording within a specified time (one year, two years, etc.), the contract can be terminated by you.

4. Changes in the Composition. If the contract includes a provision that the publisher can change the title, lyrics or music, this should be amended so that only with your previous consent can such changes be made.

5. Royalty Provisions. Basically, you should receive fifty percent (50%) of all publisher's income on all licenses issued. If the publisher prints and sells his own sheet music and folios, your royalty should be ten percent (10%) of the wholesale selling price. The royalty should not be stated in the contract as a flat rate ($.05, $.07, etc.).

6. Negotiable Deductions. Ideally, demos and all other expenses of publication should be paid 100% by the publisher. The only allowable fee is for the Harry Fox Agency collection fee, whereby the writer pays one half of the amount charged to the publisher. Today's rate charged by the Harry Fox Agency is 3.5%.

7. Royalty Statements and Audit Provision. Once the song is recorded and printed, you are entitled to receive royalty statements at least once every six months. In addition, an audit provision with no time restriction should be included in every contract.

8. Writer's Credit. The publisher should make sure that you receive proper credit on all uses of the composition.

9. Arbitration. In order to avoid large legal fees in case of a dispute with your publisher, the contract should include an arbitration clause.

10. Future Uses. Any use not specifically covered by the contract should be retained by the writer to be negotiated as it comes up.

For a thorough discussion of the somewhat complicated subject of contracts, see these two books published by Writer's Digest Books: *The Craft and Business of Songwriting*, by John Braheny and *Music Publishing: A Songwriter's Guide*, by Randy Poe.

The ripoffs

As in any business, the music industry has its share of dishonest, greedy people who try to unfairly exploit the talents and aspirations of others. Most of them use similar methods of attack which you can learn to identify and avoid. "Song sharks," as they're called, prey on beginners—those writers who are unfamiliar with ethical industry standards. Song sharks will take any songs—quality doesn't count. They're not concerned with future royalties, since they get their money upfront from songwriters who think they're getting a great deal.

Here are some guidelines to help you recognize these "song sharks":

• Never pay to have your music "reviewed" by a company that may be interested in publishing, producing or recording it. Reviewing material—free of charge—is the practice of reputable companies looking for hits for their artists or recording projects.

• Never pay to have your songs published. A reputable company interested in your songs assumes the responsibility and cost of promoting them. That company invests in your material because it expects a profit once the songs are recorded and released.

• Never pay a fee to have a publisher make a demo of your songs. Some publishers may take demo expenses out of your future royalties, but you should never pay upfront for demo costs for a song that is signed to a publisher.

• Never pay to have your lyrics or poems set to music. "Music mills"—for a price— may use the same melody for hundreds of lyrics and poems, whether it sounds good or not. Publishers recognize one of these melodies as soon as they hear it.

• Avoid CD compilation deals where a record company asks you to pay a fee to be included on a promotional CD. They ask you to supply a master recording of your act (along with a check for an amount of $500 or more), and they include your song on a CD to be sent to radio stations, producers, etc. First of all, the company is making a lot of money on this. The cost of mastering, pressing and mailing the CD is going to be a lot less than the amount of money they take in from the artists they solicit. Second, radio stations and other industry professionals just don't listen to these things to find new artists. Besides, would you want your material to be buried on a CD with 20 other acts? It would be better to spend the money making a quality demo on your own. It's one thing if a record company puts out a compilation of the artists they've signed as a promotional item—it's another when they ask you to pay to be included.

• Read all contracts carefully before signing and don't sign any contract you're unsure about or that you don't fully understand. Don't assume any contract is better than no contract at all. It is well worth paying an attorney for the time it takes him to review a contract if you can avoid a bad situation that may cost you thousands of dollars in royalties if your song becomes a hit.

• Don't pay a company to pair you with a collaborator. A better way is to contact songwriting organizations that offer collaboration services to their members.

• Don't sell your songs outright. It's unethical for anyone to offer such a proposition.

• If you are asked by a record company or some other type of company to pay expenses upfront, beware. Many expenses incurred by the record company on your behalf may be recoupable from royalties you may earn, but you should not be paying cash out of your pocket to a company that either employs you as an artist or owns your master recording. If someone offers you a "deal" that asks for cash upfront, it's a good idea to ask to speak with other artists who have signed similar contracts with them before signing one yourself. Weigh the expenses and what you have to gain by financing the project yourself, then make your decision. Read the stipulations of your contract carefully and go over them with a music business attorney. Research the company and its track record, and beware of any company that won't answer your questions or let you know what it has done in the past. If it has had successes and good working relationships with other writers and artists, it should be happy to brag about them.

● Before participating in a songwriting contest, read the rules carefully. Be sure that what you're giving up in the way of entry fees, etc., is not greater than what you stand to gain by winning the contest. See the Contests and Awards section introduction on page 497 for more advice on this.

● There is a version of the age-old chain letter scheme with a special twist just for songwriters. The letter names five songwriters whose tapes you are supposed to buy. You then add your name to the letter and mail it to five more songwriters who, in turn, are supposed to purchase your tape. Besides the fact that such chain letters or "pyramid" schemes generally fail, the five "amateur" songwriters named in the letter are known song sharks. Don't fall for it.

● Verify any situation about an individual or company if you have any doubts at all. Contact the performing rights society with which it is affiliated. Check with the Better Business Bureau in the town where it is located or the state's attorney general's office. Contact professional organizations you're a member of and inquire about the reputation of the company.

Record keeping

As your songwriting career continues to grow, you should keep a ledger or notebook containing all financial transactions relating to your songwriting. It should include a list of income from royalty checks as well as expenses incurred as a result of your songwriting business: cost of tapes, demo sessions, office supplies, postage, traveling expenses, dues to organizations, class and workshop fees and any publications you purchase pertaining to songwriting. It's also advisable to open a checking account exclusively for your songwriting activities, not only to make record keeping easier, but to establish your identity as a business for tax purposes.

Any royalties you receive will not reflect taxes or any other mandatory deductions. It is the songwriter's responsibility to keep track of income and file the appropriate tax forms. Contact the IRS or an accountant who serves music industry clients for specific information.

International markets

Everyone talks about the world getting smaller, and it's true. Modern communication technology has brought us to the point where information can be transmitted around the globe instantly. No business has enjoyed the fruits of this progress more than the music industry. American music is heard in virtually every country in the world, and having a hit song in other countries as well as in the United States can greatly increase a songwriter's royalty earnings.

Each year there has been a steady increase in the number of international companies listed in *Songwriter's Market*. While these listings may be a bit more challenging to deal with than domestic companies, they offer additional avenues for songwriters looking for places to place their songs.

If you consider signing a contract with an enthusiastic publisher from a country outside the United States, use the same criteria we referred to earlier when making a decision as to the acceptability of the contract.

Publisher's Roundtable: An Inside Look at Music Publishing

Music publishers provide the vital link between songwriters and performers, hoping to find the right combination of writer and artist to create a hit record.

Every new songwriter wants to know what publishers are looking for but unfortunately there is no simple, easy answer. *Songwriter's Market* gathered five publishing professionals from around the country to discuss some of the most common questions songwriters have about music publishing. In this roundtable discussion, they define the role a music publisher plays in the career of a songwriter and how the two work together. They also offer their views on the best ways for a songwriter to get the attention of a publisher, what publishers look for in demo submissions, and what to be aware of when signing a publishing contract. Participating in this discussion were:

Kathy Spanberger, Senior Vice President of Operations, peermusic, Los Angeles. The largest independent music publisher in the world, peermusic has 27 offices in 23 different countries. The extensive peermusic roster includes pop writer Jud Friedman, the Williams Brothers and the Church's Marty Wilson-Piper.

Carla Berkowitz, Director of Creative Affairs, Zomba Music Publishing, Los Angeles. Zomba Music Publishing is an affiliate of Zomba Enterprises, which also owns Jive Records. Some recent Zomba signings include alternative acts the Breeders, Juliana Hatfield, Sonic Youth and Dinosaur Jr.

Joey Gmerek, Vice President/Creative Services, Hit and Run Publishing, New York. Representing artists such as Genesis, Phil Collins and Julian Lennon, Hit and Run Publishing is an international publisher, with offices in London as well as New York City.

Roger Murrah, President, Murrah Music, Nashville. After having a string of hit songs recorded by Mel Tillis, Al Jarreau and the Oak Ridge Boys, songwriter Roger Murrah started his own publishing company in 1990. Currently, Murrah Music has found success with Tanya Tucker's "Two Sparrows in a Hurricane," and Alan Jackson's "Don't Rock the Jukebox."

Brian Rawlings, Creative Manager, Walt Disney Music Co., Burbank. One of the top ten publishers in the world, Walt Disney Music is more than just the publisher of Disney film scores. They now have an exclusive writing staff consisting of pop and R&B writers Will Robinson, Nate Phillips, Fabian Cooke, Ray Kennedy and Steve Diamond.

How would you define a music publisher, and what role does he play in the career of a songwriter?

Kathy Spanberger: Publishers are basically managers for songwriters. Whether you're a songwriter, a songwriter/artist or a songwriter/producer, what a publisher contributes to your career is working with you and putting you together in co-writing situations, getting recordings or usages in film and television.

Roger Murrah: The number one thing publishers do is support the writer financially while he's maturing professionally. As a writer learns his or her craft, a publisher usually advances him money to live on. The publisher's primary obligation and responsibility is to exploit and market the copyright, try to get recordings. Once there are recordings, a publisher collects the monies and distributes them to the writers.

Carla Berkowitz: The only kind of music publisher I know of is the kind of publisher I am. A publisher's job is to look out for the creative career of a songwriter or a producer and do everything they can to get them to the next level in their career.

Brian Rawlings: A music publisher is a person who almost acts like a songwriter's manager at the outset; they advise, counsel and creatively direct. A publisher in the best of circumstances is one who finds great songs, gets them recorded by great artists, and then, most importantly, gets the money out of the music user and distributes it to the right parties. A publisher really becomes a songwriter's best friend when the songwriter has a hit. When the songwriter starts making some money, he needs a great publisher because money falls through the cracks all over the world.

What is the biggest misconception about music publishers? What can/can't a music publisher do?

Carla Berkowitz: The biggest misconception is that writers don't fully understand the extent of what a publisher can do for them. A publisher should be doing a lot. Not only nurturing them and getting them to the point where they're writing really good songs, but hooking them up with other writers and producers, then getting the song cut. After that, taking the song that's recorded and trying to get a film for it. It never stops, and those are the kinds of things that are going to push along a writer's career.

Roger Murrah: Probably the biggest mistake a writer makes is thinking someone else is going to do all the work for them. Almost consistently I find that writers who have been successful over a long period of time are very involved in pitching their own songs and motivating the publisher to pitch the songs and make suggestions. In other words, these songwriters have done a good job of carrying the ball themselves and aren't waiting for someone else to do it. I've seen writers wait on someone else to do all the work and then all of a sudden you're not hearing from them again. If you expect too much out of other people, you'll be disappointed.

Joey Gmerek: Getting to a publisher isn't an answer to someone's career, because the publisher and the artist have to work together to get to the next level, which is either cutting a song or maybe a recording contract. Publishers should assist writers to the best of their ability, take the material and develop it, hone it, sharpen it up, and be aggressive in doing the song plugging for them. A publisher can be a great asset and a great stepping stone for a young writer or a young band.

What is the best way for a songwriter to get his or her songs heard by a music publisher?

Kathy Spanberger: There are some wonderful organizations around that assist songwriters, such as ASCAP, BMI, the National Academy of Songwriters (NAS) and the Los Angeles Songwriters Showcase (LASS). Every songwriter I know who's moved to Los Angeles or began their career here has gone to the forums provided by LASS and networked. Industry people attend these forums to find new writers. Our job is to find new talent, and we're out there working just as hard as the songwriter. You can be the most talented person in the world, and unless someone walks by your window and hears you playing the piano, you won't be discovered. It's important to be out there, performing or networking or meeting different people, taking chances and writing with other talented people.

Carla Berkowitz: I listen to tapes that come in through the mail, and a lot of times I hear of things through other songwriters. If you're a songwriter you should encourage your collaborators, the people you work with, to help you. Everybody needs help. Attorneys are also an option. It's easier to get to an attorney than it is to get to a publisher. I also count on ASCAP and BMI representatives to let me know about talented writers. Performing locally, making a few very professional phone calls and being persistent is important. If a writer is consistently sending me stuff, a song here, a song there, letting me know what's going on with him, I'll listen.

Joey Gmerek: I ask writers when they call to write us a letter. Be enthusiastic in your letter. Write what you've done—a little bit of a track record helps. If you've been in a band that's performed and opened up for other people, if you're being managed by somebody or if you've currently got a record out, mention that in the letter. If I see enthusiasm coming from the writer or the band then I give them permission to send a tape in. If I just get something like, "Would you listen to my songs, I think they'd be great for Phil Collins," I won't consider that because I don't think that writer's done his homework or researched my company, or thought really clearly about what he wants to do. You just don't send in a song for Phil Collins. If you're just starting out and it's your first batch of songs, that could be a little tough because there's not enough time in the day to listen to brand-new, first-time demos from writers. So the thing would be to nurture the craft on your own a bit more, so you can actually build up a little bit of something, and say, "I've been writing for six years, and I've had my music listened to by so and so, and these are my influences and this is what I do." Be determined and be enthusiastic when you approach a publisher, and you'll have more chances if you're doing it on your own to get a response. You can always do the attorney route, which can cost you money if you're a songwriter, but that's not a bad thing to do. A lot of publishers would consider listening to a tape if it's sent in by an attorney, especially if it's an attorney who has a decent reputation.

Brian Rawlings: There are several different ways; it all depends on how you define a beginning songwriter. Some beginning songwriters have great life experiences that make them really savvy in dealing with people. The biggest challenge I see with songwriters breaking in and dealing with publishers is that their people skills aren't very good. A lot of associations and organizations around the country can be helpful. The Northern California Songwriters Association does a great job of getting songwriters in touch with publishers by doing forums. Any of those types of things is good, because it's a meeting people game. Writers need to think of their craft as a business. A lot of songwriters ask, how do I get into this business? Well, how do you get in any business? Getting to know people in a positive way positions you so that when your talent is in place, somebody will be there to take advantage of it. People sometimes think publishers are not interested in meeting new young writers, and it's quite the opposite. We spend a large percentage of our time trying to find great new, young songwriters. Develop relationships wherever you possibly can. It doesn't mean you have to up and move, although you do at some point have to go where there are music publishers in order to meet them. Once you do meet them, respect who they are and what they're doing and establish relationships with them. That doesn't mean elbowing in, bugging people or calling too much, however. That doesn't work in establishing a relationship.

What do you look for in a demo submission package?

Kathy Spanberger: We look for a professional presentation on the surface, such as a neat, typed cover letter, before we actually hear anything. In the end, though, it all comes down to the tape—there's just no way around it. I don't think you have to go and spend a thousand dollars to create a demo. The best investment a songwriter can make today is in home recording equipment. It's well worth the investment, not to mention that if you have any desire to be a producer it's important to start knowing the equipment and working on your own demo.

Roger Murrah: I hate to see a new, up-and-coming songwriter spend a lot of money on demos. A real clean simple demo that's not overly done is always the best because if the song is there, it's going to be heard the simpler it's done. You can spend a lot of money on a bad song; you still just have a bad song that you spent a lot of money on.

Carla Berkowitz: A tape accompanied by a short letter—"Here's a new song, wanted to know what you think of it"—with a lyric sheet, nothing else. I don't want anything else. I don't want two songs and a bio. I just want one song.

Joey Gmerek: I feel that a songwriter who has extraordinary talent will take the time to make sure the music is presented to the best of his ability. That starts with the writer critiquing his material before he just sends it out and being sure that he or she sends out the song when it's done and not sending anything that's half-baked. I'm a big believer that writers should do a very good, clear-sounding demo. I don't even accept a four track anymore. I think the extra effort is really worth it. Going into the studio and putting in a little extra money is going to make you a better songwriter, make you understand your craft. The songwriting is always incredibly important, and I look to be convinced by the band's believability. I like to see a band that has a certain amount of confidence and has a distinct sound. I look for a band that I believe really feels what they're doing. I wait to get a little chill; it's very organic with me. I don't have to be impressed with a band that's got a huge buzz. I'm attracted to a very distinct sound, a very distinct vocalist. Those are things that go into making my decisions.

Brian Rawlings: If you've never had a song published, unless you're in the dance market particularly, you don't need to be doing a full band demo. You need to be in the studio with somebody who can play the piano really well, somebody who can play the guitar really well, and someone who can sing really well. And 99% of the time, unfortunately, that's not you. That would be bad advice for Billy Joel, but it'd be good advice to almost everyone else. Diane Warren doesn't sing any of her own demos, and she's the most successful pop writer in a long time. She gets somebody who can sing to do her demos; you need to find those people. If you ever get the chance to hear demos of songs by big writers, listen closely. You'd be surprised by how simple they are. There are some sophisticated markets that require extra skills. But if you want to be a songwriter, not a record producer who also writes, your songs should shine in a guitar or vocal demo.

Why do you reject songs? What are you hearing that you like/dislike?

Carla Berkowitz: What I consistently reject are dated songs. It seems that a lot of songwriters don't treat this as a business. Part of their job is to stay on top of what's being played. A songwriter, to me, is supposed to represent the times and that's the beauty in what they do. They're going to mark their time, our times, with their lyrics. Unfortunately a lot of writers don't really respect that that's their job. They're still rhyming "I love you, you love me, together we'll live happily." That's the biggest thing that I reject.

Roger Murrah: Everybody's looking for something fresh, but at the same time there are some silent rules that you learn after being in Nashville for a few years that set boundaries to keep us in what we call "country music." So, while you're wanting to be fresh and innovative, you can't go overboard. Creativity is trying to break the rules the right way, learning to be fresh in a subtle way. The country music market is a little more restricted than others, although at this particular point in time it's been swinging towards opening up again. We just went through our most recent phase of traditional and now we're opening up, as an industry where we can do things other than strictly traditional country. Which is good news for most all the writers these days because the real traditional country writers are becoming a dying breed. It's so much easier now for a country artist to break through.

Joey Gmerek: I'm always looking for the writer who goes the extra step when sending in material. What turns me off is when writers just send in material that doesn't show the effort it takes in getting a demo done.

If you like what you hear on a demo, what's the next step for you as a publisher?

Kathy Spanberger: You meet with the writer. The main thing in this business, perhaps more than anything, is relationships. A songwriter is going to sign a song or a deal with a publisher because he believes in the people across the desk. You have to get along, you have to really believe in each other. Before we sign songwriters to an exclusive deal, we've spent time with them.

Roger Murrah: I would be sure the lyric is finished. It may need some touching up here and there, or correcting, or maybe some suggestions made to the writer which might make it a little stronger. Once we get it in the best form we feel it can be in, we would hopefully use that demo to pitch it, but if not we might possibly demo it again, give it kind of a "Nashville Sound," and pitch it to people.

Joey Gmerek: Once I hear something that attracts me, my next step is to make a phone call and speak with the writer or the band and their manager. Then I'll try to find out a little more about the writer, and start to develop a little feel for what is going on with him. That's where you can be really impressed or really turned off. It's a step-by-step process, and you eventually make your decision either to sign them or just keep an eye on them for a while.

Brian Rawlings: If I hear a song I really like, I'll call the writer and talk with him. Not necessarily to tell him how much I like the song, but just to find out if he's an ax murderer or not! Unfortunately, there are no real qualifications, no IQ test needed to be in the entertainment business. Then I decide whether or not I'd like to work with that person, if I feel we can get along and we could work together. But it really all depends on how great the song is.

What should a songwriter look for when signing a contract with a publisher?

Kathy Spanberger: The best advice I can give any young songwriter is to check out the company and the people behind it. Make sure you're signing with a company that's reputable, that's been in the business a while, that is a real music publisher. One of the most common things I run across is a songwriter/artist, for instance, who has found a financial backer. The backer has some contacts and will put up the money to either do a record or production of some kind, and wants a large part of any profits for his support. My advice to the writer is if you feel you should take a shot at this, then take a shot at it. But limit the term of any contract and make sure these people have some delivery requirements, too. Either they have to deliver a record deal, or there's an obligation on their behalf to get your songs recorded within a certain amount of time, and if it doesn't happen, you're out. That's extremely important.

Roger Murrah: First of all, writers should always use an attorney and see that the contract is fair for both the publisher and the writer. They also need to realize that they're new in the business and they're not in the stage to demand things, yet they can certainly expect fairness at any point in the game.

Carla Berkowitz: Never sign a contract without getting an attorney. It's worth every penny. Publishing contracts and recording contracts are all different. There's no black and white; there's no standard agreement and everything is tailored to whatever the situation is. Make sure that you feel comfortable with everything in the contract.

Brian Rawlings: One of the biggest problems amateur songwriters have is they don't treat this like a business and are not willing to lose any money. And a business is a thing where you can lose all your money in order to take an opportunity to make money. A lot of writers don't put themselves in a position to win—they don't invest in themselves. Every songwriter who is signing a contract should have an attorney. There are some other things a writer can do—Randy Poe's book, *Music Publishing: A Songwriter's Guide* (Writer's Digest Books) is great. It explains what to look for, what's good, what's bad, etc. Songwriters should always ask about reversions, and I think that's fair. If someone's doing a single song deal with you, it's fair to give them about two years to place the song. Most songwriters want six months. I had a song on hold, "All the Man I Need," for two years for Whitney Houston, and she finally cut it and it was a big hit. Boy, I'm glad I waited!

What role does a publisher play in getting a record deal for a songwriter/artist?

Kathy Spanberger: It depends on the music publisher. These days most publishers are involved in artist development. We do serve an A&R function. A lot of record companies look towards outside people such as publishers to help develop artists and get them to the point where they're ready to go in the studio and do a record. Record companies used to serve that function but they're not doing that as much anymore. When we're involved with an artist, we're involved in talking with the manager and finding out how else we can support the artist, either in promotion, tour support or whatever it may be.

Roger Murrah: Through contacts an established publisher can get to see anybody at a label, so it comes down to contacts and networking once again. These days, record companies are very curious as to what's happening in any given camp of a publisher. They want to know about artists who have potential. Most all major publishers and some of the independents are involved in trying to get people on labels.

Carla Berkowitz: I think publishers, because of their connections in the business, can help get record deals for their writers. A publisher should do anything that's going to exploit the songwriter and his copyrights. And if that means getting a writer who has the potential to be an artist a record deal, then they should do that. And if the publisher is out of his league and all he can really do is secure the interests, then it's the publisher's job to get a manager for the writer and really look after him.

Joey Gmerek: The majority of people in A&R positions—the majority of people who run record companies—look at the publisher as someone who's committed and if they're interested in something, it must be good. If the publisher has a good reputation, they're able to access all those A&R people and record company heads. A good publisher is going to be able to do his best to sell the act, and it's a publisher with a good reputation for doing things and developing things that ultimately helps out the writer or band immensely.

What are the advantages/disadvantages of publishing your songs yourself? What would you say to someone who says, I don't need a publisher?

Kathy Spanberger: The disadvantages are that you're cutting out a lot of your marketplace if you're just starting out. The people at publishing companies have very strong contacts at all the record companies, and that's something that's going to be very difficult for you to get. You sign with a music publisher because you feel they're going to elevate your career, and how they elevate it is by using their contacts and opening the doors that are normally closed to you. We do this for a living so we know what we're doing. Publishing is a very specialized field. People think it's easy to do and it really isn't. You wouldn't go to somebody who doesn't know how to cut hair to cut your hair. Why would you try to publish a song when you don't know anything about publishing? That doesn't make a lot of sense to me. There's a real strong demand for very good people in any field, and there are some very good, expert people in publishing.

Carla Berkowitz: Some songwriters don't need a publisher, because they're either already established or they're very business oriented. I know writers who have both, and they are really lucky. They don't have to part with half of their income, since they don't need a publisher to get them cuts. But in the long term having a publisher is a good idea because they can take your songs and get them exploited in other areas such as commercial usages, films, get them on compilation records, get them covered by new artists in Europe. There's only so much that one person can do.

What trends do you see happening in the music industry that will affect music publishers and songwriters?

Kathy Spanberger: If I could guess the next trend we'd all be rich . . . but I think the most amazing trend going on today is the incredible changeover in the charts. It's kind of sad in a way but the careers of artists are about two albums long these days. Right now the craze in the business is signing bands, contemporary, collegy, grungy bands. There are little things I'm seeing artistically, in terms of an acoustic area, back to great songwriting. On a business level, the trend is focusing on new technology and the change in that. Once again, as a songwriter it's very important to have experts around you and to support the publishing industry by working with them. What we do is very important in protecting your rights in the future with all these new technologies. That's one of the least understood things about music publishers. We have organizations that lobby Washington, protecting copyright interests and laws and making sure that whatever happens five or ten or fifteen years down the road, you're going to get paid for it. All these advances in technology are fascinating, and I think we should look at it very positively. Everybody needs music, and the more venues there are to sell it, or to license it, the better it is for everybody. We just have to make sure we keep up with it.

Roger Murrah: There's one thing that I found that you can always depend on, and that's a very special song will jump more hurdles than anything I know of. There's nothing that will equip a person more than a great song. In a business where rules change every day, that's one rule that doesn't change. It would be really good for a writer who's just beginning, to be a little quicker to respect the people who have had experience in the industry because their educated opinion is just that — it's educated, instead of just an opinion.

Carla Berkowitz: Unfortunately, for the past few years, the tendency to sign songwriters is really diminishing, because it's becoming more of a writer/producer market. It's sad, because for most publishers it's hard to recoup an advance with just a songwriter. But I think it may be coming back to that. Country music really had a resurgence because it's made up of true songs, lyrics and melody. Hopefully that's going to be something that comes back. The alternative scene right now is really happening, so we'll see where that goes.

Joey Gmerek: The publisher is going to continue to provide and do initial A&R work. There's always going to be this reservoir of talent that publishers are going to be nurturing and developing to get to the next level. I also think the publisher is going to be involved in a lot of the new technology they're developing. You've got the information superhighway, satellite networks . . . these are all elements that are going to be involved in negotiating new statutory rates and so on and so forth, so the publisher's going to be very active, pro-songwriter, pro-copyright, when all this comes about. I think the publisher's role is actually going to increase because of the new technology, so get a good publisher!

Brian Rawlings: I think singer/songwriters are going to come back in a big way. They've always done well in Nashville but now they're really doing great. It may be some sort of a natural law, but people will always love a beautiful melody. The reason we still listen to Brahms and Beethoven and Mozart is because they wrote moving music. Or disturbing music. But it was all done with melody. People have to be moved by music. Why are singer/songwriters coming back? People are getting back to the roots of music, getting back to great lyrics, great melody. I always assume that's the trend and it's always worked.

Do you have any advice for a songwriter just starting out in the music business?

Kathy Spanberger: Keep an open mind and don't be scared away by assigning rights to your songs. You'll get something back for it.

Roger Murrah: Treat the music industry like a business because it is a business, but also stay close to that thing that gives you the magic to begin with. In other words, stay close to the creativity but be wise enough to be flexible with it once you have a song in your hands and changes need to be made. Be flexible and not so quick to think you've got it all figured out—that really works against you.

Carla Berkowitz: It's important for a songwriter to interview their publishers because it's a serious commitment. I don't think songwriters should expect a publisher to do everything, to make the publisher responsible for their careers. A publisher is someone who you work with and should be there as much as you need him to be. And a songwriter also has a responsibility to the publisher to do the same.

Brian Rawlings: Write more. A lot of songwriters spend way too much money making their demo, and when you tell them they need to go back and rewrite something, they really can't. Because they don't have enough money to go back and re-demo it. So I think songwriters should set realistic goals for themselves. They can only set goals for themselves, not for what other people are going to do. Most people say, well, I'm going to have a hit song by 1997! Well, you can't determine that, there are too many other people involved. You can say, well, I'm going to put myself in a position to have a hit song by 1995 and then I can have one by 1997. It always comes back to treating the music business like a business. It's a business with a lot of heart. You can do tremendous things, and it can be so much fun that it's unbelievable. Most people think it looks like a lot of fun, and it is. It can be incredibly gratifying, but it's also incredibly hard work. It's very common to work 18-hour days in our business. And people have to get a grip on that.

Joey Gmerek: Do it because you love it, and be as patient as possible. That is clearly the way to go. Patience is probably more important than anything, because it does take time. It really does.

Music Industry Trend Report

If the past year is any indication, the music industry is growing at a fairly healthy rate. Thanks to multi-platinum sales by both established and new artists, the record industry has been having a banner year, with profits reaching the 10 billion dollar mark. The acceptance by consumers of a myriad of musical styles and the rapid advances in technology have contributed to this recent boom.

Music trends

All types of music continue to do well on the charts, which is a good sign for songwriters. You no longer have to be a pop songwriter in order to have a hit record; the "mainstream" has opened its arms to embrace all types of music. Rock and country acts are the most popular on the *Billboard* 200, with adult contemporary, rap and soundtracks not far behind. Hard rock has been particularly successful of late, with albums by heavy rockers Soundgarden, Alice In Chains, Pantera and Pearl Jam all debuting in the number one spot on the *Billboard* album charts. The singles charts, however, are dominated by R&B and rap, further evidence of the public's acceptance of a wide range of musical styles.

The biggest musical growth seems to be occurring in the country and alternative markets. Atlantic Records announced plans to expand their Nashville division, and Sony Music restructured their country music division as well to keep up with the demand for country acts. Alternative music continues to cross over from the modern rock charts to the rock charts, and has made a large show of force on the *Billboard* 200. With the success of alternative acts, major labels are no longer just looking to independent labels to develop new talent; they're making a concentrated effort to actually work with the indies in the development of new artists. For instance, New York-based indie Matador Records and Chapel Hill's Mammoth Records recently became affiliated with Atlantic Records. Indies sign up with majors because it increases the cash flow into the marketing, promotion and distribution of their releases; majors want to tap into the intense artist development that takes place on the indie level. Further evidence of the majors wanting to tap into the independent market is shown by the fact that most of the big six record manufacturers have now established their own independent distribution arms or have bought into existing indie distribution systems. They want to make sure their releases find their way into smaller, mom and pop stores that cater to independent product in order to promote their smaller, more alternative acts.

Music formats

CDs, cassettes, MiniDiscs, Digital Compact Cassettes—what format will be the one to watch in the near future? It's hard to tell. The viability of MiniDisc and Digital Compact Cassette still remains to be seen, as sales in their first year of release were anything but impressive. With people just getting used to the idea of CDs and still in the process of converting their vinyl collections over to disk, the introduction of these new formats seems premature. CDs represent the largest and fastest growing format in the market, while vinyl LPs, 45s and cassette sales continue to decline.

As for MiniDisc (MD) and Digital Compact Cassette (DCC), most retailers feel it is too soon for either of the new configurations to catch on and have decided to wait and see. One of the key selling points of MD is that you can record on it, something that you can't do with a conventional CD. Blank MDs are currently selling better than prerecorded titles, suggesting that their recordability may be their main appeal. The main selling point with DCC seems to be the compatibility of DCC machines to play regular analog cassettes also. Currently, MD outsells DCC by about two to one; but vinyl records, considered by some to be a dinosaur of the industry, still sell better than MDs.

Even though sales are low, vinyl is hardly dead yet. Vinyl LPs made a mini comeback of sorts recently, with major labels releasing limited numbers of certain titles on vinyl a week or two before the official release on CD and cassette. Mainly to appeal to the alternative music buyer who still purchases music on vinyl from independent labels, new releases by Pearl Jam, Nirvana, Urge Overkill and Sonic Youth were released on vinyl, as was the latest Pink Floyd release.

Adding to the audio format fray is the introduction of interactive CDs, with artists like Todd Rundgren and David Bowie introducing interactive albums. These releases allow the consumer to manipulate the music on the discs to create an infinite number of versions of the songs. They also incorporate visual images that the consumer can customize. Record companies such as BMG have already set up interactive departments, making this field one to definitely keep an eye on in the near future.

Another technology is on the horizon which may eclipse all of the other formats currently being developed. Digital transmission — a process whereby the consumer can choose to have specific songs or albums beamed directly into his home via cable, telephone wire or satellite — should be available within the next few years. Although there have been no concrete advances made in actually setting up a system of delivery for the record buying public, there are a lot of issues that need to be addressed before the system is up and working. The questions posed by such technology are numerous: What will happen to retail outlets if a consumer doesn't have to leave his home to hear the latest release by his favorite artist? Will record stores become obsolete? Will there even be a need for physical product anymore? If the major conglomerates control the transmission of music, what will happen to independent releases? How will a songwriter's copyright be affected by this free flow of product? If royalty rates are no longer based on actual record "sales" but on the digital transmission of product, how will that be monitored? What will prevent a consumer from taping a digital quality broadcast and circulating it? As you can see, the questions that arise from the implementation of such a system are complex and varied, and these few questions only begin to touch upon the implications that digital transmission brings.

Changes in legislation

Issues relating to the imminent arrival of digital transmission are already under discussion in the nation's legislature. At the urging of the recording industry, bills have been introduced in both the House of Representatives and Congress that would amend the current Copyright Act. The purpose of these bills is to create a public performance right for artists for sound recordings used in digital transmission.

As the law now stands, the broadcast of a song or performance is not subject to mechanical royalties; the writer and publisher receive performance royalties whenever their song is played on the radio or in public performance. Mechanical royalties are paid to the songwriter and artist per each record sold. If future technology eventually does away with CDs, tapes, etc., there will, in effect, be nothing for the songwriter to collect mechanical royalties on. Any legislative solution to the problems raised by the advent of digital transmission must take into account the rights of all creators and copyright owners: songwriters, publishers and artists, as well as record companies. Songwriter organizations have been working together and lobbying Congress to make sure the interests of all parties involved are compensated for the digital transmission of an artist's material.

Keeping up with current trends

Keeping up with all the technological advances as well as music trends in the industry is just as important as perfecting the craft of songwriting itself. Knowing what's going on within the industry will help you figure out where you and your music fit in, and where you're most likely to be a success. Staying on top of these trends isn't as hard as it may seem. Reading trade publications, which are a great source of up-to-date information, as well as attending seminars and workshops pertaining to the music business, can help you stay informed. Songwriter organizations, whether local or national, are also helpful; many publish market newsletters to let you know what's going on in the industry and how it affects you as a songwriter.

Keeping up with trends can only take you so far, however. Knowing what's "hot" at the moment shouldn't dictate the kind of songwriter you are. If you're a writer of terrific pop songs, for instance, but the charts seem to be dominated by hard rock, that doesn't mean you should start writing music that you know nothing about. If there's one constant in this ever-changing business, it's the need for quality songs, no matter what genre. A great, well-crafted song will almost always transcend whatever seems to be the most recent trend.

Important information on market listings

- *Although every listing in* Songwriter's Market *is updated, verified or researched prior to publication, some changes are bound to occur between publication and the time you contact any listing.*
- *Listings are based on interviews and questionnaires. They are not advertisements, nor are markets reported here necessarily endorsed by the editor.*
- *A word about style: This book is edited (except for quoted material) in the masculine gender because we think "he/she," "she/he," "he/or she," "him or her" or "they" in copy is distracting. We bow to tradition for the sake of readability.*
- *Looking for a particular market? Check the Index. If you don't find it there, it is because 1) It's not interested in receiving material at this time. 2) It's no longer in business or has merged with another company. 3) It charges (counter to our criteria for inclusion) for services a songwriter should receive free. 4) It has failed to verify or update its listing annually. 5) It has requested that it not be listed. 6) We have received reports from songwriters about unresolved problems they've had with the company. Check the '94-95 Changes list at the end of each section to find why markets appearing in the 1994 edition do not appear in this edition.*
- *A word of warning. Don't pay to have your song published or to have your lyrics – or a poem – set to music. Read "Ripoffs" in the Business of Songwriting section to learn how to recognize and protect yourself from the "song shark."*
- Songwriter's Market *reserves the right to exclude any listing which does not meet its requirements.*

The Markets

Music Publishers

Finding songs and getting them recorded—that's the main function of a music publisher. Working as an advocate for you and your songs, a music publisher serves as a song plugger, administrator, networking resource and more. The knowledge and personal contacts a music publisher can provide may be the most valuable resources available for a songwriter just starting in the music business.

Music publishers attempt to derive income from a song through recordings, use in TV and film soundtracks and other areas. While this is their primary task, music publishers also handle administrative tasks such as copyrighting songs, collecting royalties for the songwriter, negotiating and issuing synchronization licenses for use of music in films, arranging and administering foreign rights, and producing new demos of the music submitted to them. In a small, independent publishing company, one or two people may provide all of these services. Larger publishing companies are more likely to be divided into the following departments: Creative (or Professional), Copyright, Licensing, Legal Affairs, Royalty, Accounting and Foreign.

The Creative department is responsible for finding talented writers and signing them to the company. Once a writer is signed, it is up to the Creative department to develop and nurture the writer so he will write songs that will create income for the company. Staff members help put writers together to form collaborative teams. And, perhaps most important, the Creative department is responsible for getting songs recorded by other artists and used in film and other media that will expose the song to the public. The head of the Creative department, usually called the professional manager, is charged with locating talented writers for the company. Once a writer is signed, the professional manager arranges for a demo to be made of the writer's songs. Even though a writer may already have recorded his own demo, the publisher will most often re-demo the songs using established studio musicians in an effort to produce the highest-quality demo possible. Many pro-quality demos are nearly indistinguishable from final master recordings.

Once a demo is produced, the professional manager begins shopping the song to various outlets. He may try to get the song recorded by a top artist on his or her next album. He may try to get the song used in an upcoming film. The professional manager uses all the contacts and leads he has to get the writer's songs recorded by as many artists as possible. Therefore, he must be able to deal efficiently and effectively with people in other segments of the music industry, including A&R personnel, producers, distributors, managers and lawyers. Through these contacts, he can find out what artists are looking for new material, and who may be interested in recording one of the writer's songs. The professional manager and those working with him must have extensive knowledge not only of his own segment of the industry, but of all the others as well.

After a writer's songs are recorded, the other departments at the publishing company come into play. The Licensing and Copyright departments are responsible for issuing any licenses for use of the writer's songs in film or TV, and for filing various forms with the copyright office. The Legal Affairs department works with the Professional department in negotiating contracts with its writers. The Royalty and Accounting departments are responsible for ensuring the writer is receiving the proper royalty rate as specified in the contract, and that statements are mailed to the writer promptly. Finally, the Foreign department's role is to oversee any publishing activities outside of the United States, and to make sure a writer is being paid for any uses of his material in foreign countries. (For a more in-depth look at music publishing see the Publisher's Roundtable on page 15.)

Locating a music publisher

How do you go about finding a music publisher that will work well for you? First, you must find out what kind of music a publisher handles. If a particular publisher works mostly with alternative music and you're a country songwriter, the contacts he has within the industry will hardly be of any use to you. You must find a publisher more suited to the type of music you write. Each listing in this section details the type of music that publisher is most interested in; the music types appear in boldface to make them easier to locate. You will also want to refer to the Category Index at the end of this section, which lists companies by the type of music they work with.

Do your research!

It's important to study the market and do research to identify which companies to submit to. Are you targeting a specific artist to sing your songs? If so, you must find out if that artist even considers outside material. Who was the publisher of the artist's latest release? Such information can be found in any issue of *Billboard*, the weekly magazine that covers the music industry and publishes charts of the best selling records each week. If there is an artist you are interested in and they have a recent hit on the *Billboard* charts, the publishing company they are signed with will be listed in the "Hot 100 A-Z" index. If an artist isn't currently charting in *Billboard*, check the liner notes of a recent release, which will list the name of the artist's publisher. Once you've located the name of the publishing company, you can attempt to get songs to the artist through the publisher. Carefully choosing which publishers will work best for the material you write may take time, but it will only increase your chances of getting your songs heard. "Shotgunning" your demo packages (sending out many packages without regard for music preference or submission policy) not only is a waste of time and money, but it may also label you as an unprofessional songwriter with no regard for the workings and policies of the music business.

Once you've found some companies that may be interested in your work, find out what songs have been successfully handled by those publishers. Most publishers are happy to provide you with this information in order to attract high-quality material. Ask the publisher for the names of some of their staff writers, and give them a call. Ask them their opinion of how the publisher works. Keep in mind as you're researching music publishers how you get along with them personally. If you can't work with a publisher on a personal level, chances are your material won't be represented as you would like it to be. A publisher can become your most valuable contact to all other segments of the music industry, so it's important to find someone you can trust and feel comfortable with.

Also consider the size of the publishing company. The publishing affiliates of the major music conglomerates are huge, handling catalogs of thousands of songs by hundreds of songwriters. Unless you are an established songwriter, your songs probably won't receive enough attention from such large companies. On the other hand, smaller, independent publishers offer several advantages. First, independent music publishers are located all over the country, making it easier for you to work face-to-face rather than by mail or phone. Smaller companies usually aren't affiliated with a particular record company, and are therefore able to pitch your songs to many different labels and acts. Independent music publishers are usually interested in a smaller range of music, allowing you to target your submissions more accurately. The most obvious advantage to working with a smaller publisher is the personal attention they can bring to you and your songs. With a smaller roster of artists to work with, the independent music publisher is able to concentrate more time and effort on each particular project.

Publishing contracts

Once you've located a publisher you like and he's interested in shopping your work, it's time to consider the publishing contract — an agreement in which a songwriter grants certain rights to a publisher for one or more songs. The contract specifies any advances offered to the writer, the rights that will be transferred to the publisher, the royalties a songwriter is to receive and the length of time the contract is valid. When a contract is signed, a publisher will ask for a 50-50 split with the writer. This is standard industry practice; the publisher is taking that 50% to cover the overhead costs of running his business and for the work he's doing to get your songs recorded. It is always a good idea to have a publishing contract (or any music business contract) reviewed by a competent entertainment lawyer. There is no "standard" publishing contract, and each company offers different provisions for their writers. Make sure you ask questions about anything you don't understand, especially if you're new in the business. Songwriter organizations such as the Songwriters Guild of America provide contract review services, and can help you learn about music business language and what constitutes a fair music publishing contract.

When signing a contract, it's important to be aware of the music industry's unethical practitioners. The "song shark," as he's called, makes his living by asking a songwriter to pay to have a song published. The shark will ask for more than the standard 50% publisher's share and may even ask you to give up all rights to a song in order to have it published. Although none of these practices is illegal, it's certainly not ethical, and no successful publisher uses these methods. *Songwriter's Market* works to contain only honest companies interested in hearing new material. (For more on "song sharks," see The Business of Songwriting on page 10.)

Submitting material to a publisher

When submitting material to a publisher, always keep in mind that a professional, courteous manner goes a long way in making a good impression. When you submit through the mail, make sure your package is neat and meets the particular needs of the publisher. Review each publisher's submission policy carefully, and follow it to the letter. Disregarding this information will only make you look like an amateur in the eyes of the company you're submitting to. (For more detailed information on submitting your material, see Getting Started on page 5.)

Listings of companies in countries other than the U.S. feature the name of the country in bold type. You will find an alphabetical list of these companies at the end of this section, along with an index of publishers in the New York, Los Angeles and Nashville metropolitan areas. This will prove helpful when planning a trip to one of these major music centers. Also included is a Category Index, which lists companies by the type of music they work with.

a HI-TEK PUBLISHING COMPANY, Opera Plaza 601, VanNess Ave., E3-141, San Francisco CA 94102. (510)455-6652. Fax: (510)455-6651. Owner: Thomas L. Wallis. Music publisher. Estab. 1989. Publishes 10-25 songs/year; publishes 5 new songwriters/year. Works with composers and lyricists; teams collaborators. Pays standard royalty.
How to Contact: Submit demo tape by mail. Unsolicited submissions are OK. Prefers cassette (or VHS videocassette) with 3-5 songs and lyric sheet. SASE. Reports in 1 month.
Music: Mostly **country**; also **MOR**. Published "Earthquake" (by Boots Tafolca/Denny Hemingson), recorded by Ray Sanders on Pacific Coast Records; "I Want To Cheat Tonight (Pay Later On)" and "The Fall," (by T.L. Wallis), both recorded by Ray Sanders on a Hi-Tek Publishing Records.
Tips: "Be original and creative. Write something that has never been written before."

*ABALONE PUBLISHING, Suite 10, 8318 Columbus, North Hills CA 91343. Music Director: Jack Timmons. Music publisher and record company (L.A. Records). Estab. 1984. Publishes 20-30 songs/year; publishes 20-30 new songwriters/year. Hires staff songwriters. Works with composers and lyricists; teams collaborators. Pays standard royalty.
Affiliate(s): BGM Publishing, AL-KY Music, Bubba Music (BMI).
How to Contact: Submit demo tape by mail. Unsolicited submissions are OK. Prefers cassette with 1-5 songs and lyric sheet. "Include cover letter describing your objective goals." SASE. Reports in 1 month.
Music: Mostly **rock, pop**, and **alternative**; also **dance, pop/rock**, and **country**. Published "Shive" (by Al Long), recorded by The Lords (rock); *Taboo* (by S. Stevens), recorded by Harry Carrike (pop); and *Love Junkie* (by K. Simmons), recorded by Slut (alternative), all on L.A. Records.
Tips: "Write what you feel, however, don't stray too far from the trends that are currently popular. Lyrical content should depict a definite story line and paint an accurate picture in the listener's mind."

*ABIGWAN, 188 Ave. de Couronne, Brussels 1050 **Belgium**. (32)2 640 34 90. Fax: (32)2 640 34 97. Managing Director: Mathieu A. Music publisher, record company. Estab. 1986. Publishes 50 songs/year; publishes 5 new songwriters/year. Works with composers and lyricists. Pays standard royalty.
How to Contact: Submit demo tape by mail. Unsolicited submissions are OK. Prefers cassette or VHS videocassette with minimum 2 songs. SASE. Reports in 3 or 4 weeks.
Music: Mostly **rock, pop** and **dance**; also **instrumentals** and **jazz**. Published *Coeur De Loup*, written and recorded by P. Lafontaine on Promax Records (French); *Too Late* (by Frantzis), recorded by Patty Burns on Abigwan Records (rock); and *Carol Ann* (by Roseman), recorded by Medford Slim on Abigwan (blues).

ABINGDON PRESS, Dept. SM, 201 Eighth Ave. S., Nashville TN 37203. (615)749-6158. Music Editor: Gary Alan Smith. Music publisher. ASCAP, BMI. Publishes approximately 300 songs/year; publishes as many new songwriters as possible.
How to Contact: Submit a manuscript and a demo tape by mail. Unsolicited submissions are OK. "Unsolicited material must be addressed with Gary Alan Smith's name on the first line." Prefers cassette with no more than 4 songs and lyric sheet. "Please assure name and address are on tapes and/or manuscripts, lyric sheets, etc." SASE. Reports in 1 month.
Music: Mostly **sacred choral and instrumental**.
Tips: "Focus material on mid-size, volunteer church choirs and musicians."

ACCENT PUBLISHING CO., Dept. SM, 3955 Folk-Ream Rd., Springfield OH 45502. (513)325-5767. President/Owner: Dave Jordan. Music publisher, record company (Dove Song Records). Estab. 1989. Publishes 4-6 songs/year; publishes 3 new songwriters/year. Works with composers and lyricists; teams collaborators. Pays negotiable royalty.
How to Contact: Submit demo tape by mail. Unsolicited submissions are OK. Prefers cassette (or VHS videocassette) with 2 songs and lyric or lead sheet. SASE. Reports in 8-10 weeks.
Music: Mostly **country, gospel** and **R&B**; also **pop, soft rock** and **rap**. Published "Am I The One," written and recorded by David Reeves; "The Only Thing Missing Is You" (by Johnson/Jordan), recorded by Chris Baldwin; and "Missing You" (by Justin Slusher), recorded by Orderly Revolution, all on Dove Song Records.

 The asterisk before a listing indicates that the listing is new in this edition. New markets are often the most receptive to unsolicited submissions.

Tips: "Write with feeling, have a catchy title and hook. Be willing to re-write until the song is good! Send a well-recorded demo."

*ACCOLADE MUSIC LTD., 25 Earlsdon Ave. N., Coventry CV5 6GX **England**. (44)203711935. Director: Graham Bradshaw. Music publisher, record company and record producer. Estab. 1979. Works with composers and lyricists.
How to Contact: Write first and obtain permission to submit. Prefers cassette. SASE. Reports in 2-3 weeks.
Music: Mostly **folk** and **country**. Published *Out of The Shadowland*, written and recorded by Jim Couza (folk); *Mocha Express* (by Ian Smith), recorded by Prego (folk); and *Camels Are Coming* (by Ian Wilson), recorded by Peeping Tom (folk), all on Folksound Records.

*ADM PUBLISHING (SA BAM/IFPI), De Singel 5, Kontich, Antwerp 2840 **Belgium**. (3)457 58 59. Fax: (3)457 58 83. A&R Manager: Mr. Martin King. Music publisher. Estab. 1991. Publishes 5-6 new songwriters/year. Hires staff songwriters. Works with composers and lyricists. Pays standard royalty.
How to Contact: Write or call first to arrange personal interview. Submit demo tape by mail. Unsolicited submissions are OK. Prefers videocassette and lyric sheet. Reports in 3 weeks.
Music: Mostly **dance, house** and **reggae**; also **R&B, soul** and **ballads**. Published "Hey You" (by Jo Bogaert), recorded by Technotronic (house); "Gorgeous" (by Nik Skorsky), recorded by Rozlyne Clarke (dance); and "Life," written and recorded by Shane (R&B), all on ARS Records.
Tips: "Don't send more than 2 tracks. Listen to current trends in dance and use them as a reference for formulating your material."

AIM HIGH MUSIC COMPANY (ASCAP), Suite #200, 1300 Division St., Nashville TN 37203. (615)242-4722. (800)767-4984. Fax: (615)242-1177. Producer: Robert Metzgar. Music publisher and record company (Platinum Plus/BMG Records). Estab. 1971. Publishes 250 songs/year; publishes 5-6 new songwriters/year. Hires staff writers. Works with composers and lyricists; teams collaborators. "Our company pays 100% to all songwriters."
Affiliate(s): Aim High Music (ASCAP), Bobby & Billy Music (BMI), Billy Ray Music (BMI), Club Platinum Music (BMI).
How to Contact: Submit a demo tape by mail. Unsolicited submissions are OK. Prefers cassette or VHS videocassette with 5-10 songs and lyric sheet. "I like to get to know songwriters personally prior to recording their songs." Does not return unsolicited material. Reports in 3 weeks.
Music: Mostly **country, traditional country** and **pop country**; also **gospel, southern gospel** and **contemporary Christian**. Published *West Texas Sam* (by B. Gerick), recorded by Billy Ray on BMG Records (country); "Two Steps" written and recorded by J. Gardner on JMH Records (country); and "Six Pac" (by Max Allen), recorded by Line-Dance Kings on BMG Records (country).
Tips: "The quality of the demo pitched to a major label is extremely important."

*ALA/BIANCA SRL, Mazzoni 34/36, Modena 41100 **Italy**. Phone: (059)223897. Fax: (059)219218. President: Toni Verona. Music publisher, record company (Bravo, Flea, River Nile), record producer (Idem) and video production (S.I.A.E.). Estab. 1978. Publishes 300 songs/year; publishes 10 new songwriters/year. Teams collaborators. Pays standard royalty.
How to Contact: Submit demo tape by mail. Unsolicited submissions are OK. Prefers cassette with 3-5 songs. Include biography. Does not return unsolicited material. Reports in 1 month.
Music: Mostly **pop, rock** and **dance**; also **instrumental**. Published "No Sad Goodbyes" (by G. Romani), recorded by the Rocking Chairs on River Nile Records (rock); "Ala Li La (Sega')", written and recorded by D. Azor on Mighty Quinn Records (sega); and "Dedicated" (by various writers), recorded by R. Roberts on River Nile Records (rock/funky soul).
Tips: "We are looking for material suitable for the European market."

*ALEXANDER SR., MUSIC (BMI), P.O. Box 8684, Youngstown OH 44507. (216)782-5031. Fax: (216)782-5955. A&R: LaVerne Alexander. Music publisher, record company (LRG Records) and record producer. Estab. 1992. Publishes 12-22 songs/year; publishes 2-4 new songwriters/year. Works with composers and lyricists; teams collaborators. Pays varying royalty.
How to Contact: Write first and obtain permission to submit. Prefers cassette with 4 songs and lyric sheet. "We will accept finished masters (cassette or CD) for review." SASE. Reports in 1 month.
Music: Mostly **contemporary jazz, contemporary Christian** and **gospel**; also **R&B, rap** and **pop**. Published *Coast to Coast* (by Darryl Alexander); *Steps of Faith* (by Stephen Allen); and *Don't Dis Me My*

Listings of companies in countries other than the U.S. have the name of the country in boldface type.

Brother (by Vince Andrews and Darryl Alexander), all recorded by Darryl Alexander on LRG Records (jazz).
Tips: "Submit your best songs and follow submission guidelines. 'If at first you don't succeed, try try again.' Finished masters open up additional possibilities. Lead sheets may be requested for material we are interested in. No profanity in rap."

ALEXIS (ASCAP), P.O. Box 532, Malibu CA 90265. (213)463-5998. President: Lee Magid. Music publisher, record company, personal management firm, and record and video producer. Member AIMP. Estab. 1950. Publishes 50 songs/year; publishes 20-50 new songwriters/year. Works with composers.
Affiliate(s): Marvelle (BMI), Lou-Lee (BMI), D.R. Music (ASCAP) and Gabal (SESAC).
How to Contact: Submit a demo tape—unsolicited submissions are OK. Prefers cassette (or VHS videocassette of writer/artist if available) with 1-3 songs and lyric sheet. "Try to make demo as clear as possible—guitar or piano should be sufficient. A full rhythm and vocal demo is always better." SASE. Reports in 6 weeks "if interested."
Music: Mostly **R&B, jazz, MOR, pop** and **gospel**; also **blues, church/religious, country, dance-oriented, folk** and **Latin**. Published "Jesus Is Just Alright" (by Reynolds), recorded by D.C. Talk on Forefront Records (pop); *A Mighty Hand* (by C. Rhone), recorded by Tramaine Hawkins on Sony (crossover gospel); and *What Shall I Do?* (by Q. Fielding), recorded by Tramaine Hawkins on Sparrow Records (gospel).
Tips: "Try to create a good demo, vocally and musically."

ALHART MUSIC PUBLISHING (BMI), P.O. Box 1593, Lakeside CA 92040. (619)443-2170. President: Richard Phipps. Music publisher. Estab. 1981. Releases 4 singles/year. Works with songwriters on contract. Pays standard royalty.
How to Contact: Write or call first and obtain permission to submit. Prefers cassette with 2 songs and lyric or lead sheets. SASE. Reports in 2-4 weeks.
Music: Mostly **country**; also **R&B**. Released "Party For One," "Don't Turn My Gold To Blue," and "Blue Lady" (by Dan Michaels), on Alhart Records (country).

ALJONI MUSIC CO. (BMI), 8010 International Village Dr., Jacksonville FL 32211. (904)765-8276. Creative Manager: Ronnie Hall. Director/Producer: Al Hall, Jr. Music publisher, record producer (Hallways to Fame Productions). Estab. 1971. Publishes 4-8 songs/year; publishes 1-2 new songwriters/year. Teams collaborators. Pays negotiated royalty.
Affiliate(s): Hallmarque Musical Works Ltd. (ASCAP).
How to Contact: Submit demo tape by mail. Unsolicited submissions are OK. Prefers cassette (or VHS videocassette) with no more than 3 songs and lead sheet. Does not return material. Reports in 2-3 months.
Music: Mostly **rap, dance/R&B** and **jazz**. Published *Buffalo Soldiers* (by Al Hall Jr.), recorded by Cosmos Dwellers on Hallway International Records (jazz/world); "Dash 4 Da Cash," written and recorded by Al Money on 1st Coast Posse/MCM (rap); and "Look Out 4 Me" (by Al and Ronnie Hall), recorded by Lady Jaye on 1st Coast Posse (R&B dance).
Tips: "Rap—rise above the rest! Dance/R&B—songs should have a good hook and a meaningful story line. Jazz—send solid straight ahead stuff as well as electronically oriented material. World, New Age and Latin welcome too!!"

***ALL NATIONS MUSIC PUBLISHING, LTD. (ASCAP)**, 8857 W. Olympic, Beverly Hills CA 90211. (310)657-9814. Fax: (310)657-2331. Contact: Creative Staff. "Call to find out if we're accepting outside submissions and to get specific name." Music publisher. Estab. 1989. Publishes 10-15 songs/year; publishes 2 new songwriters/year. Hires staff songwriters (if they have some sort of royalty earning track record). Works with composers and lyricists. Pays standard royalty.
Affiliate(s): Songs Of All Nations (BMI) and Every Song Counts (SESAC).
How to Contact: Write or call first and obtain permission to submit. Prefers cassette with 3 songs and lyric sheet. SASE. Reports in 3-4 weeks.
Music: Mostly **rock, country, A/C, R&B** and **pop**. Published "She's Got The Rhythm" (by Randy Travis), recorded by Alan Jackson on Arista Records (country); "That's What Love Is For" (by Michael Omartian), recorded by Amy Grant on A&M Records (A/C); and "Nothin' But A 'G' Thang" (by Leon Haywood), recorded by Dr. Dre on Interscope Records (rap).
Tips: "It's becoming more and more difficult to get artists to cover outside songwriters' material. Write songs customized for a particular artist. You have to write hits to make money—you have to make money to get a writer/publisher deal."

ALL ROCK MUSIC, P.O. Box 2296, Rotterdam 3000 CG **Holland**. Phone: (31) 1862-4266. Fax: (32) 1862-4366. President: Cees Klop. Music publisher, record company (Collector Records) and record producer. Estab. 1967. Publishes 50-60 songs/year; publishes several new songwriters/year. Pays standard royalty.

Affiliate(s): All Rock Music (England) and All Rock Music (Belgium).
How to Contact: Submit demo tape by mail. Unsolicited submissions are OK. Prefers cassette. SAE and IRC. Reports in 4 weeks.
Music: Mostly **'50s rock, rockabilly** and **country rock**; also **piano boogie woogie**. Published *Boogie Woogie Bill*, written and recorded by Teddy Redell on Collector Records; *Backseat Boogie*, written and recorded by EricJan Oberbeek on Down South Records; and *Grand Hotel*, written and recorded by Vincent Laurentis on Down South Records.

ALLEGED IGUANA MUSIC, 44 Archdekin Dr., Brampton, Ontario L6V 1Y4 **Canada**. President: Randall Cousins. Music publisher and record producer (Randall Cousins Productions). SOCAN. Estab. 1984. Publishes 80 songs/year. Works with composers and lyricists.
Affiliate(s): Secret Agency (SOCAN) and AAA Aardvark Music (SOCAN).
How to Contact: Write first and obtain permission to submit a tape. Prefers cassette (or VHS videocassette) with 3 songs and lyric sheet. Does not return unsolicited material. Reports in 8 weeks.
Music: Mostly **country, country-rock** and **A/C**; also **pop** and **rock**. Published *Some Rivers Run Dry* (by David Weltman), recorded by Diane Raeside; *Easy For You To Say*, written and recorded by Mark LaForme; and *Corners* (by Di Fronzo-Nollette), recorded by Ericka, all on Roto Noto Records.

ALLEGHENY MUSIC WORKS, 306 Cypress Ave., Johnstown PA 15902. (814)535-3373. Managing Director: Al Rita. West Coast A&R Consultant: Dale Siegenthaler. Music publisher, record company (Allegheny Records). Estab. 1991. Works with composers and lyricists; teams collaborators. Pays standard royalty.
Affiliate(s): Allegheny Music Works Publishing (ASCAP), Tuned on Music (BMI).
How to Contact: Submit demo tape by mail. Unsolicited submissions are OK. Prefers cassette with 3 songs and lyric or lead sheet. SASE. Reports in 2-4 weeks.
Music: Mostly **country, pop, adult contemporary, R&B**; also **gospel, MOR** and **contemporary Christian**. Published "Just Passin' Through" (by Dennis Leogrande), recorded by Mark McLelland; "All That I Need Is You" (by Dennis Leogrande), recorded by Wanda Copier and Mark McLelland; and "If It Ain't Love By Now" (by Brian McArdle, Kevin McArdle, and Gary Georgett), recorded by Tom Woodard, all on Allegheny Records.
Tips: "The song must be outstanding in both its melody and its lyric, and the demo should sparkle and shine."

ALLISONGS INC., 1603 Horton Ave., Nashville TN 37212. (615)292-9899. President: Jim Allison. Music publisher, record company (ARIA Records), record producer (Jim Allison, AlliSongs Inc.) BMI, ASCAP. Estab. 1985. Publishes more than 50 songs/year. Works with composers and lyricists.
Affiliate(s): Jims' Allisongs (BMI), d.c. Radio-Active Music (ASCAP) and Annie Green Eyes Music (BMI).
How to Contact: Send chrome cassette and lyric sheet. Does not return material. *"Will call you* if interested."
Music: Mostly **country**. Published "What Am I Gonna Do About You" (by Allison/Simon/Gilmore), recorded by Reba McEntire on MCA Records (country); "Preservation of the Wild Life" (by Allison/Young), recorded by Earl Thomas Conley on RCA Records (country); and "Against My Will" (by Hogan), recorded by Brenda Lee on Warner Bros. Records (pop).
Tips: "Send your best—we will contact you if interested."

*ALPANA MUSIK & FILM (GMBH), Am Sohonblickg, 85293 Reichouts **Germany**. 08447-84294. Fax: 08447-84280. A&R: Alain Cap. Estab. 1987. Publishes 140 songs/year; publishes 20 new songwriters/year. Works with composers and lyricists. Pays standard royalty.
How to Contact: Submit demo tape by mail. Unsolicited submissions are OK. Prefers cassette with lyric sheet. SAE and IRC. Reports in 2 months.
Music: Mostly **dance** and **rock**; also **ballroom dance**. Published "Wann Werdenmeine" (by A. Cap/Gogo), recorded by Dirk on BMG Records (rock); *Chocone* (by Gewehr), recorded by H. Strasser on EMI Records (ballroom); and *La Danza*, written and recorded by W. Tauber on Polydor Records (dance).

*ALPHA MUSIC INC. (BMI), 747 Chestnut Ridge Rd., Chestnut Ridge NY 10977. (914)356-0800. Fax: (914)356-0895. Contact: Michael Nurko. Music publisher. Estab. 1931. Pays standard royalty.
Affiliate(s): Dorian Music Corp. (ASCAP), TRF Music Inc.
How to Contact: Submit demo tape by mail. Unsolicited submissions are OK. Prefers cassette or VHS videocassette (if available). Does not return material.
Music: All categories, mainly **instrumental** and **acoustic**; also **theme music** for television and film. "Have published over 50,000 titles since 1931."

ALTERNATIVE DIRECTION MUSIC PUBLISHERS, Dept. SM, 101 Pine Trail Crescent, Ottawa, Ontario K2G 5B9 **Canada**. (613)225-6100. President and Director of Publishing: David Stein. Music publisher, record company, record producer and management firm (Alternative Direction Management). SO-CAN. Estab. 1980. Publishes 5-10 songs/year; publishes 2-3 new songwriters/year. Works with composers; teams collaborators. Pays standard royalty.
How to Contact: Submit demo tape by mail. Unsolicited submissions are OK. Prefers cassette (or VHS videocassette) with 2-4 songs. SASE if sent from within Canada; American songwriters send SAE and $2 for postage and handling. Reports in 1 month.
Music: Up-tempo rock, up-tempo R&B and up-tempo pop. Published "Big Kiss" (by David Ray), recorded by Theresa Bazaar on MCA Records (pop/dance) and Cindy Valentine on CBS Records (rock).
Tips: "Make certain your vocals are up front in the mix in the demos you submit. I am looking only for up-tempo R&B and pop songs with a strong chorus and killer hooks. Don't send me any MOR, country, blues or folk music. I don't publish that kind of material."

AMALGAMATED TULIP CORP., Dept. SM, 117 W. Rockland Rd., Box 615, Libertyville IL 60048. (708)362-4060. President: Perry Johnson. Professional Manager: Rick Johnson. Music publisher, record company and record producer. BMI. Estab. 1968. Publishes 12 songs/year; publishes 3-6 new songwriters/year. Pays standard royalty.
Affiliate(s): Mo Fo Music and Perik Music.
How to Contact: Submit a demo tape—unsolicited submissions are OK. Prefers cassette with 2-4 songs and lyric sheet. SASE. Prefers studio produced demos. Reports in 6 months.
Music: Mostly **rock, top 40/pop, dance** and **R&B**; also **country, MOR, blues, easy listening** and **progressive**. Published "This Feels Like Love to Me" (by Charles Sermay), recorded by Sacha Distel (pop); "Stop Wastin' Time" (by Tom Gallagher), recorded by Orjan (country); and "In the Middle of the Night," recorded by Oh Boy (pop).
Tips: "Send commercial material."

AMERICATONE INTERNATIONAL, 1817 Loch Lomond Way, Las Vegas NV 89102-4437. (702)384-0030. Fax: (702) 382-1926. President: Joe Jan Jaros. Estab. 1975. Publishes 25 songs/year. Pays standard royalty.
Affiliate(s): Americatone Records International, Christy Records International USA, Rambolt Music International (ASCAP).
How to Contact: Submit demo tape by mail. Unsolicited submissions OK. Prefers cassettes, "studio production with top sound recordings." SASE. Reports in 1 month.
Music: Mostly **country, jazz, R&B, Spanish** and **classic ballads**. Published *Mark Master Jazz Orchestra*, recorded by Mark Master; *I'm Coming Home*, recorded by Jim 'Bo' Evans; and *The Old West*, recorded by Patrick W. McElhoes, all on Americatone International.

AMICOS II MUSIC, LTD., P.O. Box #320-158, Brooklyn NY 11232-0158. (718)332-7427. President: Ziggy Gonzalez. Music publisher, record producer. Estab. 1989. Publishes 10-20 songs/year; publishes up to 10 new songwriters/year. Hires staff songwriters. Works with lyricists. Pays standard royalty.
Affiliate(s): Christian II Music (ASCAP).
How to Contact: Submit demo tape by mail. Unsolicited submissions are OK. Prefers cassette (or VHS videocassette) with 1-5 songs, lyric and lead sheet (if available). "Quality is stressed, submit songs on good cassettes (CRD2/high bias or metal)." SASE. Reports in 1-2 month.
Music: Mostly **R&B/pop, dance/house** and **Latin freestyle**; also **adult contemporary, Latin/salsa** and **Christian contemporary**. Published "So Far Away" (by Victor Franco), recorded by Jaidie on Cutting 4 West (dance/pop); "Lejos de ti" (by Max), recorded by Jaidie on 4 West Records (Latin/salsa); and *Que Bueno Es*, written and recorded by Alberto Lugo on El Elyon/MIM Records (contemporary/Latin Christian).
Tips: "Submit 'pretty' melodic songs with good meaningful lyrics. Would prefer songs with a decent production."

AMIRON MUSIC, Dept. SM, 20531 Plummer St., Chatsworth CA 91311. (818)998-0443. Manager: A. Sullivan. Music publisher, record company, record producer and manager. ASCAP. Estab. 1970. Publishes 2-4 songs/year; publishes 1-2 new songwriters/year. Pays standard royalty.
Affiliate(s): Aztex Productions and Copan Music (BMI).
How to Contact: Prefers cassette (or Beta or VHS videocassette) with any number songs and lyric sheet. SASE. Reports in 10 weeks.
Music: **Easy listening, MOR, progressive, R&B, rock** and **top 40/pop**. Published "Let's Work It Out" (by F. Cruz), recorded by Gangs Back; and "Try Me," written and recorded by Sana Christian, all on AKO Records (pop). Also "Boys Take Your Mind Off Things" (by G. Litvak), recorded by Staunton on Les Disques Records (pop).
Tips: "Send songs with 'good story-lyrics.' "

ANGELSONG PUBLISHING CO., 2723 Westwood Dr., Nashville TN 37204. (615)298-2826 (615)833-9678. President: Mabel Birdsong. BMI, ASCAP. Music publisher and record company (Birdsong Records). Publishes 2 albums/year; publishes 2 new songwriters/year.
Affiliate(s): Prosperous (ASCAP).
How to Contact: Write or call first and obtain permission to submit. Prefers cassette with maximum 4 songs and lyric sheet. Does not return unsolicited material. Reports in 2-3 weeks, "if requested."
Music: Mostly **gospel**, **country** and **MOR**; also **pop**. Published all CD's by Petra; "If You Died Tonight" (by G. Ashworth/D. Sigmon), recorded by Don; and "Revelations" (by Chris Fox), recorded by Abigal Corlew on Angelsong Records.

*ANODE MUSIC (BMI), 417 E. Crosstimbers, Houston TX 77021. (713)694-2971. President: Freddie Kober. Music publisher. Estab. 1982. Publishes 10-15 songs/year; publishes 1-4 new songwriters/year. Pays standard royalty.
How to Contact: Submit demo tape by mail. Unsolicited submissions are OK. Prefers cassette with 2 songs. SASE. Reports in 2 weeks.
Music: Mostly **R&B**, **gospel** and **rap**; also **pop** and **top 40**. Published *Can't Nuthin' Keep Me From You*, *Feel Me Forever* and *My Baby Can* (by Freddie Kober), recorded by Trudy Lynn on Ichiban Records (R&B).

ANOTHER AMETHYST SONG (BMI), 273 Chippewa Dr., Columbia SC 29210-6508. (803)750-5391. Contact: Manager. Music publisher, record company (Amethyst Group). Estab. 1985. Publishes 70 songs/year; publishes 20 new songwriters/year. Works with composers. Pays standard royalty.
How to Contact: Prefers cassette (or VHS videocassette) with 3-7 songs and lyric sheet; include any photos, biographical information. SASE. Reports in 5 weeks.
Music: Mostly **alternative rock**, **pop**, **new wave**, **techno**, **R&B**, **industrial** and **eclectic styles**. Published *PG-13*, recorded by Slither (industrial); *Big Neon Scream*, recorded by Silhouette (alternative); and *Welcome to America*, by various artists. Other artists include The Sages, Ted Neiland and New Fire Ceremony.
Tips: "Simplicity is the key. A hit is a hit regardless of the production. Don't 'overkill' the song! We mainly sign artist/writers. Get ready to cooperate and sign what's necessary. Send as close to an album as possible. We move fast to gain airplay, press and bookings. We also have our artists/writers do showcases."

*ANOTHER EAR MUSIC, Box 110142, Nashville TN 37222-0142. General Manager: T.J. Kirby. BMI, ASCAP. Music publisher, record company (T.J. Records), record producer (T.J. Productions) and management firm (T.J. Productions). Publishes 2 songs/year; publishes 2 new songwriters/year. Works with composers and lyricists; teams collaborators. Pays standard royalty.
Affiliate(s): Peppermint Rainbow Music (ASCAP).
How to Contact: Submit a demo tape with 1-2 songs (or VHS videocassette) by mail. One song only on video with lyric sheets.
Music: Mostly **country/pop** and **R&B**; also **gospel**, **rock** and **"concept songs."** Published "Let it Be Me Tonight" (by Tom Douglas/Bob Lee/T.J. Kirby), recorded by Kathy Ford on Prerie Dust Records; "Don't Take a Heart" (by Kirby/Smith) and "Faster Than a Speeding Bullet" (by Paul Hotchkiss), recorded by Deb Merrit on T.J. Records (country/pop).
Tips: "Videos are great to help present a writer's concept but don't let the ideas of what you would put in a video stand in the way of writing a great song."

ANTELOPE PUBLISHING INC., 23 Lover's Lane, Wilton CT 06897. (203)384-9884. President: Tony LaVorgna. Music publisher. Estab. 1982. Publishes 15-20 new songs/year; publishes 3-5 new songwriters/year. Works with composers and lyricists. Pays standard royalty.
How to Contact: Submit demo tape by mail. Unsolicited submissions are OK. Prefers cassette with lead sheet. Does not return material. Cannot guarantee a response.
Music: Mostly **acoustic jazz** and **MOR vocal**. Published *Somewhere Near* (by T. Lavorgna), recorded by Jeri Brown on Just N Time Records (MOR); *The Train* (by A. Schweitzer) and *All Star Bebop* (by T. Dean), both recorded by Swing Fever on Alto Sounds Records (MOR).

APON PUBLISHING CO. (ASCAP), Box 3082, Steinway Station, Long Island City, NY 11103. Manager: Don Zemann. Music publisher, record company (Apon, Supraphon, Panton and Love Records) and record producer. Exclusive subpublishers of Supraphon and Supraphon CDs, Prague, Czech Republic. Estab. 1957. Publishes 250 songs/year; publishes 50 new songwriters/year. Teams collaborators. Pays standard royalty or according to special agreements made with individual songwriters.
How to Contact: Write or call first and obtain permission to submit. Prefers cassette (or VHS videocassette) with 1-6 songs and lyric sheet. SASE. Reports in 3-4 weeks.
Music: New Age, classical, background music, dance-oriented, easy listening, folk and international. Published "Who Knows" (by B. Sedlacek), recorded by BRNO Radio Orchestra on Panton Records

(background music); "Operatic Arias" (by Peter Dvorsky), recorded by Slovak Symphony Orchestra; and "You Are Everywhere" (by Karel Gott), recorded by J. Staidl Orchestra.

Tips: "We are sub-publishers for pop music from overseas. We publish and record background music for the major background systems operational all over the world. Need only top quality, no synthesizer recordings."

*AQUARIUS PUBLISHING, Servitengasse 24, Vienna A-1090 **Austria.** (+43)1-707-37-10. Fax:(+43)1-707-84-22. Owner: Peter Jordan. Music publisher and record company (World Int'l Records). Estab. 1987. Publishes 100-200 songs/year; publishes 10 new songwriters/year. Works with composers and lyricists; teams collaborators.

How to Contact: Submit demo tape by mail. Unsolicited submissions are OK. Prefers cassette with up to 10 songs. "Lyric sheets not important; send photo of artist." SAE and IRC. Reports in 2-4 weeks.

Music: Mostly **country, pop** and **rock/ballads**; also **folk, instrumental** and **commercial**. Published *Dance With Me* (by S. Tisbert), recorded by Crossover on Fearless Records (country); *The Best is Yet to Come*, written and recorded by Mark McLelland on WIR Records (country); and *Reaching Out* (by M. Whitney), recorded by Insight on Insight Records (pop).

*ARC MUSIC PRODUCTIONS INTERNATIONAL LTD., P.O. Box 111, East Grinstead, West Sussex **United Kingdom.** (0342)328567. Director's Secretary: Uschi Löhle. Music publisher, record company and record producer. Estab. 1987. Works with composers and lyricists. Pays standard royalty.

How to Contact: Write first and obtain permission to submit. Prefers cassette. "Musician/composer demo tapes preferred." Does not return material. Reports in 1 month.

Music: Mostly **world, folk** and **ethnic**; also **bluegrass**. Published *Kike and Pa-Ti*, written and recorded by P. Carcamo (Latin); and *Layali Ramadan*, written and recorded by H. Ramzy (Egypt), all on ARC Productions.

ART AUDIO PUBLISHING COMPANY/TIGHT HI-FI SOUL MUSIC, 9706 Cameron Ave., Detroit MI 48211. (313)893-3406. President: Albert M. Leigh. Professional Manager: Dolores M. Leigh. Music publisher and record company. BMI, ASCAP. Pays standard royalty.

Affiliate(s): Leopard Music (London), Pierre Jaubert, Topomic Music (France), ALPHABET (West Germany), KMW Publishing (South Africa), Kitty Records, Inc. (Japan), Jimco Records (Japan).

How to Contact: Submit demo tape by mail. Unsolicited submissions are OK. Prefers cassette with 1-3 songs and lyric or lead sheets. "Keep lyrics up front on your demo." SASE. Reports in 2 weeks.

Music: House, dance, movie sound tracks and songs for TV specials for the younger generation, uptempo pop rock, mellow R&B dance, uptempo country, uptempo gospel, rap, soul and hip hop. Published "Jesus Showed Us the Way" (by Willie Ayers), recorded by The Morning Echoes of Detroit on Nashboro Records; "I'm Singing Lord," written and recorded by Willie Ayers on X-Tone Records; and "Twon Special" (by Jesse Taylor), recorded by Rock and Roll Sextet on Echoic High Fidelity Records.

Tips: "Basically we are interested only in a new product with a strong sexual uptempo title with a (hook) story. Base it on the good part of your life — no sad songs; we want hot dance and rap. Arrange your songs to match the professional recording artist."

ART OF CONCEPT MUSIC, 1374 Grove St., San Francisco CA 94117. General Manager: Trevor Levine. Music publisher, record company (Fountainhead Records). Estab. 1989. Publishes 6 songs/year; publishes 1 new songwriter/year. Works with composers and lyricists. Pays standard royalty.

How to Contact: Write first and obtain permission to submit. SASE. Does not return material. Reports back in 3 months — *only* if interested in using the material submitted.

Music: Mostly **pop/rock ballads** and "**moderate-paced meaningful rock** (not 'good time rock and roll' or dance music)." Published *6 Months to Live*, *Surrendering My Pride* and *We the People*, all written and recorded by Trevor Levine on Fountainhead Records.

Tips: "We are interested in songs with powerful melodic and lyrical hooks — songs that are beautiful, expressive and meaningful, with uniquely dissonant or dramatic qualities that really *move* the listener. Our songs deal with serious topics, from inner conflicts and troubled relationships to anthems, story songs and message songs which address social and political issues, government corruption, women's and minority issues and human and animal rights. Keep the song's vocal range within an octave, if possible, and no more than 1½ octaves. The music should convey the meaning of the words. Please only contact us if you are interested in having your songs recorded by an artist other than yourself. We listen to the tapes we receive as time permits; however, if the first 20 seconds don't grab us, we move on to the next tape. So always put your best, most emotional, expressive song first, and avoid long introductions."

*ARYLIS CORPORATION (SOCAN), 301-1042 Nelson St., Vancouver, British Columbia V6E 1H8 **Canada.** (604)669-7531. Vice President/A&R: Machiko Yamane. Music publisher, record company,

record producer, distributor. Estab. 1990. Works with performers who produce their own recordings. Pays variable royalty.
How to Contact: Submit demo tape by mail. Unsolicited submissions are OK. Prefers cassette. "Send cassette by air mail only (no couriers please)." Does not return material. Reports in 2 months. "We call only if interested. Artist should call after 2 months."
Music: Mostly **easy listening**, **A/C** and **light jazz**. Published *Lavender*, written and recorded by Christopher on Arylis Records (A/C).
Tips: "We are looking primarily for artists who produce their own recordings, including covers. Instrumental, or vocal."

ASSOCIATED ARTISTS MUSIC INTERNATIONAL (AAMI), Maarschalklaan 47, 3417 SE Montfoort, **The Netherlands**. Phone: (0)3484-72860. Fax: (31)3484-72860. General Manager: Joop Gerrits. Music publisher, record company (Associated Artists Records), record producer (Associated Artists Productions) and radio and TV promoters. BUMA. Estab. 1975. Publishes 200 songs/year; publishes 50 new songwriters/year. Works with composers; teams collaborators. Pays standard royalty.
Affiliate(s): BMC Publishing Holland (BUMA); Hilversum Happy Music (BUMA); Intermelodie and Holland Glorie Productions.
How to Contact: Submit demo tape by mail. Unsolicited submissions are OK. Prefers compact cassette (or VHS videocassette). SAE and IRC. Reports in 6 weeks.
Music: Mostly **disco**, **pop** and **Italian disco**; also **rock**, **gospel (evangelical)**, **musicals**, **MOR** and **country**. Published "U got 2 know" (by Bortolotti), recorded by Cappella on Media Records (dance); "Find the Way" (by Aventino), recorded by Mars Plastic on Zomba Records (dance); and "To Love" (by Bortolotti), recorded by Fits of Gloom on News Records (dance).
Tips: "We are looking for good dance productions."

ASTRODISQUE PUBLISHING, #1001, 6453 Conroy Rd, Orlando FL 32811. (407)295-6311. President: Richard Tiegen. Music publisher, record company (Plum Records) and record producer (Richard Tiegen/Magic Sound Productions). BMI. Estab. 1980. Publishes 15 songs/year; publishes 10 new songwriters/year. Works with composers and lyricists; teams collaborators. Pays standard royalty. "Charges recording and production fees."
How to Contact: Write first to obtain permission to submit. Prefers cassette (or VHS videocassette). Does not return unsolicited material. Reports in 2 weeks.
Music: **Rock**, **R&B** and **country**; also **New Age** and **acoustic**. Published "Star Train Express," "Too Hot to Handle" and "I Need Your Love," (by Letourneau), recorded by Dixie Train on Plum Records.
Tips: "Ask what we are currently looking for stylistically."

ASTRON MUSIC PUBLISHING, 4746 Bowes Ave., P.O. Box 22174, Pittsburgh PA 15122. Director, A&R Manager: Renee Asher. Music publisher and record company. Estab. 1991. Publishes 20 songs/year. Works with composers and lyricists. Pays standard royalty.
How to Contact: Submit demo tape by mail. Unsolicited submissions are OK. Prefers cassette (or VHS videocassette if available) with 3-5 songs and lyric sheet. "Include promotional packages for artists and list of any credits." SASE. Reports in 2 months.
Music: Mostly **rock**, **pop** and **heavy metal**; also **alternative**, **reggae** and **country**. Published *Holy War* (by Piotr Czyszanowski), recorded by Blitzkrieg on Asta Records (alt. pop); "Times to Remember" and "Little Dream Boy," both written and recorded by Steve Cicone on Astron Records (pop).
Tips: "We also sponsor Eclipse East, a regional music industry showcase. Event is annual, generally around October. Write for information."

*****AUCOURANT MUSIC**, P.O. Box 672902, Marietta GA 30067. Artistic Director: Dr. R.S. Thompson. Estab. 1986. Pays standard royalty.
How to Contact: Submit demo tape by mail. Unsolicited submissions are OK. Does not return material. Reports in 4 months.
Music: Mostly **contemporary instrumental**, **avant-garde** and **computer music**; also **experimental pop** and **ambient music**. Published *Deeper in the Dream Time*, *Ginnungagap* and *Shadow Gazing*, all on Aucourant Records (computer music).
Tips: "Know what we are interested in and don't submit material that is *not* of interest to us."

AUDIO MUSIC PUBLISHERS (ASCAP), 449 N. Vista St., Los Angeles CA 90036. (213)653-0693. Contact: Ben Weisman. Music publisher, record company and record producer. Estab. 1962. Publishes 25 songs/year; publishes 10-15 new songwriters/year. Works with composers and lyricists; teams collaborators. Pays standard royalty.
How to Contact: Submit a demo tape by mail. Unsolicited submissions are OK. "No permission needed." Prefers cassette with 3-10 songs and lyric sheet. "We do not return unsolicited material without SASE. Don't query first; just send tape." Reports in 2 weeks.
Music: Mostly **pop**, **R&B**, **rap**, **dance**, **funk**, **soul** and **rock (all types)**.

AUGUST NIGHT MUSIC, P.O. Box 676 Station U, Etobicoke (Toronto), Ontario M8Z 5P7 **Canada**. (416)233-0547. Catalog Manager: Margo Clarke. Music publisher, record company (Whippet Records), record producer. Estab. 1988. Publishes 6-10 songs/year. Publishes 2 new songwriters/year. Works with composers and lyricists. Pays standard royalty.
How to Contact: Submit demo tape by mail. Unsolicited submissions are OK. Prefers cassette with 3-4 songs and lyric sheet. "Label everything in your package: name, address, phone #; use exact time loaded cassettes if possible." SASE (usually sent back including a critique of the material). Reports in 3 weeks.
Music: Mostly **pop/rock, ballads** and **country**; also **R&B** and **New Age**. Published *Don't Let Your Heart Break* (by Dan Alksnis), recorded by Denny Doe; "Solitary Blue" (by Dan Hartland), recorded by Kathryn Eve; and *A Musical Journey* (by Knightscape), recorded by Denny Doe (Irish rock), all on Whippet Records.
Tips: "Although we can 'hear' a song, make the best demo you can afford; write, write, copyright, make your presentation 'professional.' You are competing with Don Henley, Billy Joel, Diane Warren, Lyle Lovett."

*AUM CIRCLE PUBLISHING, Otto-Seeling-Promenade 2-4, Fuerth 90762 **Germany**. (0911)773795. Fax: (0911)747305. Owner: Blazek Dalibor. Music publisher, record company (5233) and recording studio. Estab. 1993. Publishes 68 songs/year; publishes 15 new songwriters/year. Hires staff songwriters. Works with composers and lyricists.
How to Contact: Submit demo tape by mail. Unsolicited submissions are OK. Does not return material. Reports in 1 month.
Music: Mostly **independent rock/pop, rock/pop mainstream** and **industrial**; also **grunge** and **funk rock**. Published *Life Is Not Easy*, by K. Reger (soft rock); and *Misuser* (by B. Meissner), recorded by Slot (industrial), both on 5233 Records.
Tips: "We are looking for high quality material, very straight songs, no 'solo' guitarists!"

AVC MUSIC (ASCAP), Dept. SM, #200, 6201 Sunset Blvd., Los Angeles CA 90028. (213)461-9001. Fax: (213)962-0352. President: James Warsinske. Music publisher. Estab. 1988. Publishes 30-60 songs/year; publishes 10-20 new songwriters/year. Works with composers and lyricists; teams collaborators. Pays standard royalty.
Affiliate(s): Harmonious Music (BMI).
How to Contact: Submit demo tape by mail. Unsolicited submissions OK. Prefers cassette or VHS videocassette with 2-5 songs and lyric sheet. "Clearly labelled tapes with phone numbers." SASE. Reports in 1 month.
Music: Mostly **R&B/soul, pop** and **rock**; also **rap, metal** and **dance**. Published "Let It Be Right," written and recorded by Duncan Faure on AVC Records (pop/rock); "Melissa Mainframe" (by Hohl/Rocca), recorded by Rocca on Life Records (pop/rap); and "In Service" (by Michael Williams), recorded by Madrok on AVC Records (rap).
Tips: "Be yourself, let your talents shine regardless of radio trends."

AXBAR PRODUCTIONS (BMI), Box 12353, San Antonio TX 78212. (210)829-1909. Business Manager: Joe Scates. Music publisher, record company, record producer and record distributors. Member CMA. Estab. 1978. Publishes 30 songs/year; publishes 10-12 new songwriters/year. Works with composers. Pays standard royalty.
Affiliate(s): Axe Handle Music (ASCAP), Scates and Blanton (BMI).
How to Contact: Submit a demo tape by mail. Unsolicited submissions are OK. Prefers cassette (or VHS videocassette) with 1-5 songs and lyric sheet. SASE. Reports as soon as possible, but "we hold the better songs for more detailed study."
Music: Mostly **country**; also **country crossover, comedy, blues, MOR** and **rock (soft)**. Published "Like Smoke In The Wind," recorded by Billy D. Hunter on Axbar (country); "Since My Woman Set Me Free," written and recorded by Jackson Boone on Trophy Records (country); and "Heartache County" recorded by Mark Chesnutt on Axbar (country).
Tips: "Send only your best efforts. We have plenty of album cuts and flip sides. We need hit songs."

BABY HUEY MUSIC (ASCAP), P.O. Box 121616, Nashville TN 37212. (615)269-9958. President: Mark Stephan Hughes. Music publisher, record company. Estab. 1969. Publishes 100 songs/year; publishes 4-5 new songwriters/year. Hires staff writers. Pays standard royalty.
Affiliate(s): Krimson Hues Music (BMI).
How to Contact: Submit demo tape by mail. Unsolicited submissions are OK. Prefers cassette with 3 songs and lyric sheet. SASE. Reports in 4-5 months.
Music: **Christian**; focusing on praise, worship and scripture songs. Also accepting Messianic Jewish music. Published "Jesus Says," written and recorded by Lanier Ferguson; "He'll Make a Way," written and recorded by Kathy Davis; and "You Are Exalted," written and recorded by Mark Stephan Hughes, all on Fresh Start Records.

Tips: "Make a demo worthy of your song. Your presentation reflects your confidence in your material. Always give it the best consideration you can afford. Be led by the Spirit."

BABY RAQUEL MUSIC, 15 Gloria Lane, Fairfield NJ 07006. (201)575-7460. President: Mark S. Berry. Music publisher. ASCAP, BMI. Estab. 1984. Publishes 5-10 songs/year; publishes 1-2 new songwriters/ year. Teams collaborators. Pays standard royalty.
Affiliate(s): Raquels Songs (BMI).
How to Contact: Submit a demo tape by mail. Unsolicited submissions are OK. Prefers cassette with 1-3 songs and lyric sheet. SASE. Reports in 2-3 weeks.
Music: Mostly **alternative, pop/dance** and **pop/rock.** Published "Say Goodbye" (by M. Berry, M. Sukowski), recorded by Indecent Obsession on MCA Records (rock); "I Feel Love" (by M. Smith, M. Berry), recorded by Fan Club on Epic Records (pop/dance); and "Crazy for You" (by M. Berry), recorded by White Heat on Sony/Canada Records (rock). Other artists include Elvis Manson and Clutter.

*BAD HABITS MUSIC PUBLISHING, 7 Drayton Grove, London W13 0LA **England.** (+44)81 991 1516. Fax: (+44)81 566 7215. Managing Director: John S. Rushton. Music publisher, record company (Bad Habits) and record producer. Estab. 1991. Hires staff songwriters. Works with composers and lyricists; teams collaborators. Royalty varies depending upon type of contract.
Affiliate(s): Great Life Music Publishing (ASCAP), BHMP (America) (BMI).
How to Contact: Submit demo tape by mail. Unsolicited submissions are OK. Prefers cassette (or VHS or Beta videocassette) with 3 songs. "Include what the writer lyricist wants to do, brief details/ aspirations." SASE. Reports in 2 weeks.
Music: Mostly **pop/rock/dance, soul** and **jazz;** also **classical/opera, soundtracks/shows** and **New Age.** Published "Baby Jane," recorded by Lunchbox; *Silk* (by Kook), recorded by The Sway (indie); and *Green* (by Green), recorded by J. Green (soul), all on Bad Habits Records.
Tips: "Focus your talents (writing/orchestration) and make sure that it is professionally presented (music wise)."

BAL & BAL MUSIC PUBLISHING CO. (ASCAP), P.O. Box 369, LaCanada CA 91012-0369. (818)548-1116. President: Adrian P. Bal. Music publisher, record company (Bal Records) and record producer. Member AGAC and AIMP. Estab. 1965. Publishes 2-6 songs/year; publishes 2-4 new songwriters/ year. Works with composers; teams collaborators. Pays standard royalty.
Affiliate(s): Bal West Music Publishing Co. (BMI).
How to Contact: Submit a demo tape by mail. Unsolicited submissions are OK. Prefers cassette with 3 songs and lyric sheet. SASE. Reports in 6 weeks.
Music: Mostly **MOR, country, rock** and **gospel;** also **blues, church/religious, easy listening,** jazz, **R&B, soul** and **top 40/pop.** Published "Fragile" (by James Jackson), recorded by Kathy Simmons; "Circles of Time," written and recorded by Paul Richards (A/C); and "Dance to the Beat of My Heart" (by Dan Gertz), recorded by Ace Baker (medium rock), all on Bal Records.

BARKING FOE THE MASTER'S BONE, #520, 1111 Elm St., Cincinnati OH 45210-2271. Office Manager: Kevin Curtis. Music publisher. Estab. 1989. Publishes 16 songs/year; publishes 2 new songwriters/ year. Works with composers and lyricists; teams collaborators. Pays 66% royalty.
Affiliate(s): Beat Box Music (ASCAP), Feltstar (BMI).
How to Contact: Submit demo tape by mail. Unsolicited submissions are OK. Prefers cassette (or VHS videocassette) with 3 songs. SASE. Reports in 2 weeks.
Music: Mostly **country, soft rock** and **pop;** also **soul, gospel** and **rap.** Published "Stroke What Feels On Fire", "Playboy's Paradise" and "Thrill Me Easy" (by Kevin Curtis/Dave Arps), recorded by Santarr on Warner Bros. Records.
Tips: "Take a lesson from seasoned performers such as Bette Midler, Ray Charles and Chaka Khan, the noted 'Queen of R&B,' all of whom continue to allow their own brand of musical style to affect generations to come."

BARTOW MUSIC, 324 N. Bartow St., Cartersville GA 30120. (404)386-7243. Publishing Administrator: Jack C. Hill. Producer: Tirus McClendon. Music publisher and record producer (HomeBoy, Ragtime Productions). BMI. Estab. 1988. Publishes 5 songs/year; 5 new songwriters/year. Works with composers and lyricists; teams collaborators. Pays standard royalty.
How to Contact: Submit a demo tape by mail. Unsolicited submissions are OK. Prefers cassette (or VHS videocassette) with 3 songs and lyric sheets. Does not return unsolicited material. Reports in 1 month.
Music: R&B, **pop, dance** and **house.** Published "Emerson Girl" (by D. Maxwell), recorded by D.G.I. Posse (rap); "Give You All My Love" (by A. Hall), recorded by Daybreak (R&B); and "Dreaming" (by T. McClendon), recorded by The Girls, all on Bartow Music.

BEARSONGS, Box 944, Birmingham, B16 8UT **England**. Phone: 44-021-454-7020. Managing Director: Jim Simpson. Music publisher and record company (Big Bear Records). Member PRS, MCPS. Publishes 25 songs/year; publishes 15-20 new songwriters/year. Pays standard royalty.
How to Contact: Submit demo tape by mail. Unsolicited submissions are OK. Prefers reel-to-reel or cassette. Does not return material. Reports in 3 weeks.
Music: Blues and **jazz**. Published *I've Finished With The Blues* and *Blues For Pleasure* (by Skirring/Nicholls), recorded by Fins Pleasure and The Biscuit Boys; and *Side-Steppin* (by Barnes), recorded by Alan Barnes/Bruce Adams Quintet, all on Big Bear Records.

BERANDOL MUSIC LTD. (BMI), Unit 220, 2600 John St., Markham ON L3R 3W3 **Canada**. (416)475-1848. A&R Director: Ralph Cruickshank. Music publisher, record company (Berandol Records), record producer and distributor. Member CMPA, CIRPA, CRIA. Estab. 1969. Publishes 20-30 songs/year; publishes 5-10 new songwriters/year. Works with composers. Pays standard royalty.
How to Contact: Submit demo tape by mail. Unsolicited submissions are OK. Prefers cassette with 2-5 songs. Does not return unsolicited material. Reports in 2 weeks.
Music: Mostly **instrumental, children**'s and **top 40**.
Tips: "Strong melodic choruses and original sounding music receive top consideration."

HAL BERNARD ENTERPRISES, INC., P.O. Box 8385, 2612 Erie Ave., Cincinnati OH 45208. (513)871-1500. Fax: (513)871-1510. President: Stan Hertzman. Professional Manager: Pepper Bonar. Music publisher, record company and management firm. Publishes 12-24 songs/year; 1-2 new songwriters/year. Works with composers. Pays standard royalty.
Affiliate(s): Sunnyslope Music (ASCAP), Bumpershoot Music (BMI), Apple Butter Music (ASCAP), Carb Music (ASCAP), Saiko Music (ASCAP), Smorgaschord Music (ASCAP) and Clifton Rayburn Music (ASCAP), Robert Stevens Music (ASCAP).
How to Contact: Submit a demo tape by mail. Unsolicited submissions are OK. Prefers cassette with 3 songs and lyric sheet. SASE. Reports in 6 weeks.
Music: Rock, R&B and **top 40/pop**. Published "Standing In the Shadow," "Inner Revolution" and "This Is What I Believe In," all written and recorded by Adrian Belew on Atlantic Records (progressive pop), and "Angel," "Big Love Now" and "Stella," all recorded by psychodots on Strugglebaby Records.
Tips: "Best material should appear first on demo. Cast your demos. If you as the songwriter can't sing it — don't. Get someone who can present your song properly, use a straight rhythm track and keep it as naked as possible. If you think it still needs something else, have a string arranger, etc. help you, but still keep the *voice up* and the *lyrics clear*."

BEST BUDDIES, INC. (BMI), Dept. SM, 2100 8th Ave. South, Nashville TN 37204. (615)383-7664. Contact: Review Committee. Music publisher, record company (X-cuse Me) and record producer (Best Buddies Productions). Estab. 1981. Publishes 18 songs/year. Publishes 1-2 new songwriters/year. Pays standard royalty.
Affiliate(s): Swing Set Music (ASCAP), Best Buddies Music (BMI).
How to Contact: Write first and obtain permission to submit. Must include SASE with permission letter. Prefers cassette (or VHS videocassette) with maximum 3 songs. SASE. Reports in 8 weeks. Do not call to see if tape received.
Music: Mostly **country, rock** and **pop**; also **gospel** and **R&B**. Published "Somebody Wrong is Looking Right" (by King/Burkholder), recorded by Bobby Helms; "Give Her Back Her Faith in Me" (by Ray Dean James), recorded by David Speegle (country); and "I Can't Get Over You Not Loving Me" (by Misty Efron and Bobbie Sallee), recorded by Sandy Garwood, all on Bitter Creek Records (country).
Tips: "Make a professional presentation. There are no second chances on first impressions."

BETHLEHEM MUSIC PUBLICATIONS, P.O. Box 201, Tecumseh OK 74873. (405)598-6379. President/Manager: Darrell V. Archer. Music publisher, record company and record producer. Estab. 1970. Publishes 50 songs/year; publishes 8-10 new songwriters/year. Works with composers or lyricists; teams collaborators. Pays standard royalty. Print publications pay a different royalty (normally 10% of retail) that is divided between the writers.
Affiliate(s): Archer Music, Rapture Music Publications, Courier Records, Conarch Publications, Rapture Records.
How to Contact: Submit demo tape by mail. Unsolicited submissions are OK. Prefers cassette with 3 songs and lyric or lead sheet. "Make sure all lyrics are either typewritten or neatly printed and that your submissions are accompanied by a SASE." Reports in 2 months.
Music: Mostly **MOR, sacred, southern gospel** and **easy listening contemporary**; also **spirituals, choir material** and **youth/children's material**. Published *There's Not a Doubt* (by Archer), recorded by Morning Chapel Hour on Courier Records (gospel); *Lord, Wrap Me Up In You* (by Walker), recorded by Archer on Courier Records (contemporary); and *Just As I Am* (by Lehmann), recorded by Bethlehem Choir on Bethlehem Records (traditional).

Tips: "Make sure your song has good form and focus. Try to approach your subject matter in a fresh way or from a new perspective."

BETH-RIDGE MUSIC PUBLISHING CO., Dept. SM, Suite 204, 1508 Harlem, Memphis TN 38114. (901)274-2726. Professional Manager: Janelle Rachal. Music publisher, record company, record producer and recording studio. BMI. Estab. 1978. Publishes 40 songs/year; publishes 10 new songwriters/year. Pays standard royalty.
Affiliate(s): Chartbound Music Ltd. (ASCAP).
How to Contact: "Write to see what our needs are." Prefers cassette (or VHS videocassette) with 3 songs and lyric sheet. SASE for return of materials. Reports in 1 month.
Music: Mostly R&B, top 40, dance and blues; also soul and gospel. Published "Hooked on Love," written and recorded by Eddie Mayberry on Blue Town Records (blues/R&B); "Love Song" (by Steve-A), recorded by First Class Crew on GCS Records; and "Call on Jesus" (by various artists), recorded by Voices of Hope on GCS Records (gospel).

*BETTER THAN SEX MUSIC (ASCAP), Suite 3E, 140 7th Ave., New York NY 10011. (212)645-1600. Partners: James Citkovic, Wolfgang Busch. Music publisher, record company. Estab. 1993. Publishes 1-10 songs/year; publishes 1-10 new songwriters/year. Hires staff songwriters. Works with composers and lyricists; teams collaborators. Pays standard royalty.
How to Contact: Submit demo tape by mail. Unsolicited submissions are OK. "No phone calls!" Prefers cassette (or VHS videocassette) with 3-5 songs and lyric sheet. SASE for letter reply. Reports in 6 weeks.
Music: Mostly pop rock, alternative rock and R&B; also female fronted rock, female fronted alternative rock and male/female R&B. Published "S.O.S." (by James Page), recorded on Jamic Entertainment (R&B).

BETTY JANE/JOSIE JANE MUSIC PUBLISHERS, 7400 N. Adams Rd., North Adams MI 49262. (517)287-4421. Professional Manager: Claude E. Reed. Music publisher and record company (C.E.R. Records). BMI, ASCAP. Estab. 1980. Publishes 20+ songs/year; 10 new songwriters/year. Works with composers and lyricists; teams collaborators. Pays standard royalty.
Affiliate(s): Betty Jane Music Publishing Co. (BMI) and Josie Jane Music Publishing Co. (ASCAP).
How to Contact: Submit a demo tape by mail. Unsolicited submissions are OK. Prefers cassette or 7½ ips reel-to-reel with up to 5 songs and lyric or lead sheets. "We prefer typewritten and numbered lyric sheets and good professional quality demo tapes." SASE. Reports in 2-3 weeks.
Music: Mostly gospel and country western; also R&B. Published *Coming Down*, *Lambsong* and *Blessed Rock of Ages* all by Dr. Charles Cravey, recorded by Rev. C. Cravey, C.E.R. (gospel).
Tips: "Try to be original, present your music in a professional way, with accurate lyric sheets and well made demo tape. Send SASE with a sufficient amount of postage if you wish material returned."

BIG SNOW MUSIC (BMI), P.O. Box 21323, Eagan MN 55121. President: Mitch Viegut. Vice President and General Manager: Mark Alan. Music publisher. Estab. 1989. Publishes 30 new songs/year; publishes 4 new songwriters/year. Works with composers and lyricists; teams collaborators. Pays standard royalty.
How to Contact: Write first and obtain permission to submit. Prefers cassette with 3 songs and lyric sheet. SASE. Reports in 2-3 months.
Music: Mostly rock, metal and pop/rock. Published "Somewhere" (by Mitch Viegut) and "85 mph" (by Mitch Viegut, Dave Saindon, Roger Prubert), both on Curb Records and "Thief in the Night" (by Doug Dixon and Mitch Viegut), on Premiére Records (rock), all recorded by Airkraft.

BLACK STALLION COUNTRY PUBLISHING, Box 368, Tujunga CA 91043. (818)352-8142. Fax: (818)352-2122. President: Kenn Kingsbury. Music publisher and book publisher (*Who's Who in Country & Western Music*). BMI. Member CMA, CMF. Publishes 2 songs/year; publishes 1 new songwriter/year. Pays standard royalty.
How to Contact: Prefers 7½ ips reel-to-reel or cassette with 2-4 songs and lyric sheet. SASE. Reports in 1 month.
Music: Bluegrass and country.
Tips: "Be professional in attitude and presentation. Submit only the material you think is better than anything being played on the radio."

*BLUE CUE MUSIC (GEMA), Frankenholzer Str. 1, Bexbach 66450 Germany. (49)6826-80909. Fax: (49)6826-80738. General Manager: Peter Hayo. Music publisher and record producer. Estab. 1988. Publishes 25 songs/year; publishes 2-3 new songwriters/year. Teams collaborators. Pays "standard royalty as fixed by German GEMA."
How to Contact: Submit demo tape by mail. Unsolicited submissions are OK. Prefers cassette. SAE and IRC. Reports in 1 month.

Music: Mostly **pop, dance** and **ballads**; also **rock.** Published "Secret Fire"(by Kannerneier), recorded by Planet Claire on EMI-Electrola Records (pop); "Paradise"(by Merziger/Kessler), recorded by Chakra and "Pain In My Heart"(by Merziger/Branden B.), recorded by Zulu, both on Sony Music (dance).

BLUE HILL MUSIC/TUTCH MUSIC (BMI), 308 Munger Lane, Bethlehem CT 06751. Contact: Paul Hotchkiss. Music publisher, record company (Target Records, Kastle Records) and record producer (Red Kastle Records). Estab. 1975. Publishes 20 songs/year; publishes 1-5 new songwriters/year. Pays standard royalty.
How to Contact: Write first and obtain permission to submit a tape. Prefers cassette with 2 songs and lyric sheet. "Demos should be clear with vocals out in front." Does not return unsolicited material. Reports in 2 weeks.
Music: Mostly **country** and **country/pop;** also **MOR** and **blues.** Published "Destination You," written and recorded by M. Terry on Roto Noto Records (country/pop); "Midnight Dancer" (by P. Hotchkiss), recorded by Gerry King on Saddlestone Records (country); and "Memory of You" (by Jesse Lane), recorded by Stoney Edwards on Hill Country Records (country/pop).

BLUE SPUR MUSIC GROUP, INC. (ASCAP), 358 W. Hackamore, Gilbert AZ 85233. (602)892-4451. Director of A&R: Esther Burch. President: Terry Olson. A&R: Beve Rhyan Cole. Music publisher, artist development/management, promotion. Estab. 1990. Royalty varies.
How to Contact: Write or call first and obtain permission to submit. Prefers cassette with 3-5 songs and lyric sheet. "Please send only songs protected by copyright. Please be sure submissions are cassette form and call for coded submission number to insure your material will be given our full attention." Does not return unsolicited material. Reports back in 6-12 weeks.
Music: Mostly **contemporary country** and **gospel.**
Tips: "Study the market carefully, listen to the trends, attend a local songwriter's association; be committed to your craft and be persistent. Write, write and re-write!"

BOAM (ASCAP), P.O. Box 201, Smyrna GA 30081. (404)432-2454. A&R: Tom Hodges. Music publisher. Estab. 1965. Publishes 20 songs/year; publishes 4 new songwriters/year. Teams collaborators. Pays standard royalty.
Affiliate(s): Mimic Music, Stepping Stone, Skip Jack (BMI).
How to Contact: Submit demo tape by mail. Unsolicited submissions are OK. Prefers cassette (or VHS videocassette) with 6 songs and lyric or lead sheet. SASE. Reports in 3 weeks.
Music: Mostly **country, R&B** and **MOR;** also **rock, gospel** and **folk.** Published "Reborn" and "Living On Borrowed Time," written and recorded by J. McClain; and "Where Is Sundae," written and recorded by Caps, all on Trend Records.

BoDe MUSIC (ASCAP), Suite 228, 18016 S. Western Ave., Gardena CA 90248. President: Ms. Tory Gullett. Music publisher. Estab. 1990. Publishes 12-15 songs/year; publishes 6-10 new songwriters/year. Pays standard royalty.
Affiliate(s): Gullett Music (BMI).
How to Contact: Submit demo tape by mail. Unsolicited submissions are OK. Prefers cassette with 3 songs and lyric sheet. SASE. Reports in 1 month.
Music: Country. Published "How Many Times" (by Nathan Kory); "The Other Side" (by Kheri Han); and "The Best Heartache a Cheater Ever Had" (by Paul Austin and Sarah Summers).
Tips: "With country's ignited rise, the competition is stiff. You *have* to be a great songwriter and you have to follow up on every contact."

BOK MUSIC, P.O. Box 17838, Encino CA 91416. Fax: (818)705-5346. President: Monica Benson. Music publisher. Estab. 1989. Publishes 30 songs/year; 20 new songwriters/year. Works with composers and lyricists; teams collaborators. Pays standard royalty.
Affiliate(s): Wild Pink Music (ASCAP).
How to Contact: Submit demo tape by mail. "Do not call!!" Prefers cassette with 4 songs and lyric sheet. "I listen to everything I receive. I'll respond only if interested."
Music: Mostly **pop/A/C, R&B** and **rock.** Published "So Intense" (by Essra Mohawk), recorded by Lisa Fischer on Elektra Records; "Hoops of Fire" (by Nina Ossoff/Jeff Franzel/Porter Carroll), recorded by Temptations on Motown Records; and "Remember Who You Are" (by Lynn DeFino/Roxanna Ward), recorded by Phyllis Hyman on MoJazz Records (all R&B).
Tips: "I look for great lyrics."

*BOLLMAN INTERNATIONAL PUBLISHING CO. (BMI), P.O. Box 121833, Fort Worth TX 76121. (817)626-8300. Owner: B.L. Bollman. Music publisher and record company. Estab. 1972. Publishes 75-100 songs/year; publishes 7-8 new songwriters/year. Works with composers. Pays negotiable royalty.

Affiliate(s): Misty-Christy Publishing (ASCAP).
How to Contact: Submit demo tape by mail. Unsolicited submissions are OK. Prefers cassette. Does not return material.
Music: Mostly **gospel, country** and **Spanish**. Published "Have a Nice Day Comma Marge," written and recorded by Ken Powers (country); "Bear Creek Jump," written and recorded by Dale Potter (country); and "Love Personified" (by Harry T. Crawley), recorded by Wendy Nelson (gospel), all on Show Biz Records.

BONNFIRE PUBLISHING, P.O. Box 6429, Huntington Beach CA 92615-6429. (714)962-5618. Contact: Eva and Stan Bonn. Music publisher, record company (ESB Records) and record producer. ASCAP, BMI. Estab. 1987. Pays standard royalty.
Affiliate(s): Bonnfire Publishing (ASCAP) and Gather 'Round Music (BMI).
How to Contact: Submit demo cassette by mail with lyric sheet. Unsolicited submissions OK. SASE. Reports in 2 weeks.
Music: **Country (all forms)**. Published *Don't Throw Stones* (by Jack Schroeder), recorded by John P. Swisshelm on ESB Records (country); "I'll Never Know Why Love Ends" (by Rick Streitfel), recorded by Josie K on Pegasus Records (pop); and "The Sounds of the Universe" (by Stan Bonn/Eddie Sheppard), recorded by Bobby Lee Caldwell on ESB Records (pop country).

*BOURNE CO. MUSIC PUBLISHERS (ASCAP), 5 W. 37th St., New York NY 10018. (212)391-4300. Fax: (212)391-4306. President: Bebe Bourne. Professional Director: Thomas Morrison. Music publisher. Estab. 1919. Works with composers and lyricists; teams collaborators.
Affiliate(s): Murbo Music Publishing, Inc. (BMI).
How to Contact: Write or call first and obtain permission to submit. Prefers cassette with 3 songs maximum and lyric sheet. SASE. Reports in 2 months.
Music: Mostly **pop, ballads** and **R&B**; also **future standards**. Published "Unforgettable" (by Irving Gordon), recorded by Natalie Cole with Nat 'King' Cole on Elektra Records (pop); and "In The Wee Small Hours of The Morning" (by Bob Hilliard/David Mann), recorded by Carly Simon and Frank Sinatra on Capitol Records (pop/AC).

*BRANCH GROUP MUSIC, 1067 Sherwin Rd., Winnipeg MB R3H 0T8 **Canada**. (204)694-3101. President: Gilles Paquin. Music publisher, record company (Oak Street Music) and record producer (Oak Street Music). SOCAN. Estab. 1987. Publishes 10 songs/year; publishes 2 new songwriters/year. Works with composers and lyricists; teams collaborators. Pays negotiable royalty.
Affiliate(s): Forest Group Music (SOCAN).
How to Contact: Submit a demo tape by mail. Unsolicited submissions are OK. Prefers cassette or VHS videocassette with 2-3 songs and lyric and lead sheet. SAE and IRC. Reports in 1-2 months.
Music: Mostly **children's** and **novelty**. Published "Sandwiches" (by Bob King), "The Season" (by Fred Penner), and "Christmasy Kind of Day" (by Ken Whiteley); all recorded by Fred Penner on Oak Street Records.

*KITTY BREWSTER SONGS, "Norden," 2 Hillhead Rd., Newtonhill Stonehaven AB3 2PT **Scotland**. Phone: 0569 730962. MD: Doug Stone. Music publisher, record company (KBS Records), record producer and production company (Brewster & Stone Productions). Estab. 1989. Works with composers and lyricists; teams collaborators. Pays standard royalty.
How to Contact: Submit demo tape by mail. Unsolicited submissions are OK. Prefers cassette (or VHS videocassette if available) with any amount of songs and lyric or lead sheet. Does not return material. Reports in 3-4 months.
Music: Mostly **AOR, pop, R&B** and **dance**; also **country, jazz, rock** and **contemporary**. Published *Sleepin' Alone* (by R. Donald); *I Still Feel the Same* (by R. Greig/K. Mundie); and *Your Love Will Pull Me Thru* (by R. Greig), all recorded by Kitty Brewster on KBS Records (AOR).

BRONX FLASH MUSIC, INC., Suite 300, 3151 Cahuenga Blvd. W., Los Angeles CA 90068. (213)882-6127. Fax: (213)882-8414. Professional Manager: Michael Schneider. Music publisher. BMI, ASCAP. Estab. 1990. Publishes 50 songs/year; publishes 1-2 new songwriters/year. Hires staff writers. Works with composers and lyricists; teams collaborators. Royalty varies depending on particular songwriter (never less than 50%).

How to Get the Most Out of Songwriter's Market (at the front of this book) contains comments and suggestions to help you understand and use the information in these listings.

Affiliate(s): Eagles Dare Music (ASCAP) and Kenwon Music (BMI).
How to Contact: Write or call first for permission to submit. Prefers cassette with maximum of 3 songs. Does not return unsolicited material. Reports in 1 month.
Music: Mostly **pop**, **R&B** and **rock**. Published "You Are My Home" (by F. Wildhorn), recorded by Peabo Bryson/Linda Elder; and *The Scarlet Pimpernel* (by F. Wildhorn) (cast album), both on EMI.
Tips: "Keep it clever. Keep it short."

BUG MUSIC, INC., Dept. SM, 9th Floor, 6777 Hollywood, Los Angeles CA 90028. (213)466-4352. Contact: Temple Ray. Music publisher. BMI, ASCAP. Estab. 1975. Other offices: Nashville contact Dave Durocher and London contact Mark Anders. "We handle administration."
Affiliate(s): Bughouse (ASCAP).
How to Contact: Prefers cassette. Does not return unsolicited material.
Music: All genres. Published "Rollin' And Tumblin'," (by Muddy Waters), recorded by Eric Clapton; "Search And Destroy" (by Iggy Pop), recorded by Red Hot Chili Peppers; "The Nightingale" (by Jude Johnstone), recorded by Trisha Yearwood; "Raw Power" (by Iggy Pop), recorded by Guns & Roses; and "One Moment To Another" (by Jon Dee Graham), recorded by Patty Smyth.

BULLET PROOF MANAGEMENT, (formerly G Fine Sounds), Suite 13G, 2 Washington Square Village, New York NY 10012-1701. (212)995-1608. President: Jonathan P. Fine. Music publisher, record producer, artist management. Estab. 1986. Publishes 25 songs/year. Publishes 4 new songwriters. Works with composers and lyricists; teams collaborators.
How to Contact: Submit demo tape by mail. Unsolicited submissions are OK. Prefers high bias cassette (or VHS videocassette if available); 3 songs and lyric sheet. "Prefers DAT or metal cassette." SASE. Reports in 2 months only if interested.
Music: Mostly **rap**, **alternative rock** and **R&B**; also **rock** and **reggae**. Published "Ring the Alarm," "Be Bo" and "Back Off" (by Lyvio G/Fu-Schnickens), recorded by Fu-Schnickens on Jive Records.
Tips: "Send innovative material of superior quality."

BURIED TREASURE MUSIC (ASCAP), 524 Doral Country Dr., Nashville TN 37221. Executive Producer: Scott Turner. Music publisher and record producer (Aberdeen Productions). Estab. 1972. Publishes 30-50 songs/year; publishes 3-10 new songwriters/year. Works with composers and lyricists. Pays standard royalty.
Affiliate(s): Captain Kidd Music (BMI).
How to Contact: Submit a demo tape by mail. Unsolicited submissions are OK. Prefers cassette (or VHS videocassette) with 1-4 songs and lyric sheet. Reports in 2½ weeks. "Always enclose SASE if answer is expected."
Music: **Country** and **country/pop**; also **rock**, **MOR** and **contemporary**. Published "Rise Above It" (by Steve Rose), recorded by Brittany Hale on G.B.S. Records (country); *Pieces of You* (by Nanette Malher), recorded by Sheylyn Jaymes on T.B.A. Records (country); and "A Woman Can" (by Dave Travis), recorded by Jim Cartwright on Hawk Records (country).
Tips: "*Don't* send songs in envelopes that are 15"x 20", or by registered mail. It doesn't help a bit. Say something that's been said a thousand times before . . . only say it differently. A great song doesn't care who sings it. Songs that paint pictures have a better chance of ending up as videos. With artists only recording 10 songs every 18-24 months, the advice is . . . Patience!"

BILL BUTLER MUSIC (BMI), P.O. Box 20, Hondo TX 78861. (210)426-2112. President: Bill Butler. Music publisher and record producer. Estab. 1979. Publishes 75 songs/year; publishes 3-6 new songwriters/year. Works with composers or lyricists; teams collaborators. Pays standard royalty.
Affiliate(s): Republic of Texas Publishing (ASCAP) and Hill Country Publishing (BMI).
How to Contact: Submit demo tape by mail. Unsolicited submissions are OK. Prefers cassette with 3-5 songs and lyric sheet. "Must be quality demos with lyrics clearly understandable." Does not return unsolicited material. Reports in 6 weeks.
Music: Mostly **country**, **country rock** and **soul**; also **R&B** and **Tejano**. Published "Love Without End, Amen" and "Baby Blue" (by Aaron Barker), recorded by George Strait on MCA Records (country); and "Taste of Freedom," written and recorded by Aaron Barker on Atlantic Records (country).
Tips: "We look for lyrics that are different from most songs. They must say the same thing as other songs, but from a fresh perspective."

*BUZZART ENTERPRISES, Top Floor, 169 Pier Ave., Santa Monica CA 90405. (310)392-3088. Fax: (310)392-0931. Co-President: Arthur Berggren. Music publisher. Estab. 1986. Publishes 10 songs/year; publishes 1 new songwriter/year. Works with composers. Pays standard royalty.
Affiliate(s): Buzzart Music (BMI).
How to Contact: Submit demo tape by mail. Unsolicited submissions are OK. Prefers cassette with lyric and lead sheet. SASE. Reports in 1 month.

Music: Mostly A/C, **rock** and **country**. Published "Monkey In the Jungle" (by Neal Sunder), recorded by Rattling Bones on Atlantic Records.
Tips: "Have highly produced master recordings available on DAT."

*CACTUS MUSIC AND WINNEBAGO PUBLISHING (ASCAP), P.O. Box 1027, Neenah WI 54957-1027. President: Tony Ansems. Music publisher and record company (Fox Records). Estab. 1984. Publishes 5-8 songs/year; publishes 3-5 new songwriters/year. Works with composers. Pays standard royalty.
How to Contact: Submit demo tape by mail. Unsolicited submissions are OK. Prefers cassette with 3 songs maximum and lyric sheet. SASE. Reports in 1 month.
Music: Mostly **C&W** and **gospel**. Published *Wet Paint Don't Touch* (by Eugene Wellmann, Tony Ansems and Tarheel Pete); *God's Holy Hands* (by Bob Rose); and *We Don't See Eye to Eye* (by Jim Hall and Bob Rose), all recorded by Tony Ansems on Tarheel Records.

*JOHN CALE MUSIC, INC., Suite 1410, 270 Madison Ave., New York NY 10016. (212)683-5320. Fax: (212)686-2182. Contact: Christopher Whent. Music publisher, record company and record producer. Estab. 1983. Publishes 20 songs/year. Works with composers and lyricists. Pays standard royalty.
How to Contact: Write or call first and obtain permission to submit. Prefers cassette and lyric or lead sheet. Does not return material. Reports in 2 months.
Music: Mostly **rock**; also **classical**. Published *Coyote* (by John Cale/Lou Reed), recorded by Velvet Underground on Sire Records (rock); *Library of Force*, written and recorded by John Cale on Rhino Records (rock); and *23 Pieces*, written and recorded by John Cale on Crépescule Records (classical).

CALIFORNIA COUNTRY MUSIC (BMI), 112 Widmar Pl., Clayton CA 94517. (510)672-8201. Owner: Edgar J. Brincat. Music publisher, record company (Roll On Records). Estab. 1985. Publishes 30 songs/year; publishes 2-4 new songwriters/year. Works with composers and lyricists; teams collaborators. Pays standard royalty.
Affiliate(s): Sweet Inspirations Music (ASCAP).
How to Contact: Submit a demo tape by mail. Unsolicited submissions are OK. Prefers cassette with 3 songs and lyric sheet. Any calls will be returned collect to caller. SASE. Reports in 2-4 weeks.
Music: Mostly **MOR, contemporary country** and **pop**; also **R&B, gospel** and **light rock**. Published "Outskirts of Phoenix" (by Petrella Pollefeyt), "Write to P.O. Box 33" (by Michael Gooch/Susan Branding) and "Never Thought Of Losing You" (by Jeanne Dickey-Boyter/Gina Dempsey), all recorded by Edee Gordon and the Flash Band.
Tips: "Listen to what we have to say about your product. Be as professional as possible."

CALINOH MUSIC GROUP, 608 W. Iris Dr., Nashville TN 37204. (615)292-3568. Contact: Ann Hofer or Tom Cornett. Music publisher. Estab. 1992. Publishes 50 songs/year; publishes 10 new songwriters/year. Teams collaborators. Pays standard royalty.
Affiliate(s): Little Liberty Town (ASCAP) and West Manchester Publishing (BMI).
How to Contact: Submit demo tape by mail. Unsolicited submissions are OK. Prefers cassette with 3 songs and lyric sheet. "Include SASE." Does not return unsolicited material.
Music: Mostly **country, gospel** and **pop**.

CALVARY MUSIC GROUP, INC., Dept. SM, 142 Eighth Ave. N., Nashville TN 37203. (615)244-8800. President: Dr. Nelson S. Parkerson. Music publisher and record company ASCAP, BMI, SESAC. Publishes 30-40 songs/year; publishes 2-3 new songwriters/year. Pays standard royalty.
Affiliate(s): Songs of Calvary, Music of Calvary and LifeStream Music, Soldier of the Light, Torchbearer Music.
How to Contact: Accepting material at this time.
Music: **Church/religious, contemporary Christian, gospel** and **wedding music**.

CAMEX MUSIC, 535 5th Ave., New York NY 10017. (212)682-8400. A&R Director: Alex Benedetto. Music publisher, record company, record producer. Estab. 1970. Publishes 100 songs/year; publishes 10 new songwriters/year. Hires staff songwriters. Works with composers and lyricists. Query for royalty terms.
How to Contact: Submit demo tape by mail. Unsolicited submissions are OK. Prefers cassettes with 5-10 songs and lyric sheet or lead sheet. SASE. Reports in 1-3 weeks.
Music: Mostly **alternative rock, pop** and **hard rock**; also **R&B, MOR** and **movie themes**. Artists include Marmalade, SAM, Hallucination Station.

*CAP-SOUNDS PUBLISHING (GEMA), Sudetenweg 6, D-65830, Kriftel **Germany**. 6192-45861. Fax: 6192-46922. MD: Manfred Holz. Music publisher. Estab. 1989. Publishes 20 songs/year; publishes 3-4 new songwriters/year. Works with composers and lyricists; teams collaborators. Pays standard royalty.

How to Contact: Submit demo tape by mail. Unsolicited submissions are OK. Prefers cassette and lyric sheet. SASE. Reports in 3 weeks.
Music: Mostly **dance** and **pop**. Published *Breathless* (by Capony/McGae), recorded by G. McGae on Polygram Records (pop); "Amazonia," recorded by Amazonia on Polygram Records (pop); and "That's What Love Can Do For You" (by Capony), recorded by T.M.Y. on East West Records (dance).

*CAPTAIN CLICK, 47 Villa Des Tulipes, Paris 75018 **France**. (331)46 06 4721. Fax: (331)42 54 7779. A&R: Oliver Masselot. Music publisher, record producer, recording studio. Estab. 1985. Publishes 20-30 songs/year; publishes 2-3 new songwriters/year. Works with composers and lyricists. Pays standard royalty.
How to Contact: Submit demo tape by mail. Unsolicited submissions are OK. Prefers cassette and lyric sheet. Does not return material. Reports in 1 month.
Music: Mostly **rock/pop, dance** and **world music**; also **instrumentals**. Published *Africa Be One* (by Georges Seba), recorded by African Gospel Choir (world); "M' bah bah" (by Cathy Grier/B. Masseot), recorded by Shawasana on Scorpio Records (dance); and "Allez Allez" (by Vincens/Wäntier), recorded by Nightclubbers on EMI Records (dance).

CARAVELL MAIN SAIL MUSIC (ASCAP), P.O. Box 1645, Branson MO 65615. (417)334-7040. President: Keith O'Neil. Music publisher, record producer (Caravell Recording Studio). Estab. 1989. Publishes 5 new songwriters/year. Works with composers and lyricists. Pays standard royalty.
Affiliate(s): White River Valley Music (BMI).
How to Contact: Call first and obtain permission to submit. Prefers cassette with 3 songs and lyric sheet. SASE. Reports in 2 months.
Music: Mostly **country, pop** and **gospel**. Published "The Darlin' Boys" and "The Wizard of Song," by Rodney Dillard on Vanguard Records; and "In the Meadow," by Jackie Pope on Caravell Records.

CASH PRODUCTIONS, INC. (BMI), (formerly Ernie Cash Music), 744 Joppa Farm Rd., Joppa MD 21085. (301)679-2262. President: Ernest W. Cash. Music publisher, record company (Continental Records, Inc.), national and international record distributor, artist management, record producer (Vision Music Group, Inc.) and Vision Video Production, Inc. Estab. 1987. Publishes 30-60 songs/year; publishes 10-15 new songwriters/year. Works with composers and lyricists; teams collaborators. Pays standard royalty.
Affiliate(s): Big K Music, Inc. (BMI), Guerriero Music (BMI) and Deb Music (BMI).
How to Contact: Call first and obtain permission to submit. Prefers cassette (VHS videocassette if available) with 3 songs and lyric sheet. SASE. Reports in 2 weeks.
Music: Mostly **country, gospel** and **pop**; also **R&B** and **rock**. Published *Family Ties*, *Tampa* and *Party*, all written and recorded by Short Brothers on Silver City Records (C&W).
Tips: "Do the best job you can on your work—writing, arrangement and production. Demos are very important in placing material."

CASTLE MUSIC CORP., Dept. SM, Suite 201, 50 Music Square W., Nashville TN 37203. (615)320-7003. Fax: (615)320-7006. Publishing Director: Eddie Russell. Music publisher, record company, record producer. Estab. 1969. Pays standard royalty.
Affiliate(s): Castle Music Group.
How to Contact: Submit demo tape by mail—unsolicited submissions are OK. Prefers cassette with 3 songs and lyric sheet. SASE. Reports as soon as possible.
Music: Mostly **country, pop** and **gospel**.

CEDAR CREEK MUSIC (BMI), Suite 503, 44 Music Square East, Nashville TN 37203. (615)252-6916. Fax: (615)329-1071. President: Larry Duncan. Music publisher, record company (Cedar Creek Records), record producer, and artist management. Estab. 1981. Publishes 100 songs/year; publishes 30 new songwriters/year. Works with composers and/or lyricists; teams collaborators. Pays standard royalty.
How to Contact: Submit demo tape by mail. Unsolicited submissions are OK. Prefers cassette (or VHS videocassette) with 4-6 songs and lyric sheet (typed). Does not return unsolicited material. Reports in 1 month.
Music: Mostly **country, country/pop** and **country/R&B**; also **pop, R&B** and **light rock**. Published "14 Karat Gold" (by Deke Little/Joel Little), recorded by Joel Little on Interstate Records; *Bright Lights and Honky Tonk Nights* (by Tony Rast/Debra McClure/Danny Neal) and *I'm In Love* (by Sarita Wortham/Danny Neal/Debra McClure), both recorded by Kym Wortham on ADD Records.
Tips: "Submit your best songs sung by a great demo singer with vocal upfront. Submit a full demo (5 instruments) professionally done by the best musicians you can find."

*CENTROPA N.V., Lange Dreef 25, Malle 2390 **Belgium**. (+32)33117828. Fax: (+32)33123323. President: Beyers Guy. Music publisher, record company and record producer. Estab. 1990. Publishes 50 songs/year; publishes 10 new songwriters/year. Works with composers and lyricists. Pays standard royalty.

How to Contact: Submit demo tape by mail. Unsolicited submissions are OK. Prefers cassette with 5 songs and lead sheet. SAE and IRC. Reports in 2 weeks.

Music: Mostly **pop, dance** and **ballads**; also **R&B** and **country**.

CHAPIE MUSIC (BMI), Dept. SM, 228 W. Fifth, Kansas City MO 64105. (816)842-6854. Owner: Chuck Chapman. Music publisher, record company (Fifth Street Records), record producer (Chapman Recording Studios). Estab. 1977. Publishes 6 songs/year. Works with composers; teams collaborators. Pays standard royalty.

How to Contact: Call to get permission to submit tape. Prefers cassette with 1-3 songs and lyric sheet. SASE.

Music: Mostly **country, pop** and **gospel**; also **jazz, R&B** and **New Age**. Published "Lonely Country Road" and "Talkin 'Bout," both written and recorded by Mike Eisel; and "Sometimes Takes A Woman" (by Greg Camp), recorded by Rick Loveall, all recorded on Fifth Street Records (country).

Tips: "Make it commercial—with a twist on the lyrics."

CHEAVORIA MUSIC CO. (BMI), 1219 Kerlin Ave., Brewton AL 36426. (205)867-2228. President: Roy Edwards. Music publisher, record company and record producer. Estab. 1972. Publishes 20 new songwriters/year. Works with composers and lyricists; teams collaborators. Pays standard royalty.

Affiliate(s): Baitstring Music (ASCAP).

How to Contact: Write first to get permission to submit. Prefers cassette with 3 songs and lyric sheet. Does not return unsolicited material. Reports in 1 month.

Music: Mostly **R&B**, **pop** and **country**; also **good ballads**. Published "Forever and Always," written and recorded by Jim Portwood on Bolivia Records (country).

*CHERIE MUSIC (BMI), 3621 Heath Lane, Mesquite TX 75150. (214)279-5858. Contact: Jimmy Fields or Silvia Harra. Music publisher, record company. Estab. 1955. Publishes approximately 100 songs/year. Works with composers. Pays standard royalty.

How to Contact: Submit demo tape by mail. Unsolicited submissions are OK. Prefers cassette with up to 10 songs. SASE. Reports in approximately 2 months, "depending on how many new songs are received."

Music: Mostly **country** and **rock** (if not over produced—prefer 1950s type rock). Published "Cajun Baby Blues" and *Alive with Alan Dryman* (by Hank Williams/Jimmy Fields), recorded by Allen Dryman on Jamaka Records; and "Is The King Still Alive" (by Fields/McCoy/Kern), recorded by Johnny Harra on HIA Records.

*CHESTNUT MOUND MUSIC GROUP, P.O. Box 989, Goodlettsville TN 37070. (615)851-1360. (615)851-7755. Publishing Coordinator: Ray Lewis. Music publisher, record company (Morning Star, Cedar Hill, Harvest) and record producer. Estab. 1981. Publishes 200 songs/year; publishes 30 new songwriters/year. Hires staff writers. Pays standard royalty.

Affiliate(s): Pleasant View Music (ASCAP), Chestnut Mound Music (BMI), Indian Forest (SESAC).

How to Contact: Write first and obtain permission to submit or arrange personal interview. Prefers cassette with 3 songs and lyric sheet. Does not return material.

Music: Mostly **Southern gospel, country gospel** and **secular country**; also **inspirational**. Published "From the Depths of My Heart"(by Ben and Sonya Isaacs), recorded by the Isaacs on MorningStar Records (gospel); "He's All I Need" (by Sammy Easom), recorded by the Kingsmen on Horizon Records (gospel); and "Outside the Gate" (by Larry Petree), recorded by the Wilburns on Morning-Star Records (gospel).

Tips: "In Southern gospel music, emphasis is placed more on strong lyrics rather than melody. Have a clean, clear demo."

*CHRISTEL MUSIC LIMITED, Fleet House, 173 Haydons Rd., Wimbledon, London SW19 8TB **England**. (081)679-5010. Fax: (081)679-4416. Managing Director: Dennis R. Sinnott. Music publisher. Estab. 1983. Publishes 350 songs/year; publishes 50 new songwriters/year. Works with composers and lyricists. Pays 60/40 in favor of the writer.

How to Contact: Write first and obtain permission to submit. Prefers cassette with 4 songs and lyric sheet. SAE and IRC. Reports in 2 weeks.

Music: Mostly **mainstream pop, rock ballads** and **MOR**. *All music with commercial potential.* Published *Grange Hill*, written and recorded by Peter Moss on BBC1 (TV theme); "Caught Your Lie" (by Lea Hart/D. Senczak), recorded by True Brits on West Coast Productions (heavy metal); and "Ask Myself Why," written and recorded by Nick Clark on Fern Records (pop).

Tips: "I think songwriters should put a lot of emphasis on what they feel will carry commercial persuasion. Songs can be skillfully put together—indeed technically brilliant, and yet commercially poor and, of course, vice-versa. We feel the more a songwriter researches before submitting material, the greater his/her chance of success. The second point is presentation. You wouldn't, for example, go to an interview in a pair of torn jeans if you wanted a job as a bank manager!"

*CHRISTMAS & HOLIDAY MUSIC (BMI), Suite 4, 3517 Warner Blvd., Burbank CA 91505. (213)849-5381. President: Justin Wilde. Music publisher. Estab. 1980. Publishes 8-12 songs/year; publishes 8-12 new songwriters/year. Works with composers and lyricists. "All submissions must be complete songs (i.e., music and lyrics)." Pays standard royalty.
Affiliate(s): Songcastle Music (ASCAP).
How to Contact: Submit demo tape by mail. Unsolicited submissions are OK. "First class mail only. Registered or certified mail not accepted." Prefers cassette with 3 songs and lyric sheet. "Professional demos a must." SASE. Reports in 2-3 weeks.
Music: Strictly **Christmas music** (and a little Hanukkah) in every style imaginable: easy listening, rock, R&B, pop, blues, jazz, country, reggae, rap, children's secular or religious. *Please do not send anything that isn't Christmas.* Published "It Must Have Been The Mistletoe" (by Justin Wilde and Doug Konecky), recorded by Barbara Mandrell on MCA Records; by Vicki Carr on Laser Light Records; and by Kathie Lee Gifford on Warner Bros. Records. Has had several holiday songs performed by Anita Baker, Johnny Mathis, Anne Murray, Vince Gill, Tanya Tucker, Marilyn McCoo, Glen Campbell, Jack Jones and others on network TV Christmas specials.
Tips: "If a stranger can hum your melody back to you after hearing it twice, it has 'standard' potential. Couple that with a lyric filled with unique, inventive imagery, that stands on its own, even without music. Combine the two elements, and workshop the finished result thoroughly to identify weak points. Only when the song is polished to perfection, then cut a master quality demo that sounds like a record or pretty close to it. Submit positive lyrics only. Avoid negative themes like 'Blue Christmas.'"

SONNY CHRISTOPHER PUBLISHING (BMI), P.O. Box 9144, Ft. Worth TX 76147-2144. (817)595-4655. Owner: Sonny Christopher. Music publisher, record company and record producer. Estab. 1974. Publishes 20-25 new songs/year; publishes 3-5 new songwriters/year. Pays standard royalty.
How to Contact: Write first and obtain permission to submit. Prefers cassette with lyric sheet. SASE. Reports in 3 months.
Music: Mostly **country, rock** and **blues.** Published "Texas Shines Like A Diamond," written and recorded by Sonny on Sabre Records; *I'm Learning Not To Love You,* written and recorded by Ronny Collins; and "Sourmash Whiskey and Red Texas Wine," written and recorded by Howard Crockette on Texas International Records.
Tips: "Stay with it. A winner *never* quits and a quitter never *wins.*"

CIMIRRON MUSIC (BMI), 607 Piney Point Rd., Yorktown VA 23692. (804)898-8155. President: Lana Puckett. Music publisher, record company and record producer. Estab. 1986. Publishes 10-20 songs/year. "Royalty depends on song and writer."
How to Contact: Write first and obtain permission to submit. Prefers cassette and lyric sheet. SASE. Reports in 3 months.
Music: Mostly **country, acoustic, folk** and **bluegrass.** Published *Cornstalk Pony* written and recorded by L. Puckett; *Some Things Never Change,* written and recorded by K. Person; and *Farmer of Love* (by K. Person/Lana Puckett), recorded by K. Person, all on Cimirron Records.
Tips: "It needs to be a great song *musically* and *lyrically.*"

CISUM, 708 W. Euclid, Pittsburg KS 66762. (316)231-6443. Partner: Kevin Shawn. Music publisher, record company (Cisum), record producer (Cisum). BMI, SESAC and ASCAP. Estab. 1985. Publishes 100 songs/year. Works with composers and lyricists; teams collaborators. Pays standard royalty.
How to Contact: Write first and obtain permission to submit a tape. Prefers cassette (or VHS videocassette if available) and lyric sheet. "Unpublished, copyrighted, cassette with lyrics. Submit as many as you wish. We listen to everything, allow 3 months. When over 3 weeks please call."
Music: Mostly **novelty, country** and **rock;** also **pop, gospel** and **R&B.** Published "Angry Gun" (by R. Durst), recorded by Gene Straser on Antique Records (country); "Smooth Talk" (by Rhuems), recorded by Rich Rhuems on Antique Records (country); "Mailman Mailman" (by Strasser), recorded by Willie & Shawn on Cisum Records (novelty).
Tips: "Good demo, great song; always put your best effort on the tape first."

CITY PUBLISHING CO., 840 Windham Ave., Cincinnati OH 45229. (513)559-1210. President: Roosevelt Lee. Music publisher, record company and record producer. BMI. Publishes 8 songs/year. Pays standard royalty.

Affiliate(s): Carriage Publishing Co. (BMI).
How to Contact: Submit demo tape by mail. Unsolicited submissions are OK. Prefers cassette with maximum of 4 songs and lyric sheet. SASE. Reports in 1 month.
Music: Mostly **rap, gospel, pop, reggae**. Published "Instantpart," written and recorded by Gradual Taylor; "Fat Rat," written and recorded by Albert Washington; and "Hey Little Girl" (by Robert Hill), recorded by Roosevelt Lee, all on Westworld Records.
Tips: "I am looking for finished masters."

CLEAR POND MUSIC (BMI), Suite 32, 115 E Water St., Santa Fe NM 87501. (505)983-3245. Fax: (505)982-9168. Publisher: Susan Pond. Music publisher and record producer (Crystal Clear Productions). Estab. 1992. Publishes 10-20 songs/year; publishes 1-5 new songwriters/year. Works with composers and/or lyricists; teams collaborators. Pays standard royalty. "We use the Songwriters Guild Contract."
How to Contact: Write and obtain permission to submit. "We are now working exclusively with artists/songwriters." Prefers cassette with 1-3 songs and lyric sheet. Only accepting master recordings. SASE. Reports in 1 month.
Music: Mostly **pop, pop/rock** and **country/contemporary**; also **A/C**. Published "Back to Love Again" (by recording artist Erik Darling) on Folk Era Records; and "I Only Have Time for the Dance," written and recorded by J.D. Haring on Starquest Records; "Rodeo Roam" (by Darling/Strahan) on Comstock Records.
Tips: "Write very strong hook melodies with tight lyrics; know the business, do your homework. Have good studio demos. Study lyric writing and music; be realistic about your goals."

CLEARWIND PUBLISHING, P.O. Box 42381, Detroit MI 48242-0381. (313)336-9522. "A Contemporary Christian Publishing and Management Company." Contact: A&R Department Director. Music publisher and personal management company (Clearwind Management). Estab. 1983. Publishes 12-15 songs/year; publishes 2-4 new songwriters/year. Pays standard royalty.
How to Contact: Write to obtain permission to submit. "Do NOT call! Unsolicited submissions will be returned unopened." Prefers cassette (or VHS videocassette) with 2 songs and lyric sheet. (NO more than TWO songs!) Does not return unsolicited material. Reports in up to 12 weeks.
Music: Mostly **pop, highly commercial country** and **R&B**; also **highly commercial rock**. Published *Champion* and "What A Friend," written and recorded by Ron Moore on Morada Records.
Tips: "Write what the market wants because that is who will buy your music. Always try to be commercial and strive to write a hit. Most importantly, don't give up!"

R.D. CLEVÈRE MUSIKVERLAG, Postfach 2145, D-63243 Neu-Isenburg, **Germany**. Phone: (6102)51065. Fax: (6102)52696. Professional Manager: Tony Hermonez. GEMA. Music publisher. Estab. 1967. Publishes 700-900 songs/year; publishes 40 new songwriters/year. Works with composers and lyricists; teams collaborators. Pays standard royalty.
Affiliate(s): Big Sound Music, Hot Night Music, Lizzy's Blues Music, Max Banana Music, R.D. Clevère-Cocabana-Music, R.D. Clevère-Far East & Orient-Music, and R.D. Clevère-America-Today-Music.
How to Contact: "Do not send advance letter(s) asking for permission to submit your song material, just send it." Prefers cassette with "no limit" on songs and lyric sheet. SAE and a minimum of two IRCs. Reports in 3 weeks.
Music: Mostly **pop, disco, rock, R&B, country** and **folk**; also **musicals** and **classic/opera**.
Tips: "If the song submitted is already produced/recorded professionally on 16/24-multitrack-tape and available, we can use this for synchronization with artists of the various record companies/record producers."

CLIENTELE MUSIC, (ASCAP), 252 Bayshore Dr., Hendersonville TN 37075. (615)822-2364. Fax: (615)824-3400. Director: Thornton Cline. Music publisher. Estab. 1989. Publishes 15 songs/year; publishes 10 new songwriters/year. Works with composers and lyricists. Pays standard royalty.
Affiliate(s): Incline Music (BMI).
How to Contact: Submit demo tape by mail. Unsolicited submissions are OK. Prefers cassette with 1 song and lyric sheet. "Send only radio ready demos—your No. 1 songs." SASE. Reports in 6 weeks.
Music: Mostly **R&B/dance, pop/dance** and **pop/ballads**; also **soul, country** and **contemporary Christian**. Published *Desperation Time* (by T. Cline/N. Bryan), recorded by Nancy Bryan on Aerosound Records (alternative); *What's This Love Coming To* (by T. Cline/K. Tribble/J. Whiting), recorded by Darlene Shadden on Chelsea Records (country); and *Something Out of Nothing* (by T. Cline/M. Hauth), recorded by David Brett on Benson Records (gospel).
Tips: "Send me the very best you could possibly write from the heart. Listen to radio only as a format; don't write songs like those on radio unless they're standards."

CLOTILLE PUBLISHING (SOCAN), 9 Hector Ave., Toronto, Ontario M6G3G2 **Canada**. (416)588-6751. Manager: Al Kussin. Music publisher, record company (Slak Records) and record producer (Slak Productions). Estab. 1988. Publishes 5 songs/year; publishes 1 new songwriter/year. Teams collaborators. Pays standard royalty.
How to Contact: Submit a demo tape by mail. Unsolicited submissions are OK. Prefers cassette with 3 songs and lyric sheet. "Recording quality must be sufficient to convey the total impact of song." SAE and IRC. Reports in 2 months.
Music: Mostly **pop**, **R&B** and **dance**. Published "Here Comes Next" (by L. Roberts/A. Kussin), recorded by EMC² on Slak Records; "Ritmo de la Noche" (by A. Coelho), recorded by Click 2 on TJSB Records; and "Duck" (by M. Munroe), recorded by Mystah Munroe on Slak Records.
Tips: "Submit good commercial material with strong hooks and interesting form. On most submissions, lyrics are usually cliched and substandard. Production quality must be adequate to get the song across."

COFFEE AND CREAM PUBLISHING COMPANY, Dept. SM, 1138 E. Price St., Philadelphia PA 19138. (215)842-3450. President: Bolden Abrams, Jr. Music publisher and record producer (Bolden Productions). ASCAP. Publishes 20 songs/year; publishes 4 new songwriters/year. Works with composers and lyricists. Pays standard royalty.
How to Contact: Prefers cassette (or VHS videocassette) with 1-4 songs and lyric or lead sheets. Does not return unsolicited material. Reports in 2 weeks "if we're interested."
Music: Mostly **dance**, **pop**, **R&B**, **gospel** and **country**. Published "No Time for Tears" (by Bolden Abrams/Keith Batts), recorded by Gabrielle (R&B ballad); "You Are My Life" (by Seane Charger), recorded by Chuck Jackson; and "If I Let Myself Go" (by Jose Gomez/Sheree Sando), recorded by Dionne Warwick/Chuck Jackson on Ichiban Records (pop/ballad).

*COLD CHILLIN' MUSIC PUBLISHING (ASCAP), 1995 Broadway, New York NY 10023. (212)724-5000. Fax: (212)724-6018. President: Dee Garner. Record company (Cold Chillin' Records). Estab. 1987. Publishes 30-35 songs/year.
Affiliate(s): Jus' Livin' Music Publishing (BMI).
How to Contact: Write first and obtain permission to submit. Prefers cassette. SASE.
Music: Mostly **R&B** and **hip hop**.

COLLINS MUSIC GROUP, 25 Music Sq. West, Nashville TN 37203. (615)255-5550. Creative Director: Jeff Gordon. Music publisher. Estab. 1971. Publishes 400 songs/year; publishes 1 or 2 new songwriters/year. Pays standard royalty.
How to Contact: Submit demo tape by mail. Unsolicited submissions are OK. Prefers cassette and lyric sheet. "Do not call or write, send a tape and if we can use it we will call you." Does not return unsolicited submissions.
Music: Mostly **country**. Published "Only Love" (by Roger Murrah), recorded by Wynonna; "Holdin Heaven" (by Bill Kenner), recorded by Tracy Byrd, both on MCA Records; and "Jesus & Mama" (by Danny Mayo), recorded by Confederate Railroad on Atlantic Records.
Tips: "Don't send just lyrics or scattered ideas. We want well worked out great songs. If you send more than one song, put the best song you've ever written in your life first."

*COLSTAL MUSIC, 5th Floor, Parkrise, 3 Alison St., Surfer's Paradise, QLD H217 **Australia**. (075)388-911. Fax:(075)703-434. Director: Bernie Stahl. Music publisher and video distributor. Estab. 1985. Works with composers and lyricists; teams collaborators. Pays negotiable royalty.
How to Contact: Submit demo tape by mail. Unsolicited submissions are OK. Prefers cassette (or PAL videocassette if available). SAE and IRC.
Music: Mostly **country** and **comedy**. Published *Henry, Banjo and Me* (by P. Pierse); *Works Out Easier That Way* (by J. Chester); and *Smokin' Again* (by Elliott/Vincent), all recorded by Col Elliot on AIC Records (country/comedy).

JERRY CONNELL PUBLISHING CO. (BMI), 130 Pilgrim Dr., San Antonio TX 78213. (210)344-5033. Partner: Jerry Connell. Music publisher and record producer. Publishes 75 songs/year; publishes 50 new songwriters/year. Works with composers and lyricists; teams collaborators. Pays standard royalty.
Affiliate(s): Old Bob Music. (ASCAP).
How to Contact: Submit demo tape by mail. Unsolicited submissions are OK. Prefers cassette with lyric or lead sheet (if possible). Does not return unsolicited material. Reports in 1 month.
Music: Mostly **country**, **gospel/religious** and **tejano**; also **jazz**, **easy listening** and **rock**. Published "Dos Tacos de Chorito Por Favor" (by Steve Mallett), recorded by Tom Frost on Indian Grass Records; "Ride Cowboy Ride," written and recorded by Richard Wolfe; and *Chester Field Blues*, written and recorded by Jimmy Jack on Cherokee Records.
Tips: "A song should have a melody that is a grabber, a lyric that expresses familiar ideas in a new and unusual way and, most important, have a beginning, middle and end."

CONTINENTAL COMMUNICATIONS CORP., Dept. SM, P.O. Box 389, Monsey NY 10952. (914)426-1466. President: Robert Schwartz. ASCAP, BMI. Estab. 1952. Music publisher and record company (Laurie Records and 3C Records). Publishes 50 songs/year; publishes 5-10 new songwriters/year. Works with composers and lyricists; teams collaborators. Pays standard royalty.
Affiliate(s): 3 Seas Music (ASCAP) and Northvale Music (BMI).
How to Contact: Call for information.

*CONTROLLED DESTINY MUSIC PUBLISHING, P.O. Box 155191, Waco TX 76715. (817)881-1962. Owner: Kerry A. Thomas. Music publisher, record producer. Estab. 1992. Publishes 5 songs/year; publishes 3 new songwriters/year. Works with composers and lyricists; teams collaborators. Pays standard royalty.
How to Contact: Submit demo tape by mail. Unsolicited submissions are OK. Prefers cassette (or VHS videocassette) with 4 songs and lyric sheet. SASE. Reports in 3 weeks.
Music: Mostly **R&B**, **pop** and **country**; also **gospel** and **rap, instrumental**.
Tips: "We are a young company looking for hits, not B-side material or album fillers. Make sure song has a strong hook, and vocals up front. Write a song to fit today's market and believe in it. Keep it clean, clear and simple."

*COPPELIA, 21, rue de Pondichéry, 75015 Paris **France**. Phone: 45 67 30 66. Fax: 43 06 30 26. Manager: Jean-Philippe Olivi. Music publisher, record company (Olivi Records), record producer (Coppelia) and music print publisher. SACEM. Publishes 150 songs/year; publishes 80 new songwriters/year. Works with composers and lyricists. Pays standard royalty.
How to Contact: Submit a demo tape by mail. Unsolicited submissions are OK. Prefers cassette (or VHS videocassette). SAE and IRC. Reports in 1 month.
Music: Mostly **pop**, **rock** and **New Age**; also **background music** and **movies/series music**. Published "A St. Germain de Prés," written and recorded by Bodin on Olivi Records (sax); "Sagapo," and "Ambitions" (by Remy), both recorded by Ferchit on Olivi Records.

THE CORNELIUS COMPANIES, Dept. SM, Suite 5, 819 19th Ave. S., Nashville TN 37203. (615)321-5333. Owner/Manager: Ron Cornelius. Music publisher and record producer (The Cornelius Companies, Ron Cornelius). BMI, ASCAP. Estab. 1987. Publishes 60-80 songs/year; publishes 2-3 new songwriters/year. Occasionally hires staff writers. Works with composers and lyricists; teams collaborators. Pays standard royalty.
Affiliate(s): RobinSparrow Music (BMI).
How to Contact: Write or call first and obtain permission to submit a tape. Prefers cassette with 2-3 songs. SASE. Reports in 2 months.
Music: Mostly **country** and **pop**. Published "Time Off for Bad Behavior" (by Lorry Latimer), recorded by Confederate Railroad on Atlantic Records; "You're Slowly Going Out of My Mind" (by Gordon Dee), recorded by Southern Tracks, both on CBS Records; and "These Colors Never Run" (by Gordon Dee).

*CORPORATE ROCK MUSIC, 154 Grande Cote, Rosemere, Quebec J7A 1H3 **Canada**. President: Paul Levesque. Music publisher, record company (Artiste Records) and management company (Paul Levesque Management Inc.). Estab. 1971. Publishes 20 songs/year; publishes 1-2 new songwriters/year. Works with composers and lyricists; teams collaborators. Pays standard royalty.
Affiliate(s): Savoir Faire Music (ASCAP), Transfer Music (BMI).
How to Contact: Submit demo tape by mail. Unsolicited submissions are OK. Prefers cassette (or VHS videocassette if available) with 4 songs and lyric sheet. SAE and IRC. Reports in 2 months.
Music: Mostly **rock, pop** and **R&B (dance)**. Published "What Ya Do" and "She Got Me," both written and recorded by Haze & Shuffle on Arista Records (rock); and "Tu Pars," written and recorded by Bruno Pelletier on Artiste Records (pop).

COTTAGE BLUE MUSIC (BMI), P.O. Box 121626, Nashville TN 37212. (615)726-3556. Contact: Neal James. Music publisher, record company (Kottage Records) and record producer (Neal James Productions). Estab. 1971. Publishes 30 songs/year; publishes 3 new songwriters/year. Works with composers only. Pays standard royalty.
Affiliate(s): James & Lee (BMI), Neal James Music (BMI) and Hidden Cove Music (ASCAP).
How to Contact: Submit demo tape by mail. Unsolicited submissions OK. Prefers cassette with 2 songs and lyric sheet. SASE. Reports in 4-6 weeks.
Music: Mostly **country**, **gospel** and **rock/pop**; also **R&B**. Published "She Don't" (by Bill Fraser and Neal James), recorded by Bill Fraser (pop); "Who's Holding Him" (by Neal James), recorded by Cindy Lee (C&W); and *Tell Me* (by Neal James), recorded by Terry Banbaz (C&W).
Tips: "Screen material carefully before submitting."

COUNTRY BREEZE MUSIC, 1715 Marty, Kansas City KS 66103. (913)384-7336. President: Ed Morgan. Music publisher and record company (Country Breeze Records, Walkin' Hat Records). BMI, ASCAP. Estab. 1984. Publishes 100 songs/year; publishes 25-30 new songwriters/year. Teams collaborators. Pays standard royalty.
Affiliate(s): Walkin' Hat Music (ASCAP).
How to Contact: Submit a demo tape by mail. Unsolicited submissions are OK. Prefers cassette (or VHS videocassette) with 4-5 songs and lyric sheet. SASE. "The songwriter/artist should perform on the video as though on stage giving a sold-out performance. In other words put heart and soul into the project. Submit in strong mailing envelopes." Reports in 2 weeks.
Music: Mostly **country (all types), gospel (southern country and Christian country)** and **rock (no rap or metal)**. Published "Bourbon & Water," recorded by Jamie Mitchell; "Natures Law" (by J. Cox/R. Wingerter), recorded by Beverly Elliott; and "Stranger" written and recorded by Ron Bassett, all on Country Breeze Records.
Tips: "Give us time to review your material; don't call us 3 days after you send it to us, wanting to know how we like it. We'll get back with you."

*COUNTRY SHOWCASE AMERICA (BMI), 385 Main St., Laurel MD 20707. (301)725-7713. Fax: (301)604-2676. Contact: Francis Gosman. Music publisher, record company and record producer. Estab. 1971. Publishes 9 songs/year; publishes 1 new songwriter/year. Works with composers and lyricists; teams collaborators. Pays standard royalty.
How to Contact: Submit demo tape by mail. Unsolicited submissions are OK. Prefers cassette with 2 songs and lyric sheet. Does not return material.
Music: Mostly **country**. Published *Too Late For Roses, Runaway Train* and *Sweet Love's Not Forever* (by Cochran & Gusman), recorded by Johnny Anthony on CSA Records (country).

COUNTRY STAR MUSIC (ASCAP), 439 Wiley Ave., Franklin PA 16323. (814)432-4633. President: Norman Kelly. Music publisher, record company (Country Star, Process, Mersey and CSI) and record producer (Country Star Productions). Estab. 1970. Publishes 15-20 songs/year; publishes 4-6 new songwriters/year. Works with composers and lyricists; teams collaborators. Pays standard royalty.
Affiliate(s): Kelly Music Publications (BMI) and Process Music Publications (BMI).
How to Contact: Submit demo tape by mail. Unsolicited submissions are OK. Prefers cassette with 1-4 songs and typed lyric or lead sheet. SASE. Reports in 2 weeks. "No SASE no return."
Music: Mostly **country** (80%); also **rock, gospel, MOR** and **R&B** (5% each). Published *Western Dawn* (by James E. Myers), recorded by Jeffrey Connors (country); *Spinning In My Heart*, recorded by Jonie Loo on Country Star Records (country); and *God Specializes*, written and recorded by Sheryl Friend on Process Records (gospel).
Tips: "Send only your best songs—ones you feel are equal to or better than current hits. Typed or printed lyrics, please."

*COWBOY JUNCTION FLEA MARKET AND PUBLISHING CO. (BMI), Highway 44 West, Junction 490, Lecanto FL 32661. (904)746-4754. President: Elizabeth Thompson. Music publisher (Cowboy Junction Publishing Co.), record company (Cowboy Junction Records) and record producer. Estab. 1957. Publishes 5 songs/year. Pays standard royalty or other amount.
How to Contact: Submit demo tape (or VHS videocassette) by mail. Unsolicited submissions are OK. SASE. Reports as soon as possible.
Music: **Country, western, bluegrass** and **gospel**. Published "They Call Me a Cowboy," "Pretty Girls on TV" and "Pay It No Mind," all written by Boris Max Pastuch and recorded by Buddy Max on Cowboy Junction Records (country).
Tips: "You could come to our flea market on Tuesday or Friday and present your material—or come to our Country and Western Bluegrass Music Show held any Saturday."

*CQK RECORDS AND MUSIC (ASCAP), 4400-D Moulton St., Greenville TX 75401. (214)420-1971. Fax: (903)454-8524. President: Mary Dawson. Music publisher, record company. Estab. 1992. Publishes 50 songs/year. Works with composers and lyricists; teams collaborators.
How to Contact: Call first and obtain permission to submit. Prefers cassette and lyric sheet. Does not return material. Reports in 6 weeks.
Music: Mostly **positive message pop, R&B** and **country**; also **choral, instrumental** and **Christian contemporary**. Published *The Serenity Prayer* (by Mary Dawson/Bruce Greer), recorded by Cynthia Clawson (pop ballad); *A.S.A.P.* (by Mary Dawson/Bruce Greer), recorded by Babbie Mason & Jessy Dixon (R&B); and "Long Distance Christmas" (by Mary Dawson/Bruce Greer), recorded by Cynthia Clawson and Bruce Greer (pop).
Tips: "We are looking for 'positive message' music in all styles—inspirational, but not necessarily Christian or religious."

LOMAN CRAIG MUSIC, P.O. Box 111480, Nashville TN 37222-1480. (615)331-1219. President: Loman Craig. Engineer/Producer: Tommy Hendrick. Music publisher, record company (Bandit Records, HIS Records), record producer (Loman Craig Productions). BMI, ASCAP, SESAC. Estab. 1979. Publishes 15 songs/year; publishes 5 new songwriters/year. Works with composers and lyricists. Pays standard royalty.
Affiliate(s): Outlaw Music of Memphis (BMI), We Can Make It Music (BMI) and Doulikit Music (SESAC).
How to Contact: Submit a demo tape by mail. Unsolicited submissions are OK. Prefers cassette with 2-3 songs and lyric sheet. "Does not have to be a full production demo." SASE. Reports in 4-6 weeks.
Music: Mostly **country** and **pop**; also **bluegrass** and **gospel.** Published "I Can't See Me Gone" (Craig/ Craig) and "Between The Whiskey And The Beer," both recorded by James Bryan; and "One And the Same" (by Craig/Hendrick), recorded by Loman Craig, all on Bandit Records.

CREEKSIDE MUSIC, Dept. SM, 100 Labon St., Tabor City NC 28463. (910)653-2546. Owner: Elson H. Stevens. Music publisher, record company (Seaside Records) and record producer (Southern Sound Productions). BMI. Estab. 1978. Publishes 30 songs/year; publishes 5 new songwriters/year. Works with composers, lyricists; teams collaborators. Pays 25-50% royalty from record sales.
How to Contact: Submit demo tape by mail. Unsolicited submissions OK. Prefers cassette with 3 songs and lead sheets. SASE. Reports in 1 month.
Music: Mostly **country, rock** and **gospel**; also "**beach music.**" Published "I'll Never Say Never Again" (by G. Todd and S. Hart) and "Long Country Road" (by G. Taylor), both recorded by Sherry Collins (country); and "Heaven's Ready" (by E. Watson), recorded by The Watson Family (gospel), all on Seaside Records.
Tips: "Be original—search for 'the hook'."

*CROSS CULTURE PRODUCTIONS, INC. (BMI), P.O. Box 4918, Falls Church VA 22044. Contacts: Yuri Z. and Kaan A. Music publisher. Estab. 1993. Publishes 5 songs/year; publishes 5 new songwriters/ year. Teams collaborators. Pays standard royalty.
How to Contact: Submit demo tape by mail. Unsolicited submissions are OK. Prefers cassette with 3 songs. SASE. Reports in 2 weeks.
Music: Mostly **R&B, pop** and **hip hop**; also **dance.**

*CRS, 724 Winchester, Broomall PA 19008. (215)544-5920. Fax: (215)544-5921. Administrative Assistant: Caroline Hunt. Record company and record producer. Estab. 1979. Deals with artists and songwriters. Pays 10% royalty to artists on contract; varying amount to publisher per song on record.
How to Contact: Submit demo tape by mail. Unsolicited submissions are OK. Prefers cassette (or videocassette if available). SASE. Reports in 1 month.
Music: All types.

CSB KAMINSKY GMBH, Wilhelmstrasse 10, 23611 Bad Schwartau, **Germany.** Phone: (0451)21530. General Manager: Pia Kaminsky. GEMA, PRS. Music publisher and collecting agency. Estab. 1978. Publishes 2-4 songs/year; 1 new songwriter/year. Teams collaborators. Pays 50% if releasing a record; 85% if only collecting royalties.
Affiliate(s): Leosong Copyright Management, Ltd. (London, United Kingdom).
How to Contact: Write and submit material. Prefers cassette or VHS videocassette. Does not return unsolicited material. Reports in 4 weeks.
Music: Mostly **pop**; also **rock, country** and **reggae.**

*CTV MUSIC (GREAT BRITAIN), Television Centre, St. Helier, Jersey JE2 3ZD Channel Islands **Great Britain.** (534)68999. Fax: (534)59446. Managing Director: Gordon De Ste. Croix. Music publisher, music for TV commercials, TV programs and corporate video productions. Estab. 1986. Works with composers and lyricists; teams collaborators. Royalty negotiable.
How to Contact: Submit demo tape by mail. Unsolicited submissions are OK. Prefers cassette. SAE and IRC. Reports as soon as possible.

CUNNINGHAM MUSIC (BMI), Dept. SM, 23494 Lahser, Southfield MI 48034. (313)948-9787. President: Jerome Cunningham. Music publisher. Estab. 1988. Publishes 8-9 songs/year; publishes 2 new songwriters/year. Teams collaborators. Pays standard royalty.
How to Contact: Submit a demo tape by mail. Unsolicited submissions are OK. Prefers cassette (or VHS videocassette if available) with 3 songs and lyric sheet. SASE. Reports in 3-4 weeks.
Music: Mostly **R&B, gospel** and **jazz**; also **pop** and **rock.** Published "Can't Teach Old Dog Tricks," written and recorded by Vernon B. on 2-Hot Records (R&B).
Tips: Main reason for rejection of submitted material includes: "Incomplete songs, no melody involved. Overall, just poorly prepared presentations."

CUPIT MUSIC (BMI), P.O. Box 121904, Nashville TN 37212. (615)731-0100. President: Jerry Cupit. Music publisher and record producer (Jerry Cupit Productions). Publishes 30 songs/year; publishes 6 new songwriters/year. Hires staff songwriters. Works with composers and lyricists; teams collaborators. Pays standard royalty.
Affiliate(s): Cupit Memaries (ASCAP).
How to Contact: Artist/writer submissions only. Submit by mail with SASE. Reports in 4-6 weeks.
Music: Mostly **country, southern rock** and **gospel/contemporary Christian**. Published *I Know What You Got Up Your Sleeve*, recorded by Hank Williams Jr. on Warner Bros. Records; "Jukebox Junkie," recorded by Ken Mellons on Epic Records; and "For Crying Out Loud," recorded by Clinton Gregory on Step One Records.
Tips: "Keep vocals up front on demos, study correct structure, always tie all lines to hook!"

DAGENE MUSIC (ASCAP), P.O. Box 410851, San Francisco CA 94141. (415)822-1530. President: David Alston. Music publisher, record company (Cabletown Corp.) and record producer (Classic Disc Production). Estab. 1988. Hires staff songwriters. Works with composers; teams collaborators. Pays standard royalty.
Affiliate(s): 1956 Music.
How to Contact: Write or call first and obtain permission to submit a tape. Prefers cassette with 2 songs and lyric sheet. "Be sure to obtain permission before sending any material." Does not return unsolicited material. Reports in 1 month.
Music: Mostly **R&B/rap, dance** and **pop**. Published "Mind Ya Own" (by Bernard Henderson/Marcus Justice), recorded by 2wo-Dominatorz on Dagene Records; "Started Life" (by David/M. Campbell), recorded by Star Child on Dagene Records; and "Lies," written and recorded by David on Cabletown Records (all rap).
Tips: "It's what's in the groove that makes people move."

DAN THE MAN MUSIC, P.O. Box 81550, Cleveland OH 44181-0550. President: Daniel L. Bischoff. Music publisher, record company (Dan The Man Records) and management firm (Daniel Bischoff Management). ASCAP, BMI. "We have some major label connections. Always looking for top country hit material. Also interested in strong pop-rock material." Pays standard royalty.
Affiliate(s): Bischoff Music Publishing Co. (BMI). Long Island Music (ASCAP).
How to Contact: Submit a demo tape by mail. Unsolicited submissions OK. Please send cassette or VHS tape and lyrics. SASE. Reports in 1 month.
Music: **Country** and **pop/rock**. Published "Gently Break A Heart" (by C. Brumfield) and "Just a Heartache Ago" (by Al Glenn Duke), both recorded by Tommy Becker; and "High Priced Gasoline" (by Dan Bischoff), recorded by Dan the Man, all on Dan The Man Records.

DARBONNE PUBLISHING CO. (BMI), Dept. SM, Route 3, Box 172, Haynesville LA 71038. (318)927-5253. President: Edward N. Dettenheim. Music publisher and record company (Wings Record Co.). Estab. 1987. Publishes 50 songs/year; publishes 8-10 new songwriters/year. Works with composers and lyricists; teams collaborators. Pays standard royalty.
How to Contact: Submit a demo tape by mail. Unsolicited submissions are OK. Prefers cassette or 7½ ips reel-to-reel with up to 12 songs and lyric sheet. Does not return unsolicited material. Reports in 6 weeks.
Music: Mostly **country** and **gospel**. Published "Blanche" (by E. Dettenheim) and "It Don't Always Thunder" (by E. Dettenheim/T.J. Lynn), both recorded by T.J. Lynn on Wings Records (country); and "The Room" (by T.J. Lynn/E. Dettenheim), recorded by Kathy Shelby (country).
Tips: "The better the demo—the better your chances of interesting your listener."

*DE LEON PUBLISHING, 2903 S. Gen Bruce Dr., Temple TX 76504. (817)773-1775. Fax (817)773-4778. Contact: Thomas Cruz. Music publisher, record company.
How to Contact: Call first and obtain permission to submit. Prefers cassette with 4 songs and lyric or lead sheet. Does not return material. Reports in 4-6 weeks.
Music: All types.

THE EDWARD DE MILES MUSIC COMPANY (BMI), 8th Fl., 4475 Allisonville Rd., Indianapolis IN 46205. (317)546-2912. Attn: Professional Manager. Music publisher, record company (Sahara Records), management, bookings and promotions. Estab. 1984. Publishes 50-75 songs/year; publishes 5 new songwriters/year. Hires staff songwriters. Works with composers and lyricists; teams collaborators. Pays standard royalty.
How to Contact: Write first and obtain permission to submit. Prefers cassette with 1-3 songs and lyric sheet. SASE. Reports in 1 month.
Music: Mostly **top 40 pop/rock, R&B/dance** and **C&W**; also **musical scores for TV, radio, films and jingles**. Published "Dance Wit Me" and "Moments," written and recorded by Steve Lynn on Sahara Records (R&B).

Tips: "Copyright all songs before submitting to us."

*DEAD DEAD GOOD RECORDS/MUSIC LTD., 2 Witton Walk, Northwich, Cheshire CW9 5AT **United Kingdom.** (606)44559. Fax: (606)330185. A&R: Andy Wood, Music publisher, record company. Estab. 1990. Pays varying royalty.
How to Contact: Submit demo tape by mail. Unsolicited submissions are OK. Prefers cassette and lead sheet. SAE and IRC. Reports in 3 weeks.
Music: Mostly **indie/rock, dance** and **indie.** Published "Song For Me," written and recorded by Cherry on Elektra Records (rock); and "Shackled," written and recorded by Venus Beads (indie).
Tips: "US market can be very different to the UK—check out British trends as well as US!!"

DEAN ENTERPRISES MUSIC GROUP, Dept. SM, P.O. Box 620, Redwood Estates CA 95044-0620. (408)353-1006. Attn: Executive Director. Music publisher, record producer, record company. Member: CMRRA, NARAS, Harry Fox Agency. Estab. 1989. Publishes 4-6 songs/year; publishes 3-5 new songwriters/year. Pays standard royalty.
Affiliate(s): Mikezel Music Co. (ASCAP), Teenie Deanie Music Co. (BMI) and Minotaur Records.
How to Contact: "Unsolicited submissions are OK. Prefers maximum of 6 songs with typed lyric sheets and brief letter of introduction. Material must be copyrighted and unassigned. Prefers to keep tapes on file, but will return if fully paid SASE is included. A free evaluation is given with first class SASE, even if tape not returned. Reports in 2-6 weeks. PLEASE, no phone calls. Show name, address, phone number and © sign on tape and lyric sheets."
Music: Mostly **country, pop, novelty, MOR/easy listening, soft/easy rock, dance** (Hi NRG, house, pop), **folk, top 40, R&B.** No instrumental, rap music, jazz, heavy metal, punk/acid rock. Published The Memory Brothers and Bobby Petersen.
Tips: "Learn to handle rejection. Listen to the feedback you get. Learn your craft. Join songwriting organizations, read songwriting books and network as much as possible. Opportunity, talent and connections are the name of the game in the music industry. Watch out for the sharks. NEVER pay to have your song published or recorded if you're a songwriter."

DELEV MUSIC COMPANY, 7231 Mansfield Ave., Philadelphia PA 19138-1620. (215)276-8861. President: W. Lloyd Lucas. Music publisher, record company (Surprize Records, Inc.), record producer and management. BMI, ASCAP, SESAC, SGA, and CMRRA. Publishes 6-10 songs/year; publishes 6-10 new songwriters/year. Pays standard royalty.
Affiliate(s): Sign of the Ram Music (ASCAP), Gemini Lady Music (SESAC), and Delev Music (BMI).
How to Contact: Submit demo tape by mail. Unsolicited submissions OK. Prefers cassette (or VHS videocassette) with 1-3 songs and lyric sheet. Send all letter size correspondence and cassette submissions to: P.O. Box 6562, Philadelphia, PA 19138-6562. Larger than letter-size to the Mansfield Avenue address. "Video must be in VHS format and as professionally done as possible. It does not necessarily have to be done at a professional video studio, but should be a very good quality production showcasing artist's performance." SASE. "We will not accept certified mail." Reports in 1 month.
Music: **R&B ballad** and **dance-oriented, pop ballads, crossover** and **country/western.** Published "If Love Comes Again" (by Tyrone W. Brown); "Say It Again" (by Richard Hamersma & Gerry Magallan); and "Tomorrow" (by Jerry Dean Lester, Wayne Gamache & Lazlo Nemeth), which are three of eleven songs on the *Tomorrow* compact disc scheduled for release in 1994.
Tips: "Persevere regardless if it is sent to our company or any other company. Believe in yourself and send the best songs you have to any company submitted to."

FRANK DELL MUSIC, Box 7171, Duluth MN 55807. (218)628-3003. President: Frank Dell. Music publisher, record company, record producer and management. Estab. 1980. Publishes 2 songs/year. Works with composers and lyricists; teams collaborators. Pays standard royalty.
Affiliate(s): Albindell Music (BMI).
How to Contact: Submit demo tape by mail. Unsolicited submissions are OK. Prefers cassette. SASE. Reports in 6 months.
Music: Mostly **country, gospel** and **pop.** Published "Memories" and "Exodus," written and recorded by Frank Dell; and *Country Gospel* (by various), also recorded by Frank Dell, all on MSM Records.

DELPHA'S MUSIC PUBLISHERS (BMI), Box 329, Mulberry AR 72947. (501)997-1557. Fax: (501)997-1557. CEO: Delpha J. Rosson. Music publisher. Estab. 1989. "Publishes 1 (one) song per agreement—no limit." Works with lyricists; teams collaborators. Pays standard royalty.
How to Contact: Submit demo tape by mail. Unsolicited submissions are OK. Prefers cassette with 3 songs and lyric sheet. "Prefers copyrighted material." SASE. Reports in 4-6 weeks.
Music: Mostly **country, pop** and **gospel.** Published "The Liberator" (by Gibbs/Ridener), recorded by Charlie Ridener on Bolder Bluff Records.
Tips: "Make sure that your song is protected before you send it to anyone. Do not pay anyone for publishing."

DEMI MONDE RECORDS & PUBLISHING LTD., Foel Studio, Llanfair Caereinion, POWYS, **Wales**. Phone: (0938)810758. Managing Director: Dave Anderson. Music publisher, record company (Demi Monde Records & Publishing Ltd.), record producer (Dave Anderson). Member MCPS. Estab. 1983. Publishes 50-70 songs/year; publishes 10-15 new songwriters/year. Works with composers and lyricists; teams collaborators. Pays standard royalty.
How to Contact: Submit a demo tape. Unsolicited submissions are OK. Prefers cassette (or VHS videocassette) with 3-4 songs. SAE and IRC. Reports in 1 month.
Music: Mostly **rock**, **R&B** and **pop**. Published "I Feel So Lazy" (by D. Allen), recorded by Gong (rock); "Phalarn Dawn" (by E. Wynne), recorded by Ozric Tentacles (rock); and "Pioneer" (by D. Anderson), recorded by Amon Dual (rock), all on Demi Monde Records.

DENNY MUSIC GROUP, Dept. SM, 3325 Fairmont Dr., Nashville TN 37203-1004. (615)269-4847. Contact: Pandora Denny. ASCAP, BMI, SESAC. Estab. 1983. Music publisher, record company (Dollie Record Co., Jed Record Production) and record producer. "Also owns Denny's Den, a 24-track recording studio designed for songwriters, which won a Grammy in 1990." Publishes 100 songs/year; 20 new songwriters/year. Works with composer and lyricists; teams collaborators. Pays standard royalty.
How to Contact: Write or call first and obtain permission to submit. Prefers cassette with 3 songs and lyric sheet. Reports in 6 weeks.
Music: Mostly **country**, **Bluegrass** and **MOR**. Published "Angel Band" and "On the Other Side" (by Greg Homner, bluegrass).

DIAMOND WIND MUSIC (BMI), P.O. Box 311, Estero FL 33928. Fax: (813)267-6000. President: Reenie Diamond. Music publisher, record company (Diamond Wind Records) and record producer (Diamond Wind Productions). Estab. 1991. Publishes 25-50 songs/year; publishes 10 new songwriters/year. Works with composers and lyricists; teams collaborators. Pays standard royalty.
How to Contact: Write first and obtain permission to submit. Prefers cassette (or VHS videocassette) with 3 songs and lyric sheet. "Photo and bio extremely helpful." Does not return unsolicited material. Reports in 4-6 weeks.
Music: Mostly **country**, **country blues** and **country pop/rock**; also **pop** and **R&B**. Published "Thunder In My Heart" and "Mama I Love You" (by M.L. Northam), recorded by Bronze Bonneville on Continental Records (country); and "Diamond Den," written and recorded by Reenie Diamond on Diamond Wind Records (country).
Tips: "Prepare your demo thoughtfully with a clean, upfront vocal. If you are a self-contained singer/songwriter, be willing to invest in your own career."

DIRECT MANAGEMENT GROUP, #G, 947 N. La Cienega Blvd., Los Angeles CA 90069. (310)854-3535. Partners: Martin Kirkup and Steve Jensen. ASCAP, BMI. Estab. 1989. Publishes 10 songs/year; publishes 2-5 new songwriters/year. Works with composers and lyricists; teams collaborators. Pays variable royalty.
Affiliate(s): Direct World Music (ASCAP), Direct Planet Music (BMI).
How to Contact: Write first and obtain permission to submit with reply card enclosed. Prefers cassette with 3 songs and lyric and lead sheet. SASE. Reports in 3 months.
Music: **Rock**, **pop** and **alternative**. Published "Our Last Time" (by Hanes), recorded by The Robert Cray Band on Mercury Records.

DISCAPON PUBLISHING CO. (ASCAP), Box 3082, Lic NY 11103. (718)721-5599. Contact: Discapon. Music publisher. Estab. 1980. Publishes 100 songs/year. Works with composers. Pays standard royalty.
How to Contact: Write or call first and obtain permission to submit. Does not return unsolicited material. Prefers cassette with 2-6 songs. SASE. Reports in 2 months.
Music: Mostly **background music without words**; also **classical**.

D'NICO INTERNATIONAL, 1627 N. Laurel Ave., Los Angeles CA 90046. (213)650-1334. Manager: Dino Nicolosi. Music publisher. Estab. 1983. Works with composers. Pays standard royalty.
Affiliate(s): Tillandsia Music, Unche Chico Music, EP2, DYCA Music, Anahi Music (ASCAP), D'Nico Music, Amanza Music, Ben Conga Music, Axel Music, L.B. Wilde Music, Diam Music (BMI).
How to Contact: Write first and obtain permission to submit. Prefers cassette and lyric sheet. SASE. Reports in 2 months.
Music: Mostly **pop-dance**, **pop rock** and **Latin**; also **R&B**, **ballads** and **70's music**. Published *Voy A Gritana Los Cuatro Vientos* (by C. Leon/E. Londaits), recorded by Mijares on EMI Records (pop); *Too Many Tears* (by Peter Beckett), recorded by Lauriano Brizvilo on WEA (pop); and "Guajiro Man" (by A. Rubalcava), recorded by Que Pasa on Sony (rap).
Tips: "Send your best 3 songs available. We are a sound business—don't forget the principles of sound!"

DOC PUBLISHING, 10 Luanita Ln., Newport News VA 23606. (804)930-1814. A&R: Judith Guthro. Music publisher. SESAC, BMI, ASCAP, SOCAN. Estab. 1975. Publishes 30-40 songs/year; 20 new songwriters/year. Works with composers and lyricists; teams collaborators. Pays standard royalty. **Affiliate(s):** Dream Machine (SESAC), Doc Holiday Music (ASCAP).
How to Contact: Submit a demo tape by mail. Unsolicited submissions are OK. Does not return submissions. Reports in 2 weeks.
Music: Mostly **country** and **cajun**. Published "Mr. Jones—The Final Chapter," written and recorded by Big Al Downing; "Cajun Stripper," written and recorded by Doug Kershaw; and "That's The Way I Like It" (by King "B"), recorded by King "B" and the New Jack Crew, all on Tug Boat Records.

DON DEL MUSIC (BMI), 902 N. Webster, Port Washington WI 53074. (414)284-5242. Manager: Joseph C. DeLucia. Music publisher, record company (Cha Cha Records) and music promoter—"Wisconsin Singer/Songwriter Series." Works with composers and lyricists. Pays standard royalty (negotiable).
How to Contact: Write and obtain permission to submit. Prefers cassette with 4-6 songs and lyric sheet. "A simple arrangement is much better than a major production—make sure the lyrics can be heard." SASE. Reports in 3 months.
Music: Mostly **acoustic folk**, **country** and **R&B**.

DORÉ RECORDS (ASCAP), 1608 Argyle, Hollywood CA 90028. (213)462-6614. Fax: (213)462-6197. President: Lew Bedell. Music publisher and record company. Estab. 1960. Publishes 15 songs/year; publishes 15 new songwriters/year. Pays standard royalty. Artist royalties vary.
How to Contact: Submit demo tape by mail. Unsolicited submissions are OK. Prefers cassette and lyric sheet. Does not return unsolicited material. Reports in 2 weeks.
Music: Mostly **all kinds**; also **novelty** and **comedy**. Published *Percolator* (by Biden & Freeman), recorded by the Ventures on EMI Records; and *Ten-Uh-See*, written and recorded by Steve Rumph on Doré Records.
Tips: "Currently seeking an R&B group with male lead vocals. No rap."

BUSTER DOSS MUSIC (BMI), Box 13, Estill Springs TN 37330. (615)649-2577. President: Buster Doss. Music publisher and record company (Stardust). Estab. 1959. Publishes 500 songs/year; publishes 50 new songwriters/year. Teams collaborators. Pays standard royalty.
How to Contact: Write or call first and obtain permission to submit a tape. Prefers cassette with 2 songs and lyric sheets. SASE. Reports in 1 week.
Music: Mostly **country**; also **rock**. Published "Movin' Out, Movin' Up, Movin' On" (by Buster Doss), recorded by "Danny Boy" Squire; *Rainbow of Roses* (by Buster Doss), recorded by Larry C. Johnson; and "Lovin' For A Lifetime" (by Steve Ledford), recorded by Linda Wunder, all on Stardust Records.

*DPP MUSIC, Falcon Mews, Oakmead Rd., London SW12 9SJ **England**. (081)675-5584. Fax: (081)675-6313. Professional Manager: Joanna Underwood. Music publisher. Estab. 1989. Works with composers. Pays more than 50% royalty.
How to Contact: Submit demo tape by mail. Unsolicited submissions are OK. Prefers cassette with 3-4 songs and lyric sheet. Does not return unsolicited submissions. Reports in 1 month.
Music: Mostly **dance/R&B**, **pop** and **rock**; also **anything interesting**. Published "Hey Hey," written and recorded by D&S; "You're The Only One" (by Ward/Peter), both recorded by CCN on WGAF Records (dance); and *Deathroom* (by Ward/Peter), recorded by Deathroom on PMI Video (rave).

DREAM SEQUENCE MUSIC, LTD. (BMI), P.O. Box 2194, Charlottesville VA 22902. (804)295-1877. President: Kevin McNoldy. Music publisher. Estab. 1987. Publishes 12-15 songs/year; publishes 2-3 new songwriters/year. Works with composers and lyricists; teams collaborators. Usually pays standard royalty, "but everything is negotiable."
How to Contact: Submit demo tape by mail. Unsolicited submissions OK. Prefers cassette with 3-5 songs and lyric sheet. Does not return unsolicited material. Reports in 4-5 weeks.
Music: Mostly **rock**, **pop** and **R&B**. Published "Paper Dolls," written and recorded by Melissa McGinty (ballad); *Chapter 1: The Coming of Age*, written and recorded by Wendy Repass (folk/pop); and *Out of the Shadows* (by Doug Schneider/Kevin McNoldy), recorded by Doug Schneider (pop), all on DSM, Ltd. Records.

*DREZDON BLACQUE MUSIC (ASCAP), 414 N. Quaker Lane, Hyde Park NY 12538. (914)229-7580. Contact: Lisa Fairbanks. Music publisher. Estab. 1986. Publishes 20 songs/year; publishes 1 or 2 new songwriters/year. Pays standard royalty.
How to Contact: Submit demo tape by mail. Prefers cassette (or VHS videocassette if available) with up to 4 songs and lyric sheet. Does not return material. Reports only if interested. "No phone calls!"

Music: Mostly **rock, pop** and **R&B**; also **country**. Published "Angeline" (by George Fletcher); "Heart to Heart" (by Lisa Fairbanks); and "Can't You See" (by Fairbanks/Fletcher), all recorded by Drezdon Blacque on FLG Records (rock).
Tips: "We want hooky pop songs a la Heart, Alannah Myles and Fleetwood Mac. Please be professional!"

*DRIVE MUSIC, INC. (BMI), 10351 Santa Monica Blvd., Los Angeles CA 90025. (310)553-3490. Fax: (310)553-3373. Executive Vice President: Arthur Braun. Music publisher, record company (Drive Entertainment). Estab. 1993. Publishes 25 songs/year; publishes 6 new songwriters/year. Hires staff songwriters. Works with composers and lyricists; teams collaborators. Pays standard royalty.
Affiliate(s): Donunda Music (ASCAP).
How to Contact: Submit demo tape by mail. Unsolicited submissions are OK. Prefers with 3 songs and lyric sheet. "Send regular mail only." SASE. Reports in 2 weeks.
Music: Mostly **dance, pop, rock**; also **R&B**. Published all Sharon, Lois and Bram product on Rhino/W.E.A. (children's).
Tips: "Practice your craft and never give up."

DUANE MUSIC, INC. (BMI), 382 Clarence Ave., Sunnyvale CA 94086. (408)739-6133. President: Garrie Thompson. Music publisher. Publishes 10-20 songs/year; publishes 1 new songwriter/year. Pays standard royalty.
Affiliate(s): Morhits Publishing (BMI).
How to Contact: Prefers cassette with 1-2 songs. SASE. Reports in 1 month.
Music: **Blues, country, disco, easy listening, rock, soul** and **top 40/pop**. Published "Little Girl," recorded by The Syndicate of Sound & Ban (rock); "Warm Tender Love," recorded by Percy Sledge (soul); and "My Adorable One," recorded by Joe Simon (blues).

EARITATING MUSIC PUBLISHING (BMI), P.O. Box 1101, Gresham OR 97030. Owner: Steve Montague. Music publisher. Estab. 1979. Publishes 40 songs/year; publishes 5 new songwriters/year. Works with composers or lyricists; teams collaborators. Pays individual per song contract, usually greater than 50% to writer.
How to Contact: Submit demo tape by mail. Unsolicited submissions are OK. Prefers cassette with lyric sheet. "Submissions should be copyrighted by the author. We will deal for rights if interested." Does not return unsolicited material. No reply unless interested.
Music: Mostly **rock, contemporary Christian** and **country**; also **folk**.
Tips: "Melody is most important, lyrics second. Style and performance take a back seat to these. A good song will stand with just one voice and one instrument."

EARTH DANCE MUSIC, P.O. Box 241, Newbury Park CA 91320. (805)499-9912. Fax: (805)499-9047. President: Gil Yslas. Music publisher. Estab. 1990. Publishes 90-120 songs/year; publishes 6-10 new songwriters/year. Hires staff writers. Works with composers. Pays standard royalty.
How to Contact: Write first and obtain permission to submit. Prefers cassette. "Interested in master quality catalogs." Does not return unsolicited material. Reports in 1 month.
Music: Mostly **instrumental, TV-background** and **world music**; also **adult contemporary** and **new acoustic**. *The Unicorn*, written and recorded by R. Searles; and *Winter Air*, written and recorded by Aerial Logic, both on Sundown Records.

EARTHSCREAM MUSIC PUBLISHING CO. (BMI), 8377 Westview Dr., Houston TX 77055. (713)464-GOLD. Contact: Jeff Johnson. Music publisher, record company and record producer. Estab. 1975. Publishes 12 songs/year; publishes 4 new songwriters/year. Pays standard royalty.
Affiliate(s): Reach For The Sky Music Pub. (ASCAP).
How to Contact: Submit demo tapy by mail—unsolicited submissions are OK. Prefers cassette (or videocassette) with 2-5 songs and lyric sheet. SASE. Reports in 2 months.
Music: **New rock, country** and **top 40/pop**. Published "Ride of a Lifetime" (by Greg New), recorded by Billy Rutherford on Earth Records; "Goodbye Sexy Carol," written and recorded by Terry Mitchell (new age) and "Do You Remember" (by Pennington/Wells), recorded by Perfect Strangers (pop rock) on Weeny Dog Records.

ECCENTRAX MUSIC CO. (ASCAP), 80855 Coon Creek Rd., Armada MI 48005. (810)784-5745. President: Debbie Coulon. Music publisher (Multi-Music Management). Estab. 1990. Publishes 3 songs/year; publishes 2 new songwriters/year. Works with composers and lyricists; teams collaborators. Pays standard royalty.
How to Contact: Write first and obtain permission to submit. Prefers cassette with 3 songs and lyric sheet. "Please make sure lyrics are understandable." SASE. Reports in 6-8 weeks.

Music: Mostly **pop, country** and **rock**; also **children's** and **R&B**. Published "Until That Day" and "It Happens," written and recorded by Allen Bondar; and "When I'm With You" (by A. Bondar/V. Ripp), recorded by G. Worth, all on Eccentrax Records.
Tips: "Include your name and address on demo tape and typed lyrics."

*EDITIONS MUSICALES ALPHA, 5 rue Lincoln, Paris 75008 **France**. 44136161. Managing Director: Jacques Wolfsohn. Music publisher. Estab. 1959. Publishes 20 songs/year; publishes 1 new songwriter/ year. Works with composers and lyricists. Pays standard royalty.
How to Contact: Call first and obtain permission to submit. Prefers cassette with 2 songs. Does not return material. Reports in 1 week.
Music: Mostly **pop, rock** and **classical**; also **children's** and **ballet**. Published "Cactus" (by J. DuFronc), recorded by Vanessa Paradis on Remark Productions.

*EDITIONS SCIPION, 33 rue des Jeuneurs, Paris 75002 **France**. A.D.: Bialek Robert. Music publisher, management. Estab. 1983. Publishes 40 songs/year; publishes 1 new songwriter/year. Works with composers and lyricists.
How to Contact: Submit demo tape by mail. Unsolicited submissions are OK. Prefers cassette. SAE and IRC. Reports in 1 week.
Music: Mostly **rock**.

ELECT MUSIC PUBLISHING, P.O. Box 22, Underhill VT 05489. (802)899-3787. Founder: Bobby Hackney. Music publisher and record company (LBI Records). BMI. Estab. 1980. Publishes 24 songs/year; publishes 3 new songwriters/year. Works with composers and/or lyricists; teams collaborators. Pays standard royalty.
How to Contact: Submit a demo tape by mail. Unsolicited submissions are OK. Prefers cassette and VHS videocassette with 3-4 songs and lyric sheet. SASE. Reports in 1 month.
Music: Mostly **reggae, R&B** and **rap**; also **New Age**, **rock** and some **country**. Published *Reggae Mood* and *Hurry Up* (by B. Hackney), recorded by Lambsbread; and "In and Out of Love" (by Lewis Lester), recorded by Karrie Taylor, all on LBI Records.
Tips: "Send your best and remember, the amount of postage it took to get to the publisher is the same amount it will take to have your tape returned."

ELEMENT MOVIE AND MUSIC (BMI), Box 30260, Bakersfield CA 93385. Producer: Jar the Superstar. Music publisher, record company and record producer. Publishes 2 songs/year; publishes 2 new songwriters/year. Hires staff writers. Pays standard royalty.
How to Contact: Write first about your interest or to arrange personal interview. "Query with résumé of credits. Do not mail songs without permission! We are taking interviews only." Prefers 15 ips reel-to-reel or cassette with 1-3 songs. Does not return unsolicited material. Reports in 3 months.
Music: Mostly **R&B, rock, soul, gospel, jazz, progressive, easy listening** and **top 40/pop**; also **blues, children's, choral, church/religious, classical, country, dance-oriented, MOR, Spanish** and **music for feature films**. Published "God Will Post Your Bail" (by Judge A. Robertson) (Christian pop); "What Could I've Done Without Jesus Around" (by Jar the Superstar); and "Put Nothing Over God" (by Jar the Superstar) all on Element Records (church rock).

*ELLIOT MUSIC, 45 rue Vauvenargues, Paris 75018 **France**. (33)142261615. Fax: (33)146277999. A&R: Langella. Music publisher and record producer. Estab. 1991. Publishes 20 songs/year. Hires staff writers. Works with composers and lyricists; teams collaborators. Pays standard royalty.
How to Contact: Submit demo tape by mail. Unsolicited submissions are OK. Prefers cassette. SAE and IRC. Reports in 1 week.
Music: Mostly **dance** and **rap**. Published "I Wanna Be With You," written and recorded by Lena on Elliot/EMI Records (dance).

EMANDELL TUNES, 10220 Glade Ave., Chatsworth CA 91311. (818)341-2264. Fax: (818)341-1008. President/Administrator: Leroy C. Lovett, Jr. Estab. 1979. Publishes 6-12 songs/year; publishes 3-4 new songwriters. Pays standard royalty.
Affiliate(s): Ben-Lee Music (BMI), Birthright Music (ASCAP), Northworth Songs, Chinwah Songs, Gertrude Music (all SESAC); LMS Print/Publishings Co. and Nadine LTD, Music/Artist Management Company, Zurich, Switzerland.
How to Contact: Write or call first to get permission to submit tape. Prefers cassette (or videocassette) with 4-5 songs and lead or lyric sheet. Include bio of writer, singer or group. SASE. Reports in 4-6 weeks.
Music: **Inspirational, contemporary gospel** and **choral**; also **strong country and light-top 40 "rap-gospel."** Published *Something Within* (by Paul Jackson), recorded by Texas Mass Choir on Savoy Records (gospel); *If There's A Way* (by Mark Seline), recorded by Pam Tillis on Liberty Records

(country); and *Get Busy With It* (by James Jernigan), recorded by The Jamz Gang on Faith Records (rap gospel).
Tips: "Concentrate on strong lyrics and easy flowing melody. Have good 'hook' or chorus."

EMF PRODUCTIONS, Suite D, 1000 E. Prien Lake Rd., Lake Charles LA 70601. (318)474-0435. President: Ed Fruge. Music publisher, record producer. Estab. 1984. Works with composers and lyricists. Pays standard royalty.
How to Contact: Submit demo tape by mail. Unsolicited submissions are OK. Prefers cassette (or VHS videocassette) with 4 songs and lyric sheet. Does not return material. Reports in 6 weeks.
Music: Mostly **R&B**, **pop** and **rock**; also **country** and **gospel**.

*EMI MUSIC PUBLISHING, E. Plasky Laan 140B, Brussels 1860 **Belgium**. (02)735-29-02. Fax: (02)735-92-14. Professional Manager: Van Handenhove Guy. Music publisher and production company. Estab. 1970. Publishes 5-6 new songwriters/year. Works with composers and lyricists; teams collaborators. Pays standard royalty.
How to Contact: Submit demo tape by mail. Unsolicited submissions are OK. Prefers cassette (or DAT) with 3 or 4 songs. Does not return material. Reports in 3 weeks.
Music: Mostly **pop**, **dance** and **rock**; also **AOR**. Published "Love's Embrace" (by Kid Coco), recorded by Dinky Toys; and "Rain," recorded by B.C. & Basic Boom, both on Creastars/BMG (dance).

EMPEROR OF EMPERORS (ASCAP), 16133 Fairview Ave., Fontana CA 92336. (909)355-2372 (phone and fax). President/Producer: Stephen V. Mann. Music publisher, record company, record producer (Emperor Productions) and distributor. Estab. 1979. Publishes 250-1,000 songs/year; publishes 50 new songwriters/year. Hires staff writers. Works with composers and lyricists; team collaborators. Pays standard royaltys in most cases, but negotiable.
How to Contact: Submit demo tape by mail. Unsolicited submissions are OK. Prefers cassette album material with 12-15 songs and lyric or lead sheet. Quality stressed instead of quantity. Material is kept on file. Signs for minimum of 5 years.
Music: Mostly **rock**, **pop** and **country**; also **rap**, **jazz**, **soul**, **heavy metal**, **gospel**, **traditional Indian**, **New Age**, **folk**, **techno**, **blues**, and **reggae**. Published *Reminisence*, recorded by Princesita De Youngay; *All Souled Out*, recorded by Krishnautiz; and *Music of Peru*, all arranged and produced by Stephen V. Mann.
Tips: "Melody should be suitable for motion picture sound tracks and dance. Top-notch quality and serious inquiries only."

EMPTY SKY MUSIC COMPANY, 14th St., P.O. Box 626, Verplanck NY 10596. Promotional Manager: Lisa Lancaster. Music publisher, record company (Empty Sky, Yankee, Verplanck) and record producer (Rick Carbone for Empty Sky). ASCAP, BMI. Estab. 1982. Publishes 15-20 songs/year; publishes 10 new songwriters/year. Works with composers and lyricists; teams collaborators. Pays standard royalty.
Affiliate(s): Empty Sky Music (ASCAP) and Rick Carbone Music (BMI).
How to Contact: Submit a demo tape by mail. Unsolicited submissions are OK. Prefers cassette with 3-5 songs and lyric sheet. SASE. Reports in 3-4 months.
Music: Mostly **country**, **gospel** and **pop**; also **rap**, **rock** and **rap/gospel**. Published "Take Time to Love" (by B. Martinson/K. Alexander) and "Oh Lord, How Come You're Takin' Her Away" (by R. Carbone), both recorded by Bob Martinson on Empty Sky Records; and "White Water" (by E. Aldridge), recorded by Phil Coley on Verplanck Records.
Tips: "Don't send the same songs to us that ten other publishers are considering for publishing, too."

EMZEE MUSIC, Box 3213, S. Farmingdale NY 11735. (516)420-9169. President: Maryann Zalesak. Music publisher, record company (Ivory Tower Records, Avenue Records). Estab. 1970. Publishes 40 songs/year; publishes 16 new songwriters/year. Hires staff songwriters. Works with composers and lyricists; teams collaborators. Pays standard royalty.
How to Contact: Submit demo tape by mail. Unsolicited submissions are OK. Prefers cassette with 3 songs and lyric sheet. SASE. Reports in 7-8 weeks. "Press kits are preferred."
Music: Mostly **rock**, **pop** and **country**; also **R&B** and **rap**. Published *Comin' Down*, written and recorded by Emma Zale (groove rock) and *Memories Of You*, written and recorded by Tony Novarro (guitar instrumental), both on Ave. A Records; and *Reflections*, written and recorded by John Sanders on Ivory Tower Records (jazz).
Tips: "Be persistent, organized, and dedicated."

*THE ESCAPE ARTIST COMPANY, 20 Woodlands Rd., Bushey, Herts WD2 2LR **United Kingdom** 010-44-923-244673. Fax: 010-44-923-244693. CEO/Professional Manager: Barry Blue or Ian West. Estab. 1975. Publishes approximately 20 songs/year. Works with composers and lyricists; teams collaborators. Pays negotiable royalty.

Affiliate(s): Shanna Music/Sony Music (ASCAP).
How to Contact: Submit demo tape by mail. Unsolicited submissions are OK. Prefers cassette with 2-3 songs and lyric sheet. Does not return material. Reports in 3-4 weeks.
Music: Mostly **R&B/soul** and **pop/dance**. Published "Escaping" (by Blue/Smith), recorded by Asia Blue on A&M Records (R&B); *Crime To Be Cool* (by Blue/Smith), recorded by Alison Limerick on Arista Records (R&B/dance); and "Morning Noon & Night" (by Blue/Brown), recorded by Lorraine on Columbia Records (pop/dance).

ESI MUSIC GROUP (BMI), (formerly Entertainment Services Music Group), Suite 118, 9 Music Square S., Nashville TN 37203-3203. (615)297-9712. Executive Administrator: Curt Conroy. Music publisher. Estab. 1990. Publishes 50-60 songs/year. Pays standard royalty.
How to Contact: Submit a demo tape by mail. Unsolicited submissions are OK. Prefers "good quality 3-4 song demo" and lyric sheet. "Guitar or piano-vocal OK. All envelopes must meet postal requirements for content." SASE. Reports within 4-6 weeks.
Music: Mostly **country (traditional)**, **country rock** and **country pop**; also **country blues**. Published "Wine Over Matter," written and recorded by Pinto Bennett on MCM Records (country); "In the Wings," written and recorded by David Stewart on Wings Records; and "I've Been Branded," written and recorded by Hannah Onassis on Badger Records.
Tips: "Listen to current Nashville releases and match your songs to specific artists. Send the best demo tape possible."

EUDAEMONIC MUSIC, P.O. Box 371 Peck Slip Station, New York NY 10272. (212)495-6622. President: Gary Leet. Music publisher. Estab. 1992. Publishes 10 songs/year; publishes 2 new songwriters/year. Pays standard royalty.
How to Contact: Submit demo tape by mail. Unsolicited submissions are OK. Prefers cassette (or VHS videocassette) with as many songs as you feel appropriate. Does not return unsolicited material. Reports in 4-6 weeks.
Music: Mostly **progressive/alternative rock**, **new wave/punk rock** and **progressive folk**; also **off the wall**. Published "Laughing Song" and "Scratch & Claw" (by Mica), recorded by Altered Boys on URATV Records; and "Ice Ages," written and recorded by Chris Grimes on Industrial Records.
Tips: "Music always comes first, a really rockin' tune. Then clever lyrics is a nice bonus. Above all, creativity is most important."

EVER-OPEN-EYE MUSIC (PRS), Wern Fawr Farm, Pencoed, MID, Glam CF356NB **United Kingdom**. Phone: (0656)860041. Managing Director: M.R. Blanche. Music publisher and record company (Red-Eye Records). Member PPL and MCPS. Estab. 1980. Publishes 6 songs/year. Works with composers and lyricists; teams collaborators. Pays negotiable amount.
How to Contact: Submit demo tape by mail. Unsolicited submissions are OK. Prefers cassette (or VHS videocassette). Does not return unsolicited material.
Music: Mostly **R&B**, **gospel** and **pop**; also **swing**. Published "Breakdown Song," "Shadow of the Sun" and "Outside Looking In," written by Finn/Jones on Red Eye Records.

EVOPOETICS PUBLISHING (ASCAP), P.O. Box 71231, Milwaukee WI 53211-7331. (414)332-7474. President: Dr. Martin Jack Rosenblum. Music publisher and record company (Roar Records). Estab. 1969. Works with composers.
Affiliate(s): Roar Recording, American Ranger Incorporated and Lion Publishing.
How to Contact: "Writers must query in writing first before submitting. We cannot return phone calls as we have been overloaded and doing so is not cost-effective. All inquiries must be addressed to Cicero DeWestbrook, Office Manager." SASE. Reports in 1 week.
Music: **Progressive rock with a serious poetic lyric intent**. Published *Free Hand* (by Rosenblum), recorded by Blues Riders on Flying Fish Records; "Down on the Spirit Farm," recorded by Spirit Farm Band; and "Music Lingo," (by Jack Grassel).

EXCURSION MUSIC GROUP, Suite 388, 9 Music Square S., Nashville TN 37203. (800)760-4646. President: Frank T. Prins. Music publisher, record company (Excursion Records) and record producer. BMI, ASCAP. Estab. 1976. Publishes 25 songs/year; publishes 5 new songwriters/year. Hires staff writers. Works with composers and lyricists; teams collaborators. Pays standard royalty.
Affiliate(s): Echappee Music (BMI), Excursion Music (ASCAP).
How to Contact: Write or call first and obtain permission to submit. Prefers cassette or VHS videocassette with 3 songs and lyric sheet. SASE. Reports in 3 weeks.

Music: Mostly **pop**, **country** and **gospel**; also **rock** and **R&B**. Published "Jukin' Down in Mississippi" (by Ian Ballard) and "I Just Can't Stand It" (by Ron Dunivan), both recorded by Ian Ballard.

*F.E.D. PUBLISHING CO. (ASCAP), P.O. Box 101107, San Antonio TX 78201-9107. (800)846-5201. President: Fred Weiss. Music publisher and record company (Belt Drive). Estab. 1991. Publishes 6-8 songs/year; publishes 4 new songwriters/year. Works with composers and/or lyricists. Pays negotiable royalty.
How to Contact: Submit demo tape by mail. Unsolicited submissions are OK. Prefers cassette (or VHS videocassette if available) with 1-3 songs. Does not return unsolicited submissions.
Music: Mostly **rock**, **Latin** and **country**; also **dance**, **hip hop**, and **pop**. Published "Speaking in Tongues" (by Flores), recorded by Innocent Bystander; *City of Passion*, written and recorded by Carolyn Flores (video soundtrack); and *World House*, recorded by World Bizarre.

DOUG FAIELLA PUBLISHING, 19153 Paver Barnes Rd., Marysville OH 43040. (513)644-8295. President: Doug Faiella. Music publisher, record company (Studio 7 Records) and recording studio. BMI. Estab. 1984. Publishes 25 songs/year; publishes 5 new songwriters/year. Works with composers; teams collaborators. Pays standard royalty.
How to Contact: Write to obtain permission to submit a tape. SASE. Prefers cassette with 3 songs and lyric sheets. Does not return unsolicited material. Reports in 4 weeks.
Music: Mostly **country**, **gospel** and **rock**.

FAMOUS MUSIC PUBLISHING COMPANIES, Suite 300, 10635 Santa Monica Blvd., Los Angeles CA 90025. (310)441-1300. Fax: (310)441-4722. Creative Dept.: Lisa Wells-Cronin, Roanna Gillespie, Robyn Roseman, Ellie Schwimmer. Estab. 1929. Publishes 500 songs/year; publishes 5 new songwriters/year. Hires staff songwriters. Works with composers and lyricists; teams collaborators. Pays standard royalty.
Affiliate(s): Famous Music (ASCAP) and Ensign Music (BMI).
How to Contact: Write or call first and obtain permission to submit. Prefers cassette with 3 songs and lyric sheet. Reports in 2-3 months.
Music: Mostly **rock**, **R&B** and **pop**. Published "What's Up" (by 4 Non-Blondes) and "Ghetto Jam" (by Domino), recorded by Bjork (alternative).

F&J MUSIC, 23, Thrayle House, Stockwell Road, London SW9 0XU **United Kingdom**. (071)737-6681/(081)672-6158. Fax: (071)737-7881. Managing Director: Errol Jones. Music publisher and record company (Leopard Music/Jet Set International Records). PRS, BMI. Estab. 1978. Publishes 75 songs/year. Publishes 35 new songwriters/year. Works with composers and lyricists; teams collaborators. Pays standard royalty.
Affiliate(s): EURUSA Worldwide Publishing (BMI) and F&J Music Publishing (PRS).
How to Contact: Write first and obtain permission to submit. Prefers cassette and/or CD, 12" vinyl with 3 songs, or more. Include biography, résumé and picture. SAE and IRC. Reports in 2 weeks.
Music: Mostly **dance**, **soul** and **pop**; also **ballads**, **reggae** and **gospel**. Published "Time After Time," (by Guy Spell), recorded by Rico J. on Leopard Music/Jet Set International Records (disco/soul); "I Need You" (by F. Campbell/E. North Jr.), recorded by Big Africa (soul/reggae); and "God is Beauty," written and recorded by Evelyn Ladimeji (gospel), both on Leopard Music.

*FARR-AWAY MUSIC, 701 N. Graycroft, Madison TN 37115. (615)865-2639. President: Tony Farr. Music publisher. Estab. 1970.
How to Contact: Submit demo tape by mail. Unsolicited submissions are OK. Prefers cassette or videocassette with 2-3 songs and lyric sheet. Does not return material.
Music: Mostly **country**.

FAT CITY PUBLISHING, #2, 1226 17th Ave. S., Nashville TN 37212. (615)320-7678. Fax: (615)321-5382. Vice President: Noel Michael. Music publisher, record company (Fat City Artists), record producer and booking agency (Fat City Artists). Estab. 1972. Publishes 25 songs/year; publishes 10 new songwriters/year. Hires staff writers. Works with composers and lyricists; teams collaborators. Pays standard royalty.

Affiliate(s): Fort Forever (BMI).
How to Contact: Submit demo tape by mail. Unsolicited submissions are OK. Prefers cassette (or VHS videocassette) with 4-6 songs and lyric sheet. SASE. Reports in 2 weeks.
Music: Mostly **rock, country** and **blues**; also **alternative, rockabilly** and **jazz.**
Tips: "Provide as much information and material as possible."

FEZSONGS (ASCAP), Dept. SM, 429 S. Lewis Rd., Royersford PA 19468. (215)948-8228. Fax: (215)948-4175. President: Jim Femino. Vice President: Mike Moore. Music publisher. Estab. 1970. Publishes 12-15 songs/year; publishes 1-2 new songwriters/year. Works with composers and lyricists; teams collaborators. Pays standard royalty.
How to Contact: Write first and obtain permission to submit. Prefers cassette (or VHS videocassette) with 3 songs and lyric sheet. SASE. Reports in 4-6 weeks.
Music: Country.
Tips: "Write, write, re-write then write some more."

*****FILMWORKS,** P.O. Box 2363, Clarksville TN 37040. (615)647-2641. Fax: (615)645-8139. Founder/Publisher: E.A. Lawson. Music publisher, film and video production and record producer. Estab. 1990. Publishes 3-5 songs/year; publishes 5-7 new songwriters/year. Works with composers. Pays standard royalty.
How to Contact: Submit demo tape by mail. Unsolicited submissions are OK. Prefers VHS videocassette with 3 songs and lyric sheet. Does not return material. Reports in 1 month.
Music: Mostly **rock, pop** and **country**; also **children's, special** and **disco.** Published *Never Die* (by E.A. Lawson), recorded by Held Hostage (rock); *I Wish Christmas Was Like It Use to Be*, written and recorded by Barry Winslow (pop); and *Louisiana Man* (by Traci Packard), all on Filmworks.
Tips: "Send your best efforts; send 3 songs only per submission."

FIRST RELEASE MUSIC PUBLISHING, 943 N. Madison Ave., Pasadena CA 91104. (818)794-5545 (phone and fax). President: Danny Howell. Music publisher. BMI, ASCAP, SACEM, GEMA, PRS, MCPS. Publishes 30-50 songs/year. Hires staff songwriters. Pays standard royalty; co-publishing negotiable. "Very active in obtaining cover records and film and TV uses, e.g., *Arsenio Hall, Lethal Weapon III*, many others."
Affiliate(s): Fully Conscious Music, Cadillac Pink, Illegal Songs, I.R.S. Songs, Reggatta Music, Magnetic Publishing Ltd., Animal Logic Publishing and Blue Turtle Music.
How to Contact: "We *never* accept unsolicited tapes or phone calls—you must have referral or request." Returns all unsolicited material. Reports only if interested, but "retain personally written critique for every song I agree to accept."
Music: "We are interested in great songs and great writers. We are currently successful in all areas." Published "Power of Love" (by Tom Kimmel/Elizabeth Vidal), recorded by Sam Moore on Sony Records (R&B).
Tips: "Show up at one of my guest workshops and play me the last song you would ever play for a publisher; not the worst, the last! Educate yourself as to what writers we represent before pitching me (e.g., Sting, Lyle Lovett, Concrete Blonde)."

FIRST TIME MUSIC (PUBLISHING) U.K. LTD. (PRS), Sovereign House, 12 Trewartha Road, Praa Sands, Penzance, Cornwall TR20 9ST **United Kingdom.** Phone: (0736)762826. Fax: (0736)763328. Managing Director: Roderick G. Jones. Music publisher, record company (First Time Records), record producer and management firm (First Time Management and Production Co.). Member MCPS. Estab. 1986. Publishes 500-750 songs/year; 20-50 new songwriters/year. Hires staff writers. Works with composers and lyricists; teams collaborators. Pays standard royalty; "50-60% to established and up-and-coming writers with the right attitude."
How to Contact: Submit a demo tape—unsolicited submissions are OK. Prefers cassette, 1⅞ ips cassette (or VHS videocassette "of professional quality") with unlimited number of songs and lyric or lead sheets, but not necessary. Reports in 4-10 weeks. SAE and IRC. "Postal costs in the U.K. are much higher than the U.S.—one IRC doesn't even cover the cost of a letter to the U.S., let alone the return of cassettes. Enclose the correct amount for return and contact as stated." Reports in 4-10 weeks.
Music: Mostly **country** and **folk, pop/soul/top 20/rock, country with an Irish/Scottish crossover**; also **gospel/Christian.** Published "The Robinsons Ball" (by Pete Arnold), recorded by Brendan Shine on Play Records (MOR/country); "Sentimental Over You" (by Rod Jones/Colin Eade), recorded by PJ Proby on J'ace Records (pop); and "I Wouldn't Have It Any Other Way" (by Bill Allen), recorded by Kenny Paul on Luvinikind Records (country).
Tips: "Have a professional approach—present well produced demos. First impressions are important and may be the only chance you get. Remember that you as a writer/artist are in a competitive market. As an active independent-international publisher we require good writers/artists and product. As a company we seek to work with writers. If the product is good then we generally come up with something

in the way of covers. Writers are advised to join the Guild of International Songwriters and Composers in the United Kingdom."

FIVE ROSES MUSIC GROUP (BMI), P.O. Box 417, White Sulpher Springs NY 12787. (914)292-4042. President: Sammie Lee Marler. Music publisher, record company, record distributor and booking agent. Estab. 1989. Publishes 50-75 songs/year. Works with composers and lyricists. Pays standard royalty.
How to Contact: Submit a demo tape by mail. Unsolicited submissions are OK. Prefers cassette with 3 songs. SASE. Reports in 3 weeks.
Music: Mostly **country and western, bluegrass, country rock, country gospel, gospel, light rock, R&B** and **children's**. Published "I'm Missin You" (by Larry Capton) (C&W); "Still Thinkin About You" (by Tom Loughlin) (C&W); and "Low Down And Dirty" (by Bob Freedman) (rock).
Tips: "Send what you have. Be kind and not demanding."

***FLASH INTERNATIONAL (BMI)**, P.O. Box 580058, Houston TX 77258-0058. (713)488-1978. Fax: (713)488-4559. Owner: Renel L. Boudreaux. Music publisher, record company and record producer. Estab. 1981. Publishes 3 songs/year; publishes 1 new songwriter/year. Hires staff songwriters. Teams collaborators. Pays standard royalty.
How to Contact: Submit demo tape by mail. Unsolicited submissions are OK. Prefers cassette and lyric sheet. SASE. Reports in 2 weeks.
Music: Mostly **R&B, jazz** and **gospel**; also **rap** and **country**. Published "We Gone Party" (by C. Johnson), recorded by Conrad Johnson on GC Records (jazz).
Tips: "Must have a unique style and a good sound."

***FLOWSOUND LTD.**, The Cottage, 15 Overbury Rd., London N15 6RH **United Kingdom**. (081)802-2522. Fax: (081)802-3100. Managing Director: Rick Davey. Music publisher, record company (Zion Records, Universal Egg, Custer's Last Stand, Dream Addict, Interchill) and record producer. Estab. 1990. Publishes 50 songs/year; publishes 8 new songwriters/year. Works with composers and lyricists; teams collaborators. "We usually split 75%-25% artist favor but we negotiate depending on contract."
How to Contact: Submit demo tape by mail. Unsolicited submissions are OK. Prefers cassette. SAE and IRC. Reports in 2 weeks.
Music: Mostly **dub reggae, ambient** and **house**; also **experimental** and **dance**. Published "One Love" (by Cod/Tench/Perch), recorded by Molara on Big Life (Skunk) Records (pop/reggae); "Rain" (by Packett/Radford), recorded by K.O.T.O.T. on Planet Dog Records (ambient); and "Re-Evolution" (by McKenna), recorded by Shamen on One Little Indian Records (ambient).
Tips: "Be yourself and be spontaneous. Target your market. Check out the sort of music a company does before sending tapes. It saves everybody time and money. I still get heavy metal tapes sent but no matter how good, I don't do it."

***FLYING RED HORSE PUBLISHING (BMI)**, 7139 Azalea, Dallas TX 75230-3633. (214)363-5771. Contact: Beverly Houston. Music publisher, record company (Remarkable Records) and record producer. Estab. 1993. Publishes 15-30 songs/year; publishes 6-10 new songwriters/year. Works with composers and lyricists. Pays standard royalty.
How to Contact: Submit demo tape by mail. Unsolicited submissions OK. Prefers cassette with 3 songs and lyric sheet. SASE. Reports in 1 month.
Music: Mostly **children's**. Published *That's What I Like About You* (by Beverly Houston and Barbara McMillan); *The Dinosaur Rag* and *Lightning Bug Song* (both by Beverly Houston), all on Remarkable Records.
Tips: "Even when a song is written for children, it should still meet the criteria for a well-written song—and be pleasing to adults as well."

FOCAL POINT MUSIC PUBLISHERS (BMI), Dept. SM, 920 McArthur Blvd., Warner Robins GA 31093. (912)923-6533. Manager: Ray Melton. Music publisher and record company. Estab. 1964. Publishes 4 songs/year; publishes 1 new songwriter/year. Works with composers. Pays standard royalty. "Songwriters must have BMI affiliation."
How to Contact: Write first to get permission to send a tape. Prefers cassette with 2-4 songs and lead sheet. Prefers studio produced demos. SASE. Reports in 3 months.
Music: Mostly **country** and **gospel**; also **"old-style pop and humor."**
Tips: "Try it out on your friends. Go to workshops. Belong to a songwriters group."

MARK FOSTER MUSIC COMPANY, Box 4012, Champaign IL 61824-4012. (217)398-2760. Fax: (217)398-2791. President: Jane C. Menkhaus. Music publisher. Estab. 1962. Publishes 20-30 songs/year; publishes 4-5 new songwriters/year. Works with composers. Pays 5-10% over first 3,000 copies choral music sold.

Affiliate(s): Marko Press (BMI) and Fostco Press (ASCAP).
How to Contact: Submit demo tape by mail. Unsolicited submissions are OK. Prefers cassette and 1 copy choral manuscript (must be legible). Include brief bio of composer/arranger if new. SASE. Reports in 3-4 months.
Music: Mostly **sacred SATB, secular SATB** and **sacred and secular treble & male choir**; also **conducting books** and **Kodaly materials**. Published "Two Early American Hymns" (by Crawford Thoburn) (sacred SATB); "As Imperceptibly as Grief" (by Timothy Snyder) (SATB secular).
Tips: "Must be well-constructed piece to begin with, manuscript should be in decent format preferable with keyboard reduction."

FOUR NEWTON PUBLISHING (BMI), Rt. 1, Box 187-A, Whitney TX 76692. (817)694-4047. President: Allen Newton. Music publisher, record company (Pristine Records, Pleasure Records, Cactus Flats, MFN). Estab. 1980. Publishes 20 songs/year; publishes about 10 new songwriters/year. Works with composers and lyricists; teams collaborators. Pays standard royalty.
Affiliate(s): Stephash Publishing (ASCAP).
How to Contact: Submit a demo tape by mail. Unsolicited submissions are OK. Prefers cassette with 3-6 songs and lyric sheets. SASE. Reports in 4-6 weeks.
Music: Mostly **country, rock** and **R&B**; also **pop, gospel** and **New Age**. Published "Texas Mile," written and recorded by D. Nowell on Pleasure Records; "Don't Want No Strangers" (by D. Van Horne), recorded by Marcel Evans; and "Medicine Man" (by A. Martin/J. Willoughby), recorded by Jet Black Machine, both on Pristine Records.
Tips: "Study the material charting. Learn from the pros."

*FOURTH FLOOR MUSIC, P.O. Box 135, Bearsville NY 12409. (914)679-7303. Fax: (914)679-5731. A&R: Ian Kimmet. Music publisher, record company (Bearsville Records) and record producer. Estab. 1971. Works with composers and lyricists; teams collaborators.
How to Contact: Submit demo tape by mail. Unsolicited submissions are OK. Prefers cassette (or VHS videocassette if available). Does not return material.
Music: "Songs of a personalized nature; autobiographical; observed; experienced." Published *Thanks to You* (by J. Winchester), recorded by Emmylou Harris on Asylum Records (country).

FOX FARM RECORDING, 2731 Saundersville Ferry Rd., Mt. Juliet TN 37122. (615)754-2444. President: Kent Fox. Music publisher, record producer and demo production recording studio. BMI, ASCAP. Publishes 20 songs/year; publishes 5 new songwriters/year. Works with composers and lyricists; teams collaborators. Pays standard royalty.
Affiliate(s): Blueford Music (ASCAP) and Mercantile Music (BMI).
How to Contact: Submit a demo tape by mail. Unsolicited submissions are OK. Prefers cassette with 4 songs and lyric sheet. SASE. Reports in 3 months.
Music: **Country, bluegrass** and **contemporary Christian**.
Tips: "If your song is good enough to become a hit, it's worth investing money for a good demo: drums, bass, guitar, keyboard, fiddle, sax, vocals etc."

*FREKO RECORDS (BMI), 417 E. Cross Timbers, Houston TX 77022. (713)694-2971. Engineer: Freddie Kober. Music publisher, record company (Freko Records, Honeybee Records) and record producer (Freddie Kober Productions). Estab. 1976. Publishes 11 songs/year; publishes 3 new songwriters/year. Works with composers and lyricists.
Affiliate(s): Anode Music (BMI), Claudia B (ASCAP).
How to Contact: Submit a demo tape by mail. Unsolicited submissions are OK. Prefers cassette with 4-8 songs and lyric sheet. SASE. Reports in 2 weeks.
Music: Mostly **R&B, rap** and **gospel**; also **pop**. Published *Same Thang, Different Game*, recorded by Jo Jo Gunn (rap); *I Know My Baby Can* and *Feel Me, Feel You* (by Freddie Kober), recorded by Trudy Lynn on Ichiban Records (R&B).

*FRETBOARD PUBLISHING (BMI), Box 40855, Nashville TN 37204. (615)292-2047. Contact: A&R Department. Music publisher, record company (Mosrite Records), record producer (Mark Moseley). Estab. 1963. Publishes 25 songs/year; publishes 3 new songwriters/year. Works with composers and lyricists. Pays standard royalty.
Affiliate(s): Woodgrain Publishing Co. (ASCAP).
How to Contact: Submit a demo tape by mail. Prefers cassette with 2 songs and lyric sheets. Does not return unsolicited material. Reports in 6 weeks "only if we want to hear more."
Music: Mostly **country, rock** (not heavy) and **southern gospel**. Published "Even Now" (by Mark Moseley) and "Mommy's Playing Santa Claus" (by Maurice Brandon), both recorded by Marie Lester (Christmas); and "Queen For a Day" (by Billy Mize), recorded by Barbara Mandrell (country), all on Mosrite Records.
Tips: "Give us time to get to your songs before you make another contact."

FRICK MUSIC PUBLISHING CO. (BMI), 404 Bluegrass Ave., Madison TN 37115. (615)865-6380. Contact: Bob Frick. Music publisher, record company and record producer. Publishes 50 songs/year; publishes 2 new songwriters/year. Works with lyricists. Pays standard royalty.
Affiliate(s): Sugarbakers Music (ASCAP).
How to Contact: Write or call first to get permission to submit. Prefers 7½ ips reel-to-reel or cassette (or videocassette) with 2-10 songs and lyric sheet. SASE. Reports in 2 weeks.
Music: Mostly **gospel**; also **country**, **rock** and **top 40/pop**. Published "I Found Jesus in Nashville" (by Lin Butler), recorded by Bob Scott Frick; and "Good Lovin'," written and recorded by Teresa Ford, both on R.E.F. Records.

THE FRICON ENTERTAINMENT CO., INC., 1048 S. Ogden Dr., Los Angeles CA 90019. (213)931-7323. Attn: Publishing Department. Music publisher. Music supervision (Fricon Music/BMI; Fricout Music/ASCAP). Pays standard royalty.
How to Contact: Write first and obtain permission to submit. Include SASE. Prefers cassette with 1 song and lyric sheet. Does not return unsolicited material without SASE. Reports in 6 weeks.
Music: Mostly **TV** and **film**. Also **gospel**, **R&B**, **rock**, **pop**, **dance** and **country**.

FROG AND MOOSE MUSIC (BMI), Box 40784, Nashville TN 37204. (615)331-1469. Publisher: Steven R. Pinkston. Contact: Jim Chapman. Music publisher and record producer (Third Floor Productions). Estab. 1988. Publishes 10 new songwriters/year. Teams collaborators. Pays standard royalty.
How to Contact: Submit a demo tape by mail. Unsolicited submissions are OK. Prefers cassette or DAT (or VHS videocassette) with 3 songs and lyric or lead sheets. SASE. Reports in 2 months.
Music: Mostly **pop**, **gospel** and **rock**; also **R&B**, **country** and **blues**.

*FROG HAIR SONGS (BMI), 313 N. Locust, Denton TX 76201. (800)270-9297. Fax: (817)383-0756. President: Dave Patton. Music publisher, record company (VIP Records) and record producer. Estab. 1992. Publishes 80 songs/year; publishes 20 new songwriters/year. Works with composers; teams collaborators. Pays standard royalty.
How to Contact: Submit demo tape by mail. Unsolicited submissions are OK. Prefers cassette (or ½" VHS videocassette) with 3-5 songs and lyric and lead sheet. "No phone calls please." Does not return material. Reports in 1 month.
Music: Mostly **rock**, **rap/R&B** and **country**; also **gospel**, **folk** and **jazz**. Published *Talk Show*, written and recorded by James Vincent on VIP Records (jazz); *Funky Hitman* (by Kenton Paul), recorded by Oak Cliff Assassin on Lockdown/VIP Records (rap); and *Wonderful Trap* (by Chris Livingston), recorded by Impulse on VIP Records (rock).
Tips: "When sending in a song, make sure that it has some sort of commercial potential. Otherwise, it's useless. Remember, it's easier to cater your songwriting skills to an existing market than it is to try and create a new one."

FRONTLINE MUSIC GROUP, P.O. Box 28450, Santa Ana CA 92799-8450. Director of Music Publishing: Kenneth Hicks. Music publisher and record company (Frontline Records). Estab. 1987. Works with composers and lyricists; teams collaborators. Pays standard royalty.
Affiliate(s): Broken Songs (ASCAP) and Carlotta Publishing (BMI).
How to Contact: Submit demo tape by mail. Unsolicited submissions are OK. Prefers cassette with 3 songs and lyric sheet. "Address to Broken Songs." Does not return unsolicited material. Reports in 1-2 months.
Music: Mostly **pop**, **rock** and **R&B**.
Tips: "Frontline is a Christian Record Company. The songs we would publish should have lyrics that are wholesome and/or point to a relationship with Jesus."

FROZEN INCA MUSIC, Suite 333, 1800 Peachtree St., Atlanta GA 30309. (404)355-5580. Fax: (404)351-2786. President: Michael Rothschild. Music publisher, record company and record producer. Estab. 1981. Publishes 12 songs/year; publishes 3 new songwriters/year. Works with composers and lyricists; teams collaborators. Pays negotiated percentage.
Affiliate(s): Landslide Records.
How to Contact: Submit demo tape by mail. Unsolicited submissions are OK. Prefers cassette with 6-12 songs and lyric sheet. SASE. Reports in 1 month.
Music: Mostly **R&B**, **blues** and **rap**; also **rock**. Published "The Next Miss Wrong" (by T. Ellis and Eddie Cleveland); *Bad Dream #108*, written and recorded by Tinsley Ellis; and *The Hulk* (by T. Ellis/R. Keller/D. Wells/S. Meeder), recorded by Tinsley Ellis, all on Alligator Records.
Tips: "We look for strong rhythmic hooks."

*GARRIVAN MUSIC, #A7, 4715 Sullivant Ave., Columbus OH 43228. (614)851-9710. CEO: Albert VanHoose. Music publisher and record company. Estab. 1992. Publishes 10 songs/year; publishes 3 new songwriters/year. Works with composers and/or lyricists. Pays standard royalty.

Affiliate(s): Vangarr Publishing Co. (BMI).
How to Contact: Submit demo tape by mail. Unsolicited submissions are OK. Prefers cassette with 3 songs and lyric sheet. "Do not mail tape in box." SASE. Reports in 2 weeks.
Music: Mostly **country, gospel (all types)** and **contemporary**; also **pop, jazz/blues** and MOR. Published *Back at Your Altar*, written and recorded by Ralph Hanson; *Guilty*, written and recorded by Lewis D. Martin; and *No Greater Love*, written and recorded by Martin/Hanson, all on Al-Van Records.
Tips: "Write about true-to life story, make the story new, and make each word add to the story as an individual event. Have a clean sounding demo, studio quality, typed lyric sheet(s)."

ALAN GARY MUSIC, P.O. Box 179, Palisades Park NJ 07650. President: Alan Gary. Creative Director: Fran Levine. Creative Assistant: Harold Green. Music publisher. ASCAP, BMI. Estab. 1987. Publishes a varying number of songs/year. Works with composers and lyricists. Pays standard royalty.
How to Contact: Submit demo tape by mail. Unsolicited submissions are OK. Prefers cassette (or VHS videocassette) with lyric sheet. SASE.
Music: Mostly **pop, R&B** and **dance**; also **rock, A/C** and **country**. Published "Liberation" (by Gary/Julian), recorded by Les Julian on Music Tree Records (A/C); "Love Your Way Out of This One" (by Gary/Rosen), recorded by Deborah Steel on Bad Cat Records (contemporary country); and "Dueling Rappers" (by Gary/Free), recorded by Prophets of Boom on You Dirty Rap! Records (rap/R&B).

GENERAL JONES MUSIC, Dept. SM, 3252 Grenoble Lane, Memphis TN 38115. (901)365-1429. Owner: Danny Jones. Music publisher, record producer and recording engineer. Estab. 1980. BMI. Publishes 3-4 songs/year; publishes 1-2 new songwriters/year. Works with composers and lyricists; teams collaborators. Pays standard royalty.
Affiliate(s): General Jones Music (BMI) and Danny Jones Productions.
How to Contact: Write or call first and obtain permission to submit. Prefers cassette (or VHS videocassette) with 3 songs and lyric or lead sheet. SASE. Reports in 1 month.
Music: Rock, country and **R&B**. Published "King of the Cowboys" (by Larry Carney/Roy Rogers, Jr.), recorded by Roy Rogers, Jr. on RCA Records (country); "I Eat Roadkill" (by Dan Hyer), recorded by 50 FT (rock); and "Don't Cheat on Me," written and recorded by Keith Swinton and Steve Rarick (rock), all on RCA Records.

GENETIC MUSIC PUBLISHING, 10 Church Rd., Merchantville NJ 08109. (609)662-4428. Contact: Whey Cooler or Jade Starling. Music publisher, record company (Svengali) and record producer (Whey Cooler Production). ASCAP. Estab. 1982. Publishes 1-5 songs/year. Pays standard royalty.
Affiliate(s): Cooler By A Mile (ASCAP), BC Music (ASCAP) and Baggy Music (BMI).
How to Contact: Write or call first and obtain permission to submit a tape. Prefers cassette. SASE. Reports in 3 weeks.
Music: Mostly **dance, R&B** and **pop**; also **rock** and **jazz**. Published "Dial M for Murder" (by Sakura/Cooler), recorded by Malik on FTS Records (rap); "Giddy Up " (by Collins/Starling/Cooler), recorded by Aphrodesia on FTS Records (rap); and "You Should Know" (by Costa Brothers), recorded by Ton De Jon on Svengal Records.
Tips: "Submissions are reviewed and put on file for one year before being reviewed again. During that time they are regularly submitted to various projects for consideration. If they are accepted then a publishing deal between ourselves and the songwriter will result."

GIFTNESS ENTERPRISE, Dept. SM, Suite #5, 1315 Simpson Rd. NW, Atlanta GA 30314. (404)642-2645. Contact: New Song Department. Music publisher. BMI, ASCAP. Publishes 30 songs/year; publishes 15 new songwriters/year. Employs songwriters on a salary basis. Works with composers and lyricsts; teams collaborators. Pays standard royalty.
Affiliate(s): Blair Vizzion Music (BMI) and Fresh Entertainment (ASCAP).
How to Contact: Submit demo tape by mail. Unsolicited submissions are OK. Prefers cassette with 4 songs and lyric or lead sheet. SASE. Reports in 1 month.
Music: Mostly **R&B, pop** and **rock**; also **country, gospel** and **jazz**. Published "This Time" and "Always Girl" (by Cirocco), recorded by Georgio on RCA Records; and "Broken Promises" (by J. Calhoun), recorded by S.O.S. Band on Tabu/A&M Records.

GLOBEART PUBLISHING, A Division of GlobeArt Inc., #26H, 50 E. 76th St., New York NY 10021. (212)249-9220. Fax: (212)861-8130. President: Jane Peterer. Music publisher. BMI, ASCAP. Estab. 1989. Publishes 50 songs/year; publishes 2 new songwriters/year. Works with composers/lyricists. Pays standard royalty.
Affiliate(s): GlobeSound Publishing (ASCAP).
How to Contact: Submit a demo tape by mail. Unsolicited submissions are OK. Prefers cassette (or videocassette) with 3-5 songs and lyric or lead sheet. SASE. Reports in 6-8 weeks.
Music: Mostly **pop/R&B, jazz** and **gospel**; also **New Age** and **country**. Published *Urban Primitive* (by Richard Applegate), recorded by Applegate on Media Orphan Records; *Beautiful Morning*, written

and recorded by Rebbein on Pick Records; and "Coffee Song" (by Ray Smith), recorded by Cream on Polygram Records.
Tips: "Be professional."

*GO! DISCS MUSIC (PRS), 72 Black Lion Lane, London W6 9BE **England**. (081)748-7973. Fax: (081)741-2184. Contact: Bruce Craigie. Music publisher. Estab. 1984. Teams collaborators. Uses English contracts.
How to Contact: Submit demo tape by mail. Unsolicited submissions are OK. Prefers cassette (or VHS English videocassette) with 3 songs and lyric sheet. SAE and IRC. Reports in 6 weeks.

GO STAR MUSIC, Dept. SM, Suite #20, 4700 Belle Grove Rd., Baltimore MD 21225. (410)789-1005. Fax: (301)789-1006. Owner: William E. Baker. Music publisher, record company (Go Records) and record producer (International Music). Estab. 1988. Publishes 50-100 songs/year; publishes 50 new songwriters/year. Pays standard royalty.
Affiliate(s): Billy Baker and Associates, Go Records, Infinity Productions and Independent International Music Associates.
How to Contact: Submit a demo tape. Unsolicited submissions are OK. "Limit 4 songs with lyric sheets, bio and photo. SASE with phone number. List what you would like to achieve." Prefers cassette and lyric or lead sheet. SASE. Reports in 3 weeks.
Music: Mostly **rock, pop, country, R&B, New Age** and **gospel**. Published "If You're Not Here" (by Paula Anderson/Pam Bailey), recorded by Closin' Time (country); "Numbered Door" (by Roger Ware), recorded by Doug Beacham both on Go Records (country); and "Carolina Blue" (by Jim Hession), recorded by John Anthony on Go/Silver Dollar Records (country).

JAY GOLD MUSIC PUBLISHING (BMI), P.O. Box 409, East Meadow NY 11554-0409. (516)486-8699 (phone and fax). President: Jay Gold. Music publisher. Estab. 1981. Publishes 25 songs/year; publishes 6 new songwriters/year. Works with composers and lyricists; teams collaborators. Pays standard royalty.
How to Contact: Submit a demo tape by mail. Unsolicited submissions are OK. Prefers cassette with 2 songs and lyric sheets. SASE. Reports in 6 weeks. "Use only high quality chrome cassettes for submissions."
Music: Mostly **pop, rock** and **country**. Published "A Touch of the Heart," recorded by Eric Burdon; "All the Wrong Reasons," written and recorded by Jay Gold on Turbo Records (pop); and "Long Time" (by Jay Gold), recorded by Joe-Joe Bentry on Cardinal Records.
Tips: "Make the best demo you can afford. It's better to have a small publisher pushing your songs than a large one keeping them on the shelf."

S.M. GOLD MUSIC (ASCAP), % Compositions, Inc., 36 E. 22nd St., 2nd Floor, New York NY 10010. President: Steven M. Gold. Music publisher and jingle/TV/film score producer. Publishes 5 songs/year. "We employ freelance and staff songwriters/composers." Pays standard royalty or cash advance (buy-out).
How to Contact: Submit a demo tape by mail. Unsolicited submissions are OK. Prefers cassette with 2 songs "commercial composers: please send *DAT*." Does not return unsolicited material. No calls please.
Music: Mostly **dance, 'commercial' rap** and **R&B**.
Tips: "We're not looking for 'album tracks' or 'B sides.' Hits only!"

*GOLD PLATE MUSIC (BMI), 1041 W. 108th Place, Chicago IL 60643. (312)779-2384. President: Casey Jones. Music publisher, record company. Estab. 1983. Publishes 12 songs/year; publishes 12 new songwriters/year.
How to Contact: Write first and obtain permission to submit. Prefers cassette with 1 song. SASE. Reports in 1 month.
Music: Mostly **blues** and **R&B**. Published *Help Yourself* (by Casey Jones), recorded by Robert Covington (blues); *Lonesome Blues* (by Casey Jones), recorded by L.B. Blue (blues); and *I Got Troubles*, written and recorded by Casey Jones (blues), all on Airwax Records.

GORDON MUSIC CO., INC., Dept. SM, P.O. Box 2250, Canoga Park CA 91306. (818)883-8224. Owner: Jeff Gordon. Music publisher, record company (Paris Records). ASCAP, BMI. Estab. 1950. Publishes 10-20 songs/year. Works with composers and lyricists; teams collaborators. Pays standard royalty or arrangements of many kinds can be made between author and publisher.
Affiliate(s): Marlen Music (ASCAP), Sunshine Music (BMI) and Gordon Music (ASCAP).
How to Contact: Call first and obtain permission to submit. Prefers cassette (or VHS videocassette) with 3-4 songs and lyric or lead sheets. Does not return unsolicited material. Reports in 1 month.
Music: Mostly **pop, children's** and **rock**; also **jazz**. Published "Izzy, Pest of West" and "The Corsican Cat," both written and recorded by Champie (childrens); and "Alfred Hitchcock" (by D. Kahn and M. Lenard), recorded by Failsafe (TV theme); all on Paris Records.

JON GORR CUSTOM MUSIC (BMI), 828 Vista St., Pittsburgh PA 15212. (412)323-9331. President: Jon Gorr. Music publisher (MassMedia Records), record producer (Jon Gorr), advertising/jingle agency and planetarium soundtracks and film scoring. Estab. 1983. Publishes 10 songs/year; publishes 1-2 new songwriters/year. Works with composers and lyricists. Pays standard royalty.
How to Contact: Submit a demo tape by mail. Unsolicited submissions are OK. Prefers cassette with 3 songs. Does not return unsolicited material. Reports in 1 month.
Music: Mostly **rock, New Age** and **reggae**. Published "Drive By Love" (by Jon Gorr), recorded by Bill Osborne on JGCM Records (reggae); the soundtrack for ESPN's "Today's Diver"; and theme music for Pittsburgh Penguins hockey team (1993).

RICHARD E. GOWELL MUSIC (BMI), Dept. SM, 45 7th St., Auburn ME 04210. (207)784-7975. Professional Manager: Rich Gowell. Music publisher and record company (Allagash Country Records, Allagash R&B Records, Gowell Records). Estab. 1978. Publishes 10-30 songs/year; 5-10 new songwriters/year. Works with composers and lyricists. Pays standard royalty.
Affiliate(s): Global Allagash Music Co. (ASCAP).
How to Contact: Submit a demo tape by mail. Unsolicited submissions are OK. Prefers cassette with 2-4 songs and lyric sheets. SASE. Reports in 1-2 months.
Music: Mostly **country, pop** and **R&B**. Published *Colorado Rockies* (by R. Gowell), recorded by Ace Diamond on Allagash Country Records (pop/C&W); "Fireball" (by B. Lee/L. Main), recorded by The Country Line Band on Sabre Records (country rock); and *It's Love*, written and recorded by Johnnie Mandell on Allagash Country Records (MOR/country).
Tips: "Have a great song with a professional demo and keep plugging to the right people."

GREEN MEADOWS PUBLISHING (BMI), 811 W. 4th St., Beaver Dam KY 42320. (502)274-3169. Executive Director: Robert Bailey. Music publisher, record company. Estab. 1991. Publishes 10 songs/year; publishes 2-3 new songwriters/year. Works with composers and lyricists. Pays standard royalty.
How to Contact: Write or call first to obtain permission to submit. Prefers cassette with 5 songs and lyric sheet. Does not return unsolicited material. Reports in 2 months.
Music: Mostly **folk** and **gospel**. Published *Where Did Our Lovin' Go, Land up High*, and *Oh Kentucky*, all written and recorded by Robert Bailey on Beatle Records.

***GREEN ONE MUSIC (BMI)**, 3200 Peoria, Steger IL 60475. (708)754-4869. Fax: (708)754-6886. President: George J. Skupien. Music publisher, recording studio. Estab. 1992. Publishes 6-12 songs/year. Works with composers and lyricists; teams collaborators. Pays standard royalty.
How to Contact: Submit demo tape by mail. Unsolicited submissions are OK. Prefers cassette (or DAT). "We prefer 2-4 songs on each tape. No more than 6." Does not return material. Reports in 2 months.
Music: Mostly **country, MOR, light rock**; also **American polka music, waltzes** and **comedy — fun songs**. Published "Our Last Cowboy Song" (by G. Skupien), recorded by Matthew Row'd on Green Bear Records (country); "Da Bulls, Da Bears, Da Beer" (by D. Mack/G. Skupien) recorded by The Stagemen (polka); and "In the Dog House with Daisy," written and recorded by G. Skupien, both on Briar Hill Records.
Tips: "Always put your best song first on your tapes submitted. If possible, submit a professional demo of your song. We do accept home grown demo tapes — be sure your vocal is clear!"

FRANK GUBALA MUSIC, Hillside Rd., Cumberland RI 02864. (401)333-6097. Contact: Frank Gubala. Music publisher and booking agency.
How to Contact: Prefers cassette and lead sheet. Does not return unsolicited material. Reports in 3 months.
Music: Blues, disco, easy listening, MOR, top 40/pop, rock and country.

***HALGEO MUSIC**, P.O. Box 2776, Florence AL 35630-0776. (205)760-8017. Fax: (205)767-3299. Owner: George Soulé. Music publisher. Estab. 1975. Publishes 5 songs/year; publishes 1 new songwriter/year. Hires staff writers. Works with composers and lyricists; teams collaborators. Pays standard royalty.
How to Contact: Submit demo tape by mail. Unsolicited submissions are OK. Prefers cassette. Does not return material.
Music: Mostly **pop, R&B** and **country**. Published *A Woman Without Love* (by G. Soulé/A. Aldridge), recorded by Dorothy Moore on Malaco Records; *She's Too Pretty To Cry* (by G. Soulé/A. Aldridge), recorded by Percy Sledge on Monument Records; and *It's Hurting Time Again* (by G. Soulé/G. Jackson), recorded by Bobby Bland on Malaco Records.
Tips: "Expensive demos are not necessary for submission of material. A guitar and vocal, or a piano and vocal will suffice."

HALO INTERNATIONAL, P.O. Box 101, Sutton MA 01590. Professional Manager: John Gagne. Music publisher, record company (MSM Records, Hālo Records, Bronco Records), record producer; artists signed to labels only. BMI. Estab. 1979. Publishes 1-4 songs/year. Works with composers and lyricists; teams collaborators. Pays standard royalty.
Affiliate(s): Pick the Hits Music (ASCAP), Mount Scott Music (BMI).
How to Contact: Write first and obtain permission to submit a tape. Prefers cassette with 2 songs and lyric sheets. Does not return unsolicited material. Reports in 2-3 weeks.
Music: Mostly **contemporary country, traditional country, pop-rock** and **folk**. Also working with playwrights and composers for musical and theater works with incidental music. Published "Here Comes the Rain Again" (by M. Lewis/M. Brush), recorded by Gwen Newton on Halo Records (country); *The Windows* (by J.S. Gagne), recorded by Terry Michaels on Allagash Records (country); and Sound Score: "Hamlet," written and recorded by J.S. Gagne on MSM Records (theater).
Tips: "Keep writing. Like any other craft you will improve only through practice."

HAPPY HOUR MUSIC, 2410 Del Mar Ave., P.O. Box 1809, Rosemead CA 91770. (909)621-9903. Fax: (909)621-2412. President: Wan Seegmiller. Music publisher and record company (Happy Hour Music). BMI. Estab. 1985. Publishes 5 songs/year; publishes 3 new songwriters/year. Works with composers.
How to Contact: Write first and obtain permission to submit a tape. Prefers cassette. SASE. Reports in 3 weeks.
Music: Mostly **jazz** and **Brazilian contemporary**. Published "The New Lambadas" (by Loão Parahyba); "Alemão Bem Brasileiro" (by Olmir Stocker); and "Hermeto Pascoal Egrupo" (by Hermeto Pascoal and Antonio Adolfo), all on Happy Hour Records (Brazilian).

HARMONY STREET MUSIC (ASCAP), Box 4107, Kansas City KS 66104. (913)299-2881. President: Charlie Beth. Estab. 1985. Music publisher, record company (Harmony Street Records), and record producer (Harmony Street Productions). Publishes 30-50 songs/year; publishes 15 new songwriters/year. Pays standard royalty.
Affiliate(s): Harmony Lane Music (BMI).
How to Contact: Prefers cassette (or VHS videocassette) with 1-3 songs and lyric or lead sheets. SASE. "Due to the large amount of submissions that we receive we are no longer able to return unsolicited material. We will report within 6 weeks if we are interested."
Music: **Country, gospel, rockabilly, pop, R&B, bluegrass** and **rock**. Published "I Keep Comin' Back To You" (by Terry Allen and Sue Mahurin), recorded by Terry Allen on Harmony Street Records (country); "So Many Women, So Little Time" (by Edna Mae Foy and Virgil Hooks), recorded by Don Malena on Starquest Records; and "Don't Tell My Heart" (by Scott Hansgen), recorded by Tony Mantor on Harmony Street Records (country).
Tips: "Start with a good strong hook and build your song around it. A song is only as good as the hook or idea. Make each line and verse say something. Keep your lyrics and melody fairly simple but interesting. Your chorus should stand out musically (usually uplifting). Demos should be clear and clean with voice out front. Try to keep your songs 3 minutes or less. Songs must be original both musically and lyrically. Send only your best."

JOHANN HARTEL MUSIKVERLAG, Nibelungenring 1, A-3423 St. Andrä—Wörden, **Austria** 0043-2242/33-519. Contact: Hans Hartel. Music Publisher. AKM. Estab. 1985. Publishes 100 songs/year. Publishes 5 new songwriters/year. Hires staff writers. Works with composers and lyricists; teams collaborators. Pays "usual standard royalties per AKM/Austro Mechana."
Affiliate(s): Elisabeth Lindl, Edition Dum Dum, Edition Magnum, Edition Cactus.
How to Contact: Submit a demo tape by mail. Unsolicited submissions OK. Prefers cassette with 3 songs and lyric sheet. SAE and IRC. Reports in 1 month "only if interested."
Music: Mostly **pop, German pop** and **instrumental**; also **ethno** and **New Age**. Published *Manana* (by Jonny Blue), recorded by Chris White (pop); *Shine on*, written and recorded by Duncan Mlango (pop); and *Wenn du gehst*, written and recorded by Chris White (pop), all on Cactus Records.

*HAUTBOY MUSIC, Lawford House, Berrister Place, Raunds, Northants NN9 6JN **England**. (0933)460628. Proprietor: Peter Malski. Music publisher. Estab. 1988. Publishes 12 songs/year; publishes 5 new songwriters/year. Works with composers and lyricists; teams collaborators. Pays standard royalty.
How to Contact: Submit demo tape by mail. Unsolicited submissions are OK. Prefers cassette (or VHS videocassette) with 5 songs and lyric or lead sheet. SAE and IRC. Reports in 1 month.

Remember: Don't "shotgun" your demo tapes. Submit only to companies interested in the type of music you write. For more submission hints, refer to Getting Started on page 5.

Music: Mostly **dance/pop, rock/indie/A.O.R.** and **any other**; also **soundtrack/theme, MOR** and **world**. Published "Fever" (by K. Scott/K. Alner), recorded by Databass on Sunbass Records (dance); "Gonna Make You Move" (by G. Van Den Bussche), recorded by Funky Disco on Wizz Records (dance); and "Planet Irie" (by Upthegrove), recorded by I-Lab on Breakin' Loose Records (pop/reggae).

*HAVASONG MUSIC, 169 Cecil Rd., Rochester, Kent ME1 2HW **England.** (0634)815613. A&R Manager: Jim Hirst-Amos. Music publisher. Estab. 1979. Publishes 2-30 songs/year; publishes 1-2 new songwriters/year. Works with composers and lyricists. Pays standard royalty.
How to Contact: Submit demo tape by mail. Unsolicited submissions are OK. Prefers cassette with 1-2 songs. SAE and IRC. Reports in 1-2 weeks.
Music: Mostly **MOR, pop, rock, funk** or **new wave**; also **country/rock**. Published "My Dad" and "You're Just Like A Bubble in Wine," written and recorded by Mavin James on Havasong Records; and "The Good Times Are Killing Me" (by Billy Childish), recorded by Thee Headcoats on Vinyl Japan UK (funk rock).

HAWK'S BILL MUSIC, P.O. Box 910, Orange VA 22960. (703)672-9120. President: Parke Stanley. Music publisher. Estab. 1991. Works with composers and/or lyricists; teams collaborators. Pays standard royalty.
How to Contact: Submit demo tape by mail. Unsolicited submissions are OK. Prefers cassette with lyric sheet. SASE. Reports in 2 weeks.
Music: Mostly **country rock, country** and **R&B**; also **crossover** and **pop**. Published "She'd Make a Bulldog Break His Chain" (by George Allison); and "Let's Live a Little" (by Michael Lounibos/Lisa Aschman), both recorded by Gene Paul Mann on Missle Records (country rock); and "A Little More of Us" (by Parke Stanley), recorded by Lisa Doubleday on Summit Records (country).
Tips: "Learn the song techniques that artists are looking for, particularly hooks featuring play-on-words and antonyms (2 words with opposite meanings). Use vivid imagery. Constantly write down hit songs from the radio and observe their rhyming patterns. Express everyday situations in a new way. Positive, up-tempo songs have a better chance of being cut. Write us and ask for our free tip sheets to make your songs more competitive. We have Music Row connections."

HEARTBEAT MUSIC, 282 Bruce Court, Westerville OH 43081. (614)882-5919. Vice President: Stephen Bashaw. Music publisher and record company. Estab. 1987. Publishes 25-30 songs/year; publishes 5-10 new songwriters/year. Works with composers or lyricists; teams collaborators. Pays standard royalty.
Affiliate(s): RGK Heartbeat Music (ASCAP), RGK Heartlight Music (BMI).
How to Contact: Call first to arrange personal interview. Submit demo tape by mail. Unsolicited submissions are OK. Prefers cassette and lyric sheet. SASE. Reports in 3-4 weeks.
Music: Mostly **adult contemporary Christian, black gospel** and **inspirational**; also **Christian rock/pop**. Published "I Surrender" (by Milton Ruffin); "Pray" (by Bill Clemons); and "Share Love" (by Darrin Lundy), all recorded by Heartlight Studios on Pulse Records.

*HEAVEN MUSIC, P.O. Box 92, Gloucester, Gloucestershire GL4 8HW **England.** (0452)812442. Fax: (0452)812106. Contact: Vic Coppersmith. Music publisher, record producer. Estab. 1980. Publishes 20 songs/year; publishes 5 new songwriters/year. Works with composers and lyricists; teams collaborators. Pays 75% royalty but negotiable on advances required.
How to Contact: Write and obtain permission to submit. Prefers cassette (or VHS videocassette) and lyric sheet. Does not return material. Reports in 1 month.
Music: Mostly **rock** and **popular/dance**. Published "Harmony" (by Bob Appleby), recorded by Tiffany on BBC TV.

HEAVEN SONGS (BMI), C-300, 16776 Lakeshore Dr., Lake Elsinore CA 92330. Contact: Dave Paton. Music publisher, record company and record producer. Publishes 30-50 songs/year; publishes 10 new songwriters/year. Pays standard royalty.
How to Contact: Submit demo tape by mail. Unsolicited submissions are OK. Prefers 7½ ips reel-to-reel or cassette with 3-6 songs and lyric sheet. SASE. Reports in 1 month.
Music: Country, dance-oriented, easy listening, folk, jazz, MOR, progressive, R&B, rock, soul and **top 40/pop**. Published *Blizzard In the Mix* and *Solo Flight*, written and recorded by Brett Duncan (rock); and *You Betcha*, written and recorded by Linda Rae (country rock), all on Hollyrock Records.
Tips: Looking for "better quality demos."

*HEDLEY MUSIC GROUP/GET READY PUBLISHING, 75 Rutland Rd., Chesterfield 540 IND **England.** (44)246-236667. Contact: Steve Watkinson/Lee Timmins. Music publisher, record company (Rutland Records) and music business management. Estab. 1968 (reformed 1993). Publishes 50 songs/year; publishes 4 new songwriters/year. Works with composers and lyricists. Pays negotiable royalty.
How to Contact: Submit demo tape by mail. Unsolicited submissions are OK. Prefers cassette (or VHS videocassette), lyric sheet and lead sheet. Does not return material. Reports in 6-8 weeks.

Music: Mostly **commercial pop, MOR** and **rock.**

HENDERSON GROUP MUSIC, 125 Powell Mill Rd., Spartanburg SC 29301. (803)576-5832. Owner/ President: Dr. Barry Henderson. Music publisher and artist management. Estab. 1990. Publishes 10-20 songs/year; publishes 2-3 new songwriters/year. Works with composers; teams collaborators. Pays standard royalty.
Affiliate(s): HPL Communications (BMI).
How to Contact: Submit demo tape by mail. Unsolicited submissions are OK. Prefers cassette with 3-4 songs. Does not return material. Reports in 2-3 months.
Music: Mostly **country, pop** and **rock.** Published "Don't Come Crying Back to Me" and "Some Day You'll Understand," both written by John Davison.
Tips: "The song has to be commercial."

HENLY MUSIC ASSOCIATES (ASCAP), 45 Perham St., W. Roxbury MA 02132. (617)325-4594. President: Bill Nelson. Music publisher, record company (Woodpecker Records) and record producer. Estab. 1987. Publishes 5 songs/year; publishes 5 new songwriters/year. Works with composers and lyricists; teams collaborators. Pays standard royalty.
How to Contact: Submit demo tape by mail. Unsolicited submissions are OK. Prefers cassette with 4 songs and lyric sheet. Does not return material. Reports in 1 month.
Music: Mostly **country, pop** and **gospel.** Published "Big Bad Bruce" (by J. Dean), recorded by B.N.O. (pop); "Do You Believe in Miracles" (by B. Nelson), recorded by Parttime Singers (country); and "Don't Hurry with Love" (by B. Nelson and B. Bergeron), recorded by Bill Nelson (country), all on Woodpecker Records.

HEUPFERD MUSIK VERLAG GmbH, Ringwaldstr. 18, Dreieich 63303 **Germany.** Phone and fax: (06103)86970. General Manager: Christian Winkelmann. Music publisher. GEMA. Publishes 60-100 songs/year; publishes 2-3 new songwriters/year. Works with composers and lyricists. Pays "royalties after GEMA distribution plan."
Affiliate(s): Edition Payador (GEMA) and Song Bücherei (book series).
How to Contact: Write first and obtain permission to submit. Prefers cassette and lead sheet. SAE and IRC. Reports in 1 month.
Music: Mostly **folk, jazz** and **fusion;** also **New Age, rock** and **ethnic music.** Published "Valse Mélancolique," written and recorded by Rüdiger Oppermann (New Age); and "Rainy Sundays" (by Andy Irvine), recorded by Andy Irvine and others, both on Wundertüte Records.

*HI TENSION RECORDS, J.B. Tassijnstraat 52, Zwijndrecht 2070 **Belgium.** (03)252 88 82. Fax: (03)253 04 20. Managing Director: Raymond Muylle. Music publisher, record company. Estab. 1983. Publishes 50 songs/year. Works with composers and lyricists. Pays standard royalty.
How to Contact: Submit demo tape by mail. Unsolicited submissions are OK. Prefers cassette. Does not return material. Reports in 3 weeks.
Music: Mostly **dance.** Published "James Brown is Dead" (by D. Slemming), recorded by L.A. Style on Arista Records; and "Dance Your Ass Off" (by Foco), recorded by RTZ on Radikal Records.

HICKORY LANE PUBLISHING AND RECORDING (SOCAN, ASCAP), P.O. Box 2275, Vancouver, British Columbia V6B 3W5 **Canada.** (604)465-1408. President: Chris Michaels. A&R Manager: Dave Rogers. Music publisher, record company and record producer. Estab. 1988. Publishes 3 songs/year; publishes 3 new songwriters/year. Hires staff writers. Works with composers and lyricists; teams collaborators. Pays standard royalty.
How to Contact: Submit demo tape by mail. Unsolicited submissions are OK. Prefers cassette (or VHS videocassette) with 1-5 songs. SAE and IRC. Reports in 6 weeks.
Music: Mostly **country, MOR** and **gospel;** also **soft rock, musical compositions** and **children's music.** Published "Country Drives Me Wild" (by Chris Michaels); "Until Now" (by Steve Mitchell/Chris Michaels); and "Tear and Tease" (by Parmjit Pawa), all recorded by Chris Michaels on Hickory Lane Records.
Tips: "Keep the vocals up front, have feeling in your song with a strong melody, easy lyrics. Be original."

HICKORY VALLEY MUSIC (ASCAP), 10303 Hickory Valley, Ft. Wayne IN 46835. President: Allan Straten. Music publisher, record company (Yellow Jacket Records) and record producer (Al Straten Productions). ASCAP, BMI. Estab. 1988. Publishes 10 songs/year; publishes 5 new songwriters/year. Works with composers. Pays standard royalty.
Affiliate(s): Straten's Song (BMI).
How to Contact: Submit a demo tape by mail. Unsolicited submissions are OK. Prefers cassette with 3-4 songs and lyric sheets. SASE. Reports in 3-4 weeks.

Music: Mostly **country** and **MOR**. Published *A Rose and A Kiss*, *Countin' Down to Love* and *One Of A Kind* (by Grogg/Straten), all recorded by April on Yellow Jacket Records (country).
Tips: "Keep it simple—write about one single moment in time and be prepared to rewrite. Send submission in a 6×9 envelope, no staples."

HIGH DESERT MUSIC CO., 29512 Peoria Rd., Halsey OR 97348-9742. (503)491-3524. A/R: Karl V. Black. Music publisher. BMI. Estab. 1976. Publishes 10 songs/year. Works with composers and lyricists; teams collaborators. Pays standard royalty.
How to Contact: Submit demo tape by mail. Unsolicited submissions are OK. Prefers cassette with 1 song only. Demos do not have to be professional. "Be sure name is on everything submitted." Does not return material.
Music: **Holiday** only.
Tips: "Be sure lyrics make sense. After listening to a song you should not have to ask 'What's the name of that song?' "

HIGH-MINDED MOMA PUBLISHING & PRODUCTIONS (BMI), 10330 Cape Arago, Coos Bay OR 97420. Contact: Kai Moore Snyder. Music publisher and production company. Pays standard royalty.
How to Contact: Prefers 7½ ips reel-to-reel, CD or cassette with 4-8 songs and lyric sheet. SASE. Reports in 1 month.
Music: **Country, MOR, rock** (country) and **top 40/pop**.

HISTORY PUBLISHING CO., Dept. SM, Box 7-11, Macks Creek MO 65786. (314)363-5432. President: B.J. Carnahan. Music publisher, record company (BOC, History) and record producer (AudioLoft Recording Studios). BMI. Estab. 1977. Publishes 10-15 songs/year; 2 new songwriters/year. Works with composers and lyricists. Pays standard royalty.
How to Contact: Write first and obtain permission to submit a tape. Prefers cassette with 2 songs and lyric sheets. "We prefer not to keep songs on file. Send a good, clean demo with vocal up front." SASE. Reports in 1 month.
Music: Mostly **country** and **gospel**. Published "Big Texas Waltz" (by G. Terry), recorded by Merle Haggard on Curb Records (country); "Remember the Alimony" (by J.B. Haynes), recorded by Bill and Roy on Gallery II Records (country); and "Grovespring Swing" (by F. Stowe), recorded by F. Stowe on History Records (country).

HIT & RUN MUSIC PUBLISHING INC., Suite 411, 1841 Broadway, New York NY 10023. (212)956-2882. Vice President: Joey Gmerek. Assistant: Michelle De Vries. Also at Suite 414, 9229 Sunset Blvd., Los Angeles CA 90069. (310)274-0275. Vice President: Gigi Gerard. Assistant: Lisa Brown. Music publisher. ASCAP. Publishes 20-30 songs/year; publishes 2 new songwriters/year. Hires staff writers. Works with composers and lyricists; teams collaborators. Pays standard royalty.
Affiliate(s): Charisma Music Publishing USA Inc. (ASCAP), Hidden Pun Music Publishing Inc. (BMI).
How to Contact: Write or call first and obtain permission to submit a tape. Prefers cassette (or VHS videocassette) with lyric sheet. Does not return unsolicited material.
Music: Mostly **pop, rock** and **R&B**; also **dance**. Published "The Every Day," written and recorded by Phil Collins on Atlantic Records (pop); "With Your Hand on my Heart" (by B.A. Robertson), recorded by Michael Crawford and Patti Labelle on Atlantic Records (pop); and "Think I'm in Trouble (by Shelly Peiken), recorded by Exposé on Arista Records (pop).

HITSBURGH MUSIC CO. (BMI), P.O. Box 1431, 233 N. Electra, Gallatin TN 37066. (615)452-0324. President/General Manager: Harold Gilbert. Music publisher. Estab. 1964. Publishes 12 songs/year. Pays standard royalty.
Affiliate(s): 7th Day Music (BMI).
How to Contact: Submit demo tape by mail. Unsolicited submissions are OK. Prefers cassette (or quality videocassette) with 2-4 songs and lead sheet. Prefers studio produced demos. Reports in 6 weeks. Does not return unsolicited material.
Music: **Country** and **MOR**. Published "The Last Kiss" (by H. Gilbert), recorded by Jean; and "The Depth of His Love" (by H. Gilbert), recorded by Kim Gilbert, both on Southern City Records (pop).

HITSOURCE PUBLISHING (BMI), 1324 Oakton, Evanston IL 60202. (708)328-4203. President: Alan J. Goldberg. Music publisher. Estab. 1986. Publishes 12 songs/year; publishes 3-6 new songwriters/year. Works with composers. Pays standard royalty.
Affiliate(s): Grooveland Music (ASCAP).
How to Contact: Write or call first and obtain permission to submit. Prefers cassette with 2 songs and lyric sheet. Does not return material. Reports in 1 to 6 months. "No reply if we are very busy."

Music: Country, pop, rock, R&B and **dance**. Published "Hostage," written and recorded by TS Henry Webb; "Love Without End" (by H. Berkman); and "Be A Good Girl" (by Juan Lopez), recorded by Organic Theatre.

Tips: "Come up with an original idea and develop that idea with original and memorable melody and lyrics. Send me a great song, not a good song, that an established artist would want to risk his career on."

*HO-HUM MUSIC (A division of Care Free Records Group), Box 2463, Phoenix AZ 85377. (602)230-4177. Vice President: Doya Fairbanks. Music publisher, record company, distributor and promotion company. Estab. 1990. Publishes 25-35 songs/year; publishes 5-6 new songwriters/year. Hires staff songwriters. Works with composers and lyricists; teams collaborators. Pays standard royalty.
How to Contact: Submit demo tape by mail. Unsolicited submissions are OK. Prefers cassette (or VHS videocassette if available) with 4-6 songs. SASE. Reports in 1 month.
Music: Mostly **country, jazz** and **classical**; also **rock/pop, metal** and **New Age**. Published *Long Branch*, written and recorded by Ward (country); *Golden Wok*, written and recorded by Ho-Zay (rock); and *Pink Pepper*, written and recorded by Pink Pepper (pop), all on Care Free Records.

HOLY GRAIL PUBLISHING (BMI), 13313 Perthshire St., Austin TX 78729. (512)219-1355. Vice President/A&R: Gary A. Coll. Music publisher and record company (Pendragon Records). Estab. 1987. Publishes 50 songs/year; 5-10 new songwriters/year. Works with composers. Pays standard royalty.
How to Contact: Write first and obtain permission to submit a tape. Prefers cassette with 3 songs and lyric sheet. "Include a self-addressed stamped envelope." Does not return unsolicited material. Reports in 3 months. "We now (freelance) produce for artists in the Texas area. Please write for terms and prices."
Music: Mostly **rock** and **pop**. Published "Theft," written and recorded by G.A. Collier; *Charlie Chaplin's Factory* (by J. Cook), recorded by The Wallflowers; and "Leather Lord" (by Tom Kross and S. Wilcox), recorded by Young Thunder, all on Pendragon Records (metal).
Tips: "Please be better than the past 25,000 submissions!"

HOLY SPIRIT MUSIC (BMI), Box 31, Edmonton KY 42129. (502)432-3183. President: W. Junior Lawson. Music publisher. Member GMA, International Association of Gospel Music Publishers. Estab. 1973. Publishes 4 songs/year; publishes 2 new songwriters/year. Pays standard royalty. Works with composers.
How to Contact: Submit demo tape by mail. Unsolicited submissions OK. Prefers cassette with 2 songs and lyric sheet. SASE. Reports in 3 weeks.
Music: Mostly **Southern gospel**; also **MOR, progressive** and **top 40/pop**. Published "He Did It All For Me" (by Marilyn K. Bowling), recorded by De De Chalwell on Dove Records; *Excuses* (by Harold S. Leake), recorded by Knox Bros. on Knox Bros. Records; and *My God Knows What I Need* (by Jeanette Cooke), recorded by The Kingsmen on RiverSong Records.
Tips: Send "good clear cut tape with typed or printed copy of lyrics."

HOLYROOD PRODUCTIONS, 40 Sciennes, Edinburgh EH9 1NH **Scotland**. Contact: Neil Ross. PRS. Estab. 1973. Publishes 10-20 songs/year; publishes 1-2 new songwriters/year. Works with composers. Pays 60% royalty.
Affiliate(s): Ad-Chorel Music (PRS).
How to Contact: Submit a demo tape by mail. Unsolicited submissions are OK. Prefers cassette with 2-3 songs. Does not return unsolicited material. Reports in 3 weeks.
Music: Mostly **pop, dance** and **MOR**; also **traditional**. Published "Your Wish," written and recorded by Santos on Holyrood Records (dance); "Come Together," written and recorded by Howie J & Co. on REL Records (pop); and "Radio" (by Gordon Campbell), recorded by Shakin' Stevens on Epic Records.
Tips: "Rejection does not mean a bad song, only that we can't work with it at that time."

*HONK MUSIC — MUSIKVERLAG H. GEBETSROITHER, Hormayrgasse 3/25, Vienna A-1170 **Austria**. (43)1/464287 (phone and fax). MD: Herbert Gebetsroither. Mailing Address: P.O. Box 118 (Zip: A-1172). Music publisher, record company (Honk Records) and record producer. Estab. 1992. Publishes 20-50 songs/year; publishes 2-3 new songwriters/year. Works with composers and lyricists. Pays 60% mechanical right, ⅔ performing right, 50% for subpublishing.
How to Contact: Submit demo tape by mail. Unsolicited submissions are OK. Prefers cassette (or VHS or Beta videocassette) with 3-10 songs, lyric and lead sheet. SAE and IRC. Reports in 2-3 months.
Music: Mostly **instrumentals: lite jazz, fusion, Latin, New Age, album rock/acid** and **dancefloor jazz, contemporary classics**; also **R&B, country, soul** and **funk, reggae**. Published *Carnival* and *Quiet Star* (by Andy Bartosh), recorded by H.I.P. (Latin/bossa); and *Golden Days* (by J. Honk), recorded by The Honk (rock), all on Honk Records.

Tips: "We look for timeless and catchy songs that will survive at least 2 more decades. Hits are OK. The song should have pretentious lyrics and the music should already have the arrangement finished for the interpretation of another artist. Artist/songwriters preferred. Instrumentals should be so good that they fit easily in adult contemporary radio programs or jazz stations. Also background music."

*HOT LIPS MUSIC COMPANY (BMI), 498 West End Ave., New York NY 10024. (212)580-9065. Fax: (212)799-0382. President: Randy Klein. Music publisher and record producer. Estab. 1978. Publishes 2-3 songs/year; publishes 1 or 2 new songwriters/year. Works with composers and lyricists; teams collaborators. Pays standard royalty.
Affiliate(s): Zoon Tunes Music (ASCAP).
How to Contact: Write or call first and obtain permission to submit. Prefers cassette with lyric sheet. "Send 1 song - only your best." Does not accept unsolicited material. Reports in 4 weeks.
Music: Mostly **jazz (with lyrics)**, **pop ballads** and **R&B with intelligent lyrics**; also **R&B dance** and **children's songs**. Published *No, Data* and *Coffee* (by Randy Klein), all recorded by Jazzheads on JH9949 Records (jazz).

HUMANFORM PUBLISHING COMPANY, Box 158486, Nashville TN 37215. (615)373-9312. Publisher: Kevin Nairon. BMI. Music publisher. Pays standard royalty.
How to Contact: Submit demo tape by mail. Unsolicited submissions are OK. Prefers cassette with 4 songs and lyric and lead sheets. SASE. Reports in 4 weeks.
Music: Mostly **blues (traditional)**. Published "The Rain Is Falling" and "I Need Your Love" (by Kevin Nairon), recorded by Sleepy Joe on CS Records.
Tips: "Please strive for maximum quality when making your demo. Write about your own experiences in a standard blues format."

HUMONGOUS MUSIC PUBLISHING, INC. (ASCAP), Suite 308, 38 East 28th St., New York NY 10016. (212)447-6000. Fax: (212)447-6003. Executive Vice President: Bruce B. Fisher. Music publisher, record company (Big Productions Records), record producer and management company. Estab. 1992. Publishes 12 songs/year; publishes 6 new songwriters/year. Teams collaborators. Pays standard royalty. "If co-publishing with major publisher, pays less than the statutory rate."
Affiliate(s): XXL Music Publishing (BMI).
How to Contact: Submit a demo tape by mail. Unsolicited submissions are OK. Prefers cassette or VHS videocassette with 3 songs and lyric sheet. "Send the best possible representation of the material." SASE. Reports in 2 months.
Music: Mostly **R&B/dance**, **pop dance** and **alternative rock**. Published "Butt Naked" and "I Love Music" (by P. Punzone/P. Falcone/G. Sicard/B.B. Fisher), recorded by Charm on Turnstyle/Atlantic Records (hip house).
Tips: "The song has to fit in the musical styles we listed. Be professional. Listen before you submit. Does your song compare to the quality of songwriting on the radio? Be realistic. The music industry does not pat you on the back. Competition is fierce. Expect rejection. The flavor of the week makes it, not always the best song."

*GREGG HUTCHINS MUSIC (BMI), 116 Roberta Dr., Hendersonville TN 37075. (615)264-1373. Owner: Gregg Hutchins. Music publisher. Estab. 1993. Publishes 20 songs/year; publishes 10 new songwriters/year. Works with composers and lyricists; teams collaborators. Pays standard royalty.
How to Contact: Write first and obtain permission to submit. Prefers cassette with 1 song and lyric sheet. Does not return material. Reports in 1 month.
Music: All types of **gospel music**. Published *Adam's Side* (by Jesse Wilson), recorded by Billy Walker on Rejoice Records (gospel).
Tips: "Use creative lyrics to describe a familiar topic . . . i.e., say it in a different way."

*INSIDE RECORDS/OK SONGS, Bisschopstraat 25, 2060 Antwerp 6 **Belgium**. (32)03-226-77-19. Fax: (32)03-226-78-05. MD: Jean Ney. Music publisher and record company. Estab. 1989. Publishes 50 songs/year; publishes 30-40 new songwriters/year. Hires staff writers. Works with composers and lyricists. Royalty varies "depending on teamwork."
How to Contact: Submit demo tape by mail. Unsolicited submissions are OK. Prefers cassette with complete name, address, telephone and fax number. SAE and IRC. Reports in 2 months.
Music: Mostly **dance**, **pop** and **MOR contemporary**; also **country**, **reggae** and **Latin**. Published *Fiesta De Bautiza* (by Andres Manzana); *I'm Freaky* (by Maes-Predu'homme-Robinson); and *Heaven* (by KC One-King Naomi), all on Inside Records.

INTERNATIONAL MUSIC NETWORK (BMI), #300, 3151 Cahuenga Blvd. W., Los Angeles CA 90068. (213)882-6127. Fax: (213)874-4602. Professional Manager: Michael Carey Schneider. Music publisher. Estab. 1985. Publishes 30-50 songs/year; publishes 1 or 2 new songwriters/year. Works with composers and lyricists; teams collaborators. Pays standard royalty.

How to Contact: Call first and obtain permission to submit. Prefers cassette with 3 songs and lyric sheet. SASE. Reports in 2-3 months.
Music: Mostly **R&B/dance**, **pop** and **rock**. Published "Fallen," written and recorded by Lauren Wood on EMI Records (*Pretty Woman* soundtrack); and *More Than Just The Two Of Us* (by Michael Carey Schneider), recorded by Sneaker.

*INTERNATIONAL MUSIC NETWORK LIMITED, 83 Palmerston Rd., Buckhurst Hill, Essex IG9 5NS **England**. (081)505-2588. Fax: (081)559-1159. Managing Director: Ellis Rich. Music publisher. Estab. 1987. Publishes 3-4,000 songs/year; publishes 8-10 new songwriters/year. Works with composers and lyricists; teams collaborators. Pays 60-75% royalty.
Affiliate(s): Collaboration Music (ASCAP), American Music Network (BMI).
How to Contact: Submit demo tape by mail. Unsolicited submissions are OK. Prefers cassette (or VHS or Beta videocassette) with 3 songs (maximum) and lyric sheet. SAE and IRC. Reports in 1 month.
Music: Mostly **dance**, **soul** and **R&B**; also **ballads**. Published "Caught In The Middle," written and recorded by Juliet Roberts on Cool Tempo Records (dance); "Im Min' Alu" (by B. Nagari), recorded by Ofra Haza on Sire Records (dance); and "Gimme Gimme," written and recorded by Ava Cherry on Radikal Records (dance).
Tips: "Don't over produce your demo. Make certain lyrics can be clearly heard. Be patient."

INTERPLANETARY MUSIC (BMI), 584 Roosevelt, Gary IN 46404. (219)886-2003. President: James R. Hall III. Music publisher, record company (Interplanetary Records), record producer and booking agency. Estab. 1972. Publishes 10 songs/year; publishes 4 new songwriters/year. Works with composers; teams collaborators. Pays standard royalty.
How to Contact: Call first and obtain permission to submit. Prefers cassette. SASE. Reports in 5 weeks.
Music: **R&B**, **top 40/urban contemporary**. Published "In The Shade" (by J. Hall/A. Dickerson) and "I Want You" (by J. Hall/ G. Echols), both recorded by Basic Instinct on Interplanetary Records.
Tips: "Please submit a good quality cassette recording of your best work."

*IONA PUBLISHING, 27/29 Carnoustie Place, Glasgow G58PH **United Kingdom**. (+44)41-420-1881. Fax:(+44)41-420-1892. Publishing Manager: Sinclair Curdie. Music publisher and record company (Iona Records). Estab. 1973. Publishes 100 songs/year; publishes 10 new songwriters/year. Works with composers and lyricists.
How to Contact: Submit demo tape by mail. Unsolicited submissions are OK. Prefers cassette. SAE and IRC. Reports in 2 months.
Music: Mostly **adult contemporary** and **folk**.

IRON SKILLET MUSIC, B-105, Richard Jones Rd., Nashville TN 37215. (615)297-8595. Fax: (615)292-7178. Executive Vice President: Claude G. Southall. Music publisher, record company (Rustic Records Inc.), record producer. Estab. 1984. Publishes 20 songs/year. Pays standard royalty.
Affiliate(s): Covered Bridge Music (BMI), Town Square Music (SESAC).
How to Contact: Submit demo tape by mail. Unsolicited submissions are OK. Prefers cassette with 3 songs and lyric sheet. SASE. Reports in 3 months.
Music: Mostly **country**. Published "Turn off the Lights," "You Make Me Feel Like Dancin'," and "Maybe This Time," all written and recorded by Holt Wilson on Rustic Records.
Tips: "Material should be attention grabbing from start to finish with good hook."

*ISBA MUSIC PUBLISHING INC. (ASCAP), 5046 Rue Chambord, Montreal H23 3N2 **Canada**. (514)522-4722. Fax: (514)525-7550. Contact: Maurice Velenosi or Larry Mancini. Music publisher. Estab. 1983. Publishes 85 songs/year; publishes 20 new songwriters/year. Works with composers and lyricists. Pays standard royalty.
Affiliate(s): Gabbro Music (BMI).
How to Contact: Write or call first and obtain permission to submit. Prefers cassette with 3 songs and lyric sheet. Reports in 6 weeks.
Music: Mostly **pop/rock**, **rap/hip hop** and **dance**; also **R&B**, **A/C**, **MOR** and **country**.

JACLYN MUSIC, 306 Millwood Dr., Nashville TN 37217-1604. (615)366-9999. President: Jack Lynch. Music publisher, producer, recording company (Jalyn, Nashville Bluegrass and Nashville Country) and distributor (Nashville Music Sales). BMI, ASCAP. Estab. 1963. Publishes 50-100 songs/year; 25-50 new songwriters/year. Works with composers and lyricists. Pays standard royalty.
Affiliate(s): JLMG (ASCAP), Jack Lynch Music Group (parent company), Nashville Country Productions and Nashville Music Sales.
How to Contact: Submit a demo tape by mail. Unsolicited submissions are OK. Send good quality cassette recording, neat lyric sheets and SASE. Prefers 1-4 selections per tape. Reports in 1 month.

Music: Country, bluegrass, gospel and **MOR**. Published *Close Your Eyes*, written and recorded by Elaine George on Jalyn Records (country); *Life's Rugged Path* (by Otis Johnson), recorded by Glenda Rider (country); and *Too Much To Dream Last Night*, written and recorded by Lonnie Pierce (country), both on NCP Records.

*JACOB-MAXWELL, INC., (BMI), P.O. Box 61443, Ft. Myers FL 33906-1443. (813)466-0078. Fax: (813)768-1819. President: James J. Albion. Music publisher. Estab. 1992. Publishes 2-6 songs/year; publishes 2 new songwriters/year. Works with composers and lyricists; teams collaborators.
How to Contact: Submit demo tape by mail. Unsolicited submissions are OK. Prefers cassette with 2-4 songs and lyric sheet. "Include cover letter." SASE. Reports in 3-6 weeks.
Music: Mostly **pop ballads, MOR** and **country crossover**; also **pop rock** and **contemporary blues**. Published *Heart On My Sleeve* (by Warren Keller), recorded by TBD on TBD Records (ballad); *Lost Without You* (by James Albion/Ronald Jacobson), recorded by 5 O'clock Shadow (ballad); and *My Heart Keeps Saying No* (by Sheri Shepard), recorded by Lynn Richardson (blues rock), both on Spot Records.
Tips: "Present the tape clean, well, and in best performance possible. Presentation does not always include studio recordings. Still, a strong song needs a clean tape, proper label, and professional appearance. I'm presently publishing a song recorded on a pocket recorder in a music practice room."

JANA JAE MUSIC (BMI), P.O. Box 35726, Tulsa OK 74153. (918)749-1647. Secretary: Phyllis Nelson. Music publisher, record company (Lark Records) and record producer. Estab. 1977. Publishes 5-10 songs/year; publishes 1-2 new songwriters/year. Pays standard royalty.
How to Contact: Submit demo tape by mail—unsolicited submissions OK. Prefers cassette (or VHS videocassette) with 4-5 songs and lyric and lead sheet if possible. Does not return unsolicited material.
Music: Country, pop and instrumentals (classical or country). Published "Mayonnaise," "Bus 'n' Ditty" (by Steven Upfold), and "Let the Bible Be Your Roadmap" (by Irene Elliot), all recorded by Jana Jae on Lark Records.

JAELIUS ENTERPRISES, Route 2, Box 94B, Royse City TX 75189. (214)636-2600. Owner: James Cornelius. Music publisher. ASCAP, BMI. Publishes 3-5 songs/year; publishes 3 new songwriers/year. Pays standard royalty.
Affiliate(s): Jaelius Music (ASCAP), Hitzgalore Music (BMI), Air Rifle Music (ASCAP) and Bee Bee Gun Music (BMI).
How to Contact: Write first and obtain permission to submit. Prefers cassette. SASE. Reports in 3 weeks.
Music: Mostly **pop, country** and **gospel**; also **R&B**. Published "So It Shall Be" (by G. Penny/Lang), recorded by k.d. lang on Sire Records; *She's In Love*, written and recorded by J.J. Cale on Silvertone Records (rock); and *Fly Away* (by Eliot Tucker), recorded by Mark Poncy on Playback Records (country).
Tips: "Today's market requires good demos. Strong lyrics are a must."

JAMMY MUSIC PUBLISHERS LTD., The Beeches, 244 Anniesland Rd., Glasgow G13 1XA, **Scotland**. Phone: (041)954-1873. Managing Director: John D. R. MacCalman. Music publisher and record company. PRS. Estab. 1977. Publishes 45 songs/year; publishes 2 new songwriters/year. Works with composers and lyricists. Pays royalty "in excess of 50%."
How to Contact: Write first and obtain permission to submit. Does not return unsolicited material. Reports in 1 month.
Music: Mostly **rock, pop, country** and **instrumental**; also **Scottish**. Published "The Wedding Song," (by Bill Padley/Grant Mitchell), recorded by True Love Orchestra on BBC Records (pop); *The Old Button Box* (by D.McCrone), recorded by Foster & Allen on Stylus Records; and "Absent Friends" (by D. McCrone), recorded by Dominic Kirwan on Ritz Records.
Tips: "We are now working with a small writers' roster and it's unlikely we would be able to take new writers in the future."

JA/NEIN MUSIKVERLAG GMBH, Hallerstr. 72, D-20146 Hamburg **Germany**. Phone: (40)4102161. Fax: (040)448850. General Manager: Mary Dostal. Music publisher, record company and record producer. GEMA. Publishes 100 songs/year; publishes 20 new songwriters/year. Works with composers and lyricists; teams collaborators. Pays 40% royalty.
Affiliate(s): Pinorrekk Mv., Star-Club Mv., and Wunderbar Mv. (GEMA).
How to Contact: Submit a demo tape—unsolicited submissions are OK. Prefers cassette (or VHS videocassette) and lyric sheet. SAE and IRC. Reports in 2 months.
Music: Mostly **rock, pop, MOR** and **blues**. Published *Berlin Song* (by Michael Alpert), recorded by Brave New World on Pinorrekk & Rounder Records; *Bombe* (by Bernadette Hengst), recorded by Die Bravt on RCA Records; and *Prof. Boogie*, written and recorded by Axel Zwingenberger on Vagabond Records.

Tips: "Good is not good enough. Single A-Side songs only, please. Plus photo (if artist). Leave 3 seconds space between songs. Enclose lyrics."

JASPER STONE MUSIC (ASCAP)/JSM SONGS (BMI), P.O. Box 24, Armonk NY 10504. President: Chris Jasper. Vice President/General Counsel: Margie Jasper. Music publisher. ASCAP, BMI. Estab. 1986. Publishes 20-25 songs/year. Works with composers; teams collaborators. "Each contract is worked out individually and negotiated depending on terms." Pays standard royalty.
How to Contact: Submit a demo tape by mail. Unsolicited submissions are OK. Prefers cassette with maximum of 3 songs and lyric sheets. SASE. Reports in 2-3 weeks.
Music: Mostly **R&B/pop**, **rap** and **rock**. Published *Forever* and *Praise The Eternal*, written and recorded by Chris Jasper; and *Out Front*, written and recorded by Out Front, all on Gold City Records.
Tips: "Keep writing. Keep submitting tapes. Be persistent. Don't give it up. Send your best songs in the best form (best production possible.)"

JEDO INC., 5062 Calatrana Dr., Los Angeles CA 91364-1807. (818)703-0083. Fax: (818)784-5842. Vice President-Creative: Jon Devirian. Music publisher and record producer. Estab. 1978. Publishes 20 songs/year; publishes 2 new songwriters/year. Hires staff writers. Works with composers and lyricists; teams collaborators. Pays standard royalty.
Affiliate(s): J.E.D.O. Music, Worthless Music (ASCAP), SUKI Music, Pointless Music (BMI).
How to Contact: Write or submit demo tape by mail. Unsolicited submissions are OK. Prefers cassette (or VHS videocassette) with 5 songs and lyric sheet. SASE. Reports in 2 weeks.
Music: Mostly **pop/rock**, **country** and **R&B ballads**; also **alternative music**. Published "I Handle Snakes," written and recorded by Tonio K. on A&M Records (alternative rock); and "San Antonio Stroll" (by P. Noah), recorded by Tanya Tucker on MCA Records (country).
Tips: "We are partial to intriguing lyrics with strong melodies and hook chorus. Alternative writing styles are encouraged as well. Arrangement ideas and hook riffs are desired, feel free to submit more than one arrangement but keep it simple."

JENNACO-ALEXAS PUBLISHING CO. (BMI), Suite 433, 1935 S. Main St., Salt Lake City UT 84115. (801)467-2104. A&R: Patrick Melfi. Music publisher and record company (Alexas Records). Estab. 1976. Publishes 6-10 songs/year; publishes 2-3 new songwriters/year. Hires staff writers. Works with composers and lyricists. Pays standard royalty.
Affiliate(s): The Music Group (ASCAP), Alexas Music Productions (ASCAP).
How to Contact: Write first and obtain permission to submit. Prefers cassette or VHS videocassette with 1-3 songs and lyric sheet. SASE. Reports in 2 months.
Music: Mostly **country**, **pop** and **gospel**. Published *She's On Her Own* (by Melfi/Masters), recorded by Leroy Parnell on Arista Records (country); "Between Your Heart & Mine" (by Melfi), recorded by Prophesy on Atlantic Records (MOR); and *Child of God* (by Melfi/Kone), recorded by Sheri Sampson on Godley Music (gospel).
Tips: "Write from the heart! Write a good story and compliment it with a strong melody. We look for story songs like "Where Have You Been," recorded by Kathy Mattea or "Change My Mind," recorded by Oak Ridge Boys, written by AJ Masters and Jason Bloome."

JERJOY MUSIC (BMI), P.O. Box 1264, Peoria IL 61654-1264. (309)673-5755. Professional Manager: Jerry Hanlon. Music publisher. Estab. 1978. Publishes 4 songs/year; publishes 2 new songwriters/year. Pays standard royalty.
How to Contact: Submit a demo tape by mail. Unsolicited submissions are OK. Prefers cassette with 4-8 songs and lyric sheet. SASE. Reports in 2 weeks.
Music: **Country** (modern or traditional), **gospel/Christian**, **Irish music**. Published *If The Good Lord Is Willing* (by Sammie Marler/BobbyRoyce); *Jesus In the Picture* (by Rob Hull); and "The Calling" (by Jerry Hanlon), all recorded by Jerry Hanlon on UAR Records.
Tips: "Be 'real' in what you write. Don't submit any song that you don't honestly feel is strong in commercial value."

***JESTER SONG LTD.**, P.O. Box 308, London SW6 6JQ **United Kingdom**. (071)736-5520. Owner/MD: Roland B. Rogers. Music publisher, music consultant. Estab. 1988. Works with composers and lyricists; teams collaborators. Pays 50-80% royalty.
How to Contact: Submit demo tape by mail. Unsolicited submissions are OK. Prefers cassette with 3 songs and lyric sheet. SAE and IRC. Reports in 1 month.
Music: Mostly **pop** and **rock**, **country**; also **jazz**. Published *Dreams Of You* (by McGarry), recorded by Saxtet on Serendipity Records (jazz); "Good Old Coronation Street" (by Goodwin/Spodcur), recorded by Houghton Weavers on Grasmere Records (pop); and "Special Train," written and recorded by Roger Spencer on Tram Records (pop).
Tips: "Provide a clearly thought out song: lyric, music, arrangement, idea etc. on a demo where all your main ideas can be heard clearly and simply."

JOEY BOY PUBLISHING CO., 3081 NW 24th St., Miami FL 33142. (305)633-7469. Director: Allen Johnston. Music publisher. BMI. Estab. 1985. Publishes 100-150 songs/year; publishes 12-15 new songwriters/year. Works with composers and lyricists; teams collaborators. Pays standard royalty.
Affiliate(s): Beam of Light (ASCAP) and Too Soon To Tell (SESAC).
How to Contact: Submit demo tape by mail. Unsolicited submissions are OK. Prefers cassette with no more than 3 songs and lyric sheets. "Type or print lyric sheet legibly please!" SASE. Reports in 6-8 weeks.
Music: Mostly **R&B, rap**; also **dance, jazz** and **comedy**. Published "30's and Low's" and *King of Bass* by Bass Patrol, on Joey Boy Records (bass); "La Passola" (by A. Santos), recorded by Wilfrido Vargas on T.H. Ralven Records (Spanish); and "Funky ½ C" (by C. Mills and J. Hayes), recorded by The Puppies on Columbia Records.
Tips: "Be true to your trade and write about the things you know."

JOF-DAVE MUSIC (ASCAP), P.O. Box 27410, Las Vegas NV 89126. (702)735-8175. Owner: David E. Johnson. Music publisher, record company (Cymbal Records). Estab. 1984. Publishes 60 songs/year; 4 new songwriters/year. Works with composers. Pays standard royalty.
How to Contact: Write first and obtain permission to submit a tape. Prefers cassette with 3-4 songs and lyric or lead sheets. SASE. Reports in 1 month.
Music: Mostly **rock, pop** and **rap**; also **serious music, country, R&B**. Published *I Need Your Love*, written and recorded by David Wilkerson (R&B); *Handprints* and *Mindprobe*, written and recorded by Ben Sher (jazz), all on Cymbal Records.

LITTLE RICHIE JOHNSON MUSIC (BMI), 318 Horizon Vista Blvd., Belen NM 87002. (505)864-7441. Manager: Tony Palmer. Music publisher, record company (LRJ Records) and record producer. Estab. 1959. Publishes 50 songs/year; publishes 10 new songwriters/year. Works with composers. Pays standard royalty.
Affiliate(s): Little Cowboy Music (ASCAP).
How to Contact: Submit a demo tape by mail. Unsolicited submissions are OK. SASE. Reports in 6 weeks.
Music: **Country** and **Spanish**. Published "New Mexico Waltz" (by Little Richie Johnson) and "Little Children" (by Alan Godage), both recorded by Alan Godage on LRJ Records (C&W).

AL JOLSON BLACK & WHITE MUSIC, 116 17th Ave. S., Nashville TN 37203. (615)244-5656. President: Albert Jolson. Music publisher. BMI. Estab. 1981. Publishes 600 songs/year; publishes 50 new songwriters/year. Works with composers and lyricists; teams collaborators. Pays standard royalty.
Affiliate(s): Jolie House Music (ASCAP).
How to Contact: Submit a demo tape—unsolicited submissions are OK. Prefers cassette with 3 songs and lyric sheet. Send: Attn. Johnny Drake. SASE. Reports in 6 weeks.
Music: Mostly **country crossover, light rock** and **pop**. Published "Come Home to West Virginia" (by Scott Phelps), recorded by Kathy Mattea; "Ten Tiny Fingers, Ten Tiny Toes" (by David John Hanley), recorded by Kelly Dawn on ASA Jolson Records (country); and "Indiana Highway" recorded by Staggerlee on ASA Jolson Records (country).
Tips: "Make sure it has a strong hook. Ask yourself if it is something you would hear on the radio 5 times a day. Have good audible vocals on demo tape."

*JON MUSIC (BMI), P.O. Box 233, Church Point LA 70525. (318)684-2176. Owner: Lee Lavergne. Music publisher, record company (Lanor Records), record producer and recording studio (Sound Center Recorders). Estab. 1960. Publishes 30-40 songs/year; publishes 3-4 new songwriters/year. Pays standard royalty.
How to Contact: Write or call first and obtain permission to submit. Prefers cassette with 4 songs and lyric sheet. "Use a good quality cassette and make sure the vocals are above the music." SASE. Reports in 2 weeks. ("Depends how busy we are and if I am undecided.")
Music: Mostly **country**. Published *Pictures*, written and recorded by Tommy McLain (country); *Bridges* (by D. Jones/B. Cheshire), recorded by David Jones (country); and *Hey Jolie* (by R. Naquin/V. Bruce), recorded by Vin Bruce (country), all on Lanor Records.
Tips: "Write professional hit material that's fresh and different."

JOSENA MUSIC (SESAC), P.O. Box 566, Los Altos CA 94022. President: Joe Nardone. Music publisher and producer. Estab. 1983. Publishes 30 songs/year; publishes 1-2 new songwriters/year. Hires staff songwriters. Works with composers and lyricists. Pays standard royalty.
Affiliate(s): Reigninme Music (SESAC).
How to Contact: Write first and obtain permission to submit a tape. Prefers cassette with 3 songs and lyric sheet. Does not return unsolicited material. Reports in 2 months if interested.
Music: Mostly **Christian rock/pop, pop** and **gospel**; also **modern rock** and **Latin Music** as well— **flamenco, rumba style** (Spanish) and **Spanish ballads**. Published "Coming Home," (by Dino Veloz/

Joe Nardone), recorded by Joe Nardone (modern Christian rock); "Make Us One" (by Lee Kalem/ Joe Nardone); recorded by Lillie Knauls (gospel); and "Go God's Way" written and recorded by Joe Nardone (jazz).
Tips: "Make sure it is a hot marketable tune—get unbiased opinions on your song—would it be playable on the radio?"

*PATRICK JOSEPH MUSIC INC. (BMI), 2004 Wedgewood Ave., Nashville TN 37212. Contact: Steve Markland. Music publisher. Estab. 1988. Publishes 2 new songwriters/year. Works with composers and lyricists; teams collaborators.
Affiliate(s): Patrix Jamus Music (ASCAP), Second Wave Music (ASCAP), August Wind Music (BMI), PJH Music (SESAC).
How to Contact: Write first and obtain permission to submit. Does not return material.
Music: Mostly **country, pop** and A/C. Published "Rock My World" (by B. LaBounty), recorded by Brooks & Dunn on Arista Records (country); "Tell Me What You Dream" (by V. Melamed), recorded by Restless Heart on RCA Records (A/C); and "Wrong Side of Memphis" (by M. Bong), recorded by Trisha Yearwood on MCA Records (country).

JUMP MUSIC, Langemunt 71, 9420 AAIGEM, **Belgium**. Phone: (053)62-73-77. General Manager: Eddy Van Mouffaert. Music publisher, record company (Jump Records) and record producer. Member of SABAM S.V., Brussels. Publishes 100 songs/year; publishes 8 new songwriters/year. Works with composers and lyricists. Pays royalty via SABAM S.V.
How to Contact: Submit demo tape by mail. Unsolicited submissions are OK. Prefers cassette. Does not return unsolicited material. Reports in 2 weeks.
Music: Mostly **easy listening, disco** and **light pop**; also **instrumentals**. Published "Just A Friend" (by Eddy Govert), recorded by Sherly on Ideal Records (pop); "Go Go Go" (by H. Deschuyteneer), recorded by Rudy Silvester on Scorpion Records (Flemish); and *Won't You Stay With Me* (by Eddy Govert), recorded by Frank Valentino on Holy Hole Records (Flemish).
Tips: "Music wanted with easy, catchy melodies (very commercial songs)."

JUNGLE BOY MUSIC (BMI), #222, 2491 Purdue Ave., Los Angeles CA 90064. (310)452-7004. Fax: (310)452-7035. President: Robert Anderson. Music publisher. Estab. 1982. Publishes 30 songs/year; publishes 4 new songwriters/year. Hires staff songwriters. Works with composers and lyricists; teams collaborators. Pays standard royalty.
How to Contact: Submit demo tape by mail. Unsolicited submissions are OK. Prefers cassette (or DAT) with up to 5 songs. SASE. Reports in 3 weeks.
Music: Mostly **rock, pop** and **R&B**; also **country** and **rap**. Published "Can't Stand This Heat" (by Paul Sabu), recorded by Lee Aaron; "Dream Burnin' Down" and "In My Blood," written and recorded by Paul Sabu on Now & Then Records.
Tips: "Believe in your song and don't be afraid to send it in, you never know."

JUST A NOTE, 1058 E. Saint Catherine, Louisville KY 40204. (503)637-2877. General Partner: John V. Heath. Music publisher, record companies (Hillview, Estate) and record producer (MVT Productions). ASCAP and BMI. Estab. 1979. Publishes 35 songs/year; publishes 10-15 new songwriters/year. Works with composers and lyricists. Pays standard royalty.
Affiliate(s): Two John's Music (ASCAP).
How to Contact: Write or call first and obtain permission to submit. Prefers cassette, 7½ ips reel-to-reel or VHS videocassette with 3 songs and lead sheet. SASE. Reports in 1 month.
Music: Mostly **pop, country, R&B** and **MOR**; also **gospel**. Published *Old Age* and *Rose*, written and recorded by Mark Gibbs on Hillview Records; and *Area Code 502*, written and recorded by Adonis, on Estate Records.

*JUSTICE MUSIC CORPORATION, 11586 Blix St., N. Hollywood CA 91602. (818)762-6850. Fax: (818)762-6747. Acquisitions Director: Craig Herkimer. Music publisher. Estab. 1990. Publishes 200 songs/year; publishes 10 new songwriters/year. Hires staff writers. Works with composers and/or lyricists; teams collaborators. Pays standard royalty.
Affiliate(s): Equity Music Corp. (ASCAP) and Justice Artists Music Corp. (BMI).
How to Contact: Submit demo tape by mail. Unsolicited submissions are OK. Prefers cassette (or VHS ½" videocassette) with at least 1 song and lyric sheet. Does not return material. Reports in 3 weeks.
Music: Mostly **rock, pop rock** and **alternative**; also **jazz/blues** and **country**. Published *Nice & Warm*, written and recorded by Tab Benoit; and *All Come True* (by Mike Brayton), recorded by Thrillcat.

KANSA RECORDS CORPORATION, P.O. Box 1014, Lebanon TN 37088. (615)444-3865. Secretary and Treasurer/General Manager: Kit Johnson. Music publisher, record company and record producer.

Estab. 1972. Publishes 50-60 songs/year; publishes 8-10 new songwriters/year. Teams collaborators. Pays standard royalty.
Affiliate(s): Great Leawood Music, Inc. (ASCAP) and Twinsong Music (BMI).
How to Contact: Submit demo tape by mail. Unsolicited submissions are OK. Prefers cassette with 4 songs and lyric sheet. SASE. Reports in 1 month.
Music: Mostly **country, MOR** and **country rock**; also **R&B** (leaning to country) and **Christian.** Published *I Miss You* (by K. Francisco) and *Playin' the Part of a Fool* (by P. Petersen/J. Peterson), both recorded by Glen Bailey; and *Out of Sight/Out of Mind* (by Geoffrey Jacobs), recorded by Jimmy Dallas, all on Kansa Records.

KAUPPS & ROBERT PUBLISHING CO. (BMI), P.O. Box 5474, Stockton CA 95205. (209)948-8186. Fax: (209)942-2163. President: Nancy L. Merrihew. Music publisher, record company (Kaupp Records), and manager and booking agent (Merri-Webb Productions and Most Wanted Bookings). Estab. 1990. Publishes 15-20 songs/year; publishes 5 new songwriters/year. Works with composers and lyricists; teams collaborators. Pays standard royalty.
How to Contact: Write or call first and obtain permission to submit. Prefers cassette (or VHS videocassette if available) with 3 songs maximum and lyric sheet. "If artist, send PR package." SASE. Reports in 3 months.
Music: Mostly **country, R&B** and **A/C rock**; also **pop, rock** and **gospel.** Published "Willie Gee" (by Nancy Merrihew), recorded by Nanci Lynn (country); "Kick Start," written and recorded by Dan Alice (rock); and "Canadian Way," written and recorded by Stephen Bruce (pop rock), all on Kaupp Records.
Tips: "Know what you want, set a goal, focus in on your goals, be open to constructive criticism, polish tunes and keep polishing."

KAREN KAYLEE MUSIC GROUP, R.D. #11 Box 360, Greensburg PA 15601. (412)836-0966. President: Karen Kaylee. Music publisher. BMI. Estab. 1989. Publishes 15-20 songs/year; publishes 3 new songwriters/year. Works with composers and lyricists; teams collaborators. Pays standard royalty.
How to Contact: Submit demo tape by mail. Unsolicited submissions are OK; "serious submissions only." Prefers cassette (or VHS videocassette) with 3-5 songs and lyric sheet. "No phone calls please." Does not return unsolicited material. Reports in 1 month.
Music: Mostly **country, gospel** and **traditional country.** Published "Gone Again" (by Carlene Haggerty), and "Only God" (by Matt Furin), recorded by Karen Kaylee; and "There's a Reason," written and recorded by Lisa Amadio, all on Ka-De Records.
Tips: "Send only your best material — clean and professional demos. Your song must be better than the ones on the radio. Don't get discouraged. There are hits that haven't been written yet. I listen to every tape."

KEEP CALM MUSIC LIMITED, Falcon Mews, London SW12 9SJ **England.** (081)675-5584. Fax: (081)675-6313. Professional Manager: Joanna Underwood. Music publisher, record company and record producer (Don't Panic Productions Ltd.). PRS. Member MCPS. Publishes approximately 50-75 songs/year. Works with composers. Pays varying royalty.
Affiliate(s): Yo Bro, Low Spirit (UK office), The Brothers Organisation, DPP Music.
How to Contact: Submit demo tape by mail. Unsolicited submissions are OK. Prefers cassette with maximum 5 songs and lyric sheet. Does not return unsolicited material. Reports in 1 month.
Music: Mostly **R&B, black/dance** and **pop**; also **high energy** and **rock.** Published "Hey Hey" (by Ramaekers/Sas), recorded by D&S on WGAF Records; "State of Mind" (by Peter/Ward), recorded by CCN on WGAF Records; and "Everything" (by Smart/Ward), recorded by Smart on Brothers Organisation Records.

KEL-CRES PUBLISHING (ASCAP), 2525 East 12th St., Cheyenne WY 82001. (307)638-9894. A&R Manager: Gary J. Kelley. Music publisher, record company (Rough Cut Records) and record producer. Estab. 1989. Publishes 2 songs/year. Teams collaborators. Pays standard royalty.
Affiliate(s): Kelley-Kool Music (BMI).
How to Contact: Submit a demo tape by mail. Unsolicited submissions are OK. Prefers cassette, CD or DAT (or VHS videocassette) with 3 songs and lyric sheets. Guitar/piano demo with "words up front" is sufficient. SASE. Reports in 4-6 weeks.
Music: Mostly **country, country rock** and **rockabilly.** Published *Heart Mender* (by Bob Mau), recorded by Generation Gap; *Serina* and *Jail House Blues* (by Tim Anderson), both recorded by Generation Gap, all on Rough Cut Records.
Tips: "Keep songs simple, very few lyrics with strong repeated 'hook-line.' Can a stranger hum your tune after hearing it?"

GENE KENNEDY ENTERPRISES, INC., 3950 N. Mt. Juliet Rd., Mt. Juliet TN 37122. (615)754-0417. President: Gene Kennedy. Vice President: Karen Jeglum Kennedy. Music publisher, record company

(Door Knob Records), record producer, distributor and promoter. ASCAP, BMI, SESAC. Estab. 1975. Publishes 30-40 songs/year; publishes 15-20 new songwriters/year. Works with composers and lyricists. Pays standard royalty.
Affiliate(s): Chip 'n Dale Music Publishers (ASCAP), Door Knob Music Publishing (BMI) and Lodestar Music (SESAC).
How to Contact: Submit demo tape by mail. Unsolicited submissions OK. Prefers cassette or 7½ ips reel-to-reel with 1-3 songs and lyric sheet. "We will not accept anything we have to sign for." SASE. ("Please send large enough envelope for tape returns.") Reports in 3 weeks.
Music: Country and **gospel.** Published "Praise Ye The Lord" (by Linda Almond), recorded by Dave Jeglum (gospel); "Open For Suggestions" (by Wyndi Harp), recorded by Perry La Pointe (country); and "I've Had Enough of You" (by Johnette Burton), recorded by Debbie Rich (country), all on Door Knob Records.

KENO PUBLISHING, P.O. Box 4429, Austin TX 78765-4429. (512)441-2422. Owner: Keith A. Ayres. Music publisher and record company (Glitch Records). BMI. Estab. 1984. Publishes 12 songs/year; publishes 10 new songwriters/year. Works with composers and lyricists; teams collaborators. Pays standard royalty.
How to Contact: Write first and obtain permission to submit a tape. Prefers cassette (and/or VHS videocassette if available) with 2-3 songs and lyric or lead sheets. Does not return unsolicited material.
Music: Rock, rap, reggae and **pop**; also **metal, R&B** and **alternative** (all types). Published "I Wrote the Note" (by George Alistair Sanger), recorded by European Sex Machine (computerized); "Here It Is" (by John Patterson), recorded by Cooly Girls (rap); and "Kick'em in the Ass" (by Los Deflectors/Keith Ayres), recorded by Ron Rogers (rock), all on Glitch Records.

*KICKING MULE PUBLISHING/DESK DRAWER PUBLISHING, Box 158, Alderpoint CA 95511. (707)926-5312. Manager: Ed Denson. Music publisher and record company. BMI and ASCAP. Member NAIRD. Publishes 80 songs/year; publishes 5 new songwriters/year. Pays standard royalty.
How to Contact: Write first and obtain permission to submit. Prefers cassette with 1-3 songs. SASE. Reports "as soon as possible."
Music: Blues (fingerpicking) and **folk** (guitar/banjo only). Published "The Sweeper," written and recorded by George Gritzbach on KM Records (folk); "Thunder On The Run," written and recorded by Stefan Grossman on KM Records (guitar instrumental); and "Pokerface Smile" (by Robert Force), recorded by Force & D'Ossche (country).
Tips: "We publish only material released on our albums. Since we record virtuoso guitar, dulcimer and banjo players, virtually the only way to get a tune published with us is to be such a player, or to have such a player record your song. We don't publish many 'songs' per se, our entire catalog is devoted 95% to instrumentals and 5% to songs with lyrics. As publishers we are not in the market for new songs. This listing is more of a hope that people will not waste their time and ours sending us blue-sky demos of material that does not relate to our very specialized business."

KEVIN KING MUSIC, Crickhowell, Powys NP8 1LB **England.** (0873)810142. Fax: (0873)811557. Contact: Kevin King. Music publisher. Estab. 1985. Publishes 6 songs/year; publishes 3 new songwriters/year. Works with composers and/or lyricists. Pays standard royalty.
How to Contact: Submit demo tape by mail. Unsolicited submissions are OK. Prefers cassette. SAE and IRC. Reports in 1 month.
Music: Mostly **pop, easy listening** and **country.** Published "Just In Time" (by R. Ackrill), recorded by Kyro (pop); "We Got To Try" (by Laurie Thompson), recorded by Kevin Coose (pop); and "Phantom of Soap" (by Lee Carroll), recorded by Lee J. Simple (pop), all on Riviera Records.
Tips: "Don't follow current trends as it is usually too late for your publishing to catch the market. Concentrate on quality of writing."

KINGSPORT CREEK MUSIC PUBLISHING (BMI), P.O. Box 6085, Burbank CA 91510. Contact: Vice President. Music publisher and record company (Cowgirl Records). Estab. 1980. Works with composers, lyricists; teams collaborators. Pays standard royalty.
How to Contact: Submit a demo tape—unsolicited submissions are OK. Prefers cassette (or VHS videocassette) with any number of songs and lyric sheet. Does not return unsolicited material. "Include photos and bio if possible."
Music: Mostly **country** and **gospel**; also **R&B** and **MOR.** Published "Who Am I," "Golden Wedding Ring" and "Let's Give Love," all written and recorded by Melvena Kaye on Cowgirl Records.
Tips: "Videocassettes are advantageous."

KOMMUNICATION KONCEPTS, Dept. SM, Box 2095, Philadelphia PA 19103. (215)848-7475. President: S. Deane Henderson. Music publisher and management firm. Publishes 10-15 songs/year; publishes 6 new songwriters/year. Pays standard royalty.

Affiliate(s): Bill Tower Entertainment Group (ASCAP).
How to Contact: Prefers cassette (or VHS videocassette) with 4-8 songs and lyric sheets. Does not return unsolicited material. Reports in 2 weeks.
Music: Dance-oriented, easy listening, gospel, MOR, R&B, rock, soul, top 40/pop, funk and **heavy metal**. Published "Monica, Brenda and Lisa," recorded by Helen McCormick; "Hot Number" (by John Fitch), recorded by The Racers (heavy rock); and "In God's Hand" (by Verdelle C. Bryant), recorded by Verdelle & Off Spring Gospel Singers (gospel).
Tips: "We're currently looking for female and male R&B groups."

KOZKEEOZKO MUSIC (ASCAP), Suite 602, 928 Broadway, New York NY 10010. (212)505-7332. Professional Managers: Ted Lehrman and Libby Bush. Music publisher, record producer and management firm (Landslide Management). Estab. 1978. Publishes 5 songs/year; publishes 3 new songwriters/year. Pays standard royalty.
How to Contact: Write or call first and obtain permission to submit. Prefers cassette (or VHS ½" videocassette) with 2 songs maximum and typewritten lyric sheet for each song. SASE. Reports in 6 weeks.
Music: Mostly **soul/pop, dance, pop/rock** (no heavy metal), **A/C** and **country**. Published "Ain't No Cure For You" (by Ed Chalfin and Tedd Lawson), recorded by Dan Kramer on Thunder Records (pop), "We Are Now, We Are Forever" (by Ed Chalfin and Tedd Lawson), recorded by Bernard Purdy on Grand Strand Records (soul/pop); and "Music to My Eyes" (by Ed Calfin and Tedd Lawson), recorded by Jam Box (soul).
Tips: "Send unique, well-crafted, today songs on great demos."

KREN MUSIC PUBLISHING (BMI), P.O. Box 5804, Hacienda Heights CA 91745. (818)855-1692. Co-owner: Kris Clark. Music publisher, record producer (Kren Music Productions). Estab. 1985. Publishes 10-20 songs/year; publishes 5-10 new songwriters/year. Works with composers and lyricists; teams collaborators. Pays standard royalty.
How to Contact: Submit a demo tape by mail. Unsolicited submissions OK. Prefers cassette with 3 songs and lyric sheet. SASE. Reports in 2 months.
Music: Mostly **country, pop** and **rock**; also **gospel** and **New Age**. Published "Where Fools are Kings" (by Jeffrey Steele), recorded by Steve Wariner on MCA Records (country).
Tips: "Make your song the best you possibly can and present a demo tape that reflects such."

KRUDE TOONZ MUSIC (ASCAP), P.O. Box 308, Lansdale PA 19446. (215)855-8628. President: G. Malack. Music publisher. Estab. 1988.
Affiliate(s): Teeze Me Pleeze Me Music (ASCAP).
How to Contact: Write first and obtain permission to submit a tape. Prefers cassette (or VHS videocassette if available) with 3 songs. SASE.
Music: Mostly **rock** and **pop**. Published "Tonight," "Fantasy" and "Love Or Lust" (by G. Malack), recorded by Roughhouse on CBS Records (rock).

*HANS KUSTERS MUSIC, Broekstraat, Kobbegem 1730 **Belgium**. (02)452 72 03. Fax: (02)452 34 25. Managing Director: Mr. Hans Kusters. Music publisher and record producer. Estab. 1976. Publishes 100 songs/year. Pays standard royalty.
How to Contact: Submit demo tape by mail. Unsolicited submissions are OK. Prefers cassette with 3 songs and lyric sheet. SAE and IRC. Reports in 3 weeks.
Music: Mostly **Tex-Mex** and **pop/rock**. "We have mostly Dutch repertoire."

LACKEY PUBLISHING CO. (BMI), Dept. SM, Box 269, Caddo OK 74729. (405)367-2798. President: Robert F. Lackey. Music publisher and record producer. Publishes 6-8 songs/year; publishes 3-4 new songwriters/year. Pays standard royalty.
How to Contact: Submit demo tape by mail. Unsolicited submissions are OK. Prefers cassette with 1-10 songs. SASE. Reports in 2-3 months.
Music: Mostly **country** and **MOR**; also **bluegrass, blues, church/religious, easy listening, folk, gospel, progressive, R&B** and **top 40/pop**. Published "The Devil In Tight Blue Jeans," written and recorded by Franklin Lackey (country); "Teenager in Love," written and recorded by Sherry Kenae (pop/country); and "The Rose of Goodbye" (by Franklin Lackey), recorded by Sherry Kenae (progressive country), all on Uptown Records.
Tips: "Make every word count on the lyrics."

*LANTERN MUSIC/MUSIC FOR FILMS, 34 Batchelor St., London N1 0EG **United Kingdom**. (71)278-4288. Director: Rob Gold. Music publisher. Estab. 1968. Publishes 12 songs/year; publishes 4 new songwriters/year. Hires staff writers. Works with composers and/or lyricists.
How to Contact: Submit demo tape by mail. Unsolicited submissions are OK. Prefers cassette. SAE and IRC. Reports in 2 weeks.

Music: Mostly **film and TV music, hit country** and **anything good!** Published *A Dark-Adapted Eye*, written and recorded by David Ferguson (BBC TV program); "Viva" (by David Lowe/Julian Ronnie), recorded by Crazy Fan Tutti on Oval/East West Records (opera/funky world music); and *Thicker Than Water* (by Julian Wastall), recorded by various artists (BBC TV drama series).

LARI-JON PUBLISHING (BMI), 325 West Walnut, Rising City NE 68658. (402)542-2336. Owner: Larry Good. Music publisher, record company (Lari-Jon Records) and record producer (Lari Jon Productions). Estab. 1967. Publishes 20 songs/year; publishes 2-3 new songwriters/year. Teams collaborators. Pays variable royalty.
How to Contact: Submit a demo tape by mail. Unsolicited submissions are OK. Prefers cassette with 5 songs and lyric sheet. "Be professional." SASE. Reports in 2 months.
Music: Mostly **country Southern gospel** and **'50's rock.** Published *Happy Valley June*, written and recorded by Tom Campbell; "Nebraskaland," written and recorded by Larry Good; and *Between the Lies* (by Mick Kovar), recorded by Johnny Nace, all on Lari-Jon Records.

LATIN AMERICAN MUSIC CO., INC., P.O. Box 1844, Cathedral Station, New York NY 10025. (212)993-5557. Fax: (212)993-5551. Contact: D. Vera. Music Publisher. Estab. 1970. Publishes 20 songs/year; publishes 5 new songwriters/year. Works with composers and lyricists; teams collaborators. Pays standard royalty.
Affiliate(s): The International Music Co.
How to Contact: Submit demo tape by mail. Unsolicited submissions OK. Prefers cassette. Does not return unsolicited material. Reports in 3 months.
Music: Mostly **Latin American**; also **reggae.** Published "La Finquita" (G. Rosario), recorded by the Believers; "Se Me Van" (by T. Sanchez), recorded by Pupy on CBS Records; and "Te Siento," written and recorded by Lan Franco on Audio Records.

***LAURMACK MUSIC (ASCAP)**, 655 Wyona St., Brooklyn NY 11207. (718)272-1200. Fax: (718)649-1280. President: Alfred McCarther. Music publisher and record company (Alcarm Records). Estab. 1981. Hires staff songwriters. Works with composers and lyricists; teams collaborators. Pays standard royalty.
How to Contact: Submit demo tape by mail. Unsolicited submissions are OK. Prefers cassette (or VHS videocassette) with 3 songs and lyric sheet. SASE. Reports in 3 weeks to 3 months.
Music: Mostly **R&B, pop, rap** and **hip hop**; also **jazz, gospel** and **country.** Published "Teach Them" (by Michael Augustus), recorded by Jonn Gee (pop); and *Get Ready Devil It's Your Turn* (by James Spencer), recorded by Your Brother (rap), both on Alcarm Records.

LAYMOND PUBLISHING CO., INC., Box 25371, Charlotte NC 28229. (704)573-8999. A&R Director: Dwight Moody. Music publisher, record company (Panhandle Records, Lamon Records) and record producer (David and Carlton Moody). BMI, ASCAP. Publishes 60-70 songs/year; publishes 20 new songwriters/year. Works with composers. Pays standard royalty.
Affiliate(s): CDT Productions.
How to Contact: Submit demo tape by mail. Unsolicited submissions are OK. Prefers cassette. SASE. Reports in 2 months.
Music: Mostly **country, R&B** and **rock**; also **gospel.** Published *Loving Arms*, written and recorded by Chris Clothier; *Stevie the Star* (by Sammie Lee), recorded by Carlton Moody; and *Line Dancing* (by Carlton Moody), recorded by Moody Brothers, all on Lamon Records.

LCS MUSIC GROUP, INC., 6301 N. O'Connor Blvd., The Studios of Las Colinas, Irving TX 75039. (214)869-0700. Contact: Publishing Assistant. Music publisher. BMI, ASCAP, SESAC. Works with composers. Pays standard royalty.
Affiliate(s): Bug and Bear Music (ASCAP), Chris Christian Music (BMI), Court and Case Music (ASCAP), Home Sweet Home Music (ASCAP), Monk and Tid Music (SESAC), Preston Christian Music (BMI).
How to Contact: Submit a demo tape by mail. Unsolicited submissions are OK. Prefers cassette with lyric sheet (only necessary if the words are difficult to understand). "Put all pertinent information on the tape itself, such as how to contact the writer. Do not send Express!" Does not return unsolicited material. Reports in 2 months.
Music: Mostly **contemporary Christian** and **inspirational.** Published "The Me Nobody Knows" (by Vincent Grimes), recorded by Marilyn McCoo on Warner Alliance (contemporary Christian); "Calling You," written and recorded by Eric Champion on Word Records (contemporary Christian); and "Warrior for the Lord" (by Brent Tallent), recorded by Marilyn McCoo on Warner Alliance Records (inspirational).
Tips: "Listen to the cutting edge of whatever style you write—don't get caught in a rut stylistically."

LE GRANDE FROMAGE/CHEDDAR CHEESE MUSIC, 8739 Sunset Blvd., Los Angeles CA 90069. (310)659-9820. Fax: (310)652-0907. President: Jan Rhees. Estab. 1988. Publishes 30 songs/year. Publishes 5 new songwriters/year. Works with composers and lyricists; teams collaborators.
How to Contact: Call first and obtain permission to submit. Prefers cassette (or VHS videocassette if available) with 3 songs and lyric sheet. SASE. Reports in 3-4 weeks.
Music: R&B, pop/alternative and **jazz; all forms of music.** Published *A Woman Knows* (by Chris McCarty), recorded by Martina McBride on CA Records (country); "Touch" (by S. Lane), recorded by Diane Schuur on GRP Records (jazz); and "Love in the Making" (by S. Lane/D. Winzeler), recorded by Barry White and Mona Lisa on Quality Records.
Tips: "Write the best song you can—demo it to enhance the song—be tenacious and patient."

*LILLY MUSIC PUBLISHING (SOCAN), 61 Euphrasia Dr., Toronto, Ontario M6B 3V8 **Canada**. (416)782-5768. Fax: (416)782-7170. President: Panfilo DiMatteo. Music publisher and record company. Estab. 1992. Publishes 20 songs/year; publishes 8 new songwriters/year. Teams collaborators. Pays standard royalty.
Affiliate(s): San Martino Music Publishing, Paglieta Music Publishing (CMRRA).
How to Contact: Submit demo tape by mail. Unsolicited submissions are OK. Prefers cassette (or videocassette if available) with 3 songs and lyric and lead sheets. "We will contact you only if we are interested in the material." Does not return material. Reports in 1 month.
Music: Mostly **dance** and **ballads, rock;** also **country.** Published "I Can See It In Your Eyes" (by DiMatteo/Pagano/Vineiguera) and "Don't Know" (by Pagano/DiMatteo), both recorded by Angelica Castro on P&N Records.

DORIS LINDSAY PUBLISHING (ASCAP), 1203 Biltmore Ave., High Point NC 27260. (910)882-9990. President: Doris Lindsay. Music publisher and record company (Fountain Records). Estab. 1979. Publishes 20 songs/year; publishes 4 songwriters/year. Works with composers and lyricists; teams collaborators. Pays standard royalty.
Affiliate(s): Better Times Publishing (BMI).
How to Contact: Submit demo tape by mail. Unsolicited submissions are OK. Prefers cassette with 2 songs. "Submit good quality demos." SASE. Reports in 2 months.
Music: Mostly **country, pop** and **contemporary gospel.** Published *Service Station Cowboy* (by Hoss Ryder), recorded by Ace Diamond on Sabre Records; "Share Your Love," written and recorded by Mitch Snow; and "America's Song" (by Cathy Roeder), recorded by Terry Michaels, both on Fountain Records.
Tips: "Present a good quality demo (recorded in a studio). Positive clean lyrics and up-tempo music are easiest to place."

LINEAGE PUBLISHING CO. (BMI), Box 211, East Prairie MO 63845. (314)649-2211. (Branch: Apt. D., Nashboro Blvd., Nashville TN 37217. (615)366-4975.) Professional Manager: Tommy Loomas. Staff: Alan Carter and Joe Silver. Music publisher, record producer and record company. Pays standard royalty.
How to Contact: Query first. Prefers cassette with 2-4 songs and lyric sheet; include bio and photo if possible. SASE. Reports in 1 month.
Music: Country, easy listening, MOR, country rock and **top 40/pop.** Published "Yesterday's Teardrops" and "Round & Round," (by Phil and Larry Burchett), recorded by The Burchetts on Capstan Records (country).

LIN'S LINES (ASCAP), #434, 156 Fifth Ave., New York NY 10010. (212)691-5631. President: Linda K. Jacobson. Music publisher. Estab. 1978. Publishes 4 songs/year; publishes 4 new songwriters/year. Works with composers and lyricists; teams collaborators. Pays standard royalty.
How to Contact: Submit a demo tape by mail. Unsolicited submissions are OK. Prefers cassette or VHS or ¾" videocassette with 3-5 songs and lyric or lead sheet. SASE. Reports in 6 weeks.
Music: Mostly **rock, pop** and **rap;** also **world music, R&B** and **gospel.**

LION HILL MUSIC PUBLISHING CO. (BMI), P.O. Box 110983, Nashville TN 37222-0983. (615)731-6640. Publisher: Wayne G. Leinsz. Music publisher, record company (Richway Records). ASCAP. Estab. 1988. Publishes 40-50 songs/year; publishes a few new songwriters/year. Works with composers and lyricists; teams collaborators. Pays standard royalty.
How to Contact: Write or call to obtain permission to submit. Prefers cassette with 3 songs and lead sheets. SASE. Reports back in 1 month.
Music: Mostly **country;** also **gospel** and **bluegrass.** Published "What More Could I Ask For," written and recorded by Ernie Hollar; "Cold October Night," written and recorded by Phillip Clarkson; and "I Still Pretend" (by Guffnett, Pugh, Stange), recorded by Jill Michaels, all on Richway Records.

LITTLE POND PRODUCTIONS, P.O. Box 20594, Portland OR 97220. (503)254-5776. Fax: (503)254-1239. President: David Brenton-Miller. Vice President: JoAnna Burns-Miller. Music publisher, record company and record producer. Estab. 1985. Publishes 10-20 songs/year; publishes 1 or 2 new songwriters/year. Works with composers and lyricists. Pays standard royalty or flat fee.
How to Contact: Submit demo tape by mail. Unsolicited submissions are OK. Prefers cassette with 2 songs and lyric or lead sheet. "Send clear recordings." SASE. Reports in 2-3 months.
Music: Mostly **New Age, spiritual** and **MOR**; also **contemporary soft pop.** Published "Making Changes," "Remember Me" and "You Held My Hand," all written and recorded by JoAnna Burns-Miller on Little Pond Productions.
Tips: "Keep it clean, clear, obvious 'hook,' good focused message with a lesson, moral. Need good strong lyrics sung by a great singer. We like songs that offer hope, inspiration, beauty, healing. Instrumentals welcome."

*LOGICAL CHOICE MUSIC, 117 Marian St., Enmore, NSW 2042 **Australia**. 565 1562. Fax: 516 5589. Owner/Manager: Greg Grant. Production music company. Estab. 1993. Publishes 100-200 songs/year. Pays standard royalty.
How to Contact: Submit demo tape by mail. Unsolicited submissions are OK. Prefers cassette. SAE and IRC. Reports in 1 month.
Music: Mostly **production music.**
Tips: "We are only interested in production music. All styles, but the submission has to be up to a rough mix stage."

LONNY TUNES MUSIC (BMI), P.O. Box 460086, Garland TX 75046. President: Lonny Schonfeld. Music publisher, record company (G-Town Records) and record producer. Estab. 1988. Publishes 8-10 songs/year; publishes 2-3 new songwriters/year. Works with composers and/or lyricists; teams collaborators. Pays standard royalty.
How to Contact: Submit a demo tape by mail. Unsolicited submissions are OK. Prefers cassette with 3-5 songs and lyric sheet. "Professional quality only." Does not return unsolicited submissions. Reports in 6-8 weeks.
Music: Mostly **country, children's** and **rock**; also **jazz** and **comedy.** Published "Lordiness" and "Baby With You," written and recorded by Randy Stout; and "The G-Town Rap" (by The Hart Bros.), recorded by Stuart Sutcliff, all on G-Town Records.
Tips: "Make sure your lyrical content is contemporary. 'Old time' rhymes like moon and June will not work for us."

LOVEFORCE INTERNATIONAL, P.O. Box 241648, Los Angeles CA 90024. Submissions Manager: T. Wilkins. Music publisher, record company and international record promotion company. BMI. Estab. 1979. Publishes 5-10 songs/year; publishes 2 new songwriters/year. Pays standard royalty.
How to Contact: Write first and obtain permission to submit. Prefers cassette (or VHS videocassette) with 2 songs maximum and lyric sheet. "SASE a must." Reports in 1 month.
Music: Mostly **pop, rock** and **R&B**; also **ballads, country** and **gospel.** Published "I Wanna Be Good To You," written and recorded by Bandit on LoveForce International; "Betweeen Two People," written and recorded by Spiderworks on Sinbad Records; also an instrumental LP by Bandit released in the People's Republic of China on a Chinese record label.

LOVEY MUSIC, INC., P.O. Box 630755, Miami FL 33163. (305)935-4880. President: Jack Gale. Music publisher. BMI, ASCAP. Estab. 1981. Publishes 25 songs/year; publishes 10 new songwriters/year. Pays standard royalty.
Affiliate(s): Cowabonga Music, Inc. (ASCAP).
How to Contact: Submit a demo tape by mail. Unsolicited submissions are OK. Prefers cassette or VHS videocassette with 2 songs max and lyric sheets. Does not return unsolicited material. Reports in 2 weeks if interested.
Music: Mostly **country crossover** and **country.** Published "If I Could Hear My Mother Pray Again" (by C. Louvin), recorded by Charlie Louvin and Tammy Wynette; "When They Ring Those Golden Bells" (by C. Louvin), recorded by John Conlee and Charlie Louvin; and "Second Time Around" (by R. Priola), recorded by Del Reeves, all on Playback Records.

JERE LOWE PUBLISHING (BMI), 603 E. Broadway, Denver City TX 79323-3311. (806)592-8020. Fax: (806)592-9486. Owner: Jeré Lowe. Music publisher, record company (FAB 5 Records) and record producer (Loco Sounds). Estab. 1990. Publishes 10 songs/year; publishes 3 new songwriters/year. Works with composers and lyricists. Pays standard royalty.
How to Contact: Submit demo tape by mail. Unsolicited submissions are OK. Prefers cassette (or videocassette) with 3 songs and lyric sheet. "Best demos help sell songs." SASE. Reports in 1 month.

Music: Mostly **new** or **young country**, **R&B** and **Spanish**; also **pop-top 40**, **children's** and **adult contemporary**. Writer, publisher and music producer for "Imagineland," Jack Houston's children's TV program.
Tips: "I screen 300 songs a month for 6 major publishing firms in the U.S. Please send your best songs and best quality demo. I cannot do anything with a poor demo."

THE LOWERY GROUP of Music Publishing Companies, 3051 Clairmont Rd. NE, Atlanta GA 30329. (404)325-0832. General Professional Manager: Cotton Carrier. Music publisher. ASCAP, BMI. Estab. 1952. Publishes 100 songs/year; publishes varying number of new songwriters/year. Works with composers and lyricists. Pays standard royalty.
Affiliate(s): Lowery Music Co., Inc. (BMI); Low-Sal, Inc. (BMI); Low-Twi, Inc. (BMI); Low-Ab Music (BMI); Low-Bam Music (BMI); Low-Ja Music (BMI); Low-Rico Music (BMI); Low-Thom Music (BMI); Eufaula Music (BMI); Steel City Music (BMI); Wonder Music (BMI); Eternal Gold Music (BMI); New Testament Music (BMI); Songs of Faith (BMI); Brother Bill's Music (ASCAP); Miss Delta Music (ASCAP); Terri Music (ASCAP); and Holy Ground Music (ASCAP).
How to Contact: Submit a demo tape by mail. Unsolicited submissions are OK. Prefers cassette with 3 songs and lyric sheet. Does not return unsolicited material. "No response unless we wish to publish the song."
Music: **Country, MOR** and **pop**; also **gospel**, **rock** and **comedy**. Published "Rock Bottom" (by Buddy Buie/J.R. Cobb), recorded by Wynonna Judd on Curb-MCA (country rock); "If Ten Percent's Good Enough For Jesus, It Oughta Be For Uncle Sam" (by Hal Coleman/Ken Gibbons/Roger Searcy), recorded by Ray Stevens on Curb Records (comedy); and "I Love the Nightlife" (by Alicia Bridges/ Susan Hutcheson), recorded by Scooter Lee on Southern Tracks Records (dance).

HAROLD LUICK & ASSOCIATES MUSIC PUBLISHER (BMI), P.O. Box B, Carlisle IA 50047. (515)989-3748. President: Harold L. Luick. Music publisher, record producer and music industry consultant. Publishes 25-30 songs/year; publishes 5-10 new songwriters/year. Pays standard royalty.
How to Contact: Write or call first about your interest. Prefers cassette with 3-5 songs and lyric sheet. SASE. Reports in 1 month.
Music: **Traditional country** and **hard core country**. Published "Mrs. Used To Be," written and recorded by Joe E. Harris, on River City Music Records (country); and "Ballad of Deadwood S.P.," written and recorded by Don Laughlin on Kajac Records (historical country).
Tips: "Ask yourself these questions: Does my song have simplicity of lyric and melody? Good flow and feeling? A strong story line? Natural dialogue? Hook chorus, lyric hooks, melody hooks? If it doesn't, then why should a publisher or A&R person take the time to listen to it? Most material that is sent to us is also sent simultaneously to several other publishers. If we are going to publish a song, the writer must assure us that the same music submission isn't floating around out there somewhere."

M & T WALDOCH PUBLISHING, INC. (BMI), 4803 S. 7th St., Milwaukee WI 53221. (414)482-2194. VP, Creative Management: Timothy J. Waldoch. Music publisher. Estab. 1990. Publishes 2-3 songs/ year; publishes 2-3 new songwriters/year. Works with composers and lyricists; teams collaborators. Pays standard royalty.
How to Contact: Submit demo tape by mail. Unsolicited submissions are OK. Prefers cassette with 3-6 songs and lyric sheet or lead sheet. "We prefer a studio produced demo tape." SASE. Reports in 2-3 months.
Music: Mostly **country/pop**, **rock** and **top 40 pop**; also **melodic metal**, **dance** and **R&B**. Published "It's Only Me" and "Let Peace Rule the World" (by Kenny LePrix), recorded by Brigade on SBD Records (rock).
Tips: "We want songs with strong melodies and well crafted lyrics. Read *The Craft of Lyric Writing* by Sheila Davis and other books on songwriting to help you develop your craft."

JIM McCOY MUSIC, Rt. 2, Box 114 H, Berkeley Springs WV 25411. Owners: Bertha and Jim McCoy. Music publisher, record company (Winchester Records) and record producer (Jim McCoy Productions). BMI. Estab. 1973. Publishes 20 songs/year; publishes 3-5 new songwriters/year. Pays standard royalty.
Affiliate(s): New Edition Music (BMI).
How to Contact: Write first and obtain permission to submit. Prefers cassette, 7½ or 15 ips reel-to-reel (or VHS or Beta videocassette) with 6 songs. SASE. Reports in 1 month.
Music: Mostly **country, country/rock** and **rock**; also **bluegrass** and **gospel**. Published "I'm Getting Nowhere," written and recorded by J.B. Miller on Hilton Records; "One More Time" (by S. Howard), recorded by Carl Howard and *Touching Your Heart*, written and recorded by Jim McCoy, both on Winchester Records.

*McGIBONY PUBLISHING, 203 Mission Rdg. Rd., Rossville GA 30741. (706)861-2186. Music Publisher: Richard McGibony. Music publisher, record company (R.R. & R. Music) and record producer.

Estab. 1986. Publishes 20 songs/year; publishes 10-15 new songwriters/year. Works with composers and/or lyricists; teams collaborators. Pays standard royalty.
Affiliate(s): Sounds of Aicram (BMI), R.D. Wheeler Publishing (BMI).
How to Contact: Write or call first and obtain permission to submit. Prefers cassette (or VHS videocassette if available) with 2 songs and lyric sheet. "Have a clear understandable tape with legible lyric sheets." SASE. Reports in 2 months.
Music: Mostly **country, gospel** and **R&B.** Published *Monteagle Mountain* (by R. McGibony), recorded by Johnny Cash on Polygram Records (country); *Shoe Lites* (by R. McGibony/J. Welz), recorded by Joey Welz on Caprice Records (country rock); and "Dark Desert Skies" (by Artur Corey/Alton Corey), recorded by Bill Scarbrough on Legend Records (country).

DANNY MACK MUSIC, 3484 Nicolette Dr., Crete IL 60417. (708)672-6457. General Manager: Daniel H. Mackiewicz. Music publisher and independent record producer. Estab. 1984. Publishes 1-8 songs/year. Pays standard royalty.
Affiliate(s): Syntony Publishing (BMI), Briar Hill Records (1992 Label of the Year Award, CMAA).
How to Contact: Submit demo tape by mail. Unsolicited submissions OK. Prefers cassette or phonorecords with no more than 4 songs and typed lyric sheets. SASE. Reports in 2-3 weeks.
Music: Mostly **country, gospel (southern/country)** and **polka.** Published "Jesus Is The Reason For the Season" (by M. Nevers/C. Elliott), recorded by Danny Mack (Christmas); "Beer In Heaven" written and recorded by Danny Mack (country novelty); and "Afterall," (by A. Scharinger), recorded by Danny Mack and Debbie Rodriguez (country), all on Briarhill Records.
Tips: "Send me your best, don't explain to me why you think your song is commercial. This business is speculation. Most of all, get to the point, be honest and send me songs not egos. I can tell which is which."

MACMAN MUSIC, INC. (ASCAP), 10 NW Sixth Ave., Portland OR 97209. (503)221-0288. Fax: (503)227-4418. Secretary: David Leiken. Music publisher and record producer. ASCAP, BMI. Estab. 1980. Publishes 8-10 songs/year; publishes 1-2 new songwriters/year. Works with composers and lyricists; teams collaborators. Pays "deal by deal."
Affiliate(s): Fresh Force Music, Inc.
How to Contact: Submit a demo tape by mail. Unsolicited submissions are OK. Prefers cassette with lyric sheet. Does not return unsolicited material. Reports "only if we are interested."
Music: Mostly **R&B, blues/rock** and **rock.** Published *If You Were Mine* (by Larry Bell), recorded by U-Krew on Enigma/Capitol Records (rap/funk); *Corbin's Place,* written and recorded by Dennis Springer on Nastymix Records, and *I Shouted Your Name* (by Marlon McClain), recorded by Curtis Salgardo on BFE/JRS Records.

*MAGIC MESSAGE MUSIC (ASCAP), P.O. Box 9117, Truckee CA 96162. (916)587-0111. Owner: Alan Redstone. Music publisher and record company (Sureshot Records). Estab. 1979. Publishes 6 songs/year; publishes 1 new songwriter/year. Pays standard royalty.
How to Contact: Submit demo tape by mail. Unsolicited submissions are OK.
Music: Mostly **country, ballads** and **rock.** Published "Emily," "Girls" and "For Yesterday," all written and recorded by Alan Redstone on Sureshot Records (country rock).

*MAGNUM MUSIC CORP. LTD., 8607 128th Ave., Edmonton, Alberta T5E 0G3 **Canada.** (403)476-8230. Fax: (403)472-2584. General Manager: Bill Maxim. Record company. Estab. 1982.
Affiliate(s): High River Music Publishing (ASCAP), Ramblin' Man Music Publishing (BMI).
How to Contact: Write or call first and obtain permission to submit. Prefers cassette (or VHS videocassette) with 3 songs and lyric sheet. Does not return material. Reports in 6 weeks.
Music: Mostly **country, gospel** and **contemporary;** also **pop, ballads** and **rock.** Published *Pray for the Family* and *Emotional Girl,* both written and recorded by C. Greenly (country); and *Don't Worry 'Bout It,* written and recorded by T. Anderson (country), all on Magnum Records.

MAKERS MARK GOLD (ASCAP), 3033 W. Redner St., Philadelphia PA 19121. (215)236-4817. Record Producer: Paul Hopkins. Music publisher and record producer. Estab. 1991. Pays standard royalty.
How to Contact: Submit demo tape by mail. Unsolicited submissions are OK. Prefers cassette with 2-4 songs. Does not return material. Reports in 4-6 weeks if interested.
Music: Mostly **R&B, country, hip hop** and **rap;** also **pop.** Published "Busted," "Why You Want My Love" and "Something for Nothing" (by E. Monk/P. Hopkins/G. Reed), all recorded by Elaine Monk on Black Sands Records.
Tips: "Be very persistent in submitting your material, because you never know what song in the right hands can do. It only takes one song to make you a megastar. You could be next!"

*MAKIN TRACKS MUSIC, 18 Hassel Brook Rd., Nashua NH 03060-4307. Music publisher and record producer (Hank Rowe). ASCAP. Estab. 1986. Publishes 4 songs/year; publishes 2 new songwriters/

year. Works with composers and lyricists; teams collaborators. Pays standard royalty.
How to Contact: Submit a demo tape by mail. Unsolicited submissions are OK. Prefers cassette with 4-6 songs and bio. SASE. Reports in 4-6 weeks.
Music: Metal, rock, pop, fusion, jazz and **New Age.** Published "Half Life" and "Danger Zone," by Hazardous Waste (metal); and "Candle to the Magic," by Johann Smith (rock), all recorded by Makin Tracks on Hazardous Records.
Tips: "Have a solid sound and good production."

*MAMA LINDA, 93 A. Dansaert, Brussels 1000 **Belgium.** (32)2-5132772. Fax:(32)2-5113338. Owner: Linda Van Waesberge. Music publisher and management company. Estab. 1993. Publishes 10 new songwriters/year. Works with composers and lyricists. Pays standard royalty.
How to Contact: Submit demo tape by mail. Unsolicited submissions are OK. Prefers cassette with lyric sheet. SAE and IRC. Reports in 1 month.
Music: Mostly **ambient, film** and **rock.**

MANAPRO (MANAGEMENT ARTIST PRODUCTIONS), 82 Sherman St., Passaic NJ 07055. (201)777-6109. Executive Producer: Tomasito Bobadilla. Music publisher and production company. ASCAP, BMI. Estab. 1987. Publishes 2 songs/year; publishes 3-4 songwriters/year. Hires staff songwriters. Works with lyricists; teams collaborators. Pays standard royalty.
Affiliate(s): No Mas (BMI), In Che (ASCAP).
How to Contact: Submit a demo tape by mail. Unsolicited submissions are OK. Prefers cassette with 2 songs and lyric sheet. SASE. Reports in 3 months.
Music: Mostly **pop, dance** and **rock;** also **R&B** and **New Age.** Published "One Way" (by Chene Garcia), recorded by Mellow Dee on Halogram (hip house); *Lagrima* (by Opti Gomez), recorded by Munchy on Globo Records (pop); and "2 Hearts" (by Pacheso), recorded by Time Chambers on Requeslime Records (dance/pop).
Tips: "Songs should have very catchy hooks."

MANBEN MUSIC (ASCAP), 3117 SW 17 St., Miami FL 33145. (305)443-5674. President: Manny Benito. Music publisher. Estab. 1988. Publishes 20 songs/year; publishes 1-2 new songwriters/year. Teams collaborators (very seldom). Pays standard royalty.
How to Contact: Submit a demo tape by mail. Unsolicited submissions are OK. Prefers cassette with lyric sheet. Does not return unsolicited material. Reports in 4-6 weeks.
Music: Mostly **rap, country** and **pop;** also **Latin music.** Published *Quien lo Diria* (by Manny Benito), recorded by Rey Ruiz on Sonny Records (tropical); *Donde Iras,* written and recorded by Manny Benito on Biscayne Europa Records (ballad); and "Despacio" (by Manny Benito), recorded by Sophy on Sonny Records (ballad)
Tips: "Send songs with a very strong and catchy chorus."

*MANNY MUSIC, INC. (BMI), 2035 Pleasanton Rd., San Antonio TX 78221-1306. (210)924-2224. Fax: (210)924-3338. Publishing Dept.: Pete Rodriguez. Music publisher, record company (Manny Records, AMS Records). Estab. 1963. Publishes 2-3 new songwriters/year. Works with composers and lyricists. Pays standard royalty.
Affiliate(s): Rosman Music (ASCAP), Texas Latino (SESAC).
How to Contact: Submit demo tape by mail. Unsolicited submissions are OK. Prefers cassette and lyric sheet. "Allow three to four weeks before calling to inquire about prior submission." SASE. Reports in 3 weeks.
Music: Mostly **Spanish, Tejano or Tex-Mex** and **C&W;** also **Spanish gospel, ballads** and **tropical/ Caribbean/South American rhythms.** Published "No Soporto Mas" (by Graciela Goede), recorded by Mazz on Capitol-EMI Records (Tex-Mex); "Heart Over Matter" (by Harrell Moore), recorded by Shelly Lares on Sony Records (C&W); and "Adios" (by Elio Quintanilla), recorded by Ram Herrera on Sony Records (ballad).
Tips: "Songs should have a good storyline; good punchline; the melody must have a quality that can be expressed in different rhythms and still sound 'original'."

THE MARCO MUSIC GROUP INC., P.O. Box 24454, Nashville TN 37202. (615)269-7074. Director of Publishing: Jeff Hollandsworth. Music publisher. Estab. 1988. Publishes 100 songs/year; 5-10 new songwriters/year. Pays standard royalty.
Affiliate(s): Goodland Publishing Company (ASCAP), Marc Isle Music (BMI) and Gulf Bay Publishing (SESAC).
How to Contact: Submit demo tape by mail. Unsolicited submissions OK. Prefers cassette with 2 songs maximum and lyric sheet. Does not return material. Reports in 3 weeks.
Music: Country. Published "My Way Or The Highway" (by Reynolds/Fritz); "Mama's Rocking Chair" (by S. Clark); and "I'm Runnin' Out of Memories" (by F. Powers), all recorded by Debra Dudley on Concorde Records.

Tips: "Prefer songs with top-40 potential."

ROD MARTIN'S MUSIC PUBLISHING (BMI), 3585 Pinao St., Honolulu HI 96822. (808)988-4859. Owner: Rod Martin. Music publisher. Estab. 1992. Publishes 6-12 songs/year. "Payment negotiable." **How to Contact:** Submit demo tape by mail. Unsolicited submissions are OK. Prefers cassette with lyric sheet. SASE. Reports in 7 weeks. **Music:** Mostly **folk, pop, comedy, rock, blues, instrumentals**. **Tips:** "Play your songs for a group of people and ask them to suggest which are the best. We are willing to collaborate with beginning songwriters to improve any song that shows potential."

THE MATHES COMPANY, P.O. Box 22653, Nashville TN 37202. (615)252-6912. Owner: David W. Mathes. Music publisher, record company (Star Image, Heirborn, Kingdom), record producer (The Mathes Company) and music industry consultant. BMI, ASCAP, SESAC. Estab. 1962. Records 30-50 sessions/year; publishes 10-30 new songwriters/year. Pays standard royalty. Also offers home study course: "The Business Side of the Music Business" through Institute of Recording Arts & Sciences. **Affiliate(s):** Sweet Singer Music (BMI), Sing Sweeter Music (ASCAP) and Star of David (SESAC). **How to Contact:** Submit a demo tape by mail. Unsolicited submissions are OK. "Registered or certified mail refused." Prefers cassette with maximum of 3 songs and lyric sheet. "Only positive country songs (not controversial, political, demeaning or sex oriented). Only gospel songs that are not rock contemporary, and no new age music." SASE. Reports in 1 month. **Music:** Mostly **gospel (country)**, **country** and **instrumental**; also **jingle ideas**. Published "Limousine Lovers" (by Dorothy Hampton and Larry Pearre), recorded by Jeannie C. Riley on Sapphire Records (country); and *I Can't Wait To Get To Heaven* (by Cherie Mullins), recorded by The Mullins on Canaan Records (gospel). **Tips:** "Submit only your best songs and follow submission requirements."

*MCA MUSIC PUBLISHING (ASCAP), 1755 Broadway, New York NY 10019. (212)841-8000. Fax: (212)582-7340. Music publisher. Estab. 1964. "The MCA catalog contains over 100,000 copyrights." Hires staff songwriters. Works with composers and lyricists; teams collaborators. **Affiliate(s):** Music Corporation of America (BMI) and Musicor (SESAC). **How to Contact:** Write first and obtain permission to submit. Prefers cassette. SASE. **Music:** Mostly **popular**. Published "Livin On The Edge" (by Mark Hudson) and "Cryin" (by Taylor Rhodes), both recorded by Aerosmith on Geffen Records (rock); "Run To You" (by Allan Rich), recorded by Whitney Houston on Arista Records (pop); and "Insane In The Brain" (by D.J. Muggs), recorded by Cypress Hill on Columbia (rap).

MEDIA PRODUCTIONS/RESISTOR MUSIC (ASCAP), 1001½ Elizabeth St., Oak Hill WV 25901. (304)465-1298. Producer: Doug Gent. Music publisher, record company (Resistor Records) and record producer (Media Productions). Estab. 1985. Publishes 20 songs/year; publishes 3 new songwriters/year. Works with composers and lyricists; teams collaborators. Pays standard royalty. **Affiliate(s):** Capacitor Music (BMI). **How to Contact:** Submit a demo tape by mail. Unsolicited submissions are OK. Prefers cassette with 3 songs and lyric sheet. Does not return unsolicited material. Reports in 1 month. **Music:** Mostly **country, gospel** and **R&B**; also **top 40** and **rock**. Published *Love On The Line* (by Dan Bailey), recorded by Marty Dawn; *"Promises,"* written and recorded by Jeanie Woods; and *Baby I'll Try* (by Reed/Godsey), recorded by Delnora Reed, all on Resistor Records. **Tips:** "Know your craft and learn the business—be professional."

*MENACE MUSIC GROUP, 2 Park Rd., Radlett, Herts WD7 8EQ **England**. (44)+923853789. Fax:(44)+923853318. MD: Dennis Collopy. Music publisher and management company. Estab. 1992. Publishes 250-300 songs/year; publishes 3-4 new songwriters/year. Works with composers and lyricists; teams collaborators. Pays "administration deals 85/15, exclusive writer contracts 75/25." **Affiliate(s):** Menace Tunes (ASCAP), Menace Songs USA (BMI). **How to Contact:** Call first and obtain permission to submit. Prefers cassette with 3 songs and lyric sheet. "Put name and telephone number on cassette and on box." SAE and IRC. Reports in 1 month. **Music:** Mostly **soul, house** and **alternative**; also **country, blues** and **rock**. Published "Don't Lie" (by Al McKay), recorded by Sinclair on Dome/EMI Records (soul); "Sweetest Child" (by Maria McKee/Bruce Brody/Martin Glover), recorded by Maria McKee on Geffen Records (rock/dance); and "I've Got News for You," written and recorded by Feargal Sharkey on Virgin Records (rock). **Tips:** "Produce good quality demos with professional vocals. Think about contemporary production values."

*MENTO MUSIC GROUP, Box 20 33 12, Hamburg D-20223 **Germany**. General Manager: Arno H. Van Vught. Music publisher and record company. Pays standard royalty.

Affiliate(s): Auteursunie, Edition Studio CAP Music, Edition Lamplight, Edition Melodisc, Massimo Jauch Music Productions, Marathon Music.
How to Contact: Submit demo tape by mail. Unsolicited submissions are OK. Prefers cassette. SAE and IRC. Reports in 2 weeks.
Music: Mostly **instrumental, pop, MOR, country, background music** and **film music.** Published *Anytime and Anywhere* (by Massimo-Jauch/Raschner) and *Rodeo 93* (by Massimo-Jauch), both recorded by Stephan Massimo on EMI Records (pop); and *Fusión*, written and recorded by Jan Hengmith on Acoustic Music (flamenco).

MERRY MARILYN MUSIC PUBLISHING (BMI), 33717 View Crest Dr., Lake Elsinore CA 92532. (909)245-2763. Owner: Marilyn Hendricks. Music publisher. Estab. 1980. Publishes 10-15 songs/year; publishes 3-4 new songwriters/year. Pays standard royalty.
How to Contact: Submit a demo tape by mail. Unsolicited submissions are OK. No more than 2 songs per submission. "Submit complete songs only. No lyrics without music." SASE. Reports in 1-3 months (depending on volume of submissions).
Music: Mostly **country** and **MOR.** Published "God Knows" and "This Man" (by J. Hendricks); and "What Do I Drink About That" (by R. Whitaker).
Tips: "Write a *great* song! Something fresh and new!"

*MIA MIND MUSIC (ASCAP), #4B, 500½ East 84th St., New York NY 10028. (212)861-8745. Professional Manager: Ashley Wilkes. Music publisher, record company (Mindfield Records) and record producer (I.Y.F. Productions). Estab. 1986. Publishes 100 songs/year; publishes 3-4 new songwriters/year. Works with composers and lyricists; teams collaborators. Pays standard royalty.
How to Contact: Call for submission requirements. Prefers cassette or DAT with 3 songs. SASE. Reports in 6 weeks.
Music: Mostly **top 40, alternative** and **dance.** Published "Time and Time Again" (by S. Bentzel), recorded by Madonna on Merlin Records (dance); and "Cyberpunk," written and recorded by Ashley Wilkes on MMM Records (alternative rock).
Tips: "Seek out and hire professional assistance from the beginning of the recording process through the marketing process. Quality will cost, but it pays in the long run."

*MIGHTY TWINNS MUSIC (BMI), 9134 S. Indiana Ave., Chicago IL 60619. (312)737-4348. General Manager: Ron Scott. Music publisher and record producer. Member NMPA, Midwest Inspirational Writers Association. Estab. 1977. Publishes 4-10 songs/year; publishes 5 new songwriters/year. Works with composers and lyricists; teams collaborators. Pays standard royalty.
How to Contact: Submit a demo tape by mail. Unsolicited submissions are OK. Prefers cassette with 2-4 songs and lyric sheet. SASE "only if you want material returned." Reports in 1 month.
Music: Mostly **top 40, R&B, "hot" inspirational** and **gospel;** also **children's.** Published "Steady" and "Reality" (by Chuck Chu), recorded by MTM (reggae).
Tips: Looking for "good hot songs with hot hooks. Please have tapes cued up. *Do not write for permission!* Submit a cued up cassette and wait for our response. No materials returned without proper postage. Take the time to write and re-write to get the song in its best form; then make a good clear/audible demo."

MIRACLE MILE MUSIC/BLACK SATIN (BMI), P.O. Box 35449, Los Angeles CA 90035. (310)281-8599. A&R: Robert Riley. Music publisher, record company (Miles Ahead) and record producer. Estab. 1968. Publishes 75 songs/year. Hires staff writers. Works with composers and lyricists; teams collaborators. Pays standard royalty.
Affiliate(s): Family Affair (ASCAP) and Respect Music (BMI).
How to Contact: Submit demo tape by mail. Unsolicited submissions are OK. Prefers cassette with 4 songs and lyric sheet. SASE. Reports in 2 weeks, "sometimes minutes."
Music: Mostly **R&B, dance** and **pop.** Published "I'm The One" (by Keith Cobbin), recorded by Jefferson Starship on RCA Records (pop); "I Can Dream" (by Lermon Horton), recorded by The Whispers on Capitol Records (R&B); and "All My Love" (by Duane Roberts), recorded by Anita Baker on Elektra Records (R&B).

*MOMENTUM MUSIC INC., #302, 1201 Larrabee St., Los Angeles CA 90069-2033. (310)652-9142. Fax: (310)652-2729. President: Charly Prevost. Music publisher. Estab. 1976. Publishes 400 songs/year; publishes 15 new songwriters/year. Teams collaborators. Pays standard royalty.

Listings of companies in countries other than the U.S. have the name of the country in boldface type.

Affiliate(s): "Momentum Music is UK-based and is sub-published by Warner Chappell."
How to Contact: Call first and obtain permission to submit. Prefers cassette. "Keep it brief and send your best songs. Do not worry about recording quality." Does not return material.
Music: Mostly **alternative, dance** and **world music**; also **pop**. Published "Ubiquitous Mr. Lovegrove," written and recorded by Dead Can Dance on 4AD Records (alternative); "Evangeline," written and recorded by Cocteau Twins on EMI Records (alternative); and "Day You Went Away" (by Male/Batson), recorded by Wendy Matthews on Atlantic Records (pop).
Tips: "Please do not send anything that sounds like anyone you have heard on the radio."

MONTINA MUSIC (SOCAN), Box 702, Snowdon Station, Montreal, Quebec H3X 3X8 **Canada**. Professional Manager: David P. Leonard. Music publisher. Estab. 1963. Works with composers, lyricists; teams collaborators. Pays standard royalty.
Affiliate(s): Sabre Music (SOCAN).
How to Contact: Submit a demo tape by mail. Unsolicited submissions are OK. Prefers cassette, phonograph record (or VHS videocassette) and lyric sheet. Does not return unsolicited material.
Music: Mostly **top 40**; also **bluegrass, blues, country, dance-oriented, easy listening, folk, gospel, jazz, MOR, progressive, R&B, rock** and **soul**.
Tips: "Maintain awareness of styles and trends of your peers who have succeeded professionally. Understand the markets to which you are pitching your material. Persevere at marketing your talents. Develop a network of industry contacts, first locally, then regionally and nationally."

*DOUG MOODY MUSIC (BMI), Box 1596, San Marcos CA 92069. (619)945-2412. Fax: (619)630-1066. Professional Manager: Eva Watts. Music publisher, record company (Mystic Records, Clock Records), record and video producer. Publishes over 100 songs/year; publishes 100 new songwriter-artists/year. Pays standard royalty.
Affiliate(s): DM Music (BMI), Emit Music, Clock Music, Accumulated Copyrights (BMI), VIM Music Corp., and Variety In Music/New York.
How to Contact: Write first and obtain permission to submit. "Only new songs performed by new groups or local performing groups." Does not return unsolicited material.
Music: "All kinds of rock: hardcore, teen, 'thrash' and skateboard rock." Published *No FX*, recorded by The Original on Mystic Records.
Tips: "We specialize in teen-age entertainment: records, radio shows, videos. We target the 11-year-old to 27-year-old skateboard market."

MOON JUNE MUSIC (BMI), 4233 SW Marigold, Portland OR 97219. President: Bob Stoutenburg. Music publisher. Estab. 1971. Pays standard royalty.
How to Contact: Submit demo tape by mail. Unsolicited submissions OK. Prefers cassette (or VHS videocassette) with 2-10 songs. "Unable to return material due to volume of tapes received."
Music: Country.

*BRYAN MORRISON MUSIC, 1 Star St., London **England**. 071 706 7304. A&R: Karl Adams. Music publisher. Estab. 1964. Publishes 100-200 songs/year; publishes 5-10 new songwriters/year.
How to Contact: Submit demo tape by mail. Unsolicited submissions are OK. Prefers cassette. Does not return material. Reports in 1 month.
Music: "All good music."

*MOTEX MUSIC, Rt. 1, Box 70G, Dale TX 78616. (512)398-7519. Owner: Sandra Jones. Music publisher. Estab. 1980. Publishes 50 songs/year. Works with composers and lyricists; teams collaborators. Pays standard royalty.
Affiliate(s): Misty Haze Music, Clock Publishing (BMI).
How to Contact: Submit demo tape by mail. Unsolicited submissions are OK. Prefers cassette and lyric sheet. SASE. Reports in 1 month.
Music: Mostly **country, gospel** and **blues**; also **rock, folk** and **Tex-Mex**. Published "Can't Find a Way to Say Goodbye" (by Billy Jo Kirk), recorded by Stoney Edward (country); "Fall of Year" (by Billy Shafer), recorded by Winston Kirk (country); and *Hotter Than the Flame* (by Winston James), recorded by Drug Store Cowboys (country), all on MCR Records.

*MURDOCK'S MUSIC COMPANY (BMI), Suite 1, 1315 N. Sunrise, Bowling Green KY 42101. Producers: Dave Harris and John Pigg. Music Director: Rick Faulkner. Music publisher, record company and record producer. Estab. 1994. Publishes 30 songs/year; publishes 10 new songwriters/year. Works with composers and lyricists; teams collaborators. Pays standard royalty.
How to Contact: Submit demo tape by mail. Unsolicited submissions are OK. Prefers cassette with 3-4 songs and lyric sheet. "Send a clean sounding demo (good quality)." Does not return material. Reports in 1 month.

Music: Mostly **pop/rock, alternative** and **country**; also **R&B, A/C** and **heavy metal**. Published "In The Blink of An Eye" (by Mark Lennon, Bill Sacrey, Dave Harris, Steve Wood) and "Friend Are You There" (by Mark Lennon, Chad Shireman, Dave Harris, Bob Baldwin), both recorded by Mark Lennon (AC/country); and "Losing You (Life Goes On)" (by Dave Harris, Bill Sacrey, Chris Gooden), recorded by Bill Sacrey (alternative), all on Murdock Records.
Tips: "Write from the heart. Write what you know about. Don't let today's music scene stifle your creativity. Be free. Write what you feel."

MUSIC FACTORY ENTERPRISES, INC., Suite 300, Ford & Washington, Norristown PA 19401. (610)277-9550. President: Jeffrey Calhoon. Music publisher, record company (MFE Records). BMI. Estab. 1984. Publishes 8 songs/year. Works with composers and lyricists; teams collaborators. Pays standard royalty.
Affiliate(s): Robin Nicole Music (BMI).
How to Contact: Write or call first and obtain permission to submit a tape. Prefers cassette with 3-4 songs, lyric sheet and lead sheet. "Make sure notations are clear and legible." SASE. Reports in 3 weeks.
Music: Mostly **20th Century Minimalism, world beat, alternative rock/pop** and **New Age**. Published "Crazy Times" (by John Fritz); "Stillwater," and "Shamont," written and recorded by Gregory Darvis on MFE Records (New Age).
Tips: "Develop every song fully, be different, submit best quality product you can."

*MUSIC HOUSE INTERNATIONAL LIMITED, 5 Newburgh St., London WIV 1LH **England**. (071)434 9678. Fax: (071)434 1470. Creative Director: Aaron Harry. Music publisher and production music library. Estab. 1986. Hires staff writers. Works with composers and lyricists; teams collaborators. Pays standard royalty.
How to Contact: Submit demo tape by mail. Unsolicited submissions are OK. Prefers cassette with 3 songs. SAE and IRC. Reports in 3 months.
Music: Mostly **contemporary**.

MUSIC IN THE RIGHT KEYS PUBLISHING COMPANY (BMI), 3716 West 87th St., Chicago IL 60652. (312)735-3297. President: Bert Swanson. Music publisher. Estab. 1985. Member CMA. "A noted publisher." Publishes 200-500 songs/year; publishes 50-100 new songwriters/year. Works with composers. Pays standard royalty.
Affiliate(s): High 'n Low Notes (ASCAP).
How to Contact: Submit a demo tape (professionally made) by mail—unsolicited submissions are OK. Prefers cassette with 3-8 songs and lyric and lead sheets. SASE. Reports in 10 weeks.
Music: Mostly **country, gospel** and **pop**; also **R&B, blues** and **MOR**. Published "The Drinking Got A Little Out of Hand," (by B. Swanson), recorded by C. Fisher on Write Way Records; *Hometown Detour* (by O. Laufenberg); and "As Far As Love's Concerned" (by B. Swanson/C. Fisher), recorded by Robert Beckom on Sabre Records.
Tips: "Always submit a good demo for presentation. The better the demo, the better your chances for placement. Remember, Music In The Right Keys will listen to your melodies; all that I ask of you is to send me good demos please."

THE MUSIC ROOM PUBLISHING GROUP, P.O. Box 219, Redondo Beach CA 90277. (310)316-4551. President/Owner: John Reed. Music publisher and record producer. Estab. 1982. Works with composers. Pays standard royalty.
Affiliate(s): Black House Music (BMI), Music Room Productions.
How to Contact: Submit demo tape by mail. Unsolicited submissions are OK. Prefers cassette with 3 songs and lyric sheet. SASE. Reports in 2-3 weeks.
Music: Mostly **pop/rock/R&B** and **crossover**. Published "The Best," written and recorded by J. Reed/ B. Walker on Nomo Records (pop); "Snap, Crackle, Crunch" (by B. Walker), recorded by Tea Party; and "Use It" (by K. Kristen), recorded by Power 2000 on Learntech Records.

MUSIC SALES CORPORATION (ASCAP), 257 Park Ave. S., New York NY 10010. (212)254-2100. Fax: (212)254-2013. Professional/Creative Manager: Philip "Flip" Black. Music publisher. Estab. 1935. Publishes 100 songs/year; publishes 5 new songwriters/year. Works with composers and lyricists; teams collaborators. Pays standard royalty.
Affiliate(s): Embassy Music Corporation (BMI).
How to Contact: Write first and obtain permission to submit. Prefers cassette with lyric sheet. Does not return unsolicited material. Reports in 2 months.
Music: Mostly **rock, easy listening** and **country**; also **R&B**. Published "Down on the Farm" (by Harper Gibbs), recorded by Guns N' Roses on Geffen Records (rock); "Like Someone in Love" (by Burke/ VanHeusen), recorded by Björk on Elektra Records (standard); and "Come Sunday" (by Ellington), recorded by Johnny Mathis on Columbia Records (standard).

*MUSIKVERLAG K. URBANEK, Hadikg 17819, A-1440 Wien **Austria**. (+43)11894-8398. Contact: Mr. K. Urbanek. Music publisher. Estab. 1988. Works with composers and lyricists.
How to Contact: Write or call first and obtain permission to submit. Prefers cassette with lead sheet. SAE and IRC. Reports in 2 months.
Music: Mostly **instrumental choir music in middle grade difficulties.**

*MUSIKVERLAG ROSSORI, Hietzinger Hptstr 94, Vienna A-1130 **Austria**. (01)8762400. Fax: (01)876240090. Manager: Mario Rossori. Music publisher and management agency. Estab. 1990. Publishes 100 songs/year; publishes 10 new songwriters/year. Works with composers and lyricists; teams collaborators. Pays standard royalty.
How to Contact: Submit demo tape by mail. Unsolicited submissions are OK. Prefers cassette with 5 songs and lyric and lead sheets. SAE and IRC. Reports in 2 months.
Music: Mostly **pop, dance** and **rock.** Published "Loveline" (by Geppner/Freistetter/Okon), recorded by Uniquez on Sony (dance); and "Hidden in the Rain" (by Fendrich/Gabler/Madden), recorded by Joni Madden on Spray Records (pop).

MYKO MUSIC (BMI), #D203, 1324 S. Avenida, Tucson AZ 85710. (602)885-5931. President: James M. Gasper. Music publisher, record company (Ariana Records) and record producer (Future 1 Productions). BMI. Estab. 1980. Publishes 4 songs/year; 2 new songwriters/year. Works with composers. Pays standard royalty.
How to Contact: Submit a demo tape by mail. Unsolicited submissions are OK. Prefers cassette (or ½″ VHS videocassette) with 3 songs and lyric sheet. SASE. Reports in 4-6 weeks.
Music: Top 40, **dance rock,** AOR, **R&B, country rock** or **Tex-Mex.** Published "House of Gloom" (by J. Gasper/T. Privett), recorded by Love Kills for Myko Music; *Point Me To The Door* (by J. Gasper/ T. Privett), recorded by The Rakeheads; and *Better Days* (by T. Privett), recorded by Buddy System, both on Ariana Records.

CHUCK MYMIT MUSIC PRODUCTIONS (BMI), 9840 64th Ave., Flushing NY 11374. A&R: Chuck Mymit. Music publisher and record producer (Chuck Mymit Music Productions). Estab. 1978. Publishes 3-5 songs/year; publishes 2-4 new songwriters/year. Works with composers and lyricists; teams collaborators. Pays standard royalty.
Affiliate(s): Viz Music (BMI) and Tore Music (BMI).
How to Contact: Submit a demo tape by mail. Unsolicited submissions are OK. Prefers cassette or VHS videocassette with 3-5 songs and lyric and lead sheets. "Bio and picture would be helpful." SASE. Reports in 3-6 weeks.
Music: Mostly **pop, rock** and **R&B.** Published "To Love You Again" and "One Night of Love" (C. Mymit), recorded by Kim LePork on JR Records (MOR); and "Baby Me" (by M. Mymit), recorded by Diana M. on Kismet Records (rock).
Tips: "Have strong confidence in your work. Don't be afraid to write complex things."

NAMAX MUSIC PUBLISHING, P.O. Box 24162, Richmond VA 23224. President: Nanette Brown. Music publisher. BMI. Estab. 1989. Publishes 2-4 songs/year; publishes 2 new songwriters/year. Works with composers; teams collaborators. Pays standard royalty.
How to Contact: Submit demo tape by mail. Unsolicited submissions OK. Prefers cassette with 2 songs and lyric sheet. "No phone calls please." SASE. Reports in 4-6 weeks.
Music: Mostly **R&B** and **pop/top 40;** also **contemporary gospel.** Published "Love Affair" (by D. Trebor/ B. Tenan), recorded by Destiny on Xaman Records (R&B).
Tips: "Namax is looking for great songs with a strong hook. Our background is R&B music—do not send us country."

NASHVILLE MUSIC GROUP (SOCAN), P.O. Box 111416, Nashville TN 37211-1416. (615)834-4124. Manager: Cindy Brooks. Music publisher and production company. Estab. 1993. Publishes 12 songs/ year; publishes 1-2 new songwriters/year. Works with composers and lyricists; teams collaborators. Pays standard royalty.
Affiliate(s): Four Flags Music (ASCAP), Brooks Bros. Publishers (BMI), Enchantment Music (BMI).
How to Contact: Submit demo tape by mail. Unsolicited submissions are OK. Prefers cassette with 3 songs and lyric sheet. SASE. Reports in 2 weeks.
Music: Mostly **country, rock** and **gospel;** also **alternative** and **blues.** Published *100 Years Too Late,* written and recorded by Ted Scanlon on Goldust Records; *Cowboy Icon* (by E. Johnson) and "This Cowboy's Hat" (by Jake Brooks), recorded by Chris Le Doux on Liberty Records.

NASHVILLE SOUND MUSIC PUBLISHING CO. (SOCAN), P.O. Box 728, Peterborough, Ontario K9J 6Z8 **Canada**. (705)742-2381. President: Andrew Wilson Jr. Music publisher. Estab. 1985. Publishes 10 songs/year; publishes 5 new songwriters/year. Pays standard royalty.

Affiliate(s): Northern Sound Music Publishing Co. (SOCAN).
How to Contact: Submit demo tape by mail. Unsolicited submissions are OK. Prefers cassette or 7½ ips reel-to-reel with 2-4 songs and lyric sheet. "Please send only material you do not want returned. We have an open door policy." Reports in 2 weeks.
Music: Mostly **country, country/pop** and **crossover country**. Published "Just Beyond the Pain" (by Ron Simons), recorded by Charlie Louvin and Crystal Gayle; "Let An Old Race Horse Run" (by Ron Simons), recorded by Tommy Cash; and "Fallin' Out of Love Can Break Your Heart" (by Andrew Wilson, Jr/Joseph Pickering, Jr.), recorded by Mark Poncy, all on Playback Records.
Tips: "Send me a well crafted song, both lyrically and musically! You need great hooks!"

NATIONAL TALENT (BMI), P.O. Box 14, Whitehall MI 49461. (616)894-9208. 1-800-530-9255. President: Sharon Leigh. Vice President: Jay Ronn. Music publisher and record company (United Country). Estab. 1985. Publishes 7-8 songs/year. Teams collaborators. Pays standard royalty.
Affiliate(s): House of Shar (BMI).
How to Contact: Submit a demo tape by mail. Unsolicited submissions are OK. Prefers cassette with 1-10 songs and lyric sheet. SASE. Reports in 1 month.
Music: **Country** and **gospel**. Published "Mistletoe" (by Prohaska), recorded by Jay Ronn; "Blue Days" (by Duncan), recorded by Lexi Hamilton; and "I Believe in Country" (by Koone), recorded by Bobbie G. Rice, all on United Records.

NAUTICAL MUSIC CO. (BMI), Box 120675, Nashville TN 37212. (615)255-1068. Owner: Ray McGinnis. Music publisher and record company (Orbit Records). Estab. 1965. Publishes 25 songs/year; 10 new songwriters/year. Works with composers. Pays standard royalty.
How to Contact: Submit demo tape by mail. Unsolicited submissions are OK. Prefers cassette with 4 songs and lyric sheets. SASE. Reports in 6-8 weeks.
Music: Mostly **country ballads** and **country rock**. Published "I Never Stopped Loving You" and "Hometown Rodeo" (by M. Deryer), recorded by Debra Lee; and *Southern Living* (by S. McGregory), recorded by Sonny Martin, all on Orbit Records.
Tips: "The trend is back to traditional country music with songs that tell a story."

NERVOUS PUBLISHING, 4/36 Dabbs Hill Lane, Northolt, Middlesex, London, **England**. Phone: (4481)963-0352. Managing Director: Roy Williams. Music publisher, record company and record producer. MCPS, PRS and Phonographic Performance Ltd. Estab. 1979. Publishes 100 songs/year; publishes 25 new songwriters/year. Works with composers and lyricists. Pays standard royalty; royalties paid directly to US songwriters.
How to Contact: Submit a demo tape. Unsolicited submissions are OK. Prefers cassette with 3-10 songs and lyric sheet. "Include letter giving your age and mentioning any previously published material." SAE and IRC. Reports in 3 weeks.
Music: Mostly **psychobilly, rockabilly** and **rock** (impossibly fast music—ex.: Stray Cats but twice as fast); also **blues, country, R&B** and **rock** (50s style). Published *New Generation* (by Roman), recorded by The Quakes on Nervous Records; *I Sold My Soul* (by Owen), recorded by Rough Diamonds on Fury Records; and *Eastern Sun* (by Whitehouse), recorded by Frenzy on Rage Records.
Tips: "Submit *no* rap, soul, funk—we want *rockabilly*."

A NEW RAP JAM PUBLISHING, P.O. Box 683, Lima OH 45802. (419)228-0691. President: James Milligan. Music publisher, record company. Estab. 1989. Publishes 30 songs/year; publishes 2-3 new songwriters/year. Hires staff songwriters. Works with composers and lyricists; teams collaborators. Pays standard royalty.
Affiliate(s): New Experience Records/Party House Publishing (BMI), Creative Star Management, Grand Slam Records/A New Rap Jam Publishing (ASCAP).
How to Contact: Submit demo tape by mail. Unsolicited submissions are OK. Prefers cassette with 3-5 songs and lyric sheet or lead sheet. SASE. Reports in 1 month.
Music: Mostly **R&B, pop** and **rock/rap**; also **contemporary, gospel, country** and **soul**. Published "Thinking About You" (by James Milligan), recorded by James Junior (R&B); "Together Forever," written and recorded by Carl Whitner (R&B); and "Denied" (by Richard Bamberger), recorded by Rich B. (pop), all on New Experience Records.
Tips: "Establish music industry contacts, write and keep writing and most of all believe in yourself. Use a good recording studio but be very professional. And if there is interest we will contact you."

NEWCREATURE MUSIC (BMI), P.O. Box 1444, Hendersonville TN 37077-1444. President: Bill Anderson, Jr. Professional Manager: G.L. Score. Music publisher, record company, record producer and radio and TV syndicator. Publishes 25 songs/year; publishes 2 new songwriters/year. Pays standard royalty.

Affiliate(s): Mary Megan Music (ASCAP).
How to Contact: Submit demo tape by mail. Unsolicited submissions are OK. Prefers 7½ ips reel-to-reel or cassette (or videocassette) with 4-10 songs and lyric sheet. SASE. Reports in 1 month.
Music: **Country, gospel, jazz, R&B, rock** and **top 40/pop**. Published *When A Good Love Comes Along*, *The Storm Is Gone* and *I've Come Home to You*, all written and recorded by Gail Score on Landmark Records.

THE JOSEPH NICOLETTI MUSIC CO. (ASCAP), P.O. Box 2818, Newport Beach CA 92659. (714)494-0181. President A&R: Joseph Nicoletti. Music publisher. Estab. 1976. Publishes 30-60 songs/year; publishes 40 songwriters/year. Works with composers and lyricists; teams collaborators. Pays standard royalty.
Affiliate(s): Global Village Music Co. (ASCAP), Creative Network (ASCAP).
How to Contact: Submit demo tape by mail. Unsolicited submissions are OK. Prefers cassette with up to 5 songs and lyric sheet. "You may want to type a cover letter about yourself." SASE. Reports in 2-3 weeks.
Music: Mostly **country, pop** and **rock**; also **R&B, gospel** and **adult contemporary**. Published "Let's Put the Fun Back In Rock 'n Roll" (by B. Feldman/J. Nicoletti), recorded by Fabian, Frankie Avalon and Bobby Rydell on A&M Records (pop); "Step Into The Light" and "Soldiers Eyes," written and recorded by J. Nicoletti, on California Int. Records.
Tips: "Send only what you think is your best material!"

*NISE PRODUCTIONS INC. (BMI), 413 Cooper St., Camden NJ 08102. (609)963-6400. President: Michael Nise. Music publisher, record company (Power Up-Sutra), recording studio (Power House) and production company. Publishes 10 songs/year; publishes 5 new songwriters/year. Pays standard royalty.
Affiliate(s): Logo III Records, Power Up Records and Wordan Records.
How to Contact: Write first and obtain permission to submit. Prefers cassette (or videocassette) with 3 songs. Send Attention: Michael Nise. SASE a must. Reports in 1-2 months.
Music: **Dance, R&B, country rock** and **pop**, all with pop crossover potential; also **children's, church/religious, easy listening, folk, gospel, jazz**.
Tips: "Submit only well-produced demos."

NON-STOP MUSIC PUBLISHING, 915 West 100 South, Salt Lake City UT 84104. (801)531-0060. Fax: (801)531-0346. Vice President: Michael L. Dowdle. Music publisher. Estab. 1990. Publishes 50-100 songs/year; 3-4 new songwriters/year. Works with composers and lyricists; teams collaborators. Pays standard royalty.
Affiliate(s): Non-Stop Outrageous Publishing, Inc. (ASCAP), Non-Stop International Publishing, Inc. (BMI) and Airus International Publishing.
How to Contact: Submit demo tape by mail. Unsolicited submissions are OK. Prefers cassette with lyric or lead sheet, where possible. SASE. Reports in 4-6 weeks.
Music: Mostly **pop, R&B** and **country**; also **jazz** and **new age**. Published *Emerald Mist* and *Wishing Well*, written and recorded by Sam Cardon; and *A Brighter Day*, written and recorded by Mike Dondle, all on Airus Records.

*NOW & THEN MUSIC (BMI), Suite 3, 501 78th St., North Bergen NJ 07047. (201)854-6266. Owner: Shane Faber. Music publisher, record company (Now & Then Records) and record producer. Estab. 1980. Pays standard royalty.
How to Contact: Submit a demo tape by mail. Unsolicited submissions are OK. Prefers cassette with 4 songs and lyric sheet. SASE. Reports in 2 months.
Music: **Pop, rap, dance** and **R&B**.

NSP MUSIC PUBLISHING INC., (formerly Network Sound Music Publishing Inc.), 345 Sprucewood Rd., Lake Mary FL 32746-5917. (407)321-3702. Fax: (407)321-2361. President, A&R: Vito Fera. Office Manager, A&R: Rhonda Fera. Music publisher, record company (S.P.I.N. Records), record producer (NSP Inc.). ASCAP. Estab. 1980. Publishes 10 songs/year; publishes 3 new songwriters/year. Hires staff writers "on agreement terms." Pays standard royalty.
Affiliate(s): Fera Music Publishing (BMI).
How to Contact: Submit a demo tape by mail or UPS with 3 songs maximum and lyric sheet. Unsolicited submissions are OK. Prefers cassette (or VHS videocassette). "Package song material carefully. Always label (name, address and phone) both cassette and lyric sheet. Copyright songs. If you need assistance or advice on submission procedures or packaging, please contact us." SASE. Reports in 4 weeks.
Music: Mostly **dance/pop, R&B, rock/light, soundtracks, Christian music** and **children's music**. Published "Moments" (by Vito Fera, Bobby Burnett and Bill Buchanan), recorded by Bobby Burnett on Aurora Records; "Amore Infinito" (by Vito Fera, Bobby Burnett, Bill Buchanan, Franco & Maria

Russo), recorded by Angela Bacari on Aurora Records; and *The Glory of The Lord*, written and recorded by Salvatore Cristiano on S.P.I.N. Records.

Tips: "Carefully follow each music publisher's review instructions. Always include lyrics and a SASE for reply. A professional package and music production will help your songs stand out amongst the crowd. Always deliver exciting new music to the music industry. Use short intros and 'quality' vocalists to record your demo. Supply us with your best songs, commercial styling and catchy lyrics but not too personal. As you write, try to imagine a major artist singing your song. If you can't, rewrite it! If you are submitting yourself or band as the 'Artist or Act,' please specify your intentions. Finally, read every available songwriting book, music business manual and publication on the subject and inquire about songwriting organizations."

OBH MUSIKVERLAG OTTO B. HARTMANN, Box 2691, Ch-6901 Lugano **Switzerland**. Fax and phone: 0041(91)685586. President: Otto B. Hartmann. Music publisher, record company (OKAY/EXPO, Kick/OBH) and record producer. Estab. 1968. Publishes 100 songs/year; publishes 2 new songwriters/ year. Hires staff writers. Works with composers and lyricists. Pays standard royalty.
Affiliate(s): Edition Plural (classical).
Music: Mostly **rock, jazz, folk, pop** and **R&B**; also **classical**.

OH MY GOSH MUSIC (BMI), 5146 Hill Dr., Memphis TN 38109. (901)789-5296. Owner: Gerald McDade. Music publisher and record producer (Home Town Productions). Estab. 1985. Publishes 1-6 songs/year; publishes 1-6 new songwriters/year. Works with composers and lyricists; teams collaborators. Pays standard royalty.
How to Contact: Write first and obtain permission to submit. Prefers cassette (or VHS videocassette if available) with 2-4 songs and lyric sheet. Does not return unsolicited material. Reports in 2-4 months.
Music: Mostly **traditional country, country rock** and **rockabilly**; also **gospel**. Published "Get Right or Get Left," written and recorded by Janice Murry (C/W); "Hands Off" (by G. McDade), recorded by Jumpin Jerry McDade (country rock); and "Slow Down" (by B. Roberts), recorded by Bobby Lee (country rock), all on Hometown Records.

OKISHER MUSIC (BMI), P.O. Box 20814, Oklahoma City OK 73156. (405)755-0315. President: Mickey Sherman. Music publisher, record company (Seeds Records, Okart Records, Homa Records and Okie Dokie Records), record producer and management firm (Mickey Sherman's Talent Management). Estab. 1973. Member OCMA. Publishes 10-15 songs/year; publishes 2-3 new songwriters/year. Works with composers and lyricists. Pays standard royalty.
How to Contact: Submit demo tape by mail. Unsolicited submissions OK. Prefers 7½ ips reel-to-reel or cassette (or VHS videocassette) with 1-3 songs and lyric sheet. "Don't let the song get buried in the videocassette productions; a bio in front of performance helps. Enclose press kit or other background information." Does not return unsolicited material. Reports in 3 months.
Music: Mostly **blues, country** and **ballads**; also **easy listening, jazz, MOR, R&B** and **soul**. Published *Arizona Moon*, written and recorded by Ron Higdon (country); "Hush, Hush," written and recorded by Jan Jo (blues), both on Seeds Records; and *Guitar Picker's Nightmare*, written and recorded by Johnny Shackleford on Home Records (country).
Tips: "Have a 'hook' in the lyrics. Use good quality tape/lyric sheet and clean recording on demos."

OLD SLOWPOKE MUSIC (BMI), P.O. Box 52681, Tulsa OK 74152. (918)742-8087. President: Rodney Young. Music publisher, record producer. Estab. 1977. Publishes 24-36 songs/year; publishes 2-3 new songwriters/year. Works with composers and lyricists; teams collaborators. Pays standard royalty.
How to Contact: Write first and obtain permission to submit. Prefers cassette with 4 songs and lyric sheet. SASE. Reports in 6-8 weeks.
Music: Mostly **rock, country** and **R&B**; also **jazz**. Published *Blue Dancer*, written and recorded by Chris Blevins on CSR Records; *She Can't Do Anything Wrong* (by Davis/Richmond), recorded by Bob Seger on Capitol Records; and *Hardtimes*, written and recorded by Brad Absher on CSR Records.
Tips: "SASE must be sent or demo will be destroyed after 30 days."

RONNIE OLDHAM MUSIC PUBLISHING (BMI), 202 Auburn St., Florence AL 35630. (205)767-7667. President: Ronnie Oldham. Music publisher, record company (Gazebo Records) and record producer. Estab. 1990. Publishes 20-30 songs/year; publishes 3-6 new songwriters/year. Works with composers and lyricists; teams collaborators. Pays standard royalty.
How to Contact: Submit demo tape by mail. Unsolicited submissions are OK. Prefers cassette with 2-4 songs and lyric sheet. "Send as good a demo as possible." SASE. Reports in 2 months. "No response unless we wish to publish your song."
Music: Mostly **country, R&B** and **pop**; also **gospel, MOR** and **rock**. Published *Rollin' Stone* (by Ronnie and Bobby Oldham), recorded by Dick Allen on THZ Records (R&B/pop); and *Men of The Bible*, written and recorded by Barbara Staggs, on Gazebo Records (gospel).
Tips: "Be original, send as good a demo as you possibly can and also lyric sheets."

ONE FOR THE MONEY MUSIC PUBLISHING CO. (BMI), P.O. Box 18751, Milwaukee WI 53218. (414)527-4477. President: Michael W. White. Music publisher, record company (World Class Record Co.) and record producer (MW Communications). Estab. 1989. Publishes 4-6 songs/year. Works with composers and lyricists; teams collaborators. Pays standard royalty.
How to Contact: Submit demo tape by mail. Unsolicited submissions are OK. Prefers cassette or VHS videocassette with 6-8 songs and lyric sheet (if possible). SASE. Reports in 2-3 months.
Music: Mostly **country-rock, country-pop** and **country**; also **rock** and **R&B**. Published "Whoops I'm in Love Again" (by White, Kowalski, Barker, Goetzke); "Twenty Three Days" (by M.W. White); and "Just Remember I'm Still Lovin' You" (by Kowalski, White, Barker), all recorded by Sky Harbor Band on World Class Records (country rock).

ONE HOT NOTE MUSIC INC., P.O. Box 216, 454 Main St., Cold Spring Harbor NY 11724. (516)367-8544. Fax: (516)367-8507. A&R: Greg MacMillan. Music publisher, record company (Reiter Records Ltd.). Estab. 1989. Publishes 200 songs/year; publishes 10 new songwriters/year. Works with composers and lyricists; teams collaborators. "We take 100% of publishing but can be negotiated based upon track history of composer."
How to Contact: Submit demo tape by mail. Unsolicited submissions are OK. Prefers cassette. Does not return material.
Music: Mostly **pop, rock** and **jazz**; also **dance, country** and **rap**. Published "Be My Baby," written and recorded by T.C. Kross on Reiter Records; "Ready or Not" (by Lange/Bastianelli), recorded by Yolanda Yan on Cinepoly Records and by Camille Nivens on BMG Records.
Tips: "Make the song as well produced and recorded as you can."

OPERATION PERFECTION, Suite 206, 6245 Bristol Pkwy., Culver City CA 90230. Contact: Larry McGee. Vice-President: Darryl McCorkle. Music publisher. BMI. Estab. 1976. Publishes 15 songs/year; publishes 1-2 new songwriters/year. Works with composers and lyricists. Pays standard royalty.
How to Contact: Submit a demo tape by mail. Unsolicited submissions OK. Prefers cassette (or VHS videocassette) with 1-4 songs and lyric sheet. "Please only send professional quality material!" SASE. Reports in 2 months.
Music: **Rock, rap, pop, MOR/adult contemporary** and **R&B**. Published "We're Number One" (by Liz Davis), recorded by The Saxon Sisters (rock); "Captain Freedom" (by Kenny Sims), recorded by Bill Sawyer both on Boogie Band (crossover); and "Got It Going On" (by Alan Walker), recorded by Executives on Crossover Records.
Tips: "Study past, present and future trends in the music industry. Make sure your song relates to the current marketplace."

ORCHID PUBLISHING (BMI), Bouquet-Orchid Enterprises, P.O. Box 1335, Norcross GA 30091. (404)798-7999. President: Bill Bohannon. Music publisher, record company, record producer (Bouquet-Orchid Enterprises) and artist management. Member CMA, AFM. Publishes 10-12 songs/year; publishes 3 new songwriters/year. Works with composers and lyricists; teams collaborators. Pays standard royalty.
How to Contact: Submit demo tape by mail. Unsolicited submissions OK. Prefers cassette with 3-5 songs and lyric sheet. "Send biographical information if possible—even a photo helps." SASE. Reports in 1 month.
Music: Religious ("Amy Grant, etc., contemporary gospel"); **country** ("Garth Brooks, Trisha Yearwood type material"); and **top 100/pop** ("Bryan Adams, Whitney Houston type material"). Published *Blue As Your Eyes*, written and recorded by Adam Day; "Spare My Feelings" (by Clayton Russ), recorded by Terri Palmer; and "Trying to Get By" (by Tom Sparks), recorded by Bandoleers, all on Bouquet Records.

ORDERLOTTSA MUSIC (BMI), 441 E. Belvedere Ave., Baltimore MD 21212. (410)377-2270. President: Jeff Order. Music publisher and record producer (Jeff Order/Order Productions). Estab. 1986. Publishes 20 songs/year. Works with composers and lyricists. Pays standard royalty.
How to Contact: Submit demo tape by mail. Unsolicited submissions are OK. Prefers cassette with 3 songs. SASE. Reports in 1 month.
Music: Prefers **contemporary instrumental music**, but will listen to **all types**. Published "Sea of Tranquility," "Isis Unveiled," and "Keepers of the Light," written and recorded by Jeff Order on Order Records (instrumental new age).
Tips: "Submit high-quality, well-recorded and produced material. Original styles and sounds. Don't waste our time or yours copying the music of mainstream artists."

OTTO PUBLISHING CO., P.O. Box 16540, Plantation FL 33318. (305)741-7766. President: Frank X. Loconto. Music publisher, record company (FXL Records) and record producer (Loconto Productions). ASCAP. Estab. 1978. Publishes 25 songs/year; publishes 1-5 new songwriters/year. Pays standard royalty.

Affiliate(s): Betty Brown Music Co. (BMI), Clara Church Music Co. (SESAC), True Friends Music (BMI).
How to Contact: Prefers cassette with 1-4 songs and lyric sheet. SASE. Reports in 1 month.
Music: Mostly **country, MOR, religious** and **gospel.** Published "Sewing Without Pins" (TV theme) and "Safety Sam" (novelty), both by Frank X. Loconto, recorded by Loconto Productions. Theme song for "Nightly Business Reports," nationally syndicated TV show, written and recorded by Frank X. Loconto. Also published "Seminole Man" (by Loconto), recorded by James Billie on FXL Records (country).

PADRINO MUSIC PUBLISHING (BMI,SESAC), 1001 Highway 77, Bishop TX 78343. (512)584-3735. Fax: (512)584-3803. Proprietor: Jesus Gonzales Solis. Music publisher. Estab. 1993. Publishes 4 songs/year. Pays standard royalty. "Padrino Music is owned by Jesus Gonzales Solis, who is at this time the sole composer, publishing his own music."
How to Contact: Submit demo tape by mail. Unsolicited submissions are OK. Prefers cassette with lead sheet. SASE. Reports in 2 weeks.
Music: Mostly **Spanish rancheras, Latin ballads** and **cumbias.** Published *Quiero Saber Lo*, *Sabes De Mi*, "Caliente Dulce Amor" and "Quiero Besarte los Labios" (by Solis), recorded by La Sombra on Fonovisa Records.
Tips: "Write what you feel; no matter how outrageous, there is a purpose to everything that is written. Never give up if you believe in yourself, your time will come. Be persistent."

*PAISLEY PARK MUSIC, 1290 Avenue of Americas, New York NY 10019. (212)399-6971. Fax: (212)315-5590. Director of Admin./Product Development: Terri MacMillan. Music publisher. Estab. 1992. Works with composers and lyricists. Pays various amounts.
How to Contact: Submit demo tape by mail. Unsolicited submissions are OK. Prefers cassette or VHS videocassette with 3 songs and lyric sheet. "Wait 4-6 weeks for written response; we do not respond by phone." SASE. Reports in 6 weeks.
Music: Mostly **Black, street R&B, interesting funk/hip hop,** and **rich, high quality pop.** Published "Otha Fish" (by L.A. Jay), recorded by Pharcyde (jazz/hip hop).

PALMETTO PRODUCTIONS, P.O. Box 1376, Pickens SC 29671. President: Brian E. Raines. Music publisher, record company and record producer. Estab. 1985. Publishes 5 songs/year. Publishes 3 new songwriters/year. Works with composers and lyricists; teams collaborators. Pays standard royalty.
Affiliate(s): Brian Raines Music Co. (ASCAP) and Brian Song Music Co. (BMI).
How to Contact: Submit demo tape by mail. Unsolicited submissions are OK. Requires VHS tape with no more than 3 songs. Does not return unsolicited material. Reports in 3 months.
Music: Mostly **gospel, contemporary Christian** and **country.** Published *Take It To Jesus* (by Dale Cassell), recorded by Trinity on Mark V Records; "Since I Met You," written and recorded by Brian Raines, on Palmetto Records; and *From The Heart*, written and recorded by Jim Hubbard, on Hubbit Records.
Tips: "If possibly, send photo and bio information."

J. S. PALUCH COMPANY, INC./WORLD LIBRARY PUBLICATIONS, 3825 N. Willow Rd., P.O. Box 2703, Schiller Park IL 60176-0703. Music Editors: Nicholas T. Freund, Betty Z. Reiber, Ron Rendek, Laura Dankler, Mike Hay, Lorenzo Florian. Music publisher. SESAC. Estab. 1913. Publishes 50 or more songs/year; publishes varying number of new songwriters/year; recordings. Works with composers and lyricists; teams collaborators. "Pays pro-rated 5% for text or music alone; 10% for both."
How to Contact: Submit demo tape and/or manuscript by mail—unsolicited submissions are OK. Prefers cassette with any number of songs, lyric sheet and lead sheet. SASE. Reports in 3 months.
Music: **Sacred music, hymns, choral settings, descants, psalm settings, masses;** also **children's sacred music.** Published *Veni, Creator Spiritus* (by Carl Johensen); *Three Psalms* (by Mike Hay); and *Navidad, Navidad* (by Lorenzo Florian), all recorded by William Ferris Chorale on WLP (sacred).
Tips: "Make your manuscript as legible as possible, with clear ideas regarding tempo, etc. Base the text upon scripture."

*PANAMA MUSIC LIBRARY, Sovereign House, 12 Trewartha Rd., Praa Sands, Penzance, Cornwall TR20 9ST **England.** 0736-762826. Fax: 0736-763328. M.D.: Roderick G. Jones. Music publisher, library music production company (Panama Production). Estab. 1990. Publishes 100 songs/year; publishes 30 new songwriters/year. Hires staff songwriters. Works with composers. Pays standard royalty.

Refer to the Category Index (at the end of this section) to find exactly which companies are interested in the type of music you write.

Affiliate(s): Scamp Music.

How to Contact: Submit demo tape by mail. Unsolicited submissions are OK. Prefers cassette and lead sheet. "At least 5 International Reply Coupons to the value of 2 dollars for return postage/reply." SAE and IRC. Reports in 2-4 weeks.

Music: "Only interested in **instrumental theme music** and **jingles** for use in TV radio—advertising—film and audiovisual industries worldwide." Published *Shades of Mozart* (by Elon Davies), *Challenger* (by Tim Donovan) and *News Headline* (by Steve James), all recorded by Production Music on Panama Records (instrumental).

Tips: "Be professional and patient especially if you do not understand the complexities of how the music industry operates. Be prepared to work with a successful organisation with representation in many territories worldwide."

PANCHO'S MUSIC CO. (BMI), 3121 29th Ave., Sacramento CA 95820. (916)452-9144. Contact: Frank Lizarraga. Music publisher. Estab. 1980. Publishes 3 songs/year; publishes 1 new songwriter/year. Works with lyricists. Pays standard royalty.

How to Contact: Write first and obtain permission to submit. Prefers cassette (or VHS videocassette) with 3 songs, lyric sheet and brief résumé/fact sheet. SASE. Reports in 4-6 weeks.

Music: Mostly **Latin**, **pop** and **rock**; also **country**. Published "100 Miles of Bad Road" and "You Belong With Me" (by F. Lizarraga), recorded by Andre and Pancho; and "I Wonder. . . Why" (by Adam Lizarraga), recorded by Adam D, all on A.D. Records.

Tips: "We specialize in Latin music and prefer bilingual songwriters. Also, only BMI affiliated writers may contact us."

PARRAVANO MUSIC, 17 Woodbine St., Cranston RI 02910. (401)785-2677. Owner: Amy Parravano. Music publisher, record company (Peridot Records), record producer (Peridot Productions). Estab. 1986. Publishes 5 songs/year. Works with composers and lyricists. Pays standard royalty.

How to Contact: Submit demo tape by mail. Unsolicited submissions are OK. Prefers cassette with 3-4 songs and lyric sheet. Lead sheets are optional.

Music: Mostly **country, gospel, folk**; also **MOR, children's**, and **novelty**. Published "America" (by Stamm/Parravano), recorded by Amy Parravano on Stop Hunger Records; "North Hampton Line" and "Trust in Him" (by Amy Parravano), both recorded by Amy Beth on Peridot Records.

Tips: "Be sure that it is something that you would want to listen to. Not only is there a wealth of song ideas in the world around us; but within us too."

*PARSIFAL, bvba, Gulden Vlieslzan 67, Brugge 8000 **Belgium**. (32)50/339516. Fax: (32)50/333386. A&R: Nico A. Mertens. Music publisher and record company. Estab. 1974. Publishes 50 songs/year. Works with composers and lyricists. Pays standard royalty.

How to Contact: Submit demo tape by mail. Unsolicited submissions are OK. Prefers cassette. Does not return material. Reports in 2 months.

Music: Mostly **blues, R&B** and **rock**; also **singer/songwriters**. Published "Born to Win," written and recorded by Studebaker John on Double Trouble Records (rock); and "Johnny," written and recorded by Bery deConinck on Parsifal Records (singer/songwriter).

Tips: "I look for songwriters who are also performing artists."

*PAS MAL PUBLISHING SARL, 283 FBG St. Antoine, Paris 75020 **France**. (33)1 43485151. Fax: (33)1 43485753 Managing Director: Jammes Patrick. Music publisher. Estab. 1990. Publishes 5-10 songs/year. Works with composers and lyricists. Pays 60% royalty.

How to Contact: Submit demo tape by mail. Unsolicited submissions are OK. Prefers cassette (or PAL videocassette). Does not return material. Reports in 6 months.

Music: Mostly **new industrial** and **metal**. Published *Skinflowers*, *TV Sky* and *Gasoline Man* (by F. Treichler, A. Monod, U. Hiestand, R. Mosimann), all recorded by The Young Gods on Interscope Records (rock).

*PASSING PARADE MUSIC (ASCAP), P.O. Box 872, West Covina CA 91790. Owner: Kelly D. Lammers. Music publisher. Estab. 1972. Publishes 10-30 songs/year; publishes 3-6 new songwriters/year. Works with composers and lyricists; teams collaborators. Pays standard royalty.

How to Contact: Submit demo tape by mail. Unsolicited submissions are OK. Prefers cassette with 1-3 songs and lyric sheet. SASE. Reports in 6 weeks.

Music: Mostly **country/pop, children's** and **A/C**; also **MOR, New Age** and **soundtrack material**. Published "Punkline" (by K. Lammers), recorded by The Surfaris on Koinkidink Records; "The Getaway," written and recorded by K. Lammers; and "No Turning Back (by K. Lammers)," recorded by Kavaliers, both on Corby Records.

Tips: "Hone your writing skills, and learn how to get from here to there as quickly and craftily as possible. If it's a ballad, tell a good story. Also, keep our seasoned performers in mind. They need good material too! Everything old is new again, as was proven by Natalie Cole and Harry Connick,

Jr. Don't be afraid to write for that big band sound. It may be coming back to a brand new audience, loud and strong."

PDS MUSIC PUBLISHING, P.O. Box 412477, Kansas City MO 64141-2477. Contact: Submissions Department. Music publisher and record company (PDS Records, Universal Jazz, PDS Associated labels). ASCAP, BMI. Estab. 1988. Publishes 30 songs/year; publishes 3-4 new songwriters/year. Works with composers and lyricists. Pays varying royalty.
Affiliate(s): PDS Universal (ASCAP), PDS Worldwide (BMI).
How to Contact: Write first and obtain permission to submit a tape. Prefers cassette with 5-10 songs and lyric sheet. Does not return unsolicited material. Reports in 2-3 months.
Music: Mostly **rap** and **R&B.** Published "Wack M. Cee's," written and recorded by Seeds Of a Generik Kreed (hip hop); "Let's Hold On" and "The Heat of Passion" (by D. Shivers), recorded by Rajah (R&B).

PECOS VALLEY MUSIC (BMI), 2709 West Pine Lodge, Roswell NM 88201. (505)622-0244. President: Ray Willmon. Music publisher. Estab. 1989. Publishes 15-20 songs/year; publishes 4-5 new songwriters/year. Works with composers. Pays standard royalty.
How to Contact: Submit a demo tape by mail. Unsolicited submissions are OK. "No phone calls please." Prefers cassette or CD (or VHS videocassette if available) with 1-2 songs and lyric sheet. SASE. Reports in 6 weeks.
Music: Country-western. Published "More Than You," (by Sam Wells); "Move On Over" (by Ron Williams); and "Nowhere To Go" (by Jimmy Johns), all recorded by Etan Moore on SunCountry Records (country).
Tips: "Write original lyrics with an understandable story line with correct song form (i.e., AAAA, AABA, ABAB)."

PEERMUSIC, 8159 Hollywood Blvd., Los Angeles CA 90069. (213)656-0364. Fax: (213)656-3298. Assistant to the Head of Talent Acquisitions: Nicole Bahuchet. Music publisher and artist development promotional label. ASCAP, BMI. Estab. 1928. Publishes 600 songs/year (worldwide); publishes 1-2 new songwriters/year. Hires staff songwriters. Works with composers and lyricists; teams collaborators. Royalty standard, but negotiable.
Affiliate(s): Peer Southern Organization (ASCAP) and Peer International Corporation (BMI).
How to Contact: Write first and obtain permission to submit. "We do NOT accept unsolicited submissions." Prefers cassette and lyric sheet. Does not return unsolicited material. Reports in 6 weeks.
Music: Mostly **pop, rock** and **R&B.** Published "Run to You" (by Jud Friedman/Allan Rich), recorded by Whitney Houston on Arista Records (pop); "Can't Cry Hard Enough" (by Williams/Williams/Etzioni), recorded by The Williams Brothers on Warner Bros. Records (rock); and "I'm Gonna Get You" (by A. Scott/Bizarre, Inc./Toni C.), recorded by Bizarre, Inc. on Columbia Records (pop).

PEGASUS MUSIC, 27 Bayside Ave., Te Atatu, Auckland 8, **New Zealand.** Professional Manager: Errol Peters. Music publisher and record company. APRA. Estab. 1981. Publishes 20-30 songs/year; publishes 5 new songwriters/year. Works with composers and lyricists; teams collaborators. Pays 3-5% to artists on contract and standard royalty to songwriters; royalties paid directly to US songwriters.
How to Contact: Submit a demo tape—unsolicited submissions are OK. Prefers cassette with 3-5 songs and lyric sheet. SAE and IRC. Reports in 1 month.
Music: Mostly **country;** also **bluegrass, easy listening** and **top 40/pop.** Published *In the Arms of a Memory* (by Ginny Peters), and *Just a Stone's Throw From You* (by Johnny and Beverly Spears), recorded by Brian Letton on LBS Records; and "I Can Feel Him Touching You" (by Johnny and Beverly Spears), recorded by Riley Coyle on Playback Records.
Tips: "Be very direct and do not use too many words. Less is better."

*PEN COB PUBLISHING INC. (BMI). 5660 E. Virginia Beach Blvd., Norfolk VA 23502. (804)455-8454. Fax: (804)461-4669. A&R: Tres Swann. Music publisher. Estab. 1991. Publishes 100 songs/year; publishes 6 new songwriters/year. Teams collaborators. Royalty varies.
How to Contact: Write or call first to obtain permission to submit. Prefers cassette (or VHS videocassette). SASE. Reports in 3-4 weeks.
Music: Mostly **alternative/progressive, rock (heavy)** and **country.** Published *One Good Eye*, recorded by On Beyond Zee; *Vice Verses*, recorded by Psycho Johnny; and *Alone*, recorded by William A., all on Trumpeter Records.

PERFECTION MUSIC PUBLICATIONS (BMI), P.O. Box 4094, Pittsburgh PA 15201. (412)782-4477. President: Edward J. Moschetti. Music publisher and record company (Century Records). Estab. 1953. Works with composers. Pays standard royalty.

Affiliate(s): Regal Music Publications (ASCAP).
How to Contact: Write first and obtain permission to submit. Prefers cassette. Does not return unsolicited material. Reports in 1 month.
Music: Ballads, country and pop.

JUSTIN PETERS MUSIC (BMI), 3609 Donna Kay Dr., Nashville TN 37211. (615)331-6056. Fax: (615)831-0991. President: Justin Peters. Music publisher. Estab. 1981.
How to Contact: Prefers cassette with 3 songs and lyric sheet. Does not return unsolicited material.
Music: Mostly **contemporary Christian.** Published "Saved By Love," recorded by Amy Grant on A&M Records; "Love Still Changing Hearts," recorded by Imperials on Starsong Records; and "Wipe a Tear," recorded by Russ Taff and Olanda Daper on Word Records, all written by Justin Peters.
Tips: "Learn your craft and submit quality work."

PHAJA MUSIC, (formerly Mega-Star Music), a division of Mega-Star Music, P.O. Box 1427, Bayshore NY 11706. (212)713-5229. General Manager: Barry Yearwood. Music publisher, record producer (Barry Yearwood) and management firm (Yearwood Management). Estab. 1984. Publishes 4 songs/year; publishes 4 new songwriters/year. Pays standard royalty.
How to Contact: Submit demo tape by mail. Unsolicited submissions are OK. Prefers cassette with 4 songs. SASE. Reports in 1 month.
Music: Mostly **dance** and **R&B;** also **pop.** Published "Black Puddin'," recorded by SWV on RCA Records. Other artists include Paul Mitchel.

PHILIPPOPOLIS MUSIC (BMI), 12027 Califa St., North Hollywood CA 91607. President: Milcho Leviev. Music publisher. Member GEMA, NARAS. Estab. 1975. Publishes 3-5 songs/year; publishes 1-2 new songwriters/year. Works with lyricists. Pays standard royalty.
How to Contact: Submit demo tape by mail. Unsolicited submissions are OK. Prefers cassette with 1-3 songs. Prefers studio produced demos. Does not return material. Reports in 1 month.
Music: **Jazz** and **classical fusion.** Published *Monday Morning* and *California Winter* (by Leviev); and *Manipulation* (by Spassov), all recorded by Katoomi Quartet on Balicantor Records.

*PINE ISLAND MUSIC, 9430 Live Oak Place, Ft. Lauderdale FL 33324. (305)472-7757. President/A&R: Jack P. Bluestein. Music publisher, artist booking. Estab. 1974. Publishes 50-75 songs/year; publishes 10-20 new songwriters/year. Works with composers and lyricists. Pays standard royalty.
Affiliate(s): Lantana Music/Quadrant Records (BMI).
How to Contact: Submit demo tape by mail. Unsolicited submissions are OK. Prefers cassette with 3 songs and lyric or lead sheet. SASE. Reports in 2 months.
Music: Mostly **beautiful music, soft rock, country** and **soft pop;** also **movie themes, movie background** and **innovative country and pop.**

*PLATINUM BOULEVARD PUBLISHING (BMI), 523 East Prater Ave., Reno NV 89431. (702)358-7484. President: Lawrence Davis. Music publisher. Estab. 1984. Publishes 12 songs/year; publishes 1 new songwriter/year. Works with composers and lyricists. Pays standard royalty.
How to Contact: Submit demo tape by mail. Unsolicited submissions are OK. Prefers cassette (or VHS videocassette), with unlimited songs and lyric or lead sheets. Does not return unsolicited material. "We report only if interested."
Music: Mostly **rock, country** and **R&B;** also **jazz** and **New Age.** Published *Ladies In Their Mercedes*, *Do I Ever Cross Your Mind* and *When We Met*, all written and recorded by Lawrence Davis on Platinum Boulevard Records (rock).
Tips: "We own a 24-track studio and are willing to provide inexpensive recording time to qualified artists wishing to improve their demo sound. We are willing to develop and manage acts who display professional potential."

*PLAY THAT BEAT!, 38 Rue Fernand Bernier, 1060 Brussels **Belgium.** (322)534-2323. Fax: (322)534-7995. Managing Directors: Theo Linder, Marc Debouvier. Music publisher, record company, record producer and management company. Estab. 1988. Publishes 100 songs/year; publishes 4 new songwriters/year. Works with composers and lyricists; teams collaborators. Pays standard royalty.
How to Contact: Submit demo tape by mail. Unsolicited submissions are OK. Prefers cassette (or VHS videocassette if available) with lyric sheet. Does not return material. Reports in 1 week.
Music: Mostly **pop, rock** and **blues;** also **dance.** Published work by Mama's Jasje, Jo Lemaire and De Mens.

POLLYBYRD PUBLICATIONS LIMITED, P.O. Box 8442, Universal CA 91608. (818)506-8533. Fax: (818)760-8533. Branch office: 333 Proctor St., Carson City NV 89703. (818)884-1946. Fax: (818)882-6755. Professional Manager: Maxx Diamond. Music publisher. ASCAP, BMI, SESAC. Estab. 1979.

Publishes 100 songs/year; publishes 25-40 new songwriters/year. Hires staff writers. Works with composers and lyricists; teams collaborators. Pays standard royalty.
Affiliate(s): Kellijai Music (ASCAP), Pollyann Music (ASCAP), Ja'Nikki Songs (BMI), Branmar Songs International (BMI), Lonnvanness Songs (SESAC) and PPL Music (ASCAP).
How to Contact: Submit demo tape by mail. Unsolicited submissions are OK. Prefers cassette or VHS videocassette with 4 songs and lyric and lead sheet. SASE. Reports in 6 weeks.
Music: Published "Hero" (by J. Jarrett), recorded by The Band AKA (dance-R&B); "Anything" (by D. Mitchell), recorded by D.M. Groove (dance-R&B); and "Cool Fire" (by J. Jarrett), recorded by Katrina Gibson, all on Bouvier/Sony Records (dance/pop).

PORTAGE MUSIC, 16634 Gannon W., Rosemont MN 55068. (612)432-5737. President: Larry LaPole. Music publisher. BMI. Publishes 5-20 songs/year. Pays standard royalty.
How to Contact: Submit demo tape by mail. Unsolicited submissions are OK. Prefers cassette with 3 songs and lyric sheet. Does not return unsolicited material. Reports in 2 months.
Music: Mostly **country** and **country rock.** Published "King of the Surf," "My Woodie" and "A-Bone" (by L. Lapole), recorded by Trashmen.
Tips: "Keep songs short, simple and upbeat with positive theme."

PPI/PETER PAN INDUSTRIES, 88 St. Francis St., Newark NJ 07105. (201)344-4214. Senior Vice President (and songwriter): Joseph M. Porrello. Product Manager: Marianne Eggleston. Music publisher, record company (Compose Records, Current Records, Parade Video), record producer (Dunn Pearson, Jr.); also outside producers. ASCAP, BMI. Estab. 1928. Publishes over 100 songs/year. Hires staff songwriters. Works with composers and lyricists; teams collaborators. Pays standard royalty "based on negotiation."
Affiliate(s): Ironbound Publishing (ASCAP), Ina Kustik, Sweet Basil, Benco/World Music.
How to Contact: Submit a demo tape by mail. Unsolicited submissions are OK. Prefers cassette (or VHS videocassette if available) with 5-7 songs. "Please include name, address and phone numbers on all materials, along with picture, bio and contact information." SASE. Reports in 2-3 months.
Music: Mostly **children's — audio, R&B** and **jazzy;** also **exercise — video, rock** and **classical.** Published "Where Do Trolls Come From" (by Barry Hirschberg), recorded by various artists on Peter Pan Records; "Frankie Paul," written and recorded by Frankie Paul on Tassa/Compose Records (reggae); and "Manhattan Jazz Reunion," written and recorded by Manhattan Jazz Reunion on Compose/Sweet Basil Records (jazz).
Tips: "Submit materials professionally packaged with typewritten correspondence."

PREJIPPIE MUSIC GROUP, Box 2849, Trolley Station, Detroit MI 48231. (313)581-1267. Partner: Bruce Henderson. Music publisher, record company (PMG Records) and record producer (PMG Productions). BMI. Estab. 1990. Publishes 50-75 songs/year; publishes 2-3 new songwriters/year. Hires staff writers. Teams collaborators. Pays standard royalty.
How to Contact: Submit a demo tape by mail. Unsolicited submissions are OK. Prefers cassette with 3-4 songs and lyric sheet. "No phone calls please." SASE. Reports in 3 months.
Music: Mostly **techno/house, funk/rock** and **dance;** also **alternative rock** and **experimental.** Published "Evangeline," written and recorded by Bourgeoisie Paper Jam on PMG Records (alternative rock); and "We're on The Move Now," written and recorded by the Prejippies on Black Toxic Records (techno/alternative).
Tips: "Think your arrangements through carefully. Always have a strong hook (whether vocal-oriented or instrumental)."

PRESCRIPTION COMPANY (BMI), % D.F. Gasman, Apt. B-1, S. Wildwood Gardens, Port Washington NY 11050. (516)767-1929. President: David F. Gasman. Music publisher and record producer. Pays standard royalty.
How to Contact: Call or write first about your interest. Prefers cassette with any number of songs and lyric sheet. "Send all submissions with SASE (or no returns)." Reports in 1 month.
Music: **Bluegrass, blues, children's, country, dance-oriented, easy listening, folk, jazz, MOR, progressive, R&B, rock, soul** and **top 40/pop.** Published "You Came In," "Rock 'n' Roll Blues" and "Seasons" (by D.F. Gasman), all recorded by Medicine Mike on Prescription Records.
Tips: "Songs should be good and written to last. Forget fads — we want songs that'll sound as good in 10 years as they do today. Organization, communication and exploration of form are as essential as message (and sincerity matters, too)."

PRESTATION MUSIC, (formerly B. Sharp Music), 24 rue Gachard, 1050 Brussels **Belgium.** Phone: (02)649-28-47. Fax: (02)648-79-31. Music publisher, record company (B. Sharp, Selection Records) and record producer (Pletinckx). Estab. 1950. Works with composers. Pays standard royalty.

Affiliate(s): Prestation Music and Multi Sound.
How to Contact: Write or call first and obtain permission to submit. SAE and IRC. Reports in 3 months.
Music: Jazz and **instrumental music**. Published *Aftertouch*, written and recorded by Ivan Paduart; *No Wall, No War* (by Charles Loos), recorded by Charles Loos/Ali Ryerson, both on B. Sharp Records; and *Approach*, written and recorded by Bernard L'Hoir on Selection Records.

PRITCHETT PUBLICATION (BMI), P.O. Box 725, Daytona Beach FL 32114-0725. (904)252-4848. Vice President: Charles Vickers. Music publisher and record company. (Main office in California.) Estab. 1975. Publishes 21 songs/year; publishes 12 new songwriters/year. Works with composers and lyricists. Pays standard royalty.
Affiliate(s): Alison Music (ASCAP), Charles H. Vickers (BMI).
How to Contact: Write first and obtain permission to submit. Prefers cassette with 6 songs and lyric or lead sheet. SASE.
Music: **Gospel, rock-disco** and **country**. Published *Walkin On The Water*, written and recorded by Charles Vickers on King of Kings Records (gospel); and "It'll Be A Cold Day" (by Leroy Pritchett), recorded by Ray Sanders on Allagash Country Records (country).

*PROMO, Kasteelstraat 6, Tervuren 3080 **Belgium**. (2)7677567 Fax: (2) 7728445. President: Hascher Francois. Music publisher, record producer. Estab. 1986. Publishes 50 songs/year; publishes 2-3 new songwriters/year. Works with composers and lyricists. Pays standard royalty.
How to Contact: Submit demo tape by mail. Unsolicited submissions are OK. Prefers cassette and lyric sheet. SAE and IRC. Reports in 2 months.
Music: Mostly **rock** and **blues**; also **French songs**. Published *Obsession* (by F. Sterckx), recorded by M.C. Michael (French); *Marylin's Busstop* (by J. Lauwers), recorded by John Lauwers Band (rock); and *Dreammaker* (by T. Frantzis), recorded by Tuner (rock), all on Krazy Kobra Rekords.
Tips: "Make real music—no sampling. Melodious, if possible."

*PROSPECTOR THREE D PUBLISHING (BMI), 4003 Turnberry Cir., Houston TX 77025. (713)665-4676. Fax: (713)665-5576. Consultant-Owners: Dave or Peggy Davidson. Music publisher, record producer and management company. Estab. 1989. Publishes 2 or 3 new songwriters/year. Works with composers and/or lyricists; teams collaborators. Pays standard royalty.
How to Contact: Submit demo tape by mail. Unsolicited submissions are OK. (No replies unless interested in songs or singer). Prefers cassette (or VHS videocassette if available) with 4 songs and lyric sheet.
Music: Mostly **country, country/Christian** and **pop**; also **blues, pop rock** and **bluegrass**. Published *West Tx DeJaVu* (by Tadd Williams); and *Love Lightning* (by Blake Weldon), both on Triumph Records (country); and *No Time For Blues* (by Karon) on TNT Records (pop rock).
Tips: "Study your craft and write songs under 3 minutes that are complete and sound like hits you hear on radio."

PUBLISHING CENTRAL, 7251 Lowell Dr., Overland Park KS 66204. (913)384-6688. Director of Publishing: David Jackson. Music publisher. "We are also a theatrical agency." SAG, ITAA. Estab. 1961. Publishes 5 songs/year; publishes 3 new songwriters/year. Teams collaborators. Pays standard royalty.
Affiliate(s): Jac-Zang (ASCAP), Bunion (BMI), Very Cherry (ASCAP), All Told (BMI).
How to Contact: Submit a demo tape—unsolicited submissions are OK. Prefers cassette with 1-3 songs and lead sheets. Does not return unsolicited material. Reports in 3 months.
Music: Mostly **country rock, pop** and **rock**; also **gospel, reggae, alternative** and **soul (southern)**.
Tips: "Know your trade. Be able to write (manuscript) music. Learn basic music skills—theory, etc. Become more sophisticated."

PURPLE HAZE MUSIC (BMI), P.O. Box 1243, Beckley WV 25802. President: Richard L. Petry. (304)252-4836. A & R: Carol Lee. Music publisher. Estab. 1968. Publishes 50 songs/year; publishes 5-10 new songwriters/year. Pays standard royalty.
How to Contact: Submit demo tape by mail. Unsolicited submissions are OK. Prefers cassette with 3-4 songs and lyric sheet. "Separate lyric sheet for each song." SASE. Reports in 6-12 weeks.
Music: **Country, rock** and **R&B**. Published "My Old Friend," written and recorded by Chuck Paul on Rising Sun Records; and "Home Sweet W.V.," written and recorded by Dave Runyon on Country Bridge Records.
Tips: "Type up lyrics in capital letters, double-space between verses and chorus. Keep lyric sheet clean with only your name as songwriter with © year. Professional demos! Not home made!!"

PUSTAKA MUZIK EMI (Malaysia) SDN. BHD., Suite 10.01, 10th Floor, Exchange Square, off Jalan Semantan, Damansara Heights, 50490 Kuala Lumpur, **Malaysia**. Phone: 03-6277511. Contact: Publishing Manager. Music publisher and record company. Publishes 50 songs/year; publishes 15 new song-

writers/year. Works with composers and lyricists; teams collaborators. Pays standard royalty.
How to Contact: Submit demo tape by mail. Unsolicited submissions are OK. Prefers cassette and lyric or lead sheet. Does not return unsolicited material. Reports in 1 month.
Music: Mostly **MOR, country** and **commercial jazz**; also **blues** and **rock.** Published *Teringin* (by Fauzi Marzuki), recorded by Shima on Sony Records (pop rock); *Untukmu* (by Norman), recorded by Kru on EMI Records (rap); and *Lahar Cinta* (by Awang), recorded by Final List on Life Records (pop rock).
Tips: "Please send us properly recorded demo tape containing commercial pop, rock musical material."

*QMARK MUSIC (BMI), 1201 Carlisle Ave., York PA 17404. (717)843-4228. President: Lewis Quintin. Music publisher. Estab. 1985. Publishes 12 songs/year; publishes 3 new songwriters/year. Pays standard royalty.
Affiliate(s): Barquin Music (ASCAP).
How to Contact: Write first and obtain permission to submit a tape. Prefers cassette with 2 songs and lyric sheet. Does not return unsolicited material. Reports in 6 weeks.
Music: Mostly **country** and **R&B.** Published "José" (by B. Belton), "Subway Casanova" (by Barken), and "Walking Down the Avenue" (by Belton), all recorded by Spyke on Qmark Records (pop/rock).

QUEEN ESTHER MUSIC PUBLISHING (ASCAP), 449 N. Vista St., Los Angeles CA 90036. Owner: Len Weisman. Music publisher. Pays standard royalty.
Affiliate(s): House of Sound Music (BMI).
How to Contact: Submit demo tape by mail. Unsolicited submissions are OK. Prefers cassette. SASE. Reports in 2 months.
Tips: "If I send back your tape with no response, it's a reject, but please keep sending."

R. J. MUSIC, 10A Margaret Rd., Barnet, Herts. EN4 9NP **United Kingdom**. Phone: (01)440-9788. Managing Directors: Roger James and Laura Skuce. Music publisher and management firm (Roger James Management). PRS. Pays negotiable royalty (up to 50%).
How to Contact: Prefers cassette with 1 song and lyric or lead sheet. "Will return cassettes, but only with correct *full* postage!"
Music: Mostly **MOR, blues, country** and **rock**; also **chart material.** "No disco or rap!"

R.T.L. MUSIC, %Stewart House, Hillbottom Rd., Highwycombe, Buckinghamshire **United Kingdom** HP124HJ. Phone: (0630)647374. Fax: (0630)647612. Art Director: Ron Lee. Music publisher, record company and record producer. MCPS, PRS. Member MPA, PPL. Estab. 1971. Publishes 30 songs/year; publishes 10 new songwriters/year. Works with composers, lyricists; teams collaborators. Royalty negotiable.
Affiliate(s): Lee Music, Ltd., Swoop Records, Grenoville Records, Check Records, Zarg Records, Pogo Records, Ltd., R.T.F.M., Value for Money Productions, Lee Sound Productions, Le Matt Distributors, Hoppy Productions.
How to Contact: Submit demo tape by mail. Unsolicited submissions OK. Prefers 7½ or 15 ips reel-to-reel or cassette (or VHS 625/PAL system videocassette) with 1-3 songs and lyric and lead sheets; include still photo. "Make sure name and address are on reel or cassette." SAE and IRC. Reports in 2 months.
Music: All types. Published *Rumble, Traffic Jam* and *Young Power*, all recorded by Suburban Studs on Anagram Records.

*RADIANT MUSIC, 1445 Boonville Ave., Springfield MO 65802-1894. (417)862-2781, ext. 4130. Fax: (417)862-0416. National Secretary: Dan Crace. Music publisher. Estab. 1956. Works with composers and lyricists.
How to Contact: Submit demo tape by mail. Unsolicited submissions are OK. Prefers cassette with 3 songs and lyric sheet and lead sheet. SASE. Reports in 6 months.
Music: Mostly **evangelical choral, praise** and **worship choruses.**

*RAGLAND PUBLICATIONS (BMI), Box 43659, Las Vegas NV 89116. (702)794-4588. President: Lou Ragland. Music publisher, record company (Casino Records Inc., Spirit Records of Nevada) record producer (Ragland Enterprises). Estab. 1962. Publishes 10 songs/year; 2 new songwriters/year. Hires staff writers. Works with composers and lyricists; teams collaborators. Pays standard royalty.
How to Contact: Write first and obtain permission to submit. Prefers cassette with 4 songs and lyric sheets. SASE. Reports in 3 months.
Music: Mostly **pop, R&B** and **gospel**; also **rock.** Published *Which Every Way the Wind Blows* (by Lou Ragland/Gloria Copeland), recorded by Lou Ragland (pop); "Freedoms Calling," written and recorded by Laurie Buckley (pop); and *We Have It All* (by Cozzetta Ragland/Lou Ragland), recorded by Cozzetta (R&B), all on Casino Records.

Tips: "Produce the best demo that you can, and use a very very good vocalist!"

RAHSAAN PUBLISHING, P.O. Box 564, Newburyport MA 01950-0764. (800)284-1730. Fax: (508)465-7441. Owner: Tom Reeves. Music publisher, record company (Cat's Voice) and record producer. Estab. 1982. Publishes 4 songs/year; publishes 4 new songwriters/year. Hires staff writers. Works with composers and lyricists; teams collaborators. "Royalty depends on project, but standard usually applies."
Affiliate(s): Cat's Voice (ASCAP) and Black Gold (BMI).
How to Contact: Submit demo tape by mail. Unsolicited submissions are OK. Prefers cassette (or VHS videocassette) with 3 songs and lyric or lead sheet. "Songwriters must be copyrighted; send copy of form." SASE. Reports in 1 month.
Music: Mostly **rock, New Age** and **reggae;** also **country, light rock** and **R&B.** Published *Earl and Maureen* (by Fabian Kunster) and *Rodents* (by Dick D. Lox), both recorded by Mangled Ducklings on Cat's Voice Records.
Tips: "Lead sheet, copyright register form, clear cassette with guitar and voice or piano and voice."

RANA INTERNATIONAL MUSIC GROUP, INC., P.O. Box 106, Valhalla NY 10595. (914)741-2576. Fax: (914)741-2566. CEO: Giuseppe Nudo. President: Raffaele A. Nudo. Vice President: Wesley C. Kraritz. Music publisher, management firm and record company. Estab. 1990. Publishes 3-5 songs/year; publishes 1-3 new songwriters/year. Works with composers and lyricists. Pays standard royalty.
Affiliate(s): Big Z Productions (ASCAP) and CHRISMARIE Records.
How to Contact: Submit demo tape by mail. Unsolicited submissions are OK. Prefers cassette (or VHS videocassette) with 3-4 songs and lyric sheet. "Include SASE." Does not return material. Reports in 6-12 weeks.
Music: Mostly **pop, rock** and **ballads;** also **country, R&B** and **new music.** Published "Dream On," written and recorded by Niko; "Anita," written and recorded by Adamus; and "High Reality," written and recorded by DECLARATION, all on CHRISMARIE Records.
Tips: "Music should never overshadow the lyrics. Stay positive and have faith in your talent. All submissions must include name, phone number, etc. on all items."

RAVING CLERIC MUSIC PUBLISHING/EUROEXPORT ENTERTAINMENT, P.O. Box 4735, Austin TX 78765-4735. (512)452-2701. Fax: (512)452-0815. President: L.A. Evans. Music publisher, record company (RCM Productions), record producer, artist management and development. Estab. 1985. Publishes 15-20 songs/year; publishes 7-10 new songwriters/year. Works with composers and lyricists; teams collaborators. Pays standard royalty.
Affiliate(s): Tripoli Inferno Music Publishing.
How to Contact: Write first and obtain permission to submit. Prefers cassette (or VHS videocassette if available) with 3 songs maximum and lyric sheet. "Submissions of more than 3 songs will not be listened to." Does not return material. "Does not accept unsolicited material." Reports in 3-4 weeks.
Music: Prefers **alternative rock, pop, R&B;** also **country, blues, rap/urban.** Published *Do You Remember* (by Abbott/Dotin) and *Twisted and Depraved* (by Abbott/Mitchum), both recorded by Argument Clinic on RCM Productions (rock); and *Between You and I,* written and recorded by Fred Mitchum on Zombo Productions (New Age).
Tips: "Patience—our company mainly acquires songs for projects and artists we produce as a label."

RED BOOTS TUNES, 5503 Roosevelt Way NE, Seattle WA 98105. (206)524-1020. Fax: (206)524-1102. Music publisher. ASCAP. Estab. 1991. Publishes 25 songs/year; publishes 2-3 new songwriters/year. Teams collaborators. Pays standard royalty.
How to Contact: Submit a demo tape by mail; call first. Prefers cassette with 2-3 songs and lyric sheet. SASE. Reports in 6-8 weeks.
Music: Mostly **country;** also **R&B/rock.**
Tips: "Have professional looking lyric sheets and good quality tapes."

*RENT-A-SONG, 4433 Petit, Encino CA 91436. (818)906-0618. Fax: (818)907-7664. Publishing Representative: Anita Alban. Music publisher and record producer. Estab. 1980. Publishes 50 songs/year; publishes 1-2 new songwriters/year. Hires staff songwriters. Works with composers and lyricists; teams collaborators. Pays standard royalty.
Affiliate(s): Lease-A-Tune (ASCAP) and Dennis Lambert Music (BMI).
How to Contact: Write first and obtain permission to submit. Prefers cassette with 2 songs and lyric sheet. Does not return material. Reports in 2 weeks.
Music: Mostly **R&B, pop** and **rock.** Published *Finish What You Started* (by Annie Roboff), recorded by Lea Salonga on Atlantic Records (pop); *Upside* (by Pam Reswick/Steve Werfel), recorded by Girlfriend on BMG Records (dance); and *Thru My Daddy's Eyes* (by Annie Roboff), recorded by Fleetwood Mac on Warner Bros. Records (pop).
Tips: "Send only top quality, competitive hit songs."

RIDGE MUSIC CORP., 38 Laurel Ledge Court, Stamford CT 06903. President/General Manager: Paul Tannen. Music publisher and manager. Estab. 1961. BMI, ASCAP. Member CMA. Publishes 12 songs/year. Pays standard royalty.
Affiliate(s): Tannen Music Inc. and Deshufflin, Inc.
How to Contact: Submit demo tape by mail. Unsolicited submissions OK. Prefers cassette with 3 songs and lyric sheet. SASE. Reports in 2 months.
Music: Country, rock, top 40/pop and jazz.

RISING STAR RECORDS AND PUBLISHERS, (formerly Rising Star Music Publishers), 710 Lakeview Ave. NE, Atlanta GA 30308. (404)872-1431. Fax: (404)872-3104. Promotions Manager: Kevin Berg. Music publisher, record producer and record company (Rising Star Records). Estab. 1987. Publishes 40-50 songs/year; publishes 5 new songwriters/year. Works with composers and/or lyricists. Teams collaborators. Pays standard royalty.
Affiliate(s): New Rising Star Music Publications (ASCAP), Ristar Music Publications (BMI).
How to Contact: Submit demo tape by mail. Unsolicited submissions are OK. Prefers cassette (or VHS videocassette if available) with 3 songs and lyric or lead sheet. "Print music submissions must send cassette demo plus sample pages of manuscript." SASE. Reports in 1 month.
Music: Mostly New Age, jazz and classical; also print music and music instruction. Published *Dreamrunner* (by Brad Rudisail); *Breaking the Rules* (by Rick Pruett), recorded by Pruett and Davis; and *Oh Watch The Stars* (by John Krumich), all on Rising Star Records.
Tips: "We specialize in instrumental music, do not send vocal music unless it is for the classical genre. We are most interested in artist development and are looking for original acts that are willing to perform and promote themselves."

*RIVERHAWK MUSIC (BMI), 327 Highway 17 N., Surfside Beach SC 29575. (803)238-1633. President: Arthur W. Byman. Music publisher, record company (Peregrine Records) and record producer. Estab. 1994. Publishes 10 songs/year; publishes 3 new songwriters/year. Works with composers and lyricists. Pays standard royalty.
How to Contact: Submit demo tape by mail. Unsolicited submissions are OK. Prefers cassette with 3 songs and lyric sheet. "Follow submission outlines exactly. Be neat." SASE. Reports in 1 month.
Music: Mostly MOR, country and A/C; also cowboy-type western and comedy. Published "Dark Hearted Woman" (by A. Byman), recorded by Ken Jordan on NEK Records (A/C); "Just One Time" (by J. Carothers), recorded by Arthur Byman (MOR); and "Haunted" (by A. Byman), recorded by Marie Clark (pop), both on Peregrine Records.

FREDDIE ROBERTS MUSIC, P.O. Box 203, Rougemont NC 27572. (919)477-4077. Manager: Freddie Roberts. Music publisher, record company, record producer (Carolina Pride Productions), and management firm and booking agency. Estab. 1967. BMI. Publishes 45 songs/year; publishes 15 new songwriters/year. Works with composers, lyricists; teams collaborators. Pays standard royalty.
How to Contact: Write first about your interest or to arrange personal interview. Prefers 7½ ips reel-to-reel or cassette with 1-5 songs and lyric sheet. SASE. Reports in 5 weeks.
Music: Mostly country, MOR and top 40/pop; also bluegrass, church/religious, gospel and southern rock. Published "Any Way You Want It" (by B. Fann), recorded by Sleepy Creek (southern rock) on Bull City Records; "Just A Little" (by C. Justis), recorded by Dean Phillips (country) on Ardon Records; and "He Knows What I Need" (by J. Dobbs), recorded by the Roberts Family (gospel) on Bull City Records.
Tips: "Write songs, whatever type, to fit today's market. Send good, clear demos, no matter how simple."

ROB-LEE MUSIC (ASCAP), P.O. Box 1130, Tallevast FL 34270. Vice Presidents: Rodney Russen, Eric Russen, Bob Francis. Music publisher, record company (Castle Records, Rock Island Records and Jade Records), record producer and manager. Estab. 1965. Publishes 18-36 songs/year; publishes 6 new songwriters/year. Teams collaborators. Pays standard royalty.
Affiliate(s): Heavy Weather Music (ASCAP).
How to Contact: Submit a demo tape by mail. Unsolicited submissions OK. Prefers cassette (or VHS videocassette) with 4-8 songs and lyric sheet. Does not return unsolicited material. Reports in 2 weeks.
Music: Dance-oriented, easy listening, MOR, R&B, rock, soul, top 40/pop and funk. Published "Loose Cannon" (by Terry Davis), recorded by Terminator on TCB Records (rock); and "Pile Driver" (by D. Isley), recorded by The Big Cheese on Jade Records (rock).
Tips: "Submit full arrangements, not just vocals and acoustic guitar!"

ROCKER MUSIC/HAPPY MAN MUSIC, P.O. Box 73, 4501 Spring Creek Rd., Bonita Springs, FL 33923-6637. (813)947-6978. Executive Producer: Dick O'Bitts. BMI, ASCAP. Estab. 1960. Music publisher, record company (Happy Man Records, Condor Records and Air Corp Records), record producer (Rainbow Collections Ltd.) and management firm (Gemini Complex). Publishes 25-30 songs/

year; publishes 8-10 new songwriters/year. Works with composers; teams collaborators. Pays standard royalty.

How to Contact: Submit a demo tape by mail. Unsolicited submissions are OK. Prefers cassette (or VHS videocassette) with 4 songs and lyric or lead sheet. SASE. Do not call. "You don't need consent to send material." Reports in 1 month.

Music: Country, rock, pop, gospel, Christian and **off-the-wall**. Published *The Joke's On You* (by Ken Cowden), recorded by Overdue (rock); *Buying My Way to Happiness* (by Coy White), recorded by Challengers (country); and *Believing Is What It Takes*, written and recorded by Bengter Sisters (Christian), all on Happy Man Records.

ROCKFORD MUSIC CO., Suite 6-D, 150 West End Ave., New York NY 10023. Manager: Danny Darrow. Music publisher, record company (Mighty Records), record and video tape producer. BMI, ASCAP. Publishes 1-3 songs/year; publishes 1-3 new songwriters/year. Teams collaborators. Pays standard royalty.

Affiliate(s): Corporate Music Publishing Company (ASCAP) and Stateside Music Company (BMI).

How to Contact: Submit a demo tape by mail. Unsolicited submissions are OK. Prefers cassette with 3 songs and lyric sheet. "SASE a must!" Reports in 1-2 weeks. *"Positively no phone calls."*

Music: Mostly **MOR** and **top 40/pop**; also **adult pop, country, adult rock, dance-oriented, easy listening, folk** and **jazz**. Published *Impulse* and *Let There Be Peace* (by D. Darrow); *Doomsday* (by Robert Lee Lowery and Danny Darrow), all recorded by Danny Darrow on Mighty Records.

Tips: "Listen to top 40 and write current lyrics and music."

RONDOR MUSIC INTERNATIONAL, (formerly Rondor International Music Publishing), 360 N. La Cienega, Los Angeles CA 90048. (310)289-3500. Fax: (310)289-4000. Senior Vice President Creative: Brenda Andrews. Music publisher. Estab. 1965. Hires staff writers. Works with composers and lyricists. Royalty amount depends on deal.

Affiliate(s): Almo Music Corp. (ASCAP) and Irving Music, Inc. (BMI).

How to Contact: Submit demo tape by mail. Unsolicited submissions are OK. Prefers cassette with 3 songs and lyric sheet. "Send DATs if possible, discography if applicable." SASE. Reports in 3-6 weeks.

Music: A/C, R&B and **rock**. Published *Through Those Doors* (by Andrea Martin), recorded by Ce Ce Peniston on A&M Records (R&B); "Waiting," written and recorded by Peter Frampton on Relativity Records (rock/A/C)); and *Please God*, written and recorded by Ian Moore on Capricorn Records (rock).

Tips: "Give only your best, be original."

ROOTS MUSIC (BMI), Box 111, Sea Bright NJ 07760. President: Robert Bowden. Music publisher, record company (Nucleus Records) and record producer (Robert Bowden). Estab. 1979. Publishes 2 songs/year; publishes 1 new songwriter/year. Works with composers and lyricists; teams collaborators. Pays standard royalty.

How to Contact: Submit a demo tape by mail. Unsolicited submissions are OK. Prefers cassette (or VHS videocassette) with 3 songs and lyric sheet; include photo and bio. "I only want inspired songs written by talented writers." SASE. Reports in 1 month.

Music: Mostly **country** and **pop**; also **church/religious, classical, folk, MOR, progressive, rock** (soft, mellow) and **top 40**. Published "Always", "Selfish Heart" and "Hurtin' " (by Bowden), all recorded by Marco Sission on Nucleus Records (country).

ROSE HILL GROUP, 1326 Midland Ave., Syracuse NY 13205. (315)475-2936. A&R Director: V. Taft. Music publisher. Estab. 1979. Publishes 1-15 songs/year; publishes 1-5 new songwriters/year. Works with composers and lyricists; teams collaborators. Pays standard royalty.

Affiliate(s): Katch Nazar Music (ASCAP) and Bleecker Street Music (BMI).

How to Contact: Submit demo tape by mail. Unsolicited submissions are OK. Prefers cassette. "Please include typed lyric sheet. No promotional material please." SASE. Reports in 2-4 weeks.

Music: Mostly **pop/rock, pop/dance** and **contemporary country**. Published *Better Say Whatcha Mean* (by E. Jacobson), recorded by Io on StarCity Records (R&B); *Definitely In Love* (by Andrew George), recorded by Inside on Sunday Records (pop); and *We Belong Together* (by G. Davidian), recorded by Z-Team on Cherry Records (pop).

Tips: "Write concise, memorable melodies; strong, real stories."

STEVE ROSE MUSIC, #6K, 115 E. 34th St., New York NY 10016. (212)213-6100. Manager: Steve Rose. Pitches country only via Nashville co-publisher.

How to Contact: "Don't unless you've had an indie country cut. Send an unstapled, self-sealing fortified envelope with an unboxed cassette wrapped in lyric sheets. Two songs only please, up-tempo and positive preferred. You must include a SASE for return of lyric sheets. Reply ASAP."

Music: Country only. "Demo must pitch in Nashville against 5,000 others. 3:15 max, no solos needed on demos. Clean vocal mixed up."
Tips: "1) For every 500 serious writers one makes a living and she or he probably lives in Nashville. 2) Worse than no hook is a decent hook that is not set up in verse one and driven home in verse two and bridge with killer lyrics. 3) If you hear a throwaway song on radio it was probably written by the writer or producer; they've earned the right to coast. Your song must be thrice as good. 4) Do not pay money to go to expensive seminars that imply they'll open doors. Don't pay for demos unless a reliable publisher says he'll go to the wall for you, and does. Badger your performance rights agency if you have indie chart songs and they don't pay. 5) Keep your chin up."

*ROUGH TRADE PUBLISHING, 81 Wallingford Rd., Goring, Reading RG8 0HL **United Kingdom.** 011-44-491-873612. Fax: (011)44-491-873612. Director: Cathi Gibson. Music publisher. Estab. 1991. Publishes 80 songs/year; publishes 8 new songwriters/year. Works with composers and lyricists; teams collaborators. Pays 50-85% royalty depending on circumstances.
How to Contact: Submit demo tape by mail. Unsolicited submissions are OK. Prefers cassette. "Not more than 4 songs." SAE and IRC. Reports in 2 months.
Music: Mostly **indie, rock** and **pop.** Published "Marbles" (by Stuart Staples), recorded by Tindersticks on This Way Up Records (indie); "Pick Up Your Coat," written and recorded by Nicola Hitchcock on Demon Records (folk-rock); and "Happy Land" (by Robert Wyatt), recorded by Ultramarine on Blanco y Negro Records (dance).

ROYAL FLAIR PUBLISHING, Box 438, Walnut IA 51577. (712)366-1136. President: Bob Everhart. Music publisher and record producer. BMI. Estab. 1967. Publishes 5-10 songs/year; publishes 1-2 new songwriters/year. Works with composers and lyricists. Pays standard royalty.
How to Contact: Submit a demo tape by mail. Unsolicited submissions are OK. Prefers cassette with 2-6 songs. SASE. Reports in 9 months.
Music: **Traditional country, bluegrass** and **folk.** Published *Berlin Folksinger, Jack Darby* and *Fishpole John*, written and recorded by Bob Everhart on Prairie (country).
Tips: "Song definitely has to have old-time country flavor with all the traditional values of country music. No sex, outlandish swearing, or drugs-booze type songs accepted. We have an annual Hank Williams Songwriting Contest over Labor Day weekend and winners are granted publishing."

*RUSHWIN PUBLISHING (BMI), Box 1150-SM95, Buna TX 77612. (409)423-2521.Owner/General Manager: Larry Gibson. Music publisher. Estab. 1985. Works with composers and lyricists. Pays standard royalty.
How to Contact: Write first to get permission to submit a tape. "Include SASE with request for permission to submit." Does not return unsolicited material. Reports within 6 months.
Music: Southern gospel and **Christian country.**
Tips: "We are interested in the type material suited for the recording artist that appear in the music charts published by *The Gospel Voice* and *The Singing News*."

*RUSTRON MUSIC PUBLISHERS, 1156 Park Lane, West Palm Beach FL 33417-5957. (407)-686-1354. Professional Managers: Rusty Gordon, Ron Caruso and Davilyn Whims. Music publisher and record producer (Rustron Music Productions). ASCAP, BMI. Estab. 1974. Publishes 100-150 songs/year; publishes 10-20 new songwriters/year. Works with composers and lyricists; teams collaborators. Pays standard royalty.
Affiliate(s): Whimsong (ASCAP).
How to Contact: Submit a demo tape (cassette)—unsolicited submissions are OK. Prefers cassette with 1-3 songs and lyric or lead sheet. "Clearly label your tape and container. Include cover letter." SASE required for all correspondence. Reports in 2-4 months.
Music: Mostly **pop** (ballads, blues, theatrical, cabaret), **progressive country** and **folk/rock;** also **R&B** and **New Age** instrumentals. Published "City Song" (by Rusty Gordon and Ron Caruso), recorded by Jayne Margo-Reby on Rustron Records (rock/pop fusion); "When is Enough, Enough," written and recorded by Ellen Hines on Marcus Records (jazz/folk fusion); and "Moon Glow Motel" (by Vincent Meade), recorded by Boomslang on Road House Records (swamp music/folk fusion).
Tips: "Write strong hooks. Keep song length 3½ minutes or less. Avoid predictability—create original lyric themes. Tell a story. Compose definitive melody. Tune in to the trends and fusions indicative of the 90s."

*S & R MUSIC PUBLISHING CO. (ASCAP), 71906 Highway 111, Rancho Mirage CA 92270. (619)346-0075. CEO: Scott Seely. Music publisher. Estab. 1965. Publishes 25-50 songs/year; publishes 10-15 new songwriters/year. Hires staff songwriters. Works with composers and lyricists; teams collaborators. Pays standard royalty.

Affiliate(s): Boomerang Music, Meteor Music (BMI).
How to Contact: Submit demo tape by mail. Unsolicited submissions are OK. Prefers cassette with 4 songs and lyric sheet. SASE. Reports in 6 weeks.
Music: Mostly **pop-country**. Published *Hey Baby* (by Duke Dyches); *Sharin' Sharon* (by Alvie Self); and *Let's Make Love* (by Mike Williams), all recorded by The Duke on Accent Records.

*S.M.C.L. PRODUCTIONS, INC., P.O. Box 84, Boucherville, Quebec J4B 5E6 **Canada**. (514)641-2266. President: Christian Lefort. Music publisher and record company. CAPAC. Estab. 1968. Publishes 25 songs/year. Pays standard royalty.
Affiliate(s): A.Q.E.M. Ltee, Bag Enrg., C.F. Music, Big Bazaar Music, Sunrise Music, Stage One Music, L.M.S. Ltee, ITT Music, Machine Music, Dynamite Music, Danava Music, Coincidence Music, Music and Music, Cinemusic Inc., Cinafilm, Editions La Fete Inc., Groupe Concept Musique, Editions Dorimen, C.C.H. Music (PRO/SDE) and Lavagot Music.
How to Contact: Write first to get permission to submit a tape. Prefers cassette with 4-12 songs and lead sheet. SAE and IRC. Reports in 2-3 months.
Music: **Dance, easy listening, MOR, top 40/pop** and **TV and movie soundtracks**. Published *Always and Forever* (by Maurice Jarre/Nathalie Carien), recorded by N. Carsen on BMG Records (ballad); *Au Noy De La Passion*, written and recorded by Alex Stanke on Select Records; and many soundtracks of French-Canadian TV series like: Shadow of the Wolf (Maurice Jarre); The Breakthrough (Oswaldo Montes); Bethune (Alan Reeves); The First Circle (Gabriel Yared).

SABTECA MUSIC CO., Box 10286, Oakland CA 94610. (415)465-2805. A&R: Sean Herring. President: Duane Herring. Music publisher and record company (Sabteca Record Co., Andre-Romare). ASCAP, BMI. Estab. 1980. Publishes 8-10 songs/year; 1-2 new songwriters/year. Works with composers and lyricists; teams collaborators. Pays standard royalty.
Affiliate(s): Sabteca Publishing (ASCAP), Toyiabe Publishing (BMI).
How to Contact: Write first and obtain permission to submit a tape. Prefers cassette with 2 songs and lyric sheet. SASE. Reports in 3-4 weeks.
Music: Mostly **R&B, pop** and **country**. Published "I Just Ain't Right" (by Duane Herring), recorded by Johnny B. on Andre-Romare Records (country); "7 Days" by Walter Coleman (R&B); and "Lazy Day," by W. Coleman and Bill Charles (country).

SADDLESTONE PUBLISHING, 264 "H" St., Box 8110-21, Blaine WA 98230. Canada Address: 8821 Delwood Dr., Delta B.C., V4C 4A1 **Canada**. (604)582-7117. Fax: (604)582-8610. President: Rex Howard. Music publisher, record company (Saddlestone) and record producer (Silver Bow Productions). SOCAN, BMI. Estab. 1988. Publishes 100 songs/year; publishes 12-30 new songwriters/year. Hires staff writers. Works with composers and lyricists; teams collaborators. Pays standard royalty.
Affiliate(s): Silver Bow Publishing (SOCAN, ASCAP).
How to Contact: Submit a demo tape by mail. Unsolicited submissions are OK. Prefers cassette with 3 songs and lyric sheet. "Make sure vocal is clear." SASE. Reports in 6-8 weeks.
Music: Mostly **country, rock** and **pop**; also **gospel** and **R&B**. Published *Heart of the Workin' Man* (by K. Wilson, G. Murphy, D. Murphy, B. Rogers), recorded by Last Wild Sons on 9B South (rock); *Read Between the Lies* (by Frank Turner), recorded by Debbie Davis on Saber (country); and *Chicken Lady* (by Todd Butler), recorded by The Muppets on Jim Henson Records and BMG-Kidz.
Tips: "Submit clear demos, good hooks and avoid long intros or instrumentals. Have a good singer do vocals."

SAMUEL THREE PRODUCTIONS (BMI), 4056 Shady Valley Dr., Arlington TX 76013. (817)274-5530. President: Samuel Egnot. Music publisher and record company (Alpha Recording Co.). Estab. 1992. Publishes 12 songs/year; publishes 7 new songwriters/year. Works with composers and lyricists. Pays standard royalty.
How to Contact: Submit demo tape by mail. Unsolicited submissions are OK. Prefers cassette with lead sheet. SASE. Reports in 1 month.
Music: Mostly **country, country-gospel** and **gospel**; also **southern gospel**. Published "What Can I Do" (by Robert C.L. Fogle), recorded by Samuel 3 (gospel); "Havin' A Real Good Time," written and recorded by Samantha McLemore (country); and "Greatest Gift," written and recorded by Bea Egnot (gospel), all on Alpha Recording Label.

How to Get the Most Out of Songwriter's Market (at the front of this book) contains comments and suggestions to help you understand and use the information in these listings.

Tips: "Be aggressive in getting your demos out. Don't stop at one turndown, send to another and another till you feel it's going to receive recognition. If it's good to you, ask for perhaps another musical group to consider redoing your material."

TRACY SANDS MUSIC (BMI), Suite 119, 2166 W. Broadway, Anaheim CA 92804-2446. (714)992-2652. Vice President, A&R: Harold Shmoduquet. Music publisher, record company (Orange Records, Beet Records), record producer (Orange Productions). Estab. 1977. Publishes 12 songs/year; publishes 4 new songwriters/year. Pays standard royalty.
Affiliate(s): Lipstick Traces Music (BMI).
How to Contact: Submit a demo tape by mail. Unsolicited submissions are OK. Prefers cassette with 2-3 songs and lyric sheet. SASE. Reports in 2 months.
Music: All types. Published *Euradice*, written and recorded by Greg James on Beet Records; *Woman's World* (by Robert Wahlsteen), recorded by Jubal's Children on Swak Records; and *Big Noise from Mar Vista* (by T. Sands and C. Gacsi), recorded by Big Snow on Torchlite Records.
Tips: "We are mostly interested in 'sixties' themes: psychedelia, anti-establishment, etc., unsigned material from the era."

SARISER MUSIC (BMI), Box 211, Westfield MA 01086. (413)967-5395. Operations Manager: Alexis Steele. Music publisher and record company (Sweet Talk Records). Publishes 6-12 songs/year; publishes 1-2 new songwriters/year. Works with composers and lyricists; teams collaborators. Pays standard royalty.
How to Contact: Write first and obtain permission to submit. No calls. Prefers cassette or 7½ ips reel-to-reel with 3-4 songs and lyric or lead sheet. "Lyrics should be typed; clear vocal on demo." SASE. Reports in 6 weeks.
Music: Mostly **country/pop**, **country/rock** and **educational material**; also **soft rock** and **rockabilly**. "We're interested in 50s/60s style 4-part harmony." Published "One Last Kiss" (by Sparkie Allison), recorded by Moore Twinz on MMT Records (country); "Sweet Talk" and "Ride a Rainbow," written and recorded by Sparkie Allison and Ginny Cooper on Sweet Talk Records (country/pop).
Tips: "Lyrics must have positive message. No cheatin' songs. Be unique. Try something different."

WILLIAM A. SAULSBY MUSIC COMPANY, #4872, 311 W. Monroe St. Jacksonville FL 32202. Producer: Aubrey Saulsby. Estab. 1985. Publishes 8-10 songs/year. Pays standard royalty.
How to Contact: Write first and obtain permission to submit. Prefers cassette or 7½" reel and lyric sheet. Does not return unsolicited material.
Music: Mostly **R&B**, **rap** and **jazz**; also **blues**, **pop** and **top 40**. Published "Because You're Mine" and "Free" (by Willie A. Saulsby), recorded by William Icey; and "The Way That I Am" (by Willie A. Saulsby), recorded by Willie Bones, all on Hibi Dei Hipp Records.

SCI-FI MUSIC, P.O. Box 941, N.D.G., Montreal Quebec H4A 3S3 **Canada**. (514)487-8953. President: Gary Moffet (formerly guitarist/composer with April Wine). Music publisher. SOCAN. Estab. 1984. Publishes 10 songs/year; publishes 2 new songwriters/year. Works with composers; teams collaborators. Pays standard royalty.
How to Contact: Submit demo tape by mail. Unsolicited submissions OK. Submit cassette with 3-10 songs and lyric sheet. Does not return material. Reports in 1 month.
Music: Mostly **rock** and **pop**.

TIM SCOTT MUSIC GROUP, 96 St. James Ave., Springfield MA 01109. (413)746-8262. President: Timothy Scott. Music publisher. Estab. 1993. Publishes 20-50 songs/year; publishes 10 songwriters/year. Hires staff writers. Works with composers and lyricists; teams collaborators. Pays standard royalty.
Affiliate(s): Tim Scott Music (ASCAP).
How to Contact: Submit demo tape by mail. Unsolicited submissions are OK. Prefers cassette with 3-5 songs and lyric sheet. SASE. Reports in 2 months.
Music: Mostly **rap**, **R&B** and **pop**; also **country**, **rock** and **gospel**. Published "Faithful" and "Holding On" (by Johnnie Hatchett), recorded by Physical Attraction; and "Cable TV Is Just A Joke," written and recorded by Tim Scott, all on Nightowl Records.

SCRUTCHINGS MUSIC, 429 Homestead St., Akron OH 44306. (216)773-8529. Owner/President: Walter E.L. Scrutchings. Music publisher. BMI. Estab. 1980. Publishes 35 songs/year; publishes 10-20 new songwriters/year. Hires staff songwriters. Works with composers and lyricists; teams collaborators. Pays standard royalty. "Songwriters pay production costs of songs."
How to Contact: Submit a demo tape—unsolicited submissions are OK. Prefers cassette (or videocassette if available) with 2 songs, lyric and lead sheet. Does not return unsolicited material. Reports in 3-4 weeks.

Music: Mostly **gospel, contemporary** and **traditional**. Published "The Joy He Brings" (by R. Hinton), recorded by Akron City Mass; "God Has the Power" (by W. Scrutchings), recorded by Gospel Music Workshop Mass on Savoy Records (gospel); and "My Testimony" (by A. Cobb), recorded by Akron City Family Mass Choir on Scrutchings Music (gospel).
Tips: "Music must be clear and uplifting in message and music."

*SEA DREAM MUSIC, 236 Sebert Rd., Forest Gate, London E7 0NP **United Kingdom**. Phone: (081)534-8500. Senior Partner: Simon Law. PRS. Music publisher and record company (Plankton Records, Embryo Arts (Belgium), Gutta (Sweden), Wildtracks and Radio Records). Estab. 1976. Publishes 50 songs/year; publishes 2 new songwriters/year. Works with composers and lyricists; teams collaborators. Pays 66⅔% royalty.
Affiliate(s): Scarf Music Publishing, Really Free Music, Ernvik Musik (Sweden), Chain of Love Music, Crimson Flame.
How to Contact: Submit a demo tape—unsolicited submissions are OK. Prefers cassette with 3 songs and lyric sheet. "Technical information about the recording is useful, as are the songwriter's expectations of the company—i.e., what they want us to do for them." SAE and IRC. Reports in 6 weeks.
Music: Mostly **funk/rock, rock** and **blues**. Published *Bleeding for You* (by Simon Law), recorded by Fresh Claim (blues); *She Said*, written and recorded by Ben Okafar (reggae); and *Cocaine* (by Wray Powell), recorded by Out of Darkness (rock), all on Plankton Records.
Tips: "We are specifically interested in material with a Christian bias to the lyrics."

SEGAL'S PUBLICATIONS, 16 Grace Rd., Newton MA 02159. (617)969-6196. Contact: Charles Segal. Music publisher and record producer (Segal's Productions). BMI, SAMRO. Estab. 1963. Publishes 80 songs/year; publishes 6 new songwriters/year. Works with composers and lyricists. Pays standard royalty.
Affilates: Charles Segal's Publications (BMI). Charles Segal's Music (SESAC).
How to Contact: Write or call first and obtain permission to submit. Prefers cassette (or VHS videocassette) with 3 songs and lyric or lead sheet. Does not return unsolicited material. Reports in 4 months.
Music: Mostly **rock, pop** and **country;** also **R&B, MOR** and **children's songs**. Published "It's Cold Out There" (by Shelley Coburn) and "Eagle With A Broken Wing" (by Brilliant/Segal), both recorded by Rosemary Wills on Spin Records (country); and "What Is This Love" (by Pam/Chorn), recorded by Nick Chorn on AVS Records (ballad).
Tips: "Besides making a good demo cassette, include a lead sheet of music—words, melody line and chords."

SELLWOOD PUBLISHING, 170 N. Maple, Fresno CA 93702. (209)255-1717. Owner: Stan Anderson. Music publisher, record company (TRAC Record Co.) and record producer. BMI. Estab. 1972. Publishes 10 songs/year; publishes 3 new songwriters/year. Pays standard royalty.
How to Contact: Submit a demo tape—unsolicited submissions are OK. Prefers cassette (or VHS videocassette) with 2 songs and lyric sheet. SASE. Reports in 2 weeks.
Music: Mostly **traditional country** and **country rock**. Published "Whiskey Blues," "Dan" and "Night Time Places," all written by Jimmy Walker on TRAC Records.

*SEYCHELLES MUSIC, Box 13 01 44, Cologne 1 D-5000 **Germany**. (0221)97309014. Fax: (0221)97309021. Managing Director: Walther Kahl. Music publisher. GEMA. Estab. 1977. Publishes 40-50 songs/year; publishes 2-3 new songwriters/year. Pays standard royalty. Works with composers; teams collaborators.
How to Contact: Submit demo tape by mail. Unsolicited submissions are OK. Prefers cassette and lyric sheet. SAE and IRC. Reports in 1 month.
Music: **MOR, rock** and **country**. Published "Seas of Emotions" written and recorded by Prezman and Tomaszewski (classic pop); "Danson le Sega," written and recorded by Jocelyn Perreac, both on Seychelles Records; and "It All Started In Africa" (by Sonny Morgan).

SHADOWLAND PRODUCTIONS, 3 Lancet Court, Shawnee OK 74873. Music Editor: Russell Walker. Music publisher, record company and record producer. Estab. 1991. Publishes 48-60 songs/year; publishes 15-20 new songwriters/year. Works with composers and lyricists; teams collaborators. Pays standard royalty.

Listings of companies in countries other than the U.S. have the name of the country in boldface type.

Affiliate(s): Calvary's Shadow Publications, Morning Dew Publications, Shadowland Records.
How to Contact: Submit demo tape by mail. Unsolicited submissions are OK. Prefers cassette with 3 songs and lyric or lead sheet. "If lyrics are handwritten, make sure printed and legible with SASE on all submissions." SASE. Reports in 6-8 weeks.
Music: Mostly **southern gospel/spiritual, MOR, sacred, contemporary Christian**; also **choral anthems, children's songs** and **seasonal**. *The Man Called Jesus* (by Richards); *I Heard the Voice of Jesus Say* (by Stephens); and *I Can't Even Call My Soul My Own* (by Walker), all recorded by Shadowland Singers on Shadowland Records.
Tips: "We are a publisher of gospel and sacred music. We need material that specifically addresses a personal relationship with Christ, a born-again experience, the reality of God's presence, the depth of His love, a Christian's role in the world, etc. Almost any subject matter is appropriate if it is approached from a Christian perspective."

SHA-LA MUSIC, INC. (BMI), 137 Legion Place, Hillsdale NJ 07642. (201)664-1995. Fax: (201)664-1955. President: Robert Allen. Music publisher. Estab. 1987. Publishes 10-20 songs/year; publishes 1-4 new songwriters/year. Works with composers and lyricists. Pays standard royalty.
Affiliate(s): By The Numbers Music (ASCAP).
How to Contact: Submit demo tape by mail. Unsolicited submissions are OK. Prefers cassette with 3 songs and lyric sheet. "Keep package neat to make a good impression." SASE. Reports in 1-2 weeks.
Music: Mostly **R&B, pop, dance**; also **rock** and **A/C**. Published *Catch Me If You Can*, written and recorded by Jr. C on Fastland Records; and *Good Karma*, written and recorded by Monte Farber on Sconesville Music.
Tips: "Keep it simple and clean. Concentrate on quality."

SHANKMAN DE BLASIO MELINA, INC., #202, 2434 Main St. Santa Monica CA 90405. (310)399-7744. Fax: (310)399-2027. Contact: Laurent Besencon. Music publisher, personal management. Estab. 1979. Hires staff songwriters. Works with composers and lyricists; teams collaborators.
Affiliate(s): Playhard Music (ASCAP), Playfull Music (BMI).
How to Contact: Write or call first and obtain permission to submit. Prefers cassette (or VHS or Beta videocassette if available) with 3 songs and lyric sheet. SASE. Reports in 2 months.
Music: Mostly **contemporary hit songs: pop, R&B, dance, rock** and **ballads**. Published *Downtown* (by Gomez/Parker), recorded by SWV on BCA Records; *EYC* (by Lawson/Gomez), recorded by EYC on MCA Records; and *Sunday Morning* (by Reynolds), recorded by Earth, Wind & Fire on Warner Bros.
Tips: "Write hits!"

SHAOLIN MUSIC (ASCAP), P.O. Box 58547, Salt Lake City UT 84158. (801)595-1123. President: Richard O'Connor. Vice President, A&R: Michelle McCarty. Music publisher, record company (Shaolin Film and Records) and record producer (The Coyote). Estab. 1984. Pays standard royalty.
How to Contact: Prefers cassette with 3-4 songs and lyric sheet. Include bio and press kit. Does not return unsolicited material. Reports in 2 months.
Music: Mostly **rock, hard rock** and **pop**; also **soundtracks**. Published "Christ Killer," *Wishwood Bridge* and "Great Salt Lake," all written and recorded by The Coyote on Shaolin Film and Records.
Tips: "No matter how clever, cute, or pretty a song is, if it doesn't *mean something* or *create an emotion* it's just exercises."

SHU'BABY MONTEZ MUSIC (BMI), 1447 North 55th St., Philadelphia PA 19131. (215)473-5527. President: Leroy Schuler. Music publisher. Estab. 1986. Publishes 25 songs/year; publishes 15 new songwriters/year. Pays standard royalty.
How to Contact: Write first and obtain permission to submit. Prefers cassette with 3 songs and lyric sheet. SASE. Reports in 5 weeks.
Music: Mostly **R&B, pop** and **hip-hop**. Published "I Believe in Me" (by Lou Leggieri), recorded by Mark Chamberlin on Logic Records; "Secret Love Affair" (by Clint Washington/Shu'Baby), recorded by Ken Chaney; and "I Always Feel Lonely" (by Vinc Butler/Shu'Baby), recorded by Andre Procter on Logic Records.

SIEGEL MUSIC COMPANIES, 2 Hochlstr, 80 Munich 8000 **Germany**. Phone: 089-984926. Managing Director: Joachim Neubauer. Music publisher, record company, (Jupiter Records and 69-Records) and record producer. Estab. 1948. GEMA. Publishes 1,500 songs/year; publishes 50 new songwriters/year. Hires staff songwriters. Works with composers and lyricists. Pays 60% according to the rules of GEMA.
Affiliate(s): Ed. Meridian, Sound of Jupiter Ltd. (England), Sounds of Jupiter, Inc. (USA), Step Two (Austria), Step One (Holland), Step Four (France), Step Five (Brazil), Step Six (Scandinavia), Step Seven (Australia), Step Eight (Belgium) and Yellowbird (Switzerland). Gobian Music (ASCAP), Symphonie House Music (ASCAP).

How to Contact: Submit demo tape by mail. Unsolicited submissions are OK. Prefers cassette (or VHS videocassette, but not necessary). SAE and IRC. Reports in 6 weeks.
Music: Mostly **pop, disco** and **MOR**; also **"hard and heavy" rock, country** and **soul**. Published *Neon Cowboy* (by Siegel), recorded by the Bellamy Brothers on Jupiter Records (country); *Sadeness* (by Curly MC), recorded by Enigma on Virgin Records (dance pop); and "Nana" (by T. Stenzel), recorded by Nuke on LMV Records.

SILICON MUSIC PUBLISHING CO. (BMI), Ridgewood Park Estates, 222 Tulane St., Garland TX 75043. President: Gene Summers. Vice President: Deanna L. Summers. Public Relations: Steve Summers. Music publisher and record company (Domino Records, Ltd. and Front Row Records). Estab. 1965. Publishes 10-20 songs/year; publishes 2-3 new songwriters/year. Pays standard royalty.
How to Contact: Prefers cassette with 1-2 songs. Does not return unsolicited material. "We are usually slow in answering due to overseas tours."
Music: Mostly **rockabilly** and **50's material**; also **old-time blues/country** and **MOR**. Published "Black on Saturday Night" and "Ballad of Jerry Lee" (by Joe Hardin Brown), both unreleased; and "Domino" (by James McClung & Dea Summers), recorded by Gene Summers on Domino Records.
Tips: "We are very interested in 50s rock and rockabilly *original masters* for release through overseas affiliates. If you are the owner of any 50s masters, contact us first! We have releases in Holland, Switzerland, England, Belgium, France, Sweden, Norway and Australia. We have the market if you have the tapes! Sample recordings available! Send SASE for catalogue."

*SILVER BLUE MUSIC/OCEANS BLUE MUSIC, 5370 Vanalden Ave., Tarzana CA 91356. (818)345-2558. Music publisher. Estab. 1971. Publishes 25 songs/year. Teams collaborators. Pays standard royalty.
How to Contact: Submit demo tape by mail. Unsolicited submissions are OK. Prefers cassette with lead sheet. Does not return unsolicited submissions.
Music: Mostly **pop** and **R&B**; also **rap**. Published "After the Lovin" (by Bernstead/Adams), recorded by Englebert Humperdinck.

*SILVER THORN ENTERPRISES, P.O. Box 196, Panguitch UT 84759. (801)676-8055. President/Owner: John Burdick. Music publisher, record company (Jodi-Con Records, Silverthorn Records), record producer. Estab. 1981. Publishes 15-25 songs/year; publishes 5 new songwriters/year. Works with composers and lyricists; teams collaborators. Pays standard royalty.
Affiliate(s): Wild River Music (ASCAP), Luvus Music (BMI).
How to Contact: Submit demo tape by mail. Unsolicited submissions are OK. Prefers cassette or VHS videocassette with 2 songs and lyric sheet. "No phone calls." SASE. Reports in 1 month.
Music: Mostly **country, country-rock** and **folk**. Published *The Cowboy's Growin' Old* (by G. Davis/J. Burdick) and *The Angel Brought the Devil Down* (by McCormick, Burdick, Hepworth), both recorded by Gale Davis; and *Mary Hold Me*, written and recorded by Jerri Ashurst/Chris McCormick (country), all on Silver Thorn Records.
Tips: "Tune your guitar. Use quality tape and don't overload the demo with too many background effects (reverb, distortion, etc.)."

SILVER THUNDER MUSIC GROUP, P.O. Box 41335, Nashville TN 37204. (615)391-5035. President: Rusty Budde. Music publisher, record producer (Rusty Budde Productions). Estab. 1985. Publishes 200 songs/year. Publishes 5-10 new songwriters/year. Hires staff songwriters. Works with composers and lyricists. Pays standard royalty.
How to Contact: Write to obtain permission to submit. Prefers cassette (or VHS videocassette if available). Does not return material.
Music: Mostly **country, pop** and **R&B**. Published *Rock N Cowboys*, written and recorded by Jeff Chunn on NA Records; *This Ain't the Real Thing* (by Rusty Budde), recorded by Les Taylor on CBS Records; and "Feel Again" (by Rusty Budde), recorded by Keli Derring on S.T.R. Records.
Tips: "Send clear clean recording on cassette with lyric sheets."

SILVERFOOT PUBLISHING, 4225 Palm St., Baton Rouge LA 70808. (504)383-7885. President: Barrie Edgar. BMI. Music publisher, record company and record producer (Hogar Musical Productions). Estab. 1977. Publishes 20-30 songs/year; publishes 8-20 new songwriters/year. Pays standard royalty.
How to Contact: Submit a demo tape—unsolicited submissions are OK. Prefers cassette with maximum 4 songs and lyric sheet. SASE. "Patience required on reporting time." Reports in 6 months or sooner.
Music: Mostly **rock, pop, blues** ("not soul") and **country**. Published "Come Home" (by B. Meade/V. Trippe); "Hopeless Romantic" (by David Ellis); and "Rico & Lila" (by Dennis Ferado).

*SILVERHILL MUSIC (BMI), P.O. Box 39439, Los Angeles CA 90039. (213)663-8073. Fax: (213)669-1470. A&R: Diana Collette. Music publisher and record company. Estab. 1975. Pays standard royalty "in most cases."
Affiliate(s): Silver Ridge Music (ASCAP), Dwell Music (BMI), Roughage Music (BMI).
How to Contact: Submit demo tape by mail. Unsolicited submissions are OK. Prefers cassette. Does not return material. Reports in 2 months.
Music: Mostly **country, bluegrass** and **children's**; also **alternative** and **death metal**. Published *Melting Point*, written and recorded by Eddie Adcock on CMH Records (folk); *Gonna Get There Soon* (by M. Adcock) and *Champagne Break*, written and recorded by Eddie Adcock, both on Sugar Hill Records (country).

*SILVERSCAPES MUSIC, Suite 100-497, 22821 Lake Forest Blvd., Lake Forest CA 92630. (714)472-2257. Owner: John Salat. Music publisher and record company. Estab. 1992. Publishes 18 songs/year; publishes 1 new songwriter/year. Works with composers only. Pays standard royalty.
How to Contact: Write or call first and obtain permission to submit. Prefers cassette or DAT. Does not return material.
Music: Mostly **New Age, NAC/world** and **world fusion**. Published *Eratic, Silverdrops* and *Satin Dreams*, all written by John Salat on Silverscapes Records (New Age).

SIMPLY GRAND MUSIC, INC., P.O. Box 41981, Memphis TN 38174-1981. (901)272-7039. President: Linda Lucchesi. Music publisher. ASCAP, BMI. Estab. 1965. Works with composers and lyricists; teams collaborators. Pays standard royalty.
Affiliate(s): Memphis Town Music, Inc. (ASCAP) and Beckie Publishing Co. (BMI).
How to Contact: Write or call first to get permission to submit a tape. Prefers cassette with 1-3 songs and lyric sheet. SASE. Reports in 6 weeks.
Music: Mostly **pop** and **soul**; also **country** and **soft rock**.
Tips: "We are the publishing home of 'Wooly Bully'."

*SINCERITY, LTD., #4, 1358 Jefferson Ave., Redwood City CA 94062. A&R Director: Thom J. Wood. Evaluator: T. Reed. Music publisher. Estab. 1962. Publishes 10 songs/year. Teams collaborators. Pays standard royalty "initially, depending on talent and sales."
How to Contact: Submit demo tape by mail. Unsolicited submissions are OK. Prefers cassette with 2-6 songs. "Print clearly on cassette: name, address, phone number. Send in a legal size security type envelope (no case), seal well. We file good songs." Reports in 6-8 weeks if interested. Does not return material. "No certified or registered mail accepted!"
Music: Pop, pop/country, **light country, light R&B, blues, melodic (hard/soft) rock, MOR,** and **film background** (w/lyrics). No heavy metal or rap! Published "How Many Trees Make A Forest," "Everyone Knows But You" and "Measure of Love," all written and recorded by Tommy Reed and T. Wood.
Tips: "Send a clean tape and lyric sheets. Print clearly. Send only 2-6 songs. Originals only, any variety stated. Accept critiques—don't give up."

SINGING ROADIE MUSIC GROUP, 1050 Leatherwood Rd., White Bluff TN 37187-5300. (615)952-5190. General Manager: Garth Shaw. Music publisher, member CMA, BMI, ASCAP. Estab. 1984. Publishes 3-10 songs/year; publishes 1-3 new songwriters/year. Pays standard royalty.
Affiliate(s): Singing Roadie Music (ASCAP), Helioplane Music (BMI).
How to Contact: Submit a demo tape by mail. Unsolicited submissions are OK. No calls, please. Prefers cassette with 1-3 songs and lyric sheets. SASE. Reports in 1 month.
Music: **Country**, all styles, from traditional to contemporary. Co-published "She Was Wrong" (by Rod Stone/Terri Lynn Weaver), recorded by Terri Lynn on Intersound Records; "She Wins" (by Cobey Pitcher/Al Goll), recorded by Ronna Reeves on Mercury Records; and "Bed of Roses" (by Rex Benson, Steve Gillette), recorded by Kenny Rogers on Reprise Records.
Tips: "If you're a great writer and a terrible singer, find a great demo singer!"

SISKATUNE MUSIC PUBLISHING CO., 285 Chestnut St., West Hempstead NY 11552. (516)489-0738. Fax: (516)565-9425. President: Mike Siskind. Vice President Creative Affairs: Rick Olarsch. Music publisher. Estab. 1981. Publishes 20 songs/year; publishes 10 new songwriters/year. Pays standard royalty.
How to Contact: Prefers cassette with a maximum of 3 songs and lyric sheet. "Send any and all pertinent information." SASE. Reports in 2-3 months.
Music: **R&B, country; dance** and **ballads**. Published *Take It Easy* (by John C. Thomas); *Lonely* (by David Holland/Georgi Smith), recorded by Georgi Smith on Red Hand Records; and *Try And Forget Me* (by Jack Bono).
Tips: "Please be extremely selective with what you send."

SIZEMORE MUSIC (BMI), P.O. Box 23275, Nashville TN 37202. (615)385-1662. Fax: (904)799-9958. Contact: Gary Sizemore. Music publisher, record company (The Gas Co.) and record producer (Gary Sizemore). Estab. 1960. Publishes 5 songs/year; 1 new songwriter/year. Works with composers and lyricists; teams collaborators. Pays standard royalty.
How to Contact: Submit a demo tape by mail. Unsolicited submissions are OK. Prefers cassette (or VHS videocassette) with lyric sheets. SASE.
Music: Mostly **soul** and **R&B**; also **blues**, **pop** and **country**. Published "Liquor and Wine" and "The Wind," written and recorded by K. Shackleford on Heart Records (country); and "She's Tuff" (by Jerry McCain), recorded by The Fabulous Thunderbirds on Chrysalis Records (blues).

*SKY-CHILD MUSIC (BMI), 643 72nd St., Niagara Falls NY 14304. (716)283-1750. General Manager: Jack Williams. President: Alvin Dahn. Music publisher. Estab. 1976. Publishes 60-100 songs/year; publishes 6-10 new songwriters/year. Works with composers and lyricists. Pays standard royalty.
How to Contact: Write first and obtain permission to submit. Prefers cassette (or VHS videocassette) with 3-6 songs and lyric sheet and lead sheet. Does not return material. Reports in 4-6 weeks.
Music: Mostly **pop/rock, rock, country**; also **blues, novelty** and **classical**. Published "Once In A While" (by Wayne Cozad), recorded by At Large on Squire Records (rock); "Big Time Sally," written and recorded by Sam Domicolo on Pontiac Records (pop); "404" (by Alvin Dahn/Burt Fairchild), recorded by Alvin Dahn on Sky-Child Records (country/rock).
Tips: "Be sure your song is well developed and submitted in a professional manner with a full press kit (if possible)."

*SLAVIA PUBLISHING, Heilsborre 28, Asse 1730 **Belgium**. (322)452-4629. Fax: (322)452-2507. General Manager: Sergio Popovski. Music publisher, record company and record producer. Estab. 1980. Publishes 10 songs/year; publishes 2-6 new songwriters/year. Works with composers and lyricists; teams collaborators. Pays standard royalty.
How to Contact: Write first to arrange personal interview, or submit demo tape by mail. Unsolicited submissions are OK. Prefers cassette (or VHS videocassette if available) with 1 song. Does not return material. Reports in 1 month.
Music: Mostly **pop, pop/rock** and **pop/folk**. Published *Zingarella* (by D. Novkovic), recorded by E. Macias on Trella Records (pop); *Ia Ma Zuri Dimo* (by K. Buradiiev), recorded by Magical Voices From Bulgaria on Univerce Records (folk); and *C'est La Vie* (by A. Kossev), recorded by Liliane S'Pierre on Slavia Productions (pop).

*SLEEPING GIANT MUSIC INTERNATIONAL LTD., 34 Great James St., London WCIN 3HB **United Kingdom**. (071)405-3786. Fax: (071)405-5245. A&R Director: Ian Taylor King. Music publisher, record company and record producer. Works with composers and lyricists. Teams collaborators. Pays varying royalty.
How to Contact: Submit demo tape by mail. Unsolicited submissions are OK. Prefers cassette (or VHS videocassette if available) with 4 songs and lyric sheet. SAE and IRC.
Music: All types. Published "World Is So Small," recorded by Francesco Bruno and Richie Havens; "Till the Next Somewhere," recorded by Dee Bridgewater and Ray Charles; and "Shades," recorded by George Williams, all on Prestige Records Ltd.

SOCIETE D'EDITIONS MUSICALES ET ARTISTIQUES "ESPERANCE", 85 Rue Fondary, Paris 75015 **France**. Phone: (1) 45 77 30 34. Manager: Marcel Perse. Music publisher and record company (Societe Sonodisc). SACEM/SDRM. Estab. 1972. Publishes 50 songs/year; 20 new songwriters/year. Pays negotiable rates.
How to Contact: Submit a demo tape, unsolicited submissions are OK. Prefers cassette (or VHS videocassette). Does not return unsolicited material. Reports in 2-3 weeks.
Music: African, West Indian, Arabian and **salsa music**. Published "Exile" (by Ina Cesaire) and "Les Années Folles" (by Roland Brival), both recorded by Ralph Tamar on GD Production (West India); and "Diniya," written and recorded by Kante Manfila on Esperance (African).
Tips: "See that the style of your songs fits in with the music we distribute."

SONG CELLAR, 1024 16th Ave. South, Nashville TN 37212. (615)256-7507. Owner: Jack Cook. Music publisher, record producer, song production service. Estab. 1984.
Affiliate(s): Song Cellar Music (ASCAP), Juke Music (BMI), Cook In Music (SESAC).
How to Contact: Write first and obtain permission to submit. Prefers cassette with 1-3 songs and lyric sheet. Does not return material. Reports in 6 weeks.
Music: Mostly **rock/country, R&B/country** and **pop/country**; also **gospel/country** and **gospel/rock, gospel/pop.**
Tips: "Send a good, well arranged, well performed song on a good, clean cassette."

SONG FARM MUSIC (BMI), P.O. Box 24561, Nashville TN 37202. (615)742-1557. President: Tom Pallardy. Music publisher and record producer (T.P. Productions). Member NSAI. Estab. 1980. Publishes 2-5 songs/year; publishes 1-2 new songwriters/year. Pays standard royalty.
How to Contact: Call first and obtain permission to submit. Prefers cassette with maximum 2 songs and lyric or lead sheet. SASE required with enough postage for return of all materials. Reports in 4-6 weeks.
Music: Mostly **country, R&B** and **pop**; also **crossover** and **top 40**. Published "Mississippi River Rat" (by J. Hall, R. Hall, E. Dickey), recorded by Tom Powers on Fountain Records (Cajun country); "Today's Just Not the Day" (by J. Bell, E. Bobbitt), recorded by Liz Draper (country); and "In Mama's Time" (by T. Crone), recorded by Pat Tucker on Radioactive Records (country/pop).
Tips: "Material should be submitted neatly and professionally with as good quality demo as possible. Songs need not be elaborately produced (voice and guitar/piano are fine) but they should be clear. Songs must be well constructed, lyrically tight, good strong hook, interesting melody, easily remembered; i.e., commercial!"

SONG WIZARD MUSIC (ASCAP), P.O. Box 931029, Los Angeles CA 90093. (213)461-8848. Fax: (213)461-0936. Owner: Dave Kinnoin. Music publisher, record company and record producer. Estab. 1987. Publishes 12 songs/year; publishes 2 new songwriters/year. Works with composers and lyricists; teams collaborators. "We use Songwriters Guild of America contracts."
How to Contact: Submit demo tape by mail. Unsolicited submissions are OK. Prefers cassette with 3 songs and lyric sheet. SASE. Reports in 2 months.
Music: Mostly **children's**. Published *Good Friends Like Mine* (by Kinnoin/Hammer); *Children of the World* and *Dunce Cap Kelly*, (by Kinnoin), all recorded by Dave Kinnoin on Song Wizard Records.
Tips: "We like fresh, pure rhymes that tell a funny or touching story."

SONGFINDER MUSIC (ASCAP), 4 Reina Lane, Valley Cottage NY 10989. (914)268-7711. Owner: Frank Longo. Music publisher. Estab. 1987. Publishes 20 songs/year; publishes 5-10 new songwriters/year. Works with composers; teams collaborators. Pays standard royalty.
Affiliate(s): Spring Rose Music (BMI).
How to Contact: Submit a demo tape by mail. Unsolicited submissions are OK. Prefers cassette with 2 songs and lyric sheets. SASE. "No SASE—no returns." Reports in 4 weeks.
Music: Mostly **MOR, top 40/pop, soft rock, country/pop** and **uptempo country**. Published *Little White Slippers* (by F. Longo/Jay Gotney), recorded by J. D'Alessandro on Philz Records (Christmas); "You Make it Magic," written and recorded by J. Capplan on Caprice Records (country); and "Livin' On Hopes," by G. Pieper (country).
Tips: "Listen to what's being played on the radio. Be professional. Good demos get good results. Up tempo positive lyrics are always wanted. Success needs no apology—failure provides no alibi."

SONGRITE CREATIONS PRODUCTIONS (BMI), 692 S.E. Port St. Lucie Blvd., Port St. Lucie FL 34984. President: Judy Welden. Music publisher, record company and recording artist. Estab. 1990. Publishes 50 songs/year; publishes 12 new songwriters/year. Works with composers and lyricists; teams collaborators. Pays standard royalty.
Affiliate(s): Sine Qua Non Music (ASCAP).
How to Contact: Submit demo tape by mail. Unsolicited submissions are OK. "Send only your best one or two unpublished songs (with bio, press, number of songs written, releases, awards, etc.)." Prefers cassette (or videocassette) with 2-3 songs (2 each style) and lyric sheet. SASE. Reports in 6 weeks.
Music: Mostly **contemporary country, pop (AC)** and **gospel**; also **R&B, blues** and **novelty**. Published *Woman Of The 90's* (by Judy Welden, Tina Billias & Tom Little); "Hurry Up Sunrise" (by Judy Welden & Tina Billias), recorded by Judy Welden; and "His Music Is Alive" (by Tom Littleby, Judy Welden), recorded by Tony Diamond all on Treasure Coast Records.
Tips: "Demo tapes must be well-produced and current sounding. Be prepared for a re-write if lyrics are not conversational and in the best possible meter. Believe in yourself and your talent and you will not get discouraged easily!"

SOUL STREET MUSIC PUBLISHING INC. (ASCAP), 265 Main St., East Rutherford NJ 07073. (201)933-0676. President: Glenn La Russo. Music publisher. Estab. 1988. Publishes 20 songs/year; publishes 5 new songwriters/year. Works with composers. Pays standard royalty.
How to Contact: Submit a demo tape by mail. Unsolicited submissions are OK. Prefers cassette with 3 songs and lyric sheet. SASE. Reports in 2 months.
Music: Only **R&B, dance** and **rap**. Published "Touch Me" (by Carmichael), recorded by Cathy Dennis on Polydor Records (dance); "Symptoms of True Love" (by Harman/Weber), recorded by Tracie Spencer on Capitol Records (R&B); and "Thinking About Your Love," written and recorded by Skipworth and Turner on Island Records (R&B).

SOUND ACHIEVEMENT GROUP, P.O. Box 24625, Nashville TN 37202. (615)883-2600. President: Royce B. Gray. Music publisher. BMI, ASCAP. Estab. 1985. Publishes 120 songs/year; publishes 4 new songwriters/year. Works with composers and lyricists; teams collaborators. Pays standard royalty.
Affiliate(s): Song Palace Music (ASCAP) and Emerald Stream Music (BMI).
How to Contact: Submit a demo tape—unsolicited submissions are OK. Prefers cassette (or VHS videocassette if available) with 3 songs and lyric sheet. SASE. Reports in 3 months.
Music: Gospel. Published "You Are" (by Penny Strandberg Miller), recorded by Revelations on New Wind Records (gospel); "I Want My Life To Count," written and recorded by Sammy Lee Johnson on Image Records (gospel); and "The Wonder of Christmas" (by Giorgio Longdo/John Ganes), recorded by Giorgio Longdo on Candle Records (gospel).

SOUND CELLAR MUSIC, 116 N. Peoria, Dixon IL 61021. (815)288-2900. Music publisher, record company, record producer, recording studio. Estab. 1987. Publishes 15-25 songs/year. Publishes 5 or 6 new songwriters/year. Works with composers. Pays standard royalty. "No charge obviously for publishing, but if we record the artist there is a small reduced fee for rental of our studio."
How to Contact: Submit demo tape by mail. Unsolicited submissions are OK. Prefers cassette with 3 or 4 songs and lyric sheet. Does not return material. Reports in 1 month.
Music: Mostly **metal**, **country** and **rock**; also **pop**, **rap** and **blues**. Published *Windows of Pain*, written and recorded by Manic Oppression (metal); *Frolicking in the Autumn Mist*, written and recorded by Decadenza (metal); and *Break the Mold*, written and recorded by Concussion (thrash), all on Cellar Records.
Tips: "Don't worry about the style of your music. We want people who write songs from the heart. We are not concerned with music styles, just good music."

SOUND COLUMN PUBLICATIONS, Country Manor, 812 S. 890 East, Orem UT 84058. (801)225-9975. President/General Manager: Ron Simpson. Professional Manager: Kim J. Simpson. Music publisher, record company (SCP Records) and record producer (Sound Column Productions). BMI, ASCAP. Member CMA, AFM, NAS. Estab. 1968. Publishes 20 songs/year; publishes 2-3 new songwriters/year. Hires staff writers. Listens to complete songs only. Pays standard royalty.
Affiliate(s): Ronarte Publications (ASCAP), Mountain Green Music (BMI), Macanudo Music (BMI).
How to Contact: Submit demo tape (3 songs max) with lyric sheet. "We listen to everything, but with the recent volume of submissions, we do get behind. Be patient—you *will* hear from us, and you'll receive specific feedback. Please honor our request for no phone calls." SASE. Reports as time permits.
Music: Mostly **country**. Published "Norma Jean Riley" (by Rob Honey), recorded by Diamond Rio on Arista Records; "Dream with Your Name on It" (by Tom Lerners); and "Grandma's Garden" (by Gary and Robin Earl).
Tips: "We maintain a very small catalog, accepting just a few songs a year from outside writers, but work hard for the songs we sign. We always need strong material suitable for pitching to the mainline country artists. Submissions in general are getting better and better. Thanks in advance, writers, for giving us a chance to hear your work."

SOUNDS OF AICRAM (BMI), (formerly Super Rapp Publishing), Demo mailing: 9305 Dogwood Place, Gainesville GA 30506. (706)861-2186. Main office: #204, 23 Music Sq. East, Nashville TN 37203; (615)726-2571. President: Ron Dennis Wheeler. Music publisher. Estab. 1964. Publishes 100 songs/year; 20-25 new songwriters/year. "Sometimes hires staff writers for special projects." Pays standard royalty.
Affiliate(s): Do It Now Publishing (ASCAP), RR&R Music (BMI).
How to Contact: "Send a demo tape/professionally recorded—if not, response time may be delayed. If you need a tape produced or song developed, contact RR&R Music Inc. first before submitting a badly produced tape. Unsolicited submissions are OK. Send music trax with and without lead vocals. Lyric sheet and chords. Also send music score if possible. Prefers 15 ips and a cassette copy or DAT. Clarity is most important. SASE is a must if you want submission returned. Responds only if interested."
Music: Gospel, **rock** and **pop**; also **country** and **R&B**. "No New Age." Published "I Need You" (by Richard McGibony), co-published by EMI; "Reason," written and recorded by Richard McGibony; and "Two Shades of Blue" (by R. McGibony/R.D. Wheeler), recorded by Bill Scarbrough on Legends Records.

SOUNDS-VISION MUSIC, P.O. Box 3691, La Mesa CA 91944-3691. (800)447-1132. Fax: (800)447-1132. Owner: Rod Hollman. Music publisher, record company, record producer and distributor. Estab. 1986. Publishes 30 songs/year. Publishes 3-4 new songwriters/year. Works with composers and lyricists. "Royalty amount varies per contract."

Affiliate(s): Xpresh'N Series Music (BMI).
How to Contact: Submit demo tape by mail. Unsolicited submissions are OK. Prefers cassette with 1-5 songs. Does not return material. Reports in 1 month.
Music: Mostly **flamenco, gypsy music, international**; also **classical guitar**. Published *Poder Gitano*, written and recorded by Rodrigo; *Bullerias Trio* (by Rodrigo), recorded by La Familia Flores; and *Cansada de Querer*, written and recorded by Fernanda Romero, all on Sounds-Vision Records.

SOUTHERN MOST PUBLISHING COMPANY (BMI), P.O. Box 97, Climax Springs MO 65324. (314)374-1111. President/Owner: Dann E. Haworth. Music publisher, record producer (Haworth Productions), engineer. Estab. 1985. Publishes 10 songs/year; 3 new songwriters/year. Hires staff songwriters. Works with composers and lyricists; teams collaborators. Pays standard royalty.
Affiliate(s): Boca Chi Key Publishing (ASCAP).
How to Contact: Submit demo tape by mail. Unsolicited submissions are OK. Prefers cassette with 3 songs and lyric sheet. SASE. Reports in 6 weeks.
Music: Mostly **rock, R&B** and **country**; also **gospel** and **New Age**.
Tips: "Keep it simple and from the heart."

*THE SPACEK CO., P.O. Box 741506, Dallas TX 75374. (903)882-1375. President: Ed Spacek. Music publisher. Estab. 1978.
Affiliate(s): Woodcreek (ASCAP), Eagles Nest (BMI).
How to Contact: Write first and obtain permission to submit. Prefers cassette.
Music: All types.

SPHEMUSATIONS, 12 Northfield Rd., Onehouse, Stowmarket Suffolk 1P14 3HR **England**. Phone: 0449-613388. General Manager: James Butt. Music publisher. Estab. 1963. Publishes 200 songs/year; publishes 6 new songwriters/year. Works with lyricists; teams collaborators. Pays standard royalty.
How to Contact: Submit demo tape by mail. Unsolicited submissions are OK. Prefers cassette (or VHS or Beta videocassette). SAE and IRC. Reports in 3 months.
Music: Mostly **country, blues** and **jazz**, also **"serious modern music."** Published "Satyr's Song" and "The Weeper" (by J. Playford, J. Butt); and "O. Moon" (by J. Keats, J. Butt), all on Sphemusations Records.
Tips: "Present yourself with a good sense of style."

SPINWILLY MUSIC PUBLISHING, 214 State Rd., Media PA 19063. (215)565-5099. Director A&R: Rick Smith. Music publisher, record company (Radio Records, Stardiner Records). Estab. 1987. Publishes 5 songs/year. Works with composers and lyricists. Pays standard royalty.
How to Contact: Write first and obtain permission to submit. "No calls please." Prefers cassette with 3 songs and lyric sheet. Does not return material. Reports in 2 months.
Music: Published "Human Condition" and "Can't Have Me" (by D'Anjolell), recorded by Almighty Shuhorn on Radio Records (pop); and *Sally* (by D'Anjolell/Fisher), recorded by Droopy Sperm on Medical Records (rock).

SPRADLIN/GLEICH PUBLISHING (BMI), 3010 16th St., Phoenix AZ 85016. Manager: Lee Gleich. Music publisher. Estab. 1988. Publishes 4-10 songs/year; 2-4 new songwriters. Works with composers and lyricists. Pays standard royalty.
Affiliate(s): Paul Lee Publishing (ASCAP).
How to Contact: Write first to arrange personal interview. Prefers cassette with 3 songs and lyric or lead sheet. "It must be very good material, as I only have time for promoting songwriters who really care." Does not return unsolicited material. Reports in 3 weeks.
Music: Mostly **country** geared to the US and European country markets. Published *First Try Love* (by Paul Spradlin), recorded by Goosecreek on Apple Records (country).
Tips: "Send me a request letter, then send me your best song. If it is a quality song that will create interest by us for more material. We are now publishing mostly all country and rockabilly!"

*STABLE MUSIC CO. (BMI), 6503 Wolf Creek Pass, Austin TX 78749. (512)288-3370. Fax: (512)288-1926. Owner: Rex T. Sherry. Music publisher, record company (Thoroughbred Records) and record producer. Estab. 1967. Publishes 5-10 songs/year. Works with composers and lyricists; teams collaborators. Pays standard royalty.
How to Contact: Write first and obtain permission to submit. Prefers cassette with 2-4 songs and lyric sheet. SASE. Reports in 3 weeks.
Music: Mostly **country**; also **bluegrass**.
Tips: "Write material with a particular artist in mind."

*STAR SONG COMMUNICATIONS, 2325 Crestmoor Rd., Nashville TN 37215. Music publisher, record company. Estab. 1974. Publishes 50 songs/year; 2 new songwriters/year. Hires staff songwriters. Works with composers and lyricists; teams collaborators.
Affiliate(s): Ariose Music (ASCAP), Shepherd's Fold Music (BMI) and Dawn Treader Music (SESAC).
How to Contact: Submit demo tape by mail. Unsolicited submissions are OK. "No phone calls please. We call back if interested."
Music: Published "Favorite Song of All" (by Dan Dean), recorded by Phillips Craig & Dean; "Destiny," written and recorded by Twila Paris; and "Inside Out" (by David Meece), recorded by Dwight Liles/D. Meece, all on StarSong Records.
Tips: "Come to Nashville and get involved in the community with our and other songwriters."

STARBOUND PUBLISHING CO. (BMI), Dept. SM, 207 Winding Rd., Friendswood TX 77546. (713)482-2346. President: Buz Hart. Music publisher, record company (Juke Box Records, Quasar Records and Eden Records) and record producer (Lonnie Wright and Buz Hart). Estab. 1970. Publishes 35-100 songs/year; publishes 5-10 new songwriters/year. Works with composers and lyricists; teams collaborators. Pays standard royalty.
How to Contact: Submit demo tape by mail. Unsolicited submissions are OK. Prefers cassette with 3 songs and lyric sheet. SASE. Reports in 3 months.
Music: Mostly **country**, **R&B** and **gospel**. Published "Butterfly" (by Pamela Parkins/Buz Hart), recorded by Frankie Laine on Score Records; "Let it Slide" (by James Watson/Buz Hart), recorded by Stan Steel on Gallery II Records; and "Country Boy's Dream" (by Gene Thomas/Buz Hart), recorded by Charlie Louvin, Waylon Jennings, and George Jones on Playback Records.

*STATE 51 PUBLISHING INC. (BMI), P.O. Box 465, Coram NY 11727. (516)732-6672. Fax: (516)732-7125. President: Michael Ugarte. Music publisher, record company (Horizon Records), record producer and CD and cassette duplication. Estab. 1991. Publishes 12 songs/year; publishes 5 new songwriters/year. Works with composers. Pays standard royalty.
How to Contact: Submit demo tape by mail. Unsolicited submissions are OK. Prefers cassette with lyric sheet. "Be sure all pertinent info is on cassette." SASE. Reports in 1 month.
Music: Mostly **R&B**, **pop** and **dance**; also **Latin ballads**.

STELLAR MUSIC INDUSTRIES, P.O. Box 30166, Memphis TN 38130-0166. (901)458-2472. Fax: (901)458-2476. Vice President: S.D. Burks. Music publisher. Estab. 1977. Publishes 100 songs/year; publishes 3-5 new songwriters/year. Hires staff writers. Pays standard royalty.
Affiliate(s): Rodanca Music (ASCAP) and Bianca Music (BMI).
How to Contact: Submit demo tape by mail. Unsolicited submissions are OK. Prefers cassette (or VHS videocassette) with 4-6 songs and lyric sheet. SASE. Reports in 6 weeks.
Music: Mostly **R&B**, **country** and **blues**; also **rap** and **rock**. Published *Your Love* (by Laurna Moore), recorded by Lauralea (country); *Many Miles*, written and recorded by Lauralea (country); and *Time Ain't Healed The Pain* (by Beach/S. Adams), recorded by Ruby Andrews (soul), all on Goldwax Records.

JEB STUART MUSIC CO. (BMI), Box 6032, Station B, Miami FL 33123. (305)547-1424. President: Jeb Stuart. Music publisher, record producer and management firm. Estab. 1975. Publishes 4-6 songs/year. Teams collaborators. Pays standard royalty.
How to Contact: Submit a demo tape—unsolicited submissions are OK. Prefers cassette or disc with 2-4 songs and lead sheet. SASE. Reports in 1 month.
Music: Mostly **gospel**, **jazz/rock**, **pop**, **R&B** and **rap**; also **blues**, **church/religious**, **country**, **disco** and **soul**. Published "Guns, Guns (No More Guns)" and "Come On Cafidia," both written and recorded by Jeb Stuart on Esquire Int'l Records.

*STYLECRAFT MUSIC CO. (BMI), P.O. Box 802, 953 Highway 51, Madison MS 39110. (601)856-7468. Professional Manager: Style Wooten. Music publisher, record company (Style Records, Styleway Records and Good News Records), record producer and booking agency. Estab. 1964. Publishes 20-65 songs/year; publishes 20 new songwriters/year. Pays standard royalty.
How to Contact: Submit demo tape by mail. Unsolicited submissions OK. Prefers cassette with 2-4 songs and "typewritten lyric sheet." SASE. Reports in 6-8 weeks.
Music: **Country**, **R&B** and **black gospel**. Published "Let's Take a Vacation to Heaven" parts 1-4 (by Douglas Bell), all recorded by Douglas Bell on Four Winds Records (gospel).
Tips: "Do it right. Don't be one of those 'I can write a song about anything' writers."

*SUCCES, Pynderslaan, Dendermonde 9200 **Belgium**. (52)21 89 87. Fax: (52)22 52 60. Director: Deschuyteneer Hendrik. Music publisher, record company and record producer. Estab. 1978. Publishes

400 songs/year. Hires staff songwriters. Works with composers and lyricists; teams collaborators. Pays standard royalty.

How to Contact: Submit demo tape by mail. Unsolicited submissions are OK. Prefers cassette (or VHS videocassette) with 3 songs. SASE. Reports in 6 weeks.

Music: Mostly **pop, dance** and **variety**; also **instrumental** and **rock.** Published *International* (by Jimmy Towers), recorded by Le Grand Julot on RM Records (instrumental); "Go Go Go" (by H. Spider), recorded by Rudy Silvester on Scorpion Records (rock); and "Couac Couac Beat" (by Ricky Mondes), recorded by Ronald & Donald on B.M.P. Records (beat dance).

SUGAR MAMA MUSIC (BMI), #805, 4545 Connecticut Ave. NW, Washington DC 20008. (202)362-2286. President: Jonathan Strong. Music publisher, record company (Ripsaw Records) and record producer (Ripsaw Productions). Estab. 1983. Publishes 3-5 songs/year; publishes 2 new songwriters/year. Works with composers and lyricists. Pays standard royalty.

Affiliate(s): Neck Bone Music (BMI) and Southern Crescent Publishing (BMI).

How to Contact: Submit demo tape by mail. Unsolicited submissions OK. "Please do not call." Prefers cassette and lyric sheet. SASE. Reports in 1-6 months.

Music: Mostly **country, blues, rockabilly** and **traditional rock.** Published "It's Not the Presents Under My Tree" (by Billy Poore and Tex Rubinowitz), recorded by Narvel Felts on Renegade Records (country); *What Do I Hafta Do* (by R.O. Smith), recorded by Bobby Smith on Ripsaw Records (rockabilly); and *Let Me Give You Lovin'* (by Arthur Gerstein), recorded by Uptown Rhythm Kings on Ripsaw Records (blues).

Tips: "Hardcore authentic roots music only. Send no more than 3-4 songs on cassette with lyric sheet and SASE with sufficient postage. Only authentic country, blues, rockabilly or roots rock and roll."

SUGARFOOT PRODUCTIONS, P.O. Box 1065, Joshua Tree CA 92252. A&R Director: Sheila Dobson. Music publisher, record company (Sugarfoot, Babydoll, Durban), record producer (Sugarfoot Records). ASCAP. Estab. 1987. Publishes 10-15 songs/year; publishes 4 new songwriters/year. Works with composers and lyricists; teams collaborators. Pays standard royalty; statutory rate per song on records.

How to Contact: Submit a demo tape—unsolicited submissions are OK. Prefers cassette with 3 songs and lyric sheet. "Make sure tape and vocal are clear." Does not return material. Reports in 1 month.

Music: Mostly **jazz, blues, swing, country, R&B, salsa** and **dance**; also **bassas, conga; Cuban** and **easy listening.** Published "Not for Love" (by Elijah), recorded by Sugarfoot on Westways Records (R&B); "You're Blue" (by Deke), recorded by Jam'n Jo on Durban Records (jazz); and "2 Me An Yu" (by Dobby), recorded by Aleets on Breton Records (jazz).

Tips: "Listen to Irving Berlin, Cole Porter, Gershwin, Carmichael for professional music and lyrics."

SULTAN MUSIC PUBLISHING (BMI), P.O. Box 461892, Garland TX 75046. (214)271-8098. President: Don Ferguson. Music publisher, record company (Puzzle Records), record producer. Publishes 15 songs/year, including some new songwriters. Works with composers and lyricists; teams collaborators. Pays standard royalty.

Affiliate(s): Illustrions Sultan (ASCAP).

How to Contact: Prefers cassette with 3 songs and lyric sheet. SASE. Reports in 3 weeks.

Music: Mostly **country**; also **MOR.** Published "What Does It Take," written and recorded by Derek Hartis (country); "After Burn," written and recorded by Phil Rodgers (jazz); and "Ain't No Way" (by G. Duke), recorded by Flash Point (rock), all on Puzzle Records.

Tips: "The best quality demo makes the listener more receptive."

SUN STAR SONGS, P.O. Box 787, Gatlinburg TN 37738. (615)436-4121. Fax: (615)436-4017. President: Tony Glenn Rast. Music publisher. Estab. 1965, reactivated 1992. Works with composers and lyricists; teams collaborators. Pays standard royalty.

How to Contact: Submit demo tape by mail. Unsolicited submissions OK. Prefers cassette with 3 songs and lyric sheets. SASE. Reports in 2 weeks.

Music: Mostly **country, Christian country-gospel** and **bluegrass**; also **pop-rock.**

Tips: "Submit quality demos. Also interested in good lyrics for co-writing."

*SUNFLARE SONGS/RECORDS, 31 W. Church St., Fairport NY 14450. (716)223-2310. President: Garry Manuel. Music publisher, record company, record producer. Estab. 1982. Publishes 15-20 songs/year; publishes 2-4 new songwriters/year. Pays standard royalty.

How to Contact: Submit demo tape by mail. Unsolicited submissions are OK. Prefers cassette with 2-3 songs and lyric sheet. "Lyric sheets should be neat, with name, address and phone number." SASE. Reports in 3-4 months.

Music: Mostly **contemporary folk, jazz** and **adult contemporary**; also **rock, New Age** and **country.**

Tips: "Send as professional a kit as possible."

SUNFROST MUSIC, P.O. Box 231, Cedarhurst NY 11516-0231. (516)791-4795. Publisher: Steve Gold-mintz. Estab. 1985. Publishes 36 songs/year. Publishes 1-2 new songwriters/year (usually by collabora-tion). Works with composers and lyricists; teams collaborators. Pays standard royalty.
Affiliate(s): Anglo American Music, Manchester, England.
How to Contact: Write first and obtain permission to submit. Prefers cassette. SASE. Reports in 5-6 weeks.
Music: Mostly **pop, rock** and **folk**; also **children's, country** and **R&B**. Published "She Loves To Rock and Roll" (by S. Goldmintz), commissioned for MOR Music TV; "Take A Look At My Eyes" (by M. Perkins), set for 1994 republication; and "I Fell In Love At Disneyland" (by Kim Olson).
Tips: "After the song is done, the work begins and your local contacts may be just as important as the unknown publisher that you are trying to reach. Build your own network of writers. Let's put the 'R' back into 'A&R.' "

*SUNSET PRODUCTIONS (BMI), 1710 Grand Ave., Nashville TN 37212-2206. President: Mark Meckel. Music publisher, record company (M.D.M. Records), record producer (Sunset Productions), and management firm. SRS. Estab. 1978. Publishes 20 songs/year; publishes 3-4 new songwriters/year. Pays standard royalty.
Affiliate(s): Street Singer Music (BMI).
How to Contact: Prefers cassette with minimum 3 songs and lyric sheet.
Music: Mostly **country, rock, R&B** and **Christmas**; also **blues**. Published "Just Like the Rain" (by Corey Gonzales), recorded by Dave Pfeiffer (pop rock); "Showdown" (by J. Routh, B. Ronen, M. Benish), recorded by Brent Ronen (country); and "Nobody Left to Save" (by M. Benish), recorded by Bren Ronen (country), all on M.D.M. Records.
Tips: "Be willing to change and work with a producer."

SUNSONGS MUSIC/HOLLYWOOD EAST ENTERTAINMENT, 52 N. Evarts Ave., Elmsford NY 10523. (914)592-2563. Professional Manager: Michael Berman. Music publisher, record producer and talent agency. Estab. 1981. BMI, ASCAP, SESAC. Publishes 20 songs/year; publishes 10 new songwriters/ year. Pays standard royalty; co-publishing deals available for established writers.
Affiliate(s): Media Concepts Music and Dark Sun Music (SESAC).
How to Contact: Submit demo tape by mail. Unsolicited submissions OK. Prefers cassette with 3-4 songs and lyric sheet. SASE. Reports in 1 month.
Music: **Dance-oriented, techno-pop, R&B, rock (all styles)** and **top 40/pop**. Published "Paradise (Take Me Home)" (by Henderson/Riccitelli), recorded by Lisa Jarrett on Ro-Hit Records (dance); "Come Back to Me" (by Henderson/Riccitelli), recorded by The Joneses on Warner Bros. Records (R&B), and "Christmas Rappin'" by Grand Rapmasters on Essex Records.
Tips: "Submit material with strong hook, good demo, and know the market being targeted by your song."

SUPREME ENTERPRISES INT'L CORP., 3rd Fl., 12304 Santa Monica Blvd., Los Angeles CA 90025. (818)707-3481. Fax: (818)707-3482. G.M. Copyrights: Lisa Lew. Music publisher, record company and record producer. Estab. 1979. Publishes 20-30 songs/year; publishes 2-6 new songwriters/year. Works with composers and lyricists. Pays standard royalty.
Affiliate(s): Fuerte Suerte Music (BMI).
How to Contact: Submit demo tape by mail. Unsolicited submissions are OK. Prefers cassette. Does not return unsolicited material. Reports in 2-3 weeks.
Music: Mostly **Latin pop, reggae in Cumbias Spanish and English** and **ballads in Spanish**. Published "Chocolate" (by David Choy/Renato); "Cucu Bam Bam" (by David Choy), recorded by Kathy on Polydor Records (reggae/pop); and "Aprietame" (by David Choy), recorded by Wilfredo Vargas on Rodven (tropical).
Tips: "A good melody is a hit in any language."

SWEET GLENN MUSIC (BMI), P.O. Box 1067, Santa Monica CA 90406. (310)452-0116. Fax: (310)465-4287. Vice President Talent: Mr. Friedwin. Music publisher and management company. Estab. 1980. Publishes 3-5 songs/year; publishes 1 new songwriter/year. Hires staff writers. Works with composers. Royalty rate varies.
Affiliate(s): Sweet Karol Music (ASCAP).
How to Contact: Write first and obtain permission to submit. "You must write before submitting." Reports in 2 months.
Music: Mostly **hip hop/funk, retro R&B** and **country**. Published "Rhythm of Romance" (by Scott), recorded by Randy Crawford.
Tips: "Must be part of a performing act or established producer/arranger-writer only!"

*TABITHA MUSIC, LTD., 39 Cordery Rd., St. Thomas, Exeter, Devon EX2 9DJ, **United Kingdom**. Phone: 44-0392-79914. Fax: 44-392-498068. Managing Director: Graham Sclater. Music publisher,

record company (Tabitha and Willow Records) and record producer. MCPS, PRS. Member MPA. Estab. 1975. Publishes 25 songs/year; publishes 6 new songwriters/year. Works with composers. Pays standard royalty; royalties paid directly to US songwriters.
Affiliate(s): Domino Music and Dice Music.
How to Contact: Submit a demo tape by mail. Unsolicited submissions are OK. Prefers cassette with 1-4 songs and lyric sheet. SAE and IRC. Reports in 2 weeks.
Music: Mostly **MOR** and **pop**; also **country, dance-oriented, Spanish, rock, soul** and **top 40**. Published "Aliens" (by Mark Fojo), recorded by Sovereign; "Not A Chance," written and recorded by Simon Galt; and "Teenage Love," written and recorded by A. Ford, all on Tabitha Records.

DALE TEDESCO MUSIC CO., 16020 Lahey St., Granada Hills CA 91344. (818)360-7329. Fax: (818)886-1338. President: Dale T. Tedesco. General Manager: Betty Lou Tedesco. Music publisher. BMI, ASCAP. Estab. 1981. Publishes 20-40 songs/year; publishes 20-30 new songwriters/year. Works with composers and lyricists; teams collaborators. Pays standard royalty.
Affiliate(s): Tedesco Tunes (ASCAP).
How to Contact: Submit a demo tape—unsolicited submissions are OK. Prefers cassette with 1-2 songs and lyric sheet. SASE or postcard for critique. "Dale Tedesco Music hand-critiques all material submitted. Only reviews 2 songs maximum. Free evaluation."
Music: Mostly **pop, R&B** and **A/C**; also **dance-oriented, instrumentals** (for TV and film), **jazz, MOR, rock, soul** and **ethnic instrumentals.**
Tips: "Listen to current trends and touch base with the publisher."

TEK PUBLISHING (BMI), P.O. Box 1485, Lake Charles LA 70602. (318)439-8839. Administrator: Eddie Shuler. Music publisher, freelance producer. Estab. 1956. Publishes 50 songs/year; publishes 35 new songwriters/year. Teams collaborators. Pays standard royalty.
Affiliate(s): Nassetan (BMI) and EMFS Music (ASCAP).
How to Contact: Submit a demo tape by mail. Unsolicited submissions are OK. Prefers cassette with 3 songs and lyric sheet. "Return postage is required for return of material." SASE. Reports in 2 months.
Music: Mostly **country** and **R&B**; also **cajun, humorist** and **zydeco.** Published "Yesterday's News," recorded by Cari Gregory (contemporary pop); "No Lowdown Boogie" (blues) and "Breaking Down the Door" (cajun), recorded by Mickey Newman.
Tips: "KEEP WRITING. If you write a thousand songs, and even one is a hit it was all worthwhile. Concentrate on what's going on by listening to broadcasts and see what others are doing. Then try to determine where your story fits."

TENDER TENDER MUSIC (BMI), #105, 158 W. 81st St. SE, New York NY 10024. (212)724-5624. Publisher: Christopher Berg. Music publisher. Estab. 1990. Publishes 5-10 songs/year; publishes 1 new songwriter/year. Works with composers and lyricists; teams collaborators. Pay negotiable.
How to Contact: Write first and obtain permission to submit. Prefers cassette (or VHS videocassette) with 3 songs and lyric, score or lead sheet. SASE. Reports in 1 month.
Music: Mostly **concert songs, concert instrumental** and **opera**; also **musical theater, ballads** and **rock.** Published *Poem* (by Christopher Berg), recorded by Carl Halvorsen on MHS Records (serious).
Tips: "Write something which tickles the mind, not only the body. Make significant personal and musical contacts with artists who perform and record regularly."

*TENTEX MUSIC PUBLISHING (BMI), 6003 Brown Rock Trail, Austin TX 78749. (512)288-0793. Contact: George Watson. Music publisher. Estab. 1989. Publishes 3 songs/year; publishes 2 new songwriters/year. Works with composers and lyricists. Pays standard royalty.
Affiliate(s): Los-Tex Music (ASCAP).
How to Contact: Write or call first and obtain permission to submit. Prefers cassette with 2 songs and typed lyric sheet. Does not return material. Reports in 1 month.
Music: Mostly **country, R&B** and **pop.**

*TERRACE ENTERTAINMENT CORPORATION, P.O. Box 239, Las Vegas NM 87701. (505)425-5188. Fax: (505)425-5110. President: Robert John Jones. Music publisher and record company. Estab. 1970. Publishes 50 songs/year; 1 or 2 new songwriters/year. Hires staff writers. Pays standard royalty.
Affiliate(s): Terrace, Choskee Bottom (ASCAP), Blue Lake (BMI) and Lorville (SESAC).
How to Contact: Submit demo tape by mail. Unsolicited submissions are OK. Prefers cassette with 3 songs only and lyric sheet. SASE. Reports in 2-3 weeks.
Music: Mostly **country, folk** and **pop.** Published "Oh Me, Oh My Sweet Baby" (by Tom Shapiro), recorded by Diamond Rio on Arista Records (country); "Heaven's Just a Sin Away" (by Jerry Gillespie), recorded by Kelly Willis on MCA Records (country); and "Searchin' " (by Simon Fung), recorded by China Black on Polydor Records (pop/R&B).

TIKI ENTERPRISES, INC., 195 S. 26th St., San Jose CA 95116. (408)286-9840. President: Gradie O'Neal. Music publisher, record company (Rowena Records) and record producer (Jeannine O'Neal and Gradie O'Neal). BMI, ASCAP. Estab. 1967. Publishes 40 songs/year; publishes 12 new songwriters/year. Works with composers; teams collaborators. Pays standard royalty.
Affiliate(s): Tooter Scooter Music (BMI), Janell Music (BMI) and O'Neal & Friend (ASCAP).
How to Contact: Submit a demo tape by mail. Unsolicited submissions are OK. Prefers cassette with 3 songs and lyric or lead sheets. SASE. Reports in 3 weeks.
Music: Mostly **country, Mexican, rock/pop gospel, R&B** and **New Age.** Published "Yamor Indio," by Roy De Hoyos (Mexican Tex-Mex); "I See Me In Your Eyes Again" (by Kathy Bazinet/Joan Fitzpatrick), recorded by Jacque Lynn; and "Stand Firm" by Jeannine O'Neal (contemporary Christian).

TOMPAUL MUSIC CO. (BMI), 628 South St., Mount Airy NC 27030. (919)786-2865. Owner: Paul E. Johnson. Music publisher, record company, record producer and record and tape distributor. Estab. 1960. Publishes 25 songs/year. Works with composers. Pays standard royalty.
How to Contact: Submit a demo tape by mail. Unsolicited submissions are OK. Prefers cassette tapes with 4-6 songs and lyric or lead sheet. SASE. Reports in 2 months.
Music: Mostly **country, bluegrass** and **gospel**; also **church/religious, easy listening, folk, MOR, rock, soul** and **top 40.** Published *She Has Forgotten, Why Do You Week* and *Little Green Valley* (by Atkins & Hill), recorded by Bobby Lee Atkins on Stark Records (country).
Tips: "Try to write good commercial type songs, use new ideas, listen to the songs that are played on radio stations today; you could get some ideas. Don't try to make alterations in a song already established."

*TOOTH AND NAIL MUSIC, P.O. Box 140136, Nashville TN 37214. Manager: Jenny Travis. Music publisher and record producer. Estab. 1993. Publishes 30 songs/year; publishes 3 new songwriters/year. Works with composers and lyricists; teams collaborators.
Affiliate(s): 1st Page Music (BMI).
How to Contact: Submit demo tape by mail. Unsolicited submissions are OK. Prefers cassette (or VHS videocassette) with 1-10 songs and lyric sheet. "Artists send a picture with tape — even Polaroid." SASE. Reports in 3 weeks.
Music: Mostly **pop, rock** and **R&B.** Published *Always A Place* (by Billy Herzig/Anderson Page); *One Step Back* (by Kip Summers); and *Colorful Romance* (by Darryl Girard), all recorded by Daryo on Tooth and Nail Records.

*TOPS AND BOTTOMS MUSIC (BMI), P.O. Box 1545, New York NY 10013. (212)366-9079. Fax: (212)366-9078. Director: Richard Dworkin. Music publisher. Estab. 1988. Publishes 5 songs/year; publishes 1 new songwriter/year. Works with composers and lyricists; teams collaborators. Pays standard royalty.
How to Contact: Submit demo tape by mail. Unsolicited submissions are OK. Prefers cassette (or VHS videocassette if available) with 3-5 songs and lyric sheet. Does not return material. Reports in 4 weeks.
Music: Music relating to gay/lesbian life. Published "Love Don't Need A Reason"(by Peter Allen/Michael Callen/Marsha Malamet), recorded by Peter Allen on MCA Records (ballad); *Living In Wartime* and *Crazy World*, both written and recorded by Michael Callen on Significant Other Records (rock/ballad).

TOULOUSE MUSIC PUBLISHING CO., INC. (BMI), Box 96, El Cerrito CA 94530. Executive Vice President: James Bronson, Jr. Music publisher, record company and record producer. Member AIMP. Publishes 1 new songwriter/year. Hires staff writers. Pays standard royalty.
How to Contact: Prefers cassette with 2-4 songs and lyric sheet. SASE. Reports in 1 month.
Music: Bluegrass, gospel, jazz, R&B and **soul.**

*TOWER BRIDGE MUSIC, LTD., 1 Gledwood Dr., Hayes UB4 OA9 **Middle England.** MD: Stuart Johnson. Music publisher. Estab. 1972. Works with composers and lyricists. Pays standard royalty.
How to Contact: Submit demo tape by mail. Unsolicited submissions are OK. Prefers cassette (or VHS videocassette if available) with 3 songs. Does not return material. Reports in 4 weeks.
Music: Mostly **pop, dance** and **rock**; also **anything commercial.** Published "Why Can't We Be Friends" (by R. Benham), recorded by O'Chic Bros. on Magnet Records (dance).

TRANSITION MUSIC CORP., Suite 700, 6290 Sunset Blvd., Los Angeles CA 90028. Professional Manager: Kim Lyles. Music publisher and management firm. BMI, ASCAP. Member NMPA. Estab. 1982. Publishes 35 songs/year; publishes 10 new songwriters/year. Teams collaborators. Pays standard royalty.

Affiliate(s): Creative Entertainment Music (BMI), Pushy Publishing (ASCAP).
How to Contact: Submit demo tape by mail. Unsolicited submissions OK. Prefers cassette with 1 song and lyric sheet. Does not return unsolicited material. Reports in 3-4 weeks.
Music: R&B and **dance.** Published "Lead Me Into Love," recorded by Anita Baker; *House Party 3* (by David Allen Jones), recorded by various artists; and music for the television show "Doogie Howser."
Tips: "Please submit top quality radio-ready demos."

*TRI-SHE KIETA PUBLISHERS, INC. (BMI), #825, 122 W. Monroe, Chicago IL 60603. President: John Bellamy. Music publisher, record company (Source Records), record producer (Anthony Stephens). Estab. 1974. Publishes 12 new songs/year; 1-2 new songwriters/year. Works with composers and lyricists; teams collaborators. Pays standard royalty.
Affiliate(s): Light & Sound Music, Inc. (ASCAP), Source Records, Inc.
How to Contact: Submit demo tape by mail. Unsolicited submissions are OK. Prefers cassette (or VHS videocassette if available) with 3 songs and lyric sheet. Does not return unsolicited material. Reports in 3 weeks.
Music: Mostly **R&B, pop** and **gospel.** Published "Deeper in Debt" (by Spright Simpson); "Crazy for You" (by Kennedy Green), recorded by The Source (R&B); and "Greater By and By," written and recorded by Sean Williams (gospel), all on Source Records.

TRUSTY PUBLICATIONS (BMI), 8771 Rose Creek Rd., Nebo KY 42441. (502)249-3194. President: Elsie Childers. Music publisher, record company (Trusty Records) and record producer. Member CMA. Estab. 1960. Publishes 2-3 songs/year; publishes 2 new songwriters/year. Pays standard royalty.
How to Contact: Write or call first and obtain permission to submit. Prefers cassette (or VHS videocassette) with 2-4 songs and lead sheet. SASE. Reports in 6 weeks.
Music: Mostly **country, R&B, rock, contemporary Christian, Southern gospel, hip hop** and **club** and **dance;** some **rap.** Published *Can Do Man,* written and recorded by E. Childers; *Blue, Too* and *Don't Mess with the Jukebox* (by Childers and Williams), recorded by Noah Williams, all on Trusty Records.

TUFFIN MUSIC ENTERPRISES, P.O. Box 566, Naperville IL 60566. (708)416-6606. Fax: (708)416-3313. President: Paul Kurth. Music publisher. Estab. 1990. Publishes 2 songs/year. Publishes 1-2 new songwriters. Hires staff songwriters. Works with composers and lyricists; teams collaborators. Pays standard royalty.
Affiliate(s): Tuffin Music (BMI).
How to Contact: Submit demo tape by mail. Unsolicited submissions are OK. Prefers cassette or CD (or VHS videocassette) with 1-5 songs and lyric or lead sheet (if available). "We prefer copyrighted material." SASE. Reports in 3 weeks.
Music: Mostly **country, rock, alternative, adult contemporary;** also **novelty, educational, instructional.** Published "From the Heart" (by Paul and Joan Kurth), recorded by Jean Dunn on Muffaletta Records.
Tips: "Demo should be of high quality and as close to finished commercial concept as possible."

TWIN TOWERS PUBLISHING CO., Dept. SM, 8833 Sunset Blvd., Penthouse West, Los Angeles CA 90069. (310)659-9644. President: Michael Dixon. Music publisher and booking agency (Harmony Artists, Inc.). Works with composers and lyricists. Publishes 24 songs/year. Pays standard royalty.
How to Contact: Call first to get permission to submit a tape. Prefers cassette with 3 songs and lyric sheet. SASE. Will respond only if interested.
Music: Mostly **pop, rock** and **R&B.** Published "Magic," from *Ghostbusters* soundtrack on Arista Records; and "Kiss Me Deadly" (by Lita Ford) on RCA Records.

TWO/POLYGRAM MUSIC PUBLISHING, 122 McEvoy St., Alexandria NSW 2015 **Australia.** Phone: (02)518-1234. Professional Manager: Kim Green. Music publisher. Estab. 1988. Works with composers and lyricists.
How to Contact: Submit demo tape by mail. Unsolicited submissions are OK. Prefers cassette with 3 songs and lyric sheet. Does not return unsolicited material. Reports in 4-6 weeks.
Music: Mostly **top 40, pop** and **rock.** Published "Into Your Arms" (by Robyn St. Clare), recorded by Lemonheads on Atlantic Records (pop); and *Strictly Ballroom* (by David Herschfelder), recorded on Alberts Records (soundtrack).

UBM, Hohenstaufenring 43-45, 50674 Köln **Germany.** Phone: 43 13 13. President: Uwe Buschkotter. Music publisher, record company and record producer. GEMA (Germany), BMI (USA). Estab. 1968. Publishes 100 songs/year; publishes 10 new songwriters/year. Works with composers. Pays standard royalty.
How to Contact: Submit a demo tape by mail. Unsolicited submissions OK. Prefers cassette (or VHS videocassette) and lead sheets. SAE and IRC. Reports in 4 weeks.

Music: Mostly **jazz, pop, MOR, funk** and **easy listening**; also **classical.** Published *Joyrobic Song* (by McLauren Foster); *Nightwave* (by Chris Walden); and *Lovers Lane* (by Ingrid Materne), all recorded on UBM Records.

*ULTIMATE PEAK MUSIC (BMI), P.O. Box 707, Nashville TN 37076. Manager: Danny Crader. Music publisher. Estab. 1992. Publishes 35 songs/year; publishes 4 new songwriters/year. Hires staff writers. Works with composers and lyricists; teams collaborators. Pays standard royalty.
How to Contact: Submit demo tape by mail. Unsolicited submissions are OK. Prefers cassette with 1-6 songs and lyric sheet. SASE. Reports in 3 weeks.
Music: Mostly **country** and **MTV pop/rock.** Published *Better* (by Billy Herzig and Anderson Page), and *Colorful Romance* (by Darryl Girard), both recorded by Daryo on Tooth and Nail Records (dance); and "Same Ol' Same Ol'" (by Stephany Delray), recorded by Tim Murphy on Peak Records (country).
Tips: "Listen to the radio and compare your songs to the hits—not for recording quality, but for substance and content and structure—and be objective and realistic and honest with yourself."

*UNIMUSICA INC. (ASCAP), #110, 3191 Coral Way, Miami FL 33145. (305)442-7273. Fax: (305)442-1790. Manager: Maria Flores. Music publisher. Estab. 1981. Publishes 5,000 songs/year; publishes 500 new songwriters/year. Works with composers and lyricists. Pays standard royalty.
Affiliate(s): Musica Unica Publishing (BMI).
How to Contact: Submit demo tape by mail. Unsolicited submissions are OK. Prefers cassette. Does not return material. Reports in 2 months.
Music: Mostly **salsa, baladas** and **merengues.** Published *Ven devorame otra vez* (by Palmer Hernandez), recorded by Lalo Rodriguez (salsa); *Antologia De Caricias* (by Jankarlos Nunez), recorded by Altamina Banda Shaw on Rodven Records (merengue); *Madrigal* (by Don Telo), recorded by Jose Luis on Sony Records (balada).
Tips: "Listen to the records of our affiliated company Rodven and write for their styles."

VAAM MUSIC GROUP, P.O. Box 29688, Hollywood CA 90029-0688. (213)664-7765. President: Pete Martin. Music publisher and record producer. ASCAP, BMI. Estab. 1967. Publishes 9-24 new songs/year. Pays standard royalty.
Affiliate(s): Pete Martin Music.
How to Contact: Prefers cassette with 2 songs maximum and lyric sheet. SASE. Reports in 1 month. "Small packages only."
Music: **Top 40/pop, country** and **R&B.** "Submitted material must have potential of reaching top 5 on charts." Published "The Greener Years," recorded by Frank Loren on Blue Gem Records (country/MOR); "Bar Stool Rider" (by Peggy Hackworth); and "I Love a Cowboy," written and performed by Sherry Weston in the feature film "Far Out Man," with Tommy Chong (of Cheech & Chong comedy team) and also co-starring Martin Mull.
Tips: "Study the top 10 in charts in the style that you write. Stay current and up to date to today's market."

VALET PUBLISHING CO., #273, 2442 NW Market, Seattle WA 98107. (206)524-1020. Fax: (206)524-1102. Publishing Director: Buck Ormsby. Music publisher and record company (Etiquette/Suspicious Records). BMI. Estab. 1961. Publishes 5-10 songs/year. Hires staff songwriters. Pays standard royalty.
How to Contact: Submit a demo tape—call first. Prefers cassette with 3-4 songs and lyric sheets. SASE. Reports in 6-8 weeks.
Music: Mostly **R&B, rock** and **pop;** also **dance** and **country.**
Tips: "Production of tape must be top quality and lyric sheets professional."

*VELOCITY PRODUCTIONS, Box 518, Leander TX 78646-0518. (512)259-3779. Contact: Review Coordinator. Music publisher and record producer. Estab. 1986. Publishes 10-20 songs/year; publishes 2-3 new songwriters/year. Works with composers and lyricists; teams collaborators. Pays standard royalty.
Affiliate(s): Velocity Publishing (BMI).
How to Contact: Write and obtain permission to submit. Prefers cassette (or VHS videocassette) with 1-4 songs and lyric sheet. Does not return unsolicited submissions. Reports in 1 month.
Music: Mostly **children's.** Published *Going South* and "Bear Blues" (by J. Brehm-Stern), recorded by VeloCity Players on Velocity Records.

VICTORY MUSIC, P.O. Box 6132, Elberton GA 30635. Professional Manager: Dianna Kirk. Music publisher. Estab. 1991. Works with composers and lyricists. Pays standard royalty.
Affiliate(s): Wild Katt Music.
How to Contact: Write first and obtain permission to submit. Prefers cassette with 3 songs and lyric sheet. SASE. Reports in 2-3 weeks.
Music: Mostly **heavy metal, rock** and **dance.** Published "Ready To Rock" and "Ton of Fun" (by Dizzy Dale).

Tips: "Always include a SASE if you want a response."

VOICE NOTES PUBLISHING, 1225 Shallowford Rd., Chattanooga TN 37411. (615)624-0815. Music publisher, record company (GO-ROC-CO-POP Records). ASCAP. Estab. 1984. Publishes 20 songs/year; publishes 1-5 new songwriters/year. Works with composers and lyricists; teams collaborators. Pays standard royalty.
Affiliate(s): Voice Score Publishing (BMI).
How to Contact: Submit a demo tape by mail. Unsolicited submissions are OK. Prefers cassette with 3-5 songs and lyric or lead sheets. "Have melody out front, words and diction clear." SASE. Reports in 3 months.
Music: Mostly **gospel, rock, country,** pop and **R&B.** Published "Come On and Cry" (by Bruce Newman), recorded by Keith Hartline (rock ballad); "Get Your Own Money" (by Sharon Lewis), and "Ghost Of Music Row" (by Horace Hatcher and Ed Smith), recorded by RENA (country), all recorded on GO-ROC-CO-POP Records.

VOKES MUSIC PUBLISHING (BMI), Box 12, New Kensington PA 15068-0012. (412)335-2775. President: Howard Vokes. Music publisher, record company, booking agency and promotion company.
How to Contact: Submit cassette (3 songs only), lyric or lead sheet. SASE. Reports within a week.
Music: Traditional country-bluegrass and **gospel.** Published "A Million Tears" (by Duke & Null), recorded by Johnny Eagle Feather on Vokes Records; "I Won't Be Your Honky Tonk Queen" (by Vokes-Wallace), recorded by Bunnie Mills on Pot-Of Gold Records; and "Break The News" (by Vokes-Webb), recorded by Bill Beere on Oakhill Records.
Tips: "We're always looking for country songs that tell a story, and only interested in hard-traditional-bluegrass, country and country gospel songs. Please no 'copy-cat-song writers.'"

*JIMMY WALTON MUSIC PUBLISHING CO. (ASCAP), P.O. Box 501013, Malabar FL 32950-1013. (407)951-2626. Executive Producer: Jimmy Walton. P.R.: S. Hardesty. Music publisher, record company (Walton Record Productions) and record producer. Estab. 1992. Publishes 16 songs/year; publishes 5 new songwriters/year. Works with composers and lyricists; teams collaborators. Pays standard royalty or other amount "depending on the deal per artist or writer."
How to Contact: Submit demo tape by mail. Unsolicited submissions are OK. Prefers cassette (or VHS videocassette if available) with 1-4 songs and lyric sheet. "Lyric sheets must be clearly printed." SASE. Reports in 1 month.
Music: Mostly **new country/uptempo,** pop/MOR and **A/C;** also **ballads, gospel** and **country/ballads.** Published *How Many Heartaches* (by Jimmy Walton/Herman House), recorded by Sally Evans (country); *Chesapeake Girl* (by Jimmy Walton), recorded by Rich Gibson and Jimmy Walton (pop); and *Just Another Woman* (by Ken Michaels/Jimmy Walton), recorded by Barry Russell (country), all on Walton Record Productions.
Tips: "Submit a clear demo. Keep your songs under 3 minutes. Clean, simple and based on a true love story."

*WATERBURY ROAD MUSIC (BMI), P.O. Box 1517, Dublin OH 43017. (614)766-4100. President: Rick Cooper. Music publisher. Estab. 1989. Publishes 10 songs/year; publishes 3 new songwriters/year. Works with composers and lyricists; teams collaborators. Pays standard royalty.
How to Contact: Write first and obtain permission to submit. Prefers cassette or VHS videocassette with 3 songs and lyric sheet. "Submit completed songs only—no works-in-progress." SASE. Reports in 2 weeks.
Music: Mostly **rock, country** and **metal;** also **alternative.** Published *How The West Was Lost* (by Rick Cooper/John Schwab), recorded by J.D. Blackfoot on Tokala Records (rock); *The Home of Billy D.* (by Rick Cooper/George Jeffrey), recorded by Bobby Ross on Echo Summit Records (country); and *A Helping Hand* (by Rick Cooper/John Schwab/Kenny Aronoff), recorded by John Schwab on Sisapa Records (acoustic rock).
Tips: "We prefer to work with singer-songwriters, but will consider all."

*WATONKA RECORDS CO. (ASCAP), 19523 Lockridge Dr., Spring TX 77373. President: Earl The Pearl Roberts. Music publisher, record company and record producer. Estab. 1974. Publishes 1-10 songs/year. Pays standard royalty.
How to Contact: Submit demo tape by mail. Unsolicited submissions are OK. Prefers cassette or VHS videocassette with 4 songs maximum and lyric/lead sheet. SASE. Reports in 2 weeks.
Music: Country, **rock** and **Tex Mex** only. Published "Passing Seasons" and "Ecstasy" (by E. Roberts), recorded by ETP; and "Sharon's World" (by G.W. Walks), recorded by GWW, all on Watonka Records (country).
Tips: "Send demo with return postage—I'll listen and let you know one way or the other in a couple of weeks. Do not send just lyrics. Must be complete song."

WAVEWORKS (BMI), 2000 P. St. NW, Washington DC 20036. (202)861-0560. Contact: Patrick Smith. Music publisher. Estab. 1987. Produces and publishes 20 songs/year. Hires staff writers. Works with composers and lyricists; teams collaborators. Pays standard royalty.
How to Contact: Write first and obtain permission to submit. Prefers cassette (or ¾″ videocassette if available). Does not return unsolicited material.
Music: Primarily music for television, film and video. "We are interested in instrumental background music for films/TV."

WEAVER WORDS OF MUSIC (BMI), P.O. Box 803, Tazewell VA 24651. (703)988-6267. President: H. R. Cook. Music publisher and record company (Fireball Records). Estab. 1978. Publishes 12 songs/year; varying number of new songwriters/year. Works with composers and lyricists; teams collaborators. Pays standard royalty.
How to Contact: Submit a demo tape by mail. Unsolicited submissions are OK. Prefers cassette with 3 songs and lyric or lead sheets. SASE. Reports in 1 month.
Music: Mostly **country**. Published "Winds of Change," written and recorded by Cecil Surrett; "Texas Saturday Night" and "Old Flame Burning," written and recorded by H.R. Cook, all on Fireball Records (country).

*FRIEDRICH WEBER MUSIKVERLAG, P.O. B. 70, Vienna 1195 **Austria**. (1)5539773. Fax: (1)5452077. Contact: Ulrike Kühlwein-Weber. Music publisher, record producer, author, composer and musician. Estab. 1992. Publishes 50 songs/year; publishes 2-3 new songwriters/year. Works with composers and lyricists. Pays 40-60% royalty.
How to Contact: Submit demo tape by mail. Unsolicited submissions are OK. Prefers cassette and lyric sheet. Does not return material.
Music: Mostly **gospel, soul, rock-blues** and **folk**; also **jazz**. Published *My Land* (by F. Weber), recorded by Vienna Voice (folk); *First Spring of Concrete* (by F.X. Groemmer), recorded by Foggy Dew (folk); and *Listen To The Pouring Rain* (by U. Kühlwein), recorded by Freak Weber (rock), all on FRW Records.
Tips: "We are musicians, we created our labels and publishing to stay independent from the major corporations. We are looking for self confident artists."

WEEDHOPPER MUSIC (BMI), 1916 28th Ave. S., Birmingham AL 35209-2605. (205)942-3222. President: Michael Panepento. Estab. 1985. Music publisher (Chapel Lane), artist development (Chapel Lane Productions) and management firm (Airwave Production Group, Ltd.). Publishes 4-6 songs/year; publishes 3 new songwriters/year. Works with composers and lyricists. Pays standard royalty.
Affiliate(s): Panepentunes (ASCAP); Panelips (BMI).
How to Contact: Write first and obtain permission to submit. Prefers cassette or 15 ips reel-to-reel with 3 songs. SASE. Reports in 6-8 weeks.
Music: Mostly **pop/rock, AOR, R&B/jazz** and **rock**; also **all others**. Published "Home" and "Land of Kings" (by Hammrick), recorded by The Skeptics on Pandem Records (modern rock).
Tips: "Send us the best possible demo/example of your work."

WEMAR MUSIC (BMI), #416, 16200 Ventura Blvd., Encino CA 91436. President: Stuart Wiener. Music publisher. Estab. 1943. Publishes 5-10 songs/year; publishes 2-3 new songwriters/year. Works with composers and lyricists; teams collaborators. Pays standard royalty.
Affiliate(s): Grand Music (ASCAP).
How to Contact: Submit demo tape by mail. Unsolicited submissions are OK. Prefers cassette with 3 songs and lyric sheet. "Do not call to follow; we will contact writer if we can use songs." SASE. Reports in 1 month.
Music: Mostly **R&B**, **pop** and **dance**; also **rock**. Published "The Truth" (by Mike Nally), recorded by Systm X (dance); "Ride" (by Mike Jett), recorded by Fuel, both on Innerkore Records (dance); and "Shout" (by Isley, Isley, Isley), recorded by Louchie Lou, Meechie One on FFRR Records (reggae).
Tips: "We are looking for master quality demos, good vocals, contemporary and meaningful lyrics—we are very particular about the songs we choose."

BERTHOLD WENGERT (MUSIKVERLAG), Waldstrasse 27, D-76327, Pfinztal-Soellingen, **Germany**. Contact: Berthold Wengert. Music publisher. Teams collaborators. Pays standard GEMA royalty.
How to Contact: Prefers cassette and complete score for piano. SAE and IRC. Reports in 4 weeks. "No cassette returns!"
Music: Mostly **light music** and **pop**.

BOBE WES MUSIC, P.O. Box 28609, Dallas TX 75228. (214)681-0345. President: Bobe Wes. Music publisher. BMI. Publishes 20 songs/year. Pays standard royalty.
How to Contact: Submit a demo tape—unsolicited submissions are OK. Prefers cassette. "State if songs have been copyrighted and if you have previously assigned songs to someone else. Include titles,

readable lyrics and your full name and address. Give the same information for your co-writer(s) if you have one. State if you are a member of BMI, ASCAP or SESAC. Lead sheets are not required. Comments will follow only if interested." SASE. No certified mail accepted.
Music: Blues, country, disco, gospel, MOR, progressive, rock (hard or soft), soul, top 40/pop, polka, Latin dance and instrumentals. *"Special interest in Christmas songs."*

*WEST & EAST MUSIC, Hans Sachs Str. 39, Klagenfurt 9020 **Austria.** (011)43-463-516570. Fax: (011)43-463-516570-15. MD: Harry Huber. Music publisher, record company and record producer. Estab. 1989. Publishes 100-130 songs/year. Hires staff songwriters. Works with composers and lyricists. Pays standard royalty.
How to Contact: Submit demo tape by mail. Unsolicited submissions are OK. Prefers cassette. SAE and IRC. Reports in 3-4 weeks.
Music: Mostly **dance, rock, rock ballads** and **pop**; also **instrumental**. Published *Inside Out* (by various), recorded by Mindwork on Bellaphon Records (pop); *Fahrenheit* (by Ghidini/Huber), recorded by Fahrenheit on The Fab Records (rock); and *Goomoo* (by Kano), recorded by The Kano on WEM Records (dance/techno).

WESTUNES MUSIC PUBLISHING CO. (ASCAP), 167 Main St., Metuchen NJ 08840. (908)548-6700. Fax: (908)548-6748. A&R Director: Kevin McCabe. Music publisher and management firm (Westwood Entertainment Group). Publishes 15 songs/year; publishes 2 new songwriters/year. Works with composers and lyricists. Pays standard royalty.
How to Contact: Write first and obtain permission to submit. Prefers cassette with 3 songs and lyric sheet. SASE. Reports in 6 weeks.
Music: Mostly **rock**; also **pop**. Published "Fearless," written and recorded by Kevin McCabe on Westwood Records; "Lonely Hearts" and "Shooting Star" (by Jim Forest), recorded by Kidd Skruff on Azra International Records.
Tips: Submit a "neat promotional package; attach biography of the songwriter."

*WHATAPAYNE PUBLISHING, #316, 6001 Old Hickory Blvd., Hermitage TN 37076. Music Publisher: Lydia McCall. Music publisher and record producer. Estab. 1992. Publishes 1-3 songs/year; publishes 1-3 new songwriters/year. Pays standard royalty.
How to Contact: Submit demo tape by mail. Unsolicited submissions are OK. Prefers cassette with 3 songs and lyric sheet. Does not return material. Reports in 2 months.
Music: Mostly **country**; also **R&B** and **dance**. Published "Don't Leave Me Angry" (by Lee Munger), recorded by Desiree Knight on Greenwood Records (country); *Could You Learn to Love A Loser* (by Lee Munger), recorded by Steve Canyon on Blaster Records (country ballad); and *Tear Collector* (by Ken Carson), recorded by Mark Stead on Venture Records (country ballad).
Tips: "Make sure your songs relate to the person buying the product."

*WHEELER COMMUNICATIONS INC. (ASCAP), #103A, 901 Sixth St. SW, Washington DC 20024. (202)488-3266. Executive Director: George Wheeler, Jr. Music publisher and record producer. Estab. 1994. Publishes 12 songs/year. Pays standard royalty.
How to Contact: Call first and obtain permission to submit. Prefers cassette (or VHS videocassette) with 3 songs and lyric sheet. SASE. Reports in 6 weeks.
Music: Mostly **R&B, hip hop** and **dance**; also **house, club** and **jazz pop**.

*WHIMSONG PUBLISHING (ASCAP), 1156 Park Lane, West Palm Beach FL 33417-5957. (407)686-1354. Professional Managers: Rusty Gordon, Ron Caruso and Davilyn Whims. Music publisher and record producer (Rustron Music Productions). Estab. 1990. Works with composers and lyricists; teams collaborators. Pays standard royalty. Publishes 100-150 songs/year; publishes 10-20 new songwriters/year.
How to Contact: Submit a demo tape—unsolicited submissions are OK. Prefers cassette with 1-3 songs and lyric or lead sheet. "Clearly label your tape and container. Include cover letter." SASE required for all correspondence. Reports in 2-4 months.
Music: Mostly **pop** (ballads, blues, theatrical, cabaret), **progressive country** and **folk/rock**; also **New Age instrumentals** and **R&B**. Published "Money Doesn't Pay The Price," written and recorded by Bonnie Jean Johns on Whimsong Records (country/blues fusion); "I Pledge Allegiance" (by Gary Gonzalez), recorded by Relative Viewpoint on RVP Records (topical folk); and "Lady of the Lake" (by Gary Barth), recorded by Gary Jess on GJB Records (New Age fusion).
Tips: "Write for the market as it really exists, create songs for the recording artists who accept original material, read label credits. Stay tuned to the trends and fusions indicative of the '90s. Compose definitive melody."

WHITE CAR MUSIC (BMI), 11724 Industriplex, Baton Rouge LA 70809. (504)755-1400. Contact: Nelson Blanchard. Music publisher, record company (White Car Records/Techno Sound Records), record producer. BMI, ASCAP. Estab. 1988. Publishes 15 songs/year; publishes 2 new songwriters/year. Works with composers and lyricists; teams collaborators. Pays standard royalty.

Affiliate(s): Char Blanche Music (ASCAP).

How to Contact: Submit a demo tape by mail. Unsolicited submissions are OK. Prefers cassette with 4 songs. Does not return unsolicited material. Reports in 2 weeks.

Music: Mostly **country, rock** and **pop**; also **R&B**. Published "Leading Man" (by Butch Reine), recorded by Atchafalaya on White Car Records (country); "Sail On" (by Blanchard, Watts, Bullion), recorded by Johnsteve on Stebu Records (rock); and "Crazy Bound" (by Blanchard), recorded by Tareva on White Car Records (country).

*WHITE CAT MUSIC, Suite 114, 10603 N. Hayden Rd., Scottsdale AZ 85260. (602)951-3115. Fax: (602)951-3074. Professional Manager: Frank Fara. Producer: Patty Parker. Music publisher. Member CMA, CARAS, CCMA, BCCMA and BBB. Estab. 1978. Publishes 30 songs/year; publishes 20 new songwriters/year. "50% of our published songs are from non-charted and developing writers." Pays standard royalty.

Affiliate(s): Rocky Bell Music (BMI) and How The West Was Sung Music (BMI).

How to Contact: Submit a demo tape—unsolicited submissions are OK. Cassettes only with 2 songs and lyric or lead sheet. SASE. Reports in 2 weeks.

Music: Mostly **A/C, traditional country** and **contemporary country**. Published *When A Love Goes Wrong* (by Joe Radosevich), recorded by Inger Nordstrom (country); "Ain't No One in Love with Me" (by M. Ray and R. Rich), recorded by Keith Lamb (country); and "He Don't Love Me with His Eyes" (by Mari Earl), recorded by Sophie Stillman, all on Comstock Records.

Tips: "Send only 2 songs—they will be heard faster and listened to more intently! Send up-tempo songs—this will increase your chances. Don't use long instrumental intros and breaks, it detracts from listening to the song itself."

WHITEWING MUSIC (BMI), 413 N Parkerson Ave., Crowley LA 70526. (318)788-0773. Fax: (318)788-0776. Owner J.D. Miller. Music publisher and record company (Master-Trak, Showtime, Par T, MTE, Blues Unlimited, Kajun, Cajun Classics). Estab. 1946. Publishes 12-15 songs/year. Publishes 6 new songwriters/year. Pays standard royalty.

Affiliate(s): Jamil Music (BMI).

How to Contact: Submit demo tape by mail. Unsolicited submissions are OK. Prefers cassette (or videocassette) with 6 songs and lyric or lead sheets. Reports in 5-6 weeks.

Music: Mostly **country, rock, MOR**; also **cajun**. Published *Avec Amis* (by Lee Benoit).

WILCOM PUBLISHING (ASCAP), Box 4456, West Hills CA 91308. (818)348-0940. Owner: William Clark. Music publisher. Estab. 1989. Publishes 10-15 songs/year; publishes 1-2 new songwriters/year. Works with composers and lyricists. Pays standard royalty.

How to Contact: Write first and obtain permission to submit a tape. Prefers cassette with 1-2 songs and lyric sheet. SASE. Reports in 3 weeks.

Music: Mostly **R&B, pop** and **rock**; also **country**. Published "Girl Can't Help It" (by W. Clark/D. Walsh/P. Oland), recorded by Stage 1 on Rockit Records (top 40).

SHANE WILDER MUSIC (BMI), P.O. Box 3503, Hollywood CA 90078. (805)251-7526. President: Shane Wilder. Music publisher, record producer (Shane Wilder Productions) and management firm (Shane Wilder Artists Management). Estab. 1960. Publishes 25-50 songs/year; publishes 15-20 new songwriters/year. Works with composers. Pays standard royalty.

How to Contact: Submit demo tape by mail. Unsolicited submissions OK. Prefers cassette (or VHS videocassette) with 3 songs and lyric sheet. "Include SASE if you wish tape returned. Photo and résumé should be sent if you're looking for a producer." Reports in 2-4 weeks.

Music: Mostly **traditional country** and **crossover**. Published *That's the Reason God Created Men*, recorded by Annette on Playback Records (C&W); *Legend of the Daltons*, recorded by Tony Lee (C&W); and *100% Pure Texan*, recorded by Kimber Cunningham and Dorie Alexander on Saddlestone Records (C&W).

Tips: "Make sure songs are your best and commercial—songs should have strong lyrics with a good hook."

WINSTON & HOFFMAN HOUSE MUSIC PUBLISHERS (ASCAP/BMI), #318, 1680 N. Vine St., Hollywood CA 90028. President: Lynne Robin Green. Music publisher. Estab. 1958. Publishes 25 songs/year. Works with composers and lyricists. Pays standard royalty.

Affiliate(s): Lansdowne Music Publishers (ASCAP), Bloor Music (BMI), Clemitco Publishing (BMI) and Ben Ross Music (ASCAP).

How to Contact: Submit demo tape by mail. Unsolicited submissions are OK. Prefers cassette with 3 songs maximum and lyric sheet. "*Must* SASE, or *no* reply! No calls." Reports in 3½ weeks.

Music: Mostly **R&B dance, ballads, hip hop, vocal jazz, alternative rock** and **R&B**; also **pop ballads**. Published "Bad By Myself," written and recorded by Biz Markie on Warner Bros. Records; "Thoughts in the Buttermilk" (by Handy/Warfield/Huston), recorded by Justin Warfield on QWest/Warner Bros. Records; also many songs featured in *Return to Two Moon Junction* (Trimark '94).
Tips: "Be selective in what you send. Be realistic about which artist it suits! Be patient in allowing time to place songs. Be open to writing for films—be interesting lyrically and striking melodically."

WITHOUT PAPERS MUSIC PUBLISHING INC., 2366 Woodhill Rd., Cleveland OH 44106. (216)791-2100, ext. 204. Fax: (216)791-7117. President: Michele Norton. Music publisher. Estab. 1992. Publishes 4 songs/year; publishes 2 new songwriters/year. Hires staff songwriters. Works with composers and lyricists; teams collaborators. "Royalties are negotiated—songwriters currently at 50%."
How to Contact: Call first and obtain permission to submit. Prefers cassette with lyric sheet. Does not return material. Reports in 2 weeks.
Music: Mostly **rock, R&B** and **country** (with R&B or rock base); also **children's, classical, different** and **commercial**. Published *Make It Burn, Too High A Price* and *Had Another Girl* (all by Stutz Bearcat), recorded by Armstrong/Bearcat on Strange Attractor Records.
Tips: "Be patient and be willing to work with us and the song."

WONDERWAX PUBLISHING, P.O. Box 4641, Estes Park CO 80517. President: James Haber. Music publisher, record company (DG Records, Wonderwax Records). BMI. Estab. 1983. Publishes 25 songs/year; publishes 10 new songwriters/year. Pays standard royalty.
How to Contact: Submit a demo tape—unsolicited submissions are OK. "Prefers cassette with your best 2 songs and lyric sheets. Send clear demos, please." SASE. Reports in 1 week to 3 months.
Music: Mostly **pop, alternative** and **grunge**, will listen to **R&B** and **country**. Rock submissions only in the alternative genre. Published "Vain" (by J. Upham); "Boxer" (by Scott Roberts) on Wonderwax Records; and "Some Guy Named Paul" (by Slash N.F.), recorded by Degeneration on Wonderwax Records (psychodance 45).
Tips: "We prefer full demos, please keep this in mind when submitting. We are a 'writer friendly' organization, our contracts for publishing are the standard Songwriters Guild variety. Protect yourself! Have all contracts reviewed by a lawyer or by the Guild itself, do not be taken advantage of! We are especially interested in alternative rock. Submit your best efforts, bio-pictures, press kit. Show us how professional you really are, if I'm 'taken away' by your demo, I'll help you 1 step at a time, right through this monster called the music business. Is anyone out there?"

WOODRICH PUBLISHING CO. (BMI), P.O. Box 38, Lexington AL 35648. (205)247-3983. President: Woody Richardson. Music publisher and record company (Woodrich Records) and record producer. Estab. 1959. Publishes 25 songs/year; publishes 12 new songwriters/year. Works with composers; teams collaborators. Pays standard royalty.
Affiliate(s): Mernee Music (ASCAP), Melstep Music (BMI) and Tennesse Valley Music (SESAC).
How to Contact: Submit a demo tape by mail. Unsolicited submissions are OK. Prefers cassette with 2-4 songs. Prefers studio produced demos. SASE. Reports in 2 weeks.
Music: Mostly **country** and **gospel**; also **bluegrass, blues, choral, church/religious, easy listening, folk, jazz, MOR, progressive, rock, soul** and **top 40/pop**. Published *Welcome Back To Me* (by Sam Celia), recorded by Sandi Thompson on Playback Records (country); *Winding Road*, written and recorded by Darryl Alexander on LRG Records (jazz); and "I'll Say My Own Prayer," written and recorded by Wm. L. Godwin on Woodrich Records (gospel).
Tips: "Use a studio demo if possible. If not, be sure the lyrics are extremely clear. Be sure to include a SASE with *sufficient* return postage."

WORLD FAMOUS MUSIC CO., Dept. SM, 1518 Crowe Ave., Deerfield IL 60015-2122. (708)405-0806. President: Chip Altholz. Music publisher, record producer. ASCAP. Estab. 1986. Publishes 25 songs/year; 3-4 new songwriters/year. Works with composers and lyricists. Pays standard royalty.
How to Contact: Submit a demo tape—unsolicited submissions are OK. Prefers cassette with 3 songs and lyric sheet. SASE. Reports in 1 month.
Music: Mostly **pop, R&B** and **rock**. Published "Jungleman," "Automatic" and "All the Stars" (by N. Bak) recorded by Ten-28 on Pink Street Records (pop/dance).
Tips: "Have a great melody, a lyric that is visual and tells a story and a commercial arrangement."

*X PRESH'N SERIES MUSIC (BMI), P.O. Box 3691, La Mesa CA 91944. (619)460-1146. Owner/General Manager: R.L. Hollman. Music publisher. Estab. 1990. Publishes 30 songs/year; publishes 4 new songwriters/year. Works with composers and lyricists. Pays 12% retail cost of produced recording.
How to Contact: Submit demo tape by mail. Unsolicited submissions are OK. Prefers cassette (or VHS videocassette). SASE. Reports in 4-6 weeks.
Music: Mostly **flamenco, Middle Eastern** and **Latin**. Published *Poder Gitano*, written and recorded by Rodrigo (flamenco); *Granainas*, written and recorded by Alberto De Malaga (flamenco); and *Nos*

Volvemos a Querer, written and recorded by Remedios Flores (flamenco).

XMAS MUSIC (ASCAP), P.O. Box 828, Hollywood CA 90078. (213)466-4000. President: Randall Paul. Music publisher. Works with composers and lyricists. Pays standard royalty.
Affiliate(s): Xmas Songs (BMI).
How to Contact: Submit demo tape by mail. Unsolicited submissions are OK. Prefers cassette with 2 songs and lyric sheet. SASE. Reports in 1 month.
Music: Seasonal songs only. Published "Santa Claus' Spaceship" (by Maxine Manners); "Santa Claus is Goin' Country (by Andrew Glenn); and "Christmastime on the Radio" (by Randall Heddon).

*Y-NOT PRODUCTIONS, P.O. Box 902, Mill Valley CA 94942. (415)898-0027. Fax: (415)898-8580. Administrative Supervisor: Lane Lombardo. Music publisher, record company (YNP Records) and record producer. Publishes 20-30 songs/year; publishes 15-20 new songwriters/year. Hires staff songwriters. Works with composers and lyricists; teams collaborators. "Royalty varies."
Affiliate(s): Lindy Lane Music (BMI).
How to Contact: Submit demo tape by mail. Unsolicited submissions are OK. Prefers cassette or VHS videocassette with 3 songs and lyric, lead sheet. SASE. Reports in 3 weeks.
Music: Mostly **pop, dance jazz** and **contemporary**. Published *Whispering Waters*, written and recorded by Tony Saunders on YNP Records; *Hooked on You* (by Darryl Waters), recorded by Pure Essence on RCA Records; and *I Give All My Love to You* (by Tony Saunders), recorded by Paradize on MCA Records.
Tips: "If your melody is not catchy by itself the song probably is at a loss. The song has to have a strong hook."

YORGO MUSIC, 615 Valley Rd., Upper Montclair NJ 07043. (201)746-2359. President: George Louvis. Music publisher. BMI. Estab. 1987. Publishes 5-10 songs/year; publishes 3-5 new songwriters/year. Works with composers and lyricists; teams collaborators. Pays standard royalty.
How to Contact: Submit demo tape by mail. Unsolicited submissions OK. Prefers cassette with 1-3 songs and lyric or lead sheet. "Specify if you are a writer/artist or just a writer." Does not return unsolicited material. Reports in 1-3 months.
Music: Mostly **gospel, contemporary Christian, R&B, dance** and **pop**; also **ballads** and **pop metal**. Published "To the Maximum" (by S. Stone, S. McGhee, G. Louvis), recorded by Steve D the Destroyer on Q-Rap Records (rap); and "Love Me True" (by G. Louvis), recorded by Kimiesha Holmes on Quark Records (dance).
Tips: "We also own two production companies and have access to quite a few artists and labels. Be honest about your material; if you wouldn't buy it, don't send it. We are looking for songs and artists."

YOUR BEST SONGS PUBLISHING, Suite P171, 1210 Auburn Way N., Auburn WA 98002. Phone and fax: (206)939-3571. General Manager: Craig Markovich. Music publisher. Estab. 1988. Publishes 10-30 songs/year. Publishes 1-4 new songwriters/year. Works with composers and lyricists. Query for royalty terms.
How to Contact: Submit demo tape by mail. Unsolicited submissions are OK. Prefers cassette with 1-3 songs and lyric sheet. "Submit your 1-3 best songs per type of music. Use separate cassettes per music type and indicate music type on each cassette." SASE. Reports in 1-2 months.
Music: Mostly **alternative, rock/blues** and **pop/rock**; also **progressive, adult contemporary**, some **heavy metal**. Published "Hidden Gun" and "Farewell (My Love)," recorded by Brain Box on Cybervoc, Inc.
Tips: "Not necessary to have a full blown production; just require good lyrics, good melodies and good rhythm in a song."

ZAUBER MUSIC PUBLISHING (ASCAP), P.O. Box 5087, V.M.8.O., Vancouver, British Columbia V6B 4A9 **Canada**. (604)528-9194. Professional Manager: Martin E. Hamann. Music publisher and record producer. Estab. 1981. Publishes 3-5 songs/year; publishes 1-2 new songwriters/year. Hires staff writers. Works with composers and lyricists; teams collaborators. Pays minimum 50% to writer.
Affiliate(s): Merlin Productions and Zauberer Music (SOCAN).
How to Contact: Submit demo tape by mail. Unsolicited submissions are OK. Prefers cassette with lyric or lead sheet. SAE and IRC. Reports in 3 weeks.
Music: Mostly **dance, pop/R&B** and **rock**; also **techno** and **Euro-pop**. Published *Sweet Soul Reminder* and *Let Harmony Reign*, both written and recorded by Mode to Joy on Merlin Records (dance); and *Never Ever Green*, written and recorded by Katryna Rael on Merlin Records (rock).
Tips: "Send 3 songs only, the most commercial first. Hire the best singer available. Uptempo songs work best. Have a strong lyric/melodic chorus."

Geographic Index

The U.S. section of this handy Geographic Index will quickly give you the names of music publishers located in or near the music centers of Los Angeles, New York and Nashville. Of course, there are many valuable contacts to be made in other cities, but you will probably want to plan a trip to one of these established music centers at some point in your career and try to visit as many of these companies as you think appropriate. The International section lists, geographically, markets for your songs in countries other than the U.S.

Find the names of companies in this index, and then check listings within the Music Publishers section for addresses, phone numbers and submission details.

Los Angeles
Alexis
All Nations Music Publishing, Ltd.
Audio Music Publishers
AVC Music
Bok Music
Bronx Flash Music, Inc.
Bug Music, Inc.
Buzzart Enterprises
Christmas & Holiday Music
Direct Management Group
D'Nico International
Doré Records
Drive Music, Inc.
Famous Music Publishing Companies
First Release Music Publishing
The Fricon Entertainment Co., Inc.
International Music Network
Jedo Inc.
Kingsport Creek Music Publishing
Le Grande Fromage/Cheddar Cheese Music
Loveforce International
Miracle Mile Music/Black Satin
Momentum Music Inc.
The Music Room Publishing Group
Peermusic
Philippopolis Music
Queen Esther Music Publishing
Rent-A-Song
Rondor Music International
Shankman De Blasio Melina, Inc.
Song Wizard Music
Supreme Enterprises Int'l Corp.
Sweet Glenn Music
Transition Music Corp.
Twin Towers Publishing Co.
Vaam Music Group
Wemar Music

Shane Wilder Music
Winston & Hoffman House Music Publishers
Xmas Music

Nashville
Abingdon Press
Aim High Music Company
Allisongs Inc.
Angelsong Publishing Co.
Another Ear Music
Baby Huey Music
Best Buddies, Inc.
Buried Treasure Music
Calinoh Music Group
Calvary Music Group, Inc.
Castle Music Corp.
Cedar Creek Music
Clientele Music
Collins Music Group
The Cornelius Companies
Cottage Blue Music
Loman Craig Music
Cupit Music
Denny Music Group
ESI Music Group
Excursion Music Group
Fat City Publishing
Fretboard Publishing
Frog and Moose Music
Humanform Publishing Company
Gregg Hutchins Music
Iron Skillet Music
Jaclyn Music
Al Jolson Black & White Music
Patrick Joseph Music Inc.
Lion Hill Music Publishing Co.
The Marco Music Group Inc.
The Mathes Company
Nashville Music Group
Nautical Music Co.
Justin Peters Music
Silver Thunder Music Group
Sizemore Music
Song Cellar

Song Farm Music
Sound Achievement Group
Star Song Communications
Sunset Productions
Tooth and Nail Music
Ultimate Peak Music

New York
Amicos II Music, Ltd.
Apon Publishing Co.
Better Than Sex Music
Bourne Co. Music Publishers
Bullet Proof Management
John Cale Music, Inc.
Camex Music
Cold Chillin' Music Publishing
Eudaemonic Music
Globeart Publishing
Jay Gold Music Publishing
S.M. Gold Music
Hit & Run Music Publishing Inc.
Hot Lips Music Company
Humongous Music Publishing, Inc.
Jasper Stone Music/JSM Songs
Jungle Boy Music
Kozkeeozko Music
Latin American Music Co., Inc.
Laurmack Music
Lin's Lines
MCA Music Publishing
Mia Mind Music
Music Sales Corporation
Chuck Mymit Music Productions
One Hot Note Music Inc.
Paisley Park Music
Phaja Music
PPI/Peter Pan Industries
Prescription Company
Rockford Music Co.
Steve Rose Music
Siskatune Music Publishing Co.
Soul Street Music Publishing Inc.

State 51 Publishing Inc.
Sunfrost Music
Tender Tender Music
Tops And Bottoms Music

International

Australia
Colstal Music
Logical Choice Music
Two/Polygram Music Publishing

Austria
Aquarius Publishing
Johann Hartel Musikverlag
Honk Music—Musikverlag H. Gebetsroither
Musikverlag K. Urbanek
Musikverlag Rossori
Friedrich Weber Musikverlag
West & East Music

Belgium
Abigwan
ADM Publishing
Centropa N.V.
EMI Music Publishing
Hi Tension Records
Inside Records/OK Songs
Jump Music
Hans Kusters Music
Mama Linda
Parsifal
Play That Beat!
Prestation Music
Promo
Succes

Canada
Alleged Iguana Music
Alternative Direction Music Publishers
Arylis Corporation
August Night Music
Berandol Music Ltd.
Branch Group Music
Clotille Publishing
Corporate Rock Music

Hickory Lane Publishing and Recording
ISBA Music Publishing Inc.
Lilly Music Publishing
Magnum Music Corp. Ltd.
Montina Music
Nashville Sound Music Publishing Co.
S.M.C.L. Productions, Inc.
Sci-Fi Music
Zauber Music Publishing

France
Captain Click
Coppelia
Editions Musicales Alpha
Editions Scipion
Elliot Music
Pas Mal Publishing SARL
Societe D'Editions Musicales et Artistiques "Esperance"

Germany
Alpana Musik & Film
Aum Circle Publishing
Blue Cue Music
Cap-Sounds Publishing
R.D. Clevère Musikverlag
CSB Kaminsky
Heupferd Musik Verlag
Ja/Nein Musikverlag
Mento Music Group
Seychelles Music
Siegel Music Companies
UBM
Berthold Wengert

Italy
Ala/Bianca SRL

Malaysia
Pustaka Muzik EMI

The Netherlands
All Rock Music
Associated Artists Music International

New Zealand
Pegasus Music

Switzerland
OBH Musikverlag Otto B. Hartmann

United Kingdom
Accolade Music Ltd.
Arc Music Productions International Ltd.
Bad Habits Music Publishing
Bearsongs
Kitty Brewster Songs
Christel Music Limited
CTV Music
Dead Dead Good Records/Music Ltd.
Demi Monde Records & Publishing Ltd.
DPP Music
The Escape Artist Company
Ever-Open-Eye Music
F&J Music
First Time Music (Publishing) U.K. Ltd.
Flowsound Ltd.
Go! Discs Music
Hautboy Music
Havasong Music
Heaven Music
Hedley Music Group/Get Ready Publishing
Holyrood Productions
International Music Network Limited
Iona Publishing
Jammy Music Publishers Ltd.
Jester Song Ltd.
Keep Calm Music Limited
Kevin King Music
Lantern Music/Music for Films
Menace Music Group
Bryan Morrison Music
Music House International Limited
Nervous Publishing
Panama Music Library
R.J. Music
R.T.L. Music
Rough Trade Publishing
Sea Dream Music
Sleeping Giant Music International Ltd.
Sphemusations
Tabitha Music, Ltd.
Tower Bridge Music, Ltd.

Category Index

The Category Index is a good place to begin searching for a market for your songs. Below is an alphabetical list of 19 general music categories. If you write country songs and are looking for a publisher to pitch them, check the Country section in this index. There you will find a list of publishers who are interested in hearing country songs. Once you locate the entries for those publishers, read the music subheading *carefully* to determine which companies are most interested in the type of country music you write. Some of the markets in this section do not appear in the Category Index because they have not indicted a specific preference. Most of these said they are interested in "all types" of music. Listings that were very specific, or whose description of the music they're interested in doesn't quite fit into these categories, also do not appear here.

Adult Contemporary a Hi-Tek Publishing Company; All Nations Music Publishing, Ltd.; Alleged Iguana Music; Allegheny Music Works; Amalgamated Tulip Corp.; Amicos II Music, Ltd.; Amiron Music; Angelsong Publishing Co.; Antelope Publishing Inc.; Apon Publishing Co.; Arylis Corporation; Associated Artists Music International; Axbar Productions; Bal & Bal Music Publishing Co.; Bethlehem Music Publications; Blue Hill Music/Tutch Music; BOAM; Bok Music; Buried Treasure Music; Buzzart Enterprises; California Country Music; Camex Music; Christel Music Limited; Clear Pond Music; Connell Publishing Co., Jerry; Country Star Music; Dean Enterprises Music Group; Denny Music Group; Duane Music, Inc.; Earth Dance Music; Element Movie and Music; Garrivan Music; Gary Music, Alan; Green One Music; Gubala Music, Frank; Hautboy Music; Havasong Music; Heaven Songs; Hedley Music Group/Get Ready Publishing; Hickory Lane Publishing and Recording; Hickory Valley Music; High-Minded Moma Publishing & Productions; Hitsburgh Music Co.; Holy Spirit Music; Holyrood Productions; Inside Records/OK Songs; Iona Publishing; ISBA Music Publishing Inc.; Jaclyn Music; Jacob-Maxwell, Inc.; Ja/Nein Musikverlag; Joseph Music Inc., Patrick; Jump Music; Just a Note; Kansa Records Corporation; Kaupps & Robert Publishing Co.; King Music, Kevin; Kingsport Creek Music Publishing; Kommunication Koncepts; Kozkeeozko Music; Lackey Publishing Co.; Lineage Publishing Co.; Little Pond Productions; Lowe Publishing, Jere; Lowery Group, The; Magnum Music Corp. Ltd.; Mento Music Group; Merry Marilyn Music Publishing; Montina Music; Murdock's Music Company; Music House International Limited; Music In the Right Keys Publishing Company; Music Sales Corporation; New Rap Jam Publishing, A; Nicoletti Music Co., The Joseph; Nise Productions Inc.; Okisher Music; Oldham Music Publishing Company, Ronnie; Operation Perfection; Otto Publishing Co.; Parravano Music; Passing Parade Music; Pegasus Music; Pine Island Music; Prescription Company; Pustaka Muzik EMI; R. J. Music; Riverhawk Music; Roberts Music, Freddie; Rob-Lee Music; Rockford Music Co.; Rondor Music International; Roots Music; S.M.C.L. Productions, Inc.; Segal's Publications; Seychelles Music; Shadowland Productions; Sha-La Music, Inc.; Siegel Music Companies; Silicon Music Publishing Co.; Sincerity, Ltd.; Songfinder Music; Songrite Creations Productions; Sugarfoot Productions; Sultan Music Publishing; Sunflare Songs/Records; Tabitha Music, Ltd.; Tedesco Music Co., Dale; Tompaul Music Co.; Tuffin Music Enterprises; UBM; Walton Music Publishing Co., Jimmy; White Cat Music; Woodrich Publishing Co.; Your Best Songs Publishing

Alternative Abalone Publishing; Another Amethyst Song; Astron Music Publishing; AUM Circle Publishing; Baby Raquel Music; Better Than Sex Music; Bullet Proof Management; Camex Music; Dead Dead Good Records/Music Ltd.; Direct Management Group; Eudaemonic Music; Fat City Publishing; Hautboy Music; Havasong Music; Humongous Music Publishing, Inc.; Jedo Inc.; Josena Music; Justice Music Corporation; Le Grande Fromage/Cheddar Cheese Music; Menace Music Group; Mia Mind Music; Momentum Music Inc.; Murdock's Music Company; Music Factory Enterprises, Inc.; Nashville Music Group; Pas Mal Publishing Sarl; Pen Cob Publishing Inc.; Prejippie Music Group; Publishing Central; Rana International Music Group Inc.; Raving Cleric Music Publishing/Euro Export Entertainment; Rough Trade Publishing; Tuffin Music Enterprises; Waterbury Road Music; Winston & Hoffman House Music Publishers; Wonderwax Publishing; Your Best Songs Publishing

Blues Alexis; Amalgamated Tulip Corp.; Axbar Productions; Bal & Bal Music Publishing Co.; Bearsongs; Beth-Ridge Music Publishing Co.; Blue Hill Music/Tutch Music; Christopher Publishing, Sonny; Duane Music, Inc.; Element Movie and Music; Emperor of Emperors; Fat City Publishing; Frog and Moose Music; Frozen Inca Music; Gold Plate Music; Gubala Music, Frank; Humanform

Publishing Company; Jacob-Maxwell, Inc.; Ja/Nein Musikverlag; Kicking Mule Publishing/Desk Drawer Publishing; Macman Music, Inc.; Martin's Music Publishing, Rod; Menace Music Group; Motex Music; Nashville Music Group; Nervous Publishing; Okisher Music; Parsifal; Play That Beat!; Prescription Company; Promo; Prospector Three D Publishing; Pustaka Muzik EMI; R.J. Music; Raving Cleric Music Publishing/Euroexport Entertainment; Saulsby Music Co., William A.; Sea Dream Music; Silverfoot Publishing; Sincerity, Ltd.; Sizemore Music; Sky-Child Music; Songrite Creations Productions; Sound Cellar Music; Sphemusations; Stellar Music Industries; Stuart Music Co., Jeb; Sugar Mama Music; Sugarfoot Productions; Sunset Productions; Weber Musikverlag, Friedrich; Wes Music, Bobe; Woodrich Publishing Co.; Your Best Songs Publishing

Children's Berandol Music Ltd.; Bethlehem Music Publications; Branch Group Music; Eccentrax Music Co.; Editions Musicales Alpha; Element Movie and Music; Filmworks; Five Roses Music Group; Flying Red Horse Publishing; Gordon Music Co., Inc.; Hickory Lane Publishing And Recording; Hot Lips Music Company; Lonny Tunes Music; Lowe Publishing, Jere; Mighty Twinns Music; Nise Productions Inc.; NSP Music Publishing Inc.; Paluch Company, J. S./World Library Publications, Inc.; Parravano Music; Passing Parade Music; PPI/Peter Pan Industries; Prescription Company; Segal's Publications; Shadowland Productions; Silverhill Music; Song Wizard Music; Sunfrost Music; Velocity Productions; Without Papers Music Publishing Inc.

Classical Apon Publishing Co.; Bad Habits Music Publishing; Cale Music, Inc., John; Clevère Musikverlag, R.D.; CQK Records and Music; Discapon Publishing Co.; Editions Musicales Alpha; Element Movie and Music; Ho-hum Music; Jae Music, Jana; JOF-Dave Music; Musikverlag K. Urbanek; OBH Musikverlag Otto B. Hartmann; Philippopolis Music; Rising Star Records and Publishers; Roots Music; Sky-Child Music; Tender Tender Music; UBM; Without Papers Music Publishing Inc.

Country a Hi-Tek Publishing Company; Abalone Publishing; Accent Publishing Co.; Accolade Music Ltd.; Aim High Music Company; Alexis; Alhart Music Publishing; All Nations Music Publishing, Ltd.; All Rock Music; Alleged Iguana Music; Allegheny Music Works; AlliSongs Inc.; Amalgamated Tulip Corp.; Americatone International; Angelsong Publishing Co.; Another Ear Music; Aquarius Publishing; ARC Music Productions International Ltd.; Art Audio Publishing Company/ Tight Hi-Fi Soul Music; Associated Artists Music International; Astrodisque Publishing; Astron Music Publishing; August Night Music; Axbar Productions; Bal & Bal Music Publishing Co.; Barking Foe The Master's Bone; Best Buddies, Inc.; Betty Jane/Josie Jane Music Publishers; Black Stallion Country Publishing; Blue Hill Music/Tutch Music; Blue Spur Music Group, Inc.; BOAM; BoDe Music; Bollman International Publishing Co.; Bonnfire Publishing; Brewster Songs, Kitty; Buried Treasure Music; Butler Music, Bill; Buzzart Enterprises; Cactus Music and Winnebago Publishing; California Country Music; Calinoh Music Group; Caravell Main Sail Music; Cash Productions, Inc.; Castle Music Corp.; Cedar Creek Music; Centropa N.V.; Chapie Music; Cheavoria Music Co.; Cherie Music; Chestnut Mound Music Group; Christopher Publishing, Sonny; Cimirron Music; Cisum; Clear Pond Music; Clearwind Publishing; Clevère Musikverlag, R.D.; Clientele Music; Coffee and Cream Publishing Company; Collins Music Group; Colstal Music; Connell Publishing Co., Jerry; Controlled Destiny Music Publishing; Cornelius Companies, The; Cottage Blue Music; Country Breeze Music; Country Showcase America; Country Star Music; Cowboy Junction Flea Market and Publishing Co.; CQK Records and Music; Craig Music, Loman; Creekside Music; CSB Kaminsky GMBH; Cupit Music; Dan the Man Music; Darbonne Publishing Co.; De Miles Music Company, The Edward; Dean Enterprises Music Group; Delev Music Company; Dell Music, Frank; Delpha's Music Publishers; Denny Music Group; Diamond Wind Music; Doc Publishing; Don Del Music; Doss Music, Buster; Drezdon Blacque Music; Duane Music, Inc.; Earitating Music Publishing; Earthscream Music Publishing Co.; Eccentrax Music Co.; Elect Music Publishing Company; Element Movie and Music; Emandell Tunes; EMF Productions; Emperor of Emperors; Empty Sky Music Company; Emzee Music; ESI Music Group; Excursion Music Group; F.E.D. Publishing Co.; Faiella Publishing, Doug; Farr-Away Music; Fat City Publishing; Fezsongs; Filmworks; First Time Music (Publishing) U.K. Ltd.; Five Roses Music Group; Flash International; Focal Point Music Publishers; Four Newton Publishing; Fox Farm Recording; Fretboard Publishing; Frick Music Publishing Co.; Fricon Entertainment Co., Inc., The; Frog and Moose Music; Frog Hair Songs; Garrivan Music; Gary Music, Alan; General Jones Music; Giftness Enterprise; GlobeArt Publishing; Go Star Music; Gold Music Publishing, Jay; Gowell Music, Richard E.; Green One Music; Gubala Music, Frank; Halgeo Music; Halo International; Harmony Street Music; Havasong Music; Hawk's Bill Music; Heaven Songs; Henderson Group Music; Henly Music Associates; Hickory Lane Publishing and Recording; Hickory Valley Music; High-Minded Moma Publishing & Productions; History Publishing Co.; Hitsburgh Music Co.; Hitsource Publishing; Ho-hum Music; Honk Music — Musikverlag H. Gebetsroither; Inside Records/OK Songs; Iron Skillet Music; ISBA Music Publishing Inc.; Jaclyn Music; Jacob-Maxwell, Inc.; Jae Music, Jana; Jaelius Enterprises; Jammy Music Publishers Ltd.; Jedo Inc.; Jennaco-Alexas Publishing Co.; Jerjoy Music; Jester Song Ltd.; JOF-Dave Music; Jolson Black & White Music, Al; Jon Music; Joseph Music Inc., Patrick; Jungle Boy Music; Just a Note; Justice Music Corporation; Kansa Records Corporation; Kaupps & Robert Publishing Co.; Kaylee Music Group, Karen; Kel-Cres Publishing; Kennedy Enterprises, Inc., Gene; King Music, Kevin; Kingsport Creek Music Publishing; Kozkeeozko Music; Kren Music Publishing; Lackey Publishing Co.; Lantern Music/Music For Films; Lari-Jon Publishing; Laurmack Music; Laymond Publishing Co., Inc.; Lilly Music Publishing; Lindsay Publishing, Doris; Lineage Publishing Co.; Lion Hill Music Publishing Co.; Little

Richie Johnson Music; Lonny Tunes Music; Loveforce International; Lovey Music, Inc.; Lowe Publishing, Jere; Lowery Group, The; Luick & Associates Music Publisher, Harold; M & T Waldoch Publishing, Inc.; McCoy Music, Jim; McGibony Publishing; Mack Music, Danny; Magic Message Music; Magnum Music Corp. Ltd.; Makers Mark Gold; Manben Music; Manny Music, Inc.; Marco Music Group Inc., The; Mathes Company, The; Media Productions; Menace Music Group; Mento Music Group; Merry Marilyn Music Publishing; Montina Music; Moon June Music; Motex Music; Murdock's Music Company; Music In the Right Keys Publishing Company; Music Sales Corporation; Myko Music; Nashville Music Group; Nashville Sound Music Publishing Co.; National Talent; Nautical Music Co.; Nervous Publishing; New Rap Jam Publishing, A; Newcreature Music; Nicoletti Music Co., The Joseph; Nise Productions Inc.; Non-Stop Music Publishing; Oh My Gosh Music; Okisher Music; Old Slowpoke Music; Oldham Music Publishing Company, Ronnie; One for the Money Music Publishing Co.; One Hot Note Music Inc.; Orchid Publishing; Otto Publishing Co.; Palmetto Productions; Pancho's Music Co.; Parravano Music; Passing Parade Music; Pecos Valley Music; Pegasus Music; Pen Cob Publishing Inc.; Perfection Music Publications; Pine Island Music; Platinum Boulevard Publishing; Portage Music; Prescription Company; Pritchett Publication; Prospector Three D Publishing; Publishing Central; Purple Haze Music; Pustaka Muzik EMI; Qmark Music; R. J. Music; Rahsaan Publishing; Rana International Music Group Inc.; Raving Cleric Music Publishing/Euro Export Entertainment; Red Boots Tunes; Ridge Music Corp.; Riverhawk Music; Roberts Music, Freddie; Rocker Music/Happy Man Music; Rockford Music Co.; Roots Music; Rose Hill Group; Rose Music, Steve; Royal Flair Publishing; Rushwin Publishing; Rustron Music Publishers; S & R Music Publishing Co.; Sabteca Music Co.; Saddlestone Publishing; Samuel Three Productions; Sariser Music; Scott Music Group, Tim; Segal's Publications; Sellwood Publishing; Seychelles Music; Siegel Music Companies; Silicon Music Publishing Co.; Silver Thorn Enterprises; Silver Thunder Music Group; Silverfoot Publishing; Silverhill Music; Simply Grand Music, Inc.; Sincerity, Ltd.; Singing Roadie Music Group; Siskatune Music Publishing Co.; Sizemore Music; Sky-Child Music; Song Cellar; Song Farm Music; Songfinder Music; Songrite Creations Productions; Sound Cellar Music; Sound Column Publications; Sounds of Aicram; Southern Most Publishing Company; Sphemusations; Spradlin/Gleich Publishing; Stable Music Co.; Starbound Publishing Co.; Stellar Music Industries; Stuart Music Co., Jeb; Stylecraft Music Co.; Sugar Mama Music; Sugarfoot Productions; Sultan Music Publishing; Sun Star Songs; Sunflare Songs/Records; Sunfrost Music; Sunset Productions; Sweet Glenn Music; Tabitha Music, Ltd.; TEK Publishing; Tentex Music Publishing; Terrace Entertainment Corporation; Tiki Enterprises, Inc.; Tompaul Music Co.; Toulouse Music Publishing Co., Inc.; Trusty Publications; Tuffin Music Enterprises; Ultimate Peak Music; Vaam Music Group; Valet Publishing Co.; Voice Notes Publishing; Vokes Music Publishing; Walton Music Publishing Co., Jimmy; Waterbury Road Music; Watonka Records Co.; Weaver Words of Music; Wes Music, Bobe; Whatapayne Publishing; Whimsong Publishing; White Car Music; White Cat Music; Whitewing Music; Wilcom Publishing; Wilder Music, Shane; Without Papers Music Publishing Inc.; Wonderwax Publishing; Woodrich Publishing Co.

Dance Abalone Publishing; Abigwan; ADM Publishing; Ala/Bianca SRL; Alexis; Aljoni Music Co.; Alpana Musik & Film; Amalgamated Tulip Corp.; Amicos II Music, Ltd.; Apon Publishing Co.; Art Audio Publishing Company/Tight Hi-Fi Soul Music; Associated Artists Music International; Audio Music Publishers; AVC Music; Baby Raquel Music; Bad Habits Music Publishing; Bartow Music; Beth-Ridge Music Publishing Co.; Blue Cue Music; Brewster Songs, Kitty; CAP-Sounds Publishing; Captain Click; Centropa N.V.; Clevère Musikverlag, R.D.; Clientele Music; Clotille Publishing; Coffee and Cream Publishing Company; Cross Culture Productions, Inc.; Dagene Music; De Miles Music Company, The Edward; Dead Dead Good Records/Music Ltd.; Delev Music Company; D'Nico International; DPP Music; Drive Music, Inc.; Duane Music, Inc.; Element Movie and Music; Elliot Music; EMI Music Publishing; Escape Artist Company, The; F.E.D. Publishing Co.; F&J Music; Filmworks; Flowsound Ltd.; Fricon Entertainment Co., Inc., The; Gary Music, Alan; Genetic Music Publishing; Gold Music, S.M.; Gubala Music, Frank; Hautboy Music; Heaven Music; Heaven Songs; Hi Tension Records; Hit & Run Music Publishing Inc.; Hitsource Publishing; Holyrood Productions; Hot Lips Music Company; Humongous Music Publishing, Inc.; Inside Records/OK Songs; International Music Network; International Music Network Limited; ISBA Music Publishing Inc.; Joey Boy Publishing Co.; Jump Music; Keep Calm Music Limited; Kommunication Koncepts; Kozkeeozko Music; Lilly Music Publishing; M & T Waldoch Publishing, Inc.; Manapro (Management Artist Productions); Menace Music Group; Mia Mind Music; Miracle Mile Music/Black Satin; Momentum Music Inc.; Montina Music; Musikverlag Rossori; Myko Music; Nise Productions Inc.; Now & Then Music; NSP Music Publishing Inc.; One Hot Note Music Inc.; Phaja Music; Play That Beat!; Prejippie Music Group; Prescription Company; Rob-Lee Music; Rockford Music Co.; Rose Hill Group; S.M.C.L. Productions, Inc.; Sha-La Music, Inc.; Shankman De Blasio Melina, Inc.; Siegel Music Companies; Siskatune Music Publishing Co.; Soul Street Music Publishing Inc.; State 51 Music Publishing Inc.; Stuart Music Co., Jeb; Succes; Sugarfoot Productions; Sunsongs Music/Hollywood East Entertainment; Tabitha Music, Ltd.; Tedesco Music Co., Dale; Tower Bridge Music, Ltd.; Transition Music Corp.; Trusty Publications; Valet Publishing Co.; Victory Music; Wemar Music; Wes Music, Bobe; West & East Music; Whatapayne Publishing; Wheeler Communications Inc.; Winston & Hoffman House Music Publishers; Y-Not Productions; Yorgo Music; Zauber Music Publishing

Folk Accolade Music Ltd.; Alexis; Apon Publishing Co.; Aquarius Publishing; ARC Music Productions International Ltd.; Astrodisque Publishing; BOAM; Cimirron Music; Clevère Musikverlag, R.D.; Dean Enterprises Music Group; Don Del Music; Earitating Music Publishing; Earth Dance Music; Emperor of Emperors; Eudaemonic Music; First Time Music (Publishing) U.K. Ltd.; Frog Hair Songs; Green Meadows Publishing; Halo International; Heaven Songs; Heupferd Musik Verlag GmbH; Kicking Mule Publishing/Desk Drawer Publishing; Lackey Publishing Co.; Martin's Music Publishing, Rod; Montina Music; Motex Music; Nise Productions Inc.; OBH Musikverlag Otto B. Hartmann; Parravano Music; Prescription Company; Rockford Music Co.; Roots Music; Royal Flair Publishing; Rustron Music Publishers; Silver Thorn Enterprises; Slavia Pubilshing; Sunflare Songs/Records; Sunfrost Music; Terrace Entertainment Corporation; Tompaul Music Co.; Whimsong Publishing; Woodrich Publishing Co.

Jazz Abigwan; Alexander Sr. Music; Alexis; Aljoni Music Co.; Americatone International; Antelope Publishing Inc.; Arylis Corporation; Bad Habits Music Publishing; Bal & Bal Music Publishing Co.; Bearsongs; Brewster Songs, Kitty; Chapie Music; Connell Publishing Co., Jerry; Cunningham Music; Element Movie and Music; Emperor of Emperors; Fat City Publishing; Flash International; Frog Hair Songs; Garrivan Music; Genetic Music Publishing; Giftness Enterprise; GlobeArt Publishing; Gordon Music Co., Inc.; Happy Hour Music; Heaven Songs; Heupferd Musik Verlag GmbH; Ho-hum Music; Honk Music — Musikverlag H. Gebetsroither; Hot Lips Music Company; Jester Song Ltd.; Joey Boy Publishing Co.; Justice Music Corporation; Laurmack Music; Le Grande Fromage/Cheddar Cheese Music; Lonny Tunes Music; Makin Tracks Music; Montina Music; Newcreature Music; Nise Productions Inc.; Non-Stop Music Publishing; OBH Musikverlag Otto B. Hartmann; Okisher Music; Old Slowpoke Music; One Hot Note Music Inc.; Philippopolis Music; Platinum Boulevard Publishing; Prescription Company; Prestation Music; Pustaka Muzik EMI; Ridge Music Corp.; Rising Star Records and Publishers; Rockford Music Co.; Saulsby Music Company, William A.; Sphemusations; Stuart Music Co., Jeb; Sugarfoot Productions; Sunflare Songs/Records; Tedesco Music Co., Dale; Toulouse Music Publishing Co., Inc.; UBM; Weber Musikverlag, Friedrich; Weedhopper Music; Wheeler Communications Inc.; Winston & Hoffman House Music Publishers; Woodrich Publishing Co.; Y-Not Productions

Latin Alexis; Americatone International; Amicos II Music, Ltd.; Bollman International Publishing Co.; D'Nico International; Element Movie and Music; F.E.D. Publishing Co.; Happy Hour Music; Honk Music — Musikverlag H. Gebetsroither; Inside Records/OK Songs; Josena Music; Latin American Music Co., Inc.; Little Richie Johnson Music; Lowe Publishing, Jere; Manben Music; Manny Music, Inc.; Motex Music; Padrino Music Publishing; Pancho's Music Co.; Societe D'Editions Musicales Et Artistiques "Esperance"; Sounds-Vision Music; State 51 Music Publishing Inc.; Sugarfoot Productions; Supreme Enterprises Int'l Corp.; Tabitha Music, Ltd.; Unimusica Inc.; Wes Music, Bobe; X Presh'n Series Music

Metal Astron Music Publishing; AVC Music; Big Snow Music; Emperor of Emperors; Ho-hum Music; Keno Publishing; Kommunication Koncepts; M & T Waldoch Publishing, Inc.; Makin Tracks Music; Murdock's Music Company; Pas Mal Publishing Sarl; Silverhill Music; Sound Cellar Music; Victory Music; Waterbury Road Music; Yorgo Music; Your Best Songs Publishing

New Age Apon Publishing Co.; Astrodisque Publishing; August Night Music; Bad Habits Music Publishing; Chapie Music; Coppelia; Elect Music Publishing Company; Emperor of Emperors; Four Newton Publishing; GlobeArt Publishing; Go Star Music; Gorr Custom Music, Jon; Hartel Musikverlag, Johann; Ho-hum Music; Honk Music — Musikverlag H. Gebetsroither; Kren Music Publishing; Little Pond Productions; Makin Tracks Music; Manapro (Management Artist Productions); Music Factory Enterprises, Inc.; Non-Stop Music Publishing; Passing Parade Music; Platinum Boulevard Publishing; Rahsaan Publishing; Rising Star Records and Publishers; Rustron Music Publishers; Southern Most Publishing Company; Sunflare Songs/Records; Tiki Enterprises, Inc.; Whimsong Publishing

Novelty Axbar Productions; Branch Group Music; Cisum; Colstal Music; Dean Enterprises Music Group; Doré Records; Green One Music; Joey Boy Publishing Co.; Martin's Music Publishing, Rod; Parravano Music; Riverhawk Music; Sky-Child Music; Songrite Creations Productions; Tuffin Music Enterprises

Pop Abalone Publishing; Abigwan; Accent Publishing Co.; Ala/Bianca SRL; Alexander Sr. Music; Alexis; All Nations Music Publishing, Ltd.; Alleged Iguana Music; Allegheny Music Works; Alternative Direction Music Publishers; Amalgamated Tulip Corp.; Amicos II Music, Ltd.; Amiron Music; Angelsong Publishing Co.; Anode Music; Another Amethyst Song; Another Ear Music; Aquarius Publishing; Art Audio Publishing Company/Tight Hi-Fi Soul Music; Art of Concept Music; Associated Artists Music International; Astron Music Publishing; Aucourant Music; Audio Music Publishers; August Night Music; AUM Circle Publishing; AVC Music; Baby Raquel Music; Bad Habits Music Publishing; Bal & Bal Music Publishing Co.; Barking Foe The Master's Bone; Bartow Music; Berandol Music Ltd.; Bernard Enterprises, Inc., Hal; Best Buddies, Inc.; Beth-Ridge Music Publishing Co.; Better Than Sex Music; Big Snow Music; Blue Cue Music; Blue Hill Music/Tutch Music; Bok Music; Bourne Co. Music Publishers; Brewster Songs, Kitty; Bronx Flash Music, Inc.; Buried Treasure Music; California Country Music; Calinoh Music Group; Camex Music; CAP-Sounds Publishing; Captain Click; Caravell Main Sail Music; Cash Productions, Inc.; Castle Music Corp.; Cedar Creek Music; Centropa N.V.; Chapie Music; Cheavoria Music Co.; Christel Music Limited; Cisum; City Publishing Co.; Clear Pond Music; Clearwind Publishing; Clevère Musikverlag, R.D.; Clientele Music; Clotille Publishing; Coffee and Cream Publishing Company; Controlled Destiny Music Publishing; Coppelia; Cornelius Companies, The; Corporate

Rock Music; Cottage Blue Music; CQK Records and Music; Craig Music, Loman; Cross Culture Productions, Inc.; CSB Kaminsky GMBH; Cunningham Music; Dagene Music; Dan the Man Music; De Miles Music Company, The Edward; Dean Enterprises Music Group; Delev Music Company; Dell Music, Frank; Delpha's Music Publishers; Demi Monde Records & Publishing Ltd.; Diamond Wind Music; Direct Management Group; D'Nico International; DPP Music; Dream Sequence Music, Ltd.; Drezdon Blacque Music; Drive Music, Inc.; Duane Music, Inc.; Earthscream Music Publishing Co.; Eccentrax Music Co.; Editions Musicales Alpha; Element Movie and Music; EMF Productions; EMI Music Publishing; Emperor of Emperors; Empty Sky Music Company; Emzee Music; Escape Artist Company, The; ESI Music Group; Ever-Open-Eye Music; Excursion Music Group; F.E.D. Publishing Co.; Famous Music Publishing Companies; F&J Music; Filmworks; First Time Music (Publishing) U.K. Ltd.; Four Newton Publishing; Freko Records; Frick Music Publishing Co.; Fricon Entertainment Co., Inc., The; Frog and Moose Music; Frontline Music Group; Garrivan Music; Gary Music, Alan; Genetic Music Publishing; Giftness Enterprise; GlobeArt Publishing; Go Star Music; Gold Music Publishing, Jay; Gordon Music Co., Inc.; Gowell Music, Richard E.; Gubala Music, Frank; Halgeo Music; Halo International; Harmony Street Music; Hartel Musikverlag, Johann; Hautboy Music; Havasong Music; Hawk's Bill Music; Heartbeat Music; Heaven Music; Heaven Songs; Hedley Music Group/Get Ready Publishing; Henderson Group Music; Henly Music Associates; High-Minded Moma Publishing & Productions; Hit & Run Music Publishing Inc.; Hitsource Publishing; Ho-hum Music; Holy Grail Publishing; Holy Spirit Music; Holyrood Productions; Hot Lips Music Company; Humongous Music Publishing, Inc.; Inside Records/OK Songs; International Music Network; ISBA Music Publishing Inc.; Jacob-Maxwell, Inc.; Jae Music, Jana; Jaelius Enterprises; Jammy Music Publishers Ltd.; Ja/Nein Musikverlag; Jasper Stone Music/JSM Songs; Jedo Inc.; Jennaco-Alexas Publishing Co.; Jester Song Ltd.; JOF-Dave Music; Jolson Black & White Music, Al; Josena Music; Joseph Music Inc., Patrick; Jump Music; Jungle Boy Music; Just a Note; Justice Music Corporation; Kaupps & Robert Publishing Co.; Keep Calm Music Limited; Keno Publishing; King Music, Kevin; Kommunication Koncepts; Kozkeeozko Music; Kren Music Publishing; Krude Toonz Music; Kusters Music, Hans; Lackey Publishing Co.; Laurmack Music; Le Grande Fromage/Cheddar Cheese Music; Lindsay Publishing, Doris; Lineage Publishing Co.; Lin's Lines; Little Pond Productions; Loveforce International; Lowe Publishing, Jere; Lowery Group, The; M & T Waldoch Publishing, Inc.; Magnum Music Corp. Ltd.; Makers Mark Gold; Makin Tracks Music; Manapro (Management Artist Productions); Manben Music; Martin's Music Publishing, Rod; MCA Music Publishing; Media Productions/Resistor Music; Mento Music Group; Mia Mind Music; Mighty Twinns Music; Miracle Mile Music/Black Satin; Momentum Music Inc.; Montina Music; Murdock's Music Company; Music Factory Enterprises; Music In the Right Keys Publishing Company; Music Room Publishing Group, The; Musikverlag Rossori; Myko Music; Mymit Music Productions, Chuck; Namax Music Publishing; Nashville Sound Music Publishing Co.; New Rap Jam Publishing, A; Newcreature Music; Nicoletti Music Co., The Joseph; Nise Productions Inc.; Non-Stop Music Publishing; Now & Then Music; NSP Music Publishing Inc.; OBH Musikverlag Otto B. Hartmann; Oldham Music Publishing Company, Ronnie; One For the Money Music Publishing Co.; One Hot Note Music Inc.; Operation Perfection; Orchid Publishing; Paisley Park Music; Pancho's Music Co.; Passing Parade Music; peermusic; Pegasus Music; Perfection Music Publications; Phaja Music; Pine Island Music; Play That Beat!; Prescription Company; Prospector Three D Publishing; Publishing Central; Ragland Publications; Rana International Music Group Inc.; Raving Cleric Music Publishing/Euro Export Entertainment; Rent-A-Song; Ridge Music Corp.; Roberts Music, Freddie; Rob-Lee Music; Rocker Music/Happy Man Music; Rockford Music Co.; Roots Music; Rose Hill Group; Rough Trade Publishing; Rustron Music Publishers; S & R Music Publishing Co.; S.M.C.L. Productions, Inc.; Sabteca Music Co.; Saddlestone Publishing; Sariser Music; Saulsby Music Company, William A.; Sci-Fi Music; Scott Music Group, Tim; Segal's Publications; Sha-La Music, Inc.; Shankman De Blasio Melina, Inc.; Shaolin Music; Shu'Baby Montez Music; Siegel Music Companies; Silver Blue Music/Oceans Blue Music; Silver Thunder Music Group; Silverfoot Publishing; Simply Grand Music, Inc.; Sincerity, Ltd.; Sizemore Music; Sky-Child Music; Slavia Pubilshing; Song Cellar; Song Farm Music; Songfinder Music; Sound Cellar Music; Sounds of Aicram; State 51 Music Publishing Inc.; Stuart Music Co., Jeb; Succes; Sun Star Songs; Sunfrost Music; Sunsongs Music/Hollywood East Entertainment; Tabitha Music, Ltd.; Tedesco Music Co., Dale; Tentex Music Publishing; Terrace Entertainment Corporation; Tiki Enterprises, Inc.; Tompaul Music Co.; Tooth and Nail Music; Tower Bridge Music, Ltd.; Tri-She Kieta Publishers, Inc.; Twin Towers Publishing Co.; Two/Polygram Music Publishing; UBM; Ultimate Peak Music; Vaam Music Group; Valet Publishing Co.; Voice Notes Publishing; Walton Music Publishing Co., Jimmy; Weedhopper Music; Wemar Music; Wengert, Berthold (Musikverlag); Wes Music, Bobe; West & East Music; Westunes Music Publishing Co.; Wheeler Communications Inc.; Whimsong Publishing; White Car Music; Wilcom Publishing; Winston & Hoffman House Music Publishers; Wonderwax Publishing; Woodrich Publishing Co.; World Famous Music Co.; Y-Not Productions; Yorgo Music; Your Best Songs Publishing; Zauber Music Publishing

Rap Accent Publishing Co.; Alexander Sr. Music; Aljoni Music Co.; Anode Music; Art Audio Publishing Company/Tight Hi-Fi Soul Music; Audio Music Publishers; AVC Music; Barking Foe The Master's Bone; Bullet Proof Management; City Publishing Co.; Cold Chillin' Music Publishing; Controlled Destiny Music Publishing; Cross Culture Productions, Inc.; Dagene Music; Elect Music Publishing Company; Elliot Music; Emandell Tunes; Emperor of Emperors; Empty Sky Music

Company; Emzee Music; F.E.D. Publishing Co.; Flash International; Freko Records; Frog Hair Songs; Frozen Inca Music; Gold Music, S.M.; ISBA Music Publishing Inc.; Jasper Stone Music/ JSM Songs; Joey Boy Publishing Co.; JOF-Dave Music; Jungle Boy Music; Keno Publishing; Laurmack Music; Lin's Lines; Makers Mark Gold; Manben Music; New Rap Jam Publishing, A; Now & Then Music; One Hot Note Music Inc.; Operation Perfection; Paisley Park Music; PDS Music Publishing; Raving Cleric Music Publishing/Euro Export Entertainment; Saulsby Music Company, William A.; Scott Music Group, Tim; Shu'Baby Montez Music; Silver Blue Music/Oceans Blue Music; Soul Street Music Publishing Inc.; Sound Cellar Music; Stellar Music Industries; Stuart Music Co., Jeb; Sweet Glenn Music; Trusty Publications; Wheeler Communications Inc.; Winston & Hoffman House Music Publishers

R&B Accent Publishing Co.; ADM Publishing; Alexander Sr. Music; Alexis; Alhart Music Publishing; Aljoni Music Co.; All Nations Music Publishing, Ltd.; Allegheny Music Works; Alternative Direction Music Publishers; Amalgamated Tulip Corp.; Americatone International; Amicos II Music, Ltd.; Amiron Music; Anode Music; Another Amethyst Song; Another Ear Music; Art Audio Publishing Company/Tight Hi-Fi Soul Music; Astrodisque Publishing; Audio Music Publishers; August Night Music; AVC Music; Bad Habits Music Publishing; Bal & Bal Music Publishing Co.; Barking Foe The Master's Bone; Bartow Music; Bernard Enterprises, Inc., Hal; Best Buddies, Inc.; Beth-Ridge Music Publishing Co.; Better Than Sex Music; Betty Jane/Josie Jane Music Publishers; BOAM; Bok Music; Bourne Co. Music Publishers; Brewster Songs, Kitty; Bronx Flash Music, Inc.; Bullet Proof Management; Butler Music, Bill; California Country Music; Camex Music; Cash Productions, Inc.; Cedar Creek Music; Centropa N.V.; Chapie Music; Cheavoria Music Co.; Cisum; Clearwind Publishing; Clevère Musikverlag, R.D.; Clientele Music; Clotille Publishing; Coffee and Cream Publishing Company; Cold Chillin' Music Publishing; Controlled Destiny Music Publishing; Corporate Rock Music; Cottage Blue Music; Country Star Music; CQK Records and Music; Cross Culture Productions, Inc.; Cunningham Music; Dagene Music; De Miles Music Company, The Edward; Dean Enterprises Music Group; Delev Music Company; Demi Monde Records & Publishing Ltd.; Diamond Wind Music; D'Nico International; Don Del Music; Doré Records; DPP Music; Dream Sequence Music, Ltd.; Drezdon Blacque Music; Drive Music, Inc.; Duane Music, Inc.; Eccentrax Music Co.; Elect Music Publishing Company; Element Movie and Music; EMF Productions; Emperor of Emperors; Emzee Music; Escape Artist Company, The; Ever-Open-Eye Music; Excursion Music Group; Famous Music Publishing Companies; F&J Music; First Time Music (Publishing) U.K. Ltd.; Five Roses Music Group; Flash International; Four Newton Publishing; Freko Records; Fricon Entertainment Co., Inc., The; Frog and Moose Music; Frog Hair Songs; Frontline Music Group; Frozen Inca Music; Gary Music, Alan; General Jones Music; Genetic Music Publishing; Giftness Enterprise; GlobeArt Publishing; Go Star Music; Gold Music, S.M.; Gold Plate Music; Gowell Music, Richard E.; Halgeo Music; Harmony Street Music; Hawk's Bill Music; Heaven Songs; Hit & Run Music Publishing Inc.; Hitsource Publishing; Honk Music — Musikverlag H. Gebetsroither; Hot Lips Music Company; Humongous Music Publishing, Inc.; International Music Network; International Music Network Limited; Interplanetary Music; ISBA Music Publishing Inc.; Jaelius Enterprises; Jasper Stone Music/JSM Songs; Jedo Inc.; Joey Boy Publishing Co.; JOF-Dave Music; Jungle Boy Music; Just a Note; Kansa Records Corporation; Kaupps & Robert Publishing Co.; Keep Calm Music Limited; Keno Publishing; Kingsport Creek Music Publishing; Kommunication Koncepts; Kozkeeozko Music; Lackey Publishing Co.; Laurmack Music; Laymond Publishing Co., Inc.; Le Grande Fromage/Cheddar Cheese Music; Lin's Lines; Loveforce International; Lowe Publishing, Jere; M & T Waldoch Publishing, Inc.; McGibony Publishing; Macman Music, Inc.; Makers Mark Gold; Manapro (Management Artist Productions); Media Productions; Menace Music Group; Mighty Twinns Music; Miracle Mile Music/ Black Satin; Montina Music; Murdock's Music Company; Music In the Right Keys Publishing Company; Music Room Publishing Group, The; Music Sales Corporation; Myko Music; Mymit Music Productions, Chuck; Namax Music Publishing; Nervous Publishing; New Rap Jam Publishing, A; Newcreature Music; Nicoletti Music Co., The Joseph; Nise Productions Inc.; Non-Stop Music Publishing; Now & Then Music; NSP Music Publishing Inc.; OBH Musikverlag Otto B. Hartmann; Okisher Music; Old Slowpoke Music; Oldham Music Publishing Company, Ronnie; One for the Money Music Publishing Co.; Operation Perfection; Paisley Park Music; PDS Music Publishing; peermusic; Phaja Music; Platinum Boulevard Publishing; Prescription Company; Purple Haze Music; Qmark Music; Ragland Publications; Rahsaan Publishing; Rana International Music Group Inc.; Raving Cleric Music Publishing/Euro Export Entertainment; Red Boots Tunes; Rent-A-Song; Rob-Lee Music; Rondor Music International; Rustron Music Publishers; Sabteca Music Co.; Saddlestone Publishing; Saulsby Music Company, William A.; Scott Music Group, Tim; Segal's Publications; Sha-La Music, Inc.; Shankman De Blasio Melina, Inc.; Shu'Baby Montez Music; Siegel Music Companies; Silver Blue Music/Oceans Blue Music; Silver Thunder Music Group; Simply Grand Music, Inc.; Sincerity, Ltd.; Siskatune Music Publishing Co.; Sizemore Music; Song Farm Music; Songrite Creations Productions; Soul Street Music Publishing Inc.; Sounds of Aicram; Southern Most Publishing Company; Starbound Publishing Co.; State 51 Music Publishing Inc.; Stellar Music Industries; Stuart Music Co., Jeb; Stylecraft Music Co.; Sugarfoot Productions; Sunfrost Music; Sunset Productions; Sunsongs Music/Hollywood East Entertainment; Sweet Glenn Music; Tabitha Music, Ltd.; Tedesco Music Co., Dale; TEK Publishing; Tentex Music Publishing; Tiki Enterprises, Inc.; Tompaul Music Co.; Tooth and Nail Music; Toulouse Music Publishing Co., Inc.; Transition Music Corp.; Tri-She Kieta Publishers, Inc.; Trusty Publications;

Twin Towers Publishing Co.; Vaam Music Group; Valet Publishing Co.; Voice Notes Publishing; Weber Musikverlag, Friedrich; Weedhopper Music; Wemar Music; Wes Music, Bobe; Whatapayne Publishing; Wheeler Communications Inc.; Whimsong Publishing; White Car Music; Wilcom Publishing; Winston & Hoffman House Music Publishers; Without Papers Music Publishing Inc.; Wonderwax Publishing; Woodrich Publishing Co.; World Famous Music Co.; Yorgo Music; Zauber Music Publishing

Religious Abingdon Press; Accent Publishing Co.; Aim High Music Company; Alexander Sr. Music; Alexis; Allegheny Music Works; Amicos II Music, Ltd.; Angelsong Publishing Co.; Anode Music; Another Ear Music; Art Audio Publishing Company/Tight Hi-Fi Soul Music; Associated Artists Music International; Baby Huey Music; Bal & Bal Music Publishing Co.; Barking Foe The Master's Bone; Best Buddies, Inc.; Bethlehem Music Publications; Beth-Ridge Music Publishing Co.; Betty Jane/Josie Jane Music Publishers; Blue Spur Music Group, Inc.; BOAM; Bollman International Publishing Co.; Cactus Music and Winnebago Publishing; California Country Music; Calinoh Music Group; Calvary Music Group, Inc.; Caravell Main Sail Music; Cash Productions, Inc.; Castle Music Corp.; Chapie Music; Chestnut Mound Music Group; Cisum; City Publishing Co.; Clientele Music; Coffee and Cream Publishing Company; Connell Publishing Co., Jerry; Controlled Destiny Music Publishing; Cottage Blue Music; Country Breeze Music; Country Star Music; Cowboy Junction Flea Market and Publishing Co.; CQK Records and Music; Craig Music, Loman; Creekside Music; Cunningham Music; Cupit Music; Darbonne Publishing Co.; Dell Music, Frank; Delpha's Music Publishers; Earitating Music Publishing; Element Movie and Music; Emandell Tunes; EMF Productions; Emperor of Emperors; Empty Sky Music Company; Ever-Open-Eye Music; Excursion Music Group; Faiella Publishing, Doug; F&J Music; First Time Music (Publishing) U.K. Ltd.; Five Roses Music Group; Flash International; Focal Point Music Publishers; Foster Music Company, Mark; Four Newton Publishing; Fox Farm Recording; Freko Records; Fretboard Publishing; Frick Music Publishing Co.; Fricon Entertainment Co., Inc., The; Frog and Moose Music; Frog Hair Songs; Garrivan Music; Giftness Enterprise; GlobeArt Publishing; Go Star Music; Green Meadows Publishing; Harmony Street Music; Heartbeat Music; Henly Music Associates; Hickory Lane Publishing And Recording; History Publishing Co.; Holy Spirit Music; Hutchins Music, Gregg; Jaclyn Music; Jaelius Enterprises; Jennaco-Alexas Publishing Co.; Jerjoy Music; Josena Music; Just a Note; Kansa Records Corporation; Kaupps & Robert Publishing Co.; Kaylee Music Group, Karen; Kennedy Enterprises, Inc., Gene; Kingsport Creek Music Publishing; Kommunication Koncepts; Kren Music Publishing; Lackey Publishing Co.; Lari-Jon Publishing; Laurmack Music; Laymond Publishing Co., Inc.; LCS Music Group, Inc.; Lindsay Publishing, Doris; Lin's Lines; Lion Hill Music Publishing Co.; Little Pond Productions; Loveforce International; Lowery Group, The; McCoy Music, Jim; McGibony Publishing; Mack Music, Danny; Magnum Music Corp. Ltd.; Mathes Company, The; Media Productions; Mighty Twinns Music; Montina Music; Motex Music; Music In the Right Keys Publishing Company; Namax Music Publishing; Nashville Music Group; National Talent; New Rap Jam Publishing, A; Newcreature Music; Nicoletti Music Co., The Joseph; Nise Productions Inc.; NSP Music Publishing Inc.; Oh My Gosh Music; Oldham Music Publishing Company, Ronnie; Orchid Publishing; Otto Publishing Co.; Palmetto Productions; Paluch Company, J. S./World Library Publications, Inc.; Parravano Music; Peters Music, Justin; Pritchett Publication; Prospector Three D Publishing; Publishing Central; Radiant Music; Ragland Publications; Roberts Music, Freddie; Rocker Music/Happy Man Music; Roots Music; Rushwin Publishing; Saddlestone Publishing; Samuel Three Productions; Scott Music Group, Tim; Scrutchings Music; Shadowland Productions; Song Cellar; Songrite Creations Productions; Sound Achievement Group; Sounds of Aicram; Southern Most Publishing Company; Starbound Publishing Co.; Stuart Music Co., Jeb; Stylecraft Music Co.; Sun Star Songs; Tiki Enterprises, Inc.; Tompaul Music Co.; Toulouse Music Publishing Co., Inc.; Tri-She Kieta Publishers, Inc.; Trusty Publications; Voice Notes Publishing; Vokes Music Publishing; Walton Music Publishing Co., Jimmy; Weber Musikverlag, Friedrich; Wes Music, Bobe; Woodrich Publishing Co.; Yorgo Music

Rock Abalone Publishing; Abigwan; Accent Publishing Co.; Ala/Bianca SRL; All Nations Music Publishing, Ltd.; All Rock Music; Alleged Iguana Music; Alpana Musik & Film; Alternative Direction Music Publishers; Amalgamated Tulip Corp.; Amiron Music; Another Ear Music; Aquarius Publishing; Art Audio Publishing Company/Tight Hi-Fi Soul Music; Art of Concept Music; Associated Artists Music International; Astrodisque Publishing; Astron Music Publishing; Audio Music Publishers; August Night Music; AUM Circle Publishing; AVC Music; Axbar Productions; Baby Raquel Music; Bad Habits Music Publishing; Bal & Bal Music Publishing Co.; Barking Foe The Master's Bone; Bernard Enterprises, Inc., Hal; Best Buddies, Inc.; Better Than Sex Music; Big Snow Music; Blue Cue Music; BOAM; Bok Music; Brewster Songs, Kitty; Bronx Flash Music, Inc.; Bullet Proof Management; Buried Treasure Music; Butler Music, Bill; Buzzart Enterprises; Cale Music, Inc., John; California Country Music; Camex Music; Captain Click; Cash Productions, Inc.; Cedar Creek Music; Cherie Music; Christel Music Limited; Christopher Publishing, Sonny; Cisum; Clear Pond Music; Clearwind Publishing; Clevère Musikverlag, R.D.; Connell Publishing Co., Jerry; Coppelia; Corporate Rock Music; Cottage Blue Music; Country Breeze Music; Country Star Music; Creekside Music; CSB Kaminsky GMBH; Cunningham Music; Cupit Music; Dan the Man Music; De Miles Music Company, The Edward; Dead Dead Good Records/Music Ltd.; Dean Enterprises Music Group; Demi Monde Records & Publishing Ltd.; Diamond Wind Music; Direct Management Group; D'Nico International; Doss Music, Buster; DPP Music; Dream Sequence Music, Ltd.; Drezdon Blacque Music; Drive Music, Inc.; Duane Music, Inc.; Earitating Music

Publishing; Earthscream Music Publishing Co.; Eccentrax Music Co.; Editions Musicales Alpha; Editions Scipion; Elect Music Publishing Company; Element Movie and Music; EMF Productions; EMI Music Publishing; Emperor of Emperors; Empty Sky Music Company; Emzee Music; ESI Music Group; EvoPoetics Publishing; Excursion Music Group; F.E.D. Publishing Co.; Faiella Publishing, Doug; Famous Music Publishing Companies; Fat City Publishing; Filmworks; Five Roses Music Group; Four Newton Publishing; Fretboard Publishing; Frick Music Publishing Co.; Fricon Entertainment Co., Inc., The; Frog and Moose Music; Frog Hair Songs; Frontline Music Group; Frozen Inca Music; Gary Music, Alan; General Jones Music; Genetic Music Publishing; Giftness Enterprise; Go Star Music; Gold Music Publishing, Jay; Gordon Music Co., Inc.; Gorr Custom Music, Jon; Green One Music; Gubala Music, Frank; Halo International; Harmony Street Music; Hautboy Music; Havasong Music; Hawk's Bill Music; Heartbeat Music; Heaven Music; Heaven Songs; Hedley Music Group/Get Ready Publishing; Henderson Group Music; Heupferd Musik Verlag; Hickory Lane Publishing And Recording; High-Minded Moma Publishing & Productions; Hit & Run Music Publishing Inc.; Hitsource Publishing; Ho-hum Music; Holy Grail Publishing; Honk Music — Musikverlag H. Gebetsroither; International Music Network; ISBA Music Publishing Inc.; Jacob-Maxwell, Inc.; Jammy Music Publishers Ltd.; Ja/Nein Musikverlag; Jasper Stone Music/JSM Songs; Jedo Inc.; Jester Song Ltd.; JOF-Dave Music; Jolson Black & White Music, Al; Jungle Boy Music; Justice Music Corporation; Kansa Records Corporation; Kaupps & Robert Publishing Co.; Keep Calm Music Limited; Kel-Cres Publishing; Keno Publishing; Kommunication Koncepts; Kozkeeozko Music; Kren Music Publishing; Krude Toonz Music; Kusters Music, Hans; Lari-Jon Publishing; Laymond Publishing Co., Inc.; Lilly Music Publishing; Lineage Publishing Co.; Lin's Lines; Lonny Tunes Music; Loveforce International; Lowery Group, The; M & T Waldoch Publishing, Inc.; McCoy Music, Jim; Macman Music, Inc.; Magic Message Music; Magnum Music Corp. Ltd.; Makin Tracks Music; Mama Linda; Manapro (Management Artist Productions); Martin's Music Publishing, Rod; Media Productions; Menace Music Group; Montina Music; Moody Music, Doug; Motex Music; Murdock's Music Company; Music Factory Enterprises; Music Room Publishing Group, The; Music Sales Corporation; Musikverlag Rossori; Myko Music; Mymit Music Productions, Chuck; Nashville Music Group; Nautical Music Co.; Nervous Publishing; New Rap Jam Publishing, A; Newcreature Music; Nicoletti Music Co., The Joseph; Nise Productions Inc.; NSP Music Publishing Inc.; OBH Musikverlag Otto B. Hartmann; Oh My Gosh Music; Old Slowpoke Music; Oldham Music Publishing Company, Ronnie; One for the Money Music Publishing Co.; One Hot Note Music Inc.; Operation Perfection; Pancho's Music Co.; peermusic; Pen Cob Publishing Inc.; Pine Island Music; Platinum Boulevard Publishing; Play That Beat!; Portage Music; PPI/Peter Pan Industries; Prejippie Music Group; Prescription Company; Pritchett Publication; Promo; Prospector Three D Publishing; Publishing Central; Purple Haze Music; Pustaka Muzik EMI; R. J. Music; Ragland Publications; Rahsaan Publishing; Rana International Music Group Inc.; Red Boots Tunes; Rent-A-Song; Ridge Music Corp.; Roberts Music, Freddie; Rob-Lee Music; Rocker Music/Happy Man Music; Rockford Music Co.; Rondor Music International; Roots Music; Rose Hill Group; Rough Trade Publishing; Rustron Music Publishers; Saddlestone Publishing; Sariser Music; Sci-Fi Music; Scott Music Group, Tim; Sea Dream Music; Segal's Publications; Sellwood Publishing; Seychelles Music; Sha-La Music, Inc.; Shankman De Blasio Melina, Inc.; Shaolin Music; Siegel Music Companies; Silicon Music Publishing Co.; Silver Thorn Enterprises; Silverfoot Publishing; Simply Grand Music, Inc.; Sincerity, Ltd.; Sky-Child Music; Slavia Pubilshing; Songfinder Music; Sound Cellar Music; Sounds of Aicram; Southern Most Publishing Company; Stellar Music Industries; Stuart Music Co., Jeb; Succes; Sugar Mama Music; Sun Star Songs; Sunflare Songs/Records; Sunfrost Music; Sunset Productions; Sunsongs Music/Hollywood East Entertainment; Tabitha Music, Ltd.; Tedesco Music Co., Dale; Tender Tender Music; Tiki Enterprises, Inc.; Tompaul Music Co.; Tooth and Nail Music; Tower Bridge Music, Ltd.; Trusty Publications; Tuffin Music Enterprises; Twin Towers Publishing Co.; Two/Polygram Music Publishing; Ultimate Peak Music; Valet Publishing Co.; Victory Music; Voice Notes Publishing; Waterbury Road Music; Watonka Records Co.; Weber Musikverlag, Friedrich; Weedhopper Music; Wemar Music; Wes Music, Bobe; West & East Music; Westunes Music Publishing Co.; Whimsong Publishing; White Car Music; Whitewing Music; Wilcom Publishing; Without Papers Music Publishing Inc.; Woodrich Publishing Co.; World Famous Music Co.; Your Best Songs Publishing; Zauber Music Publishing

World Music ADM Publishing; Apon Publishing Co.; ARC Music Productions International Ltd.; Astron Music Publishing; Bullet Proof Management; Captain Click; City Publishing Co.; CSB Kaminsky GMBH; Earth Dance Music; Elect Music Publishing Company; Emperor of Emperors; F&J Music; Flowsound Ltd.; Gorr Custom Music, Jon; Hautboy Music; Heupferd Musik Verlag; Honk Music — Musikverlag H. Gebetsroither; Inside Records/OK Songs; Keno Publishing; Latin American Music Co., Inc.; Lin's Lines; Manny Music, Inc.; Momentum Music Inc.; Music Factory Enterprises, Inc.; Publishing Central; Rahsaan Publishing; Societe D'Editions Musicales Et Artistiques "Esperance"; Sounds-Vision Music; Supreme Enterprises Int'l Corp.; Tedesco Music Co., Dale; X Presh'n Series Music

Music Publishers/'94-'95 Changes

The following markets appeared in the 1994 edition of *Songwriter's Market* but are absent from the 1995 edition. Most of these companies failed to respond to our request for an update of their listing for a variety of reasons. For example, they may have gone out of business or they may have requested deletion from the 1995 edition because they are backlogged with material. If we know the specific reason, it appears within parentheses.

A Street Music
Abiding Love Music Publishing
Auntie Argon Music
Bad Grammar Music
Bagatelle Music Publishing Co.
Balance of Power Music
Earl Beecher Publishing
Benyard Music (unable to contact)
Better Tunes Publishing (affiliate of Doris Lindsay Publishing)
Blenheim Music
C.A.B. Independent Publishing Co.
Don Casale Music, Inc.
Catharine Courage Music Ltd.
Century City Music Publishing
Charis Music
Chestler Publishing Co.
China Groove
Cling Music Publishing
Cod Oil Productions Limited
Cosgroove Music Inc. (not accepting submissions)
Cosmotone Music
Creole Music Ltd.
Cude & Pickens (not accepting submissions)
Cumberland Music Group Inc. (unable to contact)
D.S.M. Producers Inc.
De Dan Music (out of business)
Dingo Music
Dupuy Records/Productions/Publishing, Inc.
Edition Musica
Ertis Music Company (requested deletion)
Eye Kill Music
First Million Music Inc. (unable to contact)
Flaming Star West
Foxworthy Music Inc.
Galaxia Musical S.A. De C.V.
Gift of Grace Music
Graduate Music Ltd.
Green Dog Productions (requested deletion)
Grooveland Music (affiliate of

Hitsource Publishing)
Hammer Musik GmbH
Hamstein Publishing Company, Inc.
Heavy Jamin' Music
Hicky's Music (unable to contact)
Ivory Palaces Music
Jay Jay Publishing
Jellee Works Music
Kenning Productions (unable to contact)
Keystone Music Group Inc. (unable to contact)
Koke, Moke & Noke Music (affiliate of Ichiban Records)
Lansdowne and Winston Music Publishers (affiliate of Winston and Hoffman House Music Publishers)
Lighthouse Music Company, Inc.
Lucrecia Music (unable to contact)
Majestic Control Music
Andy Marvel Music (not accepting submissions)
Moneytime Publishing Co.
Mud Cat Music (requested deletion)
Musica Arroz Publishing (unable to contact)
Nadine Music
Nasetan Publishing (affiliate of TEK Publishing)
Nebo Ridge Publishing Company
No Mas Music
O'Lyric Music
Pandisc Records (unable to contact)
Parchment Harbor Music
Placer Publishing (requested deletion)
Planet Dallas Recording Studios
Jimmy Price Music Publisher (unable to contact)
Prophecy Publishing, Inc. (not accepting submissions)

Quan-Yaa Records
Quark, Inc.
Ren Maur Music Corp.
Rhythms Productions (not accepting submissions)
Rosemark Publishing
William Seip Music Incorporated
Single Minded Music
Sinus Musik Produktion, Ulli Weigel
Sneak Tip Music
Songwriters' Network Music Publishing
Sound Resources
Star International, Inc. (not accepting submissions)
Sueño Publishing Co. (unable to contact)
Ten of Diamonds Music Publishing (unable to contact)
This Beats Workin' Music Inc. (unable to contact)
TKO Music, Inc.
Toro'na Music (unable to contact)
Transworld West Music Group (unable to contact)
Tropical Beat Records/Polygram
Two Fold Music (out of business)
Warner/Chappell Music, Inc.
Watchesgro Music
Wazuri Music
West Broadway Music
Wil-Too/Wil-So Music
Wind Haven Publishing (unable to contact)
Windswept Pacific Entertainment (not accepting submissions)
Word Music (requested deletion)
Young Bob Publishing Co.
Young Graham Music (unable to contact)
Zatco Music (unable to contact)

Music Print Publishers

The music print publisher's function is much more specific than that of the music publisher. Music publishers try to exploit a song in many different ways: on records, videos, movies and radio/TV commercials, to name a few. But, as the name implies, music print publishers deal in only one publishing medium: print.

Although the role of the music print publisher has virtually stayed the same over the years, demand for sheet music has declined substantially. Today there are only a few major sheet music publishers in operation, along with many minor ones.

Most songs and compositions fall into one of two general categories: popular or educational music. Popular songs are pop, rock, adult contemporary, country and other hits heard on the radio. They are printed as sheet music (for single songs) and folios (collections of songs). Educational material includes pieces for chorus, band, orchestra, instrumental solos and instructional books. In addition to publishing original compositions, print publishers will sometimes print arrangements of popular songs.

Most major publishers of pop music won't print sheet music for a song until a popular recording of the song has become a hit single, or at least is on the *Billboard* Hot 100 chart. Most of the companies listed here indicate the lowest chart position of a song they've published, to give you a better idea of the market.

Chart action is obviously not a factor for original educational material. What the print publishers look for is quality work that fits into their publishing program and is appropriate for the people who use their music, such as school and church choirs, school bands or orchestras.

When dealing with music print publishers, it is generally unacceptable to send out simultaneous submissions; that is, sending identical material to different publishers at the same time. Since most of the submissions they receive involve written music, whether single lead sheets or entire orchestrations, the time they invest in evaluating each submission is considerable — much greater than the few minutes it takes to listen to a tape. It would be discourteous and unprofessional to ask a music print publisher to invest a lot of time in evaluating your work and then possibly pull the deal out from under him before he has given you an answer.

Writers' royalties range from 10-15% of the retail selling price of music in print. For educational material that would be a percentage of the price of the whole set (score and parts). For a book of songs (called a folio), the 10-15% royalty would be pro-rated by the number of songs by that writer in the book. Royalties for sheet music are paid on a flat rate per sheet, which is usually about one-fifth of the retail price. If a music publisher licenses print publishing to a music print publisher, print royalties are usually split evenly between the music publisher and songwriter, but it may vary. You should read any publishing contract carefully to see how print deals fit in, and consult your attorney if you have any questions.

*A & C BLACK (PUBLISHERS) LTD., 35 Bedford Row, London WC1R 4JH **England**. Phone: (071)242-0946. Commissioning Editor: Sheena Roberts. Music print publisher. Publishes educational material. Prints 6 items/year. Pays a fee per 1,000 copies printed.
How to Contact: Query or write first and obtain permission to submit. Prefers cassette. SAE and IRC. Reports in 4-8 weeks.
Music: Instrumental/method and repertoire books and children's songs. Published "Green Umbrella," by Jill Brand (assembly stories, songs and poems); "Abracadabra Clarinet," (graded pieces for clarinet); and "Okki-Tokki-Unga" (children's song compilation).

Tips: "We keep a list of good children's songwriters whom we commission to write songs that fit the needs of our compilations. A compilation may consist of around 30-50% commissioned songs. Look at our children's catalogue (available on request) to see what sort of books we publish."

BOSTON MUSIC CO. (ASCAP), 172 Tremont St., Boston MA 02111. (617)426-5100. Contact: Editorial Department. Music print publisher. Prints 100 pieces/year, both individual pieces and music books. Pays 10% royalty.
How to Contact: Write or call first and obtain permission to submit. SASE. Reports in 6-9 months.
Music: Choral pieces, educational material, instrumental solo pieces, method books and **"piano instructional materials that piano teachers would be interested in."** Published "Gavotte and Musette" (by Frederick Werlé) (piano solo); "Concord Hymn" (by Linda Grom) (choral piece); and "Chuckles" (by Rémi Bouchard) (piano collection).
Tips: "We do not publish 'songs' and are not interested in the current 'pop' field. Any music we consider must have a teaching use and must be completely written out—no tapes please!"

BOURNE COMPANY, 5 W. 37th St., New York NY 10018. (212)391-4300. Contact: Professional Department. Music print publisher. Estab. 1917. Publishes education material and popular music.
Affiliate(s): ABC Music, Ben Bloom, Better Half, Bogat, Burke & Van Heusen, Goldmine, Harborn, Lady Mac, Murbo Music.
How to Contact: Write first and obtain permission to submit. Write first to arrange personal interview. Does not return unsolicited material. Reports in 3-6 months.
Music: Band pieces, choral pieces and handbell pieces. Published "You Can Count on Me" (by S. Cahn/N. Monath) (2 part choral); "Unforgettable" (by Gordon), recorded by Natalie Cole on Elektra Records (vocal duet); and "The Songs of Charlie Chaplin."

ECS PUBLISHING, (formerly E.C. Schirmer ● Boston), Dept. SM, 138 Ipswich St., Boston MA 02215. (617)236-1935. President: Robert Schuneman. Music print publisher. Prints 200 pieces/year, mostly individual pieces and music books. Pays 10% royalty on sales and 50% on performance/license.
Affiliate(s): Galaxy Music Corporation (ASCAP), E.C. Schirmer Music Co. Inc. (ASCAP), Ione Press, Inc. (BMI), Highgate Press (BMI).
How to Contact: Query with complete score and tape of piece. Prefers cassette. "Submit a clean, readable score." SASE. Reports in 6-8 months.
Music: Choral pieces, orchestral pieces, instrumental solo pieces, instrumental ensemble pieces, methods books, books on music, and keyboard pieces.

MARK FOSTER MUSIC COMPANY, Box 4012, Champaign IL 61824-4012. (217)398-2760. Fax: (217)398-2791. President: Jane C. Menkhaus. Music print publisher, music publisher and retail music division. Estab. 1962. Publishes 20-30 pieces/year; mostly choral music and books. Publishes 3-4 new songwriters/year. Pays 5-10% over first 3,000 copies sold.
Affiliate(s): Fostco (ASCAP) and Marko (BMI).
How to Contact: Submit demo tape by mail. Unsolicited submissions are OK. Prefers cassette with 1 song and choral manuscript. If new composer/arranger, submit bio. Returns material with SASE.
Music: Mostly sacred SATB, secular SATB and sacred and secular treble and male choir music; also conducting books and Kodaly materials. Published "Before Your Throne" (by Bradley Ellingboe); "City on the Hill" (by Marvin V. Curtis); and "Jubilant Song" (by René Clausen).
Tips: "Must be well-constructed piece to begin with, manuscript should be in decent format, preferably with keyboard reduction."

GENEVOX MUSIC GROUP, 127 9th Ave. N., Nashville TN 37234. (615)251-3770. SESAC, ASCAP and BMI affiliate. Music print publisher. Estab. 1986. Director: Mark Blankenship. Prints 75-100 songs/year; publishes 10 new songwriters/year. Pays 10% royalty.
How to Contact: Submit demo tape and choral arrangement, lead sheet or complete score. Unsolicited submissions are OK. Prefers cassette with 1-5 songs. SASE. Reports in 2 weeks acknowledging receipt, 3 months response.
Music: Choral, orchestral, instrumental solo and instrumental ensemble pieces. "We publish all forms of choral sacred music for all ages, and instrumental for handbell, organ, piano and orchestra." Published "Go, Go Jonah," by Kathie Hill (children's choral musical); "Bless the Lord," arranged by Dave Williamson (praise/worship); and "God So Loved the World," arranged by Camp Kirkland and Tom Fettke (musical).
Tips: "Most of what we publish is designed for use by church choirs and instrumentalists. Middle-of-the-road, traditional anthems, hymn arrangements, praise and worship, contemporary and inspirational songs in an SATB/keyboard choral format stand the best chance for serious consideration."

HINSHAW MUSIC, INC. (ASCAP), Box 470, Chapel Hill NC 27514-0470. (919)933-1691. Editor: Don Hinshaw. Music print publisher. Estab. 1975. Prints 100 pieces/year, both individual pieces and music books. Publishes educational material. Pays 10% royalty.
Affiliate(s): Hindon Publications (BMI) and Chapel Hill Music (SESAC).
How to Contact: Write first and obtain permission to submit. After receiving permission, "Send the complete score. Lyric sheets and/or tapes alone are not acceptable. We do not review lyrics alone. Cassette tapes may be sent in addition to the written ms. Send clear, legible photocopies, *not* the original. Submit only 2 or 3 mss at a time that are representative of your work. An arrangement of a copyrighted work will not be considered unless copy of written permission from copyright owner(s) is attached. Once a ms has been submitted, do not telephone or write for a 'progress report.' Be patient." SASE. Reports in 1-4 months.
Music: Choral pieces, organ and **instrumental music.** Published "Music to Hear" (by G. Shearing); and *Magnificat* (by J. Rutter), recorded by Collegium.
Tips: "Submit your ms to only one publisher at a time. It requires considerable time and expense for us to thoroughly review a work, so we want the assurance that if accepted, the ms is available for publication. We are unable to 'critique' rejected works. A pamphlet, 'Submitting Music for Publication' is available with SASE."

JUMP MUSIC, Langemunt 71, 9420 Aaigem, **Belgium**. Phone: (053)62-73-77. Estab. 1976. General Manager: Eddy Van Mouffaert. Music print publisher. Publishes educational material and popular music. Prints 150 songs/year, mostly individual songs. Pays 5% royalty.
How to Contact: Submit demo tape by mail. Unsolicited submissions are OK. Prefers cassette and lead sheet or complete score. Does not return unsolicited material. Reports in 2 weeks.
Music: Pop, ballads, band pieces and **instrumentals.** Published "Lief de Voor Muziek" (by Eddy Govert), recorded by Evelien on Scorpion Records (Flemish); "Just a Friend" (by Eddy Govert), recorded by Sherly on Ideal Records (pop); and "He He Nick" (by Eddy Govert), recorded by Jo Calypso on Calypso Records (Flemish).

THE LORENZ CORPORATION, Box 802, Dayton OH 45401-0802. (513)228-6118. Contact: Editorial Department. Music print publisher. ASCAP, BMI. Estab. 1890. Publishes 500 titles/year; 10 new composers/year. Hires staff writers. Works with composers and lyricists; teams collaborators. Pays standard royalty.
How to Contact: Submit manuscript (completely arranged, not songs or lead sheets); tape not necessary. SASE. Reports in 2 months.
Music: Interested in **religious/Christian choral, high school, junior high, elementary choral** and **organ/piano music;** also **sacred and educational band music,** and **handbell music.**
Tips: "Send in a legible copy, arranged for a choral market. We do not produce vocal solo collections or sheet music."

HAROLD LUICK & ASSOCIATES (BMI), Box B, Carlisle IA 50047. (515)989-3748 and 989-3676. President: Harold Luick. Prints 4-5 songs/year, mostly individual songs. Lowest chart position held by a song published in sheet form is 98. Pays 4% royalty.
How to Contact: Write and obtain permission to submit or submit through publisher or attorney. Prefers cassette or reel-to-reel and lyric sheet. SASE. Reports in 3 weeks.
Music: Mostly **traditional country;** also **novelty songs.** Published "Mrs. Used To Be," written and recorded by Joe Harris on River City Records (country).
Tips: "Send us song material that is conducive to type of market today. Good commercial songs."

PLYMOUTH MUSIC CO., INC., 170 NE 33rd St., Ft. Lauderdale FL 33334. (305)563-1844. General Manager: Bernard Fisher. Music print publisher. Estab. 1953. Prints 50 pieces/year: individual pieces, individual songs, music books and folios. Pays 10% of retail selling price.
Affiliate(s): Aberdeen Music, (ASCAP), Galleria Press (ASCAP), Walton Music (ASCAP), and Music for Percussion (BMI).
How to Contact: Call first and obtain permission to submit or to arrange personal interview. Prefers cassette and lead sheet or complete score. SASE. Reports in 3-4 weeks.
Music: Choral pieces and **percussion music.**
Tips: "Send choral music for church and school with cassette tape if available. Manuscripts should be legible."

THEODORE PRESSER CO., Dept. SM, One Presser Place, Bryn Mawr PA 19010. (215)525-3636. Fax: (215)527-7841. ASCAP, BMI and SESAC affiliate. Contact: Editorial Committee. Music print publisher. Member MPA. Publishes 90 works/year. Works with composers. Pays varying royalty.
Affiliate(s): Merion Music (BMI); Elkan-Vogel, Inc. (ASCAP); and Mercury Music Corp. (SESAC).
How to Contact: Unsolicited submissions are OK. Prefers cassette with 1-2 works and score. "Include return label and postage." Reports in 2 weeks.

Music: Serious, educational and **choral music.** "We primarily publish serious music of emerging and established composers, and vocal/choral music which is likely to be accepted in the church and educational markets, as well as gospel chorals of high musical quality. We are *not* a publisher of song sheets or pop songs."

R.T.F.M., % Stewart House, Hillbottom Rd., Highwycombe, Buckinghamshire HP124HJ **United Kingdom.** Phone: (0630)647374. Fax: (0630)647612. A&R: Ron Lee. Music print publisher, music publisher. Publishes educational material and popular music. Prints 40 songs/year, mostly individual songs. Lowest chart position held by a song published in sheet form is 140. Royalty negotiable.
Affiliate(s): Lee Music Ltd., Pogo Records Ltd. and R.T.L. Music.
How to Contact: Submit demo tape—unsolicited submissions are OK. Prefers cassette or 7½ or 15 ips reel-to-reel and lyric and lead sheets or complete score. Include photo and bio. SAE and IRC. Reports in 2 months.
Music: All types: **band, orchestral, instrumental solo** and **instrumental ensemble** pieces; also **radio, TV** and **film music** (specializes in jingles/background music). Published *I Wana Be Shot* (by Daniel Boone), recorded by Nightmare on Zarg Records (rock); *Necro* (by Arthur E. Hunt), recorded by Suburban Studs on Anagram Records (punk); and *Groovin* (by M.J. Lawson), recorded by Emmit Till on Swoop Records (rock).

*SEA DREAM MUSIC, 236 Sebert Rd., London E7 0NP **England.** Phone: (081)534-8500. Senior Partner: Simon Law. Music print publisher. Publishes educational material and popular music. Estab. 1976. Prints 20 songs/year, mostly individual songs. Has printed sheet music for uncharted songs. Pays 10% royalty per sheet sold.
Affiliate(s): Chain of Love Music, Crimson Flame, Ernvik Musik (Sweden), Really Free Music, Scarf Music Publishing.
How to Contact: Submit demo tape by mail. Unsolicited submissions OK. Prefers cassette and lyric sheet. SAE and IRC. Reports in 6 weeks.
Music: Band and **choral pieces.** Published *Walk The Talk*, written and recorded by Garth Hewitt on Myrrh Records (worship); *Jesus is Greater* (by Gill Hutchinson), recorded by Spring Harvest on ICC Records (kids praise); *123 Follow Me* (by Llewellyn/Morgan), recorded by Ian Chia on Su (Aus) (kids praise).
Tips: "We publish specifically Christian songs."

SHELLEY MUSIC, 177 Balmoral Dr., Bolingbrook IL 60440. President: Guy Shelley. Music print publisher, music publisher (Guy Smilo Music BMI). Estab. 1992. Publishes 20-50 songs/year; publishes 4 new songwriters/year. Works with composers and lyricists. Pays 10% standard sheet music royalty.
How to Contact: Write first and obtain permission to submit. Prefers cassette with 1-3 songs and lyric sheet. SASE. Reports in 6 months. "No phone calls!"
Music: Mostly **classical (educational).** Published "The Glass Leaf," "Love Theme No. 2" and "The Parade," all piano pieces written by Donna Shelley.
Tips: "Have a finished score and a clean demo. Only submit your best material."

WILLIAM GRANT STILL MUSIC (ASCAP), Suite 422, 4 S. San Francisco St., Flagstaff AZ 86001-5737. (602)526-9355. Estab. 1983. Manager: Judith Anne Still. Music print publisher. Publishes educational material and classical and popular music. Prints 2-3 arrangements/year; 2-3 new arrangers/year. Works with arrangers only. Pays 10% royalty for arrangements sold. "We publish arrangements of works by William Grant Still. This year we are especially interested in developing a catalog of clarinet arrangements, though other sorts of arrangements may be considered."
How to Contact: Write or call first and obtain permission to submit. Does not return unsolicited material. Reports in 1 month.
Music: Mostly **instrumental solo pieces.** Published "Mother and Child" by Timothy Holley (classical); "Memphis Man" by Bert Coleman, for organ (popular); and "Coquette," by Anthony Griggs (classical).
Tips: "Any arrangement of the work of William Grant Still will be considered for publication, as will be works by American Indian composers."

3 SEAS MUSIC/NORTHVALE MUSIC, P.O. Box 565, Tappan NY 10983. (914)426-1466. Fax: (914)426-1273. President: Robert Schwartz. Music print publisher. Prints mostly individual songs. Lowest chart position held by a song published in sheet form is 20. Pays 14¢/song to songwriter for each sheet sold.
How to Contact: Call first.
Music: Rock and **Top 40.** Published "Stay With Me" (by James Denton) and "Take Me" (by Peter Mechtinal) recorded by Maurice Williams; "Someday Again," written and recorded by Bill Senkel, all on Laurie Records (pop).
Tips: "Write something fresh and different."

*TPM/STUDIO, 1735 Slade Rd., Blanch NC 27212. Fax: (910)694-9846 (send fax to Terry Poteat). Owners: Terry Poteat, Shonette Pulliam. Music publisher, lead sheet service. Estab. 1993. Publishes 90-120 pieces/year; mostly individual songs and folios. Publishes 50-100 new songwriters/year. "Charge on all completed lead sheets. Average song cost about $60 to engrave (3 pages)." Pays 10% royalty on printed sheet music.
Affiliate(s): TPM/Studio Productions; SYP Enterprises (BMI).
How to Contact: Write or fax for information, or submit demo tape by mail. Unsolicited submissions are OK. Prefers cassette with 1-2 songs and lyric sheet. "Prepare a neat package. Make everything legible, send an SASE please!" Reports in 2-4 weeks.
Music: Mostly **top 40/popular, gospel (contemporary)** and **easy listening**; also **educational (vocal and instrumental)**, **modern jazz** and **chamber or solo music**. Published "Black Rain" (by Kym Holliday), recorded by Ranid Woods on Jet Records (top 40); and "Brighter Day," written by Terry Poteat.
Tips: "Send good quality music. We are a new company so we are selective. At the present we are not looking for material; however, if you have something that shows promise we'll be glad to review it. Send good recordings. We engrave about all of our lead sheet submissions, but sometimes we refuse a submission because the recording is not clear. Please try to limit your fax to 1 page. A lyric sheet should accompany submissions when appropriate."

TRANSCONTINENTAL MUSIC PUBLICATIONS (ASCAP), Dept. SM, 838 Fifth Ave., New York NY 10021. (212)249-0100. Senior Editor: Dr. Judith B. Tischler. Music print publisher. Estab. 1941. Publishes 2 new songwriters/year. Works with composers. Pays 10% royalty. "We publish serious solo and choral music. The standard royalty is 10% except for rentals—there is no cost to the songwriter."
Affiliate(s): New Jewish Music Press (BMI).
How to Contact: Write or call first and obtain permission to submit a tape. Prefers cassette. "We usually do not accept lead sheets. Most all of our music is accompanied. Full and complete arrangements should accompany the melody." Does not return material. Reports in 6-12 months.
Music: Only **Jewish vocal** and **Jewish choral**. Published "Numi Numi" by Stern (classical); "Biti" (by Isaacson) (Bat Mitzvah Solo) and "Shalom Aleichem" (by Kalmanoff), recorded by Milnes on Ross Records (choral).
Tips: "Submit clean manuscript or computer typographer with accompaniment. Suitable material of sacred or secular Jewish relevance."

VIVACE PRESS, NW 310 Wawawai Rd., Pullman WA 99163. (509)334-4660. Fax: (509)334-3551. Contact: Jonathan Yordy. Music print publisher. Estab. 1990. Publishes 25 pieces of music/year; publishes several new composers/year. Pays 10% royalty for sheet music sales.
How to Contact: Submit demo tape and sheet music—unsolicited submissions OK. Prefers cassette. SASE. Reports in 1-2 weeks.
Music: Mostly **specialty historical classical** and **contemporary classical keyboard**. Published "Concerto in E-flat Major," by Maria Hester Park (piano); "Prelude For Organ," Fanny Mendelssohn (organ); and "Toccata For Harpsichord," by Emma Lou Diemer (harpsichord).
Tips: "Know our catalog to determine our intended market. If you haven't heard any compositions we carry, don't submit."

THE WILLIS MUSIC COMPANY, 7380 Industrial Rd., Florence KY 41022-0548. (606)283-2050. Harry Fox affiliate. Estab. 1899. Editor: David B. Engle. Music print publisher. Publishes educational material. Prints 100 publications/year; "no charted songs in our catalog." Pays 5-10% of retail price or outright purchase.
How to Contact: Prefers fully notated score. SASE. Reports in 3 months.
Music: Mostly **early level piano teaching material**; also **instrumental solo pieces, method books** and "supplementary materials—educational material only."

Music Print Publishers/'94-'95 Changes

The following markets appeared in the 1994 edition of *Songwriter's Market* but are absent from the 1995 edition. Most of these companies failed to respond to our request for an update of their listing or requested deletion.

Davike Music Co.
Emandell Tunes (requested
    deletion)
Hammer Musik Gmbh

Ivory Palaces Music
Lillenas Publishing Co.
    (requested deletion)

Record Companies

The role of the record company is to record and release records, cassettes and CDs — the mechanical products of the music industry. They sign artists to recording contracts, decide what songs those artists will record, and finally determine which songs to release. They are also responsible for providing recording facilities, securing producers and musicians, and overseeing the manufacture, distribution and promotion of new releases.

The costs incurred by a record company, especially the major labels, are substantially larger than those of other segments of the music industry. The music publisher, for instance, considers only items such as salaries and the costs of making demos. Record companies, at great financial risk, pay for all those services discussed above. It's estimated that 8% of acts on the major labels are paying for the losses incurred by the remaining 92%.

This profit/loss ratio and the continuing economic crunch have forced changes in the record industry. Major labels are signing fewer new acts and dropping unprofitable ones. This means a shrinking market among the majors for new songs for their acts. Also, the continuing fear of copyright infringement suits has closed avenues to getting new material heard by the majors. Most don't listen to unsolicited submissions . . . period. Only songs recommended by attorneys, managers and producers major label employees trust and respect are being heard by A&R people, who have much of the input on what songs should be performed and recorded by a particular act.

Recommendations by key music industry people may be hard to come by, but they're not impossible. Songwriters must remember that talent alone does not guarantee success in the music business. You must be recognized through contacts, and the only way to make contacts is through networking. Networking is the process of building an interconnecting web of acquaintances within the music business. The more industry people you meet, the larger your contact base becomes, and the more your chances of meeting someone with the clout to get your demo into the hands of the right people increase. If you want to get ahead in this business, and you want to get your music heard by key A&R representatives, networking is imperative.

Networking opportunities are also available at regional and national music conferences and workshops. You should try to attend at least one or two of these events each year. It's a great way to increase the number and quality of your music industry contacts.

Because of the continuing changes and shrinking market the majors represent, independent labels take on a new significance for your work. Since they're located all over the country, they're much easier to contact and can be important in building a local base of support for your music. Independent labels usually concentrate more on a specific type of music, which will help you target those companies your submissions should be sent to. And since the staff at an indie label is smaller, there are fewer channels to go through to get your music heard by the top personnel of the company.

Independent labels are seen by many as a stepping stone to a major recording contract. Very few artists are signed to a major label at the start of their careers; usually, they've had a few independent releases that helped build their reputation in the industry. Major labels watch the independent record labels closely to locate up-

and-coming bands and new trends. But independents aren't just farming grounds for future major label acts; many bands have long-term relationships with indies, and prefer it that way. While they may not be able to provide the extensive distribution and promotion that a major label can, indie labels can help make an artist a regional success, and may even help the performer to see a profit as well. With the lower overhead and smaller production costs that an independent label operates on, it's much easier to be a "success" on an indie label than on a major.

Most of the following listings are for independent labels. They are the most receptive to new material. Just because the companies are small, however, doesn't mean you should forget professionalism. When submitting material to a record company, be specific about what you are submitting and what your goals are. If you are strictly a songwriter and the label carries a band you believe would properly present your song, state that in your cover letter. If you are an artist looking for a contract, make sure you showcase your strong points as a performer in the demo package. Whatever your goals are, follow submission guidelines closely, be as neat as possible and include a top-notch demo. If you need more information concerning a company's requirements, write or call for more details.

At the end of this section, you will find a Geographic Index listing alphabetically the record companies in the major music centers — New York, Los Angeles and Nashville — to help you plan a trip to one or more of these cities. There is also an alphabetical list of international listings appearing in this section.

You will want to refer to the Category Index, also at the end of this section. It lists companies by the type of music they're interested in hearing and will help you find those companies most receptive to the type of music you write.

*A & R RECORDS, Suite 207, 900 19th Ave. S., Nashville TN 37212. (615)329-9127. Owner/President: R. Steele/David Steele. Labels include South Side of Heaven Records, Aarrow Records. Record company, record producer, music publisher and talent development/booking. Estab. 1986. Deals with artists and songwriters. Releases 10 LPs and 10 CDs/year. Royalty varies, depending on individual agreement. Pays statutory rate to publisher per song on record.
How to Contact: Writer/artists may call first, or submit demo tape by mail. Unsolicited submissions are OK. But must be coded: Songwriter's Market. Prefers cassette with 2 songs and lyric sheet. "We are currently working with writer/artists only. We are not soliciting songs from outside writers who are not singers." SASE. Must include multiple choice reply card or letter for individual comment. Reports ASAP.
Music: Mostly **country, gospel** and **alternative/folk/bluegrass**; also **Cajun, instrumental (fiddle)** and **children's**. Released "I Want You," written and recorded by Bethany Reynolds on Aarrow Records (country); "Drivin' Me Crazy" (by Bob Delaposta), recorded by Kurt Weston on A & R Records (country); and "Coldest Night Since 1951" (by Joey Boone), recorded by Ruthie Steele on Aarrow Records. Other artists include Tricia Torline, Michael Fender, Will LeBlanc, Lollie Ellis, Nashville Nelly, Kelli Steele, David Steele, Randy Cox, Tanya West, Carl L'Amour, Mark Thomsen.
Tips: "Must have professional package in place for P.R. and promotion. Only dedicated, unique, business minded artists can be considered. Identifiable, unique voice is a must."

A.M.I. RECORDS, 394 W. Main St., Hendersonville TN 37075. (615)822-7595. Vice President: Dwight Martin. Record company, music publisher (Silver Heart Music, BMI; Silver Dust Music, ASCAP), record producer. Estab. 1981. Works with musicians/artists on record contract or songwriters on royalty contract. Pays 3-9¢ to artists on contract for each record sold; statutory rate to publisher per song on record. No advance for services.
How to Contact: Write or call first and obtain permission to submit. Prefers cassette (or VHS videocassette if available) with 5 songs and lyric sheets. Does not return material. Reports in 2 months.
Music: Mostly **country, pop** and **light rock**. Released "I Just Lost My Baby Blues" (by T. Street), recorded by Jan Beard and "How Can I Miss You" (by J. Ecret), recorded by Joe Barr, both on A.M.I. Records; and "Steppin' Stone," written and recorded by Charlie Goodman on Tamara Records.

AARSON RECORDS, % Entertainment Management Enterprises, 454 Alps Rd., Wayne NJ 07470. (201)694-3333. President: Richard Zielinski. Labels include Unicorn Records. Record company and manager. Estab. 1983. Works with musicians/artists on contract.

How to Contact: Submit demo tape by mail. Unsolicited submissions are OK. Prefers cassette (or VHS videocassette) with 4 songs and lyric sheet. SASE. Reports in 1 month.
Music: Mostly **rock**, **metal** and **urban**. Artists include Mirror's Image and Sinful.

ADOBE RECORDS, Dept. SM, Box W, Shallowater TX 79363. (806)873-3537. President: Tom Wood-ruff. Record company. Estab. 1989. Releases 5 LPs/year. Works with musicians/artists, storytellers and poets on contract. Pays statutory rate.
How to Contact: Write (attn: Sue Swinson) or call first and obtain permission to submit. Prefers cassette or VHS videocassette with 3 songs and lyric or lead sheet. Does not return unsolicited material. Reports in 3 months.
Music: Folk, **bluegrass**, **C&W**, **jazz** and **blues**. Released "The One That I Never Could Write," written and recorded by R.W. Hampton (cowboy western); "Talking To a Tennessee Moon," written and recorded by Candace Anderson; and *Moon Light on the Colorado*, arranged and recorded by Joe Stephenson, all on Adobe Records.

AIR CENTRAL RECORDINGS, 3700 S. Hawthorne, Sioux Falls SD 57105. Owners: William Prines III. Labels include Omnigram Records. Record company. Estab. 1983. Releases 2 singles, 5-6 cassettes and 2-3 CDs/year. Works with musicians/artists on contract. Pays statutory rate to publisher per song on record.
How to Contact: Write to obtain permission to submit. Prefers cassette with 3 songs. SASE. Reports in 3 months.
Music: Mostly **country**, **pop** and **gospel**; also **rock** and **R&B**.

AIRWAVE PRODUCTION GROUP, INC., 1916 28th Ave. S., Birmingham AL 35209. (205)870-3239. President/A&R: Michael Panepento. Artist development and production company and artist management company. Estab. 1985. Releases 5-15 CDs/year. Works with musicians/artists on contract and hires musicians for in-house studio work. Develops and manages new talent, secures recording contracts.
How to Contact: Submit demo tape by mail. Unsolicited submissions are OK. Prefers cassette with 3 songs and lyric sheets. SASE. Reports in 6-8 weeks.
Music: Mostly **pop/top 40**, **rock** and **R&B**; also **country** and **jazz**. Released albums by Brother Cane (Virgin Records), Slick Lilly (Zeal Records), Vallejo (Pandem Records), Rick Carter and the Loveland Orchestra (Prairie Eden Records) and Kelly Garrett (Sony/Tree).
Tips: "Make it a complete, neat package!"

ALCAZAR RECORDS, Box 429, Waterbury VT 05676. (802)244-7845. Manager: Mitch Cantor. Labels include Alcazar, Fogarty's Cove, Fretless, Alacazam!, Tara Records, Round River Records, Dunkeld Records, Audio Outings, Gadfly Records, Keltia Musique, Mark Rubin Productions, Mineral River, NSO Records, Well-N-Tune Productions and Record Rak Records. Estab. 1977. Works with musicians/artists on record contract, songwriters on royalty contract and musicians on salary for in-house studio work.
How to Contact: Prefers cassette (or VHS videocassette) with 3 songs and lyric sheet. Does not return material. Reports in 2 months.
Music: Children's, **folk** and **blues**; also **pop/soft rock**, **avant-garde** and **Celtic**. Artists include Doc Watson, Odetta, George Gritzbach, Priscilla Herdman, Rory Block, Utah Phillips, Eric Bogle, Fred Koller, Dave Van Ronk, Sara Banham, Radhika Miller and Mike and Carleen McCornack.

ALISO CREEK PRODUCTIONS INCORPORATED, Box 8174, Van Nuys CA 91409. (818)787-3203. President: William Williams. Labels include Aliso Creek Records. Record company. Estab. 1987. Releases 4 LPs and 4 CDs/year. Works with musicians/artists and songwriters on contract. Pays negotiable royalty to artists on contract. Pays statutory rate to publisher per song on record.
How to Contact: Write and obtain permission to submit. Prefers cassette with 3 songs and lyric sheet. SASE. Reports in 3-4 weeks.
Music: Mostly **New Age**, **new acoustic** and **children's music**; also **rock**, **pop** and **country**. Released *Change*, written and recorded by Steve Kenyata (new world); and *Take a Trip* (by Bob Menn), recorded by various artists (children's), both on Aliso Creek Records.
Tips: "We are looking for career singer/songwriters with well-developed material and performance skills and the desire to tour."

 The asterisk before a listing indicates that the listing is new in this edition. New markets are often the most receptive to unsolicited submissions.

INSIDER REPORT

Children's music market provides opportunities for songwriters

"There are many opportunities for songwriters in the children's market," says children's music writer and performer Terri Sigafus. "I think the old mind-set of children's music has changed a lot. It's become a real art and many serious songwriters are starting to delve into this expanding market."

Terri, along with her husband Chad, began writing children's music seven years ago. Today, they own their own recording studio and music publishing company, and have released five albums on their own Teeter-Tot Records label. The couple is enthusiastic about the growing opportunities available for children's songwriters.

They point to the number of major adult artists who are putting out children's tapes and the increasing number of radio stations programming

Chad and Terri Sigafus

strictly children's music as an indication of its increasing appeal. "The growing popularity of children's music is incredible," Terri says. "There are Grammy Awards for children's music, a column in *Billboard* about it, and major distributors specifically for children's music. There are literally hundreds of new children's artists who are looking for material. It's opened up tremendously for the songwriter."

When Chad and Terri first started in the industry, things were different—most people got into children's music because they weren't good enough to succeed in other markets. "There were stores filled with products that reflected that," Terri says. "Now it seems people have really started to take it seriously. People pay as much for our tapes as they pay for Garth Brooks's tapes."

But Chad and Terri did not tap into the children's market on purpose. The couple had been playing their own folk-style music for several years, as well as covering the work of other artists on the club circuit. Everything changed, however, when Terri became pregnant with their first child, Joshua.

"When we got into children's music, the reasons were twofold," Chad explains. "When Joshua came into the picture, we realized that music would take a lot of time away from our family. Also the types of venues you play are not always suitable for kids. So we started writing a lullaby album for Joshua, and one thing led to another. We decided to take on that style of music and go in that direction from a family point of view as well as a musical point of view."

Those lullabies became *Water Color Ponies*, Chad's and Terri's first release on Teeter-Tot Records. Many of their enchanting, folksy tunes were just as pleasing to adults as they were to children, but it was classified as children's music because the songs were lullabies. "So we kind of fell into the children's market without even realizing it," Terri says. "All of a sudden, an opportunity opened up because there was such a need in children's music. Before we knew it we had national distribution, and were putting out all kinds of material. It was just remarkable. We fit perfectly."

Today, Chad's and Terri's philosophy for the music they write remains the same—to create songs that appeal to adults as well as children. And they continue to garner inspiration from Joshua as well as his younger sisters, Addie and Rebeccah. Terri, who writes the pair's lyrics, uses real situations from her children's lives as well as her own childhood—tea parties, playing the drums on pots and pans, learning to tie your shoes. "I think some adults see themselves in these same situations when they were little and they reflect back. Or they see through the eyes of their own children. It's just such a joy, the innocence of it. We try to make sure our music keeps that innocence."

Working out of the recording studio housed in their Stockton, Illinois farmhouse, Chad and Terri are never far from their three small sources of inspiration. Terri comes up with the concept for a song. "Then I bring it to Chad, and he turns it into something wonderful," she says. "When I bring him an idea, there could be changes when he's through, but each song is a combination of both of us, and I think that's the magic in it."

Both Chad and Terri are still surprised at the response their music receives. "It's so overwhelming because there's a big need for what we do," Terri says. "I think all the children's recording artists have been doing the same songs for so long that they need something new."

"And we're looking for new artists all the time," Chad adds. "But like every independent label, we have a certain sound and a certain feel we're looking for. We think this is a great market to break into for both songwriters and performers."

Chad's and Terri's latest album, *The Bravest Little Cowboy: Lullabies for Little Cowboys*, is distributed through Silo Music and Music for Little People. But, like most children's recordings, it may be hard to find in record stores, which devote little or no space to children's music, especially independent releases. Children's bookstores, however, recognize children's audio as one of their biggest sidelines, and are usually more open to carrying independent product.

The children's music market, unlike its adult counterpart, doesn't need to depend on radio airplay, and independents do very well competing against the big labels. "When an independent's tapes move off the shelves faster than a major label's, there's something to be said for that, and it boils down to the quality of the product," Terri says. "You can't buy the public when it comes to children's music. Everyone's got an equal opportunity in this market. If you're sincere about what you're doing, and you've got a good product, people are going to buy it."

—*Alice P. Buening*

*ALL NIGHT RECORDS, 208½ N. Washington, Eldorado AR 71730. (501)862-6686. Fax: (501)862-8800. A&R Director: David Feinberg. Labels include A.N.R. Record company and record producer. Estab. 1978. Deals with artists and songwriters. Releases 10 singles, 10 12″ singles, 10 LPs, 10 EPs and 10 CDs/year. Royalty varies to artists on contract; varying amount to publisher per song on record.
How to Contact: Submit demo tape by mail. Unsolicited submissions are OK. Prefers cassette. SASE. Reports in 2-3 weeks.
Music: Mostly **rock** and **R&B**. Released "Moon Dust" (by W.D. Palmer), recorded by Rick Palmer on ANR Records (pop); "Walkout," written and recorded by T.J. Milan on All Night Records (rock); and "Monkey's," (by Group), recorded by Live Dogs on ANR Records (punk). Other artists include Billy Lee Cross & The Wildcats.

*ALL STAR PROMOTIONS, P.O. Box 1130, Tallevast FL 34270. (813)351-3253. Vice President/A&R: Bob Francis. Labels include Castle Records, TCB Records, Rock Island Records, Jade Records, Phoenix Records, Heavy Weather Records. Record company, record producer and music publisher. Estab. 1967. Deals with artists and songwriters. Releases 18 singles, 6 12″ singles, 6 LPs and 6 CDs/year. Pays 4-6% royalty to artists on contract; statutory rate to publisher per song on record.
How to Contact: Submit demo tape by mail. Unsolicited submissions are OK, "But tapes are not returned." Prefers cassette (or VHS videocassette if available) with 6 songs. Does not return material. Reports in 2 weeks.
Music: Mostly **rock**, **dance** and **R&B/funk**; also **AOR** and **MOR**. Released "Diamond Dallas" (by P. Facken), recorded by Diamond Dallas Page on Rock Island Records (heavy rock); *Nasty As They Wanna Be* (by D. Lawrence), recorded by Nasty Boys on Castle Records (rock); and "Ultimate Male" (by P. Lucic), recorded by Noelle on Jade Records (dance). Other artists include Phoenix, Derrick Dukes, The Big Cheese, Bambi, Hot Shot and TCB Band.
Tips: "Submit quality demo (not merely acoustic guitar and vocal) on quality cassette in order to give us a chance to hear the potential of the tune or the artist. Poor quality tapes get minimum consideration."

ALLAGASH COUNTRY RECORDS, 45 7th St., Auburn ME 04210. (207)784-7975. President/A&R Director: Richard E. Gowell. Labels include Gowell Records and Allagash R&B Records. Record company, music publisher (Richard E. Gowell Music/BMI) and record producer. Estab. 1986. Releases 3-5 singles and 1-3 LPs/year. Works with musicians/artists and songwriters on contract. Pays 3-25% royalty to artists on contract; statutory rate to publisher per song on record.
How to Contact: Submit demo tape by mail. Unsolicited submissions OK. Prefers cassette with 2-12 songs and lyric or lead sheet. SASE. Reports in 2-6 weeks.
Music: Mostly **country**, **pop/country** and **country rock**; also **R&B/pop**. Released "I Want to See Her Again," written and recorded by Kevin Cronin (country); "Back Home" (by J. Main), recorded by Larry Main (pop/country); and "Is It My Body You Want?" (by R.E. Gowell) recorded by Rich Gowell (50s rock), all on Allagash Records.
Tips: "We release compact discs worldwide and lease out album projects on singer/songwriters that have original unpublished masters available. 10-12 songs/masters in above styles that we accept, are contracted for this promotion. We work with many new acts with commercial material."

ALLEGHENY MUSIC WORKS, 306 Cypress Ave,. Johnstown PA 15902. (814)535-3373. Managing Director: Al Rita. West Coast A&R Consultant: Dale Siegenthaler. Labels include Allegheny Records. Record company, music publisher (Allegheny Music Works Publishing/ASCAP and Tuned on Music/BMI). Estab. 1991. Works with musicians/artists or songwriters on royalty contract. Pays 8-12% royalty to artists on contract; statutory rate to publisher per song on record.
How to Contact: Submit demo tape by mail. Unsolicited submissions are OK. Prefers cassette with 3 songs and lyric sheet or lead sheet. SASE. Reports in 2-4 weeks.
Music: Mostly **country**, **pop**, **adult contemporary** and **R&B**; also **church/religious**. "We are interested in leasing masters for overseas sub-licensing." Released "Running On Empty" (by Sterling Kodiak and Larry Evans), recorded by Tom Woodard; "Shades of Gray" (by M. Carroll), recorded by Michael Dean; and "Is She That Much Better Than Me" (by Thelma Lemons Todd and Abbie Faye Petty), recorded by Wanda Copier, all on Allegheny Records. Other artists include "Country" Joe Liptock and Mark McLelland.
Tips: "First, be talented, professional, committed, and always willing to accept constructive criticism. Second, set well defined, realistic goals for each project, and budget time and money accordingly."

*ALLIGATOR RECORDS, P.O. Box 60234, Chicago IL 60660. Fax: (312)973-2088. Contact: A&R Dept. Record company and music publisher (Eyeball Music/BMI). Estab. 1971. Pays standard royalty to artists on contract; statutory rate to publisher per song on record.
How to Contact: Submit demo tape by mail. Unsolicited submissions are OK. Prefers cassette with 3 songs and lyric sheet. Does not return material. Reports in 4 months.
Music: **Blues** only!

ALPHABEAT, Box 12 01, D-97862 Wertheim/Main, **Germany**. Phone: (09342)841 55. Owner/A&R Manager: Stephan Dehn. A&R National Manager: Marga Zimmermann. Press & Promotion: Alexander Burger. Disco Promotion: Matthias Marth. Music Service: Wolfgang Weinmann. Creative Services: Heiko Köferl. Record company and record producer. Releases vary "depending on material available." Works with musicians/artists on contract; hires musicians for in-house studio work. Also works through "license contract with foreign labels." Payment to artists on contract "depends on product." Payment: conditional on German market.
How to Contact: Submit demo tape by mail. Unsolicited submissions are OK. Prefers cassette (or PAL videocassette) with maximum of 3 songs and lyric sheet. "When sending us your demo tapes, please advise us of your ideas and conditions." SAE and IRC. Reports in 2 weeks.
Music: Mostly **dance/disco/pop**, **synth/pop** and **electronic**; also **R&B**, **hip hop/rap** and **ballads**. Artists include Red Sky, Fabian Harloff, Silent Degree, Mode Control, Mike M.C. & Master J., Skyline, Lost in the Dessert, Oriental Bazar, Voice In Your Head and Love Game.
Tips: "We are a distributor of foreign labels. If foreign labels have interest in distribution of their productions in Germany (also Switzerland and Austria) they can contact us. We distribute all styles of music of foreign labels. Please contact our department 'Distribution Service.' "

ALTERNATIVE RECORDS, P.O. Box 46, Eugene OR 97440-0046. (503)344-3616. A&R: KC Layton. Labels include Gravity, Alternative Archive. Record company. Estab. 1979. Releases 3-4 singles, 5 LPs, 1 EP and 5 CDs/year. Works with musicians/artists on record contract. Pays 17% royalty to artists on contract; statutory rate to publisher per song on record.
How to Contact: Write first and obtain permission to submit. Be sure to include SASE! Prefers cassette (or VHS videocassette if available) with 5 songs and lyric sheet. SASE. Reports in 4 weeks.
Music: Mostly **rock (alternative)**, **pop (again, alternative in nature)** and **country/rock**; also **experimental** and **industrial**. Released "Burn It Low," written and recorded by John Nau; *Trust*, written and recorded by Two Pound Planet, both on Alternative Records; and *Wes Montgomery Blues*, written and recorded by Sheep Theatre on Alternative Archives Records. Also released *Songs from the Hydrogen Jukebox* by Two Pound Planet, produced by Mitch Easter. Other artists include Robert Vaughn, 77's and Zoo People.
Tips: "Every release we've done has consistently been praised by fans and critics alike so we seek to make every album something that will hold up over the years, not just attempting to mimic trend of the day. It's important that your vision of your art be as focused as possible."

*AMERICAN MUSIC NETWORK, INC., P.O. Box 7018, Warner Robins GA 31095. (912)953-2800. President: Robert R. Kovach. Labels include Scaramouche Recordings. Record company, record producer and music marketing corp. Estab. 1986. Deals with artists and songwriters. Releases 25 singles, 12 LPs and 12 CDs/year. Pays varying royalty to artists on contract; statutory rate to publisher per song on record.
How to Contact: Submit demo tape by mail. Unsolicited submissions are OK. Prefers cassette with 4 songs and lyric sheet. "We need name, address and telephone number." SASE. Reports in 4-6 months.
Music: Mostly **country**, **A/C** and **bluegrass**; also **rock**, **gospel** and **other forms**. Released "Easy On Your Feet," written and recorded by Theresa Justus (A/C); "Real Country Livin'," written and recorded by Little Rudy (country); and "What Happens To Love," written and recorded by Wayne Little (country), all on Scaramouche Recordings. Other artists include Napoleon Starke and Dusty Shelton.

AMERICATONE RECORDS INTERNATIONAL USA, 1817 Loch Lomond Way, Las Vegas NV 89102-4437. (702)384-0030. Fax: (702)382-1926. Estab. 1975. Record company, producer and music publisher. Releases 5 12″ singles, 5 EPs and 8 CDs/year. Pays standard royalty.
Affiliate(s): The Rambolt Music International (ASCAP), Christy Records International.
How to Contact: Submit demo tape by mail. Prefers cassettes and studio production with top sound recordings and lyric sheets. SASE. Reports in 4 weeks.
Music: Mostly **country**, **jazz**, **R&R**, **Spanish** and **classic ballads**. Published *Dick Sheare and His Stan Kenton Spirit*, recorded by Dick Sheare; *Jazz in the Raine*, recorded by Raine Band; and *Big Band Jazz*, recorded by Todd McIntosh, all on Americatone International Records.

THE AMETHYST GROUP LTD./ANTITHESIS RECORDS, 273 Chippewa Dr., Columbia SC 29210-6508. Contact: A&R. Labels include Amethyst Records, Antithesis Records, Amaryllis Records, Analysis Records, Gizmo Records. Record company, music publisher (Another Amethyst Song/BMI) and management firm. Estab. 1979. Releases 10 CD's. Works with musicians/artists on contract. Pays 8-12%

Listings of companies in countries other than the U.S. have the name of the country in boldface type.

royalty to artists on contract. Pays statutory rate to publishers per song on record. International distribution, management, marketing firm. "Our forte is management, with overseas marketing."
How to Contact: Submit demo tape by mail. Unsolicited submissions are OK. Prefers cassette (or VHS videocassette) with 3-7 songs and lyric sheet. SASE. Reports within 3-5 weeks only if interested. "Always include return postage for any reply."
Music: Mostly **alternative, rock** and **R&B**; also **dance, country, techno, industrial, space, rock, new music, jazz/rap** and **heavy metal**. Released *Yesterday's News* (by Michael Yows), recorded by Safari on Analysis Records (funk); *When Love Calls My Name*, written and recorded by Toni Monet on Antithesis Records (pop); and *Speed Mama* (by Gary Weisberg), recorded by Slither on Analysis Records (industrial). Other artists include Bodyshop, Torre, Progress In April.
Tips: "Try to be realistic about someone investing in your material."

AMIRON MUSIC/AZTEC PRODUCTIONS, 20531 Plummer St., Chatsworth CA 91311. (818)998-0443. General Manager: A. Sullivan. Labels include Dorn Records and Aztec Records. Record company, booking agency and music publisher (Amiron Music). Releases 2 singles/year. Works with artists and songwriters on contract. Pays 10% maximum royalty to artists on contract; standard royalty to songwriters on contract. Pays statutory rate to publishers.
How to Contact: Prefers cassette and lead sheet. SASE. Reports in 3 weeks.
Music: **Dance, easy listening, folk, jazz, MOR, rock** ("no heavy metal") and **top 40/pop**. Released "Look In Your Eyes," by Newstreet; and "Midnight Flight," recorded by Papillon.
Tips: "Be sure the material has a hook; it should make people want to make love or fight. Write something that will give a talented new artist that edge on current competition."

*AMUSED PRODUCTIONS, P.O. Box 671, Claremont CA 91711. (909)625-3169. President: Sherban Cira. Record producer. Estab. 1988. Releases 1 single, 1 LP and 1 CD/year. Pays statutory rate to publisher per song on record.
How to Contact: Write first and obtain permission to submit. Prefers cassette with 3 songs and lyric sheet. Does not return material. Reports in 1 month.
Music: Mostly **children's music**.

*ANGEL EYES RECORDS & FILMWORKS, INC., 9900 NW 80 Place, Hialeah Gardens FL 33016. (305)558-1881. Fax: (305)826-9499. President: Joe Granda. Labels include AER, Techno-Grooves, Music for The Children of The World. Record company. Estab. 1988. Deals with artists and songwriters. Releases 10 singles, 10 12" singles, 3 LPs, 5 EPs and 10 CDs/year. Pays 6% royalty to artists on contract; statutory rate to publisher per song on record.
How to Contact: Call first and obtain permission to submit. Prefers cassette and lyric sheet. "If songwriter is also an artist, submit photo and bio." SASE. Reports in 4-5 weeks.
Music: Mostly **dance-pop, R&B/soul** and **alternative-dance**; also **rap, pop-ballads** and **alternative rock**. Released *Dubland* (by J. Bartet/A. Arzeno), recorded by Warning (dance); "Feliz Navidad" (by J. Feliciano), recorded by Mini Kidz (Christmas); and "Need A Little Love" (by J. Minnis), recorded by South Beach Dance Alliance (dance), all on Angel Eyes Records. Other artists include John Minnis, Underground Soul, Charlie, Creative Element, Elio & Juliano, Nice & Wild.
Tips: "Patience and persistence are key in this business, don't give up, keep on trying, something soon will click. We will mail response, please don't call."

ASSOCIATED ARTISTS MUSIC INTERNATIONAL, Maarschalklaan 47, 3417 SE Montfoort, **The Netherlands**. Phone and fax: 31-3484-72860. Release Manager: Joop Gerrits. Labels include Associated Artists, Disco-Dance Records and Italo. Record company, music publisher (Associated Artists International/BUMA-STEMRA, Hilversum Happy Music/BUMA-STEMRA, Intermedlodie/BUMA-STEMRA and Hollands Glorie Productions), record producer (Associated Artists Productions) and TV promotions. Estab. 1975. Releases 10 singles, 25 12" singles, 6 LPs and 6 CDs/year. Works with musicians/artists and songwriters on contract. Royalties vary.
How to Contact: Submit demo tape by mail. Unsolicited submissions OK. Prefers compact cassette or 19 cm/sec reel-to-reel (or VHS videocassette) with any number of songs and lyric or lead sheets. Records also accepted. SAE and IRC. Reports in 6 weeks.
Music: Mostly **dance, pop, house, hip hop** and **rock**. Released "U Got 2 Know" (by Bortolotti), recorded by Cappella on Media Records (dance); "To Love" (by Arduini), recorded by Fits of Gloom on News Records (dance); and "Your Love" (by Rossini), recorded by Fargetta on Arcade Records (dance). Other artists include Clubhouse, F.R. David, Mars Plastic, Naomi.
Tips: "We invite producers and independent record labels to send us their material for their entry on the European market. Mark all parcels as 'no commercial value—for demonstration only.' We license productions to record companies in all countries of Europe and South Africa. Submit good demos or masters."

ATLANTIC RECORDING CORP., 9229 Sunset Blvd., Los Angeles CA 90069. (310)205-7460. A&R Representatives: Kevin Williamson, Tom Carolan, Tim Sommer. Labels include Atco, East-West and Atlantic. "We distribute Interscope, Rhino, Matador, Mammoth and Third Stone Records." Record company, music publisher. Estab. 1948. Works with artists on contract, songwriters on royalty contract and musicians on salary for in-house studio work.
How to Contact: "We accept solicited material only by managers, attorneys, producers or publishers who are legitimately established within the industry."
Music: Blues, disco, easy listening, folk, jazz, MOR, progressive, R&B, rock, soul and **top 40/pop.** Released *Come On Feel the Lemonheads*, recorded by The Lemonheads (alternative rock); *Core*, recorded by Stone Temple Pilots (hard rock); and *Bad Boys*, recorded by Inner Circle (R&B), all on Atlantic Records. Artists include INXS, AC/DC, Pete Townsend, Bette Midler, Skid Row, Crosby, Stills, Nash & Young, Genesis, Phil Collins, Robert Plant, Laura Brannigan, Intro, The Juliana Hatfield Three, Mr. Big, The Hatters, Screamin' Cheetah Wheelies, Melissa Ferrick, Clannad, Tori Amos, Bad Religion, The Melvins and Lea Salonga.
Tips: "Make sure you research the contacts you will be making and have professional representation."

*AUCOURANT RECORDS, P.O. Box 672902, Marietta GA 30067. Artistic Director: Dr. R. S. Thompson. Estab. 1989. Deals with artists and songwriters. Releases 5 CDs/year. Pays 12% royalty to artists on contract; statutory rate to publisher per song on record.
How to Contact: Submit demo tape by mail. Unsolicited submissions are OK. Prefers cassette with lead sheet. Does not return material. Reports in 4 months.
Music: Mostly **contemporary instrumental, avant-garde** and **computer music;** also **experimental pop** and **ambient music.** Released *Deeper in the Dreamtime, Ginnungagap* and *Shadow Gazing*, all on Aucourant Records (computer music)
Tips: "Know what we are interested in and don't submit material that is *not* of interest to us."

*AUGUST RECORDS, P.O. Box 7041, Watchung NJ 07060. (908)753-1601. Executive Vice President: Meg Polterak. Labels include August Jazz, August Country and August Classics. Record company, record producer, music publisher (Humbletunes) and video production company. Estab. 1990. Deals with artists and songwriters. Releases 4 singles, 4-6 LPs and 4-6 CDs/year. Pays variable royalty to artists on contract; statutory rate to publishers per song on record.
How to Contact: Submit demo tape by mail. Unsolicited submissions are OK. Prefers cassette (or ½″ videocassette if available) with 3-5 songs and lyric sheet. "We are a small company with a huge work load so it takes us a while to review submissions." Does not return material. Reports in 3-6 months.
Music: "Each of our labels is genre specific: **pop/rock, country, jazz** and **classical.**" Released *Worlds Apart*, written and recorded by Tim Keyes (pop); *The High Places*, written and recorded by Tom Gavornik (jazz); and *Out of My Heart* (by various), recorded by Lorianna (country), all on August Records. Other artists include Tang S'Dang, Almighty ShuHorN, Q87, Chris Fischer and Serious Pilgrim.

AVANT-GARDE RECORDS CORP., 12224 Avila Dr., Kansas City MO 64145. (816)942-8861. Director A&R/President: Scott Smith. Record company, music publisher and record producer. Estab. 1983. Releases 2 CDs/year. Pays 80% royalty to artists on contract.
How to Contact: Write first and obtain permission to submit. Prefers cassette (or VHS videocassette if available) with 4 songs. SASE. Reports in 8 weeks.
Music: Mostly **themes, new standards** and **pop classical,** (no New Age) on piano only. Released *Take A Bow, Concerto Themes Nocturne in E Flat*, and *40th Anniversary Collector's Edition*, recorded by Ferrante & Teicher on Avant-Garde Records.
Tips: "Only send instrumentals—no lyrics. Piano recordings get top priority. Prefer semi-established concert-pianist caliber. No New Age type music considered. Solid melody lines a must! Prefer up tempo—no dreary depressing songs considered."

AVC ENTERTAINMENT INC., Suite 200, 6201 Sunset Blvd., Hollywood CA 90028. (213)461-9001. President: James Warsinske. Labels include AVC Records. Record company and music publisher (AVC Music/ASCAP, Harmonious Music/BMI). Estab. 1988. Releases 6-12 singles, 6-12 12″ singles, 3-6 LPs and 3-6 CDs/year. Works with musicians/artists and songwriters on contract. Pays rate of 75% to publishers.
How to Contact: Submit demo tape by mail. Unsolicited submissions OK. Prefers cassette and VHS videocassette with 2-4 songs and lyric sheet. SASE. Reports in 1 month.
Music: Mostly **R&B/rap, pop** and **rock;** also **funk/soul, dance** and **metal.** Released "In Service" (by Michael Williams), recorded by Madrok (rap); "There's a New Today," written and recorded by Duncan Faure (pop/rock); and "Melissa Mainframe" (by Hohl/Rocca), recorded by Rocca, all on AVC Records (pop/rock).

Tips: "Be original and contemporary, we take our time selecting our artists, but stay committed to them."

*AWSOM RECORD CO., 29512 Peoria Rd., Halsey OR 97348-9742. (503)491-3524. A&R: Joanne Kendall. Record company. Deals with artists only. Pays statutory royalty.
How to Contact: Submit demo tape by mail. Unsolicited submissions are OK. Prefers cassette with 3 or more songs. "Explain what your intentions and goals are, and what you expect." SASE. Reports in 1 month.
Music: All kinds. Artists include Dreamer (rock), Don McHan (gospel), Dave Cole (country), Molley McRay (country), Ted Snow (country) and Soldier (gospel rock).

AZRA INTERNATIONAL, Box 459, Maywood CA 90270. (213)560-4223. A&R: Jeff Simins. Labels include World Metal, Metal Storm, Azra, Iron Works, Not So Famous David's Records and Masque Records. Record company. Estab. 1978. Releases 10 singles, 5 LPs, 5 EPs and 5 CDs/year. Works with artists on contract. "Artists usually carry their own publishing." Pays 10% royalty to artists on contract; statutory rate to publishers for each record sold.
How to Contact: Submit demo tape by mail. Unsolicited submissions are OK. Prefers cassette (or VHS videocassette) with 3-5 songs and lyric sheet. Include bio and photo. SASE. Reports in 3 weeks.
Music: Mostly **rock, heavy metal, Christian** and **New Age;** also **novelty.** Released *Colors Of The Sun,* written and recorded by Dan James on Condor Records (New Age); *Its For You,* written and recorded by Omicron on Iron Work Records (metal); and *Gun For Hire,* written and recorded by Whiskey Train on Masque Records (rock). Other artists include Comatose, Carry Nation, Acid Face, Laughing House.
Tips: "Make sure your songs are timeless; don't follow the current trends."

AZTLAN RECORDS, P.O. Box 5672, Buena Park CA 90622. (714)826-7151. Manager: Carmen Ortiz. Record company, record distributor and music publisher. Estab. 1986. Releases 1 LP and 1 CD/year. Works with musicians/artists on record contract. Royalty paid to artist on contract varies.
How to Contact: Write first and obtain permission to submit. SASE.
Music: Mostly **alternative, industrial** and **experimental;** also **gothic, performance poetry** and **ethnic.** Released *Nirvana,* written and recorded by 12 artists (compilation); *Awaken,* written and recorded by 7 artists (compilation); and *Der Kirshenwasser,* written and recorded by Angel of the Odd (alternative), all on Aztlan Records. Other artists include Cecilia±, Stereotaxic Device, Black Tape for A Blue Girl, Dichroic Mirror, Pleasure Center and Spiderbaby.
Tips: "Die rather than compromise what you are doing. Music is your life."

*BABY SUE, P.O. Box 1111, Decatur GA 30031-1111. (404)875-8951. President/Owner: Don W. Seven. Record company. Estab. 1983. Deals with artists and songwriters. Releases 2 singles, 5 LPs, 2 EPs and 7 CDs/year. Royalty varies. Pays statutory royalty to publishers per song on record.
How to Contact: Submit demo tape by mail. Unsolicited submissions are OK. Prefers cassette with any number of songs. Does not return material. Reports in 6 months. "We only report back if we are interested in the artist or act."
Music: Mostly **rock, pop** and **gospel;** also **heavy metal, punk** and **classical.** Released *Camera-Sized Life* and *The Tiny Cupcake Dilemma,* written and recorded by LMNOP (rock); and *Ring Around the Weasel,* written and recorded by The Mommy, both on baby sue records (pop). Other artists include The Stereotypes, Mushcakes, the Shoestrings.
Tips: "Send us cash (just kidding). Actually, we're just into sincere, good stuff."

BAGATELLE RECORD COMPANY, P.O. Box 53568, Houston TX 77052-3568. (713)225-6654. President: Byron Benton. Record company, record producer and music publisher (Floyd Tillman Music Co.). Releases 20 singles and 10 LPs/year. Works with songwriters on contract; musicians on salary for in-house studio work. Pays negotiable royalty to artists on contract.
How to Contact: Prefers cassette and lyric sheet. SASE. Reports in 2 weeks.
Music: Mostly **country;** also **gospel.** Released "This is Real," by Floyd Tillman (country); "Lucille," by Sherri Jerrico (country); and "Everything You Touch," by Johnny Nelms (country). Other artists include Jerry Irby, Bobby Beason, Bobby Burton, Donna Hazard, Danny Brown, Sonny Hall, Ben Gabus, Jimmy Copeland and Johnny B. Goode.

BAL RECORDS, Box 369, La Canada CA 91012-0369. (818)548-1116. President: Adrian Bal. Record company, record producer and music publisher (Bal & Bal Music Publishing Co./ASCAP, Bal West Music Publishing Company/BMI). Estab. 1965. Releases 2-6 singles/year. Works with artists and songwriters on contract; musicians on salary for in-house studio work. Works with composers and lyricists; teams collaborators. Pays standard royalty to artists on contract; statutory rate to publishers for each record sold.

How to Contact: Submit demo tape by mail — unsolicited submissions are OK. Prefers cassette (or videocassette) with 1-3 songs and lyric or lead sheet. SASE. Reports in 6 weeks.
Music: Rock, MOR, country/western, gospel and **jazz.** Released "Fragile" and "Right to Know" (by James Jackson), both recorded by Kathy Simmons (med. rock); and "Dance to the Beat of My Heart" (by Dan Gertz), recorded by Ace Baker.
Tips: "Consider: Will young people who receive an allowance go out and purchase the record?"

BANDIT RECORDS, P.O. Box 111480, Nashville TN 37222. (615)331-1219. President: Loman Craig. Labels include HIS Records (gospel). Record company, record producer (Loman Craig Productions). Estab. 1979. Releases 5 singles, 2 LPs/year. Works with custom sessions. Pays statutory rate to publisher per song on record. "There is a charge for demo and custom sessions."
How to Contact: Submit demo tape by mail. Unsolicited submissions are OK. Prefers cassette with 2-3 songs and lyric sheet. SASE. Reports in 4-6 weeks.
Music: Mostly **country, ballads** and **gospel.** Released "Can't See Me Gone" (by Craig/Craig) and "Whiskey and Beer" (by J. Bryan), both recorded by James Bryan (country); and "Daddy" (by P. Pentell), recorded by Patty Pentell (ballad), all on Bandit Records. Other artists include Chadd D. Allen, Pat Riley, Allen Gray, Wally Jemmings.
Tips: "Send a clear sounding demo and readable lyric sheets. Since we are a small independent record label, we do have to charge for services rendered."

*BCM-USA, Box 351176, Los Angeles CA 90035. (213)278-9540. Manager: S. Kleinman. Labels include Romance Records. Record company, music publisher (BCM-USA Publishing/BMI, GEMA), record producer. Estab. 1987. Works with musicians/artists on contract. Royalty paid to artists on contract varies.
How to Contact: Submit demo tape by mail. Unsolicited submissions are OK. Prefers cassette. Does not return unsolicited material. Reports in 1 week.
Music: Mostly **dance** and **rock.** Artists include Technotronic, Stevie B., 24! 7 and LaToya Jackson.
Tips: "Persist, be professional! Clearly label cassette with telephone number."

BEACON RECORDS, P.O. Box 3129, Peabody MA 01961. (603)893-2200. Principal: Tony Ritchie. Labels include VISTA Records. Record company, music publisher. Releases 12-15 CDs/year. Works with musicians/artists on record contract, songwriters on royalty contract or musicians on salary for in-house studio work.
How to Contact: Submit demo tape by mail. Unsolicited submissions are OK. Does not return unsolicited material. Reports in 1-2 months.
Music: Mostly **folk, Celtic** and **folk-rock;** also **country, New Age** and **blues.** Recorded *New England's Daughter* (by M.L. Partington), recorded by Pendragon; *Shoes That Fit Like Sand,* written and recorded by Diane Taraz; and *Beth* (by Fowler/Shulman), recorded by Aztec Two-Step, all on Beacon Records. Other artists include Tempest, Jeff Wilkinson, David Rea, Aine Minogue and the John Michaels Group.

BELMONT RECORDS, 484 Lexington St., Waltham MA 02154. (617)891-7800. President: John Penny. Labels include Waverly Records. Record company and record producer. Works with musicians on salary for in-house studio work. Pays standard royalty to artists on contract; statutory rate to publisher per song on record.
How to Contact: Write first and obtain permission to submit. Prefers cassette with 3 songs and lyric sheet. SASE. Reports in 3 weeks.
Music: Mostly **country.** Released *One Step At a Time,* recorded by Cheri Ann on Belmont Records (C&W); and *Tudo Bens Sabe,* recorded by Familia Penha (gospel). Other artists include Stan Jr., Tim Barrett, Jackie Lee Williams, Robin Right, Mike Walker and Dwain Hathaway.

*BELT DRIVE RECORDS LTD., P.O. Box 101107, San Antonio TX 78201. (800)846-5201. President: Fred Weiss. Record company and music publisher. Estab. 1991. Deals with artists and songwriters. Releases 3 12″ singles and 1 CD/year. Pays varying royalty to artists on contract; statutory rate to publisher per song on record.
How to Contact: Submit demo tape by mail. Unsolicited submissions are OK. Prefers cassette (or VHS videocassette if available) with 1-3 songs. Does not return material. Reports in 1-2 months.
Music: Mostly **rock, Latin** and **country;** also **dance** and **hip hop.** Released *World Bizarre,* written and recorded by World Bizarre (rock); "Speaking in Tongues," written and recorded by Innocent Bystander (dance); and "Move Your Body," written and recorded by Muzic Box (dance), all on Belt Drive Records.

*BENSON MUSIC GROUP, 365 Great Grove Dr., Nashville TN 37228. (615)742-6895. Fax: (615)742-6915. Production Coordinator: Mark Quattrochi. Labels include Riversong and New Haven. Record company. Estab. 1901. Deals with artists and songwriters. Releases 130 LPs and 130 CDs/year. Pays

4-6% royalty to artists on contract; varying royalty to publishers per song on record.
How to Contact: Call first and obtain permission to submit. Prefers cassette with lyric sheet. Does not return material. Reports in 2 months.
Music: Mostly **A/C**, **pop rock** and **alternative**; also **R&B** and **gospel(Black)**. Released *Basics of Life* (by various), recorded by 4-Him (A/C); *Michael Sweet* (by various), recorded by Michael Sweet (A/C rock); and *Larnelle Harris* (by various), recorded by Beyond All the Limits (A/C), all on Benson Records. Other artists include Billy & Sarah, NewSong, Keith Dudley and Angelo & Veronica.
Tips: "Be persistent, confident, remember we are a gospel company so the content (lyrics) should be of the highest standard as well as the music."

BERANDOL MUSIC, Unit 220, 2600 John St., Markham, Ontario L3R 3W3 **Canada**. (416)475-1848. A&R: Ralph Cruickshank. Record company, music publisher (Berandol Music/SOCAN). Estab. 1947. Works with musicians/artists on record contract or songwriters on royalty contract. Pays 10-15% royalty to artists on contract; statutory rate to publisher per song on record.
How to Contact: Submit demo tape by mail. Unsolicited submissions are OK. Prefers cassette with 4 songs. Does not return material. Reports in 2 weeks.
Music: Mostly **instrumental**, **children's** and **CHR (top 40)**.

***BEST WEST PRODUCTIONS**, 1301 Morrison, Redlands CA 92374. (714)798-6449/370-1980. Contact: Deborah Harmon. Labels include Best West Records. Record company, music publisher (BMI) and record producer (Best West Records). Estab. 1988. Works with songwriters on royalty contract.
How to Contact: Submit demo tape by mail. Unsolicited submissions are OK. Prefers cassette (or any videocassette if available) with 3 songs and lyric sheet. SASE. Reports in 2 weeks to 2 months.
Music: Mostly **pop** and **country**. Looking for 5 part male harmony songs, and male and female solos.
Tips: "Send your best material only. Simple guitar/vocal or piano/vocal demo preferred. Send bio."

***BIG BEAR RECORDS**, Box 944, Birmingham, B16 8UT, **United Kingdom**. Phone: 44-021-454-7020. Fax: 44-021-454-9996. A&R Director: Jim Simpson. Labels include Truckers Delight and Grandstand Records. Record company, record producer and music publisher (Bearsongs). Releases 6 LPs/year. Works with artists and songwriters on contract; teams collaborators. Pays 8-10% royalty to artists on contract; 8¼% to publishers for each record sold. Royalties paid directly to the songwriters and artists or through US publishing or recording affiliate.
How to Contact: Submit demo tape by mail. Unsolicited submissions are OK. Prefers 7½ or 15 ips reel-to-reel, DAT, or cassette (or videocassette) and lyric sheet. Does not return material. Reports in 3 weeks.
Music: **Blues** and **jazz**. Released *I've Finished with the Blues* and *Blues for Pleasure* (by Skirving/Nicholls), both recorded by King Pleasure and the Biscuit Boys (jazz); and *Side-Steppin.'* (by Barnes), recorded by Alan Barnes/Bruce Adams Quintet (jazz), all on Big Bear Records. Other artists include Lady Sings the Blues, Bill Allred, Poorboys, Charles Brown.

***BIG POP**, P.O. Box 12870, Philadelphia PA 19108. (215)551-3191. Fax: (215)467-2048. Contact: A&R Dept. Record company. Estab. 1993. Deals with artists and songwriters. Releases 8 singles, 6 LPs/CDs and 2 EPs/year. Pays variable royalty to artists on contract; statutory rate to publisher per song on record.
How to Contact: Write first and obtain permission to submit. Prefers cassette (or VHS videocassette if available) with 3-4 songs and lyric sheet. "We are looking for artist/songwriters. None of our current artists perform other writers' material. Please send a complete press kit with bios, photos and tearsheets with submission." SASE. Reports in 1-2 months.
Music: Mostly **modern rock** and **adult album alternative**. Released *The Dust Has Come to Stay* (by M. Bund), recorded by Mexico 70; and *Space Flyer*, written and recorded by Melting Hopefuls, both on Big Pop Records. Other artists include The Holy Cows.
Tips: "We're interested in artists and songs. Your image and concept of where you fit in should be defined before we get involved. The quality of your songs—structure, hooks and lyrics—is very important to us. And generally, you shouldn't imitate others' styles. Be original!"

BIG ROCK PTY. LTD., P.O. Box, Dulwich Hill, NSW 2203 **Australia**. Phone (02)5692152. A&R Manager: Chris Turner. Labels include Big Rock Records, Sound Energy. Record company, music publisher (A.P.R.A.), record producer (Big Rock P/L). Estab. 1979. Releases 5 singles, 10 LPs and 10 CDs/year. Works with musicians/artists on record contract. Pays 5% royalty to artists on contract.
How to Contact: Submit demo tape by mail. Unsolicited submissions are OK. Prefers cassette with 6 songs and lyric sheet. SAE and IRC. Reports in 6 weeks.
Music: Mostly **rock**, **R&B**, and **pop**.

BLACK & BLUE, Suite 152, 400D Putnam Pike, Smithfield RI 02917. (401)949-4887. New Talent Manager: Larry Evileff. Record company. Releases 5-20 LPs, 3-8 EPs, 5-20 CDs/year. Works with musicians/artists on record contract. Pays statutory rate to publisher per song on record. Royalty rate varies.

How to Contact: Write first and obtain permission to submit. Prefers cassette (or VHS videocassette) with 3 songs and lyric sheet or lead sheet. Does not return material. Reports in 1 month. Replies only if interested.

Music: Mostly **eclectic, alternative rock** and **hardcore**; also **speed metal, C&W** and **grind core.** Released *Murder Junkies* (by Don McCloud), recorded by Bloody Mess (hardcore); *Peanut Butter Picnic* (by Kevin Allin), recorded by G.G. and the SFs (hardcore); and *The Seal Song* (by Steve Vieus), recorded by Richard Yoran (alternative), all on Black & Blue Records. Other artists include Blue Nouveau.

Tips: "Don't send pop or mainstream junk!"

BLACK DIAMOND RECORDS INC., P.O. Box 8073, Pittsburg CA 94565. (510)980-0893. President: Jerry "J". Labels include "In The House" Records, Hittin' Hard Records and Jairus Records. Record company, music publisher (BMI), record producer (Bo/Joe Productions, In The House Productions). Estab. 1988. Works with musicians/artists on record contracts, songwriters on royalty contract or musicians on salary for in-house studio work. Pays 5½-16% royalty to artists on contract; ½ statutory rate to publisher per song on record.

How to Contact: Submit demo tape by mail. Unsolicited submissions are OK. Prefers cassette with 2-4 songs, photo and lyric sheet. Does not return material. Reports in 4-6 weeks to 3 months.

Music: Mostly **R&B, hip hop, country/jazz** and **hip hop rap**; also **jazz, blues** and **rock.** Released "U Sold Me" (by BoJoe Productions), recorded by Jerry J (R&B); "Sneaking Through the Window" (by Aron Allatorre), recorded by D.S.C. (R&B) and "Where U From" (by Charles Mathis), recorded by C. Mae (hip hop/rap), all on Black Diamond Records. Other artists include Selec, Shejlia/Dela, Lady's of Color, T.K.T., Smoke MC Rod, Mobsters and Acyte 2.

BLACK DOG RECORDS, Rt. 2 Box 38, Summerland Key FL 33042. (305)745-3164. Executive Director: Marian Joy Ring. A&R Contact: Rusty Gordon (Rustron Music Productions), 1156 Park Lane, West Palm Beach, FL 33417. (407)686-1354. Record company. Estab. 1989. Releases 2-6 singles and 3 LPs/year. Pays standard royalty to artists on contract; statutory rate to publishers per song on record.

How to Contact: Submit demo tape by mail to W. Palm Beach address or write or call first at (407)686-1354 and obtain permission to submit. Prefers cassette with 3-6 songs and lyric or lead sheet. Does not return unsolicited material. Reports in 4-6 weeks.

Music: Mostly **pop, R&B** and **folk-rock**; also **New Age** and **cabaret.** Released *Yemanjah, Water Over the Dam* and *3 Teenage Mothers*, all written and recorded by Marian Joy Ring on Black Dog Records. Other artists include Woody Allen and Quint Lange.

*BLUE DUCK!! RECORDS, 2807 Penn Ave., Pittsburgh PA 15222. (412)261-9050. Fax: (412)232-0295. Artist Relations and Bookings: Greg Natale. Marketing and Distribution: Bree Freeman. Publicity and Promotions: Joelle Park. Labels include Anthem Records U.S.A. Record company. Estab. 1992. Deals with artists and songwriters. Releases 5 singles, 1 LP and 4 CDs/year. Pays 10-25% royalty to artists on contract; statutory rate to publisher per song on record (depends on deal).

How to Contact: Submit demo tape by mail. Unsolicited submissions are OK. Prefers cassette or VHS videocassette with 2-3 songs. "Keep it short." Does not return material. Reports in 3-8 weeks.

Music: Mostly **alternative, rock** and **world beat**; also **hip-hop, reggae** and **power pop.** Released *Cruel Sun*, written and recorded by Rusted Root (world rock); *You Can Be Replaced*, written and recorded by Steve Morrison (power pop); and *Duck Tracks*, written and recorded by various artists, all on Blue Duck!! Records. Other artists include The Means, Out of the Blue, The Affordable Floors.

Tips: "When submitting tapes, include a letter that tells us what's going on with the band . . . we aren't interested in false hype . . . tell us honestly where you're at with the band and music. No metal."

BLUE GEM RECORDS, Box 29688, Hollywood CA 90029. (213)664-7765. Contact: Pete Martin. Record company and record producer (Pete Martin Productions). Estab. 1981. Works with musicians/artists on contract. Pays 6-15% royalty to artists on contract; statutory rate to publisher per song on record.

How to Contact: Submit demo tape by mail. Unsolicited submissions are OK. Prefers cassette with 2 songs. SASE. Reports in 3 weeks.

Music: Mostly **country** and **R&B**; also **pop/top 40** and **rock.** Released "The Greener Years," written and recorded by Frank Loren (country); "It's a Matter of Loving You" (by Brian Smith), recorded by Brian Smith & The Renegades (country); and "Two Different Women" (by Frank Loren and Greg Connor), recorded by Frank Loren (country), all on Blue Gem Records. Other artists include Sherry Weston (country).

Tips: "Study top 10 on charts in your style of writing and be current!"

BLUE WAVE, 3221 Perryville Rd., Baldwinsville NY 13027. (315)638-4286. President/Producer: Greg Spencer. Labels include Blue Wave/Horizon. Record company, music publisher (G.W. Spencer Music/

ASCAP) and record producer (Blue Wave Productions). Estab. 1985. Releases 3 LPs and 3 CDs/year. Works with musicians/artists on contract. Royalty to artists on contract varies; pays statutory rate to publishers per song on records.

How to Contact: Submit demo tape by mail. Unsolicited submissions are OK. Prefers cassette (or VHS or Beta videocassette – live performance only) and as many songs as you like. SASE. "We contact only if we are interested." Reports in 6 weeks.

Music: Mostly **blues/blues rock**, **roots rock** and **roots R&B/soul**; also **roots country/rockabilly** or **anything with "soul."** Released *Love Is A Damn Good Feelin'*, written and recorded by CubKoda; *Under My Tree* (by Ron DeRollo), recorded by Kim Lembo; and *Keep Cool*, written and recorded by Built for Comfort. Other artists include Backbone Slip.

Tips: "Send it only if it's great, what you send must come from the soul. Not interested in top 40, so-called "hits" or commercial music. I'm looking for real, original artists or those who can make someone else's music their own. The singer must be convincing and be able to deliver the message. Please don't call, I listen to everything sent and I will call if you're what I'm looking for. Please, no lyric sheets or photos, I like to listen without any preconceived notions. Always looking for great blues/blues rock songs. Do not send rap, dance or heavy metal."

*BMX ENTERTAINMENT, Suite 255, 114 Broad St., Stamford CT 06902-2702. (800)853-3569. Fax: (203)961-1505. President: Mauris Gryphon. Labels include Red Tape Records. Record company. Estab. 1984. Deals with artists and songwriters. Releases 7 singles, 7 12" singles, 7 LPs, 7 EPs and 7 CDs/year. Pays 10-12% royalty to artists on contract.

How to Contact: Submit demo tape by mail. Unsolicited submissions are OK. Prefers cassette (or VHS videocassette if available) with 4 songs. "Send résumé, photo, management arrangements, if any." SASE. Reports in 2 weeks.

Music: Mostly **country**, **R&B** and **rock**; also **rap**, **pop**, **jazz** and **salsa**. Released "You & I," written and recorded by Edwin Rivera (ballad); "Hot As Fire," written and recorded by Damm Samm (rock); and "Tick Tica Tock," written and recorded by Tic Tock (reggae), all on BMX Entertainment. Other artists include K. Nice, Head Banger, Singles, Donald Murray and Tom Adams.

Tips: "When submitting make sure it's professional quality, photos, tape, background information, etc."

*BNA ENTERTAINMENT, 1 Music Circle North, Nashville TN 37203. (615)780-4400. Fax: (615)780-4464. Director of A&R: Byron Hill. Record company. Estab. 1990. Deals with artists and songwriters. Pays standard royalty to artists on contract; statutory rate to publisher per song on record.

How to Contact: Call first and obtain permission to submit. Prefers cassette or videocassette with 2 songs and lyric sheet. "We prefer that writers submit via a publisher." Refuses unsolicited submissions. Reply time "depends on the project."

Music: Mostly **country**. Released "Watch Me" (by Burr), recorded by Lorrie Morgan; "Reno" (by Doug Supernaw and others), recorded by Doug Supernaw; and "Moonlight Drive-in" (by Turner/ Nichols), all on BNA. Other artists include Lisa Stewart, Dale Daniel, Kim Hill, Jesse Hunter, Marc Beeson, John Anderson.

Tips: "Put together a presentable package and showcase."

BOGART RECORDS, Box 63302, Phoenix AZ 85082. Owner: Robert L. Bogart Sr. Record company. Estab. 1991. Works with musicians/artists and songwriters on contract and hires musicians for in-house studio work. Pays standard royalty to artists on contract; statutory rate to publisher per song on record.

How to Contact: Submit demo tape by mail. Unsolicited submissions are OK. Prefers cassette with 4 songs and lyric sheet. SASE. Reports in 1 month.

Music: Mostly **country**, **R&B** and **rock**; also **pop** and **gospel**. Released "I'd Be Ly, In" and "The Only Women," written and recorded by James Beckwith on Bogart Records (country). Other artists include Tim Tesch and Earl Eric Brown.

*BOLD 1 RECORDS, 2124 Darby Dr., Massillon OH 44646. (216)833-2061. A&R Dept.: Nick Boldi. Labels include Rox Town Records. Record company, record producer and music publisher (Bolnik Music/BMI). Estab. 1986. Deals with artists and songwriters. Releases 2 CDs/year. Pays 6% royalty on net to artists on contract; statutory rate to publisher per song on record.

How to Contact: Submit demo tape by mail. Unsolicited submissions are OK. Prefers cassette with 4 songs and lyric sheet. Does not return material. Reports in 10 weeks.

Music: Mostly **new country**, **rockabilly** and **ballads**. "We are not interested in rap, jazz, blues or heavy metal." Released "Country Boogie Band" and *He'll Always Be My Daddy To Me* (by Dan Pellegrini/ Nick Boldi), recorded by Kody Stormn (country); and "Who Do You Want Me To Be" (by Joey Welz/ Lou Mishiff), recorded by Joey Welz (rockabilly). Other artists include Dew Watson, Big Lou.

Tips: "We were awarded record label of the year by *Airplay International* May 1993 on the indie charts."

BOLIVIA RECORDS, 1219 Kerlin Ave., Brewton AL 36426. (205)867-2228. President: Roy Edwards. Labels include Known Artist Records. Record company, record producer and music publisher (Cheavoria Music Co.). Estab. 1972. Releases 10 singles and 3 LPs/year. Works with artists and songwriters on contract; musicians on salary for in-house studio work. Pays 4-5% royalty to artists on contract; statutory rate to publishers for each record sold.
How to Contact: Write first. Prefers cassette with 3 songs and lyric sheet. All tapes will be kept on file. Reports in 1 month.
Music: Mostly **R&B**, **country** and **pop**; also **easy listening**, **MOR** and **soul**. Released "You Are My Sunshine" and "If You Only Knew," written and recorded by Roy Edwards on Bolivia Records (R&B). Other artists include Bobbie Roberson and Jim Portwood.

BONAIRE MANAGEMENT INC., 7774 Torreyson Dr., Los Angeles CA 90046. (213)876-0367. President: Clive Corcoran. Labels include Bo and AVA. Record company, music publisher (ASCAP and SOCAN), record producer. Estab. 1977. Releases 2 singles, 5 LPs, 5 CDs/year. Works with musicians/artists on record contract or songwriters on royalty contract. Pays statutory royalty to publishers per song on record.
How to Contact: Submit demo tape by mail. Unsolicited submissions are OK. Prefers cassette (or VHS videocassette if available) with 3 songs and 3 lyric sheets. Does not return unsolicited material. Reports in 1 month.
Music: Mostly **rock** and **pop**. Artists include Saga, Edith Grove.

BOOGIE BAND RECORDS, Suite 206, 6245 Bristol Pkwy., Culver City CA 90230. Contact: Larry McGee. Labels include Classic Records and Mega Star Records. Record company, music publisher (Operation Perfection Publishing), record producer (Intrigue Productions) and management firm (LMP Management). Estab. 1976. Releases 6 singles, 3 12" singles, 1 LP, 4 EPs and 2 CDs/year. Works with musicians/artists and songwriters on contract; musicians on salary for in-house studio work. Pays 10% royalty to artists on contract; statutory rate to publishers per song on record.
How to Contact: Submit demo tape by mail. Unsolicited submissions are OK. Prefers cassette with 1-4 songs and lyric sheet. SASE. Reports in 2 months. "Please only send professional quality material."
Music: **Urban contemporary**, **dance**, **rock**, **MOR/A/C**, **pop**, **rap** and **R&B**. Released *Starflower* (by Joe Cacamisse), recorded by Star Flower (A/C); *Too Tough* (by Terrence Jones), recorded by En-Tux (pop); and *Got It Going On* (by Alan Walker), recorded by Executives, all on Mega Star Records. Other artists include Love Child, Revalution, The Altairs, These Gents, MGM Trio and Heavy Luv.
Tips: "Make your song as commercial, crossover and as current as possible. Be sure to use current arrangements as well as song structure."

BOUQUET RECORDS, Bouquet-Orchid Enterprises, P.O. Box 1335, Norcross GA 30091. (404)798-7999. President: Bill Bohannon. Record company, music publisher (Orchid Publishing/BMI), record producer (Bouquet-Orchid Enterprises) and management firm. Releases 3-4 singles and 2 LPs/year. Works with artists and songwriters on contract. Pays 5-8% maximum royalty to artists on contract; pays statutory rate to publishers for each record sold.
How to Contact: Submit demo tape by mail. Unsolicited submissions are OK. Prefers cassette with 3-5 songs and lyric sheet. SASE. Reports in 1 month.
Music: Mostly **religious** (contemporary or country-gospel, Amy Grant, etc.), **country** ("the type suitable for Clint Black, George Strait, Patty Loveless, etc.") and **top 100** ("the type suitable for Billy Joel, Whitney Houston, R.E.M., etc."); also **rock** and **MOR**. Released *Blue As Your Eyes* (by Bill Bohannon), recorded by Adam Day (country); *Take Care of My World* (by Bob Freeman), recorded by Bandoleers (top 40); and *Making Plans* (by John Harris), recorded by Susan Spencer (country), all on Bouquet Records.
Tips: "Submit 3-5 songs on a cassette tape with lyric sheets. Include a short biography and perhaps a photo. Enclose SASE."

*BRENTWOOD MUSIC, One Maryland Way, Brentwood TN 37027. (615)373-3950. Fax: (615)373-8612. Attn: Publishing. Labels include Brentwood Records, Brentwood Kids Co., Brentwood Bluegrass, Brentwood Jazz, Smoky Mtn. Music, Spotted Dog, Ransom, Essential. Record company, music publisher. Estab. 1981. Deals with artists and songwriters. Releases 10-15 singles, 75-100 LPs, 75-100 CDs/year. Pays various percent royalty to artists on contract; statutory rate to publisher per song on record.
How to Contact: Call first and obtain permission to submit. Prefers cassette with lyric or lead sheet. SASE. "Reports once per quarter."
Music: Mostly **contemporary Christian**, **children's** and **religious choral**; also **bluegrass** and **positive country**. Released *Smoky Mtn. Sunday*, written and recorded by various artists on Smoky Mtn. Records (acoustic); *Universal*, written and recorded by Chuckie Perez on Essential Records (pop); and *One Way*, written and recorded by Jack Jezzro on Brentwood Jazz Records (jazz).

BRIARHILL RECORDS, 3484 Nicolette Dr., Crete IL 60417. (708)672-6457. A&R Director: Danny Mack. Record company, music publisher (Syntony Publishing/BMI), record producer (The Danny Mack Music Group). Estab. 1983. Releases 3-4 singles, 1 LP, 2 EPs, and 1 CD/year. Works with musicians/artists on record contract or songwriters on royalty contract. Pays 5% royalty to artists on contract; statutory rate to publisher per song on record.
How to Contact: Submit demo tape by mail. Unsolicited submissions are OK. Prefers cassette with 3 songs and lyric sheet. SASE. Reports in 3 weeks.
Music: Mostly **country, novelty** and **polka**; also **southern gospel** and **Christmas**. Released "Heaven Bound" (by D. O'Connor/S. Fowler) and "Jesus Is The Reason For The Season" (by Nevers/Elliott), both recorded by Danny Mack (Christmas); and "After All" (by A. Scharinger), recorded by Danny Mack and Debbie Rodriguez (country), all on Briarhill Records. Other artists include The Stagemen.
Tips: "We are a small but very aggressive independent company. If we are interested in your material for recording by one of our artists we pay the costs. We will do custom recording projects and production fees are charged to client. We insist the artist/writer be specific in his query or submission. Briarhill is a 1992 recipient of Indie Label of the Year from the CMAA. Always mention the *Songwriter's Market* when contacting us."

*BRIGHT GREEN RECORDS, P.O. Box 24, Bradley IL 60915. (815)932-7455. Fax: (815)932-0933. Contact: Mykel Boyd. Record company and record producer. Estab. 1989. Deals with artists only. Releases 8 singles, 6 LPs, 4 EPs and 2 CDs/year. Royalty varies; depends on agreement.
How to Contact: Write or call first and obtain permission to submit. Prefers cassette or VHS videocassette. Does not return material. Reports in 1 month.
Music: Mostly **experimental, noise/de-composition** and **jazz**; also **techno, electronic** and **soundtrack**. Released "whitechapel," written and recorded by The Angelhood (soundtrack); *Ulcer*, written and recorded by Ulcer (techno); and "Heck's," written and recorded by TrespassersW (rock), all on Bright Green Records. Other artists include Foul Play, Oliver Magnum, Black Dahlia, Fection Fekler, Math, Juliet Armstrong, Foo, Cage.
Tips: "Don't be afraid to experiment, there is a real market for off the wall strange music, and we release it!"

BROKEN RECORDS INTERNATIONAL, 305 S. Westmore Ave., Lombard IL 60148. (708)916-6874. International A&R: Roy Bocchieri. Record company. Estab. 1984. Works with musicians/artists on contract. Payment negotiable.
How to Contact: Submit demo tape by mail. Unsolicited submissions are OK. Prefers cassette or CDs (or VHS videocassette) with at least 2 songs and lyric sheet. Does not return material. Reports in 8 weeks.
Music: Mostly **rock, pop** and **dance**; also **acoustic** and **industrial**. Released *Electric*, written and recorded by LeRoy (pop); and *Hallowed Ground*, written and recorded by Day One (alternative), both on Broken Records.

BSW RECORDS, P.O. Box 2297, Universal City TX 78148. (210)653-3987. President: Frank Wilson. Record company, music publisher (BSW Records/BMI) and record producer. Estab. 1987. Releases 12 singles, 4 LPs and 6 CDs/year. Works with musicians/artists on record contract or songwriters on royalty contract. Pays statutory rate to publisher per song on record.
How to Contact: Submit demo tape by mail. Unsolicited submissions are OK. Prefers cassette (or ¾" videocassette) with 3 songs and lyric sheet. SASE. Reports in 5 weeks.
Music: Mostly **country, rock** and **blues**. Released *I Cried My Last Tear* (by Tony Tolliver), recorded by Candee Land (country); *Bulls to Bronks*, written and recorded by Rusty Doherty (country); and *My Boss* (by D. Fleming), recorded by Paradise Canyon, all on BSW Records. Other artists include Jess DeMaine, Harold Doan, Ron Arlon, C. Howard, Stan Crawford and Mike Lord.

BULL CITY RECORDS, Box 6, Rougemont NC 27572. (919)477-4077. Manager: Freddie Roberts. Record company, record producer and music publisher (Freddie Roberts Music). Releases 20 singles and 6 LPs/year. Works with songwriters on contract. Pays standard royalty to artists on contract; statutory rate to publishers for each record sold.
How to Contact: Write or call first about your interest or to arrange personal interview. Prefers 7½ ips reel-to-reel or cassette (or videocassette) with 1-5 songs and lyric sheet. "Submit a clear, up-to-date demo." SASE. Reports in 3 weeks.
Music: Mostly **country, MOR, southern rock** and **top 40/pop**; also **bluegrass, church/religious, gospel** and **rock/country**. Released "Redeemed" (by Jane Durham), recorded by Roberts Family (southern gospel); "Almost" (by Rodney Hutchins), recorded by Billy McKellar (country) and "Not This Time" (by D. Tyler), recorded by Sleepy Creek (southern rock) on Bull City Records.

BULLET PROOF MANAGEMENT (formerly G Fine Records/Productions), Box 180 Cooper Station, New York NY 10276. (212)995-1608. President: P. Fine. Record company, music publisher and record

producer. Estab. 1986. Works with musicians/artists on contract. Pays 7-12% royalty to artists on contract; statutory rate to publisher per song on record.
How to Contact: Submit demo tape by mail. Unsolicited submissions are OK. Prefers cassette or DAT. Include SASE for return of tape. Reports in 2 months.
Music: Mostly **"undercore," college/alternative rock**, **rap**, **dance** and **R&B**. Released "Ghetto Child," featuring Main One on Select/Atlantic Records.

*BUY OR DIE CDS & LPS INC., 174 Main St., Hackettstown NJ 07840. (908)850-0688. Fax: (908)850-1190. A&R/Head of Label: Jerry Balderson. Record company. Estab. 1993. Releases 3 singles, 1 or 2 LPs, 3 CDs/year. Pays standard royalty to artists on contract; statutory rate to publisher per song on record.
How to Contact: Submit demo tape by mail. Unsolicited submissions are OK. Prefers cassette. "A bio is helpful." Does not return material. Reports in 2 weeks.
Music: Mostly **rock**, **blues** and **folk**; also **ska**, **zydeco** and **country**; "as long as we think it's good, we'll take it." Released "Luck of the Irish" (by Bill Kelly), recorded by Bill Kelly and the House of Cards (roots, country rock); "Pleasure Before Business" (by Gannon/Nodzak), recorded by The Partners (acoustic folk rock); and "Inwigcity," written and recorded by various artists, all on Buy or Die Records. Other artists include Good Reason, Sawney Bean, Jack Tannehill, Psuedo-Realists.

CACTUS RECORDS, Nibelungenring 1, A-3423 St. Andrä-Wördern, **Austria** 0043-2242/33-519. Contact: Hans Hartel. Labels include Ha Ha Soundwave. Record company, music publisher and record producer (Hans Hartel). Estab. 1985. Releases 10 singles, 2 12″ singles, 4 LPs and 2 CDs/year. Works with musicians/artists on contract, songwriters on contract and musicians on salary for in-house work.
How to Contact: Submit demo tape by mail. Prefers cassette with 3 songs and lyric sheet. Does not return unsolicited material. Reports in 1 month "only if interested."
Music: Mostly **pop**, **German pop** and **instrumentals**; also **ethno** and **New Age**. Released *Der letze Vorhang*, written and recorded by Jonny Blue on J. Robin Records; *Solang i atmen kann* (by Jonny Blue), recorded by Rudi Thaller on VM Records; and *Tabyia Mbaya*, written and recorded by Duncan Mlango on Cactus Records. Other artists include Chris White, Kids Can't Wait, Tam Tam des Damels d'Afrique, Weekend, Foxey, Johnny and the Credit Cards.
Tips: "You should have enough material for at least one album."

CAFFEINE DISK, P.O. Box 3451, New Haven CT 06515. (203)562-8239. A&R Director: John Notsure. Record company. Estab. 1992. Releases 3 singles, 3 LPs, 4 EPs and 3 CDs/year. Works with musicians/artists on record contract. "Special arrangements are often made."
How to Contact: Submit demo tape by mail. Unsolicited submissions are OK. Prefers cassette with 3-4 songs, bio and press. Does not return material. Reports in 3-6 weeks. ("Be patient!")
Music: **Alternative**, **rock** and **punk/pop**; also **noise** and **hardcore**. Released *Seized the Day*, recorded by Blind Justice; *Reunité*, recorded by SHIV; and *Crashland*, recorded by the Gravel Pit, all on Caffeine Disk Records. Other artists include Quest of the Moonbreed, Flowerland, Laurels, The Streams, The Philistines Jr. and Mighty Purple.
Tips: "If your demo percolates our ears it may be what we're looking for. Nothing is too loud or messy. Anything propelled by caffeine!"

*CALIBER RECORDS, 12754 Ventura Blvd., Studio City, CA 91604. (818)985-0009. Fax: (818)985-9292. Director, Licensing and Publishing: Su Brazie. Labels include Big City Records. Record company and music publisher. Estab. 1989. Deals with artists and songwriters. Releases 2 singles, 10 LPs, 4 EPs and 10 CDs/year. Pays varying royalty to artists on contract; statutory rate to publisher per song on record.
How to Contact: Call first and obtain permission to submit. Prefers cassette with 1-3 songs and lyric sheet. Does not return material.
Music: Mostly **pop**, **rock**, **R&B** and **country**. Released *Back to the Wonderful*, written and recorded by Crusoe on Caliber Records (A/C); *Mothers of Hope*, written and recorded by John James on Big City Records; and *Get Off*, written and recorded by Haywire on Caliber Records (rock). Other artists include Rocca, Love/Hate, Damn the Diva, Att Will, Howard Hewett and West End Girls.
Tips: "Patience. We are a small independent label whose main requirement is that the music be great and not just good."

CAMBRIA RECORDS & PUBLISHING, Box 374, Lomita CA 90717. (310)831-1322. Fax: (310)833-7442. Director of Recording Operations: Lance Bowling. Labels include Charade Records. Record company and music publisher. Estab. 1979. Releases 5 cassettes and 6 CDs/year. Works with artists on contract; musicians on salary for in-house studio work. Pays 5-8% royalty to artists on contract; statutory rate to publisher for each record sold.
How to Contact: Write first to obtain permission to submit. Prefers cassette. SASE. Reports in 2 months.

Music: Mostly classical. Released *Songs of Elinor Remick Warren* on Cambria Records. Other artists include Marie Gibson (soprano), Mischa Leftkowitz (violin), Leigh Kaplan (piano), North Wind Quintet, Sierra Wind Quintet and many others.

*CANTILENA RECORDS, 512 Meister Way, Sacramento CA 95819. (916)737-8360. A&R: Davis Lynn. Record company. Estab. 1993. Deals with artists and songwriters. Releases 5 CDs/year. Pays negotiable royalty to artists on contract; statutory rate to publishers per song on record.
How to Contact: Submit demo tape by mail. Unsolicited submissions are OK. Prefers cassette. Does not return material. Reports in 4 weeks.
Music: Mostly rock, classical and pop; also jazz. Released *Poetic Justice* (by Davis Lynn), recorded by Poetic Justice (rock); *Laurel Zucker, Virtuoso Flutist* (by various), recorded by Laurel Zucker and Robin Sutherland (classical); and *Laurel Zucker, An American Flute Recital* (by various), recorded by Laurel Zucker and Marc Shapiro (classical), all on Cantilena Records. Other artists include Tim Gorman, Prairie Prince and Dave Margen.

*CANYON RECORDS AND INDIAN ARTS, 4143 N. 16th St., Phoenix AZ 85016. (602)266-4823. Owner: Bob Nuss. Labels include Indian House, Indian Sounds. Record company, distributor of American Indian recordings. Estab. 1984. Deals with artists and songwriters. Releases 50 cassettes and 20 CDs/year.
How to Contact: Write or call first and obtain permission to submit. Prefers cassette or VHS videocassette. SASE. Reports in 1 month.
Music: Music by American Indians—any style (must be enrolled tribal members). Released *Blackstone Singers Vol. 5*, written and recorded by Blackstone (pow wow); *Emergence* (by R. Carlos Nakai), recorded by Nakai (Native American flute); and *Eyabe*, written and recorded by Eyabe (pow wow), all on Canyon Records. Other artists include Black Lodge, John Rainer, Tree Cody.
Tips: "We deal only with American Indian performers. We do not accept material from others. Please include tribal affiliation. *No* New Age 'Indian style' material."

CAPSTAN RECORD PRODUCTION, Box 211, East Prairie MO 63845. (314)649-2211. Branch: 7205 Nashboro Blvd., Apt. D, Nashville TN 37217. (615)649-2211. Contact: Joe Silver or Tommy Loomas. Labels include Octagon and Capstan Records. Record company, music publisher (Lineage Publishing Co.) and record producer (Silver-Loomas Productions). Pays 3-5% royalty to artists on contract.
How to Contact: Write first about your interest. Prefers cassette (or VHS videocassette) with 2-4 songs and lyric sheet. "Send photo and bio." SASE. Reports in 1 month.
Music: Country, easy listening, MOR, country rock and top 40/pop. Released "Country Boy" (by Alden Lambert); "Yesterday's Teardrops" and "Round & Round" (by The Burchetts). Other artists include Bobby Lee Morgan, Skidrow Joe and Fleming.

*CARE FREE RECORDS GROUP, Box 2463, Carefree AZ 85377. (602) 230-4177. Vice President: Doya Fairbanks. Labels include Blue Mesa and Tempe. Record company, record producer, music publisher, distribution and promotion company. Estab. 1990. Deals with artists and songwriters. Releases 6 singles, 4 12″ singles, 12 LPs, 5 EPs and 12 CDs/year. Pays varying royalty to artists on contract; statutory rate to publishers per song on record.
How to Contact: Submit demo tape by mail. Unsolicited submissions are OK. Prefers cassette (or VHS videocassette if available) with 4-6 songs. SASE. Reports in 1 month.
Music: Mostly country, jazz and classical; also rock, metal and New Age. Released *Pablo,* written and recorded by Pablo on Blue Mesa Records (pop); *The Totem Pole* (by Doug), recorded by Totem Pole (pop); and *Harold's Coral,* written and recorded by Harold's Coral (country), both on Care Free Records. Other artists include Paul Conseio, Arisnal and Gypsy Wind.

CARLYLE RECORDS, INC., 1217 16th Ave. South, Nashville TN 37212. (615)327-8129. President: Laura Fraser. Record company. Estab. 1986. Releases 3 12″ singles, 6 LPs/year, 4 EPs and 6 CDs. Works with musicians and artists on contract. Pays compulsory rate to publisher per song on record.
How to Contact: Submit demo tape by mail. Unsolicited submissions are OK. Prefers cassette (or VHS videocassette). Does not return unsolicited material. Reports in 1 month.
Music: Mostly rock. Released "Orange Room" (by Michael Ake), recorded by the Grinning Plowmen; *All Because of You,* written and recorded by Dorcha; and *Sun* (by John Elliot), recorded by Dessau, all on Carlyle Records.

CARMEL RECORDS, 2331 Carmel Dr., Palo Alto CA 94303. (415)856-3650. Contact: Jeanette Avenida. Label includes Edgetone, Accoustic Moods, Rainin' Records Fountain. Record company, record producer. Estab. 1987. Releases 4 singles, 4 LPs/year. Payment as negotiated, statutory rate to publisher per song on record.
How to Contact: Write first and obtain permission to submit. Prefers cassette (or VHS videocassette if available) and lyric sheet. SASE. Reports in 6 months.

Music: Mostly **AC, folk/rock** and **classical**; also **instrumental** and **rock**. Released *World's Greatest Love Songs* (by Linda Genteel); *Create the Harmony* (by Martin and Scott); and *The Time is Now* (by Martha Lorin). Other artists include Fred Clarke, Images From The Sky, Rainin' Records.
Tips: "Send a complete demo with lyric sheet. Call to follow up. Be very nice – do something to make your submission different."

CAROLINE RECORDS, INC., 11th Floor, 114 W. 26th St., New York NY 10001. (212)989-2929. Director Creative Operations: Lyle Preslar. Exclusive manufacturing and distribution of EG, Editions EG, Antler Subway Records, Herald, Astralwerks (dance) and Real World (world music). Record company and independent record distributor (Caroline Records Inc.). Estab. 1985. Releases 3-4 12" singles, 10 LPs, 1-2 EPs and 10 CDs/year. Works with musicians/artists on record contract. Pays varying royalty to artists on contract; statutory rate to publisher per song.
How to Contact: Submit demo tape by mail. Unsolicited submissions are OK. Prefers cassette with lead sheets and press clippings. SASE. Reports in 1 month.
Music: Mostly **alternative/indie rock**. Released *My Aquarium*, written and recorded by Drop Nineteens; *New Wave*, written and recorded by The Auteurs; and *Oreo Dust*, written and recorded by Fudge, all on Caroline Records. Other artists include Idaho, Action Swingers, Adrian Belew, The Buzzcocks and Peach.
Tips: "When submitting a demo keep in mind that we have never signed an artist who does not have a strong underground buzz and live track record. We listen to all types of 'alternative' rock, metal, funk and rap but do not sign mainstream hard rock or dance. We send out rejection letters so do not call to find out what's happening with your demo."

CASARO RECORDS, 932 Nord Ave., Chico CA 95926. (916)345-3027. Contact: Hugh Santos. Record company, record producer (RSA Productions). Estab. 1988. Releases 5-8 LPs/year. Works with musicians/artists and songwriters on contract; session players. Pays variable royalty to artists on contract; statutory rate to publisher per song on record.
How to Contact: Write or call first and obtain permission to submit. Prefers cassette with full project demo and lyric sheet. Does not return unsolicited material. Reports in 6 months.
Music: **Jazz** and **country**; also **R&B** and **pop**. Released "I'll Be Back" (by Borthwick), recorded by Mr. Haw (country); "Fandango Pass" (by Hamm/Santos), recorded by Steve Hamm (rock); and *Songbird* (by various), recorded by Liz Graffell (gospel), all on Casaro Records. Other artists include Lesley McDaniel, Jeff Dixon, Lory Dobbs, Charlie Robinson.
Tips: "Produce your song well (in tune – good singer). It doesn't need to be highly produced – just clear vocals. Include lyric sheet."

CAT'S VOICE PRODUCTIONS, P.O. Box 564, Newburyport MA 01950. (508)463-3028. Owners: Tom Reeves/Rosemarie Reeves. Record company, music publisher (Rahsaan Publishing/ASCAP), record producer (Boston Tom) and recording studio (Reel Adventures II). Estab. 1982. Releases 8 singles, 4 12" singles, 20 LPs, 6 EPs and 50 CDs/year. Works with musicians/artists on record contract, songwriters on royalty contract or musicians on salary for in-house studio work. Pays 15-25% royalty to artists on contract; statutory royalty to publishers per song on record.
How to Contact: Submit demo tape by mail. Unsolicited submissions are OK. Prefers cassette (or VHS videocassette) with 3 songs and lyric sheet. Does not return material. Reports in 2 weeks.
Music: Mostly **rock, R&B** and **country**; also **reggae, New Age** and **alternative**. Released *Give It Up* (by Dennis Turner), recorded by Mangled Ducklings (rock); *Time*, written and recorded by Richard Hartwell (New Age); and *Rodents* (by Dick D. Loy), recorded by Mangled Ducklings (rock). Other artists include Buddy Sullivan, Cleanshot, Andy Henry, David Hartwell, Billy DeNuzzio, CoCo, Ned Claffin and Carl Armano.

*THE CCC GROUP, INC., Box 853, Ridgeland MS 39158. Professional Manager: King Corbett. Labels include Pleasure Records. Record company. Estab. 1987. Releases 12 singles and 12 LPs/year. Works with musicians/artists and songwriters on contract. Pays 10-20% royalty to artists on contract; statutory rate to publisher per song on record.
How to Contact: Prefers cassette with 2-4 songs and lyric or lead sheet. SASE. Reports in 6 weeks.
Music: Mostly **traditional country**; also **spoken word, folk** and **jazz**.
Tips: "Send clean lyric sheets, labels on cassettes."

CEDAR CREEK RECORDS™, Suite 503, 44 Music Square E., Nashville TN 37203. (615)252-6916. Fax: (615)329-1071. President: Larry Duncan. Record company, music publisher (Cedar Creek Music/BMI), record producer (Cedar Creek Productions). Estab. 1992. Releases 20 singles, 5 LPs and 5 CDs/year. Works with musicians/artists on record contract or songwriters on royalty contract. Pays 10% royalty to artists on contract; statutory rate to publisher per song on record.
How to Contact: Submit demo tape by mail. Unsolicited submissions are OK. Prefers cassette (or VHS videocassette). Does not return material. Reports in 1 month.

Music: Mostly **country, country/pop** and **country/R&B, gospel/Christian contemporary**; also **pop, R&B** and **light rock**. Released "14 Karat Gold" (by Deke Little/Joel Little/John Moran), recorded by Joel Little on Interstate Records (country); *Bright Lights and Honky Tonk Nights* (by Tony Rast/Danny Neal/ Debra McClure) and *I'm In Love* (by Sarita Wortham/Danny Neal/Debra McClure), both recorded by Kym Wortham on ADD Records. Other artists include Dave Marshal.
Tips: "Submit your best songs on a good fully produced demo or master."

CELLAR RECORDS, 116 N. Peoria, Dixon IL 61021. (815)288-2900. Owners: Todd Joos or Bob Brady. Record company, music publisher (Sound Cellar Music/BMI), record producer (Todd Joos), recording studio (Cellar Studios). Estab. 1987. Releases 4-6 singles, 12 cassettes, 6 EPs, 2-3 CDs/year. Pays 30% royalty to artists on contract; statutory rate to publisher per song on record. Charges in advance "if they use our studio to record."
How to Contact: Submit demo tape by mail. Prefers cassette (or VHS videocassette if available) with 3-4 songs and lyric sheet. Does not return material. "If we like it we will call you."
Music: Mostly **metal, country** and **rock**; also **pop, rap** and **blues**. Released *Frolicking in the Autumn Mist*, written and recorded by Decadenza (metal); *Windows of Pain*, written and recorded by Manic Oppression (metal); and *Concussion*, written and recorded by Concussion (thrash), all on Cellar Records. Other artists include Chaotic Realm, Axen Province, Lefwitch, Blind Witness, Drastic Measures and Catacomb.
Tips: "Make sure your live act is well put together. Send a clear sounding cassette with lyrics."

*CENTURY RECORDS INC., P.O. Box 4094, Pittsburgh PA 15201. (412)782-4477. President: Edward Moschetti. Labels include Star Records. Record company and music publisher. Estab. 1958. Deals with artists and songwriters.
How to Contact: Write first and obtain permission to submit. Prefers cassette. SASE. Reports in 2 weeks.
Music: Mostly **pop, country** and **background**.
Tips: "Believe in what you are doing and make what you are doing believeable."

CEREBRAL RECORDS, 1236 Laguna Dr., Carlsbad CA 92008. (619)434-2497. Vice President: Laura Maher. Record company, music publisher (Cerebral Records/BMI), record producer (Cerebral Records), recording studio. Estab. 1991. Releases 1-3 LPs and 1-3 CDs/year. Pays negotiable royalty.
How to Contact: Write first and obtain permission to submit. Prefers cassette. SASE. Reports in 2 months.
Music: Mostly **progressive rock**. Released *Broken Hands*, *I Am Myself* and *Two Cents*, all written and recorded by State of Mind on Cerebral Records.
Tips: "Have fun. Write songs you like. Cover 'em with hooks and fill 'em with intelligence. Keep on growing as an artist."

CHA CHA RECORDS, 902 North Webster St., Port Washington WI 53074. (414)284-5242. President: Joseph C. De Lucia. Labels include Cap and Debby. Record company, record producer, and music publisher (Don Del Music/BMI). Estab. 1955. Releases 1 single and 1 LP/year. Works with artists/ musicians and songwriters on contract. Pays 50% royalty to artists on contract; statutory rate to publishers per song on record.
How to Contact: Write first and obtain permission to submit. Prefers cassette with 4-6 songs and lyric sheet. SASE. Reports in 3 months.
Music: Country, folk and religious.

CHATTAHOOCHEE RECORDS, 15230 Weddington St., Van Nuys CA 91411. (818)788-6863. Contact: Chris Yardum. Record company and music publisher (Etnoc/Conte). Member NARAS. Releases 4 singles/year. Works with artists and songwriters on contract. Pays negotiable royalty to artists on contract.
How to Contact: Submit demo tape by mail. Unsolicited submissions are OK. Prefers cassette with 2-6 songs and lyric sheet. Does not return unsolicited material. "We contact songwriters if we're interested."
Music: Rock.
Tips: "Send it in. If we're interested, we'll contact you in 6 to 8 weeks."

CHERRY RECORDS, 9717 Jensen Dr., Houston TX 77093. (713)695-3648. Vice President: A.V. Mittelstedt. Labels include AV Records, Music Creek. Record company, music publisher (Pen House Music/ BMI) and record producer (AV Mittelstedt Productions). Estab. 1970. Releases 10 singles and 5 LPs/ year. Works with musicians/artists and songwriters on contract and hires musicians for in-house studio work. Pays varying royalty to artists on contract; statutory rate to publishers per song on record.
How to Contact: Submit demo tape by mail. Unsolicited submissions are OK. Prefers cassette with 2 songs. SASE. Reports in 3 weeks.

Music: Mostly **country** and **pop**. Released "Too Cold at Home" (by B. Hardin) and "Girls Like Her" (by Wimberly-Hart), recorded by Mark Chesnutt on Cherry Records (country); and "Half of Me" (by Wimberly/Trevino), recorded by Geronimo Trevino on AV Records (country crossover). Other artists include Randy Cornor, Roy Hilad, Georgie Dearborne, Kenny Dale, Karla Taylor and Borderline.

CHERRY STREET RECORDS, Box 52681, Tulsa OK 74152. (918)742-8087. President: Rodney Young. Record company, music publisher. Estab. 1990. Releases 2 CD/year. Works with musicians/artists and songwriters on contract. Pays 5-15% royalty to artists on contract; statutory rate to publisher per song on record.
How to Contact: Write first and obtain permission to submit. Prefers cassette (or Beta or VHS videocassette) with 4 songs and lyric sheet. SASE. Reports in 6 weeks to 4 months.
Music: Rock, country and **R&B**; also **jazz**. Released *Blue Dancer* (by Chris Blevins) and *Hardtimes* (by Brad Absher), both on CSR Records (country rock); also *She Can't Do Anything Wrong* (by Davis/ Richmond), recorded by Bob Seger on Capitol Records.
Tips: "We are a songwriter label — the song is more important to us than the artist. Send only your best 4 songs."

*CHRISMARIE RECORDS, P.O. Box 106, Valhalla NY 10595. (914)741-2576. Fax: (914)741-2566. A&R Director: Peggy Conney. Producer: Joseph W. Nudo. Record company. Estab. 1990. Deals with artists and songwriters. Releases 2 singles, 2 LPs and 1 CD/year. Pays 5-10% royalty to artists on contract; statutory rate to publishers per song on record.
How to Contact: Submit demo tape by mail. Unsolicited submissions are OK. Prefers cassette (or VHS videocassette if available) with 2-4 songs and lyric sheet. Does not return material. Reports in 6-12 weeks.
Music: Mostly **pop, rock** and **ballads**; also **country, R&B** and **new music**. Released *Dream On*, written and recorded by Niko (pop); "Anita," written and recorded by Adamos (rock ballad); and *High Reality*, written and recorded by Declaration (rock), all on CHRISMARIE Records. Other artists include Tom Hughes, J.C. Amitie, Adriana, Motion, Burgandy Row and Bitterr Tides.
Tips: "We are interested in original material only! The quality of your demo projects, your talent and the music should *never* overpower the lyrics. We strongly encourage submissions of VHS videocassettes. Need not be professionally done. Stay positive! All submissions must include name, phone number and SASE for response."

CIMIRRON/RAINBIRD RECORDS, 607 Piney Point Rd., Yorktown VA 23692. (804)898-8155. President: Lana Puckett. Vice President: Kim Person. Record company. Releases at least 3 CDs and cassettes/year. Works with musicians/artists on contract. Pays variable royalty to artists on contract; statutory rate to publisher per song on record.
How to Contact: Write. Prefers cassette with 1-3 songs and lyric sheet. SASE. Reports in 3 months.
Music: Mostly **country-bluegrass, New Age** and **pop**. Released *Nutcracker Suite* and *Guitar Town*, written and recorded by Steve Bennett (guitar); and *Windows of Life* (by Lana Puckett and Kim Person), recorded by Lana & Kim (country), all on Cimirron/Rainbird Records.

CIRCLE "M" RECORDS, 289 Fergus St. S., Mount Forest, Ontario N0G 2L2 **Canada**. (519)323-2810. Contact: Clare Adlam. Labels include C.B.A. Records. Record company, music publisher (Clar-Don Publishing, Amalda Publishing), record producer (Clare Adlam Enterprises).
How to Contact: Submit demo tape by mail. Unsolicited submissions are OK. Write first to arrange personal interview. Prefers cassette and lyric sheet or lead sheet.
Music: Mostly **country, gospel** and **R&B**. Released *Lost in the Wilderness*, written and recorded by C. Adlam; *Saving To-day For To-morrow* (by C. Adlam), recorded by Bonnie Brigant; and *Country Music I Tip My Hat to You*, written and recorded by Ted Morris, all on C.M. Records.

CITA COMMUNICATIONS INC., Dept. SM, 676 Pittsburgh Rd., Butler PA 16001. (412)586-6552. A&R/Producer: Mickii Taimuty. Labels include Phunn! Records and Tropē Records. Record company. Estab. 1989. Releases 6 singles, 3 12" singles, 3 LPs, 2 EPs and 5 CDs/year. Works with musicians/ artists on record contract. Pays artists 10% royalty on contract. Pays statutory rate to publisher per song on records.
How to Contact: Call first and obtain permission to submit. Prefers cassette (or VHS, Beta or ¾" videocassette) with a maximum of 6 songs and lyric sheets. SASE. Reports in 8 weeks.
Music: Interested in **rock/dance music** and **contemporary gospel**; also **rap, jazz** and **progressive country**. Released "Forged by Fire", written and recorded by Sanxtion on Tropē Records; "I Cross My Heart" (by Taimuty/Nelson), recorded by Melissa Anne on Phunn! Records; and "Fight the Fight,"

written and recorded by M.J. Nelson on Tropē Records. Other artists include Most High, Sister Golden Hair and Countdown.

*CLEOPATRA RECORDS, Suite D-82, 8726 S. Sepulveda Blvd., Los Angeles CA 90045. (310)305-0172. Fax: (310)821-4702. Contact: A&R. Labels include Zoth Ommog, Link U.K. Record company. Estab. 1991. Releases 5 singles, 10 LPs, 5 EPs and 12 CDs/year. Pays 10-14% royalty to artists on contract; negotiable rate to publisher per song on record.
How to Contact: Submit demo tape by mail. Unsolicited submissions are OK. Prefers cassette or VHS videocassette with 5 songs and lyric sheet. Does not return material. Reports in 1 month.
Music: Mostly **industrial**, **gothic** and **ambient**; also **space rock** and **electronic**. Released *Thoth*, written and recorded by Nik Turner (electronic/space rock); *Lost Minds* (by Rozz Williams/Evao), recorded by Christian Death (gothic); and *Lucy is Red*, written and recorded by Nosferato (gothic), all on Cleopatra Records. Other artists include Controlled Bleeding, Helios Creed, Rosetta Stone, Psychic TV.
Tips: "Don't write your music thinking of a hit record for the mainstream."

CLR LABEL GROUP, 1400 Aliceanna, Baltimore MD 21231. (410)522-1001. A&R Director: Stephen Janis. Labels include Ultra-Ethereal Records, Calvert Street and CLR Records. Record company, music publisher (ASCAP). Estab. 1989. Releases 20 12″ singles, 10 LPs, 2 EPs and 12 CDs/year. Works with musicians/artists on contract or songwriters on royalty contract. Pays 10-12% royalty to artists on contract; ¾ statutory rate to publisher per song on record.
How to Contact: Write or call first and obtain permission to submit. Prefers cassette. Does not return material.

COLLECTOR RECORDS, Box 2296, Rotterdam 3000 CG **Holland**. Phone: (1862)4266. Fax: (1862)4366. Research: Cees Klop. Labels include All Rock, Downsouth, Unknown, Pro Forma and White Label Records. Record company, music publisher (All Rock Music Pub.) and record producer (Cees Klop). Estab. 1967. Releases 10 singles and 30 LPs/year. Works with musicians/artists and songwriters on contract. Pays standard royalty to artist on contract.
How to Contact: Prefers cassette. SAE and IRC. Reports in 1 month.
Music: Mostly **50's rock**, **rockabilly**, **hillbilly boogie** and **country/rock**; also **piano boogie woogie**. Released "Spring in April" (by Pepping/Jellema), recorded by Henk Pepping on Down South Records (50's rock); "Go Cat Go" (by Myers), recorded by Jimmy Myers and "Knocking On the Backside" (by T. Redell), recorded by T. Redell, both on White Label Records (50's rock).

COM-FOUR, (formerly Community 3), 7 Dunham Pl., Brooklyn NY 11211. (718)599-2205. Label Manager: Albert Garzon. Labels include Community 3 Russia, VERB. Record company. Estab. 1985. Releases 5-10 singles and 10 CDs/year. Works with musicians/artists on record contract or songwriters on royalty contract. Pays various royalties to artists on contract.
How to Contact: Submit demo tape by mail. Unsolicited submissions are OK. Prefers cassette (or VHS videocassette if available) with 5-7 songs. Does not return material. "We only respond if we like material."
Music: Mostly **rock**, **grunge** and **post-punk**; also **ethnic** and **jazz**. Released *Manres of Behavior* (by various), recorded by Kolibri on Community 3 Records (Russian pop); *Viva la Vulva* (by various), recorded by Astro Zombies on VERB Records (punk rock); and *In the Kitchen*, written and recorded by Va Bank on Community 3 Russia.
Tips: "Be original and have some talent. Be willing and ready to work hard touring, promoting, etc."

COMMA RECORDS & TAPES, Postbox 2148, 63243 Neu-Isenburg, **Germany**. Phone: (6102)52696. General Manager: Roland Bauer. Labels include Big Sound, Comma International and Max-Banana-Tunes. Record company. Estab. 1969. Releases 50-70 singles and 20 LPs/year. Works with musicians/artists and songwriters on contract. Pays 7-10% royalty to artists on contract.
How to Contact: Prefers cassette and lyric sheet. Reports in 3 weeks. "Do not send advanced letter asking permission to submit, just send your material, SAE and minimum two IRCs."
Music: Mostly **pop**, **disco**, **rock**, **R&B** and **country**; also **musicals**.

COMSTOCK RECORDS LTD., Suite 114, 10603 N. Hayden Rd., Scottsdale AZ 85260. (602)951-3115. Fax: (602)951-3074. Canadian, United States and European distribution on Paylode & Comstock Records. Production Manager/Producer: Patty Parker. President: Frank Fara. Record company, music

---

Refer to the Category Index (at the end of this section) to find exactly which companies are interested in the type of music you write.

publisher (White Cat Music/ASCAP, Rocky Bell Music/BMI, How the West Was Sung Music/BMI), Nashville Record Production and International Record Promotions. Member CMA, BBB, CCMA, BCCMA, British & French C&W Associations and CARAS. "Comstock Records, Ltd. has three primary divisions: Production, Promotion and Publishing. We distribute and promote both our self-produced recordings and outside master product." Releases 24-30 singles and 5-6 CDs/year. Works with artists and songwriters on contract; musicians on salary. Pays 10% royalty to artists on contract; statutory rate to publishers for each record sold. "Artists pay distribution and promotion fee to press and release their masters."

How to Contact: Submit demo tape by mail. Unsolicited submissions OK. Prefers cassette (or VHS videocassette) with 1-4 songs "plus word sheet. Enclose stamped return envelope if cassette is to be returned." Reports in 2 weeks.

Music: Western music, A/C and **country**. Released "Norman Rockwell," written and recorded by Ray Dean James; "Heaven Sent Country Girl," written and recorded by R.J. McClintock; and "Do You Think About Me" (by Jerry Edwards), recorded by Rick Dean, all on Comstock Records. Other artists include Keith Lamb, Kenny Hess, Michael Thomas, Colin Clark, Jess Owen, Patti Mayo and Rydin' High.

Tips: "Our international division needs songs for Europe! We specialize in producing overseas singers in Nashville as seen on CNN's 'Across America' show."

*CONCORD JAZZ, P.O. Box 845, Concord CA 94522. (510)682-6770. Fax: (510)682-3508. Director of A&R: Nick Phillips. Labels include Concerto, Picante. Record company. Estab. 1973. Deals with artists only. Releases 70 CDs/year.

How to Contact: Call first and obtain permission to submit. Does not return material.

Music: Mostly **jazz**, **Latin-jazz** and **classical**. Released *Outrageous*, recorded by Tania Maria on Picante Records (Latin jazz); *A Little Piece of Heaven*, recorded by Gene Harris (jazz); and *East of the Sun*, recorded by Scott Hamilton, both on Concord Jazz. Other artists include Howard Alden, Ray Barretto, Rosemary Clooney, Rob McConnell, Marian McPartland, Ken Peplowski, Tito Puente, Poncho Sanchez.

*CONSPIRACY RECORDS, (formerly Tongue & Groove), 625 Main St., Simpson PA 18407. (717)282-0863. Fax: (717)282-0362. Director of A&R: Diane Bassett. Record company. Estab. 1993. Deals with artists and songwriters. Releases 4 CDs/year.

How to Contact: Write or call first and obtain permission to submit. Prefers cassette (or VHS videocassette if available) with 3-5 songs and lyric sheet. SASE. Reports in 6 weeks.

Music: Mostly **alternative** and **rock**. Released *Post-Hypnotic Suggestion Box*, written and recorded by Museum of Fear (alternative); and *Matt's Altar*, written and recorded by Matt's Altar (rock), both on Conspiracy Records. Other artists include Young Turk.

CONTINENTAL RECORDS, 744 Joppa Farm Rd., Joppatowne MD 21085. (410)679-2262. General Manager: Ernest W. Cash. Record company and music publisher (Ernie Cash Music/BMI). Estab. 1986. "We cover all musical services." Pays 8% royalty to artists on contract.

How to Contact: Call first and obtain permission to submit. Prefers cassette (or VHS videocassette) with 3 songs and lyric sheet. SASE. Reports in 2 weeks.

Music: Mostly **country** and **gospel**. Published *Just-Us-Three*, written and recorded by Just Us Bros.; *Another Birthday* (by Carl Becker), recorded by Ernie C. Penn; and *The Dream*, written and recorded by Bill Michael, all on Continental Records. Other artists include Johnny Ray Anthony, Ernie Cash, Bobby Helms, Eddie Baker, Clay Price and Jimmy Buckley.

*CO-OP ARTIST RECORDINGS, Box 1794, Campbell CA 95009. Owner-Artist: Kathy V. Labels include Earth Shaker, Artsong. Record company, music publisher. Artist owned network for arts and human/animal rights, talent agent, concert promoter. Estab. 1991. Releases 1 LP and 1 CD/year. "Mostly compilations." Pays 10-50% royalty to artists on contract; statutory rate to publisher per song on record.

How to Contact: Submit demo tape by mail. Unsolicited submissions are OK. Does not return material. Reports in 1 week to 3 months.

Music: Mostly **alternative rock** and **country/gospel**; also **rap/political** and **pop/classical**. Released *Safe in the Harbor* (by Kathy V) and *Songs for Somalia* (by various artists), all recorded on Co-op Artist Recordings. Other artists include Space Angels, Angry Cows, Huckleberry's Dolphin, Communion, Stratus.

Tips: "Be patient—we give everyone an equal chance. We hope artists will help promote if they can. We urge disabled and older artists to submit. Don't give up and don't listen to people who say you can't."

COUNTRY BREEZE RECORDS, 1715 Marty, Kansas City KS 66103. (913)384-7336. President: Ed Morgan. Labels include Angel Star Records and Midnight Shadow Records. Record company, music publisher (Country Breeze Music/BMI and Walkin' Hat Music/ASCAP). Releases 15 7″ singles and 20 cassettes/year. Works with musicians/artists and songwriters on contract. Pays 25% royalty to artists on contract; statutory rate to publisher per song on record.

How to Contact: Submit demo tape by mail. Unsolicited submissions are OK. Prefers studio-produced demo with 3 songs and lyric sheet. SASE. Reports in 2 weeks.

Music: All types **country**. Released "Guess Who," written and recorded by Vergene Powell on Angel Star Records (gospel); "I'll Leave That Decision Up To You," written and recorded by Jim Cox on Country Breeze Records (country); and "Too Late To Say You're Sorry," (by E. Morgan), recorded by Mike Gravelin on Country Breeze Records (country rock). Other artists include Ken Trammell, Alexa Smith-Lambert, Susie McMillan, Rick Truett, Bill Cameron and The Mills Family, Jerry Jack Garren, Curtis Andrews.

Tips: "Do not submit material and call me three days later wanting to know if it's recorded yet. It takes time."

COUNTRY SHOWCASE AMERICA, #10, 1018 17th Ave. S., Nashville TN 37212. (301)854-2917. President: Francis Gosman. Record company. Estab. 1971. Releases 5 singles/year. Works with musicians/artists and songwriters on contract. Pays scale royalty to artists on contract; statutory rate to publishers for each record sold.

How to Contact: Submit demo tape by mail. Unsolicited submissions are OK. Prefers cassette and lyric sheet. Does not return unsolicited material.

Music: Country. Released "Runaway Train" and "Too Late for Roses" (by Cochran/Gosman); "Evening Ride" (by Vague/Gosman), all recorded by Johnny Anthony on CSA Records (country).

Tips: "Keep it simple, with words understandable."

COUNTRY STAR INTERNATIONAL, 439 Wiley Ave., Franklin PA 16323. (814)432-4633. President: Norman Kelly. Labels include CSI, Country Star, Process and Mersey Records. Record company, music publisher (Country Star/ASCAP, Process and Kelly/BMI) and record producer (Country Star Productions). Member AFM and AFTRA. Estab. 1970. Releases 5-10 singles and 5-10 LPs/year. Works with musicians/artists and songwriters on contract. Works with lyricists and composers. Pays 8% royalty to artists on contract; statutory rate to publishers for each record sold. "Charges artists in advance only when they buy records to sell on personal appearances and show dates."

How to Contact: Submit demo tape by mail. Unsolicited submissions are OK. Prefers cassette with 2-4 songs and typed lyric or lead sheet. Unsolicited submissions OK. SASE. "No SASE no return." Reports in 2 weeks.

Music: Mostly **C&W** and **bluegrass.** Released "Teardrops Still Fall" (by N. Kelly/J. Barbaria), recorded by Larry Piefer (country); "Western Dawn" (by J. E. Meyers), recorded by Jeffrey Connors, both on Country Star Records; and "God Specializes," written and recorded by Sheryl Friend on Process Records. Other artists include Junie Lou, Tammi McClean and Bob Stamper.

Tips: "Send only your best efforts."

COURIER RECORDS, P.O. Box 201, Tecumseh OK 74873. (405)598-6379. President-Manager: Darrell V. Archer. Labels include Rapture Records, Conarch Recordings. Record company, music publisher (Bethlehem Music Publications, Archer Music, Rapture Music Publications) and record producer (Conarch Productions). Estab. 1985. Releases 8-10 singles, 12-15 LPs/year. Works with musicians/artists on record contract, songwriters on royalty contract, musicians on salary for in-house studio work and lyricists. Pays .80-1.00 per unit; statutory rate to publisher per song on record.

How to Contact: Submit demo tape by mail. Unsolicited submissions are OK. Prefers cassette (or VHS videocassette) with 3 songs and lyric or lead sheet. SASE. Reports in 6-8 weeks.

Music: Mostly **MOR sacred, Southern gospel** and **easy listening contemporary;** also **spirituals, choir material** and **youth/children's material.** Released *Children of the Lord* (by Archer), *Teach the Children* (by Richards), and *Handful of Dust* (by Meade), all recorded by Archer on Courier Records. Other artists include The Chosen Few, Brush Arbor Voices, Legacy Orchestra and Vocal Bouquet Acappella Singers.

Tips: "We are especially interested in material that can be adapted to choral use. This can be songs of almost any type except heavy rock or rap. Keep this in mind when submitting your material for review."

*COWGIRL RECORDS, Box 6085, Burbank CA 91510. Contact: Vice President. Record company and music publisher (Kingsport Creek). Estab. 1980. Works with musicians/artists and songwriters on contract. Pays statutory rate to publishers for each record sold.

How to Contact: Submit demo tape by mail. Unsolicited submissions OK. Prefers cassette (or VHS videocassette) with any number of songs and lyric sheet or lead sheet. Does not return unsolicited material. "Include a photo and bio if possible."

Music: Mostly **country, R&B, MOR** and **gospel.** Released "Leading Me On," "Pick Up Your Feet" and "With Me Still," all written and recorded by Melvena Kaye on Cowgirl Records.

CYMBAL RECORDS, P.O. Box 27410, Las Vegas NV 89126. (702)735-8175. CEO/President: David E. Johnson. Record company, music publisher (JOF-Dave Music/ASCAP). Estab. 1984. Releases 2 singles, 2 LPs and 2 CDs/year. Works with musicians/artists on record contract or songwriters on royalty contract. Pays 20% royalty to artists on contract; 50% to publisher per song on record.
How to Contact: Write first and obtain permission to submit. Prefers cassette with 4 songs and lyric sheet. SASE. Reports in 1 month.
Music: Mostly **pop, rock** and **jazz**; also **country, rap** and **classical**. Released *I Need Your Love*, written and recorded by David Wilkerson (R&B); *Handprints* and *Mind Probe*, written and recorded by Ben Sher (jazz), all on Cymball Records.

DAGENE RECORDS, Box 410851, San Francisco CA 94141. (415)822-1530. President: David Alston. Labels include Cabletown Corp. Record company, music publisher (Dagene Music) and record producer (David-Classic Disc Productions). Estab. 1993. Works with musicians/artists and songwriters on contract and hires musicians on salary for in-house studio work. Pays statutory rate to publishers per song on record.
How to Contact: Write or call first and obtain permission to submit. Prefers cassette (or VHS videocassette) with 2 songs and lyric sheet. Does not return unsolicited material.
Music: Mostly **R&B/rap, dance** and **pop**; also **gospel**. Released "Mind Ya Own" (by Bernard Henderson/Marcus Justice), recorded by 2WO Dominatorz; "Started Life" (by David/M. Campbell), recorded by Star Child, both on Dagene Records; and "Lies," written and recorded by David on Cabletown Records. Other artists include Taxi and the Independents.

ALAN DALE PRODUCTIONS, 1630 Judith Ln., Indianapolis IN 46227. (317)786-1630. President: Alan D. Heshelman. Labels include ALTO Records. Record company. Estab. 1990. Works with musicians/ artists on record contract or songwriters on royalty contract.
How to Contact: Submit demo tape by mail. Unsolicited submissions are OK. Prefers cassette with 3 songs. SASE. Reports in 4-6 weeks.
Music: Mostly **adult contemporary, country, jazz, gospel** and **New Age**. Released "Better Than Before" (by Johnna Maze); "Haunting Love" (adult) and "In Love With Me" (contemporary) both by Alan Dale, all recorded by Trinia on A.D.P. Records. Other artists include Still Water.
Tips: "Create a writing style with good paraphrasing and excellent vocals."

*DANCER PUBLISHING CO., 166 Folkstone, Brampton, Ontario L6T 3M5 **Canada**. (905)791-1835. President: David Dancer. Labels include Cougar Records. Record company, music publisher. Estab. 1991. Deals with artists and songwriters. Releases 6 singles and 4 CDs/year. Pays 10% royalty to artists on contract; statutory rate to publisher per song on record.
How to Contact: Submit demo tape by mail. Unsolicited submissions are OK. Prefers cassette with 4 songs and lyric sheet. Does not return material. Reports in 1 month.
Music: Mostly **country, bluegrass** and **light rock**. Released "Lady," written and recorded by Issie Saminara; "Hometown Girl," written and recorded by Paul Pret; and "Bless My Soles," written and recorded by David Dancer, all on Cougar Records.

DAT BEAT RECORDS, INC., Suite 4303, 333 E. Ontario, Chicago IL 60611. (312)751-0906. Contact: Robert Shelist. Labels include UBAD Records. Record company. Estab. 1989. Works with musicians/ artists and songwriters on contract and hires musicians for in-house studio work. Pays 5-15% royalty to artists on contract; rate to publisher per song on record varies.
How to Contact: Write first and obtain permission to submit. Prefers cassette with 4 songs and lyric sheet or lead sheet. Does not return unsolicited material. Reports in 2 months.
Music: Mostly **rap, pop** and **dance**; also **R&B, rock** and **New Age**. Released *Fever for the Flavor*, written and recorded by O.Z. on UBAD Records; and *Strictly Soul*, recorded by 2 Damn on Dat Beat Records.

*DEADEYE RECORDS, P.O. Box 5022-347, Lake Forest CA 92630. (714)768-0644. Manager: Karen Jenkins. Labels include Thunderzone Records. Record company. Estab. 1992. Deals with artists and songwriters. Releases 3 CDs/year. Pays varying royalty to artists on contract; statutory rate to publisher per song on record.
How to Contact: Write first and obtain permission to submit. Prefers cassette (or videocassette if available) with 3 songs and lyric sheet. Does not return material. Reports in 2 months.
Music: Mostly **country, rock** and **blues**; also **R&B**. Released *Ragin' Wind* (by Frank Jenkins), recorded by Diamondback on Deadeye Records (country).

*DEJADISC, INC., 537 Lindsey St., San Marcos TX 78666. (512)392-6610. Fax: (512)754-6886. Director of Product Development: Steve Wilkison. Record company. Estab. 1992. Deals with artists and songwriters. Releases 6 LPs and 6 CDs/year. Pays 10-12% royalty to artists on contract; statutory rate to publisher per song on record.

How to Contact: Submit demo tape by mail. Unsolicited submissions are OK. Prefers cassette or VHS videocassette with 5-10 songs and lyric sheet. "Keep it simple and be neat." Does not return material. Reports in 1-2 months.
Music: Mostly **folk, rock** and **country**. Released *Love & Trust*, written and recorded by Michael Fracasso (folk); *Brand New Ways*, written and recorded by Don McCalister (country); and *Trashman Shoes* (by Slattery/Kassens), recorded by Shoulders (rock), all on Dejadisc Records. Other artists include David Rodriguez, Elliott Murphy, Sarah Elizabeth Campbell, Lisa Mednick, Coffee Sergeants.
Tips: "Our focus is primarily devoted to folk, singer-songwriter, country and rock recordings. We look for strong, unique and original songwriters."

DEMI MONDE RECORDS AND PUBLISHING, LTD., Foel Studio, Llanfair Caereinion, Powys, Wales, **United Kingdom**. Phone and fax: (0938)810758. Managing Director: Dave Anderson. Record company and music publisher (Demi Monde Records & Publishing, Ltd.) and record producer (Dave Anderson). Estab. 1983. Releases 5 12" singles, 10 LPs and 6 CDs/year. Works with musicians/artists and songwriters on contract; hires musicians for in-house studio work. Pays 10-12% royalty to artists on contract; statutory rate to publisher per song on record.
How to Contact: Submit demo tape by mail. Unsolicited submissions are OK. Prefers cassette with 3-4 songs. SAE and IRC. Reports in 1 month.
Music: **Rock, R&B** and **pop**. Released *Hawkwind* and *Amon Duul II & Gong* and *Groundhogs* (by T.S. McPhee), all on Demi Monde Records.

DETROIT MUNICIPAL RECORDINGS, P.O. Box 20879, Detroit MI 48220. (313)547-2722. Fax: (313)547-5477. Label Director: Bricee Rivers. Director A&R: Bill Laimbeer. Record company (BMI). Estab. 1992. Releases 2 LPs and 2 CDs/year. Works with musicians/artists on record contract, band and tour management. Pays 30-49% royalty to artists on contract; statutory rate to publisher per song on record.
How to Contact: Submit demo tape by mail. Unsolicited submissions are OK. Prefers cassette or CD with minimum of 4 songs. Does not return material. Reports in 1-2 months.
Music: Mostly **alternative college** or **guitar type non-dance** or **non-industrial**. Released "The Complete Works of . . ." and "Christmas Eve Get Together With . . . ," recorded by Goober and the Peas on DMR Records. Other artists include PRIM U.K.

DIAMOND WIND RECORDS, P.O. Box 311, Estero FL 33928. President: Reenie Diamond. Record company and music publisher (BMI). Estab. 1991. Pays standard royalty to artists on contract; statutory rate to publisher per song on record.
How to Contact: Write first and obtain permission to submit. Prefers cassette (or VHS videocassette) with 3 songs and lyric sheet. Does not return material. Reports in 4-6 weeks.
Music: Mostly **country, country blues** and **country pop/rock**; also **pop** and **R&B**. Released "Thunder In My Heart" and "Mama I Love You" (by M.L. Northam), recorded by Bronze Bonneville on Continental Records; and "Diamond Den," written and recorded by Reenie Diamond on Diamond Wind Records.

DIGITALIA RECORDS, 234 Columbus Drive, Jersey City NJ 07302. (201)963-1621. Vice President/A&R: Charles Farley. Record company and record producer. Estab. 1992. Releases 10 12" singles/year. Works with musicians/artists on record contract. Pays 10% royalty to artists on contract; variable rate to publisher per song on record.
How to Contact: Submit demo tape by mail. Unsolicited submissions are OK. Prefers cassette (or VHS videocassette) with 2-3 songs and lyric sheet. Reports in 3 weeks.
Music: **Rap** and **dance**. Released "Slip Slam Bam" (by B.Zeger), recorded by Just Say Yo (rap); "Skit Up" (by Barry Harris), recorded by Exxe (dance); "I'm the Man" (by Brad Turk/Mitch Moses), recorded by M.C. Sneak, all on Digitalia Records. Other artists include KXXK.
Tips: "Do your homework before submitting material. Listen to the radio, read the trades, learn what hits are and try to understand why they are."

***DISCOVERY MUSIC**, 5554 Calhoun, Van Nuys CA 91401. (818)782-7818. Fax: (818)782-7817. Chief Creative Officer: David Wohlstadter. Record company. Estab. 1985. Deals with artists and songwriters. Releases 3-4 LPs and 2-3 CDs/year. Royalty negotiated; statutory rate to publisher per song on record.
How to Contact: Submit demo tape by mail. Unsolicited submissions are OK. Prefers cassette ½" videocassette and lyric sheet. Does not return material.
Music: Mostly **children's audio & video**. Released *Jump for Joy*, written and recorded by Joanie Bartels; *Bethie's Really Silly Songs about Numbers*, written and recorded by Bethie; and *The Wooleycat's Favorite Fairy Tales*, written and recorded by Dennis Hysom, all on Discovery Music.

DISC-TINCT MUSIC, INC., 95 Cedar Lane, Englewood NJ 07631. (201)568-7066. President: Jeffrey Collins. Labels include Music Station, Echo USA, Dancefloor, Soul Creation and Soul Vibes. Record company, music publisher (Distinct Music, Inc./BMI, Distinct Echo Music/ASCAP), record producer (Echo USA Productions). Estab. 1985. Releases 50 12″ singles, 10 LPs, 4 EPs and 15 CDs/year. Works with musicians/artists on record contract or songwriters on royalty contract. Pays 5-8% royalty to artists on contract; ⅔ statutory rate to publisher per song on record.
How to Contact: Submit demo tape by mail. Unsolicited submissions are OK. Prefers cassette (or VHS videocassette) with up to 5 songs. SASE. Reports in 1 month.
Music: Mostly **R&B, dance** and **house/techno**. Released *Your Attitude* (by Jimmie Fox), recorded by Kim Cummings on Music Station Records; and "As Quiet As It's Kept" (by Elis Pacheco), recorded by Colonel Abrams on Soul Creation Records. Other artists include Debbie Blackwell/Cook, Eleanor Grant, Black Rebels, Ready for the World, Llake, George Kerr and Quincy Patrick.
Tips: "Cue your cassettes, which should be labelled clearly."

*DISQUES NOSFERATU RECORDS, C.P. 304 Succ. S, Montreal Quebec H4E 4J8 **Canada**. (514)769-9096. Promotion Director: Ginette Provost. Record company. Estab. 1986. Releases 1 12″ single and 1 cassette/year. Works with musicians/artists on contract and hires musicians for in-house studio work. Pays statutory rate to publishers per song on records.
How to Contact: Write first and obtain permission to submit. Prefers cassette or VHS videocassette with 3 songs and lyric sheet. Does not return unsolicited submissions. Reports in 3 to 6 months.
Music: Mostly **rock** and **blues**; also **instrumental** and **heavy metal**. Released "Brulée Parle Blues" (by Fee Ross); "Hollywood" (by Fee Ross); and "Barracuda Blues" (by J.J. LaBlonde), all recorded by Nosferatu (blues/rock).
Tips: "Any artist who signs with us must have stage experience."

DOMINO RECORDS, LTD., Ridgewood Park Estates, 222 Tulane St., Garland TX 75043. Contact: Gene or Dea Summers. Public Relations/Artist and Fan Club Coordinator: Steve Summers. Labels include Front Row Records. Record company and music publisher (Silicon Music/BMI). Estab. 1968. Releases 5-6 singles and 2-3 LPs/year. Works with artists and songwriters on contract. Pays negotiable royalty to artists on contract; standard royalty to songwriters on contract.
How to Contact: Prefers cassette (or VHS videocassette) with 1-3 songs. Does not return material. SASE. Reports ASAP.
Music: Mostly **50's rock/rockabilly**; also **country, bluegrass, old-time blues** and **R&B**. Released "Ready to Ride" (from the HBO Presentation *Backlot*), by Pat Minter (country); *School of Rock 'N Roll* by Gene Summers (50s) and "Cactus In The Snow" by Pat Minter (C&W).
Tips: "If you own masters of 1950s rock and rockabilly, contact us first! We will work with you on a percentage basis for overseas release. We have active releases in Holland, Switzerland, Belgium, Australia, England, France, Sweden, Norway and the US at the present. We need original masters. You must be able to prove ownership of tapes before we can accept a deal. We're looking for little-known, obscure recordings. We have the market if you have the tapes! Sample records available. Send SASE for catalogue. We are also interested in C&W and rockabilly *artists* who have not recorded for awhile but still have the voice and appeal to sell overseas. *We request a photo and bio with material submission.*"

*DRAG CITY, INC., P.O. Box 476867, Chicago IL 60647. (312)455-1015. President: Daniel Koretzky. Labels include Sea Note. Record company. Estab. 1989. Deals with artists and songwriters. Releases 10 singles, 10 LPs, 5 EPs and 10 CDs/year. Works with musicians/artists on record contract. Pays 50/50 profit split.
How to Contact: Submit demo tape by mail. Unsolicited submissions are OK. Prefers cassette. Does not return material. Does not report back on submissions "unless we're interested."
Music: Mostly **rock** and **country**. Released "Back to School," recorded by Royal Trux; *Julius Caesar*, recorded by Smog; and *Funny Farm*, recorded by King Kong, all on Drag City. Other artists include The Red Crayola, Palace Brothers, The Silver Jews, Mantis, Burnout, Gastr del Sol and Hot Toasters.

E.A.R.S. INC., Box 8132, Philadelphia PA 19101. (215)328-1619. President/General Manager: Jim Miller. Labels include Encounter Records. Record company (BMI), music publisher (Electro Jazz Music) and record producer (E.A.R.S. Inc.). Estab. 1986. Releases 3 cassettes and 3 CDs/year. Works with musicians/artists on record contract, musicians on salary for in-house studio work. Pays 10-20% royalty to artists on contract; statutory rate to publisher per song on record.
How to Contact: Submit demo tape by mail. Unsolicited submissions are OK. Prefers cassette (or VHS or Beta videocassette). SASE. Reports within 6 months.
Music: Jazz. Released *Tunnel Vision*, recorded by Reverie; *Blue Nite*, recorded by Andy Lalasis/John Mulhern; and *Street Blues*, recorded by "Father John" D'Amico, all on E.A.R.S. Inc. Records. Other artists include The Wide-Awake Club, Evelyn Simms, Leslie Savoy Burrs, Suzanne Cloud, Richard Drueding, Don Glanden and KMQ.

Tips: "Shop your stuff around. Consider us the last resort of record labels. Only contact us if you *have* to get your stuff out because you *know* it's so good it's been rejected by everyone else."

E.S.R. RECORDS, 61 Burnthouse Lane, Exeter, Devon EX2 6AZ **United Kingdom**. Phone: (0392)57880. M.D: John Greenslade. Record company (P.R.S.) and record producer (E.S.R. Productions). Estab. 1965. Releases 4 singles and 10 LPs/year. Works with musicians on salary for in-house studio work. Pays standard royalty; statutory rate to publisher per song on records.
How to Contact: Submit demo tape by mail. Unsolicited submissions are OK. Prefers cassette with 4 songs and lyric sheet. SAE and IRC. Reports in 1 month.
Music: Mostly **country** and **MOR**. Released *Can't Imagine* (by John Greenslade), recorded by Ginger Walker (MOR); "Hey Lady" (by John Greenslade), recorded by Johnny Sold (MOR); and *I Will Ask Again* (by John Greenslade), recorded by Mike Scott (MOR), all on E.S.R. Records. Other artists include Kar Barron, Barracuda, Gary Kane.

EARACHE RECORDS/EARACHE SONGS, #915, 295 Lafayette St., New York NY 10012. General Manager: Bill Wilson. Labels include Sub-Bass Records. Record company and music publisher (PRS/BMI). Estab. 1986. Releases 6 singles, 6 12" singles, 12 LPs, 6 EPs and 12 CDs/year. Works with musicians/artists on record contract. Pays various royalty; various rate to publisher per song on record.
How to Contact: Submit demo tape by mail. Unsolicited submissions are OK. Prefers cassette (or ½" VHS videocassette) with 3-4 songs. Does not return material. Reports in 3 weeks.
Music: Mostly **alternative**, **metal** and **rock**; also **techno/rave** and **industrial/experimental**. Released *Pure* (by Justin Brodrick), recorded by Godflesh on Earache Records (alternative); *Soul Sacrifice*, written and recorded by Cathedral on Earache/Columbia Records (rock/metal); and *Utopia Banished*, written and recorded by Napalm Death on Earache Records (alternative/metal). Other artists include Fudge Tunnel, Morbid Angel, Carcass, Entombed, Brutal Truth and Bolt Thrower.
Tips: "Be original!"

ELEMENT RECORDS, Box 30260, Bakersfield CA 93385-1260. President: Judge A. Robertson. Record company. Estab. 1978. Releases 5 singles and 5 EPs/year. Works with musicians/artists on contract. Pays standard royalty.
How to Contact: Write first to arrange personal interview. Prefers cassette with 1 or more songs and lyric sheet.
Music: All types. Released "I Like You The Way You Are," written and recorded by Jar The Superstar (funk); "Let the Beauty Of The Lord Come Down On Us" by Judge A. Robertson (gospel); and "Spirits of Truth," by Jar The Superstar (Christian pop).

*EMA MUSIC INC., P.O. Box 91683, Washington DC 20090-1683. (202)319-1688. Fax: (202)575-4452. President: Jeremiah N. Murphy. Director of Promotions: Benjamin R. Stukes. Record company. Estab. 1993. Deals with artists and songwriters. Releases 2 LPs and 2 CDs/year. Pays statutory rate to publisher per song on record.
How to Contact: Submit demo tape by mail. Unsolicited submissions are OK. Prefers cassette with lyric or lead sheet. "Do not call." SASE. Reports in 3 months.
Music: Mostly **gospel** and **contemporary Christian**. Released *Just Jesus* (by M. Brown); *I Must* (by J. Murphy); and *Blessed Assurance* (by P. Crosby), all recorded by J. Murphy on EMA Records (gospel).

EMPTY SKY RECORDS, P.O. Box 626, Verplanck NY 10596. Producer/Manager: Rick Carbone. Labels include Power Ranger, Verplanck, Yankee Records. Record company, music publisher and record producer (Rick Carbone-Empty Sky). Estab. 1982. Releases 15-20 singles, 2 12" singles, 2 LPs, 1 EP and 1 CD/year. Works with musicians/artists and songwriters on contract. Pays 8-10% royalty to artists on contract; statutory rate to publisher per song on record.
How to Contact: Submit demo tape by mail. Unsolicited submissions are OK. Prefers cassette with 3-5 songs and lyric sheet. SASE. Reports in 2-3 months.
Music: Mostly **country**, **gospel** and **pop**; also **rap**, **rock** and **rap/gospel**. Released "Blue Tick Hound" (by C. Hawley/B. Martinson), recorded by Bob Martinson (C&W); "Fill Me Up With Your Love," written and recorded by Lloyd Caudle (pop), both on Empty Sky Records; and "Zayed Out," recorded by Zoo Niggazs on Power Ranger Records (rap). Other artists include The Dependents, The Sweetarts, Phil Coley, Steve Mercer, Roberta Boyle, Ms. Special Tee, Bosco, Wylie and Leo Stephens.
Tips: "We are looking for songwriters/artists (all kinds). Also looking for 'Halloween' music for CD projects."

EMZEE RECORDS, Box 3213, S. Farmingdale NY 11735. (212)724-2800, (516)420-9169. President: Dawn Kendall. Labels include Avenue A Records, Ivory Tower Records. Record company, music publisher (Emzee Music/BMI). Estab. 1970. Releases 40 singles, 20 12" singles, 20 LPs, 15 EPs and 30 CDs/year. Works with musicians/artists and songwriters on contract and hires musicians for in-house studio work. Royalty to artists on contract varies; pays statutory rate to publisher per song on record.

How to Contact: Submit demo tape by mail. Unsolicited submissions are OK. Prefers cassette with 3 songs and lyric sheet. SASE. Press kit needed. Reports in 7-8 weeks.

Music: Mostly **pop, rock** and **country**; also **R&B** and **gospel**. Released "Intuition," written and recorded by Lara (jazz) and "Memories of You," written and recorded by Tony Navarro, both on Avenue A Records (guitar); and "Rhythm Moves," written and recorded by Susan Hara on Ivory Tower Records (dance). Other artists include John Sanders, Azle and Ingrid Mayi.

Tips: "Don't be influenced by what people think. Write what you *feel*."

*ENDANGERED RECORDS, Suite 104, 4 Daniels Farm Rd, Trumbull CT 06611. (203)381-0043. Owner: Tom McKee. Labels include Combustion Records. Record company, record producer. Estab. 1991. Deals with artists. Releases 1 LP and 3 CDs/year. Pays 15-50% profit share to artists on contract; statutory rate to publisher per song on record.

How to Contact: Submit demo tape by mail. Unsolicited submissions are OK. "Send any format — any video — the more background info and lyrics the better. Try to use quality tape for better sound." SASE. Reports in 2-3 weeks.

Music: Mostly **pop rock, R&B** and **blues**; also **folk, country rock** and **classical jazz fusion**. Released *A Light Went Out In New York* by Matthew Fisher and The Downliners Sect (R&B, pop); *That Ain't The Way to Go* by Del Dwyer and Robbie Ross (blues); and *On This Moment* by Michael Brown and Yvonne Vitale (pop), all on Endangered Records. Other artists include Jimmy Dewar, Peter Taylor, British All Stars and LaSetta.

Tips: "First impressions are important — you must love music first and money last — give it 110% and it will eventually come back to you — make demos sound clear and understandable."

ESB RECORDS, Box 6429, Huntington Beach CA 92615-6429. (714)962-5618. Executive Producers: Eva and Stan Bonn. Record company, music publisher (Bonnfire Publishing/ASCAP, Gather' Round/BMI), record producer (ESB Records). Estab. 1987. Releases 1 single, 1 LP and 1 CD/year. Works with musicians/artists and songwriters on contract. Pays negotiable royalty to artists; pays statutory rate to publisher per song on record.

How to Contact: Submit demo tape by mail. Unsolicited submissions are OK. SASE. Reports in 2 weeks.

Music: Country, all formats. Released "The Sounds of the Universe," (by Eddie Sheppard/Stan Bonn) and "Star Child (Why All the Tears)" (by Clayton Bonn/Eua Bonn), both recorded by Bobby Lee Caldwell; and *Don't Throw Stones* (by Jack Schroeder), recorded by John P. Swisshelm.

Tips: "Be worldwide and commercial in lyrics and present a professional package."

*ETHEREAN MUSIC/VARIENA PUBLISHING, #510, 9200 W. Cross Ave., Littleton CO 80123. (303)973-8291. Fax: (303)973-8499. Contact: A&R Department. Labels include Elation Artists, Native Spirit, EM Pop. Record company and music publisher. Estab. 1979. Deals with artists and songwriters. Releases 1-2 singles, 1-2 12″ singles and 4-10 CDs/year. Royalty negotiable.

How to Contact: Submit demo tape by mail. Unsolicited submissions are OK. Prefers cassette (or VHS videocassette if available) with all songs and lyric or lead sheet; include photo and tearsheets. "We only return recorded media. All 'promo' materials are kept." SASE. Reports in 2 months.

Music: Mostly **New Age/ethnic, jazz/contemporary** and **instrumental/world**; also **pop**. Released *Mayan Dream* (by Dik Darnell), recorded by Tze'ec & Dik Darnell on Etherean Music (new); *Saxafaction*, recorded by Bryan Savage on Elation Artists (jazz); and *Ghetto Madness*, written and recorded by Denco Set on EM Pop (rap). Other artists include Denean, Kenny Passarelli, Elk Nation Singers and Patrick Walsh.

EXCLUSIVE RECORDING CO., (formerly In-House Publishing, Inc.), 146-05 130th Ave., South Ozone Park NY 11436. President: Barry Jones. Record company. Estab. 1985. Pays negotiated royalty.

How to Contact: Submit demo tape by mail. Unsolicited submissions are OK. Prefers cassette with 4 songs and lyric sheet. "Include a music career résumé and indicate *Songwriter's Market* referral." Does not return material. Reports in 1 month.

Music: Mostly **popular** and **dance**.

Tips: "Submit a quality recording that's easy to listen to."

EXCURSION RECORDS, Suite 388, 9 Music Square S., Nashville TN 37203. (800)760-4646. President: Frank T. Prins. Labels include Echappee Records. Record company, music publisher (ASCAP/BMI). Record producer (Frank T. Prins). Estab. 1982. Releases 2-5 singles, 1 LP and 1 EP/year. Works with musicians/artists and songwriters on contract. Pays 5-6% royalty to artists on contract; statutory rate to publisher per song on record.

How to Contact: Write or call first and obtain permission to submit. Prefers cassette (or VHS videocassette if available) with 3 songs and lyric and lead sheet. SASE. Reports in 2-3 weeks.

Music: Mostly **pop, rock** and **country**; also **gospel** and **R&B**. Released "Red Roses In My Hand" and *Always*, both written and recorded by Ian Ballard; also *Time Clock Livin'* (by Wayne and Homer Osborne), recorded by Ian Ballard, all on Excursion Records. Other artists include Bittersweet.

FAME AND FORTUNE ENTERPRISES, P.O. Box 121679, Nashville TN 37212. (615)244-4898. Producers: Jim Cartwright and Scott Turner. Labels include Fame and Fortune Records and National Foundation Records. Record company, music publisher (Boff Board Music/BMI) and record producer. Estab. 1976. Releases 6 singles, 6 LPs and 6 CDs/year. Works with musicians/artists and songwriters on contract. Pays statutory rate to publisher per song on record.
How to Contact: Submit demo tape by mail. Unsolicited submissions are OK. Prefers cassette (or VHS videocassette) with 4 songs and lyric sheet. SASE (with correct postage). Reports in 6-10 weeks.
Music: Mostly **country**, **MOR, med. rock** and **pop**. Released "Rise Above It," (by Steve Rose), recorded by Brittany Hale on GBS Records (country); "Big Strong Man," written and recorded by A.C. Brooks (country rock); and *Payday* (by DeWayne Oerender/Paulette Tyler), recorded by Sheylyn Jaynes, both on Fame & Fortune Records (country). Other artists include Bryan Perrin, John Guthrie.
Tips: "We have expanded our company and now have Fame & Fortune Management (artist development and management). Potential artists *must* have financial backers in place. Contact Jim Cartwright or Susan Roach."

FARR RECORDS, P.O. Box 1098, Somerville NJ 08876. Vice President: Candace Campbell. Record company. Estab. 1973. Releases 150 singles, 12 LPs and 12 CDs/year. Works with musicians/artists on record contract, songwriters on royalty contract. Pays various royalty; statutory rate to publisher per song on record.
How to Contact: Submit demo tape by mail. Unsolicited submissions are OK. Prefers cassette (or VHS videocassette) with 4 songs and lyric sheet. SASE. Reports in 1 month.
Music: Mostly **rock, pop** and **country**; also **R&B**.

FAT CITY ARTISTS, Suite 2, 1226 17th Ave. S., Nashville TN 37212. (615)320-7678. Fax: (615)321-5382. Vice President: Rusty Michael. Record company, music publisher (Fort Forever/BMI), record producer (Creative Communications Workshop) and booking agency (Fat City Artists). Estab. 1972. Releases 4-6 singles, 4-6 LPs, 4-6 EPs and 4-6 CDs/year. Works with musicians/artists on record contract, songwriters on royalty contract and producers for demo work. Pays 12-15% royalty to artist on contract for demo work; statutory rate to publisher per song on record.
How to Contact: Submit demo tape by mail. Unsolicited submissions are OK. Prefers cassette (or VHS videocassette) with 4-6 songs and lyric sheet. SASE. Reports in 2 weeks.
Music: Mostly **rock, country** and **blues**; also **alternative, rockabilly** and **jazz**.
Tips: "Provide us with as much information as you can with regard to your material and act and we will provide you with an evaluation as soon as possible. Our advertising/promotion division specializes in developing effective artist promotional packages, including demos, videos, video press kits, photography and copy. We will evaluate your present promotional material at no cost."

FEARLESS RECORDS, P.O. Box 11111, Whittier CA 90603-0111. (310)946-9766. A&R Director: Steve James. Record company, music publisher (Shelf Music, BMI), record producer. Estab. 1990. Releases 5 LPs and 2 CDs/year. Works with musicians/artists on record contract, songwriters on royalty contract or musicians on salary for in-house studio work. Pays 12% royalty to artists on contract; statutory rate to publisher per song on record.
How to Contact: Submit demo tape by mail. Unsolicited submissions are OK. Prefers cassette (or VHS videocassette) with 4 songs and lyric sheet. Does not return material. Reports in 1 month.
Music: Mostly **country**, **pop** and **R&B**; also **rock** and **rap**. Released "Moment of Truth" and "Never Say Goodbye," both written and recorded by Crossover (country); and "Think It Over" (by B. Holly), recorded by Crossover, all on Fearless Records. Other artists include Latin Side of Soul, Hot Rod Hearts, Rod Coleman, Carol Martini and Ryan Flynn.
Tips: "Be ready to work with Steve James, who has been very consistent producing hit records for the last 10 years."

*FICTION, 850 Seventh Ave., New York NY 10019. (212)489-3717. Fax: (212)489-3743. Vice President, A&R: Randall Barbera. Record company, music publisher. Estab. 1977. Deals with artists and songwriters.
How to Contact: Submit demo tape by mail. Unsolicited submissions are OK. Prefers cassette. SASE.
Music: Mostly **alternative** and **rock**. Released *SHOW*, written and recorded by The Cure on Fiction Records; *Scenes From The Second Story*, written and recorded by The God Machine on Elektra Fiction/PLG; and *EPICURE*, written and recorded by EAT on Fiction/Polydor Records. Other artists include Die Warzau, Liquid Sky, Randy Jackson, Bleed, Oxygiene.

FIFTH STREET RECORDS, 228 West 5th St., Kansas City MO 64105. (816)842-6854. Office Manager: Gary Sutton. Record company, music publisher (Chapie Music Publishing, BMI). Estab. 1980. Releases 24 LPs and 12 CDs/year. Works with musicians/artists/artists on record contact or songwriters on royalty contract. Pays various royalties to artists on contract; statutory rate to publisher per song on record.

How to Contact: Call first and obtain permission to submit. Prefers cassette with 3 songs and lyric sheet. Does not return material. Reports in 1 month.

Music: Mostly **black gospel**, **country** and **rock/pop**; also **jazz**, **southern gospel** and **urban**. Released *Statement of Direction* (by Vic Jones), recorded by Joy Unlimited; *Don't Want 2 Be Left* (by D. Horne), recorded by John McConnell (black gospel); and *Poet & Wealthy Man*, written and recorded by Land-Hildebrand (pop gospel), all on Fifth Street Records. Other artists include Bob McCartney, Deliverence Temple and DayStar.

Tips: "Write in the style of our artists. Write meaningful lyrics with a wide range of appeal."

FINK-PINEWOOD RECORDS, P.O. Box 5241, Chesapeake VA 23324. (804)627-0957. Labels include Bay Port Records. Record company. Estab. 1954.

How to Contact: Submit demo tape by mail. Unsolicited submissions are OK. Prefers cassette with 2 songs. SASE. Reports in 3 weeks.

Music: Mostly **soul-blues** and **soul-gospel**.

Tips: "Try to work with a growing small label, one that is unknown with commercial broadcasting media!"

FIRST TIME RECORDS, Sovereign House, 12 Trewartha Rd., Praa Sands, Penzance, Cornwall TR20 9ST **England**. Phone (0736)762826. Fax: (0736)763328. Managing Director A&R: Roderick G. Jones. Labels include Pure Gold Records, Rainy Day Records and Mohock Records. Registered members of Phonographic Performance Ltd. (PPL). Record company and music publisher (First Time Music Publishing U.K. Ltd./MCPS/PRS), and record producer (First Time Management & Production Co.). Estab. 1986. Works with musicians/artists and songwriters on contract; hires musicians for in-house studio work. Royalty to artists on contract varies; pays statutory rate to publishers per song on record subject to deal.

How to Contact: Prefers cassette with unlimited number of songs and lyric or lead sheets, but not necessary. SAE and IRC. Reports in 1-3 months.

Music: Mostly **country/folk**, **pop/soul/top 20** and **country with an Irish/Scottish crossover**; also **gospel/ Christian** and **HI NRG/dance**. Released *Songwriters and Artistes Compilation Volume III*, on Rainy Day Records; "The Drums of Childhood Dreams," written and recorded by Pete Arnold on Mohock Records (folk) and *The Light and Shade of Eddie Blackstone*, written and recorded by Eddie Blackstone on T.W. Records (country).

Tips: "Writers should learn patience, tolerance and understanding of how the music industry works, and should present themselves and their product in a professional manner and always be polite. Listen to constructive criticism and learn from the advice of people who have a track record in the music business. Your first impression may be the only chance you get, so it is advisable to get it right from the start."

FLYING HEART RECORDS, Dept. SM, 4026 NE 12th Ave., Portland OR 97212. (503)287-8045. Owner: Jan Celt. Record company. Estab. 1982. Releases 2 LPs and 1 EP/year. Works with musicians/artists and songwriters on contract and hires musicians for in-house studio work. Pays variable royalty to artists on contract; negotiable rate to publisher per song on record.

How to Contact: Submit a demo tape by mail. Unsolicited submissions are OK. Prefers cassette with 1-10 songs and lyric sheets. Does not return material. "SASE required for *any* response." Reports in 3 months.

Music: Mostly **R&B**, **blues** and **jazz**; also **rock**. Released "Get Movin" and "Down Mexico Way" (by Chris Newman), recorded by Napalm Beach (rock); and "Which One Of You People" (by Jan Celt), recorded by The Esquires (R&B), all on Flying Heart Records. Other artists include Janice Scroggins, Tom McFarland, Obo Addy, Snow Bud and The Flower People.

Tips: "Express your true feelings with creative originality and show some imagination. Use high quality cassette for best sound."

FOLK ERA RECORDS, 705 S. Washington St., Naperville IL 60540. (708)305-0783. Fax: (708)305-0782. Vice President: Mike Fleischer. Record company. Estab. 1989. Releases 6-12 CDs/year. Pays negotiable rate to artist and publisher.

How to Contact: Write first and obtain permission to submit. Prefers cassette (or VHS videocassette) with 3-5 songs. Does not return material.

Music: Mostly **folk**, **bluegrass** and **acoustic country**; also **Celtic folk**, **traditional gospel** and **acoustic blues**. Released "In the Heat of the Summer," written and recorded by Ken and Reggie Harris; and

"Rising In Love," written and recorded by David Roth, all on Folk Era Records. Other artists include New St. George, Cornerstone, Glenn Yarborough and NE Winds.

FOREFRONT RECORDS, P.O. Box 1964, Hoboken NJ 07030-1308. (201)653-1990. Owner: Michael O. Young. Labels include Radcore Records. Record company. Estab. 1985. Works with musicians/artists on record contract. Pays 5-10% royalty to artist on contract; statutory rate to publisher per song on record.
How to Contact: Submit demo tape by mail. Unsolicited submissions are OK. Prefers cassette. Does not return material. Reports in 1-2 month.
Music: Mostly **punk, hard-core** and **heavy metal**; also **alternative**. Released *Cirkus Berzerkus*, recorded by the AG's; *WACT*, recorded by the Fiendz; and "Seersucker," recorded by Soda Can, all on Forefront Records.
Tips: "Have good, original material, patience and money."

FOUNTAIN RECORDS, 1203 Biltmore Ave., High Point NC 27260. (910)882-9990. President: Doris W. Lindsay. Record company, music publisher (Better Times Publishing/BMI, Doris Lindsay Publishing/ASCAP) and record producer. Estab. 1979. Releases 3 singles and 1 LP/year. Works with musicians/artists and songwriters on contract. Pays 5% royalty to artists on contract; statutory rate to publishers per song on record.
How to Contact: Submit demo tape by mail. Unsolicited submissions are OK. Prefers cassette with 2 songs and lyric sheets. SASE. Reports in 2 months.
Music: Mostly **country, pop** and **gospel**. Released "American Song" (by Roedy/Michaels), recorded by Terry Michaels; "Share Your Love" and "Back In Time," written and recorded by Mitch Snow, all on Fountain Records.
Tips: "Have a professional type demo and include phone and address on cassette."

FOUNTAINHEAD RECORDS, 1374 Grove St., San Francisco CA 94117. General Manager: Trevor Levine. Record company, music publisher (Art of Concept Music/BMI). Estab. 1989. Releases 1 single and 1 cassette/year. Works with musicians/artists and songwriters on contract. Pays negotiable royalty to artists on contract; statutory rate to publisher for each record sold.
How to Contact: Write first and obtain permission to submit. Send SASE. Does not return material. Reports in 3 months—*only* if interested in using the material submitted.
Music: Mostly **pop/rock ballads** and "**moderate-paced meaningful rock** (not 'good time rock and roll' or dance music)." Released *6 Months to Live, Surrendering My Pride* and *We The People*, written and recorded by Trevor Levine on Fountainhead Records.
Tips: "We are interested in songs with powerful melodic and lyrical hooks—songs that are beautiful, expressive and meaningful, with uniquely dissonant or dramatic qualities that really *move* the listener. Our songs deal with serious topics, from inner conflicts and troubled relationships to anthems, story songs and message songs which address social and political issues—government corruption, women's and minority issues, human and animal rights. Keep the song's vocal range within an octave, if possible, and no more than 1½ octaves. The music should convey the meaning of the words. Please only contact us if you are interested in having your songs recorded by an artist other than yourself. We listen to tapes we receive as time permits; however, if the first 20 seconds don't grab us, we move on to the next tape. So always put your best, most emotional, expressive song first, and avoid long introductions."

*FOXFIRE RECORDS, #113, 107 Music City Circle, Nashville TN 37214. (615)391-4874. Fax: (615)391-0916. Executive Vice President: Charlie Ray. Labels include Blue Denim, Golden Gate, Crystal Ram. Record company, record producer, music publisher and music trade publication. Estab. 1976. Deals with artists and songwriters. Releases 100-200 singles, 50-100 LPs and 50-100 CDs/year. Royalty varies; statutory rate to publisher per song on record.
How to Contact: Submit demo tape by mail. Unsolicited submissions are OK. Prefers cassette (or videocassette if available) with 3 songs and lyric or lead sheet. SASE. Reports in 4-6 weeks.
Music: Mostly **country, gospel** and **Southern rock**; also **R&B**. Released *Stand In Woman* (by J. Powell) and *How Far Can I Fall* (by C. Powell), both recorded by D. Richards (C&W); and *Speak The Word*, written and recorded by J. Greatorex (gospel), all on Foxfire Records. Other artists include Janie Reardon, Moore & Moore, Jesse Mears, Don Pitman, Ann Marie, Tricia Elliott.
Tips: "Submit a professional studio demo—no more than 3 songs, include photo—label cassette with name/phone number."

FRESH ENTERTAINMENT, Suite 5, 1315 Simpson Rd. NW, Atlanta GA 30314. (404)642-2645. Vice President, Marketing/A&R: Willie Hunter. Record company and music publisher (Hserf Music/ASCAP, Blair Vizzion Music/BMI). Releases 5 singles and 2 LPs/year. Works with musicians/artists and songwriters on contract. Pays 7-10% royalty to artists on contract.
How to Contact: Prefers cassette (or VHS videocassette) with at least 3 songs and lyric sheet. Unsolicited submissions accepted. SASE. Reports in 2 months.

Music: Mostly **R&B, rock** and **pop**; also **jazz, gospel** and **rap**. Released "Don't Say Goodnight" (by Cirocco/Crum), recorded by Andrew Logan on Motown Records (R&B); and "Baby Make Your Move" (by Wright/Cirocco), recorded by Linus on C-Four Records (R&B). Other artists include Sir Anthony with Rare Quality and Larion.
Tips: "Be creative in packaging material."

FRESH START MUSIC MINISTRIES, Box 121616, Nashville TN 37212. (615)269-9984. President: Mark Stephan Hughes. Record company, record producer (Mark Stephan Hughes). Estab. 1989. Releases 4 LPs/year. Works with musicians/artists and songwriters on contract. Pays various royalty to artists on contract; statutory rate to publishers per song on record.
How to Contact: Submit demo tape by mail. Unsolicited submissions are OK. Prefers cassette (or VHS videocassette) with 3 songs and lyric sheet. SASE. Reports in 3-4 months.
Music: **Christian**; also **Christian praise/worship, Christian pop/rock** and **Christian R&B**. Released *You Are Exalted*, written and recorded by Mark Stephan Hughes on Fresh Start Music Ministries Records.

FRONTLINE MUSIC GROUP, Box 28450, Santa CA 92799-8450. Contact: Kenny Hicks. Labels include Frontline Records, MYX Records, Intense Records, Alarma Records. Record company, music publisher (Broken Songs/ASCAP, Carlotta Music/BMI). Estab. 1985. Releases 50 CDs/year. Works with musicians/artists and songwriters on contract. Pays statutory rate to publishers per song on record.
How to Contact: Submit demo tape by mail. Unsolicited submissions are OK. Prefers cassette (or VHS videocassette) with 3-4 songs and typed lyric sheet. Does not return unsolicited material. "We only reply on those of interest—but if you've not heard from us within 1-2 months we're not interested."
Music: Mostly **gospel/contemporary/Christian, rock/pop** and **R&B**; also **worship** and **praise**. Released "Light of Love" (by Steve Harvey/Gary Brown), recorded by Angie and Debbie Winans on Frontline Records (R&B); *Get On Up* (by Blackwell/Massey/Dunn), recorded by Scott Blackwell on MYX Records (dance); and *Shine* (by Sprinkle/Sprinkle/Hunter/Barber), recorded by Poor Ol' Lou on Alarma Records (rock). Other artists include Pete Shambrook, David Zaffiro, Mad At the World.
Tips: "Put your best songs at the top of the tape. Submit a *brief* background/history. Listen to product on the label and try writing for a specific artist. Be professional; please don't hound the label with calls."

FULLMOON ENTERTAINMENT/MOONSTONE RECORDS, 3030 Andrita St., Los Angeles CA 90065. (213)341-5959. Fax: (213)341-5960. Contact: A&R Dept. Record company, music publisher (Taley Music, BMI, Terror Tunes/ASCAP). Estab. 1991. Releases 8 CDs/year. Works with musicians/artists on record contract, songwriters on royalty contract, musicians on salary for in-house studio work. Pays negotiable royalty to artists on contract.
How to Contact: Submit demo tape by mail. Unsolicited submissions are OK. Prefers cassette (or VHS-NTSC videocassette) with 3-5 songs and lyric sheet. SASE. Reports in 1 month.
Music: Mostly **hard rock, rock** and **alternative/dance**; also **pop** and **blues**. Released *Bad Channels* (by Blue Oyster) and *Dr. Mordrid* (by Richard Band), both recorded by Blue Oyster Cult; and *Terrified*, written and recorded by Quiet Riot, all on Moonstone Records. Other artists include David Arkenstone and Pino Donnagio.
Tips: "Your songs must be competitive (in content and presentation) with the best writers out there. We are a film and record company and work with only the best—the best old pros and the best new comers."

*FUNKY MUSHROOM RECORDS, P.O. Box 100270, Brooklyn NY 11210. (718)859-0596. A&R Rep: H. Pocus. Labels include Earth Tung. Record company. Estab. 1990. Deals with artists. Releases 10 singles, 3 LPs and 15 CDs/year. Pays flat rate to artists on contract; statutory rate to publishers per song on record.
How to Contact: Submit demo tape by mail. Unsolicited submissions are OK. Prefers cassette or VHS, ¾, 8mm, Hi-8 videocassette with 4 or less songs and lyric or lead sheet. "Send press clips and include SASE for reply. Don't call." Reports in 2-4 months.
Music: Mostly **indie/alternative rock, industrial noise** and **punk/pop**; also **folk, art-jazz** and **pop.** Released *Kissyfur*, written and recorded by Susanne Lewis (rock); *The Spitters*, written and recorded by The Spitters (punk); and *Virus-23*, written and recorded by Virus-23 (industrial), all on Funky Mushroom Records. Other artists include Azalia Snail, Barbie Complex, Hot Box, God is My Copilot.
Tips: "Keep at it and don't expect a million bucks the first year."

GANVO RECORDS, P.O. Box 36152, Oklahoma City OK 73136. (405)424-8612. A&R Director: Kathy James. Record company, music publisher (Wink Two Music, BMI), record producers (LaMarr & Ria, Steve Burks and Paul E. Paul). Estab. 1988. Releases 5 12″ singles, 3 LPs/year. Works with musicians/

artists on record contract or songwriters on royalty contract. Pays 15% royalty to artists on contract; statutory rate to publisher per song on record.

How to Contact: Submit demo tape by mail. Unsolicited submissions are OK. "No calls!" Prefers cassette with 3-5 songs and lyric sheet. Does not return material. Reports in 2 weeks.

Music: Mostly **soul/R&B**, **hip hop** and **contemporary jazz**; also **R&B/rap, house** and **dance**. Released "It All Falls Down" (by LeMarr & Ria), recorded by Ava Gardner (soul/R&B); *Techs N Effect* (by Darion Haggin and Paul Cheadle), recorded by Undecided UND (rap); and *Church of Triumphant* (by Vilot Alberty), recorded by Church of Triumphant (gospel), all on Ganvo Records. Other artists include The L&M Progect, Steve Burks, Cisco.

Tips: "Demo should be the best quality possible—it does matter. We are not looking for potential, be professional."

GENERIC RECORDS, INC., 433 Limestone Rd., Ridgefield CT 06877. (203)438-9811. President: Gary Lefkowith. Labels include Outback, GLYN. Record company, music publisher (Sotto Music/BMI), record producer. Estab. 1976. Releases 1-2 singles, 1-2 12″ singles, 1 LP and 1 CD/year. Works with musicians/artists on record contract, songwriters on royalty contract or musicians on salary for in-house studio work. Pays 5% royalty to artists on contract; statutory rate to publisher per song on record.

How to Contact: Submit demo tape by mail. Unsolicited submissions are OK. Prefers cassette with 2-3 songs. SASE. Reports in 4 weeks.

Music: Mostly **alternative rock, rock** and **pop**; also **country** and **rap**. Released *Too Much Talk* (by Jeff Soloman), recorded by Urban Symphony on D.A.I. Records (CHR); *Religious*, written and recorded by No Left Stone (alternative); and "100 Ways" (by Debbie Bux/John Cox), recorded by Metro Beat (CHR), both on Generic Records.

Tips: "Concentrate on making the music great. Everything else will fall into place if you're in the groove."

GLOBAL PACIFIC RECORDS, 270 Perkins St., Sonoma CA 95476. (707)996-2748. Fax: (707)996-2658. A&R Director: Howard Sapper. Record company and music publisher (Global Pacific Publishing). Releases 10 singles, 12 LPs and 12 CDs/year. Works with musicians/artists and songwriters on contract; hires musicians for in-house studio work. Pays 9% royalty to artists on contract; statutory rate to publishers per song on record.

How to Contact: Call first and obtain permission to submit. Prefers cassette with 3 songs. "Note style of music on envelope." Does not return material. Reports in 3 months.

Music: Mostly **New Age, pop, jazz, alternative rock** and **"pop/quiet storm"**; also **rock, blues** and **classical**. Released "Mystic Fire," written and recorded by S. Kindler (jazz); "Seasons," written and recorded by M. Johnathon and "Mango Cooler," written and recorded by C.M. Brothman, all on Global Pacific Records. Other artists include Bob Kindler, David Friesen, Georgia Kelly, Ben Tavera King, Paul Greaver and Morgan Fisher.

Tips: "Write us a hit! Know your label and market you are targeting."

*GMV MUSIC ENTERPRISES, 1650 Broadway, New York NY 10019. (212)245-3703. Vice President: Steve Camhi. Labels include GMV Records. Record company, record producer and music publisher. Estab. 1991. Deals with artists and songwriters. Releases 6 singles, 6 12″ singles, 3 LPs, 3 EPs and 6 CDs/year. Pays 5% royalty to artists on contract; statutory rate to publisher per song on record.

How to Contact: Submit demo tape by mail. Unsolicited submissions are OK. Prefers cassette with 4 songs. SASE. Reports in 1 month.

Music: Mostly **rap, R&B** and **dance**. Released "Don't Doubt the Clout," written and recorded by Elite (rap); "Tonite Tonite" (by E. Chiprut), recorded by The Ovations (dance); and "What You Think About Love" (by E. Chiprut), recorded by The Magic Triplets (dance), all on GMV Records.

*GODMAN MUSIC AND PUBLICATIONS, #408, 46 Edgeworth St., Worcester MA 01605. (508)757-1551. President: David B. Schroder. Record company, music publisher. Estab. 1992. Releases 1 LP and 1 CD/year. Pays 5-10% royalty to artists on contract; statutory rate to publisher per song on record.

How to Contact: Write or call first and obtain permission to submit. Prefers cassette or VHS video-cassette with 4 songs and lyric sheet. Does not return material. Reports in 1 month.

Music: Mostly **alternative rock, hard rock** and **techno**; also **hard core rock** and **rap**. Released *You're Soakinginit* (by Life Goes Wrong), recorded by Godman on Godman Records (alternative).

GOLD CITY RECORDS, INC., Box 24, Armonk NY 10504. (914)273-6457. President: Chris Jasper. Vice President/General Counsel: Margie Jasper. Labels include Gold City Label. Record company. Estab. 1986. Releases 5-10 singles, 5-10 12″ singles, 3-5 LPs and 3-5 CDs/year. Works with musicians/artists and songwriters on contract and hires musicians for in-house studio work. Pays statutory rate to publisher per song on record.

How to Contact: Submit demo tape by mail. Unsolicited submissions are OK. Prefers cassette with 3 songs and lyric sheets. SASE. Reports in 3-4 weeks.
Music: Mostly **R&B/gospel**. Released *Praide The Eternal* and *Forever*, written and recorded by Chris Jasper; and *Outfront*, written and recorded by Outfront, all on Gold City Records.

GOLDBAND RECORDS, Box 1485, Lake Charles LA 70602. (318)439-8839. President: Eddie Shuler. Labels include Folk-Star, Tek, Tic-Toc, Anla, Jador and Luffcin Records. Record company, music publisher (TEK Publishing) and record producer. Works with artists and songwriters on contract; musicians on salary for in-house studio work. Pays 3-5% royalty to artists on contract; statutory royalty to publishers per song on record.
How to Contact: Submit demo tape by mail. Unsolicited submissions are OK. Prefers cassette with 2-6 songs and lyric sheet. SASE. Reports in 2 months.
Music: Blues, country, easy listening, folk, **R&B,** rock and **top 40/pop**. Released "How Could You," written and recorded by Bobbie McDowell on Goldband Records; "Rock My Baby Tonight," written and recorded by Johnny Jano and "Ready Ready," written and recorded by Rockin Joe Viator, both on Ace Records.

GOLDEN TRIANGLE RECORDS, 1051 Saxonburg Blvd., Glenshaw PA 15116. Producer: Sunny James. Labels include Rockin Robin and Shell-B. Music publisher (Golden Triangle/BMI) and record producer (Sunny James). Estab. 1987. Releases 8 singles, 6 12″ singles, 10 LPs and 19 CDs/year. Works with musicians/artists and songwriters on contract and hires musicians for in-house studio work. Pays 10% royalty to artists on contract; statutory rate to publishers per song on record.
How to Contact: Submit demo tape by mail. Unsolicited submissions are OK. Prefers cassette, 15 IPS reel-to-reel (or ½″ VHS videocassette) with 3 songs and lyric or lead sheets. SASE. Reports in 1 month.
Music: Mostly **progressive R&B, rock** and A/C; also **jazz** and **country**. Released "Astor" (by S. Bittner), recorded by P. Bittner on Shell-B Records (rock); "Those No's" (by R. Cvetnick), recorded by J. Morello on Rockin Robin Records (R&B); and "Most of All" (by F. Johnson), recorded by The Marcels on Golden Triangle Records (A/C). Other artists include The original Mr. Bassman Fred Johnson of the Marcels (Blue Moon).

GOLDWAX RECORD CO., INC., Suite 325, 3181 Poplar Ave., Memphis TN 38130-0166. (901)458-2285. A&R: Jimmy Willis. Labels include Bandstand, Beale Street, Abec and Rap-N-Wax. Record company, music publisher (Bianca Music/BMI, Rodanca Music/ASCAP). Estab. 1964. Releases 50 singles, 20 12″ singles, 50 LPs and 30 CDs/year. Works with musicians/artists on record contract or songwriters on royalty contract. Pays standard royalty to artists on contract; statutory rate to publisher per song on record.
How to Contact: Submit demo tape by mail. Unsolicited submissions are OK. Prefers cassette (or VHS videocassette if available) with 3-4 songs and lyric sheet. SASE. Reports in 6 weeks.
Music: Mostly **R&B, country** and **rock;** also **blues** and **gospel**. Released "Nothing Between Us" (by Frank Longo), recorded by Lauralea; "Walk A Way" (by Ollie Hoskins), recorded by Percy Milem; and "Burn, Make It" (by Darrell Coats), recorded by Total Package, all on Goldwax Records. Other artists include Black Oak Arkansas, Ruby Andrews, Santana Milem, Black Is Black, B.C.D. Garfield.

GOPACO LIMITED, P.O. Box 664, Lombard IL 60148. Managing Director: Neale Parker. Labels include Griffin Music. Record company. Estab. 1988. Releases 15 LPs and 15 CDs/year. Works with musicians/artists on records contract. Pays 18% royalty to artists on contract; statutory rate to publisher per song on record.
How to Contact: Submit demo tape by mail. Unsolicited submissions are OK. Prefers cassette with 4-6 songs. SASE. Reports in 4-6 weeks.
Music: Mostly **classic rock, pop** and **heavy metal**. Released *Pigpen's Birthday*, written and recorded by Fish (ex-Marillion); "Close to the Hyde," written and recorded by John Anderson (ex-Yes); and *Parker's Birthday* (by D. Moug), recorded by UFO, all on Griffin Records. Other artists include Pendragon, Hawkwind, Roy Harper, Eddie Clarke (ex-Motorhead), Hugh Cornwall (ex-Stranglers), Grace, Grey Lady Down.
Tips: "We are looking mainly for groups with a good press repertoire."

How to Get the Most Out of Songwriter's Market (at the front of this book) contains comments and suggestions to help you understand and use the information in these listings.

GORDON MUSIC CO. INC., P.O. Box 2250, Canoga Park CA 91306. (818)883-8224. A&R: Barney Gordon. Labels include Paris Records. Record company, music publisher. Estab. 1981. Releases 4 singles, 2 LPs and 2 CDs/year. Works with musicians/artists on record contract or songwriters on royalty contract.
How to Contact: Call first and obtain permission to submit. Prefers cassette (or VHS videocassette if available) with 3-4 songs and lyric sheet or lead sheet. Does not return material. Reports in 1 month.
Music: Mostly **children's**, **country-western** and **pop**; also **jazz**. Released *Izzy: Pest of West*, written and recorded by Champ; *I'm a Google* (by Champ), and "Armor Woman" (by J.G. Elliot), recorded by The Googles, all on Paris Records (children's).

GRASS ROOTS RECORD & TAPE/LMI RECORDS, Box 532, Malibu CA 90265. (213)463-5998. President: Lee Magid. Record company, record producer, music publisher (Alexis/ASCAP, Marvelle/BMI, Lou-Lee/BMI) and management firm (Lee Magid Management Co.). Member AIMP, NARAS. Estab. 1967. Releases 4 LPs and 4 CDs/year. Works with musicians/artists and songwriters on contract. Pays 2-5% royalty to artists on contract; pays statutory rate to publishers per song on record.
How to Contact: Submit demo tape by mail. Unsolicited submissions are OK. Prefers cassette with 3 songs and lyric sheet. "Please, no 45s." SASE. Reports in 6-8 weeks.
Music: Mostly **pop/rock**, **R&B**, **country**, **gospel**, **jazz/rock** and **blues**; also **bluegrass**, **children's** and **Latin**. Released "A Mighty Hand" (by C. Rhone), recorded by Tramaine Hawkins on Sony Records (gospel); "Sweet & Lovely," written and recorded by Pet Cameron on LMI Records (reggae); and "He's Always There," (by J.M. Hides), recorded by Tata Vega on Quest Records (pop). Other artists include John Michael Hides, Julie Miller.

*GREEN BEAR RECORDS, 3200 Peoria, Steger IL 60475. (708)754-4869. President: George J. Skupien. Labels include Green One Records and Bear Tracks Records. Record company, music publisher (Green One Music/BMI), and record producer (George Skupien). Estab. 1992. Releases 3-4 singles, 1-10 LPs and 2-6 CDs/year. Pays 10% royalty to artists on contract; statutory rate to publisher per song on record.
How to Contact: Submit demo tape by mail. Unsolicited submissions are OK. Prefers cassette (or DAT if available) with 4-6 songs and lyric or lead sheet. Does not return material. Reports in 6-8 weeks.
Music: Mostly **polkas**, **waltzes** and **country**; also **Southern gospel**, **MOR** and **light rock**. Released "My Last Cowboy Song," written and recorded by George Skupien (country); "An American Tradition" (by George Skupien), recorded by The Stagemen (polka); and "Keep On Keepin' On," written and recorded by Matt Row'd (country), all on Green Bear Records. Other artists include D. Mack, B. Jackson, Ted Thomas, Rudy Negron and The Mystics.
Tips: "Submit a well-produced, studio quality demo of your material on cassette or DAT with a clean vocal up front. If possible, submit your demo with and without lead vocal for presentation to recording artists."

*G-TOWN RECORDS, P.O. Box 460086, Garland TX 75046. (214)497-1616. President: Lonny Schonfeld. Record company, record producer and music publisher (Lonny Tunes/BMI). Estab. 1988. Deals with artists and songwriters. Releases 8-10 singles, 8-10 LPs and 2 CDs/year. Pays 40% (of wholesale) to artists on contract; statutory rate to publisher per song on record.
How to Contact: Submit demo tape by mail. Unsolicited submissions are OK. Prefers cassette or VHS videocassette with 3-5 songs and lyric sheet. "Professional quality only." Does not return material. Reports in 6-8 weeks.
Music: Mostly **country**, **children's** and **rock**; also **jazz** and **comedy**. Released "Baby, With You" (by L. Schonfeld/R. Stout) and "Loneliness," written and recorded by Randy Stout (pop), all on G-Town Records. Other artists include Charlie Shearer, Doug Richardson.

FRANK GUBALA MUSIC, 41 Hillside Rd., Cumberland RI 02864. (401)333-6097. Contact: Frank Gubala. Music publisher and record producer. Estab. 1962. Works with musicians/artists on record contract, songwriters on royalty contract.
How to Contact: Submit demo tape by mail. Unsolicited submissions are OK. Prefers cassette with 1 song and lyric or lead sheet. Does not return material. Reports in 2 months.
Music: Mostly **pop** and **contemporary**; also **C&W**.

*GUESTSTAR RECORDS, 17321 Ritchie Ave. NE, Sand Lake MI 49343-9475. President: Raymond G. Dietz, Sr. Record company, record producer and music publisher (Sandlake Music/BMI). Estab. 1967. Deals with artists and songwriters. Releases 8 singles, 2 LPs and 2 CDs/year. Royalty varies to artist on contract, "depending on number of selections on product; 2 ½¢/song."
How to Contact: Submit demo tape by mail. Unsolicited submissions are OK. Prefers cassette (or VHS videocassette) with lyric and lead sheet. "Send a SASE with submissions." Does not return material. Reports in 1 week.

Music: Mostly **country rock** and **country**; also **religious/country** and **mountain songs**. Released *Best of Mountain Man* (by Mike Gillette/Raymond Dietz); "Old Man From the Mountain" (by Meryl Haggard); and "When Jesus Comes" (by Ray Dietz), all recorded by Mountain Man on Gueststar Records (country). Other artists include Jamie "K" and Sweetgrass Band.
Tips: "Songwriters: send songs like you hear on the radio. Keep updating your music to keep up with the latest trends. Artists: send VHS video and press kit."

*GUITAR RECORDINGS, 10 Midland Ave., Port Chester NY 10573. (914)935-5200. Fax: (914)937-0614. Contact: Label Director. Labels include Guitar Acoustic, Classic Cuts. Record company. Estab. 1989. Deals with artists and songwriters. Releases 4-6 cassettes and 4-6 CDs/year.
How to Contact: Submit demo tape by mail. Unsolicited submissions are OK. Prefers cassette with 3 songs. Include bio, photo, press kit. SASE. Reports in 6 months.
Music: Mostly **rock, classic/blues** and **jazz/acoustic**; also **alternative**. Released *HAT*, written and recorded by Mike Keneally on Guitar Recordings (rock/alternative); *Walter Ego*, written and recorded by Sy Klopps Blues Band on Classic Cuts (blues); and *Shearwater*, written and recorded by Pete Kennedy on Guitar Acoustics (jazz/acoustic). Other artists include Brad Gillis, Mark Wood, Blues Saraceno.
Tips: "Submit your best (original) material, with no excuses! We send out rejection letters, so please do not call for an update on your demo."

HALLWAY INTERNATIONAL RECORDS/1ST COAST POSSE, 8010 International Village Dr., Jacksonville FL 32211. (904)765-8276. Record company, music publisher (Aljoni Music Co./BMI, Hallmarque Musical Works, Ltd./ASCAP), record producer (Hallways to Fame Productions) and video makers (Cosmic Eye). Estab. 1971. Releases 4-6 singles, 8 12″ singles and 6 LPs/year. Works with musicians/artists on record contract, songwriters on royalty contract. Royalty negotiated per contract.
How to Contact: Submit demo tape by mail. Unsolicited submissions are OK. Prefers cassette (or VHS videocassette) with 2-4 songs and lyric or lead sheet. Does not return material. Reports in 6-8 weeks.
Music: Mostly **rap, R&B** and **jazz**; also **world** (others will be considered). Released "Dash 4 Da Cash," written and recorded by Al Money on MCM/1st Coast Posse Records (rap); and "ABAFU (Clouds)" (by Al Hall Jr.), recorded by Cosmos Dwellers on Hallway International Records (world jazz). Other artists include Akshun Jaxon, GPH₂N, Da Hood.
Tips: "Rap, R&B-dance, jazz-world is what we do best—so, send your best and we'll do the rest!!"

HALOGRAM, 23 Market St., Passaic NJ 07055. (201)777-6109. President: Tomasito Bobadilla. Record company. Estab. 1989. Releases 6 singles, 6 12″ singles, 3 LPs and 1 EP/year. Works with musicians/artists on record contract, musicians on salary for in-house studio work. Pays 6-8% royalty to artist on contract; statutory rate to publisher per song on record.
How to Contact: Submit demo tape by mail. Unsolicited submissions are OK. Prefers cassette with 3 songs and lyric or lead sheet. SASE.
Music: Mostly **dance, alternative rock** and **pop**; also **R&B** and **New Age**. Released "Invasion" (by Cool Say), recorded by Say Cees (dance); and "Dirty Laundry" (by Concept One), recorded by Dirty Laundry (dance), both on Halogram Records. Other artists include Lori Adams, Bettye Jordan and 3 Men on Moon Trip.

HAPPY MAN RECORDS, Box 73, 4501 Spring Creek Dr., Bonita Springs FL 33923. (813)947-6978. Executive Producer: Dick O'Bitts. Labels include Condor, Con Air. Record company, music publisher (Rocker Music/BMI, Happy Man Music/ASCAP) and record producer (Rainbow Collection Ltd.). Estab. 1972. Releases 4-6 singles, 4-6 12″ singles, 4-6 LPs and 4 EPs/year. Pays standard royalty to artists on contract; statutory rate to publishers per song on record.
How to Contact: Submit demo tape by mail. Unsolicited submissions are OK. Prefers cassette (or VHS videocassette) with 3-4 songs and lyric sheet. SASE. Reports in 4 weeks.
Music: **All types.** Released *You Gotta Hit Them Hard*, written and recorded by Challengers (country); *4 More For the Road*, written and recorded by Overdue (rock); and *God's Got Time to Listen* (by Archie Johnson), recorded by Bengsters, all on Happy Man Records. Other artists include Ray Pack.

*HAPPY TAILS RECORDS, P.O. Box 5467, Evanston IL 60204. (708)866-9544. President: Brent Ritzel. Labels include Crank Records. Record company and magazine (Tail Spins). Estab. 1990. Releases 2 singles, 2 LPs and 4 CDs/year.
How to Contact: Submit demo tape by mail. Unsolicited submissions are OK. Prefers cassette. Does not return material.
Music: Mostly **alternative rock, punk** and **pop**. Released *Springfield, U.S.A.*, written and recorded by the Charming Beggars (alternative rock); *Play Dead*, written and recorded by Doghouse (alternative rock); and *Free Fest 1993*, written and recorded by various artists (alternative rock), all on Happy Tails

Records. Other artists include Avocado Jungle Fuzz, Fig Dish, Rustbucket, Word of Mouth and These Days.

HARMONY STREET RECORDS, Box 4107, Kansas City, KS 66104. (913)299-2881. President: Charlie Beth. Record company, music publisher (Harmony Street Music/ASCAP and Harmony Lane Music/BMI), and record producer (Harmony Street Productions). Estab. 1985. Releases 15-30 singles, 4-6 LPs and 3-5 CDs/year. Works with musicians/artists and songwriters on contract; musicians on salary for in-house studio work. Pays 10% royalty (retail) to artists on contract; pays statutory rate to publishers per song on record.
How to Contact: Prefers cassette (or VHS videocassette) with no more than 3 songs and lyric or lead sheet. OK for artists to submit album projects, etc., on cassette. Also photo and bio if possible. "Due to the large amount of submissions that we receive we are no longer able to return unsolicited material. We will report within 6 weeks if interested. Please include a full address and telephone number in all submitted packages."
Music: Mostly **country, gospel, rockabilly, pop, R&B, bluegrass** and **rock.** Released "Smooth Talkin' Man" (by Terry Allen & Sue Mahurin), recorded by Terry Allen (country); "If She Leaves and My Heart When She Goes" (by Edna Mae Foy and Val Zudell), recorded by Tony Mantor (country); "Like the Flip of a Coin" (by Woody Waldrop), recorded by Woody Wills (country), all on Harmony Street Records. Other artists include Scott Hansgen, The Dusters, Terry Diebold and Georgia Carr.
Tips: "Songs submitted to us must be original, commercial and have a good strong hook. Submit only your best songs. Demos should be clear and clean with voice out front. We are interested in working with commercial artists with a commercial style and sound, professional attitude and career goals. Our records are released world wide and also available for sales world wide. Our standards are high and so are our goals."

HEATH & ASSOCIATES, #1058, E. Saint Catherine, Louisville KY 40204. (502)637-2877. General Partner: John V. Heath. Labels include Hillview Records and Estate Records. Record company, music publisher (Two John's Music/ASCAP), record producer (MVT Productions and Just a Note/BMI). Estab. 1979. Releases 8-10 singles, 3 12″ singles, 4-5 LPs, 3 EPs and 3 CDs/year. Pays 10% royalty to artists on contract; statutory rate to publisher per song on record.
How to Contact: Write or call first and obtain permission to submit. Prefers cassette, 7½ ips reel-to-reel or VHS videocassette with 3 songs and lead sheets. SASE. Reports in 1 month.
Music: Mostly **pop, country, R&B** and **MOR;** also **gospel.** Released "Dry Those Tears," written and recorded by Donald Dodd on Hillview Records (MOR); "Hot," written and recorded by The Word on Estate Records (gospel); and "Crazy Trucker," written and recorded by Michael Palko on Hillview Records (country). Other artists include Terry Burton, Moody and Louisville.
Tips: "Be professional in submissions."

HERITAGE MUSIC, #311, 41 Antrim Cr., Scarborough Ontario M1P4T1 **Canada.** (416)292-4724. President: Jack Boswell. Record company (Condor-Oak). Estab. 1967. Deals with artists and songwriters. Produces 10-15 cassettes/CDs/year.
How to Contact: Submit demo tape by mail. Unsolicited submissions are OK.
Music: Interested in **instrumental** fiddle, steel guitar, Dobro, piano, etc. Also **country gospel, yodel, square dance, bluegrass.**

HIBI DEI HIPP RECORDS, #4872, 311 W. Monroe St., Jacksonville FL 32202. (904)448-3534. Producer: Aubrey Saulsby. Record company, music publisher (WASMC/BMI). Estab. 1986. Releases 4-6 singles, 2 12″ singles, 1 LP, 1 EP and 1 CD/year. Works with musicians/artists and songwriters on contract and hires musicians for in-house studio work. Pays standard royalty.
How to Contact: Write and obtain permission to submit. Prefers cassette 9 or 7½″ reel with 3 songs and lyric sheet. Does not return unsolicited material.
Music: Mostly **R&B, rap** and **jazz;** also **blues, pop** and **top/40.** Released "Because You're Mine" and "Free," both recorded by William Icey; and "The Way That I Am," recorded by Willie Bones, all written by Willie A. Saulsby (R&B). Other artists include Hob Slob, King William.

HICKORY LANE PUBLISHING AND RECORDING, P.O. Box 2275, Vancouver, British Columbia V6B 3W5 **Canada.** (604)465-1408. President: Chris Michaels. A&R Manager: David Rogers. Labels include Hickory Lane Records. Record company, music publisher and record producer. Estab. 1985. Releases 3 singles, 3 LPs and 3 CDs/year. Works with musicians/artists on record contract. Pays standard rate royalty to artists on contract; statutory rate to publisher per song on record.
How to Contact: Submit demo tape by mail. Unsolicited submissions are OK. Prefers cassette (or VHS videocassette if available) with 1-5 songs and lyric sheet or lead sheet (if available). SAE and IRC. Reports in 6 weeks.
Music: Mostly **country, MOR** and **gospel;** also **soft rock, musical compositions** and **children's music.** Released *Country Drives Me Wild*, written and recorded by Chris Michaels; *Until Now* (by Steve Mitch-

ell and Chris Michaels), recorded by Chris Michaels; and *Tear and Tease* (by Parmjit Dawa), recorded by Chris Michaels and Steve Mitchell, all on Hickory Lane Records.
Tips: "Send original songs, only your best. Have a good demo with vocals up front. Write and rewrite."

HOLLYROCK RECORDS, Suite C-300, 16776 Lakeshore Dr., Lake Elsinore CA 92330. A&R Director: Dave Paton. Record company, record producer and music publisher (Heaven Songs/BMI). Releases 4 singles and 6 LPs/year. Works with artists and songwriters on contract; musicians on salary for in-house studio work. Pays negotiable royalty to artists on contract; statutory rate to publishers for each record sold.
How to Contact: Submit demo tape by mail. Unsolicited submissions are OK. Prefers 7½ ips reel-to-reel or cassette with 3-6 songs and lyric sheet. SASE. Reports in 1 month.
Music: Progressive, **top 40/pop, country, easy listening, folk, jazz, MOR** and **rock.** Released *Big Gonzo* (by Big "D"), recorded by Lunas (rock); and *Yesterday and Today*, written and recorded by Brett Duncan, both on Hollyrock Records.

*HOLOGRAPHIC RECORDS, P.O. Box 14121, Cincinnati OH 45214. (513)542-9525. Artist Relations: Brooks Jordan. Record company. Estab. 1984. Deals with artists and songwriters. Releases 2-5 singles, 3-5 LPs, 0-5 EPs and 3-5 CDs/year. Royalty is negotiable.
How to Contact: Submit demo tape by mail. Unsolicited submissions are OK. Prefers cassette with 3-4 songs and lyric sheet. "Send bio, press clippings, any other important info." SASE. Reports in 1 month.
Music: Mostly **modern rock, progressive rock** and **fusion rock;** also **country.** Released *James & The Acumen* (by James/Sfarnas),recorded by James & The Acumen (modern rock); *Think* (by James Sfarnas), recorded by Acumen; and "Deeper Green" (by Brad Stenz), recorded by Moth, all on Holographic Records. Other artists include One Mint Julep.
Tips: "Send very best songs, and place best song 1st on cassette."

HOMEBASED ENTERTAINMENT CO., 96 St. James Ave., Springfield MA 01109. (413)746-8302. President: Timothy Scott. Labels include Night Owl Records, Second Time Around Records, Southend-Essex Records. Record company. Estab. 1993. Releases 3 singles, 2 LPs and 2 CDs/year. Works with musicians/artists on record contract, songwriters on royalty contract, musicians on salary for in-house studio work. Pays 10-15% royalty to artists on contract; statutory rate to publisher per song on record.
How to Contact: Submit demo tape by mail. Unsolicited submissions are OK. Prefers cassette (or VHS videocassette) with 3-5 songs and lyric sheet. SASE. Reports in 2 months.
Music: Mostly **pop, R&B,** and **rap;** also **country, rock** and **gospel.** Released "Faithful" and "Holding On" (by Johnnie Hatchett), recorded by Physical Attraction; and "Cable TV is Just a Joke," written and recorded by Tim Scott, all on Night Owl Records. Other artists include Big Shot DoJo, D.J. Smoothe.

HOMESTEAD RECORDS, Box 800, Rockville Centre NY 11570. (516)764-6200. A&R Director: Steven Joerg. Record company. Estab. 1983. Releases 12 singles, 12 LPs, 2 EPs and 12 CDs/year. Works with musicians/artists on contract. Pays 10-13% royalty to artists on contract; ¾ of statutory rate to publisher per song on record.
How to Contact: Submit demo tape by mail. Unsolicited submissions are OK. Prefers cassette with 4 songs. Does not return material. Reports in 2-3 months.
Music: Mostly **punk rock** and **rock.** Artists include Trumans Water, Babe the Blue Ox, Sleepyhead, Pony and Tara Key.

HORIZON RECORDING STUDIO, Rt. 1 Box 306, Seguin TX 78155. (512)372-2923. Studio Manager: Mark Rubenstein. Labels include Route One Records. Record company, music publisher (BMI). Estab. 1989. Works with songwriters on royalty contract or musicians on salary for in-house studio work. Pays 5% royalty to artists on contract.
How to Contact: Submit demo tape by mail. Unsolicited submissions are OK, write first to arrange personal interview. Prefers cassette (or VHS videocassette if available) with 6 songs and lyric sheet. Does not return material. Reports in 2 months.
Music: Mostly **pop, country** and **gospel;** also **R&B** and **jazz.** Artists include Mike Lord and Tom Gruning.
Tips: "Be persistent but patient."

*HORIZON RECORDS, P.O. Box 465, Coram NY 11727. (516)732-6975. Fax: (516)732-7125. Owner: Michael Ugarte. Labels include Landford Records. Record company and music publisher (State 51 Music). Estab. 1993. Deals with artists and songwriters. Releases 2 singles, 2 12″ singles, 2 LPs, 2 EPs and 2 CDs/year. Pays statutory rate to publishers per song on record.

How to Contact: Submit demo tape by mail. Unsolicited submissions are OK. Prefers cassette (or VHS videocassette if available) with 3 songs and lyric sheet. Does not return material. Reports in 4-6 weeks.
Music: Mostly **R&B**, **pop** and **dance**; also **Latin**. Released *Over the Rainbow* (by various), recorded by The Demensions on Landford Records.

HOTTRAX RECORDS, 1957 Kilburn Dr., Atlanta GA 30324. (404)662-6661. Vice President, A&R: Oliver Cooper. Labels include Dance-A-Thon, Hardkor. Record company and music publisher (Starfox Publishing). Releases 12 singles and 3-4 CDs/year. Works with musicians/artists and songwriters on contract. Pays 5-7% royalty to artists on contract.
How to Contact: Prefers cassette with 3 songs and lyric sheet. SASE. "We will not return tapes without adequate postage." Reports in 3 months. "When submissions get extremely heavy, we do not have the time to respond/return material we pass on. We do notify those sending the most promising work we review, however."
Music: Mostly **top 40/pop**, **rock** and **country**; also **hardcore punk** and **jazz-fusion**. Released *Introducing The Feel*, written and recorded by The Feel (new rock) on Hottrax Records; "The Condom Man," recorded by Big Al Jano and "Ms. Perfection," by Larry Yates (urban contemporary). Other artists include Burl Compton (country), Michael Rozakis & Yorgos (pop), Starfoxx (rock), The Night Shadows (rock), The Bop (new wave), Secret Lover, The Bob Page Project (blues/jazz) and Roger "Hurricane" Wilson (blues rock).

*HYPERNORMAL RECORDS, P.O. Box 2384, Noroton Heights CT 06820. A&R Dept: John. Record company, music publisher (Dolce Ojo/BMI). Estab. 1991. Releases 1-2 singles, 1 LP and 1 CD/year. Pays negotiable royalty to artists on contract.
How to Contact: Write first and obtain permission to submit. Prefers cassette with 3 songs and lyric sheet. SASE. Reports in 2-3 months.
Music: Mostly **rock, pop** and **acoustic**. Released *Beat Pioneer*, *Aimlessly* and *Long Gone*, written and recorded by John Bowman on Hypernormal Records (rock). Other artists include Jon Goodloe and David Swartz.
Tips: "Be professional with submitted material! Must be willing and able to tour!"

*I WANNA RECORDS, P.O. Box 303 W.B.B., Dayton OH 45409. (513)228-4136. Label Manager: Nicholas C. Kizirnis. Record company. Estab. 1985. Deals with artists only. Releases 2 singles, 1 LPs, 2 EPs and 2 CDs/year. "Royalties are based on each project."
How to Contact: Submit demo tape by mail. Unsolicited submissions are OK. Prefers cassette or VHS videocassette with 3-4 songs. "Please include as much info on band as possible, as well as what the band is doing currently." SASE. Reports in 1 month.
Music: Mostly **alternative/underground**, **experimental** and **singer-songwriter**; also **surf/rockabilly**. Released "In Stereo," recorded by Cage (alternative); "Two Thumbs Down" and *Rock'n'Roll in the Big City*, recorded by The Obvious, all on I Wanna Records. Other artists include Sourbelly, Real Lulu, Nicky Kay and the Mulchmen, Gregg Spence.
Tips: "We are a small label working on projects that vary in scale. We listen to everything and do our best to respond by mail, so please don't call about submissions. We are also involved in booking, and helping people make contacts around the midwest."

ICHIBAN RECORDS, 3991 Royal Dr. NW, Kennesaw GA 30144. General Manager Publishing: Bryan Cole. Labels include Wrap, Wild Dog. Record company, music publisher (Koke, Moke and Noke Music, BMI), record producer. Estab. 1982. Releases 50 LPs and 50 CDs/year. Works with musicians/artists on record contract, songwriters on royalty contract. Pays various royalties to artists on contract; statutory rate to publisher per song on record.
How to Contact: Submit demo tape by mail. Unsolicited submissions are OK. Prefers cassette with 4 songs and lyric sheet. SASE. Reports in 2 months.
Music: Mostly **R&B**, **60's style soul** and **blues**; also **alternative rock** and **rock**. Released *Something Mighty Wrong*, recorded by Tyrone Davis on Ichiban Records (soul/R&B); *Party Tuff or Stay Home*, recorded by The Shadows on Wild Dog Records (blues); and *Power Stance*, recorded by Fleshtones on Naked Language (alternative).
Tips: "Research the people you're sending songs to know what they do—for example, don't send a country song to M.C. Hammer."

*IMPS MUSIC, 70 Rt. 202-N, Peterboro NH 03458. (603)924-0058. Sales/A&R: Don Fluckinger. Labels include GWE, Greener Pastures, Adventures in Music. Record company, pressing brokerage. Estab. 1960. Deals with artists and songwriters. Releases 10 EPs and 50 CDs/year. Pays 10-15% royalty to artists on contract; statutory rate to publisher per song on record.
How to Contact: Submit demo tape by mail. Unsolicited submissions are OK. Prefers CDs. Does not return material.

Music: Mostly **alternative rock, pop/rock** and **blues**; also **jazz, folk** and **New Age**. Released *Complete Scott Joplin* (by Joplin), recorded by Scott Kirby on GPR Records (ragtime); *Blacker Than That* (by various), recorded by Black Rock Coalition (funk/rock/rap); and *Larry Mitchell*, written and recorded by Larry Mitchell on IMPS Records (instrumental rock).
Tips: "We'll call you if we like it. We'll like it if it's not derivative drivel."

*INFERNO RECORDS, P.O. Box 28743, Kansas City MO 64118. (816)454-7638. A&R Director: Mark Murtha. Record company. Estab. 1989. Deals with artists and songwriters. Releases 6 LPs, 4 EPs and 4 CDs/year. Pays negotiable royalty to artists on contract; statutory rate to publishers per song on record.
How to Contact: Submit demo tape by mail. Unsolicited submissions are OK. Prefers cassette with 4 songs. SASE. Reports in 1 month.
Music: Mostly **rock, alternative** and **country**. Released *Rock Collection Vol. 3*, written and recorded by various artists (rock); *Wet*, written and recorded by Crazy River (rock); and *See Eye to Eye*, written and recorded by CI2I (dance), all on Inferno Records. Other artists include London Drive, Shadowed Fate, Lovedog, Sedition, Atomic Angel, Darkside, Forbidden Forest, Possession and Wyred.
Tips: "Be original, be yourself. Don't be afraid to be different. We're looking for unique talent and songwriting that has a message."

*INSTINCT RECORDS, #502, 26 W. 17th, New York NY 10011. Contact: A&R. Labels include Sonic Records, Liquid Music, Kickin' USA. Record company. Estab. 1989. Deals with artists only. Releases 18 singles, 18 12″ singles, 24 LPs, 6 EPs and 30 CDs/year.
How to Contact: Submit demo tape by mail. Unsolicited submissions are OK. Prefers cassette. "Name, address and phone on cassette label." Does not return material.
Music: Mostly **rave, ambient** and **house**; also **acid jazz, dance** and **pop**. Released *Moby*, written and recorded by Moby; *Plasticity*, written and recorded by Cabaret Voltaire; and *CFM Band*, written and recorded by CFM Band, all on Instinct Records. Other artists include Human Mesh Dance, Omicron, Evolve Now, Prototype 909.

INTERSTATE 40 RECORDS, 9208 Spruce Mountain Way, Las Vegas NV 89134. (702)363-8506. President: Eddie Lee Carr. Labels include Tracker Records. Record company and music publisher (Watchesgro Music/BMI and Watch Us Climb/ASCAP). Estab. 1979. Releases 12 singles, 1 LP and 2 CDs/year. Works with musicians/artists on contract. Pays 50% royalty to artists on contract; statutory rate to publisher per song on record.
How to Contact: Submit demo tape by mail. Unsolicited submissions are OK. Prefers cassette with 3 songs. SASE. Reports in 2 weeks.
Music: Mostly **country**. Movie and TV credits include "Young Guns of Texas," "Story of Evil Knievel," "Alias Smith & Jones," "The Christopher Columbus Story" and "Cochise."

*INTREPID RECORDS, Ste. 1409, 808 Travis, Houston TX 77002. Director of Operations: Rick Eyk. Record company and record producer (Rick Eyk).
How to Contact: Submit demo tape by mail. Unsolicited submissions are OK. Prefers cassette (or VHS videocassette) with maximum of 7 songs, lyric sheet and bio. SASE. Reports in 1 month.
Music: Mostly **rock, country** and **jazz**; also **classical, gospel** and **blues**. Recent recording schedule includes Downtown Bruno, E.J. Silks, Elise Ditmar, Tom Wood, Bobby Holland and Charlie Anderson.
Tips: "Currently seeking finished masters for distribution."

JALYN RECORDING CO., 306 Millwood Dr., Nashville TN 37217. (615)366-9999. President: Jack Lynch. Labels include Nashville Bluegrass and Nashville Country Recording Company. Record company, music publisher (Jaclyn Music/BMI), record producer, film company (Nashville Country Productions) and distributor (Nashville Music Sales). Estab. 1963. Releases 1-12 LPs/year. Works with musicians/artists and songwriters on contract; hires musicians for in-house studio work; also produces custom sessions. Pays 5-10% royalty to artists on contract; statutory rate to publisher per song on record.
How to Contact: Submit demo tape by mail. Unsolicited submissions are OK. Prefers cassette with 1-4 songs and lyric sheet. SASE. Reports in 1 month.
Music: Country, **bluegrass, gospel** and **MOR**. Released "Hand Me My Heart" and "The Man With All the Gold" (by Timpy/Overton); and "I Sure Did Lose A Lot" (by Chuck Timpy), all recorded by Chuck Timpy on Jalyn Records (country).
Tips: "Send good performance on cassette, bio, picture and SASE."

JAMAKA RECORD CO., 3621 Heath Ln., Mesquite TX 75150. (214)279-5858. Contact: Jimmy Fields. Labels include Felco and Kick Records. Record company, record producer and music publisher (Cherie Music/BMI). Estab. 1955. Releases 2 singles/year. Works with artists and songwriters on contract; hires musicians for in-house studio work. Works with in-house studio musicians on salary. Pays .05% royalty to artists on contract; statutory rate to publishers for each record sold.

How to Contact: Prefers cassette with lyric sheet. "A new singer should send a good tape with at least 4 strong songs, presumably recorded in a professional studio." Does not return without return postage and proper mailing package.

Music: **Country** and **progressive country**. Released "Cajun Baby Blues" and "If You Call This Loving," recorded by Steve Pride.

Tips: "Songs should have strong lyrics with a good story, whether country or pop."

J&J MUSICAL ENTERPRISES LTD., P.O. Box 575, Kings Park NY 11754. (212)691-5630. Contact: Frances Cavezza. Labels include JAJ Records. Record company and record production. Estab. 1983. Releases 2-3 singles, 1-2 12" singles, 1-2 LPs, 1-2 EPs and 1-2 CDs/year. Works with musicians/artists on contract and hires musicians for in-house studio work. Pays variable royalty.

How to Contact: Write first and obtain permission to submit. Prefers cassette with 4 songs and lyric sheet. SASE. Reports in 3-4 weeks. "Typed letters preferred."

Music: Mostly **progressive** and **jazz**. Released "Jumpers," "The Scribe" and "Clutch," all written and recorded by Jeneane Claps on JAJ Records (jazz).

Tips: "Letters should be neat, short and provide some kind of reply card."

*JK JAM MUSIC, Saratoga Mall, Rt. 50, P.O. Box 3039, Saratoga NY 12866. (518)984-9020. Director of A&R: Jamie Keats. Record company, music publisher, record producer (JK Jam Productions), C'MON = Consumers' Music Opinion Network. Estab. 1992. Releases 6 CDs/year. Pays 66% royalty to artists on contract; statutory rate to publishers per song on record.

How to Contact: Accepts unsolicited but prefers for you to write first and obtain permission to submit. Prefers master quality, well produced cassette, bio, photo. Does not return material. Reports only to interested artists or writers.

Music: Mostly **pop, rock, alternative, R&B** and **dance**. Artists include Johnny Valentine, Ellis Junction, Dog, Lonnie Park, Paul Traudt.

Tips: "Send only quality recordings, produced and mastered. If it sounds like a demo it can't be released. Mastered tracks have dollar value if released, ain't no matter how many tracks!"

JOEY BOY RECORDS INC., 3081 NW 24th St., Miami FL 33142. (305)635-5588. Contact: Hadasa Fyffe. Labels include J.R. Records, American Faith Records. Record company. Estab. 1985. Releases 50 singles, 50 12" singles, 15-20 LPs and 15-20 CDs/year. Works with musicians/artists on contract. Pays 6% royalty to artists on contract; statutory rate to publisher per song on record.

How to Contact: Write or call first and obtain permission to submit. Prefers cassette with 3 songs and lyric sheet. SASE. Reports in 6-8 weeks.

Music: Mostly **bass, rap** and **dance**; also **jazz** and **comedy**. Released *The Puppies* (by Tamara & Calvin Mills), recorded by The Puppies on Columbia Records; *Spend the Night* (by David Suggs), recorded by Ace; and *Nothin' But Bass* (by Brian Graham/Robert Lewis), recorded by Bass Patrol, both on Joey Boy Records. Other artists include Ant D & The Puppies.

Tips: "Be creative in your writing and exercise patience in your business dealings. Go through the proper channels of submission, be creative and politely persistent."

JOYFUL SOUND RECORDS, 130 87th Ave. N., St. Petersburg FL 33702. A&R: Mike Douglas. Record company and music publisher (Nite Lite Music/BMI). Releases various number of compilations/year. Pays statutory royalty to writers and publishers.

How to Contact: "When submitting, send a cassette with 4 songs and lyric or lead sheets. *Do not write asking permission to submit.* Clearly label each item you send with your name and address." Does not return material. Reports in 6-8 weeks.

Music: All types of **children's music**. Releases compilations of children's music produced by Triangle Productions.

Tips: "I'm looking for unpublished works—also am not really interested in promoting someone else's finished LP or single. Don't send me material because you like it. Send me songs that others will like."

*JUSTIN TIME RECORDS INC., Suite 101, 5455 Pare, Montreal Quebec H4P 1P7 **Canada**. (514)738-9533. A&R Director: Jean-Pierre Leduc. Labels include Just a Memory Records. Record company, music publisher (Justin Time Publishing and Janijam Music/SOCAN) and record producer (Jim West). Estab. 1982. Releases 12 LPs and 12 CDs/year. Works with musicians/artists and songwriters on contract. Pays statutory rate to publisher per song on record.

How to Contact: Submit demo tape by mail. Unsolicited submissions are OK. Prefers cassette (or VHS videocassette if available) with at least 5 songs and lyric sheet. Does not return unsolicited material. Reports in 3 months.

Music: Mostly **jazz, blues** and **gospel**; also **French pop, comedy** and **cajun**. Released *Under One Sky*, by guitarist Brian Hughes; *Stepping Out*, by pianist/vocalist Diana Krall; and *Just 88*, by pianist Oliver Jones, all on Justin Time Records.

Tips: "Include a good representation of your work, for example several different styles if applicable. Also, be prepared to *tour* and *promote*."

KAUPP RECORDS, Box 5474, Stockton CA 95205. (209)948-8186. President: Nancy L. Merrihew. Record company, music publisher (Kaupp's and Robert Publishing Co./BMI), record producer (Merri-Webb Productions). Estab. 1990. Releases 1 single and 4 LPs/year. Works with musicians/artists and songwriters on contract and hires musicians for in-house studio work. Pays standard royalty; statutory rate to publisher per song on record.

How to Contact: Write or call first and obtain permission to submit. Prefers cassette (or VHS videocassette if available) with 3 songs. SASE. Reports in 3 months

Music: Mostly **country, R&B** and **A/C rock**; also **pop, rock** and **gospel**. Released "Rose Colored Wine," "Willie Gee" and "Another Notch on Your Gun" (all by Nancy L. Merrihew), all recorded by Nanci Lynn on Kaupp Records. Other artists include David "Dude" Westmoreland, California Gold, Mike Glover, Steve Boutte, Shane "Rockin' Round Boy" Burnett and Gary Epps.

Tips: "Know what you want, set a goal, focus in on your goals, be open to constructive criticism, polish tunes and keep polishing."

KICKING MULE RECORDS, INC., Box 158, Alderpoint CA 95511. (707)926-5312. Head of A&R: Wendi Leader. Record company and music publisher (Kicking Mule Publishing/BMI and Desk Drawer Publishing/ASCAP). Member NAIRD. Releases 12 CDs/year. Works with artists on contract. Pays 10-16% royalty to artists on contract; standard royalty to songwriters on contract.

How to Contact: Query first (finished projects only). SASE. Reports in 1 month.

Music: **Bluegrass, blues** and **folk**. Released *Solo Guitar* by Tom Ball (folk); *Christmas Come Anew* by Maddie MacNeil (folk); and *Cats Like Angels* by Bob Griffin (piano folk). Other artists include Michael Rugg, Neal Hellman, Bert Jansch, John Renbourn, Stefan Grossman, John James, Happy Traum, Fred Sokolow, Bob Stanton, Bob Hadley, Leo Wijnkamp, Jr., Mark Nelson, Lea Nicholson and Hank Sapoznik.

Tips: "We are a label mostly for instrumentalists. The songs are brought to us by the artists but we contract the artists because of their playing, not their songs. First, listen to what we have released and don't send material that is outside our interests. Secondly, learn to play your instrument well. We have little interest in songs or songwriters, but we are quite interested in people who play guitar, banjo or dulcimer well."

KING KLASSIC RECORDS, P.O. Box 460173, San Antonio TX 78246. (210)822-6174. Contact: Dennis Bergeron or Phil Baker. Labels include Super God and Zoinks! Record company. Estab. 1985. Releases 5 LPs and 5 CDs/year. Works with musicians/artists on contract. Pays various royalty to artists on contract.

How to Contact: Submit demo tape by mail. Unsolicited submissions are OK. Prefers vinyl, CD or cassette. SASE. Reports in 2 weeks.

Music: "Anything good and heavy!" Released *Mirror of Sorrow* (by John Perez), recorded by Solitude; *Day In Day Out* (by Pete Toomey), recorded by Bitches' Sin; and *Landscape of Life*, written and recorded by Genocide, all on King Klassic Records.

Tips: "Please no more crappy tapes of some loser and his lame songs! Out of 1,000 tapes sent in response to last year's *Songwriter's Market* listing only maybe 20 had any business leaving the artist's home. If it's not good—throw it away and save me the trouble! If there's anybody out there with homemade vinyl albums of their music *please send those*—even if the records are 10 or 20 years old."

KING OF KINGS RECORD CO., 38603 Sage Tree St., Palmdale CA 93551-4311. (Branch office: P.O. Box 725, Daytona Beach FL 32015-0725. (904)252-4849.) President: Leroy Pritchett. A&R Director: Charles Vickers. Labels include L.A. International, Dell Records International, Charles Vickers Music Associates. Record company and music publisher (Pritchett Publications/BMI). Estab. 1978. Releases 1 single and 1 LP/year. Works with musicians/artists and songwriters on contract. Pays 5-10% royalty to artists on contract; statutory rate to publishers per song on record.

How to Contact: Write first for permission to submit. Prefers cassette and lyric sheet. SASE. Reports in 1 month.

Music: Mostly **gospel**; also **country**. Released "Walkin' On the Water," "If God Be For You" and "Let Your Light Shine," all written and recorded by Charles Vickers on King of Kings Records (gospel).

KINGSTON RECORDS, 15 Exeter Rd., Kingston NH 03848. (603)642-8493. Coordinator: Harry Mann. Record company, music publisher (Strawberry Soda Publishing/ASCAP). Estab. 1988. Releases 3-4 singles, 2-3 12″ singles, 3 LPs and 2 CDs/year. Works with musicians/artists and songwriters on contract.

Pays 3-5% royalty to artists on contract; statutory rate to publisher per song.

How to Contact: Write first and obtain permission to submit. Prefers cassette, 15 ips reel-to-reel or videocassette with 3 songs and lyric sheet. Does not return unsolicited material. Reports in 6-8 weeks.

Music: Mostly **rock, country** and **pop**; "no heavy metal." Released *Two Lane Highway*, written and recorded by Doug Mitchell Band on Kingston Records (folk/rock).

Tips: "Working only with N.E. and local talent."

KOTTAGE RECORDS, Box 121626, Nashville TN 37212. (615)726-3556. President: Neal James. Record company, music publisher (Cottage Blue Music/BMI) and record producer (Neal James). Estab. 1979. Releases 4 singles, 2 LPs and 3 CDs/year. Works with musicians/artists on contract. Pays standard royalty to artists on contract; statutory rate to publisher per song on record.

How to Contact: Submit demo tape by mail. Unsolicited submissions are OK. Prefers cassette with 2 songs and lyric sheet. SASE. Reports in 1 month.

Music: Mostly **country, rock/pop** and **gospel**; also **R&B.** Released "Maxine," written and recorded by Terry Barbay (pop); and "She Don't" (by Bill Fraser/Neal James), recorded by Bill Fraser, both on Kottage Records. Other artists include P.J. Hawk, Judie Bell.

KRYSDAHLARK MUSIC, Box 26160, Cincinnati OH 45226. President: Jeff Krys. Artist Management/production company and publisher designed to produce and shop music to record labels and producers. Estab 1986. Pays variable royalty to artists on contract; statutory rate to publisher per song on record.

How to Contact: Submit demo tape by mail. Unsolicited submissions are OK. Does not return unsolicited material. Reports in 3-6 months.

Music: Released *Road Of Miles* (by Chris Dahlgren), recorded by Ekimi on Krysdahlark Records (progressive jazz); and *Cure Of Folly*, recorded by Sleep Theatre on Vertebrae Records (alternative rock). Other artists include Sylvain Acher, Terri Cantz, SHAG and Sylvia Bullett.

*L.A. RECORDS, Suite 10, 8318 Columbus, North Hills CA 91343. Music Director: Jack Timmons. Labels include Stark Records, R.C. Records, Fearless. Record company, record producer and music publisher (Abalone Publishing). Estab. 1984. Deals with artists and songwriters. Releases 20-30 singles, 1-10 12″ singles, 20-30 LPs, 1-5 EPs and 2-15 CDs/year. Pays 10% royalty to artists on contract; statutory rate to publisher per song on record.

How to Contact: Submit demo tape by mail. Unsolicited submissions are OK. Prefers cassette with 1-10 songs and lyric sheet. "It is very important to include a cover letter describing your objective goals." SASE. Reports in 1 month.

Music: Mostly **rock/hard rock, heavy metal** and **pop/rock**; also **country/gospel, MOR/ballads, R&B, jazz, New Age, dance** and **easy listening.** Released *Tripper* (by J. Scott), recorded by The Pistol Kids (rock); "Renegade" (by Kate Smahl), recorded by Licks (dance); and *Love's Tough* (by Sam Steel), recorded by The Stars (pop/rock), all on L.A. Records. Other artists include The Simmones, Kevin Stark, The Comets, Fearless.

Tips: "Don't be afraid to indulge, PURSUE and aim forward. This means every effort on your part in terms of attitude, expenditure, taking chances, etc."

LAMAR MUSIC GROUP, Box 412, New York NY 10462. Associate Director: Darlene Barkley. Labels include Lamar, MelVern, Wilson, We-Us and Co. Pub. Record company, music publisher (BMI), and workshop organization. Estab. 1984. Releases 10-12 12″ singles and 2-4 LPs/year. Works with musicians/artists and songwriters on contract and hires musicians for in-house studio work. Pays standard royalty to artists on contract; statutory rate to publisher per song. "We charge only if we are hired to do 'work-for-hire' projects."

How to Contact: Write first and obtain permission to submit. Prefers cassette with 2 songs. Does not return material. Reports in 1 month.

Music: Mostly **R&B, rap** and **pop.** Released "So In Love" (by R. Robinson), recorded by L. Williams on Macola Records (R&B/dance); "Lose You Love" (by R. Robinson), recorded by Vern Wilson on Lamar Records (R&B/dance); and "Feel Like a Woman" (by Wilson/Johnson), recorded by S. Taylor on MelVern Records (R&B/ballad). Other artists include Barry Manderson and Co/Vern.

Tips: "Members of our company function as singers, songwriters, musicians, producers, executive producers. We basically have all graduated from college in areas related to music or the music business. We either teach about music and the music business or we perform in the business. If you sincerely want to be in this industry this is the type of work you will need to do in order to succeed. It is not as easy as you think. Many of our artists are signed to record companies through our annual showcase."

Listings of companies in countries other than the U.S. have the name of the country in boldface type.

LANDMARK COMMUNICATIONS GROUP, Box 1444, Hendersonville TN 37077. Producer: Bill Anderson, Jr. Labels include Jana and Landmark Records. Record company, record producer and music publisher (Newcreature Music/BMI and Mary Megan Music/ASCAP) and management firm (Landmark Entertainment). Releases 10 singles, 8 LPs, and 8 CDs/year. Works with musicians/artists and songwriters on contract; hires musicians for in-house studio work. Teams collaborators. Pays 5-7% royalty to artists on contract; statutory rate to publishers for each record sold.
How to Contact: Prefers 7½ ips reel-to-reel or cassette with 4-10 songs and lyric sheet. SASE. Reports in 1 month.
Music: Country/crossover, gospel, jazz, R&B, rock and **top 40/pop.** Released *Joanne Cash Yates Live . . . w/Johnny Cash,* on Jana Records (gospel); "You Were Made For Me" by Skeeter Davis and Teddy Nelson on Elli Records/Norway; and "The Tradition Continues" (by Vernon Oxford), recorded on Landmark Records (country).

LANDSLIDE RECORDS, Suite 333, 1800 Peachtree St., Atlanta GA 30309. (404)355-5580. President: Michael Rothschild. Record company, music publisher (Frozen Inca Music/BMI) and record producer. Estab. 1981. Releases 2 12″ singles, 6 LPs, 6 CDs/year. Works with musicians/artists and songwriters on contract. Pays 8-14% royalty to artists on contract; statutory rate to publishers per song on record.
How to Contact: Submit demo tape by mail. Unsolicited submissions are OK. Prefers cassette with 6-12 songs and lyric sheet. SASE. Reports in 6 weeks.
Music: Mostly **R&B, blues** and **rap;** also **techno-pop.** Released *Cut You Loose* and *Trouble Time,* both written and recorded by Tinsley Ellis on Alligator Records (blues); and *Navigator,* written and recorded by Paul McCandless on Landslide Records (jazz).

LANOR RECORDS, Box 233, 329 N. Main St., Church Point LA 70525. (318)684-2176. Contact: Lee Lavergne. Record company and music publisher (Jon Music/BMI). Releases 8-10 cassettes a year. Works with artists and songwriters on contract. Pays 3-5% royalty to artists on contract; statutory rate to writers for each record sold.
How to Contact: Prefers cassette with 2-6 songs. SASE. Reports in 2 weeks.
Music: Mostly **country;** also **rock, soul, zydeco, cajun** and **blues.** Released "*Cajun Pickin',*" recorded by L.A. Band (cajun); *Rockin' with Roy,* recorded by Roy Currier and *Zydeco All Night,* recorded by Joe Walker (zydeco), all on Lanor Records.
Tips: Submit "good material with potential in today's market. Use good quality cassettes—I don't listen to poor quality demos that I can't understand."

LARI-JON RECORDS, 325 W. Walnut, Rising City NE 68658. (402)542-2336. Owner: Larry Good. Record company, music publisher (Lari-Jon Publishing/BMI) and record producer (Lari-Jon Productions). Estab. 1967. Releases 15 singles and 5 LPs/year. Works with songwriters on royalty contract.
How to Contact: Submit demo tape by mail. Unsolicited submissions are OK. Prefers cassette with 5 songs and lyric sheet. SASE. Reports in 2 months.
Music: Mostly **country, gospel-Southern** and **'50s rock.** Released "The Greatest Star," written and recorded by Tom Campbell (country); "Nebraskaland," written and recorded by Larry Good (country); and *Her Favorite Song,* written and recorded by Johnny Nace (country), all on Lari-Jon Records. Other artists include Kent Thompson and Brenda Allen.

LARK RECORD PRODUCTIONS, INC., Suite 520, 4815 S. Harvard, Tulsa OK 74135. (918)749-1648. Vice-President: Phyllis Nelson. Record company, music publisher (Jana Jae Music/BMI) and record producer (Lark Talent and Advertising). Estab. 1980. Works with musicians/artists on contract. Payment to artists on contract negotiable; statutory rate to publishers per song on record.
How to Contact: Submit demo tape by mail. Unsolicited submissions are OK. Prefers cassette or VHS videocassette with 3 songs and lead sheets. Does not return material.
Music: Mostly **country, bluegrass** and **classical;** also **instrumentals.** Released "Fiddlestix" (by Jana Jae); "Mayonnaise" (by Steve Upfold); and "Flyin' South" (by Cindy Walker), all recorded by Jana Jae on Lark Records (country). Other artists include Syndi, Hotwire and Matt Greif.

LBJ PRODUCTIONS, 8608 W. College St., French Lick IN 47432. (812)936-7318. Director A&R: Janet S. Jones. Owner/Producer: Larry Jones. Labels include Stone Country Records, SCR Gospel, SCR Rock. Record company, music publisher (Plain Country Publishing/ASCAP, Riff-Line Publishing/BMI), record producer (LBJ Productions) and produce radio-spot ads and jingles. Estab. 1989. Releases 2-4 singles, 3-6 LPs, 2-3 EPs and 1-2 CDs/year. Works with musicians/artists on record contract, songwriters on royalty contract, musicians on salary for in-house studio work. Pays 10-15% royalty to artists on contract; statutory rate to publisher per song on record.
How to Contact: Write first and obtain permission to submit or arrange personal interview. Prefers cassette (or VHS videocassette) with 4-6 songs and lyric sheet. SASE. Reports in 8-10 weeks.

Music: Mostly **country, gospel** and **rock**; also **R&B, MOR** and **pop**. Released *Big Jim Mugombo* (by Nicholson/Purkhiser), recorded by Desert Reign; *First Time Out* (by B. Taylor), recorded by Borrowed Time; and "This Bud Ain't For You," written and recorded by Bobby Easterday, all on SCR Records. Other artists include Rosalee Bateman, T.J. Staggs, Rita White, Gordon Ray, Joy Vaughan.

Tips: "Make a good first impression. Put the song on your demo tape that you think is strongest first. If you catch our ear we'll listen to more music. We are not looking for someone that does imitations, we need new and exciting people with styles that cry out for attention. But remember make your submissions to the point and professional—we'll decide if you've got what we want."

LE MATT MUSIC LTD., % Stewart House, Hill Bottom Rd., Highwycombe, Buckinghamshire, HP12 4HJ **England**. Phone: (0630)647374. Fax: (0630)647612. Contact: Ron or Cathrine Lee. Labels include Swoop, Zarg Records, Genouille, Pogo and Check Records. Record company, record producer and music publisher (Le Matt Music, Ltd., Lee Music, Ltd., R.T.F.M. and Pogo Records, Ltd.). Member MPA, PPL, PRS, MCPS. Estab. 1972. Releases 30 12" singles, 20 LPs and 20 CDs/year. Pays negotiable royalty to artists on contract; statutory rate to publishers for each record sold. Royalties paid to US songwriters and artists through US publishing or recording affiliate.

How to Contact: Submit demo tape by mail. Unsolicited submissions are OK. Prefers 7½ or 15 ips reel-to-reel or cassette (or VHS or PAL standard videocassette) with 1-3 songs and lyric sheet. Include bio and still photo. SAE and IRC. Reports in 2 months.

Music: Mostly interested in **pop/top 40**; also interested in **bluegrass, blues, country, dance-oriented, easy listening, MOR, progressive, R&B, 50s rock, disco, new wave, rock** and **soul**. Released *Hit Man*, *Messin* and *Dirty Love*, all written by M.J. Lawson and recorded by Amazing Dark Horse on Swoop Records. Other artists include Johnny Moone, Hush, Dead Fish, Nightmare and Daniel Boone.

LEGS RECORDS, 32 White Mountain Rd., Tularosa NM 88352-9603. (414)725-4467. Executive President: Lori Lee Woods. Labels include Sand Dollar Records. Record company, music publisher (Lori Lee Woods Music/BMI) and record producer. Works with musicians/artists and songwriters on contract. Pays variable royalty to artists on contract; statutory rate to publisher per song on record.

How to Contact: Write first and obtain permission to submit. Prefers cassette (or VHS videocassette) with 3 songs and lyric or lead sheet. SASE. Reports in 2 months.

Music: Mostly **country, rock** and **gospel**.

LEOPARD MUSIC, 23 Thrayle House, Stockwell Rd., London, SW9 0XU **England**. Phone: (071)737-6681/081672-6158. Fax: (071)737-7881. Executive Producer: Errol Jones. Vice President: Terri Schiavo. Labels include Jet Set Records International (US). Record company (PRS, BMI) and record producer. Releases 15 singles and 2 LPs/year. Works with musicians/artists and songwriters on contract and hires musicians for in-house studio work. Pays 5-12% royalty to artists on contract, statutory rate to publishers per song on record.

How to Contact: Write first and obtain permission to submit. Prefers cassette and/or CD, 12" vinyl with 3 songs or more. SAE and IRC. Reports in 2 weeks.

Music: Mostly **dance music, soul** and **pop**; also **ballad, reggae** and **gospel**. Released "Time After Time" (by Guy Spell), recorded by Rico J; "I Need You" (by E. Campbell and E. North Jr.), recorded by Big Africa; and *God is Beauty*, written and recorded by Evelyn Ladimeji, all on Leopard Music Records. Other artists include Zoil Foundations and Michael Eytle.

Tips: "Create strong original songs, and artists must have good image."

*LETHAL RECORDS, P.O. Box 14868, Long Beach CA 90803-1414. (310)435-2353. Director of Operations: John Geldbach. Record company. Estab. 1993. Deals with artists only. Pays above standard royalty to artists on contract; statutory rate to publisher per song on record.

How to Contact: Submit demo tape by mail. Unsolicited submissions are OK. Prefers cassette with 3-4 songs. Does not return material. Reports in 3 weeks.

Music: Mostly **alternative, punk** and **indie rock**. Released "Stoned," recorded by Ragabash (alternative/punk); and "Friends," recorded by Rule 62 (alternative), and "Old School Pride," recorded by HFL (punk), all on Lethal Records. Other artists include Bedwetter, Dolonset and Drain Bramaged.

Tips: "Play live as often as possible. Build a loyal fan base and the labels will come find you."

LIMITED POTENTIAL RECORDS, P.O. Box 268586, Chicago IL 60626. (312)764-9636. A&R: Mike Potential. Record company. Estab. 1988. Releases 5 singles, 1 12" single, 6 LPs, 2 EPs and 6 CDs/year. Works with musicians/artists on record contract, musicians on salary for in-house studio work. Pays 8-12% royalty to artists on contract; ¾ statutory rate to publisher per song on record.

How to Contact: Submit demo tape by mail. Unsolicited submissions are OK. Prefers cassette (or VHS videocassette if available) with 3-5 songs. SASE. Reports in 1 month.

Music: Mostly **alternative rock** and **pop**. Released "Train Robber" (by Nick Eddy), recorded by OO OO WA (rock); "I Am One" (by Corgan/Iha), recorded by Smashing Pumpkins (rock); and "Then

She Fell," written and recorded by Feeble Landslide (rock), all on Limited Potential Records. Other artists include Triple Fast Action, Hushdrops and Chickenboy.
Tips: "Don't send a tape with excuses like 'Oh, we're not happy with the recording but we're really good live,' send the best possible representation of your music. We're not impressed with pages of press from local papers, your music stands or dies on its own."

LION HUNTER MUSIC, Box 110678, Anchorage AK 99511. Vice President: Clive Lock. Record company (BMI). Estab. 1989. Releases 1 single and 1 CD/year. Works with musicians/artists on contract. Pays negotiable royalty to artists on contract; statutory rate to publisher per song on record.
How to Contact: Submit demo tape by mail. Unsolicited submissions are OK. Prefers cassette with 3 songs and lyric sheet. Does not return material. Reports in 3 weeks.
Music: Mostly **rock, pop** and **R&B.** Released "That Ain't All" (by Connett/Lock), recorded by Abandon on Lion Hunter Music (alternative).

LOADING BAY RECORDS, 586 Bristol Road, Selly Oak, Birmingham B29 6BQ **England.** Phone (21)472-2463. Fax: (21)414-1540. M.D.: Duncan Finlayson. Labels include Two Bears Music, Loading Bay Classics and Time Records (Italy). Record company and record producer (Loading Bay Productions). Estab. 1988. Releases 10 12″ singles, 3 LPs and 3 CDs/year. Works with musicians/artists on contract and "negotiates one-off licensing deals." Pays variable royalty; statutory rate to publishers per song on record.
How to Contact: Submit demo tape by mail. Unsolicited submissions are OK. Prefers cassette (or D.A.T.) with several songs. Does not return material. Reports in 2-3 months.
Music: Only **Hi-NRG-dance** and **disco dance.** Released "Save Your Love" (by T. Hendrik), recorded by Bad Boys Blue on Loading Bay Records; "Diamond Eyes" (by G. Maiolini), recorded by Vanessa on Time Records; and "When You Tell Me," written and recorded by Kelly on Loading Bay Records. Other artists include Rofo, Baccara, Shot In The Dark and Ernest Kohl.

LOCONTO PRODUCTIONS/SUNRISE STUDIO, 10244 NW 47 St., Sunrise FL 33351. (305)741-7766. President: Frank X. Loconto. Labels include FXL Records. Record company, music publisher (Otto Music Publishing, ASCAP), recording studio. Estab. 1978. Releases 10 singles, 10 LPs and 5 CDs/year. Works with musicians/artists on record contract, songwriters on royalty contract and musicians on salary for in-house studio work. Pays standard royalty to artists on contract; statutory rate to publisher per song on record.
How to Contact: Write first and obtain permission to submit. Prefers cassette with lyric sheet or lead sheet. SASE.
Music: "We are a full service professional recording studio." Released "La Horida" and "Barry U," written and recorded by Frank Locanto; and "Believe In America" (by Frank Locanto), recorded by The Lane Brothers, all on FXL Records. Other artists include Connie Francis, Kenny Martin, Michael Moog and Donna Shaleff.
Tips: "Be sure to prepare a professional demo of your work and don't hesitate to seek 'professional' advice."

*LONESOME WIND CORPORATION, 111 E. Canton St., Broken Arrow OK 74012. (918)455-5850. President: Marty R. Garrett. Labels include Lonesome Wind Records. Record company, record producer, music publisher and entertainment consultant. Estab. 1988. Deals with artists who write songs only. Releases 1 LP, 3-4 EPs and 1 CD/year. Pays varying royalty to artists on contract; statutory rate to publisher per song on record.
How to Contact: Write or call first and obtain permission to submit. Prefers cassette, 7½ ips reel or VHS videocassette with 4-5 songs and lyric or lead sheet. Does not return material. Reports in 3 weeks.
Music: Mostly **country.** "Straight-up, honky tonk and ballads only, no bluegrass or gospel." Released *Too Free too Long* (by Cliff Voss), recorded by Mark Cypert on Stormy Heart Records; and *Carry Me Over,* written and recorded by The Cripple Jimmi Band on Kid Mega Records.
Tips: "We only work with artists who want to submit to major record companies with finished product as well as independent releases. Artists will need to be prepared to educate themselves as to what is required. We do not require professional demos to submit, but make sure vocals are distinct and up-to-date. I personally listen and respond to each submission I receive, so call to see if we are currently reviewing for an upcoming project."

*LONG PLAY RECORDS, P.O.Box 55233, Atlanta GA 30308. (404)681-4915. Fax: (404)577-2927. Co-Owners: Steve Pilon or Jill Kalish. Record company. Estab. 1992. Deals with artists only. Releases 6 LPs and 6 CDs/year. Royalty varies. Pays statutory rate to publisher per song on record.
How to Contact: Submit demo tape by mail. Unsolicited submissions are OK. Prefers cassette. "Send bio and press clips." Does not return material. Reports in 2 months.

Music: Mostly **alternative/indie rock**; also anything that defies categorization. Released *I Hate Parties*, written and recorded by Big Fish Ensemble; *The Love That Won't Shut Up*, written and recorded by Opal Foxx Quartet; and *Here No Evil—A Tribute to the Monkees*, written and recorded by various artists (all alternative/indie rock), all on Long Play Records. Other artists include Cicada Sings.
Tips: "We're not interested in anything mainstream. We're looking for bands with a unique sound and vision."

LRJ, Box 3, Belen NM 87002. (505)864-7441. Manager: Tony Palmer. Labels include Little Richie, Chuckie. Record company. Estab. 1959. Releases 5 singles and 2 LPs/year. Works with musicians/ artists on contract.
How to Contact: Submit demo tape by mail. Unsolicited submissions are OK. Prefers cassette. SASE. Reports in 1 month.
Music: Mostly **country**. Released "Sing Me a Love Song," written and recorded by Myrna Lorrie; "Auction of My Life" written and recorded by Joe King and "Helpless" recorded by Alan Godge, all on LRJ Records.

LUCIFER RECORDS, INC., Box 263, Brigantine NJ 08203-0263. (609)266-2623. President: Ron Luciano. Labels include TVA Records. Record company, music publishers (Ciano Publishing and Legz Music), record producers (Pete Fragale and Tony Vallo) and management firm and booking agency (Ron Luciano Music Co. and TVA Productions). Works with artists and songwriters on salary and contract. "Lucifer Records has offices in South Jersey; Palm Beach, Florida; Sherman Oaks, California; and Las Vegas, Nevada."
How to Contact: Arrange personal interview. Prefers cassette with 4-8 songs. SASE. Reports in 3 weeks.
Music: **Dance, easy listening, MOR, rock, soul** and **top 40/pop**. Released "I Who Have Nothing," by Spit-N-Image (rock); "Lucky," by Legz (rock); and "Love's a Crazy Game," by Voyage (disco/ballad). Other artists include Bobby Fisher, Jerry Denton, FM, Zeke's Choice and Al Caz.

***LUNA SEA RECORDS,** 226 E. Avondale Ave., Youngstown OH 44507. (216)788-7868. Executive Producer: Robert Graz. Producer/President: Mark Stone. Record company, record producer and music publisher (Mark My Words/ASCAP). Estab. 1989. Deals with artists and songwriters. Releases 6 singles, 5 LPs, 3 EPs and 8 CDs/year. Pays 10% royalty to artists on contract; statutory rate to publisher per song on record.
How to Contact: Submit demo tape by mail. Unsolicited submissions are OK. Prefers cassette with 3 songs and lyric sheet. "If at all possible include 8 × 10 black and white photo." SASE. Reports in 2-3 weeks.
Music: Mostly **commercial rock, pop rock** and **hard rock/metal**; also **R&B, country** and **country rock**. Released *Can We Try It Again* (by Fravel/Weber), recorded by Romeo (pop/rock); *Praise*, written and recorded by Stone Sundae (hard rock); and *Who's Holding You*, written and recorded by Frank Aledia (commercial rock/single). Other artists include Feedback, Les Blaster, Rick Blackson, Valerie Vernon and Psycho Soul.
Tips: "We listen to every demo we receive. Period. We respond with rejection or letters of interest. Please don't call us for your demo status."

***MACOLA RECORD GROUP INC.,** #202, 8831 Sunset, W. Hollywood CA 90069. (310)659-6036. Fax: (310)659-6039. President: Don Macmillan. Labels include Macola, Pacific Inland. Record company. Estab. 1983. Deals with artists only. Releases 5 singles, 8 LPs and 8 CDs/year. Pays standard royalty to artists on contract.
How to Contact: Write or call first and obtain permission to submit. Prefers cassette. Does not return material. Reports in 1 month.
Music: Mostly **alternative rock** and **rap**. Released *Friendly Dog* and *Peghead*, recorded by Black Happy; and *Marvel*, recorded by Lemons, all on Macola Records. Other artists include David Burrill, Citizen Swing, Jimmy Carslake.
Tips: "Need a strong buzz and constantly busy with club dates."

***MADFLOW RECORDINGS,** Suite 16J, 175 Prospect St., E. Orange NJ 07017. (201)674-0985. Fax: (201)673-7708. Director A&R: Maurice Nusom. Record company. Estab. 1992. Deals with artists only.
How to Contact: Write and obtain permission to submit. Prefers cassette, bio, cover letter, 8 × 10 b&w photo (complete press kit). Does not return material. Reports in 1 month.
Music: Mostly **rap/hip hop, dance** and **house**. Artists include Raw Approach.

MAKESHIFT MUSIC, P.O. Box 557, Blacktown, NSW 2148 **Australia**. Phone: (612)626-8991. Manager: Peter Bales. Record company, music publisher (Aria and Apra). Estab. 1980. Releases 10 singles and 5 CDs/year. Works with musicians/artists on record contract, songwriters on royalty contract or musicians on salary for in-house studio work. Pays statutory rate to publisher per song on record.

How to Contact: Submit demo tape by mail. Unsolicited submissions are OK. Prefers cassette (or PAL/VHS videocassette if available) with 2-3 songs and lyric sheet. SAE and IRC. Reports in 1-2 months.
Music: Mostly **rock/pop**. Released *Time Is Money* (by L. Smith), recorded by Chimps; *The Party* (by F. Seckold), recorded by The Party; and *Only Human*, recorded by Blackout. Other artists include Frank Seckold, Lance Smith.

MALACO RECORDS, (formerly Muscle Shoals Sound Gospel), 3023 W. Northside Dr., Jackson MS 39213. (601)982-4522. Executive Director: Jerry Mannery. Estab. 1986. Releases 6 LPs/year. Works with musicians/artists and songwriters on contract and hires musicians for in-house studio work. Pays 8% royalty to artists on contract; statutory rate to publisher per song.
How to Contact: Write first and obtain permission to submit. Prefers cassette (or VHS videocassette) with 4 songs. Does not return material. Reports in 8 weeks.
Music: Mostly **gospel, inspirational**. Released "Magnify Him," by Keith Pringle; and "The Promise," by Ricky Dillard (new generation chorale).

*MANNY MUSIC, INC., 2035 Pleasanton Rd., San Antonio TX 78221-1306. (210)924-2224. Fax: (210)924-3338. Publishing Dept.: Pete Rodriguez. Labels include Manny Records, RP Records and Tapes, AMS Records (gospel line). Record company, record producer and music publisher (Manny Music/BMI, Rosman Music/ASCAP, Texas Latino/SESAC). Estab. 1963. Deals with artists and songwriters. Releases 20-35 singles and 10-15 CDs/year. Pays negotiable royalty to artists on contract; statutory rate to publisher per song on record.
How to Contact: Submit demo tape by mail. Unsolicited submissions are OK. Prefers cassette and lyric sheet. "Allow three or four weeks before calling to inquire about submission." SASE. Reports in 3-4 weeks.
Music: Mostly **Spanish, Tex-Mex or Tejano** and **Spanish gospel**; also **C&W, pop** and **rock**. Released "Loco, Loco," (by Delia Gonzales), recorded by Culturas (cumbia); "Ganas de Besarte" (by Sergio Blaz), recorded by Shelly Lares (cumbia); and "Donde Quiera Que Estes," written and recorded by Elio Quintanilla (ballad), all on WEA Latina. Other artists include Oscar G., La Tropa F, Steve Diaz, Sunny Ozuna, George Rivas, Johnny Bustamante, Raul Alberto, Esmeralda, Orquesta Shati, Baby Phaze, Roel Martinez, Texas Latino, Ronny Tee & Marcos Antonio.

*JOHN MARKS RECORDS, 19 Wright Ave., Wakefield RI 02879. (401)782-6298. Fax: (401)351-3914. Owner: John Marks. Record company. Estab. 1991. Deals with artists only. Releases 1 LP and 4 CDs/year. Royalty varies.
How to Contact: Submit demo tape by mail. Unsolicited submissions are OK. Prefers cassette (analog or DAT). "Primarily interested in master tapes suitable for licensing." SASE. Reports in 2 weeks.
Music: Mostly **classical, new music** and **jazz**; also **Celtic** and **instructional**. Released *Songs My Mother Taught Me*, recorded by Arturo Delmoni (classical); and *Nathaniel Rosen In Concert*, recorded by Nathaniel Rosen (classical), both on John Marks Records. Other artists include Guy Klucevsek.
Tips: "Have something meaningful and beautiful to say, and record it with wonderful sound quality."

*MARTINI RECORDS, 1840 Colapissa St., Ole Metaire LA 70001. (504)899-5565. Owner: John Arrizza. Labels include Gin Mill Records and Al Fresco Recording Co. Record company and record producer. Estab. 1988. Deals with artists only. Releases 10 singles, 4 12″ singles, 13 LPs and 13 CDs/year. Pays 15% royalty to artists on contract; variable rate to publisher per song on record.
How to Contact: Write first and obtain permission to submit. Prefers cassette or VHS videocassette. "No phone calls." Does not return material. Reports in 2 weeks.
Music: Mostly **mod jazz, cocktail croons** and **psycho-wah-wah**; also **new jazz** with no touches of Wynton-Connick feeling. Released *More Drunken Buffoonery* (by Rik Slave), recorded by The Phantoms on Martini Records (garage); *Meet Al Fresco* (by Al Dante), recorded by Al Fresco on Gin Mill Records (cocktail croon); and *Zangolli* (by Arturo Greco), recorded by Zangolli on Martini Records (rap-Italian). Other artists include Multiple Places, Shot Down in Equador, Lump, The Black Problem, Lower Chakras and Beyond Einstein's Eulypian Bats.
Tips: "We're looking for totally refined tunes. It's not how good you play; it is the feeling that counts."

MASTER-TRAK ENTERPRISES, Dept. SM, 413 N. Parkerson, Crowley LA 70526. (318)788-0773. General Manager and Chief Engineer: Mark Miller. Labels include Master-Trak, Showtime, Kajun, Blues Unlimited, Par T and MTE Records. Recording studio and record companies. Releases 20 singles and 6-8 LPs/year. Works with musicians/artists on contract. Pays 7% artist royalty. (No studio charges to contract artists.) Studio available on an hourly basis to the public. Charges for some services: "We charge for making audition tapes of any material that we do not publish."
How to Contact: Submit demo tape by mail. Unsolicited submissions are OK. Prefers cassette and lead sheet. Does not return material.

Music: Mostly **country, rock, R&B, cajun, blues** and **zydeco**. Released "That's When I Miss You" (by J. Runyo), recorded by Sammy Kershaw; "Please Explain," written and recorded by Wade Richards, both on MTE Records; and "My Heart Is Hurting," written and recorded by Becky Richard on Kajun Records. Other artists include Al Ferrier, Fernest & The Thunders, River Road Band, Clement Bros. and Lee Benoit.

Tips: "The song is the key. If we judge it to be a good song, we record it and it sells, we are happy. If we misjudge the song and/or the artist and it does not sell, we must go back to the drawing board."

THE MATHES COMPANY, P.O. Box 22653, Nashville TN 37202. (615)252-6912. Owner: David Mathes. Labels include Rising Star (custom)/Star Image (country), Heirborn (country gospel)/Kingdom (Christian). Record company, record producer and Institute of Recording Arts & Sciences (home study course). Estab. 1962. Releases 12-15 LPs and 10 CDs/year. Works with songwriters on royalty contract and artists for custom productions. Pays statutory rate to publisher per song on record. "Charges for demo services not connected with publishing."

How to Contact: Submit demo tape by mail. Unsolicited submissions are OK. Prefers cassette (or VHS videocassette) with 2-3 songs and lyric sheet. SASE. Reports in 1 month.

Music: Mostly **gospel** and **country**; also **spoken word, MOR** and **instrumental**. Released *My Love For You* (by David & Deanna Mathes), recorded by Warner Mack on Sapphire Records (country); *I'm In Ohio Now With Georgia On My Mind* (by Don Frost), recorded by Johnny Newman on Star Image (country); and *Hello Jesus Hello* (by Craig Anderson), recorded by De Anna on Heirborn Records (country/gospel). Other artists include The Ballards and Harry Greenberg.

Tips: "Songs must be positive country or gospel, with strong messages, not out of date and not political or controversial. Artists must have unique vocal style, good stage presence, have past performances and long term commitment."

*MAUI ARTS & MUSIC ASSOCIATION, Suite 208, P.O. Box 356, Paia, Maui HI 96779. (808)573-0999. A&R Public Submissions: Jason Q. Publik. Labels include Survivor, Rough Diamond, Maui No Ka Oi, Revelation. Record company, record producer, music publisher and environmental association. Estab. 1974. Deals with artists and songwriters. Releases 1-12 singles, 1-12 LPs and 1-12 CDs/year. Pays 5% royalty to artists on contract; pays varying royalty to publisher per song on record.

How to Contact: Write first and obtain permission to submit. Prefers cassette or videocassette with 3 songs and lyric or lead sheet. Does not return material. Reports in 3-5 weeks.

Music: Mostly **pop, rock** and **blues**; also **country, jazz** and **instrumental**.

*MAXERN RECORDS, 14104 Forest Ridge, Potomac MD 20878. (301)738-3879. Fax: (703)528-2358. President: T.V. John (Langworthy). Record company and booking agent. Estab. 1992. Deals with artists and songwriters. Releases 33 singles, 1 LP, 3 EPs and 1 CD/year. Pays negotiable royalty.

How to Contact: Submit demo tape by mail. Unsolicited submissions are OK. Prefers cassette (or VHS videocassette if available) with unlimited songs and lyric sheet. "Send completed songs, instrumentals and/or just lyrics." Does not return material. Reports in 3 weeks.

Music: Mostly **country, A/C** and **light rock**; also **easy listening** and **gospel**. Released *Dream Songs, Dream Power* and *Dream Master,* all written by T.V. John (Longworthy) on Maxern Records. Other artists include Marco Delmar, David Dunbar, Jim Cupino, Robert Musser, John Harbison and Dave Campbell.

Tips: "We focus on beautiful melodies with catchy, memorable lyrics. We also produce music videos."

*MAXIM RECORDS LTD., Suite 32, 115 E. Water St., Santa Fe NM 87501. (505)983-3245. Fax: (505)982-9168. Contact: A&R Dept. Record company, record producer (Crystal Clear Productions) and music publisher (Clear Pond Music/BMI). Estab. 1992. Deals with artists and songwriters. Releases 20-25 singles and 5-8 CDs/year. Pays 10% royalty to artists on contract; 3/4 statutory rate to publishers per song on record.

How to Contact: Submit demo tape by mail. Unsolicited submissions are OK. Prefers cassette with 1-3 songs and lyric or lead sheet. "Include a bio, press kit, etc." SASE. Reports in 1 month.

Music: Mostly **contemporary country, A/C** and **alternative**; also **uptempo dance** and **R&B**. Released *Walk Right In,* written and recorded by Erik Darling on Maxim/Folk Era Records (country); "I Didn't Mean to Break Your Heart," written and recorded by Lauren Montgomery (pop); and "Fallin' Star," written and recorded by David Anthony (pop), both on Maxim Records. Other artists include George Page, Jack Clift, J.D. Haring and Bennet Strahan.

Tips: "We are only interested in professional performing artists. Be realistic about your goals and have financial backing. We don't charge a production fee, artist is only responsible for recording and promotional cost."

MCA RECORDS, 8th Floor, 1755 Broadway, New York NY 10019. (212)841-8000. East Coast A&R Director: Hans Haedelt. Vice President: Michael Rosenblatt. Labels include Costellation, Cranberry,

Curb, London, Zebra and Philly World. Record company and music publisher (MCA Music). Works with musicians/artists on contract.
How to Contact: Call first and obtain permission to submit. Prefers cassette (or VHS videocassette) and lyric or lead sheet. SASE.

MCI ENTERTAINMENT GROUP, P.O. Box 8442, Universal City CA 91608. (818)506-8533. Fax: (818)760-8533. Vice President A&R: Jaeson Effantic. Labels include Bouvier, Credence, PPL. Record company. Estab. 1979. Releases 50-60 singles, 12 12″ singles, 6 LPs and 6 CDs/year. Works with musicians/artists and songwriters on contract and hires musicians for in-house studio work. Pays 10-16% royalty to artists on contract; statutory rate to publisher per song on record.
How to Contact: Write first and obtain permission to submit. Prefers cassette or videocassette with 2 songs. SASE. Reports in 2 months.
Music: Released *Night Song* (by Gip Noble), recorded by Phuntaine on Bouvier Records (jazz); *Fynne as I can B* (by Santiono), recorded by I.B. Phyne on Credence Records (pop); and *Love Song* (by DM Groove), recorded by Dale Mitchell on Bouvier Records (R&B). Other artists include Big Daddy and Blazers, Lejenz and Condottiere.
Tips: "Don't limit yourself to just one style of music. Diversify and write other styles of songs."

*MCR, Rt. 1 Box 70G, Dale TX 78616. (512)398-7519. Owner: Don Jones. Labels include Misty, Texas Gold. Record company, record producer, music publisher and artist career development. Estab. 1968. Deals with artists and songwriters. Releases 25 singles, 15-20 LPs and 10 CDs/year. Pays varying royalty to artists on contract; statutory rate to publisher per song on record.
How to Contact: Submit demo tape by mail. Unsolicited submissions are OK. Prefers cassette with 4 songs and lyric sheet. SASE. Reports in 1 month.
Music: Mostly **country, gospel** and **blues.** Released "Dixie Sundown," (by Billy Joe Kirk), recorded by Stoney Edwards on MCR Records (country); "Can I Bring My Own Angel" (by Tommy Overstreet), recorded by Sandy Samples on Misty Records (country); and "Houston" (by Larry Valentine), recorded by Larry Bane on Texas Gold Records (country). Other artists include Becky Rolling, Drug Store Cowboys, Bud Robbins, Dennis Martin, Jan Tyson and DORON.
Tips: "Send press kit if available. MCR is a Texas-based independent record label dedicated to becoming a vehicle for the development of country talent."

MEGAFORCE WORLDWIDE ENTERTAINMENT, 210 Bridge Plaza Dr., Manalapan NJ 07726. (908)972-3456. Director A&R: Maria Ferrero. Labels include Megaforce Records Inc. Record company. Estab. 1983. Releses 5 LPs, 2 EPs and 5 CDs/year. Works with musicians/artists on record contract. Pays various royalties to artists on contract; ¾ statutory rate to publisher per song on record.
How to Contact: Submit demo tape by mail. Unsolicited submissions are OK. Prefers cassette (or ¾″ videocassette if available) with 4 songs. Does not return material. Reports in 3 months.
Music: Mostly **rock.** Released *Chemical Imbalance*, written and recorded by Skatenigs; *F Sharp*, written and recorded by Nudeswirl and *Fire in the Kitchen*, written and recorded by Warren Haynes, all on Megaforce Records.
Tips: "Don't compromise – do what you want to do creatively."

MERCURY RECORDS, (an affiliate of Polygram Records), 825 8th Ave., New York NY 10019. (212)333-8000. Contact: A&R Assistant. Record company. Works with artists on contract. Pays varying royalty.
How to Contact: Write first and obtain permission to submit. Recommends referral from a reputable industry source. Does not return material. Reports in 3-4 weeks.
Music: **Rock, top 40/pop, R&B** and **dance/urban.** Released "Steep," written and recorded by Lauren Christy (A/C); *Broken Moon*, written and recorded by Lowen & Navarro (progressive adult); and *Laid*, written and recorded by James (alternative), all on Mercury Records.
Tips: "Write the strongest material you can and try to keep it non-generic, from the heart."

MERKIN RECORDS INC., 310 E. Biddle St., Baltimore MD 21202. (410)234-0048. President: Joe Goldsborough. Labels include Protocool Records. Record company. Estab. 1988. Releases 5-6 singles, 5-10 LPs, 3-5 EPs and 5-10 CDs/year. Works with musicians/artists on record contract. Pays 9-16% royalty to artists on contract; statutory rate to publisher per song on record. "Nothing if we don't get part of publishing."
How to Contact: Submit demo tape by mail. Unsolicited submissions are OK. Prefers cassette with 3 songs. "If we don't like, you might not hear from us. If you can't say something nice don't say anything at all."
Music: Mostly **eclectic alternative rock.** Released *Lowborne*, written and recorded by Liquor Bike; "Oil Resist Soul," written and recorded by Broad; and *Anthology*, written and recorded by Reptile House, all on Merkin Records. Other artists include W.O.D. (Womyn of Destruction), Buttsteak, Meatjack and Onespot Fringehead.

Tips: "We want to hear from driven musicians doing something new. All our artists write their own songs. We are interested in unique, visionary people playing songs that mean something to them. Standard pop or metal will do better somewhere else."

METRO RECORDS, 216 3rd Ave. N., Minneapolis MN 55401. (612)338-3833. A&R Director/Staff Producer: James Walsh. Labels include Mars and Black Pearl. Record company, record producer, artist management and development/talent agency. Estab. 1991. Releases 3-4 singles, 1-2 EPs and 5-10 CDs/year. Works with musicians/artists on record contract. Pays 5-20% royalty to artists on contract; statutory rate to publishers per song on record.
How to Contact: Call first and obtain permission to submit. Prefers cassette (or VHS videocassette if available) with 3-4 songs and lyric sheet or lead sheet. SASE. Reports in 2-3 weeks.
Music: Mostly **pop**, **rock** and **country**; also **jazz**. Released *Live Buffalo* (by Wilson/Sickels/Adams), recorded by Buffalo Alice (country); *40 Thieves*, written and recorded by 40 Thieves (rock); and *The Nielsen White Band* (by Nielsen/White), recorded by Nielsen White Band (country), all on Metro Records. Other artists include Chainsaw, Mata Hari, Northcoast, One Horse, Mark Allen, Icebreaker, Natalie Allen, Legion of Boom, Trouble Shooter, Jack Richter.
Tips: "Be prepared to make a commitment to the label and your career. The level of your commitment will be mirrored by our company. As an artist, be prepared to back up your recorded product live."

MFE RECORDS, 500 E. Washington St., Norristown PA 19401. (610)277-9550. President: Jeffrey Calhoon. Record company, music publisher (BMI). Estab. 1984. Releases 5 LPs/year. Works with musicians/artists on record contract, musicians and producers on a per project basis. Pays 5-50% royalty to artists on contract; statutory rate to publishers per song on record.
How to Contact: Write or call first and obtain permission to submit. Prefers cassette with 3 songs and lyric sheet. SASE. Reports in 5 weeks.
Music: Mostly **alternative rock**, **hard rock** and **pop rock**; also **20th century** and **New Age**. Released *Bulkhead*, recorded by Naked Twister and *Rusts, Smuts & Heart Rot*, recorded by Monkey 101, both on MFE Records. Other artists include Robert Moran, Plumbing, Gregory Darvis.
Tips: "Be different, have something new or clever to say."

MIGHTY RECORDS, Suite 6-D, 150 West End, New York NY 10023. (212)873-5968. Manager: Danny Darrow. Labels include Mighty Sounds & Filmworks. Record company, music publisher, record producer (Danny Darrow). Estab. 1958. Releases 1-2 singles, 1-2 12″ singles and 1-2 LPs/year. Works with songwriters on royalty contract and hires musicians for in-house studio work. Pays standard royalty to artists on contract; statutory rate to publishers per song on record.
How to Contact: Submit demo tape by mail. Unsolicited submissions are OK. "No phone calls." Prefers cassette with 3 songs and lyric sheet. SASE. Reports in 1-2 weeks.
Music: Mostly **pop**, **country** and **dance**; also **jazz**. Released *Impulse* (by D. Darrow); *Carnival Nights* (by Vincent C. DeLucia/Raymond Squillacote); and *Falling In Love* (by Brian Dowen), all recorded by Danny Darrow on Mighty Records.
Tips: "Listen to the top 40 hits and write better songs."

MILES AHEAD RECORDS, P.O. Box 35449, Los Angeles CA 90035. (310)281-8599. A&R: Robert Riley. Record company, music publisher (BMI/ASCAP), record producer Estab. 1968. Releases 10 singles, 2 12″ singles, 10 LPs and 10 CDs/year. Works with musicians/artists on record contract, songwriters on royalty contract, musicians on salary for in-house studio work. Royalty negotiated; pays statutory rate to publisher per song on record.
How to Contact: Submit demo tape by mail. Unsolicited submissions are OK. Prefers cassette with 4 songs and lyric sheet. SASE. Reports in 2 weeks.
Music: Mostly **R&B**, **pop** and **country**; also **gospel/pop**.
Tips: "Be yourself, but above all be in touch with the heartbeat of what is true to be a commercial product."

MINDFIELD RECORDS, 4B, 500 ½ E. 84th St., New York NY 10028. (212)861-8745. A&R: Ashley Wilkes. Record company, music publisher (Mia Mind Music/ASCAP) and record producer (I.Y.F. Productions). Estab. 1985. Releases 10 singles, 6 12″ singles, 4 LPs and 4 CDs/year. Works with musicians/artists and songwriters on contract. Payment to artists on contract varies; pays statutory rate to publisher per song on record.
How to Contact: Call first and obtain permission to submit. Prefers cassette with 3 songs. SASE. Reports in 2 months.
Music: Mostly **top 40**, **alternative rock** and **dance**. Released "Cosmic Climb" and "Gods" (by Werner/Sargent), recorded by Madonna (dance); and "So Phony," written and recorded by Jade, all on Mindfield Records. Other artists include P.O.A., Metal L and Papa HaHa.
Tips: "Submit demos on DAT cassettes for best sound quality."

MIRROR RECORDS, INC., 645 Titus Ave., Rochester NY 14617. (716)544-3500. Vice President: Armand Schaubroeck. Labels include House of Guitars Records. Record company and music publisher. Works with artists and songwriters on contract and hires musicians for in-house studio work. Royalty paid to artists varies; negotiable royalty to songwriters on contract.
How to Contact: Prefers cassette or record (or videocassette). Include photo with submission. SASE. Reports in 2 months.
Music: Folk, progressive, rock, punk and **heavy metal**. Released "Don't Open Til Doomsday" and "Drunk on Muddy Water" by Chesterfield Kings; and "Through The Eyes of Youth" by Immaculate Mary.

MISSILE RECORDS, Box 5537 Kreole Station, Moss Point MS 39563. (601)475-2098. "No collect calls." President/Owner: Joe F. Mitchell. Record company, music publisher (Bay Ridge Publishing/BMI) and record producer (Missile Records; have also produced for Happy Hollow Records, Myra Records, JB Records, Tel-Star Records, Round Up Records, RCI and Wake Up Records). Estab. 1974. Releases 24 singles and 8 LPs/year. Works with artists on contract. Pays 6-10% royalty to artists on contract; statutory rate to publishers for each record sold.
How to Contact: Write first and obtain permission to submit. Include #10 SASE. "All songs sent for review must include sufficient return postage." Prefers cassette with 3-6 songs and lyric sheets. Does not return unsolicited material. Reports in 6 weeks.
Music: Mostly **country, gospel, rap, heavy metal, jazz** and **R&B**; also **soul, MOR, blues, rock, pop,** and **bluegrass**. Released "I'm So Glad We Found Each Other" and "Excuse Me Lady," written and recorded by Rich Wilson; and "I'll Always Care For You," written and recorded by Jerry Wright, all on Missile Records. Other artists include Herbert Lacey, Happy Harvey Thompson, Pam Nelson, The Sly Fox, Gene Paul Mann and The Headliners, Lori Mark, Jerry Wright and Jerry Ann. "Also considering songs on master tape for release in the US and abroad."
Tips: "If a recording artist has exceptional talent and some backing then Missile Records will give you our utmost consideration. A bio and cassette tape and picture of the artist should be submitted with his or her best 2 to 6 songs along with sufficient return postage."

MODERN BLUES RECORDINGS, Box 248, Pearl River NY 10965. (914)735-3944. Owner: Daniel Jacoubovitch. Record company. Estab. 1985. Releases 1-2 LPs and 1-2 CDs/year. Works with musicians/artists and songwriters on contract.
How to Contact: Write or call first and obtain permission to submit. Does not return material. Reports in 6-8 weeks.
Music: Blues, R&B, soul and **rock**. Released "Poison Kisses," written and recorded by Jerry Portnoy; "Ida's Song," written and recorded by J. Vaughn; and "Frances," written and recorded by Johnson/ Maloney, all on Modern Blues Recordings. Other artists include Clayton Love, Tommy Ridgley, Little Hatch.

MODERN MUSIC VENTURES, INC., 5626 Brock St., Houston TX 77023. (713)926-4431. Chief Operations Officer: Max Silver. Labels include Discos MM. Record company. Estab. 1986. Releases 12 singles, 2 12″ singles, 6 LPs, 2 EPs and 6 CDs/year. Works with musicians/artists on record contract. Pays statutory rate to publisher per song on record. Distributed by Capitol/EMI.
How to Contact: Write first and obtain permission to submit. Prefers cassette with 5 songs and lyric sheet. SASE. Reports in 6 weeks.
Music: Mostly **Latin (in Spanish), country** and **jazz**; also **rap (in Spanish)**. Released *El Poderde Una Mujer* (by Joe Martinez), recorded by The Hometown Boys; *Por Ti* (by Albert Gonzalez), recorded by The Choice; and *Todo es Gris* (by Lupe Olivares), recorded by The Basics, all on Discos MM. Other artists include Mercedez, Los Pekadores, Los Monarcas, Los Dos Gilbertos, Ellos and Dallazz.

MODERN VOICES ENTERTAINMENT, LTD., (formerly Modern Voices Productions), 22 Yerk Ave., Ronkonkoma NY 11779. (516)585-5380. President: Chris Pati. Record producer. Estab. 1991. Releases 10 singles, 5 12″ singles, 2-3 LPs, 2-3 EPs and 1 CD/year. Pays 7% royalty to artists on contract; statutory rate to publisher per song on record.
How to Contact: Write or call first to obtain permission to submit. Prefers cassette (or videocassette) with 2-3 songs and lyric sheet. Does not return material. Reports in 1 month.
Music: Mostly **dance, pop** and **R&B**; also **pop/rock, rap** and **alternative**. Released "Move It," "I Want Love" and "I Got A Notion," all written and recorded by Chris Pati on Modern Voices Records. Other artists include Deborah Ann, Tony Mascolo, Peace of Mind, Kyle Jason, Monaco, Bobby 6, J. Michael Quinn, Jeannie Manzo.
Tips: "If you are looking to get a fair shot in this industry we offer a program called 'Artist Development Program'—for a very low fee we write, produce, release, shop test press, and promote first single so new artists have a head start instead of just having a finished demo. Great exposure."

MONARCH RECORDS, (formerly Monarch Recordings), 406 Centre St., Boston MA 02130. (617)983-9999. A&R Rep: Akhil Garland. Record company. Estab. 1989. Releases 4 singles, 2 LPs, 6 EPs, 2 CDs/year. Works with musicians/artists and songwriters on contract and hires musicians for in-house studio work. Pays 9% royalty to artists on contract; statutory rate to publisher per song on record.
How to Contact: Submit demo tape by mail. Unsolicited submissions are OK. Prefers cassette or CD with lyric sheet. SASE. Reports in 2 months.
Music: Mostly **children's music**; also **reggae** and **folk**. Recorded *Sound Song*, *When I Grow Up* and *Lullabye*, written and recorded by John & Sara on Monarch Records (children's).

MONTICANA RECORDS, P.O. Box 702, Snowdon Station, Montreal, Quebec H3X 3X8 **Canada**. General Manager: David P. Leonard. Labels include Dynacom. Record company, record producer and music publisher (Montina Music/SOCAN). Estab. 1963. Works with artists and songwriters on contract. Pays negotiable royalty to artists on contract.
How to Contact: Submit demo tape by mail. Unsolicited submissions are OK. Prefers phonograph record (or VHS videocassette) and lyric sheet. Does not return material.
Music: Mostly **top 40, blues, country, dance-oriented, easy listening, folk, gospel, jazz, MOR, progressive, R&B, rock** and **soul**.

*MOONSTONE RECORDS, 3030 Andrita St., Los Angeles CA 90065. (213)341-5959. Fax: (213)341-5960. A&R: Dean Schachtel. Record company. Estab. 1990. Deals with artists and songwriters. Releases 2-5 LPs and 10-12 CDs/year. Pays statutory rate to publisher per song on record.
How to Contact: Submit demo tape by mail. Unsolicited submissions are OK. Prefers cassette or VHS videocassette with 3 songs. "We are seeking new rock, alternative and female artists as well as established acts with worldwide recognition." SASE. Reports in 2 months.
Music: Mostly **rock, alternative** and **female soloists**; also **notable score composers**. Released *Terrified* (by various), recorded by Quiet Riot (rock); *Robot Wars*, written and recorded by David Arkenstone (New Age); and *Bad Channels*, written and recorded by Blue Oyster Cult (rock), all on Moonstone Records. Other artists include David Bryan (of Bon Jovi), Pino Donaggio, Richard Band, Aman Folk Orchestra, Edgar Winter.

MOR RECORDS, 17596 Corbel Court, San Diego CA 92128. (619)485-1550. President: Stuart L. Glassman. Record company and record producer. Estab. 1980. Releases 3 singles/year. Works with musicians on salary for in-house studio work. Pays 4% royalty to artists on contract; statutory rate to publisher per song on record.
Affiliate(s): MOR Jazztime.
How to Contact: Submit demo tape by mail. Unsolicited submissions are OK. Prefers cassette (or VHS videocassette). SASE. Reports in 3 weeks.
Music: Mostly **pop instrumental/vocal MOR**; also **novelty** songs. Released *A Passion for the Piano*, written and recorded by Zach Davids; *The Hour of Love*, written and recorded by Dennis Russell; and *Sandy Taggart Sings*, written and recorded by Sandy Taggart, all on MOR Records. Other artists include Frank Sinatra Jr., Dave Racan, Dave Austin, Wally Flaherty, Mr. Piano.
Tips: "Send original work. Do not send 'copy' work. Write lyrics with 'hook.' "

MORGAN CREEK MUSIC GROUP, Suite 200, 1875 Century Park E., Los Angeles CA 90067. (310)284-8884. Contact: A&R. Labels include Morgan Creek Records. Record company. Estab. 1991. Releases 12 singles, 4 12″ singles, 12 LPs, 3 EPs and 12 CDs/year. Works with musicians/artists on record contract.
How to Contact: Submit demo tape by mail. Unsolicited submissions are OK. Prefers cassette (or VHS videocassette if available). SASE.
Music: Mostly **rock/pop/alternative, R&B** and **country**; also **soundtrack songs**. Artists include Miracle Legion, Auto & Cherokee, Little Feat, Chris Kowarko and Shelby Lynne.

*MOSRITE RECORDS, P.O. Box 40855, Nashville TN 37204. (615)292-2057. Fax: (615)386-9169. Contact: A&R Dept. Labels include Gospel Encounters Records. Record company. Estab. 1963. Deals with artists and songwriters. Releases 3-5 CDs/year. Pays varying royalty to artists on contract; statutory royalty to publishers per song on record.

How to Contact: Submit demo tape by mail. Unsolicited submissions are OK. Prefers cassette (or VHS videocassette if available) with 3 songs and lyric sheet. "Do not send if you want it back." Does not return material. Reports in 6-8 weeks.
Music: Mostly **country, gospel** and **Christmas**; also **Black gospel**. Released *Breakin' It Down*, written and recorded by Tuff Luck (country rock); *Neon Lights* (by various), recorded by Billy D. Hunter (gospel); and *Main St. Gospel* (by various), recorded by Dixie Truelors (Black gospel), all on Mosrite Records. Other artists include Mark Moseley and Marie Lester.
Tips: "Three hit songs is all you need. We want to hear you sing, not play."

*MSM RECORDS, Box 101, Sutton MA 01590. Publisher/Owner: John Scott. Labels include Hālo Records and Bronco Records. Record company and music publisher (Mount Scott Music/BMI and Pick The Hits Music/ASCAP). Estab. 1979. Releases 3-4 singles/year. Works with songwriters on contract and hires musicians for in-house studio work. Pays 4-8% royalty to artists on contract; statutory rate (or as negotiated) to publisher per song on record.
How to Contact: Write first and obtain permission to submit. Prefers cassette with 2 songs and lyric sheet. Does not return material. Reports in 1 month.
Music: Mostly **folk, traditional country, contemporary country, pop-rock** and **theater/musical works**. Released soundtracks for theater productions of *Hamlet*; *Stages* (by Lou Roberts, libretto; composed by J.S. Gagne); and *The Account, An American Musical* (libretto by S. Harris; composers J.S. George/Scott Harris). Other artists include Robin Sorensen and Roger Young.
Tips: "Follow submission guidelines. Pro demos preferred. Lead sheets best, but will accept typed lyric sheets. Will discuss acceptance of theater works for review/possible collaboration. Write and include synopsis (2 pg. maximum) if submitting theater works."

MULE KICK RECORDS, 5341 Silverlode Dr., Placerville CA 95667. (916)626-4536. Owner: Doug McGinnis, Sr. Record company and music publisher (Freewheeler Publishing/BMI). Estab. 1949. Works with musicians/artists and songwriters on contract and hires musicians for in-house studio work. Pays artists 6¢ per album; statutory rate to publisher.
How to Contact: Submit demo tape by mail. Unsolicited submissions are OK. Prefers cassette with 6-10 songs and lyric and lead sheet. SASE. Reports in 1 month.
Music: Mostly **C&W** and **c-rock**; also **pop**. Released *A Tribute to Billy Hughes*, recorded by Doug McGinnis; *Diana Blair Sings Her Songs*, recorded by Diana Blair; and *Album #207*, recorded by Toni Bellin.

*MURDOCK'S MUSIC COMPANY, Suite 1, 1315 N. Sunrise Dr., Bowling Green KY 42101. (502)842-0554 or (502)842-0334. Fax: (502)842-1136. Producers: Dave Harris, John Pigg. Music Director: Rick Faulkner. Record company, record producer and music publisher (Murdock's Music/BMI). Estab. 1994. Releases 6-10 singles, 3-10 LPs and 5-20 CDs/year. Pays 7-10% royalty to artists on contract; statutory rate to publisher per song on record.
How to Contact: Submit demo tape by mail. Unsolicited submissions are OK. Prefers cassette with 3-4 songs and lyric sheet. "Include quick bio and publicity portfolio (if available)." Does not return material. Reports in 4 weeks.
Music: Mostly **pop/rock, alternative** and **country**; also **R&B, A/C** and **heavy metal**. Released "In the Blink of an Eye"(by M. Lennon/S. Wood/D. Harris/B. Sacrey) and "Friend Are You There"(by D. Harris/C. Shireman/M. Lennon/B. Baldwin), both recorded by Mark Lennon; and "The Goodbye Song"(by S. Wood/B. Sacrey/D. Harris), recorded by Sacrey & Wood, all on Murdock Records. Other artists include Benton Edwards and Jack Lewis.
Tips: "Write from the heart and what you know about. Use your poetic license. Send only material that you would want to receive yourself. Keep it of the best quality."

*THE MUSIC COMPANY, 180 Varick St., New York NY 10014. (212)606-3748. Fax: (212)675-7168. Art Director: R. Soares. Labels include Celluloid, Subharmonic, Metrotone. Record company, record producer and music publisher. Estab. 1981. Deals with artists and songwriters. Releases 20 LPs and 20 CDs/year. Pays 15% royalty to artists on contract; varying rate to publisher per song on record.
How to Contact: Submit demo tape by mail. Unsolicited submissions are OK. Prefers cassette or VHS videocassette and lyric or lead sheet. SASE. Reports in 1 month.

How to Get the Most Out of Songwriter's Market (at the front of this book) contains comments and suggestions to help you understand and use the information in these listings.

Music: Mostly **alternative, techno** and **hardcore;** also **country, rock** and **pop.** Released *Not Alone* (by Dr. John/T.J. Kaye), recorded by T.J. Kaye on Hudson Canyon Records (rock); *Divination*, written and recorded by Bill Laswell (ambient); and *Sacrifist* (by Praxis), recorded by Bill Laswell, both on Subharmonic Records (hardcore).

*MUSIC GARDEN, INC., 3397 Renault St., Memphis TN 38118. (901)794-2776. Fax: (901)363-7750. President: Quinton M. Claunch. Labels include Soultrax Records and QMC Records. Record company, record producer and music publisher (Philtac Music Co./BMI, Music Garden Pub. Co./BMI, Quinton Music Co./ASCAP). Estab. 1975. Deals with artists and songwriters. Releases 6 singles, 8 LPs and 8 CDs/year. Pays 5% of retail to artists on contract; statutory rate to publisher per song on record.
How to Contact: Submit demo tape by mail. Unsolicited submissions are OK. Prefers cassette or videocassette with 4 songs and lyric sheet. Does not return material. Reports in 3 weeks.
Music: Mostly **R&B, blues** and **progressive R&B;** also **country, rock (Southern), gospel** and **simple pop.** Released *Soul Survivor* (by J. Ward/S. Bailey), recorded by James Carr (R&B); *Memphis After Midnight* (by Michael Floyd), recorded by "Big Boy" Floyd (R&B); and *Strangers In The Sheets* (by John Ward), recorded by Vernis Rucker (R&B), all on Soultrax Records. Other artists include The Jubilee Hummingbirds, BCD, Willie Mull, J.C. Mull.

MUSIC OF THE WORLD, Box 3620, Chapel Hill NC 27515-3620. President: Bob Haddad. Record company and music publisher (Owl's Head Music/BMI). Estab. 1982. Releases 10 CDs/year. Works with musicians/artists on contract and hires musicians for in-house studio work. Royalty paid to artists on contract varies; pays statutory rate to publisher per song on record.
How to Contact: "Do *not* submit unsolicited demos; they will be disregarded.Write first, and request permission. The label is only interested in gigging bands, *not* individual song writers."
Music: Only **world music.** Released "I Remember" and "Fieso Jaiye," written and recorded by I.K. Dairo (Afro pop); and "Grodlaten," written and recorded by Anders Rosén (jazz), all on M.O.W. Records.
Tips: "Submit only traditional world music, or ethnic-influenced modern music."

MUSIC SERVICE MANAGEMENT, P.O. Box 7171, Duluth MN 55807. (218)628-3003. President: Frank Dell. Record company, music publisher (Frank Dell Music/BMI) and record producer (MSM). Estab. 1970. Releases 2 singles, 1 LP and 1 CD/year. Works with musicians/artists on record contract, songwriters on royalty contract, musicians on salary for in-house studio work. Pays 10% royalty to artists on contract; statutory rate to publisher per song on record.
How to Contact: Submit demo tape by mail. Unsolicited submissions are OK. Write first to arrange personal interview. Prefers cassette with 2 songs. Reports in 1 week.
Music: Mostly **country** and **gospel.** Released "Memories," written and recorded by Frank Dell on MSM. Other artists include Betty Lee.

*MUSIC STATION/DANCEFLOOR, 95 Cedar Lane, Englewood NJ 07631. (201)568-7066. Fax: (201)568-8699. President: Jeffrey Collins. Labels include East Harlem, Soul Creation, Echo USA. Record company, record producer, music publisher (Disc-Tinct Music, Inc./B.M.I.) and distributor (Dancefloor Distribution). Estab. 1985. Deals with artists and songwriters. Releases 50 12" singles, 10 LPs, 10 EPs and 10 CDs/year. Pays 5% of retail to artists on contract; statutory rate to publisher per song on record.
How to Contact: Submit demo tape by mail. Unsolicited submissions are OK. Prefers cassette. SASE. Reports in 2-3 weeks.
Music: Mostly **R&B, dance** and **house.** Released "I Got This Feeling" (by Roland Clark), recorded by Urban Soul on Music Station Records (dance); "As Quiet As It's Kept" (by Elis Pacheco), recorded by Colonel Abrams on Soul Creation Records (dance); and "Non-Stop," written and recorded by Ronald Burrell on Music Station Records (dance). Other artists include Yarbrough & Peoples, Llake, Gerideau, Ready for the World.

NEP-TUNE RECORDS, INC., Box 3011, Country Club IL 60478. (708)798-9408. A&R Department: Mark Surrucci or Tony Shayne. Record company and 32 track all digital recording studio.
How to Contact: Prefers cassette, DAT (or VHS or Beta videocassette) with maximum of 3 songs; lyric sheet optional. SASE. Reports in 1 month.
Music: Mostly **dance, top-40, R&B, hip-hop** and **new metal rock.** Released "What U-Gonna Do About My Love," written and recorded by Vernon Badie; "Kiss Off" (by Tony Shayne), recorded by Ami Stewart; and *Cool Contempo*, written and recorded by Dean Davis, all on Nep-Tune Records. Other artists include Rustin' Jammin Harris, Katie-K, Nate Harris, Linda Clifford, Cool Posse, Double Trouble, Mirror Image, The The.
Tips: "Submit a legible, thoughtful presentation short and to the point. We prefer lyrics without 4 letter words."

NERVOUS RECORDS, 7-11 Minerva Rd., London NW10 6HJ, **England.** Phone: 4481-963-0352. Managing Director: R. Williams. Record company (Rage Records), record producer and music publisher (Nervous Publishing and Zorch Music). Member MCPS, PRS, PPL, ASCAP, NCB. Releases 10 CDs/year. Works with songwriters on royalty contract. Pays 8-10% royalty to artists on contract; statutory rate to publishers per song on records. Royalties paid directly to US songwriters and artists or through US publishing or recording affiliate.
How to Contact: Submit demo tape by mail. Unsolicited submissions OK. Prefers cassette with 4-15 songs and lyric sheet. SAE and IRC. Reports in 3 weeks.
Music: Psychobilly and **rockabilly.** "No heavy rock, AOR, stadium rock, disco, soul, pop—only wild rockabilly and psychobilly." Released *New Generation* (by Roman), recorded by Quakes on Nervous Records; *I Sold My Soul* (by Owen), recorded by Rough Diamonds on Fury Records; and *Eastern Sun* (by Whitehouse), recorded by Frenzy on Rage Records. Other artists include Nitros, Tim Polecati, 3 Blue Teardrops.
Tips: "Send us good rockabilly only."

NETTWERK PRODUCTIONS, 1250 W. 6th Ave., Vancouver, British Columbia V6H 1A5 **Canada.** (604)654-2929. A&R Assistant: Simon Hussey. Record company, music publisher (Nettwerk Productions/SOCAN). Estab. 1984. Releases 12-15 singles, 6 LPs, 2 EPs and 6 CDs/year. Works with musicians/artists and songwriters on contract.
How to Contact: Submit demo tape by mail. Unsolicited submissions are OK. Prefers cassette. Does not return material. Reports in 3 months.
Music: Mostly **pop, alternative rock** and **dance.** Released *Dirge* (by Hooper/Jones/Hooper), recorded by Ginger (pop); *Possession*, written and recorded by Sarah McLachlan (A/C); and *Awaiting Eternity* (by Thirsk/Miranda/Woerd/Cochrane), recorded by Rose Chronicles (pop), all on Nettwerk Records. Other artists include Mystery Machine, P.O.W.E.R., Delirium, Primordia, Single Gun Theory.
Tips: "Keep smiling and always maintain a broad perspective on life and all its possibilities."

*NEW BEGINNING RECORD PRODUCTIONS, Box 4773, Fondren Station, Jackson MS 39216-0773. A&R Manager: S. Wooten. Record company. Works with musicians/artists on contract, songwriters on royalty contracts and hires musicians for in-house studio work. "We will work with composers, lyric writers and collaborators on unusual songs. Also new unusual talent is welcome." Pays 10-20% royalty to artists on contract; statutory rate to publishers for each record sold.
How to Contact: Write. Prefers cassette with 2-4 songs. SASE. Reports in 1 month.
Music: Mostly **country;** also **bluegrass** and **black gospel.** Released "Little David," "I'm The One," and "Going Home Look," all written and recorded by Sojourners on New Beginning Records (Southern gospel).

NEW EXPERIENCE RECORDS/GRAND SLAM RECORDS, Box 683, Lima Ohio 45802. (419)228-0691. Contact: James Milligan. Record company, music publisher (A New Rap Jam Publishing/ASCAP and Party House Publishing/BMI), management (Creative Star Management) and record producer (James Milligan). Estab. 1989. Releases 15-20 singles, 5 12″ singles, 3 LPs, 2 EPs, 2-5 CDs/year. Works with musicians/artists and songwriters on contract and hire musicians for in-house studio work. Pays 8% royalty; statutory rate to publisher per song on record.
How to Contact: Submit demo tape by mail. Unsolicited submissions are OK. Address material to A&R Dept. or Carl Milligan, Talent Coordinator. Prefers cassette (or VHS videocassette) with 3-5 songs and lyric sheet. SASE. Reports in 1 month.
Music: Mostly **R&B, pop** and **rock/rap;** also **country, contemporary gospel** and **soul/top 40.** Released "Tell Me If You Still Care" (by SOS Band), recorded by T.M.C. and James Junior; "Together Forever," written and recorded by Carl Whitner; and "Jerome Black" (by D. Bacon/M.Day), recorded by Volume 10, all on New Experience Records. Other artists include Anthony Milligan (soul gospel singer), UK Fresh Crew (rap group), Carl Milligan (gospel singer) and Richard Bamberger.

NEW SOUTH RECORDS, (formerly Whitestocking Records), Box 250013, Atlanta GA 30325. (404)352-9999. A&R Department: Steve C. Hill. Estab. 1994. Releases 4 singles and 4 CDs/year. Works with musicians/artists and songwriters on contract. Pays 5% royalty to artists on contract; statutory royalty to publisher per song on record.
Affiliate(s): Whitestocking Records, Tigersteeth Records.
How to Contact: Submit demo tape by mail. Unsolicited submissions are OK. Prefers cassette with 3 songs and lyric sheets. SASE. Reports in 3 months. Do not call.
Music: Pop, rock, **soul** and **alternative.** Elaborate production not necessary—piano/guitar and vocals OK. 2-3-4 part harmonies get special attention.
Tips: "We listen for danceability, musicality and lyrical content."

*NEW TRIX RECORDS, P.O. Box 493, Rosendale NY 12472. (914)687-9573. Vice President/Artist Development: Robbie Casey. Labels include Old Dog Records. Record company. Estab. 1970. Deals

with artists and songwriters. Releases 6-10 CDs/year. Pays statutory rate to publisher per song on record.
How to Contact: Submit demo tape by mail. Unsolicited submissions are OK. Prefers cassette and lyric sheet. SASE. Reports in 2 months.
Music: Political protest. Non-violent, radical, poetic. Looking for lyrics that confront issues of human rights and social change. No religious or environmental. Released *Snake In The Grass* (by Paul Williams), recorded by Eddie Kirkland (R&B); *Chicken Raid* and *Alcatraz Blues*, written and recorded by Frank Edwards (blues), all on Trix Records. Other artists include John Cephas, Robert Lockwood, William Robertson and Dan Del Santo.

NORTH STAR RECORDS, 95 Hathaway St., Providence RI 02907. (401)785-8400. President: Richard Waterman. Record company. Estab. 1985. Releases 5-10 LPs/year. Works with musicians/artists and songwriters on contract. Pays 4-10% royalty to artists on contract; statutory rate to publisher per song on record.
How to Contact: Submit demo tape by mail. Unsolicited submissions are OK. Prefers cassette with 4-5 songs and lyric sheet. Does not return material. Reports in 2 months.
Music: Mostly **folk**; also **acoustic traditional, classical, traditional jazz, New Age** and **contemporary**. Released *Broadway Openings* (by various), recorded by Rick Johnson (jazz); *Eveningtide*, written and recorded by Bruce Foulke (contemporary); and *Prelude in Pastel*, written and recorded by Ron Murray (contemporary), all on North Star Records. Other artists include Judith Lynn Stillman, Greg Joy, Gerry Beaudoin, Cheryl Wheeler, Nathaniel Rosen, Swingshift.
Tips: "Send a professional looking, well thought-out presentation of your best material."

*NOVA RECORDS INC., Suite 41B, 235 W. 56th St., New York NY 10019. A&R: Jethro Brannigan. Record company. Estab. 1993. Deals with artists and songwriters. Pays negotiable royalty. "We work out individual deals with the artist according to his/our needs."
How to Contact: Submit demo tape by mail. Unsolicited submissions are OK. Prefers cassette. "Prefer high quality demos." SASE. Reports in 1 month.
Music: Mostly **rock, country** and **blues**. Released *Everything*, written and recorded by Josh Max on Nova Records (country/blues).
Tips: "Write songs that spark a feeling or emotion; laughter, anger, sadness, joy, etc. Don't make us work to figure out the meaning. First 10 seconds are crucial."

*NOVEMBER RECORDS, 530 Broadway, New York NY 10012. (212)343-0799. Fax: (212)343-0899. Vice President A&R and Operations: Rob Holt. Record company. Estab. 1993. Deals with artists and songwriters. Releases 4-7 singles, 8 LPs, 4 EPs and 4-7 CDs/year.
How to Contact: Submit demo tape by mail. Unsolicited submissions are OK. Prefers cassette and lyric sheet. Does not return material. Reports in 2 months.
Music: Mostly **alternative, rock** and **metal**; also **pop/rock** and **R&B**. Released *Time of Trains*, written and recorded by David Broza (adult alternative); *Offering*, written and recorded by Shrunken Head (alternative rock); and *Feel*, written and recorded by Rival Suns (rock), all on November Records. Other artists include Karen Farr, Eat, Malford Milligan.
Tips: "We're looking for live bands with very little sequences. If computer oriented—include some kind of live substance, i.e., guitars, vocals. No instrumental music."

NUCLEUS RECORDS, P.O. Box 111, Sea Bright NJ 07760. President: Robert Bowden. Record company and music publisher (Roots Music/BMI). Member AFM (US and Canada). Estab. 1979. Releases 2 singles and 1 LP/year. Works with musicians/artists on contract and hires musicians for in-house studio work. Pays up to 10% royalty to artists on contract; statutory rate to publisher per song on record.
How to Contact: Submit demo tape by mail. Unsolicited submissions are OK. Prefers cassette (or videocassette) with any number songs and lyric sheet. Prefers studio produced demos. SASE. Reports in 1 month.
Music: Mostly **country** and **pop**; also **church/religious, classical, folk, MOR, progressive, rock** (soft, mellow) and **top 40**. Released "4 O'Clock Rock," "Henrey C" and "Will You Miss Me Tonight" (by Bowden), recorded by Marco Sison, all on Nucleus Records.

OLD SCHOOL RECORDS, 179 Prospect Ave., Wood Dale IL 60191-2727. Owner/President: Peter J. Gianakopoulos. Record company, music publisher (Old School Records/Goosongs, ASCAP). Estab. 1992. Releases 1-2 singles, 1-2 LPs, 1-2 EPs, and 1-2 CDs. Pays 10% to artists on contract; statutory rate to publishers per song on record.
How to Contact: Submit demo tape by mail. Unsolicited submissions are OK. Prefers cassette with 3-5 songs and lyric sheet. SASE. Reports in 1 month.
Music: Mostly **alternative rock, blues** and **pop**; also **funk, punk** and **tribute albums**. Released *Muse* and *Delusions of Grandeur* (by Peter Gaines), recorded by The Now on Old School Records (rock).

Tips: "Be true to your craft. No matter how different the feel of music—take it to the style you feel like writing. Most artists may find their best writing style is different from their listening tastes."

ON TOP RECORDS, 3081 NW 24th St., Miami FL 33167. (305)635-5588. Contact: Hadasa Fyffe. Record company. Estab. 1985. Releases 40-50 singles, 10 LPs and 10 CDs/year. Pays 6% royalty to artists on contract; standard rate to publisher per song on record.
How to Contact: Write or call first and obtain permission to submit. Prefers cassette. SASE. Reports in 6-8 weeks.
Music: Mostly **bass**, **rap** and **dance**; also **R&B**, **gospel** and **jazz**. Released *What's My Name*, recorded by Uncle Al; and *One Leg Up* (by Dion Hamilton), recorded by Half-Pint, both on On Top Records.
Tips: "Copyright all material before submitting to anyone. Be creative and persist politely."

ORBIT RECORDS, P.O. Box 120675, Nashville TN 37212. (615)255-1068. Owner: Ray McGinnis. Record company, music publisher (Nautical Music Co.) and record producer (Ray Mack Productions). Estab. 1965. Releases 6-10 singles, 6 12" singles and 4 CD LPs/year. Works with musicians/artists on contract. Pays 5.25% royalty to artists on contract; statutory rate to publisher per song on record.
How to Contact: Submit demo tape by mail. Unsolicited submissions are OK. Prefers cassette with 4 songs and lead sheet. SASE. Reports in 6-8 weeks.
Music: Country (ballads), country rock and R&B. Released "Burning Love," written and recorded by Alan Warren (hard rock); and "No More Tears" (by D. Cannon), recorded by Debra Lee, both on Orbit Records. Other artists include Steve Wyles, Sonny Martin.
Tips: "We like artists with individual styles, not 'copy cats'; be original and unique."

*ORDER RECORDS, 441 E. Belvedere Ave., Baltimore MD 21212. (410)435-0993. Fax: (410)435-3513. General Partner: Joyce Klein. Record company, record producer (Order Productions) and music publisher (Orderlottsa Music/BMI). Estab. 1985. Deals with artists and songwriters. Releases 3 LPs and 3 CDs/year. Pays standard royalty to artists on contract; statutory rate to publisher per song on record.
How to Contact: Submit demo tape by mail. Unsolicited submissions are OK. Prefers cassette with 3 songs. SASE. Reports in 4-5 weeks.
Music: Mostly **New Age contemporary instrumental**, **reggae** and **world**. Released *Unconquered Lions*, written and recorded by Uprising on Order/Unconquered Lions Records (reggae); and *Keepers of the Light*, written and recorded by Jeff Order on Order Records (New Age).
Tips: "Don't expect any record label to invest in your career if you haven't done so first! Always include a SASE with your submissions. Make your compositions and songs interesting with clean melodies, good arrangements and well executed."

ORINDA RECORDS, P.O. Box 838, Orinda CA 94563. (510)833-7000. A&R Director: Harry Balk. Record company. Works with musicians/artists on record contract, songwriters on royalty contract. Pays negotiable rate to publishers per song on record.
How to Contact: Submit demo tape by mail. Unsolicited submissions are OK. Prefers cassette and lead sheet. Does not return material. Reports in 3 months.
Music: Mostly **pop**, **rock** and **jazz**.

*P. & N. RECORDS, 61 Euphrasia Dr., Toronto, Ontario M6B 3V8 **Canada**. (416)782-5768. Fax: (416)782-7170. Presidents: Panfilo Di Matteo and Nicola Di Matteo. Record company, record producer and music publisher. Estab. 1993. Deals with artists and songwriters. Releases 10 singles, 20 12" singles, 15 LPs, 20 EPs and 15 CDs/year. Pays statutory rate to publisher per song on record.
How to Contact: Submit demo tape by mail. Unsolicited submissions are OK. Prefers cassette or videocassette with 3 songs and lyric or lead sheet. "We only contact if we are interested in the material." Reports in 1 month if interested.
Music: Mostly **dance**, **ballads** and **rock**. Released "I Can See It In Your Eyes," (by Pagano/Vinciguerra/DiMatteo) and "Don't Know" (by Pagano/DiMatteo), both recorded by Angelica Castro on P. & N. Records. Other artists include Dynamite David and Suddy.

PACIFIC ARTISTS RECORDS INTERNATIONAL, (formerly Pacific Artists Records), 246 Esperanza, Tiburon CA 94920. (415)435-2772. Fax: (415)435-6417. President: Alexandra Morriss. Record company, music publisher and record producer. Estab. 1980. Pays 20% royalty to artists on contract.
How to Contact: Call first and obtain permission to submit. Prefers cassette (or VHS videocassette) with 3 songs and lyric or lead sheet. Does not return unsolicited material. Reports in 2-3 months.
Music: Mostly **jazz/New Age**, **world** and **children's**; also **country** and **orchestral**. Released *The Circle*, written and recorded by Alexandra Randolph on Pacific Artists Records (New Age). Artists include The Alexandra Quartet, Peggy Monaghan, Doug Gittens and Randi Morriss.

*PAINT CHIP RECORDS, P.O. Box 12401, Albany NY 12212. (518)765-4027. President: Dominick Campana. Record company. Estab. 1992. Releases 6 singles, 2 EPs and 4 CDs/year. Pays negotiable royalty; statutory rate to publisher per song on record. Mainly provides promotion and distribution deals.

How to Contact: Submit demo tape by mail. Unsolicited submissions are OK. Prefers cassette with 4 songs. "Please don't send anything 'metal-like,' 'funky' or keyboard driven." Does not return material. Reports in 6 weeks.

Music: Mostly **"alternative" guitar rock** (bands). 1993 releases included: *Lead Into Gold* (by various artists); "Crush" (by R. Crist), recorded by Bloom; and "Corner Of This Bar" (by H. Glassman), recorded by The Dugans, all on Paint Chip Records. Other artists include North Again, Dara Albro, Dryer, Disciples of Agriculture, 100 Acre Wood, Crawdad, All Fall Down, Topper, Billy Riley.

Tips: "Be honest. Don't depend on your music to generate steady income right away. Pour your soul and guts into every song."

PAJER RECORDS, 23 Forest Lane, Black Mountain NC 28711. (704)669-7290. Owner: Jerry Caldwell. Record company, music publisher (Hazewell Music Pub/BMI), record producer (Pajer Music Production). Estab. 1973. Releases 3 singles and 3 EPs/year. Works with musicians/artists on record contract, songwriters on royalty contract. Pays 15% royalty to artists on contract; statutory rate to publishers per song on record.

How to Contact: Submit demo tape by mail. Unsolicited submissions are OK, but not more than 4 at a time on cassette. SASE a must, otherwise tapes not returned. Prefers cassette with 4 songs and lyric sheet. Reports in 2 weeks. Works with Canadian and European producers and record companies.

Music: Mostly **contemporary country, pop/crossover** and **MOR**. Released "Bring Me Down Slow," recorded by Ann Beaman; "Don't Send Me No Rosebuds" and "Little Soldier Boy," recorded by C.B. Ryan, all on Pajer Records. Other artists include Max Berry, J. Thomas, Johnny House, Wayne Dorlan, Norman Mays, Sue Stover.

Tips: "Productions MUST be professional studio cuts. SASE a MUST or tapes will not be returned."

*PARADE, 88 St. Francis St., Newark NJ 07105. (201)344-4214. Senior Vice President, Product Development/A&R Director: Joey Porello. Labels include Peter Pan, Power, Compose Records and Compose Memories. Record company. Estab. 1928. Releases 10-20 singles and 5-10 12″ singles, 10-20 LPs, and 10-20 CDs/year. Works with artists and songwriters on contract. Pays varying royalty to artists on contract; statutory rate to publishers for each record sold.

How to Contact: Prefers cassette with 1-3 songs and lyric sheet. SASE. Reports in 2 months.

Music: Mostly **dance, children's** and **MOR**; also **country, R&B, New Age rock, novelty** and **classical**. Released *Aerobics*, by Joanie Greggains (exercise). Other artists include Morton Downey, Jr. (country) and Gilead Limor (New Age).

PARAGOLD RECORDS & TAPES, Box 292101, Nashville TN 37229-2101. (615)865-1360. Director: Teresa Parks Bernard. Record company, music publisher (Rainbarrel Music Co./BMI) and record producer. Estab. 1972. Releases 3 singles and 3 LPs/year. Works with musicians/artists and songwriters on contract. Pays statutory rate to publishers per song on record.

How to Contact: Write first and obtain permission to submit. Prefers cassette (or VHS videocassette) with 2 songs and lyric or lead sheet. SASE (#10 envelope not acceptable). Reports in 2 months.

Music: Country. Released "Rose & Bittercreek" and "Bottle of Happiness," written and recorded by Johnny Bernard; and "Daddy's Last Letter" (by J. Bernard), recorded by JLyne, all on Paragold Records (country). Other artists include Sunset Cowboys.

Tips: "We are only accepting limited material of the highest quality."

PARC RECORDS INC., Suite 205, 5104 N. Orange Blossom Trail, Orlando FL 32810. (407)292-0021. Executive Assistant: Leslie A. Schipper. Record company (Mister Sunshine Music/BMI). Estab. 1985. Releases 4+ singles, 2 12″ singles, 2 LPs and 2 CDs/year. Works with musicians/artists and songwriters on contract.

How to Contact: Prefers cassette (or VHS videocassette) with 3-5 songs and lyric sheet. SASE. Reports in 6-8 weeks.

Music: Mostly **rock/metal, dance** and **jazz/new wave**; also **A/C** and **R&B**. Released *Lighting Strikes*, recorded by Molly Hatchet on Parc/Capitol Records (rock); *China Sky*, recorded by China Sky on Parc/CBS Records (rock); and *Ana*, recorded by Ana on Parc/CBS Records (dance). Other artists include Glen Kelly and Deryle Hughes.

Tips: "Quality songs with good hooks are more important than great production. If it's good, we can hear it."

*PATTY LEE RECORDS, 6034 Graciosa Place, Hollywood CA 90068. (213)469-5431. Assistant to the President: Susan Neidhart. Record company and record producer. Estab. 1985. Deals with artists and songwriters. Releases 1-2 singles, 1-2 EPs and 2-3 CDs/year. Pays negotiable royalty to artists on contract.

How to Contact: Write first and obtain permission to submit. Does not return material.

Music: Mostly **New Orleans rock, bebop jazz** and **cowboy poetry**; also **eclectic, folk** and **country**. Released *Alligator Ball, Be Your Own Parade* and "Must Be the Mardi Gras," all written and recorded by Armand St. Martin on Patty Lee Records (New Orleans rock). Other artists include Too Tall Timm, James T. Daughtry, Jim Sharpe, Curt Warren, Kevin Atkinson and John Jordan.

Tips: "Our label is small, which gives us the ability to develop our artists at their own rate of artistry. We are interested in quality *only*, regardless of the genre of music or style. Keep in mind that Patty Lee Records is not Warner Bros.! So patience and a good query letter are great starts."

*PAVEMENT MUSIC, INC., 17W703A Butterfield Rd., Oakbrook Terrace IL 60181. (708)916-1155. Fax: (708)916-1159. President: Mark Nawara. Record company and music publisher (NMG Music). Estab. 1993. Deals with artists and songwriters. Releases 2 EPs and 30 CDs/year. Pays varying royalty to artists on contract; statutory rate to publisher per song on record.

How to Contact: Submit demo tape by mail. Unsolicited submissions are OK. Prefers cassette (or VHS videocassette if available) with 3 songs. "Include photo." SASE. Reports in 1 month.

Music: Mostly **metal, alternative** and **rock**; also **death metal**. Released *Crowbar*, written and recorded by Crowbar; *Stressball*, written and recorded by Stressball; and *183.85*, written and recorded by Tungsten, all on Pavement Music. Other artists include Demented Ted and Hinge.

Tips: "Make sure you put your phone number on the cassette itself. Everything sent will be listened to."

*PBM RECORDS, P.O. Box 1312, Hendersonville TN 37077-1312. (615)865-1696. Owner: Michele Gauvin. Labels include Nashville Rocks! Records. Record company. "PBM also independently produces 2 television shows from Nashville." Estab. 1990. Deals with artists and songwriters. Releases 1-4 singles, 1-4 12″ singles and 8-10 LPs/year. Pays statutory rate to publisher per song on record.

How to Contact: Submit demo tape by mail. Unsolicited submissions are OK. Prefers cassette or VHS videocassette with 3-5 songs and lyric sheet. SASE. Reports in 2-4 months.

Music: Mostly **country, rock** and **gospel**; also **bluegrass, country/gospel** and **Christian rock**. Released "Don't Touch Me" (by Hank Cochran) and "You're Not the Only Heart In Town" (by Lonnie Wilson), both recorded by Michele Gauvin on PBM Records (country). Other artists include Jim Woodrum.

Tips: "Send your best material and be persistent."

PDS RECORDS, Box 412477, Kansas City MO 64141. (800)473-7550. Contact: A&R, Dept. 100. Labels include Universal Jazz, PDS Associated labels. Record company, music publisher (PDS Music Publishing/ASCAP/BMI) and record producer (PDS Productions). Estab. 1988. Releases 8-10 singles, 8-10 12″ singles, 3-5 LPs, 8-10 EPs and 3-5 CDs/year. Works with musicians/artists on contract.

How to Contact: Write first and obtain permission to submit. Prefers cassette (or VHS videocassette) with 4-5 songs and lyric sheet. Does not return material. Reports in 2-3 months.

Music: Released "Let's Hold On" and "The Heat of Passion (by D. Shivers), recorded by Rajah; and "Wack M. Cee's," written and recorded by Seeds of a Generik Kreed, all on PDS Records.

PENGUIN RECORDS, INC., #2, 3031 SW 27th Ave., Miami FL 33133. Product Manager: Michael J. McNamee. Operation Manager: Gregory J. Winters. Labels include Straitgate Records and Kinetic Records. Record company, music publisher. Estab. 1990. Releases 6 singles, 6 12″ singles, 3 LPs and 3 CDs/year. Pays varying royalty.

How to Contact: Submit demo tape by mail. Unsolicited submissions are OK. Prefers cassette (or VHS videocassette) with 3 songs and lyric sheet. SASE. Reports in 2 months.

Music: Mostly **dance, pop, rock, R&B/rap** and **alternative/dance**. Artists include Razor, The Maxxturs, Final Demand, Bananas on Fire.

Tips: "Be patient! There's a lot of music out there. Everyone will get a chance."

PERIDOT RECORDS, P.O. Box 8846, Cranston RI 02920. Owner/President: Amy Parravano. Record company, music publisher (Peridot/ASCAP), record producer (Peridot Productions). Estab. 1992. Releases 2 singles, 2 12″ singles, 1 LP/year. Works with musicians/artists on record contract. Pays 10% royalty to artists on contract; statutory rate to publisher per song on record.

How to Contact: Write first and obtain permission to submit. Prefers cassette with 3-4 songs and lyric sheet or lead sheet. SASE.

Music: Mostly **country, gospel** and **folk**; also **MOR, children's** and **novelty**. Released "Grandma's Attic" (by Amy Parravano and Ellen Smith); "North Hampton Line" and "Trust In Him" (by Amy Parravano), all recorded by Amy Beth on Peridot Records.

Tips: "Send finished demo, completed master reel or DAT ready for record release."

PHOENIX RECORDS, INC., Dept. SM, Box 121076, Nashville TN 27212-1076. (615)244-5357. President: Reggie M. Churchwell. Labels include Nashville International Records and Monarch Records. Record company and music publisher (BMI/ASCAP). Estab. 1971. Releases 5-6 CDs/year. Works with musicians/artists and songwriters on contract. Pays standard royalty to artists on contract; statutory rate to publisher per song on record.
How to Contact: Write first and obtain permission to submit. "You must have permission before submitting any material." Prefers cassette with lyric sheets. Does not return material. Reports in 2-3 weeks.
Music: Mostly **country, rock** and **pop**; also **gospel**. Released "Left of Center Line" (by Howard Lips), recorded by Catfish on Phoenix Records (country/rock); and "Littlest Cowboy," written and recorded by Sonny Shroyer on Hazzard Records (children's). Other artists include Conrad Pierce and Clay Jerrolds.
Tips: "We are looking for songs with strong hooks and strong words. We are not simply looking for songs, we are looking for hits."

PILOT RECORDS AND TAPE COMPANY, 628 S. South St., Mount Airy NC 27030. (919)786-2865. President and Owner: Paul E. Johnson. Labels include Stork, Stark, Pilot, Hello, Kay, Sugarbear, Southcoast, Songcraft, Bell Sounds, Blue Ridge, Joy, Red Bird and Tornado and Blue Jay. Record company, music publisher (Tompaul Music Company/BMI) and record producer. Estab. 1960. Releases 12 singles and 75 LPs/year. Works with songwriters on contract; musicians on salary for in-house studio work. Pays 30% royalty to artists on contract; statutory rate to publishers per song on record.
How to Contact: Submit demo tape by mail. Unsolicited submissions are OK. Prefers cassette with 6 songs and lyric sheet. SASE. Reports in 2 months. "The songwriters should give their date of birth with submissions. This information will be used when copyrighting a songwriter's song."
Music: Mostly **country, gospel** and **bluegrass**; also **rock, folk** and **blues**. Released "Call Me Baby" and "You're the One I Love," written and recorded by Alan Westmoreland (pop); and "I'm So Lonesome," written and recorded by Bobby Bumgarner (country), all on Pilot Records. Other artists include Thurman Holder, Lee Martin, Clyde Johnson, Bobby Atkins, Carl Tolbert, Early Upchurch and Sanford Teague.
Tips: "Try to write commercial-type songs and use the best backup musicians possible."

*PINECASTLE/WEBCO RECORDS, 5108 S. Orange Ave., Orlando FL 32809. (407)856-0245. Fax: (407)858-0007. President: Tom Riggs. Record company. Estab. 1991. Deals with artists and songwriters. Releases 10-15 CDs/year. Pays varying rate to artists on contract.
How to Contact: Submit demo tape by mail. Unsolicited submissions are OK. Prefers cassette. Does not return material. Reports in 2 months.
Music: Mostly **bluegrass** and **related acoustic**. Released *When the Roses Bloom in Dixie Lane*, recorded by Osborne Brothers on Pinecastle Records; *Carolina Blue*, recorded by Lou Reid, Terry Baucom and Carolina on WEBCO Records; and *A Touch of the Past*, recorded by Larry Perkins on Pinecastle Records. Other artists include Chubby Wise, Larry Stephenson, Reno Brothers, Rarely Herd, Wild & Blue.
Tips: "We listen to traditional bluegrass as well as contemporary bluegrass and try to keep a balance between them. We send out rejection letters so please don't call inquiring of the status of your demo."

*PLANKTON RECORDS, 236 Sebert Rd., Forest Gate, London E7 0NP **England**. Phone: (081)534-8500. Senior Partner: Simon Law. Labels include Sea Dream, Embryo Arts (licensed, Belgium), Gutta (licensed, Sweden), Wildtracks (licensed, United Kingdom) and Radio (licensed, United Kingdom). Record company and music publisher (Sea Dream Music, Chain of Love Music, Crimson Flame, Scarf Music Publishing and Really Free Music). Estab. 1977. Releases 1 CD, 4 LPs, and 1 EP/year. Works with musicians/artists and songwriters on contract. Pays 10% royalty to artists on contract; statutory royalty to publishers per song on record.
How to Contact: Submit demo tape by mail. Unsolicited submissions OK. Prefers cassette with 3 songs and lyric sheet. SAE and IRC. Reports in 6 weeks.
Music: Mostly **funk/rock, R&B** and **gospel**; also **blues**. Released *Half My Life* (by Simon Law), recorded by Fresh Claim (rock); *Generation*, written and recorded by Ben Okafor (reggae); and *Mould Me Lord* (by Dixon/Catley), recorded by Marc Catley (folk), all on Plankton Records. Other artists include Vatten, Trevor Speaks, Out of Darkness, Ruth Turner, Geoff Mann.
Tips: "We specialize in bands with a Christian bias, regardless of their musical style."

PLAYBACK RECORDS, Box 630755, Miami FL 33163. (305)935-4880. Producer: Jack Gale. Labels include Gallery II Records, Ridgewood Records. Record company, music publisher (Lovey Music/ BMI and Cowabonga Music/ASCAP) and record producer. Estab. 1983. Releases 20 CDs/year. Pays statutory rate to publisher per song on record.

How to Contact: Submit demo tape by mail. Unsolicited submissions are OK. Prefers cassette (VHS videocassette if available) with 2 songs and lyric sheet. Does not return materials. Reports in 2 weeks if interested.
Music: Mostly **country**. Released "Next of Kin" (by Wills-Mize), recorded by Johnny Paycheck; *Let An Old Racehorse Run* (by Ron Simons), recorded by Tommy Cash; and *My Love Belongs To You* (by R. Rogers), recorded by Del Reeves, all on Playback Records. Other artists include Jimmy C. Newman, Jeannie C. Riley, Charlie Louvin, Melba Montgomery and Margo Smith.
Tips: "Send only your best. Be open to suggestion. Remember . . . this is a business, not an ego trip."

PLEASURE RECORDS, Rt. 1, Box 187-A, Whitney TX 76692. (817)694-4047. Fax: (817)694-5155. President: Allen Newton. Labels include Cactus Flats, Pristine, MFN, Seneca VII. Record company and music publisher (Four Newton Publishing/BMI, Stethash/ASCAP). Estab. 1986. Releases 12 singles, 3 12″ singles and 1 LP/year. Pays up to 50% royalty to artists on contract; statutory rate to publisher per song on record.
How to Contact: Submit demo tape by mail. Unsolicited submissions are OK. Prefers cassette with 3 songs and lyric or lead sheets. SASE. Reports in 4-6 weeks.
Music: Mostly **country**, **gospel** and **rock**; also **rockabilly**, **R&B** and **Spanish**. Released "Partying With My Pop" and "Hard Drugs For Me" (by Baumgartner/Dwyer/Arnold), recorded by Zen Butcher; and "Memories Of Love," written and recorded by Eric Moberly, all on Pristine Records. Other artists include Rhonda Jones, Sissy Padilla, David Dancer, Eric Matthews, Devarne Thomas, James David, Zen Butcher, Chi Louis, James David and Voices of Joy.
Tips: "Don't give up the dream."

PMG RECORDS, Box 2849, Trolley Station, Detroit MI 48231. President: Bruce Henderson. Record company, music publisher (Prejippie Music Group/BMI) and record producer (PMG Productions). Estab. 1990. Releases 6-12 12″ singles, 2 LPs and 2 EPs/year. Works with musicians/artists on contract. Pays variable royalty to artists on contract; statutory rate to publisher per song on record.
How to Contact: Submit demo tape by mail. Unsolicited submissions are OK. Prefers cassette (or VHS videocassette) with 3-4 songs and lyric sheet. Include photo if possible. No calls please. SASE. Reports in 3 months.
Music: Mostly **funk/rock**, **techno/house** and **dance**; also **alternative rock** and **experimental**. Released *Personality Disorder* by the Prejippies (techno/alternative) and *Frankfather* by Bourgeoisie Paper Jam (alternative rock). Other artists include Urban Transit (house) and Deep Six Honey (alternative/experimental).
Tips: "A strong hook and melody line are your best weapons! We also look for originality."

POP RECORD RESEARCH, 17 Piping Rock Dr., Ossining NY 10562. (914)762-8499. Director: Gary Theroux. Labels include Surf City, GTP and Rock's Greatest Hits. Record company, music publisher (Surf City Music/ASCAP), record producer and archive of entertainment-related research materials (files on hits and hitmakers since 1877). Estab. 1962. Works with musicians/artists and songwriters on contract and writers/historians/biographers, radio, TV and film producers requiring research help or materials. Pays statutory rate to publisher per song on record.
How to Contact: Submit demo tape, press kits or review material by mail. Unsolicited submissions are OK. Prefers cassette (or VHS videocassette). Does not return material.
Music: Mostly **pop**, **country** and **R&B**. Released "The Declaration" (by Theroux-Gilbert), recorded by An American on Bob Records; "Thoughts From a Summer Rain," written and recorded by Bob Gilbert on Bob Records; and "Tiger Paws," written and recorded by Bob Gilbert on BAL Records; all pop singles. Other artists include Gary and Joan, The Nightflight Singers and Ruth Zimmerman.
Tips: "Help us keep our biographical file on you and your career current by sending us updated bios/press kits, etc. They are most helpful to writers/researchers in search of accurate information on your success."

*POSITIVE MUSIC RECORDS, INC., P.O. Box 1521, Columbia MO 21044. (410)750-3813. Fax: (410)750-1897. Director of Promotion: David Robinson. Record company. Estab. 1991. Deals with artists only. Releases 10 LPs and 10 CDs/year. Pays 15% royalty to artists on contract; statutory rate to publisher per song on record.
How to Contact: Submit demo tape by mail. Unsolicited submissions are OK. Prefers cassette. Does not return material. Reports in 1 month.

Remember: Don't "shotgun" your demo tapes. Submit only to companies interested in the type of music you write. For more submission hints, refer to Getting Started on page 5.

Music: Mostly **contemporary jazz** and **straight ahead jazz**. Released *I Can't Complain*, written and recorded by Ken Navarro; *Summerhouse*, written and recorded by Gregg Karulou; and *Easy to Love*, written and recorded by Bobby Militello, all on Positive Records. Other artists include Don Reynolds, Mike Gealer, Rain-Bo Tribe, Philip Mathieu.
Tips: "We are looking for music that can achieve major market radio airplay on contemporary jazz radio stations such as WNUA (Chicago), WQCD (New York), KXSF (San Francisco), KIFM (San Diego)."

POWERCOAT RECORDS, P.O. Box 1791, Bensalem PA 19020. (215)639-5823. Fax: Call first. PR/A&R: Kathy J. Vulgamott. Record company, music publisher (Powercoat Records/BMI). Estab. 1990. Releases 2 singles, 2 LPs, 1 EP/year. Works with musicians/artists on record contract. Pays 40-60% royalty to artists on contract; statutory rate to publishers per song on record.
How to Contact: Write first and obtain permission to submit. "Also include cover letter, bio, photo, explain demo recording, detail equipment." Prefers cassette with 3-4 songs and lyric sheet. Does not return material. Reports in 4-6 weeks.
Music: Mostly **contemporary New Age pop**, **contemporary New Age pop instrumental** and **New Age rock**; also **soft rock**, **pop rock instrumental** and **soundtrack**. Released *Phylogeny*, written and recorded by Phantom Phorty (contemporary New Age pop instrumental); *Distress Sense* and *The World Is Never Enough*, written and recorded by Civil Allen (contemporary New Age pop). Other artists include Visionari.
Tips: "Be meticulous, melodic, but not mainstream. You must be truly dedicated to socially conscious and environmental reform. Quality, sincerity and just plain great music is what must accompany this. We are a contemporary New Age pop label. Follow submission instructions to the letter, and always send SASE if you want a reply."

PPI/PETER PAN INDUSTRIES, 88 St. Francis St., Newark NJ 07105. (201)344-4214. Product Manager: Marianne Eggleston. Labels include Compose Records, Current Records, Parade Video, Iron Bound Publishing/Compose Memories. Record company, music publisher, record producer (Dunn Pearson, Jr.) Estab. 1928. Releases more than 200 cassettes and CDs and 75-80 videos/year. Works with musicians/artists and songwriters on contract. Pays royalty per contract. "All services are negotiable!"
How to Contact: Write to obtain permission to submit. Prefers cassette (or VHS videocassette if available) with 10 songs (full cassette) and lyric sheet. SASE. Reports in 3 months.
Music: **Pop** and **R&B**; also **jazz** and **New Age**. Released "Color Tapestry," written and recorded by Dunn Pearson, Jr. on Compose Records; "A Different Light," by David Friedman; and "The Trollies," by Dennis Scott, Grammy Award winner.
Tips: "Make sure all submissions are presented typed and professional. All recording must be mastered."

PRAVDA RECORDS, 3823 N. Southport, Chicago IL 60613. (312)549-3776. Director of A&R: Mark Luecke. Labels include Bughouse. Record company. Estab. 1985. Releases 3-6 singles, 1 EP and 5-6 CDs/year. Works with musicians/artists on record contract. Pays 10-15% royalty to artists on contract; statutory rate to publishers per song on record.
How to Contact: Submit demo tape by mail. Unsolicited submissions are OK. Prefers cassette with 3-4 songs. Does not return material. Reports in 1-3 months.
Music: Mostly **rock**, **C&W** and **metal**; also **polka**, **big band** and **spoken word**. Released *Wish to the West*, written and recorded by Susan Voelz (pop); *Cannot Love You Enough* (by Willie Wisely), recorded by Willie Wisely Trio (pop); and "Stand on Fire," written and recorded by Mercy Rule (rock), all on Pravda Records. Other artists include Wake OOLOO, New Duncan Imperials, The Service.
Tips: "Perform live in Chicago."

*PREMIÉRE RECORDS, P.O. Box 21323, Eagan MN 55121-0323. (612)686-5094. President: Mitch Viegut. VP and General Manager: Mark Alan. Record company. Estab. 1988. Releases 6 singles, 2-3 LPs, 2-3 cassettes and 2-3 CDs/year. Works with musicians/artists and songwriters on contract. Pays standard royalty to artists on contract; statutory rate to publisher per song on record.
How to Contact: Write or call first to obtain permission to submit. Prefers cassette (or VHS videocassette) with 3-4 songs. Does not return unsolicited material. Reports in 2-3 months.
Music: Mostly **rock**, **pop** and **black contemporary**. Released "Someday You'll Come Running" (by Judith Randall, Robin Randall, Tony Sciuto) (rock); "Somewhere" (by Mitch Viegut) (pop); and *85 MPH* (Mitch Viegut, David Sainden, Roger Probert) (rock), all recorded by Airkraft on Premiére Records. Other artists include Crash Alley, Zwarté, Lost Horizon and The Stellectrics.

PRESENCE RECORDS, 67 Candace Lane, Chatham NJ 07928-1115. (201)701-0707. President: Paul Payton. Record company, music publisher (Paytoons/BMI), record producer (Presence Productions). Estab. 1985. Pays 1-2% royalty to artists on contract; statutory rate to publisher per song on record.

How to Contact: Write and obtain permission to submit. "No phone calls." Prefers cassette with 2-3 songs and lyric sheet. SASE. Reports in 1 month.
Music: Mostly **Doo-wop (50s)**, **rock, new wave rock** and **New Age**. Released "Davilee/Go On" (by Paul Payton/Peter Skolnik), recorded by Fabulous Dudes (doo-wop); and "Boys Like Girls/Relate 2U," written and recorded by Paul Payton (rock), both on Presence Records.

*PROSPECTIVE RECORDS, P.O. Box 6425, Minneapolis MN 55406. (612)871-9533. A&R: John Kass. Labels include Susstones, Pig's Eye, Art Midget, Flurry, Ten Pop. Record company. Estab. 1985. Deals with artists only. Releases 15 singles, 5 LPs, 2 EPs and 5 CDs/year. Pays 50% of profit to artists on contract for each record sold. Pays mechanical rate.
How to Contact: Submit demo tape by mail. Unsolicited submissions are OK. Prefers cassette. "Only bands/artists interested in independent small scale releases should contact us." SASE. Reports in 2 weeks to 2 months.
Music: Released *Flight Of . . .*, written and recorded by The Romulans (rock); "Into Your World," written and recorded by Azalia Snail (psych/rock); and "Super Slinky," written and recorded by Spare Snare (rock), all on Prospective Records. Other artists include Big Red Ball, Green Machine, Green Pyramids, Fauna, Boiled in Lead, Hang Ups.
Tips: "We are into energetic, passionate and thoughtful rock — artists must have drive and the willingness to play live."

PUZZLE RECORDS, Box 461892, Garland TX 75046. A&R Director: Don Ferguson. Record company, music publisher (Sultan Music Publishing/BMI and Illustrious Sultan/ASCAP) and record producer. Estab. 1972. Releases 7-8 singles and 2-3 CDs/year. Works with artists and songwriters on contract.
How to Contact: Accepts unsolicited material.
Music: Mostly **country**; also **MOR, jazz** and **light rock**. Released "Leave Me Right Now," written and recorded by Bobby Teesdale (MOR); "Ain't No Way" (by Duke/Osborn/Fox), recorded by Flash Point (rock); and "I'm Hurtin" (by Roy Orbison/Joe Melson), recorded by Mary Craig (country), all on Puzzle Records.

*QUALITY SOUND RECORDING, 135 Fairmont Lane, Pearl MS 39208. (601)932-5886. Engineer: Chuck Young. Labels include Ancy Records, Norman Records and Street Beat Records. Record company, record producer, music publisher and recording studio. Estab. 1990. Deals with artists and songwriters. Pays 6% royalty to artists on contract; statutory rate to publisher per song on record.
How to Contact: Submit demo tape by mail. Unsolicited submissions are OK. Prefers cassette and lyric sheet. SASE. Reports in 6 weeks.
Music: Mostly **country, blues/rock** and **rock**; also **gospel**. Released *Take Care of the Little Children* (by C.J. Quincy), recorded by C.J. Quincy and the All Stars on Norman Records (gospel); "Spring, TX," written and recorded by E.D. Trammell on Ancy Records (country); and "Christmas Rap" (by DeBra Lewis), recorded by Damian Addison on Street Beat Records (rap). Other artists include Willie Foster and the Jackson All Stars.

R.E.F. RECORDS, 404 Bluegrass Ave., Madison TN 37115. (615)865-6380. Contact: Bob Frick. Record company, record producer and music publisher (Frick Music Publishing Co./BMI). Releases 10 LPs/year. Works with artists and songwriters on contract.
How to Contact: Submit demo tape by mail. Unsolicited submissions are OK. Prefers 7½ ips reel-to-reel or cassette with 2 songs and lyric sheet. SASE. Reports in 2 weeks.
Music: Country, gospel, rock and top 40/pop. Released "I Love You In Jesus," "Warm Family Feeling" and "Our Favorites," all by Bob Scott Frick. Other artists include Larry Ahlborn, Francisco Morales, Candy Coleman, Peggy Beard, Bob Myers, The Backwoods Quartet, Jim Mattingly, David Barton, Jim Pommert, The Vision Heirs, Eddie Issacs, Tereasa Ford, Scott Frick & The Prairie Playboys, Steven Lee Caves and Craig Steele.

*R.E.X. MUSIC, INC., Suite A-23, 229 Ward Cr., Brentwood TN 37027. (615)370-8813. Fax: (615)370-8793. Director of Marketing and A&R: Tyler Bacon. Labels include Storyville Records, Rex pop-u-li. Record company. Estab. 1989. Deals with artists and songwriters. Releases 5 singles, 2 12″ singles, 24 LPs, 4 EPs and 24 CDs/year. Royalty varies.
How to Contact: Submit demo tape by mail. Unsolicited submissions are OK. Prefers cassette or VHS videocassette with 3-5 songs and lyric or lead sheet. "Include any press clippings." Does not return material. Reports in 2 months.
Music: Mostly **alternative**, **metal** and **indie rock**; also **folk, pop** and **gospel**. Released *Brainchild* (by Scott Albert), recorded by Circle of Dust on R.E.X. Records (industrial); *The Fatherless and the Widow* (by Matt Slocum), recorded on Sixpence None the Richer on Rex pop-u-li (alternative); and *Paler Shade* (by P.M. Hall), recorded by Pam Mark Hall on Storyville Records (folk). Other artists include Believer, PASSAFIST, Jan Krist, Nicholas Giaconia, Living Sacrifice, Hot Pink Turtle, Eden Burning, Mo Leverett, Charlotte Modeliene.

Tips: "We are big on creativity . . . be artful."

RAGE-N-RECORDS, Suite #3, 212 N. 12th St., Philadelphia PA 19107. (215)977-9777. Vice President, A&R: Vincent Kershner. Record company, music publisher (Cornea Publishing/ASCAP) and record producer (David Ivory). Estab. 1986. Releases 3 singles, 2 12″ singles and 6 CDs/year. Works with musicians/artists on record contract, songwriters on royalty contract, musicians on salary for in-house studio work. Pays various royalty to artist; statutory rate to publisher per song on record.
How to Contact: Submit demo tape by mail. Unsolicited submissions are OK. Prefers cassette (or VHS videocassette) with 3-5 songs and lyric sheet. SASE. Reports in 6-8 weeks.
Music: Mostly **rock**, **pop** and **R&B**; also **blues**. Released *Blues Guitar Inside & Out*, written and recorded by Stevie Larocca on Rage-N-Records.

*RAILROAD RECORDS, P.O. Box 54325, Atlanta GA 30308-0325. Owner: Paul Cornwell. Record company, music publisher. Estab. 1991. Deals with artists and songwriters. Releases 2 12″ singles, 2 EPs and 5 CDs/year. Pays 11-13% royalty to artists on contract; statutory rate to publisher per song on record.
How to Contact: Submit demo tape by mail. Unsolicited submissions are OK. Prefers cassette with 3 songs and lyric or lead sheet. Does not return material. Reports in 1 month.
Music: Mostly **rock**, **alternative** (**college**) and **reggae**; also **gothic-dance** and **heavy metal**. Released *I Luv Human Rights* (by Paul Hudson), recorded by Human Rights (reggae); *Our Faith* (by Randy Choice), recorded by Human Rights (reggae); and *Mosaic*, written and recorded by Month of Sundays (college) all on Railroad Records. Other artists include Liers In Wait, GG Allin, Drop Circus.
Tips: "Please wait for a reply from us. It is advisable to call first to see if it arrived, but constant calling is not necessary."

RAP-A-LOT RECORDS, INC., #105, 12337 Jones Rd., Houston TX 77070. (713)890-8486. President: James A. Smith. Labels include Face-To-Face Records, Jungle Style Music, Inc. Record company, music publisher (Rap-A-Lot Records/N-The Water Publishing, Inc./ASCAP). Estab. 1985. Works with musicians/artists on record contract, songwriters on royalty contract, musicians on salary for in-house studio work.
How to Contact: Write first and obtain permission to submit. Prefers cassette with 4 songs. Does not return material. Reports in 2-3 months.
Music: Mostly **rap** and **R&B**.

*RASTAMAN WORK ETHIC PRODUCTIONS, Suite 300, 5615 Morningside, Houston TX 77005. (713)LASTGOD. Fax: (713)824-1082. Producer: Nick Cooper. Labels include Groovin' Elixir and Lorenzo Llama-Ass Records. Record company and record producer. Estab. 1988. Releases 1 single, 1 LP, 1 EP and 2 CDs/year. "We work on many more than that, but that's how many are released by RWE. Other labels release our records." Pays 10% royalty to artists on contract; statutory rate to publisher per song on record. "Many contracts include artists or other labels paying for part or all of studio expenses."
How to Contact: Submit demo tape by mail. Unsolicited submissions are OK. Prefers cassette (or VHS videocassette if available) with 1-3 songs. "DATs are preferred at 44.1." Does not return material. Reports in 6 weeks.
Music: Mostly **hip-hop**, **funk** and **jazz**; also **instrumental**. No pop, dance or country. Released *The Man With the Yellow Hat*, written and recorded by Sprawl (funk); *Texas Funk*, written and recorded by various artists (funk); and *Dance Hall Killing*, written and recorded by The Presidents (reggae), all on Rastaman Work Ethic Productions. "For Rap-A-Lot Records, RWE has done post production for the Geto Boys, album cover design for Scarface, The Odd Squad and Too Much Trouble."
Tips: "RWE is much more established in recording/post production/album cover design than in distribution/management. We often work toward getting an album together and have it released by another label."

*RAVE RECORDS, INC., 14750 Puritan Ave., Detroit MI 48227. (810)540-RAVE. Production Dept.: Derrick. Record company and music publisher (Magic Brain Music/ASCAP). Estab. 1992. Deals with artists and songwriters. Releases 2-4 singles, 2 12″ singles, 2 LPs, 2 EPs and 2 CDs/year. Pays various royalty to artists on contract; statutory rate to publisher per song on record.
How to Contact: Submit demo tape by mail. Unsolicited submissions are OK. Prefers cassette with lyric or lead sheet. "Be sure to include all press/promotional information currently used." Does not return material. Reports in 2-4 months.
Music: Mostly **alternative/indie**, **industrial dance** and **techno/rave**; also **A/C** and **R&B**. Released *Wonderful* (by M. Hoffmeyer/S. Sholtes) and "Mindblow" (by M. Hoffmeyer), recorded by Bukimi 3 (alternative); and "It's My Life" (by D. Hakim), recorded by Nicole Hakim (A/C), all on Rave Records. Other artists include Cyber Cryst.

Tips: "We are interested in artists who are new to the market place, but please include at least 4 songs on your demo. Also, if we have information regarding your demo, we will call you. Please do not call us about your submission."

RAZOR & TIE MUSIC, #5A, 214 Sullivan St., New York NY 10012. (212)473-9173. President: Cliff Chenfeld. Labels include Razor Edge Records. Record company. Estab. 1990. Releases 15-20 CDs/ year. Works with musicians/artists on contract.
How to Contact: Write first and obtain permission to submit. Prefers cassette with 3 songs and lyric sheet. SASE. Reports in 3 weeks.
Music: Mostly singer/songwriter oriented **rock, pop/R&B** and **country**. Released "Everything," by the Ghost Poets; "Sicily," by Elliott Murphy; and "She's My Everything," by Joe Grushecky, all on Razor and Tie Records (rock).

*RBW, INC., P.O. Box 14187, Parkville MO 64152. (816)587-5358. Fax: (816)421-6095. President: Russ Wojtkiewicz. Labels include RBW Record Co. and Blue City Records. Record company and production/recording/CD/cassette broker. Estab. 1990. Deals with artists and songwriters. Releases 3-5 CDs/year. Pays varying royalty to artists on contract; statutory rate to publishers per song on record.
How to Contact: Submit demo tape by mail. Unsolicited submissions are OK. Prefers cassette (or VHS videocassette if available) and lyric or lead sheet. "If no video, send recent b&w photo." Does not return material. Reports in 6-12 weeks.
Music: Mostly **blues, classical** and **New Age**; also **jazz/big band, gospel** and **country**. Released *Jehan Alain, Vol. I* (by Jehan Alain), recorded by James Higdon (classical); *Grand Organ of Princeton* (by various), recorded by Douglas Cleveland (classical); and *French Music from St. Michael's* (by various), recorded by Thomas Brown (classical). Other artists include Dr. John Obetz.
Tips: "Looking for artists with strong regional following, with or without recording track record. RBW/ Blue City is looking for unique talent and sound—especially in the New Age/new classical genre. Will listen to all music submitted. Rejection letters will be sent. Do not call."

*RED BUS RECORDS (INT.) LTD., Red Bus House, 48 Bradley Terrace, London NW1, **England**. (071) 258-0324. Fax: (071) 724-2361. Director: Ellis Elias. Record company and music publisher. Estab. 1969. Releases 7 singles, 3 CDs and 3 LPs/year. Works with musicians/artists on contract. Pays 6-10% royalty to artists on contract.
How to Contact: Submit demo tape by mail. Unsolicited submissions are OK. Prefers cassette. SAE and IRC. Reports in 5 weeks.
Music: Mostly **dance**. Artists include Room 101.

RED DOT/PUZZLE RECORDS, 1121 Market, Galveston TX 77550. (409)762-4590. President: A.W. Marullo, Sr. Record company, record producer and music publisher (A.W. Marullo Music/BMI). Estab. 1952. "We also lease masters from artists." Releases 14 12" singles/year. Works with artists and songwriters on contract; musicians on salary for in-house studio work. Pays 8-10% royalty to artists on contract; statutory rate to publishers for each record sold.
How to Contact: Prefers cassette with 4-7 songs and lyric sheet. "Cassettes will not be returned. Contact will be made by mail or phone." Reports in 2 months.
Music: **Rock/top 40 dance songs.** Released "Do You Feel Sexy," (by T. Pindrock), recorded by Flash Point (Top 40/rock); "You Put the Merry in My Christmas," (by E.Dunn), recorded by Mary Craig (rock/pop country); and "Love Machine," (by T. Pindrock), recorded by Susan Moninger, all on Puzzle/Red Dot Records.

RED SKY RECORDS, Box 7, Stonehouse, Glos. GL10 3PQ **United Kingdom**. Phone: 0453-826200. Producer: Johnny Coppin. Record company (PRS) and record producer (Red Sky Records). Estab. 1985. Releases 2 singles, 3 albums (CD and tape) per year. Works with musicians/artists and songwriters on contract and hires musicians for in-house studio work. Pays 8-10% to artists on contract; statutory rate to publisher per song on record.
How to Contact: Submit demo tape by mail. Unsolicited submissions are OK. Prefers cassette or CD with 3 songs and lyric sheet. SAE and IRC. Reports in 6 months.
Music: Mostly **rock/singer-songwriters, modern folk** and **roots music**. Released *Dead Lively!* written and recorded by Paul Burgess; *Force of the River* and "Reach Out For You," written and recorded by Johnny Coppin, all on Red Sky Records. Other artists include Phil Beer and Laurie Lee.

RED-EYE RECORDS, Wern Fawr Farm, Pencoed, Mid-Glam CF35 6NB **United Kingdom**. Phone: (0656)86 00 41. Managing Director: M.R. Blanche. Record company, music publisher (Ever-Open-Eye Music/PRS). Estab. 1979. Releases 4 singles and 2-3 LPs/year. Works with musicians/artists on contract.

How to Contact: Submit demo tape by mail. Unsolicited submissions are OK. Prefers cassette (or VHS videocassette) or 7½ or 15 ips reel-to-reel with 4 songs. SAE and IRC. Does not return material. **Music:** Mostly **R&B**, **rock** and **gospel**; also **swing**. Released "River River" (by D. John), recorded by The Boys; "Billy" (by G. Williams), recorded by The Cadillacs; and "Cadillac Walk" (by Moon Martin), recorded by the Cadillacs, all on Red-Eye Records. Other artists include Cartoon and Tiger Bay.

*REJOICE RECORDS OF NASHVILLE, 116 Roberta Dr., Nashville TN 37075. (615)264-1373. Owner: Gregg Hutchins. Record company and music publisher. Estab. 1993. Deals with artists and songwriters. Releases 3 CDs/year. Pays statutory rate to publisher per song on record.
How to Contact: Write first and obtain permission to submit. Prefers cassette with up to 3 songs and lyric sheet. Does not return material. Reports in 1 month.
Music: Mostly **southern gospel**, **country gospel** and **Christian country**; also **bluegrass gospel**. Released *Adam's Side* (by Jesse Wilson), recorded by Billy Walker (gospel); *Jordan's Banks*, written and recorded by Donnie & Vicky Clark (gospel); and *When I Can't Take It Anymore* (by Renee Smith), recorded by Heritage (gospel), all on Rejoice Records. Other artists include The Redeemed and The McGlothlins.

*RESISTOR RECORDS, 1001½ Elizabeth St., Oak Hill WV 25901. (304)465-1298. Director of A&R: Hope Stapleton. Record company, record producer and music publisher (Resistor Music/ASCAP). Estab. 1985. Deals with artists and songwriters. Releases 2-3 singles, 4-5 LPs and 4-5 CDs/year. Pays statutory rate to publisher per song on record.
How to Contact: Submit demo tape by mail. Unsolicited submissions are OK. Prefers cassette or ½" videocassette with 3 songs and lyric or lead sheet. Does not return material. Reports in 1 month.
Music: Mostly **country**, **rock** and **gospel**. Released *Delnora* (by various), recorded by Delnora Reed (country); and *Bitter Creek*, written and recorded by Bitter Creek, both on Resistor Records. Other artists include Preston Lee, Jeanie Woods and Marty Dawn.

*REVELATION RECORDS, P.O. Box 5232, Huntington Beach CA 92615. (714)375-4264. Owner: Jordan Cooper. Labels include Crisis. Record company. Estab. 1987. Deals with artists only. Releases 2 singles, 2 12" singles, 6 LPs, 4 EPs and 10 CDs/year. Royalty varies. Pays various amounts to publisher per song on record.
How to Contact: Submit demo tape by mail. Unsolicited submissions are OK. Prefers cassette or VHS videocassette with 3 songs and lyric sheet. "Send photos and bio/press sheet if you have one." Does not return material. Reports in 2 weeks.
Music: Mostly **rock**, **hardcore/punk** and **thrash**; also **country**, **rap** and **disco**. Released *Faster*, written and recorded by Onion on Crisis Records (alternative); *Sights* (by Mike Ferraro), recorded by Mike Judge & Old Smoke on Revelation Records (country-folk-blues); and "Looking Back," written and recorded by Bold on Revelation Records (hardcore). Other artists include Farside, Into Another, Sense Field, Iceburn, ORANGE 9mm, Function.
Tips: "Don't be inhibited when sending songs, we listen to everything. Don't be discouraged, our taste is not anything more than opinion."

*RICHWAY RECORDS INTERNATIONAL, P.O. Box 110983, Nashville TN 37222. (615)731-6640. President: Wayne G. Leinsz. Record company, record producer and music publisher. Estab. 1991. Releases 4 LPs and 4 CDs/year. Pays 10% royalty to artists on contract; statutory rate to publisher per song on record.
How to Contact: Write or call first and obtain permission to submit. Prefers cassette (or VHS videocassette if available) with 3 songs and lyric sheet. SASE. Reports in 1 month.
Music: Mostly **country**, **bluegrass** and **gospel**. Released "Cold October Night," written and recorded by Phillip Clarkson (country); *I Still Pretend* (by Guffnett/Pugh/Stange), recorded by Jill Michaels (country); and "Ghost of Simon Dill" (by R. Madison), recorded by Bobby Atkins (country). Other artists include Ernie Hollar, Gates Millay, Michael Hollomon, Michael Harrelson, Texas Heat, Clay Bonham, Larry Elliott.

RIGHTEOUS RECORDS, 429 Richmond Ave., Buffalo NY 14222. (716)884-0248. Manager, A&R: Dale Anderson. Record company (Blizzard Records), music publisher (Righteous Babe Music/BMI). Estab. 1991. Releases 2 LPs and 2 CDs/year. Works with musicians/artists on record contract, musicians on salary for in-house studio work. Pays 10-80% to artists on contract; statutory rate to publisher per song on record.
How to Contact: Submit demo tape by mail. Unsolicited submissions are OK. Prefers cassette with 3 or more songs. Does not return material. Reports in 4-6 weeks.
Music: Mostly **folk/acoustic**, **alternative rock** and **jazz**. Released *Puddle Dive*, *Imperfectly* and *Out of Range*, all written and recorded by Ani DiFranco on Righteous Records.
Tips: "Make honest, uncomplicated music with a strong personal point of view."

RIPSAW RECORD CO., Suite 805, 4545 Connecticut Ave. NW, Washington DC 20008. (202)362-2286. President: Jonathan Strong. Record company, record producer and music publisher (Southern Crescent Publishing/BMI and Sugar Mama Music/BMI). Estab. 1976. Releases 1-2 albums/year. Works with musicians/artists and songwriters on contract. Pays negotiable royalty to songwriters on contract; statutory rate to publishers for each record sold.
How to Contact: Submit demo tape by mail. Unsolicited submissions are OK. Prefers cassette and lyric sheet. SASE. "Invite us to a club date to listen." Reports as soon as possible, generally 1-6 months.
Music: Country, blues, rockabilly and **"traditional" rock**. Released *Oooh-Wow!*, by the Uptown Rhythm Kings on Ripsaw Records (jump blues); *Christmas In Tennessee* (by Billy Hancock) on Run Wild Records; and "Hot Rod Man" (by Tex Rubinowitz) on Rhino Records (rockabilly). Other artists include Bobby Smith and Kid Tater & The Cheaters.
Tips: "Keep it true roots rock 'n' roll."

RISING STAR RECORDS INC., 710 Lakeview Ave. NE, Atlanta GA 30308. (404)872-1431. President: Barbara Taylor. Record company, music publisher (Rising Star Music Publishers). Estab. 1987. Releases 3-4 LPs and 3-4 CDs/year. Pays negotiated royalty to artists on contract; negotiated rate to publishers per song on record.
How to Contact: Submit demo tape by mail. Unsolicited submissions are OK. Prefers cassette with 3 songs and lyric or lead sheet. SASE. Reports in 1 month.
Music: Mostly **New Age, instrumental jazz** and **classical**; also **new world, children's** and **other forms of instrumental music**. Released *Breaking the Rules*, written and recorded by Pruett & Davis (jazz); *Seashore Solitude* and *Forest Cathedrals*, written and recorded by various artists (New Age/classical), all on RSR Records. Other artists include Rob Albertson, Sylvia Carroll, Michael Thomas, Mark Davis, Rick Pruett, George Skaroulis, Brad Rudisail, Barbara Taylor and Tim Wheeler.

*RMA MUSIC, Suite 1265, 11012 Ventura Blvd., Studio City CA 91604. (818)842-4450. Marketing Director: William R. Simonsen. Record company. Estab. 1993. Deals with artists and songwriters. Releases 2 LPs and 2 CDs/year.
How to Contact: Submit demo tape by mail. Unsolicited submissions are OK. Prefers cassette. "We accept full or condensed scores. All submissions must be copyrighted." SASE. Reports in 2 months.
Music: Classical and **pops/light classical**. Released *A New Light Christmas* and *Somewhere Over . . .*, both written and recorded by Richard Audd on RMA Records.
Tips: "We are an independent record company seeking serious classical composers who write American music. All works are performed by the East Pacific Symphony, Richard Audd conducting. The EPS is the complete electronic duplication of a full symphony orchestra with all the necessary subtleties. We work directly with the composer in performing and recording his/her music to their satisfaction. All payments and agreements are negotiable."

ROAD RECORDS, 429 S. Lewis Rd., Royersford PA 19468. (215)948-8228. Fax: (215)948-4175. President: Jim Femino. Vice President: Mike Moore. Record company and music publisher (Fezsongs/ASCAP, Feminosongs/BMI). Estab. 1980. Releases 1-3 singles, 1 LP and 1 CD/year. Works with musicians/artists and songwriters on contract. Pays varying royalty to artists on contract; statutory rate to publisher per song on record.
How to Contact: Write first and obtain permission to submit. Prefers cassette (or VHS videocassette) with 1-3 songs and lyric sheets. SASE. Reports in 4-6 weeks.
Music: Country. Released "Party Tonight," *Just The Good Stuff* and "Nancy's Song," all written and recorded by Jim Femino on Road Records (rock). Other artists include Certain Flightless Birds.

ROCK DOG RECORDS, P.O. Box 3687, Hollywood CA 90028. (213)661-0259. A&R Director: Gerry North. Record company, record producer. Estab. 1987. Releases 3 singles, 1-3 12″ singles, 3-5 LPs, 1-3 EPs and 3 CDs/year. Works with musicians/artists on record contract, songwriters on royalty contract, musicians on salary for in-house studio work. Pays negotiable royalty to artists on contract.
How to Contact: Call first and obtain permission to submit. Prefers CD (or VHS videocassette) with 3-5 songs and lyric sheet. SASE. Reports in 1 month.
Music: Mostly **contemporary instrumental, jazz** and **New Age**; also **R&B** and **rap**. Released *Break in the Routine*, written and recorded by Brain Storm (New Age); *The New Air*, written and recorded by Patt Connolly; and *Nasty Day*, written and recorded by Souplex Slam, all on Rock Dog Records. Other artists include Kenny Gray, Ian Ashley, Johnathen Hall, Robert Louden and Steve Smith.
Tips: "It's the music, not the package that is important."

ROLL ON RECORDS®, 112 Widmar Pl., Clayton CA 94517. (510)672-8201. Owner: Edgar J. Brincat. Record company. Estab. 1985. Releases 2-3 LPs/cassettes/year. Works with musicians/artists and songwriters on contract and hires musicians for in-house studio work. Pays 10% royalty to artists on contract; statutory rate to publisher per song on record.

How to Contact: Submit demo tape by mail. Unsolicited submissions are OK. Prefers cassette with 3 songs and lyric sheet. SASE. Reports in 2-4 weeks.
Music: Mostly **contemporary/country, MOR** and **R&B**; also **pop, light rock** and **modern gospel**. Released "Outskirts of Phoenix" (by Pettrella Pollefeyt); "Write to P.O. Box 33" (by Michael Gooch/Susan Branding) and "Never Thought Of Losing You" (by Jeanne Dicky-Boyter/Gina Dempsey), all recorded by Edee Gordon and the Flash Band.
Tips: "Be professional, write clearly and always enclose an SASE (many people don't)."

*ROTTEN RECORDS, P.O. Box 2157, Montclair CA 91763. (909)624-2332. Fax: (909)624-2392. President: Ron Peterson. Record company. Estab. 1985. Deals with artists only. Releases 3 LPs, 3 EPs and 3 CDs/year.
How to Contact: Submit demo tape by mail. Unsolicited submissions are OK. Prefers cassette. SASE. Reports in 2 months.
Music: Mostly **rock, alternative** and **commercial**; also **punk** and **heavy metal**. Released *No Longer Human*, recorded by STG on Rotten Records (industrial).
Tips: "Don't call and keep bugging us to listen to your demo—very annoying!"

*ROUND FLAT RECORDS, 63 Lennox Ave., Buffalo NY 14226. President: Curt Ippolito. Record company and distributor. Estab. 1989. Deals with artists only. Releases 10 singles and 6 CDs/year. Pays varying royalty to artists on contract; statutory rate to publisher per song on record.
How to Contact: Submit demo tape by mail. Unsolicited submissions are OK. Prefers cassette (or VHS videocassette if available) with 5 songs and lyric sheet. Does not return material. Reports in 2-4 weeks.
Music: Mostly **alternative, hardcore** and **ska**; also **industrial**. Released "1st Mission," recorded by Cropdogs (alternative); "Powertrip," recorded by Don't Pet Me (ska); and "Purity," recorded by Foundation (hardcore), all on Round Flat Records. Other artists include Against All Hope, Discontent.
Tips: "I also like to see news clippings, fliers, etc."

*ROWENA RECORDS, 195 S. 26th St., San Jose CA 95116. (408)286-4091. Fax: (408)286-9845. A&R Director: G.J. O'Neal and Jeannine O'Neal. Labels include Chance Records and Jan-Ell Records. Record company. Releases 4 singles, 4 12" singles and 4 CDs/year. Works with musicians/artists and songwriters on contract; hires musicians for in-house studio work. Pays 10% royalty to artists on contract; pays statutory rate to publishers per song on record.
How to Contact: Submit demo tape by mail. Unsolicited submissions are OK. Prefers cassette with 4 or more songs and lyric sheet. SASE. Reports in 3 weeks.
Music: Mostly **gospel, country, R&B** and all styles of **Mexican**; also **pop, rock** and **New Age**. Released *Counting Down The Days*, recorded by Randal Max Mower (contemporary country); *Always Chasing Rainbows*, recorded by Floyd Malone (adult contemporary); and *Little Child*, recorded by Adrienne (Black contemporary/pop).

RR&R RECORDS, Demos mailed to: 9305 Dogwood Place, Gainesville GA 30506. (706)861-2186. Also Suite 204, 23 Music Sq. E., Nashville TN 37203. (615)726-2571. A&R and Producer: Ron Dennis Wheeler. Labels include Rapture Records, Ready Records and Y'Shua Records. Record company, music publisher (Sounds of Aicram/BMI, Do It Now Publishing/ASCAP), record producer (Ron Dennis Wheeler). Estab. 1966. Releases 5 singles, 5 12" singles, 5 LPs, 5 EPs and 5 CDs/year. Works with musicians/artists and songwriters on contract; hires musicians for in-house studio work. Pays artists 5-15% of sales; statutory rate to publishers per song on record.
How to Contact: Submit demo tape by mail. Unsolicited submissions are OK. Prefers cassette and DAT with and without lead vocals (or VHS videocassette) or 15 ips reel-to-reel with lyric and lead sheet. SASE. Reports if interested.
Music: Mostly **gospel, rock, pop, country** and **R&B**. Released "There's Someone for Each of Us" and "One Perfect Man" (by R. McGibony), "He's Keeping Me Strong" (by Irene Gaskings), all recorded by Ron Dennis Wheeler on RR&R Records. Other artists include Patty Weaver, Mike Brookshire, Jez Davidson, Linda Marr.
Tips: "Do not try to copy another artist or style of music. Better production masters (if possible) get more attention quicker. If you send demos only please have vocals clear and out front of music."

 The asterisk before a listing indicates that the listing is new in this edition. New markets are often the most receptive to unsolicited submissions.

RUFFCUT RECORDS, 6472 Seven Mile, South Lyon MI 48178. (313)486-0505. Producer: J.D. Dudick. Record company, music publisher (AL-KY Music/ASCAP, Bubba Music/BMI). Estab. 1991. Releases 5 singles and 4 CDs/year. Pays 12% royalty to artists on contract; statutory rate to publisher per song on record.
How to Contact: Submit demo tape by mail. Unsolicited submissions are OK. Prefers cassette with 2 songs and lyric sheet. Does not return material. Reports in 6 weeks.
Music: Mostly **rock, pop** and **country**; also **alternative**. Released "Passion's Fire" (by W. Bradley), recorded by Sassy on Fearless Records (country); and "Breakin Down The Wall" (by Chris Pierce), recorded by Flavour Mouse on Rockit Records (rock). Other artists include Q, Wild Blue and Laya.
Tips: "Write songs that mean something, and if other people like it (sincerely) let's hear it. Records sell on musical expression, not marketing hype. Remember to keep the vocals above the music."

*RUSTRON MUSIC PRODUCTIONS, 1156 Park Lane, West Palm Beach 33417-5957. (407)686-1354. Fax: (407)684-0226. Executive Director: Rusty Gordon. Labels include Rustron Records and Whimsong Records. "Rustron administers 22 independent labels for publishing and marketing." Record company, record producer and music publisher (Whimsong/ASCAP and Rustron Music/BMI). Estab. 1970. Releases 5-10 CDs/year. Pays variable royalty to artists on contract. "Artists with history of product sales get higher % than those who are 1st product with no sales track record." Pays statutory rate to publisher per song on record.
How to Contact: Submit demo tape by mail. Unsolicited submissions are OK. Prefers cassette with 3 songs and lyric sheet. "If singer/songwriter has independent product (cassette or CD) produced and sold at gigs—send this product." SASE required for all correspondence, no exceptions. Reports in 2-4 months.
Music: Mostly **mainstream** and **women's music**, **A/C, electric acoustic, pop (cabaret, blues)** and **blues (R&B, country folk)**; also **New Age fusions** (instrumentals), **modern folk fusions, environmental** and **socio-political**. Released *Jayne Margo-Reby* (by Rusty Gordon, Vic Paul, Ron Caruso, Debbie Tyson, Jayne Margo-Reby), recorded by Jayne Margo-Reby on Rustron Records (fusion); *Marian Joy Ring: Third Time*, written and recorded by Marian Joy Ring on Rustron Records (folk-jazz fusion); and *Bonnie Jean Johns: Pay The Price*, written and recorded by Bonnie Jean Johns on Whimsong Records (country fusion). Other artists include Boomslang, Deb Criss, Lynn Thomas, Flash Silvermoon, Sue Embler.
Tips: "Find your own unique style, write well crafted songs with unpredictable concepts, strong hooks and definitive melody. New Age composers: evolve your themes and add multi-cultural diversity with instruments. Don't be predictable. Don't over-produce your demos and don't drown vocals."

*SABRE PRODUCTIONS, P.O. Box 10147, San Antonio TX 78210. (210)533-6910. Producer: E.J. Henke. Labels include Fanfare, Satin, Legacy. Record company, record producer. Estab. 1965. Deals with artists and songwriters. Releases 48 singles, 5 LPs and 4 CDs/year. Pays 10% royalty to artists on contract; statutory rate to publisher per song on record.
How to Contact: Submit demo tape by mail. Unsolicited submissions are OK. Prefers cassette with 4 songs and lyric sheet. SASE. Reports in 3 weeks.
Music: Mostly **country** (all styles), **gospel** and **rock/R&B**. Released *Take A Number* (by Staggs/Norton/Wharton), recorded by Robert Beckom on Sabre (country); *Borderline Crazy* (by Betty Kay Miller), recorded by Darnell Miller on Fanfare Records (country); and "Hypnotized," (by Ted Snyder), recorded by Ace Diamond on Legacy (rockabilly). Other artists include Joe Terry, Suzie Rowles and Sunglows.
Tips: "Submit only your best material. Be patient and don't irritate your publisher, record label, etc."

SABTECA RECORD CO., Box 10286, Oakland CA 94610. (510)465-2805. President: Duane Herring. Creative Manager: Sean Herring. Record company and music publisher (Sabteca Music Co./ASCAP, Toyiabe Music Co./BMI). Estab. 1980. Releases 3 singles and 1 12" single/year. Works with songwriters on contract and hires musicians for in-house studio work. Pays statutory rate to publisher per song on record.
Affiliate(s): Andre Romare Records.
How to Contact: Write or call first and obtain permission to submit. Prefers cassette with lyric sheet. SASE. Reports in 2-4 weeks.
Music: Mostly **R&B, pop** and **country**. Released "It Just Ain't Right" and "Sleeping Beauty" (by Duane Herring), recorded by Johnny B on Andre Romare Records (country); and *Hooray For You, Girl* (by Walt Coleman/Bill Charles), recorded by Lee Coleman on Sabteca Records (pop). Other artists include Walt Coleman and Lois Shayne.
Tips: "Improve your writing skills. Keep up with music trends."

SADDLESTONE RECORDS, 264 "H" Street Box 8110-21, Blaine WA 98230. Canada address: 8821 Delwood Drive N. Delta British Columbia V4C 4A1 **Canada**. (604)582-7117. Fax: (604)582-8610. President: Candice James. Labels include Silver Bow Records. Record company, music publisher

(PROCAN, SOCAN, Saddlestone/BMI) and record producer (Silver Bow Productions). Estab. 1988. Releases 50 singles, 30 LPs and 30 CDs/year. Works with musicians/artists on contract. Pays 10% royalty to artists on contract; statutory rate to publishers per song on record.
How to Contact: Submit demo tape by mail. Unsolicited submissions are OK. Prefers cassette with 3-5 songs and lyric sheet. SASE. Reports in 3 months.
Music: Mostly **country, pop, rock**; also **R&B, gospel** and **children's**. Released *Pardon Me* (by John McLaughlin), recorded by Clancy Wright on Saddlestone Records (country); *Chicken Lady* (by Todd Butler), recorded by The Muppets on Jim Henson Records (children's); and *Listen to the Rain*, written and recorded by Doug Pettigrew on Saddlestone Records (pop). Other artists include Gary MacFarlane, Sunny & Houserockers, Randy Friskie, Tracy Todd, Joe Lonsdale, Blackwater Jack, Robert Rigby, John McCabe and Clancy Wright.
Tips: "Send original material, studio produced, with great hooks."

SAHARA RECORDS AND FILMWORKS ENTERTAINMENT, 8th Floor, 4475 Allisonville Rd., Indianapolis IN 46205. (317)546-2912. President: Edward De Miles. Record company, music publisher (EDM Music/BMI) and record producer. Estab. 1981. Releases 15-20 12″ singles and 5-10 LPs/year. Pays 9½-11% royalty to artists on contract; pays statutory rate to publishers per song on record.
How to Contact: Write first and obtain permission to submit. Prefers cassette with 3-5 songs and lyric sheet. SASE. Reports in 1 month.
Music: Mostly **R&B/dance, top 40 pop/rock** and **contemporary jazz**; also **TV-film themes, musical scores** and **jingles**. Released "Hooked on U," "Dance Wit Me" and "Moments," written and recorded by Steve Lynn (R&B), all on Sahara Records. Other artists include Lost in Wonder, Dvon Edwards and Multiple Choice.
Tips: "We're looking for strong mainstream material. Lyrics and melodies with good hooks that grab people's attention."

*SANITY CHECK MUSEC, INC., P.O. Box 527, Front Royal VA 22630. (703)636-7587. A&R: Christina Orr. Labels include Big Sky Country Records. Record company, record producer and music publisher. Estab. 1989. Deals with artists and songwriters. Releases 5 LPs, 2 EPs and 5 CDs/year. Pays varying royalty to artists on contract; statutory rate to publisher per song on record.
How to Contact: Submit demo tape by mail. Unsolicited submissions are OK. Prefers cassette (or VHS videocassette if available) with 4 songs and lyric sheet. Does not return material. Reports in 1 month.
Music: Mostly **rock (alternative** or **other), blues** and **experimental rock**; also anything but New Age, gospel and country. Released *Alive in the Valley/Dead in the Water*, written and recorded by Blue (rock); *In Wonderland*, written and recorded by Dirty Deal (rock); and *17 Year Locust Tour*, written and recorded by The Agency (alternative), all on Sanity Check Records. Other artists include Erik & the Dragtones, Naked House, Shield, Savage Garden, Ralph Fortune and Michael Dowell.

SCENE PRODUCTIONS, Box 1243, Beckley WV 25802. (304)252-4836. President/Producer: Richard L. Petry. A&R: Carol Lee. Labels include Rising Sun and Country Bridge Records. Record company, record producer and music publisher (Purple Haze Music/BMI). Member of AFM. Releases 1-2 singles and 1-2 LPs/year. Works with musicians/artists on contract. Pays 4-5% minimum royalty to artists on contract; standard royalty to songwriters on contract; statutory rate to publishers for each record sold. Charges "initial costs, which are conditionally paid back to artist."
How to Contact: Submit demo tape by mail. Unsolicited submissions are OK. Prefers cassette with 2-5 songs and lyric sheet. Prefers studio produced demos. SASE. Reports in 4-8 weeks.
Music: Mostly **country, top 40, R&B/crossover** and **pop/rock**; also **MOR, light** and **commercial rock**. Released "My Old Friend," written and recorded by Chuck Paul (pop) on Rising Sun Records; and "Home Sweet W.V.," written and recorded by Dave Runion on Country Bridge Records.
Tips: "Prepare ahead of time with a very good demo tape presenting your talent. Don't spend a lot on a taping and video. You need some kind of initial financial backing to get your career started. Remember you're investing in yourself. You'll need around $10,000 to get the proper exposure you need. Major labels require around 10 times this to sign you. Deal with a company that is reputable and has music with the trade people, *Billboard, Cashbox, R&R* and *Gavin*".

SCP RECORDS, Country Manor, 812 S. 890 East, Orem UT 84058. (801)225-9975. President/General Manager: Ron Simpson. Record company, music publisher and record producer (Sound Column Productions). Member CMA, AFM. Estab. 1968. Releases 3 singles and 5 albums/year. Works with artists and songwriters on contract; hires musicians for in-house studio work. Pays negotiable royalty to artists on contract; statutory rate to publishers for each record sold.
How to Contact: Submit demo tape (3 songs max) with lyric sheet. "We listen to everything, but with the volume of submissions, we do get behind. Be patient—you *will* hear from us, and you'll receive specific feedback. Please honor our request for no phone calls."

Music: All styles except rap. Released *Destination* and "Doom Carousel," both written and recorded by Kim Simpson; and "Mister Music Maker" (by Ron Simpson), recorded by Randy Porter.
Tips: "Sound Column Publications is currently seeking acoustic-style adult contemporary songs for SCP Records artist Gary Voorhees."

*SCRATCHED RECORDS, 1611 Arcade Dr., Richardson TX 75081. (214)680-1830. President: Gerard LeBlanc. Labels include Spectre. Record company. Estab. 1990. Deals with artists only. Releases 6 singles and 3 CDs/year. Pays 50% royalty to artists on contract; statutory rate to publisher per song on record. "We split all expenses 50/50."
How to Contact: Submit demo tape by mail. Unsolicited submissions are OK. Prefers cassette. "Will respond if interested." Does not return material. Reports in 2 weeks.
Music: Mostly **alternative**, **punk** and **hard core**; also **girl bands**. Released *A Reason to Care*, written and recorded by Humungus (punk); *Phurly*, written and recorded by Third Leg (hard core); and *We're From Texas*, written and recorded by 21 different bands (alternative), all on Scratched Records. Other artists include Caulk.

SEALED WITH A KISS, INC., Suite 119, 2166 W. Broadway, Anaheim CA 92804-2446. (714)992-2652. Vice President A&R: Tracy Sands. Labels include SWAK Records. Record company and music publisher (Lipstick Traces Music Publishing/BMI). Estab. 1989. Releases 6-12 singles, 4 LPs, 2 EPs and 4 CDs/year. Works with musicians/artists and songwriters on contract. Pays 1-9% royalty to artists on contract; negotiable rate to publisher per song.
How to Contact: Submit demo tape by mail. Unsolicited submissions are OK. Prefers cassette. SASE. Reports in 2 months.
Music: Mostly **rock** and **psychedelic**. Released "The Bomb" (by Robert Wahlsteen), recorded by Jubal's Children (psychedelic); "Dance Time" (by Jeff Schreibman), recorded by The Royalites (rock); and "My Silver Lining" (by David Rangel and Harry Watkins), recorded by The Yorkshires (rock), all on SWAK Records. Other artists include Tracy Sands.
Tips: "If you own unsigned masters, demos, live recordings, garage rehearsal tapes of 1960's rock and psychedelic, contact us first! We're looking for obscure, little known groups from any region. Must prove ownership and authenticity. Then we talk."

SEASIDE RECORDS, 100 Labon St., Tabor City NC 28463. (910)653-2546. Owner: Elson H. Stevens. Labels include JCB. Record company, music publisher and record producer. Estab. 1978. Releases 10 singles and 15 LPs/year. Works with musicians/artists and songwriters on contract; musicians on salary for in-house studio work, and producers. Pays 3-10% royalty to artists on contract; statutory rate to publisher per song on record.
How to Contact: Submit demo tape by mail. Unsolicited submissions are OK. Prefers cassette with 3 songs and lyric or lead sheet. SASE. Reports in 1 month.
Music: Mostly **country**, **gospel** and **rock**; also **beach music**." Released "I'll Never Say Never Again" (by G. Todd/T. Everson), recorded by Sherry Collins (country); "Faith of a Tiny Seed" (by R. Lynn), recorded by Randa Lynn (contemporary gospel); and "Long Lonesome Road" (by G. Taylor), recorded by Sherry Collins (country); all on SeaSide Records.
Tips: "Send only unpublished material. Songs must have strong hook."

SEEDS RECORDS, Box 20814, Oklahoma City OK 73156. (405)755-0315. Labels include Homa and Okart Records. Record company, record producer, music publisher (Okisher Publishing/BMI), and Mickey Sherman Talent Management. Estab. 1973. Releases 6-12 12" singles, 3 LPs and 3 CDs/year. Works with songwriters on contract and hires in-house studio musicians. Pays 10% royalty to artists on contract; statutory rate to publishers for each record sold.
How to Contact: Submit demo tape by mail. Unsolicited submissions OK. Prefers cassette (or video-cassette) with 1-3 songs and lyric sheet. Does not return unsolicited material. Reports in 3 months.
Music: Mostly **blues**, **country** and **ballads**; also **easy listening**, **jazz**, **MOR**, **R&B** and **soul**. Released "Loose As A Goose," written and recorded by Rod Higdon; "Thank You For the Favor" (by M. Sherman) and "Hush Hush" (by Jan Jo), both recorded by Jan Jo, all on Seeds Records. Other artists include Charley Shaw and Benny Kubiak.

*SHAKEFORK RECORDS, P.O. Box 9711, Downers Grove IL 60515. (708)960-0973. Contact: A&R. Record company. Estab. 1989. Deals with artists only. Releases 12 singles, 3 12" singles, 6 LPs, 5 EPs and 4 CDs/year. Royalty is negotiable. Pays statutory rate to publisher per song on record.
How to Contact: Submit demo tape by mail. Unsolicited submissions are OK. Prefers cassette with lyric sheet. SASE. Reports in 1 month.
Music: Mostly **punk rock**, **alternative** and **grunge**; also **heavy metal**, **rap** and **country**. Released *It's a Punk Thing . . .*, written and recorded by various artists (punk); "Friction" (by Nanna), recorded by Friction (punk); and "Gauge" (by Gub), recorded by Gauge (punk), all on Shakefork Records. Other artists include Billingsgate, Target, Ivy League, Mannequin Head, Dickey MO.

SHAKY RECORDS, Box 71, Stn "C", Winnipeg Manitoba R3M 3X3 **Canada**. (204)932-5212. President: Shaky. Record company, music publisher (Shaky Publishing Co./SOCAN). Estab. 1984. Releases 2 LPs, 2 EPs and 1 CD/year. Works with musicians/artists on record contract, songwriters on royalty contract, musicians on salary for in-house studio work.
How to Contact: Submit demo tape by mail. Unsolicited submissions are OK. Prefers cassette (or VHS videocassette if available) with 4-5 songs and lyric sheet. SASE. Reports in 1 month.
Music: Mostly **hard rock, heavy metal** and **rock**. Released *Strictly Business, Three The Hard Way* and *Bad Boys of Rock* (by B. Johnston), recorded by Lawsuit on Shaky Records. Other artists include The Shake.
Tips: "Build up your song catalog, look to other genres of music to expand your ideas in your type of music. Demo quality is important but songs come first. Write lots, choose wisely."

SHAOLIN FILM & RECORDS, Box 58547, Salt Lake City UT 84158. (801)595-1123. President: Richard O'Connor. A&R: Michelle McCarty. Labels include Shaolin Communications. Record company, music publisher (Shaolin Music/ASCAP) and record producer (The Coyote). Estab. 1984. Releases 2 singles, 1 LP, 1 CD and 1 EP/year. Works with musicians/artists on record contract.
How to Contact: Submit demo tape by mail. Unsolicited submissions are OK. Prefers cassette with 3-4 songs and lyric sheet. Include bio and press kit. Does not return material. Reports in 6 weeks.
Music: Mostly **rock, hard rock** and **pop**; also **soundtracks**. Released "Christ Killer," "Great Salt Lake" and *Wishwood Bridge*, all written and recorded by Coyote on Shaolin Film and Records.

SHORE RECORDS, P.O. Box 161, Hazlet NJ 07730. (908)888-1846. Director of A&R: Paul Bonanni. Record company, music publisher (BMI), record producer (Bobby Monroe). Estab. 1991. Releases 3 singles and 3 12″ singles/year. Works with musicians/artists on record contract, songwriters on royalty contract. Pays standard rate to artists on contract; statutory rate to publishers per song on record.
How to Contact: Submit demo tape by mail. Unsolicited submissions are OK. Prefers cassette (or VHS videocassette if available) with 3-4 songs and lyric sheet or lead sheet. Does not return material. Reports in 2 to 6 months.
Music: Mostly **rock/techno, alternative** and **hard rock/metal**; also **country, R&B** and **dance**. Released *Tri-State's* (by 16 different artists); and "What Do All the People Know?" (by Monroes), recorded by Bobby Monroe, both on Shore Records (rock). Other artists include Leap of Faith, Fallon, King for a Day, Simon Quiss, Eric Denton Dog.
Tips: "Provide me with good quality music at more of a commercial/mainstream sound."

*SHOW BIZ PRODUCTIONS, P.O. Box 121833, Fort Worth TX 76121. (817)626-8300. Owner: B.L. Bollman. Labels include Gospel City and BI Records. Record company, record producer and music publisher (Bollman Int'l Publishing Co./BMI, Misty-Christy Publishing/ASCAP). Estab. 1972. Deals with artists and songwriters. Releases 26 LPs/year. Pays variable royalty to publishers per song on record.
How to Contact: Submit demo tape by mail. Unsolicited submissions are OK. Prefers cassette. Does not return material.
Music: Mostly **gospel, country** and **Spanish**. Released "Who Makes the Rain," written and recorded by Homer Ferrell (gospel); "Road Train Driver," written and recorded by Michael Gant (country); and "Tears Dim My Eyes" (by Clarence E. Jones), recorded by Full Sail (gospel), all on Show Biz Records. Other artists include Ken Powers, 2 Days Later, Larry Demoron, Al Turner, Cindy Woolet, Harry T. Crawley, Wade Chandler, Fern Borrelli and Jerry House.

*SIGNIFICANT OTHER RECORDS, P.O. Box 1545, New York NY 10013. (212)366-9078. President: Richard Dworkin. Record company. Estab. 1988. Deals with artists and songwriters. Pays varying royalty to artists on contract; statutory rate to publisher per song on record.
How to Contact: Submit demo tape by mail. Unsolicited submissions are OK. Prefers cassette (or VHS videocassette if available) with 3-5 songs and lyric sheet. Does not return material. Reports in 1 month.
Music: Music by gay/lesbian artists. Released *Purple Heart* and *Legacy,* both written and recorded by Michael Callen; and *The Flirtations,* written and recorded by The Flirtations, all on Significant Other Records.

SILENT RECORDS, #206, 101 Townsend St., San Francisco CA 94107. (415)957-1320. Fax: (415)957-0779. President: Kim Cascone. Record company and record producer (Kim Cascone). Estab. 1986. Releases 20 CDs/year. Works with musicians/artists on contract. Accepts LPs and CDs for consideration and distribution. Pays 15% of wholesale as royalty to artists on contract; negotiable rate to publishers per song on record.
Affiliate(s): Furnace, Sulphur.
How to Contact: Write first and obtain permission to submit. Prefers cassette (or VHS videocassette) with press kit (press clips, bio, etc.). Does not return material. Reports in 6 months.

Music: Mostly **ambient.** Released *In A Garden of Eden* (by Kim Cascone), recorded by The Heavenly Music Corporation; *Ritual Ground* (by Steve Roach), recorded by Solitaire; and *Poplar Regions*, written and recorded by Cosmic Trigger, all on Silent Records. Other artists include 303 Terrorists, Deeper Than Space, 23°, Michael Mantra.
Tips: "Give up all hope of being rich and famous and create music because you love it."

*SILVER WAVE RECORDS, P.O. Box 7943, Boulder CO 80306. (303)443-5617. Fax: (303)443-0877. General Manager: Greg Fisher. Labels include Silver Planet Productions. Record company. Estab. 1986. Deals with artists only. Releases 6-8 LPs and 6-8 CDs/year. Pays varying royalty to artists on contract; statutory rate to publisher per song on record.
How to Contact: Submit demo tape by mail. Unsolicited submissions are OK. Prefers cassette. "Call us two weeks after submitting to make sure it has been received. We will call if interested." SASE. Reports in 1 month.
Music: Mostly **world, New Age** and **contemporary instrumental.** Released *How the West Was Lost*, recorded by Peter Kater and R. Cralos Nakai (New Age/world); *Globalarium*, recorded by James Asher (New Age/world); and *Skeleton Woman*, recorded by Flesh & Bone (New Age/world), all on Silver Wave Records. Other artists include Danny Heines, Tom Wasinger and Jim Harvey, Peter Kater, Davol, Steve Haun Wind Machine.
Tips: "Realize we are primarily an instrumental music label, though we are always interested in good music. Songwriters in the genres of world, New Age and contemporary instrumental are welcome to submit demos. Please include radio and press info, along with bio."

SIRR RODD RECORD & PUBLISHING CO., 2453 77th Ave., Philadelphia PA 19150-1820. President: Rodney J. Keitt. Record company, music publisher, record producer and management and booking firm. Releases 5 singles, 5 12″ singles and 2 LPs/year. Works with musicians/artists and songwriters on contract. Pays 5-10% royalty to artists on contract; statutory rate to publishers for each record sold.
How to Contact: Prefers cassette (or videocassette) with 3-5 songs and lyric sheet. SASE. Reports in 1 month.
Music: **Top 40, pop, gospel, jazz, dance** and **rap.** Released "All I Want For Christmas," by The Ecstacies; "Guess Who I Saw Today," by Starlene; and "Happy Birthday Baby," by Rodney Jerome Keitt.

*SKENE! RECORDS, P.O. Box 4522, St. Paul MN 55104. (612)645-6361. Fax: (612)645-1592. Director/ Label Manager: Jeff Spiegel. Record company. Estab. 1988. Deals with artists only. Releases 5 singles, 5 LPs and 5 CDs/year. Royalty varies. Pays statutory rate to publisher per song on record.
How to Contact: Submit demo tape by mail. Unsolicited submissions are OK. Prefers cassette. Does not return material. Reports in 1 month.
Music: Mostly **alternative rock, slacker rock** and **pokey rock.** Released *Inside the Future*, written and recorded by Trenchmouth (indie); *Jersey Barrier*, written and recorded by Bob Evans (indie); and *Candy Machine*, written and recorded by Candy Machine (slacker rock), all on Skene! Records. Other artists include Hard Ons, Shades Apart, Gneissmaker.
Tips: "We sign what we like (obviously) but because we're a small label, we're only interested in working with groups who will work as hard as we do."

*SKY-CHILD RECORDS, 643 72nd St., Niagara Falls NY 14304. (716)283-1750. President: Alvin Dahn. General Manager and Director of A&R: Edward Parker. Labels include Lucy-V Records. Record company. Estab. 1976. Deals with artists and songwriters. Releases 6 singles, 3 LPs and 3 CDs/year. Pays 5% (or more, % is negotiable) royalty to artists on contract. "We only release material published by our affiliated publishers."
How to Contact: Write first and obtain permission to submit. Prefers cassette (or VHS videocassette if available) with 3-6 songs and lyric or lead sheet. Does not return material. Reports in 4-6 weeks.
Music: Mostly **pop/rock, rock** and **country;** also **blues, ballads** and **classical.** Released *It's Time*, written and recorded by Alvin Dahn (pop/rock); "Cold Spring Harbor," written and recorded by Don Watson (pop/rock); and "Tonight" (by Barry McCaffrey), recorded by The Barry James Band (rock), all on Sky-Child Records. Other artists include The A.D. Sky-Child Band and Al & Jim.
Tips: "Make sure your material is well developed and submitted in a professional manner with a full press kit (if possible)."

SLAK RECORDS, 9 Hector Ave., Toronto, Ontario M6G3G2 **Canada.** (416)588-6751. President: Al Kussin. Record company, music publisher (Clotille Publishing/PROCAN) and record producer (Slak Productions). Estab. 1986. Releases 2 singles, 2 12″ singles and 1 LP/year. Works with musicians/ artists on contract. Pays 8-14% per record sold. Pays statutory rate to publisher per song on record.
How to Contact: Submit demo tape by mail. Unsolicited submissions are OK. Prefers cassette with 3 songs and lyric sheet. SAE and IRC. Reports in 2 months.

Music: Mostly **pop, R&B** and **dance.** Released "Duck" (by M. Munroe), recorded by Mystah Munroe; "Hell Comes Next" (by L. Roberts/A. Kussin), recorded by EMC², both on Slak Records; and "Big Yellow Taxi" (by J. Mitchell), recorded by Lorraine Scott on Intrepid Records.
Tips: "Most of the material on Slak has been written by me. However, I wish to expand. A small label needs commercial, solid songwriting with good hooks and interesting lyrics."

SONIC GROUP, LTD., 15 Gloria Lane, Fairfield NJ 07006. (201)575-7460. President: Mark S. Berry. Record company, music publisher (Baby Raquel Music/ASCAP) and record producer (Mark S. Berry). Estab. 1984. Releases 1-2 12" singles and 1-2 CDs/year. Works with musicians/artists on contract. Pays 10-14% royalty to artists on contract; statutory rate to publishers per song on record.
How to Contact: Submit demo tape by mail. Unsolicited submissions are OK. Prefers cassette or VHS videocassette with 3 songs and lyric sheet. SASE. Reports in 2-4 weeks.
Music: Mostly **alternative rock/dance.** Current acts include Clutter, Voivod and Elvis Manson.

SOUND ACHIEVEMENT GROUP, INC., P.O. Box 24625, Nashville TN 37202. (615)883-2600. President: Royce B. Gray. Labels include New Wind Records, Sugar Mountain Records, Palace Records, Candle Records, Heart Reign Records, Image Records. Record company. Estab. 1985. Releases 15 singles, 15 LPs and 4 CDs/year. Pays 5-12% royalty to artists on contract; statutory rate to publishers per song on record.
How to Contact: Submit demo tape by mail. Unsolicited submissions are OK. Prefers cassette (or VHS videocassette) with 3 songs and lyric sheet. SASE. Reports in 3 months.
Music: Mostly **southern gospel, country gospel** and **MOR/inspirational;** also **contemporary gospel** and **Christmas songs.** Released *Whatever It Takes* (by Sam Johnson), recorded by Darla McFadden and *Glorious Hymns of Praise,* recorded by Giorgio Longdo, both on Candle Records; and *Sam's Songs III,* written and recorded by Sam Johnson on Image Records. Other artists include New Spirit Singers, Revelations, Paradise, Heather Stemann and Impact Brass & Singers.
Tips: "Submit quality demos with lyric sheets on all works."

*SOUND DESIGNS OF ARIZONA, P.O. Box 30605, Phoenix AZ 85046-0605. (602)992-6106. Executive Director: Gregory Zduniak. Record company. Estab. 1988. Deals with artists and songwriters. Releases 4-5 cassettes and 4-5 CDs/year. Pays 8% royalty to artists on contract; statutory rate to publisher per song on record.
How to Contact: Submit demo tape by mail. Unsolicited submissions are OK. Prefers cassette. Does not return material. Reports in 1 month.
Music: Mostly **New Age, new adult contemporary** and **new classical.** Released *The Odyssey* (by Joe Lo Presti), recorded by Midnight Skye (New Age); *Runaway* (by various), recorded by Esteban; and *Streams of Consciousness* (by Zduniak & Frassetti), recorded by Mirage (New Age), all on SDA.
Tips: "We produce music with strong melodic and/or rhythmic content. Please include any P/R with submittal."

*SOUNDS-VISION MUSIC, P.O. Box 3691, La Mesa CA 91944. (619)460-1146. Fax: (800)447-1132. Owner: R.L. Hollman. Labels include Gypsy Power Records. Record company, record producer, music publisher and record distributor. Estab. 1985. Deals with artists and songwriters. Releases 3 LPs and 3 CDs/year. Pays 10% royalty to artists on contract; varying amount to publisher per song on record.
How to Contact: Submit demo tape by mail. Unsolicited submissions are OK. Prefers cassette (or videocassette if available) with 1 song. SASE. Reports in 6 weeks.
Music: Mostly **flamenco, Latin jazz** and **classical;** also **middle eastern.** Released *La Familia Flores,* written and recorded by La Familia Flores; *The Gypsy Four,* written and recorded by Rodrigo; and *El Arte Inolvidable De Fernanda Romero,* written and recorded by Fernando Romero, all on Sounds-Vision Records. Other artists include Remedios Flores, Angelita Agujetas, Alberto de Malaga, Daniel de Malaga, Angelita, Luana Moreno, Carlos Montoya, Manitas de Plata.
Tips: "Be open to our opinions and suggestions."

*SOURCE RECORDS, INC., #825, 39 S. LaSalle St., Chicago IL 60603. (312)287-2227. President: John Bellamy. Record company. Estab. 1974. Releases 2 singles, 3 12" singles and 2 LPs/year. Works with musicians/artists and songwriters on contract. Pays statutory rate to publisher per song on record.
How to Contact: Submit demo tape by mail. Unsolicited submissions are OK. Prefers cassette (or VHS or ¾" videocassette if available) with 2 songs and lyric sheet. SASE. Reports in 3 weeks.
Music: Mostly **R&B, pop** and **gospel.** Released "Deeper in Debt" (by Spright Simpson); "Crazy for You" (by Kennedy Green); and "Greater By & By" (by Sean Williams), all recorded by The Source on Source Records.

*SOUTHERN TRACKS RECORDS, 3051 Clairmont Rd. NE, Atlanta GA 30329. (404)325-0832. Contact: Mr. Carrier. Record company and record producer. Releases 10 singles and 3 LPs/year. Works

with musicians/artists and songwriters on contract. Pays 5% royalty to artists on contract.
How to Contact: Write first and obtain permission to submit. Prefers cassette with 3 unpublished songs and lyric sheet. Does not return unsolicited material.
Music: Interested in **all types.** Released "I Love the Nightlife" (by Alicia Bridges), recorded by Scooter Lee (country dance); "My Little Jalapeno," written and recorded by Mike Dyche (country dance); and "Garth Brooks Has Ruined My Life," written and recorded by Tim Wilson (comedy), all on Southern Tracks Records. Other artists include Bertie Higgins, Sammy Johns, Milton Crabapple and Lewis Grizzard.

*SPHEMUSATIONS, 12 Northfield Rd., Onehouse, Stowmarket Suffolk 1P14 3HF **England.** Contact: General Manager. Record company and music publisher. Estab. 1963. Releases 8 singles, 8 LPs, 8 EPs and 8 CDs/year. Works with musicians/artists and songwriters on contract and hires musicians for in-house studio work. Pays variable royalty to artists on contract; statutory rate to publisher per song on record.
How to Contact: Write first and obtain permission to submit. Prefers cassette. SAE and IRC. Reports in 3 months.
Music: Mostly **country, blues** and **jazz;** also "**serious modern.**" Released "The Weeper" (by J. Playford and J. Butt), recorded by K. Van Kampen; "The Lark" (by J. Playford and J. Butt), recorded by Simon Dresorgmer and "O Moon" (by J. Kears and J. Butt), recorded by Lorraine Anderson, all on Sphemusations Records (light music).

*SPINART RECORDS, P.O. Box 1798, New York NY 10156-1798. (212)343-9644. Fax: (212)343-1970. Co-owners: Jeff Price or Joel Morowitz. Record company. Estab. 1992. Deals with artists only. Releases 10 singles, 10 LPs, 3 EPs and 10-13 CDs/year. Pays statutory rate to publisher per song on record.
How to Contact: Submit demo tape by mail. Unsolicited submissions are OK. Prefers cassette. Does not return material. Reports in 6 weeks.
Music: Mostly **indie-pop.** Released *Suddenly, Tammy!*, written and recorded by Suddenly, Tammy! (indie-pop); *I Do Not Love You,* written and recorded by Small Factory (indie-pop); and *Cool,* written and recorded by Throw That Beat In The Garbage Can (indie-pop), all on SpinART Records. Other artists include Lotion, Poole, Technical Jed, Trampoline, Barnabys, Lilys, Monsterland, Dambuilders, Zeke Fiddler, Sneetches.
Tips: "Just send us a sample of your music. Please do not worry about photos, press kits, etc. We will get in touch with you if we would like to work with you (and hopefully you would like to work with us)."

*SPIRITUAL WALK RECORDS, #1, 4007 23rd Pkwy., Temple Hills MD 20748. (301)894-5467. Fax: (301)894-8016. Marketing Director: Yolanda Weir. Labels include Obadiah Records. Record company, concert/promotional company (GTB Productions). Estab. 1993. Deals with artists and songwriters. Releases 4-5 singles, 5 LPs and 5 CDs/year. Pays 2-5% royalty to artists on contract; statutory rate to publisher per song on record.
How to Contact: Write first and obtain permission to submit. Prefers cassette (or VHS videocassette if available) with 3 songs and lyric sheet. "Include biography sheet with 8×10 color photo. Demo— 3 songs, 1 which must be a cappella, unless artist's music is a cappella." Does not return material. Reports in 3-4 weeks.
Music: Strictly **gospel** (all styles). Released *I Wanna Be Like Christ Jesus* (by Yolanda Weir), recorded by Natalie Masterson (traditional); *Somewhere Down the Road You're Gonna' Need Jesus* and *Be At Peace* (by Yolanda Weir), recorded Rea Allen-Brent (traditional), all on Spiritual Walk Records.
Tips: "Songwriter: Strong lyrics and diversity in style is a big plus. Experiment in your songwriting. Artist: Must have a strong desire to be in the gospel music industry. Have your own style; be original."

*SPOT RECORDS, P.O. Box 61443, Ft. Myers FL 33906-1443. (813)466-0078. Fax: (813)768-1819. President, A&R Director: James Albion. Record company. Estab. 1993. Deals with artists and songwriters. Releases 2 singles and 2 CDs/year. Pays negotiable royalty to artists on contract; statutory rate to publishers per song on record.
How to Contact: Submit demo tape by mail. Unsolicited submissions are OK. Prefers cassette (or VHS videocassette if available) with 3-4 songs and lyric sheet. "Please include bio and credentials." SASE. Reports in 3-6 weeks.
Music: Mostly **A/C, pop rock** and **ballads;** also **MOR** and **blues.** Artists include Lynn Richardson and 5 O'clock Shadow.
Tips "Submit your best. As an artist, you get one chance to make a great first impression. With so many submissions, and so little time, the initial impression is all you get; make the most of it."

*STAPLEGUN RECORDS, P.O. Box 867262, Plano TX 75086. Owner: Kris McLauchlan. Record company. Estab. 1990. Deals with artists only. Releases 4 singles and 6-8 CDs/year. Pays variable royalty to artists on contract; other amount to publisher per song on record.
How to Contact: Submit demo tape by mail. Unsolicited submissions are OK. Prefers cassette and lead sheet. "Send press clippings if possible." Reports in 4-6 weeks.
Music: Mostly **alternative rock, alternative pop** and **just plain good music**. Released "Hole In My Eye," written and recorded by Grover; "Splendid," written and recorded by Smile; and "Martin Scorcese," written and recorded by King Missile, all on Staplegun Records. Other artists include Combine and Andrew King.
Tips: "Send as much info on your band as possible."

*STARDANCER RECORDS, 2509½ Everett, Kinston NC 28501. Owners: Gene or Deanna David. Record company and music publisher (Poco Lago Publishing). Estab. 1989. Deals with artists and songwriters. Releases 6-8 singles/year. Pays variable royalty to artists on contract; statutory rate to publisher per song on record.
How to Contact: Submit demo tape by mail. Unsolicited submissions are OK. Prefers cassette or videocassette with 2-4 songs and lyric sheet. Does not return material. Reports in 2 months.
Music: Mostly **country, gospel** (traditional and contemporary). Released "Don't Look Back," "Honey I Like What You Got," and "Ain't No Love," all written and recorded by Deanna David on Stardancer Records.

STARDUST, 341 Billy Goat Hill Rd., Winchester TN 37398. (615)649-2577. President: Buster Doss. Labels include Stardust, Wizard, Doss, Kimbolon, Flaming Star. Record company, music publisher (Buster Doss Music/BMI) and record producer (Colonel Buster Doss). Estab. 1959. Releases 50 singles and 25 LPs/year. Works with musicians/artists and songwriters on contract and hires musicians for in-house studio work. Pays 8-10% royalty to artists on contract; statutory rate to publisher per song on record.
How to Contact: Write or call first and obtain permission to submit. Prefers cassette with 2 songs and lyric sheet. SASE. Reports in 1 week.
Music: Mostly **country**; also **rock**. Released *Rainbow of Roses* (by Buster Doss), recorded by Larry Johnson on Stardust Records; "Something In Genes" (by Buddy Hart), recorded by Al Ross on Doss Records; and *Never Find Another You* (by Buster Doss), recorded by "Danny Boy" Squire on Stardust Records. Other artists include Linda Wunder and Buck Cody.

STARGARD RECORDS, Box 138, Boston MA 02101. (617)696-7474. Artist Relations: Janice Tritto. Labels include Oak Groove Records. Record company, music publisher (Zatco Music/ASCAP and Stargard Publishing/BMI) and record producer. Estab. 1985. Releases 9 singles and 1 LP/year. Works with musicians/artists on contract; hires musicians for in-house studio work. Pays 5-6% royalty to artists on contract; statutory rate to publishers per song on record.
How to Contact: Submit demo tape by mail. Unsolicited submissions are OK. Prefers cassette and lyric sheet. SASE. Reports in 6-7 weeks. "Sending bio along with picture or glossies is appreciated but not necessary."
Music: Mostly **R&B** and **dance/hip hop**. Released "What About Me" (by U-Nik Approach) and "Let Me Give It to You" (by Floyd Wilcox), both recorded by U-Nik Approach (R&B/hip hop); and "What I Did 4 Love" (by Addison Martin), recorded by Mixed Emotions (club), all on Stargard Records. Other artists include Andre Dubose, Penny Love.

*STARTRAK RECORDS, INC., 2200 Evergreen St., Baltimore MD 21216. (410)225-7600. Fax:(410)225-9651. Vice President, A&R: Jimmie McNeal. Labels include Moe Records, D&L Records and JLM Records. Record company. Estab. 1989. Deals with artists and songwriters. Releases 3-4 singles, 3-4 12" singles, 4 LPs, 3 EPs and 6 CDs/year. Pays varying royalty.
How to Contact: Write or call to arrange personal interview, or submit demo tape by mail. Unsolicited submissions are OK. Prefers cassette (or VHS videocassette if available). SASE. Reports in 2 weeks.
Music: Mostly **R&B, rap** and **jazz**; also **gospel, rock/pop** and **country**. Released *Love Goddess* and *Magic Lady*, both recorded by Lonnie L. Smith on Startrak Records (jazz); and *Club Jazz*, recorded by Pieces of a Dream on Startrak/Capitol Records (jazz). Other artists include Terry Burrus, Dee D. McNeal and Tony Guy.
Tips: "Be original—we always look for new and fresh material with a new twist."

*STATIC NETWORK & RECORDS, Suite 2-A, 9139 Cadieux Rd., Detroit MI 48224-3617. (313)886-7860. Fax: (313)886-8479. President: Sue Summers. Record company, management and promoter. Estab. 1990. Deals with artists only. Releases 3 singles, 3 LPs and 3 CDs/year.
How to Contact: Submit demo tape by mail. Unsolicited submissions are OK. Prefers cassette and lyric sheet. SASE. Reports in 3 weeks.

Music: Mostly **alternative, pop** and **industrial**; also **rock, experimental** and **funk**. Released *A Fist Full of Chaos*, recorded by various artists on Chaos Records (alternative); and "Mental Landscape," written and recorded by Mental Landscape on Static Records (alternative). Other artists include Skinhorse, Tickweasel, Red September.
Tips: "Anything new and interesting will get our attention!"

STATUE RECORDS, 2810 McBain St., Redondo Beach CA 90278. President: Jim Monroe. A&R Director: Lisa Raven. Record company. Releases 50 singles and 100 LPs/year. Works with musicians/artists and songwriters on contract. Pays 5-10% or negotiable royalty to artists on contract.
How to Contact: Submit demo tape by mail. Unsolicited submissions are OK. Prefers "high quality" cassette with 3-5 songs and lyric sheet. Reports in 1 month. "Please include glossy photo(s) if you are a group looking for a recording deal."
Music: Mostly "**up-tempo rock,** with *strong* hooks," **new wave, rap, pop** and **alternative.** Artists include Rude Awakening, Cruella D'Ville, LA Riot, New Dynasty, The Lyming Brothers, Chosin Few, Wolfgang Elvis, The Hollywood Bears, England 402 and Bill Bream.

*STEAM RECORDS, #300, 741 Piedmont Ave., Atlanta GA 30308. A&R Director: Harvey Schwartz. Record company, promotions company. Estab. 1993. Deals with artists and songwriters. Releases 4 singles, 4 LPs, 5 CDs/year. Pays variable amount to artists on contract.
How to Contact: Submit demo tape by mail. Unsolicited submissions are OK. Prefers cassette or VHS videocassette. Does not return material. Reports in 1 month.
Music: Mostly **alternative, rock** and **jazz**; also **rap.** Released *Pleasures of the Past*, written and recorded by Steve Ellis (alternative); *Slick Night Out*, written and recorded by Donkey (alternative); and *Naked Rhythm*, written and recorded by various artists (rock), all on Steam Records. Other artists include Nasty Poets.
Tips: "Have local/regional support."

*STINC RECORDS AMERICA, 26 Mead Ave., Byram CT 06830. (203)531-4190. Fax: (203)532-0379. President: Jon Bonci. Record company. Estab. 1992. Deals with artists and songwriters. Releases 1 EP and 2 CDs/year. Pays statutory rate to publisher per song on record.
How to Contact: Submit demo tape by mail. Unsolicited submissions are OK. Prefers cassette or VHS videocassette with 3-4 songs. SASE. Reports in 1-2 months.
Music: Mostly **rock, folk** and **dance**; also **singer/songwriters** and **jazz.** Released *Charlie's Dilemma* (by Charlie Mangold), recorded by Dilemma (rock); *Vulvaticans* (by various), recorded by Vulvaticans (rock); and *A New Moon* (by various), recorded by Lillian Fitzgerald (folk), all on Stinc Records. Other artists include Shelly Finkelstein Trio.

*STREETS OF GOLD RECORDS, P.O. Box 1467, Brookshire TX 77423. (713)280-8000. A&R Director: Wayne Allen. Record company and record producer. Estab. 1993. Deals with artists and songwriters. Releases 2-5 singles, 2-5 LPs and 4-5 CDs/year. Pays varying royalty to artists on contract; statutory rate to publisher per song on record.
How to Contact: Submit demo tape by mail. Unsolicited submissions are OK. Prefers cassette (or VHS videocassette if available) with 3 songs and lyric sheet. "Be professional, even if only vocals and one instrument." Does not return material. Reports in 2-4 weeks.
Music: Mostly **Christian country, southern gospel** and **positive country**. Released "Special Rainbow" and "Headin' Home," written and recorded by Buddy Scherff on Streets of Gold Records (Christian country). Other artists include Darrel Lake, John Gould and Allen Hebert.
Tips: "When writing, twist the lyrics so they will grab the listener, and he will remember the song, tell a great story! The artist must learn to deliver words, the way George Foreman delivers a punch!"

*STRUGGLEBABY RECORDING CO., 2612 Erie Ave., Cincinnati OH 45208. (513)871-1500. Fax: (513)871-1510. A&R/Professional Manager: Pepper Bonar. Record company. Estab. 1983. Releases 2-3 LPs and 3-4 CDs/year. Pays negotiable royalty to artists on contract; statutory (per contract) rate to publisher per song on record.
How to Contact: Submit demo tape by mail. Unsolicited submissions are OK. Prefers cassette with 3 songs and lyric sheet. SASE. Reports in 3-4 weeks.
Music: Mostly **modern rock, rock** and **R&B.** Released *On The Grid*, written and recorded by Psychodots (modern rock); *The Blue Birds*, written and recorded by The Blue Birds (R&B); and *Water* (by Jim Orr), recorded by Groovy Cools (modern pop rock), all on Strugglebaby Recording Co. Other artists include Prizoner, America Smith, The Raisins.

*SUN DANCE RECORDS, 907 Baltimore St., Mobile AL 36605. Branch: P.O. Box 173, Berkeley Heights NJ 07050. Record company. Estab. 1987. Releases 12-15 singles, 8-10 12″ singles, 10 LPs and 10 CDs/year. Works with musicians/artists/songwriters on contract and in-house studio musicians on salary. Pays negotiated royalty to artists on contract.

How to Contact: Submit demo tape by mail. Unsolicited submissions are OK. Prefers cassette (or VHS videocassette if available) with 2 songs, photo and lyric sheets. SASE. Reports in 4-6 weeks.
Music: Mostly **R&B, pop** and **rap**; also **rock, gospel** and **jazz**. Released *Messenger* (by David Trippe), recorded by Messenger (contemporary Christian); "2 the Groove" (by Domonic Laforce), recorded by Da Force (dance); "The Funk" (by Cornelius Sinar), recorded by Red Rum (hip hop), all on Sun Dance Records. Other artists include Travone, Showers of Blessing Mass Choir, Regina Adams.
Tips: "He that can have patience can have what he will."

***SUNCOUNTRY RECORDS,** 2709 W. Pine Lodge, Roswell NM 88201. (505)622-0244. President: Ray Willmon. Record company and music publisher (Pecos Valley Music). Estab. 1989. Deals with artists and songwriters. Releases 2-4 singles, 3-5 LPs and 3 CDs/year. Pays 2-10% royalty to artists on contract; statutory rate to publisher per song on record.
How to Contact: Submit demo tape by mail. Unsolicited submissions are OK. "No phone calls please—we will accept or reject by mail." Prefers cassette or VHS videocassette with 3 songs maximum and lyric sheet. SASE. Reports in 8-10 weeks.
Music: Mostly **C&W, soft rock** and **gospel (country)**. Released "Why Me" and "There It Goes" (by Jimmy Maples), recorded by Will Anderson (country); and "I Guess Its Over," written and recorded by Ray Willmon (country), all on SunCountry Records. Other artists include Jessie Wayne.
Tips: "Listen to what's being aired on TV and radio. Write your songs with these in mind. No sexually suggestive lyrics. Write with proper form, i.e., AAAA ABAA ABAB etc."

***SURESHOT RECORDS,** Box 9117, Truckee CA 96162. (916)587-0111. Owner: Alan Redstone. Record company, record producer and music publisher. Estab. 1979. Releases 1 single and 1 LP/year. Works with songwriters on contract. Pays statutory royalty to publisher per song on record.
How to Contact: Submit demo tape by mail. Unsolicited submissions OK. SASE. Reports in 2 weeks.
Music: Mostly **country**, A/C and **rock**; also **ballads**. Released "Love & Life," "Emily" and "Family History," all written and recorded by Alan Redstone on Sureshot Records (country).

SURPRIZE RECORDS, INC., 7231 Mansfield Ave., Philadelphia PA 19138-1620. (215)276-8861. President: W. Lloyd Lucas. Director of A&R: Darryl L. Lucas. Labels include SRI. Record company and record producer (Surprize Records, Inc.). Estab. 1981. Releases 4-6 singles, 1-3 12″ singles and 2 LPs/year. Works with musicians/artists and songwriters on contract. Pays 6-10% royalty to artists on contract; statutory rate to publisher per song on record.
How to Contact: Submit demo tape by mail. Unsolicited submissions are OK. Prefers cassette or VHS videocassette with 3 songs and lyric or lead sheet. SASE. Reports in 1 month. "We will *not* accept certified mail!"
Music: Mostly **R&B ballads, R&B dance oriented** and **crossover country**. Released "If Love Comes Again" (by T. Brown); "Say It Again" (by R. Hamersma/G. Magahan); and "Tomorrow" (by Lester Camache/Nemeth), all recorded by Jerry Dean (R&B). Other artists include Lamar (R&B), Rosella Clemmons-Washington (jazz).
Tips: "Be dedicated and steadfast in your chosen field whether it be songwriting and/or performing. Be aware of the changing trends. Watch other great performers and try to be as good, if not better. 'Be the best that you can be.' And as Quincy Jones says, 'Leave your egos at the door' and take all criticisms as being positive, not negative. There is always something to learn."

SWEET TALK RECORDS, Box 211, Westfield MA 01086. (413)967-5395. Operations Manager: Alexis Steele. Record company and music publisher (Sariser Music/BMI). Estab. 1987. Releases 2 LPs/year. Works with musicians/artists and songwriters on contract. Pays statutory rate to publisher per song on record.
How to Contact: Write first and obtain permission to submit. No phone calls. Prefers cassette or 7½ ips reel-to-reel (or VHS #¼″ videocassette) with 3-4 songs and lyric or lead sheet. SASE. Reports in 6 weeks.
Music: Mostly **country/pop, country/rock** and **educational material**; also **soft rock** and **rockabilly**. Released "Magic & Music," written and recorded by Sparkie Allison on Sweet Talk Records (jazz); and "One Last Kiss" (by Sparkie Allison), recorded by The Moore Twins on MMT Records (country).
Tips: "Be unique. Try something different. Avoid the typical love songs. We look for material with a universal positive message. No cheatin' songs, no drinkin' songs."

SWOOP RECORDS, Stewart House, Hillbottom Rd., Highwycombe, Bucks, HP124HJ **England**. Phone: (0630)647374. Fax: (0630)647612. A&R Director: Xavier Lee. Labels include Grenoullie, Zarg, RTFM, Pogo and Check. Record company, music publisher (R.T.L. Music) and record producer (Ron Lee). Estab. 1976. Releases 50 singles, 50 12″ singles, 60 LPs and 60 CDs/year. Works with musicians/artists and songwriters on contract. Royalty paid to artists varies; statutory rate to publishers per song on record.

How to Contact: Submit demo tape by mail. Unsolicited submissions OK. Prefers cassette, (or PAL videocassette) with 3 songs and lyric or lead sheet and still photos. SAE and IRC. Reports in 2 months.
Music: Interested in **all types**. Released *Street Fighters*, *One More Night* and *Sweet Conversation*, all written and recorded by Daniel Boone on Swoop Records. Other artists include Orphan, Nightmare, Groucho, Amazing Dark Horse and The Chromatics.
Tips: "Be original."

T.O.G. MUSIC ENTERPRISES, 2107 S. Oakland St., Arlington VA 22204. (703)685-0199. President: Teo Graca. Record company, music publisher (T.O.G. Publishing), record producer (T.O.G. Productions). Estab. 1988. Releases 6 singles, 10 LPs and 2 CDs/year. Works with musicians/artists on record contract, songwriters on royalty contract, musicians on salary for in-house studio work. Pays 5-15% royalty to artists on contract; statutory rate to publishers per song on record. Charges in advance for promotion and recording services.
How to Contact: Write first and obtain permission to submit. Prefers cassette with 3 songs, lyric sheet and lead sheet are optional. Does not return material. Reports in 2-6 weeks.
Music: All styles. Released *Missions for the Money* (by Stuck-N-Tyme) on Nasty Plastic Records (hip hop); *The Wisemen Looked Like Hippies* (by Teo Grace/John Rustad); and *The Angels Sing* (by Cobb Ervin/Teo Graca/Alex Krause), both on T.O.G. Recordings (pop). Other artists include Fusion Hackers, Double Time, Martin Connell, Rev. Nate, Impulse.
Tips: "We are currently breaking into the CD ROM, CDI market. All songs, styles and formats will be considered. Please send inquiry."

*TAKEOVER RECORDS, P.O. Box 40116, St. Paul MN 55104. (612)642-9738. New Talent Coordinator: Kevin Morse. Labels include Factor-Evil Recording. Record company. Estab. 1989. Deals with artists only. Releases 2 singles, 1 12″ single, 2 LPs and 1 CD/year. Pays varying royalty to artists on contract.
How to Contact: Submit demo tape by mail. Unsolicited submissions are OK. Prefers cassette or VHS videocassette with 3 songs and lyric or lead sheet. Does not return material. Reports in 3 weeks.
Music: Mostly **alternative, metal** and **rock**; also **hip-hop**. Released "Waiting Game," written and recorded by Bloodline; *Soul Reaction*, written and recorded by Soul Reaction, both on Takeover Records; and *Endless*, written and recorded by Emaciated Corpse on Factor-Evil Records. Other artists include Billingsgate, The King Mob Echo, Doggman.
Tips: "Presentation is of utmost importance in all aspects of your submission. An attractive package shows us that you are serious and organized."

TANDEM RECORDS, #191, 842 Stanton Rd., Burlingame CA 94010. (415)692-2866. Fax: (415)692-8800. A&R Representative: Dave Christian. Record company, music publisher (Atherton Music/ASCAP, Atherton Road Music/BMI). Estab. 1985. Pays statutory rate to publishers per song on record.
Affiliate(s): Speed Records.
How to Contact: Submit demo tape by mail. Unsolicited submissions are OK. Prefers cassette and lyric sheet. Does not return material. Reports in 1 month.
Music: Mostly **rap, R&B** and **gospel**; also **modern** and **techno**. Released *Anyway You Bless Me* (by Steven Roberts), recorded by Rev. Fleetwood Irving; *Faith* (by Dave Sears), recorded by 7 Red 7; and *Marked for Death*, (by Dave Christian), recorded by Chunk, all on Tandem Records. Other artists include Funklab All Stars, Van Damme, Rated X and Tenda Tee, What The Hell, Tabb Doe.
Tips: "Don't submit until you are sure you are submitting your best work."

TARGET RECORDS, Box 163, West Redding CT 06896. President: Paul Hotchkiss. Labels include Kastle Records. Record company (BMI), music publisher (Tutch Music/Blue Hill Music) and record producer (Red Kastle Prod.). Estab. 1975. Releases 6 singles and 4 compilation CDs/year. Works with songwriters on contract. Pays statutory rate to publisher per song on record.
How to Contact: Write first and obtain permission to submit. Prefers cassette with 2 songs and lyric sheet. Does not return unsolicited material. Reports in 3 weeks.
Music: Country and **crossover**. Released "Love Walked Thru My Door" (by P. Hotchkiss), recorded by Jett; "Dancing in the Kitchen," written and recorded by M. Terry, both on Roto-Noto Records; and "Slow Dance" (by Dee Crandall), recorded by D. Raeside on Target Records. Other artists include Susan Rose Manning and Rodeo.
Tips: "Write songs people want to hear over and over. Strong commercial material."

*TEETER-TOT RECORDS, 6331 E. Center Rd., Stockton IL 61085. (815)947-3137. President/A&R Directors: Chad Sigafus/Terri Sigafus. Record company, record producer and music publisher. Estab. 1988. Deals with artists and songwriters. Releases 4 LPs/year. Pays negotiable royalty to artists on contract; statutory rate to publisher per song on record.
How to Contact: Submit demo tape by mail. Unsolicited submissions are OK. Prefers cassette with 4 songs. Does not return material. Reports in 1 month.

Music: Mostly **children's, all styles** and **Christian/children's.** Released *Water Color Ponies, Orange Tea & Molasses* and *The Bravest Little Cowboy*, all written and recorded by Chad and Terri Sigafus on Teeter-Tot Records. Other artists include "Mr. Steve."
Tips: "In children's music, you must be sincere. It's not an easy market. It requires just as much in terms of quality and effort as any other music category. Your heart must be in it."

TEN SQUARED, INC., P.O. Box 865, N. Hollywood CA 91603. (818)506-3143. President: Michael Wenslow. Record company, music publisher (Ten Squared Music/BMI), record producer (Michael Wenslow). Estab. 1990. Releases 6 singles, 2 12″ singles, 4 LPs, 4 CDs/eyar. Works with musicians/artists on record contract, songwriters on royalty contract. Pays 7-10% royalty to artists on contract; negotiable rate to publishers per song on record.
How to Contact: Write first and obtain permission to submit. Prefers cassette and lyric sheet. Does not return material. Reports in 2 weeks.
Music: Mostly **A/C, country** and **urban contemporary**; also **CHR** and **NAC.** Released *No Majik On My Johnson* (by Al Brown/M. Wenslow/J. Rando), recorded by Al Baby on Urban Jungle Records (urban contemporary); *Secret Love* (by Jeff and Jane Kozuch), recorded by Standard Deviation; and *Mike and Mark* (by various), recorded by Mike Fahn on Burnin' Jazz Records (jazz). Other artists include Dr. Geek, Geary Hanley, Joe Lano, Mark Waggoner, Branchwater and Nancy Rando.
Tips: "Letters full of hype go directly to the wastebasket."

*THIRD LOCK RECORDS AND MANAGEMENT, P.O. Box 25523, Charlotte NC 28229. (704)379-3407. Fax: (704)391-9392. Owner: Mitchell Cooper. Labels include Stendeck, Prismic, Rambler. Record company, record producer, music publisher (Roamas A Gloomas), artist. Estab. 1983. Deals with artists and songwriters. Releases 8 singles, 3 LPs and 3 CDs/year. Pays 20% royalty to artists on contract; varying amount to publisher per song on record.
How to Contact: Write first and obtain permission to submit. Prefers cassette or VHS videocassette with 3 songs and lyric or lead sheet. Also include press kit and 8 × 10 photo. Does not return material. Reports in 2 weeks.
Music: Mostly **psy/pop, country** and **alternative**; also **bluegrass, soul** and **jazz.** Released *The Inn* (by Cooper), recorded by The Inn; *Todd Rundgren* (by Mitch Easter), recorded by various artists; and *Statements III*, written and recorded by various artists, all on Third Lock Records. Other artists include Don Dixon, Inmailers, Scott Hatfield.

*TIMBRELINE MUSIC, P.O. Box 40493, Tucson AZ 85717. (602)624-5812. President: Michael Gulezian. Record company, record producer and music publisher (Now That's Music/BMI). Estab. 1987. Deals with artists and songwriters. Releases 1 LP and 1 CD/year. Pays varying royalty to artist on contract; statutory rate to publisher per song on record.
How to Contact: Submit demo tape by mail. Unsolicited submissions are OK. Prefers cassette. Does not return material. Reports in 1-2 months.
Music: Only **original instrumental acoustic music.** "Please don't send any mushy, meandering New Age." Released *The Dare of an Angel*, written and recorded by Michael Gulezian on Timbreline Music.
Tips: "Be sure to have a distinct, individual voice on your instrument."

T-JAYE RECORD COMPANY, 923 Main St., P.O. Box 60412, Nashville TN 37206. (615)226-1004. President A&R: Ted Jarrett. Labels include TRJ Records, Signull Records. Record company, music publisher (Poncello Music/ASCAP), record producer. Estab. 1980. Works with musicians/artists on record contract. Pays varying royalty to artists on contract; statutory rate to publishers per song on record.
How to Contact: Write or call first and obtain permission to submit. Prefers cassette with 2 songs and lyric sheet. SASE. Reports in 1 month.
Music: Mostly **R&B, dance** and **black gospel.** Released "Peace in the World," recorded by The Dynamic Dixie Travelers; *By and By*, written and recorded by Christian Crusaders (gospel); and *On the Road Again* (by Sandis Cooper), recorded by Sons of Glory (gospel), all on T-Jaye Records.
Tips: "Write, rewrite, rewrite and rewrite."

TOP RECORDS, Gall. del Corso, 4 Milano 20122 **Italy.** Phone: (02)76021141. Fax: (0039)276021141. Manager/Director: Guido Palma. Labels include United Colors Productions, Dingo Music, KIWI Record, Smoking Record and Tapes. Estab. 1979. Record company and music publisher. Releases 20 12″ singles, 30 LPs, 15 EPs and 40 CDs/year. Works with musicians/artists and songwriters on contract and hires in-house studio musicians. Pays standard royalty to artists on contract.
How to Contact: Write first to arrange personal interview. Prefers cassette (or videocassette) with 5 songs and lyric sheet. Does not return unsolicited material. Reports in 1 month with IRC.
Music: Mostly **pop** and **dance**; also **soundtracks.** Released *Una Vecchia Cantone Italiana* (by Marrocchi), recorded by Rosanna Fratello; *Morning Has Broken* (by Roussel), recorded by Demis Roussos;

and *Giovani Leoni*, written and recorded by Paolo Luciani; all on Top Records. Other artists include Daiano, Morelli, Gianni Dei, Diego D'Aponte, Santarosa.

*TOP TEN HITS RECORDS INC., 925 S. Semoran, Winter Park FL 32792. (407)672-0101. Fax: (407)672-5742. President: Hector L. Torres. Labels include T.R., New Generation, Rana and CEG. Record company, music publisher and independent record distributor. Estab. 1979. Deals with artists and songwriters. Releases 20 singles, 15 LPs and 15-20 CDs/year. Pays varying royalty to artists on contract; statutory royalty to publishers per song on record.
How to Contact: Submit demo tape by mail. Unsolicited submissions are OK. Prefers cassette with lead sheet. SASE. Reports in 1 month.
Music: Mostly **Spanish: tropical/pop, salsa,** and **merengue;** also **Latin-jazz** and **cumbia.** Released *15 to Aniversario* (by Ringo Martinez), recorded by Datrullal 15 (merengue); *Now is the Time* (by Martin Arroyo), recorded by MAQ (jazz); and *Grupomania* (by various), recorded by Grupomania (merengue), all on Top Ten Hits Records. Other artists include Zona Roja, Bronx Horns, Bobby Valenin, Gran Daneses, Alfa 8 and Magnificos.
Tips: "We are an independent Latin record company specializing mostly in tropical rhythms and Latin jazz."

TOUCHÉ RECORDS, Box 96, El Cerrito CA 94530. Executive Vice President: James Bronson, Jr. Record company, record producer (Mom and Pop Productions, Inc.) and music publisher (Toulouse Music Co./BMI). Member AIMP. Releases 2 LPs/year. Works with artists and songwriters on contract; musicians on salary for in-house studio work. Pays statutory rate to publishers per song on record.
How to Contact: Prefers cassette with 2-4 songs and lyric sheet. SASE. Reports in 1 month.
Music: Mostly **jazz;** also **bluegrass, gospel, R&B** and **soul.** Released *Bronson Blues* (by James Bronson), *Nigger Music* and *Touché Smiles* (by Smiley Winters), all recorded by Les Oublies du Jazz Ensemble on Touché Records. Other artists include Hi Tide Harris.

TRAC RECORD CO., 170 N. Maple, Fresno CA 93702. (209)255-1717. Owner: Stan Anderson. Record company and music publisher (Sellwood Publishing/BMI). Estab. 1972. Releases 5 singles, 5 LPs and 2 CDs/year. Works with musicians/artists on contract, songwriters on royalty contract and in-house musicians on contract. Pays 13% royalty to artists on contract; statutory rate to publisher per song on record.
How to Contact: Submit demo tape by mail. Unsolicited submissions are OK. Prefers cassette (or VHS videocassette) with 2-4 songs and lyric sheet. SASE. Reports in 3 weeks.
Music: **Traditional country** and **country rock.** Released *Whiskey Blues, Dan* and *Night Time Places,* all written and recorded by Jimmy Walker on TRAC Records. Other artists include Gil Thomas, Jessica James, The Country Connection.

*TRAVELER ENTERPRISES, P.O. Box 3234, Wichita Falls TX 76309. (817)855-6710. Vice President: Paul Palmer. Labels include Traveler Records. Record company, music publisher (Cooter Bug Music/BMI), record producer (Croslec Promotions). Estab. 1976. Releases 2-4 singles, 2-4 12" singles, 2 LPs. Pays lease rate to publisher per song on record.
How to Contact: Write first and obtain permission to submit. Prefers cassette with 2 songs and lyric sheet. SASE. Reports in 6 weeks.
Music: Mostly **country.** Released *Handin' It Down* (by Slim Clark), recorded by Slim Clark and Mike Preston; *Live In Japan*, recorded by The Travelers; and *California Wine*, recorded by Mark Murphey and the Class Band, all on Traveler Records. Other artists include Bonnie Rairdon, Mike Preston, Gary Bean, Gary Lee Hale, Texas Heat, Hired Gun, Rusty Rodgers, David Clark.
Tips: "Be very selective on material you submit."

TREASURE COAST RECORDS, 692 SE Port St. Lucie Blvd., Port St. Lucie FL 34984. President: Judy Welden. Record company, music publisher (Songrite Creations Productions/BMI, Sine Qua Non Music/ASCAP), record producer and recording artist/songwriter. Estab. 1992. Releases 6-8 singles, 2 LPs, 4 EPs and 2 CDs/year. Works with musicians/artists on record contract, songwriters on royalty contract, songwriters/artists with masters ready for release. Pays 10-15% royalty to artists on contract; statutory rate to publisher per song on record.
How to Contact: Submit demo tape by mail. Unsolicited submissions are OK. "Send only your best unpublished songs (1 or 2 max), send bio, press, number of songs written, releases, awards, etc." Prefers cassette with 1 or 2 songs and lyric sheet. SASE. Reports in 6 weeks.

Listings of companies in countries other than the U.S. have the name of the country in boldface type.

Music: Mostly **contemporary country, pop (A/C)** and **gospel**; also **R&B, blues** and **novelty**. Released *Woman Of The 90s*, written and recorded by Judy Welden/Tina Billias/Tom Littleby (AC crossover); "Hurry Up Sunrise" (by Judy Welden/Tina Billias), recorded by Judy Welden (AC crossover); and "Please Get Off Your Soapbox" (by Judy Welden/Tina Billias), recorded by Alita Marie Davis (country). Other artists include Charlotte, Ron Michael, Ellen James, Larry La Vey, Alesia Panajota, Kimberly Vonne.

Tips: "Demo must be well-produced and current sounding. Be prepared for a re-write if lyrics are not conversational and in the best possible meter. Believe in yourself and your talent and you will not get discouraged easily!"

TREND RECORDS, P.O. Box 201, Smyrna GA 30081. (404)432-2454. President: Tom Hodges. Labels include Trendsetter, Atlanta's Best, Trend Star, Trend Song, British Overseas Airways Music and Stepping Stone Records. Record company, music publisher (Mimic Music/BMI, Skipjack Music/BMI and British Overseas Airways Music/ASCAP), record producer and management firm. Estab. 1965. Releases 4 singles, 14 LPs and 3 CDs/year. Works with musicians/artists and songwriters on contract, songwriters on royalty contract and musicians on salary for in-house studio work. Pays 15% royalty to artists on contract; standard royalty to songwriters on contract; statutory rate to publisher per song on records.

How to Contact: Submit demo tape by mail. Unsolicited submissions are OK. Prefers cassette (or VHS videocassette) with 8-10 songs and lyric lead sheet. SASE. Reports in 3 weeks.

Music: Mostly **R&B, country** and **MOR**; also **gospel, light rock** and **jazz**.. Released *Thank You For the Roses*, written and recorded by Bill Clayton; *Unshed Tears* (by Tomich), recorded by J.L. Carlyle; and *Desert Rd.*, written and recorded by Dave Sanborn, all on Trend Records. Other artists include The Cads, "Little" Jimmy Dempsey, Candy Chase.

*TRF MUSIC INC., 747 Chestnut Ridge Rd., Chestnut Ridge NY 10477. (914)356-0800. Fax: (914)356-0895. Contact: Michael Nurko. Music publisher. Estab. 1931. Deals with songwriters only.

How to Contact: Submit demo tape by mail. Unsolicited submissions are OK. Prefers cassette. Does not return material.

Music: Mostly **instrumental** recordings.

*TRIPLE X RECORDS, P.O. Box 862529, Los Angeles CA 90086-2529. (213)221-2204. Fax: (213)221-2778. A&R: Bruce Duff. Record company. Estab. 1986. Deals with artists and songwriters. Releases 5 singles, 10 LPs, 4 EPs and 25 CDs/year. Royalties not disclosed.

How to Contact: Call first and obtain permission to submit. Prefers cassette. "Photo and bio are helpful." Does not return material. Reports in 1 month.

Music: Mostly **rock, industrial/goth** and **rap**; also **blues, roots** and **noise**. Released *This Should Not Be*, written and recorded by Bo Diddley (blues/rock); *Lucky Jim* (by J.L. Pierce), recorded by Gun Club (rock); and *Curb Your Dogma*, written and recorded by Spongehead (rock), all on Triple X Records. Other artists include Rozz Williams, Vandals, Jeff Dahl, Die Haut, Lydia Lunch, Miracle Workers.

Tips: "Looking for self-contained units that generate their own material and willing and able to tour."

*TRUMPETER RECORDS INC., 5660 E. Virginia Beach Blvd., Norfolk VA 23502. (804)455-8454. Fax: (804)461-4669. A&R: Tres Swann. Subsidiary labels include Peacetime Records. Record company. Estab. 1991. Deals with artists and songwriters. Releases 2 singles, 10 LPs, 2 EPs and 10 CDs/year. Pays varying royalty to artists on contract; statutory rate to publisher per song on record.

How to Contact: Call first and obtain permission to submit. Prefers cassette or VHS videocassette. SASE. Reports in 3 weeks.

Music: Mostly **alternative/progressive, rock (heavy)**, and **country**. Released *One Good Eye*, recorded by On Beyond Zee (alternative/progressive); *Vice Verses*, recorded by Psycho Johnny (rock); and *Alone*, recorded by William A., all on Trumpeter Records. Other artists include The Mundahs (alternative), Hickey Necklace (alternative) and Sea of Souls (alternative/metal).

TRUSTY RECORDS, 8771 Rose Creek Rd., Nebo KY 42441. (502)249-3194. President: Elsie Childers. Record company and music publisher (Trusty Publications/BMI). Member NSAI, CMA. Estab. 1950. Releases 2 singles and 2 LPs/year. Works with musicians/artists and songwriters on contract. Pays various royalty to artists on contract; statutory rate to publishers for each record sold.

How to Contact: Write first and obtain permission to submit. Prefers cassette with 2-4 songs and lead sheet. SASE. Reports in 1 month.

Music: Mostly **country**; also **blues, church/religious, dance, easy listening, folk, gospel, MOR, soul** and **top 40/pop**. Released *Blue, Too, It Didn't Take Long* and *Time After Time* (by E. Childers/N. Williams), recorded by Noah Williams on Trusty Records (country).

TUG BOAT RECORDS, 10 Luanita Lane, Newport News VA 23606. (804)930-1814. A&R: Judith Guthro. Record company, music publisher (Doc Publishing/BMI, Dream Machine/SESAC) and record producer (Doc Holiday Productions). Estab. 1967. Releases 12 singles, 15 12″ singles, 15 LPs, 15 EPs and 8 CDs/year. Works with musicians/artists and songwriters on contract and hires musicians for in-house studio work. Pays varying royalty to artists on contract; statutory rate to publisher per song on record.
How to Contact: Submit demo tape by mail. Unsolicited submissions are OK. Prefers cassette with 1 song and lyric sheet. Does not return material.
Music: Mostly **country**, **top 40** and **rock**. Released "Mr. Jones," written and recorded by Big Al Downing; "Cajun Baby" (by Hank Williams, Jr. and Sr.), recorded by Doug Kershaw and Hank Jr., and "Don't Mess with My Toot Toot" (by Fats Domino), recorded by Fats Domino and Doug Kershaw, all on Tug Boat Records (country). Other artists include Ronn Craddock, Tracy Wilson, Doc Holiday, Jolene, Eagle Feather, John Lockhart M.D., Narvel Felts, Wyndi Renee, The Showmen, King B & The New Jack Crew, Jon Washington of The Fortunes, Paula Pritchard, Cory Sparks, J.B. Johnson, Matt Farington & Outlaw Country.

*TVT RECORDS, 23 East 4th St., New York NY 10003. (212)979-6410. Fax: (212)979-6489. Director of A&R: Tommy Sarig. Labels include Tee Vee Toons, Wax Trax! Records, 1001 Sundays, Blunt Recordings, Fuel Records. Record company and music publisher (TVT Music). Estab. 1986. Deals with artists and songwriters. Releases 25 singles, 20 12″ singles, 40 LPs, 5 EPs and 40 CDs/year. Pays varying royalty to artists on contract; statutory rate to publisher per song on record.
How to Contact: Submit demo tape by mail. Unsolicited submissions are OK. Prefers cassette (or VHS videocassette if available). Does not return material. Reports in 6 weeks.
Music: Mostly **alternative rock**, **rap** and **techno**; also **jazz/R&B**. Released *Pretty Hate Machine* (by Trent Reznor), recorded by Nine Inch Nails (industrial rock); *Ring* (by Mike Connell), recorded by The Connells (alternative rock); and *Spirits*, written and recorded by Gil Scott-Heron (jazz/soul/rap), all on TVT Records. Other artists include Catherine, Mic Geronimo, Kinsui, D*Note Cords, KM-FDM, Psykosonik, Rise Robots Rise, Jester, Chris Connelly, AFX, Autechre, EBN.
Tips: "We look for seminal, ground breaking, genre-defining artists of all types with compelling live presentation. Our quest is not for hit singles but for enduring important artists."

*TWIN SISTERS PRODUCTIONS, INC., Suite D, 1340 Home Ave., Akron OH 44310. (800)248-TWIN. President: Kim Thompson. Record company. Estab. 1986. Deals with artists and songwriters. Releases 4-6 LPs/year. Negotiable royalty.
How to Contact: Call first and obtain permission to submit. Prefers cassette (or VHS videocassette if available). Does not return material. Reports in 1 month.
Music: Children's only (video and audio). Released *Letter & Numbers*, *Colors & Shapes* and *Phonics*, all written and recorded by Thompson/Hildebrand on Twin Sisters Productions.
Tips: "We are mainly interested in children's educational and entertaining audio. Artists wishing to become children's performers and songwriters skilled in children's audio are asked to call first before submitting. A demo will be required."

TYPETOKEN RECORDS, 1211 Arlington Place, Warrensburg MO 64093. (816))747-5578. Director of Talent Acquisition: Phil Easter. Record company, music publisher (Typetoken Music/BMI). Estab. 1990. Releases 2-3 CDs/year. Works with musicians/artists on record contract. Pays 10-15% royalty to artists on contract; statutory rate to publishers per song on record.
How to Contact: Submit demo tape by mail. Unsolicited submissions are OK. Prefers cassette with 3 or more songs and promo-materials, including brief bio and personal photo. Does not return unsolicited material. Reports in 1-2 months.
Music: Mostly **ambient-industrial**, **electronic-experimental** and **industrial/cyber**; also **acid-house/rave**, **ambient/space-music** and **gothic**. Released *Industrial Icon* and *Signal Tower Red*, written and recorded by Stone Glass Steel (ambient-industrial); and *House of Garbar*, written and recorded by Death in Arcadia (experimental-electronic), all on Typetoken Records. Other artists include Black Beach Moonrise (ambient-space music).
Tips: "Have a familiarity with the ambient, industrial and experimental genres. Have an awareness of other small international independent labels and artists. Embrace technology. Blur the line between songwriter and recording artist. Experiment continually."

*UMBRELLA RECORDS, #424, 23391 Mulholland Dr., Woodland Hills CA 91364. (818)222-0774. Fax: (213)876-2552. President: Michael Wyner. Vice President: Derek Smalls. Record company, music publisher and production company. Estab. 1992. Deals with artists and songwriters. Releases 1-4 CDs/year. Pays negotiable royalty to artists on contract; statutory rate to publisher per song on record.
How to Contact: Submit demo tape by mail. Unsolicited submissions are OK. Prefers cassette with 2-3 songs. SASE. Reports in 2-4 weeks.

Music: Mostly **R&B**, **rock** and **rap**. Released *Reggie Morris*, written and recorded by Reggie Morris on Umbrella Records (R&B). Other artists include Pepper, Centerfold, Girlfriends, Section 8 and Rosie Pazzaro.

UNIVERSAL-ATHENA RECORDS, Box 1264, Peoria IL 61654-1264. (309)673-5755. A&R Director: Jerry Hanlon. Record company and music publisher (Jerjoy Music/BMI). Estab. 1978. Releases 1-2 singles and 1 LP/year. Works with musicians/artists on contract; hires musicians on salary for in-house studio work. Pays statutory rate to publishers for each record sold.
How to Contact: Submit demo tape by mail. Unsolicited submissions are OK. Prefers cassette with 4-8 songs and lyric sheet. SASE. Reports in 2-3 weeks.
Music: Country. Released *Chevrolet Express* (by R. Priolo); *Words Great Grandpa Said* (by J. Hanlon); and *I Can't Remember To Forget* (by Rex Bell).
Tips: "Be extremely critical and make realistic comparisons of the commercial and professional value of your work before submission."

*URGE RECORDING CO., Suite 220, 208 SW First Ave., Portland OR 97201. (503)226-8196. Fax: (503)227-3953. President: Russell Ziecker. Record company. Estab. 1993. Deals with artists and songwriters. Releases 3 singles, 4 LPs, 1 EP and 4 CDs/year. Pays statutory rate to publishers per song on record.
How to Contact: Submit demo tape by mail. Unsolicited submissions are OK. Prefers cassette (or VHS videocassette if available) with 2 songs and lyric and lead sheet. Does not return material. Reports in 2 weeks.
Music: Mostly **rock** and **adult alternative**. Released *Wild Place*, recorded by the Violets (rock); *Klaatu Verata Nikru*, recorded by Forehead (rock); and *Little Boy Underrant*, recorded by Boohouse Boys (rock), all on Urge Recordings. Other artists include Prawn.
Tips: "Write the best songs you possibly can, and remember that music is the most powerful and subjective form of expression in the universe."

VELVET PRODUCTIONS, 517 W. 57th St., Los Angeles CA 90037. (213)753-7893. Manager: Aaron Johnson. Labels include Velvet, Kenya, Normar and Stoop Down Records. Record company, booking agency and promoter. Estab. 1965. Releases 5 singles, 2 12″ singles and 3 EPs/year. Works with artists and songwriters on contract. Pays 5% royalty to artists on contract.
How to Contact: Submit demo and/or lead sheet by mail. Prefers cassette with 3-5 songs and lead sheet. SASE. Reports in 2 months.
Music: **Blues**, **gospel**, **rock**, **soul** and **top 40/pop**. Released "How I Wish You" (by Arlene Bell/Delais Ene), recorded by Arlene Bell on Velvet Records.

VENTURE BEYOND RECORDS, Box 3662, Santa Rosa CA 95402-3662. (707)528-8695. Record company, music publisher (BMI, ASCAP), record producer, licensed for export and import, sub publisher for NSK, Russia, Estab. 1989. Releases 2 CDs/year. Works with "people we like." Pays all except 2% royalty to artists on contract; all except 2% to publishers per song on record. "Songwriters/artists pay our cost."
How to Contact: Submit demo tape by mail. Unsolicited submissions are OK. Prefers cassette (or VHS videocassette). Does not return material. "We get so many, it's difficult to spend our time returning, but we try." Reports in 1 month.
Music: Only **underground** and **alternative**. Released *Veer and Tringe* (by Davis Smith), recorded by Prairie Sun; *Just Touching It* (by P. Vampire), recorded by VBR; and *Pulsators* (by Campbell), recorded by Prairie Sun, all on Venture Beyond Records.
Tips: "We're looking for good songs and repeatable live performance (as good as the CD). We're not interested in taking the money that's rightfully yours."

*THE VICTORY LABEL, Suite P, 1321 Commerce St., Petaluma CA 94954. Director of A&R: Shelly Trumbo. Record company, music publisher. ASCAP affiliate. Estab. 1985. Deals with artists and songwriters. Produces 5 singles, 2 12″ singles, 7 LPs, 10 EPs and 10 CDs/year.
How to Contact: Write first and obtain permission to submit. Prefers cassette (or VHS videocassette if available) with 3 songs and lyric sheet. Does not return unsolicited material. Reports in 3 months.
Music: Mostly **rock**, **pop** and **Christian rock**; also **dance**. Produced "Out of Control" and "Shelly T," both recorded by Shelly T. on Victory Records (rock).

*VICTORY RECORDS, 1122 N. Milwaukee Ave., Chicago IL 60622. (312)862-4442. Fax: (312)862-4441. Victory Europe: Gönninger Str. 3 72793 Pfullingen Germany. Contact: Tony Brummel. Record company, distributor. Estab. 1989. Deals with artists only. Releases 4 singles, 4 LPs, 2 EPs and 4 CDs/year. Royalty varies; pays statutory rate to publisher per song on record.
How to Contact: Submit demo tape by mail. Unsolicited submissions are OK. Prefers cassette with lyric sheet. "Send us as much information as possible." Does not return material. Reports in 2 weeks.

Music: Mostly **hardcore** and **indie rock/punk**; also **rockabilly**. Released *Firestorm*, recorded by Earth Crisis; *Live at CBGB*, recorded by Warzone; and *Only the Strong*, recorded by various artists, all on Victory Records (hardcore). Other artists include Snapcase, Strife, Hi Fi and the Roadburners.
Tips: "Don't waste your time and ours with poorly produced submissions. If you're not familiar with the label, odds are we won't be interested in you."

*VIP RECORDS, 313 N. Locust, Denton TX 76201. (800)270-9297. Fax: (817)383-0756. President: David G. Patton. Vice President: Jim Vincent. Labels include Lockdown/VIP. Record company, record producer and music publisher (Frog Hair Songs/BMI). Estab. 1992. Deals with artists and songwriters. Releases 8-10 singles, 6 12″ singles, 8-10 LPs, 8-10 EPs and 8-10 CDs/year. Pays negotiable royalty to artists on contract; statutory rate to publisher per song on record.
How to Contact: Submit demo by mail. Unsolicited submissions are OK. Prefers cassette or ½″ VHS videocassette with 3-5 songs and lyric or lead sheet. "No phone calls please." Does not return material. Reports in 1 month.
Music: Mostly **rock**, **rap/R&B** and **country**; also **folk**, **jazz** and **gospel**. Released *Lost Highway* (by Jimmy R.), recorded by Jimmy R Band (rock); and *Fresh Off The Farm*, written and recorded by Impulse, both on VIP Records (rock); and *A Hit On Da Hitman* (by Kenton Paul), recorded by Oak Cliff Assassin on Lockdown/VIP (rap). Other artists include Infra Red.
Tips: "We are looking for solid, marketable groups. If you can sell records, we'll talk. Take time to learn the business so you don't embarrass yourself."

*VITAL MUSIC, 2591 Pomona Blvd., Pomona CA 91768. (909)613-1323. Fax: (909)594-9652. Sales Manager: Kathleen Cherrier. Labels include Friends of Vital and Vital Classique. Record company and record producer. Estab. 1991. Deals with artists and songwriters. Releases 15 LPs and 25 CDs/year. Pays 6.25% to artists on contract; statutory rate to publishers per song on record.
How to Contact: Call first and obtain permission to submit or arrange personal interview. Prefers cassette (or VHS videocassette if available) with 3 songs and lyric and lead sheets. "Include current bio, photo and reviews." SASE. Reports in 3 months.
Music: Mostly **blues**, **jazz** and **world**; also **gospel**, **classical** and **hip hop jazz**. Released *Munyungo*, written and recorded by Munyungo Jackson (world); *James*, written and recorded by James Leary (traditional jazz); and *The Poetic List* (by Frank Liszt), recorded by Gert Hecher (classique), all on Vital Music. Other artists include Todd Cochran, Sekou Bunch, Doc Powell, Louis Verdieu, David Garfield, Karen Briggs, Bill Summers, Lazaro Galarrago, Lesley Olsher, Vickie Leigh, Jimmy Cleveland, Kate McGarry, Karen Knowles, Josh Sklair, Jim Dawson, Brown Burnett, Jim Christopher, Sam Sklair and Janet Cleveland.

VOKES MUSIC PUBLISHING & RECORD CO., Box 12, New Kensington PA 15068. (412)335-2775. President: Howard Vokes. Labels include Vokes and Country Boy Records. Record company, booking agency and music publisher. Releases 8 singles and 5 LPs/year. Works with artists and songwriters on contract. Pays 2½-4½¢/song royalty to artists and songwriters on contract.
How to Contact: Submit cassette only and lead sheet. SASE. Reports in 2 weeks.
Music: **Country**, **bluegrass** and **gospel-old time**. Released "Cherokee Trail Of Tears" and "City Of Strangers" by Johnny Eagle Feather and "Portrait Of An Angel" by Lenny Gee, all on Vokes Records.

*VONDY MUSIC PUBLISHING, P.O. Box 351, Liberty IN 47353. (317)458-5144. Fax: (317)458-7559. Publisher: James Hensley. Music publisher. Estab. 1992. Deals with songwriters only. Pays statutory rate to publisher per song on record.
How to Contact: Submit demo tape by mail. Unsolicited submissions are OK. Prefers cassette with no more than 3 songs and lyric sheet. SASE. Reports in 4-6 weeks.
Music: Mostly **traditional country**, **modern country** and **gospel**; also **MOR**, **country rock** and **A/C**.
Tips: "Studio quality demos with upfront vocals. Simple, clean and clear. Typed lyric sheets. Serious writers only."

*WALL STREET MUSIC, 1189 E. 14 Mile Rd., Birmingham MI 48009. (810)646-2054. Fax: (810)646-1957. A&R Director: Joe Sanders. Record company and music publisher (Burgundy Bros.). Estab. 1985. Deals with artists only. Releases 6 singles, 4 12″ singles, 4 LPs, 4 EPs and 8 CDs/year. Pays 12% royalty to artists on contract; statutory rate to publisher per song on record.
How to Contact: Call first and obtain permission to submit. Prefers cassette (or VHS videocassette if available) with 2 songs and photo. "Label all items completely." Does not return material. Reports in 6 weeks.
Music: Mostly **rap**, **hip hop** and **house**; also **rave**, **trance** and **R&B**. Released *Outta Bounds*, written and recorded by A.N.G. (rap); "UR So Good 2 Me," written and recorded by Drueada — Queen of House (house); and "On A Serious Tip," written and recorded by Stevie C. (rave), all on Wall Street Music.

Tips: "Be professional and realistic. If we sign you, we'll be looking for someone with a cooperative, partnership attitude."

WATCH MUSIC COMPANY LTD., 121 Logan Ave., Toronto, Ontario M4M 2M9 **Canada**. President: Ross Munro. Record company, music publisher (Watch The Watch Music/Stinky Pete Publishing) and record producer. Estab. 1992. Works with musicians/artists on record contract. Pays statutory royalty to publishers per song on record.
How to Contact: Submit demo tape by mail. Unsolicited submissions are OK. Prefers cassette (or VHS videocassette) with 4-6 songs and lyric sheet. Does not return material. Only responds if interested.
Music: Mostly **rock**, **pop** and **country**. Released *Scribblehead* and *Thrash Waltz* (by Alun Piggins), recorded by The Morganfields; and *A Soap Bubble and Inertia*, written and recorded by The Grandharvas (rock), all on Watch Records.

*WEDGE RECORDS, Box 290186, Nashville TN 37229-0186. (615)754-2950. President: Ralph D. Johnson. Labels include Dome Records and Fleet Records. Record company, music publisher (Big Wedge Music/BMI and Pro-Rite Music/ASCAP), record producer (Ralph D. Johnson) and Pro-Star Talent Agency. Estab. 1960. Releases 10 singles, 2 LPs and 2 CDs/year. Works with musicians/artists and songwriters on contract. Pays 10% royalty to artists on contract; statutory rate to publisher per song on record.
How to Contact: Submit demo tape by mail. Unsolicited submissions OK. Prefers cassette and lyric or lead sheet. SASE. Reports in 2 weeks.
Music: Mostly **country** and **country crossover**; also **rock**, **gospel**, **pop** and **R&B**. Released "I'm Gonna Leave You Now" (by Roy August), recorded by Cindy Jackson (country); "Boogie Man Is Gonna Get You" (by Roy August), recorded by Stacy Edwards (country); and "On the Other Side of Midnight" (by Jesse Cupp), recorded by Dean Mitchell (country), all on Wedge Records (country).

WENCE SENSE MUSIC/BILL WENCE PROMOTIONS, P.O. Box 110829, Nashville TN 37222. Contact: Kathy Wence. Labels include Six-One-Five Records and Skyway Records. Record company, music publisher (Wence Sense Music/ASCAP), record producer (Bill Wence). Estab. 1984. Releases 4-8 singles, 4 CDs/year. Pays statutory rate to publishers per song on record.
How to Contact: Call first and obtain permission to submit. Prefers cassette with 1 song. Does not return material. Reports in 3 weeks.
Music: Prefers **country**. Released *Who's Foolin' Who*, written and recorded by Allen Borden on PlayMe Records; *Looking on the Outside* (by Gil Caballero), recorded by Caballero on 615 Records; and *You Can Always*, written and recorded by Leon Seiter on Skyway Records. Other artists include Trena and Lanada Cassidy.
Tips: "Send only one song until we request more of you and be patient."

*WESTPARK MUSIC - RECORDS, PRODUCTION & PUBLISHING, Box 260227, Rathenauplatz 4 50515 Cologne **Germany**. Phone: (49)221 247644. Fax: (49)221 231819. Contact: Ulli Hetscher. Labels distributed by BMG Ariola and Indigo. Estab. 1986. Releases 3-4 singles and 10-12 CDs/year. Works with musicians/artists on contract; tape lease. Pays 8-14% royalty to artists on contract.
How to Contact: Submit demo tape by mail. Unsolicited submissions are OK. Prefers cassette with 5-6 songs and lyric sheets. Does not return unsolicited material. Reports in 2-3 months.
Music: Everything apart from mainstream-pop, jazz, classical. "The only other criterion is: we simply should love it." Released "Lovers in a Dangerous Time" (by B. Cockburn), recorded by Barenaked Ladies (folk); "Wonderin' Where Lions Are," recorded by B-Funn (pop/dance) on Westpark Records; and "Man Overboard," written and recorded by P. Millins on SM/Ariola Records (rock ballad).
Tips: "Mark cassette clearly. No high quality cassettes expected. We only send letters back!!"

*WESTWORLD RECORD CO., 840 Windham Ave., Cincinnati OH 45229. (513)559-1210. President: Roosevelt Lee. Labels include Roosevelt Lee International Records. Record company, record producer and music publisher (City/BMI, Carnage Music/BMI). Estab. 1985. Deals with artists and songwriters. Releases 5 singles, 5 12" singles, 5 LPs and 5 CDs/year. Pays 10% royalty to artists on contract; negotiable rate to publisher per song on record.
How to Contact: Submit demo tape by mail. Unsolicited submissions are OK. Prefers cassette with lead sheet. SASE. Reports in 3 months.
Music: Mostly **rock**, **blues**, **pop**, **country**, **R&B**, **rap**, **jazz** and **reggae**.

WHITE CAR RECORDS, 10611 Cal Rd., Baton Rouge LA 70809. (504)755-1400. Owner: Nelson Blanchard. Labels include Techno Sound Records. Record company, music publisher (White Car Music/BMI, Char Blanche/ASCAP) and independent record producer. Estab. 1980. Releases 6 singles, 4 12" singles, 6 LPs, 1 EP and 2 CDs/year. Works with musicians/artists and songwriters on contract. Pays 7½-20% royalty to artists on contract; statutory rate to publisher per song.

How to Contact: Submit demo tape by mail. Unsolicited submissions are OK. Prefers cassette with 4 songs. Does not return material. Reports in 2 weeks.
Music: Mostly **country, rock** and **pop**; also **R&B.** Released "Time, You're No Friend of Mine" written and recorded by Howard Austin; "Closer to Heaven" written and recorded by Joey Dupuy, both on Techno Sound Records; and "I Read Between the Lines (by Stan Willis) recorded by Nelson Blanchard on White Car Records. Other artists include John Steve, B.J. Morgan and Bayon Country Band.

*WIDELY DISTRIBUTED RECORDS, 1412 W. Touhy, Chicago IL 60626. (312)465-2558. President: Jack R. Frank. Record company. Estab. 1988. Deals with artists only. Releases 3 EPs and 6 CDs/year. Pays 10-14% royalty to artists on contract; negotiable amount to publisher per song on record.
How to Contact: Submit demo tape by mail. Unsolicited submissions are OK. Prefers cassette. Does not return material. Reports in 4 months.
Music: Mostly **pop** and **rock;** also **spoken word.** Released *Pathetique* (by Jeff Lesher), recorded by Green; *Make a Wish,* written and recorded by Skull Fish Cactus (rock); and *Little Dark Mansion* (by Will Merriman), recorded by Harvest Ministers (pop), all on Widely Distributed Records. Other artists include Algebra Suicide, The Lilacs, The Wake (UK).

*WILD PITCH RECORDS LTD., 231 West 29th St., New York NY 10001. (212)594-5050. Fax: (212)268-4968. Vice President, A&R: Stu Fine. Record company. Estab. 1988. Deals with artists and songwriters. Releases 15 singles, 1-2 EPs and 6-8 CDs/year. Pays ¾ of statutory rate to publishers per song on record.
How to Contact: Submit demo tape by mail. Unsolicited submissions are OK. Prefers cassette or ½" videocassette with 3 songs. Does not return material.
Music: Mostly **rap.** Released "Raise It Up" and *Unleashed,* both recorded by Ultramagnetic MCs; and *Kill My Landlord,* recorded by The Coup, all on Wild Pitch Records. Other artists include Main Source, Large Professor, N-Tyce, Street Military, Super Lover C & Casanova Rud.

WINCHESTER RECORDS, (formerly Alear Records), % McCoy, Route 2, Box 114, Berkeley Springs WV 25411. (304)258-9381. Labels include Master Records and Real McCoy Records. Record company, music publisher (Jim McCoy Music, Clear Music, New Edition Music/BMI), record producer and recording studio. Releases 20 singles and 10 LPs/year. Works with artists and songwriters on contract; musicians on salary. Pays standard royalty to artists; statutory rate to publishers for each record sold.
How to Contact: Write first and obtain permission to submit. Prefers 7½ ips reel-to-reel or cassette with 5-10 songs and lead sheet. SASE. Reports in 1 month.
Music: Bluegrass, church/religious, country, folk, gospel, progressive and **rock.** Released *Touch Your Heart,* written and recorded by Jim McCoy; "Leavin'," written and recorded by Red Steed, both on Winchester Records; and "The Taking Kind" (by Tommy Hill), recorded by J.B. Miller on Hilton Records. Other artists include Carroll County Ramblers, Bud Arnel, Nitelifers, Jubilee Travelers and Middleburg Harmonizers.

*WINGS RECORD COMPANY, Route 3, Box 172, Dept. SM, Haynesville LA 71038. (318)927-5253. President: E. Dettenheim. Record company and music publisher (Darbonne Publishing Co./BMI). Estab. 1987. Releases 4 singles and 4-8 LPs/year. Works with musicians/artists on record contract. Pays 5-10% royalty to artists on contract; statutory rate to publishers per song on record.
How to Contact: Submit demo tape by mail. Unsolicited submissions are OK. Prefers cassette, 7½ ips reel-to-reel with at least 3 songs and lyric sheeet. Does not return unsolicited material.
Music: Mostly **country, rock** and **gospel;** also **pop** and **R&B.** Released "Man in the Mirror" written and recorded by Leon Martin (country); "Still Haven't Let You Go," written and recorded by Kate Chandler (contemporary country); and "Turner Hotel" (by E. Dettenheim), performed by Skidrow Joe, all on Wings Records.

WIZMAK PRODUCTIONS, P.O. Box 477, Wingdale NY 12594. (914)877-3943. Manager: Geri White. Record company and recording studio (Fulfillment House). Estab. 1986. Releases 4 cassettes and CDs/year. Works with musicians/artists on record contract. "Musicians receive a set fee per track for in house studio work." Pays 12% royalty to artists on contract; statutory rate to publisher per song on record.
How to Contact: Submit demo tape by mail. Unsolicited submissions are OK. Prefers cassette with 3 songs and lyric sheet. "Also include news article or review of a recent performance." SASE. Reports in 6-12 weeks.
Music: Mostly **dulcimer/folk, traditional (American & Irish)** and **gospel, children's (folk);** also **contemporary, acoustic** and **singer/songwriter.** Released *Home For The Harvest,* written and recorded by Rich Bala (traditional folk); *Acre Bay,* written and recorded by Jim Pospisil (acoustic folk and blues); and *The Rainbow Dragon,* written and recorded by Jonathan Kruk (children's), all on Wizmak Records. Other artists include Jerry Rockwell and Peter Sutherland.

Tips: "Know your direction, establish yourself as a performer on a regional level."

WOODRICH RECORDS, Box 38, Lexington AL 35648. (205)247-3983. President: Woody Richardson. Record company and music publisher (Woodrich Publishing Co./BMI, Mernee Music/ASCAP and Tennessee Valley Music/SESAC) and record producer (Woody Richardson). Estab. 1959. Releases 12 singles and 12 LPs/year. Works with songwriters on contract. Pays 10% royalty to writers on contract; statutory rate to publisher per song on record.
How to Contact: Submit demo tape by mail. Unsolicited submissions are OK. Prefers cassette with 4 songs and lyric sheet. "Be sure to send a SASE (not a card) with sufficient return postage." Reports in 2 weeks. "We prefer a good studio demo."
Music: Mostly **country**; also **gospel, comedy, bluegrass, rock** and **jazz**. Released *Welcome Back to Me* (by Sam Celia), recorded by Sandi Thompson on Playback Records (country); *Winding Road*, written and recorded by Darryl Alexander on LRG Records (jazz); and "I'm on the Right Road Again" (by Mack/Murks), recorded by Danny Mack on Dynamite Records (country).
Tips: "Use a good studio with professional musicians. Don't send a huge package. A business envelope will do. It's better to send a cassette *not in a box.*"

*WORLD DISC PRODUCTIONS INC., 915 Spring St., Friday Harbor WA 98250. (206)378-3979. Fax: (206)378-3977. Executive Producer: Richard Hooper. Labels include World Disc Music and Nature Recordings. Record company and record producer. Estab. 1985. Deals with artists only. Releases 20 CDs/year. Pays 9% royalty to artists on contract; statutory rate to publisher per song on record.
How to Contact: Submit demo tape by mail. Unsolicited submissions are OK. Prefers cassette (or VHS videocassette if available). SASE. Reports in 4-6 weeks.
Music: Mostly **world** and **New Age**. Released *All One Tribe*, written and recorded by Scott Fitzgerald (world); *In The Spirit of Play*, written and recorded by Richard Musk and Wendy (neo classical); and *Passion*, written and recorded by Rafael Aragon, et. al. (Latin jazz), all on World Disc Records. Other artists include Gary Richard Pickus, Carol Cole, Jim Centorino.
Tips: "We know how to sell music. Listen to us."

YELLOW JACKET RECORDS, 10303 Hickory Valley, Ft. Wayne IN 46835. President: Allan Straten. Record company. Estab. 1985. Releases 8-10 singles, 1 LP and 1 CD/year. Works with musicians/ artists and songwriters on contract; hires musicians for in-house studio work. Pays 7-10% royalty to artists on contract; statutory rate to publisher per song on record.
How to Contact: Submit demo tape by mail. Unsolicited submissions are OK. Prefers cassette with 3-4 songs and typed lyric sheet. SASE. Reports in 3-4 weeks.
Music: **Country** and **MOR**. Released *I See Everything In You*, *One of A Kind*, and *Call Me* (by Gregg/ Straten), recorded by April on Yellow Jacket Records (country). Other artists include Roy Allan and Mike Vernaglia.
Tips: "Be professional—be prepared to rewrite—when sending material use 6×9 envelope—no staples."

YOUNG COUNTRY RECORDS/PLAIN COUNTRY RECORDS, P.O. Box 5412, Buena Park CA 90620. (909)371-2973. Owner: Leo J. Eiffert, Jr. Labels include Eiffert Records and Napoleon Country Records. Record company, music publisher (Young Country Music Publishing Co./BMI, Eb-Tide Music/ BMI), record producer (Leo J. Eiffert, Jr). Releases 10 singles and 5 LPs/year. Works with musicians/ artists on record contract, songwriters on royalty contract, musicians on salary for in-house studio work. Pays negotiable royalty to artists on contract; negotiable rate to publishers per song on record.
How to Contact: Submit demo tape by mail. Unsolicited submissions are OK. "And please make sure your song or songs are copyrighted." Prefers cassette with 2 songs and lyric sheet. Does not return material. Reports in 3-4 weeks.
Music: Mostly **country, easy rock** and **gospel music**. Released *Like A Fool*, written and recorded by Pam Bellows; *Something About Your Love* (by Leo J. Eiffert, Jr.), recorded by Chance Waite Young (country); and *Cajunland*, written and recorded by Leo J. Eiffert, Jr., all on Plain Country Records. Other artists include Brandi Holland, Crawfish Band, Larry Settle.

YOUNGHEART MUSIC, Box 6017, Cypress CA 90630. (714)995-7888. President: James Connelly. Record company. Estab. 1975. Releases 1-2 LPs/year. Works with musicians/artists and songwriters on contract. Pays statutory rate.
How to Contact: Submit demo tape by mail. Unsolicited submissions are OK. SASE. Reports in 4 weeks.
Music: Mostly **children's** and **educational**. Released "Three Little Pig Blues" and "A Man Named King," written and recorded by Greg Scelsa and Steve Millang, both on Youngheart Records.
Tips: "We are looking for original, contemporary, motivating music for kids. Songs should be fun, educational, build self-esteem and/or multicultural awareness. New original arrangements of classic songs or nursery rhymes will be considered."

*ZEBRAOVERGROUND RECORDS, P.O. Box 7441, Santa Cruz CA 95061. (408)459-7947. Fax: (408)458-2384. Contact: A&R Department. Labels include Skateboard and Govinda. Record company and music publisher. Estab. 1982. Deals with artists and songwriters. Negotiable royalty.
How to Contact: Submit demo tape by mail. Unsolicited submissions are OK. Prefers cassette (or VHS videocassette if available) with 2 songs and lyric sheet. "Do not call to follow up, we contact all submitters." SASE. Reports in 1 month.
Music: Mostly **rock, reggae** and **pop**; also **folk, singer/songwriter** and **modern classical**. Released *Beauty For Ashes* (by Rāmākar), recorded by RAM (rock); "Give Us Love," written and recorded by Beat Scientists (pop); and "Home," written and recorded by The Gathering (rock/reggae), all on Zebraoverground Records. Other artists include Damayanti, The Fruithedz and Dayglo Rainbow.
Tips: "Be real with your music—let it be your own—we're not into copyists."

ZEROBUDGET RECORDS, P.O. Box 2044, La Crosse WI 54602. (608)783-5818. President/Director A&R: Stephen Harm. "We distribute some titles on the Boat Records label." Record company. Estab. 1982. Works with musicians/artists on record contract. Pays negotiable royalty to artists on contract; negotiable rate to publisher per song on record.
How to Contact: Submit demo tape by mail. Unsolicited submissions are OK. Prefers cassette (or VHS ½″ videocassette if available) and lyric sheet. SASE. Reports in 3 months.
Music: Mostly **alternative, industrial, rockabilly** and **techno**; also **rock** and **pop**. Released *Full Moon, Bad Weather*, written and recorded by Rousers on Boat/Zerobudget Records (rockabilly); *Altered* (by Platz/Niedfelt/Ed), recorded by 0Dark:30 (industrial); and *Silent Dreams*, written and recorded by Victims, both on Zerobudget Records. Other artists include Memory Whip, Space Bike, Flying Tigers.
Tips: "Don't follow trends—set 'em. No cliché is ever OK."

ZONE RECORD CO., 2674 Steele, Memphis TN 38127. (901)357-0064. Owner: Marshall E. Ellis. Releases 4 singles/year. Record company, music publisher and record producer. Works with songwriters on contract; musicians paid by song. Pays 4¢/side royalty to artists on contract.
How to Contact: Call first to arrange personal interview. Submit demo tape by mail. Unsolicited submissions are OK. Prefers cassette with 4 songs. "Be sure the words are clear. Don't try to make a master—just a good clean tape." SASE. Reports in 3 weeks.
Music: **Country** and **country/pop**. Released "My Last Hurrah" by Susan Magee and "She Was the Only One" by Al Hansen, both on Zone Records. Other artists include Buddy Fletcher and Larry Manual.

*ZOOM EXPRESS, Suite 1106, 578 Broadway, New York NY 10012. (212)274-0200. Fax: (212)274-9776. President: Bob Hinkle. Record company. "We are a joint venture of BMG Kidz, a division of the Bertelsmann Music Group (BMG)." Estab. 1992. Releases 12 LPs and 12 CDs/year. Royalty varies.
How to Contact: Submit demo tape by mail. Unsolicited submissions are OK. Prefers cassette. SASE Reports in 5 months.
Music: Mostly **children's** and **family** only. Released *Brother For Sale*, recorded by Mary-Kate and Ashley Olsen (children's); *Where In the World Is Carmen Sandiego?*, recorded by various artists (family); and *I Must Be Growing*, written and recorded by Glenn Bennett (children's), all on Zoom Express. Other artists include Roger Daltrey.
Tips: "Research what our company already has on the market. This is a children's and family entertainment company."

ZYLON RECORDS & TAPES, P.O. Box 39A16, Los Angeles CA 90039. (213)668-2213. Director of A&R: K. Slater. Record company. Estab. 1985. Works with musicians/artists on record contract, songwriters on royalty contract, musicians on salary for in-house studio work. Pay varies; pays statutory rate to publisher per song on record.
How to Contact: Submit demo tape by mail. Unsolicited submissions are OK. Prefers casette with 3-12 songs and lyric sheet. Does not return material. Reports in 3-4 weeks.
Music: Mostly **rock, alternative** and **pop**; also **R&B (urban)** and **country**. Released "Up On Solid Ground," written and recorded by Kim Allen; "No One Gets Out Alive" (by Russo/Orr), recorded by Lucrecia; and *Rocks*, written and recorded by Straightjacket, all on Zylon Records. Other artists include Blood Beach, Children At Play.
Tips: "Listen to what college radio is doing. Write mainstream hit songs as well as alternative cuts. Write visual songs."

Geographic Index

The U.S. section of this handy Geographic Index will quickly give you the names of record companies located in or near the music centers of Los Angeles, New York and Nashville. Of course, there are many valuable contacts to be made in other cities, but you will probably want to plan a trip to one of these established music centers at some point in your career and try to visit as many of these companies as you think appropriate. The International section lists, geographically, markets for your songs in countries other than the U.S.

Find the names of companies in this index, and then check listings within the Record Company section for addresses, phone numbers and submission details.

Los Angeles
Aliso Creek Productions Incorporated
Atlantic Recording Corp.
AVC Entertainment Inc.
Azra International
BCM-USA
Blue Gem Records
Caliber Records
Chattahoochee Records
Cleopatra Records
Cowgirl Records
Discovery Music
Fullmoon Entertainment/
    Moonstone Records
Grass Roots Record & Tape/
    LMI Records
Lethal Records
Macola Record Group Inc.
MCI Entertainment Group
Miles Ahead Records
Moonstone Records
Morgan Creek Music Group
Patty Lee Records
Rock Dog Records
Statue Records
Ten Squared, Inc.
Triple X Records
Velvet Productions
Zylon Records & Tapes

Nashville
A&R Records
A.M.I. Records
Bandit Records
Benson Music Group
BNA Entertainment
Brentwood Music
Carlyle Records, Inc.
Cedar Creek Records™
Country Showcase America
Excursion Records
Fame and Fortune Enterprises
Fat City Artists
Foxfire Records
Fresh Start Music Ministries

Jalyn Recording Co.
Kottage Records
The Mathes Company
Mosrite Records
Orbit Records
Paragold Records & Tapes
PBM Records
Phoenix Records, Inc.
R.E.X. Music, Inc.
Rejoice Records of Nashville
Richway Records International
T-Jaye Record Company
Wedge Records
Wence Sense Music/Bill Wence
    Promotions

New York
Bullet Proof Management
Caroline Records, Inc.
Com-Four
Digitalia Records
Earache Records/Earache
    Songs
Emzee Records
Fiction
Funky Mushroom Records
GMV Music Enterprises
Gold City Records, Inc.
Homestead Records
Instinct Records
J&J Musical Enterprises Ltd.
Lamar Music Group
MCA Records
Mercury Records
Mighty Records
Mindfield Records
Modern Voices Entertainment,
    Ltd.
The Music Company
Nova Records Inc.
November Records
Parade
PPI/Peter Pan Industries
Razor & Tie Music
Significant Other Records
SpinART Records

TVT Records
Wild Pitch Records Ltd.
Zoom Express

International

Australia
Big Rock Pty. Ltd.
Makeshift Music

Austria
Cactus Records

Canada
Berandol Music
Circle "M" Records
Dancer Publishing Co.
Disques Nosferatu Records
Heritage Music
Hickory Lane Publishing and
    Recording
Justin Time Records Inc.
Monticana Records
Nettwerk Productions
P. & N. Records
Shaky Records
Slak Records
Watch Music Company Ltd.

Germany
Alphabeat
Comma Records & Tapes
Westpark Music—Records,
    Production & Publishing

Italy
Top Records

The Netherlands
Associated Artists Music International
Collector Records

United Kingdom
Big Bear Records
Demi Monde Records and Publishing, Ltd.
E.S.R. Records
First Time Records

Le Matt Music Ltd.
Leopard Music
Loading Bay Records
Nervous Records
Plankton Records
Red Bus Records (Int.) Ltd.

Red Sky Records
Red-Eye Records
Sphemusations
Swoop Records

Category Index

The Category Index is a good place to begin searching for a market for your songs. Below is an alphabetical list of 19 general music categories. If you write rock music and are looking for a record company to submit your songs to, check the Rock section in this index. There you will find a list of record companies interested in hearing rock songs. Once you locate the entries for those record companies, read the Music subheading *carefully* to determine which companies are most interested in the type of rock music you write. Some of the markets in this section do not appear in the Category Index because they have not indicated a specific preference. Most of these said they are interested in "all types" of music. Listings that were very specific, or whose description of the music they're interested in doesn't quite fit into these categories, also do not appear here.

Adult Contemporary All Star Promotions; Allegheny Music Works; American Music Network, Inc.; Amiron Music/Aztec Productions; Atlantic Recording Corp.; Benson Music Group; Bolivia Records; Boogie Band Records; Bouquet Records; Capstan Record Production; Carmel Records; Comstock Records Ltd.; Courier Records; Cowgirl Records; Dale Productions, Alan; Goldband Records; Golden Triangle Records; Green Bear Records; Hickory Lane Publishing and Recording; Hollyrock Records; Kaupp Records; L.A. Records; LBJ Productions; Le Matt Music Ltd.; Lucifer Records, Inc.; Maxern Records; Maxim Records Ltd.; Monticana Records; Murdock's Music Company; Pajer Records; Parade; Parc Records Inc.; Peridot Records; Rave Records, Inc.; Roll On Records®; Rustron Music Productions; Seeds Records; Sound Designs Of Arizona; Spot Records; Sureshot Records; Ten Squared, Inc.; Treasure Coast Records; Trend Records; Trusty Records; Vondy Music Publishing

Alternative A & R Records; Alternative Records; Amethyst Group Ltd., The; Angel Eyes Records & Filmworks, Inc.; Aztlan Records; baby sue; Benson Music Group; Big Pop; Black & Blue; Blue Duck!! Records; Bullet Proof Management; Caffeine Disk; Caroline Records, Inc.; Cat's Voice Productions; Chrismarie Records; Cleopatra Records; Com-Four; Conspiracy Records; Co-op Artist Recordings; Detroit Municipal Recordings; Earache Records/Earache Songs; Fat City Artists; Fiction; Forefront Records; Fullmoon Entertainment/Moonstone Records; Funky Mushroom Records; Generic Records, Inc.; Global Pacific Records; Godman Music and Publications; Guitar Recordings; Halogram; Happy Tails Records; Holographic Records; Homestead Records; Hottrax Records; I Wanna Records; Ichiban Records; IMPS Music; Inferno Records; Instinct Records; JK Jam Music; Lethal Records; Limited Potential Records; Long Play Records; Macola Record Group Inc.; Maxim Records Ltd.; Merkin Records Inc.; MFE Records; Mindfield Records; Mirror Records, Inc.; Modern Voices Entertainment, Ltd.; Moonstone Records; Morgan Creek Music Group; Murdock's Music Company; Music Company, The; Nettwerk Productions; New South Records; November Records; Old School Records; Paint Chip Records; Pavement Music, Inc.; Penguin Records, Inc.; PMG Records; R.E.X. Music, Inc.; Railroad Records; Rave Records, Inc.; Revelation Records; Righteous Records; Rotten Records; Round Flat Records; Ruffcut Records; Sanity Check Musec, Inc.; Scratched Records; Shakefork Records; Shore Records; Skene! Records; Sonic Group, Ltd.; SpinART Records; Staplegun Records; Static Network & Records; Statue Records; Steam Records; Strugglebaby Recording Co.; Takeover Records; Tandem Records; Third Lock Records and Management; Trumpeter Records Inc.; TVT Records; Urge Recording Co.; Venture Beyond Records; Victory Records; Zerobudget Records; Zylon Records & Tapes

Blues Adobe Records; Alligator Records; Atlantic Recording Corp.; Beacon Records; Big Bear Records; Black Diamond Records Inc.; Blue Wave; BSW Records; Buy or Die CDs & LPs Inc.; Cellar Records; Deadeye Records; Disques Nosferatu Records; Domino Records, Ltd.; Endangered Records; Fat City Artists; Fink-Pinewood Records; Flying Heart Records; Folk Era Records; Goldband Records; Goldwax Record Co., Inc.; Grass Roots Record & Tape/LMI Records; Guitar Recordings; Hibi Dei Hipp Records; Ichiban Records; IMPS Music; Intrepid Records; Justin Time Records Inc.; Kicking Mule Records; Landslide Records; Lanor Records; Le Matt Music Ltd.; Master-Trak Enterprises; Maui Arts & Music Association; MCR; Missile Records; Modern Blues Recordings; Music Garden, Inc.; Nova Records Inc.; Old School Records; Pilot Records and Tape Company; Plankton Records; Quality Sound Recording; RBW, Inc.; Ripsaw Records; Rustron Music Productions; Sanity Check Musec, Inc.; Seeds Records; Sky-Child Records; Sphemusations; Spot Records; Treasure Coast Records; Triple X Records; Velvet Productions; Vital Music; Westworld Record Co.

Children's A & R Records; Aliso Creek Productions Incorporated; Amused Productions; Berandol Music; Brentwood Music; Courier Records; Discovery Music; Gordon Music Co. Inc.; Grass Roots Record & Tape/LMI Records; G-Town Records; Hickory Lane Publishing and Recording; Joyful Sound Records; Monarch Records; Pacific Artists Records International; Parade; Peridot Records; Rising Star Records Inc.; Teeter-Tot Records; Twin Sisters Productions, Inc.; Wizmak Productions; Youngheart Music; Zoom Express

Classical Avant-Garde Records Corp.; baby sue; Cambria Records & Publishing; Cantilena Records; Care Free Records Group; Carmel Records; Concord Jazz; Co-op Artist Recordings; Cymbal Records; Global Pacific Records; Intrepid Records; Lark Record Productions, Inc.; Marks Records, John; North Star Records; Nucleus Records; Pacific Artists Records International; Parade; RBW, Inc.; Rising Star Records Inc.; RMA Music; Sky-Child Records; Sounds-Vision Music; Vital Music; Zebraoverground Records

Country A & R Records; A.M.I. Records; Adobe Records; Air Central Recordings; Airwave Production Group, Inc.; Aliso Creek Productions Incorporated; Allagash Country Records; Allegheny Music Works; Alternative Records; American Music Network, Inc.; Americatone Records International USA; Amethyst Group Ltd., The; Bagatelle Record Company; BAL Records; Bandit Records; Beacon Records; Belmont Records; Belt Drive Records Ltd.; Best West Productions; Black & Blue; Black Diamond Records Inc.; Blue Gem Records; BMX Entertainment; BNA Entertainment; Bogart Records; Bold 1 Records; Bolivia Records; Bouquet Records; Brentwood Music; Briarhill Records; BSW Records; Buy or Die CDs & LPs Inc.; Caliber Records; Capstan Record Production; Care Free Records Group; Casaro Records; Cat's Voice Productions; CCC Group, Inc., The; Cedar Creek Records™; Cellar Records; Century Records Inc.; Cha Cha Records; Cherry Records; Cherry Street Records; Chrismarie Records; Cimirron/Rainbird Records; Circle "M" Records; CITA Communications Inc.; Collector Records; Comma Records & Tapes; Comstock Records Ltd.; Continental Records; Co-op Artist Recordings; Country Breeze Records; Country Showcase America; Country Star International; Cowgirl Records; Cymbal Records; Dale Productions, Alan; Dancer Publishing; Deadeye Records; Dejadisc, Inc.; Diamond Wind Records; Domino Records, Ltd.; Drag City, Inc.; E.S.R. Records; Empty Sky Records; Emzee Records; Endangered Records; ESB Records; Excursion Records; Fame and Fortune Enterprises; Farr Records; Fat City Artists; Fearless Records; Fifth Street Records; First Time Records; Folk Era Records; Fountain Records; Foxfire Records; Generic Records, Inc.; Goldband Records; Golden Triangle Records; Goldwax Record Co., Inc.; Gordon Music Co. Inc.; Grass Roots Record & Tape/LMI Records; Green Bear Records; G-Town Records; Gubala Music, Frank; Gueststar Records; Harmony Street Records; Heath & Associates; Heritage Music; Hickory Lane Publishing and Recording; Hollyrock Records; Holographic Records; Homebased Entertainment Co.; Horizon Recording Studio; Hottrax Records; Inferno Records; Interstate 40 Records; Intrepid Records; Jalyn Recording Co.; Jamaka Record Co.; Kaupp Records; Kicking Mule Records, Inc.; King of Kings Record Co.; Kingston Records; Kottage Records; L.A. Records; LBJ Productions; Landmark Communications Group; Lanor Records; Lari-Jon Records; Lark Record Productions, Inc.; Le Matt Music Ltd.; Legs Records; Lonesome Wind Corporation; LRJ; Luna Sea Records; Manny Music, Inc.; Master-Trak Enterprises; Mathes Company, The; Maui Arts & Music Association; Maxern Records; Maxim Records Ltd.; MCR; Metro Records; Mighty Records; Miles Ahead Records; Missile Records; Modern Music Ventures, Inc.; Monticana Records; Morgan Creek Music Group; Mosrite Records; MSM Records; Mule Kick Records; Murdock's Music Company; Music Company, The; Music Garden, Inc.; Music Service Management; New Beginning Record Productions; New Experience/Grand Slam Records; Nova Records Inc.; Nucleus Records; Orbit Records; Pacific Artists Records International; Pajer Records; Parade; Paragold Records & Tapes; Patty Lee Records; PBM Records; Peridot Records; Phoenix Records, Inc.; Pilot Records and Tape Company; Pincastle/WEBCO Records; Playback Records; Pleasure Records; Pop Record Research; Pravda Records; Puzzle Records; Quality Sound Recording; R.E.F. Records; Razor & Tie Music; RBW, Inc.; Rejoice Records Of Nashville; Resistor Records; Revelation Records; Richway Records International; Ripsaw Record Co.; Road Records; Roll On Records®; Rowena Records; RR&R Records; Ruffcut Records; Sabre Productions; Sabteca Record Co.; Scene Productions; Seaside Records; Seeds Records; Shakefork Records; Shore Records; Show Biz Productions; Sky-Child Records; Sphemusations; Stardancer Records; Stardust; Startrak Records, Inc.; SunCountry Records; Sureshot Records; Surprize Records, Inc.; Sweet Talk Records; Target Records; Ten Squared, Inc.; Third Lock Records and Management; Touche Records; Trac Record

Co.; Traveler Enterprises; Treasure Coast Records; Trend Records; Trumpeter Records Inc.; Trusty Records; Tug Boat Records; Universal-Athena Records; VIP Records; Vokes Music Publishing & Record Co.; Vondy Music Publishing; Watch Music Company Ltd.; Wedge Records; Wence Sense Music/Bill Wence Promotions; Westworld Record Co.; White Car Records; Winchester Records; Wings Record Company; Woodrich Records; Yellow Jacket Records; Young Country Records/Plain Country Records; Zone Record Co.; Zylon Records & Tapes

Dance All Star Promotions; Alpha-Beat; Amethyst Group Ltd., The; Amiron Music/Aztec Productions; Angel Eyes Records & Filmworks, Inc.; Associated Artists Music International; Atlantic Recording Corp.; AVC Entertainment Inc.; BCM-USA; Belt Drive Records Ltd.; Boogie Band Records; Broken Records; Bullet Proof Management; CITA Communications Inc.; Comma Records & Tapes; Dagene Records; Dat Beat Records, Inc.; Digitalia Records; Disc-tinct Music, Inc.; Exclusive Recording Co.; First Time Records; Fullmoon Entertainment/Moonstone Records; Ganvo Records; GMV Music Enterprises; Halogram; Horizon Records; Instinct Records; JK Jam Music; Joey Boy Records Inc.; L.A. Records; Le Matt Music Ltd.; Leopard Music; Loading Bay Records; Lucifer Records, Inc.; Madflow Recordings; Maxim Records Ltd.; Mercury Records; Mighty Records; Mindfield Records; Modern Voices Entertainment, Ltd.; Monticana Records; Music Station/Dancefloor; Nep-Tune Records, Inc.; Nettwerk Productions; On Top Records; P. & N. Records; Parade; Parc Records Inc.; Penguin Records, Inc.; PMG Records; Railroad Records; Rave Records, Inc.; Red Bus Records Ltd.; Red Dot/Puzzle Records; Revelation Records; Shore Records; Sirr Rodd Record & Publishing Co.; Slak Records; Stargard Records; Stinc Records America; T-Jaye Record Company; Top Records; Trusty Records; Typetoken Records; Victory Label, The; Wall Street Music

Folk A & R Records; Adobe Records; Amiron Music/Aztec Productions; Beacon Records; Black Dog Records; Buy or Die CDs & LPs Inc.; Carmel Records; CCC Group, Inc., The; Cha Cha Records; Dejadisc, Inc.; Endangered Records; First Time Records; Folk Era Records; Funky Mushroom Records; Goldband Records; Hollyrock Records; Kicking Mule Records, Inc.; Mirror Records, Inc.; Monarch Records; Monticana Records; MSM Records; North Star Records; Nucleus Records; Patty Lee Records; Peridot Records; Pilot Records and Tape Company; R.E.X. Music, Inc.; Red Sky Records; Righteous Records; Rustron Music Productions; Stinc Records America; Trusty Records; VIP Records; Winchester Records; Wizmak Productions; Zebraoverground Records

Jazz Adobe Records; Airwave Production Group, Inc.; Americatone Records International USA; Amethyst Group Ltd., The; Amiron Music/Aztec Productions; Atlantic Recording Corp.; August Records; BAL Records; Big Bear Records; Black Diamond Records Inc.; BMX Entertainment; Bright Green Records; Cantilena Records; Care Free Records Group; Casaro Records; CCC Group, Inc., The; Cherry Street Records; CITA Communications Inc.; Com-Four; Concord Jazz; Cymbal Records; Dale Productions, Alan; E.A.R.S. Inc.; Endangered Records; Etherean Music/ Variena Publishing; Fat City Artists; Fifth Street Records; Flying Heart Records; Fresh Entertainment; Funky Mushroom Records; Ganvo Records; Global Pacific Records; Golden Triangle Records; Gordon Music Co. Inc.; Grass Roots Record & Tape/LMI Records; G-Town Records; Guitar Recordings; Hallway International Records/1st Coast Posse; Hibi Dei Hipp Records; Hollyrock Records; Horizon Recording Studio; IMPS Music; Instinct Records; Intrepid Records; J&J Musical Enterprises Ltd.; Joey Boy Records Inc.; L.A. Records; Landmark Communications Group; Marks Records, John; Martini Records; Maui Arts & Music Association; Metro Records; Mighty Records; Missile Records; Modern Music Ventures, Inc.; Monticana Records; North Star Records; On Top Records; Orinda Records; Pacific Artists Records International; Parc Records Inc.; Patty Lee Records; Positive Music Records, Inc.; PPI/Peter Pan Industries; Puzzle Records; Rastaman Work Ethic Productions; RBW, Inc.; Righteous Records; Rising Star Records Inc.; Rock Dog Records; Sahara Records and Filmworks Entertainment; Seeds Records; Sirr Rodd Record & Publishing Co.; Sphemusations; Startrak Records, Inc.; Steam Records; Stinc Records America; Sun Dance Records; Third Lock Records and Management; Touche Records; Trend Records; TVT Records; VIP Records; Vital Music; Westworld Record Co.; Woodrich Records

Latin Americatone Records International USA; Belt Drive Records Ltd.; BMX Entertainment; Grass Roots Record & Tape/LMI Records; Horizon Records; Manny Music, Inc.; Modern Music Ventures, Inc.; Pleasure Records; Show Biz Productions; Sounds-Vision Music; Top Ten Hits Records Inc.

Metal Aarson Records; Amethyst Group Ltd., The; AVC Entertainment Inc.; Azra International; baby sue; Black & Blue; Care Free Records Group; Cellar Records; Disques Nosferatu Records; Earache Records/Earache Songs; Forefront Records; Gopaco Limited; L.A. Records; Luna Sea Records; Missile Records; Murdock's Music Company; Nep-Tune Records, Inc.; November Records; Pavement Music, Inc.; Pravda Records; R.E.X. Music, Inc.; Railroad Records; Rotten Records; Shaky Records; Shore Records; Takeover Records

New Age Aliso Creek Productions Incorporated; Beacon Records; Black Dog Records; Cactus Records; Care Free Records Group; Cat's Voice Productions; Dale Productions, Alan; Dat Beat Records, Inc.; Etherean Music/Variena Publishing; Global Pacific Records; Halogram; IMPS Music; L.A. Records; MFE Records; North Star Records; Order Records; Pacific Artists Records International; Parade; Powercoat Records; PPI/Peter Pan Industries; Presence Records; RBW, Inc.; Rising Star Records Inc.; Rock Dog Records; Rowena Records; Silver Wave Records; Sound Designs Of Arizona; World Disc Productions Inc.

Novelty Azra International; Briarhill Records; MOR Records; Parade; Peridot Records; Treasure Coast Records

Pop A.M.I. Records; Air Central Recordings; Airwave Production Group, Inc.; Aliso Creek Productions Incorporated; Allagash Country Records; Allegheny Music Works; Alphabeat; Alternative Records; Amiron Music/Aztec Productions; Angel Eyes Records & Filmworks, Inc.; Associated Artists Music International; Atlantic Recording Corp.; August Records; AVC Entertainment Inc.; baby sue; Benson Music Group; Berandol Music; Best West Productions; Big Rock Pty. Ltd.; Black Dog Records; Blue Duck!! Records; Blue Gem Records; BMX Entertainment; Bogart Records; Bolivia Records; Bonaire Management Inc.; Boogie Band Records; Broken Records; Cactus Records; Caffeine Disk; Caliber Records; Cantilena Records; Casaro Records; Cedar Creek Records™; Cellar Records; Century Records Inc.; Cherry Records; Chrismarie Records; Cimirron/Rainbird Records; Comma Records & Tapes; Co-op Artist Recordings; Cymbal Records; Dagene Records; Dat Beat Records, Inc.; Demi Monde Records and Publishing, Ltd.; Diamond Wind Records; Empty Sky Records; Emzee Records; Endangered Records; Etherean Music/Variena Publishing; Exclusive Recording Co.; Excursion Records; Fame and Fortune Enterprises; Farr Records; Fearless Records; Fifth Street Records; First Time Records; Fountain Records; Fountainhead Records; Fresh Entertainment; Frontline Music Group; Fullmoon Entertainment/Moonstone Records; Funky Mushroom Records; Generic Records, Inc.; Global Pacific Records; Goldband Records; Gopaco Limited; Gordon Music Co. Inc.; Grass Roots Record & Tape/LMI Records; Gubala Music, Frank; Halogram; Happy Tails Records; Harmony Street Records; Heath & Associates; Hibi Dei Hipp Records; Hollyrock Records; Homebased Entertainment Co.; Horizon Recording Studio; Horizon Redords; Hottrax Records; Hypernormal Records; IMPS Music; Instinct Records; JK Jam Music; Justin Time Records Inc.; Kaupp Records; Kingston Records; Kottage Records; L.A. Records; LBJ Productions; Lamar Music Group; Landmark Communications Group; Landslide Records; Le Matt Music Ltd.; Leopard Music; Limited Potential Records; Lion Hunter Music; Lucifer Records, Inc.; Luna Sea Records; Makeshift Music; Manny Music, Inc.; Maui Arts & Music Association; Mercury Records; Metro Records; Mighty Records; Miles Ahead Records; Missile Records; Modern Voices Entertainment, Ltd.; Monticana Records; MOR Records; Morgan Creek Music Group; MSM Records; Mule Kick Records; Murdock's Music Company; Music Company, The; Music Garden, Inc.; Nettwerk Productions; New Experience/Grand Slam Records; New South Records; November Records; Nucleus Records; Old School Records; Orinda Records; Pajer Records; Penguin Records, Inc.; Phoenix Records, Inc.; Pop Record Research; Powercoat Records; PPI/Peter Pan Industries; Premiére Records; R.E.F. Records; R.E.X. Music, Inc.; Rage-N-Records; Razor & Tie Music; Red Dot/Puzzle Records; Roll On Records®; Rowena Records; RR&R Records; Ruffcut Records; Rustron Music Productions; Sabteca Record Co.; Sahara Records and Filmworks Entertainment; Scene Productions; Shaolin Film & Records; Sirr Rodd Record & Publishing Co.; Sky-Child Records; Slak Records; Source Records, Inc.; SpinART Records; Spot Records; Staplegun Records; Stark Records and Tape Company; Startrak Records, Inc.; Static Network & Records; Statue Records; Sun Dance Records; Sweet Talk Records; Third Lock Records and Management; Top Records; Top Ten Hits Records, Inc.; Trusty Records; Tug Boat Records; Velvet Productions; Victory Label, The; Watch Music Company Ltd.; Wedge Records; Westworld Record Co.; White Car Records; Widely Distributed Records; Wings Record Company; Zebraoverground Records; Zerobudget Records; Zone Record Co.; Zylon Records & Tapes

Rap Alpha-Beat; Amethyst Group Ltd., The; Angel Eyes Records & Filmworks, Inc.; Associated Artists Music International; AVC Entertainment Inc.; Belt Drive Records Ltd.; Black Diamond Records Inc.; Blue Duck!! Records; BMX Entertainment; Boogie Band Records; Bullet Proof Management; Cellar Records; CITA Communications Inc.; Co-op Artist Recordings; Cymbal Records; Dagene Records; Dat Beat Records, Inc.; Digitalia Records; Empty Sky Records; Fearless Records; Fresh Entertainment; Ganvo Records; Generic Records, Inc.; GMV Music Enterprises; Godman Music and Publications; Hallway International Records/1st Coast Posse; Hibi Dei Hipp Records; Homebased Entertainment Co.; Joey Boy Records Inc.; Lamar Music Group; Landslide Records; Macola Record Group Inc.; Madflow Recordings; Missile Records; Modern Music Ventures, Inc.; Modern Voices Entertainment; Nep-Tune Records, Inc.; New Experience Rec/Grand Slam Records; On Top Records; Penguin Records, Inc.; Rap-A-Lot Records, Inc.; Rastaman Work Ethic Productions; Revelation Records; Shakefork Records; Sirr Rodd Record & Publishing Co.; Stargard Records; Statue Records; Steam Records; Sun Dance Records; Takeover Records; Tandem Records; Triple X Records; TVT Records; Umbrella Records; VIP Records; Wall Street Music; Westworld Record Co.; Wild Pitch Records Ltd.

R&B Air Central Recordings; Airwave Production Group, Inc.; All Night Records; All Star Promotions; Allagash Country Records; Allegheny Music Works; Alpha-Beat; Amethyst Group Ltd., The; Angel Eyes Records & Filmworks, Inc.; Atlantic Recording Corp.; AVC Entertainment Inc.; Benson Music Group; Big Rock Pty. Ltd.; Black Diamond Records Inc.; Black Dog Records; Blue Gem Records; Blue Wave; BMX Entertainment; Bogart Records; Bolivia Records; Boogie Band Records; Bullet Proof Management; Caliber Records; Casaro Records; Cat's Voice Productions; Cedar Creek Records™; Cherry Street Records; Chrismarie Records; Circle "M" Records; Comma Records & Tapes; Cowgirl Records; Dagene Records; Dat Beat Records, Inc.; Deadeye Records; Demi Monde Records and Publishing, Ltd.; Diamond Wind Records; Disc-tinct Music, Inc.; Domino Records, Ltd.; Emzee Records; Endangered Records; Excursion Records; Farr Records; Fearless Records; Fifth Street Records; Fink-Pinewood Records; First Time Records; Flying Heart Records; Foxfire Records; Fresh Entertainment; Fresh Start Music Ministries; Frontline Music Group; Fullmoon Entertainment/Moonstone Records; Ganvo Records; GMV Music Enterprises; Gold City Records, Inc.; Goldband Records; Golden Triangle Records; Goldwax Record Co., Inc.; Grass Roots Record & Tape/LMI Records; Hallway International Records/1st Coast Posse; Halogram; Harmony Street Records; Heath & Associates; Hibi Dei Hipp Records; Homebased Entertainment Co.; Horizon Recording Studio; Horizon Records; Ichiban Records; Kaupp Records; Kottage Records; L.A. Records; LBJ Productions; Lamar Music Group; Landmark Communications Group; Landslide Records; Lanor Records; Le Matt Music Ltd.; Lion Hunter Music; Lucifer Records, Inc.; Luna Sea Records; Master-Trak Enterprises; Maxim Records Ltd.; Mercury Records; Miles Ahead Records; Missile Records; Modern Blues Recordings; Modern Voices Entertainment, Ltd.; Monticana Records; Morgan Creek Music Group; Murdock's Music Company; Music Garden, Inc.; Music Station/Dancefloor; Nep-Tune Records, Inc.; New Experience/Grand Slam Records; New South Records; November Records; Orbit Records; Parade; Parc Records Inc.; Penguin Records, Inc.; Plankton Records; Pleasure Records; Pop Record Research; PPI/ Peter Pan Industries; Premiére Records; Rage-N-Records; Rap-A-Lot Records, Inc.; Rave Records, Inc.; Razor & Tie Music; Red-Eye Records; Rock Dog Records; Roll On Records®; Rowena Records; RR&R Records; Rustron Music Productions; Sabre Productions; Sabteca Record Co.; Sahara Records and Filmworks Entertainment; Scene Productions; Seeds Records; Shore Records; Slak Records; Source Records, Inc.; Stargard Records; Startrak Records, Inc.; Strugglebaby Recording Co.; Sun Dance Records; Surprize Records, Inc.; Tandem Records; Third Lock Records and Management; T-Jaye Record Company; Touche Records; Treasure Coast Records; Trend Records; Trusty Records; TVT Records; Umbrella Records; Velvet Productions; VIP Records; Wall Street Music; Wedge Records; Westworld Record Co.; White Car Records; Wings Record Company; Zylon Records & Tapes

Religious Air Central Recordings; Allegheny Music Works; American Music Network, Inc.; Azra International; baby sue; Bagatelle Record Company; BAL Records; Bandit Records; Benson Music Group; Bogart Records; Bouquet Records; Brentwood Music; Briarhill Records; Cedar Creek Records™; Cha Cha Records; Circle "M" Records; CITA Communications Inc.; Continental Records; Co-op Artist Recordings; Courier Records; Cowgirl Records; Dagene Records; Dale Productions, Alan; EMA Music Inc.; Empty Sky Records; Emzee Records; Excursion Records; Fifth Street Records; Fink-Pinewood Records; First Time Records; Folk Era Records; Fountain Records; Foxfire Records; Fresh Entertainment; Fresh Start Music Ministries; Frontline Music Group; Gold City Records, Inc.; Goldwax Record Co., Inc.; Grass Roots Record & Tape/LMI Records; Green Bear Records; Gueststar Records; Harmony Street Records; Heath & Associates; Heritage Music; Hickory Lane Publishing and Recording; Homebased Entertainment Co.; Horizon Recording Studio; Intrepid Records; Jalyn Recording Co.; Justin Time Records Inc.; Kaupp Records; King of Kings Record Co.; Kottage Records; L.A. Records; LBJ Productions; Landmark Communications Group; Lari-Jon Records; Legs Records; Leopard Music; Malaco Records; Manny Music, Inc.; Mathes Company, The; Maxern Records; MCR; Miles Ahead Records; Missile Records; Monticana Records; Mosrite Records; Music Garden, Inc.; Music Service Management; New Beginning Record Productions; New Experience/Grand Slam Records; Nucleus Records; On Top Records; PBM Records; Peridot Records; Phoenix Records, Inc.; Plankton Records; Pleasure Records; Quality Sound Recording; R.E.F. Records; R.E.X. Music, Inc.; RBW, Inc.; Red-Eye Records; Rejoice Records Of Nashville; Resistor Records; Richway Records International; Roll On Records®; Rowena Records; RR&R Records; Sabre Productions; Seaside Records; Show Biz Productions; Sirr Rodd Record & Publishing Co.; Sound Achievement Group, Inc.; Source Records, Inc.; Spiritual Walk Records; Stardancer Records; Startrak Records, Inc.; Streets of Gold Records; Sun Dance Records; SunCountry Records; Tandem Records; T-Jaye Record Company; Touche Records; Treasure Coast Records; Trend Records; Trusty Records; Velvet Productions; Victory Label, The; VIP Records; Vital Music; Vokes Music Publishing & Record Co.; Vondy Music Publishing; Wedge Records; Winchester Records; Wings Record Company; Woodrich Records; Young Country Records/Plain Country Records

Rock A.M.I. Records; Aarson Records; Air Central Recordings; Airwave Production Group, Inc.; Aliso Creek Productions Incorporated; All Night Records; All Star Promotions; Allagash Country Records; Alternative Records; American Music Network, Inc.; Americatone Records International USA; Amethyst Group Ltd., The; Amiron Music/Aztec Productions; Associated Artists Music International; Atlantic Recording Corp.; August Records; AVC Entertainment Inc.; Azra International; baby sue; BAL Records; BCM-USA; Beacon Records; Belt Drive Records Ltd.; Benson Music Group; Big Pop; Big Rock Pty. Ltd.; Black & Blue; Black Diamond Records Inc.; Black Dog Records; Blue Duck!! Records; Blue Gem Records; Blue Wave; BMX Entertainment; Bogart Records; Bold 1 Records; Bonaire Management Inc.; Boogie Band Records; Bouquet Records; Broken Records; BSW Records; Buy or Die CDs & LPs Inc.; Caffeine Disk; Caliber Records; Cantilena Records; Capstan Record Production; Care Free Records Group; Carlyle Records, Inc.; Carmel Records; Cat's Voice Productions; Cedar Creek Records™; Cellar Records; Cerebral Records; Chattahoochee Records; Cherry Street Records; Chrismarie Records; CITA Communications Inc.; Cleopatra Records; Collector Records; Com-Four; Comma Records & Tapes; Conspiracy Records; Cymbal Records; Dancer Publishing Co.; Dat Beat Records, Inc.; Deadeye Records; Dejadisc, Inc.; Demi Monde Records and Publishing, Ltd.; Diamond Wind

Records; Disques Nosferatu Records; Domino Records, Ltd.; Drag City, Inc.; Earache Records/ Earache Songs; Empty Sky Records; Emzee Records; Endangered Records; Excursion Records; Fame and Fortune Enterprises; Farr Records; Fat City Artists; Fearless Records; Fiction; Fifth Street Records; Flying Heart Records; Fountainhead Records; Foxfire Records; Fresh Entertainment; Fresh Start Music Ministries; Fullmoon Entertainment/Moonstone Records; Generic Records, Inc.; Global Pacific Records; Godman Music and Publications; Goldband Records; Golden Triangle Records; Goldwax Record Co., Inc.; Gopaco Limited; Grass Roots Record & Tape/ LMI Records; Green Bear Records; G-Town Records; Gueststar Records; Guitar Recordings; Harmony Street Records; Hickory Lane Publishing and Recording; Hollyrock Records; Holographic Records; Homebased Entertainment Co.; Homestead Records; Hottrax Records; Hypernormal Records; I Wanna Records; Ichiban Records; IMPS Music; Inferno Records; Intrepid Records; JK Jam Music; Kaupp Records; Kingston Records; Kottage Records; L.A. Records; LBJ Productions; Landmark Communications Group; Lanor Records; Lari-Jon Records; Le Matt Music Ltd.; Legs Records; Lion Hunter Music; Lucifer Records, Inc.; Luna Sea Records; Makeshift Music; Manny Music, Inc.; Master-Trak Enterprises; Maui Arts & Music Association; Maxern Records; Megaforce Worldwide Entertainment; Mercury Records; Metro Records; MFE Records; Mirror Records, Inc.; Missile Records; Modern Blues Recordings; Modern Voices Entertainment, Ltd.; Monticana Records; Moonstone Records; Morgan Creek Music Group; MSM Records; Mule Kick Records; Murdock's Music Company; Music Company, The; Music Garden, Inc.; Nep-Tune Records, Inc.; Nervous Records; New Experience/Grand Slam Records; New South Records; Nova Records Inc.; November Records; Nucleus Records; Old School Records; Orbit Records; P. & N. Records; Parade; Parc Records Inc.; Patty Lee Records; Pavement Music, Inc.; PBM Records; Penguin Records, Inc.; Phoenix Records, Inc.; Pilot Records and Tape Company; Plankton Records; Pleasure Records; PMG Records; Powercoat Records; Pravda Records; Premiére Records; Presence Records; Puzzle Records; Quality Sound Recording; R.E.F. Records; Rage-N-Records; Railroad Records; Razor & Tie Music; Red Dot/Puzzle Records; Red Sky Records; Red-Eye Records; Resistor Records; Revelation Records; Ripsaw Record Co.; Rotten Records; Rowena Records; RR&R Records; Ruffcut Records; Sabre Productions; Sanity Check Musec, Inc.; Scene Productions; Sealed With A Kiss, Inc.; Seaside Records; Shaky Records; Shaolin Film & Records; Shore Records; Skene! Records; Sky-Child Records; Spot Records; Stardust; Startrak Records, Inc.; Static Network & Records; Statue Records; Steam Records; Stinc Records America; Strugglebaby Recording Co.; Sun Dance Records; SunCountry Records; Sureshot Records; Sweet Talk Records; Takeover Records; Trac Record Co.; Trend Records; Triple X Records; Trumpeter Records Inc.; Tug Boat Records; Umbrella Records; Urge Recording Co.; Velvet Productions; Victory Label, The; Victory Records; VIP Records; Vondy Music Publishing; Watch Music Company Ltd.; Wedge Records; Westworld Record Co.; White Car Records; Widely Distributed Records; Winchester Records; Wings Record Company; Woodrich Records; Young Country Records/ Plain Country Records; Zebraoverground Records; Zerobudget Records; Zylon Records & Tapes

World Music Blue Duck!! Records; Cat's Voice Productions; Com-Four; Etherean Music/Variena Publishing; Hallway International Records/1st Coast Posse; Leopard Music; Monarch Records; Music of the World; Order Records; Pacific Artists Records International; Railroad Records; Rising Star Records Inc.; Silver Wave Records; Sounds-Vision Music; Vital Music; Westworld Record Co.; World Disc Productions Inc.; Zebraoverground Records

Record Companies/'94-'95 Changes

The following markets appeared in the 1994 edition of *Songwriter's Market* but are absent from the 1995 edition. Most of these companies failed to respond to our request for an update of their listing for a variety of reasons. For example, they may have gone out of business or they may have requested deletion from the 1995 edition because they are backlogged with material. If we know the specific reason, it appears within parentheses.

A Company Called W (no longer releasing records)
Acoustic Disc
Alternative Records
Alyssa Records (not accepting submissions)
Angry Neighbor Records
Another Approach Recording Company (did not respond)
Antelope Records Inc.
Arion Records
Artifex Records

Attack Records
Auburn Records and Tapes (unable to contact)
Autogram Records
Beau-Jim Records Inc.
Beyond Records Corp.
BGM Records (not accepting submissions)
Big Productions Records
Bovine International Record Company
Carousel Records, Inc.

Challedon Records (out of business)
Cosmotone Records
Cowboy Junction Flea Market and Publishing Co.
Creative Life Entertainment, Inc.
Crown Music Company
Cuca Record Co.
Duke Street Records
Dupuy Records/Productions/ Publishing, Inc.

Etiquette/Suspicious Records
Evolving Recording Productions (requested deletion)
Eye Kill Records
Flaming Star West (unable to contact)
Fretboard Publishing (requested deletion)
Gateway
Genesee Records, Inc.
Go-Roc-Co-Pop Records (requested deletion)
Greenlee Records (unable to contact)
H&S Records
Helion Records
Hot Records (requested deletion)
I'll Call You Records
Jimmy Jangle Records (not accepting submissions)
Jump Records & Music (out of business)
John Headley Lennon Music
M.R.E. Recording Productions
March Records
Mariah Records
Mega Records APS.
Moneytime Records (unable to contact)
Mountain Railroad Records, Inc. (unable to contact)
Ms'que Records Inc.
Musica Schallplatten Vertrieb
Narada Productions (requested deletion)
Nephelim Record
Nickel Records

Nickle Plate Records
Nightflite Records Inc.
Now & Then Records (requested deletion)
Ocean Records Inc.
One-Eyed Duck Recording and Publishing
Outstanding & Morrthythm Records (backlogged with material)
P.I.R.A.T.E. Records/H.E.G. Music Publishing
Palmetto Productions (out of business)
Paradigm Distribution (unable to contact)
Parsifal PVBA
Paula Records/Jewel Records/ Ronn Records (requested deletion)
Platinum Boulevard Records
Play Records (unable to contact)
Prairie Music Records Ltd. (unable to contact)
Presto Records (requested deletion)
Prodisc
Rainforest Records (not accepting submissions)
Raspberry Records (requested deletion)
Reca Music Production
Reveal
Rhino Records Ltd.
Roach Records (unable to contact)
Robbins Records, Inc.

Rock In Records
Rockit Records, Inc.
Rock'N'Roll Records
Rooart Records
Rosie Records
Roto-Noto Music
San-Sue Recording Studio (out of business)
Skylyne Records (out of business)
Sound Masters (affiliate of Cherry Records)
Starcrest Productions, Inc.
Stark Records and Tape Company (affiliate of Pilot Records and Tape Company)
Stop Hunger Records International
Studio B. Records
Sun-Ray/Sky-Vue Records
Sunshine Records Ltd.
Survivor Records (unable to contact)
Susan Records
Tawas Records
Terock Records
This Charming Record Co.
Vibe Records (unable to contact)
Windham Hill Productions
Wingate Records
Write Key Records
Xemu Records
Young Star Productions, Inc.
Zanzibar Records
Zulu Records

Record Producers

The independent producer can best be described as a creative coordinator. He's usually the one with the most creative control over a recording project and is ultimately responsible for the finished product. Although some larger record companies have their own in-house producers, it's common for a record company today to contract out-of-house, independent producers for recording projects.

Producers can be valuable contacts for songwriters because they work so closely with the artists whose records they produce. They usually have a lot more freedom than others in executive positions, and they are known for having a good ear for hit song potential. Many producers are songwriters, musicians and artists themselves. Since they have the most influence on a particular project, a good song in the hands of the right producer at the right time stands a good chance of being cut. And even if a producer is not working on a specific project, he is well-acquainted with record company executives and artists, and can often get material through doors not open to you.

Even so, it can be difficult to get your tapes to the right producer at the right time. Many producers write their own songs and even if they don't write, they might be involved in their own publishing companies so they have instant access to all the songs in their catalogs. It's important to understand the intricacies of the producer/publisher situation. If you pitch your song directly to a producer first, before another publishing company publishes the song, the producer may ask you for the publishing rights (or a percentage thereof) to your song. You must decide whether the producer is really an active publisher who will try to get the song recorded again and again, or whether he merely wants the publishing because it means extra income for him from the current recording project. You may be able to work out a co-publishing deal, where you and the producer split the publishing of the song. That means he will still receive his percentage of the publishing income, even if you secure a cover recording of the song by other artists in the future. But, even though you would be giving up a little bit initially, you may benefit in the future.

The listings that follow outline which aspects of the music industry each producer is involved in, what type of music he is looking for, and what records and artists he's recently produced. Study the listings carefully, noting the artists he works with, and consider if any of your songs might fit a particular artist's or producer's style.

A & R RECORDING SERVICES, 71906 Highway 111, Rancho Mirage CA 92270. (619)346-0075. Producer-Engineer: Robert Braverman. Record producer. Estab. 1978. Deals with artists. Fee derived from sales royalty when song or artist is recorded or outright fee from recording artist and record company.
How to Contact: Submit demo tape by mail—unsolicited submissions are OK. Prefers cassette (or VHS videocassette if available) with 4 songs and lyric or lead sheets. SASE. Reports in 1 month.
Music: Mostly **pop, country** and **gospel**; also **rock**. Produced *It's In Your Hands*, written and recorded by Gloria Weigand; and "Nothing's Missing," written and recorded by John C. Shipley, both on Accent Records. Other artists include Steve Henderson, Cherie Hall and Jon Kodi.

"A" MAJOR SOUND CORPORATION, Suite 421, 49 Thorncliffe Park Dr., Toronto, Ontario M4H 1J6 **Canada**. (416)423-9046. Record Producer: Paul C. Milner. Record producer and recording engineer. Estab. 1985. Deals with artists and songwriters. Fee derived from sales royalty when song or artist is recorded, or outright fee from recording artist or record company.

A producer's job goes beyond the recording process

"I much prefer working with singer/songwriters, rather than with people who only perform," says San Francisco-based producer Scott Mathews. "It seems like most of my projects are geared towards artists who also write their own material."

Perhaps the preference to work with writers has something to do with the fact that Mathews is an accomplished songwriter as well as a successful producer. He has co-written songs with John Hiatt, Al Anderson (of NRBQ), Huey Lewis and Ron Nagle, with whom he had a song cut by Barbra Streisand. Some of his current production projects include singer/songwriter John Wesley Harding, Booker T. Jones (of Booker T. and the MG's) and surf guitar king Dick Dale. "I do a lot of co-writing with the people I work with," says Mathews, "and

Scott Mathews

often the process of recording and writing is sort of balled into one."

Mathews sees a producer's job as much more than just sitting behind the recording console. "The role of the producer is to get to the heart of a song and make sure the song is ready," he explains. "It's not uncommon for me as a producer to say to an artist, 'The songs are 70% there, there's this or that missing,' or 'This is great, why don't you expand this?'—and send the writer back for a little more fine tuning. Usually I'm the first person who hears a songwriter's work. These are new songs that they're bringing out for the first time, and it's a heavy position to be that first ear. Your opinion means a lot to the writer."

Since a producer has such a large influence on the sound of an artist's product, it's important to select one who works well with the artist. "You really have to get along with a producer and have a rapport with him so you feel he really understands your work," Mathews says. "His feedback is really touching the nerve of the song you wrote; perhaps you're learning more about your work through his impression of it. The role of the producer is to boil it down to the essence of the artist and be the keeper of that vision."

A producer can also be a vital link in getting songs heard by others in the industry. "I may hear something that I just have to be involved with," says Mathews. "I end up working with the artist, and although I'm not officially the shopper of the project, I can chat it up with a lot of people, such as A&R people I've worked with before. Every day I'm in contact with these people and they're asking me what I'm working on."

Even with the influence a producer can provide, Mathews says the success or failure of an artist is ultimately up to the artist himself. "You have to be your own salesperson, and that's the hardest part," he says. "Get your material out there, and if you can't, find somebody who can. And always remember that everybody counts. The small-time critic of the local paper may be working for *Billboard* next year. The person who's working in the mail room at some small label could be working at Capitol Records. It just happens."

— Cindy Laufenberg

How to Contact: Submit demo tape by mail—unsolicited submissions are OK. Prefers cassette (or DAT) with 3-4 songs and lyric sheet. Reports in 2 months.
Music: Mostly **rock, pop** and **metal**; also **R&B** and **gospel**. Produced *Assimilation* (by D. Mal/I. Ritchie), recorded by Paul Milner on Current/MCA Records; "Resurrection" (by A. Pricesmith) and *Heroes and Legends* (by K. Herdman/B. Boychick), both recorded by Paul Milner on INDI Records. Other artists include Hokus Pick Manouver, The Burns, Freshwater Drum, Rosanne Baker and Headstones.
Tips: "Strong pre-production is the key to developing a strong product."

ABERDEEN PRODUCTIONS, (a.k.a. Scott Turner Productions), 524 Doral Country Dr., Nashville TN 37221. (615)646-9750. President: Scott Turner. Record producer and music publisher (Buried Treasure/ASCAP, Captain Kidd/BMI). Estab. 1971. Deals with artists and songwriters. Works with 30 new songwriters/year. Produces 10 singles, 15-20 12″ singles, 8 LPs and 8 CDs/year. Fee derived from production fee and minimal royalty after all monies are recouped.
How to Contact: Submit demo tape by mail—unsolicited submissions OK. Prefers cassette with maximum 4 songs and lead sheet. SASE. Reports in 2 weeks.
Music: Mostly **country, MOR** and **rock**; also **top 40/pop**. Produced "Rise Above It" (by S. Rose) and "Please Mr. Music Man" (by Audie Murphy/Scott Turner), recorded by Brittany Hale on GBS Records; and "Your Star's Still Shining" (by S. Turner/B. McNaul), recorded by Bret McNaul. Other artists include Martha Carson, Stevie Maynard and Tommy Sands.
Tips: "Be unique. A great song doesn't care who sings it . . . but there is a vast difference between a good song and a great song."

ACR PRODUCTIONS, P.O. Box 5236, Lubbock TX 79408-5236. (806)792-3804. Owner: Dwaine Thomas. Record producer, music publisher (Joranda Music/BMI) and record company (ACR Records). Estab. 1986. Deals with artists and songwriters. Produces 120 singles, 8-15 12″ singles, 25 LPs, 25 EPs and 25 CDs/year. Fee derived from sales royalty. "We charge for in-house recording only. Remainder is derived from royalties."
How to Contact: Submit demo tape by mail. Unsolicited submissions are OK. Prefers cassette (or VHS videocassette if available) with 5 songs and lyric sheet. Does not return unsolicited material. Reports in 6 weeks.
Music: Mostly **country swing, pop** and **rock**; also **R&B** and **gospel**. Produced *Shattered Dreams* and *Rodeo Cowboy* (by Dwaine Thomas); also *Break The Fall* (by Jerry Brownlow), all on ACR Records. Other artists include Rodeoactive (country).

AKO PRODUCTION, Dept. SM, 20531 Plummer, Chatsworth CA 91311. (818)998-0443. President: A. Sullivan. Record producer and music publisher (Amiron). Deals with artists and songwriters. Produces 2-6 singles and 2-3 LPs/year. Fee derived from sales royalty when song or artist is recorded.
How to Contact: Write first and obtain permission to submit. Prefers cassette (or Beta or VHS videocassette) and lyric sheet. SASE. Reports in 1 month.
Music: **Pop/rock** and **modern country**. Produced *Ladies in Charge*, written and recorded by C. Ratliff on AKO Records.

ALLEN-MARTIN PRODUCTIONS INC., Dept. SM, 9701 Taylorville Rd., Louisville KY 40299. (502)267-9658. Contact: Producer. Record producer and music publisher (Always Alive Music, Bridges Music/ASCAP, BMI). Estab. 1965. Deals with artists. Produces 10 singles, 5 12″ singles, 20 LPs, 5 EPs and 20 CDs/year. Fee derived from sales royalty when song or artist is recorded or outright fee from recording artist or record company.
How to Contact: Write first and obtain permission to submit. Prefers cassette (or ¾ or ½ videocassette) with several songs and lyric sheet. Artist photo is desirable. SASE. Reports in 2 months.

Music: Mostly **country, gospel** and **pop**; also **rock, R&B** and **rap**. Produced *Delta*, written and recorded by Duke Robillaro on Rovrene Records (R&B); *Exquisite Fashion*, written and recorded by Duke Robillaro (rock); and *More Praise* (by Harold Moore), recorded by Duke Robillaro, both on X Mode Records (gospel). Other artists include J.P. Pennington, Larnelle Harris, Turley Richards, Shaking Family and Michael Jonathon.

STUART J. ALLYN, Skylight Run, Irvington NY 10533. (212)486-0856. Associate: Jack Walker. Record producer. Estab. 1972. Deals with artists and songwriters. Produces 6 singles, 3-6 LPs and 3-6 CDs/year. Fee derived from sales royalty and outright fee from recording artist and record company.
How to Contact: Write first and obtain permission to submit. Prefers DAT, CD, cassette or 15 ips reel-to-reel (or VHS videocassette) with 3 songs and lyric or lead sheet. Does not return unsolicited material. Reports in 12 months.
Music: Mostly **pop, rock, jazz** and **theatrical**; also **R&B** and **country**. Produced *Mel Lewis & Jazz Orchestra* on Atlantic Records (jazz); *Me & Him*, on Columbia Records (film score); and "Set Sail & Sea Fans," on Passage Home Records (video release); also hundreds of commercials and industrials, all recorded by S. Allyn. Other artists include Billy Joel, Aerosmith, Carole Demas, Harry Stone, Bob Stewart, The Dixie Peppers, Nora York, Buddy Barnes and various video and film scores.

ALPHA MUSIC PRODUCTIONS, Box 14701, Lenexa KS 66285. (913)768-1033. President: Glenn Major. Record producer, music publisher (Alpha House Publishing/BMI) and record company (AMP Records). Estab. 1982. Deals with artists and songwriters. Produces 5 singles, 2 LPs and 1 CD/year. Fee derived from sales royalty when song or artist is recorded.
How to Contact: Submit demo tape by mail—unsolicited submissions are OK. Prefers cassette (or VHS videocassette if available) with 3-5 songs and lyric sheet. Include cover letter, bio and pictures. Does not return unsolicited material. Reports in 2 months.
Music: Mostly **country, rock** and **folk**. Produced *Repossesed My Heart* (by Jerry Dowell), recorded by 7 Thunders Band on Thunderhorse Records; *Scared Out of My Shoes* (by Chubby Smith), recorded by Chubby Smith Orchestra; and "Never Been to Nashville" (by Rick Hasley), recorded by Cowboy X, both on AMP Records. Other artists include the Jolly Rogers and Tall Tales.
Tips: "Be realistic in your expectations. Get lots of opinions from your peers."

*ALSTATT ENTERPRISES, Suite 273, 4255 E. Charleston, Las Vegas NV 89104. (702)431-9424. Fax: (702)641-5124. President: Albert J. Statti. Record producer, music publisher. Estab. 1989. Deals with artists and songwriters. Produces 3-4 singles, 1-2 LPs and 1-2 CDs/year. Fee derived from sales royalty or outright fee from record company.
How to Contact: Submit demo tape by mail—unsolicited submissions are OK. Prefers cassette with 3 songs and lyric or lead sheets. SASE. Reports in 2-3 months.
Music: Mostly **R&B, pop** and **MOR/rock**.

BUZZ AMATO, 2310-D Marietta Blvd., Atlanta GA 30318. (404)355-0909. Producer: Buzz Amato. Record producer and record company (Ichiban, Gold Key, Curton, J&S). Estab. 1987. Deals with artists. Produces 8 singles, 4 12″ singles, 10 LPs and 4 CDs/year. Fee derived from sales royalty when song or artist is recorded.
How to Contact: Write first and obtain permission to submit. Prefers cassette with 3 songs and lyric or lead sheet. "List how material was cut—instruments, outboard, tape format, etc." SASE. Reports in 2 months.
Music: Mostly **R&B (urban), blues** and **pop**; also **jazz**. Produced "The Magic in Your Heart," recorded by Bob Thompson; "Headed Back to Hurtsville," written and recorded by Theodis Ealey, both on Ichiban Records; and *TSOP* (by Gambol/Hoff), recorded by Three Degrees on Sony Music. Other artists include The Impressions, Vernon Garrett, Ben E. King and Scott Topper.
Tips: "Pay attention to the artist and styles when sending demos. Too many times a writer will send material that has nothing to do with what that artist is about."

AMETHYST RECORDS, INC., Box 82158, Oklahoma City OK 73148. (405)794-2481. General Manager: Russell Canaday. Record producer and record company. Estab. 1988. Deals with artists and songwriters. Produces 10 singles, 25 LPs, 3 EPs and 3 CDs/year. Recording cost derived from recording artist or Amethyst record company. "If artist is unknown, we sometimes charge an outright fee. It depends on exposure and work."

The asterisk before a listing indicates that the listing is new in this edition. New markets are often the most receptive to unsolicited submissions.

How to Contact: Submit demo tape by mail—unsolicited submissions are OK. Prefers cassette with 3 songs and lyric or lead sheets. SASE. Reports in 3 months.
Music: Mostly **country, gospel** and **easy listening**; also **R&B**. Produced "Going on With My Jesus," recorded by Wanda Jackson; *Blues Man* (by Hank Williams, Jr.), recorded by Henson Cargi (country); and "Higher" (by Mark Bryan), recorded by Sherman Andrus (gospel), all on Amethyst Records. Other artists include Cissie Lynn, Rita King and several Oklahoma Opry artists.
Tips: "Have one or two of your best songs professionally recorded so the prospective listener will understand more about the song and its production style."

ANCIENT FUTURE MUSIC, P.O. Box 264, Kentfield CA 94914-0264. (415)459-1892. Producer: Matthew Montfort. Record producer. "Ancient Future is a world music group and publishes books on world music instruction." Estab. 1979. Deals with artists and songwriters. Produces 1 LP and 1 CD/year. Fee derived from sales royalty when song or artist is recorded, outright fee from recording artist or record company.
How to Contact: Submit demo tape by mail. Unsolicited submissions are OK. Prefers cassette. "Recording quality not important, but musicianship and performance is." Does not return unsolicited material. Reports in 4 months.
Music: Mostly **world music, cross-cultural music** and **foreign language songs** *if* instrumentally excellent. Produced *Dusk Song of the Fishermen* (traditional), recorded by Zhao Hui on Narada Equinox Records; *El Gatillo of El Amadillo*, written and recorded by Ancient Future on Narada Collection Records; and *Amber*, written and recorded by Matthew Montfort on Narada Lotus Records.
Tips: "Only submit material based on world music. High quality musicianship is important."

ANDREW & FRANCIS, P.O. Box 882, Homewood IL 60430-0882. (708)258-3312. (708)755-1323. Contact: Brian Kalan. Record producer and management agency. Estab. 1984. Deals with artists and songwriters. Produces 4 LPs, 5 EPs and 1 CD/year. Fee derived from sales royalty when song or artist is recorded, or outright fee from recording artist or record company.
How to Contact: Submit demo tape by mail—unsolicited submissions are OK. Prefers cassette (or VHS videocassette if available) with 1-3 songs and lyric sheet. "Don't be afraid to submit! We are here to help you by reviewing your material for possible representation or production." Does not return unsolicited material. Reports in 2 months.
Music: Mostly **rock (commercial), hard rock** and **dance rock**; also **classical guitar, instrumental rock** and **solo guitar.** Produced "Silo-Servo," written and recorded by Larry Lipkovitch; "End of My Road" (by B.F. Clifford), recorded by Blake; and "Grandma Russell" (by M. Talkington), recorded by Reenie. Other artists include Scott Reed, T.J. and Alexander Harrison, James Glowiak (disco/dance).
Tips: "Song content is *very* important, whether it be a catchy hook/riff or a great story. If we can find a saleable element within your song, we will put our experience into bringing that element to the forefront. Focus on content, we will focus on displaying it."

ANGEL FILMS COMPANY, 967 Hwy 40, New Franklin MO 65247-9778. (314)698-3900. Vice President Production: Matthew Eastman. Record producer and record company (Angel One). Estab. 1980. Deals with artists and songwriters. Produces 5 LPs, 5 EPs and 5 CDs/year. Fee derived from sales royalty when song or artist is recorded.
How to Contact: Submit demo tape by mail—unsolicited submissions are OK. Prefers cassette (or VHS videocassette if available) with 3 songs. "Send only original material, not previously recorded, and include a bio sheet on artist." SASE. Reports in 1 month.
Music: Mostly **pop, rock** and **rockabilly**; also **jazz** and **R&B**. Produced *Inner Limits*, written and recorded by Nick Martin; *Faeries* (by Stephanie Joyce), recorded by Jerri Lee; and *Uttland*, written and recorded by Wilhelm Herman, all on Angel One Records. Other artists include Julian James, Kello So, Cat Arkin.
Tips: "Send us your best work. It doesn't need to be overworked. Just keep it simple, because expense to produce something doesn't make it better. We are looking for female artists to work with. Also, if you do not wish to promote what you have recorded via film, video or television and public appearances, there is little need to send material to us."

*ANONYMOUS PRODUCTIONS, P.O. Box 867121, Plano TX 75086. (214)517-7664. Co-owner: Keith Hays. Production company. Estab. 1992. Fee derived from studio costs and production fee. "We are a production company, set up to record artists and charge them for the service—not a publisher."
How to Contact: Submit demo tape by mail. Unsolicited submissions are OK. Prefers cassette with 3 songs and lyric sheet. SASE. Reports in 2 months.
Music: Mostly **A/C, rock** and **country**; also **instrumental** and **folk.** Produced *Howard & White* (by Ken White/Mike Howard), recorded by The Howard & White Band (country); *Wall of Skiffle* (by various), recorded by The Sutcliffes on Skiffle Beat Records(folk/rock); and *Oval Window* (by various), recorded by Akoustik Nerve on Blah, Blah, Blah Records (eclectic A/C).

Tips: "We're looking for artists that are ready to present their work to major labels. We only work with performers of the highest caliber."

APON RECORD COMPANY, INC., P.O. Box 3082, Steinway Station, Long Island City NY 11103. (718)721-5599. Manager: Andrew M. Poncic, Jr. Record producer and music publisher (Apon Publishing). Estab. 1957. Deals with artists and songwriters. Produces 100 singles, 50 LPs and 50 CDs/year. Fee derived from sales royalty and outright fee from recording artist.
How to Contact: Write or call first and obtain permission to submit. Prefers cassette with 2-6 songs and lyric sheet. Does not return unsolicited material. Reports in 1-2 months.
Music: **Classical, folk, Spanish, Slavic, polka** and **Hungarian gypsy (international folk music).** Produced *Czech Polkas* (by Slavko Kunst), recorded by Prague Singers; "Hungarian Gypsy" (by Deki Lakatos), recorded by Budapest; and "Polka - Dance With Me" (by Slavko Kunst), recorded by Prague, all on Apon Records.

AROUND SOUNDS PUBLISHING (ASCAP), 4572 150th Ave. NE, Redmond WA 98052. (206)881-9322. Fax: (206)881-3645. Contact: Lary 'Larz' Nefzger. Estab. 1981. Deals with artists and songwriters. Produces 8 LPs and 8 CDs/year. Fee depends on negotiated agreement.
How to Contact: Write or call first and obtain permission to submit.

aUDIOFILE TAPES, 209-25 18th Ave., Bayside NY 11360. Sheriff, aT County: Carl Howard. Cassette-only label of alternative music. Estab. 1984. Deals with artists and songwriters. Produces about 25 cassettes/year. "Money is solely from sales. Some artists ask $1 per tape sold."
How to Contact: Write first to obtain permission to submit. Prefers cassette. "Relevant artist information is nice. Master copies accepted on metal cassette." SASE. Reports in 3-5 weeks.
Music: Mostly **psych/electronic rock, non-rock electronic music** and **progressive rock;** also **free jazz** and **world music.** Produced *The Three Logos,* written and recorded by William Hooker; *Silent Decay,* written and recorded by Doug Michael and The Outer Darkness; and *Mugged by Life,* written and recorded by The Land of Guilt & Blarney, all on audiofile Tapes. Other artists include Through Black Holes Band, Sphinx, The Conspiracy, Liquid Sound System, Nomuzic, Alien Planetscapes and Mental Anguish.
Tips: "Please, no industrial music, no deliberately shocking images of racism and sexual brutality. And no New Age sleeping pills. Unfortunately, we are not in a position to help the careers of aspirant pop idols. Only true devotees *really* need apply. I mean it—money does not exist here."

AURORA PRODUCTIONS, 7415 Herrington N.E., Belmont MI 49306. Producer: Jack Conners. Record producer, engineer/technician, and record company (Big Rock Records and Ocean Records). Estab. 1984. Deals with artists and songwriters. Produces 2 singles, 2 LPs and 1 CD/year. Fee derived from outright fee from recording artist.
How to Contact: Write first and obtain permission to submit. Prefers cassette with 1 song. Does not return unsolicited material. Reports in 6 weeks.
Music: Mostly **classical, folk** and **jazz;** also **pop/rock** and **New Age.** Produced "Peace On Earth" (by John & Danny Murphy), recorded by The Murphy Brothers on Ocean Records; "Acousma," written and recorded by S.R. Turner on North Cedar Records; and *The Burdons,* written and recorded by The Burdons on Big Rock Records.

*AUSTIN RECORDING STUDIO, 4606 Clawson, Austin TX 78745. (512)444-5489. President: Wink Tyler. Record producer, music publisher. Estab. 1971. Deals with artists and songwriters. Produces 1 12″ single, 2 LPs and 2 CDs/year. Fee derived from outright fee from recording artist or record company, recording and producer fees and engineering.
How to Contact: Call first and obtain permission to submit or to arrange personal interview. Prefers cassette with 4 songs and lyric sheet. SASE. Reports in 3 weeks.
Music: Mostly **country.** Produced *Rusty Dougherty,* recorded by Rusty; and *Candee Land,* recorded by Candee, both on BSW Records (country).

BAL RECORDS, Box 369, LaCanada CA 91012-0369. (818)548-1116. President: Adrian Bal. Record producer and music publisher (Bal & Bal Music). Estab. 1965. Deals with artists and songwriters. Produces 3-6 singles/year. Fee derived from sales royalty when song or artist is recorded.
How to Contact: Submit demo tape by mail—unsolicited submissions are OK. Prefers cassette with 3 songs and lyric sheet. SASE. Reports in 6 weeks.
Music: Mostly **MOR, country, jazz, R&B, rock** and **top 40/pop;** also **blues, church/religious, easy listening** and **soul.** Produced "Fragile" (by James Jackson), recorded by Kathy Simmons (rock); "Dance To The Beat of My Heart" (by Dan Gertz), recorded by Ace Baker (rock); and "You're A Part of Me," written and recorded by Paul Richards (A/C), all on BAL Records.
Tips: "Write and compose what you believe to be commercial."

BARTOW MUSIC, 324 N. Bartow St., Cartersville GA 30120. (404)386-7243. A&R: "Decky D" Maxwell. Record producer. Estab. 1988. Deals with artists and songwriters. Produces 3 singles, 1 12″ single and 1 LP/year. Fee derived from sales royalty when song or artist is recorded.
How to Contact: Submit demo tape by mail. Unsolicited submissions are OK. Prefers cassette with 3 songs and lyric sheet. Does not return material. Reports in 1 month.
Music: Mostly **R&B, dance, rap, house** and **pop**. Produced "I'll Always Be Here For You" (by Scott Milner/Gerald Hall), recorded by Da'Break (R&B); "Rub That Thang," written and recorded by D.G.I. Posse (rap); and "Farewell My Love," written and recorded by Alice Johnson (R&B), all on Westview Records.

*BASEMENT BOYS, INC., 510 Jasper St., Baltimore MD 21201. (410)383-8437. Fax: (410)383-9103. Vice President: Teddy Douglas. Record producer and music publisher (Basement Boys Music). Estab. 1986. Deals with artists and songwriters. Produces 20 singles, 10 12″ singles, 3 LPs, 2 EPs and 3 CDs/year. Fee derived from sales royalty when song or artist is recorded.
How to Contact: Submit demo tape by mail. Unsolicited submissions are OK. Prefers cassette (or VHS videocassette if available) with 4 songs and lyric sheet (if possible). SASE.
Music: Mostly **dance, R&B** and **underground music**. Produced "Gypsy Woman" (by Crystal Waters/ Neal Conway) and *Storyteller* (by various), both recorded by Crystal Waters on Mercury Records (dance/R&B); and *One Woman's Insanity* (by various), recorded by Ultra Nate on Warner Bros. Records (dance/R&B). Other artists include Martha Wash and Mass Order.
Tips: "Be innovative and write meaningful, catchy, strong songs and hooks."

BAY FARM PRODUCTIONS, Box 2821, Duxbury MA 02364. (617)585-9470. Producer: Paul Caruso. Record producer and in-house 8, 16, 24 or 32 track recording availability. Estab. 1985. Deals with artists and songwriters. Produces 6 singles, 4 LPs, 2 EPs and 6 CDs/year. Fee derived from sales royalty when song or artist is recorded or outright fee from recording artist or record company.
How to Contact: Submit demo tape by mail—unsolicited submissions are OK. Prefers cassette or VHS videocassette with 3 songs and lyric sheet. "Please use a high quality cassette." SASE. Reports in 6 weeks.
Music: A/C, **folk, pop, dance** and **R&B**. Produced *Sweet Perfume*, written and recorded by Les Sambon (A/C); *Yates Hope*, written and recorded by John Parsley (A/C); and *Waiting For The Moon*, recorded by Kathy Hayden (A/C).
Tips: "We specialize in producing individual solo artists in the new acoustic, folk, pop, A/C vein. Our clients benefit from intensive pre-production and outstanding studio musicians."

BELL RECORDS INTERNATIONAL, Box 725, Daytona Beach FL 32115-0725. (904)252-4849. President: LeRoy Pritchett. Record producer, music publisher and record company (Bell Records International). Estab. 1985. Deals with artists and songwriters. Produces 12 singles, 12 LPs and 12 CDs/year. Fee derived from sales royalty when song or artist is recorded.
How to Contact: Write first and obtain permission to submit. Prefers cassette.
Music: Mostly **R&B, gospel** and **rock**; also **country** and **pop**. Produced *Hot In The Gulf* (by Billy Brown) and *Hold To God's Hand* (by James Martin), both recorded by Charles Vickers on Bell Records. Other artists include Bobby Blue Blane and Little Anthony.

HAL BERNARD ENTERPRISES, INC., P.O. Box 8385, Cincinnati OH 45208. (513)871-1500. Fax: (513)871-1510. President: Stan Hertzman. Record producer and music publisher (Sunnyslope Music Inc. and Bumpershoot Music Inc.). Deals with artists and songwriters. Produces 5 singles and 3-4 LPs/year. Fee derived from sales royalty.
How to Contact: Prefers cassette with 1-3 songs and lyric sheet. SASE. Reports in 1 month.
Music: Produced *Inner Revolution*, by Adrian Belew on Atlantic Records; *On The Grid*, recorded by psychodots; and *Young and Rejected*, recorded by Prizoner, both on Strugglebaby Records.

RICHARD BERNSTEIN, 2170 S. Parker Rd., Denver CO 80231. (303)755-2613. Contact: Richard Bernstein. Record producer, music publisher (M. Bernstein Music Publishing Co.) and record label. Deals with artists and songwriters. Produces 6 singles, 2 12″ singles, 6 LPs and 6 CDs/year. Fee derived from sales royalty or outright fee from songwriter/artist and/or record company.
How to Contact: Prefers cassette and lyric or lead sheet. Does not return unsolicited material. Reports in 6-8 weeks.
Music: **Rock, jazz** and **country**.
Tips: "No telephone calls *please*."

BIG BEAR, Box 944, Birmingham, B16 8UT, **United Kingdom**. Phone: 44-21-454-7020. Managing Director: Jim Simpson. Record producer, music publisher (Bearsongs) and record company (Big Bear Records). Works with lyricists and composers; teams collaborators. Produces 10 LPs/year. Fee derived from sales royalty.

How to Contact: Write first about your interest, then submit demo tape and lyric sheet. Does not return material. Reports in 2 weeks.
Music: Blues and jazz.

BIG PICTURE RECORD CO., #7A, 101 E. Ninth Ave., Anchorage AK 99501. (907)279-6900. Producer/ Owner: Patric D'Eimon. Record producer and record company (Big Picture Records). Estab. 1983. Deals with artists and songwriters. Produces 5 LPs/year. Fee derived from outright fee from recording artist or record company.
How to Contact: Submit demo tape by mail. Unsolicited submissions are OK. Prefers cassette or VHS videocassette with 4 songs and lyric sheet. SASE. Reports in 1 month.
Music: Mostly **country**, **pop/rock** and **R&B**; also **folk**, **New Age** and "in between styles." Produced *Sky is Blu* (by Hoppi Hopkins), recorded by Sky is Blu; *A Klezmer in Alaska* (by Marcus Brittco), recorded by Alaska Klezmer Band; and *PBL*, written and recorded by PBL.
Tips: "Educate yourselves in the recording/production process."

BIG PRODUCTIONS AND PUBLISHING CO. INC., Suite 308, 37 E. 28th St., New York NY 10016. (212)447-6000. Fax: (212)447-6003. President: "Big" Paul Punzone. Record producer, music publisher (Humongous Music Publishing/ASCAP). Estab. 1989. Deals with artists and songwriters. Produces 12 12″ singles/year. Fee derived from sales royalty when song or artist is recorded, and outright fee from recording artist or record company. Charges upfront "only when hired for independent projects."
How to Contact: Submit demo tape by mail. Unsolicited submissions are OK. Prefers cassette with 3 songs and lyric sheet. "Artists will be signed as a production deal to shop to other labels." SASE. Reports in 2 months.
Music: Mostly **house**, **R&B dance crossover** and **pop/dance**. Produced "Butt Naked," "I Love Music" and *Atrophy* (by P. Punzone/B. Fisher/G. Sicard/P. Falcone), all recorded by Charm on Atlantic Records (hip house).
Tips: "Be competitive. Make sure your songs can compete with what is on the radio. Listen!"

BLAZE PRODUCTIONS, 103 Pleasant Ave., Upper Saddle River NJ 07458. (201)825-1060. Record producer, music publisher (Botown Music) and management firm. Estab. 1978. Deals with artists and songwriters. Fee derived from sales royalty or outright fee from recording artist or record company.
How to Contact: Submit demo tape by mail—unsolicited submissions are OK. Prefers cassette (or VHS videocassette) with 1 or more songs and lyric sheet. Does not return unsolicited material. Reports in 3 weeks.
Music: **Pop**, **rock** and **dance**. Produced *Anything Can Happen*, by Voices; "Point of Attack" (by Peace/ Stevens), recorded by AK Peace; and "Up On Blocks" (by Gearhead), all on Botown Records.

*BONGO BOY, 15 Idora, San Francisco CA 94127. (415)681-5822. Producers: Jimmy Foot or Susie Foot. Record producer, record company, music publisher (Afro/Ska Publishing/BMI). Estab. 1985. Deals with artists and songwriters. Produces 2 LPs, 2 CDs/year. Fee derived from sales royalty when song or artist is recorded or outright fee from recording artist or record company.
How to Contact: Submit demo tape by mail. Unsolicited submissions are OK. Prefers cassette with 4 songs and lyric sheet. "All material must be copywritten and include year." SASE. Reports in 2 months.
Music: Mostly **world beat**, **African** and **Ska**; also **rock**, **reggae** and **alternative**. Produced *Truth and Rights* (by Rod Deal); *Afroskalypso* (by Joni Haastrop); and *MR Rhythm & Blues* (by Linda Imperial), all recorded by J & S Foot on Bongo Boy Records. Other artists include Jimmy Foot.
Tips: "Complex production not important—submit simple demos of strong material."

PETER L. BONTA, 2200 Airport Ave., Fredericksburg VA 22401. (703)373-6511. Studio Manager: Buffalo Bob. Record producer. Estab. 1980. Deals with artists and songwriters. Produces 8-12 singles, 5-8 LPs and 4-6 CDs/year. Fee derived from sales royalty or outright fee from recording artist or record company.
How to Contact: Write or call first and obtain permission to submit. Prefers cassette with 3-4 songs and lyric sheet. SASE. Reports in 6 weeks.
Music: Mostly **roots rock**, **country rock** and **blues**; also **country** and **bluegrass**. Produced *Dealin' The Blues* (by Ross/Browne), recorded by Queen Bee and the Blue Hornet Band on Sharktooth Records (blues); *American Crime* (by Buffalo Bob), recorded by Buffalo Bob & The Heard on Greek Bros Records; and *Get Used to It* (by M. Davis), recorded by Kid Davis Band on Like Cowboys Do Music (roots rock). Other artists include Billy Hancock, Lovesake, Tattoo Tribe, Little Ronnie & The Bluebeats, On Edge, Donnie Preston, Angry Young Pachyderms, Alan Maitland, Adgie Lou Davidson, Sallie Foster.

ROBERT BOWDEN, Box 111, Sea Bright NJ 07760. President: Robert Bowden. Record producer, music publisher (Roots Music/BMI) and record company (Nucleus Records). Estab. 1979. Deals with artists and songwriters. Produces 3 singles and 1 LP/year. Fees derived from sales royalty when song or artist is recorded.

How to Contact: Submit demo tape by mail. Unsolicited submissions are OK. Prefers cassette (or VHS videocassette if available) with 3 songs and lyric sheet. SASE. Reports in 1 month.

Music: Mostly **country**; also **pop**. Produced "Henrey C," "4 O'Clock Rock" and "Will You Miss Me Tonight" (by Bowden), all recorded by Marco Sisison on Nucleus Records.

BREADLINE PRODUCTIONS, Studio #3, 133 W. 14th St., New York NY 10011. (212)741-0165. Producer/Engineer: Gene Lavenue. Record producer. Estab. 1986. Deals with artists, labels and management. Produces 4 singles, 3 LPs and 3 CDs/year. Fee derived from sales royalty when song or artist is recorded.

How to Contact: Submit demo tape by mail. Unsolicited submissions are OK. Prefers cassette with 3 songs. "Send the best quality tape. Portastudio recordings acceptable if they are of good quality." SASE. Reports in 3 weeks.

Music: Mostly **alternative** and **rock**. Produced "Are You Sleeping" (by Karen Ires); "The Perfect Crime" (by Please); and "Postcards and Aeroplanes" (by Fido).

Tips: "Be creative."

BRIEFCASE OF TALENT PRODUCTIONS, Suite 52, 1124 Rutland, Austin TX 78758. (512)832-1254. Owner: Kevin Howell. Record producer and live/recording engineer. Deals with artists. Produces 1 LP, 2 EPs and 1 CD/year. Fee derived from outright fee from recording artist.

How to Contact: Submit demo tape by mail. Unsolicited submissions OK. Prefers cassette (or VHS videocassette if available) with 4 songs and lyric sheet. Does not return unsolicited material. Reports in 2 months.

Music: Mostly **alternative progressive rock (classic)** and **heavy metal**; also **R&B**. Produced *Long Way Home* (by Chris Smith), recorded by Black Smith (rock); *Rainbow* (by Chaz), recorded by US (country); and *This Time* (by Mike Forte), recorded by Outlaw Circus (rock), all on Briefcase Records.

Tips: "Eighty percent of the people listening to your submission are engineers of some sort, so a poor quality demo will not get past the first 30 seconds. Make it sound professional and as good as budget allows!"

BULLET PROOF MANAGEMENT, (formerly G Fine), Box 180, Cooper Station, New York NY 10276. (212)995-1608. Record producer, music publisher and record company. Estab. 1986. Fee derived from sales royalty.

How to Contact: Submit demo tape by mail. Unsolicited submissions are OK. Prefers high bias cassette or DAT with 3 or more songs. "Send photo, if possible." SASE. Reports in 2-3 months.

Music: "Undercore" **alternative rock, dance, rap** and **R&B**. Artists include Ghetto Child featuring Main One (Select/Atlantic).

C.S.B. MIX INC., #11, 50 Donna Court, Staten Island NY 10314. Contact: Carlton Batts. Record producer (The Bat Cave Recording Studio). Estab. 1989. Deals with artists only. Produces 15 singles, 4 12″ singles, 2 LPs and 1 EP/year. Fee derived from sales royalty when song or artist is recorded and outright fee from record company.

How to Contact: Submit demo tape by mail—unsolicited submissions are OK. Prefers DAT with 3 songs. "A picture and a bio are a must!" Does not return unsolicited material. Reports in 2 weeks if interested. "No home recorded demo tapes please. Your DAT should be of professional studio quality."

Music: Mostly **R&B, dance** and **hip-hop**; also **rap, jazz** and **reggae**. Produced "Let It Flow" (by C. Batts), recorded by Troy Taylor on Motown Records (R&B/single); "Primetime" (by C. Batts), recorded by Jocelyn Brown on RCA Records (dance single); and "Thrills & Chills" (by C. Batts), recorded by Whitney Houston on Arista Records (R&B single). Other artists include Leslie Fine, The Boys Club, One on One and Alan Rules.

Tips: "Be ready to work your butt off."

CAPITOL AD, MANAGEMENT & TALENT, Suite 200, 1300 Division St., Nashville TN 37203. (615)242-4722, (615)244-2440, (800)767-4984. Fax: (615)242-1177. Senior Producer: Robert Metzgar. Record producer, record company (Aim High Records, Hot News Records, Platinum Plus Records, SHR Records) and music publisher (Aim High Music Co./ASCAP, Bobby & Billy Music Co./BMI). Estab. 1971. Deals with artists and songwriters. Produces 35 singles, 12-15 12″ singles, 20 LPs, 15 EPs and 35 CDs/year. Fee derived from sales royalty when song or artist is recorded, outright fee from recording artist or record company, or from financial backer or investment group.

How to Contact: Submit demo tape by mail. Unsolicited submissions are OK. Prefers cassette (or videocassette) with 3-5 songs and lyric sheet. "We are interested in hearing only from *serious* artist/songwriters." Does not return unsolicited material. Reports in 3 weeks to 2 months.

Music: Mostly **country music, gospel music, pop** and **R&B**; also **jazz, contemporary Christian, rock** and **pop-rock**. Produced *There's Another Man* (by Johnny Cash), recorded on Time/Warner Brothers; *Break Out The Good Stuff* (by Alan Jackson), recorded on Amherst Records; and *Half A Man* (by Willie Nelson), recorded on Time/Warner Brothers. Other artists include Carl Butler (CBS/Sony), Tommy Cash (Columbia), Mickey Jones (Capitol), Tommy Overstreet (MCA Records), Warner Mack (MCA Records), Bobby Enriquez (Sony/New York) and others.
Tips: "Getting Capitol Management on your team is the best thing you could ever do!"

*CARE FREE RECORDS GROUP, P.O. Box 2463, Carefree AZ 85377. (602)230-4177. Vice President: Doya Fairbanks. Record producer, record company, music publisher (Ho-Hum Music), distributor and promotions company. Estab. 1990. Deals with artists and songwriters. Produces 6 singles, 4 12" singles, 12 LPs, 5 EPs and 12 CDs/year. Fee derived from sales royalty when song or artist is recorded.
How to Contact: Submit demo tape by mail. Unsolicited submissions are OK. Prefers cassette (or VHS videocassette) with 4-6 songs. Reports in 1 month.
Music: Mostly **country, jazz** and **classical**; also **rock/pop, metal** and **New Age**. Produced *Pablo*, written and recorded by Pablo on Blue Mesa Records (pop); *The Totem Pole*, written and recorded by Totem Pole (pop); and *Harold's Coral*, written and recorded by Harold's Coral (country), both on Care Free Records. Other artists include Paul Conceio, Arsinal and Gypsy Wind.

*CARLOCK PRODUCTIONS, 1013 Lions Park Dr., St. Joseph MI 49085. (616)982-1000. Fax: (616)982-1001. Producer: Dave Carlock. Record producer. Estab. 1990. Deals with artists and songwriters. Produces 6 LPs and 5 EPs/year. Fee derived from sales royalty when song or artist is recorded or outright fee from recording artist or record company.
How to Contact: Write first and obtain permission to submit. Prefers cassette (or VHS videocassette if available) with 3-5 songs and lyric sheet. Does not return material. Reports in 3-5 weeks.
Music: Mostly **pop/rock, A/C** and **rock (alternative)**; also **contemporary Christian** and **gospel**. Produced *Whatever It Takes*, recorded by Gunshy.
Tips: "Write with soul, write with experience."

CARLYLE PRODUCTIONS, 1217 16th Ave. South, Nashville TN 37212. (615)327-8129. President: Laura Fraser. Record producer, record company (Carlyle Records) and production company. Estab. 1986. Deals with artists and songwriters. Produces 6 singles and 6 LPs/CDs per year.
How to Contact: Submit demo tape by mail—unsolicited submissions are OK. Prefers cassette with 3 songs and lyric sheet. Does not return unsolicited material. Reports in 1 month.
Music: Mostly **rock, pop** and **country**. Produced "Orange Room" (by Michael Ake), recorded by The Grinning Plowman (pop/rock); *Sun* (by John Elliott), recorded by Dessau (dance); and *All Because of You*, written and recorded by Dorcha (rock), all on Carlyle Records.

CAROLINA PRIDE PRODUCTIONS, Dept. SM, Box 6, Rougemont NC 27572. (919)477-4077. Manager: Freddie Roberts. Record producer, music publisher (Freddie Roberts Music/BMI), record company, management firm and booking agency. Estab. 1967. Deals with artists, songwriters and session musicians. Produces 12 singles, 7 LPs, 2 EPs and 3 CDs/year. Fee derived from sales royalty.
How to Contact: Call or write first. Prefers 7½ ips reel-to-reel or cassette with 1-5 songs and lyric sheet. SASE. Reports in 5 weeks.
Music: Mostly **country, MOR** and **top 40/pop**; also **bluegrass, church/religious, gospel** and **country rock**. Produced "Restless Feeling," written and recorded by Rodney Hutchins (country/rock) on Catalina Records; "Empty" (by David Laws), recorded by Jerry Harrison (country) on Celebrity Circle Records; and "Redeemed" (by Jane Durham), recorded by The Roberts Family (Southern gospel) on Bull City Records. Other artists include Sleepy Creek, Lady Luck, Billy McKellar and C.J. Jackson.

STEVE CARR, % Hit & Run Studios, 18704 Muncaster Rd., Rockville MD 20855. (301)948-6715. Owner/Producer: Steve Carr. Record producer (Hit & Run Studios). Estab. 1979. Deals with artists and songwriters. Produces 10 singles, 2 12" singles, 8 LPs, 4 EPs and 10 CDs/year. Fee derived from outright fee from recording artist.
How to Contact: Write or call first and obtain permission to submit. Prefers cassette with 3 songs. "Do NOT send unsolicited material! Write name and phone number on cassette shell. Will call back if I can do anything with your material."
Music: Mostly **pop, rock** and **R&B**; also **country**. Produced/recorded *Billy Kemp* (by Billy Kemp) on Essential Records; *Classic Rock*, written and recorded by various artists (oldies digital remaster) on Warner Bros. Records; and "Bomb Squad" (by Lorenzo), on Their Own Records (single); all recorded by Hit & Run. Other artists include Beyond Words, Steve Nally/Deep End, Oho, Voodoo, Love Gods, Necrosis, Debra Brown and Universe. Produces and digitally remasters Time-Life Music's Rock n' Roll, Country Classics and R&B Series.

CEDAR CREEK PRODUCTIONS, Suite 503, 44 Music Square E., Nashville TN 37203. (615)252-6916. Fax: (615)329-1071. President: Larry Duncan. Record producer, record company (Cedar Creek Records™), music publisher (Cedar Creek Music/BMI) and artist management. Estab. 1981. Deals with artists and songwriters. Produces 20 singles, 5 LPs and 5 CDs/year. Fee derived from outright fee from recording artist.
How to Contact: Submit demo tape by mail. Unsolicited submissions are OK. Prefers cassette (or VHS videocassette) with 4-6 songs and lyric sheet (typed). "Put return address and name on envelope. Put telephone number in packet." Does not return unsolicited material. Reports in 1 month.
Music: Mostly **country, country/pop** and **country/R&B**, also **pop, R&B, gospel/Christian contemporary** and **light rock**. Produced "14 Karat Gold" (by Deke Little/Joel Little/John Moran), recorded by Joel Little on Interstate Records (country); *Bright Lights and Honky Tonk Nights* (by Tony Rast/Debra McClure/Danny Neal) and *I'm In Love* (by Sarita Wortham/Danny Neal/Debra McClure), recorded by Kym Wortham on ADD Records (country).
Tips: "Submit your best songs on a good fully produced demo or master."

JAN CELT, 4026 NE 12th Ave., Portland OR 97212. (503)287-8045. Owner: Jan Celt. Record producer, music publisher (Wiosna Nasza Music/BMI) and record company (Flying Heart Records). Estab. 1982. Deals with artists and songwriters. Produces 2 LPs, 1 EP and 2 CDs/year.
How to Contact: Submit demo tape by mail—unsolicited submissions are OK. Prefers cassette with 1-10 songs and lyric sheet. SASE. Reports in 4 months. "If calling, please check time zone."
Music: Mostly **R&B, rock** and **blues**; also **jazz**. Produced "Voodoo Garden," written and recorded by Tom McFarland (blues); "Bong Hit" (by Chris Newman), recorded by Snow Bud & the Flower People (rock); and "She Moved Away" (by Chris Newman), recorded by Napalm Beach, all on Flying Heart Records. Other artists include The Esquires and Janice Scroggins.
Tips: "Be sure your lyrics are heartfelt; they are what makes a song your own. Abandon rigid stylistic concepts and go for total honesty of expression."

CHUCK CHAPMAN, Dept. SM, 228 W. Fifth St., Kansas City MO 64105. (816)842-6854. Office Manager: Gary Sutton. Record producer and music publisher (Fifth Street Records/BMI). Estab. 1973. Deals with artists and songwriters. Fee derived from sales royalty when song or artist is recorded or outright fee from recording artist or record company. "Charges upfront for recording only."
How to Contact: Write or call first and obtain permission to submit. Prefers cassette (or ½" or ¾" videocassette) with 3 songs and lyric sheet. SASE. Does not return material. Reports in 1 month.
Music: Mostly **country, gospel** and **rock**; also **rap, jazz** and **spoken word**. Produced "Rumor Has It" (by Sheli), recorded by Freddie Hart on Fifth Street Records (country); and "Cold As Ashes" (by Lee Bruce), recorded by Montgomery Lee on Opal Records (country). Other artists include Conrad Morris and Eisel & The Haymakers.

CHROME DREAMS PRODUCTIONS, 5852 Sentinel St., San Jose CA 95120. (408)268-6066. Owner: Leonard Giacinto. Record producer. Estab. 1982. Deals with artists and songwriters. Produces 15 singles and 8 12" singles/year. Fee derived from outright fee from recording artist or record company.
How to Contact: Submit demo tape by mail. Unsolicited submissions are OK. Prefers cassette (or ½" VHS videocassette if available). Does not return unsolicited material. Reports in 1 month.
Music: Mostly **rock, New Age, avant-garde** and **college radio**. Produced "Gabriella It's True," written and recorded by Paula Azure (Latin); "Determined Peg Head," written and recorded by B. Leni (rock); and "House On Stilts," written and recorded by Gary Remick (rock). Other artists include Bay Area Group.

COACHOUSE MUSIC, P.O. Box 1308, Barrington IL 60011. (312)822-0305. Fax: (312)464-0762. President: Michael Freeman. Record producer. Estab. 1984. Deals with artists and songwriters. Produces 4 LPs and 4 CDs/year. Fees vary with project.
How to Contact: Write first and obtain permission to submit. Prefers cassette (or VHS videocassette if available) with 3-5 songs and lyric sheet. Does not return material. Reports in 1 month.
Music: Mostly **pop, rock** and **blues**; also **alternative rock** and **progressive country**. Produced *Eat At Godot's*, written and recorded by Ralph Covert on Waterdog Records (pop/folk); *Dance All Night*, written and recorded by Chubby Carrier (zydeco); and *Sideways In Paradise* (by various), recorded by Jim Thackeray and John Mooney (folk/blues), both on Blind Pig Records. Other artists include Maybe/ Definitely, Bad Examples, Arranmore, Eleventh Dream Day, Eddie Clearwater, Magic Slum, Amarillo Kings and Mick Freon.
Tips: "Be honest, be committed, strive for excellence."

COLLECTOR RECORDS, Box 2296, Rotterdam Holland 3000 CG **The Netherlands**. Phone: 1862-4266. Fax: 1862-4366. Research: Cees Klop. Record producer and music publisher (All Rock Music). Deals with artists and songwriters. Produces 8-10 singles and 30 LPs/year. Fee derived from sales royalty.

How to Contact: Submit demo tape—unsolicited submissions OK. Prefers cassette. SAE and IRC. Reports in 1 month.
Music: Mostly **50s rock, rockabilly** and **country rock**; also **piano boogie woogie**. Produced *Eager Boy* (by T. Johnson), recorded by Lonesome Orifier; *Tehm Saturday*, written and recorded by Malcolm Yelvington, both on Collector Records; and *All Night Rock*, written and recorded by Bobby Hicks on White Label Records (all 50s rock). Other artists include Teddy Redell, Gene Summers, Benny Joy and the Hank Pepping Band.

COPPELIA, 21 rue de Pondichery, Paris 75015 **France**. Phone: (1)45673066. Fax: (1)43063026. Manager: Jean-Philippe Olivi. Record producer, music publisher (Coppelia/SACEM), record company (Olivi Records) and music print publisher. Deals with artists and songwriters. Produces 4 CDs/year. Fee derived from sales royalty or outright fee from recording artist or record company.
How to Contact: Prefers cassette. SAE and IRC. Reports in 1 month.
Music: Mostly **pop, rock** and **New Age**; also **background music** and **film/series music**. Produced "Voce Di Corsica" and "Corsica," recorded by Petru Guelfucci, both on Olivi Records. Other artists include Pino Lattuca, Christian Chevallier and Robert Quibel.

JOHNNY COPPIN/RED SKY RECORDS, Box 7, Stonehouse, Glos. GL10 3PQ **UK**. Phone: 0453-826200. Record producer, music publisher (PRS) and record company (Red Sky Records). Estab. 1985. Deals with artists and songwriters. Produces 2 singles and 3 albums (CD & tape) per year. Fee derived from sales royalty when song or artist is recorded.
How to Contact: Submit demo tape by mail—unsolicited submissions are OK. Prefers cassette with 3 songs and lyric sheet. SASE. Reports in 6 months.
Music: Mostly **rock, modern folk** and **roots music**. Produced "West Country Christmas" and "Force of the River," written and recorded by Johnny Coppin; and "Dead Lively" by Paul Burgess, all on Red Sky Records. Other artists include Laurie Lee, David Goodland and Phil Beer.

CORE PRODUCTIONS, Suite 254, 14417 Chase St., Van Nuys CA 91402. (818)909-0846. Fax: (818)780-4592. President: C. Marlo. Record producer, record company (Blue Rain Records) and music publisher (Cocoloco Toons/ASCAP). Estab. 1986. Deals with artists and songwriters. Produces 2 LPs and 2 CDs/year. Fee derived from sales royalty when song or artist is recorded, outright fee from recording artist or record company or publishing royalty.
How to Contact: Write first to obtain permission to submit. Prefers cassette with 3-4 songs and lyric sheet. "If you are an artist please send a promo pack (pictures/tape/bio)." Does not return unsolicited material. Reports in 2 months.
Music: Mostly **pop, R&B** and **dance**; also **rock** and **jazz**. Produced *Speaking In Melodies*, written and recorded by Michael Ruff on Sheffield Labs Records; *The Last Protest Singer*, written and recorded by Harry Chapin on Dunhill Records; and *Antigua Blue* (by Russ Freeman), recorded by Kilavea on Brainchild Records. Other artists include Paul Gordon and Ace Baker.
Tips: "Don't try to follow trends—be who you are."

DANO CORWIN, 5839 Silvercreek Rd., Azle TX 76020. (817)560-3546. Record producer, music video and sound production company. Estab. 1986. Works with artists and songwriters. Produces 6 singles, 3 12″ singles, 5 EPs and 2 CDs/year. Fee usually derived from sales royalty, but negotiated on case-by-case basis.
How to Contact: Submit demo tape by mail. Unsolicited submissions are OK. Prefers cassette (or VHS videocassette if available) with 3 songs and lyric sheet. "Keep songs under 5 minutes. Only copyrighted material will be reviewed. Please do not send material without copyright notices." SASE, "but prefers to keep material on file." Reports in 6-8 weeks.
Music: Mostly **rock**; also **pop, New Age** and **dance**. Produced "Gone Crazy" (by M. Howard), recorded by W-4's on Big D Records (rock); "Rocket" (by Craig Cole/Kenny McClurg), recorded by Double Dog on MLM Records (rock); and *Finished* (by Billy Biesel), recorded by Complete on WW Records (rock). Other artists include Squalor, Tomidy and Drune.
Tips: "Keep songs simple and melodic. Write as many songs as possible. Out of a large quantity, a few quality songs may emerge."

COUNTRY STAR PRODUCTIONS, Box 569, Franklin PA 16323. (814)432-4633. President: Norman Kelly. Record producer, music publisher (Country Star Music/ASCAP, Kelly Music/BMI and Process Music/BMI) and record company (Country Star, Process, Mersey and CSI Records). Estab. 1970.

Refer to the Category Index (at the end of this section) to find exactly which companies are interested in the type of music you write.

Deals with artists and songwriters. Produces 5-8 singles and 5-8 LPs/year. Works with 3-4 new songwriters/year. Works with composers and lyricists; teams collaborators. Fee derived from outright fee from recording artist or record company.
How to Contact: Submit demo tape—unsolicited submissions OK. Prefers cassette with 2-4 songs and typed lyric or lead sheet. SASE. Reports in 2 weeks.
Music: Mostly **country** (80%); also **rock** (5%), **MOR** (5%), **gospel** (5%) and **R&B** (5%). Produced "Western Dawn" (by J.E. Myers), recorded by Jeffrey Alan Connors and "Tear Drops Still Fall" (by N. Kelly/J. Barbaria), recorded by Larry Peifer, both on Country Star Records; and "God Specializes," written and recorded by Sheryl Friend on Process Records. Other artists include Bob Stamper, Randy Miles, Jonie Loo, Debbie Sue and Vince Smith.
Tips: "Submit only your best efforts."

*COWBOY JUNCTION FLEA MARKET AND PUBLISHING CO., Hwy. 44 and Jct. 490, Lecanto FL 32661. (904)746-4754. Contact: Elizabeth Thompson. Record producer and music publisher (Cowboy Junction/BMI). Deals with artists and songwriters. Produces 3-4 singles and 2 12″ singles/year. Works with 6 new songwriters/year. Works with lyricists and composers; teams collaborators.
How to Contact: Submit demo tape by mail. Unsolicited submissions are OK. Prefers 7½ ips reel-to-reel or cassette with 3 songs and lyric sheet. SASE. Reports ASAP.
Music: **C&W**, **country gospel** and **bluegrass**. Produced "I Love Miss America," "One More Time" and "Alabama" (by Boris Max Pastuch), recorded by Buddy Max on Cowboy Junction Records (C&W). Other artists include Leo Vargason, Charlie Floyd, Lloyd Stevens, Troy Holliday and Wally Jones.
Tips: "Come to our Flea Market on Tuesday or Friday and show to the public, and who knows? Also, if possible, come to our Music Show at Cowboy Junction on Saturday at 2 p.m. and ask to be placed on stage to present your material to the public. (We are closed and on tour July and August of each year.)"

CREATIVE MUSIC SERVICES, 838 Fountain St., Woodbridge CT 06525. Owner: Craig Calistro. Record producer (Ace Record Company). Estab. 1989. Deals with artists and songwriters. Produces 50 singles, 20 12″ singles, 15 LPs and 15 CDs/year. Fee derived from sales royalty when song or artist is recorded or outright fee from recording artist or record company.
How to Contact: Submit demo tape by mail—unsolicited submissions are OK. Prefers cassette (or VHS videocassette if available) and 1-3 songs and lyric and lead sheets. "Send photo if available." Does not return material. Reports in 3 weeks.
Music: Mostly **pop/top 40** and **dance**; also **jazz**. Produced "Tell Me" (by Craig Calistro), recorded by J. Lord; *Don't Throw This Love Away*, written and recorded by Brenda Lee; and *Pillow Talk* (by H.L. Reeves), recorded by Tanya, all on Ace Records. Other artists include Mike Grella.

*CROSS CULTURE PRODUCTIONS, INC., P.O. Box 4918, Falls Church VA 22044. Producers: Kaan A. and Yuri Z. Record producer. Estab. 1993. Deals with artists and songwriters. Produces 2 12″ singles, 4 LPs and 4 CDs/year. Fee derived from sales royalty when song or artist is recorded or outright fee from recording artist or record company. "All depends on the situation of the artist."
How to Contact: Submit demo tape by mail. Unsolicited submissions are OK. Prefers cassette with 3 songs. SASE. Reports in 2 weeks.
Music: Mostly **R&B**, **pop**, and **hip hop**; also **dance**. Produced "A Man Is What I Need" (by John Copeland and Yuri Z), recorded by Tammy Michelle on Studio Records (house). Other artists include Embrace.

CRYSTAL CLEAR PRODUCTIONS, Suite #32, 115 E. Water St., Santa Fe NM 87501. (505)983-3245. Fax: (505)982-9168. Publisher/Producer: Susan Pond/David Anthony. Record producer and music publisher (Clear Pond Music/BMI). Estab. 1991. Deals with artists and songwriters. Produces 20 singles and 5-7 CDs/year. Fee derived from sales royalty when song or artist is recorded or outright fee from artist and record company.
How to Contact: Write first and obtain permission to submit. Prefers cassette with 1-3 songs and lyric sheet. Include cover letter stating your intentions. Always include SASE. Reports in 1 month.
Music: Mostly **pop/rock**, **country** (contemporary) and **A/C**. Produced new version of #1 Billboard Hit "Walk Right In," written and recorded by Erik Darling on Folk Era Records; "Didn't Mean to Break Your Heart," written and recorded by Lauren Montgomery on Maxim Records; and "I Only Have Time for the Dance," written and recorded by J.D. Haring on Starquest Records. Other artists include Bennett Strahan, George Page, G.J. Morse, Jack Clift and Kate Hanley.
Tips: "Have backing, do your homework, know the business, read as much as possible regarding music, composition, lyric writing, etc."

*JERRY CUPIT PRODUCTIONS, Box 121904, Nashville TN 37212. (615)731-0100. Producer: Jerry Cupit. Record producer and music publisher. Estab. 1984. Develops artists and songwriters. Fee

derived from sales royalty or outright fee from record company or artist.
How to Contact: Send demo, bio, photo and SASE. Does not return material.
Music: Mostly **country**, **rock** and **gospel**; also **R&B**. Produced "Lookin' In The Same Direction" (by Ken Mellons/Dale Dodson/Jimmy Melton) and "Jukebox Junkie" (by Ken Mellons/Jerry Cupit/Janice Honeycutt), both recorded by Ken Mellons for Epic Records; and "What's My World Coming To" (by Jerry Cupit), recorded by Jack Robertson on Step One Records.

CYBORTRONIK RECORDING GROUP, 8927 Clayco Dr., Dallas TX 75243. (214)343-3266. Owner: David May. Record producer, record company. Estab. 1990. Deals with artists and songwriters. Produces 4 12″ singles, 8 LPs, 4 EPs and 2 CDs/year. Fee derived from sales royalty when song or artist is recorded.
How to Contact: Submit demo tape by mail. Unsolicited submissions are OK. Prefers cassette or DAT (or VHS videocassette) with 4 songs. SASE. Reports in 2 months.
Music: Mostly **dance**, **techno** and **house**; also **hip-hop** and **industrial**. Produced "Thoratic/Glider Mix" (by Digital One), recorded by David May on Excel Records; "Traumatized" (by Liquid 25), recorded by David May; and "Axioms" (by Axiomatic), recorded by E.J., both on Cybortronik Records. Other artists include Proxima, Lift, Waveform, KBD, CWM, Sector 7 and Noise Matrix.
Tips: "Be patient and send decent recordings."

D.S.M. PRODUCERS, INC., (formerly Suzan Bader/D.S.M. Producers), 161 W. 54th St., New York NY 10019. (212)245-0006. Director of A&R: Ms. E.T. Toast. Contact: Associate Producer. Record producer, music publisher (ASCAP/BMI) and music library. Estab. 1979. Deals with artists and songwriters. Produces 20 CDs/year. Fee derived from sales royalty and production fee.
How to Contact: Write first and obtain permission to submit. Prefers cassette (or VHS videocassette) with 2 songs and lyric or lead sheet. SASE. Reports in 2-3 months.
Music: All styles. Produced *Rock America*, *Dance America* and *Weekend Party USA II*, written and recorded by various artists on AACL Records. "We represent over 400 American composers."
Tips: "Have your manager or lawyer contact us to produce you. If you are a new artist, follow the above procedure. It's getting more difficult for an artist who cannot present a master demo to a label. You're going to need financing for your demos/masters, but it's worth having a professional produce your first demos as they do it for a living. They can help you become an established artist/songwriter. Invest in yourself, and when you have the right product, you will be heard and you're on your way to success."

S. KWAKU DADDY, Box 424794, San Francisco CA 94142-4794. (707)769-9479. President: S. Kwaku Daddy. Record producer and record company (African Heritage Records Co.). Deals with artists and songwriters. Produces 6 LPs/year.
How to Contact: Write first and obtain permission to submit. Prefers cassette. SASE. Reports in 2 weeks.
Music: Mostly **African pop**, **R&B** and **gospel**. Produced *Times of Change*, *Life's Rhythms* and *Heritage IV*, all by S. Kwaku Daddy on African Heritage Records.
Tips: "Place emphasis on rhythm."

*DALIVEN MUSIC, P.O. Box 398, Nolensville TN 37135. (615)776-5686. Owner Operator: R. Steve Cochran. Record producer, music publisher. Produces 4 singles, 2 LPs, 2 CDs/year. Fee derived from outright fee from recording artist.
How to Contact: Submit demo tape by mail. Unsolicited submissions are OK. Prefers cassette or videocassette with 3 songs and lyric or lead sheet. "Can also send standard MIDI files of songs." SASE. Reports in 2 months.
Music: Mostly **A/C**, **R&B** and **rock**; also **jazz**, **dance** and **country**. Produced *Chicken Eater Stommp* (by T. Hannum), recorded by The Shelltones on Clam Records (country); *Just Relax* (by Tim Hayden), recorded by Dalia Garcia on Ned Records (jazz); and *Spaceman* (by Greg Wetzel), recorded on Wetzel Records (blues). Other artists include Jimmy Markham.

DANNY DARROW, Suite 6-D, 150 West End Ave., New York NY 10023. (212)873-5968. Manager: Danny Darrow. Record producer, music publisher (BMI, ASCAP), record company (Mighty Records) and Colley Phonographics—Europe. Estab. 1958. Deals with songwriters only. Produces 1-2 singles, 1-2 12″ singles and 1-2 LPs/year. Fee derived from royalty.
How to Contact: Submit demo tape by mail—unsolicited submissions are OK. "No phone calls." Prefers cassette with 3 songs and lyric sheet. SASE. Reports in 1-2 weeks.
Music: Mostly **pop**, **country** and **dance**; also **jazz**. Produced "Wonderland of Dreams" (by Phil Zinn); "Telephones" (by R.L. Lowery/D. Darrow); and "Better Than You Know" (by M. Greer), all recorded by Danny Darrow on Mighty Records.
Tips: "Listen to the hits and write better songs from the heart!"

*DATURA PRODUCTIONS, #22, 4400 Sara St., Burbank CA 91505. (818)558-1329. Owner: William Hanifan. Record producer. Estab. 1990. Deals with artists and songwriters. Fee derived from outright fee from recording artist.
How to Contact: Submit demo tape by mail. Unsolicited submissions are OK. Prefers cassette (or VHS videocassette if available) with lyric and lead sheet. Does not return material. Reports in 3 months.
Music: Mostly **R&B, rock** and **alternative**; also **metal, country** and **pop**.

DAVIS SOTO ORBAN PRODUCTIONS, #E3425, 601 Van Ness, San Francisco CA 94102. (415)775-9785. Fax: (415)775-3082. CEO: Glenn Davis. Record producer. Estab. 1984. Deals with artists and songwriters. Produces 3 LPs and 1 CD/year. Fee derived from outright fee from record company.
How to Contact: Submit demo tape by mail. Unsolicited submissions are OK. Prefers cassette (or VHS videocassette) with 4 songs and lyric sheet. Send full demo kit (bio, tape, tearsheets, pics, etc.) if possible. Does not return unsolicited material. Reports in 2 weeks.
Music: Mostly **world beat, infusion** and **modern**; also **rock, classical/poetry** and **pop**. Produced *Where Heaven Begins* (by Orban/Davis), *Transparent Empire* (by Orban) and *Summertime* (by Gershwin), all recorded by DSO on On The Wing Records.

EDWARD DE MILES, 8th Floor, 4475 Allisonville Rd., Indianapolis IN 46205. (317)546-2912. President: Edward De Miles. Record producer, music publisher (Edward De Miles Music Co./BMI), record company (Sahara Records). Estab. 1981. Deals with artists and songwriters. Produces 15-20 singles, 15-20 12″ singles, 5-10 LPs and 5-10 CDs/year. Fee derived from sales royalty when song or artist is recorded.
How to Contact: Write first and obtain permission to submit. Prefers cassette (or VHS or Beta ½″ videocassette if available) with 1-3 songs and lyric sheet. SASE. Reports in 1 month.
Music: Mostly **R&B/dance, top 40 pop/rock** and **contemporary jazz**; also **country, TV and film themes — songs and jingles**. Produced "Hooked on U," "Dance Wit Me" and "Moments," written and recorded by Steve Lynn (R&B), all on Sahara Records. Other artists include Lost in Wonder, D'von Edwards and Multiple Choice.
Tips: "Copyright all material before submitting. Equipment and showmanship a must."

*DEEP SPACE RECORDS, #307, 1576 Great Highway, San Francisco CA 94122. (415)566-6701. Owner/Producer: Kenn Fink. Record producer. Estab. 1985. Deals with artists and songwriters. Produces 12 singles and 1 LP/year. Fee derived from sales royalty when song or artist is recorded or outright fee from recording artist and record company.
How to Contact: Write or call first and obtain permission to submit. Prefers cassette with 3-5 songs and lyric sheet. SASE. Reports in 2-3 weeks.
Music: Mostly **hard rock, electronic** (not necessarily New Age) and **blends of the two**. Produced *Hitlist*, written and recorded by UKTMS (punk); and *Lifesigns* (by Kenn Fink), recorded by the Outcast on Deep Space Records (electronic/rock).

AL DELORY AND MUSIC MAKERS, #11, 3000 Hillsboro Rd., Nashville TN 37215. (615)292-2140. Fax: (615)292-1634. President: Al DeLory. Record producer and career consultant (DeLory Music/ASCAP). Estab. 1987. Deals with artists and songwriters. Produces 10 singles, 5 12″ singles, 5 LPs, 5 EPs and 5 CDs/year. Fee derived from outright fee from record company, career consultant fees.
How to Contact: Write first and obtain permission to submit or to arrange personal interview. Prefers cassette (or VHS videocassette). Does not return unsolicited material. Reports in 1 month.
Music: Mostly **pop, country** and **Latin**. Produced "Forever Friend," written and recorded by Steve Sutherland (pop).

DEMI MONDE RECORDS & PUBLISHING LTD., Foel Studio, Llanfair Caereinion, Powys, SY21 0RZ **Wales**. Phone: 0938-810758. Managing Director: Dave Anderson. Record producer, music publisher (PRS & MCPS) and record company (Demi Monde Records). Estab. 1982. Deals with artists and songwriters. Produces 5 singles, 15 12″ singles, 15 LPs and 10 CDs/year. Fee derived from sales royalty and outright fee from recording artist or record company.
How to Contact: Submit demo tape by mail — unsolicited submissions are OK. Prefers cassette with 3 or 4 songs and lyric sheet. SAE and IRC. Reports in 1 month.
Music: Mostly **rock, pop** and **blues**. Produced *Average Man*, recorded by Mother Gong (rock); *Frozen Ones*, recorded by Tangle Edge (rock); and *Blue Boar Blues* (by T.S. McPhee), recorded by Groundhogs (rock), all on Demi Monde Records. Other artists include Gong and Hawkwind.

WARREN DENNIS, 540 B. E. Todd Rd., Santa Rosa CA 95407. (707)585-1325. President/Owner: Warren Dennis Kahn. Record producer and independent producer. Estab. 1976. Deals with artists. Produces 10 LPs and 10 CDs/year. Fee derived from sales royalty when artist is recorded or outright fee from recording artist or record company. Does not return unsolicited submissions.

How to Contact: Write or call first and obtain permission to submit. Prefers cassette with 2-3 songs and lyric sheet. Reports in 1 month. Does not return unsolicited submissions.
Music: Mostly **New Age** or **world fusion**, also **pop**, **country**, **Christian** and **rock**. Produced *Music to Disappear in 2* (by Rafael), recorded by WDK on Hearts of Space Records (New Age); and *Ocean of Mercy* (by M. Poirier) on Peartree Records (Christian). Engineer and Production Assistant for "Asian Fusion" by Ancient Future for Narada/MCA (World Fusion), and many others. Other artists include Cedella Marley Booker, Ladysmith Black Mambazo, Constance Demby, Georgia Kelly, Radhika Miller and UMA.
Tips: "I'm only interested in working with artists who have a clear sense of social and moral contribution to the planet. I'm looking for artists who compose and perform at an exceptional level and whose music has a well defined and original style."

DETROIT PRODUCTIONS, Box 265, N. Hollywood CA 91603-0265. (818)569-5653. President/Executive Producer: Randy De Troit. Vice President: Ciara Dortch. Co-Producer: Jade Young. Independent television producer of network TV shows, cable-TV series. Works with freelance producers/promoters for local and national broadcast on assignment basis only; gives unlimited assignments per year. Fee derived from outright fee from recording artist or record company.
How to Contact: Submit demo tape by mail. Unsolicited submissions are OK. "Send edited version of work on VHS or broadcast quality tape. All categories of music plus surrealism, new concept, idealistic or abstract material by mail for consideration; provide résumé/bio with photos (if available) for filing for possible future assignments." SASE. Reports within 2 months.
Music: Produces weekly Cable-TV series – "Inner-Tube Presents." Features actors, actresses, singers, bands, models, dancers, rappers and whole independent production companies for all National Access Network channels. Produces documentaries, industrials, commercials, musicals, talent showcases (new performers), news, plays, lectures, concerts, talk-show format with host, music-videos, contests. Uses all types of programming; formats are color Super-VHS, broadcast quality ¾", or film to video/video to film.
Tips: "An imaginative freelance producer is an invaluable asset to any production house, not only as a constant source of new and fresh ideas, but also for pre- and post-production supportive elements, contributing just as much as any staffer. Because of the nature of the business, we tend to be more open to outside sources, especially when it is to our benefit to keep new blood flowing. Indies tend to lean towards seeking unknowns, because their styles are usually, in our opinion, more unique."

JOEL DIAMOND ENTERTAINMENT, Dept. SM, 5370 Vanalden Ave., Tarzana CA 91356. (818)345-2558. Executive Vice President: Scott Gootman. Contact: Joel Diamond. Record producer, music publisher and manager. Deals with artists and songwriters. Fee derived from sales royalty.
How to Contact: Prefers cassette with 1-3 songs and lyric sheet. Does not return material.
Music: **Dance**, **easy listening**, **country**, **R&B**, **rock**, **soul** and **top 40/pop**. Produced "One Night In Bangkok," by Robey; "Love is the Reason" (by Cline/Wilson), recorded by E. Humperdinck and G. Gaynor on Critique Records (A/C); and "After the Loving," recorded by E. Humperdinck.

COL. BUSTER DOSS PRESENTS, Box 13, Estill Springs TN 37330. (615)649-2577. Producer: Col. Buster Doss. Record producer, record company (Stardust, Wizard) and music publisher (Buster Doss Music/BMI). Estab. 1959. Deals with artists and songwriters. Produces 100 singles, 10 12" singles, 20 LPs and 10 CDs/year. Fee derived from sales royalty when song or artist is recorded.
How to Contact: Write or call first and obtain permission to submit. Prefers cassette with 2 songs and lyric sheet. SASE. Reports in 1 week.
Music: **Pop**, **country** and **gospel**. Produced *My Hacienda* (by Buster Doss), recorded by Rooster Quantrell on Stardust Records; "Women and Wine," written and recorded by Benny Ray on Thunderhawk Records; and "Messin' Around" (by Buster Doss), recorded by Tommy D on Doss Records. Other artists include Johnny Buck, Bronco Buck Cody, R.B. Stone, Cliff Archer, Linda Wunder, Mick O'Reilly, Mike Montana and Honey James.

*DOUBLETIME PRODUCTIONS, P.O. Box 710925, San Diego CA 92072. (619)448-1717. Producer: Jeff Forrest. Record producer, engineer. Estab. 1980. Deals with artists only. Produces 15 singles, 20 12" singles, 12 LPs, 18 EPs and 20 CDs/year. Fee derived from outright fee from recording artist.
How to Contact: Call first and obtain permission to submit. Prefers cassette with 3 songs and lyric sheet. SASE. Reports in 3 weeks.
Music: Mostly **alternative**, **punk** and **rock**. Produced *Home Improvements*, written and recorded by Fluf on Cargo/Head Hunter Records (alternative); *hat*, written and recorded by Mike Keneally on Guitar Recordings (alternative); and *Shrunken Head*, written and recorded by Dead Bolt on Cargo/Head Hunter Records (alternative). Other artists include aMiniature (Restless), Further (BMG) and 3 Mile Pilot (Cargo).
Tips: "Know what direction you are going in and be able to take constructive criticism."

DUANE MUSIC, INC., 382 Clarence Ave., Sunnyvale CA 94086. (408)739-6133. President: Garrie Thompson. Record producer and music publisher. Deals with artists and songwriters. Fee derived from sales royalty.
How to Contact: Prefers cassette with 1-2 songs. SASE. Reports in 1 month.
Music: **Blues, country, rock, soul** and **top 40/pop.** Produced "Wichita," on Hush Records (country); and "Syndicate of Sound," on Buddah Records (rock).

J.D. DUDICK, 6472 Seven Mile, South Lyon MI 48178. (313)486-0505. Producer: J.D. Dudick. Record producer. Estab. 1990. Deals with artists and songwriters. Produces 10 singles, 1 EP and 3 CDs/year. Fee derived from sales royalty when song or artist is recorded or outright fee from recording artist or record company.
How to Contact: Submit demo tape by mail. Unsolicited submissions are OK. Prefers cassette (or VHS videocassette) with 3 songs and lyric sheet. Does not return material. Reports in 6 weeks.
Music: Mostly **modern rock, country rock** and **alternative;** also **funk/pop** and **country.** Produced "Tonight" (by Chris Pierce), recorded by Q on Rocket Records (rock); *Buick City* (by Bill Toll), recorded by Wild Blue on Fine Line Records (blues); and *Itchin;* written and recorded by Laya on Rocket Records (alternative).

E.S.R. PRODUCTIONS, 61 Burnthouse Lane, Exeter Devon EX2 6AZ **UK.** Phone: (0392)57880. Contact: John Greenslade. Record producer and record company (E.S.R.). Estab. 1965. Deals with artists and songwriters. Produces 4 singles and 10 LPs/year. Fee derived from sales royalty when song or artist is recorded.
How to Contact: Submit demo tape by mail. Unsolicited submissions are OK. Prefers cassette with 4 songs and lyric sheet. SAE and IRC. Reports in 1 month.
Music: Mostly **country, pop** and **R&B.** Produced "There's You" (by J. Greenslade), recorded by Johnny Solo (MOR); "May I Please" (by J. Greenslade), recorded by Geraldine (MOR); and *Now and Forever* (by June Greenslade), recorded by Ginger Walker (MOR), all on E.S.R. Records. Other artists include Paul Walker, Kaz Barron and Johnny Ramone.

EARMARK AUDIO, P.O. Box 196, Vashon WA 98070. (206)463-1980. Owner: Jerry Hill. Record producer. Estab. 1991. Deals with artists and songwriters. Produces 2 LPs and 1 CD/year. Fee derived from outright fee from recording artist.
How to Contact: Submit demo tape by mail. Unsolicited submissions are OK. Prefers cassette (or VHS videocassette) with 1 song and lead sheet. Does not return unsolicited material. Reports in 2 months.
Music: Mostly **contemporary Christian, rock** and **country.** Produced *A New Day,* written and recorded by Randy Greco on Angel Wing Records; *Gloria* (by P.D./Ron Feller), recorded by Ron & Marsha Feller on Art Factory Records; and *A Mighty Fortress* (by P.D.), recorded by Grace Church. Other artists include Smelter/Neves.
Tips: "Be willing to focus your music on a specific target market."

LEO J. EIFFERT, JR., Box 5412, Buena Park CA 90620. (909)371-2973. Owner: Leo J. Eiffert, Jr. Record producer, music publisher (Eb-Tide Music/BMI, Young Country Music/BMI) and record company (Plain Country). Estab. 1967. Deals with artists and songwriters. Produces 15-20 singles and 5 LPs/year. Fee derived from sales royalty when song or artist is recorded.
How to Contact: Submit demo tape by mail. Unsolicited submissions are OK. Prefers cassette with 2-3 songs, lyric and lead sheet. SASE. Reports in 3-4 weeks.
Music: Mostly **country** and **gospel.** Produced "Daddy I Know," written and recorded by Pam Bellows on Plain Country Records; "Little Miss," written and recorded by Johnny Horton; and "My Friend," written and recorded by Leo J. Eiffert Jr., both on Young Country Records. Other artists include Crawfish Band, Brandi Holland and David Busson.
Tips: "Just keep it real country."

8TH STREET MUSIC, 204 E. Eighth St., Dixon IL 61021. Producer: Rob McInnis. Record producer. Estab. 1988. Deals with artists and songwriters. Fee derived from sales royalty when song or artist is recorded.
How to Contact: Submit demo tape by mail. Unsolicited submissions are OK. Prefers cassette with 3-6 songs and lyric sheet. "No phone calls please. Just submit material and we will contact if interested." SASE. Reports in 4-6 weeks.
Music: Mostly **top 40/pop, dance** and **new rock;** also **R&B, country** and **teen pop.** Produced "Black Roses," written and recorded by Michelle Goeking (alternative); and "Legend of Leo Mongorin," written and recorded by Jim Henkel (folk). Other artists include Jason Kermeen (country), Bob's Night Off (techno-dance), Jeff Widdicombe (country) and J&J (teen pop).
Tips: "Our current focus is on keyboard-oriented dance material, à la Information Society/Human League (male and/or female)."

ELEMENT & SUPERSTAR PRODUCTION, Box 30260, Bakersfield CA 93385-1260. Producer: Jar the Superstar. Record producer, record company (Element Records, International Motion Pictures), music publisher (BMI). Estab. 1987. Deals with artists and songwriters. Produces 40 singles and 5 LPs/year. Fee derived from standard record sales.
How to Contact: Write first to arrange personal interview. Prefers cassette (or VHS videocassette if available) with 1 or more songs, lyric and lead sheet. Does not return material.
Music: Mostly **Christian/gospel, C/W** and **R&B**; also **pop, rap** and **rock**. Produced "Where You Are" (by Judge A. Robertson), recorded by Jar the Superstar (pop); "No One Wants to be Sad," written and recorded by Jar (R&B), both on Element Records; and "Brite & Morning Lite," written and recorded by Jar the Superstar (Christian).

*EMPTY STREET PRODUCTIONS, P.O. Box 813, Champaign IL 61824. (217)352-1437. Producer: Pat Ortman. Record producer, music publisher (Winglet Music/ASCAP) and multimedia company. Estab. 1993. Deals with artists and songwriters. Produces 4 singles, 3 LPs, 1 EP and 3 CDs/year. Fee derived from sales royalty when song or artist is recorded.
How to Contact: Write or call first and obtain permission to submit, or e-mail at pattrex@aol.com. Prefers cassette (or VHS videocassette if available) with 2 songs and lyric sheet. Does not return material. Reports in 4-6 weeks.
Music: Mostly **pop/rock** and **alternative.** Produced *Pattrex* (by Pat Ortman), recorded by Pattrex on Shy Records (alternative); "Jane 7" (by Jane 7/Pat Ortman), recorded by Jane 7 on Status Records (pop); and *Official Beatles* (by Pat Ortman/Bill Whitehorse), recorded by Pat Ortman on Gizmo Records (pop). Other artists include Simon Huggs and The Biggest Guitars.
Tips: "Confidence is important. Believe in what you have because if you do not, how can anyone else? And get onto the electronic frontier. I always answer e-mail at pattrex@aol.com."

GEOFFREY ENGLAND, 2810 McBain, Redondo Beach CA 90278. (213)371-5793. Contact: Geoffrey England. Record producer. Deals with artists and songwriters. Produces 100 singles/year. Fee derived from sales royalty and/or outright fee from record company.
How to Contact: Submit demo tape by mail. Unsolicited submissions are OK. Prefers cassette and photo. SASE. Reports in 2 weeks.
Music: Mainstream melodic rock. Produced Rude Awakening, Wolfgang Elvis, Cruella D'Ville, LA Riot, New Dynasty.

*ERGO COMMUNICATIONS, P.O. Box 302, Hyde Park, VT 05655. (802)888-7063. Fax: (802)888-3531. Producer/Arranger: Peter B. Wilder. Record producer. Estab. 1985. Deals with artists and songwriters. Produces 6 CDs/year. Fee derived from outright fee from recording artist.
How to Contact: Write first and obtain permission to submit. Prefers cassette with 4 songs and lyric sheet. SASE. Reports in 2 weeks.
Music: Mostly **progressive rock, new folk** and **new country.** Produced *Flying: Home to You* and *Hooked on Flight*, written and recorded by Ken Dravis on AV Music; and *Brotherly Love*, written and recorded by Isaacson Bros. on Isonia Records. Other artists include Meg Chambers and P. Bruce Wilder.

ESQUIRE INTERNATIONAL, Box 6032, Station B, Miami FL 33101-6032. (305)547-1424. President: Jeb Stuart. Record producer, music publisher and management firm. Deals with artists and songwriters. Produces 6 singles and 2 LPs/year. Fee derived from sales royalty or independent leasing of masters and placing songs.
How to Contact: Submit demo tape. Unsolicited submissions OK. Prefers cassette or disc with 2-4 songs and lead sheet. SASE. Reports in 1 month.
Music: Blues, church/religious, country, dance, gospel, jazz, rock, soul and **top 40/pop.** Produced "Guns Guns (No More Guns)" and "No One Should Be Alone on Christmas," both written and recorded by Jeb Stuart on Esquire Int'l Records. Other artists include Moments Notice, Cafidia and Night Live.
Tips: "When sending out material make sure it is well organized, put together as neatly as possible and it is of good sound quality."

EXCELL PRODUCTIONS, Suite 404, 10930 Ashton Ave., Westwood CA 90024. (310)477-1166. Fax: (310)479-5579. Production Coordinator: Ruth Maehara. Record producer, music publisher. Estab. 1990. Deals with artists and songwriters. Produces 12 CDs/year. Fee derived from sales royalty when song or artist is recorded.
How to Contact: Submit demo tape by mail. Unsolicited submissions are OK. Prefers cassette (or videocassette if available) and lyric sheet. SASE. Reports in 2 months.
Music: Mostly **pop, ballads** and **A/C.** Produced *Mom* (by Barry Fasman) and *All You Have To Do* (by Cami Ellen), both recorded by Tomoe Sawa on BMG Victor Records; and *Lonely Mystery* (by Shun Suzuki), recorded by Shirley Kwan on Apollon Records. Other artists include Yumi Matsutoya, Nagabuchi, Takanaka, & Honda-Japan.

SHANE FABER, Dept. SM, #3, 501 78th St., North Bergen NJ 07047. (201)854-6266. Fax: (201)662-9017. Contact: Shane Faber. Record producer, music publisher (Now & Then Music/BMI) and record company (Now & Then Records). Estab. 1980. Deals with artists and songwriters. Produces 6 singles and 2 LPs/year. Fee derived from sales royalty or outright fee from recording artist or record company.
How to Contact: Submit demo tape by mail. Unsolicited submissions are OK. Prefers cassette with 4 songs and lyric sheet. SASE. Reports in 2 months.
Music: Mostly **pop, dance, R&B** and **rap**. Produced "Partyline," recorded by 5th Platoon and "Turtle Power," recorded by Partners In Krime, both on SBK Records; also produced gold album by Pendulum Records artist Digable Planets and gold single "Cool Like Dat." Regularly works with Atlantic Records, East West Records, London Records, Polygram Records, etc.

*DOUG FAIELLA PRODUCTIONS, 19153 Paver Barnes Rd., Marysville OH 43040-8838. (513)644-8295. President: Doug Faiella. Record producer, music publisher (Doug Faiella Publishing/BMI), record company (Studio 7 Records) and recording studio. Estab. 1984. Deals with artists and songwriters. Produces 10 singles and 5 LPs/year. Fee derived from outright fee from recording artist. "Charges a flat rate per song."
How to Contact: Write first and obtain permission to submit. Include SASE. Prefers cassette with 3 songs and lyric sheets. Does not return unsolicited material. Reports in 4 weeks.
Music: Mostly **country, gospel** and **rock**. Produced *Yesterday Country*, recorded by Dago Red on Studio 7 Records (country LP).

THE FEMINO-MOORE MUSIC GROUP INC., (formerly Jim Femino Productions), 429 South Lewis Rd., Royersford PA 19468. (215)948-8228. Fax: (215)948-4175. Branch: 1713 Beechwood Ave., Nashville TN 37212. (615)297-3171. President: Jim Femino. Vice President: Mike Moore. Record producer, music publisher (Fezsongs/ASCAP, Feminosongs/BMI), record company (Road Records) and independent producer/engineer with own 24-track facility. Estab. 1970. Fee derived from sales royalty when song or artist is recorded, or outright fee from record company.
How to Contact: Write first and obtain permission to submit. Prefers cassette with two songs only. SASE. Replies in 4-6 weeks.
Music: **Country**. Produced "One Too Many Days," written and recorded by Jim Femino; "Waiting in the Wings," written and recorded by Jim Femino and Kingsley Brock; and "Don't You Wanna Dance," written and recorded by Jim Femino and F.C. Collins, all on Road Records.

*VITO FERA PRODUCTIONS, 345 Sprucewood Rd., Lake Mary FL 32746-5917. (407)321-3702. Fax: (407)321-2361. President, A&R: Vito Fera. Office Manager: Rhonda Fera. Record producer, music publisher (NSP Publishing/ASCAP, Fera Music Publishing/BMI). Estab. 1980. Produces 5 singles, 1 LP and 4 EPs/year. Fee derived from outright fee from recording artist or record company.
How to Contact: Submit demo tape by mail. Unsolicited submissions are OK. Prefers cassette or VHS videocassette with 3 songs maximum and lyric sheet. "Package song material carefully. To avoid damage to your tape, stamp or write *Please Hand Cancel* on the package. Always label (name, address and phone) both cassette and lyric sheets. Bio and photo helpful." SASE. Reports in 1 month.
Music: Mostly **contemporary, R&B** and **rock/light**; also **children's, Christian** and **soundtracks**. Produced *The Glory of the Lord*, written and recorded by Salvatore Cristiano on Spin Records; "Sunoco Ultra 94" (by Vito Fera), radio ad for Sunoco Marketing Division; and "Rab-byte's 3D Professional Tapes," Volume 1 soundtrack for graphic animation video.
Tips: "The competition is extremely tough today. You've got to look and sound professional. Plan a strategy and put your heart and soul into it. Listen to those with good advice and don't give up."

DON FERGUSON PRODUCTIONS, Box 461892, Garland TX 75046. (214)271-8098. Producer: Don Ferguson. Record producer (Sultan Music/BMI and Illustrious Sultan/ASCAP), record company (Puzzle Records). Estab. 1972. Deals with artists and songwriters. Produces 10-15 singles, 4-5 cassettes and 2-3 CDs/year. "Fees are negotiated."
How to Contact: Submit demo tape by mail—unsolicited submissions are OK. Prefers cassette with 3 songs and lyric sheet. "Include bio." SASE. Reports in 2 weeks.
Music: **Country, pop** and **MOR**. Produced "Knock on Wood" (by S. Cropper, E. Floyd), recorded by Diane Elliott (country); "The Woman on Your Mind" (by L. Schonfeld), recorded by Lonny Jay (pop); and "Eight Days a Week" (by Lennon, McCartney), recorded by Mary Craig (country), all on Puzzle Records. Other artists include Heartland (band), Flashpoint (band), Charlie Shearer, Derek Hartis, Phil Rodgers and Jimmy Massey.

FESTIVAL STUDIOS, Dept. SW, 3413 Florida Ave., Kenner LA 70065. (504)469-4403. Engineer/Producer: Rick Naiser. Record producer and recording studio (Festival Studios). Estab. 1988. Deals with artists and songwriters. Produces 12 singles, 6 12" singles, 15 LPs, 10 EPs and 5 CDs/year. Fee derived from sales royalty or outright fee from recording artist or record company.

How to Contact: Submit demo tape by mail. Unsolicited submissions are OK. Prefers cassette, DAT (or ½″ VHS or Beta videocassette) with 4 songs. "Send any pictures, press clips, reviews and any promo material available."
Music: Mostly **rock, pop** and **New Age**; also **rap, R&B** and other. Produced *In It To Win It* (by Def Boyz) on Big T Records (rap); *EHG* (by EHG) on Intellectual Convulsion Records (sludge metal); and *Red Headed Step Children of Rock* (by Force of Habit) on Riffish Records (pop), all recorded by Festival. Other artists include Ice Mike, Ice Nine, RSBR, Common Knowledge and Mooncrikits.
Tips: "Concentrate on songwriting as a craft—don't spend time or money on embellishing demos. Raw demos leave room for the producer's creative input. Record demos quickly and move on to the next project."

FISHBOWL PRODUCTIONS, #3, 89 Clinton St., Everett MA 02149. (617)389-5816. President: Joe Miraglilo. Record producer. Estab. 1985. Deals with artists and songwriters. Produces 8 LPs/year. Fee derived from outright fee from recording artist.
How to Contact: Submit demo tape by mail. Unsolicited submissions are OK. Prefers cassette with 3-4 songs and lyric sheet. Does not return unsolicited material. Reports in 2-3 weeks.
Music: Mostly **electronic dance, funk/pop** and **pop/rap**; also **pop/rock, rock** and **jazz**. Produced "Snow" (by Cleopatra Jones) and "Dreamin'" (by Whirling Virtigo), both recorded by Joe Miraglilo on Fishbowl Productions Records; and "Slip Away" (by Billy Ward), recorded by Joe Miraglilo on Hipshake Records. Other artists include Bill Hartzell, Mutiny, Minus One.

FOX FARM RECORDING, 2731 Saundersville Ferry Rd., Mt. Juliet TN 37122. (615)754-2444. President: Kent Fox. Record producer (Mercantile Productions) and music publisher (Mercantile Music/BMI and Blueford Music/ASCAP). Estab. 1970. Deals with artists and songwriters. Produces 20 singles/year. Fee derived from sales royalty when song or artist is recorded.
How to Contact: Submit demo tape by mail. Unsolicited submissions are OK. Prefers cassette (or VHS videocassette if available). SASE. Reports in 3 months.
Music: **Country, bluegrass, gospel** and **contemporary Christian**.

BOB SCOTT FRICK, 404 Bluegrass Ave., Madison TN 37115. (615)865-6380. Contact: Bob Scott Frick. Record producer and music publisher (R.E.F.). Estab. 1958. Deals with artists and songwriters only. Produces 12 singles, 30 12″ singles and 30 LPs.
How to Contact: Submit demo tape by mail. Unsolicited submissions are OK. Write first and obtain permission to submit.
Music: Produced "I Found Jesus in Nashville," recorded by Bob Scott Frick; "Love Divine," recorded by Backwoods; and "A Tribute," recorded by Visionheirs on R.E.F. (gospel). Other artists include Larry Ahlborn, Bob Myers Family, David Barton, The Mattingleys and Jim Pommert.

THE FRICON ENTERTAINMENT CO., INC., 1048 S. Ogden Dr., Los Angeles CA 90019. (213)931-7323. Attention: Publishing Department. Music publisher (Fricon Music Co./BMI, Fricon Music Co./ASCAP) and library material. Estab. 1981. Deals with songwriters only. Fee derived from sales royalty.
How to Contact: Write first and obtain permission to submit. Include SASE. Prefers cassette with 1 song and lyric and lead sheet. SASE. Reports in 8 weeks.
Music: Mostly **TV/film, R&B** and **rock**; also **pop, country** and **gospel**.
Tips: "Ask for permission, submit 1 song with typed lyrics and be patient."

JACK GALE, Box 630755, Miami FL 33163. (305)935-4880. Contact: Jack Gale. Record producer, music publisher (Cowabonga Music/ASCAP) and record company (Playback Records). Estab. 1983. Deals with artists and songwriters. Produces 48 singles and 20 CDs/year. Fee derived from sales royalty when song or artist is recorded.
How to Contact: Submit demo tape by mail. Unsolicited submissions are OK. Prefers cassette (or VHS videocassette if available) with 2 songs maximum and lyric sheets. Does not return unsolicited material. Reports in 2 weeks if interested.
Music: Mostly **contemporary country** and **country crossover**. Produced "Back In Harmony" (by Silverstein/Fagen), recorded by Tanya Tucker and Charlie Louvin; "Guess Things Happen That Way" (by Clement), recorded by Johnny Cash and Tommy Cash; and *Do You Know Where Your Man Is?* (by Chase/Gibson/Smith), recorded by Melba Montgomery, all on Playback Records (country). Other artists include Jeannie C. Riley, Johnny Paycheck, Mary Smith and Del Reeves.
Tips: "Don't expect miracles—be patient!"

THE GLAND PUPPIES, INC., 120 Highview, Yorkville IL 60560. (708)355-0161. President: Rikki Rockett. Record producer. Estab. 1989. Deals with artists and songwriters. Produces 7-10 singles and 2 LPs/year. Fee derived from sales royalty.

How to Contact: Write or call first and obtain permission to submit. Prefers cassette with 4-8 songs and lyric sheet. "Send *your* favorite songs, not a rip-off of what's being played on the radio." SASE. Reports in 1-2 months.
Music: Mostly **New Age, pop/dance** and **folk** songs; also **comedy, gypsy/dance** and **thrash metal.** Produced *Cyber Christ* (by Phineas 4), recorded by Joe's Mom on Sick Dog Records (R&B); "Take This Dog & Shove It" (by Bill Harris), recorded by Big Poo Generation (novelty); and *Sally was a Re-Terd* (by Nikki Arrow), recorded by The Narcoleptics (folk), both on Spoo Disk Records. Other artists include Eschaton, Four Arm Mildew Freaks, Doug Takes Five, Spray Monkey, Your Mom and the Dog Catchers.
Tips: "Destroy the musical boundaries separating stupidity, comedy, hate and revenge!"

GLOBAL ASSAULT MANAGEMENT AND CONSULTING, (formerly David Norman Productions), #1632, 639 Garden Walk Blvd., College Park GA 30349. (404)994-1770. Producer/Engineer: David Norman. Record producer. Estab. 1986. Deals with artists and songwriters. Produces 6 singles, 5 LPs, 5 EPs and 4 CDs/year. Fee derived from outright fee from recording artist or record company.
How to Contact: Submit demo tape by mail—unsolicited submissions are OK. Prefers cassette with 5 songs. "Please send photo." Does not return material. Reports in 2 weeks.
Music: Mostly **funk** and **R&B**; also **techno-music.** Produced AC Black on Motown Records (dance/rock); and "Wages of Syn," recorded by Synical on Kudzu Records (techno). Engineer for Peabo Bryson—Sony Records, and Arrested Development—EMI Records.

*GO JO PRODUCTIONS, 195 S. 26th St., San Jose CA 95116. (408)286-4091. Fax: (408)286-9845. Owners: G.J. O'Neal and J. O'Neal. Estab. 1980. Deals with artists and songwriters. Fee derived from outright fee from recording artist or record company. Charges for arranging.
How to Contact: Submit demo tape by mail—unsolicited submissions are OK. Prefers cassette. SASE. Reports in 2-3 weeks.
Music: Mostly **country, gospel** and **Mexican**; also **rock, pop** and **urban contemporary.** Produced "Counting Down The Days," by Randal Max Mower (country); "Su Exito Diosito Santo," by Los Metalicos (Mexican); and "Living On Barroom Time," by Xandria (country).

GRAFFITI PRODUCTIONS INC., Suite 205, 3341 Towerwood, Dallas TX 75234. (214)243-3735. Fax: (214)243-4477. Vice President: Dennis Lowe. Contact: Barry Dickey. Record producer, record company (Graffiti Records) and music publisher (Writing On The Wall Music Publishing). Estab. 1989. Deals with artists and songwriters. Fee derived from outright fee from recording artist or record company.
How to Contact: Call first to arrange personal interview. Submit demo tape by mail. Unsolicited submissions are OK. Prefers cassette with 4 songs and lyric sheet. Also include bio and photos. Does not return unsolicited material. Reports in 2 weeks.
Music: Mostly **rock, industrial** and **R&B**; also **rap, country** and **New Age.** Produced *Time For Terror*, *Love You To Death* and *Call Me Devil*, (by WWIII), recorded by Heaven on Graffiti Records (rock). Other artists include Bryan Robertson (Thin Lizzy), Yoko and Ralph The Dog.

*GRASS RECORDING AND SOUND, 800 Arbor Place, Del Rey Oaks CA 93940. (408)394-1065. Owner: Michael Grass. Record producer, record company (Blackend Earth, Rabid Records) and recording studio (Live Sound Service). Estab. 1989. Deals with artists and songwriters. Produces 2 singles, 1 LP and 4 EPs/year. Fee derived from sales royalty when song or artist is recorded and outright fee from recording artist. "We sometimes require 50% cash deposit for recording only."
How to Contact: Submit demo tape by mail—unsolicited submissions are OK. Prefers cassette (or VHS videocassette if available) with 1-5 songs and lyric sheet. "Don't be overly persistent. I will listen to *all* tapes, and if I like you, I'll call you." SASE. Reports in 2 months.
Music: Mostly **thrash metal, mainstream metal** and **hard rock**; also **punk** and **fusion.** Produced *Resurrector* (by E. Garland), recorded by Resurrector (metal); *Threshold* (by B. Gillis), recorded by Pain, both on R. Records (metal); and *Pinchaloaf* (by M.A. Grass) recorded by Shithead on B. Earth (metal). Other artists include MPAA, Angst.
Tips: "Don't worry about talking me into listening. If your tape sounds good, and the songs are strong—I'll listen."

*GREEN DREAM PRODUCTIONS, P.O. Box 872, West Covina CA 91790. Owner: Kelly D. Lammers. Record producer and music publisher (Passing Parade Music/ASCAP). Estab. 1989. Deals with artists and songwriters. Produces 3-6 singles and 24 LPs/year. Fee derived from sales royalty when song or artist is recorded or outright fee from record company.
How to Contact: Submit demo tape by mail. Unsolicited submissions are OK. Prefers cassette with 1-3 songs and lyric sheet. SASE. Reports in 6 weeks.

Music: Mostly **children's, country** and **pop**; also **holiday** and **New Age**. Produced "Let Me Be a Kid" (by K.D. Lammers), recorded by Neighborhood Kids; and "Punkline" (by K.D. Lammers), recorded by The Surfaris, both on Koinkidink Records.
Tips: "When writing for children, keep the message positive and uplifting. When writing for adults, keep the lyrics either fun or sophisticated, but please not corny, especially in country. The children's market has shifted from a subsidiary market to a strong market of its own and needs to be fed. When writing, keep our children in mind."

*ALFRED B. GRUNWELL/THE O.C. CHADWICK CO., 274 Gray Road, Ithaca NY 14850. Producer/ Engineer: Alfred B. Grunwell. Record producer. Estab. 1977. Deals with artists and songwriters. Produces 5 LPs and 5 CDs/year. Fee is negotiable.
How to Contact: Submit demo tape by mail. Unsolicited submissions are OK. Prefers cassette. "Make sure name, address and phone are on tape." Does not return material. Reports in 2 weeks.
Music: Mostly **industrial, country** and **pop**. Artists include Claire Harrison.

GUESS WHO?? PRODUCTIONS, 140-23 Einstein Loop North, Bronx NY 10475-4973. (212)465-3355. Director: David Pellot. Record producer. Estab. 1988. Deals with artists and songwriters. Produces 10-15 singles/year. Fee derived from sales royalty or outright fee from recording artist or record company. "May charge in advance for services, depending on deal made with artist or songwriter."
How to Contact: Submit demo tape by mail. Unsolicited submissions are OK. Include biography, résumé and picture if available. Prefers cassette and lyric sheet. Does not return unsolicited material. Reports in 4-6 weeks.
Music: Mostly **house, techno** and **ballads**; also **rap, R&B** and **top 40/dance**.

R L HAMMEL ASSOCIATES,INC., P.O. Box 531, Alexandria IN 46001-0531. Contact: Randal L. Hammel. Record producer/arranger, music publisher (Ladnar Music/ASCAP and Lemmah Music/BMI) and consultants. Estab. 1973. Deals with artists and songwriters. Produces 4 singles, 4 LPs, 2 EPs and 4 CDs/year. Fee derived from sales royalty, outright fee from artist/songwriter or record company, or negotiable fee per project.
How to Contact: Write first and obtain permission to submit, include brief résumé (including experience, age, goal). Prefers cassette with 3 songs maximum. "Lyrics (preferably typed) *must* accompany tapes." SASE. Reports as soon as possible.
Music: Blues, church/religious, country, easy listening, gospel, MOR, progressive, R&B, rock (usually country), soul and top 40/pop.

HANSEN PRODUCTIONS, 6531 S. Owensboro, West Jordan UT 84084. Producer: R. Mark Hansen. Estab. 1989. Deals with artists and songwriters. Produces 2-3 LPs and 1 EP/year. Fee derived from sales royalty, outright fee from songwriter/artist and/or record company. Member Independent Musician's Co-op.
How to Contact: Submit demo tape by mail. Unsolicited submissions are OK. Prefers cassette with 3-4 songs and lyric sheet. Does not return unsolicited material.
Music: Any, especially **rock, country, rap** and **music in Spanish**. Produced *Outlaw*, written and recorded by Lash LaRue on Free Spirit Records; *A Joyful Noise*, written and recorded by Mark Hansen on HP Records; and *The Mixx*, recorded by various artists. Other artists include Bill Dent, Justin Naylor, Pollyanna.
Tips: "I have a particular interest at this time in material with an anti-drug or anti-gang message."

STEPHEN A. HART/HART PRODUCTIONS, Dept. SM, 171 King Rd., Petaluma CA 94954. (707)762-2521. Executive Producer: Stephen A. Hart. Record producer. Estab. 1975. Deals with artists and songwriters. Produces 8 LPs and 8 CDs/year. Fee derived from outright fee from recording artist or record company.
How to Contact: Submit demo by mail—unsolicited submissions are OK. Prefers cassette with 3 songs and lyric sheet. SASE. Reports in 3 months.
Music: Mostly **pop, rock** and **instrumental**. Produced *Continuum*, written and recorded by Ira Stein on MCA Records (instrumental); *Flora Purim*, written and recorded by Flora Purim on B&W Records; and *Over The Top*, written and recorded by Jim Chappell on Real Music Records (instrumental).

HAWORTH PRODUCTIONS, Box 97, Climax Springs MO 65324. (314)374-1111. President/Producer: Dann E. Haworth. Record producer and music publisher (Southern Most Publishing/BMI). Estab. 1985. Deals with artists and songwriters. Produces 5 singles, 3 12" singles, 10 LPs, 5 EPs and 10 CDs/ year. Fee derived from sales royalty or outright fee from recording artist or record company.
How to Contact: Submit demo tape by mail—unsolicited submissions are OK. Prefers cassette or 7½ ips reel-to-reel with 3 songs and lyric or lead sheets. SASE. Reports in 6-8 weeks.

Music: Mostly **rock, country** and **gospel**; also **jazz**, **R&B** and **New Age**. Produced *Christmas Joy* (by Esther Kreak) on Serene Sounds Records. Other artists include The Hollowmen, Jordan Border, Jim Wilson, Tracy Creech and Tony Glise.
Tips: "Keep it simple and from the heart."

HEART CONSORT MUSIC, 410 First St. W., Mt. Vernon IA 52314. (319)895-8557. Manager: Catherine Lawson. Record producer, record company, music publisher. "We are a single in-house operation." Estab. 1980. Deals with artists and songwriters. Produces 2-3 CDs/year. Fee derived from sales royalty or outright fee from recording artist or record company.
How to Contact: Submit demo tape by mail—unsolicited submissions are OK. Prefers cassette (or VHS videocassette if available) with 3 songs and 3 lyric sheet. SASE. Reports in 1-2 months.
Music: Mostly **jazz, New Age** and **contemporary.** Produced "Across the Borders," "Persia," and "Freedom Train," all written and recorded by James Kennedy on Heart Consort Music (jazz).
Tips: "Be original, don't copy someone else's style. We are interested in jazz/New Age artists with quality demos and original ideas. We aim for an international market."

HEARTBEAT MUSIC, 282 Bruce Ct., Westerville OH 43081. (614)882-5919. Vice President: Stephen Bashaw. Record producer, record company and music publisher. Estab. 1987. Deals with artists and songwriters. Produces 3-5 LPs/year. Fee derived from sales royalty when song or artist is recorded or outright fee from recording artist or record company.
How to Contact: Submit demo tape by mail. Unsolicited submissions are OK. Prefers cassette with 3-4 songs and lyric sheet. SASE. Reports in 4-6 weeks.
Music: Mostly **adult contemporary Christian, black gospel** and **inspirational;** also **Christian rock/pop** and **children's.** Produced *The Word Is* (by Freedom); "This Ain't Make Believe," recorded by King's Crew; and *Church, Do You Have It,* recorded by Keith Dobbins and the Resurrection Mass Choir, all recorded at Heartlight Studios on Pulse Records.

HICKORY LANE PUBLISHING AND RECORDING, P.O. Box 2275, Vancouver, British Columbia V6B 3W5 **Canada.** (604)465-1408. President: Chris Michaels. A&R Manager: David Rogers. Record producer, record company, music publisher. Estab. 1988. Deals with artists and songwriters. Produces 3 singles, 3 LPs and 3 CDs/year. Fee derived from sales royalty when song or artist is recorded.
How to Contact: Submit demo tape by mail. Unsolicited submissions are OK. Prefers cassette (or VHS videocassette if available) with 1-5 songs and lyric or lead sheet if available. "Be patient!" SASE. Reports in 4-6 weeks.
Music: Mostly **country, MOR** and **gospel;** also **soft rock, musical compositions** and **children's music.** Produced "Until Now" (by Steve Mitchell); *Tear and Tease* (by Chris Michaels/Parmjit Pawa); and "Cross My Heart" (by Chris Michaels/Steve Mitchell), all recorded by Chris Michaels on Hickory Lane Records. Other artists include Marina Rose, Steven James, Rick Kinderly, Rodney Austin.
Tips: "Send only original material, send your best. Keep vocals up front and make a professional presentation. Be patient."

*MAX HIGHSTEIN MUSIC, 5 Herrada Place, Santa Fe NM 87505. Proprietor: Max Highstein. Record producer, music publisher. Deals with artists and songwriters. Produces 4 CDs/year. Fee derived from outright fee from recording artist.
How to Contact: Submit demo tape by mail. Unsolicited submissions are OK. Prefers cassette with 4 songs and lyric sheet. "Clearly recorded, professional demos are a preference." Does not return material. Reports in 2 months.
Music: Mostly **contemporary folk** and **New Age.** Produced *Spiritual Healing* (by A. Getty), recorded on Serenity Records. Other artists include Chance.

HORRIGAN PRODUCTIONS, Box 41243, Los Angeles CA 90041. (213)256-0215. President/Owner: Tim Horrigan. Record producer and music publisher (Buck Young Music/BMI). Estab. 1982. Deals with artists and songwriters. Produces 5-10 singles, 3-5 LPs, 3-5 EPs and 3-5 CDs/year. Fee derived from sales royalty or outright fee from recording artist or record company. "We do some work on spec but the majority of the time we work on a work-for-hire basis."

How to Get the Most Out of Songwriter's Market (at the front of this book) contains comments and suggestions to help you understand and use the information in these listings.

How to Contact: Submit demo tape by mail. Unsolicited submissions are OK. Prefers cassette (or VHS videocassette if available) with 1-3 songs and lyric sheets. SASE. "Please do not call first; just let your music do the talking. Will reply if interested."
Music: Mostly **pop, rock** and **country**. Produced *Slap Your Catfish* (by Don Fenceton), recorded by The Nashville Cookin' Show Band on Country Heritage Records. Other artists include Mama Says (country), Vicki Silver (alternative) and Juilet Lane (1994 "Star Search" winner).
Tips: "Write from the heart with eyes on the charts."

*HORSEFEATHERS MUSIC COMPANY INC., 121 Logan Ave., Toronto, Ontario M4M 2M9 **Canada**. (416)406-4121. (416)406-0319. Contact: Melinda Skinner. Record producer and record company (Duke Street Records). Estab. 1980. Deals with artists and songwriters. Produces 5 LPs and 5 CDs/year. Fee derived from sales royalty when song or artist is recorded.
How to Contact: Submit demo tape by mail. Unsolicited submissions are OK. Prefers cassette with lyric sheet. Does not return material. Reports in 6 weeks.
Music: Mostly **alternative** and **rock/unique**. Produced *Zelig Belmondo*, written and recorded by John Cody (alternative/pop); *Rough, Raw and Simple*, written and recorded by Danny Brooks (R&B/rock); and *Monkeywalk*, written and recorded by Monkeywalk (alternative), all on MCA Records.
Tips: "Submit your best 3 songs on cassette. Do not submit unless you actively perform live."

*HOUSE OF RHYTHM, Suite 416, 16200 Ventura Blvd., Encino CA 91436. (818)501-4985. Fax: (818)501-8090. President: Joe LaChance. Record producer, production company. Estab. 1991. Deals with artists and songwriters. Produces 3-5 singles, 3-5 12″ singles, 2 LPs, 2 EPs and 2 CDs/year. Fee derived from sales royalty when song or artist is recorded.
How to Contact: Submit demo tape by mail. Unsolicited submissions are OK. Prefers cassette with 3 songs and lyric sheet. "Do not call to follow up; if we like it we will call you." SASE. Reports in 1 month.
Music: Mostly **dance, R&B** and **rock**; also **new artists** and **new producers**. Produced "The Truth" (by Mike Nally), recorded by SYSTM X on Innerkore Records (dance); "Nasty Groove" and "Lift Em" (by Mike Jett), both recorded by Cold Automatic Eyes on Crap Records (dance). Other artists include Natasha, Richard Grieco, L'Simone.

*HOWE PRODUCTIONS, 45 Budd Ave., Campbell CA 95008. (408)379-0632. Producer/Engineer: Matthew C. Howe. Record producer. Estab. 1992. Deals with artists and songwriters. Produces 8 singles, 1-2 12″ singles, 4 LPs, 4 EPs and 2-10 CDs/year. Fee derived from sales royalty when song or artist is recorded.
How to Contact: Submit demo tape by mail. Unsolicited submissions are OK. Prefers cassette (or VHS videocassette if available) with 3-4 songs and lyric sheet. "Include pictures and bio if possible." Does not return material. Reports in 1 month.
Music: Mostly **rock, pop** and **country**; also **R&B/dance**, **alternative** and **jazz**. Produced "No Rules," written and recorded by W. Mills (rock); *Holland*, written and recorded by Holland (rock); and *What Took Ya?*, written and recorded by M. Howe (pop), all on DBR Records. Other artists include No Rules, Millhouse, Robert Johnson, Alex Knight, Paul Crane, Mitchell Rymer and Christopher Jacobs.
Tips: "We are very critical of material submitted. Looking for 'great' songs and unique styles."

I.Y.F. PRODUCTIONS, 4B, 500½ E. 84th St., New York NY 10028. (212)861-8745. A&R: Steven Bentzel. Record producer, music publisher (Mia Mind Music/ASCAP) and record company (Mindfield Records). Estab. 1990. Deals with artists and songwriters. Produced 30 singles, 8 12″ singles, 6 LPs and 8 CDs/year. Fee derived from outright fee from artist or record company.
How to Contact: Call first and obtain permission to submit. Does not return material. Reports in 6 weeks.
Music: Mostly **rap, house** and **hip hop**; also **dance, top 40** and **AOR**. Produced "Shelter" (by Ashley Wilkes), recorded by Jade on MMM Records (top 40); "Toxic Man," written and recorded by Tommy Mod on Modern Records (rock); and "Time and Time Again" (by Bentzel), recorded by Madonna on Merlin Records (pop). Other artists include Kym Alex and Tonya Hurley.
Tips: "Submit demos on DAT cassettes for best sound quality."

*INDEPENDENT AUDIO SERVICES, #10-C, 235 W. 76th St., New York NY 10023. (212)580-9825. Producer-Engineer: Stephen Fitzstephens. Record producer and production and engineering service. Estab. 1977. Deals with artists and songwriters. Fee derived from outright fee from recording artist.
How to Contact: Write first and obtain permission to submit. Prefers cassette, 15 or 7.5 ips reel-to-reel (or VHS or U-matic videocassette if available) with 3 songs and lyric sheets. "Save your money and write first. I don't need much material to start off a project." SASE. Reports in 1 month.
Music: Produced *In the Key of Z* (by Lance Tait) on Tait Records; and "Traditional Tunes" (by Bill Mulligan) on Prime Records (folk rock); both recorded by Fitz. Other artists include Steven Sacher, Steven Farzan and Memphis Pilgrims.

Tips: "Write to book a presentation (performance or listening interview) at a studio of mutual choice. No synths, drum synths or sequencers."

INNER SOUND PRODUCTIONS, 5205 44th Ave. S., Minneapolis MN 55417-2211. (612)721-5647. General Partners: Sa'id Q. 'Ubaydah and Lamonte Turner. Record producer and project studio. Estab. 1989. Deals with artists and songwriters. Fee derived from outright fee from recording artist.
How to Contact: Submit demo tape by mail. Unsolicited submissions are OK. Prefers cassette with 3 songs and lyric sheet. Does not return unsolicited material. Reports in 1 month.
Music: Mostly **hip-hop, R&B** and **house/club**; also **dancehall**. Produced "In My World" (by S. 'Ubaydah/L. Turner), recorded by Twinkles (R&B); "Remember When?" (by S. 'Ubaydah/L. Turner), recorded by Rare Quality (jazz); and "Red-Tight Madness" (by S. 'Ubaydah/L. Turner), recorded by Quadir (fusion/hip hop). Other artists include Sunni Morrocan Warrior, Down to Earth, K-Smooth, L.O.D., X-Government.
Tips: "This company is like family. No pressure, no games, no B.S."

*INSIGHT RECORDS, Dept. SM, P.O. Box 30869, Seattle WA 98103-0869. Label President/Producer: Peter Fosso. Record producer, record company. Estab. 1992. Deals with artists and songwriters. Produces 2 EPs and 2 CDs/year. Fee derived from sales royalty when song or artist is recorded or outright fee from recording artist if project is a nationally released compilation CD.
How to Contact: Write first and obtain permission to submit. Prefers cassette with 2-3 songs. "Unsolicited material will be unopened and discarded." Does not return material. Reports in 1 month.
Music: Mostly **rock, alternative rock** and **AOR**; also **hard rock** and **progressive rock**. Executive producer for the full-length compilation CDs "Seattle Music Scene" (Vol. 1 & 2) and "Seattle Women In Rock." Produced "Taste of Reality" (by Shinn, Scattergood, Castor), recorded by Melody Rain (heavy rock); "Sedation" (by Clay World/Iob), recorded by Clay World (alternative rock); and "Universal Mother" (by B. Baronne), recorded by Brigitte Baronne Band (AOR), all on Insight Records. Other artists include What Happened, Jill Cohn and Life Like Feel.
Tips: "Be professional. Learn all you can about the recording industry."

INTRIGUE PRODUCTION, Suite 206, 6245 Bristol Pkwy., Culver CA 90230. (213)417-3084, ext. 206. Producer: Larry McGee. Record producer and record company (Intrigue Productions). Estab. 1986. Deals with artists and songwriters. Produces 6 singles, 3 12″ singles, 1 LP, 4 EPs and 2 CDs/year. Fee derived from sales royalty when song or artist is recorded.
How to Contact: Submit demo tape by mail. Unsolicited submissions are OK. Prefers cassette or reel-to-reel (or VHS videocassette if available) with 1-4 songs and lyric sheets. "Please put your strongest performance upfront. Select material based on other person's opinions." SASE. Reports in 2 months.
Music: Mostly **R&B, pop, rap** and **rock**; also **dance** and **A/C**. Produced "Starflower" (by Joe Cacamisse), recorded by Starflower (A/C); "Too Tough" (by Terrence Jones), recorded by En-Tux (pop); and "Got It Going On" (by Alan Walker), recorded by Executives (R&B), all on Mega Star Records.
Tips: "Make sure your song has a strong melody and a catchy chorus."

IVORY PRODUCTIONS, INC., Suite #3, 212 N. 12th St., Philadelphia PA 19107. (215)977-9777. Contact: Vincent Kershner, David Ivory. Record producer. Estab. 1986. Deals with artists/labels and managers/attorneys. Produces 10 CDs/year. Fee derived from "varying proportions of outright fee and royalties."
How to Contact: Submit demo tape by mail. Unsolicited submissions are OK. Prefers cassette with 3 songs. SASE. Reports in 6 weeks.
Music: Mostly **rock** and **pop**. Produced *Big Magic Blue*, written and recorded by Peter's Cathedral on 7 Records; *Reindeer Games*, written and recorded by Pat Godwin and *It's A Tough Town*, written and recorded by The Cutaways!, both on Rage-N-Records. Other artists include The Spelvins, Crossbone Pie, Chuck Treece, Anthrophobia, Tony Reyes, Don Himlin, The Roots, Jimmy Bruno, Waiting For Rain, Iota, Keiran Kaci and Do Or Die.

J.L. PRODUCTIONS, 4303 Teesdale Ave., Studio City CA 91604. Owner: Jeff Lorenzen. Record producer and engineer. Estab. 1988. Deals with artists only (no songwriters). Produces 5 singles, 5 12″ singles, 2 CDs/year.
How to Contact: Write first for permission to submit. Solicited material only. Reports in 6 weeks.
Music: Pop, **R&B, alternative pop** and **alternative rock**. Produced "Too Young To Love You," written and recorded by Timmy T. on Quality Records (pop). Mixed "Sweet November" (by Babyface), recorded by Troop on Atlantic Records (pop/R&B); and "Love Never Dies" (by Sami McKinney), recorded by Patti LaBelle on MCA Records (pop/R&B). Other artists include Go West, Curt Smith (from Tears for Fears), Paul Young, Martin Page, Clannad, Fine Young Cannibals, Jody Watley, The Whispers, The Isley Bros., New Edition, The Jacksons, and many more.

Tips: "When writing songs, always start with a simple, memorable melody based on chords that capture a particular mood. Also, make sure the vocal performance is strong. These are the two most important presentations on a tape. No amount of bells and whistles or production will make up for them."

JAG STUDIO, LTD., 3801-C Western Blvd., Raleigh NC 27606. (919)821-2059. Record producer, music publisher (Electric Juice Tunes/BMI), record company (JAG Records) and recording studio. Estab. 1981. Deals with artists and songwriters. Produces 10 singles, 12 LPs and 6 CDs/year. Fee derived from outright fee from recording artist or record company.
How to Contact: Write first and obtain permission to submit. Does not return unsolicited material. Reports in 1-2 months.
Music: Mostly **pop/dance, rap** and **rock**; also **country** and **gospel**. Produced *un-named* (by John Custer), recorded by DAG on Columbia Records (alternative); *Sweet Little Lass*, written and recorded by Cry of Love on Columbia Records (rock); and *Mindhorse*, written and recorded by Mindhorse on Uninhibited Productions (rock). Other artists include Johnny Quest, Bad Checks, John Custer, COC, Ellen Harlow, Stacy Jackson, Doug Jervey, Larry Hutcherson and Automatic Slim.
Tips: "Be prepared. Learn something about the *BUSINESS* end of music first."

NEAL JAMES PRODUCTIONS, P.O. Box 121626, Nashville TN 37212. (615)726-3556. President: Neal James. Record producer, music publisher (Cottage Blue Music/BMI, Neal James Music/BMI) and record company (Kottage Records). Estab. 1971. Produces 16 singles and 4 CDs and LPs/year. Deals with artists and songwriters. Fee derived from sales royalty when song or artist is recorded or outright fee from recording artist or record company.
How to Contact: Submit demo tape by mail. Unsolicited submissions are OK. Prefers cassette (or VHS videocassette if available) with 2 songs and lyric sheet. SASE. Reports in 1 month.
Music: Mostly **country, pop/rock** and **R&B**; also **gospel**. Produced "I Close My Eyes," written and recorded by Judie Bell; "Texas Eyes" (by Neal James), recorded by Terry Barbay; and "Tell Me," written and recorded by Bill Fraser, all on Kottage Records. Other artists include P.J. Hawk and Jeremiah Hedge.

SUNNY JAMES, 1051 Saxonburg Blvd., Glenshaw PA 15116. (412)487-6565. Producer: Sunny James. Record producer, music publisher, record company (Golden Triangle). Estab. 1987. Deals with artists only. Produces 2 singles, 8 12″ singles, 18 LPs and 9 CDs/year. Fee derived from sales royalty or outright fee from record company.
How to Contact: Submit demo tape by mail—unsolicited submissions are OK. Prefers cassette, 15 ips reel-to-reel (or ½″ VHS videocassette if available) with 3 songs and lyric or lead sheet. SASE. Reports in 2 months.
Music: Mostly **R&B, country** and **rock**; also **A/C** and **jazz**. Produced "Baby Blue," written and recorded by F. Johnson; "Dear Don't Wait For Me" (by F. Johnson), recorded by The Marcels; and "After You," written and recorded by F. Johnson. Other artists include Joe DeSimone, Steve Grice (The Boxtops), The Original Marcels, Bingo Mundy, Cornelius Harp, Fred Johnson, Richard Harris, Brian (Badfinger) McClain and City Heat.

*JAMLAND STUDIOS, 10988 Noble Ave., Mission Hills CA 91345. (818)361-2224. Owner: Roger Curley. Record producer, record company (Hipnautical) and music publisher. Estab. 1984. Deals with artists and songwriters. Produces 6 CDs/year. "Every deal is different."
How to Contact: Write or call first and obtain permission to submit. Prefers cassette or DAT with lyric sheet. SASE. Reports in 1 month.
Music: Mostly **songs about sailing and the ocean, New Age, soft rock** and **modern jazz**; also **world beat, innovative** and **reggae/island sound**. Produced *A Sailing Adventure*, *The Sensations of Sailing* and *Which Wayz Out* (by Roger Curley), recorded by The Monday Buds on Hipnautical Records. Other artists include Zarley, Bob Youngblood and Trade Winds.
Tips: "Don't be a copycat band, be sure it grooves more than flashes."

ALEXANDER JANOULIS PRODUCTIONS, 1957 Kilburn Dr., Atlanta GA 30324. (404)662-6661. President: Alex Janoulis. Record producer. Deals with artists and songwriters. Produces 6 singles and 2 CDs/year. Fee derived from sales royalty or outright fee from recording artist or record company.
How to Contact: Write first and obtain permission to submit. "Letters should be short, requesting submission permission." Prefers cassette with 1-3 songs. "Tapes will not be returned without SASE." Reports in 2 months.
Music: Mostly **top 40, rock** and **pop**; also **black** and **disco**. Produced "He's A Rebel" (by Gene Pitney), recorded by Secret Lover on HotTrax Records (pop); *Stop!*, written and recorded by the Chesterfield Kings on Mirror Records (rock); and *P is For Pig*, written and recorded by The Pigs on HotTrax Records (pop). Other artists include Night Shadows, Starfoxx, Splatter and Big Al Jano. "Album produced for Chesterfield Kings was reviewed in *Rolling Stone*."

JAY JAY PUBLISHING & RECORD CO., 35 NE 62nd St., Miami FL 33138. (305)758-0000. Owner: Walter Jagiello. Record producer, music publisher (BMI) and record company (Jay Jay Record, Tape and Video Co.). Estab. 1951. Deals with artists and songwriters. Produces 12 singles, 12 LPs and 12 CDs/year. Fee derived from sales royalty when song or artist is recorded.
How to Contact: Submit demo tape by mail. Unsolicited submissions are OK. Prefers cassette (or VHS videocassette if available) with 6 songs and lyric and lead sheet. "Quality cassette or reel-to-reel, sheet music and lyrics." SASE. Reports in 2 months.
Music: Mostly **ballads**, **love songs**, **country music** and **comedy**; also **polkas** and **waltzes**. Produced *Donna, I Really Wanna*; *Looking for You* and *You're Always In My Dreams* (by W.E. Jagiello), all recorded by Li'L Wally on Jay Jay Records. Other artists include Mil-Eu Duo, Eddie Kuta and Orchestra.

JAZZAND, 12 Micieli Place, Brooklyn NY 11218. (718)972-1220. President: Rick Stone. Record producer, music publisher (BMI) and record company. Estab. 1984. Deals with artists only. Produces 1 LP/year. Fee derived from outright fee from recording artist or record company.
How to Contact: Write or call first and obtain permission to submit. Prefers cassette. Does not return unsolicited material. Reports in 2 weeks.
Music: Mostly **jazz (straight ahead)**, **bebop** and **hard bop**. Produced *Blues for Nobody*, *Lullaby For Alex* and *Far East*, written and recorded by Rick Stone on Jazzand Records (jazz).
Tips: "We are only interested in acoustic, straight ahead jazz. Please do not send unsolicited demos. Call or write first!"

JERICHO SOUND LAB, Box 407, Jericho VT 05465. (802)899-3787. Owner: Bobby Hackney. Record producer, music publisher (Elect Music/BMI) and record company (LBI Records). Estab. 1988. Deals with artists and songwriters. Produces 5 singles, 2 12″ singles and 3 LPs/year. Fee derived from sales royalty or outright fee from record company.
How to Contact: Submit demo tape by mail. Unsolicited submissions are OK. Prefers cassette or VHS videocassette with 3-4 songs and lyric sheet. SASE. Reports in 6 weeks.
Music: Mostly **reggae**, **R&B** and **pop**; also **New Age** and **rock**. Produced "Let's Go Flying" (by B. Hackney), recorded by Lambsbread (reggae); "This Love" (by B. Hackney), recorded by Hackneys; and "Like An Ocean" (by B. Hackney), recorded by Carrie Taylor, all on LBI Records.
Tips: "Make it clear what you want. We look for labels to distribute our songs, so we like finished product to present. We record it, or you record it, as long as it's a professional presentation."

JGM RECORDING STUDIO, 4121 N. Laramie, Chicago IL 60641. Producer: Lito Manlucu. Record producer. Estab. 1991. Deals with artists and songwriters. Produces 1 single, 1 LP and 1 CD/year. Fee derived from sales royalty.
How to Contact: Submit demo tape by mail. Unsolicited submissions OK. Prefers cassette with 3 songs and lyric sheet. SASE. Reports in 1 month.
Music: Mostly **pop**, **R&B** and **rock**; also **foreign music**, **dance**. Produced "Blue Jean" (by Lito Manlucu), recorded by Jane Park on Independent Records (dance/pop).

*JK JAM PRODUCTIONS, Saratoga Mall, Saratoga NY 12866. (518)584-9020. Director of A&R: Jamie Keats. Record producer and music publisher. Estab. 1990. Deals with artists and songwriters. Produces 6 CDs/year. Fee derived from sales royalty when song or artist is recorded, or outright fee from recording artist.
How to Contact: Call first and obtain permission to submit. Prefers cassette with 4 songs and lyric sheet. "Mastered quality recordings only." Does not return material. Reports in 1-2 months.
Music: Mostly **alternative**, **R&B/dance** and **rock**; also **pop/country**. Produced *Paul Traudt*, written and recorded by Paul Traudt (alternative); *Doug Lawler*, written and recorded by Doug Lawler (pop/country); and *Tommy Higgins*, written and recorded by Tommy Higgins (rock), all on JK Jam Productions. Other artists include Alan Dunham and Mark Bombard.
Tips: "Maintain originality. Don't be conditioned by proven formulas. Master your timing and performance. Let us tailor your sound for today's market."

*LITTLE RICHIE JOHNSON, Box 3, Belen NM 87002. (505)864-7441. Contact: Tony Palmer. Record producer, music publisher (BMI) and record company (LRJ). Estab. 1959. Deals with artists only. Produces 6 singles, 3 12″ singles, 6 CDs and 6 LPs/year. Fee derived from outright fee from recording artist.
How to Contact: Submit demo tape by mail. Unsolicited submissions are OK. Prefers cassette with 4 songs. SASE. Reports in 1 month.
Music: Mostly **country**. Produced "Keeper of the Keys" (by Wayne Steward), recorded by Jerry Jaramillo (country) and "Mario & the General" written and recorded by Joe King, both on LRJ Records. Other artists include Sam West IV, Elmer Fudpucker, Tommy Thompson, Rowe Bros., Bonnie Lou Bishop and Lacy Salazas.

RALPH D. JOHNSON, Dept. SM, 114 Catalpa Dr., Mt. Juliet TN 37122. (615)754-2950. President: Ralph D. Johnson. Record producer, music publisher (Big Wedge Music) and record company. Estab. 1960. Deals with artists and songwriters. Produces 10 singles/year. Fee derived from sales royalty.
How to Contact: Submit demo tape by mail. Unsolicited submissions are OK. Prefers cassette with maximum of 4 songs. Does not return unsolicited material. Reports in 2 weeks.
Music: Mostly **country** and **novelty**. Recorded "In the Middle of the Nighttime" (by Ralph D. Johnson), recorded by Joey Welz on Caprice Records (country); "Shot in the Dark," written and recorded by Stacy Edwards; and "The Other Side of Midnight," written and recorded by Dean Mitchell, both on Wedge Records. Other artists include Cindy Jackson, Calmus Sisters and Kathy Johnson.
Tips: "Be critical of your own material before submitting."

JUMP PRODUCTIONS, 71 Langemunt, 9420 Aaigem **Belgium**. Phone: (053)62-73-77. General Manager: Eddy Van Mouffaert. Record producer and music publisher (Jump Music). Estab. 1976. Deals with artists and songwriters. Produces 25 singles and 2 LPs/year. Fee derived from sales royalty when song or artist is recorded.
How to Contact: Submit demo tape by mail. Unsolicited submissions are OK. Prefers cassette. Does not return unsolicited material. Reports in 2 weeks.
Music: Mostly **ballads, up-tempo, easy listening, disco** and **light pop**; also **instrumentals**. Produced "Liefde Voor Muziek" (by Eddy Govert), recorded by Evelien on Scorpion Records (Flemish); "Just A Friend" (by Eddy Govert), recorded by Sherly on Ideal Records (pop); and *Nostalgic Dreams* (by Jimmy Towers), recorded by Le Grand Julot on BMP Records (accordion).

JUNE PRODUCTIONS LTD., "Toftrees," Church Rd., Woldingham, Surrey CR3 7JH **England**. Managing Director: David Mackay. Record producer, music producer (Sabre Music) and record company (Tamarin, PRT Records). Estab. 1970. Produces 6 singles, 3 LPs and 3 CDs/year. Deals with artists and songwriters. Fee derived from sales royalty.
How to Contact: Submit demo tape by mail—unsolicited submissions are OK. Prefers cassette with 1-2 songs and lyric sheet. SAE and IRC. Reports in 8-10 weeks.
Music: MOR, **rock** and **top 40/pop**. Produced *If I Love You*, recorded by Sarah Jory on Roxy Records (country rock); *Best of Joe Fagin*, recorded by Joe Fagin on Westmere Records (adult rock); and *Sunshine Girl*, written and recorded by Jeff Turner on K-tel Records (country rock). Other artists include Jon English and John Parr.

GENE KENNEDY ENTERPRISES, INC., 3950 N. Mt. Juliet Rd., Mt. Juliet TN 37122. (615)754-0417. President: Gene Kennedy. Vice President: Karen Jeglum Kennedy. Record producer, independent distribution and promotion firm and music publisher (Chip 'N' Dale Music Publishers, Inc./ASCAP, Door Knob Music Publishing, Inc./BMI and Lodestar Music/SESAC). Estab. 1975. Deals with artists and songwriters. Produces 5-10 CDs/year. Fee derived from sales royalty or outright fee from recording artist or record company.
How to Contact: Submit demo tape by mail. Unsolicited submissions are OK. Prefers cassette with up to 3 songs and lyric sheet. "Do not send in a way that has to be signed for." SASE (appropriate size for tapes). Reports in 3 weeks.
Music: Country and **gospel**. Produced "Lord Knows I'm Trying" (by R. Preston/L. Preston), recorded by Bo Harrison (country); and "It Should Have Been Me" (by David Parr), recorded by David Reed (gospel), both on Door Knob Records.

*****KINGSPORT CREEK MUSIC,** Box 6085, Burbank CA 91510. Contact: Vice President. Record producer and music publisher. Deals with artists and songwriters.
How to Contact: Submit demo tape by mail. Unsolicited submissions are OK. Prefers cassette (or VHS videocassette). Does not return unsolicited material. "Include photo and bio if possible."
Music: Mostly **country, MOR, R&B, pop** and **gospel**. Produced "Leading Me On," "Pick Up Your Feet" and "With Me Still," all written and recorded by Melvena Kaye on Cowgirl Records.

KINGSTON RECORDS AND TALENT, 15 Exeter Rd., Kingston NH 03848. (603)642-8493. Coordinator: Harry Mann. Record producer, music publisher (Strawberry Soda Publishing/ASCAP) and record company (Kingston Records). Estab. 1988. Deals with artists and songwriters. Produces 3-4 singles, 2-3 12″ singles, 2-3 LPs and 1-2 CDs/year. Fee derived from sales royalty. Deals primarily with NE and local artists.
How to Contact: Write first and obtain permission to submit. Prefers cassette with 1-2 songs and lyric sheet. Does not return material. Reports in 6-8 weeks.
Music: Mostly **rock, country** and **pop**; "no heavy metal." Produced *5¢ Strawberry Soda* and "Message To You," written and recorded by Doug Mitchell; and *Songs Piped from the Moon*, written and recorded by S. Pappas, all on Kingston Records. Other artists include Bob Moore, Candy Striper Death Orgy, Pocket Band, Jeff Walker, J. Evans, NTM and Miss Bliss.

Tips: "I believe electronic music is going a bit too far and there is an opportunity for a comeback of real as opposed to sequenced music."

KMA, Suite 900, 1650 Broadway, New York NY 10019-6833. (212)265-1570. A&R Director: Morris Levy. Record producer, music publisher (Block Party Music/ASCAP). Estab. 1987. Deals with artists and songwriters. Produces 2 12″ singles, 3 LPs and 3 CDs/year. Fee derived from sales royalty or outright fee from recording artist or record company.
How to Contact: Submit demo tape by mail. Prefers cassette. SASE. Reports in 3 months.
Music: Mostly **R&B, dance** and **rap**; also **movie** and **ethnic**. Produced *In The Blood* (by Kissel/Halbreich), recorded by various artists on Rykodisc Records (African); *Let It Rain, Let It Pour* (by Kissel), recorded by Robin Clark and the David Bowie Band on HME/CBS Records; and *Street Jazz* (by Kissel), recorded by various artists on MicMac Records.
Tips: *"Original* lyrics a huge plus."

KNOWN ARTIST PRODUCTIONS, 1219 Kerlin Ave., Brewton AL 36426. (205)867-2228. President: Roy Edwards. Record producer, music publisher (Cheavoria Music Co./BMI, Baitstring Music/ASCAP) and record company (Bolivia Records, Known Artist Records). Estab. 1972. Deals with artists and songwriters. Produces 10 singles and 3 LPs/year. Fee derived from sales royalty when song or artist is recorded.
How to Contact: "Write first about your interest." Prefers cassette with 3 songs and lyric sheet. Reports in 1 month. "All tapes will be kept on file."
Music: Mostly **country, R&B** and **pop**; also **easy listening, MOR** and **soul**. Produced "Got To Let You Know," "You Are My Sunshine" and "You Make My Life So Wonderful," all written and recorded by Roy Edwards on Bolivia Records (R&B). Other artists include Jim Portwood, Bobbie Roberson and Brad Smiley.
Tips: "Write a good song that tells a good story."

*KOOL BREEZE PRODUCTIONS, N. 81 Lane, P.O. Box 120, Loxahatchee FL 33470. (407)795-4232. Executive Director: Kevin Reeves. Marketing Manager: Debbie Reeves. Record producer, music publisher. Estab. 1991. Deals with artists and songwriters. Produces 10 singles, 6 LPs and 6 CDs/year. Fee derived from sales royalty when song or artist is recorded or outright fee from record company.
How to Contact: Submit demo tape by mail. Unsolicited submissions are OK. Prefers cassette and lyric sheet (typed and full size). "Commercially viable to industry standards. Strong hooks, definitive melody, uplifting lyrical concepts, SASE required for all correspondence, don't be predictable." SASE. Reports in 2 months.
Music: Mostly **pop contemporary (dance), rock (pop, blues, folk, soft, jazz), A/C, electric acoustic**; also **country (pop, blues)** and **blues (R&B, urban)**. Produced *Natural Love*, written and recorded by Jayne Margo-Reby on Rustron Records (A/C); *Dynamic Derrick* (by Kevin Reeves), recorded by Dynamic Derrick on Kool Breeze Records (A/C dance pop); and *City Song* (by Ron Caruso/Rusty Gordon), recorded by Jayne Margo-Reby on Rustron Records (pop rock). Other artists include Andy Atkins, Kevin Reeves, Catfish and Boogie Brigade.
Tips: "Seek collaborating partner(s) if you are 60%+ lyric dominant or 60%+ melody dominant. Non-performing songwriters encouraged to submit. Write for performing artists who accept original songs and do not record exclusively their own originals. Read record labels for credit."

*ROBERT R. KOVACH, Box 7018, Warner Robins GA 31095-7018. (912)953-2800. Producer: Robert R. Kovach. Record producer. Estab. 1976. Deals with artists and songwriters. Produces 6 singles, 2 cassettes and 1 CD/year. Works with composers. Fee derived from sales royalty.
How to Contact: Submit demo tape—unsolicited submissions are OK. Prefers cassette with 4 songs and lyric sheet. SASE. Reports in 3 months.
Music: Mostly **country** and **pop**; also **easy listening, R&B, rock** and **gospel**.
Tips: "Be simple and sincere with your songs. Write in the form of normal conversation with a twist."

KREN MUSIC PRODUCTIONS, P.O. Box 5804, Hacienda Heights CA 91745. (818)855-1692. Co-owner: Kris Clark. Record producer, music publisher (BMI). Estab. 1985. Deals with artists and songwriters. Produces 10 singles and 4 LPs/year. Fee derived from sales royalty when song or artist is recorded.
How to Contact: Submit demo tape by mail. Unsolicited submissions are OK. Prefers cassette with 3 songs and lyric sheet. SASE. Reports in 2 months.
Music: Mostly **country, pop** and **rock**; also **gospel, R&B** and **New Age**. Produced *Twinkle, Twinkle Lucky Star* and *Chill Factor*, both written and recorded by Merle Haggard on Epic/CBS Records; and

---

The types of music each listing is interested in are printed in boldface.

"Where Fools Are Kings" (by Jeffrey Steele), recorded by Steve Wariner on CBS Records.
Tips: "The demo tape must show the best of the song you've got to offer."

L.A. ENTERTAINMENT, 6367 Selma Ave., Hollywood CA 90028. (213)467-1411. Fax: (213)462-8562. Vice President/A&R: Glen D. Duncan. Record Producer (Jim Ervin Productions), record company (Livin' Large Records) and music publisher (Songbroker Publishing/ASCAP). Estab. 1988. Deals with artists and songwriters. Fee derived from sales royalty when song or artist is recorded.
How to Contact: Submit demo tape by mail. Unsolicited submissions are OK. Prefers cassette (or videocassette if available) with 3 songs, lyric and lead sheet if available. "All written submitted materials (i.e. lyric sheets, letter, etc.) should be typed." SASE. Reports in 4-6 weeks.
Music: Mostly **alternative** and **R&B**; also **New Age, pop/rock** and **country**.
Tips: "A hit song is a hit song, whether it is recorded in a professional environment or at your home. Concentrate first on the writing of your material and then record it to the best of your ability. A professional sounding recording may help the presentation of a song, but it will not make or break a true hit."

LANDMARK COMMUNICATIONS GROUP, (formerly Landmark Audio of Nashville), P.O. Box 1444, Hendersonville TN 37077. Producer: Bill Anderson Jr. Record producer, music publisher (Newcreature Music/BMI) and TV/radio syndication. Deals with artists and songwriters. Produces 12 singles and 12 LPs/year. Works with 9 new songwriters/year. Works with composers and lyricists; teams collaborators. Fee derived from sales royalty.
How to Contact: Write first and obtain permission to submit. Prefers 7½ ips reel-to-reel or cassette (or videocassette) with 4-10 songs and lyric sheet. SASE. Reports in 1 month.
Music: Mostly **country crossover**; also **blues, country, gospel, jazz, rock** and **top 40/pop**. Produced "Good Love," written and recorded by Gail Score (R&B); "A Hero Never Dies," written and recorded by Joanne Cash Yates on Jana Records (gospel); and "Nothin' Else Feels Quite Like It" (by B. Nash/K. Nash/B. Anderson), recorded on TV Theme Records (country). Other artists include Skeeter Davis and Vernon Oxford.

LARI-JON PRODUCTIONS, 325 W. Walnut, Rising City NE 68658. (402)542-2336. Owner: Larry Good. Record producer, music publisher (Lari-Jon Publishing/BMI) and record company (Lari-Jon Records). Estab. 1967. Deals with artists and songwriters. Produces 10 singles and 5 LPs/year. "Producer's fees are added into session costs."
How to Contact: Submit demo tape by mail—unsolicited submissions are OK. "Must be a professional demo." SASE. Reports in 2 months.
Music: **Country, gospel-Southern** and **50's rock**. Produced *Glory Bound Train*, written and recorded by Tom Campbell; *Hanging From the Bottom*, written and recorded by Johnny Nace; and "Pick Me Up On Your Way Down" (by Harlan Howard), recorded by Larry Good, all on Lari-Jon Records. Other artists include Kent Thompson.
Tips: "Be professional in all aspects of the music business."

LARK TALENT & ADVERTISING, Box 35726, Tulsa OK 74153. (918)749-1648. Owner: Jana Jae. Record producer, music publisher (Jana Jae Music/BMI) and record company (Lark Record Productions, Inc.). Estab. 1980. Deals with artists and songwriters. Fee derived from sales royalty when song or artist is recorded.
How to Contact: Submit demo tape by mail. Unsolicited submissions are OK. Prefers cassette or VHS videocassette with 3 songs and lead sheet. Does not return unsolicited material.
Music: Mostly **country, bluegrass** and **classical**; also **instrumentals**. Produced "Fiddlestix" (by Jana Jae); "Mayonnaise" (by Steve Upfold); and "Flyin' South" (by Cindy Walker), all recorded by Jana Jae on Lark Records. Other artists include Sydni, Hotwire and Matt Greif.

JOHN LEAVELL, 2045 Anderson Snow, Spring Hill FL 34609. (904)799-6102. Producer: John Leavell. Record producer and recording studio. Estab. 1980. Deals with artists and songwriters. Produces 10-12 singles/year. Fee derived from outright fee from recording artist and record company. Charges artist upfront for demo production.
How to Contact: Submit demo tape—unsolicited submissions are OK. Prefers cassette (or VHS videocassette if available) with 4-5 songs and lyric sheet. SASE. Reports in 1 month.
Music: Mostly **Christian rock, Christian contemporary** and **gospel**; also **rock** and **country**. Produced "Sons of Thunder" (by Tom Butler), recorded by Sons of Thunder; *Mr. Hyde*, recorded by Mr. Hyde; and *Morning Star*, recorded by Morning Star, all on Leavell Records. Other artists include Greg Eadler, Jim Butler, Tom Martin, Final Stand and One Eyed Jack.
Tips: "Make the best first impression you can! Always keep writing new material."

LEE SOUND PRODUCTIONS, RON LEE, VALUE FOR MONEY, HOPPY PRODUCTIONS, Stewart House, Hill Bottom Road, Sands-Ind. Est., Highwycombe, Buckinghamshire HP12-4HJ **England**.

Phone: (0630)647374. Fax: (0630)647612. Contact: Catherine Lee. Record producer. Estab. 1971. Deals with artists and songwriters. Fee is negotiable.

How to Contact: Submit demo tape by mail. Unsolicited submissions are OK. Prefers cassette (or VHS/PAL videocassette if available) and still photos (8×10) with 3 songs and lyric sheet or lead sheets. SAE and IRC. Reports in 2 months.

Music: All types. Produced *Hit & Run*, *Necro* and *I Hate School*, all written and recorded by Suburban Studs on Anaeram Records (punk).

LEEWAY ENTERTAINMENT GROUP, (formerly Wilshire Artists), Suite 870, 100 Wilshire Blvd., Santa Monica CA 90401. (310)917-5666. Fax: (310)917-5646. Producer: Daniel Leeway. Record producer, recording studios (The Leeway Studios, 32 Track Digital). Estab. 1991. Deals with artists and songwriters. Fee derived from sales royalty when song or artist is recorded, or outright fee from recording artist, unless other arrangements have been made.

How to Contact: Write or call first to arrange personal interview, or submit demo tape by mail. Unsolicited submissions are OK. Prefers cassette, DAT or CD with 2 songs and lyric sheet. SASE. Reports in 1 month minimum.

Music: Mostly **dance, pop** and **New Age.**

Tips: "Send all submissions as though you were submitting a business proposal to an investor. We are not going to invest in you or your material if you are not willing to invest in yourself. Be well prepared, patient, and confident about your talents. We will contact you if we are interested."

LETHAL AUDIO WORK("LAW"), 2610 Mackenzie St., Vancouver, B.C. V6K4A1 Canada. (604)738-0569. Producer: Mark Charpentier. Record producer, consulting. Estab. 1991. Deals with artists and songwriters. Produces 3 CDs/year. Fee derived from outright fee from recording artist.

How to Contact: Submit demo tape by mail. Unsolicited submissions are OK. Prefers DAT or TDK SA-X cassette (or VHS/SVHS videocassette if available). "Include equipment used in demo." SASE. Reports in 2 weeks.

Music: Video, film, scoring and **post production.** Produced *Why Be Normal*, written and recorded by Spinal Chord on VAMS Records.

LINEAR CYCLE PRODUCTIONS, Box 2608, Sepulveda CA 91393-2608. Producer: R. Borowy. Record producer. Estab. 1980. Deals with artists and songwriters. Produces 15-25 singles, 6-10 12″ singles, 15-20 LPs and 10 CDs/year. Fee derived from sales royalty when song or artist is recorded.

How to Contact: Submit demo tape—unsolicited submissions are OK. Prefers cassette or 7⅜ ips reel-to-reel (or ½″ VHS or ¾″ videocassette if available). Does not return unsolicited material. Reports in 6 weeks to 6 months.

Music: Mostly **rock/pop, R&B/blues** and **country**; also **gospel** and **comedy.** Produced "Last Laff" (by McPwee), recorded by Melvin O'Twist on Nu-Age Records; "I Cannot Find the Tree" (by E. Link), recorded by Smelly Overhaul on Forget It Records; and "Shee . . ." (by N.C. Jail), recorded by N'Gill'E on Jail Records.

Tips: "Send materials on high quality tapes or CDs. We cannot accept anything poorly recorded."

*LJG PRODUCTIONS, P.O. Box 47, Mt. Meigs AL 36057-0047. (215)272-4883. Owner: James Grayson. Record producer and music publisher (LJG Publishing/BMI). Estab. 1993. Deals with artists and songwriters. Fee derived from sales royalty when song or artist is recorded or outright fee from record company.

How to Contact: Submit demo tape by mail. Unsolicited submissions are OK. Prefers cassette with 3-4 songs and lyric sheet. "Include short bio, possible goals to achieve in music industry." SASE. Reports in 2-4 weeks.

Music: Mostly **funk, R&B** and **rap**; also **pop** and **jazz.** Produced "My Love Is Gone" and "I Miss You" (by Louis J. Grayson), recorded by Stacy Bryant on SNA Records (R&B); and "Real Funk"(by Louis J. Grayson/Eric Davis), recorded by Eric D on LJG Records (rap). Other artists include Jaymes & the Chadeau, Florence Barnes and Billy Simpson.

Tips: "Artists should send music representative of the genre they wish to work in. All songwriters and performers should be specific in what they wish LJG Productions to accomplish for them."

LOCO SOUNDS, 603 E. Broadway, Denver City TX 79323-3311. (806)592-8020. Fax: (806)592-9486. Producer/Owner: Jere' Lowe. Record producer, record company and music publisher (Fab 5 Records, Jere' Lowe Publishing/BMI). Estab. 1978. Deals with artists and songwriters. Produces 10 singles and 3 CDs/year. Fee derived from sales royalty when song or artist is recorded or outright fee from recording artist or record company.

How to Contact: Submit demo tape by mail. Unsolicited submissions are OK. Prefers cassette (or videocassette) with 3 songs and lyric sheet. "Best songs only—better quality demos sell songs." Reports in 1 month.

Music: Mostly **new** or **young country**, **R&B** and **Spanish**; also **pop/top 40**, **children's** and **adult contemporary**. Writer, publisher and music producer for "Imagineland," Jack Houston's children's TV program.

Tips: "On demos please be very word strong—we need to hear your voice."

LOCONTO PRODUCTIONS, Box 16540, Plantation FL 33318. (305)741-7766. President: Frank X. Loconto. Record producer and music publisher. Estab. 1978. Deals with artists and songwriters. Produces 20 singles and 20 LPs/year. Fee derived from sales royalty or outright fee from songwriter/artist and/or record company.

How to Contact: Write first and obtain permission to submit. Prefers cassette. SASE.

Music: Produced "Calypso Alive and Well," written and recorded by Obediah Colebrock (island music); "Standing on the Top" (by various artists), recorded by Mark Rone (country); and "Walking on Air" (by Ken Hatch), recorded by Frank Loconto (motivational), all on FXL Records. Other artists include Bruce Mullin, Bill Dillon, James Billie (folk music) and the Lane Brothers.

*LONDON BRIJJ PRODUCTIONS, 817 E. Locust Ave., Philadelphia PA 19138. (215)438-9882. Producer/engineer: Jae London. Record producer, music publisher (Amaj Int'l Music/BMI) and production company. Estab. 1984. Deals with artists and songwriters. Produces 7 singles, 3 12" singles, 3 LPs and 2 CDs/year. Fee derived from sales royalty when song or artist is recorded or outright fee from record company.

How to Contact: Submit demo tape by mail. Unsolicited submissions are OK. Prefers cassette (or VHS videocassette if available) with 3 songs and lyric sheet. SASE. Reports in 2-4 weeks.

Music: Mostly **R&B**, **reggae** and **ballads**; also **hip hop**, **club/house** and **rap**. Produced "Dancing the Nite Away"(by Altamont Arthurs Jr.), recorded by Jamvin (hip hop reggae); *Jump, Dance, More* (by Rob Weird/M.C. Ray), recorded by M.C. Ray (club/house), both on In Effect Records; and "You Say You Love" (by K. Arthurs), recorded by Jamvin on Amaj Records (New Age). Other artists include Kenny Brown, Saidel, Jae London, Darryl Ray and Drexx Int'l.

HAROLD LUICK & ASSOCIATES, Box B, Carlisle IA 50047. (515)989-3748. Record producer, music industry consultant and music publisher. Deals with artists and songwriters. Produces 20 singles and 6 LPs/year. Fee derived from sales royalty, outright fee from artist/songwriter or record company, and from consulting fees for information or services.

How to Contact: Call or write first. Prefers cassette with 3-5 songs and lyric sheet. SASE. Reports in 3 weeks.

Music: **Traditional country**, **gospel**, **contemporary country** and **MOR**. Produced Bob Everhart's *Everhart*; Don Laughlin's *Ballads of Deadwood S.D.*; and Darrell Thomas' singles and LPs. "Over a 12-year period, Harold Luick has produced and recorded 412 singles and 478 albums, 7 of which charted and some of which have enjoyed independent sales in excess of 30,000 units."

Tips: "We are interested in helping the new artist/songwriter make it 'the independent way.' This is the wave of the future. As music industry consultants, our company sells ideas, information and results. Songwriters can increase their chances by understanding that recording and songwriting is a business. 80% of the people who travel to large recording/publishing areas of our nation arrive there totally unprepared as to what the industry wants or needs from them. Do yourself a favor. Prepare, investigate and only listen to people who are qualified to give you advice. Do not implement anything until you understand the rules and pitfalls."

JIM McCOY PRODUCTIONS, Rt. 2, Box 114, Berkeley Springs WV 25411. President: Jim McCoy. Record producer and music publisher (Jim McCoy Music/BMI). Estab. 1964. Deals with artists and songwriters. Produces 12-15 singles and 6 LPs/year. Fee derived from sales royalty.

How to Contact: Submit demo tape—unsolicited submissions are OK. Prefers cassette or 7½ or 15 ips reel-to-reel (or Beta or VHS videocassette if available) with 6 songs and lyric or lead sheets. Does not return unsolicited material. Reports in 1 month.

Music: Mostly **country**, **rock** and **gospel**; also **country/rock** and **bluegrass**. Produced "Dyin' Rain" and "I'm Gettin Nowhere," both written and recorded by J.B. Miller on Hilton Records (country). Other artists include Mel McQuain, Red Steed, R. Lee Gray, John Aikens and Jim McCoy.

*MADISON STATION PRODUCTIONS, 953 Highway 51, Box 1951, Madison MS 39130-1951. (601)856-7468. Producer: Style Wooten. Record producer and record company (Madison Station Records). Estab. 1988. Works with artists and songwriters. Produces 15 singles and 12 LPs/year. Fee derived from sales royalty or outright fee from record company.

How to Contact: Write or call first and obtain permission to submit. Prefers cassette with 1-3 songs and lyric sheet. SASE.

Music: **Modern country** and **R&B**.

*MAGIC APPLE RECORDS, (formerly Tough Guys Productions, Inc.), Box 530605, Miami FL 33238. (305)758-1903. Chairman: Clancy. Estab. 1986. Deals with artists and songwriters. Fee derived from sales royalty when song or artist is recorded.
How to Contact: Submit demo tape by mail. Unsolicited submissions are OK. Prefers cassette (or VHS videocassette if available) with 2-3 songs and lyric sheet. "Pictures and/or bios are recommended, but not necessary." SASE. Reports in 3 weeks.
Music: Mostly **pop/dance, R&B/dance** and **rap**; also **pop/rock**. Produced "Without Your Love," written and recorded by Nardy (dance); "Chunky, Chunky," written and recorded by Down 2 Deep (rap); and "Hardcore Rebel," written and recorded by Rio and Cap (rap), all on Magic Apple Records.
Tips: "Know your field and also your business."

LEE MAGID PRODUCTIONS, Box 532, Malibu CA 90265. (213)463-5998. President: Lee Magid. Record producer and music publisher (Alexis Music, Inc./ASCAP, Marvelle Music Co./BMI, Gabal Music Co./SESAC), record company (Grass Roots Records and LMI Records) and management firm (Lee Magid Management). Estab. 1950. Deals with artists, songwriters and producers. Produces 4 singles, 4 12″ singles, 8 LPs and 8 CDs/year. Publishes 10-15 new songwriters/year. Works with artists and songwriters; teams collaborators. Fee derived from sales royalty and outright fee from recording artist.
How to Contact: "Send cassette giving address and phone number; include SASE." Prefers cassette (or VHS videocassette) with 3-6 songs and lyric sheet. "Please only one cassette, and photos if you are an artist/writer." Reports only if interested, "as soon as we can after listening."
Music: Mostly **R&B, rock, jazz** and **gospel**; also **pop, bluegrass, church/religious, easy listening, folk, blues, MOR, progressive, soul, instrumental** and **top 40**. Produced "What Shall I Do?" and "I Got Joy" (by Quincy Fielding, Jr.) and "Whenever You Call" (by Calvin Rhone), all recorded by Tramaine Hawkins on Sparrow Records (gospel rock). Other artists include Julie Miller, John M. Hides and Perry "The Prince" Walker.
Tips: "Stick with your belief and a good melody and lyric."

MAJA MUSIC, 335 Lyceum Ave., Philadelphia PA 19128. (215)487-1359. Owners: Michael Aharon and John Anthony. Record producer. Estab. 1984. Deals with artists. Produces 3 LPs, 4 EPs and 3 CDs/year. Fee derived from outright fee from recording artist or record company. "Fee covers arrangement, production, pre-production and programming. For demos, fee also covers all recording costs."
How to Contact: Submit demo tape—unsolicited submissions are OK. Prefers cassette with 3-6 songs. Artists should include photo. Does not return unsolicited material. Reports in 3 weeks.
Music: Mostly **folk-rock** and **pop/urban contemporary**; also **New Age, world-beat** and **experimental**. Produced *I Will Stand Fast* and *Jaguar*, written and recorded by Fred Small; (folk/rock); and *Out of the Darkness*, written and recorded by Tom Juravich (folk/rock), all on Flying Fish Records. Other artists include Heather Mullen, Charlie Cooper Project and Julia Haines.
Tips: "Send material which exhibits your personal style and creativity, even if it is not 'commercial' material. Individuality is starting to matter again. Lyrics are starting to matter again. Singer-songwriters are on the radio again."

*MAKERS MARK MUSIC PRODUCTIONS (ASCAP), 3033 W. Redner St., Philadelphia PA 19121. (215)236-4817. Producer: Paul E. Hopkins. Record producer. Estab. 1991. Deals with artists and songwriters. Produces 15 singles, 5 12″ singles and 4 LPs/year. Fee derived from sales royalty or outright fee from recording artist or record company (depending on situation).
How to Contact: Submit demo tape by mail. Unsolicited submissions are OK. Prefers cassette with 2-4 songs and lyric sheet. "Explain concept of your music and/or style, and your future direction as an artist or songwriter." Reports in 2-4 weeks (if interested).
Music: Mostly **R&B, dance/hip house, country** and **rap**. Produced "Baby I Want U" (by Romano/ Hopkins), recorded by Andy Romano on A/R Records; "Busted" and "Silent Love" (by Monk/Hopkins/Reed), recorded by Elain Monk on Black Sands Records.

*MAKING TEXAS MUSIC, INC., P.O. Box 1971, Longview TX 75606. (903)236-3205. Fax: (903)236-3206. Business Manager: Gary Beckworth. Record producer, record company, music publisher. Estab. 1987. Deals with artists and songwriters. Produces 10 singles, 1-2 LPs and 1 CD/year. Fee derived from sales royalty when song or artist is recorded; we pay for recording, production and mailing.
How to Contact: Submit demo tape by mail. Unsolicited submissions are OK. Prefers cassette or videocassette with 3 songs and lyric sheet. Does not return material. Reports in 3-4 weeks.
Music: Mostly **country/western, rockabilly** and **rock**. Produced "I Don't Mind Keeping Up With the Jones as Long as the Jones Is George," written and recorded by Gary Lee Hale; "Because I Care," written and recorded by John Secord, both on Making Texas Music; and "Where There's A Willie There's a Way" (by Whitey Elmer), recorded by Jerry Kilgore on Code of the West Records. Other artists include Denise Nowak, B.W. Davis, Annie Laurie Hyde, Jean Marlowe, John "Big Bubba" Sharp, Jim Thompson and Ralph Wood.

Tips: "Be brief. Send cassette and picture (if artist) with good permanent address and telephone number."

PETE MARTIN/VAAM MUSIC PRODUCTIONS, Box 29688, Hollywood CA 90029-0688. (213)664-7765. President: Pete Martin. Record producer, music publisher (Vaam Music/BMI, Pete Martin Music/ASCAP) and record company (Blue Gem Records). Estab. 1982. Deals with artists and songwriters. Produces 12 singles and 5 LPs/year. Fee derived from sales royalty.
How to Contact: Prefers cassette with 2 songs and lyric sheet. SASE. Reports in 1 month.
Music: Mostly **top 40/pop, country** and **R&B**. Producer of country acts: Sherry Weston, Frank Loren, Brian Smith & The Renegades. Pop acts: Victoria Limon, Cory Canyon.
Tips: "Study the market in the style that you write. Songs must be capable of reaching top 5 on charts."

MASTERPIECE PRODUCTIONS & STUDIOS, 7002 O'Neil, Wichita KS 67212-3353. (316)943-1190. Owner/Producer: Tim M. Raymond. Record producer (Masterpiece Productions), studio owner (Masterpiece Studio), music publisher (ArtUnique Music/ASCAP). Estab. 1980. Deals with artists and songwriters. Produces 200 singles, 10 12″ singles, 25 LPs, 5 EPs and 20 CDs/year. Fee derived from sales royalty when song or artist is recorded or outright fee from recording artist or record company.
How to Contact: Submit demo tape by mail. Unsolicited submissions are OK. Prefers cassette (or VHS videocassette) with 4-6 songs and lyric sheet. "Please send a complete promo pack (photos, tapes and bio). Prefers audio submissions on DAT tape, if available." Does not return material. Reports in 6 weeks.
Music: Mostly **gospel (Christian), pop (top 40)** and **country**; also **R&B, vocal jazz** and **rap**. Produced *Cat Paws, Rhinos at Rest* and *Colors of America* (by Lee Campbell-Towell), recorded by Cat Paws in Motion (children's). Other artists include Kim Karr, Tim Enloe and Terri Messner.
Tips: "Emphasize your uniqueness! It's what makes the difference. We are always looking for a unique talent, whether it be an artist or songwriter."

DAVID MATHES PRODUCTIONS, P.O. Box 22653, Nashville TN 37202. (615)252-6912. President: David W. Mathes. AF-FM licensed. Record producer. Estab. 1962. Deals with artists and songwriters. Produces 6-10 singles, 4-16 12″ singles and 4-6 LPs/year. Fee derived from outright fee from recording artist.
How to Contact: Submit demo tape by mail. Unsolicited submissions are OK. Prefers 7½ or 15 ips reel-to-reel or cassette (or videocassette) with 2-4 songs and lyric sheet. "Enclose correctly stamped envelope for demo return." Reports in 1 month.
Music: Mostly **country** and **gospel**; also **bluegrass, R&B** and **top 40/pop**. Produced *Memory Lane* (by Randy Hall) and *Every Once in Awhile*, written and recorded by Johnny Newman on Nesak Int'l Records (line dance); and *When I Reach Home* (by Ann Ballard), recorded by The Ballards on Heirborn Records (gospel). Other artists include Nashville Sidemen & Singers, David Mathes.
Tips: "We look for professional material and presentations. Don't expect miracles on the first song released. Try to be different in style."

SCOTT MATHEWS/HIT OR MYTH PRODUCTIONS, (formerly Proud Pork Productions), 230 Montcalm St., San Francisco CA 94110. (415)648-9099. President: Scott Mathews. Record producer and music publisher (Hang On to Your Publishing/BMI). Estab. 1975. Deals with artists and labels. Produces 6 singles and 6 CDs/year. Fee derived from sales royalty when song or artist is recorded or outright fee from recording artist on demo recordings.
How to Contact: Submit demo tape by mail. Unsolicited submissions are OK. Prefers cassette. SASE. Reports in 2-3 months. "Please, no phone calls."
Music: Mostly **rock/pop, country** and **R&B**. Produced *Riding With the King*, written and recorded by John Hiatt on Geffen Records (rock); *The Loved Ones*, written and recorded by The Loved Ones on Hightone Records (R&B); and *Tribal Thunder*, written and recorded by Dick Dale on Hightone Records (rock). Has produced Roy Orbison, Rosanne Cash, Chuck Prophet and many more. Has recorded with everyone from Barbra Streisand to Sammy Hagar, including The Beach Boys, Keith Richards, John Lee Hooker, Van Morrison, Huey Lewis and Bonnie Raitt, to name but a few.
Tips: "I am looking for singer/songwriters with emphasis on great songs and great voices of any style. I am no longer placing songs or publishing outside material. If you feel your act is ready to make records, send a tape now!"

*MEDIA PRODUCTIONS, 1001 1/2 Elizabeth St., Oak Hill WV 25901. (304)465-1298. Manager/Engineer: Hope Stapleton. Recording studio. Estab. 1984. Produces 8-12 singles, 2 12″ singles, 30-40 LPs, 20 EPs and 10 CDs/year. Fee derived from sales royalty when song or artist is recorded or outright fee from recording artist or record company.
How to Contact: Write or call first and obtain permission to submit. Prefers cassette with lyric sheet and lead sheet. "No unsolicited material please!" Does not return material. Reports in 1 month.

Music: Mostly **country**, **rock** and **gospel**; also **rap**. Produced *The Virgins*, written and recorded by the Virgins on Resistor Records (rock); *Tickle Your Fancy*, written and recorded by Diamonds & Gold on Rockhouse Records (rock); and *Dream Stealer* (by Jeanie Woods), recorded by Jeanie on T&J Records (rock). Other artists include Mark Lilly, Lee Johnson, Preston Lee, Uncle Scam, Soul Survivor and Mike Starr.

PATRICK MELFI, Suite 433, 7935 S. Main St., Salt Lake City UT 84115. (801)467-2104. Contact: Patrick Melfi. Record producer, music publisher (BMI) and record company (Alexas Records). Estab. 1984. Deals with artists and songwriters. Produces 6 singles, 2 LPs, 1 EP and 2 CDs/year. Fee derived from outright fee from record company.
How to Contact: Submit demo tape by mail. Unsolicited submissions are OK. Prefers cassette (or VHS videocassette if available) with 1-6 songs and lyric or lead sheet. SASE. Reports in 2 months.
Music: Mostly **country** and **pop**; also **soundtrack scores**. Produced "She's On Her Own" (by P. Melfi/AJ Masters), recorded by AJ Masters; "Between Your Heart & Mine" (by Melfi), recorded by Prophesy on Atlantic Records (MOR); and "Child of God" (by Melfi/Kone), recorded by Sheri Sampson on Godley Music Records (gospel). Other artists include Ellis & Franklin, Billy Swan, Alan Rich, Randy Meisner (Eagles).
Tips: "Write from the heart! Write a good story and compliment it with a strong melody. Good production is a must. Always start with a great hook!"

MIDWEST RECORDS, 3611 Cleveland Ave., Lincoln NE 68504-2452. (402)466-1446. Producer: Harold Dennis. Record producer, music publisher (Cornhusker/BMI) record company (Midwest Records) and Country Music Promotions. Estab. 1983. Deals with artists and songwriters. Produces 2 singles, 2 12" singles and 2-3 LPs/year. Fee derived from outright fee from recording artist. "We do not charge songwriters; but we do charge artists."
How to Contact: Submit demo tape by mail. Unsolicited submissions are OK. Prefers cassette with 2 songs and lyric sheets. Does not return unsolicited material. Reports in 2 months.
Music: Mostly **country** and **crossover country**. Produced *Never Think for a Moment* and "Making a Life of Your Own," both written and recorded by Ricky Spains; and "Walk Me to the Door" (by Conway Twitty), recorded by Ron Royer, all on Midwest Records.

*JAY MILLER PRODUCTIONS, 413 N. Parkerson Ave., Crowley LA 70526. (318)783-1601 or 788-0773. Contact: Jay Miller. Record producer and music publisher. Deals with artists and songwriters. Produces 50 singles and 15 LPs/year. Fee derived from sales royalty.
How to Contact: Write or call first to arrange personal interview. Prefers cassette for audition.
Music: Mostly **country**; also **blues, Cajun, disco, folk, gospel, MOR, rock, top 40/pop** and **comedy**. Produced *Zydecajun*, by Wayne Toups on Mercury Records; *Business Is Pleasure* (by Sammy Kershaw); and *Avec Amis* (by Lee Benoit). Other artists include Tammy Lynn, John Fred and Camey Doucet.

*MÍMÁC PRODUCTIONS, 6520 Sunset Blvd., Hollywood CA 90028. (213)962-3400. Artist Services: Robyn Whitney. Record producer and studio-TRAX recording. Estab. 1979. Deals with artists and songwriters. Fee derived from outright fee from record company. "If not a spec deal, we are for hire for production services."
How to Contact: Submit demo tape by mail. Unsolicited submissions are OK. Prefers cassette (or VHS videocassette if available) with 4 songs and lyric sheet. "Not interested in rap, pop/dance or country. We specialize in hard rock, heavy metal, unique R&B and some mature pop." Does not return material. Reports in 5 weeks.
Music: Mostly **hard rock, heavy metal** and **funk/rock**; also **unique R&B, mature pop** and **mature Latin pop**. Produced *Total Eclipse*, written and recorded by Total Eclipse on A&M Records (rock); *Juicy Talk*, written and recorded by Jerry Riopelle on Warner Bros. Records (country rock); and *Music Speaks Louder than Words* (by G. Abbot/A. Barykin), recorded by Emmanuel on Sony Records (Latin pop).
Tips: "Have your act totally developed: exact genre of music, detailed image, perfected songs. We don't want to teach you your craft."

MR. WONDERFUL PRODUCTIONS, INC., 1730 Kennedy Rd., Louisville KY 40216. (502)774-1066. President: Ronald C. Lewis. Record producer, music publisher (Ron "Mister Wonderful" Music/BMI and 1730 Music/ASCAP) and record company (Wonderful Records and Ham Sem Records). Estab. 1984. Deals with artists and songwriters. Produces 2 singles and 3 12" singles/year. Fee is derived from sales royalty when song or artist is recorded. "We also promote records of clients nationwide to radio stations for airplay."
How to Contact: Submit demo tape by mail. Unsolicited submissions are OK. Prefers cassette with 4 songs and lyric sheet. SASE. Reports in 2 weeks.

Music: Mostly **R&B, black gospel** and **rap**. Produced "Am I Good" (by Ron Lewis) and "Just Another In My Past" (by Pam Layne), both recorded by Amanda Orch (R&B); and "Just Hold Me Close," written and recorded by Jerry Green, all on Wonderful Records.

A.V. MITTELSTEDT, 9717 Jensen Dr., Houston TX 77093. (713)695-3648. Producer: A.V. Mittelstedt. Record producer and music publisher (Sound Masters). Works with artists and songwriters. Produces 100 singles, 10 LPs and 20 CDs/year. Fee derived from sales royalty and outright fee from recording artist.
How to Contact: Prefers cassette. SASE. Reports in 3 weeks.
Music: Mostly **country, gospel** and **crossover**; also **MOR** and **rock**. Produced "Too Cold at Home" (by Bobby Harding), recorded by Mark Chestnutt on Cherry Records (country); "Two Will Be One," written and recorded by Kenny Dale on Axbar Records (country); and "Shake Your Hiney" (by Gradual Taylor), recorded by Roy Head on Cherry Records (crossover country). Other artists include Randy Cornor, Bill Nash, Ron Shaw, Borderline, George Dearborne and Good, Bad and Ugly.

MJM PRODUCTIONS, Box 654, Southbury CT 06488. Owner: Michael McCartney. Record producer and music publisher (On The Button/BMI). Estab. 1988. Deals with artists and songwriters. Produces 5 singles/year. Fee derived from sales royalty or outright fee from recording artist.
How to Contact: Submit demo tape by mail. Unsolicited submissions are OK. Prefers cassette with 1-3 songs and lyric sheet. "Give details as to what your goals are: artist in search of deal or writer wishing to place songs." SASE. Reports in 1-2 months.
Music: Mostly **country/rock, pop rock** and **R&B**. Produced "Could've Been," "Movin' On" and "Separate Ways," all singles on Giant Records.

MODERN MINSTREL MIXING, P.O. Box 19112, Minneapolis MN 55419. (612)824-4135. Fax: (612)332-6663. Contact: C.W. Frymire. Record producer. Estab. 1988. Deals with artists and songwriters. Fee derived from sales royalty when song or artist is recorded or outright fee from recording artist or record company.
How to Contact: Submit demo tape by mail. Unsolicited submissions are OK. Prefers cassette (or videocassette) with 3 or more songs and lyric sheet. "Please include any press or previous airplay information along with photo and tour schedule." SASE.
Music: Mostly **acoustic, folk (contemporary)** and **folk/rock**; also **ethnic/world** and **blues (acoustic)**. Produced *Three Legged Dawg*, written and recorded by Pigs Eye Landing on Pigs Eye Records (contra); *Blue Earth*, written and recorded by Jamie Gans on Yodelahee Records (fiddle tunes); and *Live Demos*, written and recorded by Greg Brown on Red House Records (folk).
Tips: "Make your music 'speak' to me."

MOM AND POP PRODUCTIONS, INC., Box 96, El Cerrito CA 94530. Executive Vice President: James Bronson, Jr. Record producer, record company and music publisher (Toulouse Music/BMI). Deals with artists, songwriters and music publishers. Fee derived from sales royalty.
How to Contact: Prefers cassette with 2-4 songs and lyric sheet. SASE. Reports in 1 month.
Music: **Bluegrass, gospel, jazz, R&B** and **soul**. Artists include Les Oublies du Jazz Ensemble.

MONTICANA PRODUCTIONS, P.O. Box 702, Snowdon Station, Montreal, Quebec H3X 3X8 **Canada**. Executive Producer: David Leonard. Record producer. Estab. 1963. Deals with artists, songwriters and artists' managers. Fee negotiable.
How to Contact: Submit demo tape by mail. Unsolicited submissions are OK. Prefers cassette, phonograph record (or VHS videocassette) with maximum 10 songs and lyric sheet. "Demos should be as tightly produced as a master." Does not return unsolicited material.
Music: Mostly **top 40**; also **bluegrass, blues, country, dance-oriented, easy listening, folk, gospel, jazz, MOR, progressive, R&B, rock** and **soul**.

GARY JOHN MRAZ, 1324 Cambridge Dr., Glendale CA 91205. (818)246-PLAY. Producer: Gary Mraz. Record producer. Estab. 1984. Deals with artists and songwriters. Produces 6-12 12″ singles and 2-6 LPs/year. Fee derived from sales royalty or outright fee from record company.
How to Contact: Submit demo tape by mail. Unsolicited submissions are OK. Prefers cassette (or VHS videocassette if available) with 3 songs and lyric sheet. Does not return unsolicited material.
Music: Mostly **dance, pop** and **R&B**. Produced "Too Kind," recorded by Tara King on Radio Magic Records. Other artists include Bush Baby.
Tips: "Get your finished product to the untapped college radio market."

MSH PRODUCTIONS, P.O. Box 121616, Nashville TN 37212. (615)269-9984. Producer: Mark Stephan Hughes. Record producer, record company, music publisher (Fresh Start Music Ministries, Baby Huey/Krimson Hues Music Publishing). Estab. 1969. Deals with artists and songwriters. Produces 4 LPs/year. Fee derived from sales royalty when song or artist is recorded.

How to Contact: Submit demo tape by mail. Unsolicited submissions are OK. Prefers cassette with 3 songs and lyric sheet. "Send only professional submissions." SASE. Reports in 3 months.
Music: Mostly **Christian, praise** and **worship**; also **scripture songs** and **most other Christian material**. Produced *Call Jesus*, written and recorded by Kathy Davis; *Worthy Alone*, written and recorded by Lanier Ferguson; and *You Are Exalted*, written and recorded by Mark Stephen Hughes, all on Fresh Start Records. Other artists include Fresh Start Ministries Worship Band.

*MULBERRY STREET RECORDERS, 409 Mulberry St., Coraopolis PA 15108. (412)264-6649. Fax: (412)264-2110. President: David Granati. Record producer. Estab. 1991. Deals with artists and songwriters. Produces 6 singles, 6 12″ singles, 6 EPs and 12 CDs/year. Fee derived from outright fee from recording artist or record company.
How to Contact: Call first and obtain permission to submit. Prefers cassette (or VHS videocassette) with 4 songs and lyric sheet. Does not return material. Reports in 2-3 weeks.
Music: Mostly **rock, alternative** and **pop**; also **R&B, country** and **rap**. Produced "True History," recorded by G-Force on Silvertooth Records (rock); "Trip," recorded by the Distractions on Blue Duck Records (alternative); and "Kelly Affair," recorded by Kelly Affair (alternative). Other artists include the Nomads, Racquel, TKO, The Spuds and Triage.
Tips: "Take advantage of the affordable 4 and 8 track recorders and pre-produce your product!"

*MULTI SOUND IMAGES, 601 N. Sixth St., Allentown PA 18102. (215)432-4040. Producer/Publisher: Mark Stocker. Record producer, music publisher (Multi Sound Images Music/BMI, Minnow Music/ASCAP, Little Apple Music/BMI) and record company (Little Apple Records). Estab. 1988. Deals with artists and songwriters. Produces 6 singles, 1 LP and 1 EP/year. Fee derived from sales royalty or outright fee from recording artist or record company.
How to Contact: Call first and obtain permission to submit. Prefers cassette with 3 songs and lead sheet. "I want fresh, interesting material that is well-recorded and which directly competes with the top Billboard singles." SASE. Reports in 6 weeks.
Music: Mostly **country, pop** and **gospel**; also **New Age, R&B** and **rock**. Produced "Don't Lose the Magic" (by Mark Stocker/Susan Fredericks/Carole Silvcy), recorded by Valley Voices (pop/top 40); "Baby Hold On To Me" (by Mark Stocker), recorded by Jay Proctor, both on MSI Records (R&B); and "Love's Not for Sale" (by Rick Levy), recorded by Jay Proctor on Forevermore Records (R&B). Other artists include Marian Himes.
Tips: "Keep material fresh, innovative. Lyrics must be intelligent and interesting — have good vocalists for your demo. Positively NO RAP."

*ROSS MUNRO/RANDOM ENTERTAINMENT INC., 121 Logan Avenue, Toronto Ontario M4M 2M9 Canada. (416)406-4121. Fax: (416)406-0319. Producer: Ross Munro. Record producer, music publisher (Toon Town Music/CAPAC, ASCAP). Estab. 1980. Deals with artists and songwriters. Produces 4-6 singles and 3-4 albums/year. Fee derived from artist or record company.
How to Contact: Submit demo tape by mail. Unsolicited submissions are OK. Prefers cassette (or VHS videocassette if available) with 2-4 songs and lyric sheets. "Does not return unsolicited material." Only reports if interested.
Music: Mostly **rock, pop** and **country**. Produced *Thrash Waltz*, written and recorded by The Morganfields (rock) and *Monkeywalk*, written and recorded by Monkeywalk (rock).

*MUSIC FACTORY ENTERPRISES, INC., Suite 300, Ford & Washington Sts., Norristown PA 19401. (215)277-9550. Producer: Jeffrey Calhoun. Record producer, music publisher and record company (MFE Records). Estab. 1984. Deals with artists only. Produces 3-10 singles, 1-5 12″ singles, 20 LPs and 1-5 CDs/year. Fee derived from sales royalty or outright fee from recording artist or record company. "Charges on project basis for independents; deal contingent upon artists contract with label."
How to Contact: Write first and obtain permission to submit. Prefers cassette (or ½″ VHS videocassette if available) with 3-4 songs and lyric sheet. SASE. Reports in 2-3 weeks.
Music: Mostly **alternative rock/pop, world beat** and **20th century classical**. Produced "Alien Babies," written and recorded by Steve Pullara (childrens/novelty); "Bulkhead," written and recorded by Naked Twister (alternative); and "Fusebox," written and recorded by Plumbing (rock), all on MFE Records. Other artists include Robert Moran and Gregory Darvis.
Tips: "Send fully developed material. Be different. For distribution deals, submission of finished masters is the easiest way for a band to 'get signed.'"

MUST ROCK PRODUCTIONZ WORLDWIDE, Suite 5C, 167 W. 81st St., New York NY 10024. (212)DOC-0310. President: Ivan "DJ/DOC" Rodriguez. Record producer, recording engineer. Estab. 1980. Produces 5 singles, 5 12″ singles, 2 LPs, 3 EPs and 2 CDs/year. Fee derived from sales royalty.
How to Contact: Call first and obtain permission to submit. Prefers cassette (or VHS videocassette) and lyric sheet. Does not return unsolicited material. Reports in 2 weeks.

Music: Mostly **hip-hop**, **R&B** and **pop**; also **soul**, **ballads** and **soundtracks**. Produced "Poor Georgie" (by MC Lyte/DJ DOC), recorded by MC Lyte on Atlantic Records (rap); "Mama Said Knock You Out," recorded by LL Cool J on Def Jam (rap); and *Criminal Minded*, recorded by Boogie Down Productions on Jive/RCA (rap). Engineered and mixed EPMD, Redman, Dr. Dre & Ed-Lover, Das-EFX, The Flava-Unit, Shahliv, The Mysfits.

NASHVILLE COUNTRY PRODUCTIONS, 306 Millwood Dr., Nashville TN 37217. (615)366-9999. President/Producer: Colonel Jack Lynch. Record producer, music publisher (Jaclyn Music/BMI), record companies (Jaclyn and Nashville Country Productions) and distributor (Nashville Music Sales). Estab. 1987. Works with artists and songwriters. Produces 1-12 LPs/year. Fee derived from sales royalty or outright fee from recording artist. "We do both contract and custom recording."
How to Contact: Submit demo tape, by mail. Unsolicited submissions are OK. Prefers cassette with 1-4 songs and lyric or lead sheet. SASE. Reports in 1 month.
Music: Mostly **country**, **bluegrass**, **MOR** and **gospel**; also **comedy**. "We produced Keith Whitley and Ricky Skaggs' first albums." Produced *Looking at Love* (by Drake/Kraelin); *Somewhere Along the Line* (by V. Watts); and *Let Me Dream* (by E. George), all recorded by Elaine George on NCP Records (country).
Tips: "Prepare a good quality cassette demo, send to us along with a neat lyric sheet for each song and a résumé, picture and SASE."

NASHVILLE INTERNATIONAL ENTERTAINMENT GROUP, Box 121076, Nashville TN 37212-1076. (615)244-5357. President: Reggie M. Churchwell. Vice President: Mark Churchwell. General Manager, Music Group: Ben Haynes. Record producer, music publisher (Sir Winston Music/BMI and Four Seasons Music/ASCAP) and Reggie M. Churchwell Artist Management, Nashville International Talent and Nashville International Concerts. Labels include Phoenix Records and Nashville International Records. Deals with songwriters only. Produces 6 singles, 2 LPs and 2 CDs/year. Fee derived from sales royalty.
How to Contact: Write first about your interest. Prefers cassette with 1-4 songs and lyric sheet. Does not return unsolicited material "unless prior contact has been made and SASE included."
Music: Country, MOR, pop and gospel (contemporary); also **R&B (crossover)**, **rock (country, pop, power pop)**, **soul (crossover)** and **top 40/pop**. Produced *A Little Left of Center Line*, written and recorded by Howard Lips on Phoenix Records; "Unluckiest Songwriter in Nashville," written and recorded by Sonny Shroger on Hazzard Records (single); and "Please," recorded by Howard Lips Christian Blues on Phoenix Records (single).

NEBO RECORD COMPANY, Box 194 or 457, New Hope AL 35760. Manager: Jim Lewis. Record producer, music publisher (Nebo Ridge Publishing/ASCAP) and record company (Nebo Record Company). Estab. 1985. Deals with artists and songwriters. Fee derived from sales royalty when song or artist is recorded.
How to Contact: Submit demo tape by mail—unsolicited submissions are OK. Prefers cassette (or VHS videocassette) with 1 song and lyric sheet. "It is OK to send a videocassette, but not a must. Songwriters should be sure to send a SASE. Send a neat professional package. Send only 1 song." Does not return unsolicited material. Reports "as soon as possible."
Music: Mostly **modern country**, **traditional country** and **gospel**; also **rock**, **R&B** and **pop**. Produced "I'll Be There" (by Ann Jones), recorded by Ann Hart; "Sweet Memories" (by Jill Clark), recorded by May Rose; and "Heartache" (by Tim Morgan), recorded by Lester Hill, all on Nebo Records. Other artists include Flint Paint Rock, Mary Martin, Ann Hill, Anita Dudley and Clark Love.
Tips: "Send a quality song that produces an emotion in the listener."

BILL NELSON, 45 Perham St., W. Roxbury MA 02132. Contact: Bill Nelson. Record producer and music publisher (Henly Music/ASCAP). Estab. 1987. Deals with artists and songwriters. Produces 6 singles and 6 LPs/year. Fee derived from outright fee from recording artist.
How to Contact: Submit demo tape by mail. Unsolicited submissions are OK. Prefers cassette with 3-4 songs and lyric sheet. Does not return material. Reports in 3-4 weeks.
Music: Mostly **country**, **pop** and **gospel**. Produced "Big Bad Bruce" (by J. Dean), recorded by B.N.O.; "Do You Believe in Miracles" (by B. Nelson), recorded by Part-Time Singers; and "Don't Hurry With Love" (by B. Bergeron), recorded by B.N.O., all on Woodpecker Records.

Market conditions are constantly changing! If you're still using this book and it is 1996 or later, buy the newest edition of Songwriter's Market at your favorite bookstore or order directly from Writer's Digest Books.

NEMESIS MEDIA LABS, (formerly Tavares Teleproductions), 487 Pittsfield, Columbus OH 43085. (614)841-9980. Producer: Loren Moss. Record producer, full broadcast production facility (Tamareco Artist Management, Danmo Publishing). Estab. 1988. Deals with artists and songwriters. Produces 6 singles, 2 LPs and 2 EPs/year. Fee derived from sales royalty when song or artist is recorded or outright fee from record company.
How to Contact: Submit demo tape by mail. Unsolicited submissions are OK. Prefers DAT or cassette (or ¾″ videocassette) with 4 songs and lyric sheet. "Include pictures and biographical information." Does not return material. Reports in 2 weeks.
Music: Mostly **corporate/post scoring, reggae** and **hip hop/rap**; also **world beat, dance/house** and **R&B/ top 40**. Produced "Chill" (by Tamara Straughter), recorded by Teddy B on Tamarcco Records (rap); *Learning to Walk*, written and recorded by Poets of Heresy on Private Records (alternative); and "Do You Miss Me," written and recorded by Misti Tuffs on Artists Label (jazz).
Tips: "I offer 3 words of advice: professionalism, organization and integrity."

NEO SYNC LABS, 20 Colpitts Dr., Windsor NY 13865. (607)775-0200. Owner: Bob Damiano. Record producer, engineer/recording studio operator. Estab. 1987. Deals with artists and songwriters. Produces 2-3 LPs, 2-3 EPs and 1 CD/year. Fee derived from outright fee from recording artist or record company.
How to Contact: Submit demo tape by mail. Unsolicited submissions are OK. Prefers DAT or cassette with 1-10 songs. Include SASE for response. Does not return unsolicited material. Reports in 2 weeks.
Music: Mostly **progressive rock, hard rock** and **country**; also **jazz** and **dance**. Produced "On My Way," written and recorded by Joe Rose on Up Front Music (light rock); *Folk Hue*, written and recorded by P.C. Mantree on Pure Water Records (light rock); and *AKA*, written and recorded by AKA (rock). Other artists include Tanya Rushanski.
Tips: "Be original. Don't just jump on the 'grunge wagon.' Let us bring out strengths and downplay weaknesses."

THE NETWORK PRODUCTION GROUP, P.O. Box 28816, Philadelphia PA 19151. (215)473-5527. General Manager: Leroy Schuler. Record producer. Estab. 1990. Deals with artists and songwriters. Produces 6 singles, 25 12″ singles and 3 LPs/year. Fee derived from outright fee from record company.
How to Contact: Write first and obtain permission to submit. Prefers cassette with 4 songs and lyric sheet. SASE. Reports in 5 weeks.
Music: Mostly **R&B, hip-hop** and **funk**. Produced "I Always Feel Lonely" (by V. Butter/L. Schuler), recorded by Ken Chaney; "Pulsation" (by L. Leggieri/L. Schuler), recorded by Lou Leggieri, both on Logic Records; and "It's My Fantasy," written and recorded by Swayza on Cantrell Records.

NEU ELECTRO PRODUCTIONS, P.O. Box 1582, Bridgeview IL 60455. (708)257-6289. Owner: Bob Neumann. Record producer, record company. Estab. 1984. Deals with artists and songwriters. Produces 16 singles, 16 12″ singles, 20 LPs and 4 CDs/year. Fee derived from outright fee from recording artist or record company.
How to Contact: Submit demo tape by mail. Unsolicited submissions are OK. Prefers cassette (or VHS videocassette if available) with 3 songs and lyric sheet or lead sheet. "Accurate contact phone numbers and addresses, promo packages and photos." Does not return material. Reports in 2 weeks.
Music: Mostly **dance, house, techno, rap** and **rock**; also **experimental, New Age** and **top 40**. Produced "Juicy," written and recorded by Juicy Black on Dark Planet International Records (house); "Make Me Smile," written and recorded by Roz Baker (house); and *Take My Love* (by Bob Neumann), recorded by Beatbox-D on N.E.P. Records (dance).
Tips: "Quality of production will influence profitability."

NEW EXPERIENCE RECORDS, Box 683, Lima OH 45802. (419)228-0691. Music Publisher: James L. Milligan Jr. Record producer, music publisher, management (Creative Star Management) and record company (New Experience Records, Grand-Slam Records). Estab. 1989. Deals with artists and songwriters. Produces 15-20 12″ singles, 2 LPs, 3 EPs and 2-5 CDs/year. Fee derived from sales royalty when song or artist is recorded or outright fee from recording artist or record company, "depending on services required."
How to Contact: Write or call first and obtain permission to submit. Address material to A&R Dept. or Talent Coordinator (Carl Milligan). Prefers cassette with a minimum of 3 songs and lyric or lead sheet (if available). "If tapes are to be returned, proper postage should be enclosed and all tapes and letters should have SASE for faster reply." Reports in 1 month.
Music: Mostly **pop, R&B** and **rap**; also **gospel, contemporary gospel** and **rock**. Produced *Kayo* and *Sandy Beach Cove*, written and recorded by Richard Bamberger on New Experience Records (pop); and "The N.E.R. Rap Song," written and recorded by Thomas Roach on Grand-Slam Records (rap). Other artists include Venesta Compton, Samantha Bishop, Melvin Milligan.

Tips: "Believe in yourself. Work hard. Keep submitting songs and demos. Most of all, be patient; if there's interest you will be contacted."

NEW HORIZON RECORDS, 3398 Nahatan Way, Las Vegas NV 89109. (702)732-2576. President: Mike Corda. Record producer. Deals with singers preferably. Fee derived from sales royalty when song or artist is recorded.
How to Contact: Submit demo tape by mail. Unsolicited submissions are OK. Prefers cassette with 1-3 songs and lyric sheet. SASE. Reports in 3 weeks.
Music: Blues, easy listening, jazz and **MOR**. Produced "Lover of the Simple Things," "Offa the Sauce" (by Corda & Wilson) and "Go Ahead and Laugh," all recorded by Mickey Rooney on Prestige Records (London). Artists include Bob Anderson, Jan Rooney, Joe Williams, Robert Goulet and Bill Haley and the Comets.
Tips: "Send good musical structures, melodic lines, and powerful lyrics or quality singing if you're a singer."

NIGHTSTAR RECORDS INC., P.O. Box 602, Yarmouthport MA 02675 (508)362-3601. President: David M. Robbins. Record producer, music publisher (Dact Production/BMI) and record company (Nightstar Records Inc.). Estab. 1990. Deals with artists and songwriters. Produces 3-4 LPs and 3-4 CDs/year. Fee derived from sales royalty when song or artist is recorded. "May charge artists in advance. Monies could be used to cover studio time and pre-album costs. Nightstar covers all manufacturing and promotional costs."
How to Contact: Write first and obtain permission to submit. Prefers cassette (or VHS videocassette if available) with several songs. Include biography. SASE. Reports in 2-3 weeks.
Music: Mostly **movie soundtrack**, **New Age** and **acoustic**. Produced *Daydreams*, *By the Water's Edge* and *Dancing with the Moon*, all written and recorded by Deborah T. Robbins on Nightstar Records.
Tips: "Send us music from the heart, don't clutter the music. We primarily deal in instrumental music. The time is right for the reception of non-vocal music, both on the radio and at retail levels. There is a growing market for relaxing music. New Age music, as it is known, is losing its appeal, because of some of the monotonous songs that artists create. Keep songs to 3-5 minutes, and let it flow."

*NIGHTWORK RECORDS, 355 W. Potter Dr., Anchorage AK 99502. (907)562-3754. Contact: Kurt Riemann. Record producer and music licensor (electronic). Deals with artists and songwriters. Produces 2 singles, 8 LPs and 2 CDs/year. Fee derived from sales royalty.
How to Contact: Submit demo tape by mail. Unsolicited submissions are OK. Prefers cassette or 15 ips reel-to-reel with 2-3 songs "produced as fully as possible. Send jingles and songs on separate reels." Does not return unsolicited material. Reports in 1-2 months.
Music: Mostly **electronic** and **electronic jingles**. Produced *Alaska*, written and recorded by Kurt Riemann (New Age); *Aracus*, written and recorded by Jennifer Stone, both on Nightworks Records (New Age); and *Into the Night*, written and recorded by Jeanene Walker on Windsong Records (country).

*NISE PRODUCTIONS, INC., 413 Cooper St., Camden NJ 08102. (609)963-6400. Contact: Director A&R. Record producer, music publisher (Nise Productions Inc./BMI) and record company (Power Up, Euro-American Int'l). Estab. 1981. Deals with artists and songwriters. Produces 1-5 singles and 1-5 LPs/year.
How to Contact: Submit demo tape by mail. Unsolicited submissions are OK. Prefers cassette with 3 songs and lyric sheet. SASE. Reports in 1-2 months.

ORDER PRODUCTIONS, 441 E. Belvedere Ave., Baltimore MD 21212. (410)377-2270. President: Jeff Order. Record producer and music publisher (Order Publishing/ASCAP and Orderlottsa Music/BMI). Estab. 1986. Deals with artists and songwriters. Fee derived from sales royalty and outright fee from recording artist and record company.
How to Contact: Submit demo tape—unsolicited submissions are OK. "Lyric sheets without recorded music are unacceptable." Prefers cassette with 3 songs and lyric sheet. SASE. Reports in 1 month.
Music: Works with **all types**. Produced "Won't You Dance With Me" (by Jeff Order), recorded by Tiny Tim (dance); *Isis Unveiled* and *Keepers of the Light*, written and recorded by Jeff Order (New Age). Other artists include Stephen Longfellow Fiske, Higher Octave and Boulevard.
Tips: "We only work with songwriters and artists who are seriously committed to a career in music. Submissions must be professionally recorded. Learn as much about the business of music as possible. Don't expect someone to invest in your art if you haven't done it first!"

JOHN "BUCK" ORMSBY/ETIQUETTE PRODUCTIONS, Suite 273, 2442 NW Market, Seattle WA 98107. (206)524-1020. Fax: (206)524-1102. Publishing Director: John Ormsby. Record producer (Etiquette/Suspicious Records) and music publisher (Valet Publishing). Estab. 1980. Deals with artists and songwriters. Produces 1-2 singles, 3-5 LPs, and 3-5 CDs/year. Fee varies.

How to Contact: Submit demo tape by mail—"always looking for new material but please call first." Prefers cassette (or VHS videocassette if available) with lyric or lead sheet. SASE. Reports in 6-8 weeks.

Music: R&B, rock, pop and **country**.

Tips: "Tape production must be top quality; lead or lyric sheet professional."

PANAMA MUSIC LIBRARY, (formerly First Time Management & Production Co.), Sovereign House, 12 Trewartha Rd., Praa Sands, Penzance, Cornwall TR20 9ST **England**. Phone: (0736)762826. Fax: (0736)763328. Managing Director: Roderick G. Jones. Record producer, music publisher (First Time Music Publishing U.K. Ltd. MCPS/PRS), record company (First Time, Mohock Records, Rainy Day Records and Pure Gold Records) and management firm (First Time Management & Production Co.). Estab. 1986. Deals with artists and songwriters. Produces 5-10 singles and 5 LPs/year. Fee derived from sales royalty.

How to Contact: Prefers cassette with unlimited number of songs and lyric or lead sheet. SAE and IRC. Reports in 10 weeks.

Music: Mostly **country/folk, pop/top 40, country** with an Irish/Scottish crossover, **rock, soul, jazz funk, fusion, dance** and **reggae**. Produced "Yours Forever" (by Rod Jones/Colin Eade), recorded by Colin Eade (instrumental); "Shades of Blue," written and recorded by Laurie Thompson (instrumental theme music); and "Baristoned," written and recorded by Simon Hipps, all on Panama Music Productions. Other artists include Rod Jones and Willow.

MICHAEL PANEPENTO/AIRWAVE PRODUCTION GROUP INC., 1916 28th Ave. South, Birmingham AL 35209. (205)870-3239. Producer: Michael Panepento. Record producer, music publisher (Panelips Music/BMI) and artist development company (ChapelLane Productions). Estab. 1985. Deals with artists and songwriters. Produces 5 singles, 2 12″ singles, 4 LPs, 5 EPs and 3 CDs/year. Fee derived from sales royalty when song or artist is recorded.

How to Contact: Write or call first and obtain permission to submit. Prefers cassette with 3 songs and lyric sheet. SASE. Reports in 6-10 weeks.

Music: Mostly **rock, R&B** and **pop**; also **jazz** and **country**. Produced "Another Wheel" and "Take A Step," written and recorded by Kelly Garrett on Sony Records (country); and *House of Love* (by A.J. Vallejo), recorded by Vallejo (rock). Other artists include Parousia, 4 AM and Elvis' Grave.

PANIO BROTHERS LABEL, Box 99, Montmartre, Saskatchewan S0G 3M0 **Canada**. Executive Director: John Panio, Jr. Record producer. Estab. 1977. Deals with artists and songwriters. Produces 1 single and 1 LP/year. Works with lyricists and composers, teams collaborators. Fee derived from sales royalty or outright fee from artist/songwriter or record company.

How to Contact: Submit demo tape—unsolicited submissions are OK. Prefers cassette with any number of songs and lyric sheet. SAE and IRC. Reports in 1 month.

Music: Country, dance, easy listening and **Ukrainian**. Produced *Ukranian Country*, written and recorded by Vlad Panio on PB Records.

PATTY PARKER, Suite 114, 10603 N. Hayden Rd., Scottsdale AZ 85260. (602)951-3115. Fax: (602)951-3074. Producer: Patty Parker. Record producer, record company (Comstock, Paylode). Estab. 1978. Deals with artists and songwriters. Produces 18 singles and 4-5 CDs/year. Fee derived from outright fee from recording artist or recording company. "We *never* charge songwriters!! Artist's fee for studio production/session costs."

How to Contact: Submit demo tape—unsolicited submissions are OK. Prefers cassette (or VHS videocassette if available) with 4 songs and lyric sheet. Voice up front on demos. SASE. Reports in 2 weeks.

Music: Mostly **country**—traditional to **crossover, western** and some **A/C**. Produced "Every Love Needs A Fool Now And Then" (by Joe Radosevich), recorded by Claudia Zimmerman; "It's Time I Settled Down" (by Paul Gibson), recorded by Colin Clark; and "There's No Gold" (by Roy Ownbey), recorded by Sophie Stillman, all on Comstock Records (country). Other artists include Paul Gibson, Keith Lamb, Abby & Johnny, Patti Mayo and Claudia.

Tips: "Writers should strive to write medium to up-tempo songs—there's an abundance of ballads. New artists should record medium to up-tempo material as that can sometimes better catch the ear of radio programmers."

DAVE PATON, The Idea Bank, C-300, 16776 Lakeshore Dr., Lake Elsinore CA 92330. Contact: Dave Paton. Record producer and music publisher (Heaven Songs/BMI). Deals with artists and songwriters. Produces 20 singles and 3-5 LPs/year. Fee negotiable.

How to Contact: Submit demo tape by mail. Unsolicited submissions are OK. Prefers 7½ ips reel-to-reel or cassette with 3-6 songs and lyric sheet. SASE. Reports in 4 weeks.

Music: Country, dance, easy listening, jazz, MOR, progressive, R&B, rock, top 40/pop and comedy. Produced "Steal My Heart," "Heartache Highway" and "Love is a State of Mind," all written by A.J. Masters and recorded by Linda Rae on Hollyrock Records (country).

MARTIN PEARSON MUSIC, Seestrasse 91, Zurich, CH 8002 **Switzerland**. (01)202-4077. Contact: Martin Pearson. Record producer, music publisher and record company. Works with artists and songwriters. Produces 2 singles, 2 12″ singles, 1 LP and 1 CD/year. Fee derived from sales royalty or outright fee from record company, artist, publisher or manager.
How to Contact: Submit demo tape—unsolicited submissions are OK. Prefers cassette (or PAL videocassette) with 6 songs and lyric sheet. Does not return unsolicited material. Reports in 2 months.
Music: Mostly **pop**, **rock** and **R&B**; also **disco/rock, disco** and **techno**. Produced *Jig's Dream* (by Andre) and *Basta* (by Barnard), both recorded by The Barking Dogs on Woof Trade Records (street); and *Do You Remember* (by Bunomo/Hachler), recorded by Odd'N'Even on Odd Records (pop/rock). Other artists include Ashantis, Meanviles and Rick Braun.

PERENNIAL PRODUCTIONS, Box 109, 73 Hill Rd., Redding CT 06875. (203)938-9392. Owner: Sean McNamara. Record producer. Estab. 1992. Deals with artists and songwriters. Fee derived from outright fee from recording artist.
How to Contact: Submit demo tape by mail. Unsolicited submissions are OK. Prefers cassette (or VHS videocassette) with 4-8 songs and lyric sheet or lead sheet. "Include a promo pack." Does not return unsolicited material. Reports in 1 month.
Music: Mostly **pop, contemporary jazz,** and **alternative rock**; also **R&B, rock** and **adult contemporary**. Produced "Staten Island Rain" and "Open the Door," written and recorded by Flashpoint on Flight Path Records (fusion jazz); and "Dischord," written and recorded by John Nutscher on Caffeine Disk Records (alternative).
Tips: "Send a bio about yourself and explain your intentions for the music submitted."

PERIDOT PRODUCTIONS, 17 Woodbine St., Cranston RI 02910. (401)785-2677. President: Amy Parravano. Record producer, record company, music publisher, performing artist. Estab. 1992. Deals with artists and songwriters. Produces 2 singles, 2 12″ singles and 1 LP/year. Fee derived from outright fee from recording artist.
How to Contact: Submit demo tape by mail. Unsolicited submissions are OK. Prefers cassette with 3-4 songs and lyric sheet. SASE.
Music: Mostly **country, gospel** and **folk**; also **MOR, children's** and **novelty**. Produced "America" (by Stamm/Parravano), recorded by Amy Parravano (country); "North Hampton Line" (country) and "Trust in Him" (gospel), both by Amy Parravano and recorded by Amy Beth.
Tips: "Lyrics with good messages are still getting listeners attention."

*PERL PRODUCTIONS, 3029 Prospect Ave., Cleveland OH 44115. (216)464-4646. Fax: (216)831-9863. Professional Manager: Howard Perl. Record producer and music publisher. Estab. 1988. Deals with artists and songwriters. Produces 15 singles/year. Fee derived from sales royalty when song or artist is recorded.
How to Contact: Submit demo tape by mail. Unsolicited submissions are OK. Prefers cassette (or videocassette if available) with 1-4 songs and lyric sheet. "Label every part of submission—especially with phone number and name." Does not return material. Reports in 5 weeks.
Music: Mostly **R&B/urban, rap** and **dance/house**; also **pop** and **country**. Produced "I Wanna Luv Ya" (by Howard Perl), recorded by Allison Benton on Hyperactive Records (R&B); *Drop That Mace* (by various), recorded by MPS on Rainbo Records (rap); and "Distant Love" (by H. Perl), recorded by Ed Wilson on Reel Records (pop). Other artists include Jeffrey Charles, Forecast.
Tips: "Be patient. Be yourself, but be marketable to today's society."

*PERSON TO PERSON PRODUCTIONS, 342 Norfolk Rd., Litchfield CT 06759-0546. (203)567-9012. Fax: (203)567-7001. President: Chris Brown. Record producer. Estab. 1979. Deals with artists and songwriters. Produces 4-5 LPs/year. Fee derived from outright fee from recording artist or record company.
How to Contact: Write first and obtain permission to submit. Prefers cassette with 3 songs and lyric sheet. Does not return material. Reports in 1 month.
Music: Mostly **jazz, folk** and **ethnic**; also **pop** and **rock**. Produced *Zingaro* (by Jobim), recorded by Searles & Allen; and *Alleluia* (by Mozart), recorded by Gloria Blanco. Other artists include Paul Winter Consort.

PAUL PETERSON CREATIVE MANAGEMENT, #309, 9005 Cynthia, Los Angeles CA 90069. (310)273-7255. Contact: Paul Peterson. Record producer, music publisher and personal management firm. Estab. 1983. Deals with artists and songwriters. Produces 2 LPs and 2 CDs/year. Fee derived from sales royalty when song or artist is recorded.

How to Contact: Submit demo tape by mail. Unsolicited submissions are OK. Prefers cassette and lyric sheet. SASE. Reports in 3 weeks.
Music: Mostly **rock, pop** and **jazz**; also **country**. Produced "Lost Cabin" (by Steve Cash), recorded by Ozark Mountain Daredevils on Legend Records (country/rock); "Country Pride" (by Paul Peterson and John Boylan), recorded by The Chipmunks on Epic Records (kids, novelty); and *Everything's Alright*, written and recorded by Priscilla Bowman on Legend Records (blues/rock).

PHILLY BREAKDOWN, 216 W. Hortter St., Philadelphia PA 19119. (215)848-6725. President: Matthew Childs. Record producer, music publisher (Philly Breakdown/BMI) and record company (Philly Breakdown). Estab. 1974. Deals with artists and songwriters. Produces 3 singles and 2 LPs/year. Fee derived from sales royalty when song or artist is recorded.
How to Contact: Submit demo tape—unsolicited submissions are OK. Prefers cassette with 4 songs and lead sheet. Does not return material. Reports in 6-8 weeks.
Music: Mostly **R&B, hip hop** and **pop**; also **jazz, gospel** and **ballads**. Produced "What Do I Do" (by M. Childs/G. Clark) and "Love Slave," both recorded by Gloria Clark; and "Come Home" (by Leroy Christy), recorded by Mark Adam, all on Philly Breakdown Records. Other artists include Leroy Christy, Killroy, Jerry Walker and Emmit King.
Tips: "Be original and creative and stay current. Be exposed to all types of music."

JIM PIERCE, 101 Hurt Rd., Hendersonville TN 37075. (615)824-5900. Fax: (615)824-8800. President: Jim Pierce. Record producer, music publisher (Strawboss Music/BMI, Pier-Jac Music/ASCAP) and record company (Round Robin Records). Estab. 1974. Deals with artists and songwriters. Produces 50 singles, 5-6 EPs and 2-3 CDs/year. Fee derived from sales royalty or outright fee from recording artist. "Some artists pay me in advance for my services." Has had over 200 chart records to date.
How to Contact: Write first and obtain permission to submit or to arrange personal interview. Prefers cassette with any number of songs and lyric sheet. Does not return material. Reports in 2-3 months.
Music: Mostly **country, contemporary, country/pop** and **traditional country**. Produced "Don't Call Us, We'll Call You," written and recorded by Harlen Helgeson; "You Can't Keep a Good Love Down" (by Jerry Fuller), recorded by Lenny Valenson; and "If I Live To Be A Hundred" (by Mae Borden Axton), recorded by Arne Benoni, all on Round Robin Records (country). Other artists include Jimmy C. Newman, Margo Smith, Bobby Helms, Sammi Smith, Tim Gillis, Roy Drusky, Charlie Lowin, Melba Montgomery and Harlan Craig.
Tips: "Don't let a 'no' stop you from trying."

*PIGMY PRODUCTIONS, Suite 104, 4 Daniels Farm Rd., Trumbull CT 06611. (203)381-0043. Owner/producer: Tom McKee. Record producer, record company. Estab. 1991. Deals with artists only. Produces 1 LP and 3 CDs/year. "I produce only for Endangered Records and split net profits with artist. Artist pays for CD pressing and I distribute and sell product."
How to Contact: Submit demo tape by mail. Unsolicited submissions are OK. "Any format is OK—video is fine. The more background info and lyrics the better (use good tape, it sounds better)." SASE. Reports in 2-3 weeks.
Music: Mostly **pop rock, R&B** and **blues**; also **country rock, folk** and **classical/jazz fusion**. Produced "A Light Went Out in New York," written and recorded by Matthew Fisher and The Downliners Sect (R&B pop); "Ease the Pain," written and recorded by Del Dwyer and Robbie Ross (blues); and "On This Moment," written and recorded by Michael Brown and Yvonne Vitale (pop), all on Endangered Records.
Tips: "Love music first, love money and fame last—be professional in your drive. Give it 110% and it will pay you back."

PINE ISLAND MUSIC, #308, 9430 Live Oak Place, Ft. Lauderdale FL 33324. (305)472-7757. President: Jack P. Bluestein. Record producer and music publisher. Estab. 1973. Deals with artists and songwriters. Produces 5-10 singles/year. Fee derived from sales royalty.
How to Contact: Artist: query, submit demo tape. Songwriter: submit demo tape and lead sheet. Prefers cassette or 7½ ips reel-to-reel with 1-4 songs. SASE. Reports in 1-2 months.
Music: Mostly **blues, country, easy listening, folk, gospel, jazz, MOR, rock, soul** and **top 40/pop**. Produced "Drivin' Nails," written and recorded by Gary Oakes and *An Old Old Man* (by Beth Thliveris), recorded by Bernice Boyce, both on Quadrant Records. Other artists include Jeffrey Cash and Praise (gospel) and Paula Ma Yu-Fen.
Tips: "Write good saleable material and have an understandable demo made."

*PLUG PRODUCTIONS, 273 Chippewa, Columbia SC 29210. (803)750-5391. Contact: Marketing. Record producer, production, promotion and manufacturer. Estab. 1992. Deals with artists and songwriters. Produces 9 CDs/year. Fee derived from sales royalty when song or artist is recorded or outright fee from recording artist or record company.

How to Contact: Submit demo tape by mail. Unsolicited submissions are OK. Prefers cassette (or VHS videocassette) with 4 songs and lyric sheet. SASE. Reports in 5 weeks.
Music: All types. Produced *Airtrax Vols. 4, 5, 6* by various artists and *Bodyshop*, both on Antithesis Records; and *Naked Ape*, on Analysis Records. Other artists include Ted Neiland, Blue Rooster, Toni Monet, Safari.
Tips: "Plug Productions also test markets new artists in U.S. and overseas. We also manufacture CDs, records, tapes and accessories. We contract with record companies, studios and talent agencies to promote and market singers, songwriters, recording artists, producers and other companies."

POKU PRODUCTIONS, 176-B Woodridge Cres, Nepran, Ontario K2B 759 **Canada.** (613)820-5715. President: Jon E. Shakka. Record producer (SOCAN). Estab. 1988. Deals with artists and songwriters. Produces 1 single and 1 12″ single/year. Fee derived from outright fee from recording artist or record company.
How to Contact: Write or call first and obtain permission to submit. Prefers cassette (or VHS videocassette if available) with 4 songs and lyric sheet. SAE and IRC. Reports in 3 months.
Music: Mostly **funk, rap** and **house music**; also **pop, ballads** and **funk-rock**. Produced "Money," "Dear 'O' " and "Love-One Way" (by Poku), recorded by Jon E. Shakka on Poku Records.

POMGAR PRODUCTIONS, Box 707, Nashville TN 37076-0707. Manager: Don Pomgar. Record producer, music publisher (One Time Music/BMI, Two Time Music/ASCAP). Estab. 1989. Deals with artists and songwriters. Produces 1 12″ single, 1 EP and 4 CDs/year. Fee derived from sales royalty when song or artist is recorded, outright fee from record company.
How to Contact: Submit demo tape by mail. Unsolicited submissions are OK. Prefers cassette with 1-10 songs and lyric sheet. "If you're an artist send a picture and your best vocal songs. If you're a writer don't send a picture—just your best songs." SASE. Reports in 3 weeks.
Music: Mostly **country, pop** and **rock**. Produced *Always a Place*, written and recorded by Darrell Worrell on Tooth & Nail Records (pop); *Nevermind* (by Danny Crater), recorded by Full Blown Oatmeal on Crazee Records (alternative); and *News to Me* (by Shannon/Jenkins), recorded by Sheila Shannon on CCR Records (country). Other artists include Jimmy Sampson (country).
Tips: "Here's what we're about. We try to find great songs to use with the artists we produce. Our artists are released on independent labels with the goal of shopping them to a major label for re-release or distribution. We also pitch songs regularly to major artists through our publishing company. We're growing fast—we need songs."

POPS NEON ENTERPRISES, P.O. Box 4125, West Hills CA 91308. (818)712-9046. Fax: (818)712-9338. Director: Steve Hobson. Record producer and music publisher (Auntie Argon Music/BMI, MaMa Freon/ASCAP). Estab. 1988. Deals with artists and songwriters. Produces 2 singles/year. Fee derived from sales royalty or outright fee from recording artist. Retainer required for production services.
How to Contact: Write first and obtain permission to submit. Prefers cassette with 1-3 songs and lyric sheet. Reports in 2 weeks. "Type lyric sheets. Don't overproduce demos. Piano/vocal or guitar/vocal are OK. Unsolicited tapes go straight in the trash, unopened and unheard."
Music: Mostly **mainstream** and **pop/top 40.**
Tips: "Submit songs that best represent your direction and best showcase your talents as an artist."

*POST MODERN PRODUCTIONS, P.O. Box 64980-418, Dallas TX 75206. (214)504-6743. Fax: (214)443-9422. Music Producer: Jim Gasewicz. Record producer, music publisher (Couch Trout Music/ASCAP). Estab. 1990. Deals with artists and songwriters. Produces 10 singles, 2 12″ singles, 10 LPs, 4 EPs and 10 CDs/year. Fee derived from sales royalty when song or artist is recorded or outright fee from recording artist or record company.
How to Contact: Submit demo tape by mail. Unsolicited submissions are OK. Prefers cassette or VHS videocassette with 2-4 songs and lyric sheet. "Bands may include photo and press kit if available." SASE. Reports in 3-4 weeks.
Music: Mostly **alternative, pop** and **rock**; also **dance**. Produced "Acid Is Groovy" (by Joe Christ), recorded by Bigger Than God on Reliable Records (alternative); *This Product Is Not A Toy* (by Stephen Nutt), recorded by A Thousand Words on Virelai Records (alternative); and *Stop* (by Chris Peay), recorded by Pasty Face on Pasty Face Records (alternative). Other artists include The Healing Faith, The Hemingways, The Lawless.
Tips: "Don't copy what you hear on the radio now because in six months it will be outdated. Be original. Be refreshing. We want something new and exciting."

PRAIRIE MUSIC LTD., P.O. Box 438, Walnut IA 51577. (712)366-1136. President: Robert Everhart. Record producer, music publisher (BMI) and record company (Prairie Music). Estab. 1964. Deals with artists and songwriters. Produces 2 singles and 2 LPs/year. Fee derived from sales royalty when song or artist is recorded.

How to Contact: Submit demo tape by mail. Unsolicited submissions are OK. Prefers cassette. SASE. Reports in 6 months.

Music: Mostly **traditional country, bluegrass** and **folk**. Produced *Time After Time* and *No One Comes Near*, written and recorded by Bob Everhart on Prairie Records (country); and "Home On The Range," recorded by Sons of San Joaquim on IPJV Records (country). Other artists include Bonnie Sanford, Sarah Davison, Tom Wills, Happy Valley June, Sheila Everhart and Grandad Kephart.

PREJIPPIE MUSIC GROUP, Box 2849, Trolley Station, Detroit MI 48231. President: Bruce Henderson. Record producer, music publisher (Prejippie Music Group/BMI) and record company (PMG Records). Estab. 1990. Deals with artists and songwriters. Produces 6-12 12" singles, 2 LPs and 2 EPs/year. Negotiates between sales royalty and outright fee from artist or record company.

How to Contact: Submit demo tape—unsolicited submissions are OK. No phone calls please. Prefers cassette with 3-4 songs and lyric sheet. SASE. Reports in 6 weeks.

Music: Mostly **funk/rock** and **techno/house**; also **alternative rock**, and **experimental music** (for possible jingle/scoring projects). Produced "Lolita" by Bourgeoisie Paper Jam and "Supermarket Obscene" by Prejippies; all by PMG Productions. Other artists include Urban Transit (house), Deep Six Honey (alternative/experimental) and Jezebel (house).

Tips: "We're looking for songwriters who have a good sense of arrangement, a fresh approach to a certain sound and a great melody/hook for each song."

THE PRESCRIPTION CO., % D.F. Gasman, Apt. B-1, 5 Wildwood Gardens, Port Washington NY 10050. (516)767-1929. President: David F. Gasman. Vice President A&R: Kirk Nordstrom. Tour Coordinator/Shipping: Bill Fearn. Secretary: Debbie Fearn. Record producer and music publisher (Prescription Co./BMI). Deals with artists and songwriters. Fee derived from sales royalty when artist or song is recorded or outright fee from record company.

How to Contact: Write or call first about your interest then submit demo. Prefers cassette with any number of songs and lyric sheet. Does not return unsolicited material. Reports in 1 month. "Send all submissions with SASE or no returns."

Music: Mostly **bluegrass, blues, children's, country, dance, easy listening, jazz, MOR, progressive, R&B, rock, soul** and **top 40/pop.** Produced "You Came In," "Rock 'n' Roll Blues," and *Just What the Doctor Ordered*, all recorded by Medicine Mike.

Tips: "We want quality—fads mean nothing to us. Familiarity with the artist's material helps too."

*PRIMAL PRODUCTIONS, INC., Suite 133, 3701 Inglewood Ave., Redondo Beach CA 90278. (213)214-0370. President/Producer: Jeffrey Howard. Record producer, music publisher (Primal Visions Music/BMI) and record company (Primal Records). Estab. 1985. Deals with artists and songwriters. Produces 6 singles and 3 CDs/year. Production charges vary from artist to writer. Charges in advance for services. "This doesn't always apply, but generally we get 50% production fees in advance on projects we produce, 50% on delivery of finished masters."

How to Contact: Write or call first and obtain permission to submit or to arrange personal interview. Prefers (DAT) cassette (or VHS videocassette if available) with 1-5 songs and lyric sheet. "Send only your best and strongest material. Demos are OK but use of high quality cassettes and packaging does reflect on your level of professionalism." SASE. Reports in 6 weeks.

Music: Mostly **rock, hard rock, pop** and **R&B/dance/rap**; also **country, New Age** and **heavy metal**. Produced *The Passion*, written and recorded by Jeffrey Howard on Primal Records (rock/hard-rock); and *Keeper of the Flame*, written and recorded by Jeff Laine. Other artists include Larisa Stow and Virtual Reality.

Tips: "Always believe in yourself and your material. Don't write what you think *we* want to hear. We're interested in strong material performed by people with a passion for what they do."

RAINBOW RECORDING, 113 Shamrock Dr., Mankato MN 56001. (507)625-4027. Contact: Michael Totman. Record producer, recording studio. Estab. 1986. Deals with artists and songwriters. Produces 4 singles, 4 LPs and 1 EP/year. Fee derived from outright fee from recording artist or record company.

How to Contact: Submit demo tape by mail. Unsolicited submissions are OK. Prefers cassette, DAT (or VHS videocassette) with 4 songs and lyric sheet or lead sheet. Does not return unsolicited material. Reports in 2 weeks.

Music: Mostly **rock, country** and **top 40**; also **old time, punk-alternative** and **R&B**. Produced *Middle Bridge* (by John Weber), recorded by Middle Bridge (rock); and *JBTW*, written and recorded by Stephen Houze and Terry Moore (rap).

RANDALL PRODUCTIONS, Box 265, N. Hollywood CA 91603-0265. (312)509-2945 and (818)569-5653. President: Ashley Brown. Record producer, video producer and musical services to artists/songwriters. Produces 5 singles, 2 LPs and 2 music videos/year. Fee derived from sales royalty or outright fee from artist or record company.

How to Contact: Submit demo tape by mail—unsolicited submissions are OK. Prefers cassette (or VHS videocassette if available) with 3-5 songs and lyric sheet. "Clearly label each item you send. Include photo/bio if available." SASE. Does not return material without return postage. Reports in 2 months, "but be patient."
Music: Mostly **R&B**, **soul**, **funk**, **pop**, **blues** and **gospel**; also accepting finished masters of these and **rock** (**heavy**, **hard**, **metal**) for Grandville Rock Sampler album. Produced "Black Hills Madam" (by Frank Leonard), recorded by Paree (R&B); "Crossroads" (by C. Rubin), recorded by Randy DeTroit (pop); and *Poetry of You*, written and recorded by Jade (R&B), all on Grandville Records.

*RED KASTLE PRODUCTIONS, Box 163, West Redding CT 06896. President: Paul Hotchkiss. Record producer and music publisher. Deals with artists and songwriters. Produces 10 singles, 2 EPs, 2 LPs and 2 CDs/year. Fee derived from sales royalty.
How to Contact: Prefers cassette with 2 songs and lyric sheet. Include bio. SASE. Reports in 3 weeks.
Music: Mostly **country** and **country/pop**. Produced "Honky Tonk Darlin" and "Thinking About You" (by P. Hotchkiss), recorded by Susan Rose Manning on Target Records (country); and "Destination You," written and recorded by Michael Terry on Roto Noto Records (country). Other artists include Big John Hartman, Beverly's Hill-Billy Band, Susan Rose, Jett and Road Dawgs.

REEL ADVENTURES, 9 Peggy Lane, Salem NH 03079. (603)898-7097. Chief Engineer/Producer: Rick Asmega. Estab. 1972. Produces 45 singles, 1 12" single, 20 LPs, 2 EPs and 6 CDs/year. Fee derived from outright fee from recording artist or record company.
How to Contact: Submit demo tape by mail. Unsolicited submissions are OK. Prefers cassette (or VHS/8mm videocassette) and lyric sheet. Include photos and résumé. SASE. Reports in 2-3 weeks.
Music: Mostly **pop**, **funk** and **country**; also **blues**, **reggae** and **rock**. Produced "New Crowd" (by Ned Claflin) on Touch Tone Records; *Hot-Hot-Hot* (by Jazz Hamilton) on Real Records; and "One Change" (by Buddy Sullivan) on Rock'n Records, all recorded by Reel Adventures. Other artists include Larry Sterling, Broken Men, Melvin Crockett, Fred Vigeant, Monster Mash, Carl Armand, Cool Blue Sky, Ransome, Backtrax, Too Cool for Humans and Burn Alley.

*RICHMOND ST. RECORDINGS, INC., 169 Railroad St., Huntington Station, NY 11746. (516)423-3246. President: Bill Falvey. Record producer. Estab. 1987. Deals with artists and songwriters. Produces 100 singles, 3-5 12" singles, 20 LPs, 50 EPs and 3-5 CDs/year. Fee derived from outright fee from recording artist or record company and investors.
How to Contact: Write or call first to arrange personal interview. Prefers cassette (or 1/2" VHS videocassette if available). SASE. Reports in 1-2 weeks.
Music: **All types**. Produced *Head Cleaners*, written and recorded by Marc Berge on Nickel Records (rock); *Laughing Boy* (by Carey Palmer/Kursh Kale), recorded by Rewind on LB Records (rock); and *Coronation* (by Matt Rothstein), recorded by Kig Box on R&R Records (rap). Other artists include Pure Dog, Smok'n Mirrors, Colt Daniel, Lenny Cocco & Chimes, Eileen Alexander, Gravity, Revisions and Jim Kohler.

RIGEL MEDIASOUND, Box 678, Baird TX 79504. (915)893-2616. Producer/Engineer: Randy B. McCoy. Record producer. Estab. 1985. Deals with artists and songwriters. Produces 10 singles and 4 LPs/year. Fee derived from outright fee from artist. Charges artist up front for "all phases of project from start to finish, including production, arrangements, presentation, etc."
How to Contact: Submit demo tape by mail. Unsolicited submissions are OK. Prefers cassette with 3-4 songs and lyric sheet. "Make sure vocals can be clearly heard, and keep the arrangements simple and basic." SASE. Reports in 3-4 weeks.
Music: Produced "Texas Gold," written and recorded by various on Code of the West Records (country); "Annex" (by various), recorded by Annex on Annex Records (rock); and "2 Days Later" (by Stevens/Walker), recorded by 2 Days Later (contemporary Christian).
Tips: "Craft lyrics carefully, keep music production simple."

RIPSAW PRODUCTIONS, #805, 4545 Connecticut Ave. NW, Washington DC 20008. (202)362-2286. President: Jonathan Strong. Record producer, music publisher (Sugar Mama Music/BMI) and record company (Ripsaw Records). Deals with artists and songwriters. Produces 4 singles and 3 LPs/year.
How to Contact: Submit demo tape by mail. Unsolicited submissions are OK. "Do not call." Prefers cassette and lyric sheet. SASE. Reports in 1-6 months.
Music: Mostly **country**, **blues**, **rockabilly** and **roots rock**. Helped produce "It's Not the Presents Under My Tree," recorded by Narvel Felts on Renegade Records; produced *Two Sides*, written and recorded by Bobby Smith; and "Christmas In Tennessee," recorded by Billy Hancock on Run Wild Records.

ROCK & TROLL PRODUCTIONS, 19 Chase Park, Batavia NY 14020. (716)343-1722. Vice President: Guy E. Nichols. Record producer, music publisher and record company (Rock & Troll Records).

Estab. 1981. Deals with artists and songwriters. Produces 25 singles and 2 LPs/year. Fee derived from sales royalty or outright fee from recording artist.
How to Contact: Submit demo tape—unsolicited submissions are OK. Prefers cassette with 4 songs and lyric sheet. SASE. Reports in 4 weeks.
Music: Mostly **rock, pop** and **R&B**. Produced *Heartbreaker*, written and recorded by Lost Angels; and *Little Trolls*, written and recorded by Little Trolls; both on R&T Records (rock).

ROCKSTAR PRODUCTIONS, P.O. Box 131, Southeastern PA 19399. (215)3379556. Executive Vice President: Jeffrey Sacks. Director of Marketing: Roni Sacks. Record producer. Estab. 1988. Deals with artists and songwriters. Produces 5 singles/year. Fee derived from sales royalty when song or artist is recorded.
How to Contact: Submit demo tape—unsolicited submissions are OK. Prefers cassette with 2 songs and lyric sheet. Does not return unsolicited material. Reports in 6 weeks.
Music: Mostly **rock** and **pop**. Produced "Stage Name" and "I Love You Goodbye" (by Scot Sax), recorded by Wänderlust; and "I Ain't Worth You" (by Scot Sax), recorded by Nancy Falkow, all on RKS Records.
Tips: "Make a good clean recording. The words must be clearly heard."

ROCKY MOUNTAIN HEARTLAND PRODUCTIONS, Box 6904, Denver CO 80206. (303)841-8208. Executive Producer: Steve Dyer. Record and video producer and advertising firm (full service—brochures, demo kits, promo packs, graphics, photography). Deals with artists and songwriters. Fee derived from sales royalty or outright fee from songwriter/artist.
How to Contact: Submit demo tape by mail. Unsolicited submissions are OK. Prefers cassette (or videocassette if available) with 3-5 songs and lyric sheet or lead sheet. Does not return unsolicited material. Reports in 1 month.
Music: Mostly **gospel, top 40** and **rock**; also **jazz** and **country**. "Music open and not limited to these types." Produced *The Best Is Yet to Come*, by Kent Parry (big band and orchestra gospel); *From Here to Kingdom Come*, by Heart Song (mild gospel/top 40); and *Going, Going, Gone*, by Heart Song (gospel rock); all on Record Harvest Records. Also produced music for *Tom Slick* TV show and a Best Western Hotel promotional video.
Tips: "Contact us for specific suggestions relating to your project."

ROSE HILL GROUP, 1326 Midland Ave., Syracuse NY 13205. (315)475-2936. A&R Director: Vincent Taft. Record producer and music publisher (Katch Nazar Music/ASCAP, Bleecker Street Music/BMI). Produces 5 singles and 2 LPs/year. Fee derived from sales royalty when song or artist is recorded.
How to Contact: Submit demo tape by mail. Unsolicited submissions are OK. Prefers cassette with 3 songs maximum. SASE. Reports in 2-4 weeks.
Music: Mostly **top 40/pop, rock** and **dance**; also **jazz** and **MOR**. Produced *Better Say Whatcha Mean* (by E. Jacobson), recorded by Io on StarCity Records (R&B); *Definitely In Love* (by Andrew George), recorded by Inside on Sunday Records (pop); and *We Belong Together* (by G. Davidian), recorded by Z-Team on Cherry Records (pop).
Tips: Write concise, simple, memorable melodies; strong, convincing stories."

MIKE ROSENMAN, 45-14 215 Place, Bayside NY 11361. (718)229-4864. Producer: Mike Rosenman. Record producer and arranger. Estab. 1984. Deals with artists and songwriters. Produces 2-4 singles and 1 EP/year. Fee derived from sales royalty or outright fee from recording artist.
How to Contact: Call first and obtain permission to submit. Prefers cassette (or VHS videocassette if available), with 2-4 songs and lyric sheet. Include address and phone number. Put phone number on cassette. Will not return any tapes without SASE. Reports in 2-3 months.
Music: Mostly **pop, R&B, dance/rap** and **rock**. Produced "Don't Bite the Hand That Feeds You" (by Ellen Parker), recorded by Dope Enough For Ya (rap/R&B); "My Love Is Deep" (by M. Rosenman/E. Parker), recorded by Ellen Parker (dance); and "Child's Play," written and recorded by D.E.F. (rap/R&B) on Homebase Records.
Tips: "Send simple demos of good songs with lyrics that make sense. Include SASE if you want your tape back."

RR & R MUSIC PRODUCTIONS INC., 9305 Dogwood Place, Gainesville GA 30506. (706)861-2186; also Suite 204, 23 Music Square East, Nashville TN 37203. (615)726-2571. Owner/President: Ron Dennis Wheeler. Record producer, music publisher (Sounds of Aicram/BMI and Do It Now Publishing/ASCAP) and record company (RR&R, Rapture, Ready Records and Yshua Records). Estab. 1964. Works with artists and songwriters. Produces 10-20 compilation CDs and 10-20 CDs/year. Fee derived from sales royalty when song or artist is recorded, or outright fee from recording artist or record company.
How to Contact: Call first and obtain permission to submit. Prefers cassette (Type II) or 15 or 30 ips reel-to-reel (or VHS videocassette if available) with lyric chords and lead sheet. "Demo should

have lead vocal and music and also a recording of music tracks without vocals." SASE. Reports only if interested – must be clearly produced.

Music: All types except rap or New Age and satanic. Produced "Take Me Home, Tie Me Down And Set Me Free" (by RD Wheeler/Louis Brown), recorded by Confederate Railroad and Mike Brookshire; "She Knows About Me," written and recorded by Jez Davidson; and *Bob's Nite Off*, written and recorded by Bob's Nite Off, all on RR&R Records. Other artists include Theresa Morton, Jennifer Lynn, Tanya Tucker.

*RUSTRON MUSIC PRODUCTIONS, 1156 Park Lane, West Palm Beach FL 33417-5957. (407)686-1354. A&R Directors: Rusty Gordon, Ron Caruso and Kevin Reeves. Record producer, manager and music publisher (Rustron Music Publishers/BMI, Whimsong Publishing/ASCAP). Estab. 1970. Works with artists and songwriters. Produces 6-10 LP/cassettes and 2 CDs/year. Fee derived from sales royalty or outright fee from distributorship. "This branch office reviews all material submitted for the home office in Ridgefield, CT."
How to Contact: Submit demo tape by mail. Unsolicited submissions are OK. Prefers cassette with 1-3 songs and lyric or lead sheet. "Songs should be 3½ minutes long or less and must be commercially viable for today's market. Exception: New Age fusion compositions 3-10 minutes each, ½ hour maximum. Singer/songwriters and collaborators are preferred." SASE required for all correspondence. Reports in 2-4 months.
Music: Mostly **progressive country, pop** (ballads, blues, theatrical, cabaret) and **folk/rock**; also **R&B, New Age folk fusion** and **New Age**. Produced "May Day" (by Rusty Gordon and Ron Caruso), recorded by Jayne Margo-Reby on Rustron Records (adult contemporary fusion); "What Are You Doing" (by Gary Gonzalez and Rick Groom), recorded by Relative Viewpoint on RVP Records (socio-environmental folk rock); and "Yemanjah," written and recorded by Marian Joy Ring on Black Dog Records (adult contemporary jazz/folk fusion). Other artists include Ellen Hines, Deb Criss, Robin Plitt, Lynn Thomas, Gary Jess and Roop Verma.
Tips: "Write from the heart. Don't be redundant. Develop lyrical themes, be unpredictable. Compose definitve melodies. Develop your own unique sound, don't sound like anyone else."

JOJO ST. MITCHELL, 273 Chippewa Dr., Columbia SC 29210-6508. (803)750-5391. Executive Producer and Manager: Jojo St. Mitchell. Record producer. Deals with artists and songwriters. Produces 10 singles and 4 LPs/year. Fee derived from sales royalty, booking and licensing.
How to Contact: Prefers cassette (or VHS videocassette if available) with 5-10 songs; include any photos, biography. SASE. Reports in 5 weeks, if interested. Enclose return postage.
Music: Mostly **mainstream, pop, R&B, rock, new music, country, industrial, dance** and **jazz/rap**. Produced *Big Neon Scream*, written and recorded by Silhouette; *Yesterday's News*, written and recorded by Safari; and *These Dirty Hands*, written and recorded by Blue Rooster. Other artists include Progress In April, Body Shop, Political Asylum, Slither, Max Hewitt, Marshall Plan Kids, Naked Ape.

SAS CORPORATION/SPECIAL AUDIO SERVICES, Suite 520, 503 Broadway, New York NY 10012. (212)226-6271. Fax: (212)226-6357. Owner: Paul Special. Record producer. Estab. 1988. Deals with artists and songwriters. Produces 3 singles, 1 12" single, 5 LPs, 1 EP and 5 CDs/year. Fee derived from sales royalty when song or artist is recorded or outright fee from recording artist or record company.
How to Contact: Submit demo tape – unsolicited submissions are OK. Prefers cassette with 1-10 songs and lyric sheet. SASE. Reports in 6-8 weeks.
Music: Hard rock, funk rock and **metal**; also **alternative, industrial** and **rap**. Produced "Color Of Darkness," written and recorded by Maria Excommunikata on Megaforce Records (alternative); "Love U/Duke," written and recorded by Heads Up! on Emergo Records (funk rock); and "Hope/Emelda" (by Van Orden/Hoffman), recorded by The Ordinaires on Bar None Records (alternative). Other artists include Central Europe, Band Of Weeds, Peter Moffit and Kablama Chunk.
Tips: "Don't be afraid to bring up new and unusual ideas."

*ALWIN SAUERS AUDIO PRODUCTIONS AND RECORDING, P.O. Box 548, Springfield OR 97477. (503)746-8901. Producer/Engineer: Alwin Sauers. Record producer and recording engineer. Estab. 1991. Deals with artists only. Produces 4-8 LPs and 2-4 CDs/year. Fee derived from sales royalty when song or artist is recorded or outright fee from record company.
How to Contact: Submit demo tape by mail. Unsolicited submissions are OK. Prefers cassette (or VHS videocassette if available) with 4 songs. "Include contact information: name, address, phone, best time of day to contact, bio and photo if available." SASE. Reports in 3-6 weeks.
Music: Mostly **dance/funk, rock** and **pop/New Age**; also **gospel, R&B** and **country**. Produced *Gathering Spirit*, written and recorded by Bryan Lloyd on Harmony Music (New Age); *Ethnic Utopia*, written and recorded by Onomatopoeia on 13 Records (alternative); and *International Anthem Live*, written and recorded by International Anthem on ASAP-1 Records (rock). Other artists include Intensity and John Hargett.

SEGAL'S PRODUCTIONS, 16 Grace Rd., Newton MA 02159. (617)969-6196. Contact: Charles Segal. Record producer, music publisher (Segal's Publications/BMI, Samro South Africa) and record company (Spin Records). Works with artists and songwriters. Produces 6 singles and 6 LPs/year. Fee derived from sales royalty.
How to Contact: Write or call first and obtain permission to submit. Prefers cassette (or videocassette) with 3 songs and lyric sheet or lead sheet of melody, words, chords. "Please record keyboard/voice or guitar/voice if you can't get a group." Does not return unsolicited material. Reports in 4 months.
Music: Mostly **rock, pop** and **country**; also **R&B** and **comedy**. Produced "What is This Love" (by Paul/Motou), recorded by Julia Manin (rock); "Lovely Is This Memory" (by Segal/Paul), recorded by Nick Chosn on AU.S. (ballad); and *There'll Come A Time* (by Charles Segal), recorded by Rosemary Wills on Spin Records (ballad). Other artists include Art Heatley, Dan Hill and Melanie.
Tips: "Make a good and clear production of cassette even if it is only piano rhythm and voice. Also do a lead sheet of music—words—chords."

SHADOWLAND PRODUCTIONS, 3 Lancet Court, Shawnee OK 74801. Music Editor: Russell Walker. Record producer, record company, music publisher (Calvary's Shadow Publications, Morning Dew). Estab. 1991. Deals with artists and songwriters. Produces 15-20 singles and 20-24 LPs/year. Fee derived from outright fee from recording artist.
How to Contact: Submit demo tape by mail. Unsolicited submissions are OK. Prefers cassette (or VHS videocassette) with 3 songs and lyric or lead sheet. SASE. Reports in 6-8 weeks.
Music: Mostly **Southern gospel, MOR sacred** and **contemporary Christian**; also **choral anthems, children's songs** and **seasonal**. Produced *Lord, Lift Me Up*, written and recorded by Archer on Conarch Records (gospel); *The Power Line* (by Archer), recorded by Brashear on Courier Records (Southern gospel); and *Love Beyond All Measure* (by Walker), recorded by Bethlehem Choir on Bethlehem Records (contemporary). Other artists include Great Gospels Guitars, Bethlehem Brass.
Tips: "Be willing to accept constructive criticism and rewriting. Be open to recording songs suggested by an arranger/producer. Communicate with audience."

SHARPE SOUND PRODUCTIONS, Box 140536, Nashville TN 37214. (615)391-0650. Producer/Engineer: Ed Sharpe. Record producer. Estab. 1990. Deals with artists and songwriters. Fee derived from sales royalty or outright fee from recording artist or record company.
How to Contact: Submit demo tape by mail. Unsolicited submissions are OK. Prefers cassette (or VHS videocassette if available) with 4 songs and lyric sheet. SASE. Reports in 1 month.
Music: Mostly **alternative, country** and **storytelling**. Produced *Wheels and Gears and Spinning Things*, recorded by Velocipede (alternative); *David Parks*, recorded by David Parks (country); and *Legends II*, recorded by Kathy Smith (storytelling). Other artists include Noisy Neighbors, Teren Bosz, Kay & the Kees, JoAnn Havlilko, Jim Casey, Nick Palncci.
Tips: "Look for a unique angle that sets your music apart."

SILENT PARTNER PRODUCTIONS, 14954 Tulipland Ave., Canyon Country CA 91351. (805)251-7509. Producer: Mark Evans. Record producer, Christopher Paris Productions (Instrumental Division), Canyon Studios (24 track audio studio). Estab. 1988. Deals with artists and songwriters. Produces 5-10 singles, 4-8 LPs, 5 EPs and 4-8 CDs/year. Fee derived from sales royalty when song or artist is recorded or outright fee from recording artist or record company.
How to Contact: Submit demo tape by mail. Unsolicited submissions are OK. Prefers cassette (or VHS videocassette) with 3-5 songs and lyric sheet. Does not return unsolicited material.
Music: Mostly **R&B, country** and **New Age**; also **instrumental**. Produced "Freeks Anthem" (by M. Evans), recorded by Mark Free on Tommy Productions; *L.A. Girl*, written and recorded by Mark Richard on Private Music Records; and *Butterflies*, written and recorded by Deborah Baxter on Aurel Arts Records. Other artists include Patti Principal.
Tips: "Never give up. Nothing is free. Love what you do."

*SILVER THORN ENTERPRISES, P.O. Box 196, Panguitch UT 84759. (801)676-8055. President/Owner: John Burdick. Record producer, record company (Silver Thorn Records, Jodi Con Records), music publisher. Estab. 1981. Deals with artists and songwriters. Produces 2 singles and 2-3 CDs/year. Fee derived from sales royalty when song or artist is recorded.
How to Contact: Submit demo tape by mail. Unsolicited submissions are OK. Prefers cassette or VHS videocassette with 2 songs. "No phone calls." SASE. Reports in 1 month.
Music: Mostly **country, country-rock** and **folk**; also **talented singers**. Produced *Rodeo Dreams* (by Jerri Ashurst), recorded by Chris McCormick and Gale Davis (country); *They Call Me The Outlaw* (by Tim Johnson), recorded by Gale Davis (country); and *Never Shared Love*, written and recorded by Debbie Davis (country), all on Silver Thorn Records. Other artists include John Burdick.

Tips: "Be humble. Be serious and dedicated. We want talent, not ego."

SLAVESONG CORPORATION, INC., P.O. Box 41233, Dallas TX 75241-0233. (214)225-1903. Chief Executive Officer: Keith Hill. Record producer, music publisher. Estab. 1991. Deals with artists and songwriters. Produces 2 singles, 2 12″ singles, 1 LP, 1 EP and 1 CD/year. Fee derived from sales royalty when song or artist is recorded or outright fee from recording artist.
How to Contact: Submit demo tape by mail. Unsolicited submissions are OK. Prefers cassette (or VHS videocassette) with 3-5 songs and lyric sheet. Send photo. SASE. Reports in 1 month.
Music: Mostly **R&B/dance**, **reggae** and **jazz**; also **world beat**. Produced "Oil Spill" and "Hi In My Hello" (by S.W./G.C.), recorded by George Clinton on Warner Bros. Records (R&B); and "Why?" (by S.W./K.H./2 Pos.), recorded by Two Positive M.C. on Slavesong Records (rap). Other artists include X-Slave and Gold Tee.

*SNEAK TIP RECORDS INC./HIP WRECKIN RECORDS LTD., Suite 3A, 98-05 67th Avenue, Rego Park NY 11374. (718)459-0334. Record producer, music publisher (Sneak Tip Music/Uncle J Music) and record company. Estab. 1990. Deals with artists and songwriters. Produces 10-20 singles/year. Fee derived from sales royalty.
How to Contact: Submit demo tape by mail. Unsolicited submissions are OK. Prefers cassette. SASE. Reports in 4 weeks.
Music: Mostly **house**, and **club**; also **pop**, **R&B** and **freestyle**. Produced "Make It Better" (by Norty Cotto and BB Keys), recorded by Nite Life; "The Way U Groove Me" (by Big & Bold), recorded by Groove Legion; "This Will Be Mine" (by Peter Presta), recorded by Network 109, all on Sneak Tip Records. Other artists include Rhingo and Zavier.
Tips: "Dance music or R&B only please! Be patient on response."

SOUND ARTS RECORDING STUDIO, 8377 Westview Dr., Houston TX 77055. (713)464-GOLD. President: Jeff Wells. Record producer and music publisher (Earthscream Music). Deals with artists and songwriters. Estab. 1974. Produces 12 singles and 3 LPs/year. Fee derived from outright fee from recording artist.
How to Contact: Submit demo tape – unsolicited submissions are OK. Prefers cassette with 2-5 songs and lyric sheet. SASE. Reports in 6 weeks.
Music: Mostly **pop/rock** and **dance**. Produced "Ride of a Lifetime" (by Greg New), recorded by Tim Nichols on Earth Records (country); "Love Is" (by Gary Wade), recorded by Beat Temple (R&B/funk); and "Life in the Jungle" (by Boss), recorded by 4-Deep (rap). Other artists include Perfect Strangers, Third Language and Pauline Knox.

SOUND COLUMN PRODUCTIONS, Country Manor, 812 S. 890 East, Orem UT 84058. (801)225-9975. President/General Manager: Ron Simpson. Record producer, media producer, music publisher (Ronarte Publications/ASCAP, Mountain Green Music/BMI) and record company (SCP Records). Estab. 1970. Fee derived from sales royalty or outright fee on media productions, demos and albums produced for outside labels.
How to Contact: Submit demo tape – unsolicited submissions are OK. Prefers cassette with 3 songs. SASE. "We promise to listen to everything. We've had a big year in publishing, so we honestly do get behind. We cannot return materials or correspondence without SASE. No phone calls, please."
Music: **All styles** except metal or rap; "needs vary according to artists we are working with." Produced *Destinations* and *Doom Carousel*, written and recorded by Kim Simpson on SCP Records; and "I Will Lead You" (by Clive Romney/Ron Simpson), recorded by Cody Hale. Other artists include Gary Voorhees.
Tips: "We respond to clean production and must have current-styled, well-crafted songs, targeted toward industry needs."

*SOUND CONTROL PRODUCTIONS, 2813 Azalea Place, Nashville TN 37204. (615)269-5638. Producer: Mark. Record producer and record company (Mosrite Records). Estab. 1982. Deals with artists and songwriters. Produces 30 singles, 8 LPs and 2 CDs/year. Fee derived from sales royalty or outright fee from recording artist or record company – "sometimes all or a combination of these." Charges 50% in advance for services.
How to Contact: Submit demo tape by mail. Unsolicited submissions are OK. Prefers cassette with 3 songs and lyric sheet. "Don't submit anything in which you need to explain what the song or you

---

Remember: Don't "shotgun" your demo tapes. Submit only to companies interested in the type of music you write. For more submission hints, refer to Getting Started on page 5.

are trying to say—let the performance do that." Does not return unsolicited material. Reports in 8 weeks.

Music: Mostly **country, gospel** and **bluegrass**; also **Christmas**. Produced *Paddy Kelly* (by various artists), recorded by Paddy Kelly (country); *The Thorntons* (by various), recorded by Thorntons on Bridge Records (gospel); and *The Lewis Family* (by various), recorded by The Lewistown on Benson Records (gospel bluegrass).

SOUND PLANET, (formerly E P Productions), 7455 Lorge Cr., Huntington Beach CA 92647. (714)842-5524. Studio Manager: Nici Ashton. Record producer and record company (Venue Records, Branden Records). Estab. 1987. Deals with artists and songwriters. Produces 5-10 singles, 1-2 12″ singles, 2-5 LPs, 1-5 EPs and 1 CD/year. Fee derived from sales royalty when song or artist is recorded or outright fee from recording artist and record company. (All terms are negotiable.) "Some artists come to us for production work only—not on our label. For this we charge a flat fee. We *never* charge songwriters unless for demos only."
How to Contact: Submit demo tape by mail—unsolicited submissions are OK. Prefers cassette with 1-3 songs and lyric sheet. SASE. Reports in 2 months.
Music: Mostly **pop, R&B** and **contemporary Christian**; also **country** and **rock**. Produced *Surrounded By Angels*, written and recorded by Michelle Goodwin on Angelic Records; *Gift of Love*, written and recorded by Bob Hardy on Ocean Records; and *For An Evening* (by Bill and Kim Connors), recorded by The Look.
Tips: "Be professional—typed lyric sheets and cover letter are so much easier to work with along with a well-produced demo. Don't compromise on the quality of your songs or your package."

SOUND SERVICES, Apt. 505, 39867 Fremont Blvd., Fremont CA 94538. (510)657-3079. Owner: Curtis Autin. Record producer. Estab. 1986. Deals with artists and songwriters. Produces 1 single and 2 LPs/year. Fee derived from outright fee from recording artist.
How to Contact: Submit demo tape by mail. Unsolicited submissions are OK. Prefers cassette (or VHS videocassette) with 1 song and lyric or lead sheet. SASE. Reports in 1 week.
Music: Mostly **rock, R&B** and **pop**; also **jazz**. Produced "People" (by Cardell Porter); "Lone Wolf" and *Night Ryder*, both by Dave Hamlett, all on Sound Services Records.
Tips: "I'm looking for artists and artists/songwriters."

*SOUNDHOUSE RECORDING/SCOTT CRANE, 7023 15th Ave. NW, Seattle WA 98117. (206)764-4848. Producer/President: Scott Crane. Record producer. Estab. 1992. Deals with artists and songwriters. Produces 4 singles, 20 LPs, 1 EP and 20 CDs/year. Fee is "negotiated on a per album basis."
How to Contact: Call first and obtain permission to submit. Prefers cassette. Does not return material. Reports in 3 weeks.
Music: Mostly **hard rock** (but not heavy metal), **industrial** and **avant-garde**; also **punk, grunge** and **some dance remixes**. Produced *Time to Make the Doughnuts*, written and recorded by Alcohol Funny Car on C/Z Records (rock); *Devil Head*, written and recorded by Devil Head on Sony Records (rock); and *The Gits*, written and recorded by The Gits on C/Z Records (punk). Other artists include Zipgun, Tiny Hat Orchestra, Drill, Gashuffer, Seven Year Bitch, Atomic 61 and Spinanes.
Tips: "Strong music with strong hooks, no immature attitudes, no rock star attitudes, just plain good friendly musicianship."

*SOUNDMAX MEDIA SERVICES, P.O. Box 179, Cameron Park CA 95682. (916)676-3342. Producer: Eric Brandon. Estab. 1972. Deals with artists and songwriters. Fee derived from "license fees, studio time, resale of completed programs, etc."
How to Contact: Write or call first and obtain permission to submit "or interview, or see our studio." Prefers any format tape or videocassette if available. "Call first so we can let you know about studio availability as well as time we'll need to respond to demo. We are very punctual once we make a scheduling commitment."
Music: Mostly **commercial production music, high energy dance** (aerobics) and **progressive/alternative, New Age, country** for fashion shows; also **voice over talent, sound effects** and **strings, bridges, audio logos**. Produced *Videotrax*, written and recorded by Matt Neri on Soundmax Records (production); *Scream When It Hertz* (by Nick Maglaras), recorded by Tape Heads on Noah's Ark Records (rave/dance); and *Gone But Still Here*, written and recorded by George Sehkia on Soundmax Records (Native American). Other artists include Lindsay Wright, various voice over artists and various production music packages.
Tips: "Be unique! Be versatile! Know your market."

*SOUNDSTAGE SOUTH, 5183 Darlington Dr., Memphis TN 38118. (901)363-3345. President: Fred B. Montgomery. Rock & "New" country production and artist development. Estab. 1990. Deals with artists and songwriters. Fee derived from sales royalty when song or artist is recorded. "SoundStage intends to provide a Rehearsal/Production Facility to area contemporary musicians and songwriters

on a daily and monthly rental basis—to include a demo recording studio, private rehearsal studios and showcase room."
How to Contact: Submit demo tape by mail. Unsolicited submissions are OK. Prefers cassette (or VHS videocassette if available) with 3 songs and lyric sheet. Does not return unsolicited material.
Music: Mostly **rock**, **blues rock** and **contemporary country**; also **country/rock**.
Tips: "I have represented selected songwriters/artists in the Memphis/Mid-South area in development, pre-production, demo production and general support in shopping original material to publishers and labels." Music trends: "Continued crossover occurring in contemporary country music—ballad rock and country will continue to merge. Another 'Eagles' type group will complete this transition."

SPHERE PRODUCTIONS, Box 991, Far Hills NJ 07931-0991. (908)781-1650. Fax: (908)781-1693. President: Tony Zarrella. Talent Manager: Louisa Pazienza. Record producer, artist development, management and placement of artists with major/independent labels. Produces 5-6 singles and 3 CDs/year. Estab. 1988. Deals with artists and songwriters. Fee derived from percentage royalty of deal, outright fee from record company.
How to Contact: Submit demo tape—unsolicited submissions are OK. Prefers cassette or CD (or VHS videocassette) with 3-5 songs and lyric sheets. "Must include: photos, press, résumé, goals and specifics of project submitted, etc." Does not return unsolicited material. Reports in 2 months.
Music: Specializes in **pop/rock (mainstream)**, **progressive/rock**, **New Age** and **crossover country/pop**. Also **film soundtracks**. Produced *Take This Heart*, *It's Our Love* and *You and I (Are Dreamers)* (by T. Zarrella), recorded by 4 of Hearts (pop/rock) on Sphere Records. Also represents Oona Falcon, Sky-King, Traveller and Forever More.
Tips: "Be able to take direction and have trust and faith in your producer or manager. Currently seeking artists/groups incorporating various styles into a focused mainstream product."

STARK RECORDS AND TAPE CO., 628 S. South St., Mount Airy NC 27030. (919)786-2865. Contact: Paul E. Johnson. Record producer and music publisher (TomPaul Music Company/BMI). Estab. 1960. Deals with artists, songwriters, publishers and recording companies. Produces 8 singles and 3 LPs/year. Works with 80 new songwriters/year. Fee derived from sales royalty when song or artist is recorded.
How to Contact: Submit demo tape by mail. Unsolicited submissions are OK. Prefers cassette with 4-6 songs and lyric sheet. SASE. "Return address should be on the SASE." Reports in 2 months.
Music: **Country**, **bluegrass**, **pop** and **gospel**. Produced *She Has Forgotten*, *Why Do You Weep* and *Little Green Valley* (by Atkins & Hill), all recorded by Bobby Lee Atkins on Stark Records. Other artists include Carl Tolbert, Lee Martin, Early Upchurch, Clyde Johnson, Sanford Teague, Ralph E. Hill, Wesley Easter, Ray Bryant, Leo Gravely and Don Sawyers.

MIKE STEWART PRODUCTIONS, P.O. Box 2242, Austin TX 78768. (512)476-8067. A&R: Shannon Setcik. Record producer, music publisher and management company. Estab. 1985. Deals with artists and songwriters. Produces 10 singles, 6 LPs and 6 EPs/year. Fee derived from sales royalty when song or artist is recorded or outright fee from recording artist or record company.
How to Contact: Submit demo tape by mail. Unsolicited submissions are OK. Prefers cassette (or videocassette). Does not return unsolicited material. Reports in 2 weeks.
Music: **All types**. Produced "Run to Me," written and recorded by J. Tittle (pop) and "I Woke Up" (by A. Tyler), recorded by Rockingbirds (pop), both on Sony Records; and *Avalande Drive* (by B. Giddens), recorded by Illegal Artist on Avslavter Liebe Records (rock). Other artists include Susan Voelz and Calvin Russell.

STUART AUDIO SERVICES, 342 Main St., Gorham ME 04038. (207)839-3569. Producer/Owner: John A. Stuart. Record producer, music publisher, musical consultant/arranger. Estab. 1979. Deals with artists and songwriters. Produces 1-2 singles, 3 LPs and 3 CDs/year. Fee derived from sales royalty when song or artist is recorded, outright fee from recording artist or record company, or demo and consulting fees.
How to Contact: Write or call first and obtain permission to submit or to arrange a personal interview. Prefers cassette with 4 songs and lyric sheet. SASE. Reports in 3-4 weeks.
Music: Mostly **alternative folk-rock**, **rock** and **country**; also **contemporary Christian**, **children's** and **unusual**. Produced *Hungry Eyes*, written and recorded by Noel Paul Stookey on Gold Castle Records (new folk); *Winter to Summer* written and recorded by John A. Stuart on C.T.W. Records (soundtrack); and *Signs of Home* (by Romanow/Rowe), recorded by Schoonner Fare on OuterGreen Records (folk).

The asterisk before a listing indicates that the listing is new in this edition. New markets are often the most receptive to unsolicited submissions.

Other artists include Bates Motel, Chris Heard, Al Mossberg, Bodyworks, Jim Newton, Rick Charette, music for *Sesame Street* (soundtrack work).

STUDIO A, 87 Sherry Ave., Bristol RI 02809. (401)253-4183. Fax: (401)253-7421. Owners: Jim Wilson Jr., and Jack Anderson. Recording studio, music production. Estab. 1988. Deals with artists and songwriters. Produces 2 singles, 4-6 LPs and 1-2 CDs/year. Fee derived from small fee from artist and standard royalties.
How to Contact: Write first and obtain permission to submit. Prefers cassette with 3 songs and lyric sheet or lead sheet. "Use good quality tape for demo." Does not return material. Reports in 1 month.
Music: Mostly **jazz, rock** and **fusion**; also **top 40**. Produced *Windharp*, written and recorded by Windharp; *Chili Bros. Band* (by T. Medeiros), recorded by Chili Bros. Band on Studio A Records (rock); and *Can't Let Go* (by Wilson), recorded by Cathy DeBurro on Make Mine Music Records (top 40). Other artists include Joe Parillo, Jack Anderson, Nan Michaels, Mike Zavoski, Prestige and Steppin' Out.

SUCCESSFUL PRODUCTIONS, 1203 Biltmore Ave., High Point NC 27260. (910)882-9990. President: Doris Lindsay. Record producer, music publisher (Better Times Publishing/BMI) and record company (Fountain Records). Estab. 1979. Deals with artists and songwriters. Produces 2 LPs/year. Fee derived from sales royalty.
How to Contact: Submit demo tape—unsolicited submissions are OK. Prefers cassette with 2 songs and lyric sheet. "Send a professional demo." SASE. Reports in 2 months.
Music: Mostly **country, pop** and **contemporary gospel**; also **blues, children's** and **Southern gospel**. Produced "American Song" (by K. Roeder/M. Terry), recorded by Terry Michaels (country); "Back In Time," written and recorded by Mitch Snow (country); and "Crossroads of My Life" (by Larry La Vey/Dave Right) recorded by Larry La Vey (blues), all on Fountain Records. Other artists include Pat Repose.
Tips: "Use a professional demo service."

PRESTON SULLIVAN ENTERPRISES, Dept. SM, 1217 16th Ave. S., Nashville TN 37212. (615)327-8129. President: Preston Sullivan. Record producer. Deals with artists and songwriters. Produces 10 singles and 4 LPs/year.
How to Contact: Submit demo tape—unsolicited submissions are OK. Prefers cassette (or videocassette) and lyric sheet. Does not return unsolicited material. Reports in 3 weeks.
Music: Mostly **hard rock, alternative rock, pop** and **R&B**. Produced "The Grinning Plowman" (by Michael Ake), recorded by The Grinning Plowmen (pop/rock); "Dessau" (by John Elliott), recorded by Dessau (dance) and "Dorcha," recorded by Dorcha (rock), all on Carlyle Records.

SURPRIZE RECORDS, INC., P.O. Box 6562, Philadelphia PA 19138-6562. (215)276-8861. President: W. Lloyd Lucas. Record producer, music publisher (Delev Music Co./BMI, Sign of the Ram Music/ASCAP, Gemini Lady Music/SESAC) and management firm. Estab. 1981. Deals with artists, songwriters and publishers. Produces 3-6 singles, 2-3 12″ singles and 3-6 LPs/year. Fee derived from sales royalty when song or artist is recorded.
How to Contact: Submit demo tape by mail—unsolicited submissions are OK. Prefers cassette with 1-3 songs and lyric or lead sheet. SASE. "We do not and will not accept certified mail." Reports in 1 month.
Music: Mostly **R&B, soul, top 40/pop, dance-oriented** and **MOR**. Produced *4U* and *Not In Love*, written and recorded by Jerry Dean; and *Since I Found You* (by Darryl Lucas), recorded by Lamar (R&B), all on Surprize Records. Other artists include Briheem X.
Tips: "Write songs that are what's happening on radio now, but try to visualize the next trend level so as not to copy old ideas. Send us good songs, we'll do the rest."

SYNDICATE SOUND, INC., 475 Fifth St., Struthers OH 44471. (216)755-1331. President: Jeff Wormley. Audio and video production company and record and song promotion company. Estab. 1987. Deals with artists and songwriters. Produces 6-10 singles, 3-4 12″ singles, 15-20 LPs, 10-15 EPs and 4-5 CDs/year. Fee derived from combination of sales royalty when song or artist is recorded, outright fee from recording artist or record company or production fee.
How to Contact: Submit demo tape—unsolicited submissions are OK. "Please send a promo package or biography (with pictures) of band, stating past and present concerts and records." SASE. Reports in 1 month.
Music: Mostly **rock, pop** and **Christian rock**; also **country, R&B** and **alternative**. Produced *The Swinging Johnsons* (by John Yuhas/John Massucco), recorded by The Johnsons on Hairy Discs (alternative); *25th Anniversary Collection* (by Bob Noble), recorded by Bob Noble & The Lost Then Found on LTF Records (Christian); and *Fact to Feet*, written and recorded by Tim Luman (Christian). Other artists include Mathew Gold, Rambling Reck, Medicine Train, Shilleleagh, the Ascensions, the Magpies, Terry Barrett.

GARY TANIN, 2139 N. 47th St., Milwaukee WI 53208. (414)444-2477. Producer: G. Tanin. Record producer. Estab. 1970. Deals with artists and songwriters. Produces 4 singles and 2 LPs/year. Fee derived from outright fee from recording artist or record company.
How to Contact: Write or call first and obtain permission to submit. Prefers cassette with 3 songs and lyric sheet. "On demos, piano line and vocals are OK. Prefer as complete a submission as possible." Does not return unsolicited material. Reports in 2 months.
Music: Mostly **rock, pop** and some **New Age**. Produced "The Holy Trinity," written and recorded by G. Tanin; *Empty Chairs*, written and recorded by Junior Brantley; and co-produced 1993 CD project by Sublime Nation, including tracks with Jerry Harrison (Talking Heads) and Victor DeLorenzo (ex-Violent Femmes), on Multimusica U.S.A.

TEXAS MUSIC MASTERS/WRIGHT PRODUCTIONS, 11231 Hwy. 64 E., Tyler TX 75707. Record producer. 30 years in business. Fee derived from outright fee from record company.
How to Contact: Submit demo tape—unsolicited submissions are OK. Prefers cassette with 3 songs and lyric sheet. SASE. Reports in 1 month.
Music: Mostly **country, gospel** and **blues**. Produced "The Road" (by Gene LeDoux), recorded by David Darst on Starquest Records; "Neon Glow," written and recorded by Jim Needham on Jukebox Records; and *Blue Jean* (by Alan Greene), recorded by Glen English on Starquest Records.

*TEXAS URBAN UNDERGROUND, 1118 #C, W. 10th St., Austin TX 78703. (512)476-6752. CEO: John Patterson AKA "PhD". Record producer. Estab. 1988. Deals with artists only. Produces 6-10 singles, 2-3 LPs and 1 CD/year. Fee derived from sales royalty when song or artist is recorded or outright fee from recording artist.
How to Contact: Submit demo tape by mail. Unsolicited submissions are OK. Prefers cassette with lyric sheet. "I prefer receiving demos in the mail to phone calls." Does not return material. Reports in 2-4 weeks.
Music: **Hip hop** and **dancehall reggae** only. Looking for dancehall singers and male/female rap vocalists. Produced *My Fuckin' Beeper* (by Papa Chuk/Patterson), recorded by Papa Chuk on EMI Records (hip hop); *Here It Is* and *Safe Sex Tip* (by Rogers/Patterson), recorded by Cooly Nation (hip hop).
Tips: "Send me wicked tapes, and no half-stepping."

THIRD FLOOR PRODUCTIONS, P.O. Box 40784, Nashville TN 37204. (615)331-1469. Producer: Steven Ray Pinkston. Record producer. Estab. 1982. Deals with artists and songwriters. Produces 3 singles, 10 LPs and 10 CDs/year. Fee derived from sales royalty or outright fee from recording artist and/or record company.
How to Contact: Submit demo tape by mail. Unsolicited submissions are OK. Prefers cassette (or VHS videocassette if available) or DAT with 2 songs. SASE. Reports in 2 months. Send to attention of Jim Chapman, A&R.
Music: Mostly **pop, rock, country** and **contemporary Christian**. Artists include Graham Man, CRH, Brian White, Justice, Lazenby.
Tips: "Looking for artists now!"

STEVE THOMPSON PRODUCTIONS INC., P.O. Box 623, Centerport NY 11721. (516)754-5438. Business Manager: Andrew Kipnes (212-924-2929). Record producer, music publisher, production company ("sign acts and place songs"), Thompson and Barbiero Productions (ASCAP, NARAS). Estab. 1986. Deals with artists and songwriters. Fee derived from sales royalty when song or artist is recorded or outright fee from record company.
How to Contact: Submit demo tape by mail. Unsolicited submissions are OK. Prefers cassette (or VHS videocassette) with 4 songs and lyric sheet. SASE. Reports in 3-4 weeks.
Music: Mostly **rock, alternative** and **pop**; also **R&B, dance** and **country**. Produced all Tesla LPs on Geffen Records; Expose on Arista Records and Snakeyedsue on Giant/WB Records. Other artists include Guns 'N' Roses, Metallica and Soundgarden.
Tips: "Make your music stand out from the competition. Music must be contemporary and not corporate!!"

TMC PRODUCTIONS, P.O. Box 12353, San Antonio TX 78212. (210)829-1909. Producer: Joe Scates. Record producer, music publisher (Axbar Productions/BMI, Scates & Blanton/BMI and Axe Handle Music/ASCAP), record company (Axbar, Trophy, Jato, Prince and Charro Records) and record distribution and promotion. Deals with artists and songwriters. Produces 8-10 singles, 3-4 LPs and 4-6 CDs/year. Fee derived from sales royalty or outright fee from recording artist or record company.
How to Contact: Write or call first and obtain permission to submit. Prefers cassette with 1-5 songs and lyric sheet. SASE. Reports "as soon as possible, but don't rush us."
Music: Mostly **traditional country**; also **blues, comedy** and **rock (soft)**. Produced "Wake Up Heart" (by June Fox), recorded by Denise Trapani; "Like Smoke In The Wind" (by Jerry Dove), recorded by Billy D. Hunter; and *Texas Talent Vol. 3*, written and recorded by various artists. Other artists

include Kenny Dale, George Chambers, Wayne Carter, Ed Guinn, Carroll Gilley.
Tips: "Great lyrics, good hook line. Give us a good, well thought out song and we will arrange it, but we don't have time to teach you the basics of songwriting."

TOMSICK BROTHERS PRODUCTIONS, 21271 Chardon Rd., Dept. SM, Euclid OH 44117. (216)481-8380. President: Ken Tomsick. Record producer. Estab. 1982. Produces 2-5 LPs/year. Also produces original music for TV, radio, video and ad jingles. Fee derived from outright fee from recording artist.
How to Contact: Submit demo tape by mail—unsolicited submissions are OK. Prefers cassette. Does not return unsolicited material. Reports in 1 month.
Music: Mostly **ethnic, polka** and **New Age/experimental**. Produced "A Brand New Beginning," written and recorded by David M. Lynch on T.B.P. Records; *Teacher's Pet* and *Sweet 16*, recorded by Nancy Hlad. Other artists include Matt Traum Trio (jazz) and The Polka-Poppers (polkas and waltzes).

TRAC RECORD CO., 170 N. Maple, Fresno CA 93702. (209)255-1717. Owner: Stan Anderson. Record producer, music publisher (Sellwood Publishing/BMI) and record company (Trac Records). Estab. 1972. Works with artists and songwriters. Produces 5 12" singles, 5 LPs and 5 CDs/year. Fee derived from outright fee from recording artist.
How to Contact: Submit demo tape by mail. Unsolicited submissions are OK. Prefers cassette with 3 songs and lyric sheet. "Studio quality." SASE. Reports in 3 weeks.
Music: Mostly **traditional country** and **country rock**. Produced "Whiskey Blues," "Dan" and "Night Time Places," all written and recorded by Jimmy Walker on Trac Records. Other artists include Jessica James and The Country Connection.

THE TRINITY STUDIO, P.O. Box 1417, Corpus Christi TX 78403. (512)880-9268. Owner: Jim Wilken. Record company (TC Records) and recording studio. Estab. 1988.
How to Contact: Submit demo tape by mail—unsolicited submissions are OK. Prefers cassette (or VHS videocassette if available). Does not return material. Reports in 2 weeks.
Music: Mostly **Christian-country**. Recently produced Leah (singer), Merrill Lane (singer/songwriter) and Lofton Kline (singer/songwriter).
Tips: "You must maintain a positive attitude about your career. Have faith in your work and don't get discouraged—keep at it."

*TRIPLANE PRODUCTION, 325 Winter Cress Dr., Henderson NV 89015. (702)564-3794. Producer: Vales Crossley. Record producer and music publisher. Estab. 1978. Deals with artists and songwriters. Produces 6 singles, 2 12" singles, 3 LPs, 3 EPs and 2 CDs/year. Fee derived from sales royalty when song or artist is recorded, outright fee from recording artist or record company.
How to Contact: Write or call first and obtain permission to submit. Prefers cassette (or VAC videocassette if available) with 3-6 songs and lyric sheet. Does not return unsolicited material. Reports in 4-6 weeks.
Music: Mostly **top 40, R&B, soul** and **rap**; also **New Age** and **rock**. Produced *Check Mates Live* (by various), recorded by Vales Crossley on Checkmate Records (dance); and *Street Wise* (by L. Thomas), recorded by Vales Crossley on Street Records (rap). Other artists include Plattels, Chrissie Zastzow and Mipori Powels.
Tips: "Be as ready to take care of business as you are to record."

* TUMAC ENTERTAINMENT, 4014 Colfax Ave., Studio City CA 91604. (818)769-0076. Fax: (818)769-2522. President: Paul McKenna. Record producer, record company and music publisher. Estab. 1987. Deals with artists and songwriters. Produces 10 LPs and 10 CDs/year. Fee derived from sales royalty when song or artist is recorded or outright fee from record company.
How to Contact: Submit demo tape by mail. Unsolicited submissions are OK. Prefers cassette with 4 songs. SASE. Reports in 1 month.
Music: Mostly **alternative, rock** and **spoken word**; also **rap, pop** and **country**. Produced Wall of Voodoo on IRS Records; Thin White Rope on Frontier Records; and Hammerbox on A&M Records. Other artists include Tori Amos, Sting and Elton John.

*TUNEWORKS RECORDS INC., 4433 Petit Dr., Encino CA 91436. (818)906-0618. Fax: (818)907-7664. General Manager: Anita Alban. Record producer and music publisher. Estab. 1980. Deals with artists and songwriters. Produces 6-10 singles and 2-4 LPs/year. Fee derived from sales royalty when song or artist is recorded.
How to Contact: Write first and obtain permission to submit. Prefers cassette with 3 songs and lyric sheet. Does not return material. Reports in 2-4 weeks.
Music: Mostly **R&B, pop** and **rock**; also **jazz** and **alternative**. Produced "Baby Be Still," written and recorded by Coming of Age on Zoo Entertainment (R&B); "Lucky Man," written and recorded by Dave Koz on Capitol Records (pop); and *Angel of the Night*, written and recorded by Phil Perry on GRP Records (jazz). Other artists include For Real (A&M), Volume III (Sony) and Riff (EMI).

Tips: "Submit hit songs that have a character and style, regardless of type of music."

TURBO RECORDS, Box 409, East Meadow NY 11554. (516)486-8699. President: Jay Gold. Record producer, music publisher (Jay Gold Music/BMI) and record company. Estab. 1981. Deals with artists and songwriters. Produces 5 singles and 2 12″ singles/year. Fee derived from sales royalty or outright fee from recording artist or record company.
How to Contact: Submit demo tape by mail—unsolicited submissions are OK. Prefers cassette with 3 songs and lyric sheet. Reports in 5 weeks.
Music: Mostly **pop** and **rock.** Produced "All the Wrong Reasons"; "Better Love"; and "Radio Riot," all written and recorded by Jay Gold on Turbo Records.
Tips: "Review your lyrics and be open to changes."

12 METER PRODUCTIONS, 7808 Green Lake Rd., Fayetteville NY 13066. (315)637-6656. Producers: Matt Tucker and Chris Horvath. Record producer. Estab. 1988. Deals with artists and songwriters. Produces 1-5 singles, 1-5 12″ singles 1-2 LPs and 1-2 CDs/year. Fee derived from sales royalty or outright fee from recording artist or record company.
How to Contact: Submit demo tape by mail. Unsolicited submissions are OK. Prefers cassette (or VHS videocassette if available) with 1-5 songs and lyric sheet. "Send photo, press kit or bio if available. No calls." SASE. Reports in 2-3 months.
Music: Mostly **top 40/pop, dance** and **rock**; also **rap** and **R&B**. Produced "How Can I Forget You," recorded by Jodi Bilotti and "Hello, America," recorded by Blue Steel, both on CCD Records; and "It Had All Just Been A Dream" (by Murray/Tucker), recorded by Love Is Blue, all written by Horvath/Tucker.
Tips: "Send what you feel is your best work. Don't restrict yourself to one type of music. We listen to everything. Be professional and be patient."

27TH DIMENSION INC., P.O. Box 8495, Jupiter FL 33468-8495. (800)634-6091. President: John St. John. Record producer, music publisher (ASCAP, BMI) and music library. Estab. 1986. Deals with composers and songwriters. Produces 10 CDs/year.
How to Contact: Write or call first and obtain permission to submit. Prefers cassette. Does not return unsolicited submissions. Reports in 1 month.
Music: Mostly **industrial, pop jazz** and **industrial fusion**; also **pop, impressionism** and **descriptive**. "Instrumentals only!" Produced *Country Xmas*, recorded by Generic (country) and *Angelic Xmas*, recorded by Michele Amato (New Age), both on Madaay Records; and *Dimension 10*, written and recorded by various artists on Dimensional Records (dance). Other artists include Mary Hart, Morgan Brittany, Strickly Blakk.

CHARLES VICKERS MUSIC ASSOCIATION, Box 725, Daytona Beach FL 32015-0725. (904)252-4849. President/Producer: Dr. Charles H. Vickers D.M. Record producer, music publisher (Pritchett Publication/BMI, Alison Music/ASCAP) and record company (King of Kings Records and L.A. International Records). Deals with artists and songwriters. Produces 3 singles and 6 LPs/year. Fee derived from sales royalty.
How to Contact: Write first and obtain permission to submit. Prefers 7½ ips reel-to-reel or cassette with 1-6 songs. SASE. Reports in 1 week.
Music: Mostly **church/religious, gospel** and **hymns**; also **bluegrass, blues, classical, country, easy listening, jazz, MOR, progressive, reggae (pop), R&B, rock, soul** and **top 40/pop**. Produced "Always Depend on Jesus," "The Lord is My Proctor" and "Everyday is a Holy Day," all written and recorded by C. Vickers on King of King Records.

WILLIAM F. WAGNER, Dept. SM, Suite 218, 14343 Addison St., Sherman Oaks CA 91423. (818)905-1033. Contact: Bill Wagner. Record producer. Estab. 1957. Deals with artists and songwriters. Produces 4-6 singles, 2-4 LPs and 2-4 CDs/year. Works with 25 new songwriters/year. Fee derived from sales royalty or outright fee from recording artist or record company.
How to Contact: Submit demo tape by mail—unsolicited submissions are OK. Prefers cassette with 1-5 songs and lead sheets. "No lyric sheets. Material should be copyrighted." SASE. Reports in 1 month.
Music: Mostly **top 40, pop, country** and **jazz**; also **blues, choral, gospel, easy listening, MOR, progressive, rock** and **soul**. Produced *Julie Is Her Name* (by Bobby Troup), recorded by H.A. Kratzsch on Four Freshmen Society Records; *What'll I Do* (by I. Berlin), recorded by Sandy Graham on Muse Records; and *All The Things You Are* (by Kern/Hammerstein), recorded by Page Cavanaugh on Starline Records.
Tips: "Either send a simple tune demo, or a finished record—but not both in the same track."

*WALL STREET PRODUCTIONS, 1189 E. 14 Mile, Birmingham MI 48009. (810)646-2054. Fax: (810)646-1957. Executive Producers: Tim Rochon and Joe Sanders. Record producer, record company, music publisher. Estab. 1985. Deals with artists and songwriters. Produces 6 singles, 4 12" singles, 3 LPs and 6 CDs/year. Fee derived from sales royalty when song or artist is recorded or outright fee from record company.

How to Contact: Write or call first and obtain permission to submit. Prefers cassette (or videocassette if available) with 2 songs and lyric sheet. "Label all materials completely." Reports in 3 weeks.

Music: Mostly **rap, hip hop** and **dance**; also **R&B** and **jazz**. Produced *Outtabounds*, written and recorded by ANG (rap); "UR So Good 2 Me," written and recorded by Drueada (house); and "Do U Luv Me" (by CFT & The Wave), recorded by Stevie C. (rave), all on WSM Records. Other artists include Greg C. Brown and Jay Lyles.

Tips: "If you're able to produce great songs to near master quality, we'll do business."

WATERBURY PRODUCTIONS, 6833 Murietta Ave., Van Nuys CA 91405. (818)909-9092. Owner: David. Record producer, record company (Ultimate of Cool Records). Estab. 1987. Deals with artists and songwriters. Produces 15 LPs and 3 CDs/year. Fee derived from royalty when song or artist is recorded, outright fee from recording artist or record company.

How to Contact: Submit demo tape by mail. Unsolicited submissions are OK. Prefers cassette with 3-4 songs and lyric sheet. SASE. Reports in 2-5 weeks.

Music: Mostly **modern rock, dance** and **pop rock**; also **techno, alternative** and **blues rock**. Produced *Unexpected Discoveries* and *Secrets of California*, compilations of unsigned L.A. Bands; and *Earthquake*, written and recorded by Dave Shavu, all on Ultimate of Cool Records. Other artists include Holy Soldier (A&M), Tony Bazurto, Ultramatix, X-OT-X and Lisa Shea.

Tips: "Be creative, unique."

WAVE GROUP SOUND, P.O. Box 424, San Leandro CA 94577. (510)522-6463. Producer/Engineer: James Allen. Record producer. "Staff engineer for Skywalker Sound North, a division of Lucas Digital Services." Estab. 1981. Deals with artists and songwriters. Produces 2 singles, 4 LPs and 2 CDs/year. Fee derived from sales royalty when song or artist is recorded, outright fee from recording artist or record company.

How to Contact: Submit demo tape by mail. Unsolicited submissions are OK. Prefers cassette (or VHS videocassette if available) with 3 songs and lyric or lead sheet. SASE. Reports in 2 months.

Music: Mostly **New Age, jazz** and **rock**; also **country, blues** and **R&B**. Co-produced *Half Moon Bay* and *Fantasy* (by William Aura), recorded by William Aura and James Allen on Higher Octave Records; and *Traveler* (by Paul Horn), recorded by Christopher Hedge and James Allen on CBS Records. Other artists include Pacific Heights, Bombay Heat and Dan Vicrey.

Tips: "Looking for very melodic material. Excellent hooks. Memorable. Visual. Impressionistic."

THE WEISMAN PRODUCTION GROUP, 449 N. Vista St., Los Angeles CA 90036. (213)653-0693. Contact: Ben Weisman. Record producer and music publisher (Audio Music Publishers). Estab. 1965. Deals with artists and songwriters. Produces 10 singles/year. Fee derived from sales royalty.

How to Contact: Prefers cassette with 3-10 songs and lyric sheet. SASE. "Mention *Songwriter's Market*. Please make return envelope the same size as the envelopes you send material in, otherwise we cannot send everything back. Just send tape." Reports in 1 month.

Music: Mostly **R&B, soul, dance, rap** and **top 40/pop**; also **all types of rock**.

Tips: "Work on hooks and chorus, not just verses. Too many songs are only verses."

*WESTWIRE PRODUCTIONS, 1042 Club Ave., Allentown PA 18103. (610) 435-1924. Contacts: Wayne Becker and Larry Dix. Record producer and production company. Deals with artists and songwriters. Fee derived from sales royalty or outright fee from record company.

How to Contact: Submit demo tape by mail. Unsolicited submissions are OK. Prefers cassette (or VHS videocassette if available) with 3 songs and lyric sheet. SASE. Reports in 1 month.

Music: R&B, dance, alternative and **improvisation**. Produced *Flying Discs of Luv*, recorded by Trap Door on Interstellar Discs. Other artists include Danielle Lubene.

Tips: "We're interested in artists who have performance value. Songwriters must capture the young vibe."

WILBUR PRODUCTIONS, #10, 159 W. Fourth St., New York NY 10014. (212)727-3450. President: Will Schillinger. Record producer, recording engineer/studio owner, Wilbur Systems Inc. Estab. 1989. Deals with artists and songwriters. Produces 50 singles, 20 LPs and 20 CDs/year. Fee derived from sales royalty when song or artist is recorded or outright fee from record company.

How to Contact: Submit demo tape by mail. Unsolicited submissions are OK. Prefers cassette with 3-5 songs. Does not return unsolicited material. Reports in 2 weeks.

Music: Mostly **rock** and **country**. Produced "Something in Her Laughter," written and recorded by Marshall Crenshaw on WSL Records; *Walking On The Moon* (by Katie Moffit), recorded by Janet Burgan on WSL Records; and *5 Tunes*, written and recorded by Jon Herrington on Pioneer Records.

*WILLOW SHADE RECORDS, 685 Millikens, Woodburn KY 42170. Business Manager: Susan Webber. Record producer, record company. Estab. 1986. Deals with artists and songwriters. Produces 3-4 LPs and 3-4 CDs/year. Fee derived from sales royalty when song or artist is recorded.
How to Contact: Submit demo tape by mail. Unsolicited submissions are OK. Prefers cassette with 2-4 songs and lead sheet, score. SASE. Reports in 2 months.
Music: Mostly **instrumental, acoustic** and **classical**; also **New Age, jazz** and **electronic**. Produced *New Interpretations*, written and recorded by Kevin Gallagher (classical); *Cumberland Consort*, written and recorded by Sharon Law, David Kelsey and Stephen Webber (instrumental); and *Sampler '93*, written and recorded by various artists (classical/jazz), all on Willow Shade Records. Other artists include Brenda Stuart, Martha Kelsey, John Martin and Doug Woodson.
Tips: "High quality original or classical instrumental music is what we are looking for. Submit on high quality high-bias tape."

FRANK WILLSON, Box 2297, Universal City TX 78148. (512)653-3989. Producer: Frank Willson. Record producer and record company (BSW Records). Deals with artists and songwriters. Estab. 1987. Produces 4 singles, 12-15 12″ singles, 10-12 LPs, 3 EPs and 5 CDs/year. Fee derived from sales royalty.
How to Contact: Submit demo tape by mail. Unsolicited submissions are OK. Prefers cassette with 3-4 songs and lyric sheets. SASE. Reports in 5 weeks.
Music: Mostly **country**. Produced "My Boss" (by D. Fleming), recorded by Paradise Canyon; "I Cried My Last Tear" (by Tony Tolliver), recorded by Candee Land; and "Bulls to Bronks," written and recorded by Rusty Doherty, all on BSW Records. Other artists include Mike Lord, Jess DeMaine, Harold Dean, Ron Arlen, C. Howard, Stan Crawford and Bobby Lloyd.

WIR (WORLD INTERNATIONAL RECORDS), A-1090 Vienna, Servitengasse 24, **Austria**. 707-37-10. Fax: 707-84-22. Contact: Peter Jordan. Record producer, music publisher (Aquarius) and record company (WIR). Estab. 1986. Deals with artists and songwriters. Produces 5-10 singles and 5-8 LPs/year. Fee derived from outright fee from recording artist or record company.
How to Contact: Write or call first and obtain permission to submit. Prefers cassette. SASE. Reports in 2-4 weeks.
Music: Produced *We're In Love* (by Steve Haggard), *The Best Is Yet to Come* (by M. McLelland) and *Eight Eyes* (by Claudia Robot), all recorded by Aquarius on WIR Records. Other artists include Crossover, ABC Guitars, The Cones, Diana Blair, Doug McGinnis, Dale Davis and Harry Bonanza and Band.

WLM MUSIC/RECORDING, 2808 Cammie St., Durham NC 27705-2020. (919)471-3086. Owner: Watts Lee Mangum. Recording studio (small), also Clay Man Productions. Estab. 1980. Deals with artists and songwriters. Produces 6-8 singles/year. Fee derived from outright fee from recording artist. "In some cases — an advance payment requested for demo production."
How to Contact: Submit demo tape — unsolicited submissions are OK. Prefers cassette with 2-4 songs and lyric or lead sheet (if possible). SASE. Reports in 4 months.
Music: Mostly **country, country/rock** and **blues/rock**; also **pop, rock** and **R&B**. Produced "High Time" and "Heart of Stone," written and recorded by Clayton Wrenn; and "Crown Royal Nights," written and recorded by Alan Dunn, all on WLM Records. Other artists include Barry Hayes, Pamela Rhea, Ron Davis, John Davis and Clint Clayton.
Tips: "Submit good demo tapes with artist's ideas, words, and music charted if possible."

MARK WOLFSON PRODUCTIONS, Suite 134, 11684 Ventura Blvd., Studio City CA 91604. (818)506-5467. Fax: (818)980-9756. Producer/Engineer: Mark Wolfson. Record producer, engineer/music supervisor (Tape Registry). Estab. 1972. Deals with artists and songwriters. Produces 12 singles, 2 12″ singles and 2 CDs/year. Fee derived from sales royalty when song or artist is recorded or outright fee from record company. "Will co-write with other established writers or artists."
How to Contact: Submit demo tape by mail. Unsolicited submissions are OK. SASE. Reports in 6 weeks.
Music: Produced *Mary Down the Street* (by Deleo), recorded by Stone Temple Pilots on Savage/MCA Records.
Tips: "Write phone number on all materials (cassette and box), send lyrics, and send no more than 4 songs at a time. Request verbal or written reply."

STEVE WYTAS PRODUCTIONS, Dept. SM, 11 Custer St., West Hartford CT 06110. (203)953-2834. Contact: Steven J. Wytas. Record producer. Estab. 1984. Deals with artists and labels. Produces 4-8 singles, 6 12″ singles, 3 LPs, 3 EPs and 2 CDs/year. Fee derived from outright fee from recording artist or record company.
How to Contact: Submit demo tape by mail. Unsolicited submissions are OK. Prefers cassette (or VHS-¾″ videocassette) with several songs and lyric or lead sheet. "Include live material if possible." Does not return unsolicited material. Reports in 3 months.

Music: Mostly **rock, metal, pop, top 40** and **country/acoustic**. Produced *Black* (by B. Whitten), recorded by St. Johnny on Caroline Records (rock); "Sports," written and recorded by Jon Aley on TM's Records (rock); and *Butterfly*, written and recorded by All the Voices on Turnip Records (rock). Other artists include Flying Nuns, Sons of Bob, MG's, Mud Solo, Stupe, Tom Hughes, Savage Brothers and Those Melvins.

ZEKE PRODUCTIONS, INC., 15H, 345 E. 80th St., New York NY 10021. (212)744-2312. President: Chuck Dembrak. Record producer and music publisher (Cool One Music/ASCAP). Estab. 1978. Deals with artists and songwriters. Produces 3-6 12" singles and 1-2 LPs/year. Fees derived from sales royalty and outright fee from record company. "Charges for consultation."
How to Contact: Submit demo tape by mail. Unsolicited submissions are OK. Prefers cassette (or VHS videocassette if available) with 3-4 songs and lyric sheet. SASE. Reports in 4 weeks.
Music: Mostly **R&B, pop** and **rock**. Produced *Surrender* (by J. Roach), recorded by Double Digit, and "Just A Touch" (by M. Ervin), recorded by Break-Uv-Dawn, both on Spy Records; and "Warmth" (by D. Oliver), recorded by Mesa on Esquire Records. Other artists include Larry Caldwell.

Category Index

The Category Index is a good place to begin searching for a market for your songs. Below is an alphabetical list of 19 general music categories. If you write dance music and are looking for a record producer to submit your songs to, check the Dance section in this index. There you will find a list of record producers who work with dance music. Once you locate the entries for those producers, read the music subheading *carefully* to determine which companies are most interested in the type of dance music you write. Some of the markets in this section do not appear in the Category Index because they have not indicated a specific preference. Most of these said they are interested in "all types" of music. Listings that were very specific, or whose description of the music they're interested in doesn't quite fit into these categories, also do not appear here.

Adult Contemporary Aberdeen Productions; Alstatt Enterprises; Amethyst Records, Inc.; Anonymous Productions; Bal Records; Bay Farm Productions; Carlock Productions; Carolina Pride Productions; Country Star Productions; Daliven Music; Diamond Entertainment, Joel; Excell Productions; Ferguson Productions, Don; Hammel Associates, Inc. R L; Hickory Lane Publishing and Recording; Intrigue Production; James, Sunny; Jump Productions; June Productions Ltd.; Kingsport Creek Music; Known Artist Productions; Kool Breeze Productions; Kovach, Robert R.; Loco Sounds; Luick & Associates, Harold; Magid Productions, Lee; Miller Productions, Jay; Mittelstedt, A.V.; Monticana Productions; Nashville International Entertainment Group; New Horizon Records; Panio Brothers Label; Parker, Patty; Paton, Dave; Perennial Productions; Peridot Productions; Pine Island Music; Prescription Co., The; Rose Hill Group; Surprize Records, Inc.; The; Vickers Music Association, Charles; Wagner, William F.
Alternative Basement Boys, Inc.; Bongo Boy; Breadline Productions; Briefcase of Talent Productions; Bullet Proof Management; Carlock Productions; Chrome Dreams Productions; Coachouse Music; Datura Productions; Davis Soto Orban Productions; Doubletime Productions; Dudick, J.D.; Empty Street Productions; Grunwell/The O.C. Chadwock Co., Alfred B.; Horsefeathers Music Company Inc.; Howe Productions; Insight Records; J.L. Productions; JK Jam Productions; L.A. Entertainment; Mulberry Street Recorders; Music Factory Enterprises, Inc.; Perennial Productions; Post Modern Productions; Prejippie Music Group; Rainbow Recording; SAS Corporation/ Special Audio Services; Soundhouse Recording/Scott Crane; Soundmax Media Services; Stuart Audio Services; Sullivan Enterprises, Preston; Thompson Productions Inc., Steve; Tumac Entertainment; Tuneworks Records Inc.; Waterbury Productions; Westwire Productions
Blues Amato, Buzz; Bal Records; Big Bear; Bonta L, Peter; Celt, Jan; Coachouse Music; Demi Monde Records & Publishing Ltd.; Duane Music, Inc.; Esquire International; Hammel Associates, Inc. R L; Kool Breeze Productions; Landmark Communications Group; Linear Cycle Productions; Magid Productions, Lee; Miller Productions, Jay; Modern Minstrel Mixing; Monticana Productions; New Horizon Records; Pigmy Productions; Pine Island Music; Prescription Co., The; Ran-

ductions; Bay Farm Productions; Big Picture Record Co.; Coppin, Johnny/Red Sky Records; Ergo Communications; Gland Puppies, Inc., The; Highstein Music, Max; Magid Productions, Lee; Maja Music; Miller Productions, Jay; Modern Minstrel Mixing; Monticana Productions; Nightstar Records Inc.; Peridot Productions; Person to Person Productions; Pigmy Productions; Pine Island Music; Prairie Music Ltd.; Rustron Music Productions; Silver Thorn Enterprises; Stuart Audio Services

Jazz Allyn, Stuart J.; Amato, Buzz; Angel Films Company; audiofile Tapes; Aurora Productions; Bal Records; Bernstein, Richard; Big Bear; C.S.B. Mix Inc.; Capitol Ad, Management & Talent; Care Free Records Group; Celt, Jan; Chapman, Chuck; Core Productions; Creative Music Services; Daliven Music; Darrow, Danny; De Miles, Edward; Esquire International; Fishbowl Productions; Haworth Productions; Heart Consort Music; Howe Productions; James, Sunny; Jamland Studios; Jazzand; Landmark Communications Group; LJG Productions; Magid Productions, Lee; Masterpiece Productions & Studios; Mom and Pop Productions, Inc.; Monticana Productions; Neo Sync Labs; New Horizon Records; Panama Music Library; Panepento, Michael/Airwave Production Group Inc.; Paton, Dave; Perennial Productions; Person to Person Productions; Peterson Creative Management, Paul; Philly Breakdown; Pigmy Productions; Pine Island Music; Prescription Co., The; Rocky Mountain Heartland Productions; Rose Hill Group; St. Mitchell, Jojo; Slavesong Corporation, Inc.; Sound Services; Studio A; Tuneworks Records Inc.; 27th Dimension Inc.; Vickers Music Association, Charles; Wagner, William F.; Wall Street Productions; Wave Group Sound; Willow Shade Records

Latin Apon Record Company, Inc.; DeLory And Music Makers, Al; Go Jo Productions; Hansen Productions; Loco Sounds; Mīmác Productions

Metal "A" Major Sound Corporation; Briefcase of Talent Productions; Care Free Records Group; Datura Productions; Gland Puppies, Inc., The; Grass Recording And Sound; Mīmác Productions; Primal Productions, Inc.; Randall Productions; SAS Corporation/Special Audio Services; Wytas Productions, Steve

New Age Aurora Productions; Big Picture Record Co.; Care Free Records Group; Chrome Dreams Productions; Coppelia; Corwin, Dano; Dennis, Warren; Festival Studios; Gland Puppies, Inc., The; Graffiti Productions Inc.; Green Dream Productions; Haworth Productions; Heart Consort Music; Highstein Music, Max; Jamland Studios; Jericho Sound Lab; Kren Music Productions; L.A. Entertainment; Leeway Entertainment Group; Maja Music; Multi Sound Images; Neu Electro Productions; Nightstar Records Inc.; Primal Productions, Inc.; Rustron Music Productions; Sauers Audio Productions and Recording, Alwin; Silent Partner Productions; Soundmax Media Services; Sphere Productions; Tanin, Gary; Tomsick Brothers Productions; Triplane Production; Wave Group Sound; Willow Shade Records

Novelty Gland Puppies, Inc., The; Jay Jay Publishing And Record Co.; Johnson, Ralph D.; Linear Cycle Productions; Miller Productions, Jay; Nashville Country Productions; Paton, Dave; Peridot Productions; TMC Productions

Pop A & R Recording Services; "A" Major Sound Corporation; Aberdeen Productions; ACR Productions; AKO Production; Allen-Martin Productions Inc.; Allyn, Stuart J.; Alstatt Enterprises; Amato, Buzz; Angel Films Company; Aurora Productions; Bal Records; Bartow Music; Bay Farm Productions; Bell Records International; Big Picture Record Co.; Big Productions and Publishing Co. Inc.; Blaze Productions; Bowden, Robert; Capitol Ad, Management & Talent; Care Free Records Group; Carlock Productions; Carlyle Productions; Carolina Pride Productions; Carr, Steve; Cedar Creek Productions; Coachouse Music; Coppelia; Core Productions; Corwin, Dano; Creative Music Services; Cross Culture Productions, Inc.; Crystal Clear Productions; Darrow, Danny; Datura Productions; Davis Soto Orban Productions; De Miles, Edward; DeLory And Music Makers, Al; Demi Monde Records & Publishing Ltd.; Dennis, Warren; Diamond Entertainment, Joel; Doss Presents, Col. Buster; Duane Music, Inc.; Dudick, J.D.; E.S.R. Productions; 8th Street Music; Element & Superstar Production; Empty Street Productions; Esquire International; Excell Productions; Faber, Shane; Ferguson Productions, Don; Festival Studios; Fishbowl Productions; Fricon Entertainment Co., Inc., The; Gland Puppies, Inc., The; Go Jo Productions; Green Dream Productions; Grunwell/The O.C. Chadwock Co., Alfred B.; Guess Who?? Productions; Hammel Associates, Inc. R L; Hart/Hart Productions, Stephen A.; Horrigan Productions; Howe Productions; I.Y.F. Productions; Intrigue Production; Ivory Productions, Inc.; J.L. Productions; Jag Studio, Ltd.; James Productions, Neal; Janoulis Productions, Alexander; Jericho Sound Lab; JGM Recording Studio; JK Jam Productions; Jump Productions; June Productions Ltd.; Kingsport Creek Music; Kingston Records and Talent; Known Artist Productions; Kool Breeze Productions; Kovach, Robert R.; Kren Music Productions; L.A. Entertainment; Landmark Communications Group; Leeway Entertainment Group; Linear Cycle Productions; LJG Productions; Loco Sounds; Magic Apple Records; Magid Productions, Lee; Maja Music; Martin/Vaam Music Productions, Pete; Masterpiece Productions & Studios; Mathes Productions, David; Mathews/Hit Or Myth Productions, Scott; Melfi, Patrick; Miller Productions, Jay; Mīmác Productions; MJM Productions; Monticana Productions; Mraz, Gary John; Mulberry Street Recorders; Multi Sound Images; Munro/Random Entertainment Inc., Ross; Music Factory Enterprises, Inc.; Must Rock Productionz Worldwide; Nashville International Entertainment Group; Nebo Record Company; Nelson, Bill; Nemesis Media Labs; Neu Electro Productions; New Experience Records; Ormsby, John "Buck"/Etiquette Productions; Panama Music Library; Panepento, Michael/Airwave Production Group Inc.; Paton, Dave; Pearson Music, Martin; Perennial Productions; PERL Productions; Person to

Person Productions; Peterson Creative Management, Paul; Philly Breakdown; Pierce, Jim; Pigmy Productions; Pine Island Music; Poku Productions; Pomgar Productions; Pops Neon Enterprises; Post Modern Productions; Prescription Co., The; Primal Productions, Inc.; Rainbow Recording; Randall Productions; Red Kastle Productions; Reel Adventures; Rock & Troll Productions; Rockstar Productions; Rocky Mountain Heartland Productions; Rose Hill Group; Rosenman, Mike; Rustron Music Productions; St. Mitchell, Jojo; Sauers Audio Productions and Recording, Alwin; Segal's Productions; Sneak Tip Records Inc.; Sound Arts Recording Studio; Sound Planet; Sound Services; Sphere Productions; Stark Records and Tape Co.; Successful Productions; Sullivan Enterprises, Preston; Surprize Records, Inc.; Syndicate Sound, Inc.; Tanin, Gary; Third Floor Productions; Thompson Productions Inc., Steve; Triplane Production; Tumac Entertainment; Tuneworks Records Inc.; Turbo Records; 12 Meter Productions; 27th Dimension Inc.; Vickers Music Association, Charles; Wagner, William F.; Waterbury Productions; Weisman Production Group, The; WLM Music/Recording; Wytas Productions, Steve; Zeke Productions, Inc.

Rap Allen-Martin Productions Inc.; Bartow Music; Bullet Proof Management; C.S.B. Mix Inc.; Chapman, Chuck; Cross Culture Productions, Inc.; Cybortronik Recording Group; Element & Superstar Production; Faber, Shane; Festival Studios; Fishbowl Productions; Graffiti Productions Inc.; Guess Who?? Productions; Hansen Productions; I.Y.F. Productions; Inner Sound Productions; Intrigue Production; Jag Studio, Ltd.; KMA; LJG Productions; London Brijj; Magic Apple Records; Makers Mark Music Productions; Masterpiece Productions & Studios; Media Productions; Mr. Wonderful Productions, Inc.; Mulberry Street Recorders; Must Rock Productionz Worldwide; Nemesis Media Labs; Network Production Group, The; Neu Electro Productions; New Experience Records; PERL Productions; Philly Breakdown; Poku Productions; Primal Productions, Inc.; Rosenman, Mike; St. Mitchell, Jojo; SAS Corporation/Special Audio Services; Triplane Production; Tumac Entertainment; 12 Meter Productions; Wall Street Productions; Weisman Production Group, The

R&B "A" Major Sound Corporation; ACR Productions; Allen-Martin Productions Inc.; Allyn, Stuart J.; Alstatt Enterprises; Amato, Buzz; Amethyst Records, Inc.; Angel Films Company; Bal Records; Bartow Music; Basement Boys, Inc.; Bay Farm Productions; Bell Records International; Big Picture Record Co.; Big Productions and Publishing Co. Inc.; Briefcase of Talent Productions; Bullet Proof Management; C.S.B. Mix Inc.; Capitol Ad, Management & Talent; Carr, Steve; Cedar Creek Productions; Celt, Jan; Core Productions; Country Star Productions; Cross Culture Productions, Inc.; Cupit Productions, Jerry; Daddy, S. Kwaku; Daliven Music; Datura Productions; De Miles, Edward; Diamond Entertainment, Joel; Duane Music, Inc.; E.S.R. Productions; 8th Street Music; Element & Superstar Production; Esquire International; Faber, Shane; Fera Productions, Vito; Festival Studios; Fricon Entertainment Co., Inc., The; Global Assault Management and Consulting; Go Jo Productions; Graffiti Productions Inc.; Guess Who?? Productions; Hammel Associates, Inc. R L; Haworth Productions; House of Rhythm; Howe Productions; Inner Sound Productions; Intrigue Production; J.L. Productions; James Productions, Neal; James, Sunny; Janoulis Productions, Alexander; Jericho Sound Lab; JGM Recording Studio; JK Jam Productions; Kingsport Creek Music; KMA; Known Artist Productions; Kool Breeze Productions; Kovach, Robert R.; Kren Music Productions; L.A. Entertainment; Linear Cycle Productions; LJG Productions; Loco Sounds; London Brijj; Madison Station Productions; Magic Apple Records; Magid Productions, Lee; Makers Mark Music Productions; Martin/Vaam Music Productions, Pete; Masterpiece Productions & Studios; Mathes Productions, David; Mathews/Hit Or Myth Productions, Scott; Mïmác Productions; Mr. Wonderful Productions, Inc.; MJM Productions; Mom and Pop Productions, Inc.; Monticana Productions; Mraz, Gary John; Mulberry Street Recorders; Multi Sound Images; Must Rock Productionz Worldwide; Nashville International Entertainment Group; Nebo Record Company; Nemesis Media Labs; Network Production Group, The; New Experience Records; Ormsby, John "Buck"/Etiquette Productions; Panama Music Library; Panepento, Michael/Airwave Production Group Inc.; Paton, Dave; Pearson Music, Martin; Perennial Productions; PERL Productions; Philly Breakdown; Pigmy Productions; Pine Island Music; Prescription Co., The; Primal Productions, Inc.; Rainbow Recording; Randall Productions; Rock & Troll Productions; Rosenman, Mike; Rustron Music Productions; St. Mitchell, Jojo; Sauers Audio Productions and Recording, Alwin; Segal's Productions; Silent Partner Productions; Slavesong Corporation, Inc.; Sneak Tip Records Inc.; Sound Planet; Sound Services; Sullivan Enterprises, Preston; Surprize Records, Inc.; Syndicate Sound, Inc.; Thompson Productions Inc., Steve; Triplane Production; Tuneworks Records Inc.; 12 Meter Productions; Vickers Music Association, Charles; Wagner, William F.; Wall Street Productions; Wave Group Sound; Weisman Production Group, The; Westwire Productions; WLM Music/Recording; Zeke Productions, Inc.

Religious A & R Recording Services; "A" Major Sound Corporation; ACR Productions; Allen-Martin Productions Inc.; Amethyst Records, Inc.; Bal Records; Bell Records International; Capitol Ad, Management & Talent; Carlock Productions; Carolina Pride Productions; Cedar Creek Productions; Chapman, Chuck; Country Star Productions; Cowboy Junction Flea Market and Publishing Co.; Cupit Productions, Jerry; Daddy, S. Kwaku; Dennis, Warren; Doss Presents, Col. Buster; Earmark Audio; Eiffert, Jr., Leo J.; Element & Superstar Production; Esquire International; Faiella Productions, Doug; Fera Productions, Vito; Fox Farm Recording; Fricon Entertainment Co., Inc., The; Go Jo Productions; Hammel Associates, Inc. R L; Haworth Productions; Heartbeat Music; Hickory Lane Publishing and Recording; Jag Studio, Ltd.; James Productions, Neal; Kennedy Enterprises, Inc., Gene; Kingsport Creek Music; Kovach, Robert R.; Kren Music Productions; Landmark Communications Group; Lari-Jon Productions; Leavell, John; Linear Cycle Productions; Luick & Associates, Harold; McCoy Productions, Jim; Magid Productions, Lee; Masterpiece Productions & Studios; Mathes Productions, David; Media Productions; Miller Productions, Jay; Mr. Wonderful Productions, Inc.; Mittelstedt, A.V.; Mom and Pop Productions, Inc.; Monticana Productions; MSH Productions; Multi Sound Images; Nashville Country Productions; Nashville International Entertainment Group; Nebo Record Company; Nelson, Bill; New Experience Records; Peridot Productions; Philly Breakdown; Pine Island Music; Randall Productions; Rocky Mountain Heartland Productions; Sauers Audio Productions and Recording, Alwin; Shadowland Productions; Sound Control Productions; Sound Planet; Stark Records and Tape Co.; Stuart Audio Services; Successful Productions; Syndicate Sound, Inc.; Texas Music Masters; Third Floor Productions; Trinity Studio, The; Vickers Music Association, Charles; Wagner, William F.

Rock A & R Recording Services; "A" Major Sound Corporation; Aberdeen Productions; ACR Productions; AKO Production; Allen-Martin Productions Inc.; Allyn, Stuart J.; Alpha Music Productions; Alstatt Enterprises; Andrew & Francis; Angel Films Company; Anonymous Productions; audiofile Tapes; Aurora Productions; Bal Records; Bell Records International; Bernstein, Richard; Big Picture Record Co.; Blaze Productions; Bongo Boy; Bonta L, Peter; Breadline Productions; Briefcase of Talent Productions; Capitol Ad, Management & Talent; Care Free Records Group; Carlock Productions; Carlyle Productions; Carr, Steve; Cedar Creek Productions; Celt, Jan; Chapman, Chuck; Chrome Dreams Productions; Coachouse Music; Collector Records; Coppelia; Coppin, Johnny/Red Sky Records; Core Productions; Corwin, Dano; Country Star Productions; Crystal Clear Productions; Cupit Productions, Jerry; Daliven Music; Datura Productions; Davis Soto Orban Productions; Deep Space Records; De Miles, Edward; Demi Monde Records & Publishing Ltd.; Dennis, Warren; Diamond Entertainment, Joel; Doubletime Productions; Duane Music, Inc.; Dudick, J.D.; Earmark Audio; 8th Street Music; Element & Superstar Production; Empty Street Productions; England, Geoffrey; Ergo Communications; Esquire International; Faiella Productions, Doug; Fera Productions, Vito; Festival Studios; Fishbowl Productions; Fricon Entertainment Co., Inc., The; Go Jo Productions; Graffiti Productions Inc.; Hammel Associates, Inc. R L; Hansen Productions; Hart/Hart Productions, Stephen A.; Haworth Productions; Heartbeat Music; Hickory Lane Publishing and Recording; Horrigan Productions; Horsefeathers Music Company Inc.; House of Rhythm; Howe Productions; I.Y.F. Productions; Insight Records; Intrigue Production; Ivory Productions, Inc.; Jag Studio, Ltd.; James Productions, Neal; James, Sunny; Jamland Studios; Janoulis Productions, Alexander; Jericho Sound Lab; JGM Recording Studio; JK Jam Productions; June Productions Ltd.; Kingston Records and Talent; Kool Breeze Productions; Kovach, Robert R.; Kren Music Productions; L.A. Entertainment; Landmark Communications Group; Lari-Jon Productions; Leavell, John; Linear Cycle Productions; McCoy Productions, Jim; Magic Apple Records; Magid Productions, Lee; Maja Music; Making Texas Music, Inc.; Mathews/Hit Or Myth Productions, Scott; Media Productions; Miller Productions, Jay; Mīmác Productions; Mittelstedt, A.V.; MJM Productions; Modern Minstrel Mixing; Monticana Productions; Mulberry Street Recorders; Multi Sound Images; Munro/Random Entertainment Inc., Ross; Nashville International Entertainment Group; Nebo Record Company; Neo Sync Labs; Neu Electro Productions; New Experience Records; Ormsby, John "Buck"/Etiquette Productions; Panama Music Library; Panepento, Michael/Airwave Production Group Inc.; Paton, Dave; Pearson Music, Martin; Perennial Productions; Person to Person Productions; Peterson Creative Management, Paul; Pigmy Productions; Pine Island Music; Poku Productions; Pomgar Productions; Post Modern Productions; Prejippie Music Group; Prescription Co., The; Primal Productions, Inc.; Rainbow Recording; Randall Productions; Reel Adventures; Ripsaw Productions; Rock & Troll Productions; Rockstar Productions; Rocky Mountain Heartland Productions; Rose Hill Group; Rosenman, Mike; Rustron Music Productions; St. Mitchell, Jojo; SAS Corporation/Special Audio Services; Sauers Audio Productions and Recording, Alwin; Segal's Productions; Silver Thorn Enterprises; Sound Arts Recording Studio; Sound Planet; Sound Services; Soundhouse Recording/Scott Crane; Soundstage South; Sphere Productions; Stuart Audio Services; Studio A; Syndicate Sound, Inc.; Tanin, Gary; Third Floor Productions; Thompson Productions Inc., Steve; TMC Productions; Trac Record Co.; Triplane Production; Tumac Entertainment; Tuneworks Records Inc.; Turbo Records; 12 Meter Productions; Vickers Music Association, Charles; Wagner, William F.; Waterbury Productions; Wave Group Sound; Weisman Production Group, The; Wilbur Productions; WLM Music/Recording; Wytas Productions, Steve; Zeke Productions, Inc.

World Ancient Future Music; Apon Record Company, Inc.; audiofile Tapes; Bongo Boy; C.S.B. Mix Inc.; Daddy, S. Kwaku; Davis Soto Orban Productions; Dennis, Warren; Jamland Studios; Jericho Sound Lab; JGM Recording Studio; KMA; London Brijj; Maja Music; Modern Minstrel Mixing; Music Factory Enterprises, Inc.; Nemesis Media Labs; Panama Music Library; Person to Person Productions; Reel Adventures; Slavesong Corporation, Inc.; Tomsick Brothers Productions; Vickers Music Association, Charles

Record Producers/'94-'95 Changes

The following markets appeared in the 1994 edition of *Songwriter's Market* but are absent from the 1995 edition. Most of these companies failed to respond to our request for an update of their listing for a variety of reasons. For example, they may have gone out of business or they may have requested deletion from the 1995 edition because they are backlogged with material. If we know the specific reason, it appears within parentheses.

A Street Music
Active Sound Productions
Warren Anderson
August Night Music
The Beau-Jim Agency, Inc.
Bony "E" Productions, Inc. (unable to contact)
Boom Productions, Inc. (out of business)
Rafael Brom
Peter Cardinali
Eddie Carr (unable to contact)
Challedon Productions (out of business)
Continental Communications Corp.
Dave Cottrell (requested deletion)
Country Reel Enterprises
Creative Life Entertainment, Inc.
Wade Curtiss
D.B. Productions/Promotions
Mike De Leon Productions (requested deletion)
Dino M. Production Co.
The Eternal Song Agency
Ezra Gold Productions (unable to contact)
Goodknight Productions
Happy Days Music/Jeremy McClain
Hard Hat Productions (only produces in-house material)
Heading North Music

Hearing Ear
Hobar Production
Hogar Musical Productions (requested deletion)
Horizon Recording Studio
Innersounds Productions
Inspire Productions, Inc.
Intensified Productions
Jazmin Productions
Jet Laser Productions (requested deletion)
Tyrone Jones Productions (unable to contact)
Karen Kane Producer/Engineer
Matthew Katz Productions
Greg Knowles
Frank E. Koehl (unable to contact)
John Latimer (unable to contact)
Lemon Square Productions
Leopard Music
Live Productions Inc.
M.R. Productions
Cookie Marenco
Moon Productions and Recording Studio (out of business)
Musiplex (unable to contact)
Chuck Mymit Music Productions (did not respond)
Narada Productions (requested deletion)
Not Records Tapes (not accepting submissions)

Rick Nowels Productions, Inc. (requested deletion)
Nucleus Records (affiliate of Robert Bowden)
Chris Pati Productions, Inc. (unable to contact)
Pegmatite Productions
Persia Studios
Rockit Records, Inc.
Sagittar Records (out of business)
Sherwood Productions
Silver-Loomas Productions
S'N'M Recording Hit Records
Songwriters' Network (requested deletion)
Sounds of Winchester (affiliate of Jim McCoy Productions)
Spunk Productions
Jack Stang
Stepbridge Studios (requested deletion)
Stone Cold Productions
Studio City Productions (affiliate of Geoffrey England)
System (requested deletion)
Toro'na Int'l. (unable to contact)
Visual Music
Cornell Ward (unable to contact)
Ray Woods Production (not accepting submissions)

Managers and Booking Agents

Managers and booking agents are part of the circle of music industry professionals closest to the artists themselves. Working for and with their clients, they are a vital part of an aspiring artist's career.

The artist manager is a valuable contact, both for the songwriter trying to get songs to a particular artist and for the songwriter/performer. Often the manager is the person closest to the artist, and he may have heavy influence in what type of material the performer uses. Managers of nationally known acts are not the easiest people to approach. Many songwriters are trying to get songs to these people, and in most cases they only accept material from music publishers or producers they know personally or professionally.

You need not go further than your own hometown, however, to find artists hungry for new material. Managers of local acts often have more to say in the choice of material their clients perform and record than managers in major hubs, where the producer often makes the final decision on what songs are included in a particular project. Locally, it could be the manager who not only chooses songs for a recording project, but also selects the producer, the studio and the musicians.

If you are an artist or artist/songwriter seeking management, take care in selecting your representation. A manager must know about all aspects of the music industry. His handling of publicity, promotion and finances, plus his contacts within the industry will shape your career. Look for a manager or agency who will take an interest in your development. This can be worked into a management agreement to help insure management is working on your behalf. Above all, don't be afraid to ask questions about any aspects of the relationship between you and a prospective manager. He should be willing to explain any confusing terminology or discuss plans with you before taking action. Remember: A manager works *for the artist*. His main function is advising and counseling his clients, not dictating to them.

Another function of the manager is to act as liaison between the artist and the booking agent. Some management firms may also handle booking. However, it may be in your interest to look for a separate booking agency. It will give you another member of the team working to get your work heard in live performance, and adds to the network necessary to make valuable contacts in the industry. Since their function is mainly to find performance venues for their clients, booking agents represent many more acts than a management firm, and have less contact with individual acts. A booking agent will charge a commission for his services, as will a management firm. Managers usually ask for a 15-20% commission on an act's earnings; booking agents charge less.

Talent, originality, credits, dedication, self-confidence and professionalism are qualities that will attract a manager to an artist — and a songwriter. Before submitting to a manager or booking agent, be sure he's searching for the type of music you offer. And, just as if you were contacting a music publisher or producer, always be as organized and professional as possible. *Billboard* also publishes a list of managers/

booking agents in *Billboard's International Talent and Touring Directory*, published annually.

The firms listed in this section have provided information about the types of acts they currently work with and the type of music they're interested in (you will also want to refer to the Category Index at the end of this section). Each listing contains submission requirements and information about items to include in a press kit, and will also specify whether the company is a management firm, a booking agency or both.

aaLN INTERNATIONAL, PB15, Antwerp 17, B-2018, Antwerp **Belgium**. (0)32480376. Fax: (0)32483186. President: Luc Nuitten. Management firm, booking agency. Estab. 1991. Represents artists from anywhere; currently handles 6 acts. Receives 15% commission. Reviews material for acts.
How to Contact: Submit demo tape by mail. Unsolicited submissions are OK. Prefers cassette (or VHS videocassette) with 3 songs. If seeking management, press kit should include VHS video, CD or demo cassette, references, photos, bio, press book. "Always looking for new talent — please present a complete neat and self-explanatory promo kit." Does not return material. Reports in 1 month.
Music: Mostly **jazz, world music** and **contemporary**; also **blues** and **Latin**. Works primarily with concert tour bands and festival bands.

*ACR PRODUCTIONS, Box 5236, Lubbock TX 79408. (806)792-3804. Owner: Dwaine Thomas. Mangement firm, booking agency and music publisher (Jordana Music). Estab. 1986. Represents individual artists, groups and songwriters from anywhere; currently handles 4 acts. Receives 10% commission. Reviews material for acts.
How to Contact: Submit demo tape by mail. Unsolicited submissions are OK. Prefers cassette or VHS videocassette with 5 songs and lyric sheet. If seeking management, press kit should include picture, bio, press releases, etc. in addition to tape. Does not return material. Reports in 8 weeks.
Music: Mostly **country** and **rock**; also **R&B**. Works primarily with vocalists and bands. Current acts include Rodeoactive (country show band), Crystal Creek (country dance band), Aaron Miller (songwriter).

*ADELAIDE ROCK EXCHANGE, 186 Glen Osmond Rd., Fullarton SA **Australia** 5063. Phone: (08)338-1844. Managing Editor: Brian Gleeson. Management firm and booking agency. Estab. 1982. Represents national and international artists and groups. Receives 5-10% commission. Reviews material for acts.
How to Contact: Submit demo tape by mail — unsolicited submissions are OK. Prefers cassette (or VHS videocassette if available). SAE and IRC. Reports in 2 months.
Music: Mostly **rock, pop** and **R&B**; also **duos, solos** and **sight artists**. Primarily works with recording bands, dance and concept bands. Current acts include Zep Boys (Led Zeppelin concept band), High Voltage (AC/DC concept band), Chunky Custard (70's glam rock show band) and Ian Polites (pianist/vocalist).
Tips: "Please have all demo tapes, bios and photos with a track list and, most importantly, contact numbers and addresses."

AFTERSCHOOL PUBLISHING COMPANY, P.O. Box 14157, Detroit MI 48214. (313)571-0363. President: Herman Kelly. Management firm, booking agency, record company (Afterschool Co.) and music publisher (Afterschool Pub. Co.). Estab. 1978. Represents individual artists, songwriters, producers, arrangers and musicians. Currently handles 10 acts. Receives 5-50% commission. Reviews material for acts.
How to Contact: Submit demo tape by mail — unsolicited submissions are OK. Prefers cassette with 3 songs and lyric or lead sheet. If seeking management, include résumé with demo tape and bio in press kit. SASE. Reports in 3-4 weeks.
Music: Mostly **pop, jazz, rap, country** and **folk**. Works primarily with small bands and solo artists. Current acts include William T. Stevenson (writer/producer), Shawn Spicer (writer/producer/singer), Judi Robinson (writer/singer/producer).

The asterisk before a listing indicates that the listing is new in this edition. New markets are often the most receptive to unsolicited submissions.

Artists and managers must work together to succeed

"The role of a manager is incredibly diverse," explains Karen Gibson, VP of Creative Operations at Gibson Management, Inc. "One moment you are making career decisions that can affect your clients for the rest of their lives, the next you may be trying to find them an apartment and the next you are playing the role of psychiatrist/friend/advisor."

Karen Gibson

Gibson provides such diverse services for all her clients, which include Patriot Records recording artist Bryan Austin and SBK Records recording artist (and Gibson's sister) Debbie Gibson. Gibson entered the management field after working as an assistant for several years at Polygram Publishing and at Atlantic Records as an A&R rep. "My mother had started a management company to manage recording artists, including my sister Debbie. Having worked in large corporations for four years, I thought it would be a good experience to move into the family business and try my hand at something more diverse and hands on."

In her role as manager, Gibson sees herself as helping to define an artist's image. "What we can do for our clients is try to help them define who they are — both musically and artistically," she explains, "and help them decide what they want their image to be. We help select songs, arrange demos, photo shoots, styling sessions, collaborators, producers, etc."

Gibson says an artist should be extremely careful and selective when shopping for a manager. "The most important thing is to find someone they click with personally and who really believes in them," she says. "A manager has to be the world's best salesman, and needs to believe in what he/she is selling. A manager doesn't have to be one of the 'biggies' to be right for you. Every manager starts off somewhere, and most of the time it's working with someone they absolutely love and would go the distance for. That's the person you want to find — whether they are big or small."

If you're a songwriter but not a performer, managers can help get your songs heard and perhaps recorded by the artists they represent. "When putting together a demo or album for our artists, I always keep my ears open for outside songs that are right for them," says Gibson. "The best way to get songs to the manager is to call and introduce yourself. If you don't have any luck getting through personally, try faxing. I may not always pick up the phone, but I always read my faxes! Let the manager know that you would like to send some material for him to listen to. Unfortunately, if you don't have some sort of industry recognition, your tape doesn't get the highest priority. Be polite and persistent in following up, but be careful to not become too pushy or annoying. I never mind getting a follow-up call or two as a reminder to listen to a tape."

Even if a songwriter is not trying to sell himself as a performer, demo quality is just as important. "When pitching songs, only send songs that are at least as good or better than the songs you've heard the artist record," Gibson advises. "Don't send a tape of ten songs which are all inappropriate and/or poorly demoed and recorded. Demos don't need to be done in a big 24 or 48 track studio to sound professional and catch someone's ear. Some of my favorite songs have come to me with simple guitar/vocal or piano/vocal arrangements. If you have a song that you think is brilliant, but may not be right for the artists the manager is working with, consider sending it anyway with a note explaining that they might be interested in it for another artist they have in development. Working in A&R and in management, very often I would get songs that I loved so much I would hold on to them until the right artist came along."

While managers provide numerous services for an artist, they can't be expected to do all the work—it's up to the artist or songwriter to be just as hard working and enthusiastic. "We can't make someone who doesn't have an absolute burning desire to make it wake up one day suddenly motivated," Gibson says. "That drive and motivation are equally as important as talent." Also important to Gibson is a certain quality that sets one artist apart from all others. "Most importantly," she says, "they must have that elusive thing called charisma. They must be able to get up on stage and really sell it! That makes the difference between a moderately successful act and a superstar."

—*Cindy Laufenberg*

*AKO PRODUCTIONS, 20531 Plummer, Chatsworth CA 91311. (818)998-0443. President: A.E. Sullivan. Management firm, booking agency, music publisher and record company (AKO Records, Dorn Records, Aztec Records). Estab. 1980. Represents local and international artists, groups and songwriters; currently handles 6 acts. Receives 15% commission. Reviews material for acts.
How to Contact: Submit demo tape by mail. Unsolicited submissions are OK. Prefers cassette with maximum of 5 songs and lyric sheet. If seeking management, include cassette, picture and lyrics in press kit. SASE. Reports in 6 weeks.
Music: Mostly **pop, rock** and **top 40**. Works primarily with vocalists, dance bands and original groups. No heavy metal. Current acts include Loop, Perfect Tommy, El Chicano.

MARK ALAN AGENCY, P.O. Box 21323, Eagan MN 55121. President: Mark Alan. Management firm and booking agency. Represents individual artists, groups and songwriters; currently handles 8 acts. Personal management commission 20%; booking, 15%. Reviews material for acts.
How to Contact: Submit demo tape by mail—unsolicited submissions are OK. Prefers cassette (or VHS videocassette if available) with 3 songs. If seeking management, include photo and bio in press kit. Does not return material. Reports in 1 month.
Music: Rock, pop, black contemporary and **alternative**. Works primarily with groups and solo artists. Current acts include Airkraft (rock band), Zwarté (rock band), Crash Alley (rock band), the Stellectrics (alternative band), Saturn Cats (rock band), Lost Horizon (rock), John Doe (rock) and Tyrant (rock).
Tips: "We work with bands that tour nationally and regionally and record their original songs and release them on major or independent labels. We book clubs, colleges and concerts."

ALEXAS MUSIC PRODUCTIONS, Suite 433, 1935 S. Main St., Salt Lake City UT 84115. (801)467-2104. President: Patrick Melfi. Management firm, booking agency (BMI) and record company (Alexas Records/ASCAP). Estab. 1976. Represents local, regional or international individual artists, groups and songwriters; currently handles 6 acts. Receives 15-20% commission. Reviews material for acts.

How to Contact: Write or call first and obtain permission to submit. Submit VHS videocassette only with 1-3 songs and lyric sheets. If seeking management, include bio, video and demo. SASE. Reports in 10 weeks.
Music: Mostly **country** and **pop**; also **New Age** and **gospel**. Represents well-established bands and vocalists. Current acts include A.J. Masters (singer/songwriter), Meisner, Rich & Swan, The Virgin River Band, The Drifters and The Crests.
Tips: "Be strong, be straight and be persistent/no drugs."

*ALL STAR MANAGEMENT, 1229 S. Prospect St., Marion OH 43302-7267. (614)382-5939. President: John Simpson. Management firm, booking agency. Estab. 1990. Represents individual artists, groups and songwriters artists from anywhere; currently handles 9 acts. Receives 10-15% commission. Reviews material for acts.
How to Contact: Submit demo tape by mail. Unsolicited submissions are OK. Prefers cassette, videocassette with 3 songs and lyric or lead sheet. If seeking management, press kit should include audio with 3 songs — bio, 8×10 photo or any information or articles written on yourself or group, video if you have one. Does not return unsolicited material. Reports in 2 months.
Music: Mostly **country, country rock** and **Christian country**; also **gospel** and **rock**. Works primarily with bands — singers, songwriters. Current acts include Leon Seiter (country singer/songwriter); The Mast Bros. (country Christian — band songwriters); Crimson River (gospel — songwriters).
Tips: "Don't give up and write what you like. The industry will look at close to the heart songs."

*ALL STAR TALENT AGENCY, Box 82, Greenbrier TN 37073. (615)643-4208. Agent: Joyce Kirby. Booking agency. Estab. 1966. Represents professional individuals, groups and songwriters; currently handles 6 acts. Receives 10% commission. Reviews material for acts.
How to Contact: Submit demo tape by mail — unsolicited submissions are OK. Prefers cassette with 4 songs and lead sheet (VHS videocassette if available). SASE. Reports in 1 month. If seeking management, press kit should include bios and photos.
Music: Mostly **country**; also **bluegrass, gospel, MOR, rock (country)** and **top 40/pop**. Works primarily with dance, show and bar bands, vocalists, club acts and concerts. Current acts include Alex Houston (MOR/country), Ronnie Dove (country/MOR) and Jack Greene (country).

MICHAEL ALLEN ENTERTAINMENT DEVELOPMENT, P.O. Box 111510, Nashville TN 37222. (615)754-0059. Contact: Michael Allen. Management firm and artist development, public relations. Represents individual artists, groups and songwriters; currently handles 3 acts. Receives 15-25% commission. Reviews material for acts.
How to Contact: Submit demo tape by mail — unsolicited submissions are OK. Prefers cassette (or VHS videocassette) with 3 songs and lyric or lead sheets. If seeking management, press kit should include photo, bio, press clippings, letter, tape. Does not return unsolicited material. Reports in 3 months.
Music: Mostly **country, pop** and **R&B**; also **rock** and **gospel**. Works primarily with vocalists and bands. Currently doing public relations for Shotgun Red, Ricky Lynn Gregg and Easy Street.

ALOHA ENTERTAINMENT, P.O. Box 2204, Suite #14, 193 W. Genesee St., Auburn NY 13021. (315)252-8579. Publicist/Manager: Art Wenzel. Public relations firm. Estab. 1982. Represents local, Central New York, international and national touring acts and groups. Currently handles 5 acts. Receives 10-25% commission. Reviews material for acts.
How to Contact: Submit demo tape by mail — unsolicited submissions are OK. Prefers CD or cassette. Does not return unsolicited material. Include biography, photograph, clips, and CD or cassette.
Music: **Rock, metal** and **blues**; also **jazz** and **R&B**. Current acts include Prison City Rockers (rock), Paul Quinzi Project (pop), Bad Image (rock).
Tips: "Keep the faith!"

AMAZING MAZE PRODUCTIONS, P.O. Box 282, Cranbury NJ 08512. (609)426-1277. Fax: (609)426-1217. Contact: Michael J. Mazur II. Management firm. Estab. 1987. Represents groups from anywhere. Currently handles 1 act. Commission varies.
How to Contact: Submit demo tape by mail. Unsolicited submissions are OK. Prefers cassette (or VHS videocassette) with 2 songs. If seeking management, press kit should include CD/K7, photo, bio, video. Does not return material. Current artists include Harmzway (rock).

*AMERICAN ARTIST BOOKING & MANAGEMENT, P.O. Box 292546, Nashville TN 37229. (615)758-3500. Fax: (615)754-4329. Vice President: John Milam. Management firm, booking agency, music publisher. Estab. 1973. Represents individual artists and/or groups, songwriters from anywhere; currently handles 5 acts. Receives 15% commission. Reviews material for acts.
How to Contact: Submit demo tape by mail. Unsolicited submissions are OK. Prefers cassette or videocassette with 5 songs maximum and lyric sheet. If seeking management, press kit should include

photo, tape, bio, work references. Does not return material. Reports in 2 weeks.
Music: Country only. Works primarily with artist groups that have potential of being national acts—
no one that doesn't currently work. Current acts include Canyon (national artists), Tracy Adkins
(currently signing to label), Terry Henry and Rockin' Rowdy Country Band (a big Las Vegas favorite).
National artists who have previously worked through agency include Clay Walker, Doug Supernaw
and Toby Keith.

THE AMETHYST GROUP LTD., 273 Chippewa Dr., Columbia SC 29210-6508. (803)750-5391. Manage-
ment and marketing firm. Represents individual artists, groups and songwriters; currently handles 29
acts. Receives 15-25% commission. "Signs original artists, producers, studios and composers."
How to Contact: Prefers cassette (or VHS videocassette if available) with 5-7 songs and lyric sheet.
"Be creative, simple and to the point." SASE. Reports in 5 weeks if interested.
Music: Mostly **alternative, industrial, techno, dance, rock, metal** and **pop**; also **R&B** and **new music.**
Current acts include Political Asylum, Bodyshop, Silhouette, The Sages, New Fire Ceremony, Progress
In April, Naked Ape, Blue Rooster, Ted Neiland, Slither, Toni Monét, Max Hewitt, Safari, Torre, J.
Blues.
Tips: "Be prepared to sign, if we're interested. We won't spend a lot of time convincing anyone what
we can do for them. We are way too busy with current recording artists. We help organize radio and
retail promotion for four record labels in the U.S. We develop recording artists and market them for
further distribution, promotion. Our resources cover booking agencies, major and independent record
companies, distributors, TV and radio stations, newspapers and trade publications, independent talent, record promoters and producers—all on national level. Most artists we represent *are not* in S.C.
The Amethyst Group Ltd. is an entertainment holding company which represents the interests of
various contracted companies. We also manufacture CDs, records, cassettes, photographs and other
items to enhance an artist's career. Recently signed distribution and licensing with many territories
in Europe."

ANJOLI PRODUCTIONS, 24 Center Square Rd., Leola PA 17540. (717)656-8215. President: Terry
Gehman. Management firm, booking agency and music publisher (Younger Bros. Music). Estab.
1984. Represents individual artists, groups and songwriters; currently handles 20 acts. Receives 15%
commission. Reviews material for acts.
How to Contact: Prefers cassette or VHS videocassette (preferably a live show video, good quality.
Segments of a variety of material with 15-minute maximum length) with 5 songs and lyric sheet. Does
not return unsolicited material.
Music: Country, pop and **R&B.** Works primarily with vocalists and show groups. Current acts include
Shucks (country show), Crossover (country shows), Latigo Smith (country show) and Anita Stapleton
(country vocalist).

*ARDENNE INT'L INC., Suite 423, 1800 Argyle St., Halifax, N.S. B3J 3N8 **Canada**. (902)492-8000.
Fax: (902)423-2143. President: Michael Ardenne. Management firm, record company (Ardenne Int'l
Music). Estab. 1988. Represents local, individual artists and songwriters from anywhere; currently
handles 3 acts. Receives 15-20% commission. Reviews material for acts.
How to Contact: Call first and obtain permission to submit. Prefers cassette with lyric sheet. "Put
name, address, phone number and song list on the tape. Send maximum 3 songs." If seeking management, include b&w photo, bio, chart placings. Does not return material. Reports in 2-6 weeks.
Music: Mostly **country, pop** and **soft rock.** Works primarily with vocalists/songwriters. Current acts
include Joan Kennedy (country), Annick Gagnon (pop/soft rock), Trena Fredricks (country).
Tips: "Be sure to listen to what the artist does before you send material specifically for their consideration. Be prepared to commit to your art—don't be afraid of hard, hard work and be prepared to wait
for results. For songwriters—don't send it if you don't think I can use it."

*ARE, THE ENTERTAINMENT COMPANY, 186 Glen Osmond Rd., Fullarton 5063 **South Australia**.
(08)3381844. Fax: (08)3381793. Director: Brian Gleeson. Booking agency. Estab. 1982. Represents
individual artists and/or groups from anywhere. Receives 10% commission. Reviews material for acts.
How to Contact: Submit demo tape by mail. Unsolicited submissions are OK. Prefers cassette or
VHS videocassette with 2 songs. Does not return material. Reports in 2 weeks.
Music: Mostly **rock, pop** and **show bands.** Current acts include Chunky Custard (70s glam cover
band), New Romantics (80s cover band), Soul Commitments (featuring music from the movie *The
Commitments*).

*ARISE MUSIC, 106 Windcrest Cove, Round Rock TX 78664. (512)251-7810. Fax: (512)343-6010.
Owner: Rick Odell. Management firm, booking agency. Estab. 1992. Represents individual artists
and/or groups from anywhere; currently handles 2 acts. Commission varies. Reviews material for acts.
How to Contact: Submit demo tape by mail. Unsolicited submissions are OK. Prefers cassette. Does
not return material. Reporting time varies.

Music: Mostly **Christian**, **country** and A/C. Current acts include Arise (a cappella group).

ARKLIGHT MANAGEMENT CO., P.O. Box 261, Mt. Vernon VA 22121. (703)780-4726. Manager: Vic Arkilic. Management firm. Estab. 1986. Represents local individual artists and groups; currently handles 1 act. Receives 15% commission. Reviews material for acts.
How to Contact: Submit demo tape by mail—unsolicited submissions are OK. Prefers cassette (or VHS videocassette) with 4 songs and lyric sheet. If seeking management, include photo, bio, tape, video and lyric sheets. SASE. Reports in 3 months.
Music: Mostly **rock**, **pop** and **folk**. "We work with self-contained groups who are also songwriters."
Tips: "Please submit finished demos only!"

*ARSLANIAN & ASSOCIATES, INC., #1502, 6671 Sunset Blvd., Hollywood CA 90028. (213)465-0533. Management firm. Deals with local individual artists and groups; currently handles 3 acts. Receives 20% commission.
How to Contact: Write first and obtain permission to submit. Prefers cassette with 3 songs. If seeking management, press kit should include photo and bio. SASE. Reports in 1 month.
Music: Mostly **alternative** and **rock**. Works primarily with singer/songwriters in bands. Current acts include Farm Animals (roots rock led by singer/songwriter Jerold Aram).

ARTISTE RECORDS/PAUL LEVESQUE MANAGEMENT INC., 154 Grande Cote, Rosemere QC J7A 1H3 **Canada**. President/A&R Director: Paul Levesque. Record company, management firm and music publisher. Estab. 1987. Represents local, regional and international individual artists, groups and songwriters; currently handles 6 acts. Reviews material for acts.
How to Contact: Submit demo tape by mail—unsolicited submissions are OK. Prefers cassette (or VHS videocassette if available) with 3-6 songs and lyric sheet. "Send photos and bio if possible." SAE and IRC. Reports in 2 months.
Music: Mostly **rock**, **pop** and **dance**. Current acts include Haze & Shuffle (rock band), Michael Dozier (pop/R&B singer), Sonya Papp (pop singer/songwriter) and Judith Berard (singer/songwriter).

ARTISTIC DEVELOPMENTS INTERNATIONAL, INC. (A.D.I.), P.O. Box 250400, Glendale CA 91225. (818)501-2838. Management Director: Lisa Weinstein. Management firm. Estab. 1988. Represents local, regional and international individual artists, groups and songwriters. Reviews material for acts.
How to Contact: Call or write first and obtain permission to submit. Prefers cassette with unlimited number of songs and lyric sheet. Does not return unsolicited material. Reports in 4-6 weeks.
Music: Mostly **cross-over artists**, **AC/pop** and **alternative/rock**; also **world beat/pop** and **R&B/dance**. Works primarily with singer/songwriters, bands and performance artists.
Tips: "A songwriter should have a professional quality tape that highlights his versatility and artistic vision. Lyric sheets should be included. An artist should submit a recent 8×10 photo that reflects his/her musical vision. Name and phone number should be on everything! Both artist and songwriter should include a cover letter stating intent and artistic vision."

*THE ARTISTS ONLY MANAGEMENT COMPANY, INC., Suite 12-S, 152-18 Union Turnpike, Flushing NY 11367. (718)380-4001. Fax: (718)591-4590. President: Bob Currie. Management firm, music publisher (ASCAP/Sun Face Music, BMI/Shaman Drum), record producer. Estab. 1986. Represents individual artists and/or groups, songwriters, producers, engineers from anywhere; currently handles 6 acts. Receives 20% commission. Reviews material for acts.
How to Contact: Submit demo tape by mail. Unsolicited submissions are OK. Prefers cassette or VHS videocassette with 2 songs and lyric sheet. If seeking management, press kit should include 3 song demo, photo, contact information. "If you want material returned, include stamped, self-addressed envelope." Reports in 2-3 weeks.
Music: Mostly **urban contemporary**, **dance** and **rap/rock**; also **popular (ballads)**, **Spanish** and **rock**. Works primarily with singer/songwriters, self-contained bands. Current acts include Tony Terry (singer/songwriter), Sweet Sensation (group), 2 Dreds an' a Ballhead (writers/group).
Tips: "We only want your best, and be specific with style. Quality, not quantity."

*ARTISTS'/HELLER AGENCY, Ste. 100, 21860 Burbank Blvd., Woodland Hills CA 91367. (818)710-0060. President: Jerry Heller. Management firm. Represents artists, groups and songwriters; currently handles 5 acts. Reviews material for acts. Receives 15-25% commission.
How to Contact: Write first and obtain permission to submit. Prefers cassette with 4-7 songs. Does not return material. Reports in 3 months.
Music: Mostly **R&B**, **rap** and **jazz**; also **rock**, **soul** and **progressive**. Works primarily with concert groups. Current acts include Rose Royce (R&B), Eazy E (rap), N.W.A. (rap) and H.W.A. (rap).

ASA PRODUCTIONS MANAGEMENT, P.O. Box 244, Yorba Linda CA 92686. (714)998-5575. President: Craig Seitz. Management firm. Estab. 1986. Represents local, regional and international individ-

ual artists and groups; currently handles 1 act. Receives 20% commission. Reviews material for acts.
How to Contact: Submit demo tape by mail—unsolicited submissions are OK. Prefers cassette (or VHS videocassette if available). Include photo. SASE. Reports in 1 month.
Music: Mostly **country** and **bluegrass**. Works primarily with show/concert groups.

*ASIA ARTS MANAGEMENT, 8 Bracken Ave., Montrose, Victoria 3765 **Australia**. (613)728-5446. Fax: (613)728-5353. Director: Lesley Hammond. Management firm, booking agency. Estab. 1991. Represents individual artists and/or groups, drama, dance and film and TV production from anywhere; currently handles 7 acts. Receives 20% commission. Reviews material for acts.
How to Contact: Submit demo tape by mail. Unsolicited submissions are OK. Prefers cassette or PAL/VHS videocassette with 4 songs and lyric or lead sheet. If seeking management, press kit should include photographs, bios, reviews, cassette, if possible also a videocassette (PAL-VHS format). Also, list previous engagements for past 3 years. Does not return material. Reports in 6-8 weeks.
Music: Mostly **pop, classical** and **children's**; also **country, rock** and **world music**. Current acts include Michael Easton (composer), Len Vorstir (pianist), Little Fed Flowers (children).
Tips: "Send only your best examples of your work and give as much background material as possible."

ATCH RECORDS AND PRODUCTIONS, Suite 380, Fondren, Houston TX 77096-4502. (713)981-6540. President: Charles Atchison. Management firm, record company. Estab. 1989. Represents local, regional and international individual artists, groups and songwriters; currently handles 3 acts. Receives 20% commission. Reviews material for acts.
How to Contact: Submit demo tape by mail. Unsolicited submissions are OK. Prefers cassette with 2 songs and lyric sheet. If seeking management, include bio, photo, demo and lyrics. Does not return unsolicited material. Reports in 3 weeks.
Music: Mostly **R&B, country** and **gospel**; also **pop, rap** and **rock**. Works primarily with vocalists and groups. Current acts include B.O.U. (rap) and Blakkk Media (rap).
Tips: "Send a good detailed demo with good lyrics. Looking for wonderful love stories, also songs for children."

ATI MUSIC, 75 Parkway Ave., Markham, Ontario L3P 2H1 **Canada**. (905)294-5538. President: Scoot Irwin. Management firm (ATI Music/SOCAN), music publisher, record company (ATI). Estab. 1983. Represents individual artists, groups from everywhere. Currently handles 14 acts. Reviews material for acts.
How to Contact: Submit demo tape by mail. Unsolicited submissions are OK. Prefers cassette (or VHS videocassette) with 2-3 songs and lyric sheet. If seeking management, press kit should include photo (2 different), bio and background. Does not return material. Reports in 1-2 weeks.
Music: Mostly **country, easy listening** and **gospel**. Current acts include Dick Damron (country, singer/writer award winner), Brad Bayley (country singer/songwriter), The Harcourts (gospel group).
Tips: "Material should be compatible with today's market."

*ATLANTIC ENTERTAINMENT GROUP, #700, 1125 Atlantic Ave., Atlantic City NJ 08401-4806. (609)264-0515. Fax: (609)345-8683. Director of Artist Services: Scott Sherman. Management firm, booking agency. Represents individual artists and groups from anywhere; currently handles over 30 acts. Receives 10-20% commission. Reviews material for acts.
How to Contact: Submit demo tape by mail. Unsolicited submissions are OK. Prefers cassette or VHS videocassette with 3 songs and lyric or lead sheet. If seeking management, press kit should include bio reviews. Does not return material.
Music: Mostly **dance, R&B** and **contemporary**; also **house, rock** and **specialty**. Current acts include Jennifer Holliday (singer), Candace Jourdan (singer/writer), Candy J (singer/songwriter).

*AVAILABLE MANAGEMENT, #4, 1260 Nikings Rd., W. Hollywood CA 90069. (213)650-4318. Partner: Alan Oken. Management firm. Estab. 1988. Represents individual artists, groups and songwriters from anywhere; currently handles 3-5 acts. Reviews material for acts.
How to Contact: Submit demo tape by mail. Unsolicited submissions are OK. Prefers cassette or VHS videocassette with 3 songs. If seeking management, press kit should include photos, demo, lyrics. SASE. Reports in 2 weeks.
Music: Mostly **rock, pop (CHR)** and **R&B (urban)**. Current acts include Clover, Eric Kellogg.

BABY SUE, P.O. Box 1111, Decatur GA 30031-1111. (404)288-2073. President: Don W. Seven. Management firm, booking agency, record company (baby sue). "We also publish a magazine which reviews music." Estab. 1983. Represents local, regional or international individual artists, groups and songwriters; currently handles 3 acts. Receives 10% commission. Reviews material for acts.
How to Contact: Submit demo tape by mail—unsolicited submissions are OK. Prefers cassette (or VHS videocassette if available) with 4 songs and lyric sheets. Does not return unsolicited material. Reports in 2 weeks.

Music: Mostly **rock, pop** and **alternative**; also **country** and **religious**. Works primarily with multi-talented artists (those who play more than 1 instrument). Current acts include LMNOP (rock), the Stereotypes (pop) and the Mommy (heavy metal).

BANDSTAND (INTERNATIONAL) ENTERTAINMENT AGENCY, P.O. Box 1010, Simcoe, Ontario N3Y 5B3 **Canada.** (519)426-0000. Fax: (519)426-3799. Florida Address: Unit 392, 1475 Flamingo Drive, Englewood FL 34224. President: Wayne Elliot. Management firm, booking agency. Estab. 1965. Represents individual artists and groups from anywhere. Currently handles 1 act. Receives 10-15% commission. Reviews material for acts.
How to Contact: "Not interested at present time in material from songwriters." If seeking management, press kit should include promo, video and demo. Does not return material. Reports in 2 weeks.
Music: Mostly **rock** and **country**; also **novelty acts.** Works primarily with vocalists and bands. Current acts include Peggy Pratt.

BARNARD MANAGEMENT SERVICES (BMS), 1443 Sixth St., Santa Monica CA 90401. (310)587-0771. Agent: Russell Barnard. Management firm. Estab. 1979. Represents artists, groups and songwriters; currently handles 4 acts. Receives 10-20% commission. Reviews material for acts.
How to Contact: Write first and obtain permission to submit. Prefers cassette with 3-10 songs and lead sheet. Artists may submit VHS videocassette (15-30 minutes) by permission only. Does not return unsolicited material. Reports in 2 months.
Music: Mostly **country crossover**; also **blues, country, R&B, rock** and **soul.** Works primarily with country crossover singers/songwriters and show bands. Current acts include Helen Hudson (singer/songwriter), Mark Shipper (songwriter/author) and Mel Trotter (singer/songwriter).
Tips: "Semi-produced demos are of little value. Either save the time and money by submitting material 'in the raw,' or do a finished production version."

*****DICK BAXTER MANAGEMENT,** P.O. Box 1385, Canyon Country CA 91386. (805)268-1659. Owner: Dick Baxter. Management firm and music publisher. Estab. 1963. Represents individual artists and groups from anywhere. Currently handles 1-5 acts. Reviews material for acts.
How to Contact: Write first and obtain permission to submit. Prefers cassette (or VHS videocassette if available) with 3 or more songs and lyric sheet. If seeking management, press kit should include photos, bio, press clips, audio and video if available. Does not return material. Reports in 2-3 weeks.
Music: Mostly **country, gospel** and **pop.** Current acts include Robert Hart (pop singer/songwriter), Ted & Ruth Reinhart (cowboy/western) and The Reinsmen (western).

*****BEACON KENDALL ENTERTAINMENT,** 238 Broadway, Cambridge MA 01239. Contact: Warren Scott. Management firm, booking agency. Estab. 1988. Represents individual artists, groups, songwriters from anywhere; currently handles 12 acts. Receives 15-25% commission. Reviews material for acts.
How to Contact: Submit demo tape by mail. Unsolicited submissions are OK. Prefers cassette or VHS videocassette with 6 songs and lyric sheet. If seeking management, press kit should include tape, picture, bio, video, press, etc. Does not return material. Reports in 2 months.
Music: Mostly **rock, alternative** and **R&B.** Works primarily with bands. Current acts include Heavy Metal Horns (R&B, jazz), Mighty Sam McClain (R&B) and Tree (hardcore).

*****BEASLEY & ASSOCIATES,** 1372 Pulaski Rd., East Northport NY 11731. (516)757-8128. Managing Partner: Dennis Beasley. Accounting and business management firm. Estab. 1992. Represents individual artists, groups, songwriters, management firms and independent record labels from anywhere. Fees vary.
How to Contact: Write or call first to arrange personal or phone interview.
Music: Mostly **alternative, hard rock** and **heavy metal**; also **pop, dance** and **rap.** Works primarily with artists and groups.
Tips: "We provide many services, such as preparing tax returns and assisting with contracts, and can play an important role as a member of your team."

*****MICHAEL BERKLEY MANAGEMENT,** 917 SE 42nd, Portland OR 97215. (503)239-0552. Contact: Michael Berkley. Management firm, record company. Estab. 1987. Represents individual artists and/or groups from anywhere; currently handles 2 acts. Receives 15% commission.
How to Contact: Submit demo tape by mail. Unsolicited submissions are OK. Prefers cassette with 4 songs and lyric or lead sheet. If seeking management, press kit should include full promo kit. Does not return material. Reports in 2 months.
Music: Mostly **rock** and **alternative.** Works primarily with vocalists, bands. Current acts include Brydge®, Black Pearl, Doggett.

*NIGEL BEST MANAGEMENT INC., 835 Westney Rd. S., Unit 10, Ajax, Toronto, Ontario L1S 3M4 **Canada**. President: Nigel Best. Management firm. Estab. 1992. Represents local groups and producers; currently handles 1 act.
How to Contact: Submit demo tape by mail. Unsolicited submissions are OK. Prefers cassette with 3-4 songs. If seeking management, press kit should include photo, cassette (3 songs maximum), bio. SASE.
Music: Mostly **pop** and **jazz**. Current acts include Barenaked Ladies.

*BIG BEAT PRODUCTIONS, INC., 1515 University Dr., Coral Springs FL 33071. (305)755-7759. Fax: (305)755-8733. President: Richard Lloyd. Management firm, booking agency. Estab. 1986. Represents individual artists, groups, songwriters from anywhere; currently handles 5 acts. Receives 15-20% commission. Reviews material for acts.
How to Contact: Submit demo tape by mail. Unsolicited submissions are OK. Prefers cassette or videocassette with 5 songs and lyric or lead sheet. If seeking management, press kit should include promo materials. Does not return material. Reports in 1 month.
Music: Mostly **rock** and **pop**. Current acts include Anna Collins (singer/comic/songwriter), Drew Farrell (singer/songwriter), The Alternatives.

BIG J PRODUCTIONS, 16-B Winnie Court, Laplace LA 70068. (504)652-2645. Agent: Frankie Jay. Booking agency. Estab. 1968. Represents individual artists, groups and songwriters; currently handles over 50 acts. Receives 15-25% commission. Reviews material for acts.
How to Contact: Write or call first and obtain permission to submit. Prefers cassette (or VHS videocassette if available) with 3-6 songs and lyric or lead sheet. "It would be best for an artist to lip-sync to a prerecorded track. The object is for someone to see how an artist would perform more than simply assessing song content." Does not return unsolicited material. Reports in 2 weeks.
Music: Mostly **rock, pop** and **R&B**. Works primarily with groups with self-contained songwriters. Current acts include Zebra (original rock group), Lillian Axe (original rock group), Kyper (original dance) and Top Cats (original pop group).
Tips: "Have determination. Be ready to make a serious commitment to your craft because becoming successful in the music industry is generally not an 'overnight' process."

*BISCUIT PRODUCTIONS INC., H-117, 3315 E. Russell Rd., Las Vegas NV 89120. (702)896-3600 or (702)387-3836. President: Steve Walker. Management firm. Estab. 1989. Represents individual artists and groups from anywhere; currently handles 3 acts. Receives 20% commission. Reviews material for acts.
How to Contact: Submit demo tape by mail. Prefers cassette or VHS videocassette. Does not return material. Reports in 2 months.
Music: Mostly **rap, R&B** and **dance**; also **pop** and **alternative**. Current acts include Mr. Freeze, Biscuit, Brand X.
Tips: "Believe in yourself and your work. If we can believe in you as well, it may work."

J. BIVINS' PRODUCTIONS, P.O. Box 966, Desoto TX 75123-0966. (214)869-3231. Management firm and record company (Avonna Records, Inc.). Estab. 1991. Represents individual artists, groups and songwriters from anywhere; currently handles 16 acts. Receives 15% commission. Reviews material for acts.
How to Contact: Submit demo tape by mail—unsolicited submissions are OK. Prefers cassette (or VHS videocassette if available) with 3 songs. Does not return unsolicited material. Reports in 2 weeks.
Music: Mostly **R&B, rock** and **gospel (top 40)**. Works primarily with vocalists and dance bands. Current acts include Sajo, Little Mike and TBA.

BLACK STALLION COUNTRY PRODUCTIONS, INC., P.O. Box 368, Tujunga CA 91043. (818)352-8142. President: Kenn E. Kingsbury, Jr.. Management firm, production company and music publisher (Black Stallion Country Publishing/BMI). Estab. 1979. Represents individual artists from anywhere; currently handles 5 acts. Receives 15-25% commission. Reviews material for acts.
How to Contact: Submit demo tape by mail—unsolicited submissions are OK. Prefers cassette with 3 songs and lyric sheet. SASE. Reports in 2 months.
Music: Mostly **country, R&B** and **A/C**. Works primarily with country acts, variety acts and film/TV pictures/actresses. Current acts include Lane Brody (singer country), Thom Bresh (musician), Gene Bear (TV host), Jenifer Green and Wayne Cornell, Australia (big band revue and act).
Tips: "Be professional in presentation. Make sure what you present is what we are looking for (i.e., don't send rock when we are looking for country)."

BLANK & BLANK, Suite 308, 1530 Chestnut St., Philadelphia PA 19102. (215)568-4310. Treasurer, Manager: E. Robert Blank. Management firm. Represents individual artists and groups. Reviews material for acts.

How to Contact: Submit demo tape by mail—unsolicited submissions are OK. Prefers videocassette. Does not return material.

*BLAZE PRODUCTIONS, 103 Pleasant Ave., Upper Saddle River NJ 07458. (201)825-1060. Fax: (201)825-4949. Office Manager: Toni Lynn. Management firm, music publisher (Botown Music), production company, record company (Wild Boar Records). Represents local, individual artists, groups, songwriters from anywhere; currently handles 6 acts. Receives 15-20% commission. Reviews material for acts.
How to Contact: Submit demo tape by mail. Unsolicited submissions are OK. Prefers cassette or VHS videocassette with 3-5 songs and lyric sheet. If seeking management, press kit should include tape, lyrics, picture, bio and "something that gets across the band's vibe." Does not return material. Reports in 1 month.
Music: Mostly **modern rock** and **all music**; also **tribute acts**. "If you're the *best* we want to represent you. The best band, kazoo orchestra, tribute act, etc. Any type of music or act." Works primarily with bands and solo artists. Current acts include Gearhead (modern rock), Voices (regional touring act), R&R Game Show (tribute act).
Tips: "Be persistent, yet polite, and be as creative as possible with your materials. A press kit should contain the band's vibe, not just a bio."

*THE BLUE CAT AGENCY/EL GATO AZUL AGENCY, 64 Mill St., Chico CA 95928. (916)345-6615. Fax: (916)891-0638. Owner/agent: Karen Kindig. Management firm and booking agency. Estab. 1989. Represents individual artists and/or groups from anywhere; currently handles 5 acts. Receives 15% commission.
How to Contact: Write or call first and obtain permission to submit. Prefers cassette. If seeking management, press kit should include demo tape, bio and press clippings. SASE. Reports in 2-3 weeks.
Music: Mostly **jazz**, **blues** and **pop-rock**; also **"new" country, rock/pop "en español"** and any other style "en español." Works primarily with singer/songwriters, instrumentalists and bands. Current acts include Ylonda Nickell (alto saxophonist), Mark Little (pianist), Alejandro Santos (flutist/composer).
Tips: "Never lose sight of your musical goals and persevere until you reach them."

*BLUE OX TALENT AGENCY, #121, 4130 N. Goldwater Blvd., Scottsdale AZ 85251. Agent: Barry Gross or David Bach. Booking agency. Estab. 1982. Represents individual artists, groups, variety acts and comedians from anywhere. Receives 10-20% commission. Reviews material for acts.
How to Contact: Submit demo tape by mail. Unsolicited submissions are OK. Prefers cassette or ½" VHS videocassette with 4 songs and lyric sheet. If seeking management, press kit should include photo, demo tape, song list, lyric sheet (if original material), cover letter. SASE. Reports ASAP, generally within 2 weeks.
Music: Mostly **rock, country** and **contemporary/top 40 style**; also **comedians** and **distinctive variety acts**. Works primarily with bands, comedians. Current acts include Lester Lanin Orchestra, Sanar Alixandyr (vocalist), Sam Moore (vocalist, Sam & Dave).

*GEOFFREY BLUMENAUER ARTISTS, #204, 11846 Balboa Blvd., Granada Hills CA 91344. (818)366-8117. Fax: (818)366-2890. President: Geoffrey Blumenauer. Management firm, booking agency. Estab. 1989. Represents national individual artists, groups, songwriters; currently handles 12 acts. Receives 10-15% commission. Reviews material for acts.
How to Contact: Submit demo tape by mail. Unsolicited submissions are OK. Prefers cassette with 3 songs and lyric or lead sheet. If seeking management, press kit should include picture, bio, history. Does not return material. "We contact if interested only."
Music: Mostly **rock/blues, country** and **jazz**; also **folk, bluegrass** and **pop**. Current acts include Robby Krieger (Doors), Nicolette Larson, Jim Messina.
Tips: "Submit 3 of your best songs and follow up with additional materials."

BOJO PRODUCTIONS INC., 3935 Cliftondale Place, College Park GA 30349. (404)969-1913. Management firm and record company (Bojo Records). Estab. 1982. Represents local, regional or international individual artists, groups and songwriters; currently handles 4 acts. Receives 20% commission. Reviews material for acts.
How to Contact: Submit demo tape by mail. Unsolicited submissions are OK. Prefers cassette (or videocassette if available) with 3 songs and lyric or lead sheets. SASE. Reports in 3 weeks.
Music: Mostly **R&B, gospel** and **country**; also **MOR**. Works primarily with vocalists and dance bands. Current acts include Ray Peterson (country), Jimmy Jordan (R&B) and George Smith (R&B/MOR).
Tips: "Send clean recording tape with lead sheets."

*BON TON WEST, P.O. Box 8406, Santa Cruz CA 95061. (408)425-5885. Fax: (508)426-6866. Contact: Ice Cube Slim. Management firm, booking agency. Estab. 1984. Represents individual artists and/or

groups from anywhere; currently handles 12 acts. Receives 10-25% commission.
How to Contact: Call first and obtain permission to submit. Prefers cassette or VHS videocassette with lyric sheet. If seeking management, press kit should include 8×10 photo, bio, performance history. Does not return material. Reports in 3 weeks.
Music: Mostly **New Orleans music**, **blues** and **zydeco**; also **jazz**. Current acts include Katie Webster (boogie piano), Robert Lowery and Virgil Thrasher (acoustic country blues), Sunpie and the Louisiana Sunspots (zydeco and blues).

BOUQUET-ORCHID ENTERPRISES, P.O. Box 1335, Norcross GA 30091. President: Bill Bohannon. Management firm, booking agency, music publisher (Orchid Publishing/BMI) and record company (Bouquet Records). Represents individuals and groups; currently handles 4 acts. Receives 10-15% commission. Reviews material for acts.
How to Contact: Submit demo tape by mail—unsolicited submissions are OK. Prefers cassette (or videocassette if available) with 3-5 songs, song list and lyric sheet. Include brief résumé. Press kits should include current photograph, 2-3 media clippings, description of act, and background information on act. SASE. Reports in 1 month.
Music: Mostly **country**, **rock** and **top 40/pop**; also **gospel** and **R&B**. Works primarily with vocalists and groups. Current acts include Susan Spencer, Jamey Wells, Adam Day and the Bandoleers.

*BRIER PATCH MUSIC, 3825 Meadowood Lane, Grandville MI 49418. (616)534-6571. Fax: (616)534-1113. Manager: Dave Vander Molen. Management firm, booking agency, music publisher, record company (Brier Patch Records), record producer. Represents individual artists from anywhere; currently handles 2 acts. Receives 20% commission. Reviews material for acts.
How to Contact: Call first and obtain permission to submit and arrange personal interview. Prefers cassette or VHS videocassette with 4 songs, lyric and lead sheets. If seeking management, press kit should include letter on letterhead, typed, photo, brochure. "If it doesn't look good we won't look at it!" Does not return material. Reports in 3 weeks.
Music: Mostly **peace and justice**, **Christian** and **alternative**; also **multicultural** and **folk**. Current acts include Ken Medema (songwriter/storyteller), John Fischer (author/singer/preacher).
Tips: "The tape must be professionally produced and the packet must look good."

BROADWEST MANAGEMENT, 17711 176th Ave. NE, Woodinville WA 98072. (206)487-4012. Fax: (206)485-8670. President: Luke L. Denn. Management firm, record producer. Estab. 1989. Represents individual artists, groups and songwriters from anywhere; currently handles 3 acts. Receives 15-20% commission. Reviews material for acts.
How to Contact: Submit demo tape by mail. Unsolicited submissions are OK. Prefers cassette (or VHS videocassette) with 4 songs and lyric sheet. If seeking management, press kit should include 1 cassette, 1 picture and 1-page bio. "Be sure to list what you are submitting tape for." SASE. Reports in 6 weeks.
Music: Mostly **alternative**, **dance-soul** and **R&B-rap**; also **songwriters** and **soundtracks**. Works primarily with vocalists, singer/songwriters and bands. Current acts include Jackie Young (pop-adult contemporary), Makia (hip hop/rock artist, songwriter, producer), Blackened Kill Symphony (alternative) and Jackie Young, Arthur Kohtz and Wayne Perkins (songwriters).
Tips: "Have music with lyrics typed out for review and a brief letter explaining what you are hoping to obtain, music to be sold? or to be produced? or to be used by?"

*BROCK & ASSOCIATES, Suite 200, 7106 Moores Land, Brentwood TN 37027. (615)370-4447. Fax: (615)370-4446. Contact: Darlene Brock. Management firm. Represents local individual artists and/or groups and songwriters; currently handles 2 acts. Reviews material for acts.
How to Contact: Submit demo tape by mail. Unsolicited submissions are OK. Prefers cassette. If seeking management, press kit should include bio, picture, demo, recommendations. Does not return material. Reports in 1-3 months.
Music: Mostly **contemporary Christian**. Works primarily with bands, vocalists/songwriters. Current acts include Geoff Moore and The Distance (contemporary Christian band), Eddie DeGarmo.

DAVID BRODY PRODUCTIONS, 4086 Royal Crest, Memphis TN 38115. (901)362-1719. President: David or Gina Brody. Management firm and music publisher (Brody-Segerson Publishing/BMI). Estab. 1986. Represents international individual artists, groups and songwriters; currently handles 5 acts. Reviews material for acts.
How to Contact: Call first and obtain permission to submit. Prefers cassette (or VHS videocassette if available) with 3 songs and lyric sheet. If seeking management, include audio tape, bio and photos in press kit. SASE.
Music: Interested in **all music**. Works primarily with comedians, announcers, singers and actors. Current acts include Corinda Carford (country singer), Rick Landers (singer/songwriter) and Jimmy Segerson (R&B singer).

BROTHERS MANAGEMENT ASSOCIATES, 141 Dunbar Ave., Fords NJ 08863. (201)738-0880 or 738-0883. President: Allen A. Faucera. Management firm and booking agency. Estab. 1972. Represents artists, groups and songwriters; currently handles over 50 acts. Receives 15-20% commission. Reviews material for acts.
How to Contact: Write first and obtain permission to submit. Prefers cassette (or VHS videocassette if available) with 3-6 songs and lyric sheets. Include photographs and résumé. If seeking management, include photo, bio, tape and return envelope in press kit. SASE. Reports in 2 months.
Music: Mostly **pop**, **rock**, **MOR** and **R&B**. Works primarily with vocalists and established groups. Current acts include Waterfront (R&B), Masquerade (dance) and 80 West (alternative).
Tips: "We need very commercial, chart-oriented material."

*BSA INC., P.O. Box 1516, Champaign IL 61824. (217)352-8700. Fax: (217)352-9227. Contact: Bill Stein. Management firm and booking agency. Estab. 1983. Represents groups from anywhere; currently handles 3-4 acts. Receives 10-20% commission. Reviews material for acts.
How to Contact: Submit demo tape by mail. Prefers cassette or videocasette with 2-4 songs. SASE.
Music: Mostly **rock**, **alternative** and **country**. Works primarily with bands, singer/songwriters. Current acts include Just For Kicks (pop rock), Pink Flamingoes (nostalgia), Delta Kings (alternative).

*BULLSEYE ENTERTAINMENT, Suite 340, 507 N. Sam Houston Pkwy. E., Houston TX 77060. (713)448-5694. Fax: (713)448-5696. Contact: Lee Bowley, Jr. Management firm and music publisher (K-Bowley Publishing/ASCAP, Bowley's Red Snapper Publishing/SESAC). Estab. 1991. Represents individual artists and songwriters from anywhere; currently handles 2 acts. Reviews material for acts.
How to Contact: Submit demo tape by mail. Unsolicited submissions are OK. Prefers cassette (or VHS videocassette) with 3 songs and lyric sheet. If seeking management, press kit should include bio, photo and tape. Does not return material. Reports in 3 months.
Music: Mostly **country** and **tejano**. Works primarily with vocalists, singer/songwriters and bands. Current acts include C.J. Edwards (country singer) and Staiton Brothers (singer/songwriter), reviews material for Doug Supernaw (singer/songwriter).

C & M PRODUCTIONS MANAGEMENT GROUP, 5114 Albert Dr., Brentwood TN 37027. (615)371-5098. Fax: (615)371-5317. Manager: Ronald W. Cotton. Management firm, booking agency and music publisher. Represents international individual artists; currently handles 4 acts on Polygram Records. Receives 15-25% commission. Reviews material for acts.
How to Contact: Submit demo tape by mail—unsolicited submissions are OK. Prefers cassette (or VHS videocassette if available) with 3 songs and lead sheets. If seeking management, include picture, tape and bio in press kit. Does not return material. Reports in 2 weeks.
Music: Mostly **country**, **gospel** and **pop**. Current acts include Ronna Reeves (country), Brittany Allyn (country) and Jeff Knight (country).

CAHN-MAN, Suite 201, 5273 College Ave., Oakland CA 94618. (510)652-1615. Contact: Elliot Cahn/Jeff Saltzman/David Hawkins. Management and law firm. Estab. 1986. Represents local, regional and international individual artists, groups and songwriters. Receives 20% commission; $200/hour as attorneys.
How to Contact: Submit demo tape by mail—unsolicited submissions are OK. Prefers cassette (or videocassette). If seeking management, include tape, photo, relevant press and bio in press kit. Does not return material. Artist should follow up with a call after 4-6 weeks.
Music: **All types**, with an emphasis on **alternative rock**. Current alternative acts include Primus (Interscope), Mudhoney (Warner Bros.), Hammerbox (A&M), Melvins (Atlantic), Green Day (Warner/Reprise) and The Muffs (Warner Bros.). Current singer/songwriters include Jesse Colin Young, Henry Gross, Kate Jacobs, Andy Milton and Neal Casal.
Tips: "As callous as it sounds, write great songs; but write songs for yourself, not for the industry."

CAM MUSIC ENTERTAINMENT, Suite #7, 4011 N. Mulford Rd., Rockford IL 61111. (815)877-9678. Fax: (815)877-7430. CEO and General Manager: Chip Messiner. Management firm, booking agent, producer and publisher. Estab. 1983. Represents local and regional individual artists, groups and songwriters; currently handles 28 acts. Receives 15-25% commission. Reviews material for acts.
How to Contact: Write first and obtain permission to submit. Prefers cassette (or videocassette of performance, if available) with 3 songs, lyric sheets and SASE. If seeking management, include a cover letter, up to date info on writer or artist, photo (if looking to perform), bio, tape or CD. "Do not send full songs. 60-90 seconds is enough." SASE. Reports in 2-3 months.
Music: Mostly **country**, **bluegrass** and **folk**; also **MOR**, **jazz** and **children's**. Works primarily with concert tour bands, show bands and festival bands. Current acts include Special Consensus (bluegrass), Cumberland Mountain Band (country), The Truesdells (country) and Sharon Polidan (children's).
Tips: "You have a lot of competition. Make sure your songs, promo kit, cover letter, etc. are neat. Your first impression on me will help me to take a serious look at your material."

CAPITOL MANAGEMENT, Suite 200, 1300 Division St., Nashville TN 37203. (800)767-4984; (615)244-2440; (615)244-3377. Fax: (615)242-1177. Producer: Robert Metzgar. Management firm, booking agency, music publisher (Aim High Music Co., Bobby & Billy Music) and record company (Stop Hunger Records International, Aim High Records, Hot News Records, Platinum Plus Records, SHR Records). Estab. 1971. Represents local, regional or international individual artists, groups and songwriters; currently handles 24 acts. Receives 15% commission. Reviews material for acts.
How to Contact: Submit demo tape by mail. Unsolicited submissions are OK. Prefers cassette (or videocassette of live performance, if available). If seeking management, include photo, bio, résumé and demo tape. Does not return unsolicited material. Reports in 2 weeks.
Music: Mostly **traditional country, contemporary country** and **southern gospel**; also **pop rock, rockabilly** and **R&B**. Works primarily with major label acts and new acts shopping for major labels. Current acts include Carl Butler (CBS records), Tommy Cash (CBS Records), Tommy Overstreet (CBS Records), Mark Allen Cash, Mickey Jones, The Glen Campbell Band (Warner Bros.) and Billy Walker (MCA Records).
Tips: "Call us on our toll-free line for advice before you sign with anyone else."

*CARLYLE MANAGEMENT, 1217 16th Ave. South, Nashville TN 37212. (615)327-8129. Fax: (615)321-0928. President: Laura Fraser. Management firm. Estab. 1987. Represents individual artists and groups from anywhere. Currently handles 3 acts. Reviews material for acts.
How to Contact: Submit demo tape by mail. Unsolicited submissions are OK. Prefers cassette or videocassette with 3 songs. If seeking management, press kit should include tape, photo, bio, press. Does not return material. Reports in 3 weeks.
Music: Mostly **all types**. Current acts include Robert Weston (country), The Vegas Cocks (rock), Owen's Ashes (rock).

CARMAN PRODUCTIONS, INC., 15456 Cabrito Rd., Van Nuys CA 91406. (213)873-7370. A&R: Tom Skeeter. Management firm, music publisher (Namrac/BMI, Souci/ASCAP) and record production company. Estab. 1969. Represents local, regional and international individual artists, groups, songwriters, producers and actors. Currently handles 5 acts. Receives 15-20% commission. Reviews material for acts.
How to Contact: Submit demo tape by mail—unsolicited submissions are OK. Prefers cassette with 5 songs and lyric sheet. Does not return unsolicited material. Reports in 6 weeks.
Music: Mostly **rock, dance, R&B, pop** and **country**. Current acts include Richard Carpenter, J.J. White and Jimmy DeMar.

*ERNIE CASH ENTERPRISES, 744 Joppa Farm Rd., Joppa Towne MD 21085. (301)679-2262. Fax: (301)687-4102. President: Ernest W. Cash. Management firm, music publisher (Ernie Cash Music/BMI), record company (Confidential Records Inc.). Estab. 1988. Represents local, regional or international individual artists, groups, songwriters. Currently represents 1 act. Receives 20% commission. Reviews material for acts.
How to Contact: Write or call first to obtain permission to submit. Prefers cassette (or VHS videocassette if available) with 3 songs and lyric and lead sheet. SASE. Reports in 2 weeks.
Music: Mostly **country, pop** and **gospel**; also **contemporary, light rock** and **blues**. Works primarily with individual country artists and groups. Current acts include The Short Brothers.
Tips: "Above all be honest with me and I will work with you. Please give me time to review your material and give it a justifiable chance with our music group."

CAVALRY PRODUCTIONS, P.O. Box 70, Brackettville TX 78832. (512)563-2759 and (512)563-2236 (studio). Contact: Rocco Fortunato. Management firm and record company. Estab. 1979. Represents regional (Southwest) individual artists and groups; currently handles 3 acts. Receives 10-30% comission. Reviews material for acts.
How to Contact: Submit demo tape—unsolicited submissions are OK. Prefers cassette with 3 songs and lyric sheet. SASE. If seeking management, press kit should include picture, tape (cassette), experience. Reports in 1-2 months.
Music: Mostly **country** and **Hispanic**; also **gospel** and **novelty**. Works primarily with single vocalists and various vocal groups "2 to 4 voices." Current acts include Darryl Earwood (country), Jose Lujan (Tejano), Ezpuma (Hispanic).

How to Get the Most Out of Songwriter's Market (at the front of this book) contains comments and suggestions to help you understand and use the information in these listings.

Tips: "Material 'in the raw' is OK if you are willing to work with us to develop it. Make songs available to our artists for review from our library of possibilities. Songs not used immediately may be useable in the future. (We will indicate un-useable material by returning it.)"

CEDAR CREEK PRODUCTIONS AND MANAGEMENT, Suite 503, 44 Music Square East, Nashville TN 37203. (615)252-6916. Fax: (615)329-1071. President: Larry Duncan. Management firm, music publisher (Cedar Creek Music/BMI), record company (Cedar Creek Records) and record producer. Estab. 1992. Represents individual artists, groups and songwriters from anywhere; currently handles one act. Receives 20% of gross. Reviews material for acts.
How to Contact: Submit demo tape by mail. Unsolicited submissions are OK. Prefers cassette (or VHS videocassette) with 4-6 songs and lyric sheet. If seeking management, press kit should include 8×12 color or b&w picture, bio, 4-6 songs on cassette tape, VHS video if available. Does not return material. Reports in 1 month.
Music: Mostly **country, country/pop** and **country/R&B**; also **pop, gospel/Christian contemporary, R&B** and **light rock**. Works primarily with vocalists, singer/songwriters and groups. Current acts include Dave Marshal (country/pop singer). "Looking for artists to represent now."
Tips: "Submit your best songs and a good full demo with vocal upfront with 5 instruments on tracks backing the singer; use a great demo singer."

PAUL CHRISTIE MANAGEMENT, Box 96, Avalon NSW 2107 **Australia**. Phone: (02)415-2722. Managing Director: Paul Christie. Management firm (Paul Christie Management/APRA). Estab. 1982. Represents local, regional and international individual artists, groups and songwriters; currently handles 4 acts. Receives 20% commission. Reviews material for acts.
How to Contact: Submit demo tape by mail—unsolicited submissions are OK. Prefers cassette or VHS videocassette with 3 songs and lyric or lead sheet. If seeking management, press kit should include photo and bio. Does not return material. Reports in 2 weeks.
Music: Mostly **rock, pop/rock** and **pop/R&B**. Works primarily with rock acts, singer/writers, composers. Current acts include Party Boys (2-guitar power rock) and Zillian and the Zig Zag Men (surf punk/thrash).

CLASS ACT PRODUCTIONS/MANAGEMENT, P.O. Box 55252, Sherman Oaks CA 91413. (818)980-1039. President: Peter Kimmel. Management firm, music publisher, production company. Estab. 1985. Represents local, regional or international artists, groups, songwriters, actors and screenwriters. Currently handles 2 acts. Receives 20% commission. Reviews material for acts.
How to Contact: Submit demo tape by mail—unsolicited submissions are OK. Include pictures, bio, lyric sheets (essential), and cassette tape or CD in press kit. SASE. Reports in 1-2 months.
Music: Mostly **rock, pop** and **alternative**; also **R&B** and **new country (western beat)**.

*****CLASS ACTS**, Box 641, Freeport ME 04032. (207)865-6600. Northeast Marketing Coordinator: Bill Simpson. Management firm and booking agency. Estab. 1979. Represents East Coast/South West individual artists and groups; currently handles 12 acts. Receives 15% commission. Reviews material for acts.
How to Contact: Submit demo tape by mail. Unsolicited submissions are OK. Prefers cassette (or VHS videocassette if available) with 3-4 songs and lyric sheet. If seeking management, press kit should include song list, bio, cassette or video, picture. Does not return unsolicited material. Reports in 6 weeks.
Music: Mostly **modern contemporary, rock contemporary** and **R&B**; also **comedy**. Works primarily with bands. Current acts include Lime Rockets (alternative), Definately Smooth (dance/hip hop), The Sense (modern contemporary) and Bicycle Thieves (modern contemporary).
Tips: "Understand that the business is weak—if you're expecting miracles, call someone else."

CLOCKWORK ENTERTAINMENT MANAGEMENT AGENCY, 227 Concord St., Haverhill MA 01830. (508)373-5677. President: Bill Macek. Management firm. Represents groups and songwriters throughout New England. Receives 15% commission.
How to Contact: Query or submit demo tape. Prefers cassette or CD with 3-12 songs. "Also submit promotion and cover letter with interesting facts about yourself." Does not return unsolicited material unless accompanied by SASE. Reports in 1 month.
Music: **Rock (all types)** and **top 40/pop**. Works primarily with bar bands and original acts.

THE NEIL CLUGSTON ORGANIZATION PTY. LTD., P.O. Box 387 Glebe, Sydney, N.S.W. 2037 **Australia**. (02)5523277. Fax: (02)5523713. Managing Director: Neil Clugston. Management firm. Estab. 1989. Represents individual artists, groups and actors from anywhere; currently handles 4 acts. Reviews material for acts.

How to Contact: Submit demo tape by mail. Unsolicited submissions are OK. Prefers cassette (or PAL VHS videocassette) with 2 songs and lyric sheet. If seeking management, press kit should include bio, photo, cassette. SAE and IRC. Reports in 1 month.
Music: Mostly **rock**, **pop** and **dance**; also **A/C**. Current acts include Craig McLachlan (rock singer/ songwriter), Alyssa-Jane Cook (rock/pop singer), Robyn Loau (pop/dance singer/songwriter).
Tips: "Only send your best material."

*CMS MANAGEMENT, 625 Main St., Simpson PA 18407. (717)282-0863. Fax: (717)282-0362. Management firm. Estab. 1988. Represents individual artists and/or groups from anywhere; currently handles 3 acts. Reviews material for acts.
How to Contact: Submit demo tape by mail. Unsolicited submissions are OK. Prefers cassette or VHS videocassette with 3 songs and lyric sheet. SASE. Reports in 6 weeks.
Music: Mostly **alternative** and **country**. Current acts include Young Turk, Museum of Fear and Matt's Altar.

RAYMOND COFFER MANAGEMENT, 26 Park Road, Bushey Herts WD2 3EQ **UK**. (081)420-4430. Fax: (081)950-7617. Contact: Raymond Coffer. Branch: Suite 310, 8330 Melrose Ave., Los Angeles CA 90069. (213)653-8281. Fax: (213)658-7041. Contact: Andy Gershon. Management firm. Estab. 1984. Represents local, regional and international individual artists and groups; currently handles 7 acts. Receives 20% commission.
How to Contact: Submit demo tape by mail—unsolicited submissions are OK. Prefers cassette (or PAL or VHS videocassette if available) with 3 songs and lyric sheet. If seeking management, press kit should include 3 songs and publicity photos. Does not return unsolicited material. Reports in 2 months.
Music: Mostly **rock** and **pop**. Works primarily with bands. Current acts include Love & Rockets, Daniel Ash, David J, Cocteau Twins, Swell, Ian McCulloch, Smashing Pumpkins, Curve, and The Sundays.

COLWELL ARTS MANAGEMENT, RR#1, New Hamburg, Ontario N0B 2G0 **Canada**. (519)662-3499. Fax: (519)662-2777. Director: Jane Colwell. Management firm, booking agency. Estab. 1985. Represents individual artists, groups from anywhere. Currently handles 20 acts. Receives 10-20% commission. Reviews material for acts.
How to Contact: Submit demo tape by mail. Unsolicited submissions are OK. Prefers cassette (or VHS videocassette) with 4 contrasting songs. If seeking management, press kit should include tape, photo, résumé, reviews, 2 letters of recommendation. SASE. Reports in 3 weeks.
Music: Mostly **classical**, some **cross-over**, **children's classical music**, **choral**. Works primarily with singers. Current acts include Henriette Schellenberg (soprano) and Laughton & Humphreys (trumpet/ soprano).
Tips: "Be prepared. Be honest. Have something special to offer."

*COMMUNITY MUSIC CENTER OF HOUSTON, 5613 Almeda, Houston TX 77004. (712)523-9710. Managing Director: Ron Scales. Management firm and booking agency. Estab. 1979. Represents international individual artists and groups; currently handles 6 acts. Receives 10-20% commission. Reviews material for acts.
How to Contact: Submit demo tape by mail. Unsolicited submissions are OK. Prefers cassette (VHS videocassette if available) with 4 songs and lyric or lead sheet. Does not return material. Reports in 2 months.
Music: **Jazz**, **R&B** and **blues**; also **gospel** and **folk**. Works primarily with solo vocalists, vocal groups and jazz bands. Current acts include Rhapsody (jazz vocal ensemble), Scott Joplin Chamber Orchestra (classical music by African-American composers) and Diedre Curnell (folk singer/songwriter).

*BURT COMPTON AGENCY, P.O. Box 160373, Miami FL 33116. (305)271-6880. Contact: Burt Compton. Booking agency. Estab. 1978. Represents groups; currently handles 46 acts. Receives 10-20% commission. Reviews material for acts.
How to Contact: Write first and obtain permission to submit. Prefers cassette (or videocassette) with 3-6 songs. "Include complete repertoire, 8×10 photo and résumé." Does not return unsolicited material.
Music: Mostly **top 40/nostalgia** ('50, '60s). Works primarily with dance bands. Current acts include Heroes (dance band), Fantasy (recording/concert group) and Wildlife (recording/concert group).
Tips: "Have your promotional materials professionally packaged. We don't like having to decipher handwritten résumés with misspelled words and incomplete sentences."

CONCEPT 2000 INC., 2447 W. Mound St., Columbus OH 43204. President: Brian Wallace. Management firm and booking agency (Concept 2000 Music/ASCAP). Estab. 1981. Represents international individual artists, groups and songwriters; currently handles 7 acts. Receives 10-20% commission. Reviews material for acts.

How to Contact: Submit demo tape by mail—unsolicited submissions are OK. Prefers cassette with 4 songs. If seeking management, include photo and bio. Does not return unsolicited material. Reports in 2 weeks.

Music: Mostly **country**, **gospel** and **pop**; also **jazz**, **R&B** and **soul**. Current acts include Bryan Hitch (gospel), The Breeze (country), The Andrew Jackson Piano Forte, Shades of Grey (R&B/soul), Ras Matunji and Earth Force (reggae), Marilyn Cordial (pop) and Gene Walker (jazz).

Tips: "Send quality songs with lyric sheets. Production quality is not necessary."

CORVALAN-CONDLIFFE MANAGEMENT, Suite 5, 1010 Fourth St., Santa Monica CA 90403. (213)393-6507. Manager: Brian Condliffe. Management firm. Estab. 1982. Represents local and international individual artists, groups and songwriters; currently handles 3 acts. Receives 15% commission.

How to Contact: Write or call first and obtain permission to submit. Prefers cassette with 4-6 songs. If seeking management, include bio, professional photo and demo. Does not return unsolicited material. Reports in 2 months.

Music: Mostly **R&B**, **pop** and **rock**; also **Latin** and **dance**. Works primarily with alternative rock and pop/rock/world beat club bands.

Tips: "Be professional in all aspects of your kit and presentation. Check your grammar and spelling in your correspondence/written material. Know your music and your targeted market (rock, R&B, etc.).'"

COUNTDOWN ENTERTAINMENT, 109 Earle Ave., Lynbrook NY 11563. (516)599-4157. President: James Citkovic. Management firm, consultants. Estab. 1983. Represents local, regional and international individual artists, groups, songwriters and producers; currently handles 2 acts. Receives 20-30% commission. Reviews material for acts, and for music publishing.

How to Contact: Submit demo tape by mail—unsolicited submissions are OK. "Please, no phone calls." Prefers cassette (or VHS, SP speed videocassette) if available with songs and lyric sheet. If seeking management, include cassette tape of best songs, 8×10 pictures, VHS video, lyrics, press and radio playlists in press kit. Does not return material. Reports in 6 weeks.

Music: Mostly **pop/rock**, **nu-music** and **alternative/dance**; also **R&B**, **pop/dance**, **industrial/techno** and **hard rock**. Deals with all styles of artists/songwriters/producers. Current acts include: World Bang (alternative/industrial rock), Martin/Vonn/Jewel (pop/rock songwriter/producers), John Ward Piser, Ken Kushner, Drew Miles (producers).

Tips: "Send hit songs, only hit songs, nothing but hit songs."

COUNTRY MUSIC SHOWCASE INTERNATIONAL, INC., P.O. Box 368, Carlisle IA 50047. (515)989-3676 or (515)989-3748. President: Harold L. Luick. Vice President: Barbara A. Lancaster. Management firm and booking agency "for acts and entertainers that are members of our organization." Estab. 1984. Represents individual artists, groups and songwriters; currently handles 15 acts. Receives 15-20% commission.

How to Contact: Write first and obtain permission to submit. Prefers cassette with 3 songs and lyric sheet (or VHS videocassette showing artist on the job, 3 different venues). If seeking management, include 8×10 pictures, résumé, past performance, audio tape and video tape of act in press kit. SASE. Reports in 3 weeks. "Must be paid member of Country Music Showcase International, Inc., to receive review of work."

Music: Mostly **contemporary**, **hard core country** and **traditional country**; also **bluegrass**, **western swing** and **comedy**. Works primarly with "one person single acts, one person single tape background acts and show bands." Current acts include Mr. Elmer Bird (banjo virtuoso), Country Classics USA (12-piece stage show), Joe Harris Country Music Show, Cheryl Wayne & Witchita Band.

Tips: "We want artists who are willing to work hard to achieve success and songwriters who are skilled in their craft. Through educational and informative seminars and showcases we have helped many artist and songwriter members achieve a degree of success in a very tough business. For information on how to become a member of our organization, send SASE to the above address. Memberships cost $40.00 per year for artist or songwriter."

COUNTRY STAR ATTRACTIONS, 439 Wiley Ave., Franklin PA 16323. (814)432-4633. Contact: Norman Kelly. Management firm, booking agency, music publisher (Country Star Music/ASCAP) and record company (Country Star, Process, Mersey and CSI Records). Estab. 1970. Represents artists and musical groups; currently handles 6 acts. Receives 15% commission. Reviews material for acts.

How to Contact: Submit demo tape by mail. Unsolicited submissions are OK. Prefers cassette with 2-4 songs and typed lyric or lead sheet; include photo. SASE. Reports in 2 weeks.

Music: Mostly **country** (85%); **rock** (5%), **gospel** (5%) and **R&B** (5%). Works primarily with vocalists. Current acts include Junie Lou, Sheryl Friend and Jeffrey Alan Connors, all country singers.

Tips: "Send only your very best efforts."

COUNTRYWIDE PRODUCERS, 2466 Wildon Dr., York PA 17403. (717)741-2658. President: Bob Englar. Booking agency. Represents individuals and groups; currently handles 8 acts. Receives 10-15% commission. Reviews material for acts.
How to Contact: Query or submit demo with videocassette of performance, if available. Include photo. SASE. Reports in 1 week.
Music: Bluegrass, blues, classical, country, disco, folk, gospel, jazz, polka, rock (light), soul and **top 40/pop.** Works primarily with show bands. Current acts include Carroll County Ramblers (bluegrass), Ken Lightner (country), Rhythm Kings (country), Junction (variety), the Bruce Van Dyke Show (variety) and Big Wheeley & the White Walls (country rock).

COURTRIGHT MANAGEMENT INC., 201 E. 87th St., New York NY 10128. (212)410-9055. Contacts: Hernando or Doreen Courtright. Management firm. Estab. 1984. Represents local, regional and international individual artists, groups, songwriters and producers. Currently handles 2 acts. Receives 20% commission. Reviews material for acts.
How to Contact: Write first and obtain permission to submit. Prefers cassette (or VHS videocassette if available) with 3 or 4 songs and lyric sheet. If seeking management, include photos, bio, video, tape and press in press kit. Does not return material. Reports in 1 month.
Music: Mostly **rock** and **metal**; also **pop** and **blues.** Current acts include Deena Miller (alternative), Smash Gladys (rock) and various producers.

CRASH PRODUCTIONS, P.O. Box 40, Bangor ME 04402-0040. (207)794-6686. Manager: Jim Moreau. Booking agency. Estab. 1967. Represents individuals and groups; currently handles 9 acts. Receives 10-25% commission.
How to Contact: Submit demo tape by mail—unsolicited submissions are OK. Prefers cassette (or VHS videocassette if available) with 4-8 songs. "To all artists who submit a video: We will keep it on file for presentation to prospective buyers of talent in our area—no longer than 15 minutes please. The quality should be the kind you would want to show a prospective buyer of your act." Include résumé and photos. "We prefer to hear groups at an actual performance." If seeking management, include 8×10 b&w photos, résumé, cassette, press clips and a videocassette in press kit. Does not return unsolicited material. Reports in 3 weeks.
Music: Mostly **50s-60s** and **country rock, top 40**; also **rock** and **Polish.** Works primarily with groups who perform at night clubs (with an average of 150-200 patrons) and outdoor events (festivals and fairs). Current acts include Coyote (country rock), Dakota (rock) and Airfare (top 40).
Tips: "My main business is booking acts to entertainment buyers. To sell them I must have material that tells potential buyers you are great and they need you. A photocopy press kit does not do it."

*CRAWFISH PRODUCTIONS, Box 5412, Buena Park CA 90620. (909)371-2973. Producer: Leo J. Eiffert, Jr. Music publisher (Young Country/BMI) and record company (Plain Country Records). Estab. 1968. Represents local and international individual artists and songwriters; currently handles 4 acts. Commission received is open. Reviews material for acts.
How to Contact: Submit a demo tape by mail—unsolicited submissions are OK. Prefers cassette with 2-3 songs and lyric sheet. SASE. Reports in 3 weeks.
Music: Mostly **country** and **gospel.** Works primarily with vocalists. Current acts include Brandi Holland, Teeci Clarke, Joe Eiffert (country/gospel) and Crawfish Band (country).

*CREATIVE ACTION MUSIC GROUP, Suite E12, 865 Bellevue Rd., Nashville TN 37221. (615)646-7940. Fax: (615)646-8061. President: Doc Field. Management firm. Represents individual artists and/or groups, songwriters from anywhere; currently handles 5 acts. Receives 20% commission. Reviews material for acts.
How to Contact: Call first and obtain permission to submit. Prefers cassette or VHS videocassette with 4 songs. If seeking management, press kit should include photo, bio, video (if possible). Does not return material. Reports in 1 month.
Music: Mostly **rock, pop** and **R&B**; also **country.** Current acts include Warren Haynes (singer/guitarist/songwriter), Prayin' For Rain (rock band), Gary "Mudbone" Cooper (vocalist/drummer).

CREATIVE STAR MANAGEMENT, 1331 E. Washington Blvd., Ft. Wayne IN 46803. (419)228-0691. Department of Creative Services: James Milligan. Management firm, booking agency, music publisher (Party House Publishing/BMI), record company (New Experience Records/Grand Slam Records). Estab. 1989. Represents individual artists, groups, songwriters from anywhere. Currently handles 10 acts. Receives 15-20% commission. Reviews material for acts.
How to Contact: Write or call first and obtain permission to submit. Prefers cassette (or VHS videocassette) with 3-5 songs and lyric sheet. If seeking management, press kit should include press clippings, bios, résumé, 8×10 glossy photo, any information that will support material and artist. SASE. Reports in 1 month.

Music: Mostly **R&B, pop** and **country**; also **rap, contemporary gospel** and **soul/funk**. Current acts include T.M.C. (R&B/group), Richard Bamberger, Carl Whitner, Floyed Sanders (solo artist), One Vision (group) and James Junior.
Tips: "Develop your own musical style. Believe in yourself—keep submitting updates and most of all be patient. If there's interest you will be contacted. We are seeking touring bands and solo artists."

*CRISS-CROSS INDUSTRIES, #191, 4708 Park Granada Blvd., Calabasas CA 91302. (818)222-4362. Fax: (818)222-7649. President: Doc Remer. Management firm and music publisher (Menachan's Music/ASCAP, Eyenoma Music/BMI). Estab. 1984. Represents individual artists, groups and songwriters from anywhere; currently handles 1 act. Receives 15-20% commission. Reviews material for acts.
How to Contact: Write or call first and obtain permission to submit. Prefers cassette (or VHS videocassette if available) with 3 songs and lyric sheet. SASE. Reports in 3-6 weeks.
Music: Mostly **R&B** and **pop**. Works primarily with vocalists and self contained bands. Current acts include Chill Factor (band).
Tips: "You must currently be a working act. Make the words to the songs so they can be understood. The music should not be as loud as the vocals."

*CROWE ENTERTAINMENT INC., 1020 16th Ave. S., Nashville TN 37212. (615)742-0922. Fax: (615)742-8879. President: Jerry Crowe. Management firm, booking agency, music publisher (Midnight Crow/ASCAP, Cro Jo/BMI). Estab. 1986. Represents individual artists and/or groups, songwriters from anywhere; currently handles 6 acts. Receives 20% commission. Reviews material for acts.
How to Contact: Submit demo tape by mail. Unsolicited submissions are OK. Prefers DAT, CD or cassette with no more than 3 songs and lyric sheet. If seeking management, press kit should include bio, picture, tape. SASE. Reports in 2-3 weeks.
Music: Mostly **country**. Current acts include Darryl and Don Ellis (Sony/Epic recording artists), Six-Gun (country band), Lori Smith (country singer), Karen Donovan (country), Michael Lee Jones (country), Dusty Martin (Americana Records).

BOBBY LEE CUDE'S GOOD AMERICAN MUSIC/TALENT/CASTING AGENCY, 519 N. Halifax Ave., Daytona Beach FL 32118-4017. Fax: (904)252-0381. CEO: Bobby Lee Cude. Music publisher (BMI) and record company (Hard Hat). Estab. 1978. Represents international individual artists. Receives 15% commission. Reviews material for acts.
How to Contact: Write first and obtain permission to submit. Prefers cassette (or videocassette) with 2 songs, lyric and lead sheets. "No unsolicited material reviewed."
Music: Mostly **pop** and **country**. Current acts include Frederick the Great and "Pic" Pickens.
Tips: "Read music books for the trade."

CURLY MAPLE MEDIA, P.O. Box 543, Santa Monica CA 90406. (310)396-1664. Fax: (310)396-1884. President: Matt Kramer. Management firm. Estab. 1973. Represents individual artists, groups and songwriters from anywhere; currently handles 2 acts. Receives 15-20% commission. Reviews material for acts.
How to Contact: Submit demo tape by mail. Unsolicited submissions are OK. Prefers cassette (or VHS videocassette) with 4 songs and lead sheet. If seeking management, press kit should include bio. SASE. Reports in 1 month.
Music: Mostly **pop, R&B** and **world beat**; also **folk, folk rock** and **Latin**. Current acts include Lauren Wood (performer/songwriter) and Robin Goodrow (children's entertainer).
Tips: "Enjoy your craft without being dependent upon the industry."

*CURRENT RECORDS/MANAGEMENT, 418 Ontario St., Toronto, Ontario, M5A 2W1 **Canada**. (416)921-6535. Rammit Records/Management: 414 Ontario St., Toronto, Ontario M5A 2W1 **Canada**. (416)923-7611. Fax: (416)923-3352. A&R-New Projects: Trevor G. Shelton. Management firm (The Shelton Group), music publisher (Current Sounds/CAPAC, PROCAN) and record company (Current Records, Rammit Records). Estab. 1987. Represents local, regional or international individual artists, groups and songwriters; currently handles 5 acts. Reviews material for acts.
How to Contact: Submit demo tape by mail—unsolicited submissions are OK. Prefers cassette (or VHS videocassette if available) with 4-5 songs and lyric sheets. If seeking management, include demo tape with 3-4 songs, history on band/artist and "letter explaining what it is you're looking for" in press kit. SASE. Reports in 1-6 weeks.
Music: Mostly **dance, pop** and **rock**; also **R&B, alternative, rap/hip, house**, etc. Works primarily with dance, pop and rock bands. Current acts include Line Up in Paris, Cleopatra, Sunforce.
Tips: "If you have a videocassette of your performance, please send it, but it's not a necessity. Performances can be simple. No need for big-budget videos."

*CYCLE OF FIFTHS MANAGEMENT, INC., Suite H, 331 Dante Ct., Holbrook NY 11741-3800. (516)467-1837. Fax: (516)467-1645. VP/Business Affairs: James Reilly. Management firm. Represents individual artists and/or groups from anywhere; currently handles 2 acts. Receives 15-20% commission. Reviews material for acts.

How to Contact: Write first and obtain permission to submit. Prefers cassette. Does not return material. Reports in 4-6 weeks.

Music: Mostly **rock, rap** and **alternative.** Works primarily with established groups. Current acts include Da King & I (Rowdy/Arista), Psychosis (Massacre Records) and Blackjack Bomber.

D & M ENTERTAINMENT AGENCY, P.O. Box 19242, Johnston RI 02919. (401)944-6823. President and Manager: Ray DiMillio. Management firm and booking agency. Estab. 1968. Represents local groups; currently handles 27 acts. Receives 15% commission. Reviews material for acts.

How to Contact: Submit demo tape by mail. Unsolicited submissions are OK. Prefers cassette (or VHS videocassette) with 3 songs and lyric or lead sheet. SASE. Reports in 2 weeks.

Music: Mostly **R&B** and **pop;** also **rock.** Current acts include XPO, Sunshyne and Trilogy.

D&D TALENT ASSOCIATES, P.O. Box 308, Burkeville VA 23922. (804)767-4150. Owner: J.W. Dooley, Jr. Booking agency. Estab. 1976. Currently handles 2 acts. Receives 15% commission. "Reviews songs for individuals in the jazz and 40s-50s field only."

How to Contact: Write first and obtain permission to submit. Prefers cassette (or videocassette) with 1-6 songs and lead sheet. If seeking management, press kit should include bio and demo tape, and lead sheets if available. SASE. Reports in 2 weeks.

Music: Mostly **jazz** and **40s-50s music.** Works primarily with vocalists, comics. Current acts include Johnny Pursley (humorist) and David Allyn (vocalist).

Tips: "Just submit the demo and I will do my best to give it a judgement. Since I am tied up in other things, my time allows me only to listen and give some adivce. I cannot make any follow-ups regarding contacts, etc."

*DAS COMMUNICATIONS, LTD., 83 Riverside Dr., New York NY 10024. (212)877-0400. Management firm. Estab. 1975. Represents individual artists, groups and producers from anywhere. Receives 20% commission. Reviews material for acts.

How to Contact: Call first to obtain permission to submit. Does not return material.

Music: Mostly **rock, pop** and **dance;** also **alternative.** Current acts include Spin Doctors (rock), The Hatters (rock), Mantussa (metal), Milo Z (funk-rock), Jimmy Cliff (reggae), Jim Steinman (producer/songwriter).

BRIAN de COURCY MANAGEMENT, Box 96, South Yarra, Melbourne, Victoria 3141 **Australia.** Phone: (03)836-9621. Fax: (03)867-7182. C.E.O.: Brian de Courcy. Management firm, music consultant. Estab. 1974. Represents local, regional or international individual artists, groups, songwriters, DJ's, music journalists and TV performers; currently handles 10 acts. Receives 20-25% commission. Reviews material for acts.

How to Contact: Call first and obtain permission to submit. Prefers cassette, CD (or videocassette if available) with lyric and lead sheet. SAE and IRC. Reports in 2 weeks.

Music: Mostly **rock** and **pop.** Works primarily with rock/pop acts and movie/stage music.

THE EDWARD DE MILES COMPANY, Vantage Point Towers, 4475 N. Allisonville Rd., 8th Floor, Indianapolis, IN 46205. (317)546-2912. President & CEO: Edward De Miles. Management firm, booking agency, entertainment/sports promoter and TV/radio broadcast producer. Estab. 1984. Represents film, television, radio and musical artists; currently handles 15 acts. Receives 10-20% commission. Reviews material for acts. Regional operations in Chicago, Dallas, Houston and Nashville through marketing representatives. Licensed A.F. of M. booking agent.

How to Contact: Write first and obtain permission to submit or to arrange personal interview. Prefers cassette with 3-5 songs, 8x10 b&w photo and lyric sheet. "Copyright all material before submitting." If seeking management, include demo cassette with 3-5 songs, 8 × 10 b&w photo and lyric sheet in press kit. SASE. Reports in 1 month.

Music: Mostly **country, dance, R&B/soul, rock, top 40/pop** and **urban contemporary;** also looking for material for television, radio and film productions. Works primarily with dance bands and vocalists. Current acts include Lost in Wonder (progressive rock), Steve Lynn (R&B/dance) and Multiple Choice (rap).

Tips: "Performers need to be well prepared with their presentations (equipment, showmanship a must)."

Refer to the Category Index (at the end of this section) to find exactly which companies are interested in the type of music you write.

DEMORE MANAGEMENT, P.O. Box 36152, Oklahoma City OK 73136. (405)424-8612. President: Kerwin James. Management firm (Wink Two Music/BMI), record company (Ganvo Records). Estab. 1988. Represents individual artists from anywhere. Currently handles 4 acts. Receives 20% commission. Reviews material for acts.
How to Contact: Submit demo tape by mail. Unsolicited submissions are OK. Prefers cassette with 3-5 songs and lyric sheet. If seeking management, press kit should include bio, publicity print and demo tape. Does not return material. Reports in 4-6 weeks.
Music: Mostly **soul/R&B, hip hop** and **gospel**; also **soft rock** and **contemporary jazz**. Works primarily with soul/R&B vocalists, singer/songwriters. Current acts include Ava Gardner (soul/R&B), Church of Triumphant (gospel), Undecided/UND (rap), Steve Burks (jazz/hip hop).
Tips: "Don't call and ask to send a demo and then never send it. Have your mind made up that this is really what you want to do. Don't start if you're not serious."

*DERI PROMOTIONS USA-UK, 3220 Ellington Circle, Nashville TN 37211. (615)832-6117. Fax: (615)832-6177. Managing Director: Len Jinks. Management firm, booking agency. Estab. 1979. Represents individual artists and groups from anywhere; currently handles 6-12 acts. Receives 10% commission. Reviews material for acts.
How to Contact: Submit demo tape by mail. Prefers cassette with 3 songs max (less OK) and lyric or lead sheet. If seeking management, press kit should include bio, photo, cassette recorded in studio. Does not return material. Reports in 1-2 months.
Music: Mostly **country, rock 'n country** and **rock**. Works primarily with vocalists and bands. Current acts include Steve Woods (country), Sylvie (country), Stu Page (country/rock).
Tips: "Keep all work and directions in focus. Listen to advice. Sort the good from the bad. But always keep your targets in focus."

*DIAMOND LITERARY, Box 48114-35 Lakewood Blvd., Winnipeg, Manitoba R2J 4A3 **Canada**. President: Bryan/preliminary screening. Management firm. Estab. 1989. Represents individual artists and songwriters from anywhere; currently handles 3 acts. Receives 15% commission. Reviews material for acts.
How to Contact: Submit demo tape by mail. Unsolicited submissions are OK. Prefers cassette with lyric or lead sheet. Does not return material. Reports in 1 month.
Music: Mostly **country, rock** and **pop/rock**; also **classical**.

DIETROLEQUINTE ART COMPANY, Via Orti 24, Milano 20122 **Italy**. (+39)2-55184004. Fax: (+39)2-59902676. Managing Director: Francesco Fontana. Management firm and booking agency. Represents individual artists and groups from anywhere; currently handles 5-7 acts. Receives 20% commission. Reviews material for acts.
How to Contact: Submit demo tape by mail. Unsolicited submissions are OK. Prefers cassette (or PAL videocassette) with 3 songs. If seeking management, press kit should include 2 b&w photos and tape. Does not return material. Reports in 2 months.
Music: Mostly **world music, Latin rock** and **new projects**. Works primarily with bands. Current acts include Les Pires (gypsy music), Cheb Kader (räi music) and Les Vrp (cabaret rock).
Tips: "Be original, friendly, ready to travel a lot."

*LIESA DILEO MANAGEMENT, P.O. Box 414731, Miami Beach FL 33141. President: Liesa DiLeo. Management firm, booking agency, music publisher. Estab. 1984. Represents individual artists, groups, songwriters, and actors from anywhere. Receives 20-30% commission.
How to Contact: Submit demo tape by mail. Unsolicited submissions are OK. Prefers cassette with 2 songs and lyric sheet. If seeking management, press kit should include photo, bio, press clippings, video, cassette. SASE. Reports in 2 weeks.
Music: Mostly **rock, pop, Latin, salsa** and **R&B**.

ANDREW DINWOODIE MANAGEMENT, Box 1936, Southport, QLD **Australia** 4215. Phone: (075)376222. Manager: Andrew Dinwoodie. Management firm, booking agency. Estab. 1983. Represents regional (Australian) individual artists, groups and songwriters; currently handles 3 acts. Receives 10-20% commission. Reviews material for acts.
How to Contact: Submit demo tape by mail—unsolicited submissions are OK. Prefers cassette (VHS PAL if available) with lyric sheet. SAE and IRC. Reports in 6 weeks.
Music: Mostly **country, R&B** and **rock/pop**; also **bluegrass, swing** and **folk**. Current acts include Bullamakanka, Donna Heke and the Moderation Band.
Tips: "Be imaginative and stay your own individual; don't try to conform to the norm if you are different."

*DIRECT MANAGEMENT, P.O. Box 121759, Arlington TX 76012. (817)451-4946. Owner: Danny Wilkerson. Management firm and booking agency. Estab. 1986. Represents individual artists and/or groups from anywhere; currently handles 5 acts. Receives 10-20% commission.

How to Contact: Submit demo tape by mail. Unsolicited submissions are OK. Prefers cassette (or VHS videocassette) with 3 songs. If seeking management, press kit should include bio, cassette or CD, photo, reviews. Does not return material. Reports in 1 month.

Music: Mostly **college rock, Christian** and **children's**. Current acts include Waltons (pop/rock), Generation Rumble (alternative) and EP[5] (rock).

DMR AGENCY, Suite 250, Galleries of Syracuse, Syracuse NY 13202-2416. (315)475-2500. Contact: David M. Rezak. Booking agency. Represents individuals and groups; currently handles 24 acts. Receives 15-20% commission.

How to Contact: Submit demo tape by mail—unsolicited submissions are OK. Submit cassette (or videocassette) with 1-4 songs and press kit. Does not return material.

Music: Mostly **rock (all styles), pop** and **blues**. Works primarily with cover bands.

Tips: "We do very little with groups that feature their own material."

COL. BUSTER DOSS PRESENTS, Drawer 40, Estill Springs TN 37330. (615)649-2577. Producer: Col. Buster Doss. Management firm, booking agency, record company (Stardust Records) and music publisher (Buster Doss Music/BMI). Estab. 1959. Represents individual artists, groups, songwriters and shows; currently handles 12 acts. Receives 15% commission. Reviews material for acts.

How to Contact: Write or call first and obtain permission to submit. Prefers cassette with 2-4 songs and lyric sheet. If seeking management, press kit should include demo, photos and bio. SASE. Reports in 1 week.

Music: **Country, gospel** and **progressive**. Works primarily with show and dance bands, single acts and package shows. Current acts include "Danny Boy" Squire (country rock), Larry C. Johnson (country), "Bronco" Buck Cody (western swing).

Tips: "Write good songs—send only your best."

*EARTH TRACKS ARTISTS AGENCY, Suite 286, 4809 Avenue N, Brooklyn NY 11234. Managing Director-Artist Relations: David Krinsky. Management firm. Estab. 1990. Represents individual artists, groups and songwriters from anywhere; currently handles 2 acts. Receives 15% commission. Reviews material for acts.

How to Contact: Submit demo tape by mail—unsolicited submissions are OK, accompanied by release form and SASE. "Do not call to submit tapes. Mail in for review. No calls will be returned, unsolicited or accepted, under any conditions." Prefers cassette (or VHS and/or ¾" videocassette) with 3-6 songs and lyric sheet. If seeking management, include 1 group photo, all lyrics with songs, a cassette/CD of 3-6 original songs and the ages of the artists. "We do not return unsolicited material if international." Reports in 1-2 months.

Music: Mostly **commercial rock** (all kinds), **pop/dance/rap** and **post modern rock/folk rock**. Works primarily with commercial, original, solo artists and groups, songwriters in the rock, pop, dance areas (no country, thrash or punk). Current acts include Heavy Connection (rock), Bella (pop/dance artist) and Bi-Coastals (comedy/satire artist). "We're looking for original acts who wish to be signed to record labels in the rock, pop and rap categories. (No 'show bands' 'cover bands', etc.)."

Tips: "Submit a package of completed songs along with lyrics, photo of artist/group, or songwriter credits if any. A video on VHS accepted if available. If no package available send a cassette of what you as an artist consider best represents your style. Strong meaningful songs are preferred, as well as light pop rock for top 40 release. Will submit quality songwriter's material to name artists. All materials must be accompanied by a release form and all songs must be copyrighted."

ECI, INC., 1646 Bonnie Dr., Memphis TN 38116. (901)346-1483. Vice President: Bernice Turner. Management firm, booking agency, music publisher and record company (Star Trek). Estab. 1989. Represents local, regional and international individual artists and groups; currently handles 3 acts. Receives 25% commission. Reviews material for acts.

How to Contact: Submit demo tape by mail—unsolicited submissions are OK. Prefers cassette with 2 songs. If seeking management, include videotape, photos, complete press kit. SASE. Reports in 5 weeks.

Music: Mostly **R&B** and **country**. Works primarily with show groups. Current acts include Kool and The Gang, Robby Turner and Ashley Allison.

*ELKO'S TALENT AGENCY, INC., #408, 150 Powell St., San Francisco CA 94102. (415)398-8830. Fax: (707)539-4707. President: Mrs. Elko Tusa. Booking agency. Estab. 1971. Represents individual artists and groups from anywhere. Receives 15% commission. Reviews material for acts.

How to Contact: Call first to arrange personal interview. Submit demo tape by mail. Unsolicited submissions are OK. Prefers cassette or VHS videocassette with 4 songs, photograph and song list. If seeking management, press kit should include career goals, photos, etc. "No amateurs please!" SASE. Reports in 6 weeks.

Music: Mostly **jazz, oldies** and **R&B (black)**; also **Hispanic, pop** and **show bands**. "We book Hawaii, Japan, California, Tahiti, etc." Works primarily with vocalists and self-contained bands. Current acts include The Ronettes, Eddie Fisher, Connie Francis.
Tips: "Be honest, drug free and reliable."

*ELLIPSE PERSONAL MANAGMENT, % Boxholder 665, Manhattan Beach CA 90267. (310)546-2224. Contact: Mr. L. Elsman. Management firm. Represents local individual artists, vocalists and vocalist/songwriters. Receives 15% commission and up (P.M. contract). Reviews material for acts.
How to Contact: Submit demo by mail. Prefers cassette with 3 songs. Does not return material. Reports in 5 weeks.
Music: Mostly **pop/rock**, **R&B/dance** and **AOR**. Current acts include Eric Tage Trio.
Tips: "If you are a songwriter only the songs would have to be suitable for our act. If you are a local songwriter and a vocalist and you are looking for a Personal Manager send a snapshot, your age and a tape (vocalist only, send cover songs), along with your goals and ambitions. If you call, do it when phone rates are down. Saturdays are OK."

EMARCO MANAGEMENT, Mail: P.O. Box 867, Woodland Hills CA 91365. Office Address: 23241 Ventura Blvd. #218, Woodland Hills CA. President: Mark Robert. (818)225-0061. Fax: (818)225-0069. Management firm and publishing company. Estab 1982. Represents local, regional or individual artists, groups and songwriters and professional baseball players. Currently handles 12 acts. Receives 15% commission. Reviews material for acts.
How to Contact: Call first and obtain permission to submit. Prefers cassette with 3 songs or less and lyric sheets. Returns with SASE. Reports in 2 months.
Music: Mostly **pop, rock** and **dance**. Current acts include Robbie Rist, Gabriela Rozzi, and Wonderboy.
Tips: "Don't send material in until it is ready to be heard. We generally give an act *one* best shot to pitch us. If invited, we try and send a rep out to view a band's show (L.A., San Francisco, Las Vegas only)."

ENCORE TALENT, INC., 2137 Zercher Rd., San Antonio TX 78209. (512)822-2655. President: Ronnie Spillman. Management firm and booking agency. Estab. 1978. Represents regional individual artists and groups from Texas. Currently handles 5 acts. Receives 15% commission. Reviews material for acts.
How to Contact: Submit demo tape by mail—unsolicited submissions are OK. Prefers cassette with 4 songs. If seeking management, press kit should include photo, bio and tape. SASE. Reports in 2 weeks.
Music: Mostly **country**. Works primarily with bands. Current acts include Jay Eric (writer/country singer), Bounty Hunters and Jody Jenkins (country singer/writer).

*THE ENTERTAINMENT COMPANY, P.O. Box 860096, Plano TX 75086. (214)423-1869. Fax: (214)424-2395. Contact: Debbie Meyers. Booking agency. Estab. 1987. Represents individual artists and/or groups from anywhere; currently handles 600 acts. Receives 20% commission. Reviews material for acts.
How to Contact: Submit demo tape by mail. Unsolicited submissions are OK. Prefers cassette or VHS videocassette with 5-7 songs. Does not return material. Reports in 1-4 weeks.
Music: Mostly **top 40/dance**, **R&B** and **country**; also **variety bands**, **metal** and **jazz**. Works primarily with top 40, R&B dance bands (high energy). Current acts include Bill Tillman Band (top 40/AC/R&B), Ex Mortuus (metal), Robert Lee Kobb (R&B).

THE ENTERTAINMENT GROUP, (formerly REM Management), 9112 Fireside Dr., Indianapolis IN 46250. President: Bob McCutcheon. Management firm. Estab. 1987. Represents local, regional and international individual artists and groups; currently handles 3 acts. Receives 20% commission. Reviews material for acts.
How to Contact: Write first and obtain permission to submit. Prefers cassette with 3 songs. If seeking management include photo and tape. SASE. Reports in 6 weeks.
Music: Mostly **hard rock** and **R&B**. Current acts include Beautiful Authentic Zoo Gods (alternative), Pushin Up Daisies (alternative), The Hush (alternative) and Signal (Capitol Records).
Tips: "Be patient while you're developing your skills and make sure you have something else to fall back on."

*ENTERTAINMENT INTERNATIONAL USA, P.O. Box 7189, Canton OH 44705-0189. (216)454-4843. A&R: Paulette Winderl. Management firm, booking agency, music publisher. Estab. 1969. Represents individual artists and/or groups, songwriters from anywhere; currently handles 8 acts. Receives 10% commission. Reviews material for acts.

How to Contact: Submit demo tape by mail. Unsolicited submissions are OK. Prefers cassette or VHS/Beta videocassette with 4 songs and lyric sheet. If seeking management, press kit should include bio, demo, photos. SASE. Reports in 3 weeks.
Music: All types. Current acts include Sirene (R&B), Mary White (country), Unique (folk).
Tips: "Put your package together carefully in a professional manner."

*ENTERTAINMENT MANAGEMENT ENTERPRISES, 454 Alps Rd., Wayne NJ 07470. (201)694-3333. President: Richard Zielinski. Management firm. Estab. 1982. Represents artists and musical groups; currently handles 2 acts. Receives minimum of 20% commission. Reviews material for acts.
How to Contact: Prefers cassette (or VHS videocassette) with 4-6 songs and lyric sheet. Include 8×10 glossy and bio. "Let us know, by mail or phone, about any New York area performances so we can attend." SASE. Reports in 2 weeks.
Music: Mostly **rock**. Works primarily with rock groups with vocals, synthesized rock, contemporary singers and club bands. Current acts include Voyager (progressive rock) and Mirrors' Image (metal).
Tips: "A good press kit is important."

*ENTERTAINMENT SERVICES INTERNATIONAL, 6400 Pleasant Park Dr., Chanhassen MN 55317. (612)474-5800. Fax: (612)474-4449. Owner: Randy Erwin. Booking agency. Estab. 1988. Represents groups from anywhere; currently handles 20 acts. Receives 10-20% commission. Reviews material for acts.
How to Contact: Submit demo tape by mail. Unsolicited submissions are OK. Prefers cassette or VHS videocassette. If seeking management, press kit should include photos, biography, instrumentation, references, list of places performed, reviews, video, cassette or CD. SASE. Reports in 1-2 weeks.
Music: Mostly **rock, R&B** and **alternative rock**. Works primarily with bands.

*ENTERTAINMENT WORKS, 2400 Poplar Dr., Baltimore MD 21207. (410)265-6519. President: Nancy Lewis. Management firm, booking agency and public relations/publicity firm. Estab. 1989. Represents local, regional and international groups. Receives 10-15% commission. Reviews material for acts.
How to Contact: Call first and obtain permission to submit. Prefers cassette with 3 songs "plus biography/publicity clips/photo." If seeking management, include group biography, individual biographies, 8×10 black & white glossy, all press clips/articles, PA requirements list and stage plot in press kit. Does not return material. Reports in 1 month.
Music: Reggae. Works primarily with vocalists/dance bands. Current acts include Uprising, Third Eye, Unity and Winston Grennan Ska Rocks Band.
Tips: "Start with a phone call to introduce yourself, followed by a well-recorded 3-song demo, band member biographies, photo and all publicity clips."

*ENTOURAGE ENTERTAINMENT, 21453 Alamo St., Woodland Hills CA 91364. (818)340-4165. Partner: Julie Shy. Management firm. Estab. 1987. Represents individual artists and groups from anywhere. Currently handles 5 acts. Reviews material for acts.
How to Contact: Call first and obtain permission to submit. Prefers cassette. If seeking management, press kit should include cassette and bio. SASE. Reports in 6 weeks.
Music: Mostly **rock, pop** and **country**; also **children's**. Works primarily with singer/songwriters. Current acts include Becky Barksdale (singer/songwriter), Prick, Custer & Logan (singer/songwriters).

ETERNAL TALENT/SQUIGMONSTER MANAGEMENT, 1598 E. Shore Dr., St. Paul MN 55106-1121. (612)771-0107. Fax: (612)774-8319. President/Owner: Robert (Squiggy) Yezek. Management firm, booking agency, record company (PMS Records). Estab. 1983. Represents groups from anywhere. Handles 17 acts. Receives 10% commission. Reviews material for acts.
How to Contact: Submit demo tape by mail—unsolicited submissions are OK. Prefers CD (if available) with songs (no limit) and lead sheet. If seeking management, press kit should include CD or tape, bio, promo package and any press. SASE. Reports in 2-8 weeks.
Music: Mostly **alternative rock, heavy metal** and **hard rock**; also **comedy** and **new pop**. Works primarily with alternative hard rock and heavy metal acts for nationwide concert and showcase nite clubs. Current acts include No Man's Land (alternative metal), Drop Hammer (metal), Style Monkeez and Fat Tuesday (rock).
Tips: "You must be willing to work hard and be dedicated to your goal of success."

*SCOTT EVANS PRODUCTIONS, (formerly DSI Theatrical Productions), #112, 4747 Hollywood Blvd., Hollywood FL 33021-6503. (305)963-4449 or (305)967-8890. Artistic Director: Scott Evans. Management firm and booking agency. Estab. 1979. Represents local, regional or international individual artists, groups, songwriters, comedians, novelty acts, dancers and theaters; currently handles more than 200 acts. Receives 10-25% commission. Reviews material for acts.

How to Contact: Submit demo tape by mail—unsolicited submissions are OK. Prefers cassette (or ½″ videocassette if available) with 3 songs. If seeking management, include picture, résumé, fliers, cassette or video tape. Does not return unsolicited material.
Music: Mostly **pop, R&B** and **Broadway.** Deals with "all types of entertainers; no limitations." Current acts include Scott Evans and Company (variety song & dance), Dori Zinger (female vocalist), Jeff Geist, Perfect Parties and Joy Deco (dance act).
Tips: "Submit neat, well put together, organized press kit."

*FAME INTERNATIONAL, 939 Kimball St., Philadelphia PA 19147. (215)629-0709. Exec. V.P. Productions: Albert R. Bauman. Management firm and music publisher (Jazz Lady Publishing/ASCAP). Estab. 1986. Represents individual artists, groups, songwriters and specialty acts from anywhere; currently handles 11 acts. Receives 10-25% commission. Reviews material for acts.
How to Contact: Submit demo tape by mail. Unsolicited submissions are OK. Prefers cassette or VHS videocassette with 3 songs. If seeking management, press kit should include head shot, bio, reviews, list of previous years engagements, contracted future dates and commitments. Does not return material. Reports in 2 weeks.
Music: Mostly **jazz** and **country**; also **specialty acts for casinos and cruises.** Works primarily with vocalists, singer/songwriters, big bands, comedy acts. Current acts include Nancy Kelly (jazz singer), Rich Szabo (orchestra) and Spatz Donovan (vaudeville specialty show).
Tips: "On cover letter, be as specific as possible in describing your career goals and what has prevented you from attaining them thus far. Be honest."

FAT CITY ARTISTS, Suite #2, 1226 17th Ave. South, Nashville TN 37212. (615)320-7678. Fax: (615)321-5382. President: Rusty Michael. Management firm, booking agency, lecture bureau and event management consultants. Estab. 1972. Represents international individual artists, groups, songwriters and authors; currently handles over 100 acts. Receives 20% commission. Reviews material for acts.
How to Contact: Submit demo tape and any other promotional material by mail—unsolicited submissions are OK. Prefers cassette, CD or video with 4-6 songs. Does not return unsolicited material. Reports in 2 weeks.
Music: Mostly **rock, top 40, country** and **blues**; also **rockabilly, alternative** and **jazz.** "To date our company has agreements with 140 artists that represent every genre of music." Current acts include Big Brother & The Holding Co., Duane Eddy (rock), Doug Clark & The Hot Nuts, Poo Nanny & The Stormers (top 40), The Belmont Playboys (rockabilly), Michael Dillon & Guns, Del Reeves (country), West Willie (blues), Nina Simone, Stanley Turrentine (jazz).
Tips: "Send all available information including audio, video, photo and print. Creative Communications Workshop, our advertising/promotion division, specializes in developing effective artist promotional packages, including demos, videos, photography and copy. We will evaluate your present promotional material at no cost."

S.L. FELDMAN & ASSOCIATES, #200, 1505 W. Second Ave., Vancouver, British Columbia V6H 3Y4 **Canada.** (604)734-5945. Fax: (604)732-0922. Contact: Janet York. Management firm, booking agency. Estab. 1970. Represents individual artists and groups from anywhere; currently handles over 100 acts.
How to Contact: Submit demo tape by mail. Unsolicited submissions are OK. Prefers cassette and lyric sheet. If seeking management, include photo, bio, cassette, video (if available) in press kit. SAE and IRC. Reports in 6-8 weeks.
Music: Current acts include Bryan Adams, The Chieftains, Mae Moore, Rush, Odds, Sarah McLachlan, Spirit of the West, Boy on a Dolphin.

FRED T. FENCHEL ENTERTAINMENT AGENCY, 2104 S. Jefferson Avenue, Mason City IA 50401. (515)423-4177. General Manager: Fred T. Fenchel. Booking agency. Estab. 1964. Represents local and international individual artists and groups. Currently handles 8 acts. Receives 15% commission. Reviews material for acts.
How to Contact: Submit demo tape by mail (videocassette if available). Unsolicited submissions are OK. Does not return unsolicited material. Reports in 3 weeks.
Music: Mostly **country, pop** and some **gospel.** Works primarily with dance bands, show groups; "artists we can use on club dates, fairs, etc." Current acts include The Memories, "Hot" Rod Chevy, The Sherwin Linton Show, Convertibles and Cadillac. "We deal primarily with established name acts with recording contracts, or those with a label and starting into popularity."
Tips: "Submit good material with universal appeal and be informative on artist's background."

FIRST TIME MANAGEMENT, Sovereign House, 12 Trewartha Rd., Praa Sands-Penzance, Cornwall TR20 9ST **England.** Phone: (0736)762826. Fax: (0736)763328. Managing Director: Roderick G. Jones. Management firm. Estab. 1986. Represents local, regional and international individual aritsts, groups and songwriters. Receives 20% commission. Reviews material for acts.

How to Contact: Submit demo tape by mail—unsolicited submissions are OK. Prefers cassette or 15 ips reel-to-reel (or VHS videocassette) with 3 songs and lyric sheets. SAE and IRC. Reports in 4-8 weeks.
Music: Mostly **dance, top 40, rap, country, gospel** and **pop**; also **all styles**. Works primarily with songwriters, composers, vocalists, groups and choirs. Current acts include Pete Arnold (folk) and Willow.
Tips: "Become a member of the Guild of International Songwriters and Composers. Keep everything as professional as possible. Be patient and dedicated to your aims and objectives."

*FIVE STAR ENTERTAINMENT, 10188 Winter View Dr., Naples FL 33942. (813)566-7701. Fax: (813)566-7702. Co-owner: Sid Kleiner. Booking agency. Estab. 1976. Represents local and regional individual artists and groups; currently handles 400 acts. Commission varies. Reviews material for acts.
How to Contact: Submit demo tape by mail. Unsolicited submissions are OK. Prefers cassette or VHS videocassette with 4 songs and lyric or lead sheet. If seeking management, press kit should include song list, demo, video equipment list, references. SASE. Reports in 2 months.
Music: Mostly **MOR, country** and **folk.** Current acts include Dave Kleiner (folk singer), Magic Diamond (magic act), Gents of Jazz (jazz).

FLASH ATTRACTIONS AGENCY, 38 Prospect St., Warrensburg NY 12885. (518)623-9313. Agent: Wally Chester. Management firm and booking agency. Estab. 1952. Represents artists and groups; currently handles 10 exclusive and 96 non-exclusive acts. Receives 15-20% commission. Reviews material for acts. "We are celebrating 40 years in business, and are fully licensed by the American Federation of Musicians and the State of New York."
How to Contact: Submit demo tape by mail—unsolicited submissions are OK. Prefers cassette for singers, VHS videocassette for acts, with 1-6 songs with lead and lyric sheets. Songwriters and artists may submit "professionally done" videocassettes. If seeking management, entertainers should include professionally-done videotape or cassette, 8×10 photo, résumé, song list and history of the act in press kit. Songwriters should include professionally-done cassette, lead sheet, lyrics and music. SASE. Reports in 1 month.
Music: Mostly **country, calypso, Hawaiian** and **MOR**; also **blues, dance, easy listening, jazz, top 40, country rock** and **Latin,** plus **American Indian Shows.** Works primarily with vocalists, dance bands, lounge acts, floor show groups and ethnic shows. Current acts include Mirinda James (Nashville recording artist and her country crossover show band), Loi Afo and "Island Call," The Country Belles (all girl variety band), N.C. Preservation Dixieland Jazz Band, The Robin Right Country Music (voted New England's #1 entertainer and band), Wally Chester's "Spark and a Flame Duo" (lounge act), Eagle Feather (country music band and Canadian Indian dancers) and Kit McClure and her all female 17 piece big band sound.
Tips: "Submit songs that have public appeal, good story line and simplicity."

FLEMING ARTISTS MANAGEMENT, 5975 Park Ave., Montreal, Quebec H2V 4H4 **Canada.** (514)276-5605. Contact: Director. Management firm, booking agency, record producer. Estab. 1986. Represents local and regional individual artists, groups and songwriters. Currently handles 10 acts. Receives 15-20% commission.
How to Contact: Write or call first and obtain permission to submit. Prefers CD. Does not return material. Replies in 2 weeks.
Music: Mostly **jazz, folk** and **ethnic**; also **blues, gospel** and **country.** Works primarily with jazz and folk artists. Current artists include Lorraine Desmarais (jazz), Penny Lang (folk/blues), Tricycle (jazz) and Trio François Bourassa (jazz).

*FLETCHER ENTERTAINMENT GROUP, 11504 Sonnet, Dallas TX 75229. (214)956-8130. Fax: (214)956-8156. Owner: Terry Fletcher. Management firm and music publisher. Estab. 1981. Represents individual artists and/or groups, songwriters from anywhere; currently handles 3 acts. Receives 20% commission. Reviews material for acts.
How to Contact: Submit demo tape by mail. Unsolicited submissions are OK. Prefers cassette (or VHS videocassette) with 3 (max.) songs. If seeking management, press kit should include photo, bio and cassette. Does not return material. Reports in 3 weeks.
Music: Mostly **country, rock** and **pop**; also **folk.** Works primarily with singer/songwriters. Current acts include Rory Lee (country singer/songwriter), Patsy Meyer (pop/jazz singer/songwriter) and Jan Krist (folk singer/songwriter).

*FOLEY ENTERTAINMENT, P.O. Box 642, Carteret NJ 07008. (908)541-1862. Fax: (908)541-1862. President: Eugene Foley, J.D., Ph.D. Director of Creative Services: M. Bartolo. Management firm, booking agency, music publisher and record company. Estab. 1989. Represents individual artists and/or groups, songwriters from anywhere. Receives 20% commission. Reviews material for acts.

How to Contact: "Call or write first to obtain a submission code number, which is to be written on the envelope when you send your material. Songwriters, send a tape with up to 5 songs and lyric sheets. Artists and groups, send your demo, biography and a photo. Reports back by letter or postcard in 3 to 5 weeks. However, if you want your material returned, please enclose a SASE with sufficient postage. Copyright all material before you send it." Reports in 3-5 weeks.
Music: Mostly **R&B, country** and **pop**; also **rock** and **alternative**.
Tips: "We are a national firm with clients from all across the United States. Our staff is comprised of friendly, experienced, and highly educated people who are eager to work hard for you and your career. Other services include: tape shopping, career and business advice, financial planning, music industry contracts (drafted-reviewed-negotiated), biography and press kit designing, national publicity and promotion, merchandise, 8 × 10 photo reproduction, national booking and tour coordination, tour buses and much more. Please write or call for more information."

PETER FREEDMAN ENTERTAINMENT, 1775 Broadway, 7th Floor, New York NY 10019. (212)265-1776. Fax: (212)265-3678. President: Peter Freedman. Management firm. Estab. 1986. Represents individual artists, groups and songwriters from anywhere. Currently handles 3 acts. Receives 15-20% commission. Reviews material for acts.
How to Contact: Write or call first and obtain permission to submit. Prefers cassette (or VHS videocassette) with 1-2 songs. If seeking management, press kit should include 3-4 song demo/ short bio and picture. Does not return material. Reports in 3-4 weeks.
Music: Mostly **alternative/pop, dance**, and **R&B/pop**. Works primarily with bands, solo artists. Current acts include +Live+ (alternative/pop), The Ocean Blue (alternative/pop) and The Spelvins (alternative/pop).
Tips: "Write, write and write some more."

BOB SCOTT FRICK ENTERPRISES, 404 Bluegrass Ave., Madison TN 37115. (615)865-6380. President: Bob Frick. Booking agency, music publisher (Frick Music Publishing Co./BMI and Sugarbaker Music Publishing/ASCAP) and record company (R.E.F. Recording Co). Represents individual artists and songwriters; currently handles 5 acts. Reviews material for acts.
How to Contact: Submit demo tape by mail, or write or call first to arrange personal interview. Prefers cassette with 3 songs and lyric sheet. SASE. Reports in 1 month.
Music: Mostly **gospel, country** and **R&B**. Works primarily with vocalists. Current acts include Bob Scott Frick (guitarist/singer), Larry Ahlborn (singer), Bob Myers (singer), Teresa Ford, Eddie Isaacs, Scott Frick, Jim and Ruby Mattingly and David Barton.

KEN FRITZ MANAGEMENT, 648 N. Robertson Blvd., Los Angeles CA 90069. (310)854-6488. Fax: (310)854-1015. Associate Managers: Pamela Byers, Martha Hertzberg. Management firm. Represents individual artists and groups from anywhere. Currently handles 5 acts. Receives 15% commission. Reviews material for acts.
How to Contact: Write first and obtain permission to submit. Prefers cassette (or VHS videocassette) with 2-3 songs and lyric sheet. "Submissions should be short and to the point." SASE. Reports in 1-3 months.
Music: Mostly **alternative, rock** and **pop**; also **jazz** and **kids**. Current acts include George Benson (jazz guitar/vocalist) and Peter, Paul & Mary (folk singer/songwriters).

*FRONT ROW MANAGEMENT CORP., 504 Candlewood Rd., Fort Worth TX 76103-1146. (817)654-0120. (817)457-0829. President: Tony Jones. Management firm. Estab. 1975. Represents individual artists and groups from anywhere; currently handles 5 acts. Receives 15-25% commission. Reviews material for acts.
How to Contact: Submit demo tape by mail. Unsolicited submissions are OK. Prefers cassette or VHS videocassette with 3 or more songs. If seeking management, press kit should include photo, tape, bio. Does not return material. Reports in 1-4 weeks.
Music: Mostly **pop, R&B** and **gospel**; also **comedy**. Works primarily with bands.

*FUDPUCKER ENTERTAINMENT, P.O. Box 6593, Branson MO 61615. (417)336-4188. President: Wes Ranstad. Management firm, music publisher (Fudpucker Publishing), record company (Vista Int'l). Estab. 1965. Represents individual artists from anywhere; currently handles 3 acts. Receives 15% commission. Reviews material for acts.
How to Contact: Submit demo tape by mail. Unsolicited submissions are OK. Prefers cassette or VHS videocassette with 4 songs and lyric sheet. If seeking management, send full press kit with all available information. SASE. Reports in 3-4 weeks.
Music: Mostly **country, comedy** and **novelty songs**. Works primarily with singers, comedians, bands. Current acts include Elmer Fudpucker (comedian, singer), James Walls (band), Dexter (comedian, singer).

Tips: "Be professional on and off stage. A good image and reputation is 50% of success. The other 50% is talent and hard work."

*GALLUP ENTERTAINMENT, 93-40 Queens Blvd., Rego Park NY 11374. (718)897-6428. Fax: (718)997-7531. President: A. Gallup. Management firm. Estab. 1986. Represents individual artists and/or groups from anywhere; currently handles 4 acts. Receives 10-15% commission. Reviews material for acts.
How to Contact: Write first and obtain permission to submit. Prefers cassette and lyric or lead sheet. If seeking management, press kit should include bio, photo, clippings. Does not return material. Reports in 2-3 months.
Music: Mostly **rock** and **country**. Current acts include Tommy Sands (singer), Cathy Jean & Roommates (vocal group), Shirelles (vocal group).

GANGLAND ARTISTS, 707-810 W. Broadway, Vancouver, British Columbia V5Z 1J8 **Canada**. (604)872-0052. Contact: Allen Moy. Management firm, production house and music publisher. Estab. 1985. Represents artists and songwriters; currently handles 3 acts.
How to Contact: Write first and obtain permission to submit. Prefers cassette (or VHS videocassette if available) and lyric sheet. "Videos are not entirely necessary for our company. It is certainly a nice touch. If you feel your audio cassette is strong—send the video upon later request. Something wildly creative and individual will grab our attention." Does not return material.
Music: **Rock, pop** and **R&B**. Works primarily with "original rock/left of center" show bands. Current acts include 54-40 (rock/pop), Herald Nix (singer/songwriter) and Mae Moore (pop).

*GIBSON MANAGEMENT INC., #201, 300 Main St., Huntington NY 11743. (516)942-8500. Fax: (516)385-1878. Vice President: Karen Gibson. Management firm, music publisher (ASCAP/Hats Off Music, BMI/Hats On Music). Estab. 1987. Represents individual artists and songwriters from anywhere; currently handles 7 acts. Receives 20% commission. Reviews material for acts.
How to Contact: Write first and obtain permission to submit. Prefers cassette with 3 songs and lyric sheet. If seeking management, press kit should include photo, bio, cassette, press (if any) and lyrics. Does not return material. Reports in 2 months.
Music: Mostly **country, pop** and **R&B**. Works primarily with vocalists and singer/songwriters. Current acts include Debbie Gibson (pop singer/songwriter; SBK Records/EMI Publishing), Bryan Austin (country singer/songwriter; Patriot Records/EMI Publishing) and Chris Taylor (country singer/songwriter; Warner Chappell Publishing).

*GLICKMAN QUINN COMPANY, P.O. Box 570815, Tarzana CA 91357-0815. (818)708-1300. Partner: Zach Glickman. Management firm, music publisher. Estab. 1968. Represents individual artists, groups, songwriters from anywhere; currently handles 4 acts. Reviews material for acts.
How to Contact: Write first and obtain permission to submit. Prefers cassette with lyric sheet. If seeking management, press kit should include as much information as possible. Does not return material. Reports in 2 months.
Music: **All types**. Works primarily with bands, singer/songwriters. Current acts include Dion, Russ Taff, Mighty Clouds of Joy.

GLOBAL ASSAULT MANAGEMENT, Suite 1632, 639 Gardenwalk Blvd., College Park GA 30349. (404)994-1770. Contact: David Norman. Management firm and booking agency. Represents groups and production teams. Currently handles 5 acts. Receives 15-20% commission. Reviews material for acts or available on consultant basis.
How to Contact: Submit demo tape by mail—unsolicited submissions are OK. Send bio, 8×10 photos, VHS videocassette (if possible), tape with 4 songs, cover letter, songlist. SASE. Reports in 2 weeks.
Music: Mostly self-contained **R&B** groups. Current acts include Fonzo-S, Shyrod, AC Black, Ales Gaye, Synical.
Tips: "Be open-minded, optimistic, think large. Be confident, organized and have lofty goals."

GOLDEN BULL PRODUCTIONS, P.O. Box 81153, Chicago IL 60681-0153. (312)604-1673. Manager: Jesse Dearing. Management firm. Estab. 1984. Represents local and regional (Midwest) individual artists, groups and songwriters; currently handles 3 acts. Receives 12-30% commission. Reviews material for acts.
How to Contact: Write first and obtain permission to submit. Prefers cassette (or VHS videocassette) with 4-5 songs and lyric or lead sheet. If seeking management, include demo tape, bio and 8×10 black and white photo in press kit. Does not return unsolicited material. Reports in 8-10 weeks.
Music: Mostly **R&B, pop** and **rock**; also **gospel, jazz** and **blues**. Works primarily with vocalists, bands. Current acts include Lost and Found (R&B band), Keith Stewart (songwriter) and A. Lock (singer).

*GOLDEN CITY INTERNATIONAL, Box 410851, San Francisco CA 94141. (415)822-1530. Manager: Mr. Alston. Management firm, booking agency and record company (Dagene Records, Cabletown). Estab. 1993. Represents regional (Bay area) individual artists, groups and songwriters; currently handles 3 acts. Receives 25% commission. Reviews material for acts.
How to Contact: Write or call first and obtain permission to submit. Prefers cassette with 2 songs and lyric sheet. Does not return unsolicited material. Reports in 3 weeks.
Music: Mostly **R&B/dance,** rap and **pop;** also **gospel.** Current clients include Billie Ross (songwriter), The Independents (artist) and David Alston (producer).

GOLDEN GURU ENTERTAINMENT, 301 Bainbridge St., Philadelphia PA 19147. (215)574-2900. Fax: (215)440-7367. Co-Owner: Eric J. Cohen, Esq. Management firm, music publisher, record company. Estab. 1988. Represents individual artists, groups and songwriters from anywhere; currently handles 5 acts. Reviews material for acts.
How to Contact: Write first and obtain permission to submit. Prefers cassette (or VHS videocassette) with 3-6 songs. If seeking management, press kit should include tape, press, photo, etc. Does not return material. Reports in 3-4 weeks.
Music: Mostly **rock, singer/songwriters, urban** and **pop;** "anything that is excellent!" Current acts include Jeffrey Gaines, Ben Arnold and Susan Werner (all 3 are national recording artists).
Tips: "Be patient for a response. Our firm also renders legal and business affairs services. We also do bookings for the *Tin Angel*, the premier acoustic venue (200 capacity) in Philadelphia."

*GOOD MUSIC MANAGEMENT, 216 Third Ave. N., Minneapolis MN 55401. (612)338-3833. Fax: (612)338-4235. Manager/President: Doug Brown. Management firm, booking agency, record company (Metro Records). Estab. 1978. Represents individual artists and/or groups, songwriters from anywhere; currently handles 3 acts. Receives 5-15% commission. Reviews material for acts.
How to Contact: Submit demo tape by mail. Prefers cassette or VHS videocassette with 3-4 songs and lyric or lead sheet. If seeking management, press kit should include bio, tour information, press, chart history. SASE. Reports in 3 weeks.
Music: Mostly **country, rock** and **R&B;** also **rap** and **jazz.** Current acts include Buffalo Alice (band/songwriters), Nielsen White Band (band/songwriters), Trouble Shooter (band).

*TOM GOODKIND MANAGEMENT, 355-16L S. End Ave., New York NY 10280. Contact: Tom Goodkind. Management firm and record producer. Estab. 1983. Represents individual artists from anywhere; currently handles 3 acts. Receives 10% commission. Reviews material for acts.
How to Contact: Submit demo tape by mail. Unsolicited submissions are OK. Prefers cassette. If seeking management, press kit should include tape and phone number. Does not return material. Reports in 2 weeks.
Music: Mostly **folk** and **alternative rock.** Works primarily with bands. Current acts include The Washington Squares, Loose Leg Larry Finklestone, Boring Birth Bombs.
Tips: "Lyrics, lyrics, lyrics—listen to Leonard Cohen's 'I'm Your Man' and then try to top it."

*GOODWIN MOORE & ASSOCIATES, P.O. Box 120426, Nashville TN 37212. (615)298-1689. Fax: (615)298-1446. Partner: Martha Moore. Management firm. Estab. 1993. Represents individual artists and/or groups from anywhere; currently handles 2 acts. Receives 15% commission. Reviews material for acts.
How to Contact: Write first and obtain permission to submit. Prefers cassette or VHS videocassette with 3 songs maximum and lyric sheet. If seeking management, press kit should include bio, photo, any newspaper clips available. "Send 3 songs only." Does not return material. Reports in 4-6 weeks.
Music: Mostly **country;** also **pop/rock** and **New Age.** Works primarily with vocalists, singer/songwriters. "We are looking for acts with TV and film potential." Current acts include Sonny Shroyer (actor), Randy Franks (actor/country-folk singer/songwriter).
Tips: "Follow the above instructions—don't be impatient or pushy!"

*GRAMERCY PARK ENTERTAINMENT, Suite 200, 1425 Spruce St. , Philadelphia PA 19102. President: Linda D. Coffee. Management firm. Estab. 1993. Represents individual artists from anywhere; currently handles 2 acts. Receives 25% commission. Reviews material for acts.
How to Contact: Submit demo tape by mail. Unsolicited submissions are OK. Prefers cassette. If seeking management, press kit should include promo package. SASE. Reports in 2 months.
Music: Mostly **R&B** and **New Age.** Works primarily with vocalists and songwriters. Current acts include Michele René.

*GRASS MANAGEMENT, 13546 Cheltenham Dr., Sherman Oaks CA 91423. (818)788-1777. Fax: (818)783-1542. Vice President: Barak Grass. Management firm. Estab. 1976. Represents individual artists, groups, songwriters from anywhere; currently handles 5 acts. Receives 15% commission. Reviews material for acts.

How to Contact: Submit demo tape by mail. Unsolicited submissions are OK. Prefers cassette or VHS videocassette with 1-6 songs and lyric sheet. If seeking management, press kit should include tape, photo, press and bio. "Material is not returned." Reports in 2-4 weeks.
Music: Mostly **country**, **rock** and **R&B**; also **pop/rock** and **new world**. Works primarily with singer/songwriters, bands, writers. Current acts include Blessing & The Prophets of Swing (country/rock), The Hoodstas (rap), Diamond (female singer/songwriter).
Tips: "Make submissions timely, cleanly with the adage 'less is more' in mind. Be honest and leave out all 'hype'. It's on the page or it isn't."

*GREAT LAKES COUNTRY TALENT AGENCY, 167 Sherman, Rochester NY 14606. (716)647-1617. President: Donald Redanz. Management firm, booking agency, music publisher, record company and record producer. Estab. 1988. Represents individual artists and/or groups, songwriters from anywhere; currently handles 5 acts. Receives 20% commission. Reviews material for acts.
How to Contact: Submit demo tape by mail. Unsolicited submissions are OK. Prefers cassette with 4 songs. If seeking management, press kit should include picture, places played, tape. Does not return material. Reports in 1 month.
Music: Mostly **country**, **gospel** and **top 40**; also **bluegrass**. Works primarily with vocalists, singer/songwriters, bands. Current acts include Donnie Lee Baker (country), Tony Starr (songwriter), Jimmy C (top 40).

CHRIS GREELEY ENTERTAINMENT, P.O. Box 593, Bangor ME 04402-0593. (207)827-4382. General Manager: Christian D. Greeley. Management firm, shopping/contract service. Estab. 1986. Represents local, regional and international individual artists, groups and songwriters; currently handles 6-12 acts. Receives 10% commission. Reviews material for acts.
How to Contact: Submit demo tape by mail—unsolicited submissions are OK. Prefers cassette (or VHS videocassette if available) with 1-4 songs. SASE. Reports in 1 month.
Music: Mostly **rock**, **country** and **pop**. "I'm open to anything marketable." Wide range of musical styles. Current acts include Hey Mister (acoustic duo).
Tips: "Treat your music interests as a business venture. Don't be afraid to work hard and spend money to get where you want to go."

*LAW OFFICES OF GARY GREENBERG, 4240 Vanetta Dr., Studio City CA 91604. (818)508-5867. Fax: (818)508-5965. Owner/Attorney: Gary Greenberg. Management firm, attorney. Estab. 1989. Represents individual artists and/or groups, songwriters, labels from anywhere; currently handles 40 acts. Receives 15% commission, $175/hour as attorney. Reviews material for acts.
How to Contact: Submit demo tape by mail. Unsolicited submissions are OK. Prefers cassette. Does not return material. Reports in 2 weeks.
Music: Mostly **R&B**, **rap**, **jazz** and **rock**; also **New Age** and **pop**. Current acts include The Whispers, The Rippingtons, Sergio Mendes.

*GREIF-GARRIS MANAGEMENT, 2112 Casitas Way, Palm Springs CA 92264. (619)322-8655. Fax: (619)322-7793. Vice President: Sid Garris. Management firm. Estab. 1961. Represents individual artists and/or groups, songwriters from anywhere; currently handles 2 acts. Commission varies. Reviews material for acts.
How to Contact: Submit demo tape by mail. Unsolicited submissions are OK. Prefers cassette. SASE. Reports in 3 weeks.
Music: **All types.** Current acts include The New Christy Minstrels (folk) and The Crusaders (jazz fusion).

*GUESTSTAR ENTERTAINMENT AGENCY, 17321 Ritchie Ave. NE, Sand Lake MI 49343-9475. (616)636-5068. President: Raymond G. Dietz, Sr. Management firm, booking agency, music publisher (Sandlake Music/BMI), record company (Gueststar Records, Inc.), record producer and record distributor (Gueststar Music Distributors). Represents individual artists, groups, songwriters, bands from anywhere; currently handles 3 acts. Receives 20% commission. Reviews material for acts.
How to Contact: Submit demo tape by mail. Unsolicited submissions are OK. Prefers cassette or VHS videocassette with unlimited songs, but send your best with lyric or lead sheet. If seeking management, press kit should include photo, demo tape, music résumé and VHS videocassette tape if possible. "We do not return material, but evaluate and reply if a SASE is submitted." Reports in 1 week.
Music: Mostly **contemporary country**, **hit country** and **traditional country**; also **contemporary Christian**, **MOR** and **mountain songs**. Current acts include Mountain Man (singer), Jamie "K" (singer), Sweetgrass (band).
Tips: "Bring your songs up to date, compatible with today's radio."

*H.L.A. MUSIC, 313 N. 36th St., Belleville IL 62223. (618)236-1651. Fax: (618)277-9425. President: Randy Forker. Management firm. Estab. 1987. Represents groups from anywhere; currently handles 3 acts. Receives 15-20% commission. Reviews material for acts.
How to Contact: Submit demo tape by mail. Unsolicited submissions are OK. Prefers cassette or VHS videocassette with 2 songs and lyric sheet. If seeking management, press kit should include photo, bio, tape, contact number. Does not return material. Reports in 6 weeks.
Music: Mostly **rock, metal** and **rap/hip hop**. Works primarily with bands. Current acts include Bronx Zoo (rock/metal), Phatal Burth (rap/hip hop), Busgy (rock).

*BILL HALL ENTERTAINMENT & EVENTS, 138 Frog Hollow Rd., Churchville PA 18966. (215)357-5189. Fax: (215)357-0320. Contact: William B. Hall III. Booking agency and production company. Represents individuals and groups; currently handles 30 acts. Receives 15% commission. Reviews material for acts.
How to Contact: Submit demo tape by mail. Unsolicited submissions are OK. Prefers cassette (or videocassette of performance) with 2-3 songs "and photos, promo material and record or tape. We need quality material, preferably before a 'live' audience." Does not return unsolicited material. Reports in 1 month.
Music: **Marching band, circus** and **novelty**. Works primarily with "unusual or novelty attractions in musical line, preferably those that appeal to family groups." Current acts include Fralinger and Polish-American Philadelphia Championship Mummers String Bands (marching and concert group), Erwin Chandler Orchestra (show band), "Mr. Polynesian" Show Band and Hawaiian Revue (ethnic group), the "Phillies Whiz Kids Band" of Philadelphia Phillies Baseball team, Phillies organist-entertainer Paul Richardson, Wm. (Boom-Boom) Browning Circus Band (circus band), Circus Kingdom Brass Band (circus band), Philadelphia German Brass Band (marching band) and numerous solo pianists and vocalists.

*DUSTIN HARDMAN MANAGEMENT, 3020 W. Patterson St., Tampa FL 33614-3470. (813)932-3555. Fax: (813)876-5140. President: Dustin Hardman. Management firm. Estab. 1990. Represents groups from anywhere; currently handles 4 acts. Receives 20% commission. Reviews material for acts.
How to Contact: Submit demo tape by mail. Unsolicited submissions are OK. Prefers cassette with 3 songs and lyric sheet. If seeking management, press kit should include a photo, biography that is current but to the point, tape and contact info. "Make all submissions to the Attn. of Dustin Hardman." Does not return material. Reports in 2 weeks.
Music: Mostly **hard music, alternative** and **pop/dance rock**. "All artists are worked on a level to achieve international acceptance, so only serious artists need apply." Current acts include Brutality, Kamelot, Darknes.
Tips: "My organization looks for serious and professional clients that want to achieve only the best in their genre. Represent yourself as you would want to be recognized."

*HARDWAY MUSIC MANAGEMENT, P.O. Box 540, Dearborn Heights MI 48127. (313)278-6068. Owner: Mark S. Shearer. Management firm. Estab. 1987. Represents individual artists and groups from anywhere; currently handles 2 acts. Receives 20% commission. Reviews material for acts.
How to Contact: Submit demo tape by mail. Unsolicited submissions are OK. Prefers cassette (or VHS videocassette) with 4 songs. "We will contact you if interested." Does not return material.
Music: Mostly **rock, alternative** and **dance**. Works primarily with bands. Current acts include Sex, Love and Money (on Rockworld/Sony) and Love & War (local artist).
Tips: "Have the best possible sounding demo tape you can, and always present your material in a professional manner."

*M. HARRELL & ASSOCIATES, 5444 Carolina, Merrillville IN 46410. (219)887-8814. Owner: Mary Harrell. Management firm, booking agency. Estab. 1984. Represents individual artists, groups, songwriters, all talents—fashion, dancers, etc. Currently handles 40-50 acts. Receives 10-15% commission. Reviews material for acts.
How to Contact: Submit demo tape by mail. Unsolicited submissions are OK. Prefers cassette or videocassette with 2-3 songs. If seeking management, press kit should include résumé, bio, picture. "Keep it brief and current." Does not return material. Reports in 2 weeks.
Music: Mostly **country** and **R&B**. Current acts include Bill Shelton and 11th Ave. (50s music singer and band), Kent Cleveland (country) and Stormy Weather (singers).
Tips: "Try to study the commercial market and be honest in pursuing same; write what you feel."

PAUL HAWKINS MANAGEMENT ASSOCIATES, 222 Stratford Ave., Pittsburgh PA 15206. President: Paul Hawkins. Management firm. Estab. 1992. Represents local and mid-Atlantic states individual artists and groups. Currently handles 2 acts. Commission varies. Reviews material for acts.
How to Contact: Write first and obtain permission to submit or arrange personal interview. If seeking management, press kit should include a clear description of group/artist background, philosophy and

goals. "We respond to written inquiry only and will provide submission instructions at that time." Does not return material. Reports in 1-2 weeks.
Music: Mostly **R&B, pop**, and **hip hop**. Works primarily with young adult vocalists/groups with strong visual/audio appeal.
Tips: "Present your material professionally. State what you are looking for and why."

*KEVIN HELLMAN PRODUCTIONS, Suite 223, 4490 Fanuel St., San Diego CA 92109. (619)270-0505. Fax: (619)272-4606. Owner: Kevin Hellman. Management firm, booking agency, record company. Estab. 1981. Represents local groups, artists from anywhere; currently handles 2 acts. Receives 20% commission. Reviews material for acts.
How to Contact: Submit demo tape by mail. Unsolicited submissions are OK. Prefers cassette. If seeking management, press kit should include bio, photo. Does not return material. Reports in 1 month.
Music: Mostly **rock, blues** and **reggae**; also **jazz** and **country**. Works primarily with bands. Current acts include Natasha's Ghost (pop-alternative), Rockola (classic rock).

HENDERSON GROUP MUSIC, 125 Powell Mill Rd., Spartanburg SC 29301. (803)576-0226. President: Dr. Barry Henderson. Management firm, music publisher (HPL Communications/BMI). Estab. 1990. Represents individual artists, groups and songwriters from anywhere. Currently handles 3 acts. Receives 15-25% commission. Reviews material for acts.
How to Contact: Submit demo tape by mail. Unsolicited submissions are OK. Prefers cassette (or VHS videocassette) with 3 songs. If seeking management, press kit should include photo, bio, song demo. Does not return material. Reports in 2-3 months.
Music: Mostly **country, pop** and **rock**. Current acts include Joe Bennett (songwriter), Jeff Stone (singer/songwriter), Streamliner and Stephanie Bouchard.
Tips: "Must be polished and professional with commercial songs. Must have desire to work hard and travel."

*HIDDEN STUDIOS, P.O. Box 355, Roundup MT 59072. (406)947-5866. A&R: David Ramirez. President: A. Ditonno. Management firm, record company (Wild Country Records) and record producer. Estab. 1978. Represents individual artists, groups and songwriters from anywhere; currently handles 9 acts. Receives 15% commission. Reviews material for acts.
How to Contact: Submit demo tape by mail. Unsolicited submissions are OK. Prefers cassette or VHS videocassette with 2-4 songs (not more than 4 songs per tape) and lead sheet. If seeking management, press kit should include photos, demo, résumé. SASE. Reports in 2 months.
Music: Mostly **country, pop** and **rock**; also **gospel, A/C** and **MOR**. Current acts include Tony Michael (singer/songwriter), Scott Stevens Band (rock group) and Pat Martinez (singer/songwriter).
Tips: "Don't be afraid to submit your material, what you might think is your worst could end up being your finest."

DOC HOLIDAY PRODUCTIONS, 10 Luanita Lane, Newport News VA 23606. (804)930-1814. President: Doc Holiday. Management firm, booking agent, music publisher (Doc Holiday Productions and Publishing/ASCAP, Doc Publishing/BMI and Dream Machine Publishing/SESAC), record producer and record company (Tug Boat International). Estab. 1985. Represents international individual artists, groups and songwriters; currently handles 171 acts. Receives 10-15% commission. Reviews material for acts.
How to Contact: Submit demo tape by mail. Unsolicited submissions are okay. Prefers cassette (or VHS videocassette if available) with 1 song and lyric sheet. If seeking management, include 8×10 photo, press clippings, bio, VHS, performance history, press experiments and demo tape in press kit. Does not return unsolicited material. Reports in 2 weeks.
Music: Mostly **country, pop** and **R&B**; also **gospel** and **rap**. Works primarily with vocalist dance bands. Current acts include Doug "The Ragin Cajun" Kenshaw (cajun), Big Al Downing (country).

HORIZON MANAGEMENT INC., 659 Westview Station, Binghamton NY 13905. (607)772-0857. Contact: New Talent Department. Management firm includes booking agency and concert promotion. Estab. 1967. Represents regional, national and international artists, groups and songwriters; currently handles 1,500 acts. Receives 20% commission. Reviews material for acts.
How to Contact: Call first and obtain permission to submit. Prefers cassette (or VHS videocassette if available) with 1-4 songs and 1 lyric or lead sheet. Send photo, bio, song list, equipment list, audio and/or video, press clippings, reviews, etc. Does not return unsolicited material. Reports in 1 week.
Music: Mostly **top 40 lounge** and **show, top 40 country** and **top 40 rock**; also **classic rock, oldies** and **original**. Works primarily with bands (all styles). Current acts include Beatlemania (Broadway show), The Boxtops (60s recording act), Joey Dee & Starlighters (50s recording artist), Xavier (rock), Blue

Norther (jazz), Kevie Kev (R&B), Leighton Watts (folk), Kimberly Carter (country), Steinhardt/Moon (tribute).

*KATHY HOWARD MANAGEMENT, Box 477, Rozelle N5W **Australia** 2106. Estab. 1985. Represents local individual artists and groups; currently handles 2 acts. Commission fluctuates. Reviews material for acts.
How to Contact: Submit demo tape by mail—unsolicited submissions are OK. Prefers cassette. Does not return unsolicited material. If seeking management, press kit should include bio and demo. Reports in 2-3 weeks.
Music: Rock and **pop/rock** groups. Current acts include Happy House (pop/dance), Dreamseed (pop/rock).
Tips: "Please send only rough demos, produced demos not essential, lyric sheet preferred. Send commercial, radio-friendly compositions."

HULEN ENTERPRISES, Suite 2-2447, Falcon Ave., Ottawa, Ontario K1V 8C8 **Canada**. (613)738-2373. Fax: (613)526-3481. President, General Manager: Helen Lenthall. Management firm, record producer. Represents individual artists, groups, songwriters from anywhere. Commission negotiable. Reviews material for acts.
How to Contact: Write first and obtain permission to submit. Prefers cassette (or VHS videocassette) with 3-8 songs maximum and lyric sheet or lead sheet. If seeking management, press kit should include bio, media package, photos, reviews, tracking if available. SAE and IRC. Reports in 3-8 weeks.
Music: Mostly **soul, pop/rock** and **country**; also **hip hop, rap** and **gospel**. Primarily works with bands, vocalists.

IMANI ENTERTAINMENT INC., P.O. Box 150-139, Brooklyn NY 11215. (718)622-2132. Directors: Guy Anglade and Alfred Johnston. Management firm, music publisher (Imani Hits/BMI). Estab. 1991. Represents individual artists, groups, songwriters, producers and remixers from anywhere; currently handles 3 acts. Receives 15-20% commission. Reviews material for acts.
How to Contact: Submit demo tape by mail. Unsolicited submissions are OK. Prefers cassette (or VHS videocassette) with 3 songs and lyric sheet. If seeking management, press kit should include a bio, photograph, demo tape and any press received. SASE. Reports in 1 month.
Music: Mostly **pop/dance, R&B** and **hip-hop**; also **alternative rock, country** and **New Age**. Works primarily with vocalists, singer/songwriters. Current acts include Robyn Celia (pop/rock singer), Wonda Lenee (R&B vocalist), Tucka (rapper) and Shandi (producer/remixer).
Tips: "Be specific and to the point."

*PAUL INSINNA MANAGEMENT, 5th Floor, 1700 Broadway, New York NY 10019. Contact: Paul Insinna. Management firm. Estab. 1993. Represents individual artists and/or groups, songwriters from anywhere. Receives 15-20% commission. Reviews material for acts.
How to Contact: Write or call first and obtain permission to submit. Prefers cassette with lyric sheet. If seeking management, press kit should include photo, bio, press clips. SASE. Reports in 6 weeks.
Music: Mostly **A/C** and **acoustic** (singer/songwriter); also **dance**. Works primarily with singer/songwriters. Current acts include Sean Suillivan (A/C artists), Jim Dawson (A/C artists), Tommy West (producer).

INTERMOUNTAIN TALENT, P.O. Box 942, Rapid City SD 57709. (605)348-7777. Owner: Ron Kohn. Management firm, booking agency and music publisher (Big BL Music). Estab. 1978. Represents individual artists, groups and songwriters; currently handles 30 acts. Receives 10-20% commission. Reviews material for acts.
How to Contact: Submit demo tape by mail—unsolicited submissions are OK. Prefers cassette with 3 songs and lyric sheet. Artist may submit videocassette. If seeking management, include tape, video and photo in press kit. SASE. Reports in 1 month.
Music: Mostly **rock**; also **country/rock**. Works with solo acts, show bands, dance bands and bar bands. Current acts include Croswinds (band), Curtis Knox (solo) and Cheap Thrills (band).

Market conditions are constantly changing! If you're still using this book and it is 1996 or later, buy the newest edition of Songwriter's Market at your favorite bookstore or order directly from Writer's Digest Books.

INTERNATIONAL TALENT NETWORK, 17580 Frazho, Roseville MI 48066. Executive Vice President of A&R: Ron Geddish. Booking agency. Estab. 1980. Represents Midwest groups; currently handles 3 acts. Receives 25% commission. Reviews material for acts.
How to Contact: Submit demo tape by mail—unsolicited submissions are OK. Prefers cassette (or VHS videocassette of performance if available) with 3-5 songs and lyric sheet. Does not return unsolicited material. Reports in 1 month.
Music: Works primarily with **rock, pop** and **alternative-college acts.** Current acts include His Name Is Alive (group/alternative), Elvis Hitler (rock group) and The Look (A&M/Canada rock group).
Tips: "If we hear a hit tune—rock, pop, alternative college—we are interested."

ISSACHAR MANAGEMENT, Suite 10F, 111 Third Ave., New York NY 10003. (212)477-0407. Fax: (212)477-1469. President: Jack Flanagan. Management firm specializing in tour consulting. Represents international individual artists and groups and studio engineers and musicians.
How to Contact: Submit demo tape by mail—unsolicited submissions are OK. If seeking management, include tape, lyrics, photo, bio and press clips in press kit. Reports in 3 weeks.
Music: Mostly **rock, R&B** and **reggae;** also **pop** and **funk.** Current acts include Chuck Valle, Todd Youth, Murphy's Law (rock).

ITS HAPPENING PRESENT ENTERTAINMENT, P.O. Box 222, Pittsburg CA 94565. (510)427-1314. Fax: (510)458-0915. President: Bobellii Johnson. Management firm, booking agency and record company (Black Diamond Records, Hitting Hard Records and D. City Records). Estab. 1989. Represents local, regional or international individual artists and songwriters; currently handles 6 acts. Receives 15% commission. Reviews material for acts.
How to Contact: Submit demo tape by mail—unsolicited submissions are OK. If seeking management, include bio and 8×10 b&w photo. Prefers cassette with 2 songs and lyric sheet. Does not return unsolicited material. Reports in 3 weeks to 2 months.
Music: Mostly **pop, R&B** and **jazz;** also **rap, country** and **classical.** Works primarily with vocalist songwriters, rap groups, bands, instrumentalists. Current acts include Jerry "J" (vocalist jazz/R&B), Della (vocal R&B) and D.S.C. (vocal group R&B).
Tips: "Please, copyright all your material as soon as possible. Don't let anyone else hear it until that's done first. You have to be swift about hearing, slow about speaking and slow about giving. Be true to your art or craft."

J & V MANAGEMENT, 143 W. Elmwood, Caro MI 48723. (517)673-2889. Management: John Timko. Management firm, booking agency. Represents local, regional or international individual artists, groups and songwriters; currently handles 2 acts. Receives 20% commission. Reviews material for acts.
How to Contact: Write first and obtain permission to submit. Prefers cassette with 3 songs maximum and lyric sheet. If seeking management, include cassette or video tape, lyric sheet, photo and short reference bio in press kit. SASE. Reports in 1 month.
Music: Mostly **country.** Works primarily with vocalists and dance bands. Current acts include John Patrick Timko (songwriter) and John Patrick Band (entertainers).

JACKSON ARTISTS CORP., (Publishing Central), Suite 200, 7251 Lowell Dr., Shawnee Mission KS 66204. (913)384-6688. CEO: Dave Jackson. Booking agency (Drake/Jackson Productions), music publisher (All Told Music/BMI, Zang/Jac Publishing/ASCAP and Very Cherry/ASCAP), record company and record producer. Represents artists, groups and songwriters; currently handles 12 acts. Receives 15-20% commission from individual artists and groups; 10% from songwriters. Reviews material for acts.
How to Contact: Call first and obtain permission to submit or submit demo tape by mail. Prefers cassette (or VHS videocassette of performance if available) with 2-4 songs and lead sheet. "List names of tunes on cassettes. May send up to 4 tapes. Although it's not necessary, we prefer lead sheets with the tapes—send 2 or 3 that you are proud of. Also note what 'name' artist you'd like to see do the song. We do most of our business by phone. We prefer good enough quality to judge a performance, however, we do not require that the video or cassettes be of professional nature." Will return material if requested with SASE. Reports in 3 months.
Music: Mostly **gospel, country** and **rock;** also **bluegrass, blues, easy listening, disco, MOR, progressive, soul** and **top 40/pop.** Works with acts that work grandstand shows for fairs as well as bar bands that want to record original material. Current acts include Dixie Cadillacs (country/rock), Impressions (50's and 60's), The Booher Family (bluegrass/pop/country), Paul & Paula, Bill Haley's Comets, Max Groove (jazz) and The Dutton Family (classical to pop).
Tips: "Be able to work on the road, either as a player or as a group. Invest your earnings from these efforts in demos of your originals that have been tried out on an audience. And keep submitting to the industry."

*JACOBS MANAGEMENT, 382-C Union, Campbell CA 95008. (408)559-1669. Fax: (408)559-6664. Owner: Mitchell Jacobs. Management firm. Estab. 1988. Represents individual artists and groups from anywhere; currently handles 3 acts. Receives 15% commission. Reviews material for acts.
How to Contact: Write or call first and obtain permission to submit. Prefers cassette with 3 songs and lyric sheet. SASE. Reports in 1 month.
Music: Mostly **country**, **R&B** and **roots**. Works primarily with singer/songwriters, bands. Current acts include Rosie Flores, Loved Ones, Karen Hazel.
Tips: "Send your 3 best songs. Write from the heart and be professional."

*JAMES GANG MANAGEMENT, P.O. Box 121626, Nashville TN 37212. (615)726-3556. Contact: Neal James. Management firm, music publisher, record company (Kottage Records) and record producer. Estab. 1991. Represents individual artists and/or groups, songwriters from anywhere; currently handles 3 acts. Receives 10-30% commission.
How to Contact: Submit demo tape by mail. Unsolicited submissions are OK. Prefers cassette and lyric sheet. If seeking management, press kit should include full bio, photo and cassette. SASE. Reports in 1 month.
Music: Mostly **country**, **pop** and **gospel**; also **R&B**, **beach** and **blues**. Works primarily with vocalists, singer/songwriters, bands. Current acts include P.J. Hawk (country), Terry BarBay (contemporary), Judie Bell (contemporary/country).

ROGER JAMES MANAGEMENT, 10A Margaret Rd., Barnet, Herts EN4 9NP **England**. Phone: (01)440-9788. Professional Manager: Laura Skuce. Management firm and music publisher (R.J. Music/PRS). Estab. 1977. Represents songwriters. Receives 50% commission (but negotiable!). Reviews material for acts.
How to Contact: Submit demo tape by mail—unsolicited submissions are OK. Prefers cassette with 3 songs and lyric sheet. Does not return unsolicited material.
Music: Mostly **pop**, **country** and "any good song."

JAMPOP LTD., 27 Parkington Plaza, Kingston 10 W.I. **Jamaica**. Phone: (809)968-9235. Fax: (809)968-2199. President: Ken Nelson. Management firm and booking agency. Estab. 1990. Represents local, regional and international individual artists, groups and songwriters; currently handles 30 acts. Receives 10% commission. Reviews material for acts.
How to Contact: Submit demo tape by mail. Unsolicited submissions are OK. Prefers cassette with lyric sheet. Does not return material. Reports in 4 weeks.
Music: Mostly **R&B** and **pop**; also **gospel**. Works primarily with vocalists. Current artists include Chalice, Charles Hyatt and Fab 5.

JANA JAE ENTERPRISES, #520, 4815 S. Harvard, Tulsa OK 74135. (918)749-1647. Vice President: Diana Robey. Booking agency, music publisher (Jana Jae Publishing/BMI) and record company (Lark Record Productions, Inc.). Estab. 1979. Represents individual artists and songwriters; currently handles 12 acts. Receives 15% commission. Reviews material for acts.
How to Contact: Submit demo tape by mail. Prefers cassette (or videocassette of performance if available). SASE. Reports in 1 month.
Music: Mostly interested in **country**, **classical** and **jazz instrumentals**; also **pop**. Works with vocalists, show and concert bands, solo instrumentalists. Represents Jana Jae (country singer/fiddle player), Matt Greif (classical guitarist), Sydni (solo singer) and Hotwire (country show band).

*JAN-A-LOU ENTERPRIZES, RR #1, Clive, Alberta T0C 0Y0 **Canada**. (403)784-2071. Fax: (403)346-1230. Manager: Jan Howden-Paul. Management firm, record company company (ATI). Estab. 1990. Represents individual local artists; currently handles 1 act. Receives 20% commission. Reviews material for acts.
How to Contact: Submit demo tape by mail. Unsolicited submissions are OK. Prefers cassette with lyric or lead sheet. SASE. Reports in 4-6 weeks.
Music: Mostly **country**; also **country/gospel**. Represents Lou Paul (singer/songwriter).

*JAS MANAGEMENT, Suite 512, 5645 Hillcroft, Houston TX 77036. (713)266-3106. Fax: (713)266-3009. Manager: Tony Randle. Management firm, booking agency. Estab. 1988. Represents individual artists and/or groups, songwriters from anywhere; currently handles 20 acts. Receives 10-20% commission. Reviews material for acts.
How to Contact: Submit demo tape by mail. Unsolicited submissions are OK. Prefers cassette with 4 songs. If seeking management, press kit should include cassette, bio, pictures, press (if any). Does not return material. Reports in 2 months.
Music: Mostly **rap**, **R&B** and **gospel**. Works primarily with rapper/songwriters. Current acts include Scarface/Geto Boys, Dana Dane (rapper), Odd Squad (rapper).

*JCHC MUSIC, No. 3, 145 E. 36th St., New York NY 10016. Partner: Josh Connell. Management firm, music publisher. Estab. 1893. Represents songwriters from anywhere; currently handles 12 acts. Receives 15-20% commission. Reviews material for acts.
How to Contact: Call first and obtain permission to submit. Prefers cassette with 3 songs and lyric or lead sheet. Does not return material. If seeking management, include cassette, photos and any published reviews. Reports in 4-6 weeks.
Music: Mostly **pop/rock**, **country** and **folk**; also **gospel**, **jazz** and **children's**. Current acts include Seedless Grapes, Alternate Arrows, Mamma-Laid.

*JFK ENTERTAINMENT PRODUCTION INC., 2266 Fifth Ave., New York NY 10037. (212)905-9049. Director of Operations: Barbara Slater. Management firm. Estab. 1992. Represents individual artists and/or groups, songwriters; currently handles 5 acts. Receives 20% commission. Reviews material for acts.
How to Contact: Call first and obtain permission to submit. Prefers cassette and lyric sheet. If seeking management, press kit should include demo, biography, photo. SASE. Reports in 6-7 weeks.
Music: Mostly **R&B**, **rap** and **gospel**. Works primarily with vocalists, producers, writers. Current acts include Trevon Donovan (rapper), Scoob Lover (rapper), Larry Miller (vocalist).

*NEVILLE L. JOHNSON AND ASSOCIATES, Suite 418, 11726 San Vicente Blvd., Los Angeles CA 90049. (310)826-2410. Fax: (310)846-5450. Director of A&R: Claire Fullerton. Entertainment law firm. Estab. 1978. Represents individual artists and/or groups from anywhere; currently handles 4 acts. Receives 20% commission, $125-175/hour for legal work.
How to Contact: Call first and obtain permission to submit. Prefers cassette or CD. If seeking management, press kit should include picture, bio, press clippings. SASE. Reports in 1-3 weeks.
Music: Mostly **alternative rock**, **singer/songwriter** and **contemporary American rock**; open to suggestion. Currently represents (as an attorney) Patrick Moraz (keyboard), Bug Music, Academy of Country Music.
Tips: "We are part of a team and it's a lot of hard work. Be diplomatic at all times."

C. JUNQUERA PRODUCTIONS, P.O. Box 393, Lomita CA 90717. (213)325-2881. Co-owner: C. Junquera. Management consulting firm and record company (NH Records). Estab. 1987. Represents local, regional and international individual artists and songwriters; currently handles 3 acts. Receives a flat fee, depending on project costs. Reviews material for acts.
How to Contact: Write first and obtain permission to submit. Prefers cassette with 1-3 songs and lyric sheet. If seeking management, include 8 × 10 photo, bio, photocopies of news articles and sample of product. SASE. Reports in 1-2 months.
Music: Mostly **traditional country** and **country pop**; also **easy listening**. Works primarily with vocalists. Current recording acts include Nikki Hornsby (singer/songwriter), N. Kelel (songwriter) and Tom Wayne (singer/songwriter).
Tips: "Set goal to obtain as artist or songwriter—submit sample of product and *don't* give up! Obtain financial support for your productions."

*JUPITER PRODUCTIONS, 7751 Greenwood Dr., St. Paul MN 55112. (612)784-9654. C.E.O.: Lance King. Management firm, booking agency, record company (Nightmare). Estab. 1983. Represents individual artists, groups, songwriters from anywhere; currently handles 3 acts. Receives 10-15% commission. Reviews material for acts.
How to Contact: Call first to arrange personal interview. Prefers cassette or VHS videocassette with 4 songs and lyric sheet. If seeking management, press kit should include 8 × 10 photo, poster (if available), song list, if self contained production or not, press clippings. "Send only important information." Does not return material. Reports in 2-4 weeks.
Music: Mostly **cutting edge rock**, **melodic metal** and **grunge**; also **rap metal** and **progressive rock**. Works primarily with vocalists, singer/songwriters, bands. Current acts include Gemini (metal band), Dream Machine (heavy rock band), Boneyard (grunge groove band).

R.J. KALTENBACH PERSONAL MANAGEMENT, P.O. Box 510, Dundee IL 60118-0510. (708)428-4777. President: R.J. Kaltenbach. Management firm. Estab. 1980. Represents national touring acts only (individual artists and groups); currently handles 3 acts. Receives 15% commission. Reviews material for acts.
How to Contact: Submit demo tape by mail—unsolicited submissions are OK. Prefers cassette (or VHS ½" videocassette) with 3 songs and lyric sheet. Does not return unsolicited material. Reports in 6-8 weeks "if we are interested in material."
Music: **Country** and **rock/pop**. Works primarily with "national acts with recording contracts or deals pending." Current acts include T.G. Sheppard (national recording artist), Magazine (Chicago-based rock act) and Joe K (NY based rock act/alternative).
Tips: "We deal only with professionals who are dedicated to their craft and show lots of promise."

KAUFMAN MANAGEMENT, 333 S. State St., Chicago IL 60604. (312)427-3241. Contact: Don Kaufman or Derek Mason. Estab. 1982. Represents individual artists, groups and songwriters; currently handles 2 acts. Receives 20% commission. Reviews material for acts.
How to Contact: Submit demo tape by mail—unsolicited submissions are OK. Prefers cassette (or VHS videocassette if available) with 2-6 songs and photo. If seeking management, include photo, cassette, note as to why submitting. Does not return material. Reports back only if interested.
Music: **Rock** and **pop**. Works primarily with singer/songwriters, bands, groups and vocalists. Current acts include Steve James (pop/rock singer/songwriter) and Psycho Circus (hard rock group).
Tips: "Submit by mail. If we can help you, we will be in touch."

*CLAUDIA KEMMERER MANAGEMENT, P.O. Box 50752, Nashville TN 37205. (615)352-9135. Fax: (615)352-3631. Owner: Claudia Kemmerer. Management firm, music publisher (BMI/Sendero), record company (Neo Billy). Estab. 1988. Represents individual artists, songwriters from anywhere; currently handles 2 acts. Receives 15-20% commission. Reviews material for acts.
How to Contact: Submit demo tape by mail. Unsolicited submissions are OK. Prefers cassette or VHS videocassette with 3 songs and lyric sheet. If seeking management, press kit should include bio, photo, cassette, VHS, lyric sheets. Does not return material. Reports in 1 month.
Music: Mostly **country**. Works primarily with singer/songwriters. Current acts include Clay Blaker (singer/songwriter), Chris Rivers (singer/songwriter).

*HOWARD KING AGENCY, INC., 481 Sierra Madre Villa Ave., Pasadena CA 71107-2966. President: Howard King. Management firm and booking agency. Estab. 1962. Represents artists, groups and songwriters; currently handles 4 acts. Receives 10-20% commission. Reviews material for acts.
How to Contact: Write or call first and obtain permission to submit. Prefers cassette or VHS videocassette with maximum 3 songs, photo, publicity material and lyric sheet. If seeking management, include photos, tapes and video (if possible), and well-written résumé, song lists and good writers. Does not return material. Reports in 2 months.
Music: Mostly **top 40**; also **country**, **dance-oriented**, **easy listening**, **jazz**, **MOR**, **rock** and **pop**. Works primarily with top 40 artist singles, duos and groups. Current acts include Waylon Pickard (conductor), Elizabeth Carlisle and Page Cavanaugh.

JEFF KIRK, 7108 Grammar Rd. SW, Fairview TN 37062. (615)799-8674. Owner/President: Jeff Kirk. Management firm and booking agency. Estab. 1981. Represents regional (mid-South) individual artists; currently handles 3 acts. Commission varies. Reviews material for acts.
How to Contact: Submit demo tape by mail—unsolicited submissions are OK. Prefers cassette (or VHS videocassette if available) with 1-3 songs and lyric or lead sheet. If seeking management, include bio, recent performance, recent recordings and picture (optional). Does not return unsolicited material. Reports in 1 month.
Music: Mostly **jazz**, **pop** and **rock**. Works primarily with jazz groups (4-6 members), instrumental and vocal. Current acts include Jeff Kirk Quartet (mainstream jazz) and New Vintage (jazz fusion).
Tips: "Please submit brief demos with as high audio quality as possible."

*KKR ENTERTAINMENT GROUP, 6th Floor, 1300 Clay St., Oakland CA 94612. (510)464-8024. Fax: (510)763-9004. Administrator: Keith Washington. Management firm. Estab. 1989. Represents individual artists, groups, producers from anywhere. Reviews material for acts.
How to Contact: Call first and obtain permission to submit. Prefers cassette. If seeking management, press kit should include tape and photo (if available). "We do not accept unsolicited material." SASE. Reports in 2 weeks.
Music: Mostly **R&B**, **rap** and **rock**. Current acts include E-A-Ski & CMT (producer/artist), Spice One (jive recording artist) and Christion (R&B group).
Tips: "Always learn who you are working with and stay involved in everything."

*JOANNE KLEIN, 130 W. 28 St., New York NY 10001. Phone and fax: (212)741-3949. Contact: Joanne Klein. Management firm and music publisher. Estab. 1982. Represents individual artists and songwriters from anywhere. Currently handles 4 acts. Receives 15-20% commission. Reviews material for acts.
How to Contact: Write first and obtain permission to submit. Prefers cassette or CD. If seeking management, press kit should include bio, photos, press/reviews, discography, information on compositions. Does not return material. Reports in 1 month.
Music: Mostly **jazz**. Works primarily with instrumentalist/composers. Current acts include Kenny Barron (jazz); Victor Lewis (jazz) and Terell Stafford (jazz).

BOB KNIGHT AGENCY, 185 Clinton Ave., Staten Island NY 10301. (718)448-8420. President: Bob Knight. Management firm, booking agency, music publishing and royalty collection firm. Estab. 1971. Represents artists, groups and songwriters; currently handles 5 acts. Receives 10-25% commission. Reviews material for acts and for submission to record companies and producers.

How to Contact: Submit demo tape by mail—unsolicited submissions are OK. Prefers cassette (or videocassette) with 5 songs and lead sheet "with bio and references." If seeking management, include bios, videocassette and audio cassette in press kit. SASE. Reports in 1 month.
Music: Mostly **top 40/pop**; also **easy listening, MOR, R&B, soul** and **rock (nostalgia 50s and 60s)**. Works primarily with recording and name groups and artists—50s, 60s and 70s acts, high energy dance, and show groups. Current acts include The Elegants (oldie show); Bob Gengo (top 40); and The AD-LIBS (oldies show).

*KRC RECORDS & PRODUCTIONS, HC 73, Box 5060, Harold KY 41635. (606)478-2169. President: Keith R. Carter. Management firm, booking agency, music publisher, record company. Estab. 1987. Represents local, regional individual artists; currently handles 1 act. Receives 25% commission.
How to Contact: Submit demo tape by mail. Unsolicited submissions are OK. Prefers cassette, videocassette with 1-10 songs and lyric sheet. "Feel free to send any material." SASE.
Music: Mostly **country**; also **gospel, bluegrass**. Current acts include Kimberly Carter (singer).

KUPER-LAM MANAGEMENT, P.O. Box 66274, Houston TX 77266. (713)520-5791. Fax: (713)529-0810. President: Ivan Kuper. Management firm, music publisher (Kuper-Lam Music/BMI). Estab. 1988. Represents individual artists, groups and songwriters from anywhere. Currently handles 1 act. Receives 20% commission. Reviews material for acts.
How to Contact: Submit demo tape by mail. Unsolicited submissions are OK. Prefers cassette. If seeking management, press kit should include photo, bio, one-sheet, tearsheets (reviews, etc.), cassette. Does not return material. Reports in 1 month.
Music: Mostly **rap, urban contemporary** and **alternative college rock**. Works primarily with rap groups (self contained and self produced). Current acts include Def Squad (rap), Champ X (activist).
Tips: "Create a market value for yourself, produce your own master tapes, create a cost-effective situation."

*L & R MANAGEMENT, 11231 Hwy. E., Tyler TX 75707. (903)566-5653. Vice President: Ronny Redd. Management firm. Estab. 1988. Represents individual artists, groups, songwriters from anywhere; currently handles 3 acts. Receives 25% commission. Reviews material for acts.
How to Contact: Submit demo tape by mail. Unsolicited submissions are OK. Prefers cassette or VHS videocassette with 3 songs and lyric sheet. SASE. Reports in 1 month.
Music: Mostly **gospel, country** and **bluegrass**; also **blues**. Works primarily with self sustaining acts. Current acts include David Darst (country), Ronny Redd (gospel), Jennifer Wright (musicals).

L.D.F. PRODUCTIONS, P.O. Box 406, Old Chelsea Station, New York NY 10011. (212)925-8925. President: Mr. Dowell. Management firm and booking agency. Estab. 1982. Represents artists and choirs in the New York area. Currently handles 2 acts. Receives 20% commission. Reviews material for acts.
How to Contact: Write first and obtain permission to submit. Prefers cassette (or videocassette of performance—well-lighted, maximum 10 minutes) with 2-8 songs and lyric sheet. SASE. Reports in 1 month. "Do not phone expecting a return call unless requested by L.D.F. Productions. Videos should be imaginatively presented with clear sound and bright colors." Reports in 1 month.
Music: Mostly **gospel, popular, rock** and **jazz**. Works primarily with inspirational and contemporary pop artists. Current acts include L.D. Frazier (gospel artist/lecturer) and Andrew Hall (bassist/composer).
Tips: "Those interested in working with us must be original, enthusiastic, persistent and sincere."

LANDSLIDE MANAGEMENT, 928 Broadway, New York NY 10010. (212)505-7300. Principals: Ted Lehrman and Libby Bush. Management firm and music publisher (Kozkeeozko Music). Estab. 1978. Represents singers, singer/songwriters and actor/singers; currently handles 15 acts. Receives 15% commission. Reviews material for acts.
How to Contact: Write first or call to obtain permission to submit."Potential hit singles only." SASE. "Include picture, résumé and (if available) ½" videocassette if you're submitting yourself as an act." Reports in 6 weeks.
Music: **Dance-oriented, MOR, rock (soft pop), soul, top 40/pop** and **country/pop**. Current acts include Deborah Dotson (soul/pop/jazz), Sara Carlson (pop/rock) and Fay Rusli (pop/R&B).

*LANESTAR * MANAGEMENT, P.O. Box 4017, Prescott AZ 86302. (602)771-0490. President: Elaine Spinelli. Management firm. Estab. 1992. Represents individual artists, groups from anywhere; currently handles 3 acts. Receives 10-20% commission. Reviews material for acts.
How to Contact: Write first and obtain permission to submit. Prefers cassette. If seeking management, press kit should include current bio, current press clippings, photo, recorded materials. Does not return material. Reports in 1 month.

Music: Mostly **instrumental, instrumental/vocal** and **jazz**; also **New Age**. Works primarily with instrumentalists, songwriters. Current acts include Liz Story (solo pianist), Liz Story/Joel Dibartolo (piano-bass duet), Terry Furlong (singer/songwriter).

LARI-JON PROMOTIONS, 325 W. Walnut, P.O. Box 216, Rising City NE 68658. (402)542-2336. Owner: Larry Good. Music publisher (Lari-Jon Publishing Co./BMI) and record company (Lari-Jon Records). "We also promote package shows." Represents individual artists, groups and songwriters; currently handles 5 acts. Receives 15% commission. Reviews material for acts.
How to Contact: Submit demo tape by mail—unsolicited submissions are OK. Prefers cassette with 5 songs and lyric sheet. If seeking management, include 8 × 10 photos, cassette and bio sheet in press kit. SASE. Reports in 2 months.
Music: Mostly **country, gospel** and **50s rock**. Works primarily with dance bands and show bands. Represents Kent Thompson (singer), Nebraskaland 'Opry (family type country show) and Brenda Allen (singer/comedienne).
Tips: "Be professional in all aspects of the business."

*LEFT FIELD PRODUCTIONS/POGGI PROMOTIONAL SERVICES, 1458 Union St., San Francisco CA 94109. (415)567-4706. Fax: (415)567-0195. CEO: Pietro Giacomo Poggi. Management firm, booking agency. Represents individual artists and/or groups, songwriters from anywhere; currently handles 3 acts. Receives 10-20% commission. Reviews material for acts.
How to Contact: Call first and obtain permission to submit. Prefers cassette or VHS videocassette and lyric sheet. Does not return material. Reports in 2-3 weeks.
Music: Only interested in **world music** especially **African, Caribbean** and **Latin**. Current acts include Kotoja (modern Afro-Beat), Jungular Grooves (reggae/calypso/blues "international soul"), Cool Breeze (musique tropique).
Tips: "Be innovative, speak with an original voice, be authentic, be dedicated and willing to go all out."

THE LET US ENTERTAIN YOU CO., Suite 204, 900 19th Ave. S., Nashville TN 37212-2125. (615)321-3100. Administrative Assistant: Katie. Management firm, booking agency and music publisher (ASCAP/SESAC/BMI). Estab. 1968. Represents groups and songwriters; currently handles 75-80 acts. Receives 15-20% commission. Reviews material for acts.
How to Contact: Submit demo tape by mail—unsolicited submissions are OK. Prefers cassette or videocassette and lyric sheet. If seeking management, include bio, video and/or audio demo, songlist and photo in press kit. Does not return unsolicited material. Reports only if interested.
Music: Mostly **country, pop** and **R&B**; also **rock** and **new music**. Works with all types of artists/groups/songwriters. Current acts include The Christy Brothers (group), C.N. Dubble (show group), Inception (R&B group).

LEVINSON ENTERTAINMENT VENTURES INTERNATIONAL, INC., Suite 650, 1440 Veteran Avenue, Los Angeles CA 90024. (213)460-4545. President: Bob Levinson. Management firm. Estab. 1978. Represents national individual artists, groups and songwriters; currently handles 6 acts. Receives 15-20% commission. Reviews material for acts.
How to Contact: Write first and obtain permission to submit or to arrange personal interview. Prefers cassette (or VHS videocassette) with 6 songs and lead sheet. "Inquire first. Don't expect tape to be returned unless SASE included with submission and specific request is made." Reports in 2-3 weeks.
Music: **Rock, MOR, R&B** and **country**. Works primarily with rock bands and vocalists.
Tips: "Should be a working band, self-contained and, preferably, performing original material."

RICK LEVY MGT, #715, 1881 S. Kirkman Rd., Orlando FL 32811. (407)521-6135. Fax: (407)521-6153. President: Rick Levy. Management firm, booking agency, music publisher (Flying Governor Music/BMI) and record company (Luxury Records). Estab. 1985. Represents local, regional or international individual artists and groups; currently handles 4 acts. Receives 10-20% commission. Reviews material for acts.
How to Contact: Submit demo tape by mail—unsolicited submissions are OK. Prefers cassette (or VHS videocassette if available) with 3 songs and lyric sheet. If seeking management, include tape, VHS video, photo and press. SASE. Reports in 1 month.
Music: Mostly **R&B** (no rap), **pop, country** and **oldies**. Current acts include Jay & Techniques (60s hit group), Rock Roots (variety-classic rock, rockabilly), Levy/Stocker (songwriters), Clarence Palmer Trio (jazz).
Tips: "In this business, seek out people better and more successful than you. Learn, pick their brains, be positive, take criticism and keep pluggin' no matter what."

*DORIS LINDSAY PRODUCTIONS/SUCCESSFUL PRODUCTIONS, 1203 Biltmore Ave., High Point NC 27260. (910)882-9990. President: Doris Lindsay. Management firm, music publisher (Doris Lindsay

Publishing/ASCAP, Better Times/BMI). Estab. 1979. Represents individual artists and/or songwriters from anywhere; currently handles 3 acts. Receives 10% commission. Reviews material for acts.
How to Contact: Submit demo tape by mail. Unsolicited submissions are OK. Prefers cassette or VHS videocassette with 2-3 songs and lyric sheet. If seeking management, press kit should include photo, cassette, bio. SASE. Reports in 2 months.
Music: Mostly **country contemporary Christian**, and **pop**; also **children's**. Primarily works with singers, songwriters. Current acts include Mitch Snow, Larry La Vey, Pat Repose.
Tips: "Have a professional studio type demo. Don't send too many songs at one time. Be patient."

*THE LINHARDT GROUP, 360 E. 72nd St., New York NY 10021. Fax: (212)717-5640. Owner: Si Berlin. Management firm. Estab. 1979. Represents individual artists and/or groups from anywhere. Receives 15% commission. Reviews material for acts.
How to Contact: Submit demo tape by mail. Unsolicited submissions are OK. Prefers cassette or videocassette. If seeking management, press kit should include photo, cassette or video. Does not return material.
Music: Mostly **dance**. Current acts include Lime (dance).

*LITTLE RICHIE JOHNSON AGENCY, Box 3, Belen NM 87002. (505)864-7441. Fax: (505)864-7442. Manager: Tony Palmer. Management firm, music publisher and record company. Estab. 1958. Represents individual artists from anywhere; currently handles 4-6 acts.
How to Contact: Submit demo tape by mail. Unsolicited submissions are OK. Prefers cassette. If seeking management, press kit should include tape, bio and any other important information. SASE. Reports in 3-5 weeks.
Music: Mostly **country**; also **Spanish**. Works primarily with vocalists and singers. Current acts include Alan Godage, Faron Young and Kim Frazee.

LMP MANAGEMENT FIRM, Suite 206, 6245 Bristol Pkwy., Culver City CA 90230. Contact: Larry McGee. Management firm, music publisher (Operation Perfection, Inc.) and record company (Boogie Band Records Corp.). Represents individual artists, groups and songwriters; currently handles 10 acts. Receives 15% commission. Reviews material for acts.
How to Contact: Submit demo tape—unsolicited submissions are OK. Prefers cassette (or videocassette of performance) with 1-4 songs and lead sheet. "Try to perform one or more of your songs on a local TV show. Then obtain a copy of your performance. Please only send professional quality material. Keep it simple and basic." If seeking management, include audio cassette, videocassette, photo and any additional promotional materials in press kit. SASE. Reports in 2 months.
Music: Mostly **pop-oriented R&B**; also **rock** and **MOR/adult contemporary**. Works primarily with professionally choreographed show bands. Current acts include Love Child (vocal group), The Executives (vocal group), Alan Walker (producer).
Tips: "Make sure your work is produced at a professional level."

LOWELL AGENCY, 4043 Brookside Court, Norton OH 44203. (216)825-7813. Contact: Leon Seiter. Booking agency. Estab. 1985. Represents regional (Midwest and Southeast) individual artists; currently handles 3 acts. Receives 10% commission. Reviews material for acts.
How to Contact: Submit demo tape by mail—unsolicited submissions are OK. Prefers cassette with 4 songs and lyric sheet. If seeking management, include demo cassette tape in press kit. SASE. Reports in 2 months.
Music: Mostly **country**. Works primarily with country vocalists. Current acts include Leon Seiter (country singer/entertainer/songwriter), Ford Nix (bluegrass singer and 5 string banjo picker) and Tom Durden (country singer, co-writer of "Heartbreak Hotel").

LUSTIG TALENT ENTERPRISES, INC., P.O. Box 32005, Palm Beach Gardens FL 33420-2005. (407)863-5800. President: Richard Lustig. Booking agency. Estab. 1986. Represents local, regional and international individual artists and groups. Reviews material for acts.
How to Contact: Submit demo tape by mail. Unsolicited submissions are OK. Prefers cassette or VHS videocassette. Include pictures, résumé, song list, audio cassette demo tape, and video demo tape in press kit. Does not return unsolicited material.
Music: **All types**. Works primarily with national acts, dance bands and disc jockeys. Current acts include Nightfall, Richard Lustig (disc jockey), Joey Dee and the Starliters, Bill Haley's Comets.
Tips: "Have good promo kit. Be easy to work with. Do a professional job."

RICHARD LUTZ ENTERTAINMENT AGENCY, 5625 0 St., Lincoln NE 68510. (402)483-2241. General Manager: Cherie Worley. Management firm and booking agency. Estab. 1964. Represents individuals and groups; currently handles 200 acts. Receives 15-20% commission.
How to Contact: Submit demo tape by mail—unsolicited submissions are OK. Prefers cassette (or videocassette) with 5-10 songs "to show style and versatility" and lead sheet. "Send photo, résumé,

tape, partial song list and include references. Add comedy, conversation, etc., to your videocassette. Do not play songs in full—short versions preferred." If seeking management, include audio cassette and photo in press kit. SASE. Reports in 1 week.
Music: Mostly **top 40** and **country**; also **dance-oriented** and **MOR**. Works primarily with bar and dance bands for lounge circuit. "Acts must be uniformed." Current acts include Dave Sommer Duo (variety), Addisons (country pop), Imposters (nostalgia).

THE McDONNELL GROUP, 27 Pickwick Lane, Newtown Square PA 19073. (215)353-8554. Contact: Frank McDonnell. Management firm. Estab. 1985. Represents local, regional or international individual artists, groups and songwriters; currently handles 5 acts. Receives 20-25% commission. Reviews material for acts.
How to Contact: Submit demo tape by mail—unsolicited submissions are OK. Prefers cassette (or VHS videocassette if available) with 4 songs and lyric sheet. If seeking management, include press, tape or video, recent photos, bio. SASE. Reports in 1 month.
Music: Mostly **rock, pop** and **R&B**; also **country**. Current acts include Johnny Bronco (rock group), Mike Forte (producer/songwriter) and Jim Salamone (producer/songwriter/arranger).

ANDREW MCMANUS MANAGEMENT, Suite 101, 3 Smail St., Ultimo NSW 2007 **Australia.** Phone: (02)211-3044. Fax: (02)211-3057. Manager: Andrew McManus. Management firm. Estab. 1986. Represents local, regional and international individual artists, groups and songwriters; currently handles 4 acts. Receives 15-20% commission. Reviews material for acts.
How to Contact: Call first to obtain permission to submit demo tape. Prefers cassette (or VHS videocassette if available) with several songs. If seeking management, press kit should include photo, bio, tape and VHS (if possible). SAE and IRC. Reports in 2-3 weeks.
Music: Mostly **rock, pop** and **dance.** Works primarily with rock bands and dance artists. Current acts include Divinyls (rock), Inner Circle (reggae).

MAGIANˢᵐ (a div. of Universal World Unlimited, Inc.), 6733 Rhode Island Dr., E., Jacksonville FL 32209. (904)766-1181 or (904)764-3685. Founder & President: Morris King, Jr.. Management firm. Estab. 1985. Represents local, regional and national individual artists, groups, songwriters and producers; currently handles 6 acts. Receives negotiable commission. Reviews material for acts.
How to Contact: Submit demo tape by mail—unsolicited submissions are OK. Prefers cassette (or VHS videocassette if available) with 3-5 songs and lyric sheet. If seeking management, include bio, press, photos. SASE. Reports in 2 weeks.
Music: Mostly **pop, R&B** and **jazz**; also **rock, gospel** and **country.** Works primarily with vocalists, message rappers, top 40 bands. Current acts include Vedia (vocalist/songwriter), Just Twoˢᵐ (vocal duo) and Mike Hughes (vocalist/musician/songwriter).
Tips: "Do not approach MAGIANˢᵐ if you are not dedicated, patient, and if you are looking for a miracle."

MAGNUM MUSIC CORPORATION LTD., 8607-128 Avenue, Edmonton Alberta **Canada** T5E 0G3. (403)476-8230. Fax: (403)472-2584 Manager: Bill Maxim. Booking agency, music publisher (Ramblin' Man Music Publishing/PRO, High River Music Publishing/ASCAP) and record company (Magnum Records). Estab. 1984. Represents international individual artists, groups and songwriters; currently handles 4 acts. Receives 15% commission. Reviews material for acts.
How to Contact: Write first and obtain permission to submit. Prefers cassette with 3-4 songs. If seeking management, include tape or CD, photo and bio in press kit. SAE and IRC. Reports in 6-8 weeks.
Music: Mostly **country** and **gospel.** Works primarily with "artists or groups who are also songwriters." Current acts include Catheryne Greenly (country), Thea Anderson (country) and Cormier Country (country).
Tips: "Prefers finished demos."

*MAINE-LY COUNTRY MUSIC, 212 Stillwater Ave., Old Town ME 04468. (207)827-2185. Owner/Manager: Jeff Simon. Booking agency, music publisher (Maine-ly Music/BMI, Maine-ly Country Music/SESAC) and record company (Maine-ly Country Records). Estab. 1988. Represents international individual artists, groups and songwriters; currently handles 3 acts. Receives 15-25% commission. Reviews material for acts.
How to Contact: Submit demo tape by mail. Unsolicited submissions are OK. Prefers cassette (or VHS videocassette or performance) with 3-5 songs and lyric or lead sheet. If seeking management, include song list, artist bio and demo tape (professional quality). SASE. Reports in 2 months.
Music: Mostly **country-country rock, pop** and **gospel.** Works primarily with country, country rock vocalists and dance bands. Current acts include Jeff Simon (vocalist/songwriter), Maine-ly Country (country-country rock band) and Kristi Buchanan (vocalist/performer).
Tips: "Think positive and be prepared to work."

*MALLA ENTERTAINMENT, #907, 701 W. Imperial Hwy., Lahabra CA 90631. President: Jay Malla. Management firm. Estab. 1985. Represents individual artists, groups, songwriters, producers, directors from anywhere. Receives 20% commission. Reviews material for acts.
How to Contact: Write first and obtain permission to submit. Prefers cassette or VHS videocassette with 3 songs and lyric sheet. If seeking management, press kit should include bio, photo overview and personal goals. SASE. Reports in 2 weeks.
Music: Mostly **rock, rap, metal** and **R&B/urban**. Works primarily with bands, singer/songwriters. Current acts include Paul Sanchez (house hip hop), Jose Antonio (director), Frank Roszak (producer).

*THE MANAGEMENT TRUST LTD., #100, 219 Dufferin St., Toronto, Ontario M6K 3J1 **Canada**. (416)532-7080. Fax: (416)532-8852. Contact: Jake Gold, Allan Gregg, Shelley Stertz. Management firm. Estab. 1986. Represents local, regional (Canada), individual artists and/or groups; currently handles 4 acts.
How to Contact: Write or call first and obtain permission to submit. If seeking management, press kit should include CD or tape, bio, photo, press. SAE and IRC. Reports in 4-6 weeks.
Music: **All types.** Current acts include The Tragically Hip (MCA), The Watchmen (MCA Canada), Andrew Cash (MCA/SUMO) and David Gogo (EMI Music Canada).

*MANAPRO ENTERTAINMENT, 82 Sherman St., Passaic NJ 07055. (201)777-6109. Fax: (201)458-0303. President: Tomasito Bobadilla. Management firm, record company, record producer. Estab. 1988. Represents individual artists and/or groups from anywhere; currently handles 3 acts. Reviews material for acts.
How to Contact: Submit demo tape by mail. Unsolicited submissions are OK. Prefers cassette (or VHS videocassette if available) with 3 songs and lyric sheet. If seeking management, press kit should include bio. SASE. Reports in 3-4 months.
Music: Mostly **dance, pop** and **contemporary**; also **R&B** and **alternative**. Works primarily with vocalists and bands. Current acts include Giovanni Irepante (singer), Opty Gomez (songwriter) and Tanya Solis (singer).

*MARBLE ENTERTAINMENT CO., P.O. Box 2330, Arlington TX 76004. (817)265-8541. President: Gary L. Drumm, Jr. Management firm, music publisher (Fuzzy Duck Productions) and record company (Marble Records). Estab. 1990. Represents individual artists and groups from anywhere. Reviews material for acts.
How to Contact: Submit demo tape by mail. Unsolicited submissions are OK. Prefers cassette (or VHS videocassette if available) with lyric sheet. If seeking management, "a full standard press kit is needed." Does not return material. Reports in 3 weeks.
Music: Mostly **progressive rock, rock** and **pop**; also **country, R&B** and **rap**. Current acts include Requiem (rock band/Marble Records), Art of War (rock band/Marble Records) and Gary Drumm (songwriter).
Tips: "Never give up on your dreams! Just because someone out there may not like what you do doesn't mean no one will. There is a market for EVERYTHING!"

MARK ONE-THE AGENCY, P.O. Box 62, Eastwood 5063 **South Australia**. (08)340-1661. Fax: (08)364-1206. Owner: Mark Draper. Management firm, booking agency, music publisher. Estab. 1981. Represents individual artists, groups, songwriters from anywhere; currently handles 20 acts. Receives 10-20% commission. Reviews material for acts.
How to Contact: Submit demo tape by mail. Unsolicited submissions are OK. Prefers cassette (or VHS videocassette) with 3 songs and lyric sheet. If seeking management, press kit should include photograph, 1 page bio, comprehensive contact list. SAE and IRC. Reports in 1 month.
Music: Mostly **rock, pop, dance**. Works primarily with bands. Current acts include Capacity Max (contemporary rock), Unwired (acoustic rock) and Jungle Alley (rock band).
Tips: "Be honest, reliable and available."

*MARSUPIAL LTD., Roundhill Cottage, The Ridge, Cold Ash, Newbury, Berks R616 9HZ **United Kingdom**. (0635)862200. Record Producer, Artist Manager: John Brand. Management firm, music publisher, record producer. Estab. 1990. Represents individual artists and/or groups, songwriters, producers and remixers from anywhere; currently handles 3 acts. Receives 20% commission. Reviews material for acts.
How to Contact: Submit demo tape by mail. Unsolicited submissions are OK. Prefers cassette or PAL videocassette with 4 songs and lyric sheet. If seeking management, press kit should include tape, photos, video (if possible), any press. Does not return material. Reports in 6 weeks.
Music: **All types.** Past productions have included The Cult, The Waterboys and Aztec Camera. Current acts include Jan Johnston (A&M Records singer/songwriter), DTOX (Famous Music/pop), Sacred Cows (alternative/heavy band) and Sunscreem (Sony Music/dance/pop).

RICK MARTIN PRODUCTIONS, 125 Fieldpoint Road, Greenwich CT 06830. (203)661-1615. President: Rick Martin. Personal manager and independent producer. Holds the Office of Secretary of the National Conference of Personal Managers. Represents groups, artists/songwriters, actresses/vocalists. Currently handles 5 acts. Receives 15-25% commission. "Occasionally, we are hired as consultants, production assistants or producers of recording projects." Reviews material for acts.
How to Contact: Submit demo tape by mail—unsolicited submissions are OK. "Enclose an SASE if you want tape back. Do not write for permission—will not reply, just send material." Prefers cassette (or VHS videocassette) with 2-4 songs. "Don't worry about an expensive presentation to personal managers or producers; they'll make it professional if they get involved." Artists should enclose a photo. "We prefer serious individuals who will give it all they have for a music career." Reports in 2 weeks.
Music: Top 40, dance and **easy listening**. No rock or folk music. Produces dance groups, female vocalists and songwriters. Current acts include Babe, Marisa Mercedes (vocalist/pianist/songwriter), Rob and Steve (songwriters/vocalists), the Gonzalez Family (vocal group) and McKenna Breed.
Tips: "The tape does not have to be professionally produced—it's really not important what you've done—it's what you can do now that counts."

MASTER ENTERTAINMENT, 245 Maple Ave. W., Vienna VA 22180. (703)281-2800. Owner/Agent: Steve Forssell. Booking agency. Estab. 1989. Represents local and regional (mid-Atlantic) individual artists and groups. Receives 10-20% commission.
How to Contact: Write for permission to submit. Will not return unsolicited material. Prefers cassette (or VHS/Beta videocassette) with 4 songs and lyric or lead sheet. Reports in 1 month.
Music: Mostly **hard rock/metal, progressive/alternative** and **R&B/dance**; also **variety/covers**. Current acts include disappear fear (progressive), Blues Saraceno (guitar rock), Asante (African), Carl Filipiak (jazz) and Randy Coven (bass instrumental rock).
Tips: "Submit only best work when it's *ready*. We're looking for professionally managed groups/artists with good publicist/promotion. Product in market is a plus."

PHIL MAYO & COMPANY, P.O. Box 304, Bomoseen VT 05732. (802)468-5011. President: Phil Mayo. Management firm and record company (Thrust Records). Estab. 1981. Represents international individual artists, groups and songwriters. Receives 15-20% commission.
How to Contact: Submit demo tape by mail—unsolicited submissions are OK. Prefers cassette (or VHS videocassette) with 3 songs and lyric or lead sheet. If seeking management, include bio, photo and lyric sheet in press kit. Does not return unsolicited material. Reports in 1-2 months.
Music: Mostly **rock, pop** and **R&B**; also **gospel**. Works primarily with dance bands, vocalists, rock acts. Current acts include The Drive (R&B) and Blind Date.

***MC PROMOTIONS & PUBLIC RELATIONS**, #6, 8504 Willis Ave., Panorama City CA 91402. (818)892-1741. Promotes local country artists. Receives 10% commission. Reviews material for acts.
How to Contact: Submit demo tape by mail—unsolicited submissions are OK. Prefers cassette (or videocassette). If seeking management, include videocassette or cassette demo with bio and picture in press kit. Does not return material. Reports in 3 weeks.
Music: Mostly **country**. Works primarily with vocalists.

***MEGALOPOULOS MANAGEMENT**, #321, 1173A Second Ave., New York NY 10021. President: Andrew R. Stephanopoulos. Management firm. Estab. 1991. Represents individual artists and groups from anywhere; currently handles 3 acts. Receives 20% commission. Reviews material for acts.
How to Contact: Prefers cassette or VHS videocassette with 4 songs and lyric sheet. If seeking management, press kit should include photo, video, press clippings, past touring info. Does not return material. Reports in 3 weeks months.
Music: Mostly **alternative rock, vocal** and **pop**. Works primarily with bands, producer-performers. Current acts include Gumball (alternative rock), Mercury Rev (alternative rock), Don Fleming (producer).
Tips: "Be willing to work hard and never expect anything without hard work."

MERRI-WEBB PRODUCTIONS, P.O. Box 5474, Stockton CA 95205. (209)948-8186. President: Nancy L. Merrihew. Management firm, music publisher (Kaupp's & Robert Publishing Co./BMI), record company (Kaupp Records). Represents regional (California) individual artists, groups and songwriters; currently handles 10 acts. Receives 10-15% commission. Reviews material for acts.
How to Contact: Write or call first and obtain permission to submit. Prefers cassette (or VHS videocassette if available) with 3 songs maximum and lyric sheet. SASE. Reports in 3 months.
Music: Mostly **country, A/C rock** and **R&B**; also **pop, rock** and **gospel**. Works primarily with vocalists, dance bands and songwriters. Current acts include Rick Webb (singer/songwriter), Nanci Lynn (singer/songwriter), Steve Boutte (singer/songwriter).

Tips: "Know what you want, set a goal, focus in on your goals, be open to constructive criticism, polish tunes and keep polishing."

JOSEPH C. MESSINA, CARTOON RECORDS, INC., 424 Mamaroneck Avenue, Mamaroneck NY 10543. (914)381-2565. Attorney/Manager. Represents artists, groups, songwriters, movie directors and screen writers; currently handles 3 acts. Receives negotiable commission.
How To Contact: Prefers cassette with 1-2 songs and lead sheet. Does not return unsolicited material.
Music: Works primarily with male and female vocal/dance. Current acts include Andrea (top 40 dance).

MILESTONE MEDIA, P.O. Box 869, Venice CA 90291. (310)396-1234. Co-President: Mr. Sverdlin. Management firm. Estab. 1985. Represents individual artists, groups and songwriters from anywhere. Currently handles 3 acts. Receives 20% commission. Reviews material for acts.
How to Contact: Submit demo tape by mail. Unsolicited submissions are OK. Prefers cassette (or videocassette) with 3 songs. Does not return material. Reports in 2-3 weeks.
Music: Mostly **rap**, **rock** and **dance**; also **country**, **house** and **movie**. Works primarily with singers, producers and composers. Current acts include Zap-A-Thon (alternative rock), Ray Rae Goldman (producer) and Aussie Menace (alternative rock).

THOMAS J. MILLER & COMPANY, 1802 Laurel Canyon Blvd., Los Angeles CA 90046. (213)656-7212. Fax: (213)656-7757. Artist Relations: Karen Deming. Management firm, music publisher, record company (Wilshire Park Records). Estab. 1975. Represents individual artists, groups and songwriters from anywhere; currently handles 12 acts. Reviews material for acts.
How to Contact: Submit demo tape by mail. Unsolicited submissions are OK. Prefers cassette (or NTSC videocassette) and lyric sheet. If seeking management, press kit should include photos, bio, video. Does not return material. Reports in 2-3 weeks.
Music: Mostly **pop**, **rock** and **jazz**; also **stage** and **country**. Current acts include Manowar, Fury in the Slaughterhouse and Champaign.

*MONOPOLY MANAGEMENT, 162 N. Milford, Highland MI 48357. Vice President: Bob Zilli. Management firm. Estab. 1984. Represents songwriters from anywhere. Commission is negotiable. Reviews material for acts.
How to Contact: Submit demo tape by mail. Unsolicited submissions are OK. Prefers cassette or VHS videocassette with 4 songs and lyric sheet. If seeking management, press kit should include tape, photo, bio, résumé of live performances. Does not return material. Reports in 1 month.
Music: Mostly **country**, **alternative** and **top 40**. Works primarily with singer/songwriters. Current acts include Robbie Richmond (songwriter).

*MONSTER COMMUNICATIONS, INC., 83 Riverside Dr., New York NY 10024. (212)877-0400. Management firm. Estab. 1991. Represents individual artists and groups from anywhere. Receives 20% commission.
How to Contact: Call first to obtain permission to submit. Does not return material.
Music: Mostly **rap**. Current acts include Biz Markie (rap), Poco Loco (rap), Clean Cut Craig (rap), Son of Eve (alternative rap) and Jungle Brothers (rap).

MOORE ENTERTAINMENT GROUP, 11 Possum Trail, Saddle River NJ 07458. (201)327-3698. President: Barbara Moore. Estab. 1984. Represents individual artists and groups; currently handles 8 acts. Receives 10% commission. Reviews material for acts.
How to Contact: Submit demo tape by mail—unsolicited submissions are OK. Prefers cassette (or videocassette if available) and lyric sheet. "Include photo and bio." If seeking management, include tape, photo and bio in press kit. SASE. Reports in 6 weeks.
Music: Mostly **dance**, **rock**, **R&B** and **pop**. Works primarily with vocalists. Current acts include Mike Giorgio (rock/pop), Mike Tyler (R&B), Paradise (dance/R&B), Rene Rollins (country/pop), Katani (R&B), Sue Oriavong (dance/pop) and Susan Moss (country/crossover).
Tips: "Have dedication and drive to accomplish what you want out of your career."

*THOMAS MORELLI ENTERPRISES, 15 Brimmer St., Brewer ME 04412. (207)989-2577. Owner: Thomas Morelli. Management firm, booking agency. Estab. 1980. Represents individual artists, groups, models from anywhere; currently handles 5 acts. Receives 10-20% commission. Reviews material for acts.
How to Contact: Submit demo tape by mail. Unsolicited submissions are OK. Prefers cassette. If seeking management, press kit should include tape, bio, photo. SASE. Reports in 1 month.
Music: Mostly **country** and **rock**; also, single entertainer acts for comedy/small bar circuit in New England. 90% bands, some duets, some single. Current acts include Allison Ames (country singer/ songwriter), The Flames (5 piece country band), Choice (high energy rock band).

Tips: "Since our main function is booking acts into club venues, we need quality country and rock acts who are honest and willing to work hard. The proof is in the performance!"

*MOXIE MANAGEMENT, 2180 Bryant St., San Francisco CA 94110. (415)648-7088. Fax: (415)826-5881. Co-Managers: Rina Neiman or Debbie Gordon. Management firm. Estab. 1993. Represents individual artists, groups and producers from anywhere; currently handles 4 acts. Receives 10-15% commission.
How to Contact: Write or call first and obtain permission to submit. Prefers cassette or CD and bio. If seeking management, press kit should include complete history. Does not return material.
Music: Mostly **alternative**. Works primarily with bands. Current acts include Cop Shoot Cop (band), Victims Family (band) and Gary Floyd (singer/songwriter).

*MUSIC MAN PROMOTIONS, 1st Floor, 50 Melville Parade, South Perth 6151 **Western Australia**. (09)4742300. Fax: (09)4741779. Managing Director: Eddie Robertson. Management firm and booking agency. Estab. 1983. Represents local, regional, national or international individual artists and/or groups, songwriters; currently handles 150 acts. Receives 20% commission. Reviews material for acts.
How to Contact: Submit demo tape by mail. Unsolicited submissions are OK. Prefers cassette with lyric or lead sheet. SASE. Reports in 2-3 weeks.
Music: Mostly **dance pop music**, **rock** and **jazz**; also **country**, **blues** and **hip hop**. Works primarily with show bands, jazz bands and blues bands. Current acts include Faces (show band), Sweet Blue Midnights (jazz band) and Annie Niel Band (blues/rock).

MUSIC MANAGEMENT ASSOCIATES, (formerly Ron Simpson Music Office), Country Manor, 812 S. 890 E., Orem UT 84058. President: Ron Simpson. Estab. 1991. Management company. Represents individual artists, bands and songwriters. "Our specialty is helping our clients take the 'significant next step,' i.e. market focus, material selection, demo recordings, image/photos, contacting industry on artist's behalf, etc." Various fee structures include commission, project bid, hourly rate. Currently handles 2 acts. Receives 10-20% commission. Reviews materials for acts.
How to Contact: Submit demo tape by mail—unsolicited submissions are OK. Should include cassette, VHS video (optional), photos. No returned materials or correspondence without SASE and sufficient postage. "No phone calls, please." Reports in 3 months.
Music: **Country** and **pop**. Current artists include Kim Simpson (singer/songwriter), Randy Boothe (songwriter/arranger) and Gary Voorhees (singer).
Tips: "We're looking for one or two artists or writers. We'll know it when we hear it."

MUSIC MATTERS, P.O. Box 3773, San Rafael CA 94912-3773. (415)457-0700. Management firm. Estab. 1990. Represents local, regional or international individual artists, groups and songwriters; currently handles 3 acts. Receives 15% commission. Reviews material for acts.
How to Contact: Submit demo tape by mail—unsolicited submissions are OK. Prefers cassette (or VHS videocassette if available) with lyric sheet. If seeking management, include history, bio and reviews. Does not return unsolicited material.
Music: Mostly **rock**, **blues** and **pop**; also **jazz** and **R&B**. Works primarily with songwriting performers/bands (rock). Current acts include Canned Heat (rock/blues group), Olivia Rosestone (singer/songwriter) and Sam Andrew (singer/songwriter from Big Brother and The Holding Company).
Tips: "Write great *radio-friendly* songs."

*MUSIC SERVICES, 3940 Apache Trail, Antioch TN 37013. (615)832-9920. Owner/manager: Doug Deneke. Management firm and booking agency. Estab. 1984. Represents individual artists, groups and songwriters from anywhere; currently handles 2 acts. Receives 15% commission. Reviews material for acts.
How to Contact: Submit demo tape by mail. Unsolicited submissions are OK. Prefers cassette (or VHS videocassette if available) with 4-5 songs and lyric sheet. If seeking management, press kit should include cassette, pictures (at least 4 or 5), bio, references (club or business) and lyric sheets. Does not return material. "Artist will receive mailed response or they can call within 2 weeks." Reports in 7 weeks.
Music: Mostly **contemporary Christian**, **country** and **light rock/pop**; also **Southern gospel**, **gospel rap** and **70's pop**. Current acts include Joann Scaife (contemporary Christian singer/songwriter) and Cory James (country artist/songwriter).
Tips: "Have radio ready material and a complete press kit with video if available upon request."

*MUSICA MODERNA MANAGEMENT, 5626 Brock St., Houston TX 77023. (713)926-4436. Fax: (713)926-2253. President: Max Silva. Management firm, booking agency. Represents individual artists and/or groups from anywhere; currently handles 6 acts. Receives 20-25% commission. Reviews material for acts.

How to Contact: Call first to arrange personal interview. Submit demo tape by mail. Unsolicited submissions are OK. Prefers cassette or VHS videocassette with 3 songs and lyric sheet. If seeking management, press kit should include bio, photo, demo tape. Does not return material. Reports in 2-3 weeks.

Music: Mostly **Tejano**. Works primarily with bands. Current acts include The Hometown Boys, Los Pekadorez, Estilo.

FRANK NANOIA PRODUCTIONS, 1999 N. Sycamore Ave., Los Angeles CA 90068. (213)874-8725. President: Frank Nanoia. Production firm. Represents artists, groups and songwriters. Produces TV specials and concerts. Currently handles 15 acts. Receives 15-25% commission. Reviews material for acts.

How to Contact: Submit demo tape by mail—unsolicited submissions are OK. Prefers 7½, 15 ips reel-to-reel or cassette (or videocassette of live performance, if available) with 3-5 songs and lyric and lead sheet. "Professional quality please. Check sound quality as well." If seeking management, include photo, bio, clippings and résumé. Does not return unsolicited material. Reports "only if material is above average. No phone calls please."

Music: Mostly **R&B** and **dance**; also **top 40/pop, jazz fusion, country, easy listening, MOR, gospel** and **soul**. Works primarily with soloists, Latin jazz and R&B groups. Current acts include Marc Allen Trujillo (vocalist/songwriter); Paramour (R&B show group), and Gilberto Duron (recording artist). Current productions include The Golden Eagle Awards, The Caribbean Musical Festival and The Joffrey Ballet/CSU Awards.

Tips: "No phone calls!"

NASON ENTERPRISES, INC., 2219 Polk St. NE, Minneapolis MN 55418-3713. (612)781-8353. Fax: (612)781-8355. President: Christopher Nason. Management firm, record label, video production, music publisher/ASCAP. Estab. 1989. Represents individual artists, groups and songwriters from anywhere; currently handles 5 acts. Commission rate varies. Reviews material for acts.

How to Contact: Submit demo tape by mail. Unsolicited submissions are OK. Prefers cassette (or VHS videocassette) with 1-3 songs and lyric sheet. If seeking management, press kit should include photo, bio, lyric sheets, cassette and/or CD, clubs and regions performed. "Label everything." SASE. Reports in 2 weeks to 2 months.

Music: Mostly **commercial radio, rock/heavy metal** and **crossover/pop**; also **country**. Current acts include Billy Gramer (singer/songwriter), Ron Gramer (composer), Karl Kaiser (singer/songwriter), Dan Carleen (composer), Hanz Everett (singer/songwriter).

*BRIAN NELSON ENTERTAINMENT INC., P.O. Box 3008, Long Branch NJ 07740. (908)870-6911. Fax: (908)870-9664. President: Brian Nelson. Management firm. Estab. 1991. Represents individual artists and groups, songwriters from anywhere (specializes in local artists). Currently handles 4 acts. Receives 15-25% commission. Reviews material for acts.

How to Contact: Submit demo tape by mail. Unsolicited submissions are OK. Prefers cassette or VHS videocassette with 3 or less songs and lyric sheet. If seeking management, press kit should include cassette or CD, bio, photo, letter stating what artist is looking for in mgmt. company, contact name and number. Artist will only be contacted if accepted. Does not return material. Reports in 1 month.

Music: Mostly **rock, alternative** and **country**; also **rap, R&B** and **A/C**. Works primarily with bands. Current acts include Mr. Reality (band), Outcry (band), Sal Marra (guitarist), Mars Need Women (band).

Tips: "Use great musicians to present your songs."

NETWORK ENTERTAINMENT SERVICE INC., Suite 245, 1280 Winchester Pkwy., Atlanta GA 30080. (404)319-8822. President: Mike Hooks. Management firm, booking agency. Estab. 1985. Represents local and regional individual artists and groups. Currently handles 10 acts. Receives 10-20% commission. Reviews material for acts.

How to Contact: Write or call first and obtain permission to submit. Prefers cassette. If seeking management, press kit should include whatever is available. Does not return material. Reports in 1 week.

Music: Mostly **rock** and **country**. Works primarily with bands. Current acts include Wet Willie (rock), Normaltown Flyers (country) and Metal Rose (college alternative).

Tips: "Develop your talent and skills. Rewrite your songs often. Listen to the radio and compare your material with successful artists."

*NEW SOUND ATLANTA, INC., 3245 Irish Lane, Decatur GA 30032. (404)284-5463. Vice President/Management-Promotions: Mark Willis. Management firm. Estab. 1987. Represents regional groups; currently handles 3 acts. Receives 20% commission. Reviews material for acts.

How to Contact: Submit demo tape by mail. Unsolicited submissions are OK. Prefers cassette. If seeking management, press kit should include picture, bio, 3 song tape or CD, a list of upcoming performance dates. Does not return material. Reports in 3 weeks.
Music: Mostly **rock, alternative rock** and **blues rock.** Works primarily with rock bands, all original, able to tour. Current acts include Stonehart (hard rock), Stuck Mojo (metal rap), Lush Life (blues rock).

NIC OF TYME PRODUCTIONS, INC., P.O. Box 2114, Valparaiso IN 46384. (219)477-2083. Fax: (219)477-4075. President: Tony Nicoletto. Management firm, record promoter, music publisher (Twin Spin Publishing/BMI). Estab. 1990. Represents individual artists, groups and songwriters from anywhere. Currently represents 12 acts. Receives 20-25% commission. Reviews material for acts.
How to Contact: Submit demo tape by mail. Unsolicited submissions are OK. Prefers cassette (or videocassette) with 3 songs and lyric sheet. If seeking management, press kit should include picture, demo tape, words and autobiography on the artist. "Must be original and copyright material." Does not return material. Reports in 1-3 months.
Music: Mostly **country, R&B** and **pop;** also **rock, jazz, contemporary** and **gospel.** Works primarily with singers, bands and songwriters. Current acts include Bobby Lewis (R&B singer/songwriter), John Kontol (pop singer/songwriter), Images (gospel group), Valerie James (pop/country singer/songwriter) and Dawn O'Day (country singer/songwriter).
Tips: "Review your material for clean-cut vocals. Keep trying hard and don't give up. We work primarily as a record promoter for the artist in mind. We pre-solicit labels that are interested in your style of music."

*NIGHT ART RECORD CO., P.O. Box 472035, Tulsa OK 74147-2035. (918)663-9828. President: Vaughn Lanter. Management firm, music publisher, record company. Estab. 1988. Represents groups from anywhere; currently handles 8 acts. Receives 10% commission.
How to Contact: Submit demo tape by mail. Unsolicited submissions are OK. Prefers cassette or VHS videocassette with 2-4 songs and lyric sheet. If seeking management, press kit should include head shot/group shot with résumé, any print media articles. Does not return material. Reports in 6-8 weeks.
Music: Mostly **rock of any kind.** Works primarily with rock bands with original material. Current acts include Tramp, A.K.A., Project FORTE.
Tips: "High dollar productions are not necessary. Clean vocals are important. Believe in yourself and write for yourself. NARC leans toward the garage band sound and feeling."

CHRISTINA NILSSON PRODUCTION, (formerly Cat Production AB), Rörstrandsgatan 21, Stockholm 11340 **Sweden.** Phone: (08)317-277. Managing Director: Christina Nilsson. Management firm and booking agency. Estab. 1972. Represents individual artists, groups and songwriters; currently handles 3 acts. Receives 15% commission. Reviews material for acts.
How to Contact: Submit demo tape by mail—unsolicited submissions are OK. Prefers cassette (or VHS videocassette if available) with 4-6 songs and lyric or lead sheet. If seeking management, include cassette tape or VHS videocassette, brief reviews, press clippings. Does not return material. Reports in 1 month.
Music: Mostly **R&B, rock** and **gospel;** also "texts for stand-up comedians." Works primarily with "concert bands like Janne Schaffer's Earmeal. Rock-blues-imitation shows." Current acts include Jan Schaffer (lead guitar, songwriter), Ted Ashton (singer, blues/rock guitar and harmonica player, stand up comedian) and Malou Berg (gospel singer).

*SAM J. NOLE, CPA, 230 Park Ave., New York NY 10169-0049. (212)682-0180. Fax: (212)370-4310. Owner: Sam J. Nole. Management firm. Estab. 1985. Represents individual artists from anywhere; currently handles 2 acts. Receives 10% commission. Reviews material for acts.
How to Contact: Submit demo tape by mail. Unsolicited submissions are OK. Prefers cassette. If seeking management, press kit should include biography. Does not return material. Reports in 1 month.
Music: Mostly **South African;** also **folk rock.** Works primarily with singers and band leaders. Current acts include Hugh Masekela, Miriam Makeba.

NORTHSTAR ARTIST MANAGEMENT, (formerly Northstar Management Inc.), 21742 Nowlin Rd., Dearborn MI 48124. (313)274-7000. President: Angel Gomez. Management firm. Estab. 1979. Represents local and international individual artists, groups and songwriters; currently handles 8 acts. Receives 10-20% commission. Reviews material for acts.
How to Contact: Write first and obtain permission to submit. Prefers cassette (or videocassette of performance) with 3-5 songs. If seeking management, include photo, tape, bio and schedule. Does not return unsolicited material. Reports in 6-8 weeks.

Music: Mostly **rock, pop** and **top 40**; also **metal**. Works primarily with individual artists, groups (bar bands) and songwriters. Current artists include Craig Elliott (new music), Slyboy (rock), RH Factor (rock), Hunter Brucks (rock), Reckless Youth (rock), General Clusterfunk (funk rock), Beggars Can't Be Choosers (rock) and Planet Of Fun (rock).
Tips: "Listen to your tape before sending. Is it special?"

*NOTEWORTHY PRODUCTIONS, 124½ Archwood Ave., Annapolis MD 21401. (410)268-8232. Fax: (410)268-2167. President: McShane Glover. Management firm, booking agency. Estab. 1985. Represents individual artists, groups and songwriters from everywhere; currently handles 13 acts. Receives 15-20% commission. Reviews material for acts.
How to Handle: Write first and obtain permission to submit. Prefers cassette with lyric sheet. If seeking management, press kit should include cassette (no CDs), photo, bio, venues played and press clippings (preferably reviews). "Follow up with a phone call 3-5 weeks after submission." SASE. Reports in up to 3 weeks.
Music: Mostly **country, folk,** and **bluegrass**; also **pop**. Works primarily with performing singer/songwriters. Current acts include Hard Travelers (acoustic folk/country), Tim Malchak (singer/songwriter) and Fred Koller (singer/songwriter).
Tips: "Always write from your heart because honesty is the most important ingredient in any good song. Refine your skills through contact with writers you admire and by researching the literature."

*NOVA PRODUCTIONS & MANAGEMENT, P.O. Box 6005, St. Charles MO 63302. (314)946-9609. CEO/A&R: A. Howard. Management firm, booking agency, record company (Quantum Records) and record producer. Estab. 1957. Represents individual artists, groups, songwriters from anywhere; currently handles 35-50 acts. Receives 18% commission. Reviews material for acts.
How to Contact: Submit demo tape by mail. Unsolicited submissions are OK. Prefers cassette with lyric or lead sheet. If seeking management, press kit should include demo, photo, bio. SASE. Reports in 1 month.
Music: Mostly **jazz, blues, new country**. Works primarily with vocalists, singer/songwriters, bands. Current acts include Gypsy Eden (singer), Tory Thimes (singer), Jeanie Tremont (singer).
Tips: "Send professional looking promo kit—professionally recorded demo—I want to take you seriously."

NOVEAU TALENT, 430 W. Mable Ave., Odessa TX 79763. Also: 1006 S. Marshall, Midland TX 79701. (915)335-9021, (915)682-6333, (915)699-3009. Producer/Manager: Amelio Hinojos. Artist development and an independent songwriter/producer. Represents local, regional and international individual artists, groups, songwriters and musicians. Currently handles 3 acts. Receives 15% commission. Reviews material for acts.
How to Contact: Submit demo tape by mail. Unsolicited submissions are OK ($10 fee must be included). Prefers cassette with 2-4 songs and lyric or lead sheet (if possible). If seeking management, press kit should include 5×7 photos, bio, demo tape. SASE. Reports in 2 weeks.
Music: Mostly **pop, R&B, Spanish** and **soul**; also **new styles**. Works primarily with vocalists and bands. Current artists include Nostalgia (Spanish pop), Nino (international/Spanish), Sonic (pop/ballad).
Tips: "Never quit. Success is defined 'persistence!' "

CRAIG NOWAG'S NATIONAL ATTRACTIONS, 6037 Haddington Drive, Memphis TN 38119-7423. (901)767-1990. Owner/President: Craig Nowag. Booking agency. Estab. 1958. Represents local, regional and international individual artists and groups; currently handles 27 acts. Receives 20-25% commission.
How to Contact: Submit demo tape by mail—unsolicited submissions are OK. Prefers cassette (or VHS videocassette if available) with 3-5 songs. Does not return unsolicited material. Reports in 4-6 weeks.
Music: Mostly **R&B, pop** and **blues**; also **pop/rock, crossover country** and **re-makes**. Works primarily with oldies record acts, dance bands, blues bands, rock groups, R&B dance bands and nostalgia groups. Current acts include Famous Unknowns, Dianne Price, and The Coasters.
Tips: "If the buying public won't buy your song, live act or record you have no saleability, and no agent or manager can do anything for you."

OB-1 ENTERTAINMENT, P.O. Box 22552, Nashville TN 37202. (615)672-0307. Partners: Jim O'Baid and Karen Hillebrand. Management firm, artist development and songplugging. Estab. 1990. Represents local, regional and international individual artists, groups and songwriters; currently handles 3 acts. Receives 10-20% commission. Reviews material for acts.
How to Contact: Submit demo tape by mail—unsolicited submissions are OK. Prefers cassette (or VHS videocassette if available) with 3 songs. If seeking management, include cassette with 3 songs, 8×10 photo, bio and video cassette (if possible) in press kit. Does not return unsolicited material. Reports in 2 months.

Music: Primarily **country**, but **pop** and **rock** also. Current acts include Jeannie Cruz, Tom Stanko and Rosilee.

Tips: "Make sure your ideas are as strong as possible before making a submission. You've got about about 15 seconds to make an impression."

THE OFFICE, INC., 54 Skyline Ridge Rd., Bridgewater CT 06752-1727. President: John Luongo. Management firm, music publisher (ASCAP/BMI) and production company. Estab. 1983. Represents local, regional and international individual artists, groups, songwriters and producer/engineers. Currently handles 4 acts. Receives 25% commission. Reviews material for acts.

How to Contact: Write or call first and obtain permission to submit. Prefers cassette (or VHS videocassette if available) with 2 songs and lyric sheet. If seeking management, press kit should include photo, bio, 2 songs. SASE. Reports in 4 weeks.

Music: Mostly **hard rock/pop**, **R&B** and **CHR/top 40**; also **dance**. Works primarily with groups—female vocalists; solo R&B, male or female. Current acts include Joy Winter (pop), Traci Blue (rock) and Oliver Who? (R&B).

Tips: "Do your homework before you submit. I am not a screening agency. If it's not great don't send it in to see what I think!!"

*ON STAGE MANAGEMENT, P.O. Box 679, Bronx NY 10469. (718)798-6980. President: Paul M. Carigliano. Management firm, record producer. Estab. 1988. Represents individual artists and/or groups, songwriters from anywhere; currently handles 11 acts. Receives 20% commission. Reviews material for acts.

How to Contact: Write first and obtain permission to submit. Prefers cassette or VHS videocassette with at least 2 songs, "the more the better." If seeking management, press kit should include cassette or VHS video tape, picture and bio. Does not return material. Reports in 2 weeks.

Music: Mostly **dance music**, **rock** and **pop**; also **R&B**. Current acts include Lil' Suzy (dance artist), Hi-Tech (dance, pop group), Strings of Time (rock group).

Tips: "Our artists sing songs with positive messages. We don't want songs that glorify violence, or are too risque."

OPERATION MUSIC ENTERPRISES, 1400 E. Court St., Ottumwa IA 52501. (515)682-8283. President: Nada C. Jones. Management firm and booking agency. Represents artists, groups and songwriters; currently handles 4 acts. Receives 15% commission. Reviews material for acts.

How to Contact: Submit demo tape by mail. Unsolicited submissions are OK. Prefers cassette (or VHS videocassette if available) and lyric sheet. "Keep material simple. Groups—use *only group* members—don't add extras. Artists should include references." Does not return unsolicited material. Reports in 4-6 weeks.

Music: Mostly **country**; also **blues**. Works primarily with vocalists and show and dance groups. Current acts include Reesa Kay Jones (country vocalist and recording artist), John Richards Show and White River Country (country/bluegrass).

OREGON MUSICAL ARTISTS, P.O. Box 122, Yamhill OR 97148. (503)662-3309. Contact: Michael D. LeClair. Management firm and production agency. Estab. 1982. Represents artists, groups and songwriters; currently handles 4 acts. Receives 10-25% commission. Reviews material for acts.

How to Contact: Submit demo tape by mail—unsolicited submissions are OK. Prefers cassette with 3-10 songs and lyric sheet (or videocassette if available). Does not return unsolicited material.

Music: Mostly **top 40/pop** and **R&B**; also **blues**, **church/religious**, **country**, **dance**, **easy listening**, **gospel**, **jazz**, **MOR**, **progressive**, **hard** and **mellow rock** and **soul**. Works primarily with writers and bar bands "with excellent vocalists." Current acts include The Hoyt Brothers (easy country ballads), Lee Garrett (songwriter) and Boomer Band (50's bar band).

*DEE O'REILLY MANAGEMENT, LTD., 112 Gunnersbury Ave., London W54HB **England**. Phone: (01)993-7441. Contact: Carol Wilmot. Management firm, booking agency (Central Booking Agency), music publisher (Orestes Music Publishing, Ltd.) and record company (Orestes Recording Company). Represents individual artists, groups and songwriters; currently handles 18 acts. Receives variable commission. Reviews material for acts.

How to Contact: Call first and obtain permission to submit. Prefers cassette with 2-3 songs and lyric sheet. Does not return material. Reports in 1 month.

Music: Mostly **pop** and **rock**; also "special music projects for recording and/or television." Works primarily with pop vocalists and bands. Current acts include Gary Wilmot (actor/singer), Hannah Jones (singer) and Ria (singer/composer).

*ORPHEUS ENTERTAINMENT, P.O. Box 647, Orange NJ 07051. (201)375-5671. President: Chuck Brownley. Contact: A&R Department. Management firm and production company. Estab. 1978. Represents music and variety artists, producers and songwriters; currently handles 3 acts. Receives 10-

20% commission. Reviews material for acts. Produces live concerts and sound and video recordings.
How to Contact: Submit demo tape by mail. Unsolicited submissions are OK. Prefers cassette (or videocassette) with 1-3 songs and lead sheet. If seeking management, include photo, tape, clippings, bio. Does not return material. Reports in 4-6 weeks.
Music: Mostly **pop**; also **jazz**, **comedy**, **MOR**, **progressive**, **R&B**, **rock**, **soul**, **top 40** and **fusion**. Works primarily with original recording and concert artists.

PACIFIC RIM PRODUCTIONS, P.O. Box 635 Wynnum, Brisbane 4178 Queensland **Australia**. (07)3962861. Fax: (07)3962992. Managing Director: Jon Campbell. Management firm. Estab. 1988. Represents individual artists; currently handles 1 act. Receives 15-20% commission. Reviews material for acts.
How to Contact: Submit demo tape by mail. Unsolicited submissions are OK. Prefers cassette with lyric sheet. SAE and IRC. Reports in 2 months.
Music: Mostly **folk**, **MOR** and **A/C**; also **country ballads** and **classical**. Current acts include Suzanne Clachair (singer/songwriter, recording artist).

*PALMETTO PRODUCTIONS, P.O. Box 1376, Pickens SC 29671. Owner/President: Brian E. Raines. Management firm, booking agency, music publisher (Brian Raines Music/ASCAP, Brian Song Music/BMI) and record company (Palmetto Records, Rosada Records). Estab. 1985. Represents Southeast regional artists, local individual artists, groups and songwriters; currently handles 2 acts. Receives 20% commission. Reviews material for acts.
How to Contact: Submit demo tape by mail. Unsolicited submissions are OK. VHS required for acts with 1 song and lyric sheet. Songwriters, send cassette with one song only. Does not return unsolicited material. Reports in 1-2 months.
Music: Mostly **country**, **gospel** and **novelty**. Works primarily with artists who already have some regional airplay or recorded material. Current acts include Brian Raines (country vocalist) and Jim Hubbard (gospel vocalist).

*PAQUIN ENTERTAINMENT GROUP, 1067 Sherwin Rd., Winnipeg, Manitoba R3H 0T8 **Canada**. (204)694-3104. Contact: Artist Relations. Management firm and booking agency. Estab. 1984. Represents local, regional and international individual artists; currently handles 4 acts. Reviews material for acts.
How to Contact: Submit demo tape by mail. Unsolicited submissions are OK. Prefers cassette or VHS videocassette with 3 songs and lyric sheet. Does not return material. Reports in 4-6 months.
Music: Mostly **children's**, **folk** and **comedy**; also **New Age** and **classical**. Works primarily with family performers. Current acts include Fred Penner (family entertainer/songwriter), Valdy (entertainer/songwriter) and Al Simmons (family entertainer/songwriter).

*PARADISE PRODUCTIONS, Box 29367, Honolulu HI 96820. (808)924-3301. General Manager: Kathy Koran. Management firm and booking agency. Estab. 1971. Represents artists, groups and songwriters. Currently handles 25 acts. Receives minimum 15% commission. Reviews material for acts.
How to Contact: Prefers cassette (or VHS videocassette if available) with minimum 4 songs and lyric sheet. SASE. Reports in 1 week.
Music: Mostly **rock**, **top 40/pop**, **soul**, **easy listening** and **Las Vegas style show groups**; also **dance**, **jazz**, **MOR**, **progressive**, **R&B** and **light rock**. Works primarily with Las Vegas show groups, dance bands, vocalists and high energy rock concert groups. Current acts include Rod Young (Las Vegas show band), Triple X (concert rock group), Bobby Hutton (soul/pop show group) and Alexander Butterfield (soul/show/pop group).
Tips: "Top notch polished material is what we need."

DAVE PATON MANAGEMENT, Suite C-300, 16776 Lakeshore Dr., Lake Elsinore CA 92530. (714)699-9339. Contact: Dave Paton. Management firm and record company (Hollyrock Records). Estab. 1973. Represents local, regional or international individual artists; currently handles 3 acts. Receives 20% commission. Reviews material for acts. "Associated with 'Artist Viability Research' placing acts with major labels."
How to Contact: Submit demo tape by mail—unsolicited submissions are OK. Prefers cassette (or VHS videocassette if available) with 4 songs and lyric sheet. If seeking management, press kit should include tape, bio, background info and photo. SASE. Reports in 1 month.

Refer to the Category Index (at the end of this section) to find exactly which companies are interested in the type of music you write.

Music: Mostly **country, country/rock** and **rock**; also **pop**. Works primarily with vocalists. Current acts include Linda Rae (country artist), Dylan Paton (drum tracks) and Brett Duncan (rock).

JACKIE PAUL ENTERTAINMENT GROUP, INC., (formerly Jackie Paul Management and Consultant Firm), 559 Wanamaker Rd., Jenkintown PA 19046. (215)884-3308. Fax: (215)884-1083. President: Jackie Paul. Management and promotion firm (Terrance Moore Music, Inc./BMI). Estab. 1985. Represents local and national artists, groups, producers and musicians. Currently handles 3 acts. Receives 15-30% commission. Reviews material for acts.
How to Contact: Call first and obtain permission to submit. Prefers cassette (or VHS videocassette if available) with 1-3 songs and lyric or lead sheets. "It's not mandatory but if possible, I would prefer a videocassette. A video simply helps get the song across visually. Do the best to help portray the image you represent, with whatever resources possible." If seeking management, include no more than 3 copyrighted songs, photo, bio (short and to the point), video (if possible), contact name, telephone number and address in press kit. SASE. Reports in 4-6 weeks.
Music: Mostly **rap, AC/pop** and **R&B/dance**. Works primarily with vocalists (all original acts). Current acts include Blue Eagle (pop/AC singer/songwriter, producer/musician) and Terrance T. (R&B-dance singer/songwriter/producer), Redhead Kingpin (rap artist/songwriter/producer).

***PEARSON MANAGEMENT**, P.O. Box #188, Lawndale NC 28090. (704)538-9735. Fax: (704)538-0861. Contact: Larry Pearon (President) or Carolyn Pearson. Management firm, booking agency, music publisher. Estab. 1991. Represents individual artists and/or groups, songwriters from anywhere; currently handles 4 acts. Receives 20-25% commission. Reviews material for acts.
How to Contact: Submit demo tape by mail. Unsolicited submissions are OK. Prefers cassette or videocassette with 3-5 songs and lyric or lead sheet. If seeking management, press kit should include photo, bio, cassette tape or video with 3-5 songs. SASE. Reports in 3-4 weeks.
Music: Mostly **country, country rock** and **beach music**. Works primarily with singers, songwriters and bands. Current acts include Roger Hammond (singer/songwriter).

***PERFORMANCE GROUP**, P.O. Box 40825, Washington DC 20016. (301)270-3599. President: Dennis Oppenheimer. Management firm. Estab. 1984. Represents local, regional and international individual artists, groups and songwriters; currently handles 6 acts. Receives 20% commission. Reviews material for acts.
How to Contact: Submit demo tape by mail. "Performance videos preferred." Unsolicited submissions are OK. Prefers cassette with 3-5 songs. SASE. Reports in 2 weeks.
Music: Mostly **rock, pop** and **dance**. Works primarily with vocalists and original bands. Current acts include Judy Bats, Patricia Kaas, Riverside, Swansong, Horseflies.
Tips: "Include bio and photo."

***PERFORMERS OF THE WORLD INC. (P.O.W.)**, Suite #215, 14011 Ventura Blvd., Sherman Oaks CA 91423. (818)995-2475. President: Terry Rindal. Agent: Nita Scott. Booking agency. Estab. 1989. Represents national and international individual artists and groups. Currently handles 60 acts; receives 10-15% commission.
How to Contact: Write or call first and obtain permission to submit. Prefers cassette (or VHS videocassette if available) with several songs and lyric sheet. If seeking management, include photo, bio, press clippings and recorded material in press kit. Does not return unsolicited material. Reports in 1 month. "Send SASE or portrait for reply."
Music: Mostly **world music, alternative, jazz** and **R&B**; also **folk** and **pop**. Current acts include David Wilcox (singer/songwriter), Eliza Gilkyson (singer/songwriter), Zachary Richard (Louisiana rocker), Hugh Masekela (South African trumpeter/vocalist), Echo and the Bunnymen, John Cale and Willy DeVille.
Tips: "No lounge acts, no psychopaths, nothing boring!"

RONNIE PERKINS PRODUCTION AND MANAGEMENT INC., Suite A-1, 1986 Dallas Dr., Baton Rouge LA 70806. (504)924-5922. Fax: (504)927-1638. Contact: Ronnie Perkins. Management firm, music publisher (RonPerk/BMI), record company and record producer. Estab. 1982. Represents individual artists and groups from anywhere; currently handles 5 acts. Receives 20% commission. Reviews material for acts.
How to Contact: Submit demo tape by mail. Unsolicited submissions are OK. Prefers cassette with lyric sheet. If seeking management, press kit should include presentation letter of interest with cassette and picture if available. SASE. Reports in 2 weeks.
Music: Mostly **dance, R&B** and **rap**; also **gospel**. Current acts include Gregory D. and DJ Mannie Fresh, Ronnie "Rude Boy," Egyptian Lover and Lori K.
Tips: "Make sure everything is in proper order. Submit the material with some type of musical arrangement."

PERSONAL MANAGEMENT, INC., P.O. Box 88225, Los Angeles CA 90009. (310)677-4415. CEO: Debbie DeStafano. Management firm (BMI and ASCAP affiliated). Estab. 1981. Represents individual artists, bands, songwriters, producers, recording studio musicians. Currently handles 8-12 individual artists and groups. Reviews material for acts, artist direction and consultation, music supervision, album project coordination and production, publishing management.
How to Contact: Submit demo tape by mail. Unsolicited submissions are OK. Prefers cassette (or VHS videocassette) with 2-3 songs and lyric or lead sheet. If seeking management, press kit should include bio, cassette demo tape, photos, videotape. "Not necessary to write or phone first!!" Does not return material. Reports in less than 30 days.
Music: Mostly **rock, pop** and **folk;** also **country cross-over, alternative** and **blues/soul.** Works primarily with vocalists, singer/songwriters, bands.
Tips: "Great writing/extraordinary material—be sure the songs and the voice are there."

*MICHELE PETERS MANAGEMENT, #20N, 185 West End Ave., New York NY 10023. (212)721-4731. Principle: Michele Peters. Personal management firm. Estab. 1989. Represents individual artists and/or groups, songwriters from anywhere; currently handles 2 acts. Receives 20% commission. Reviews material for acts.
How to Contact: Submit demo tape by mail. Unsolicited submissions are OK. Prefers cassette or VHS videocassette with 4 songs and lyric or lead sheet. If seeking management, press kit should include audiotape and/or video, photo, bio, reviews. SASE. Reports in 1 month.
Music: Mostly **alternative, rock** and **jazz;** also **classical** and **New Age.** Works primarily with instrumentalists, songwriters. Current acts include Premik Russell Tubbs (wind player/composer), Hampton String Quartet (rock/arrangers).

*PAUL PETERSON CREATIVE MANAGEMENT, #309, 9005 Cynthia, Los Angeles CA 90069. (213)273-7255. Contact: Paul Peterson. Management firm. Represents artists and groups from the Midwest and West Coast; currently handles 3 acts. Receives 15-20% commission. Reviews material for acts.
How to Contact: Submit demo tape by mail—unsolicited submissions are OK. Prefers cassette (or ¾″ or VHS videocassette if available) with 2-4 songs and lyric sheet. If seeking management, include photo, brief bio and touring/recording experience in press kit. SASE. Reports in 1 month.
Music: Mostly **pop/rock** and **rock;** also **jazz** and **alternative rock.** Works with rock bands doing original material. Current acts include Brian Savage (jazz/New Age), 3 Norwegians (pop/rock), Ted Anderson (country), Brewer & Shipley (country/rock) and National Lampoon's Lost Tapes (comedy).

*PHIL'S ENTERTAINMENT AGENCY LIMITED, 889 Smyth Rd., Ottawa Ontario K1G 1P4 **Canada.** (613)731-8983. President: Phyllis Woodstock. Booking agency. Estab. 1979. Represents artists and groups; currently handles 50 acts. Receives 10-15% commission. Reviews material for acts.
How to Contact: Write or call first and obtain permission to submit. Prefers cassette (or videocassette) with 4-7 songs. "Be sure the name of artist and date of completion are on the video." Does not return unsolicited material. Reports in 2-3 weeks.
Music: Mostly **country;** also **country/rock, MOR** and **old rock 'n' roll.** "We work with show bands, male and female vocalists, bar bands and dance bands on a regular basis." Current acts include Elvis Aaron Presley Jr., The Valley Legends (country), Eddy & The Stingrays (50s and 60s dance band).
Tips: "Be professional and business-like. Keep agency supplied with up-to-date promo material and develop entertainment ability. Videotape your live performance, then give yourself an honest review."

*PHUSION, P.O. Box 91507, Portland OR 97291-0507. (503)297-8720. Fax: (503)297-0699. President: Mark O. Paul. Management firm. Estab. 1979. Represents local, regional (Pacific Northwest), individual artists and/or groups; currently handles 10 acts. Receives 20-35% commission. Reviews material for acts.
How to Contact: Write first and obtain permission to submit. Prefers cassette or VHS videocassette with 2-5 songs and lyric sheet; also bio and purpose of submission (cover letter). "Submit what you think best represents you and your material." Does not return material. Reports in 1 month, "if we feel music is what we're looking for, otherwise, we don't provide a report."
Music: Mostly **jazz/rock** and **folk/acoustic/rock.** Current acts include Julie Jones (jazz/funk/rock), The Things You Are (eclectic), Lonesome Taxi (acousto-rock).
Tips: "Be unique and listenable."

*PIPELINE ARTIST MANAGEMENT, 620 16th Ave. S., Hopkins MN 55343. (612)935-0445. Fax: (612)935-5923. President: Gordon Singer. Management firm. Estab. 1990. Represents individual artists and/or groups from anywhere; currently handles 10 acts. Receives 15-20% commission. Reviews material for acts.
How to Contact: Write first and obtain permission to submit. Prefers cassette or VHS videocassette with 3 songs. Does not return material. Reports in 2-3 weeks.

Music: Mostly **rock** and **country**. Works primarily with bands. Current acts include Lovin' Spoonful, Buckinghams, Happenings.

GREGORY PITZER ARTIST MANAGEMENT, P.O. Box 460527, Houston TX 77056. (713)223-4806. President: Gregory Pitzer. Estab. 1987. Represents local, regional or national individual artists, groups and songwriters; currently handles 6 acts. Receives 15-30% commission. Reviews material for acts.
How to Contact: Submit demo tape by mail—unsolicited submissions are OK. Prefers cassette (or VHS videocassette if available) with 3-5 songs and lyric or lead sheets. If seeking management, include photo, tape, bio, VHS video. SASE. Reports in 2 weeks.
Music: Mostly **rock, pop** and **alternative**; also **country**. Works primarily with bands/vocalists. Current acts include Inside Out (pop alternative), Valentino (Latin/dance—BMG international recording artist).

PLATINUM EARS LTD., 285 Chestnut St., West Hempstead NY 11552. (516)489-0738. Fax: (516)565-9425. President: Mike Siskind. Vice President: Rick Olarsch. Management firm, music publisher (Siskatune Music Publishing Co./BMI). Estab. 1988. Represents national and international individual artists, groups and songwriters; currently handles 3 acts. Receives 20% commission.
How to Contact: Write first and obtain permission to submit. "No calls!" Prefers cassette with 1-3 songs and lyric sheet. If seeking management, include tape, photo, bio and tearsheets in press kit. SASE only. Reports in 3 months.
Music: **Rock, pop** and **R&B**. Current acts include Georgi Smith (rock), Velcro Headlock (rock) and Michael Ellis (songwriter).
Tips: "If a deal seems too good to be true, many times it is."

PLATINUM GOLD MUSIC, Suite 1220, 9200 Sunset Blvd., Los Angeles CA 90069. Managers: Steve Cohen/David Cook. Management firm, production company and music publisher. ASCAP. Estab. 1978. Represents local or regional (East or West coasts) individual artists, groups and songwriters; currently handles 4 acts. Receives 20% commission. Reviews material for acts.
How to Contact: Write or call first and obtain permission to submit. Prefers cassette (or VHS videocassette if available) with 3 songs and lyric sheets. If seeking management, include photo, cassette or videocassette, bio and press clip if available in press kit. Does not return unsolicited material. Reports in 1-2 months.
Tips: "No ballads. We do not look for potential; be prepared and professional before coming to us— and ready to relocate to West Coast if necessary."

***P-M STREET ARTIST DEVELOPMENT**, 14016 Evers Ave., Compton CA 90222. President: Robert E. Miles. Management firm, music publisher. Estab. 1989. Represents individual artists from anywhere; currently handles 1 act. Receives 20% commission. Reviews material for acts.
How to Contact: Submit demo tape by mail. Unsolicited submissions are OK. Prefers cassette or videocassette. SASE. Reports in 1 months.
Music: Mostly **rap, R&B** and **alternative rock**. Works primarily with rappers/vocalists. Current acts include Nū Dress (rap).

POWER STAR MANAGEMENT, #618, 6981 N. Park Dr., Pennsauken NJ 08109. (609)486-1480. President: Brian Kushner. Management firm. Estab. 1981. Represents international individual artists and groups; currently handles 9 acts. Receives 20% commission. Reviews material for acts.
How to Contact: Submit demo tape by mail—unsolicited submissions are OK. Prefers cassette with 4 songs and lyric sheet. SASE. Reports in 3 weeks.
Music: Mostly **pop/dance, rock** and **R&B**. Current acts include Britny Fox, Tuff, Andrea Mychaels, Divine Judgement, Stuttering John, Hit N' Run, Karen Daughtry, G.T., Derek Coile.
Tips: "Send me smash hits!"

***PRECISION MANAGEMENT**, P.O. Box 4752, Newport News VA 23604-5000. (804)887-8836. Fax: (804)728-0046. Representative: Cappriccieo Scates. Management firm, music publisher (Mytrell/ BMI). Estab. 1990. Represents individual artists and/or groups, songwriters from anywhere; currently handles 3 acts. Receives 20% commission. Reviews material for acts.
How to Contact: Write first and obtain permission to submit. Prefers cassette or VHS videocassette with 3-4 songs and lyric sheet. If seeking management, press kit should include photo, bio and all relevant press information. SASE. Reports in 4-6 weeks.
Music: Mostly **R&B, rap** and **gospel**; also **all types**. Current acts include Men of Our Time (hip hop R&B act), Lady d'Amour (rapper), Jenal Alexander (singer/songwriter).
Tips: "Send us what you have and we will determine if it is marketable or not. Just put your best foot forward, and we will help you the rest of the way."

PRESTIGE ARTISTES, (formerly New Stars Entertainment Agency), "Foxhollow," West End, Nailsea Bristol BS19 2DB **United Kingdom**. Proprietor: David Rees. Management firm and booking agency. Associate company: Lintern Rees Organisation. Estab. 1983. Represents individual artists, groups, songwriters, comedians and specialty acts—all types. Currently handles over 200 acts. Receives 15% commission. Reviews material for acts.
How to Contact: Submit demo tape by mail. Unsolicited submissions are OK. Prefers cassette with 3 songs and lyric sheet. If seeking management, press kit should include good demo tape, bio, publicity photos, video if available (UK format). SAE and IRC. Reports in 1 month.
Music: Mostly **MOR, pop, 60s style, country** and **rock**. Works primarily with vocal guitarists/keyboards, pop groups, pub/club acts, guitar or keyboard duos. Current acts include Legend (duo), Ocean (four-piece group), Elvis Presley JNR (American artiste), Andy Claridge (keyboard/vocalist).
Tips: "Do not send more than 3 songs, your best available."

*PRO STAR TALENT AGENCY, P.O. Box 290 186, Nashville TN 37229. (615)754-2950. President: Ralph Johnson. Booking agency. Estab. 1960. Represents individual artists and/or groups. Currently handles 18 acts. Receives 20% commission.
How to Contact: If seeking management, press kit should include photo, demo and bio. Reports in 2 weeks.
Music: All types. Works primarily with vocalists and bands. Current acts include Stacy Edwards (country pop), Cindy Jackson (R&B) and Kid Lester Band (rock).

PRO TALENT CONSULTANTS, P.O. Box 1192, Clearlake Oak CA 95423. (707)998-3587. Coordinator: John Eckert. Assistant General Manager: Bryan Hyland. Management firm and booking agency. Estab. 1979. Represents individual artists and groups; currently handles 9 acts. Receives 8½-9% commission. Reviews material for acts.
How to Contact: Submit demo tape—unsolicited submissions are OK. Prefers cassette (or VHS videocassette if available) with at least 4 songs and lyric sheet. "We prefer audio cassette (4 songs). Submit videocassette with live performance only." If seeking management, include an 8×10 photo, a cassette of at least 4-6 songs, a bio on group/artist, references and business card or a phone number with address to contact in press kit. Does not return unsolicited material. Reports in 3 weeks.
Music: Mostly **country, country/pop** and **rock**. Works primarily with vocalists, show bands, dance bands and bar bands. Current acts include Jon Richard (country singer), Glenn Elliott Band (country group) and Just Us (country).
Tips: "Keep working hard and place yourself with as many contacts as you can—you will succeed with strong determination!"

*PROPAS MANAGEMENT CORPORATION, 1407 Mount Pleasant Rd., Toronto, Ontario M4N 2T9 **Canada**. Manager: Steve Propas. Management firm and record company (Spy Records). Estab. 1984. Represents mostly Canadian individual artists, groups and songwriters. Currently handles 5 acts. Receives 20% commission. Reviews material for acts.
How to Contact: Write first and obtain permission to submit. Prefers cassette with at least 4 songs and lyric sheets. Does not return unsolicited material. Reports in 2-4 months.
Music: Mostly **rock** and **A/C**. Works primarily with vocalists and bands. Current acts include Dan Hill, Lee Aaron, TBTBT, Andy Curran.

GARY RABIN MANAGEMENT, 42 Spencer Rd., Cremorne NSW 2090 **Australia**. (02)908-3192. Fax: (02)908-3697. Director: Gary Rabin. Management firm. Represents individual artists, groups, songwriters, producers/engineers etc. from anywhere; currently handles 4 acts. Receives 15-20% commission. Reviews material for acts.
How to Contact: Submit demo tape by mail. Unsolicited submissions are OK. Prefers cassette with lyric sheet. If seeking management, press kit should include photos, bio, reviews and copies of press. Does not return material. Reports in 2-3 months.
Music: Mostly **rock, heavy rock** and **contemporary pop**; also **pop rock, indie** and **country**. Works primarily with singer/songwriters and bands. Current acts include Ross Wilson (singer/songwriter), The Poor Boys (heavy rock band).

RAINBOW COLLECTION LTD., 4501 Spring Creek Rd., Bonita Springs FL 33923. (813)947-6978. Executive Producer: Richard (Dick) O'Bitts. Management firm, record company (Happy Man Records) and music publisher (Rocker Music, Happy Man Music). Represents individual artists, groups, songwriters and producers; currently handles 7 acts. Receives 10-20% commission. Reviews material for acts.
How to Contact: Submit demo tape by mail—unsolicited submissions are OK. Prefers cassette (or VHS videocassette of live performance, if available) with 4 songs and lyric sheet. If seeking management, include photos, bio and tapes in press kit. SASE. Reports in 1 month.

Music: Mostly **country, pop** and **rock**. Works primarily with writer/artists and groups of all kinds. Current acts include Holly Ronick, Colt Gipson (traditional country), Overdue (rock), Flo Carter and the Bengter Sisters (gospel) and The Challengers (country pop).

*THE RAINBOW COLLECTION, LTD., Box 300, Solebury PA 18963. (215)838-2295. President: Herb Gart. Management, record production and publishing firm. Represents artists, groups and songwriters; currently handles 10 acts. Reviews material for acts.
How to Contact: Prefers cassette (or VHS videocassette) with 3 songs. "Be true to the intent of the song, and don't hide the performer. Simple and straightforward preferred." Enclose lyrics. Does not return unsolicited material. Reports in 6 weeks.
Music: Mostly **rock, pop** and **heavy metal**; also **R&B, rap, country** and **dance-oriented**. Works "almost exclusively with strong songwriters whether they are solo artists or bands." Current acts include Rattling Bones, Mighty Manatees, Marc Berger and The Headcleaners, 2%, Chain of Fools, Headsoup and Sugar Blue.
Tips: "Don't necessarily worry about current trends in music. Just do what you do to the best of your ability. With our company the song is the thing even if production-wise it's in its infant stages. If you feel you have a great and unique talent, contact us."

*RAINBOW ENTERTAINMENT, #248, 11311 Audelia, Dallas TX 75243. (214)503-1220. Booking agency. Estab. 1985. Represents regional (Texas) groups; currently handles 12 acts. Receives 10-25% commission.
How to Contact: Submit demo tape by mail. Unsolicited submissions are OK. Prefers cassette or VHS videocassette. Does not return material.
Music: Mostly **children's, jazz** and **comedy**. Works primarily with children's entertainers, bands, comedians. Current acts include Morris Brothers (children's singers), Freddie Jones (jazz), Chuck Cason (comedian).
Tips: "We only manage established regional groups."

RANA INTERNATIONAL MUSIC GROUP, INC., P.O. Box 106 Fox Hill Rd., Valhalla NY 10595. (914)741-2576. Fax: (914)741-2566. President: Raffaele A. Nudo. Vice President: Wesley C. Kranitz. Creative Director: John Gaglione. Management firm, music publisher and record company (CHRIS-MARIE Records). Estab. 1990. Represents individual artists, groups and songwriters from anywhere; currently represents 7 acts. Receives 15-20% commission. Reviews material for acts.
How to Contact: Submit demo tape by mail. Unsolicited submissions are OK. Prefers cassette (or VHS videocassette) with 3-4 songs and lyric sheet. If seeking management, press kit should include bio and photos. Include SASE. Does not return material. Reports in 6-12 weeks.
Music: Mostly **pop, rock** and **ballads**; also **country, R&B** and **new music**. Primarily works with singer/songwriters, bands and performance artists. Current acts include Niko (singer/songwriter), DECLA-RATION (rock), Tom Hughes (singer/songwriter) and Adamos (singer/songwriter).
Tips: "We are working both in the USA and Europe. Our European offices in Milan and Reggio Emlia, Italy, have featured our clients on regional/national radio and television. So if you are serious about this business and want to pursue your dream, send in the material as we've requested, stay positive and have faith in your talent. All submissions must include name, phone number, etc. on all items. Ciao!"

RON RANKE & ASSOCIATES, LTD., P.O. Box 852, Barrington IL 60011. Managing Director: Ron Ranke. Management firm, music publisher, record company (Hallmark). Represents "name" and international individual artists and groups. Currently handles 6 acts. Receives 10-25% commission.
How to Contact: Submit demo tape by mail. Unsolicited submissions are OK. "Please no calls!" Prefers cassette (or VHS videocassette) and lyric sheet. If seeking management, press kit should include whatever materials best describe your overall capabilities. Does not return material. Reports in 1 month.
Music: Mostly **country, pop** and **cross-over**; also **patriotic** and **international**. Works primarily with vocalists. Current acts include Roy Clark (country), Pia Zadora (pop), Krystof Kranczyk (Eastern Europe's number one recording artist).
Tips: "Focus on a single category of music!"

*RAZ MANAGEMENT CO., Suite 1203, 161 West 54 St., New York NY 10019. (212)757-1289. Fax (212)265-5726. President: Ron Zeelens. Management firm. Estab. 1983. Represents individual artists and/or groups from anywhere; currently handles 3 acts. Receives 20% commission. Reviews material for acts.
How to Contact: Submit demo tape by mail. Unsolicited submissions are OK. Prefers cassette. If seeking management, press kit should include demo, photo, bio, press. SASE. Reports in 1-2 months.

Music: Mostly **rock, pop** and **metal.** Works primarily with bands and singer/songwriters. Current acts include Tom Lavin (blues singer/songwriter), Kim Masters (pop singer/songwriter), Mike Hickey (metal songwriter).

RED GIANT RECORDS AND PUBLISHING, 3155 South, 764 East, Salt Lake City UT 84106. (801)486-4210. President: Anthony Perry. Music publisher (Red Giant Records) and record company (Red Giant). Estab. 1982. Represents local, regional and international individual artists, groups and songwriters. Curently represents 6 artists and groups. Receives 15% commission. Reviews material for acts.
How to Contact: Submit demo tape by mail—unsolicited submissions are OK. Prefers cassette (or ½ VHS videocassette if available) with 3-4 songs and lyric or lead sheet. If seeking management, include tape or CD, press kit and cover letter. Does not return unsolicited material. Reports in 2 months.
Music: Mostly **jazz, avant rock, country/R&B** and **R&B.** Works primarily with instrumentalists, vocalists and bands. Current acts include House of Cards (blues/rock), Armed & Dangerous (R&B), Roger Nichols (jazz/New Age songwriter).

REED SOUND RECORDS, INC., 120 Mikel Dr., Summerville SC 29485. (803)873-3324. Contact: Haden Reed. Management firm. Represents artists and groups; currently handles 2 acts. Receives 60% commission. Reviews material for acts.
How to Contact: Write first to obtain permission to submit. Prefers cassette with 1-4 songs. Does not return unsolicited material.
Music: Mostly **country;** also **church/religious, easy listening** and **gospel.** Current acts include Haden Reed (country songwriter), Vocalettes (gospel) and Happy Jack Band (country).

*WALT REEDER PRODUCTIONS, INC., P.O. Box 27641, Philadelphia PA 19150. (215)276-9936. Fax: (215)276-0985. Vice President: Walt Reeder, Jr. Management firm. Estab. 1983. Represents individual artists and/or groups from anywhere; currently handles 72 acts. Receives 20-30% commission. Reviews material for acts.
How to Contact: Submit demo tape by mail. Unsolicited submissions are OK. Prefers cassette. If seeking management, press kit should include tape, bio, picture. SASE. Reports in 3 weeks.
Music: Mostly **R&B, hip-hop** and **rap;** also **pop ballads.** Works primarily with vocalists. Current acts include Jean Carne (R&B), Marion Meadows (jazz), Pieces of a Dream (jazz).

RENAISSANCE ENTERTAINMENT GROUP, Suite 3A, 21 Mohawk Ave., Middlesex NJ 08846. (908)627-0651. Fax: (908)627-0147. Directors: Kevin A. Joy and Anthony Tucker. Management firm, booking agency, record company (Suburan Records), record producer (Onyx Music, Bo^{2}Legg Productions). Estab. 1992. Represents local and regional individual artists, groups, songwriters. Currently handles 4 acts. Receives 20% commission. Reviews material for acts.
How to Contact: Submit demo tape by mail. Unsolicited submissions are OK. Prefers cassette with 3 songs and lyric or lead sheet. If seeking management, press kit should include pictures and bio. SASE. Reports in 5 weeks.
Music: Mostly **R&B, rap** and **club.** Works primarily with R&B groups, rap and vocalists. Current acts include Below Zero (rap), Papa Larg (reggae) and Truth & Honesty (rap).
Tips: "Hard work doesn't guarantee success, but without it you don't have a chance."

*RIGHT TIME PRODUCTIONS, 382 N. Lemon Ave., Walnut CA 91789. (909)594-1841. Fax: (909)594-9652. President/Manager: Kathleen Barlow. Management firm, music publisher, record company (Vital Music) and record producer (Port Barlow/Studio Trax). Estab. 1989. Represents local and regional individual artists and/or groups, songwriters; currently handles 15 acts. Receives 15% commission. Reviews material for acts.
How to Contact: Write or call first and obtain permission to submit. Prefers cassette or VHS videocassette with lyric or lead sheet. If seeking management, press kit should include brief bio, photo and recent reviews, recorded material (if available). SASE. Reports in 1-3 months.
Music: Mostly **blues, country, jazz** and **swing;** also **world** and **alternative.** Works primarily with singer/songwriters. Current acts include Floyd "Hey Bartender" Dixon (blues, R&B/songwriter), Bill "Honky Tonk" Doggett (jazz R&B/songwriter), Rosco "Just A Little Bit" Gordon (blues R&B/songwriter).
Tips: "Be well prepared and rehearsed, believe in yourself and be seriously willing to commit to a goal to further your craft."

RIOHCAT MUSIC, P.O. Box 764, Hendersonville TN 37077-0764. (615)824-1435. Contact: Robert Kayne. Management firm, booking agency, record company (Avita Records) and music publisher (Riohcat Music/BMI). Estab. 1975. Represents individual artists and groups; currently handles 4 acts. Receives 20% commission. Reviews material for acts.

How to Contact: Submit demo tape by mail—unsolicited submissions are OK. Prefers cassette and lead sheet. If seeking management, include résumé, previous experience, tape, photo and press clippings in press kit. Does not return unsolicited material. Reports in 2 weeks.
Music: Mostly **contemporary jazz** and **fusion**. Works primarily with jazz ensembles. Current acts include Jerry Tachoir Quartet, Marlene Tachoir and Jerry Tachoir/Van Manakas Duo.
Tips: "Be organized, neat and professional."

*RIOT MANAGEMENT, 3210 21st St., San Francisco CA 94116. (415)282-3600. Fax: (415)282-1476. Assistant to President: Danielle Winograd. Management firm, music publisher (Mission District/ASCAP, Snapping Turtle Music/ASCAP, Motin/BMI), record company and record producer. Estab. 1991. Represents individual artists and/or groups, songwriters from anywhere; currently handles 10 acts. Receives 20% commission. Reviews material for acts.
How to Contact: Write or call first and obtain permission to submit. Prefers cassette (or VHS videocassette) with 3-4 songs. If seeking management, press kit should include demo, photo, bio, press. Does not return material. Reports in 4-6 weeks.
Music: Mostly **contemporary hits, urban** and **rap/hip hop;** also **alternative** and **metal.** Works primarily with singer/songwriters, rappers, bands. Current acts include Indonesia (R&B), El Salsero (Latin), Studio 69 (rap/dance), Erik Hicks (R&B), Greg Kihn Band (rock).
Tips: "You have to do it because it's the only thing that's important to you. It's got to be your life."

A.F. RISAVY, INC., 1312 Vandalia, Collinsville IL 62234. (618)345-6700. Divisions include Artco Enterprises, Golden Eagle Records, Swing City Music and Swing City Sound. Contact: Art Risavy. Management firm and booking agency. Estab. 1960. Represents artists, groups and songwriters; currently handles 75 acts. Receives 10% commission. Reviews material for acts.
How to Contact: Submit demo tape by mail—unsolicited submissions are OK. Prefers 7½ ips reel-to-reel or cassette (or VHS videocassette if available) with 2-6 songs and lyric sheet. If seeking management, include pictures, bio and VHS videocassette in press kit. SASE. Reports in 2 weeks.
Music: Mostly **rock, country, MOR** and **top 40.** Current acts include Baby Boomers (variety), Fanfare (MOR), Lang and McClain (rock).

PETER RIX MANAGEMENT P/L, P.O. Box 144 Milsons Point, NSW 2061 **Australia.** (612)922-6077. Fax: (612)922-6603. M.D.: Peter Rix. Assistant to M.D.: Leah Ashton. Management firm, music publisher, record company. Estab. 1970. Represents local individual artists; currently handles 3 acts. Receives 20% commission. Reviews material for acts.
How to Contact: Submit demo tape by mail. Unsolicited submissions are OK. Prefers cassette (PAL videocassette) with lyric sheet. SAE and IRC. Reports in 4-5 weeks.
Music: Mostly **rock/pop, R&B** and **dance.** Primarily works with vocalists. Current acts include Deni Hines, Marcia Hines and Jon English (all singer/songwriter/actors).
Tips: "All artists require quality lyric content."

RNJ PRODUCTIONS, INC., 11514 Calvert St., North Hollywood CA 91606. (818)762-6105. President: Rein Neggo, Jr. Management firm. Estab. 1974. Represents individual artists; currently handles 10 acts. Receives 10-25% commission. Reviews material for acts.
How to Contact: Submit demo tape by mail—unsolicited submissions are OK. Prefers cassette with 3 songs and lead sheet. Does not return unsolicited material. Reports in 1 month.
Music: Mostly **A/C, country, pop** and **folk.** Works primarily with vocalists and concert artists. Current acts include Glenn Yarbrough, Arizona Smoke Review, Limeliters, Bill Zorn, Jon Benns, The Kingston Trio and The New Christy Minstrels.

*ROCK WHIRLED MUSIC MANAGEMENT, 1423 N. Front St., Harrisburg PA 17102. (717)236-2386. Director: Philip Clark. Management firm, booking agency, publicists. Estab. 1987. Represents individual artists and/or groups from anywhere; currently handles 12 acts. Receives 10-25% commission. Charges $25/hour for public relations consultation, representation. Reviews material for acts.
How to Contact: Submit demo tape by mail. Unsolicited submissions are OK. Prefers cassette. If seeking management, press kit should include bio, tape, letter describing act, goals, previous experience and photo. SASE. Reports in 3 weeks.
Music: Mostly **rock** and **alternative, folk.** Works primarily with soloist singer/instrumentalists, duo acoustic acts, bands. Current acts include Dezire (original hard rock), Sterling Cooke (3-piece instrumentalist—blues/rock), The Eves (female lyricist duo—contemporary folk/satire).
Tips: "Send complete info package: tape, bio, goals, photos. Check a variety of firms—decide what approach and style of working he or she would prefer. We prefer clients who wish to work specifically with us, not just any firm."

ROGUE MANAGEMENT, 109 Earle Ave., Lynbrook NY 11563. (516)599-4157. President: James Citkovic. Partner: Ralph Beauchamp. Management firm. Estab. 1986. Represents local, regional or inter-

national individual artists, groups, songwriters and producers; currently handles 4 acts. Receives 10-30% commission. Reviews material for acts.
How to Contact: Submit demo tape by mail—unsolicited submissions are OK. "Please, no phone calls." Prefers CD or cassette (or VHS videocassette if available), 8 × 10 pictures, press, bio, tape with 4 songs and lyric sheet. SASE. Reports in 4-5 weeks.
Music: Mostly **alternative, rock** and **pop/dance**; also **industrial, rave** and **techno**. Current acts include The Fiction Scene (major label pop/dance music), Jeff Gordon (folk), Spiritual Loveaffair (alternative rock) and Requiem (4 parts man and 1 part machine).

CHARLES R. ROTHSCHILD PRODUCTIONS INC., 330 E. 48th St., New York NY 10017. (212)421-0592. President: Charles R. Rothschild. Booking agency. Estab. 1971. Represents local, regional and international individual artists, groups and songwriters; currently handles 10 acts. Receives 15-25% commission. Reviews material for acts.
How to Contact: Write first and obtain permission to submit. Prefers cassette or CD (or VHS videocassette if available) with 1 song and lyric and lead sheet. If seeking management, include cassette, photo, bio and reviews. SASE. Reports in 3 months.
Music: Mostly **rock, pop** and **folk**; also **country** and **jazz**. Current acts include Judy Collins (pop singer/songwriter), Leo Kottke (guitarist/composer) and Emmylou Harris (country songwriter).

RUSTRON MUSIC PRODUCTIONS, Send all artist song submissions to: 1156 Park Lane, West Palm Beach FL 33417-5957. (407)686-1354. Main Office: 42 Barrack Hill Rd., Ridgefield CT 06877. ("Main office does not review new material—only South Florida Branch office does.") Artists' Consultants: Rusty Gordon and Davilyn Whims. Composition Management: Ron Caruso. Management firm, booking agency, music publisher (Rustron Music Publishers/BMI and Whimsong Publishing/ASCAP) and record producer (Rustron Music Productions). Estab. 1970. Represents individuals, groups and songwriters; currently handles 25 acts. Receives 10-25% commission for management and/or booking only. Reviews material for acts.
How to Contact: Submit demo tape by mail. Unsolicited submissions are OK. Prefers cassette with 3-6 songs and lyric or lead sheet. "SASE required for all correspondence." Reports in 2-4 months.
Music: Blues (**country folk/urban, Southern**), **country (rock, blues, progressive), easy listening (ballads), women's music, R&B, folk/rock, New Age instrumentals** and **New Age folk fusion**. Current acts include Relative Viewpoint (socio/environmental folk), Gary Jess (New Age fusion) and Boomslang (swamp music, contemporary folk and humorous songs).
Tips: "Send cover letter, typed lyric sheets for all songs. Carefully mix demo, don't drown the vocals, 3-6 songs in a submission. Send photo if artist is seeking marketing and/or production assistance. Very strong hooks, definitive melody, evolved concepts, unique and unpredictable themes."

*MIKE RYMKUS MANAGEMENT AND PROMOTIONS, 21610 Park Wick Lane, Katy TX 77450. (713)492-0423. President: Mike Rymkus. Management firm. Estab. 1970. Represents local and regional (Texas) individual artists and songwriters; currently handles 1 act. Receives 20% commission. Reviews material for acts.
How to Contact: Submit demo tape by mail. Unsolicited submissions are OK. Prefers cassette. If seeking management, press kit should include a good bio, a good picture, 3 of your best songs on cassette. "Can not have any management ties or record deals." SASE "and I reserve the right to keep anything I receive." Reports back around 2 months on received material.
Music: Mostly **country**. Works primarily with singer/songwriters. Current acts include Tommy Lee (country singer/songwriter).

S.T.A.R.S. PRODUCTIONS, 2nd Floor, 1 Professional Quadrangle, Sparta NJ 07871. (201)729-7242. Fax: (201)729-2979. President: Steve Tarkanish. Booking agency. Estab. 1983. Represents individual artists, groups, songwriters from anywhere; currently handles 35-40 acts. Receives 15-20% commission. Reviews material for acts.
How to Contact: Submit demo tape by mail. Unsolicited submissions are OK. Prefers cassette with lyric or lead sheet. If seeking management, press kit should include biography, photo, cassette, list of clubs played and upcoming dates. Does not return material. Reports in 6-8 weeks.
Music: Mostly **rock, alternative** and **country**; also **singles/duos** and **folk**. Primarily works with bands. Current acts include The Nerds (rock band, songwriters), Voices (rock band, songwriters) The Jox, Stuttering John (of the Howard Stern Show), Who Brought the Dog, Good Girls Don't!, The Willies, Cats on a Smooth Surface, Love Pumps, Rev. Sole and the Saviors and Koz McDawgz. Bookings include the Spin Doctors, Air Supply, Meatloaf, Clarence Clemons, Buster Poindexter and Kansas.

*SA'MALL MANAGEMENT, P.O. Box 8442, Universal City CA 91608. (818)506-8533. Fax: (818)760-8533. Manager: Nikki Ray. Management firm. Estab. 1990. Represents local, regional and international individual artists, groups and songwriters; currently handles 5 acts. Receives 25% commission. Reviews material for acts.

How to Contact: Write first and obtain permission to submit. Prefers cassette with 2 songs and lyric and lead sheet. SASE. Reports in 6 weeks.
Music: All types. Current acts include I.B. Phyne, Rick Hendrix, LeJenz.
Tips: "Do your homework and learn your craft."

*SANDCASTLE PRODUCTIONS, 236 Sebert Road, Forest Gate, London E7 ONP **United Kingdom**. Phone: (081)534-8500. Senior Partner: Simon Law. Management firm, music publisher (Sea Dream Music/PRS, Scarf Music Publishing and Really Free Music/PRS, Chain of Love Music, Crimson Flame) and record company (Plankton Records, Embryo Arts/Belgium, Wildtracks and Gutta/Sweden) and record producers. Estab. 1980. Represents individual artists, groups and songwriters; currently handles 6 acts. Receives 10% commission. Reviews material for acts.
How to Contact: Submit demo tape—unsolicited submissions are OK. Prefers cassette with 3 songs and lyric sheet. SAE and IRC. Reports in 6 weeks.
Music: Mostly funk/rock, blues and rock. Works primarily with bands or artists with a Christian bias to their material. Current acts include Fresh Claim (funk rock), Ben Okafor (reggae), Marc Catley (folk).
Tips: "Have a commitment to communication of something real and honest in 'live' work."

*SAVVY BLONDE MANAGEMENT, 1717 Whitney Way, Austin TX 78741. (512)385-1465. Fax: (512)338-1808. Owner: Tammy Moore. Management firm. Estab. 1990. Represents individual artists, groups and songwriters from anywhere; currently handles 2 acts. Receives 15% commission. Reviews material for acts.
How to Contact: Submit demo tape by mail. Unsolicited submissions are OK. Prefers cassette or VHS videocassette with 4 songs and lyric and lead sheet. If seeking management, press kit should include photo, song list, press, bio and tape. SASE. Reports in 2 weeks.
Music: Mostly rock, alternative rock and country; also blues rock. Current acts include Jason Farmer (songwriter/vocalist), Phillip Mishae (guitarist/songwriter) and Seth Drell (drummer/guitarist/songwriter).

LONNY SCHONFELD AND ASSOCIATES, P.O. Box 460086, Garland TX 75046. (214)497-1616. President: Lonny Schonfeld. Management firm (G-Town Entertainment), promotions, public relations and music publisher (Lonny Tunes/BMI). Estab. 1988. Represents local, regional or international individual artists, groups and songwriters; currently handles 5 acts. Receives 15% commission. Reviews material for acts.
How to Contact: Submit demo tape—unsolicited submissions are OK. Prefers cassette with 3-5 songs and lyric sheet. If seeking management, include 8 × 10 head shot, bio, studio demo, live demo. Does not return unsolicited material. Reports in 6-8 weeks.
Music: Mostly country, pop, and rock. Works primarily with vocal groups and comedians. Current acts include Randy Stout (singer/songwriter), Owl Creek Band (pop) and Doug Richardson (comedian).
Tips: "Make sure your songs are commercial. Listen to the current 'hits' to see how your song stacks up, because that's what you're competing with."

DEBBIE SCHWARTZ MANAGEMENT, 7 E, 211 W. 56th St., New York NY 10019. (212)586-1514. Fax: (212)586-0139. President: Debbie Schwartz. Partner: Dennis Colligan. Management firm. Estab. 1980. Represents individual artists, groups and songwriters from anywhere; currently handles 3 acts. Receives 15-20% commission. Reviews material for acts.
How to Contact: Submit demo tape by mail. Unsolicited submissions are OK. Prefers cassette with 4-6 songs and lyric sheet. If seeking management, press kit should include demo tape and picture with bio and/or press. Does not return material. Reports in 3-4 weeks "with artist making the follow-up call."
Music: Mostly rock, alternative/folk and pop. Primarily works with singer/songwriters and bands with main songwriter lead vocalist. Current acts include Doug James (singer/songwriter, wrote "How Am I Supposed to Live Without You" with Michael Bolton), Wanderlust (alternative rock) and Dara Stewart (singer/songwriter).
Tips: "Submit demo tape by mail with follow-up 3-4 weeks after submission. Keep package simple."

*CRAIG SCOTT ENTERTAINMENT, P.O. Box 1722, Paramus NJ 07653-1722. (201)587-1066. Fax: (201)587-0481. Management firm. Estab. 1985. Represents individual artists and/or groups from anywhere; currently handles 2 acts. Commission varies. Reviews material for acts.
How to Contact: Submit demo tape by mail. Unsolicited submissions are OK. Prefers cassette. If seeking management, press kit should include tape/CD, bio, picture, relevant press. Does not return material. Reports in 3-4 weeks.
Music: Mostly jazz. Current acts include Glenn Alexander, Carol Grey.
Tips: "Remember, if it was easy everybody would be successful!"

DICK SCOTT ENTERTAINMENT, 888 7th Ave., 29th Floor, New York NY 10019. (212)581-2500. Fax: (212)581-3596. President: Dick Scott. Contact: Diane Richard. Management firm and record company. Estab. 1975. Represents individual artists and groups from anywhere; currently handles 7 acts. Reviews material for acts.
How to Contact: Call first and obtain permission to submit or submit demo tape by mail. Unsolicited submissions are OK. Prefers cassette. If seeking management, press kit should include tape, photo and bio. Does not return material.
Music: Mostly **pop, R&B** and **rap.** Current acts include Marky Mark, Boyz II Men and NKOTB.

*SHAPIRO & COMPANY, C.P.A. (A Professional Corporation), Suite 620, 9255 Sunset Blvd., Los Angeles CA 90069. (213)278-2303. Certified Public Accountant: Charles H. Shapiro. Business management firm. Estab. 1979. Represents individual recording artists, groups and songwriters. Commission varies.
How to Contact: Write or call first to arrange personal interview.
Music: Mostly **rock** and **pop.** Works primarily with recording artists as business manager.
Tips: "We assist songwriters with administration of publishing."

MICKEY SHERMAN ARTIST MANAGEMENT & DEVELOPMENT, P.O. Box 20814, Oklahoma City OK 73156. (405)755-0315. President: Mickey Sherman. Management firm. Estab. 1974. Represents individual artists and songwriters; currently handles 3 acts. Receives 10-15% commission. Reviews material for acts.
How to Contact: Submit demo tape—unsolicited submissions are OK. Prefers cassette (or VHS videocassette of live performance, if available) with 3 songs and lyric sheet or lead sheet. If seeking management, include thumbnail biography/picture/press clippings and résumé in press kit. "Keep videos simple. Use good lighting." Does not return unsolicited material. Reports in 3 months.
Music: Mostly **blues, pop** and **country;** also **R&B, rock** and **easy listening.** Works primarily with vocalists and showbands. Current acts include Jan Jo (singer/harmonica), Benny Kubiak (fiddler) and Red Higdon (country).

*PHILL SHUTE MANAGEMENT PTY. LTD., Box 273, Dulwich Hill NSW 2203 **Australia**. Phone: (02)5692152. Managing Director: Phill Shute. Management firm, booking agency and record company (Big Rock Records). Estab. 1979. Represents local individual artists and groups; currently handles 3 acts. Receives 25% commission. Reviews material for acts. Charges fee for reviewing material.
How to Contact: Submit demo tape by mail—unsolicited submissions are OK. Prefers cassette with 4 songs and lyric sheet. SASE. Reports in 2 months.
Music: Mostly **rock, pop** and **R&B;** also **country rock.** Works primarily with rock bands, pop vocalists and blues acts (band and vocalists). Current acts include Chris Turner (blues/guitarist/vocalist), Collage (pop/rock band) and Big Rock Band (rock'n'roll).
Tips: "Make all submissions well organized (e.g. bio, photo and experience of the act). List areas in which the act would like to work, complete details for contact."

*SILVER BOW MANAGEMENT, 8821 Delwood Dr., Delta BC V4C 4A1 **Canada**. (604)582-7117. Fax: (604)582-8610. C.E.O.: Candice James. Mangement firm and music publisher. Estab. 1988. Represents individual and songwriters from anywhere; currently handles 5 acts. Receives 10-20% commission. Reviews material for acts.
How to Contact: Submit demo tape by mail. Unsolicited submissions are OK. Prefers cassette with 3 songs and lyric sheet. If seeking management, press kit should include 8 × 10 photo, bio, demo tape or CD with lyric sheet and itinerary. "Visuals are everything—submit accordingly." SAE and IRC. Reports in 2 months.
Music: Mostly **country, MOR** and **children's;** also **pop, rock** and **swing.** Works primarily with vocalists. Current acts include Clancy Wright (vocalist), Stan Giles (vocalist) and Rex Howard (vocalist and instrumentalist).
Tips: "Must be creative, ambitious and enterprising."

*SIMMONS MANAGEMENT GROUP, Box 18711, Raleigh NC 27619. (919)851-8321. Fax: (919)851-8441. President: Harry Simmons. Management firm and music publisher. Represents producers, art-

How to Get the Most Out of Songwriter's Market (at the front of this book) contains comments and suggestions to help you understand and use the information in these listings.

ists, groups and songwriters; currently handles 10 acts. Receives 15-20% commission. Reviews material for acts.

How to Contact: Submit demo tape by mail—unsolicited submissions are OK. Prefers cassette or DAT (or VHS videocassette of performance) with 3-6 songs and lyric sheet; also submit promotional material, photos and clippings. "Videocassette does not have to be professional. Any information helps." If seeking management, include wide range of photos in press kit. SASE. Reports in 6 weeks.

Music: Mostly **modern pop**; also **modern rock, new wave, rock, metal, R&B** and **top 40/pop.** Works primarily with "original music recording acts or those that aspire to be." Current acts include Don Dixon (producer, songwriter and recording artist), Marti Jones (recording artist), The Woods (recording artists, songwriters), Billy C. Wirtz (recording artist), Jim Brock (recording artist), Terry Anderson (songwriter, recording artist), Kyle Davis (songwriter, recording artist) PERALTA (original music band), Jeff Finlin (songwriter, recording artist), The Ottoman Empire (recording artists).

*SINCERE MANAGEMENT, 421 Harrow Rd., London **England** W1O 4RD. (081)960-4438. Fax: (081)968-8458. Head of A&R: Mushy Jenner. Management firm. Estab. 1982. Represents individual artists and/or groups from anywhere; currently handles 12 acts. Reviews material for acts.

How to Contact: Submit demo tape by mail. Unsolicited submissions are OK. Prefers cassette with 4 songs. If seeking management, press kit should include bio, photo and cassette. SAE and IRC. Reports in 2 months.

Music: Mostly **all types.** Works primarily with singer/songwriters.

SINGERMANAGEMENT, INC., Suite 1403, 161 W. 54th St., New York NY 10019. (212)757-1217. President: Robert Singerman. Management consulting firm. Estab. 1982. Represents local, regional or international individual artists and groups; currently handles 5-10 acts. Receives hourly fee, plus 5% commission. Reviews material for acts.

How to Contact: Submit demo tape by mail—unsolicited submissions are OK. Prefers cassette (or VHS videocassette if available). Does not return unsolicited submissions. If seeking management, include tape, lyric sheet and bio in press kit. Reports in 2 weeks.

Music: Current acts include Jamie Block (grunge folk), Black Rain (cyber punk) and John McDowell (world rock).

Tips: "Be clear on your target performers and know if you are ready to enter into a representation agreement."

*SIRIUS ENTERTAINMENT, P.O. Box 66575, Portland OR 97290. (503)657-1813. Fax: (503)656-1476. Owners: Dan Blair, Rhonda Ellis. Management firm, booking agency. Estab. 1991. Represents individual artists and/or groups, songwriters from anywhere; currently handles 10 acts. Receives 10-15% commission. Reviews material for acts.

How to Contact: Submit demo tape by mail. Unsolicited submissions are OK. Prefers cassette with 3 songs and lyric sheet. If seeking management, press kit should include 8 × 10 photo, résumé, cassette, video if available. "Résumé should include total career progress from beginning with all schooling listed." SASE. Reports in 2-3 weeks.

Music: Mostly **R&B, country** and **rock;** also **jazz, blues** and **classical.** Current acts include Dorothy Moore (R&B/blues), James Van Buren (jazz/blues), Mark Olmstead (international artist).

Tips: "Be totally honest with yourself about your talent and what you want to achieve from it. If you wouldn't be proud to hear your material on radio, don't send to us. Write songs about your experiences."

*SIROCCO PRODUCTIONS, INC., #104, 5660 E. Virgina Beach Blvd., Norfolk VA 23502. (804)461-8987. Fax: (804)461-4669. Contact: Leonard A. Swann, Jr.. Management firm. Estab. 1991. Represents groups from anywhere; currently handles 3 acts. Commission varies. Reviews material for acts.

How to Contact: Write first to obtain permission to submit and arrange personal interview. Prefers VHS videocassette. If seeking management, press kit should include video, audio cassette, publicity material, photos and reviews. SASE.

Music: Mostly **nostalgia.** Current acts include The TFC Band (sounds of the Fifties and Sixties), On Beyond Zee (reggae funk).

T. SKORMAN PRODUCTIONS, INC., Suite 250, 3660 Maguire Blvd., Orlando FL 32803. (407)895-3000. Fax: (407)895-1422. President: Ted Skorman. Management firm and booking agency. Estab. 1983. Represents groups; currently handles 40 acts. Receives 10-25% commission. Reviews material for acts.

How to Contact: "Phone for permission to send tape." Prefers cassette with 3 songs (or videocassette of no more than 15 minutes). "Live performance—no trick shots or editing tricks. We want to be able to view act as if we were there for a live show." SASE. Reports in 6 weeks.

Music: Top 40, techno, dance, MOR and **pop.** Works primarily with high-energy dance acts, recording acts, and top 40 bands. Current acts include Ravyn (country rock), Tim Mikus (rock), Gibralter (R&B), Dana Kamioe and Wildheart (rock).
Tips: "We have many pop recording acts, and are looking for commercial material for their next albums."

SKYLINE MUSIC CORP., P.O. Box 31, Lancaster NH 03584. (608)586-7171. Fax: (603)586-7078. President: Bruce Houghton. Management firm (Skyline Management), booking agency (Skyline Music Agency), record company (Adventure Records) and music publisher (Campfire Music and Skyline Music). Estab. 1984. Currently handles 12 acts. Receives 10-20% commission. Reviews material for acts.
How to Contact: Submit demo tape by mail—unsolicited submissions are OK. Prefers cassette (or videocassette if available) with 3 songs. "Keep it short and sweet." If seeking management, include photo, booking history, bio and reviews. Does not return unsolicited material. Reports in 2 months.
Music: Mostly **rock** and **folk**; also **pop.** Works primarily with concert rock and folk attractions. Current acts include The Outlaws (rock), Rick Danko, New Riders of the Purple Sage, Billy Davis (singer/songwriter) and the Boneheads (rock).

***SMASH POP INTERNATIONAL,** #201, 11908 Ventura Blvd., Studio City CA 91604. (818)762-5648. Fax: (818)762-8224. Manager: Frank Volpe. Assistant Manager: Lynda Stenge. Management firm. Estab. 1992. Represents individual artists and/or groups, songwriters from anywhere; currently handles 4 acts. Reviews material for acts.
How to Contact: Submit demo tape by mail. Unsolicited submissions are OK. Prefers cassette or CD with 5 songs. If seeking management, press kit should include tape, photo, bio. "Please do not call—will contact artist back." Does not return material.
Music: Mostly **alternative rock, rock** and **R&B;** also **dance.** Current acts include Concrete Blonde (band), Definition FX (band), Casey Scott (singer/songwriter).

***MICHAEL SMITH AND ASSOCIATES,** 1110 Brentwood Point, Brentwood TN 37027. (615)377-3647. Fax: (615)371-9702. President: Mike Smith. Management firm. Estab. 1979. Represents individual artists and/or groups from anywhere; currently handles 5 acts. Receives 15-20% commission. Reviews material for acts.
How to Contact: Call first and obtain permission to submit. Prefers cassette or VHS videocassette with 3-4 songs and lyric sheet. If seeking management, press kit should include cassette, picture, bio. Does not return material. Reports in 2-3 months.
Music: Mostly **positive country, Christian country** and **country;** also **comedy.** Works primarily with singer/songwriters. Current acts include Mid South (positive country group), Terri Lynn (positive country), Brian Barrett (Christian country, A/C).
Tips: "Submissions should include original songs, not cover tunes. Positive country/Christian country is a new developing music."

SOPRO, INC., P.O. Box 227, Chicago Ridge IL 60415. (312)425-0174. Contact: Bud Monaco or Red Rose. Management firm and artist development firm. Represents artists and groups in the local region; currently handles 5 acts. Receives maximum 15-20% commission. Reviews material for acts.
How to Contact: Write first and obtain permission to submit. Prefers cassette with 2-3 songs and lead sheet. Does not return material. Reports in 1 month.
Music: Mostly **rock, blues** and **top 40;** also **R&B, MOR** and **progressive rock.** Works primarily with concert rock, blues and dance-oriented bands. Current acts include Don Griffin and The Griff Band (rock/blues), The Midwest Expedition (rock), Jody Noa & The Sho'Nuff Blues Band (blues), Joe Jammer & The Kissing Bandits (rock) and Tommy Biondo (rock).

***SOUND DIRECTION INC.,** 227 E. 31st St., New York NY 10016. (212)545-1440. Fax: (212)779-1458. President: Olga Gerrard. Management firm. Estab. 1988. Represents individual artists and/or groups from anywhere; currently handles 4 acts. Receives 20% commission. Reviews material for acts.
How to Contact: Submit demo tape by mail. Unsolicited submissions are OK. Prefers cassette or VHS videocassette with 3 songs and lyric sheet. If seeking management, press kit should include photograph, bio, press clippings, etc. SASE. Reports in 8-10 weeks.
Music: Mostly **rock, alternative** and **soundtrack.** Current acts include Michael Kamen (film composer), Monster Magnet (rock), Black Market Flowers (rock).
Tips: "Submit your best work, recognizing what's appropriate for our artists and areas of expertise. Persistence in all areas of the music business is of paramount importance!"

SOUND '86 TALENT MANAGEMENT, P.O. Box 222, Black Hawk SD 57718. Management firm. Estab. 1974. Represents 5-10 artists and groups. Receives 20% commission. Reviews material for acts.

How to Contact: Submit demo tape by mail—unsolicited submissions are OK. Prefers cassette (or VHS videocassette-professional) with 3-8 songs and lyric sheet. SASE. Reports in 1 month.
Music: Rock (all types); also **bluegrass, country, dance, easy listening** and **top 40/pop.** Works primarily with single artists. Current artists include Bold Lightning (band), Dr. K. (band) and Jim Kirst (songwriter).

*SOUTHERN CONCERTS, 8665 Oakwood, Olive Branch MS 38654. (601)895-8333. President: Buddy Swords. Management firm, record company (SCR Records), record producer and music publisher (Buddy Swords Music and Swamp Fox Music). Represents artists; currently handles 4 acts. Receives 20% commission. Reviews material for acts.
How to Contact: Submit demo tape by mail. Unsolicited submissions are OK. Prefers cassette (or videocassette) with maximum 4 songs. Reports in 2 weeks.
Music: Mostly **country, country rock** and **blues.** Works primarily with groups at festivals, concerts and bars. Current acts include Jerry Lee Lewis, Wendel Adkins, Tony Joe White and Don McMinn.

SP TALENT ASSOCIATES, P.O. Box 475184, Garland TX 75047. Talent Coordinator: Richard Park. Management firm and booking agency. Represents individual artists and groups; currently handles 7 acts. Receives negotiable commission. Reviews material for acts.
How to Contact: Prefers VHS videocassette with several songs. Also, send photo and bio with material submitted. SASE. Reports back as soon as possible.
Music: Mostly **rock, nostalgia rock** and **country;** also **specialty acts** and **folk/blues.** Works primarily with vocalists and self-contained groups. Current acts include Joe Hardin Brown (country), Rock It! (nostalgia), Renewal (rock group), Jaun Medaris and Supple Grain Seeds.
Tips: "Appearance and professionalism are *musts!*"

*SPHERE PRODUCTIONS, P.O. Box 991, Far Hills NJ 07931-0991. (908)781-1650. Fax: (908)781-1693. President: Tony Zarrella. Talent Manager: Louisa Pazienza. Management firm, record producer. Estab. 1987. Represents individual artists and/or groups, songwriters from anywhere; currently handles 5 acts. Receives 20-25% commission. Reviews material for acts.
How to Contact: Submit demo tape by mail. Unsolicited submissions are OK. Prefers cassette or VHS videocassette with 3-5 songs. If seeking management, press kit should include tape, photo a must, bio, all press, video if available. Does not return material. Reports in 6-10 weeks.
Music: Mostly **pop/rock, pop/country** and **New Age;** also **R&B.** Works primarily with bands and solo singer/songwriters. Current acts include 4 of Hearts (pop/rock), Oona Falcon (pop/rock), Jaded Heart (pop/rock).
Tips: "Develop and create your own style, focus on goals and work on maintaining good chemistry with all artists and business relationships. All works together toward success."

*SPORTSMAN MUSIC ENTERTAINMENT GROUP, 1207 17th Ave. S., Nashville TN 37212. (615)320-1900. Fax: (615)327-2070. Manager: John Bumgardner. Management firm, record company (Majestic Records). Estab. 1990. Represents individual artists from anywhere; currently handles 2 acts. Reviews material for acts.
How to Contact: Call first and obtain permission to submit. Prefers cassette or VHS videocassette with 3 songs and lyric sheet. If seeking management, press kit should include press photo, cassette and bio. Does not return material. Reports in 6 weeks.
Music: Mostly **country, country rock** and **pop;** also **western music.** Works primarily with vocalists, singer/songwriters and bands. Current acts include Paulette Carlson.
Tips: "Write songs for yourself, not the industry. Great songs will find their way."

SQUAD 16, P.O. Box 65, Wilbraham MA 01095. (413)599-1456. President: Tom Najemy. Booking agency. Estab. 1990. Represents Northeast individual artists, groups and songwriters; currently handles 11 acts. Receives 15-20% commission. Reviews material for acts.
How to Contact: Submit demo tape by mail—unsolicited submissions are OK. Prefers cassette with 4 songs. SASE. Reports in 1 month.
Music: Mostly **contemporary, funk/hiphop** and **rock;** also **reggae, world beat** and **jazz & blues;** also **contemporary rock, funk,** or **dance bands** and **acoustic performers.** Current acts include Chuck (funk/hip hop/rap), Letters to Cleo (progressive rock band), The Search Party (calypso) and Voice In Time (pop rock).
Tips: "Do as much on your own so as to impress and put a buzz in the ears of those who can help you go further in the business."

*BERNIE STAHL ENTERTAINMENT, Suite 17, 5th Floor, Parkrise, Three Alison St., Surfers Paradise Old Australia 4217. (075)388911. Fax: (075)703434. Managing Director: Bernie Stahl. Director: Suzanne Stahl. Management firm, booking agency, music publisher. Estab. 1963. Represents individual

artists (including comedy) and/or groups, songwriters from anywhere; currently handles 12 acts. Commission varies. Reviews material for acts.
How to Contact: Prefers cassette or VHS videocassette with lyric sheet. If seeking management, press kit should include VHS video, photos, bios, posters, cassette-audio. SAE and IRC.
Music: Mostly **country** and **comedy.** Works primarily with comedians, bands, solo artists. Current acts include Col Elliott (comedian/country).

*STAR ARTIST MANAGEMENT INC., 17580 Frazho, Roseville MI 48066. (313)778-6404. President: Ron Geddish. Chairman: Joe Sgroi. Executive VP: Tony Pasqualone. Director of Canadian Operations: Brian Courtis. Director of West Coast Operations: S.D. Ashley. Director of East Coast Operations: Nat Weiss. Management firm (business and personal). Estab. 1972. Represents solo rock performers and rock groups. Receives 5% (business management), 15-20% (personal management). Reviews material for acts.
How to Contact: Submit demo tape by mail—unsolicited submissions are OK. Prefers cassette (or videocassette if available) with 2 songs. Does not return material. Reports in 1 month.
Music: Rock and **alternative/college.** Works primarily with alternative music and rock groups. Current acts include His Name is Alive (4AD/Warner Bros. Records), The Look (A&M/Canada), Splatter (Sector II Records) and Trash Brats (Track Records).

*STAR VEST MANAGEMENT ASSOCIATES INC., 102 Ryders Ave., East Brunswick NJ 08816. (908)846-0077. Fax: (908)846-7205. Vice President: Bob Knight. Management firm. Estab. 1984. Represents individual artists and/or groups, songwriters from anywhere; currently handles 4 acts. Receives 15-25% commission. Reviews material for acts.
How to Contact: Submit demo tape by mail. Unsolicited submissions are OK. Prefers cassette with 4 songs. If seeking management, press kit should include videocassette, audio cassette, bio, pictures, songlist. SASE. Reports in 1 month.
Music: Mostly **top 40, R&B** and **rock**; also **country** and **gospel.** Works primarily with bands. Current acts include Delfonics (vocal), Big Smoothies (vocal/band), The Clovers (vocal group).

*STARCREST PRODUCTIONS, INC., 209 Circle Hills Dr., Grand Forks ND 58201. (701)772-6831. President: George J. Hastings. Management firm and booking agency. Estab. 1970. Represents artists, groups and songwriters; currently handles 4 acts. Receives 15% commission. Reviews material for acts.
How to Contact: Submit demo tape by mail—unsolicited submissions are OK. Prefers 7½ ips reel-to-reel or cassette with 2-10 songs with lyric and lead sheet. Does not return unsolicited material. Reports in 6 months.
Music: Mostly **country/gospel.** Works primarily with vocalists and dance bands. Current acts include Mary Joyce (country/gospel), The Pioneers (country/country rock) and Gene Wyles (country).

STEELE MANAGEMENT, 2818 Seventh Ave. N., St. Petersburg FL 33713-6714. (813)327-2818. President: Brett R. Steele. Management firm. Estab. 1987. Represents local, regional or international individual artists, groups and songwriters; currently handles 1 act. Receives 20% commission. Reviews material for acts.
How to Contact: Call first and obtain permission to submit. Prefers cassette (or VHS videocassette if available) with 5 songs and lyric sheet. If seeking management, include bio and photo. SASE. Reports in 2 months.
Music: Mostly **rock** and **pop**; also **dance pop** and **R&B.** Works primarily with rock bands, songwriters. Current acts include Roxx Gang (glam rock) and Kevin Steele (songwriter).
Tips: "Send only your best songs, make a *quality* recording and include a lyric sheet."

*HARRIET STERNBERG MANAGEMENT, 15250 Ventura Blvd., Sherman Oaks CA 91403. (818)906-9600. Fax: (818)906-1723. President: Harriet Sternberg. Management firm. Estab. 1987. Represents individual artists and/or groups, songwriters from anywhere; currently handles 5 acts. Receives 15% commission. Reviews material for acts.
How to Contact: Write first and obtain permission to submit. Prefers cassette or VHS videocassette with 3 songs and lyric sheet. If seeking management, press kit should include detailed history of the artist and professional experience. "Industry referrals are crucial." SASE. Reports in 1 month.
Music: "Great songs." Works primarily with signed acts. Current acts include Delbert McClinton, Little Jimmy Scott, Spinal Tap.
Tips: "Be knowledgeable about my artists and/or roster."

*STEVE STEWART MANAGEMENT, #303, 6161 Santa Monica Blvd., Los Angeles CA 90038. (213)468-0255. Fax: (213)468-0355. President: Steve Stewart. Management firm. Estab. 1993. Represents individual artists and/or groups from anywhere; currently handles 2 acts. Receives 20% commission. Reviews material for acts.

How to Contact: Submit demo tape by mail. Unsolicited submissions are OK. Prefers cassette. If seeking management, press kit should include tape, photo, bio. "Mail first, call 4-6 weeks later. Cannot return any material." Reports in 2 months.
Music: Mostly **alternative** and **rock**. Works primarily with bands. Current acts include Stone Temple Pilots and Wiskey Biscuit.

STRICTLEY BIZINESS MUSIC MANAGEMENT, 691½ N. 13th St., Philadelphia PA 19123. (215)281-6514 or (215)765-1382. CEO: Justus. President: Corey Hicks. Management and consulting firm/booking agency. Estab. 1989. Represents local, regional and international individual artists, groups, songwriters and producers; currently handles 5-10 acts. Receives 20-25% commission. Reviews material for acts.
How to Contact: Submit demo tape by mail—unsolicited submissions are OK. Prefers cassette or VHS videocassette with 3-5 songs, lyric sheet and photo. Does not return unsolicited material. Reports in 1 month.
Music: Mostly **R&B, pop, rock** and **rap**; also **gospel**. Current acts include Ron Ali (vocalist), Rich Tucker (producer/writer) and Gary Writer (movie/songs).

SUMMIT PRODUCTIONS/STELLAR PRODUCTIONS, 1025 Airport Rd., Bellefonte PA 16823. (814)355-4325. Fax: (814)237-9237. President: Michael Gryctko. Management firm, booking agency and record company (Arctic Records). Estab. 1982. Represents local, regional and international individual artists and groups; currently handles 5 acts. Receives 15-20% commission. Reviews material for acts.
How to Contact: Submit demo tape by mail—unsolicited submissions are OK. Prefers cassette (or VHS videocassette if available) with 3 songs and lyric sheet. SASE. Reports in 1-2 months.
Music: Mostly **rock, pop/top 40** and **R&B**. Current acts include Bashful (rock), Ripper Jack (rock), Bast Rachet (modern rock) and Savage Bliss (rock).
Tips: "Be persistent, devoted and believe in yourself."

SUNRIZE BAND, P.O. Box 3322, Darwin, N.T. 0801 **Australia.** (61)089819561. Fax: (089)795931. Manager: Denise Brewster. Management firm. Estab. 1990. Represents local and regional individual artists; currently handles 1 act. Receives 10% commission. Reviews material for acts.
How to Contact: Submit demo tape by mail. Unsolicited submissions are OK. Prefers cassette (or VHS/PAL converted videocassette) with 2-3 songs and lyric sheet. SAE and IRC. Reports in 2 months.
Music: Mostly **rock, heavy rock** and **blues**; also **traditional**. Works primarily with singer/songwriters and bands. Current acts include Sunrize Band, Ben Pascoe.

*SUNSET PROMOTIONS OF CHICAGO, INC., P.O. Box 42877, Evergreen Park IL 60642. (312)581-9009. Fax: (312)581-8869. President/CEO: Neil J. Cacciottolo. Management firm, music publisher (Sunset Publishing Division/ASCAP), record company (Sunset Records-America). Estab. 1981. Represents individual artists and/or groups, songwriters from anywhere; currently handles 7 acts. Receives 15% commission. Reviews material for acts.
How to Contact: Write first and obtain permission to submit. Prefers cassette or videocassette with 1 song and lyric or lead sheet. If seeking management, press kit should include bio, 5×7 or 8×10 b&w photo, general information, clippings. "All submissions are non returnable." Reports in 1 month.
Music: Mostly **country, gospel** and **pop/easy listening/A/C**; also **blues, classical** and **lite rock**. Current acts include Howard Burke (pop/jazz artist), Sally Holmes (gospel artist), Neil Cacci (country artist).
Tips: "Make absolutely sure that material is first quality."

*T.J. BOOKER LTD., Box 969, Rossland, B.C. V0G 1YO **Canada.** (604)362-7795. Contact: Tom Jones. Management firm, booking agency and music publisher. Estab. 1976. Represents local, regional or international individual artists, groups and songwriters; currently handles 25 acts. Receives 10-15% commission. Reviews material for acts.
How to Contact: Submit demo tape by mail—unsolicited submissions are OK. Prefers cassette (or videocassette if available) with 3 songs. If seeking management, include demo tape, picture and bio in press kit. Does not return unsolicited material.
Music: Mostly **MOR, crossover, rock, pop** and **country**. Works primarily with vocalists, show bands, dance bands and bar bands. Current acts include Kirk Orr (comedian), Tommy and T Birds (50s show band), Zunzee (top 40/pop), Mike Hamilton and Eclipse.
Tips: "There is always a market for excellence."

Listings of companies in countries other than the U.S. have the name of the country in boldface type.

THE T.S.J. PRODUCTIONS INC., 422 Pierce St. NE, Minneapolis MN 55413-2514. (612)331-8580. Vice President/Artist Manager: Katherine J. Lange. Management firm and booking agency. Estab. 1974. Represents artists, groups and songwriters; currently handles 1 international act. Receives 20% commission. Reviews material for acts.
How to Contact: Submit demo tape by mail—unsolicited submissions are OK. Prefers "cassette tapes only for music audio with 4-6 songs and lyric sheets." SASE. Reports in 1 month.
Music: Mostly **country rock, symphonic rock, easy listening** and **MOR**; also **blues, country, folk, jazz, progressive, R&B** and **top 40/pop.** Currently represents Thomas St. James (songwriter/vocalist).
Tips: "We will view anyone that fits into our areas of music. However, keep in mind we work only with national and international markets. We handle those starting out as well as professionals, but all must be marketed on a professional level, if we work with you."

TALENT ASSOCIATES OF WISCONSIN, INC., P.O. Box 588, Brookfield WI 53008. (414)786-8500. President: John A. Mangold. Booking agency. Estab. 1971. Represents local groups; currently handles 20 acts. Receives 15-20% commission. Reviews material for acts.
How to Contact: Write first and obtain permission to submit. Prefers cassette (or VHS videocassette if available) with 3 songs. Does not return unsolicited material. Reports in 1 month.
Music: Mostly **variety shows, rock/pop** and **dance**; also **R&B** and **jazz.** Works primarily with variety, rock and dance bands. Current acts include Mirage (top 40 dance band), Catch A Wave (Beach Boys show & more), Backbeat X, (alternative-pop-rock) and Hat Trick (Tex-Mex, zydeco, cajun).
Tips: "We're always looking for bands with high energy and a good stage presence, who enjoy what they're doing and radiate that through the audience, leaving all parties involved with a good feeling."

TAS MUSIC CO./DAVE TASSE ENTERTAINMENT, N2467 Knollwood Dr., Lake Geneva WI 53147-9731. Contact: David Tasse. Booking agency, record company and music publisher. Represents artists, groups and songwriters; currently handles 21 acts. Receives 10-20% commission. Reviews material for acts.
How to Contact: Submit demo tape by mail—unsolicited submissions are OK. Prefers cassette with 2-4 songs and lyric sheet. Include performance videocassette if available. If seeking management, include tape, bio, photo. Does not return unsolicited material. Reports in 3 weeks.
Music: Mostly **pop** and **jazz**; also **dance, MOR, rock, soul** and **top 40.** Works primarily with show and dance bands. Current acts include Dave Hulburt (blues), David Tasse (jazz) and Major Hamberlin (jazz).

*TCA GROUP, INC., P.O. Box 23329, Nashville TN 37202. (615)292-6666. Fax: (615)292-6756. Vice President: Frank Callari. Management firm. Estab. 1990. Represents individual artists and/or groups, songwriters from anywhere; currently handles 3 acts. Receives 20% commission. Reviews material for acts.
How to Contact: Write or call first and obtain permission to submit. Prefers cassette or VHS videocassette with 3 songs and lyric or lead sheet. If seeking management, press kit should include photo, bio, press. Does not return material. Reports in 2-4 weeks.
Music: Mostly **country, alternative rock** and **reggae.** Current acts include The Mavericks (country), Marilyn Manson (alternative) and Le Coup (reggae).

TEXAS MUSIC MASTERS, 11231 State Hwy. 64 E., Tyler TX 75707-9587. (903)566-5653. Fax: (903)566-5750. Vice President: Lonnie Wright. Management firm, music publisher and record company (TMM, Juke Box, Quazar). Estab. 1970. Represents international individual artists, groups and songwriters; currently handles 3 acts. Receives 20% commission. Reviews material for acts.
How to Contact: Submit demo tape by mail. Unsolicited submissions are OK. Prefers cassette with 3 songs. If seeking management, include short bio and photo with press kit. SASE. Reports in 1 month.
Music: Mostly **country, gospel** and **blues.** Works primarily with vocalists, writers and dance bands. Current acts include Aubrey T. Heird (singer), Ronny Redd (singer), Jim Needham and David Darst.

THEATER ARTS NETWORK/STEPHEN PRODUCTIONS, 15 Pleasant Dr., Lancaster PA 17602. (717)394-0970. Fax: (717)394-2783. Promotions: Stephanie Lynn Brubaker. Management firm and booking agency. Estab. 1977. Represents East Coast individual artists and groups; currently handles 5 acts. Receives 10-20% commission. Reviews material for acts.
How to Contact: Submit demo tape by mail—unsolicited submissions are OK. Prefers cassette (or VHS videocassette if available). If seeking management, press kit should include 8 × 10 photo, tape, video and tour schedule. Does not return unsolicited material. Reports in 2 weeks if interested.
Music: Mostly **comedy/music, Christian contemporary** and **rock.** Current acts include Stephen and Other Dummies (comedy/music/ventriloquism), Bryan Wilder (comedy) and The Following (Christian contemporary).
Tips: "We book live acts only."

*THREE E ENTERTAINMENT, Suite 3-E, 140 Seventh Ave., New York NY 10011. (212)645-1600. Partners: James Citkovic, Gaye Carleton and Wolfgang Busch. Management firm, music publisher (Better Than Sex Music/ASCAP), record company (Better Than Sex Records). Estab. 1993. Represents individual artists and/or groups, songwriters, producers from anywhere; currently handles 1 act. Receives 25% commission. Reviews material for acts.
How to Contact: Submit demo tape by mail. Unsolicited submissions are OK. Prefers cassette (or VHS videocassette if available) with 3 songs and lyric sheet. If seeking management, press kit should include picture, tape or CD, bio, press, radio playlists, etc. "No tapes and/or packages will be returned. Include SASE for letter reply. Please no calls." Does not return material. Reports in 6 weeks.
Music: Mostly **alternative rock—female vocals, R&B** and **dance**; also **industrial, techno** and **acid house.** Current acts include Lord K & Princess Klaudia (alternative rock).
Tips: "Please don't tell us how great you are. Have record companies, radio stations, booking agents/promoters state in writing that you have great songs."

*315 BEALE STUDIOS/TALIESYN ENTERTAINMENT, 315 Beale St., Memphis TN 38103. (901)523-0056. President: Eddie Scruggs. Management firm, music publisher. Estab. 1972. Represents individual artists and/or groups, songwriters from anywhere; currently handles 6 acts. Receives 20% commission. Reviews material for acts.
How to Contact: Submit demo tape by mail. Unsolicited submissions are OK. Prefers cassette. If seeking management, press kit should include bio, picture, tape, clippings. Does not return material. Reports in 3 weeks.
Music: Mostly **rock, urban** and **country.**

TERRI TILTON MANAGEMENT, Suite 601, 7135 Hollywood, Los Angeles CA 90046. (213)851-8552. Fax: (213)850-1467. Personal Manager: Terri Tilton Stewart. Management firm. Estab. 1984. Represents individual artists and groups from anywhere; currently handles 3 acts. Receives 15-20% commission. Reviews material for acts.
How to Contact: Write or call first and obtain permission to submit. Prefers cassette. SASE. If seeking management, include bio, letter, tape and résumé. Reports in 2 months.
Music: Mostly **jazz, pop** and **R&B.** Current acts include Jimmy Stewart (guitarist/producer), Dan Walker (composer) and Terry Howarth (singer/songwriter).

A TOTAL ACTING EXPERIENCE, Suite 112, Dept. Rhymes-1, 20501 Ventura Blvd., Woodland Hills CA 91364. Agent: Dan A. Bellacicco. Talent agency. Estab. 1984. Represents vocalists, lyricists, composers and groups; currently handles 27-30 acts. Receives 10% commission. Reviews material for acts. Agency License: TA-0698.
How to Contact: Submit demo tape by mail—unsolicited submissions are OK. Prefers cassette (or VHS videocassette if available) with 3-5 songs and lyric or lead sheets. Please include a revealing "self talk" at the end of your tape. "Singers or groups who write their own material must submit a VHS videocassette with photo and résumé." If seeking management, include VHS videotape, 5 8 × 10 photos, cover letter, professional typeset résumé and business card in press kit. Does not return material. Reports in 3 months only if interested.
Music: Mostly **top 40/pop, jazz, blues, country, R&B, dance** and **MOR**; also "theme songs for new films, TV shows and special projects."
Tips: "No calls please. We will respond via your SASE. Your business skills must be strong. Please use a new tape and keep vocals up front. We welcome young, sincere talent who can give total commitment, and most important, *loyalty*, for a long-term relationship. We are seeking female vocalists (a la Streisand or Whitney Houston) who can write their own material, for a major label recording contract. Your song's story line must be as refreshing as the words you skillfully employ in preparing to build your well-balanced, orchestrated, climactic last note! Try to eliminate old, worn-out, dull, trite rhymes. A new way to write/compose or sing an old song/tune will qualify your originality and professional standing."

TRANSATLANTIC MANAGEMENT, P.O. Box 2831, Tucson AZ 85702. Phone and fax: (602)881-5880. Owner: English Cathy. Management firm. Estab. 1979. Represents individual artists, groups and songwriters from anywhere; currently handles 15 acts. Receives 20% commission. Reviews material for acts.
How to Contact: Write or call first and obtain permission to submit. Prefers cassette or CD (or VHS videocassette) with 3-4 songs and lyric sheet. If seeking management, press kit should include tape/CD/bio/photo. Does not return material. Reports in 3 weeks.
Music: Mostly **all types** from **New Age to country to hard rock.** Current acts include Z City Dragons (dance/rock), Peter Subway (singer/songwriter) and John Good (poet/songwriter).

*TRIANGLE TALENT, INC., 10424 Watterson, Louisville KY 40299. (502)267-5466. President: David H. Snowden. Booking agency. Represents artists and groups; currently handles 92 acts (80 booking,

12 management). Receives 10-20% commission. Reviews material for acts.
How to Contact: Submit demo tape by mail—unsolicited submissions are OK. Prefers cassette (or VHS videocassette) with 2-4 songs and lyric sheet. If seeking management, include photo, audio cassette of at least 3 songs, and video if possible in press kit. SASE. Reports in 3-4 weeks.
Music: Rock/top 40 and **country**. Current acts include Lee Bradley (contemporary country), Karen Kraft (country) and House Marys (rock).

TSMB PRODUCTIONS, P.O. Box 1388, Dover DE 19903. (302)734-2511. Chief Executive Officer: Terry Tombosi. Management firm, booking agent, music publisher (BMI) and record company (TSMB Records). Estab. 1983. Represents local, regional or international individual artists, groups and songwriters; currently handles 25 acts. Receives 15% commission. Reviews material for acts.
How to Contact: Submit demo tape by mail—unsolicited submissions are OK. Prefers cassette (or VHS videocassette if available) with 3 songs and lyric or lead sheets. SASE. If seeking management, include photo, demo, newspaper articles, schedule. Reports in 2 weeks.
Music: Mostly **rock, blues** and **country**; also **Xmas songs**. Works primarily with show bands and bands with 3 year longevity. Current acts include The Hubcaps, The Roadsters and Jim Purdy.
Tips: "Put your best foot forward, know what you want, ask yourself, are you ready for management and advice?"

*214 ENTERTAINMENT, P.O. Box 720159, Dallas TX 75372. (214)823-3744. Fax: (214)823-5864. President: Mike Swinford. Management firm, booking agency and record company (RainMaker Records). Estab. 1993. Represents individual artists and/or groups from anywhere; currently handles 15 acts. Receives 15% commission. Reviews material for acts.
How to Contact: Submit demo tape by mail. Unsolicited submissions are OK. Prefers cassette or VHS videocassette with 3 songs and lyric sheet. If seeking management, press kit should include photo, bio, cassette and history (what have you done)—"Don't lie." "Wait for 4 weeks before calling for response." Does not return material. Reports in 1 month.
Music: Mostly **alternative rock, hard rock** and **R&B**; also **good songs**. Current acts include The Nixons (American rock), Tabula Rasa (jazz/classical/rock) and 2 Minutes Hate (alternative rock).
Tips: "Evaluate yourself constantly—are you really good enough yet to warrant representation. You must be able to look at your music objectively."

UMBRELLA ARTISTS MANAGEMENT, INC., P.O. Box 8385, 2612 Erie Ave., Cincinnati OH 45208. (513)871-1500. Fax: (513)871-1510. President: Stan Hertzman. Management firm. Represents artists, groups and songwriters; currently handles 7 acts.
How to Contact: Submit demo tape by mail—unsolicited submissions are OK. Prefers cassette with 3 songs and lyric sheet. SASE. If seeking management, press kit should include a short bio, reviews, photo and cassette. Reports in 2 months.
Music: Progressive, rock and **top 40/pop.** Works with contemporary/progressive pop/rock artists and writers. Current acts include Psychodots (modern band), Prizoner (rock band), The Blue Birds (blues-rock band), Water (modern band), Hawkins Brothers (modern band) and Adrian Belew (artist/producer/songwriter/arranger whose credits include Frank Zappa, David Bowie, Talking Heads, Nine Inch Nails, Tom Tom Club, King Crimson, Cyndi Lauper, Laurie Anderson, Paul Simon, The Bears and Mike Oldfield).

UNIVERSAL MUSIC MARKETING, P.O. Box 2297, Universal City TX 78148. (210)653-3989. Contact: Frank Willson. Management firm, booking agency, music publisher, record producer. Estab. 1987. Represents individual artists, groups from anywhere. Currently handles 6 acts. Receives 15% commission. Reviews material for acts.
How to Contact: Submit demo tape by mail—unsolicited submissions are OK. Prefers cassette (or ¾" videocassette) with 3 songs and lyric sheet. If seeking management, include tape, bio, photo, background. SASE. Reports in 3 weeks.
Music: Mostly **country** and **light rock**; also **blues**. Works primarily with vocalists, singer/songwriters and bands. Current acts include Paradise Canyon, Candee Land and Rusty Doherty.

*UPFRONT MANAGEMENT, 4 Windmill Lane, Dublin 2 Ireland. 671-4344. 671-4151. Management Assistant: Tony Strickland. Management firm. Estab. 1982. Represents individual artists and/or groups from anywhere; currently handles 2 acts. Reviews material for acts.
How to Contact: Submit demo tape by mail. Unsolicited submissions are OK. Prefers cassette. If seeking management, press kit should include bio, photo. "3 songs would be sufficient." Does not return material. Reports in 1 month.
Music: Mostly **folk** and **rock**. Works primarily with bands, solo artists. Current acts include Clannad (folk), Máire Brennan (folk).
Tips: "Submit your best songs with cassette, inlay card, etc. clearly labeled."

HANS VAN POL MANAGEMENT, P.O. Box 9010, Amsterdam HOL 1006AA **Netherlands**. Phone: (31)20610-8281. Fax: (31)20610-6941. Managing Director: Hans Van Pol. Management firm, booking agency and music publisher (Blue & White Music). Estab. 1984. Represents regional (Holland/Belgium) individual artists and groups; currently handles 7 acts. Receives 20-30% commission. Reviews material for acts.
How to Contact: Submit demo tape by mail—unsolicited submissions are OK. Prefers cassette or VHS videocassette with 3 songs and lyric sheets. If seeking management, include demo, possible video (VHS/PAL), bio, photo, release information. SASE. Reports in 1 month.
Music: Mostly **dance: rap/swing beat/hip house/R&B/soul/c.a.r.** Current acts include Tony Scott (rap), Erica (house/pop) and Twenty 4 Seven (house).

RICHARD VARRASSO MANAGEMENT, P.O. Box 387, Fremont CA 94537. (510)792-8910. Fax: (510)792-0891. President: Richard Varrasso. Management firm. Estab. 1976. Represents individual artists, groups and songwriters from anywhere; currently handles 12 acts. Receives 20% commission. Reviews material for acts.
How to Contact: Submit demo tape by mail. Unsolicited submissions are OK. Prefers cassette. Does not return material. Reports in 3 months.
Music: Mostly **rock**. Works primarily with concert headliners and singers. Current acts include Greg Kihn, Jimmy Lyon, Chaz Ross, Rattleshake and Susan Steele.

***VAULT MANAGEMENT**, #310, 9157 Sunset Blvd., Los Angeles CA 90069. (310)278-3815. Fax: (310)278-3870. Office Manager: Nina Meerstein. Management firm. Estab. 1990. Represents individual artists and/or groups from anywhere; currently handles 7 acts. Receives 10-20% commission. Reviews material for acts.
How to Contact: Submit demo tape by mail. Unsolicited submissions are OK. Prefers cassette with lyric sheet. If seeking management, press kit should include tape, picture, press (if any). SASE. Reports in 1 month.
Music: Mostly **rock, R&B** and **reggae**; also **alternative**. Works primarily with bands. Current acts include Red Devils (blues), Nazareth (rock), Blasters (rockabilly).

VOKES BOOKING AGENCY, P.O. Box 12, New Kensington PA 15068-0012. (412)335-2775. President: Howard Vokes. Represents individual traditional country and bluegrass artists. Books name acts in on special occasions. For special occasions books nationally known acts from Grand Ole Op'ry, Jamboree U.S.A., Appalachian Jubliee, etc. Receives 10-20% commission.
How to Contact: New artists send 45 rpm record, cassette, LP or CD. Reports back within a week.
Music: Traditional **country, bluegrass, old time** and **gospel**; definitely no rock or country rock. Current acts include Howard Vokes & His Country Boys (country) and Mel Anderson.
Tips: "We work mostly with traditional country bands and bluegrass groups that play various bars, hotels, clubs, high schools, malls, fairs, lounges, or fundraising projects. We work at times with other booking agencies in bringing acts in for special occasions. Also we work directly with well-known and newer country, bluegrass and country gospel acts not only to possibly get them bookings in our area, but in other states as well. We also help 'certain artists' get bookings in the overseas marketplace."

WEEKES WRITES, (formerly Illuminati Group), 37 Bennett Village Terrace, Buffalo NY 14214-2201. (716)832-5894. Partners: Ron Weekes/Donnell Mueller. Public relations and marketing communications for the entertainment industry. Represents solo artists, groups, TV, film and variety artists; currently handles 4 acts. Retainer and/or fee-per-project basis.
How to Contact: Submit demo tape by mail or send brief, one paragraph description on you and your goals and career needs. Unsolicited submissions are OK. "Do not call." Prefers professional quality cassette (VHS ¾" videocassette if available) with 4 songs and lyric sheet. SASE. Reports "as soon as humanly possible. Like to see headshots and any print publicity."
Music: Mostly **top 40/pop** and **R&B**; also **alternative, urban contemporary** and some **MOR**. Works primarily with vocalists/instrumentalists but open to other promising actors, etc.
Tips: "Words and images are important to us. Know how to construct a sentence, spell, communicate in professional manner. Know what publicists do. Read Sherry Eaker's *Back Stage Handbook for Performing Artists*. Artists with no prior contract should have funding for promotion. It's not enough to only invest time and money in your demo. Make all aspects of your career a priority—including promotion. High degree of professionalism and winning attitude vital. Read about visualization in Claude Bristol's book *The Magic of Believing*. We're interested in long-term relationships, not a flash in the pan. Prefer to deal through accredited personal managers but will consider artists with knowledge of the business. We specialize in desktop publishing, media kit concept/production/distribution. Especially seek to work with promising artists desiring total press/print identity. More than 15 years of marketing/PR experience."

WESTWOOD ENTERTAINMENT GROUP, 167 Main St., Metuchen NJ 08840. (908)548-6700. Fax: (908)548-6748. President: Victor Kaplij. VP of Artist Development/A&R: Kevin McCabe. Artist management agency (Westunes Music/ASCAP). Estab. 1985. Represents regional artists and groups; currently handles 4 acts. Receives 15% commission. Reviews material for acts.
How to Contact: Write first and obtain permission to submit. Prefers cassette with 3 songs, lyric sheet, bio, press clippings, and photo. SASE. Reports in 6 weeks.
Music: Mostly **rock**; also **pop**. Works primarily with singer/songwriters, show bands and rock groups. Current acts include Kevin McCabe (acoustic pop), Ground Zero (rock), Kidd Skruff (rock) and Tradia (rock).
Tips: "Present a professional promotional/press package with 3 song limit."

*****WILD MANAGEMENT**, Suite 207, 326 Kensal Rd., London WIO 5BZ **United Kingdom**. (081)964-2939. Fax: (081)960-8826. Manager: David Roberts. Management firm. Estab. 1989. Deals with groups from anywhere; currently handles 1 act. Receives 20% commission.
How to Contact: Submit demo tape by mail. Unsolicited submissions are OK. Prefers cassette with 3 songs. If seeking managment, press kit should include photo, bio and press clippings. Does not return material. Reports in 6 weeks.
Music: Mostly **alternative rock** and **indie**. Works primarily with bands. Current act is Kerosene (alternative rock).

SHANE WILDER ARTISTS' MANAGEMENT, P.O. Box 3503, Hollywood CA 90078. (818)508-1433. President: Shane Wilder. Management firm, music publisher (Shane Wilder Music/BMI) and record producer (Shane Wilder Productions). Represents artists and groups; currently handles 10-12 acts. Receives 15% commission. Reviews material for acts.
How to Contact: Submit demo tape by mail—unsolicited submissions are OK. Prefers cassette (or videocassette of performance if available) with 4-10 songs and lyric sheet. If seeking management, include good 8 × 10 glossy prints, résumé and press releases in press kit. SASE. Reports in 1 month.
Music: Country. Works primarily with single artists and groups. Current acts include Inez Polizzi, Billy O'Hara and Melanie Ray (songwriters).
Tips: "Make sure your work is highly commercial. We are looking for strong female country songs for major artists. Material should be available for publishing with Shane Wilder Music/BMI. We do not accept any songs for publishing with a reversion clause."

WOLFTRACKS MANAGEMENT, 3909 Spruell Court, Kensington MD 20895. (301)942-5420. Director: David J. Galinsky. Management firm. Estab. 1986. Represents local, regional and international artists and groups; currently handles 4 acts. Receives 15-20% commission. Reviews material for acts.
How to Contact: Submit demo tape by mail. Unsolicited submissions are OK. Prefers cassette (or videocassette if available) with 4 songs and lyric sheet. If seeking management, press kit should include tape, photo and bio. Does not return unsolicited material. Reports in 6 weeks.
Music: Mostly **country, jazz, rock** and **songwriters**. Current acts include A La Carte Brass Band, Kiss Tyler and Scott Young, Hothouse.

RICHARD WOOD ARTIST MANAGEMENT, 69 North Randall Ave., Staten Island NY 10301. (718)981-0641. Contact: Richard Wood. Management firm. Estab. 1974. Represents musical groups; currently handles 2 acts. Receives 20% commission. Reviews material for acts.
How to Contact: Submit demo tape—unsolicited submissions are OK. Prefers cassette and lead sheet. If seeking management, press kit should include demo tape, photo and bio. SASE. Reports in 1 month.
Music: Mostly **dance, R&B** and **top 40/pop**; also **MOR**. Works primarily with "high energy" show bands, bar bands and dance bands. Current acts include Positive Vibe (R&B) and Rainbow Slice (rap).
Tips: "Strive to be on the cutting edge no matter what your category is, be it R&B, jazz, pop, etc."

WORLD WIDE MANAGEMENT, Box 599, Yorktown Heights NY 10598. (914)245-1156. Director: Steve Rosenfeld. Management firm and music publisher (Neighborhood Music/ASCAP). Estab. 1971. Represents artists, groups, songwriters and actors; currently handles 6 acts. Receives 20-25% commission. Reviews material for acts.
How to Contact: Write or call first and obtain permission to submit or to arrange personal interview. Prefers CD or cassette (or videocassete of performance) with 3-4 songs. Does not return material. Reports in 2 months.
Music: Mostly **contemporary pop, folk, folk/rock** and **New Age**; also **A/C, rock, jazz, bluegrass, blues, country** and **R&B**. Works primarily with self-contained bands and vocalists. Current acts include Bill Popp & The Tapes, M,M,M&S, Syncope, Small Things Big, Rising Sun and Rex Baile.

WYATT MANAGEMENT WORLDWIDE, INC., 10797 Onyx Circle, Fountain Valley CA 92708. (714)839-7700; Fax: (714)775-4300. President: Warren Wyatt and Julie Hines. Management firm. Estab. 1976. Represents regional and international individual artists, groups and songwriters; currently handles 5 acts. Receives 10-20% commission. Reviews material for acts.
How to Contact: Submit demo tape by mail—unsolicited submissions are OK. Prefers cassette (or ½" VHS videocassette) with 2-10 songs and lyric sheet. If seeking management, include band biography, photos, video, members' history, press and demo reviews in press kit. SASE. Reports in 4 weeks.
Music: Mostly **rock, pop** and **R&B**; also **heavy metal**, **hard rock** and **top 40**. Works primarily with pop/rock groups. Current acts include Saigon Kick (hard rock), Bad Moon Rising (alternative/hard rock) and Broken Silence (Christian rock).
Tips: "Always submit new songs/material, even if you have sent material that was previously rejected; the music biz is always changing."

Y-NOT PRODUCTIONS, P.O. Box 902, Mill Valley CA 94942. (415)898-0027. Administrative Asst.: Lane Lombardo. Management firm and music publisher (Lindy Lane Music/BMI). Estab. 1989. Represents West Coast-USA individual artists, groups and songwriters; currently handles 6 acts. Receives 10-20% commission. Reviews material for acts.
How to Contact: Submit demo tape by mail—unsolicited submissions are OK. Prefers cassette (or VHS videocassette if available) with 3 songs. SASE. Reports in 1 month.
Music: Mostly **contemporary jazz, pop** and **R&B/rock**. Works primarily with instrumental groups/vocalists. Current acts include Tony Saunders (bassist/songwriter), Jennifer Youngdahl (pop songwriter) and Poppy & Brenda Hollaway (R&B).

*ZAR MANAGEMENT, Dreilinden Str. 42, St. Gallen CH 9011 **Switzerland.** Holder: Victor Waldburger. Management firm, music publisher (Zar Musikverlag), record label and record producer. Estab. 1980. Represents individual artists, groups, songwriters and producers; currently handles 5 acts. Reviews material for acts. Receives 20% commission.
How to Contact: Write or call to obtain permission to submit or to arrange a personal interview. Prefers cassette (or European VHS videocassette). Reports only if interested.
Music: Mostly **pop, dance, hard rock** and **heavy metal**. Current acts include Taboo, Admirals Bridge Club and Sens Unik.

Category Index

The Category Index is a good place to begin searching for a market for your songs. Below is an alphabetical list of 19 general music categories. If you write pop songs and are looking for a manager or booking agent to submit your songs to, check the Pop section in this index. There you will find a list of managers and booking agents who work with pop performers. Once you locate the entries for those managers and booking agents, read the Music subheading *carefully* to determine which companies are most interested in the type of pop music you write. Some of the markets in this section do not appear in the Category Index because they have not indicated a specific preference. Most of these said they are interested in "all types" of music. Listings that were very specific, or whose description of the music they're interested in doesn't quite fit into these categories, also do not appear here.

Adult Contemporary All Star Talent Agency; Arise Music; Artistic Developments International, Inc.; ATI Music; Atlantic Entertainment Group; Black Stallion Country Productions, Inc.; Brothers Management Associates; Cam Music Entertainment; Clugston Organization Pty. Ltd., The Neil; Five Star Entertainment; Flash Attractions Agency; Gueststar Entertainment Agency; Insinna Management, Paul; Jackson Artists Corp.; Junquera Productions, C.; King Agency, Inc., Howard; Knight Agency, Bob; Landslide Management; Levinson Entertainment Ventures International, Inc.; LMP Management Firm; Lutz Entertainment Agency, Richard; Manapro Entertainment; Martin Productions, Rick; Merri-Webb Productions; Nanoia Productions, Frank; Nelson

Entertainment Inc., Brian; Oregon Musical Artists; Orpheus Entertainment; Pacific Rim Productions; Paradise Productions; Paul Entertainment Group, Inc., Jackie; Phil's Entertainment Agency Limited; Prestige Artistes; Propas Management Corporation; Reed Sound Records, Inc.; Risavy, Inc., A.F.; RNJ Productions, Inc.; Rustron Music Productions; Sherman Artist Management & Development, Mickey; Silver Bow Management; Skorman Productions, Inc., T.; Sopro, Inc.; Sound '86 Talent Management; Sunset Promotions of Chicago Inc.; T.J. Booker Ltd.; T.S.J. Productions Inc., The; Tas Music Co./Dave Tasse Entertainment; Total Acting Experience, A; World Wide Management

Alternative Alan Agency, Mark; Amethyst Group Ltd., The; Arslanian & Associates, Inc.; Artistic Developments International, Inc.; baby sue; Beacon Kendall Entertainment; Beasley & Associates; Berkley Management, Michael; Biscuit Productions Inc.; Blaze Productions; Brier Patch Music; Broadwest Management; BSA Inc.; Cahn-Man; Class Act Productions/Management; CMS Management; Countdown Entertainment; Current Records/Management; Cycle Of Fifths Management, Inc.; DAS Communications, Ltd.; Direct Management; Entertainment Services International; Eternal Talent/Squigmonster Management; Fat City Artists; Foley Entertainment; Freedman Entertainment, Peter; Fritz Management, Ken; Goodkind Management, Tom; Hardman Management, Dustin; Hardway Music Management; Imani Entertainment Inc.; International Talent Network; Kuper-Lam Management; Let Us Entertain You Co., The; Manapro Entertainment; Master Entertainment; Megalopoulos Management; Monopoly Management; Moxie Management; Nelson Entertainment Inc., Brian; New Sound Atlanta, Inc.; Performers of the World Inc.; Personal Management, Inc.; Peters Management, Michele; Peterson Creative Management, Paul; Pitzer Artist Management, Gregory; P-M Street Artist Development; Rabin Management, Gary; RANA International Music Group; Right Time Productions; Riot Management; Rock Whirled Music Management; Rogue Management; S.T.A.R.S. Productions; Savvy Blonde Management; Schwartz Management, Debbie; Simmons Management Group; Smash Pop International; Sound Direction Inc.; Star Artist Management Inc.; Stewart Management, Steve; TCA Group, Inc.; Three E Entertainment; 214 Entertainment; Vault Management; Weekes Writes; Wild Management

Blues aaLN International; Aloha Entertainment; Barnard Management Services; Blue Cat Agency/El Gato Azul Agency, The; Blumenauer Artists, Geoffrey; Bon Ton West; Cash Enterprises, Ernie; Community Music Center of Houston; Countrywide Producers; Courtright Management Inc.; DMR Agency; Fat City Artists; Flash Attractions Agency; Fleming Artists Management; Golden Bull Productions; Hellman Productions, Kevin; Jackson Artists Group; James Gang Management; L & R Management; Music Man Promotions; Music Matters; New Sounds Atlanta Inc.; Nova Productions & Management; Nowag's National Attractions, Craig; Operation Music Enterprises; Oregon Music Enterprises; Right Time Productions; Rustron Music Productions; Sandcastle Productions; Savvy Blonde Management; Sherman Artist Management & Development, Mickey; Sirius Entertainment; Sopro, Inc.; Southern Concerts; SP Talent Associates; Squad 16; Sunrize Band; Sunset Promotions of Chicago Inc.; T.S.J. Productions Inc., The; Texas Music Masters; Total Acting Experience, A; TSMB Productions; Universal Music Marketing

Children's Asia Arts Management; Cam Music Entertainment; Colwell Arts Management; Direct Management; Entourage Entertainment; Fritz Management, Ken; JCHC Music; Lindsay Productions, Doris/Successful Productions; Rainbow Entertainment; Silver Bow Management

Classical Asia Arts Management; Colwell Arts Management; Countrywide Producers; Diamond Literary; Its Happening Present Entertainment; Jana Jae Enterprises; Pacific Rim Productions; Paquin Entertainment Group; Peters Management, Michele; Sirius Entertainment; Sunset Promotions of Chicago Inc.

Country ACR Productions; Afterschool Publishing Company; Alexas Music Productions; All Star Management; All Star Talent Agency; Allen Entertainment Development, Michael; American Artist Booking & Management; Anjoli Productions; Ardenne Int'l Inc.; Arise Music; ASA Productions Management; Asia Arts Management; Atch Records and Productions; ATI Music; baby sue; Bandstand (International) Entertainment Agency; Barnard Management Services; Baxter Management, Dick; Black Stallion Country Productions, Inc.; Blue Cat Agency/El Gato Azul Agency, The; Blue Ox Talent Agency; Blumenauer Artists, Geoffrey; Bojo Productions Inc.; Bouquet-Orchid Enterprises; BSA Inc.; Bullseye Entertainment; C & M Productions Management Group; Cam Music Entertainment; Capitol Management; Carman Productions, Inc.; Cash Enterprises, Ernie; Cavalry Productions; Cedar Creek Productions and Management; Class Act Productions/Management; CMS Management; Concept 2000 Inc.; Country Music Showcase International, Inc.; Country Star Attractions; Countrywide Producers; Crash Productions; Crawfish Productions; Creative Action Music Group; Creative Star Management; Crowe Entertainment Inc.; Cude's Good American Music/Talent/Casting Agency, Bobby Lee; De Miles Company, The Edward; Deri Promotions USA-UK; Diamond Literary; Dinwoodie Management, Andrew; Doss Presents, Col. Buster; ECI Inc.; Encore Talent, Inc.; Entertainment Company, The; Entourage Entertainment; Fame International; Fat City Artists; Fenchel Entertainment Agency, Fred T.; First Time Management; Five Star Entertainment; Flash Attractions Agency; Fleming Artists Management; Fletcher Entertainment Group; Foley Entertainment; Frick Enterprises, Bob Scott; Fudpucker Entertainment; Gallup Entertainment; Gibson Management Inc.; Good Music Management; Goodwin Moore & Associates; Grass Management; Great Lakes Country Talent Agency; Greeley Entertainment, Chris; Gueststar Entertainment Agency; M. Harrell & Associates; Hellman Productions,

Kevin; Henderson Group Music; Hidden Studios; Holiday Productions, Doc; Horizon Management Inc.; Hulen Enterprises; Imani Entertainment Inc.; Intermountain Talent; Its Happening Present Entertainment; J & V Management; Jackson Artists Corp.; Jacobs Management; James Gang Management; James Management, Roger; Jana Jae Enterprises; Jan-A-Lou Enterprizes; JCHC Music; Junquera Productions, C.; Kaltenbach Personal Management, R.J.; Kemmerer Management, Claudia; King Agency, Inc., Howard; KRC Records & Productions; L & R Management; Landslide Management; Lari-Jon Promotions; Let Us Entertain You Co., The; Levinson Entertainment Ventures International, Inc.; Levy Mgt, Rick; Lindsay Productions, Doris/Successful Productions; Little Richie Johnson Agency; Lowell Agency; Lutz Entertainment Agency, Richard; McDonnell Group, The; MAGIAN; Magnum Music Corporation Ltd.; Maine-ly Country Music; Marble Entertainment Co.; MC Promotions & Public Relations; Merri-Webb Productions; Milestone Media; Miller & Company, Thomas J.; Monopoly Management; Morelli Enterprises, Thomas; Music Man Promotions; Music Management Associates; Music Services; Nanoia Productions, Frank; Nason Enterprises, Inc.; Nelson Entertainment Inc., Brian; Network Entertainment Service Inc.; NIC Of Tyme Productions, Inc.; Noteworthy Productions; Nova Productions & Management; Nowag's National Attractions, Craig; OB-1 Entertainment; Operation Music Enterprises; Oregon Musical Artists; Pacific Rim Productions; Palmetto Productions; Paton Management, Dave; Pearson Management; Personal Management, Inc.; Phil's Entertainment Agency Limited; Pipeline Artist Management; Pitzer Artist Management, Gregory; Prestige Artistes; Pro Talent Consultants; Rabin Management, Gary; Rainbow Collection Ltd.; Rainbow Collection, Ltd., The; RANA International Music Group, Inc.; Ranke & Associates, Ltd., Ron; Red Giant Records and Publishing; Reed Sound Records, Inc.; Right Time Productions; Risavy, Inc., A.F.; RNJ Productions, Inc.; Rothschild Productions Inc., Charles R.; Rustron Music Productions; Rymkus Management and Promotions, Mike; S.T.A.R.S. Productions; Savvy Blonde Management; Schonfeld and Associates, Lonny; Sherman Artist Management & Development, Mickey; Shute Management Pty. Ltd., Phill; Silver Bow Management; Sirius Entertainment; Smith and Associates, Michael; Sound '86 Talent Management; Southern Concerts; SP Talent Associates; Sphere Productions; Sportsman Music Entertainment Group; Stahl Entertainment, Bernie; Star Vest Management Associates Inc.; Starcrest Productions, Inc.; Sunset Promotions of Chicago Inc.; T.J. Booker Ltd.; T.S.J. Productions Inc., The; TCA Group, Inc.; Texas Music Masters; 315 Beale Studios/Taliesyn Entertainment; Total Acting Experience, A; Triangle Talent, Inc.; TSMB Productions; Universal Music Marketing; Vokes Booking Agency; Wilder Artists' Management, Shane; World Wide Management

Dance Amethyst Group Ltd., The; Artiste Records/Paul Levesque Management Inc.; Artistic Developments International, Inc.; Artists Only Management Company, Inc., The; Atlantic Entertainment Group; Beasley & Associates; Biscuit Productions Inc.; Broadwest Management; Carman Productions, Inc.; Clugston Organization Pty. Ltd., The Neil; Corvalan-Condliffe Management; Countdown Entertainment; Countrywide Producers; Current Records/Management; DAS Communications, Ltd.; De Miles Company, The Edward; Earth Tracks Artists Agency; Ellipse Personal Management; Emarco Management; Entertainment Company, The; First Time Management; Flash Attractions Agency; Freedman Entertainment, Peter; Golden City International; Hardman Management, Dustin; Hardway Music Management; Imani Entertainment Inc.; Insinna Management, Paul; Jackson Artists Corp.; King Agency, Inc., Howard; Landslide Management; Linhardt Group, The; Lutz Entertainment Agency, Richard; McManus Management, Andrew; Manapro Entertainment; Mark One-The Agency; Martin Productions, Rick; Master Entertainment; Milestone Media; Moore Entertainment Group; Music Man Promotions; Nanoia Productions, Frank; Office, Inc., The; On Stage Management Inc.; Oregon Musical Artists; Paradise Productions; Paul Entertainment Group, Inc., Jackie; Performance Group; Perkins Production and Management Inc., Ronnie; Power Star Management; Rainbow Collection, Ltd., The; Renaissance Entertainment Group; Rix Management P/L, Peter; Rogue Management; Skorman Productions, Inc., T.; Smash Pop International; Sound '86 Talent Management; Squad 16; Steele Management; Talent Associates of Wisconsin, Inc.; Tas Music Co./Dave Tasse Entertainment; Three E Entertainment; Total Acting Experience, A; Van Pol Management, Hans; Wood Artist Management, Richard; Zar Management

Folk Afterschool Publishing Company; ArkLight Management Co.; Blumenauer Artists, Geoffrey; Brier Patch Music; Cam Music Entertainment; Community Music Center of Houston; Countrywide Producers; Curly Maple Media; Dinwoodie Management, Andrew; Five Star Entertainment; Fleming Artists Management; Fletcher Entertainment Group; Goodkind Management, Tom; JCHC Music; Nole, CPA, Sam J.; Noteworthy Productions; Pacific Rim Productions; Paquin Entertainment Group; Performers of the World Inc.; Personal Management, Inc.; Phusion; RNJ Productions, Inc.; Rock Whirled Music Management; Rothschild Productions Inc., Charles R.; Rustron Music Productions; S.T.A.R.S. Productions; Schwartz Management, Debbie; Skyline Music Corp.; SP Talent Associates; Squad 16; T.S.J. Productions Inc., The; Upfront Management; World Wide Management

Jazz aaLN International; Afterschool Publishing Company; Aloha Entertainment; Artists'/Heller Agency; Best Management Inc., Nigel; Blue Cat Agency/El Gato Azul Agency, The; Blumenauer Artists, Geoffrey; Bon Ton West; Cam Music Entertainment; Community Music Center of Houston; Concept 2000 Inc.; Countrywide Producers; D&D Talent Associates; DeMore Management; Elko's Talent Agency, Inc.; Entertainment Company, The; Fame International; Fat City Artists;

Flash Attractions Agency; Fleming Artists Management; Fritz Management, Ken; Golden Bull Productions; Good Music Management; Greenberg, Law Offices Of Gary; Hellman Productions, Kevin; Its Happening Present Entertainment; Jana Jae Enterprises; JCHC Music; King Agency, Inc., Howard; Kirk, Jeff; Klein, Joanne; L.D.F. Productions; Lanestar * Management; MAGIAN; Miller & Company, Thomas J.; Music Man Promotions; Music Matters; Nanoia Productions, Frank; NIC Of Tyme Productions, Inc.; Nova Productions & Management; Oregon Musical Artists; Orpheus Entertainment; Paradise Productions; Performers of the World Inc.; Peters Management, Michele; Peterson Creative Management, Paul; Phusion; Rainbow Entertainment; Red Giant Records and Publishing; Right Time Productions; Riohcat Music; Rothschild Productions Inc., Charles R.; Scott Entertainment, Craig; Sirius Entertainment; Squad 16; T.S.J. Productions Inc., The; Talent Associates of Wisconsin, Inc.; Tas Music Co./Dave Tasse Entertainment; Tilton Management, Terri; Total Acting Experience, A; World Wide Management; Y-Not Productions

Latin aaLN International; Artists Only Management Company, Inc., The; Blue Cat Agency/El Gato Azul Agency, The; Cavalry Productions; Corvalan-Condliffe Management; Curly Maple Media; Dietrolequinte Art Company; DiLeo Management, Liesa; Elko's Talent Agency, Inc.; Flash Attractions Agency; Left Field Productions/Poggi Promotional Services; Musica Moderna Management; Noveau Talent

Metal Aloha Entertainment; Amethyst Group Ltd., The; Beasley & Associates; Courtright Management Inc.; Entertainment Company, The; Eternal Talent/Squigmonster Management; H.L.A. Music; Jupiter Productions; Master Entertainment; Nason Enterprises, Inc.; Northstar Artist Management; Rainbow Collection, Ltd., The; Raz Management Co.; Riot Management; Simmons Management Group; Wyatt Management Worldwide, Inc.; Zar Management

New Age Alexas Music Productions; Goodwin Moore & Associates; Gramercy Park Entertainment; Greenberg, Law Offices Of Gary; Imani Entertainment Inc.; Lanestar * Management; Paquin Entertainment Group; Peters Management, Michele; Rustron Music Productions; Sphere Productions; World Wide Management

Novelty Bandstand (International) Entertainment Agency; Cavalry Productions; Class Acts; Front Row Management Corp.; Fudpucker Entertainment; Hall Entertainment & Events, Bill; Palmetto Productions; Paquin Entertainment Group; Smith and Associates, Michael; Stahl Entertainment, Bernie

Pop Adelaide Rock Exchange; Afterschool Publishing Company; AKO Productions; Alan Agency, Mark; Alexas Music Productions; All Star Talent Agency; Allen Entertainment Development, Michael; Amethyst Group Ltd., The; Anjoli Productions; Ardenne Int'l Inc.; Are, The Entertainment Company; ArkLight Management Co.; Artiste Records/Paul Levesque Management Inc.; Artistic Developments International, Inc.; Artists Only Management Company Inc., The; Asia Arts Management; Atch Records and Productions; Available Management; baby sue; Baxter Management, Dick; Beasley & Associates; Best Management Inc., Nigel; Big Beat Productions, Inc.; Big J Productions; Biscuit Productions Inc.; Blue Cat Agency/El Gato Azul Agency, The; Blue Ox Talent Agency; Blumenauer Artists, Geoffrey; Bouquet-Orchid Enterprises; Brothers Management Associates; C & M Productions Management Group; Capitol Management; Carman Productions, Inc.; Cash Enterprises, Ernie; Cedar Creek Productions and Management; Christie Management, Paul; Class Act Productions/Management; Clockwork Entertainment Management Agency; Clugston Organization Pty. Ltd., The Neil; Coffer Management, Raymond; Concept 2000 Inc.; Corvalan-Condliffe Management; Countdown Entertainment; Countrywide Producers; Courtright Management Inc.; Crash Productions; Creative Action Music Group; Creative Star Management; Criss-Cross Industries; Cude's Good American Music/Talent/Casting Agency, Bobby Lee; Curly Maple Media; Current Records/Management; D & M Entertainment Agency; DAS Communications, Ltd.; de Courcy Management, Brian; De Miles Company, The Edward; Diamond Literary; DiLeo Management, Liesa; DMR Agency; Earth Tracks Artists Agency; Ellipse Personal Management; Emarco Management; Entertainment Company, The; Entourage Entertainment; Eternal Talent/Squigmonster Management; Evans Productions, Scott; Fat City Artists; Fenchel Entertainment Agency, Fred T.; First Time Management; Flash Attractions Agency; Fletcher Entertainment Group; Foley Entertainment; Freedman Entertainment, Peter; Fritz Management, Ken; Front Row Management Corp.; Gangland Artists; Gibson Management Inc.; Golden Bull Productions; Golden City International; Golden Guru Entertainment; Goodwin Moore & Associates; Grass Management; Great Lakes Country Talent Agency; Greeley Entertainment, Chris; Greenberg, Law Offices Of Gary; Hardman Management, Dustin; Hawkins Management Associates, Paul; Henderson Group Music; Hidden Studios; Holiday Productions, Doc; Howard Management, Kathy; Hulen Enterprises; Imani Entertainment Inc.; International Talent Network; Issachar Management; Its Happening Present Entertainment; Jackson Artists Corp.; James Gang Management; James Management, Roger; Jampop Ltd.; Jana Jae Enterprises; JCHC Music; Junquera Productions, C.; Kaltenbach Personal Management, R.J.; Kaufman Management; King Agency, Inc., Howard; Kirk, Jeff; Knight Agency, Bob; Landslide Management; Let Us Entertain You Co., The; Levy Mgt, Rick; Lindsay Productions, Doris/Successful Productions; LMP Management Firm; Lutz Entertainment Agency, Richard; McDonnell Group, The; McManus Management, Andrew; MAGIAN; Maine-ly Country Music; Manapro Entertainment; Marble Entertainment Co.; Mark One-The Agency; Martin Productions, Rick; Mayo & Company, Phil; Megalopoulos Management; Merri-Webb Productions; Miller & Company, Thomas J.; Monopoly Management; Moore Entertainment Group; Music Man Promotions; Music Management Associates; Music Matters; Music

Services; Nanoia Productions, Frank; Nason Enterprises, Inc.; NIC Of Tyme Productions, Inc.; Northstar Artist Management; Noteworthy Productions; Noveau Talent; Nowag's National Attractions, Craig; OB-1 Entertainment; Office, Inc., The; On Stage Management Inc.; Oregon Musical Artists; O'Reilly Management, Ltd., Dee; Orpheus Entertainment; Paradise Productions; Paton Management, Dave; Paul Entertainment Group, Inc., Jackie; Performance Group; Performers of the World Inc.; Personal Management, Inc.; Peterson Creative Management, Paul; Pitzer Artist Management, Gregory; Platinum Ears Ltd.; Platinum Gold Music; Power Star Management; Prestige Artistes; Pro Talent Consultants; Rabin Management, Gary; Rainbow Collection Ltd.; Rainbow Collection, Ltd., The; RANA International Music Group, Inc.; Ranke & Associates, Ltd., Ron; Raz Management Co.; Reeder Productions, Inc., Walt; Riot Management; Risavy Inc. R.F.; Rix Management P/L, Peter; RNJ Productions, Inc.; Rogue Management; Rothschild Productions Inc., Charles R.; Schonfeld and Associates, Lonny; Schwartz Management, Debbie; Scott Entertainment, Dick; Shapiro & Company, C.P.A.; Sherman Artist Management & Development, Mickey; Shute Management Pty. Ltd., Phill; Silver Bow Management; Simmons Management Group; Skorman Productions, Inc., T.; Skyline Music Corp.; Sopro, Inc.; Sound '86 Talent Management; Sphere Productions; Sportsman Music Entertainment Group; Star Vest Management Associates Inc.; Steele Management; Strictley Biziness Music Management; Summit Productions/Stellar Productions; Sunset Promotions of Chicago Inc.; T.J. Booker Ltd.; T.S.J. Productions Inc., The; Talent Associates of Wisconsin, Inc.; Tas Music Co./Dave Tasse Entertainment; Tilton Management, Terri; Total Acting Experience, A; Triangle Talent, Inc.; Umbrella Artists Management, Inc.; Weekes Writes; Westwood Entertainment Group; Wood Artist Management, Richard; World Wide Management; Wyatt Management Worldwide, Inc.; Y-Not Productions; Zar Management

Rap Afterschool Publishing Company; Artists Only Management Company, Inc., The; Artists'/Heller Agency; Atch Records and Productions; Beasley & Associates; Biscuit Productions Inc.; Broadwest Management; Creative Star Management; Current Records/Management; Cycle Of Fifths Management, Inc.; DeMore Management; Earth Tracks Artists Agency; First Time Management; Good Music Management; Greenberg, Law Offices Of Gary; H.L.A. Music; Hawkins Management Associates, Paul; Holiday Productions, Doc; Hulen Enterprises; Imani Entertainment Inc.; Its Happening Present Entertainment; JAS Management; JFK Entertainment Production Inc.; Jupiter Productions; KKR Entertainment Group; Kuper-Lam Management; Malla Entertainment; Marble Entertainment Co.; Milestone Media; Monster Communications, Inc.; Music Man Promotions; Music Services; Nelson Entertainment Inc., Brian; Paul Entertainment Group, Inc., Jackie; Perkins Production and Management Inc., Ronnie; P-M Street Artist Development; Precision Management; Rainbow Collection, Ltd., The; Reeder Productions, Inc., Walt; Renaissance Entertainment Group; Riot Management; Scott Entertainment, Dick; Squad 16; Strictley Biziness Music Management; Van Pol Management, Hans

R&B ACR Productions; Adelaide Rock Exchange; Alan Agency, Mark; Allen Entertainment Development, Michael; Aloha Entertainment; Amethyst Group Ltd., The; Anjoli Productions; Artistic Developments International, Inc.; Artists Only Management Company, The; Artists'/Heller Agency; Atch Records and Productions; Atlantic Entertainment Group; Available Management; Barnard Management Services; Beacon Kendall Entertainment; Big J Productions; Biscuit Productions Inc.; Bivins' Productions, J.; Black Stallion Country Productions, Inc.; Bojo Productions Inc.; Bouquet-Orchid Enterprises; Broadwest Management; Brothers Management Associates; Capitol Management; Carman Productions, Inc.; Cedar Creek Productions and Management; Christie Management, Paul; Class Act Productions/Management; Class Acts; Community Music Center of Houston; Concept 2000 Inc.; Corvalan-Condliffe Management; Countdown Entertainment; Country Star Attractions; Countrywide Producers; Creative Action Music Group; Creative Star Management; Criss-Cross Industries; Curly Maple Media; Current Records/Management; D & M Entertainment Agency; De Miles Company, The Edward; DeMore Management; DiLeo Management, Liesa; Dinwoodie Management, Andrew; ECI Inc.; Elko's Talent Agency, Inc.; Ellipse Personal Management; Entertainment Company, The; Entertainment Group, The; Entertainment Services International; Evans Productions, Scott; Foley Entertainment; Freedman Entertainment, Peter; Frick Enterprises, Bob Scott; Front Row Management Corp.; Gangland Artists; Gibson Management Inc.; Global Assault Management; Golden Bull Productions; Golden City International; Good Music Management; Gramercy Park Entertainment; Grass Management; Greenberg, Law Offices Of Gary; M. Harrell & Associates; Hawkins Management Associates, Paul; Holiday Productions, Doc; Hulen Enterprises; Imani Entertainment Inc.; Issachar Management; Its Happening Present Entertainment; Jackson Artists Corp.; Jacobs Management; James Gang Management; Jampop Ltd.; JAS Management; JFK Entertainment Production Inc.; KKR Entertainment Group; Knight Agency, Bob; Kuper-Lam Management; Landslide Management; Let Us Entertain You Co., The; Levinson Entertainment Ventures International, Inc.; Levy Mgt, Rick; LMP Management Firm; McDonnell Group, The; MAGIAN; Malla Entertainment; Manapro Entertainment; Marble Entertainment Co.; Master Entertainment; Mayo & Company, Phil; Merri-Webb Productions; Moore Entertainment Group; Music Matters; Nanoia Productions, Frank; Nelson Entertainment Inc., Brian; NIC Of Tyme Productions, Inc.; Nilsson Production, Christina; Noveau Talent; Nowag's National Attractions, Craig; Office, Inc., The; On Stage Management Inc.; Oregon Musical Artists; Orpheus Entertainment; Paradise Productions; Paul Entertainment Group, Inc., Jackie; Performers of the World Inc.; Perkins Production and Management Inc., Ronnie; Personal Management, Inc.; Platinum Ears Ltd.; P-M Street Artist Development; Power Star Management;

Precision Management; Rainbow Collection, Ltd., The; RANA International Music Group, Inc.; Red Giant Records and Publishing; Reeder Productions, Inc., Walt; Renaissance Entertainment Group; Riot Management; Rix Management P/L, Peter; Rustron Music Productions; Scott Entertainment, Dick; Sherman Artist Management & Development, Mickey; Shute Management Pty. Ltd., Phill; Simmons Management Group; Sirius Entertainment; Smash Pop International; Sopro, Inc.; Sphere Productions; Star Vest Management Associates Inc.; Steele Management; Strictley Biziness Music Management; Summit Productions/Stellar Productions; T.S.J. Productions Inc., The; Talent Associates of Wisconsin, Inc.; Tas Music Co./Dave Tasse Entertainment; Three E Entertainment; 315 Beale Studios/Taliesyn Entertainment; Tilton Management, Terri; Total Acting Experience, A; 214 Entertainment; Van Pol Management, Hans; Vault Management; Weekes Writes; Wood Artist Management, Richard; World Wide Management; Wyatt Management Worldwide, Inc.; Y-Not Productions

Religious Alexas Music Productions; All Star Management; All Star Talent Agency; Allen Entertainment Development, Michael; Arise Music; Atch Records and Productions; ATI Music; baby sue; Baxter Management, Dick; Bivins' Productions, J.; Bojo Productions Inc.; Bouquet-Orchid Enterprises; Brier Patch Music; Brock & Associates; C & M Productions Management Group; Capitol Management; Cash Enterprises, Ernie; Cavalry Productions; Cedar Creek Productions and Management; Community Music Center of Houston; Concept 2000 Inc.; Country Star Attractions; Countrywide Producers; Crawfish Productions; Creative Star Management; DeMore Management; Direct Management; Doss Presents, Col. Buster; Fenchel Entertainment Agency, Fred T.; First Time Management; Fleming Artists Management; Frick Enterprises, Bob Scott; Front Row Management Corp.; Golden Bull Productions; Golden City International; Great Lakes Country Talent Agency; Gueststar Entertainment Agency; Hidden Studios; Holiday Productions, Doc; Jackson Artists Corp.; James Gang Management; Jampop Ltd.; Jan-A-Lou Enterprizes; JAS Management; JCHC Music; JFK Entertainment Production Inc.; KRC Records & Productions; L & R Management; L.D.F. Productions; Lari-Jon Promotions; Lindsay Productions, Doris/Successful Productions; MAGIAN; Magnum Music Corporation Ltd.; Maine-ly Country Music; Mayo & Company, Phil; Merri-Webb Productions; Music Services; Nanoia Productions, Frank; NIC Of Tyme Productions, Inc.; Nilsson Production, Christina; Oregon Musical Artists; Palmetto Productions; Perkins Production and Management Inc., Ronnie; Precision Management; Reed Sound Records, Inc.; Smith and Associates, Michael; Star Vest Management Associates Inc.; Starcrest Productions, Inc.; Strictley Biziness Music Management; Sunset Promotions of Chicago Inc.; Texas Music Masters; Theater Arts Network/Stephen Productions; Vokes Booking Agency

Rock ACR Productions; Adelaide Rock Exchange; AKO Productions; Alan Agency, Mark; All Star Management; All Star Talent Agency; Allen Entertainment Development, Michael; Aloha Entertainment; Amethyst Group Ltd., The; Ardenne Int'l Inc.; Are, The Entertainment Company; ArkLight Management Co.; Arslanian & Associates, Inc.; Artiste Records/Paul Levesque Management Inc.; Artistic Developments International Inc.; Artists Only Management Company, Inc., The; Artists'/Heller Agency; Asia Arts Management; Atch Records and Productions; Atlantic Entertainment Group; Available Management; baby sue; Bandstand (International) Entertainment Agency; Barnard Management Services; Beacon Kendall Entertainment; Beasley & Associates; Berkley Management, Michael; Big Beat Productions, Inc.; Big J Productions; Bivins' Productions, J.; Blue Cat Agency/El Gato Azul Agency, The; Blue Ox Talent Agency; Blumenauer Artists, Geoffrey; Bouquet-Orchid Enterprises; Brothers Management Associates; BSA Inc.; Capitol Management; Carman Productions, Inc.; Cash Enterprises, Ernie; Cedar Creek Productions and Management; Christie Management, Paul; Class Act Productions/Management; Class Acts; Clockwork Entertainment Management Agency; Clugston Organization Pty. Ltd., The Neil; Coffer Management, Raymond; Corvalan-Condliffe Management; Countdown Entertainment; Country Star Attractions; Countrywide Producers; Courtright Management Inc.; Crash Productions; Creative Action Music Group; Curly Maple Media; Current Records/Management; Cycle Of Fifths Management, Inc.; D & M Entertainment Agency; DAS Communications, Ltd.; de Courcy Management, Brian; De Miles Company, The Edward; DeMore Management; Deri Promotions USA-UK; Diamond Literary; DiLeo Management, Liesa; Dinwoodie Management, Andrew; DMR Agency; Earth Tracks Artists Agency; Ellipse Personal Management; Emarco Management; Entertainment Group, The; Entertainment Management Enterprises; Entertainment Services International; Entourage Entertainment; Eternal Talent/Squigmonster Management; Fat City Artists; Flash Attractions Agency; Fletcher Entertainment Group; Foley Entertainment; Fritz Management, Ken; Gallup Entertainment; Gangland Artists; Golden Bull Productions; Golden Guru Entertainment; Good Music Management; Goodwin Moore & Associates; Grass Management; Greeley Entertainment, Chris; Greenberg, Law Offices Of Gary; H.L.A. Music; Hardman Management, Dustin; Hardway Music Management; Hellman Productions, Kevin; Henderson Group Music; Hidden Studios; Horizon Management Inc.; Howard Management, Kathy; Hulen Enterprises; Insinna Management, Paul; Intermountain Talent; International Talent Network; Issachar Management; Jackson Artists Corp.; JCHC Music; Johnson and Associates, Neville L.; Jupiter Productions; Kaltenbach Personal Management, R.J.; Kaufman Management; King Agency, Inc., Howard; Kirk, Jeff; KKR Entertainment Group; Knight Agency, Bob; L.D.F. Productions; Landslide Management; Lari-Jon Promotions; Let Us Entertain You Co., The; Levinson Entertainment Ventures International, Inc.; LMP Management Firm; McDonnell Group, The; McManus Management, Andrew; MAGIAN; Maine-ly Country Music; Malla Entertainment; Marble Entertainment Co.; Mark One-The Agency; Master Entertainment; Mayo & Company, Phil; Merri-Webb Productions; Milestone Media; Miller & Company, Thomas J.; Moore Entertainment Group; Morelli Enterprises, Thomas; Music Man Promotions; Music Matters; Music Services; Nason Enterprises, Inc.; Nelson Entertainment Inc., Brian; Network Entertainment Service Inc.; New Sound Atlanta, Inc.; NIC Of Tyme Productions, Inc.; Night Art Record Co.; Nilsson Production, Christina; Nole CPA, Sam J.; Northstar Artist Management; Nowag's National Attractions, Craig; OB-1 Entertainment; Office, Inc., The; On Stage Management Inc.; Oregon Musical Artists; O'Reilly Management, Ltd., Dee; Orpheus Entertainment; Paradise Productions; Paton Management, Dave; Pearson Management; Performance Group; Personal Management, Inc.; Peters Management, Michele; Peterson Creative Management, Paul; Phil's Entertainment Agency Limited; Phusion; Pipeline Artist Management; Pitzer Artist Management, Gregory; Platinum Ears Ltd.; Power Star Management; Prestige Artistes; Pro Talent Consultants; Propas Management Corporation; Rabin Management, Gary; Rainbow Collection Ltd.; Rainbow Collection, Ltd., The; RANA International Music Group, Inc.; Raz Management Co.; Red Giant Records and Publishing; Risavy, Inc., A.F.; Rix Management P/L, Peter; Rock Whirled Music Management; Rogue Management; Rothschild Productions Inc., Charles R.; Rustron Music Productions; S.T.A.R.S. Productions; Sandcastle Productions; Savvy Blonde Management; Schonfeld and Associates, Lonny; Schwartz Management, Debbie; Shapiro & Company, C.P.A.; Sherman Artist Management & Development, Mickey; Shute Management Pty. Ltd., Phill; Silver Bow Management; Simmons Management Group; Sirius Entertainment; Skyline Music Corp.; Smash Pop International; Sopro, Inc.; Sound Direction Inc.; Sound '86 Talent Management; Southern Concerts; SP Talent Associates; Squad 16; Star Artist Management Inc.; Star Vest Management Associates Inc.; Steele Management; Stewart Management, Steve; Strictley Biziness Music Management; Summit Productions/Stellar Productions; Sunrize Band; Sunset Promotions of Chicago Inc.; T.J. Booker Ltd.; T.S.J. Productions Inc., The; Talent Associates of Wisconsin, Inc.; Tas Music Co./Dave Tasse Entertainment; Theater Arts Network/Stephen Productions; 315 Beale Studios/Taliesyn Entertainment; Transatlantic Management; Triangle Talent, Inc.; TSMB Productions; 214 Entertainment; Umbrella Artists Management, Inc.; Universal Music Marketing; Upfront Management; Varrasso Management, Richard; Vault Management; Westwood Entertainment Group; Wolftracks Management; World Wide Management; Wyatt Management Worldwide, Inc.; Y-Not Productions; Zar Management

World aaLN International; Asia Arts Management; Curly Maple Media; Dietrolequinte Art Company; Entertainment Works; Flash Attractions Agency; Fleming Artists Management; Grass Management; Hellman Productions, Kevin; Issachar Management; Left Field Productions/Poggi Promotional Services; Nole, CPA, Sam J.; Right Time Productions; Squad 16; TCA Group, Inc.; Vault Management

Managers and Booking Agents/'94-'95 Changes

The following markets appeared in the 1994 edition of *Songwriter's Market* but are absent from the 1995 edition. Most of these companies failed to respond to our request for an update of their listing for a variety of reasons. For example, they may have gone out of business or they may have requested deletion from the 1995 edition because they are backlogged with material. If we know the specific reason, it appears within parentheses.

Absolute Entertainment Inc. (unable to contact)
The Agency
Greg Aliferis Management
American Concert
American Family Entertainment
American Family Talent
Artist Alexander/Miracle Records (unable to contact)
Artist Representation and Management
Back Porch Blues
Backstage Productions International
Bause Associates
Bill Boyd Productions
Bright Spark Songs Pty. Ltd.
Caramba Art
CFB Productions, Inc.
Circuit Rider Talent & Management Co.

CLE Management Group/NY-Concert Event
D&R Entertainment
Debbie Dean and Assoc. (unable to contact)
Direct Box Music
Michael Dixon Management
Driven Rain Management
EME International
Entertainment Productions Co.
Entertainment Unlimited Artist Inc.
Events Unlimited
Freade Sounds Entertainment & Recording Studio
Full Tilt Management
Future Star Entertainment
Gayle Enterprises, Inc.
Great South Artists/GSA Music Management
Hale Enterprises
Hawkeye Attractions

Heavyweight Productions & Up Front Management
High Tide Management (unable to contact)
Holiday Productions
Iron John Management
Jackson/Jones Management
Jam Presents
Sheldon Kagan Productions
Kooch Management
Line-Up Promotions, Inc.
Loconto Productions
M&M Talent Agency Inc.
McLavene & Associates
Magic Management and Productions
Management Associates, Inc.
Mardi Gras Music Fest, Inc.
MCI Music Group
Media Promotion Enterprises
Alex Mellon Management
Greg Menza & Associates

Metropolitan Talent Authority (requested deletion)
M-5 Management, Inc.
Midcoast, Inc.
Mighty Management
Mt. High Entertainment
Music City Co-op, Inc.
Muskrat Productions, Inc.
Nash Angeles Inc.
National Entertainment, Inc. (unable to contact)
Jack Nelson & Associates
Nelson Road Management
New Artist's Productions
Oak Street Music
On The Level Music! (unable to contact)
Ontario Bluegrass Inc.
The Perception Works Inc.

Placer Publishing (requested deletion)
Raw Entertainment Revel Management
Rock-A-Billy Artist Agency
Jay B. Ross Entertainment
Round Robin
Rusch Entertainment Agency
Brandon Saul Management
William Seip Management, Inc.
770 Music Inc.
Sheils/Campbell and Associates
Shoe String Booking Agency
Silver Creek Partnership
Brad Simon Organization, Inc.
Skyscraper Entertainment
Southern Nights Inc.
Spider Entertainment Co.

State of the Art Entertainment
Steele Production
Bill Stein Associates Inc.
Al Straten Enterprises
Triage International (requested deletion)
Tryclops Ltd.
Valex Talent Agency
Velvett Recording Company
Victory Artists
Vision Management
Warren Pro-Motions (unable to contact)
Wave Digital/Grif Musik/Producer Eric "Griffy" Greif-Solvbjerg (unable to contact)
Wow Management

Advertising, AV and Commercial Music Firms

The music used in commercial and audiovisual presentations is secondary to the picture (for TV, film or video) or the message being conveyed. Commercial music must enhance the product. It must get consumers' attention, move them in some way and, finally, motivate them—all without overpowering the message or product it accompanies. Songwriters in this area are usually strong composers, arrangers and, sometimes, producers.

More than any other market listed in this book, the commercial music market expects composers to have made an investment in their material before beginning to submit. When dealing with commercial music firms, especially audiovisual firms and music libraries, high quality production is very important. Your demo may be kept on file at one of these companies and used or sold as you sent it. Also, a list of your credits should be part of your submission to give the company an idea of your experience in this field. In general, it's important to be as professional as you can in your submissions to these markets. Fully produced demo tapes and complete press kits will get your product recognized and heard.

Commercial music and jingle writing can be a lucrative field for the composer/ songwriter with energy, a gift for strong hook melodies, and the ability to write in many different styles. The problem is, there are many writers and few jobs—it's a very competitive field.

Advertising agencies

Ad agencies work on assignment as their clients' needs arise. They work closely with their clients on radio and TV broadcast campaigns. Through consultation and input from the creative staff, ad agencies seek jingles and music to stimulate the consumer to identify with a product or service.

When contacting ad agencies, keep in mind they are searching for music that can capture and then hold an audience's attention. Most jingles are quick, with a strong, memorable hook that the listener will easily identify with. Remember, though, that when an agency listens to a demo, it is not necessarily looking for a finished product so much as for an indication of creativity and diversity. Most composers put together a reel of excerpts of work from previous projects, or short pieces of music which show they can write in a variety of styles.

Audiovisual firms

Audiovisual firms create a variety of products. Their services may range from creating film and video shows for sales meetings (and other corporate gatherings) and educational markets, to making motion pictures and TV shows. With the increase of home video use, how-to videos are a big market now for audiovisual firms, as are spoken word educational videos.

Like advertising firms, AV firms look for versatile, well-rounded songwriters. The key to submitting demos to these firms is to demonstrate your versatility in writing specialized background music and themes. Listings for companies will tell what facet(s) of the audiovisual field they are involved in and what types of clients they serve.

Commercial music houses and music libraries

Commercial music houses are companies which are contracted (either by an advertising agency or the advertiser himself) to compose custom jingles. Since they are neither an ad agency nor an audiovisual firm, their main concern is music. And they use a lot of it—some composed by inhouse songwriters and some contributed by outside writers.

Music libraries are a bit different in that their music is not custom composed for a specific client. They provide a collection of instrumental music in many different styles that, for an annual fee or on a per-use basis, the customer can use however he chooses (most often in audiovisual and multi-media applications).

Commercial music houses and music libraries are identified as such in the following listings by **bold** typeface.

The commercial music market is similar to most other businesses in one aspect: experience is important. Until you develop a list of credits, pay for your work may not be high. Don't pass up work opportunities if the job is non- or low paying. These assignments will help make contacts, add to your experience and improve your marketability.

Many of the companies listed in this section pay by the job, but there may be some situations where the company asks you to sign a contract that will specify royalty payments. If this happens, research the contract thoroughly, and know exactly what is expected of you and how much you'll be paid.

Sometimes, depending on the particular job and the company, a composer/songwriter will be asked to sell one-time rights or all rights. One-time rights entail using your material for one presentation only. All rights means that the buyer can use your work any way he chooses for as long as he likes. Again, be sure you know exactly what you're giving up, and how the company may use your music in the future.

For additional names and addresses of advertising agencies who may use jingles and/or commercial music, refer to the *Standard Directory of Advertising Agencies* (National Register Publishing Co.). For a list of audiovisual firms, check out the latest edition of *Audiovisual Marketplace* (published by R.R. Bowker).

THE AD AGENCY, Box 2316, Sausalito CA 94965. Creative Director: Michael Carden. Advertising agency and **jingle/commercial music production house**. Clients include business, industry and retail. Estab. 1971. Uses the services of music houses, independent songwriter/composers and lyricists for scoring of videos and commercials, background music for videos, jingles for radio and commercials for radio and TV. Commissions 20 composers and 15 lyricists/year. Pays by the job or by the hour.
How to Contact: Query with résumé of credits. Prefers cassette with 5-8 songs and lyric sheet. SASE, but prefers to keep materials on file. Reports in 2 weeks.
Music: Uses variety of musical styles for commercials, promotion, TV, video presentations.
Tips: "Our clients and our needs change frequently."

THE AD TEAM, Suite 620, 11900 Biscayne Blvd., Miami FL 33181. (305)899-2030. President: Zevin Auerbach. Advertising agency. Clients include automobile dealerships, radio stations, TV stations, retail. Seeking background music for commercials and jingles. Commissions 4-6 songwriters. Pays by the job.
How to Contact: Submit demo tape of previously aired work. Prefers cassette. Does not return material.
Music: Uses all styles of music for all kinds of assignments. Most assignments include writing jingles for radio and television campaigns.

ADVANCE ADVERTISING AGENCY, #207, 606 E. Belmont, Fresno CA 93701. (209)445-0383. Manager: Martin Nissen. Advertising agency. Clients include various retail, general services. Estab. 1952. Uses the services of music houses and independent songwriters/composers for background music and jingles for radio and TV commercials. Pays by the job. Buys all rights.

How to Contact: Submit demo tape of previous work. Prefers cassette with any number of songs. Does not return material; but prefers to keep on file. Include business card.
Music: Uses nostalgic, Dixieland and traditional jazz for commercials.
Tips: "Listen carefully to the assignment. Don't be too sophisticated or abstract. Stay simple and translatable. Aim toward individual listener."

ALEXIS MUSIC INC. (ASCAP), MARVELLE MUSIC CO. (BMI), GABAL MUSIC (SESAC), Box 532, Malibu CA 90265. (213)463-5998. President: Lee Magid. Music publishing and production. Clients include all types—record companies and advertising agencies. Estab. 1960. Uses the services of independent songwriters and composers for jingles, commercials for radio and TV and manufacturers, events, conventions, etc. Commissions 5 composers and 5 lyricists/year. Pays by the job or by royalty. Buys all rights.
How to Contact: Submit demo tape of previous work or tape demonstrating composition skills or query with résumé of credits. Prefers cassette (or VHS videocassette) with 3 pieces and lyric sheets. "If interested, we will contact you." Does not return material. Include phone number and address on tape. Reports in 6 weeks.
Music: Uses R&B, gospel, blues, jazz, Latin, Afro-Cuban, country; anything of substance.
Tips: "Stay with it and keep your ears to the melody."

ALLEGRO MUSIC, 6500-4 Vanalden Ave., Reseda CA 91316. (818)708-1917. Owner: Daniel O'Brien. Scoring service, **jingle/commercial music production house.** Clients include film-makers, advertisers, network promotions and aerobics. Estab. 1991. Uses the services of independent songwriters/composers and lyricists for scoring of feature films and commercials, background music for aerobics, jingles for ad agencies and promotions, and commercials for radio and TV. Commissions 3 composers and 1 lyricist/year. Pays $500-2,000/job; or 50% royalty (composers).
How to Contact: Query with résumé of credits or write first to arrange personal interview. Prefers cassette and lyric sheet. SASE. Reports in 6 weeks (if interested). Please, no phone calls.
Music: Varied: Contemporary pop to orchestral.
Tips: "Don't over-hype your abilities. Be able to deliver on your claims. Be persistent. Accept that your success is up to you alone."

ANDERSON COMMUNICATIONS, Dept. SM, 2245 Godby Rd., Atlanta GA 30349. (404)766-8000. President: Al Anderson. Producer: Vanessa Vaughn. Advertising agency and syndication operation. Estab. 1971. Clients include major corporations, institutions and media. Uses the services of music houses for scoring and jingles for TV and radio commercials and background music for TV and radio programs. Commissions 5-6 songwriters or composers and 6-7 lyricists/year. Pays by the job. Buys all rights.
How to Contact: Call first and obtain permission to submit. Prefers cassette. SASE, but prefers to keep material on file. Reports in 2 weeks or "when we have projects requiring their services."
Music: Uses a variety of music for music beds for commercials and jingles for nationally syndicated radio programs and commercials targeted at the black consumer market.
Tips: "Be sure that the composition plays well in a 60 second format."

ANGEL FILMS COMPANY, 967 Hwy. 40, New Franklin MO 65274-9778. Phone/Fax: (314)698-3900. President: Arlene Hulse. Motion picture and record production company (Angel One Records). Estab. 1980. Uses the services of music houses, independent songwriters/composers and lyricists for scoring of feature films, TV programs and commercials, background music for feature films, television productions and commercials, and jingles. Commissions 12-20 composers and 12-20 lyricists/year. Payment depends upon budget; each project has a different pay scale. Buys all rights.
How to Contact: Submit demo tape of previous work, query with résumé of credits. Prefers cassette (or VHS videocassette) with 3 pieces and lyric and lead sheet. "Do not send originals." SASE, but prefers to keep material on file. Reports in 1 month.
Music: Uses basically MOR, but will use anything (except C&W and religious) for record production, film, television and cartoon scores.
Tips: "Don't copy others, just do the best that you can. We freelance all our work for our film and television production company, plus we are always looking for that one break-through artist for Angel One Records."

Listings of companies within this section which are either commercial music production houses or music libraries will have that information printed in boldface type.

ANGLE FILMS, Suite 240, 1341 Ocean Ave., Santa Monica CA 90401. President: John Engel. Motion picture production company and freelance producer. Estab. 1985. Clients include advertising agencies and motion picture production/distribution companies. Uses the services of independent songwriters/ composers for scoring of feature films and short dramas. Pays by the job. Buys all rights.
How to Contact: Submit demo tape of previous work. Prefers cassette with 5 pieces and lyric sheet. Does not return material; prefers to keep on file. Reports only if interested.
Music: Uses all genres for short drama and feature films.
Tips: "Present varied composition talents. Broad composition background and orchestration are important."

APON PUBLISHING COMPANY, INC., Dept. SM, Box 3082 Steinway Station, Long Island City NY 11103. (718)721-5599. Manager: Don Zeemann. **Jingle/commercial music production house, classical music library, music sound effect library.** Clients include background music companies, motion picture companies and advertising agencies. Estab. 1957. Uses the services of music houses for background music, jingles for advertising agencies and commercials for radio and TV. Payment is negotiated. Buys all rights.
How to Contact: Query with résumé of credits, or call first to arrange personal interview. Send demo cassette with background music, no voices. Prefers cassette with 2-5 pieces. Does not return unsolicited material. Reports in 2 months. No certified or registered mail accepted.
Music: Uses only background music, no synthesizer life instruments.

ATLANTIC FILM AND VIDEO, Dept. SM, 171 Park Lane, Massapequa NY 11758. (516)798-4106. Sound Designer: Michael Canzoneri. Motion picture production company. Clients include industrial/ commercial. Estab. 1986. Uses the services of independent songwriters/composers for background music for films. Commissions 1 composer and 1 lyricist/year. Pays $250/job. Buys one-time rights.
How to Contact: Submit demo tape of previous work. Prefers cassette or 7½ ips reel-to-reel. "Please specify what role you had in creating the music: composer, performer, etc." SASE, but prefers to keep material on file. Reports in 2 months.
Music: Uses jazz—modern, classical for films.

*AUTHENTIC MARKETING, 25 W. Fairview Ave., Dover NJ 07801. (201)366-9326. Director: Dan Kassell. Advertising agency. Estab. 1986. Represents independent songwriters/composers, lyricists and arrangers. Also provides services as a jazz artist's rep, business consultant or promotion consultant in New York City.
How to Contact: Query with résumé of credits or submit demo tape of previous work. Does not return unsolicited material. Reports in 6 weeks.
Music: Uses jazz for background music for videoscripts.
Tips: "Blindly mailing stuff is a waste of time. Send a letter stating what is on your tape along with a résumé."

AUGUSTUS BARNETT ADVERTISING/DESIGN, Dept. SM, 632 St. Helens Ave., Tacoma WA 98402. (206)627-8508. President/Creative Director: Augustus Barnett. Advertising agency/design firm. Clients include food and service, business to business and retail advertisers. Estab. 1981. Uses the services of independent songwriters/composers for scoring of and background music for corporate video work, and commercials for radio. Commissions 1-2 composers and 0-1 lyricist/year. Buys all rights, one-time rights or for multiple use.
How to Contact: Query with résumé of credits; write first to arrange personal interview. Prefers cassette. Does not return unsolicited material; prefers to keep on file. Reports in 4 months.
Music: Uses up-tempo, pop and jazz for educational films and slide presentations.

BASSET & BECKER ADVERTISING, Box 2825, Columbus GA 31902. (706)327-0763. Partner: Bill Becker. Advertising agency. Clients include medical/health care, banking, auto dealers, industrial, family recreation/sporting goods, business to business advertisers. Estab. 1972. Uses the services of music houses and independent songwriters/composers for scoring of and background music for TV spots and AV presentations, jingles for TV spots, AV presentations and radio, and commercials for radio and TV. Commissions 2 composers/year. "Prefers to work with engineer/producer, not directly with composer." Pays by the job. Buys all rights.

The asterisk before a listing indicates that the listing is new in this edition. New markets are often the most receptive to unsolicited submissions.

How to Contact: Submit demo tape of previous work. Prefers cassette, 7.5/15 ips reel-to-reel, or ¾ or VHS videocassette. Does not return unsolicited material; prefers to keep on file.

RON BERNS & ASSOCIATES, 520 N. Michigan Ave., Chicago IL 60611. (312)527-2800. President: Ron Berns. Advertising agency. Uses services of independent songwriters for jingles. Pays by the job. Buys all rights.
How to Contact: Submit demo tape of previous work. Prefers cassette. Prefers studio produced demo. Does not return unsolicited material; prefers to keep on file. Reports when needed.

THE BLACKWOOD AGENCY, INC., 2125 University Park Dr., Okemos MI 48864. (517)349-6770. Production Manager: Steven Gaffe. Advertising agency. Estab. 1979. Clients include financial and package goods firms. Uses services of music houses for scoring of commercials and training films, background music for slide productions, jingles for clients and commercials for radio and TV. Commissions 3 composers/year. Pays by the job. Buys all rights.
How to Contact: Submit demo tape of previous work. Prefers cassette (or ¾" videocassette) with 6-10 songs. SASE, but prefers to keep material on file.
Tips: "Give us good demo work."

BLATTNER/BRUNNER INC., 814 Penn Ave., Pittsburgh PA 15222. (412)263-2979. Broadcast Production Coordinator: Nan Quatchak. Clients include retail/consumer, service, high-tech/industrial/medical. Estab. 1975. Uses the services of music houses and independent songwriters/composers for background music for TV and radio spots and jingles for TV and radio spots. Commissions 2-3 composers/year. Pays by the job. Buys all rights or one-time rights, depending on the job.
How to Contact: Submit demo tape of previous work demonstrating background music or jingle skills. Prefers clearly labeled cassette (or VHS or ¾" videocassette) with 3-5 songs. Does not return material. Reports in 1-2 months.
Music: Uses up-beat, "unique-sounding music that stands out" for commercials and industrial videos.
Tips: "Send relevant work in conjunction to the advertising business—i.e., jingles."

*BLUE EARTH RECORDINGS CORP., 210 Blue Earth Lane, Harrisburg IL 62946. (618)252-6434. Director: Richard Banks. Advertising agency, audiovisual firm and **jingle/commercial music production house.** Clients include musicians, artists, radio stations. Estab. 1989. Uses the services of independent songwriters/composers and lyricists for background music and jingles for radio and TV. Commissions 4 composers/year. Pays by the job. Buys all rights and one time rights.
How to Contact: Write or call first and obtain permission to submit. Prefers cassette. Does not return material; prefers to keep on file.
Music: Uses all types.
Tips "We are currently forming a library of bed music on speculation. Any inquiries welcome."

BRAUNCO VIDEO, INC., Dept. SM, Box 236, Warren IN 46792. (219)375-3148. Producer: Magley Tocsin. Video production company. Estab. 1988. Clients include industrial manufacturing, service companies, factories, United Way agencies, entertainers, songwriters, etc. Uses the services of independent songwriters/composers and house studio bands for jingles and background music for corporate video presentations. Commissions composers. Pays by the job. Buys all rights.
How to Contact: Submit demo tape of previous work or write to arrange personal interview. Prefers cassette or 15 ips reel-to-reel (or ¾" videocassette) with many pieces. "We have no use for lyric or vocals." Does not return unsolicited material.
Music: Uses up-tempo, heavy metal, R&B with a bit of jazz influence and soft music for promotional corporate demos.
Tips: "Believe in yourself."

BUTWIN & ASSOCIATES, INC., Suite 120, 7515 Wayzata Blvd., Minneapolis MN 55426. (612)546-0203. President: Ron Butwin. Clients include corporate and retail. Estab. 1977. Uses the services of music houses, lyricists and independent songwriters/composers for scoring, background music, jingles and commercials for radio, TV. Commissions 3-5 composers and 1-3 lyricists/year. Pays varying amount/job. Buys all rights.
How to Contact: Submit demo tape of previous work. Prefers cassette, ¼" videocassette. "We are only interested in high-quality professional work." Does not return material. Replies only if interested.
Music: Uses easy listening, up-tempo, pop and jazz for slide presentations and commercials.

CALDWELL VANRIPER, 1314 N. Meridian, Indianapolis IN 46202. (317)632-6501. Vice President/Executive Producer: Sherry Boyle. Advertising agency and public relations firm. Clients include industrial, financial and consumer/trade firms. Uses the services of music houses for scoring of TV commercials and video presentations, jingles and background music for commercials.

How to Contact: Submit demo tape of previously aired work. Prefers standard audio cassette. Does not return material. Prefers to keep materials on file. "Sender should follow up on submission. Periodic inquiry or reel update is fine."
Tips: "We do not use the services of independent songwriters. Due to the nature of our work, we go through music production houses for jingles, original scoring, or other music needs."

THE CAMPBELL GROUP, 326 N. Charles St., Baltimore MD 21201. (410)547-0600. Associate Creative Director: Dennis Boss. Advertising agency. Clients include hotels, restaurants, destinations, automobile dealerships, publications. Estab. 1986. Uses the services of music houses and independent songwriters/composers for scoring of video sales presentations, background music for radio and TV, jingles and commercials for radio and TV. Commissions 10 composers/year. Pays $3,000-6,000/job. Buys all rights or one-time rights.
How to Contact: Submit demo tape of previous work. Prefers cassette (or ½" VHS or ¾" cassette) with 5-10 songs. Does not return unsolicited material; prefers to keep on file. Reports in 2-3 weeks.
Music: Uses up-tempo, pop, jazz and classical for commercials.
Tips: "Send demo of work, rates, brochure if available."

CANARY PRODUCTIONS, Box 202, Bryn Mawr PA 19010. (215)825-1254. President: Andy Mark. **Music library.** Estab. 1984. Uses the services of music houses and independent songwriters for background music for AV use, jingles for all purposes, and commercials for radio and TV. Commissions 10 composers/year. Pays $100 per job. Buys all rights. "No songs, please!"
How to Contact: Submit demo tape of previous work. Prefers cassette with 5-10 pieces. Does not return material. Reports in 1 month.
Music: All styles, but concentrates on industrial. "We pay cash for produced tracks of all styles and lengths. Production value is imperative. No scratch tracks accepted."
Tips: "Be persistent and considerate of people's time."

CANTRAX RECORDERS, Dept. SM, 2119 Fidler Ave., Long Beach CA 90815. (310)498-6492. Owner: Richard Cannata. Recording studio. Clients include anyone needing recording services (i.e. industrial, radio, commercial). Estab. 1980. Uses the services of independent songwriters/composers and lyricists for background music for video, jingles for radio and TV. Commissions 10 composers/year. Pays by the job.
How to Contact: Query with résumé of credits or write to arrange personal interview. Submit demo tape of previous work. Prefers cassette or 7½/15 ips reel-to-reel (or DAT) with lyric sheets. "Indicate noise reduction if used. We prefer reel to reel." SASE, but prefers to keep material on file. Reports in 3 weeks.
Music: Uses jazz, New Age, rock, easy listening and classical for slide shows, jingles and soundtracks.
Tips: "Send a 7½' or 15 ips reel or DAT tape for us to audition; you must have a serious, professional attitude."

CASANOVA-PENDRILL PUBLICIDAD, Suite 300, 3333 Michelson, Irvine CA 92715. (714)474-5001. Production: Kevan Wilkinson. Advertising agency. Clients include consumer and corporate advertising—Hispanic markets. Estab. 1985. Uses the services of music houses, independent songwriters/ composers and lyricists for radio, TV and promotions. Pays by the job or per hour. Buys all rights or one-time rights.
How to Contact: Submit demo tape of previous work, tape demonstrating composition skills and manuscript showing music scoring skills. Prefers cassette (or ¾ videocassette). "Include a log indicating spot(s) titles." Does not return unsolicited material; prefers to keep on file.
Music: All types of Hispanic music (e.g., salsa, merengue, flamenco, etc.) for TV/radio advertising.

*CHANNEL 3 VIDEO, Box 8781, Warwick RI 02888. (401)461-1616. President: Jeffrey B. Page. Audiovisual firm and video production/post production services. Clients include educational, commercial, industrial, retail firms and others. Uses the services of music houses, independent songwriters/composers and lyricists for scoring of documentary works, background music for industrials, jingles for product presentations, commercials for radio and TV and multimedia events. Commissions 5 composers and 2 lyricists/year. Pays $50-500/job. Buys all rights or one-time rights; depends on the job.
How to Contact: Submit demo tape of previous work, tape demonstrating composition skills or manuscript showing music scoring skills. Prefers cassette or 15 ips reel-to-reel (or ¾" or ½" VHS videocassette) with 3-5 pieces and lyric or lead sheets. "All submissions will be put in permanent file and not returned. At the artist's request they will be destroyed if requested in writing." Reports back in 5 weeks.
Music: Uses all styles of music.

CHAPMAN RECORDING STUDIOS, 228 W. Fifth, Kansas City MO 64105. (816)842-6854. Contact: Chuck Chapman. Custom music and production. Clients include video and music producers, musicians

and corporations. Estab. 1973. Uses the services of independent songwriters/composers and arrangers for background music for video productions; jingles for radio, TV, corporations; and commercials for radio and TV. Commissions 4 composers and 4 lyricists/year. Buys all rights.
How to Contact: Call to arrange submission of tape demo. Prefers cassette. SASE, but prefers to keep material on file. Reports in 2 months.
Music: Uses all styles, all types for record releases, video, TV and radio productions; and up-tempo and pop for educational films, slide presentations and commercials.

CINEVUE, Box 428, Bostwick FL 32007. (904)325-5254. Director/Producer: Steve Postal. Motion picture production company. Estab. 1955. Serves all types of film distributors. Uses the services of independent songwriters and composers for scoring of and background music for films. Commissions 10 composers and 5 lyricists/year. Pays by the job. Buys all rights.
How to Contact: Submit demo tape of previous work. Prefers cassette with 10 pieces and lyric or lead sheet. SASE, but prefers to keep material on file. "Send good audio-cassette, then call me in a week." Reports in 3 weeks.
Music: Uses all styles of music for features (educational films and slide presentations). "Need horror film music on traditional instruments—no electronic music."
Tips: "Be flexible, fast—do first job free to ingratiate yourself and demonstrate your style."

CLEARVUE/eav INC., Dept. SM, 6465 N. Avondale, Chicago IL 60631. (312)775-9433. Chairman of the Board: William T. Ryan. President: Mark Ventling. Audiovisual firm. Serves the educational market. Estab. 1969. "We only produce core curriculum and enrichment videos for pre-primary through high school students." Uses the services of music houses and independent songwriters. Commissions 3 songwriters or composers/year. Pays by the job.
How to Contact: Query with résumé of credits, then submit demo tape of previous work. "We are seeking original video proposal and finished product focusing on the teaching of music skills." SASE. Reports in 2 weeks.
Tips: "Submit a résumé and demo tape. Follow up with a phone call in 3 weeks. Be sure to send SASE for a reply."

COAKLEY HEAGERTY, 1155 N. First St., San Jose CA 95112. (408)275-9400. Creative Director: Susann Rivera. Advertising agency. Clients include consumer, business to business and high tech firms. Estab. 1966. Uses the services of music houses for jingles for commercials. Commissions 15-20 songwriters/year. Pays by the job. Buys all rights.
How to Contact: Submit demo tape of previously aired work. Prefers cassette or 7½ ips reel-to-reel with 8-10 pieces. Does not return material; prefers to keep on file. Reports in 6 months.
Music: All kinds of music for jingles and music beds.
Tips: "Don't be pushy and call. I'll call when I find something I want. I'm turned off by aggressive behavior from vendors."

COMMUNICATIONS CONCEPTS INC., Box 661, Cape Canaveral FL 32920. (407)783-5320. Manager: Jim Lewis. Audiovisual firm. Clients include resorts, developments, medical and high tech industries. Uses the services of music houses, independent songwriters, lyricists and music libraries, background music and jingles for radio, TV and trade shows. Commissions 2-3 composers/year and 1-2 lyricists/year. Buys all rights or one-time rights.
How to Contact: Submit demo tape of previous work. Prefers cassette. Does not return material; prefers to keep on file.
Music: Corporate, contemporary and commercial.

COMMUNICATIONS FOR LEARNING, 395 Massachusetts Ave., Arlington MA 02174. (617)641-2350. Executive Producer/Director: Jonathan L. Barkan. Audiovisual and design firm. Clients include multinationals, industry, government, institutions, local, national and international nonprofits. Uses services of music houses and independent songwriters/composers for scoring and background music for TV, audiovisual and video soundtracks. Commissions 1-2 composers/year. Pays $2,000-3,000/job. Buys one-time rights of "library" music.
How to Contact: Submit demo tape of previous work or tape demonstrating composition skills. Prefers cassette or 7½ or 15 ips reel-to-reel (or ½" or ¾" videocassette). Does not return material; prefers to keep on file. "For each job we consider our entire collection." Reports "depending on needs."
Music: Uses all styles of music for all sorts of assignments.
Tips: "Please don't call. Just send good material and when we're interested, we'll be in touch."

CONTINENTAL PRODUCTIONS, Box 1219, Great Falls MT 59405. (406)761-5536. Production Sales/Marketing: Ken Cathey. Video production house. Clients include advertising agencies, business, industry and government. Uses the services of independent songwriters/composers and music houses for

TV commercials. Commissions 1-6 composers/year. Pays $85-500/job. Buys all rights or one-time rights.
How to Contact: Query with résumé of credits. Prefers cassette (or ½" VHS videocassette). Does not return material. Reports in 2 weeks.
Music: Uses contemporary music beds and custom jingles for TV and non-broadcast video.
Tips: "Songwriters need to build a working relationship by providing quality product in short order at a good price."

CORPORATE COMMUNICATIONS INC., Main St., Box 854, N. Conway NH 03860. (603)356-7011. President: Kimberly Beals. Advertising agency. Estab. 1983. Uses the services of music houses, independent songwriters/composers for background music, jingles and commercials for radio and TV. Commissions 2 or more composers/year. Pays by the job. Buys all rights or one-time rights.
How to Contact: Submit demo tape of previous work demonstrating composition skills. Prefers cassette (or ½" videocassette) with 5 songs. Does not return material; prefers to keep on file.
Music: Uses varying styles of music for varying assignments.

CREATIVE ASSOCIATES, Dept. SM, 44 Park Ave., Madison NJ 07940. (201)377-4440. Production Coordinator: Susan Graham. Audiovisual/multimedia firm. Clients include commercial, industrial firms. Estab. 1975. Uses the services of music houses and independent songwriters/composers for scoring of video programs, background music for press tours and jingles for new products. Pays $300-5,000/job. Buys all or one-time rights.
How to Contact: Submit demo tape of previous work demonstrating composition skills or query with résumé of credits. Prefers cassette or ½" or ¾" VHS videocassette. Prefers to keep material on file.
Music: Uses all styles for many different assignments.

CREATIVE AUDIO PRODUCTIONS, 326 Santa Isabel Blvd., Laguna Vista, Port Isabel TX 78578. (210)943-6278. Owner: Ben McCampbell. **Jingle/commercial music production house.** Serves ad agencies, broadcast stations (TV and radio), video/film production houses and advertisers. Uses the services of independent songwriters/composers and lyricists for jingles for commercials for radio and TV. Commissions 1 composer and 2 lyricists/year. Fees negotiable. Buys one-time or all rights.
How to Contact: Submit demo tape of previous work. Prefers cassette with 3-5 songs. Does not return material; prefers to keep on file. Reports in 1 month.
Music: Uses pop, up-tempo, country, rock and reggae for commercials.

CREATIVE HOUSE ADVERTISING, INC., Suite 301, 30777 Northwestern Hwy., Farmington Hills MI 48334. (313)737-7077. Senior Vice President/Executive Creative Director: Robert G. Washburn. Advertising agency and graphics studio. Serves commercial, retail, consumer, industrial, medical and financial clients. Uses the services of songwriters and lyricists for jingles, background music for radio and TV commercials and corporate sales meeting films and videos. Commissions 3-4 songwriters/year. Pays $1,500-10,000/job depending on job involvement. Buys all rights.
How to Contact: Query with résumé of credits or submit tape demo showing jingle/composition skills. Submit cassette (or ¾" videocassette) with 6-12 songs. SASE, but would prefer to keep material on file. "When an appropriate job comes up associated with the talents/ability of the songwriters/musicians, then they will be contacted."
Music: "The type of music we need depends on clients. The range is multi: contemporary, disco, rock, MOR and traditional."
Tips: "Be fresh, innovative and creative. Provide good service and costs."

THE CREATIVE IMAGE GROUP, 780 Charcot Ave., San Jose CA 95131. (408)434-0490. Fax: (408)434-0284. CEO: Ed Mongievi. Clients include video game developers/publishers, corporations, retail outlets. Estab. 1988. Uses the services of music houses, independent songwriters/composers for background music for commercials for radio, TV and video games. Commissions 10 composers and fewer than 10 lyricists/year. Pays per job. Buys all rights or one-time rights, depends on project.
How to Contact: Submit letter and demo tape. Include cassette (or VHS or Beta SP videocassette) with 3 songs. Prefers to keep submitted material on file.
Music: Uses hard rock, classical rock, pop, hip hop, rap, up-tempo, modern/alternative rock, any new/trendy sound for video games.

CREATIVE SUPPORT SERVICES, 1950 Riverside Dr., Los Angeles CA 90039. (213)666-7968. Contact: Michael M. Fuller. **Music/sound effects library.** Clients include audiovisual production houses. Estab. 1978. Uses the services of independent songwriters and musicians for background music for TV commercials. Commissions 3-5 songwriters and 1-2 lyricists/year. Buys all rights.
How to Contact: Submit demo tape of previous work. Prefers cassette ("chrome or metal only") or 7½ ips reel-to-reel with 3 or more pieces. Does not return material; prefers to keep on file. "Will call if interested."

Music: Uses "industrial music predominantly, but all other kinds or types to a lesser degree."
Tips: "Don't assume the reviewer can extrapolate beyond what is actually on the demo."

*CROSS THE ROAD PRODUCTIONS, 269 W. Alameda, Burbank CA 91504. (818)954-0214. Fax: (805)255-6015. Owner: Ron Lewis. Advertising agency, audiovisual firm, **jingle/commercial music production house.** Clients include advertisers, radio and TV, motion pictures. Estab. 1988. Uses the services of music houses, independent songwriters/composers, lyricists for scoring of radio, TV, movies and tape programs; background music for audiovisual; jingles and commercials for radio and TV. Commissions 20-30 composers and 20-30 lyricists/year. Pay negotiable. Buys all rights.
How to Contact: Submit demo tape of previous work. Prefers cassette or reel-to-reel. Does not return material; prefers to keep on file. Reports in 1 month.
Music: Uses all types.

dbF A MEDIA COMPANY, Box 2458, Waldorf MD 20604. (301)843-7110. President: Randy Runyon. Advertising agency, audiovisual and media firm and audio and video production company. Clients include business and industry. Estab. 1981. Uses the services of music houses, independent songwriters/composers and lyricists for background music for industrial videos, jingles and commercials for radio and TV. Commissions 5-12 composers and 5-12 lyricists/year. Pays by the job. Buys all rights.
How to Contact: Submit demo tape of previous work. Prefers cassette or 7½ ips reel-to-reel (or VHS videocassette) with 5-8 songs and lead sheet. SASE, but prefers to keep material on file. Reports in 1 month.
Music: Uses up-tempo contemporary for industrial videos, slide presentations and commercials.
Tips: "We're looking for commercial music, primarily A/C."

DELTA DESIGN GROUP, INC., Dept. SM, 409 Washington Ave., Greenville MS 38701. (601)335-6148. President: Noel Workman. Advertising agency. Serves industrial, health care, agricultural, casino and retail commercial clients. Uses the services of music houses for jingles and commercials for radio and TV. Commissions 3-6 pieces/year. Pays by the job. Buys "rights which vary geographically according to client. Some are all rights; others are rights for a specified market only. Buy out only. No annual licensing."
How to Contact: Submit demo tape showing jingle/composition skills. Prefers 7½ ips reel-to-reel with 3-6 songs. "Include typed sequence of cuts on tape on the outside of the reel box." Does not return material. Reports in 2 weeks.
Music: Needs "30- and 60-second jingles for agricultural, health care, gambling casinos, vacation destinations, auto dealers and chambers of commerce."

DISK PRODUCTIONS, 1100 Perkins Rd., Baton Rouge LA 70802. (504)343-5438. Director: Joey Decker. **Jingle/production house.** Clients include advertising agencies, slide production houses and film companies. Estab. 1982. Uses independent songwriters/composers and lyricists for scoring of TV spots and films and jingles for radio and TV. Commissions 7 songwriters/composers and 7 lyricists/year. Pays by the job. Buys all rights.
How to Contact: Submit demo tape of previous work. Prefers cassette or 7½ ips reel-to-reel (or ½" videocassette) and lead sheet. Does not return material. Reports "immediately if material looks promising."
Music: Needs all types of music for jingles, music beds or background music for TV and radio, etc.
Tips: "Advertising techniques change with time. Don't be locked in a certain style of writing. Give me music that I can't get from pay needle-drop."

*DORSEY ADVERTISING/PUBLIC RELATIONS, P.O. Box 270942, Dallas TX 75227-0942. (214)941-7796. Fax: (214)941-7798. President: Mr. Dorsey. Advertising agency. Clients include corporate businesses. Some retail clientele. Estab. 1977. Uses the services of music houses and/or independent songwriters/composers, lyricists for scoring, background music and jingles for commercials for radio and TV; also theme songs/music. Commissions under 10 lyricists/year. Pays by the job. Buys all rights, one-time rights.
How to Contact: Query with résumé of credits or write to arrange personal interview. "No phone or fax inquiries please!" Prefers cassette. "We need song ideas about the super information highway in conjunction with the videophone for Futuretalk Telecom account." SASE. Prefers to keep submitted material on file. Reports in 3 weeks.
Music: Uses all styles with commercialism in mind. Hi-tech. Must be able to furnish professional quality with lyrics, production, originality, creative.
Tips: "The Futuretalk account needs songwriters who can help us set up a network which will result in the sales of videophones, the next wave of the future. Futuretalk is an equipment sales company. Talent, company or individual accepted will be paid for all rights to production upon acceptance. Due to workload, all submissions on this project will be filed, or returned by request with SASE only.

No queries answered without return postage. Address this project to: Futuretalk Account (to above address)."

DSM PRODUCERS INC., Suite 803, 161 W. 54th St., New York NY 10019. (212)245-0006. President, CEO: Suzan Bader. CFO, CPA: Kenneth R. Wiseman. Submit to: E.T. Toast, Director A&R. Vice President, National Sales Director: Doris Kaufman. Scoring service, **jingle/commercial music production house** and original stock library called "All American Composers Library," record producers. Clients include networks, corporate, advertising firms, film and video, book publishers (music only). Estab. 1979. Uses the services of independent songwriters/composers and "all signed composers who we represent" for scoring of film, industrial films, major films—all categories; background music for film, audio cassettes, instore video—all categories; jingles for advertising agencies and commercials for radio and TV. Pays from royalty of sales. Publishes 25 new composers annually.
How to Contact: Write first to arrange personal interview. Enclose SASE for response. Prefers cassette (or VHS videocassette) with 2 songs and lyric or lead sheet. "Use a large enough return envelope to put in a standard business reply letter." Reports in 3-4 months.
Music: Uses dance, New Age, country and rock for adventure films and sports programs.
Tips: "Keep the vocals up in the mix. We can only sell masters at this time. dsm producers Inc. is administered worldwide by Warner/Chappell Music."

ROY EATON MUSIC INC., 595 Main St., Roosevelt Island NY 10044. (212)980-9046. President: Roy Eaton. **Jingle/commercial music production house**. Clients include advertising agencies, TV and radio stations and film producers. Estab. 1982. Uses the services of independent songwriters/composers and lyricists for scoring of TV commercials; and jingles for commercials for radio and TV. Commissions 10 composers and 1 lyricist/year. Pays $50-3,000/job. Buys all rights.
How to Contact: Submit demo tape of previous work. Prefers cassette with 3-5 pieces. SASE. Reports in 6 months.
Music: Uses jazz fusion, New Age and rock/pop for commercials and films.

ELITE VIDEO PRODUCTIONS, 1612 E. 14th St., Brooklyn NY 11229. (718)627-0499. President: Kalman Zeines. Video production company. Clients include educational and industrial. Estab. 1978. Uses the services of music houses, lyricists and independent songwriters/composers for background music for narration and commercials for TV. Commissions 2 lyricists and 5 composers/year. Pays $35-1,800/job. Buys all rights.
How to Contact: Call first to obtain permission to submit. Prefers cassette. Does not return material; prefers to keep on file. Reports back in 2 weeks. Assignments include work on educational films.

EMERY & MARTINEZ ADVERTISING, (formerly Emery Advertising), 1519 Montana, El Paso TX 79902. (915)532-3636. Producer: Steve Osborn. Advertising agency. Clients include automotive dealerships, banks, hospitals. Estab. 1977. Uses the services of music houses, independent songwriters/composers and lyricists for jingles and commercials for TV and radio. Commissions 6 composers and 4 lyricists/year. Pays $250-1,000/job. Buys all rights and one-time rights.
How to Contact: Submit demo tape of previous work. Prefers cassette. Does not return unsolicited material; prefers to keep on file. Reports in 2 weeks.
Music: Uses up-tempo and pop for commercials.

ENSEMBLE PRODUCTIONS, Box 2332, Auburn AL 36831. (205)826-3045. Owner: Barry J. McConatha. Audiovisual firm and video production/post production. Clients include corporate, governmental and educational. Estab. 1984. Uses services of music houses and independent songwriters/composers for background music for corporate public relations and training videos. Commissions 0-5 composers/year. Pays $25-250/job depending upon project. Buys all rights.
How to Contact: Submit demo tape of previous work demonstrating composition skills. "Needs are sporadic, write first if submission to be returned." Prefers cassette or 7½ or 15 ips reel-to-reel (or VHS videocassette) with 3-5 songs. "Most needs are up-beat industrial sound but occasional mood setting music also. Inquire for details." Does not return material; prefers to keep on file. Reports in 3 months if interested."
Music: Uses up-beat, industrial, New Age, and mood for training, film, PR, education and multimedia.

ENTERTAINMENT PRODUCTIONS, INC., #744, 2210 Wilshire Blvd., Santa Monica CA 90403. (310)456-3143. President: Edward Coe. Motion picture and television production company. Clients include motion picture and TV distributors. Estab. 1972. Uses the services of music houses and songwriters for scores, production numbers, background and theme music for films and TV and jingles for promotion of films. Commissions/year vary. Pays by the job or by royalty. Buys all rights.

How to Contact: Query with résumé of credits. Demo should show flexibility of composition skills. "Demo records/tapes sent at own risk—returned if SASE included." Reports by letter in 1 month, "but only if SASE is included."
Tips: "Have résumé on file. Develop self-contained capability."

ALAN ETT MUSIC, Suite 1470, 3500 W. Olive Ave., Burbank CA 91505. (818)248-7105. Fax: (818)955-7067. Vice President: Scott Liggett. Scoring service and **jingle/commercial music production house** for TV/advertising/corporate. Estab. 1990. Uses the services of independent songwriters/composers and lyricists for scoring of background music for jingles for commercials for radio and TV. Commissions 6 composers/year. "Pays negotiable amount." Buys all or one-time rights.
How to Contact: Query with résumé of credits. "Write first . . . no unsolicited submissions accepted." Does not return material.

F.C.B., INC., Dept. SM, 200 S. Broad St., Philadelphia PA 19102. (215)790-4100. Broadcast Business Manager: Valencia Tursi. Advertising agency. Serves industrial and consumer clients. Uses music houses for jingles and background music in commercials. Pays creative fee asked by music houses.
How to Contact: Submit demo tape of previously aired work. "You must send in previously published work. We do not use original material." Prefers cassette. Will return with SASE if requested, but prefers to keep on file.
Music: All types.

FILM CLASSIC EXCHANGE, 143 Hickory Hill Circle, Osterville MA 02655. (508)428-7198. Vice President: Elsie Aikman. Motion picture production company. Clients include motion picture industry/TV networks and affiliates. Estab. 1916. Uses the services of music houses, independent songwriters/composers and lyricists for scoring and background music for motion pictures, TV and video projects. Commissions 10-20 composers and 10-20 lyricists/year. Pays by the job. Buys all rights.
How to Contact: Submit demo tape of previous work. Prefers cassette (or VHS videocassette). SASE, but prefers to keep material on file. Reports in 3 weeks to 2 months.
Music: Uses pop and up-tempo for theatrical films/TV movies.
Tips: "Be persistent."

FINE ART PRODUCTIONS, 67 Maple St., Newburgh NY 12550. (914)561-5866. Producer/Researcher: Richard Suraci. Advertising agency, audiovisual firm, scoring service, **jingle/commercial music production house,** motion picture production company and **music sound effect library.** Clients include corporate, industrial, motion picture, broadcast firms. Estab. 1987. Uses services of music houses, independent songwriters/composers and lyricists for scoring, background music and jingles for various projects and commercials for radio and TV. Commissions 1-10 songwriters or composers and 1-10 lyricists/year. Pays by the job. Buys all rights.
How to Contact: Submit demo tape of previous work or tape demonstrating composition skills or query with résumé of credits. Prefers cassette (or ½", ¾", or 1" videocassette) with as many songs as possible and lyric or lead sheets. SASE, but prefers to keep material on file. Reports in 6 months.
Music: Uses all types of music for all types of assignments.

FITZMUSIC, (formerly Gary Fitzgerald Music Productions), Suite B29, 37-75 63rd St., Woodside NY 11377. (718)446-3857. Producer: Gary Fitzgerald. Scoring service, **commercial music production house and music/sound effects library.** "We service the advertising community." Estab. 1987. Uses the services of music houses, independent songwriters, vocalists, lyricists and voice-over talent for scoring of TV, radio and industrials; background music for movies; jingles for TV, radio and industrials; and commercials for radio and TV. Commissions 4-5 composers and 2 lyricists/year. Tri-state talent only. Pays per project. Rights purchased depends on project.
How to Contact: Call first to obtain permission to submit demo tape of previous work. Prefers cassette. Does not return material; prefers to keep on file. "A follow-up call must follow submission."
Music: Uses all styles of music.
Tips: "Complete knowledge of how the advertising business works is essential."

*THE FRANKLYN AGENCY, #312, 1010 Hammond St., Los Angeles CA 90069. (213)272-6080. President: Audrey Franklyn. Advertising agency, audiovisual firm and cable production company. Clients include "everything from holistic health companies to singers." Estab. 1960. Uses the services of independent songwriters/composers and singers for live performances for TV. Commissions 4 composers and 2 lyricists/year. Pays flat fee per job.
How to Contact: Query with résumé of credits. Prefers cassette or videocassette. Does not return material. Reports in 1 month.
Music: Uses all types for cable background, live performance.

FREDRICK, LEE & LLOYD, 235 Elizabeth St., Landisville PA 17538. (717)898-6092. Vice President: Dusty Rees. **Jingle/commercial music production house.** Clients include advertising agencies. Estab. 1976. Uses the services of independent songwriters/composers and staff writers for jingles. Commissions 2 composers/year. Pays $650/job. Buys all rights.
How to Contact: Submit tape demonstrating composition skills. Prefers cassette or 7½ ips reel-to-reel with 5 jingles. "Submissions may be samples of published work or original material." SASE. Reports in 3 weeks.
Music: Uses pop, rock, country and MOR.
Tips: "The more completely orchestrated the demos are, the better."

FREED & ASSOCIATES, Suite 220, 3600 Clipper Mill Rd., Baltimore MD 21211. (410)243-1421. Contact: Senior Writer. Advertising agency. Clients include a variety of retail and nonretail businesses. Estab. 1960. Uses the services of music houses and independent songwriters/composers for background music for TV commercials, jingles for TV/radio commercials and commercials for radio and TV. Commissions 4-5 composers and 2-4 lyricists/year. Pays $2,000-10,000/job. Buys all rights or one-time rights, depending on the project.
How to Contact: Submit demo tape of previous work. Prefers cassette (or ½" or ¾" videocassette). Does not return unsolicited material; prefers to keep on file. Reports in 1 month.
Music: Uses varying styles for commercials and corporate videos.

PAUL FRENCH AND PARTNERS, 503 Gabbettville Rd., LaGrange GA 30240. (706)882-5581. Contact: Charles Hall. Audiovisual firm. Uses the services of music houses and songwriters for musical scores in films and original songs for themes; lyricists for writing lyrics for themes. Commissions 20 composers and 20 lyricists/year. Pays minimum $500/job. Buys all rights.
How to Contact: Submit demo tape of previous work. Prefers reel-to-reel with 3-8 songs. SASE. Reports in 2 weeks.

FRONTLINE VIDEO & FILM, 243 12th St., Del Mar CA 92014. (619)481-5566. Production Manager: Bonnie Kristell. Television and video production company. Clients include sports programming in jetskiing, surfing, yachting, skiing, skateboarding, boardsailing; medical patient education; and various industrial clients. Estab. 1983. Uses the services of music houses and independent songwriters/composers for background music for sports programming. Commissions 5 composers/year. Pays by $35-150/job. Buys all rights.
How to Contact: Submit demo tape of previous work. Prefers cassette. Does not return material; prefers to keep on file. "We contact artists on an 'as needed' basis when we're ready to use one of their pieces or styles."
Music: Uses up-tempo, jazzy, rock. "We buy works that come to us for national and international TV programming."
Tips: "Be patient, because when we need a 'sound' yours may be the 'one.'"

BOB GERARDI MUSIC PRODUCTIONS, 160 W. 73rd St., New York NY 10023. (212)874-6436. President: Bob Gerardi. Scoring service and **jingle/commercial music production house.** Clients include feature film producers, television producers, advertising agencies. Estab. 1975. Uses the services of independent songwriters/composers, lyricists and sound designers for scoring for film and TV; background music for industrials, commercials for radio and TV. Commissions 2 composers and 2 lyricists/year. Pays by the job. Buys all rights.
How to Contact: Write or call first to arrange personal interview. Prefers cassette with 3 songs. "Keep demo short." Does not return unsolicited material; prefers to keep on file.
Music: Uses pop, easy listening and jazz for commercials, education film, feature and TV.

GK & A ADVERTISING, INC., Suite 510, 8200 Brookriver Dr., Dallas TX 75247. (214)634-9486. Advertising agency. Clients include retail. Estab. 1982. Uses the services of music houses, independent songwriters/composers and lyricists for jingles for commercials for radio and TV. Commissions 1 composer and 1 lyricist/year. Buys all rights.
How to Contact: Submit demo tape of previous work. Prefers cassette (or VHS videocassette). Does not return material; prefers to keep on file. Reports in 2 weeks.
Music: Uses all types for commercials.

*GOLD COAST ADVERTISING ASSOCIATION INC., 3625 NW 82nd Ave., Miami FL 33166. (305)592-1192. President/Creative Director: Stuart Dornfield. Advertising agency. Clients include retail/beer/financial/automotive/business-to-business/package goods. Estab. 1982. Uses the services of music houses and independent songwriters/composers for scoring of TV commercials, background music for radio and TV spots, jingles and commercials for radio and TV. Commissions 5 composers/year. Pays by the job. Buys all rights or 1 year licenses and/or buyouts.

How to Contact: Submit demo tape of previous work. Prefers cassette. "Include approximate cost of music pieces." Does not return unsolicited material; prefers to keep on file. Reports "when the need of a project arises."
Music: Uses all for commercials.
Tips: "Know what sells in advertising and make the melody memorable!"

GOODRUM LEONARD & ASSOC. INC., 4301 Hillsboro Rd., Nashville TN 37215. (615)292-4431. President, Creative Director: Mil Leonard. Advertising agency. Estab. 1970. Serves retail, service businesses and manufacturers. Uses independent songwriters and music houses for jingles and background music for commercials. Commissions 4-6 composers and 4-6 lyricists/year. Pays by the job. Buys all rights or one-time rights.
How to Contact: "Send a demo; send address and phone number." SASE. Reports "when we need them."
Music: Needs vary.

*DENNIS GREEN ADVERTISING, (formerly The Dennis Group), Suite 149, 31275 Northwestern Hwy. Farmington Hills MI 48334. (810)851-8134. President: Dennis R. Green. Advertising agency. Clients include retail and industrial firms. Estab. 1991. Uses the services of music houses and independent songwriters/composers for jingles and commercials for radio and television. Commissions 6 composers/year. Buys all rights.
How to Contact: Submit a demo tape of previous work or query with résumé of credits. Prefers cassette or 7.5 ips reel to reel (or VHS videocassette) with 6-10 songs. SASE, but prefers to keep submitted material on file. Reports back in 2 weeks.
Music: All kinds, depending on clients' needs.
Tips: "Send a demo reel and keep in touch."

GREINKE, EIERS AND ASSOCIATES, 2448 N. Lake Dr., Milwaukee WI 53211-4509. (414)962-9810. Fax: (414)964-7479. Staff: Arthur Greinke, Patrick Eiers, Lora Nigro. Advertising agency and public relations/music artist management and media relations. Clients include small business, original music groups, special events. Estab. 1984. Uses the services of independent songwriters/composers, lyricists and music groups, original rock bands and artists for scoring of video news releases, other video projects, jingles for small firms and special events and commercials for radio and TV. Commissions 4-6 composers and 4-6 lyricists/year. Paid by a personal contract.
How to Contact: Query with résumé of credits or submit demo tape of previous work. Prefers CD or cassette (or DAT tape or VHS videocassette) with any number of songs and lyric sheet. "We will contact only when job is open—but will keep submissions on file." Does not return material.
Music: Uses original rock, pop, heavy rock for recording groups, commercials, video projects.
Tips: "Try to give as complete a work as possible without allowing us to fill in the holes. High energy, be creative, strong hooks!"

GRS, INC., 13300 Broad St., Pataskala OH 43062. (614)927-9566. Manager: S.S. Andrews. Teleproduction facility. Estab. 1969. Varied clients. Uses the services of music houses and independent songwriters/composers for jingles and background music. Pays by the job. Buys all rights.
How to Contact: Submit demo tape of previous work. Prefers cassette. Does not return material; prefers to keep on file.
Music: All styles for commercials.
Tips: "Follow our instructions exactly."

*HAMMOND & ASSOCIATES, 11307 Tawinee, Houston TX 77065. (713)955-5029. Fax: (713)890-8784. Owner: Michael Hammond. Audiovisual firm, **jingle/commercial music production house,** motion picture production company. Clients include food store chains, land development, auto dealers, television stations. Estab. 1985. Uses the services of independent songwriters/composers and lyricists for jingles for TV, auto dealers, commercials for radio and TV. Pays per job. Buys one-time rights.
How to Contact: Query with résumé of credits. Prefers cassette (or VHS videocassette) with 3 songs and lyric sheet. SASE. Prefers to keep submitted material on file. Reports in 3 weeks.
Music: Uses up tempo, R&B, country and gospel for jingles, educational and commercial songs.

HEPWORTH ADVERTISING CO., 3403 McKinney Ave., Dallas TX 75204. (214)526-7785. President: S.W. Hepworth. Advertising agency. Clients include financial, industrial and food firms. Estab. 1952. Uses services of songwriters for jingles. Pays by the job. Buys all rights.
How to Contact: Write first to arrange personal interview. Prefers cassette. Does not return material. Reports as need arises.

HEYWOOD FORMATICS & SYNDICATION, 1103 Colonial Blvd., Canton OH 44714. (216)456-2592. Owner: Max Heywood. Advertising agency and consultant. Clients include radio, TV, restaurants/

lounges. Uses the services of independent songwriters/composers for jingles and commercials for radio and TV. Payment varies per project. Buys all rights.
How to Contact: Submit demo tape of previous work. Prefers cassette or 7½ or 15 ips reel-to-reel (or VHS/Beta videocassette). Does not return material.
Music: Uses pop, easy listening and CHR for educational films, slide presentations and commercials.

HILLMANN & CARR INC., 2121 Wisconsin Ave. NW, Washington DC 20007. (202)342-0001. President: Alfred Hillmann. Vice President/Treasurer: Ms. Michal Carr. Audiovisual firm and motion picture production company. Estab. 1975. Clients include corporate, government, associations and museums. Uses the services of music houses and independent songwriters/composers for scoring of films, video productions and PSA's for radio and TV. Commissions 2-3 composers/year. Payment negotiable.
How to Contact: Query with résumé of credits, or submit demo tape of previous work or tape demonstrating composition skills, or write to arrange personal interview. Prefers cassette (or ¾″ VHS or Beta videocassette) with 5-10 pieces. Does not return material; prefers to keep on file. Reports only when interested. SASE.
Music: Uses contemporary, classical, up-tempo and thematic music for documentary film and video productions, multi-media exposition productions, public service announcements.

THE HITCHINS COMPANY, 22756 Hartland St., Canoga Park CA 91307. (818)715-0510. President: W.E. Hitchins. Advertising agency. Estab. 1985. Uses the services of music houses, independent songwriters/composers and lyricists for commercials for radio and TV. Commissions 1-2 composers and 1-2 lyricists/year. Will negotiate pay.
How to Contact: Query with résumé of credits. Prefers cassette or VHS videocassette. "Check first to see if we have a job." Does not return material; prefers to keep on file.
Music: Uses variety of musical styles for commercials.

HODGES ASSOCIATES, INC., P.O. Box 53805, 912 Hay St., Fayetteville NC 28305. (919)483-8489. President/Production Manager: Chuck Smith. Advertising agency. Clients include industrial, retail and consumer ("We handle a full array of clientele."). Estab. 1974. Uses the services of music houses and independent songwriters/composers for background music for industrial films and slide presentations, and commercials for radio and TV. Commissions 1-2 composers/year. Pays by the job. Buys all rights.
How to Contact: Submit demo tape of previous work. Prefers cassette. Does not return unsolicited material; prefers to keep on file. Reports in 2-3 months.
Music: Uses all styles for industrial videos, slide presentations and TV commercials.

HOME, INC., 731 Harrison Ave., Boston MA 02118. (617)266-1386. Director: Alan Michel. Audiovisual firm and video production company. Clients include cable television, nonprofit organizations, pilot programs, entertainment companies and industrial. Uses the services of independent songwriters/composers and lyricists for background music and jingles for TV commercials. Commissions 2-5 songwriters/year. Pays up to $1,000/job. Buys all rights or one-time rights.
How to Contact: Query with résumé of credits. Prefers cassette with 6 pieces. Does not return material; prefers to keep on file. Reports as projects require.
Music: Mostly synthesizer. Uses all styles of music for educational videos.
Tips: "Have a variety of products available and be willing to match your skills to the project and the budget."

*FRANK HOOPER & ASSOCIATES, #103, 13706 Research Blvd., Austin TX 78750. (512)258-3759. Fax: (512)331-6148. Contact: Alan Pernado. Advertising agency. Clients are varied. Estab. 1981. Uses the services of music houses and/or independent songwriters/composers for background music, jingles and commercials for radio, TV; also sales videos. Pays songwriters/composers per job.
How to Contact: Query with résumé of credits or submit demo tape of previous work. Prefers cassette. SASE. Reports in 2 weeks.
Music: Uses varied styles, depending on job.
Tips: "Let your work stand on its own merit. Don't be too pushy."

IZEN ENTERPRISES, INC., Dept. SM, 26 Abby Dr., East Northport NY 11731. (516)368-0615. President: Ray Izen. Video services. Clients are various. Estab. 1980. Uses the services of music houses and independent songwriters/composers for background music. Commissions 2 composers and 2 lyricists/year. Pay is open. Buys all rights.
How to Contact: Submit demo tape of previous work. Prefers cassette or VHS videocassette. Does not return material, prefers to keep on file.

THE JAYME ORGANIZATION, 25825 Science Park Dr., Cleveland OH 44122. (216)831-0110. Senior Art Director: Debbie Klonk. Advertising agency. Uses the services of songwriters and lyricists for jingles and background music. Pays by the job. Buys all rights.
How to Contact: Query first; submit demo tape of previous work. Prefers cassette with 4-8 songs. SASE. Responds by phone as needs arise.
Music: Jingles.

*KA PRODUCTIONS, 1515 Haskin, San Antonio TX 78209. (210)822-2106. Fax: (210)822-9148. Owner: Keith A. Harter. **Jingle/commercial music production house**. Clients include advertising and record companies. Estab. 1983. Uses the services of music houses and/or independent songwriters/composers and lyricists for scoring, background music and jingles for radio and TV. Commissions 2-3 composers and 2-3 lyricists/year. Pays per job. Buys all rights.
How to Contact: Query with résumé of credits or submit demo tape of previous work. Prefers cassette. Prefers to keep submitted material on file. Reports in 2 weeks.
Music: Uses rock, country, New Age, pop, jazz, dramatic music for jingles, AV shows and educational.

*KAMSTRA COMMUNICATIONS, INC., Suite 320, 5914 W. Courtyard, Austin TX 78730. (512)343-8484. Fax: (512)343-6010. Contact: Broadcast Producer. Advertising agency. Estab. 1963. Uses the services of music houses for jingles for radio and TV. Pays by the job. Buys all rights, one-time rights.
How to Contact: Submit demo tape of previous work. Prefers cassette. Does not return material.

K&R'S RECORDING STUDIOS, 28533 Greenfield, Southfield MI 48076. (313)557-8276. Contact: Ken Glaza. Scoring service and **jingle/commercial music production house**. Clients include commercial, industrial firms. Services include sound for pictures (music, dialogue). Uses the services of independent songwriters/composers for scoring of video. Commissions 1 composer/month. Pays by the job, royalty or hour. Buys all rights.
How to Contact: Submit demo tape of previous work. Prefers cassette (or ¾" or VHS videocassette) with 5-7 pieces minimum. "Show me what you can do in 5 to 7 minutes." Does not return material. Reports in 2 weeks.
Music: "Be able to compose with the producer present."

KAUFMANN ADVERTISING ASSOCIATES, INC., Dept. SM, 1626 Frederica Rd., St. Simons Island GA 31522. (912)638-8678. President: Harry Kaufmann. Advertising agency. Clients include resorts. Estab. 1964. Uses the services of independent songwriters/composers and lyricists for scoring of videos; background music for videos, radio, TV; jingles for radio; and commercials for radio and TV. Commissions 0-2 composers and 0-2 lyricists/year. Pays by the job.

KEATING MAGEE LONG ADVERTISING, 2223 Magazine, New Orleans LA 70130. (504)523-2121. President: Thomas J. Long. Advertising agency. Clients include retail, consumer products and services, business-to-business. Estab. 1981. Uses the services of music houses and independent songwriters/composers for scoring of videos, commercials and jingles for radio and TV. Commissions 4 composers/year. Pays by the job. Buys all rights.
How to Contact: Submit demo tape of previous work. Prefers cassette (or VHS videocassette). Does not return material; prefers to keep on file.
Music: Uses all for commercials, presentations.
Tips: "Send reel of actual work and references."

KEN-DEL PRODUCTIONS INC., First State Production Center, 1500 First State Blvd., Wilmington DE 19804-3596. (302)999-1164. Fax: (302)999-1656. Estab. 1950. A&R Director: Shirl Lotz. General Manager: Edwin Kennedy. Clients include publishers, industrial firms and advertising agencies, radio/TV. Uses services of songwriters for radio/TV commercials and jingles. Pays by the job. Buys all rights.
How to Contact: Submit demo of work in any format. Does not return material. Reports in 1 month.

SID KLEINER MUSIC ENTERPRISES, 10188 Winter View Dr., Naples FL 33942. (813)566-7701 and (813)566-7702. Managing Director: Sid Kleiner. Audiovisual firm. Serves the music industry and various small industries. Uses the services of music houses, songwriters and inhouse writers for background music; lyricists for special material. Commissions 5-10 composers and 2-3 lyricists/year. Pays $25 minimum/job. Buys all rights.

Listings of companies within this section which are either commercial music production houses or music libraries will have that information printed in boldface type.

How to Contact: Query with résumé of credits or submit demo tape of previously aired work. Prefers cassette with 1-4 songs. SASE. Reports in 5 weeks.
Music: "We generally need soft background music with some special lyrics to fit a particular project. Uses catchy, contemporary, special assignments for commercial/industrial accounts. We also assign country, pop, mystical and metaphysical. Submit samples—give us your very best demos, your best prices and we'll try our best to use your services."

KTVU RETAIL SERVICES, Box 22222, Oakland CA 94623. (510)874-0228. TV station and retail Marketing Director: Richard Hartwig. Retail TV commercial production firm. Estab. 1974. Clients include local, regional and national retailers. Uses the services of music houses and independent songwriters/composers for commercials, background music and jingles for radio and TV. Commissions 50 composers and 4 lyricists/year. Pays by the job. Buys all rights.
How to Contact: Submit demo tape of previous work. Prefers cassette or 7½ ips reel-to-reel with 6 pieces. Does not return material. Reports in 1 week.
Music: All styles for TV and radio commercials.

LANGE PRODUCTIONS, 7661 Curson Terrace, Hollywood CA 90046. (213)874-4730. Production Co-ordinator: Ken Sargent. Medical video production company. Clients include doctors, hospitals, corporations. Estab. 1987. Uses services of music houses and independent songwriters/composers for background music for medical videos. Commissions 6 composers/year. Pays by the job, $300-700. Buys all rights.
How to Contact: Submit demo tape of previous work. Does not return material; prefers to keep on file. Reports in 1 month.

LAPRIORE VIDEOGRAPHY, 86 Allston Ave., Worcester MA 01604. (508)755-9010. Owner: Peter Lapriore. Video production company. Clients include corporations, retail stores, educational and sports. Estab. 1985. Uses the services of music houses, independent songwriters/composers and lyricists for scoring of independent programming, background music for corporate videos, jingles for retail chains and commercials for TV. "We also own several music libraries." Commissions 2 composers/year. Pays $150-1,000/job. Buys all rights, one-time rights and limited use rights.
How to Contact: Submit demo tape of previous work. Prefers cassette or VHS videocassette with 5 songs and lyric sheet. Does not return material, but prefers to keep on file. Reports in 3 weeks.
Music: Uses slow, medium, up-tempo, jazz and classical for marketing, educational films and commercials.

WALTER P. LUEDKE & ASSOCIATES, INC., 5633 E. State St., Rockford IL 61108. (815)398-4207. Secretary: Joan Luedke. Advertising agency. Estab. 1959. Uses the services of independent songwriters/composers and lyricists for background music, jingles for clients and commercials for radio and TV. Commissions 1-2 composers and 1-2 lyricists/year. Pays by the job. Buys all rights.
How to Contact: Submit demo tape of previous work demonstrating composition skills, or write first to arrange personal interview. Prefers cassette. "Our need is infrequent, best just let us know who you are." SASE, but prefers to keep material on file. Reports in 1 month.
Music: Uses various styles.

LYONS PRESENTATIONS, 715 Orange St., Wilmington DE 19801. (302)654-6146. Audio Producer: Gary Hill. Audiovisual firm. Clients include mostly large corporations: Dupont, ICI, Alco Standard. Estab. 1954. Uses the services of independent songwriters/composers and lyricists for scoring of multi-image, film and video. Commissions 8-12 composers/year. Pays by the job. Buys all rights.
How to Contact: Submit demo tape of previous work. Prefers cassette, 15 IPS reel-to-reel, (or VHS or ¾" videocassette) with 3-4 songs. "No phone calls please, unless composers are in local area." SASE, but prefers to keep submitted materials on file.
Music: Usually uses up-tempo motivational pieces for multi-image, video or film for corporate use.
Tips: "Pay close attention to the type of music that is used for current TV spots."

MCCAFFREY AND MCCALL ADVERTISING, 117 E. Washington, Indianapolis IN 46204. (317)686-7800. V.P./Creative Director: William Mick. Advertising agency. Serves consumer electronics, technical education, retail and commercial developers. Estab. 1984. Uses the services of music houses for scoring, background music and jingles for radio and TV commercials. Commissions 3 composers/year; 1 lyricist/year. Pays $3,000-5,000/job. Buys all rights.
How to Contact: Submit demo tape of previous work and write to arrange personal interview. Prefers cassette (or ¾" videocassette) with 6 songs. SASE, but prefers to keep submitted materials on file.
Music: High-energy pop, sound-alikes and electronic for commercials.
Tips: "Keep in touch, but don't be a pest about it."

McCANN-ERICKSON WORLDWIDE, Dept. SM, Suite 1900, 1360 Post Oak Blvd., Houston TX 77056. (713)965-0303. Creative Director: Jesse Caesar. Advertising agency. Serves all types of clients. Uses services of songwriters for jingles and background music in commercials. Commissions 10 songwriters/ year. Pays production cost and registrated creative fee. Arrangement fee and creative fee depend on size of client and size of market. "If song is for a big market, a big fee is paid; if for a small market, a small fee is paid." Buys all rights.
How to Contact: Submit demo tape of previously aired work. Prefers 7½ ips reel-to-reel. "There is no minimum or maximum length for tapes. Tapes may be of a variety of work or a specialization. We are very open on tape content; agency does own lyrics." SASE, but prefers to keep material on file. Responds by phone when need arises.
Music: All types.

*MALLOF, ABRUZINO & NASH MARKETING, 477 E. Butterfield Rd., Lombard IL 60148. (708)964-7722. President: Ed Mallof. Advertising agency. Works primarily with auto dealer jingles. Estab. 1980. Uses music houses for jingles. Commissions 5-6 songwriters/year. Pays $600-2,000/job. Buys all rights.
How to Contact: Submit demo tape of previous work. Prefers cassette with 4-12 songs. SASE, but prefers to keep material on file. Reports "when we feel a need for their style."
Tips: "Send samples that are already produced and can be relyricized."

MARK CUSTOM RECORDING SERVICE, INC., 10815 Bodine Rd., Clarence NY 14031-0406. (716)759-2600. Vice President: Mark J. Morette. **Jingle/commercial music production house**. Clients include ad agencies. Estab. 1962. Uses the services of independent songwriters/composers for commercials for radio and TV. Commissions 2 composers/year. Pays $25/hour.
How to Contact: Write. Prefers cassette with 3 songs. Does not return material; prefers to keep on file.
Music: Uses pop and jazz for radio commercials.

MAXWELL ADVERTISING INC., Dept. SM, 444 W. Michigan, Kalamazoo MI 49007. (616)382-4060. Creative Director: Greg Miller. Advertising agency. Uses the services of lyricists and music houses for jingles and background music for commercials. Commissions 2-4 lyricists/year. Pays by the job. Buys all rights or one-time rights.
How to Contact: Submit demo tape of previously aired work or tape demonstrating composition skills. Prefers cassette (or VHS videocassette). Does not return material; prefers to keep on file. Reports in 1-2 months.
Music: Uses various styles of music for jingles and music beds.

MEDIA ASSOCIATES ADVERTISING, 3808 W. Dorian St., Boise ID 83705. (208)384-9278. President: Mr. Danny Jensen. Advertising agency. Clients include radio-TV commercial accounts, corporate and industrial video production. Uses the services of music houses and independent songwriters/composers for background music for video productions and commercials for radio and TV. Commissions 2-5 composers and 2-5 lyricists/year. "Pay is negotiable." Buys all rights.
How to Contact: Submit demo tape of previous work. Prefers cassette and lyric sheet. Prefers to keep submitted material on file. Reports in 2 months.
Music: Uses up-tempo, adult contemporary, contemporary hits for radio and TV commercials, jingles.
Tips: "A good demo says it all."

MEDIA CONSULTANTS, Box 130, Sikeston MO 63801. (314)472-1116. Owner: Richard Wrather. Advertising agency. Clients are varied. Estab. 1979. Uses the services of music houses, independent songwriters/composers and lyricists for background music for videos, jingles for clients and commercials for radio and TV. Commissions 10-15 composers and 10-15 lyricists/year. Pays varying amount/ job. Buys all rights.
How to Contact: Submit a demo tape of previous work demonstrating composition skills. Prefers cassette (or ½" or ¾" videocassette). Does not return material; prefers to keep on file.
Music: Uses all styles of music for varied assignments.

JON MILLER PRODUCTION STUDIOS, 7249 Airport Rd., Bath PA 18014. (215)837-7550. Executive Producer: Jon Miller. Audiovisual firm, **jingle/commercial music production house** and video production company. Clients include industrial, commercial, institutional and special interest. Estab. 1970. Uses the services of independent songwriters/composers and lyricists for scoring of themes, background music for audio and video production and live presentations and commercials for radio and TV. Commissions 5-15 composers and 2-5 lyricists/year. Buys all rights or one-time rights.
How to Contact: Query with résumé of credits and references. Prefers cassette with 7 songs and lyric or lead sheets. SASE. Reports in 2-3 weeks.
Music: Uses up-tempo and title music, introduction music for industrial marketing and training videos.
Tips: "Provide professional product on time and within budget."

MITCHELL & ASSOCIATES, Dept. SM, 7830 Old Georgetown Rd., Bethesda MD 20814. (301)986-1772. President: Ronald Mitchell. Advertising agency. Serves food, high-tech, transportation, financial, real estate, professional services, automotive and retail clients. Uses independent songwriters, lyricists and music houses for background music for commercials, jingles and post-TV scores for commercials. Commissions 3-5 songwriters and 3-5 lyricists/year. Pays by the job. Buys all rights.
How to Contact: Submit demo tape of previously aired work. Prefers cassette or 7½ ips reel-to-reel. Does not return material; prefers to keep on file.
Music: "Depends upon client, audience, etc."

MONTEREY BAY PRODUCTION GROUP, INC., Suite C, Scotts Valley Dr., Scotts Valley CA 95066. (408)438-6440. Fax: (408)728-2709. President: Larry W. Eells. Audio/video production services. Clients include industrial business and broadcast. Estab. 1985. Uses the services of independent songwriters/composers for scoring of promotional, educational and commercial videos and for CD-ROM and CD-I authors. Commissions 3-10 composers/year. Pays negotiable royalty.
How to Contact: Submit demo tape of previous work. Query with résumé of credits. Prefers cassette (or VHS videocassette) with 5 songs. SASE, but prefers to keep material on file. Reports in 1 month.
Music: Uses all types for promotional, training and commercial.

MORRIS MEDIA, P.O. Box 3249, Torrance CA 90503. (310)533-4800. Acquisitions Manager: Roger Casas. TV/video production company. Estab. 1984. Uses the services of music houses, independent songwriters/composers and lyricists for jingles for radio and TV commercials. Commissions 5 composers and 2 lyricists/year. Pays by the job or by the hour. Buys all rights.
How to Contact: Query with résumé of credits. "Write first with short sample of work." Does not return unsolicited material; prefers to keep submitted material on file. Reports in 2 weeks.
Music: Uses classical, pop, rock and jazz for music video/TV.
Tips: "Persist with good material, as we are very busy!"

MOTIVATION MEDIA, INC., 1245 Milwaukee Ave., Glenview IL 60025. (708)297-4740. Production Manager: Glen Peterson. Audiovisual firm, video, motion picture production company and business meeting planner. Clients include business and industry. Estab. 1969. Uses the services of music houses, independent songwriters/composers for business meetings video, multi-image production and motivational pieces. Commissions 3-5 composers/year. Payment varies. Buys one-time rights.
How to Contact: Submit demo tape of previous work. Prefers cassette with 5-7 songs. Does not return material. Responds in 3-4 weeks.
Music: Uses "up-beat contemporary music that motivates an audience of sales people."
Tips: "Be contemporary."

ERIC MOWER & ASSOCIATES, Dept. SM, 96 College Ave., Rochester NY 14607. (716)473-0440. Creative Director: John Conelly. Advertising agency. Member of AFTRA, SAG, ASCAP. Serves consumer and business-to-business clients. Uses independent songwriters, lyricists and music houses for jingles. Commissions 12 songwriters and 4 lyricists/year. Pays $5,000-40,000/job.
How to Contact: Query. Prefers cassette with 3-5 songs. SASE.
Music: "We're seriously interested in hearing from good production sources. We have some of the world's best lyricists and songwriters working for us, but we're always ready to listen to fresh, new ideas."

MULTI IMAGE PRODUCTIONS, Dept. SM, 8849 Complex Dr., San Diego CA 92123. (619)560-8383. Sound Editor/Engineer: Jim Lawrence. Audiovisual firm and motion picture production company. Serves business, corporate, industrial, commercial, military and cultural clients. Uses the services of music houses, independent songwriters/composers and lyricists for scoring of corporate films and videos. Commissions 2-10 composers and 2-5 lyricists/year. Pays per job. Buys all rights.
How to Contact: Submit demo tape of previous work. Prefers 7½ or 15 ips reel-to-reel with 2-5 pieces. SASE. Reports "on same day if SASE."
Music: Uses "contemporary, pop, specialty, regional, ethnic, national and international" styles of music for background "scores written against script describing locales, action, etc. We try to stay clear of stereotypical 'canned' music and prefer a more commercial and dramatic (film-like) approach."
Tips: "We have established an ongoing relationship with a local music production/scoring house with whom songwriters would be in competition for every project; but an ability to score clean, full, broad, contemporary commercial and often 'film score' type music, in a variety of styles would be a benefit."

MUSIC LANE PRODUCTIONS, Dept. SM, Box 3829, Austin TX 78764. (512)476-1567. Owner: Wayne Gathright. Music recording, production and **jingle/commercial music production house**. Estab. 1980. Serves bands, songwriters and commercial clients. Uses the services of music houses and independent songwriters/composers for jingles and commercials for radio and TV. Pays by the job. Buys one-time rights.

How to Contact: Submit demo tape of previous work or tape demonstrating composition skills; or query with résumé of credits. Prefers cassette. Does not return unsolicited material; prefers to keep on file. Reports in 6 weeks.
Music: Uses all styles.

MUSIC MASTERS, 2322 Marconi Ave., St. Louis MO 63110. (314)773-1480. Producer: Greg Trampe. **Commercial music production house** and **music/sound effect library**. Clients include multi-image and film producers, advertising agencies and large corporations. Estab. 1976. Uses the services of independent songwriters/composers for background music for multi-image and film, and commercials for radio and TV. Commissions 6 composers and 2 lyricists/year. Pays by the job. Buys all rights.
How to Contact: Submit demo tape of previous work. Prefers DAT, cassette or 7½ or 15 ips reel-to-reel with 3-6 pieces. Does not return material. Reports in 2-4 months.
Music: "We use all types of music for slide presentations (sales & motivational)."
Tips: "Resume should have at least 3 or 4 major credits of works completed within the past year. A good quality demo is a must."

MYERS & ASSOCIATES, Dept. SM, Suite 203, 3727 SE Ocean Blvd., Stuart FL 34996. (407)287-1990. Senior Vice President: Doris McLaughlin. Advertising agency. Estab. 1973. Serves financial, real estate, consumer products and hotel clients. Uses music houses for background music for commercials and jingles. Commissions 2-3 songwriters/year and 2-3 lyricists/year. Pays by the job. Buys all rights.
How to Contact: Submit demo tape of previously aired work. Prefers cassette. Does not return unsolicited material; prefers to keep on file.
Music: Uses "various styles of music for jingles, music beds and complete packages depending on clients' needs."

FRANK C. NAHSER, INC., Dept. SM, 18th Floor, 10 S. Riverside Plaza, Chicago IL 60606. (312)845-5000. Contact: Bob Fugate. Advertising agency. Serves insurance, telecommunications, toys, bicycles, hotels, and other clients. Uses the services of independent songwriters/composers, lyricists and music houses for scoring of TV commercials, background music for commercials for radio and TV and music for industrial/sales presentations and meetings. Commissions 6-10 songwriters and 4 lyricists/year. Pays $5,000-15,000 for finished production or varying royalty. Buys one-time rights.
How to Contact: Submit demo tape of previous work. Prefers cassette. Does not return unsolicited material; prefers to keep on file. "No phone calls, please. When a cassette is submitted we listen to it for reference when a project comes up. We ignore most cassettes that lack sensitivity toward string and woodwind arrangements unless we know it's from a lyricist."
Music: "We mostly use scores for commercials, not jingles. The age of the full sing jingle in national TV spots is quickly coming to an end. Young songwriters should be aware of the difference and have the expertise to score, not just write songs."
Tips: "The writing speaks for itself. If you know composition, theory and arrangement it quickly becomes evident. Electronic instruments are great tools; however, they are no substitute for total musicianship. Learn to read, write, arrange and produce music and, with this book's help, market your music. Be flexible enough to work along with an agency. We like to write and produce as much as you do."

NEW & UNIQUE VIDEOS, 2336 Sumac Dr., San Diego CA 92105. (619)282-6126. Contact: Candace Love. Production and worldwide distribution of special interest videotapes to varied markets. Estab. 1981. Uses the services of independent songwriters for background music in videos. Commissions 2-3 composers/year. Pays by the job. Buys all rights.
How to Contact: Query with résumé of credits or submit demo tape of previous work. Prefers cassette. SASE. Reports in 1-2 months.
Music: Uses up-tempo, easy listening and jazz for educational film and action/adventure, nature and love stories.
Tips: "We are seeking upbeat, versatile music, especially for fast action sports videos (among others)."

NOBLE ARNOLD & ASSOCIATES, Dept. SM, Suite 740, 1515 Woodfield Rd., Schaumburg IL 60173. (708)605-8808. Creative Director: John Perkins. Advertising agency. Clients include communication and health care firms. Estab. 1970. Uses the services of independent songwriters/composers for jingles. Commissions 1 composer and 1 lyricist/year. Pays by the job. Buys all rights.
How to Contact: Submit demo tape of previous work. Prefers cassette. Does not return unsolicited material. Reports in 4 weeks.

NORTHLICH STOLLEY LAWARRE, INC., 200 W. Fourth St., Cincinnati OH 45202. (513)421-8840. Broadcast Producer: Diane Frederick. Advertising agency. Clients include banks, hospitals, P&G, Cintas, ChoiceCare, 5/3 Bank, Mead Paper. Estab. 1949. Uses the services of independent songwriters

and music houses for jingles and background music for commercials. Commissions 3-5 composers/
year. Pays by the job. Rights purchased vary.
How to Contact: Submit demo tape of previous work demonstrating composition skills. Prefers
cassette. SASE, but prefers to keep materials on file.
Music: Uses all kinds for commercials.

NORTON RUBBLE & MERTZ, INC. ADVERTISING, Suite 206, 156 N. Jefferson, Chicago IL 60661.
(312)441-9500. President: Sue Gehrke. Advertising agency. Clients include consumer products, retail,
business to business. Estab. 1987. Uses the services of music houses and independent songwriters/
composers for jingles and background music for radio/TV commercials. Commissions 2 composers/
year. Pays by the job.
How to Contact: Submit tape of previous work; query with résumé of credits. Prefers cassette. Does
not return materials; prefers to keep on file.
Music: Uses up-tempo and pop for commercials.

OMNI COMMUNICATIONS, Dept. SM, 655 W. Carmel Dr., P.O. Box 302, Carmel IN 46032-0302.
(317)844-6664. President: W. H. Long. Television production and audiovisual firm. Estab. 1978. Serves
industrial, commercial and educational clients. Uses the services of music houses and songwriters for
scoring of films and television productions; background music for voice overs; lyricists for original
music and themes. Pays by the job. Buys all rights.
How to Contact: Query with résumé of credits. Prefers reel-to-reel, cassette (or videocassette). Does
not return material. Reports in 2 weeks.
Music: Varies with each and every project; from classical, contemporary to commercial industrial.
Tips: "Submit good demo tape with examples of your range to command the attention of our producers."

ON-Q PRODUCTIONS, INC., 618 Gutierrez St., Santa Barbara CA 93103. (805)963-1331. President:
Vincent Quaranta. Audiovisual firm. Clients include corporate accounts/sales conventions. Uses the
services of music houses, independent songwriters/composers and lyricists for scoring, background
music and jingles for AV shows. Commissions 1-5 composers and 1-5 lyricists/year. Buys all or one-
time rights.
How to Contact: Query with résumé of credits. Prefers cassette or 15 ips reel-to-reel (or VHS
videocassette). SASE, but prefers to keep material on file. Reports in 1 month.
Music: Uses up-tempo music for slide and video presentations.

OWENS ASSOCIATES, (formerly Owens & Anna Mendivil Associates), Suite 1500, 2800 N. Central,
Phoenix AZ 85004. (602)230-7557. Broadcast Producer: Lamar Owens. Advertising agency. Clients
include health care, automotive aftermarket and newspapers. Estab. 1986. Uses the services of music
houses for scoring of background music and jingles for commercials for radio/TV. Commissions 4-10
composers/year; 4-10 lyricists/year. Pays $2,000/job. Buys all rights.
How to Contact: Submit demo tape of previous work. Prefers cassette or ¾" videocassette. Does
not return material; prefers to keep on file. Reports in 6-8 weeks.
Music: Up-tempo, jazz and classical for commercials.

PANCOM LTD., (formerly Telecine Services & Production Ltd.), 23 Seapoint Ave., Blackrock, Co.
Dublin **Ireland.** Phone: 353 1 2808744. Fax: 353 1 808679. Director: Keith Nolan. Audiovisual firm
and video production house. Estab. 1977. Clients include advertising and commercial business. Uses
the services of songwriters and music houses for scoring of corporate and broadcast programs. Commissions 5 songwriters/composers and 3 lyricists for 20 pieces/year. Pays $5,000-10,000/job. Buys all
rights or rights within one country.
How to Contact: Submit demo tape of previous work. Prefers 15 ips reel-to-reel/DAT cassette with
3-10 songs. Does not return material. Reports in 1 month.
Tips: "Understand our marketing needs; know the difference between European and U.S. tastes."

PDS COMMUNICATIONS, INC., P.O. Box 412477, Kansas City MO 64141-2477. (800)473-7550. Vice
President/General Manager: Derrick Shivers. **Jingle/commercial music production house.** Clients include ad agencies, radio, TV, film and broadcast companies. Estab. 1990. Uses the services of music
houses, independent songwriters/composers, lyricists and voice talent for scoring of motion picture
sound tracks, background music for industrial films, jingles and commercials for radio and TV and
voice-overs. Commissions 4-5 composers and 10-12 lyricists/year. Pays union scale + percentage of
royalty. Buys all rights.
How to Contact: Query with résumé of credits. Prefers cassette (or VHS videocassette) with 2-3
songs and lyric sheet. "Follow directions and be patient." Does not return material. Reports in 2-3
months.

Music: Uses pop, R&B, jazz, classical, dance/house for jingles, commercials, soundtracks, voice-overs.
Tips: "Quality is the key. To produce the best, you accept no excuses, only results."

PHD VIDEO, 143 Hickory Hill Circle, Osterville MA 02655. (508)428-7198. Acquisitions: Violet Atkins. Motion picture production company. Clients include business and industry, production and post-production video houses and ad agencies. Estab. 1985. Uses the services of music houses, independent songwriters/composers and lyricists for background music for motion pictures. Commissions 10-12 composers and 10-12 lyricists/year. Pay is negotiable. Buys all rights.
How to Contact: Submit demo tape of previous work. Prefers cassette (or VHS videocassette). SASE but prefers to keep material on file. Reports in 1-2 months.
Music: Uses up-tempo and pop for commercials, motion pictures and TV shows.
Tips: "Be persistent. Constantly send updates of new work. Update files 1-2 times per year if possible. We hire approximately 25% new composers per year. Prefer to use composers/lyricists with 2-3 years track record."

PHILADELPHIA MUSIC WORKS, INC., Box 947, Bryn Mawr PA 19010. (215)825-5656. President: Andy Mark. **Jingle producers/music library producers**. Uses independent composers and music houses for background music for commercials and jingles. Commissions 20 songwriters/year. Pays $100-300/job. Buys all rights.
How to Contact: Submit demo tape of previous work. Prefers cassette. "We are looking for quality jingle tracks already produced, as well as instrumental pieces between 2 and 3 minutes in length for use in AV music library." Does not return material; prefers to keep on file. Reports in 4 weeks.
Music: All types.
Tips: "Send your best and put your strongest work at the front of your demo tape."

PHOTO COMMUNICATION SERVICES, INC., Box 508, Acme MI 49610. (616)922-3050. President: M'Lynn Hartwell. Audiovisual firm and motion picture production company. Serves commercial, in-dustrial and nonprofit clients. Uses services of music houses, independent songwriters, and lyricists for jingles and scoring of and background music for multi-image, film and video. Negotiates pay. Buys all or one-time rights.
How to Contact: Submit demo tape of previous work, tape demonstrating composition skills or query with résumé of credits. Prefers cassette or 15 ips reel-to-reel (or VHS videocassette). Does not return material; prefers to keep on file. Reports in 6 weeks.
Music: Uses mostly industrial/commercial themes.

PLAYERS MUSIC INC., 216 Carlton St., Toronto, Ontario M5A 2L1 **Canada**. (416)961-5290. Fax: (416)961-7754. Operations Manager: Jennifer Ward. Scoring service, **jingle/commercial music produc-tion house, production music library**, post audio production. Clients include advertising industry. Estab. 1980. Uses the services of independent songwriters/composers and lyricists for background music, jingles and commercials for radio and TV. Commissions 5 lyricists/year. Payment negotiable. Buys all rights.
How to Contact: Submit demo tape of previous work. Prefers cassette (or VHS videocassette). Does not return material; prefers to keep on file. Reports in 1 month.
Music: Uses all types for jingles.
Tips: "Have a talent at songwriting, not just programming."

PPI (PETER PAN INDUSTRIES), PARADE VIDEO, CURRENT RECORDS, COMPOSE RECORDS, 88 St. Frances St., Newark NJ 07105. (201)344-4214. Director of A&R: Marianne Eggleston. Video, record label, publishing. Clients include songwriters, music and video. Estab. 1928. Uses the services of music houses, independent songwriters/composers, for scoring of video and audio products and background music. Commissions hundreds of composers and lyricists/year. Pays by the job, royalty and per agreement. Rights negotiable.
How to Contact: Submit demo tape and manuscript showing previous work, composition and scoring skills, or write to arrange personal interview. Prefers cassette (or ½ or ¾ videocassette) with 6 songs and lyric sheet. Also include a picture and bio of the artist. SASE. Prefers to keep material on file "if we like it for possible reference when we're looking for new materials. Completed projects preferred!" Reports in 3 weeks to 3 months (if we like it, immediately!)

Market conditions are constantly changing! If you're still using this book and it is 1996 or later, buy the newest edition of Songwriter's Market at your favorite bookstore or order directly from Writer's Digest Books.

Music: Uses all musical styles, including children's and health and fitness.
Tips: "Make your presentation as professional as possible and include your name, address and phone number on the tape/cassette in case it gets separated from the package."

PREMIER VIDEO, FILM AND RECORDING CORP., Dept. SM, 3033 Locust St., St. Louis MO 63103. (314)531-3555. President: Robert R. Heuermann. Audiovisual firm, video producer and motion picture production company. Estab. 1931. Uses the services of music houses and independent songwriters for scoring of commercial productions for retail sales, background music for video productions and commercials for radio/TV. Commissions 6-10 pieces and 5-10 lyricists/year. Pays by royalty or by contracted services. Buys all rights.
How to Contact: Submit demo tape of previous work. Prefers VHS or cassette with any number of songs. Does not return material. Reports in 3 weeks.
Music: "As we serve every area of human development, all musical art forms are occasionally used."
Tips: "Send us your best work but show diversification."

PRICE WEBER MARKETING COMMUNICATIONS, INC., Dept. SM, Box 99337, Louisville KY 40223. (502)499-9220. Producer/Director: Kelly McKnight. Advertising agency and audiovisual firm. Estab. 1968. Clients include Fortune 500, consumer durables, light/heavy industrials and package goods. Uses services of music houses and independent songwriters/composer for scoring, background music and jingles for industrial and corporate image films and commercials for radio and TV. Commissions 6-8 composers/year. Pays by the job ($500-2,000). Buys all or one-time rights.
How to Contact: Submit demo tape of previous work demonstrating composition skills. Prefers cassette with 10 pieces. "Enclose data sheet on budgets per selection on demo tape." Does not return unsolicited material; prefers to keep on file. "We report back only if we use it."
Music: Uses easy listening, up-tempo, pop, jazz, rock and classical for corporate image industrials and commercials.
Tips: "Keep us updated on new works or special accomplishments. Work with tight budgets of $500-2,000. Show me what you're best at—show me costs."

QUALLY & COMPANY INC., #3, 2238 Central St., Evanston IL 60201-1457. (708)864-6316. Creative Director: Robert Qually. Advertising agency. Uses the services of music houses, independent songwriters/composers and lyricists for scoring, background music and jingles for radio and TV commercials. Commissions 2-4 composers and 2-4 lyricists/year. Pays by the job or by royalty. Buys various rights depending on deal.
How to Contact: Submit demo tape of previous work or query with résumé of credits. Prefers cassette (or ¾" Beta videocassette). SASE, but prefers to keep material on file. Reports in 2 weeks.
Music: Uses all kinds of music for commercials.

BILL QUINN PRODUCTIONS, 710 Cookman Ave., Asbury Park NJ 07712. (908)775-0500. Production Manager: Pat McManus. Audiovisual firm and motion picture production company. Estab. 1983. Clients include corporate, advertisers on cable and network TV and production companies. Uses the services of independent songwriters/composers and music houses for scoring of original productions and industrial films, background music for client accounts, commercials for radio and TV and video/film production. Commissions 15-20 composers/year. Pays by the job or approximately $25/hour. Buys one-time rights or all rights.
How to Contact: Submit demo tape of previous work or query with résumé of credits. Call first to arrange personal interview. Prefers cassette. Will return unsolicited material accompanied by an SASE, but prefers to keep on file. "We respond by phone whenever we find music that fits a particular need."
Music: "We don't use one type of music more than another because our client list is rather lengthy and varied. We use rock, pop, MOR, country, etc. Most often we commission music for TV and radio commercials. Interested in doing business with people in the New York and New Jersey area."
Tips: "Be flexible, able to work quickly and possess a working knowledge of all types of music."

RAMPION VISUAL PRODUCTIONS, 316 Stuart St., Boston MA 02116. (617)574-9601. Director/Camera: Steven V. Tringali. Motion picture multi media production company. Clients include educational, independent producers, corporate clients and TV producers. Estab. 1982. Uses the services of independent songwriters/composers for jingles, background music and scoring to longer form programming. Commissions 4-6 composers/year. Pays by the job. Buys all rights.
How to Contact: Submit demo tape of previous work or query with résumé of credits. Prefers cassette with variety of pieces. Does not return material; prefers to keep on file.
Music: Uses all styles for corporate, educational and original programming.
Tips: "Submit a varied demo reel showing style and client base."

RED HOTS ENTERTAINMENT, 813 N. Cordova St., Burbank CA 91505-2924. (818)954-0065. Director/ Music Videos: Chip Miller. Motion picture and music video production company. Clients include record labels, network/cable TV, MTV and motion picture studios. Estab. 1987. Uses the services of independent songwriters/composers for scoring of films, industrials and shorts, background music for commercials. Commissions 3-12 composers and 1-3 lyricists/year. Pay commensurate with film budget allocation. Rights bought depends on project.
How to Contact: Query with résumé of credits. Does not return material. Report back depends on project deadline and needs.
Music: Music depends upon the project.

*RED RIVER PRODUCTIONS, P.O. Box 2363, Clarksville TN 37042. (615)647-2641. Fax: (615)645-8139. Founder/Publisher: Ed Lawson. **Jingle/commercial music production house**, film and video production company. Estab. 1992. Uses the services of independent songwriters/composers, lyricists, film and video talent for background music for short films, commercials for radio, TV, books on tape production. Commissions 5-10 composers and 3-5 lyricists/year. Pay varies/job. Buys one-time rights.
How to Contact: Query with résumé of credits. Submit demo tape of previous work. Prefers cassette or VHS videocassette with 2 songs and lyric sheet. Prefers to keep submitted material on file. Reports in 1 month.
Music: Uses pop, rock, country, comedy, gospel, topical, children's for film, video, advertising, jingles, live performance, records and CDs.

REED PRODUCTIONS, INC., Box 977, Warsaw IN 46580. (219)267-4199. President: Howard Reed. Audiovisual firm and motion picture production company. Serves medical-industrial clients. Uses the services of music houses, independent songwriters/composers and lyricists for background music for audiovisual and video and commercials for TV. Commissions 1 composer and 1 lyricist/year. Pays $100-500/job. Buys all rights or one-time rights.
How to Contact: Submit demo tape of previous work. Prefers cassette (or VHS videocassette). SASE. Reports in 3 weeks.
Music: Uses traditional music for industrial, medical, audiovisual and video projects.

RS MUSIC PRODUCTIONS, (formerly RS Music), 378 Brooke Ave., Toronto, Ontario M5M 2L6 **Canada**. (416)787-1510. President: Richard Samuels. Scoring service, **jingle/commercial music production house**. Clients include songwriters (private sector), ad agencies, direct retailers, communications companies. Estab. 1989. Uses the services of music houses and independent songwriters/composers and lyricists for background music for film and commercials for radio and TV. Commissions 2-3 composers and 4-6 lyricists/year. Buys all or one-time rights.
How to Contact: Write first to arrange personal interview or submit demo tape of previous work. Prefers cassette (or VHS videocassette) with 4 songs and lyric sheet. Does not return material; prefers to keep on file. Reports in 1 month.
Music: Uses up-tempo and pop for jingles, corporate video underscore.
Tips: "Be exact in what you want to accomplish by contacting our company, i.e., what area of composition your forté is."

RTG PUBLISHING, INC., 130 E. 6th St., Cincinnati OH 45202. President: John Henry. Music Publisher. Clients include network TV (US), foreign TV and syndicated television producers. Uses services of MIDI composers to supply background and feature music and songs. Writers paid performance royalties through BMI/ASCAP.
How to Contact: Composers should submit résumé and demo cassette of appropriate material (i.e. examples of TV background scoring only). Songwriters should send no more than three songs on one cassette. SASE. Do not call. Reports as time allows.
Music: Song should be pop or A/C. No country, heavy metal, or rap.
Tips: "Listen to what the marketplace is using. Study TV music before submitting material."

CHARLES RYAN ASSOCIATES, Dept. SM, Box 2464, Charleston WV 25329. (304)342-0161. Vice President/Advertising Division: Harry Peck. Advertising agency. Clients in a variety of areas. Uses the services of music houses for scoring, background music, jingles and commercials for radio and TV. Commissions 2-3 songwriters/composers/year. Pays by the job. Buys all rights.
How to Contact: Submit demo tape of previous work or tape demonstrating composition skills; query with résumé of credits; or write to arrange personal interview. Prefers cassette with 15-20 songs. SASE, but prefers to keep on file.
Music: Uses easy listening, pop, jazz, classical for educational films, slide presentations and commercials.
Tips: "The first 2 songs/samples on demo tape better be good or we'll listen no further."

CARL SCHURTZ MUSIC, #1437, 3000 Olympic Blvd., Santa Monica CA 90404-5041. Contact: Carl Schurtz. **Jingle/commercial music production house**. Corporate clients, TV, cable, film, radio, recorded books and museum tours. Uses the services of independent songwriters/composers for scoring of film and TV. Commissions 1 composer/year. Pays by the job. Buys all rights.
How to Contact: Query with résumé of credits. Prefers cassette. Does not return material; prefers to keep on file. Reports in 2 months.
Music: Pop to classical, copy cats or pop tunes for industrials, multi image, videos (corporate) and jingles.

SHAFFER SHAFFER SHAFFER, INC., Dept. SM, 1070 Hanna Bldg., Cleveland OH 44115. (216)566-1188. President: Harry Gard Shaffer, Jr. Advertising agency. Clients include consumer and retail. Uses services of songwriters, lyricists and music houses for jingles and background music. Commissions 6 songwriters/year. Pays $2,000-15,000/job. Buys all rights.
How to Contact: Query with résumé of credits. Prefers cassette with 6-12 songs. Prefers to keep material on file. Responds as needs arise.

*SIGNATURE MEDIA GROUP, INC., Suite 100, 888 S. Greenville, Richardson TX 75081. (214)680-4300. Fax: (214)907-8273. Vice President: Chuck Murphy. Advertising agency. Uses the services of music houses and/or independent songwriters/composers for background music and jingles for commercials for radio and TV. Commissions 2-5 composers and 2-5 lyricists/year. Pays per job or by the hour. Buys all rights or one-time rights.
How to Contact: Submit demo tape of previous work. Prefers cassette. Does not return material. Reports in 2-3 weeks.
Music: Uses all styles, mostly for jingles.

SINGER ADVERTISING & MARKETING, INC., 1035 Delaware Ave., Buffalo NY 14209. (716)884-8885. Senior Vice President: Marilyn Singer. Advertising agency. Clients include health care, professional football, travel service and industrial. Estab. 1969. Uses the services of music houses, independent songwriters/composers and lyricists for background music for slide presentations, industrial videos, jingles for health care and professional football and commercials for radio and TV. Commissions 1-2 composers and 1-2 lyricists/year. Pay varies. Buys all rights.
How to Contact: Submit demo tape of previous work. Prefers cassette or 15 ips reel-to-reel (or ½" videocassette). SASE. "We will hold some material if we think there may be an appropriate upcoming opportunity." Reports in 3-4 weeks.
Music: Uses up-tempo pop and New Age jazz for commercial jingles and slide presentations.
Tips: "Study our client list and their current work and then submit."

ROBERT SOLOMON AND ASSOCIATES ADVERTISING, Dept. SM, Suite 1000, 505 N. Woodward, Bloomfield Hills MI 48304. (313)540-0660. Creative Director: Neil Master. Advertising agency. Clients include food service accounts, convenience stores, retail accounts and small service businesses. Uses independent songwriters, lyricists and music houses for jingles and special presentations. Commissions 1-10 songwriters and 1-10 lyricists/year. Pays by the job. Buys all rights.
How to Contact: Submit demo tape of previously aired work. Prefers cassette or 7½ ips reel-to-reel with 1-5 pieces and lyric or lead sheets. "Submissions must be up-to-date and up to industry standards." Does not return unsolicited material; prefers to keep on file.
Music: MOR, pop or rock jingles describing specific products or services.
Tips: "Please make sure all information presented is CURRENT!"

SORIN PRODUCTIONS, INC., Freehold Executive Center, 4400 Route 9 S., Freehold NJ 07728. (908)462-1785. President: David Sorin. Audiovisual firm. Serves corporate and industrial clients. Uses services of music houses and independent songwriters/composers for background music for industrials. Commissions 1-3 composers and 1-3 lyricists/year. Pays by the job. Buys all rights.
How to Contact: Query with résumé of credits. "No submissions with initial contact." Does not return unsolicited material; prefers to keep solicited materials on file. Reports in 1 month.
Music: Uses up-tempo and pop for audio, video and slides.

SOTER ASSOCIATES INC., 209 North 400 W., Provo UT 84601. (801)375-6200. President: N. Gregory Soter. Advertising agency. Clients include financial, health care, municipal, computer hardware and software. Estab. 1970. Uses services of music houses, independent songwriters/composers and lyricists for background music for audiovisual presentations and jingles for radio and TV commercials. Commissions 1 composer, 1 lyricist/year. Pays by the job. Buys all rights.
How to Contact: Submit tape demonstrating previous work and composition skills. Prefers cassette or VHS videocassette. Does not return unsolicited submissions; prefers to keep materials on file.

414 Songwriter's Market '95

SOUND IDEAS, Suite #4, 105 W. Beaver Creek Rd., Richmond Hill, Ontario L4B 1C6 **Canada**. (416)886-5000. Fax: (416)866-6800. President: Brian Nimens. **Music/sound effect library**. Clients include broadcast, post-production and recording studios. Estab. 1978. Uses the services of music houses. Commissions 5-10 composers/year. Pays by the job. Buys all rights.
How to Contact: Submit demo tape of previous work. Prefers cassette with 5-10 songs. Does not return material; prefers to keep on file. Reports in 1 month.
Music: Uses full range for all kinds of assignments.

SOUND WRITERS PUBLICATIONS, INC., Dept. SM, 223-225 Washington St., Newark NJ 07102. (201)642-5132. Producer/Engineer: Kevin Ferd. Advertising agency, audiovisual firm and **jingle/commercial music production house**. Clients include major labels and large corporations. Estab. 1980. Uses the services of independent songwriters/composers and lyricists for scoring of jingles and TV commercials. Most writing, producing and engineering done inhouse. Buys all rights and one-time rights.
How to Contact: Submit demo tape of previous work. Prefers cassette or ¾″ videocassette. "We have a no return policy on all material." Prefers to keep material on file. Reports back in 4 weeks.
Music: Uses all types of music for commercials, training tapes and music videos.
Tips: "We don't like big egos."

THE STRATEGIC GROUP, (formerly Strategic Promotions, Inc.), Suite 250, 2602 McKinney, Dallas TX 75204. (214)871-1016. President: Grahame Hopkins. Promotional marketing agency. Clients include fast food, retail food, food service, beverage, beer. Estab. 1978. Uses the services of independent songwriters/composers and lyricists for scoring of music tracks for TV commercials and background music for TV & radio commercials. Commissions 2-3 composers/year. Pays by the job. Buys all rights.
How to Contact: Submit demo tape of previous work. Prefers cassette (or ¾″ videocassette) with 4-5 songs. "No phone calls please." Does not return material; prefers to keep on file. Reports in 6 weeks.
Music: Uses all types of music for industrial videos, slide presentations and commercials.
Tips: "Be flexible, creative and open to input."

*STUDIO WORKS, 7911 Capri Circle, Houston TX 77095. (713)550-3550. Fax: (713)550-3596. Owner: Danny Erdeljac. Audiovisual firm, **jingle/commercial music production house** and multimedia production. Clients include engineering, legal, medical, commerical and industrial companies. Estab. 1986. Uses the services of independent songwriters/composers for scoring, background music and jingles for commericals for radio and TV. Commissions 3 composers and 2 lyricists/year. Pays by the job.
How to Contact: Write or call first to arrange personal interview, or submit demo tape of previous work. Prefers cassette (or VHS/Beta SP videocassette if available) with 3 songs. Prefers to keep material on file. Reports in 2 weeks.
Music: Uses all types of music (except rap) for all types of assignments.

SULLIVAN & FINDSEN ADVERTISING, Dept. SM, 2165 Gilbert Ave., Cincinnati OH 45206. (513)281-2700. Director of Broadcast Production: Kirby Sullivan. Advertising agency. Clients include consumer and business-to-business firms. Uses the services of music houses and independent songwriters/composers for jingles and commercials for radio and TV. Commissions 3 composers and 3 lyricists/year. Pays by the job. Buys all rights.
How to Contact: Submit demo tape of previous work. Prefers cassette. Does not return material; prefers to keep on file. "We report back when we need some work."
Music: Uses all styles for commercials.
Tips: "Don't call!"

*THE TAPE REGISTRY, #134, 11684 Ventura Blvd., Studio City CA 91604. (818)506-5467. Fax: (818)980-9756. Music Supervisor: Mark Wolfson. Music song library. Clients include: Warner Bros., TriStar, Orion and others. Estab. 1989. Uses the services of independent songwriters/composers for scoring and background music for films. Pays 50% royalty or flat rights publishing. Buys one-time rights.
How to Contact: Write or call first to arrange personal interview. Prefers cassette and lyric sheet. SASE. Prefers to keep submitted material on file. Reports in 6 weeks.
Music: Uses all types particularly quirky odd types for film scores.

Listings of companies within this section which are either commercial music production houses or music libraries will have that information printed in boldface type.

TEXAS AFFILIATED PUBLISHING COMPANY, "STREETPEOPLES WEEKLY NEWS," Box 270942, Dallas TX 75227-0942. (214)941-7796. Contact: Editor. Advertising agency and newspaper publisher. Clients are corporate and retail. Estab. 1977. Uses the services of independent songwriters/composers and lyricists for jingles and commercials for radio and TV. Pays negotiable amount. Buys all rights.
How to Contact: Query with résumé of credits. "No phone calls please. Send *no* originals, include SASE for returns. Our current project is about the problems of the homeless. Persons writing songs about this may want to send for a copy of 'Streetpeoples Weekly News' to get an idea of what's involved. Send $2 to cover handling/postage." SASE, but prefers to keep materials on file. Reports in 1 week.
Music: Uses easy listening, up-tempo for commercials. "We're interested in many types/styles according to job need of our clients. Also need music production for intros on radio talk shows."
Tips: "We're also looking for individuals and companies desiring to invest in a poetic anthology and music review on homelessness as well as displaying works in this new publication in 1995."

TPS VIDEO SVC., Box 1233, Edison NJ 08818. (201)287-3626. President: R.S. Burkt. Audiovisual firm, motion picture production company and **music/sound effects library**. Clients include AT&T, IBM and Xerox (industrial firms). Uses the services of independent composers and arrangers for scoring of industrials, background music and jingles for radio and TV commercials. Does not buy songs. Commissions 20-100 composers/year. Pays by the job. Buys all rights or one-time rights.
How to Contact: Submit demo tape of previous work demonstrating composition skills. Prefers cassette. SASE for response. Reports in 3 weeks.
Music: Considers all types of music for advertising.

TRF PRODUCTION MUSIC LIBRARIES, Dept. SM, 747 Chestnut Ridge Rd., Chestnut Ridge NY 10977. (914)356-0800. President: Michael Nurko. **Music/sound effect libraries.** Estab. 1931. Uses services of independent composers for jingles, background and theme music for all media including films, slide presentations, radio and TV commercials. Pays 50% royalty.
How to Contact: Submit demo tape of new compositions. Prefers cassette with 3-7 pieces.
Music: Primarily interested in instrumental music for assignments in all media.

TULLYVISION STUDIOS INC., Dept. SM, 914 Forest Grove Rd., Furlong PA 18725-1360. Producer: Michelle A. Powell. Audiovisual firm. Clients include corporate/industrial. Estab. 1983. Uses the services of independent songwriters/composers for marketing, training and corporate image videotapes. Commissions 3 composers/year. Pays $500/job. Buys all rights.
How to Contact: Submit demo tape of previous work. Prefers cassette (or ¾" VHS videocassette) with 3 songs. Does not return material; prefers to keep on file.
Music: Uses up-tempo and pop for educational films and slide presentations.

24 CARAT PRODUCTIONS–LITTLE GEMSTONE MUSIC, P.O. Box 1703, Fort Lee NJ 07024. (201)488-8562 or 488-7216. Owner: Kevin Noel. **Jingle/commercial music production house**, motion picture soundtracks company, corporate theme songs. Clients include commercial and independent clients. Estab. 1983. Uses the services of independent songwriters/composers (inhouse) for scoring of background music for jingles for commercials for radio and TV. Commissions 15 composers and 12 lyricists/year. Pays flat-rate or percentage royalty.
How to Contact: Query with résumé of credits, write first to arrange personal interview or submit demo tape of previous work. Prefers cassette. Prefers to keep submitted material on file. Reports in 2 weeks.
Music: Uses contemporary rock, pop, R&B, New Age music for commercial and private sources.

27TH DIMENSION INC., Box 1149, Okeechobee FL 34973-1149. (800)634-0091. President: John St. John. Scoring service, **jingle/commercial music production house** and music sound effect library. Clients include audiovisual producers, video houses, recording studios and radio and TV stations. Estab. 1986. Uses the services of independent songwriters/composers for scoring of library material and commercials for radio and TV. Commissions 10 composers/year. Pays $100-1,000/job; publishing (performance fees). "We buy the right to use in our library exclusively." Buys all rights except writer's publishing. Writer gets all performance fees (ASCAP or BMI).
How to Contact: Submit tape demonstrating composition skills or call. Prefers cassette. "Call before sending." SASE, but prefers to keep on file. Reports in 1 month.
Music: Uses industrial, pop jazz, sports, contemporary and New Age for music library.
Tips: "Follow style instructions carefully."

UNITED ENTERTAINMENT PRODUCTIONS, 3947 State Line, Kansas City MO 64111. (816)756-0288. Operations Manager: Dave Maygers. Recording studio, artist management, publishing company and record company. Serves musical groups, songwriters and ad clients. Estab. 1972. Uses the services of independent songwriters, lyricists and self-contained groups for scoring of album projects, background music for ads and industrial films, jingles and commercials for radio and TV. Pays negotiable royalty. Buys all rights or one-time rights.

How to Contact: Submit demo tape of previous work demonstrating composition skills. "Send cassette of material and lyric sheet when applicable." Does not return unsolicited material; prefers to keep material on file.

Music: Rock, pop, R&B, jazz, country to be used in music projects.

*VIDEO I-D, INC., Dept. SM, 105 Muller Rd., Washington IL 61571. (309)444-4323. Manager, Marketing Services: Gwen Wagner. Post production/teleproductions. Clients include industrial and business. Estab. 1978. Uses the services of music houses and independent songwriters/composers for background music for video productions. Pays per job. Buys one-time rights.

How to Contact: Submit demo tape of previous work. Prefers cassette or VHS videocassette with 5 songs and lyric sheet. SASE, but prefers to keep submitted materials on file. Reports in 3-4 weeks.

Music: "The music styles we look for are based solely on our clients' needs and preferences. When submitting material be sure to include different types."

VINEBERG COMMUNICATIONS, Dept. SM, Suite B-408, 61-20 Grand Central Pkwy., Forest Hills NY 11375. (718)760-0333. President: Neil Vineberg. **Jingle/commercial music production house.** Clients include TV/film producers. Estab. 1986. Uses the services of independent songwriters/composers and lyricists for background music for TV/film, corporate videos/film and commercials for radio and TV. Commissions 5 composers and 2 lyricists/year. Pays by the job. Buys all rights and one-time rights.

How to Contact: Submit demo tape of previous work. Submit tape demonstrating composition skills. Query with résumé of credits. Write first to arrange personal interview. Prefers cassette or VHS videocassette with 4 songs and lead sheet (if possible). "No calls. Write only." SASE, but prefers to keep material on file. Reports in 1 month.

Music: Uses all types except classical.

VIP VIDEO, Film House, 143 Hickory Hill Circle, Osterville MA 02655. (508)428-7198. President: Jeffrey H. Aikman. Audiovisual firm. Clients include business, industry and TV stations. Estab. 1983. Uses the services of music houses, independent songwriters/composers and lyricists for scoring of and background music for motion pictures and home video. Commissions 15-20 composers and 15-20 lyricists/year. Pays by the job, amounts vary depending on the length and complexity of each project. Buys all rights.

How to Contact: Submit demo tape of previous work. Prefers cassette with 1-2 songs. SASE, but prefers to keep material on file unless specifically stated. Reports in 6-8 weeks.

Music: Uses easy listening, pop and up-tempo for feature films, TV series, TV pilots and background for videotapes. Currently working on scoring series of 26 feature length silent films. If project is successful, this series will be added to at the rate of 13 per year.

Tips: "Constantly update your files. We like to hear from songwriters, lyricists and composers at least 3-4 times/year."

VISION STUDIOS, 3765 Marwick Ave., Long Beach CA 90808. (310)429-1042. Proprietor: Arlan H. Boll. Audiovisual firm, scoring service, **jingle/commercial music production house, music sound effect library.** Clients include ad agencies, film and video directors, producers, etc. Estab. 1989. Uses the services of independent songwriters/composers and lyricists for scoring of background music for all media: film, radio and TV. Commissions 2-4 composers and 2-4 lyricists/year. "Payment is negotiable." Buys all rights or one-time rights.

How to Contact: Write first to arrange personal interview. Does not return material.

Music: Uses all types of music for all types of assignments.

*WARD AND AMES, #350, 7500 San Felipe, Houston TX 77063. (713)266-9696. Fax: (713)266-2481. Partners: Danny Ward or Nancy Ames. Scoring service, **jingle/commercial music production house,** event design and consultant. Clients include corporations, ad agencies, political entities, TV markets, production houses. Estab. 1982. Uses the services of independent songwriters/composers and audio recording studios for scoring of background music, jingles and commercials for radio; also industrials. Pays per job. Buys all rights.

How to Contact: Submit demo tape of previous work. Prefers cassette with lead sheet. SASE.

Music: Uses all types, excluding heavy metal, for custom show production, jingles and industirals.

WEBER, COHN & RILEY, 444 N. Michigan Ave., Chicago IL 60611. (312)527-4260. Executive Creative Director: C. Welch. Advertising agency. Serves real estate, business, financial and food clients. Estab. 1960. Uses music houses for jingles and background music for commercials. Commissions 2 songwriters and 2 lyricists/year. Pays $500 minimum/job. Buys all rights or one-time rights, "open to negotiation."

How to Contact: Write a letter of introduction to creative director. SASE. "We listen to and keep a file of all submissions, but generally do not reply unless we have a specific job in mind." Songwriters may follow up with a phone call for response.

Music: "We use music for a variety of products and services. We expect highly original, tight arrangements that contribute to the overall concept of the commercial. We do not work with songwriters who have little or no previous experience scoring and recording commercials."

Tips: "Establish credentials and get experience on small local work, then go after bigger accounts. Don't oversell when making contacts or claim the ability to produce any kind of 'sound.' Present a work that is creative and meets our strategies and budget requirements."

WEST COAST PROJECTIONS, #100, 11245 W. Bernardo Court, San Diego CA 92127. (619)452-0041. Producer: David Gibbs. Video production. Estab. 1980. Uses the services of independent songwriters/composers for scoring and background music. Commissions 3 composers/year. Pays by the job. Buys one-time rights.

How to Contact: Submit demo tape of previous work. Prefers cassette (or any videocassette). Does not return material; prefers to keep on file. Reports only if interested.

Music: Uses up-tempo pop for rock videos and corporate image presentations.

WHITE PRODUCTION ARCHIVES, INC., Dept. SM, 5525 W. 159th St., Oak Forest IL 60452. (708)535-1540. President: Matthew White. Motion picture production company. Produces home video entertainment programs. Estab. 1987. Uses the services of independent songwriters/composers for scoring documentaries; videogame tapes. Commissions 5 composers/year. Pays by the job. Buys all rights.

How to Contact: Submit demo tape of previous work. Prefers cassette. Does not return unsolicited material. Prefers to keep submitted materials on file.

Music: Uses material for home videos.

EVANS WYATT ADVERTISING, 346 Mediterranean Dr., Corpus Christi TX 78418. (512)939-7200. Owner: E. Wyatt. Advertising agency. Clients are general/all types. Estab. 1975. Uses the services of music houses and independent songwriters/composers for background music for soundtracks, jingles for advertising and commercials for radio and TV. Commissions 10-12 composers/year. Pays by the job. Buys all rights.

How to Contact: Submit demo tape of previous work demonstrating composition skills, query with résumé of credits or write first to arrange personal interview. Prefers cassette. SASE, but prefers to keep material on file. Reports in 2 months.

Music: Uses all types for commercials plus videos mostly.

GREG YOUNGMAN MUSIC, Box 381, Santa Ynez CA 93460. (805)688-1136. Advertising agency/audio production. Serves all types of clients. Local, regional and national levels. Uses the services of music houses and independent composers/lyricists for commercials, jingles and audiovisual projects. Commissions 12-20 composers/year. Pays $500-10,000/project. Buys all or one-time rights.

How to Contact: Submit demo tape of previously aired work. Prefers cassette, R-DAT or reel-to-reel. Does not return material; prefers to keep on file. Reports in 1 month.

Music: Uses all types for radio commercials, film cues.

Tips: "Keep demos to 10 minutes."

Advertising, AV and Commercial Music Firms/'94-'95 Changes

The following markets appeared in the 1994 edition of *Songwriter's Market* but are absent from the 1995 edition. Most of these companies failed to respond to our request for an update of their listing for a variety of reasons. For example, they may have gone out of business or they may have requested deletion from the 1995 edition because they are backlogged with material. If we know the specific reason, it appears within parentheses.

Paul Anand Music
Ball Communications, Inc.
B&C Productions
Ted Barkus Company, Inc.
Capitol-OGM Production
Carleton Productions Inc.
ETV
Leisure-For-Pleasure
Luna Tech, Inc.

Master Management Music
Mid-Ocean Recording Studio
Paisano Publications/Easyriders Home Video
Pullin Productions Ltd.
Response Graphics
Right Tracks Productions Ltd.
Ruffcut Recording
S.A. Productions, Inc.

Schembri Vision
Spivack Advertising, Inc.
Station Break Productions
Strauchen Associates, Inc.
Teeman/Sleppin Enterprises
Transworld West Music Group
Tri Video Teleproduction
Video Arts
Weston Woods

Play Producers
and Publishers

Writing music for the stage is a considerable challenge in the theater of the 1990s. Conventional wisdom says that if a composer or playwright doesn't have a production to his credit, he will have a difficult time establishing himself. Play producers in the major markets, especially Broadway, won't often take a chance on unproven talent when productions routinely cost millions of dollars and a show must run for several years to break even. It's a classic catch-22; the aspiring playwright needs experience to get his work produced, but can't get that experience without production.

Fortunately, the conventional wisdom about musical theater may not be accurate. Many venues for new musical works do exist, and are listed here. Contained within are listings of theater companies, producers, dinner theaters, and publishers of musical theater works. We've separated this section into two subsections: one for producers and one for publishers. All these markets are interested in and actively seeking new musical theater works of all types for their stages or publications.

Many of these listings are for small theaters run on a nonprofit basis. Their budgets for production and rehearsal time are, by necessity, limited. Keep this in mind when preparing to submit your work. When submitting, ask about other opportunities available for your work. Some companies or theaters may like your work, but may wish to present it in revue form. Others may be looking for incidental music for a spoken word play. Research each company or theater carefully and learn about their past performances, the type of work they present, and the kinds of material they're looking for. The more knowledgeable you are about the workings of a particular company or theater, the easier it is to tailor your work to fit their style and the more responsive they will be to you and your work.

Use research and further education to help you enrich your personal experience and therefore your work. Attend as many performances as possible; know exactly what kind of work a particular theater presents. Volunteer to work at a theater, whether it be moving sets or selling tickets. This will give you valuable insight into the day to day workings of a theater and the building of a new show. Look into professional internships at theaters and attend any theater workshops in your area (for more information, see the Workshops section of this book). As a composer for the stage, you need to know as much as possible about the theater and how it works, its history and the different roles played by the people involved in it. Flexibility is a key to successful productions, and having a knowledge of how the theater works will only aid you in cooperating and collaborating with the work's director, producer, technical people and actors.

Read the following listings carefully for information on each market, the type of work being sought, and their submission procedures. Research further the markets that you believe will be interested in your work. And when you've decided on the best markets for your work, follow submission procedures meticulously.

INSIDER REPORT

Musical playwrights need to focus on storyline

Michael Koppy, producer of the Ten-Minute Musicals Project in West Hollywood, estimates that he's read more than 600 musicals in the last few years, submitted from every continent except Antarctica. He has received ideas from well-known songwriters such as Barry Manilow and Toni Tennille, as well as beginning playwrights. And yet he is often surprised by how little writers understand musical theater.

Michael Koppy

"There's such a dearth of knowledge about how intense the musical theater format is," he says. "This is extra difficult material to do, which is why there are so few successful musicals."

Koppy feels the most important element of a good musical is a strong storyline. "Too often people disparage the importance of the spoken dialogue and storyline," he notes. "The story is the armature on which the musical is built. You can't have a good musical without a good story." Koppy suggests that writers try adapting works that are in the public domain: short stories, plays or poems. Many of the Project's musicals have been based on short stories, by authors from O. Henry to Ambrose Bierce.

The Ten-Minute Musicals Project was founded in 1984 by New York producer Joseph Papp, and one of the first productions was *The Mystery of Edwin Drood,* which later ran on Broadway. Koppy took over the Project in 1988, "because I believe in the format," he says. "I believe in what you can accomplish in musical theater."

Koppy points out that most successful musicals have a dramatic flair, what he calls a "sense of event" that makes the musical stand out. He says musicals like *Cats* or *Godspell* have dramatic sequences that provide much of the power of a production. But he cautions writers against getting too wrapped up in the technicalities of staging a production. "Don't worry about the sense of event," he advises. "Don't worry about how you are going to send 100 semi-trucks flying underneath the arches of the Golden Gate Bridge. If it's important enough to the story, the choreographers and designers can figure out how to make it work. Just be sure the story works."

Koppy has guidelines for submissions, but very few hard-and-fast rules. He looks for short, contemporary pieces, usually 7 to 14 minutes long. Any genre or musical style can be used effectively, but some formats work better than others. Fast-paced comedy material usually has an advantage, while fairy tales can easily become too cute and trite. He warns writers to "be wary of writing only introspective musical 'moments,' as they usually stop the progression of the plot." He also finds that devices like narrators and long solo ballads tend to slow things down.

There are no rules cast in stone, however, and many of the most effective pieces he's worked with have broken one or more of these rules. "This is not some obnoxious academic arts bureaucracy!" he says. "We're looking for quality ideas, not somebody who dots the i's."

Many pieces need some reworking before they're ready to be produced, and Koppy is willing to work with writers to fine-tune a piece. The Ten-Minute Musicals Project holds regular workshops, which feature six or seven of the best pieces. In recent years Koppy has conducted workshops in San Francisco, New York and Nashville, and is selecting new material for a workshop in Los Angeles during the 1994-95 season. Koppy has taken some of the finest pieces from the first four seasons and compiled them into a full-length musical entitled *Stories*, and is negotiating with several theaters to bring this show to the stage.

Koppy firmly believes that short musical theater is an important, if somewhat neglected, format. Like poetry, it packs a lot of meaning into a small space, which means the writing has to be of the highest caliber. "There's no wasted motion," he says. "Every sentence and every lyric has to have meaning, to develop the story. It's such an efficient form."

—Alison Holm

Play Producers

A.D. PLAYERS, 2710 W. Alabama, Houston TX 77098. (713)526-2721. Dramaturg: Martha Doolittle. Play producer. Estab. 1967. Produces 4-5 full-length, 4 children's and approximately 20 1 acts in repertory and 1-2 musicals/year. General public tend to be conservative—main stage shows, children/families—children's shows; churches schools, business—repertory shows. Payment varies.
How to Contact: Query with synopsis, character breakdown and set description. Reports in 6-12 months.
Musical Theater: We prefer musicals for family and/or children, comedy or drama, full-length, original or classic adaptations with stories that reflect God's relevence and importance in our lives. Any style. Maximum 10 actors. No fly space required. Minimum wing space required. No New Age; anything contradictory to a Christian perspective; operatic; avant garde cabaret. Music should be simple, easy to learn and perform, we utilize a broad range of musical ability; will consider musical revue to musical comedy, play with music.
Productions: *Narnia*, by Jules Tasca (children, family, fantasy, musical); *Smoke on the Mountain*, by Connie Ray and Alan Bailey (family gospel, hymn heritage); *Galley Proof*, by Jeanette Cliff George (musical comedy, biblical characters, and storyline).
Tips: "Learn the craft, structure and format of scriptwriting before submitting. Then be flexible and open to learning from any producing theatre which takes an interest in your work."

THE ACTING COMPANY, Dept. SM, Box 898, Times Square Station, New York NY 10108. (212)564-3510. Play producer. Estab. 1972. Produces 2-3 plays/year. "Have done musicals in the past. We are a national touring company playing universities and booking houses." Pays by royalty or negotiated fee/commission.
How to Contact: Submit through agent only. SASE. Reports in 12 weeks.
Musical Theater: "We would consider a wide variety of styles—although we remain a young, classical ensemble. Most of our classical plays make use of a lot of incidental music. Our company consists of 17 actors. All productions must be able to tour easily. We have no resident musicians. Taped sound is essential. Actors tend to remain active touring members for 2-3 seasons. Turnover is considerable. Musical ability of the company tends to vary widely from season to season. We would avoid shows which require sophisticated musical abilities and/or training."

*THE ACTORS' THEATRE, P.O. Box 780, Talent OR 97540. (503)535-5250. New Plays Director: Becky Jones. Play producer. Estab. 1982. Produces 6 plays and 1 new musical/year. "99 seat flexible thrust, 2 chorus dressing rooms, with modest tech capabilities. Unit sets work best." Pay is negotiable.
How to Contact: Query with synopsis, character breakdown, set description, 10 page dialogue and tape of songs. SASE. Reports in 4 months.
Musical Theater: "Adaptations of classics, especially children's books/stories. Emphasis on contemporary understanding of myth, i.e., Joseph Campbell, Carl Jung, C.S. Lewis. Not necessarily politically correct. Definitely not cute. Native Americans especially sought. Cast size limit: 15. Unit set best, though not mandatory. Minimal furniture and prop best. No formulas."
Productions: *Tale of Two Cities*, by Harrison; *Fellowship of the Ring*, by Haliburtorn; and *Snow Queen*, by Coyne/Mansfield.
Tips: "Send only what you feel passionate about."

ALLEGHENY HIGHLANDS REGIONAL THEATRE, 526 West Ogle St., Ebensburg PA 15931. (814)472-4333. Managing Director: Noel Feeley. Play producer. Estab. 1974. Produces 4 plays and 2 musicals/year. "Rural audience, many elderly, many families; 200 seat arena." Pays $40-50/performance.
How to Contact: Query with synopsis, character breakdown and set description. SASE. Reports in 6 months.
Musical Theatre: "Small cast, full-length musicals, preferably orchestrated for no more than 6 musicians. Anything set in Pennsylvania about Pennsylvanians is of particular interest. Especially interested in musicals for children, up to 60 minutes in length. Roles for children are a plus. We have difficulty finding men to audition. Few men's roles are a plus. No more than 19-20 including chorus, no more than 2-3 settings. We had original music scored for scene changes and intermission music for *She Stoops To Conquer*. Perhaps some underscoring for a mystery would be fun. Also pieces for young performers."
Productions: *Meet Me In St. Louis*, by Benson/Martin/Blane; and *Waiting for the Parade*, by Murrell.

AMERICAN LIVING, History Theater, Box 2677, Hollywood CA 90078. (213)876-2202. President and Artistic Director: Dorene Ludwig. Play producer. Estab. 1975. Produces 1-2 plays/year. All over U.S., but mostly Southern California—conventions, schools, museums, universities, libraries, etc. Pays by royalty.
How to Contact: Query first. SASE. Reports in 6 months.
Musical Theater: "We use only primary source, historically accurate material: in music—*Songs of the Civil War* or *Songs of the Labor Movement*, etc.—presented as a program rather than play would be the only use I could foresee. We need music historians more than composers."
Tips: "Do not send fictionalized historical material. We use primary source material only."

AMERICAN STAGE FESTIVAL, Box 225, Milford NH 03055. (603)673-4005. Producing Director: Matthew Parent. Play producer. Estab. 1975. Produces 5 mainstage plays, 10 children's and 1-2 musicals/year. Plays are produced in 496 seat proscenium stage for a general audience.
How to Contact: Query with synopsis, character breakdown and set description. SASE. Reports in 1 month.
Musical Theater: "We seek stories about interesting people in compelling situations. Besides our adult audience we have an active children's theater. We will not do a large chorus musical if cast size is over 18. We use original music in plays on a regular basis, as incidental music, pre-show and between acts, or as moments in and of themselves."
Productions: *Little Shop of Horrors*, by Howard Ashman and Alan Menken; the Tony Award-nominated *Starmites* and the musical version of the classic comedy *Peg O' My Heart*.
Tips: "Submit tape of songs. Quality of music is most important in selecting musicals. We are most attracted to 'book' musicals."

ARDEN THEATRE COMPANY, P.O. Box 779, Philadelphia PA 19105. (215)829-8900. Fax: (215)829-1735. Producing Artistic Director: Terrence J. Nolen. Play producer. Estab. 1988. Produces 5 plays and 1-2 musicals/year. Adult audience—diverse. 150-175 seats, flexible. Pays 5% royalty.
How to Contact: Submit complete ms, score and tape of songs. SASE. Reports in 6 months.
Musical Theater: Full length plays and musicals. Intimate theater space, maximum cast approximately 15, minimum can be smaller. Not interested in children's music. Will consider original music for use in developing or pre-existing play. Composers should send samples of music on cassette.

 The asterisk before a listing indicates that the listing is new in this edition. New markets are often the most receptive to unsolicited submissions.

Productions: *Sweeney Todd*, by Sondheim/Wheeler (musical thriller); *Change Partners & Dance*, by Dennis Raymond Smeal (romantic comedy); *The Tempest*, by Shakespeare (classic).
Tips: "Send cassette."

ARIZONA THEATRE COMPANY, P.O. Box 1631, Tucson AZ 85702. (602)884-8210. Artistic Director: David Goldstein. Professional regional theater company. Members are professionals. Performs 6 productions/year, including 1 new work. Audience is middle and upper-middle class, well-educated, aged 35-64. "We are a two-city operation based in Tucson, where we perform in a 603-seat newly renovated, historic building, which also has a 100-seat flexible seating cabaret space. Our facility in Phoenix, the Herberger Theater Center, is a 712-seat, proscenium stage." Pays 4-10% royalty.
How to Contact: Query first. Reports in 5 months.
Musical Theater: Musicals or musical theater pieces. 15-16 performers maximum including chorus. Instrumental scores should not involve full orchestra. No classical or operatic.
Productions: Barbara Damashek's *Quilters* (musical theater piece); Sondheim/Bernstein's *Candide* (musical); and Anita Ruth/American composer's *Dreamers of the Day* (musical theater piece).
Tips: "As a regional theater, we cannot afford to produce extravagant works. Plot line and suitability of music to further the plot are essential considerations."

ARKANSAS REPERTORY THEATRE, 601 Main, P.O. Box 110, Little Rock AR 72203. (501)378-0445. Contact: Brad Mooy. Play producer. Estab. 1976. Produces 7 plays and 4 musicals (1 new musical)/year. "We perform in a 354-seat house and also have a 99 seat blackbox." Pays 5-10% royalty or $75-150 per performance.
How to Contact: Query with synopsis, character breakdown and set description. SASE. Reports in 6 months.
Musical Theater: "Small casts are preferred, comedy or drama and prefer shows to run 1:45 to 2 hours maximum. Simple is better; small is better, but we do produce complex shows. We aren't interested in children's pieces, puppet shows or mime. We always like to receive a tape of the music with the book."
Productions: *Sing, Baby Sing*, by Don Jones/Jack Heifner (original swing musical); *Nunsense II*, by Dan Goggin (Catholicism Revue); *Always . . . Patsy Cline*, by Ted Swindley (bio-musical).
Tips: "Include a *good* cassette of your music, *sung well*, with the script."

ASHLAWN-HIGHLAND SUMMER FESTIVAL, Box 37, Route 6, Charlottesville VA 22902. (804)293-4500. General Manager: Judith H. Walker. Play producer. Estab. 1977. Produces 1 musical and 2 operas/year. "Our operas and musicals are performed in a casual setting. The audience is composed of people from the Charlottesville area."
How to Contact: Query first. SASE. "We try to return items after review but depending on the time of year response time may vary."
Musical Theater: "We are very open to new ideas and young artists. Included in our season is a summer Saturday program designed for children. We enjoy puppet shows, story tellers and children-related plays. We are a small company with a limited budget. Our cast is usually 12 performers and a volunteer local chorus. Minimal scenery is done. Our audience is composed of families with children and retired adults. Material should suit their tastes." Would consider original music for use in a play being developed.
Productions: Rossini's *Cinderella (La Ceneventola)*; Mozart's *Cosi Fan Tutte*; and Rogers and Hammerstein's *The Sound of Music*.

ASOLO THEATRE COMPANY, (formerly Asolo Center for the Performing Arts), Dept. SM, 5555 N. Tamiami Trail, Sarasota FL 34243. (813)351-9010. Literary Manager: Bruce E. Rodgers. Play producer. Produces 7-8 plays (1 musical)/year. Plays are performed at the Asolo Mainstage (500-seat proscenium house). Pays 5% minimum royalty.
How to Contact: Query with synopsis, character breakdown, set description and one page of dialogue. SASE. Reports in 3 months.
Musical Theater: "We want small to mid-size non-chorus musicals only. They should be full-length, any subject. There are no restrictions on production demands; however, musicals with excessive scenic requirements or very large casts may be difficult to consider."
Productions: Julie Boyd's *Sweet and Hot*; Boyd, Wildhorn and Bettis' *Svengali* and Warrender and Luis's *Das Barbecü*.

BAILIWICK REPERTORY, Dept. SM, 1225 W. Belmont, Chicago IL 60657. (312)883-1091. Executive Director: David Zak. Play producer. Estab. 1982. Produces 5 mainstage, 5 one-act plays and 1-2 new musicals/year. "We do Chicago productions of new works on adaptations that are politically or thematically intriguing and relevent. We also do an annual director's festival which produces 50-75 new short works each year." Pays 5-8% royalty.

How to Contact: "Send SASE (business size) first to receive manuscript submission guidelines. Material returned if appropriate SASE attached."
Musical Theater: "We want innovative, dangerous, exciting and issue-oriented material."
Productions: *Nebraska*, by Logan; *Blues in the Night* (musical); and *Songs of the Season* (musical).
Tips: "Be creative. Be patient. Be persistent. Make me believe in your dream."

*BARTER THEATRE, P.O. Box 867, Abingdon VA 24210. (703)628-2281. Fax: (703)628-4551. Artistic Director: Richard Rose. Play producer. Estab. 1933. Produces 15 plays and 2-3 musicals/year, including 1 new musical. Audience "varies; middle American, middle age, tourist and local mix." 400 seat proscenium stage, 150 seat thrust stage. Pays by fee or royalty.
How to Contact: Query with synopsis, character breakdown and set description. SASE. Reports in 4-6 months.
Musical Theater: "We investigate all types. We are not looking for any particular standard. Prefer sellable titles with unique use of music. Prefer small cast musicals, although have done large scale projects with marketable titles or subject matter. We use original music in almost all of our plays." Does not wish to see "political or very urban material, or material with very strong language."
Productions: *The Last Leaf*, by Peter Ekstron (world premiere/O. Henry); *Peter Pan*, by Stevan Jackson (J.M. Barrie story); and *Man of LaMancha*, by Mitchell Leigh (Don Quixote story).
Tips: "Be patient. Be talented. Don't be obnoxious. Be original."

BERKSHIRE PUBLIC THEATRE, P.O. Box 860, 30 Union St., Pittsfield MA 01202. (413)445-4631. Artistic Director: Frank Bessell. Play producer. Estab. 1976. Produces 9 plays (2 musicals)/year. "Plays are performed in a 285-seat proscenium thrust theatre for a general audience of all ages with wide-ranging tastes." Pays negotiable royalty or amount per performance.
How to Contact: Query with synopsis, character breakdown and set description. SASE. Reports in 3 months.
Musical Theater: Seeking musicals with "no more than 3 acts (2½ hours). We look for fresh musicals with something to say. Our company has a flexible vocal range. Cast size must be 2-50, with a small orchestra." Would also consider original music "for a play being developed and possibly for existing works."
Productions: *Jesus Christ Superstar*, by Rice/Lloyd-Webber (gospel/life of Christ); *The Fantasticks*, by Tom Jones/Harvey Schmidt (youth and love); *You're Gonna Love Tom*, by Sondheim (revue of Sondheim).
Tips: "We are a small company. Patience is a must. Be yourself—open, honest. Experience is not necessary but is helpful. We don't have a lot of money but we are long on nurturing artists! We are developing shows with commercial prospects to go beyond the Berkshires, i.e., a series of rock music revues is now in its fifth year."

BRISTOL RIVERSIDE THEATRE, Dept. SM, Box 1250, Bristol PA 19007. (215)785-6664. Artistic Director: Susan D. Atkinson. Play producer. Estab. 1986. Produces 5 plays, 2 musicals/year (1 new musical every 2 years). "302-seat proscenium Equity theater with audience of all ages from small towns and metropolitan area." Pays by royalty 6-8%.
How to Contact: Submit complete ms, score and tape of songs. SASE. Reports in 6 months.
Musical Theater: "No strictly children's musicals. All other types with small to medium casts and within reasonable artistic tastes. Prefer one-set; limited funds restrict. Do not wish to see anything catering to prurient interests."
Productions: *Sally Blane, World's Greatest Girl Detective*, by David Levy/Leslie Eberhard (spoof of teen detective genre); *Moby Dick*, by Mark St. Germain, music by Doug Katsarous; and *Alive and Well*, by Larry Gatlin.
Tips: "He or she should be willing to work with small staff, open to artistic suggestion, and aware of the limitations of newly developing theaters."

WILLIAM CAREY COLLEGE DINNER THEATRE, William Carey College, Hattiesburg MS 39401. (601)582-6218. Managing Director: O.L. Quave. Play producer. Produces 2 plays (2 musicals)/year. "Our dinner theater operates only in summer and plays to family audiences." Payment negotiable.
How to Contact: Query with synopsis, character breakdown and set description. Does not return material. Reports in 1 month.
Musical Theater: "Plays should be simply-staged, have small casts (8-10 maximum), and be suitable for family viewing; two hours maximum length. Score should require piano only, or piano, synthesizer."
Productions: *Ernest in Love*; *Rodgers and Hart: A Musical Celebration*; and *Side by Side*, by Sondheim.

CENTENARY COLLEGE, THEATRE DEPARTMENT, Shreveport LA 71134-1188. (318)869-5011. Chairman: Robert R. Buseick. Play producer. Produces 6 plays (1-2 new musicals)/year. Plays are presented in a 350-seat playhouse to college and community audiences.

How to Contact: Submit manuscript and score. SASE. Reports in 1 month.
Productions: *Man of La Mancha*; *Nunsense*; *Chicago*; *Broadway Bound*; *Into the Woods*; *Little Shop of Horrors*; and *Jerry's Girls*, by Todd Sweeney.

*CENTER THEATER, 1346 W. Devon, Chicago IL 60660. (312)508-0200. Contact: Literary Manager. Play producer. Estab. 1984. Produces 6 plays and 1 musical (1 new musical)/year. "Our 80 seat modified thrust theater has produced 3 original musicals, based on novels or plays." Pays 3-10% royalty.
How to Contact: Query with synopsis, character breakdown and set description. SASE. Reports in 3 months.
Musical Theater: 12 person maximum.
Productions: *The Black Tulip*, by Tracy Friedman/Brian Lasser (adaptation of Dumas novel); *Two Many Bosses*, by Dan La Morte/Donald Coates (musical adaptation of "Servant of Two Masters"); and *Lysistrata 2411 A.D.*, by Dale Calandra/Donald Coates (futuristic musical adaptation).

CIRCA' 21 DINNER PLAYHOUSE, Dept. SM, Box 3784, Rock Island IL 61204-3784. (309)786-2667. Producer: Dennis Hitchcock. Play producer. Estab. 1977. Produces 1-2 plays, 4-5 musicals (1 new musical)/year. Plays produced for a general audience. Two children's works/year, concurrent with major productions. Pays by royalty.
How to Contact: Query with synopsis, character breakdown and set description or submit complete manuscript, score and tape of songs. SASE. Reports in 8 weeks.
Musical Theater: "We produce both full length and one act children's musicals. Folk or fairy tale themes. Works that do not condescend to a young audience yet are appropriate for entire family. We're also seeking full-length, small cast musicals suitable for a broad audience." Would also consider original music for use in a play being developed.
Productions: *Smoke on the Mountain*, by Allen Bailey; *A Closer Walk with Patsy Cline*, by Dean Regan; and *Sleeping Beauty*, by Jim Eiler.
Tips: "Small, upbeat, tourable musicals (like *Pump Boys*) and bright musically-sharp children's productions (like those produced by Prince Street Players) work best. Keep an open mind. Stretch to encompass a musical variety—different keys, rhythms, musical ideas and textures."

CIRCLE IN THE SQUARE THEATRE, Dept. SM, 1633 Broadway, New York NY 10019. (212)307-2700. Literary Advisor: Nancy Bosco. Play producer. Estab. 1951. Produces 3 plays/year; occasionally produces a musical. Pays by royalty.
How to Contact: Query with synopsis, character breakdown and set description. Reports in 3-6 months.
Musical Theater: "We are looking for original material with small cast and orchestra requirements. We're not interested in traditional musical comedies." Will consider original music for use in a play being developed or in a pre-existing play at the option of the director.
Productions: *Pal Joey*, *Sweeney Todd* and *Anna Karenina*.
Tips: "The material has to be 'do-able' in our unique arena space."

*CITIARTS THEATRE, A-20, 1975 Diamond Blvd., Concord CA 94520. (510)671-3066. Artistic Director: Richard H. Elliott. Play producer. Estab. 1973. Produces 8 plays and 4 musicals (0-4 new musicals)/year. "CitiArts/Theatre Concord is the resident theater in the 203-seat Willows Theatre, a proscenium stage, in Concord, located in suburban San Francisco." Pays variable royalty.
How to Contact: Query first. SASE. Reports in 6 months.
Musical Theater: "Full-length musicals addressing contemporary themes or issues, small to mid-size cast (maximum 15 characters) with maximum 15 instruments. Topics which appeal to an educated suburban and liberal urban audience are best. Maximum 10 cast members, 9 musicians, prefer unit set (we have no fly loft or wing space)."
Productions: *Smoke On The Mountain*, by Ray/Bailey (white southern gospel); *Nunsense II*, by Goggin (religious satire); *Grease*, by Jacobs/Casey (50s rock).

CITY THEATRE COMPANY, INC., 57 S. 13th St., Pittsburgh PA 15203. (412)431-4400. General Manager: Adrienne Keriotis. Play producer. Estab. 1974. Produces 5 plays/year. "Plays are performed in a 225 seat thrust-stage or proscenium configuration theater to an adventurous subscriber base."
How to Contact: Query with synopsis, character breakdown and set description. "We select plays through Play Showcases (Louisville, Denver and Rochester), Summer Workshop Programs (Shenandoah, New Harmony and Carnegie Mellon University) and local playwright centers and organizations from new dramatists in New York, Chriog Dramatists Workshop and Southeast Playwrights project. Also various scriptshare and play catalogue newsletters."
Musical Theater: "We want sophisticated plays with music. We prefer a small cast with no more than 10 (including musicians) and single set because we have small stage capabilities only. We don't want traditional, large cast musical comedies."

Productions: *Painting It Red*, by Steven Dietz (modern romance); *Lovers and Keepers*, by Irene Fornes (failed romance); *Maybe I'm Doing It Wrong*, by Randy Newman (musical review); *Evelyn and the Polka King*, by John Olive (light comedy); and *Cabaret Verboten*, by Jeremy Lawrence (historical political cabaret).

*THE CLEVELAND PLAY HOUSE, P.O. Box 1989, Cleveland OH 44106. (216)795-7010. Literary Manager: Scott Kanoff. Play producer. Estab. 1915. Uses Dramatists Guild contracts.
How to Contact: Submit through agent only. SASE. Reports in 4-6 months.
Productions: *Heartbeats*, by Amanda McBroom (marriage); and *Heart's Desire*, by Glen Roven (modern relationships).

COCKPIT IN COURT SUMMER THEATRE, 7201 Rossville Blvd., Baltimore MD 21237. (410)780-6534. Managing Director: F. Scott Black. Play producer. Estab. 1973. Produces 6-8 plays and 5-7 musicals/year. "Plays are produced at four locations: Mainstage (proscenium theater), Courtyard (outdoor theater), Cabaret (theater-in-the-round) and Lecture Hall (children's theater)."
How to Contact: Query with synopsis, character breakdown and set description. SASE. Reports in 1 month.
Musical Theater: "Seeking musical comedy and children's shows. We have the capacity to produce large musicals with up to 50 cast members."
Productions: *I Remember Mama*, by Richard Rodgers; *Chicago*, by Kander and Ebb; and *Heidi*, by Johanna Spyri.
Tips: "We look for material that appeals to a community theater audience."

THE COTERIE, 2450 Grand Ave., Kansas City MO 64108. (816)474-6785. Artistic Director: Jeff Church. Play producer. Estab. 1979. Produces 7-8 plays/year. Plays produced at Hallmark's Crown Center in downtown Kansas City in The Coterie's resident theater (capacity 240). A typical performance run is one month in length. "We retain some rights on commissioned plays. Writers are paid a royalty for their work per performance or flat fee."
How to Contact: Query with synopsis and character breakdown. Submit complete manuscript and score "if established writer in theater for young audiences. We will consider musicals with smaller orchestration needs (3-5 pieces), or a taped score." SASE. Reports in 6 months.
Musical Theater: "Types of plays we produce: pieces which are universal in appeal; plays for all ages. They may be original or adaptations of classic or contemporary literature. Limitations: Typically not more than 12 in a cast—prefer 5-9 in size. No fly space or wing space. No couch plays. Prefer plays by seasoned writers who have established reputations. Groundbreaking, and exciting scripts from the youth theater field welcome. It's perfectly fine if your musical is a little off center."
Productions: *Animal Farm*, by Sir Peter Hall; *The Wind in the Willows*, (adapted), by Doug Post; and *The Ugly Duckling*, by Pamela Sterling, music by Chris Limber.
Tips: "Make certain your submitted musical to us is very theatrical and not cinematic. Writers need to see how far the field of youth and family theater has come—the interesting new areas we're doing—before sending us your query or manuscript. We LIKE young protagonists in our plays, but make sure they're not romanticized or stereotyped good-and-bad like the children's theater playwrights of yesterday would have them."

CREATIVE PRODUCTIONS, INC., 2 Beaver Pl., Aberdeen NJ 07747. (908)566-6985. Director: Walter L. Born. Play producer. Estab. 1970. Produces 3 musicals (1-2 new musicals)/year. "Our audience is the general community with emphasis on elderly and folks with disabilities. We use local public school theater facilities." Pays $2,000 for outright purchase.
How to Contact: Submit complete ms, score and tape of songs. SASE. Reports in 1 month.
Musical Theater: "We want family type material (i.e. *Brigadoon*, *Charlie Brown*) with light rock to classical music and a maximum running time of two hours. The subject matter should deal with older folks or folks with disabilities. We have no flying capability in facility; cast size is a maximum 10-12; the sets are mostly on small wagons, props aren't anything exotic; the orchestra is chamber size with standard instruments. We don't want pornographic material or children's shows. We want nothing trite and condescending in either the material or the treatment. We like the unusual treatment well-structured and thought out, with minimal sets and changes. We can't handle unusual vocal requirements. We prefer an integrated piece with music a structural part from the beginning."
Productions: *Gifts of Magi*, by O. Henry (unselfish love); *Reluctant Dragon*, by Rone/Anderson; *For Love Or Money*, by M. Lombardo/J. Callis (based on O. Henry).
Tips: "Prepare/send representative script and music based on above criteria and follow up with phone call after our response."

CREATIVE THEATRE, 102 Witherspoon St., Princeton NJ 08540. (609)924-3489. Artistic Director: Eloise Bruce. Play producer. Estab. 1969. Produces 5 plays, all with music (1 new musical)/year. "Plays are performed for young audiences grades K-6. The plays are always audience participation and done in schools (45 minute format)." Pays a fee for writing and production and royalty for two seasons, then per performance royalty fee.

How to Contact: Query with synopsis, character breakdown and set description. SASE. Reports in 1 month.

Musical Theater: "Audience participation plays, 45 minutes in length, 4-6 performers, usually presentational style. Topics can range from original plots to adaptations of folk and fairytales. Staging is usually in the round with audience of no more than 300/seating on the floor. No lighting and usually piano accompaniment. Actor is focus with strong but very lean set and costume design." Does not wish to see plays without audience participation. "We are not doing as many 'heavy musicals,' but are looking for light plays with less music."

Productions: *The Bremen Town Musicians*, by Joan Prall (fairy tale); *Where Snow Falls Up*, by Mark Schaeffer (holiday show); and *The Island of Yaki Yim Bamboo*, by Fred Rohan Vargas.

Tips: "Develop child centered work which encourages the imagination of the audience and is centered in child play."

CREEDE REPERTORY THEATRE, P.O. Box 269, Creede CO 81130. (719)658-2541. Producing/Artistic Director: Richard Baxter. Play producer. Estab. 1966. Produces 6 plays and 1 musical/year. Performs in 243-seat proscenium theatre; audience is ½ local support and ½ tourist base from Texas, Oklahoma, New Mexico and Colorado. Pays 7% royalty.

How to Contact: Query first. SASE. Reports in 1 year.

Musical Theater: "We prefer historical Western material with cast no larger than 11. Staging must be flexible as space is limited."

Productions: *Baby Doe Tabor*, by Kenton Kersting (Colorado history); *A Frog in His Throat*, by Feydeau, adapted by Eric Conger, (French farce); and *Tommyknockers*, by Eric Engdahl, Mark Houston and Chris Thompson (mining).

Tips: "Songwriter must have the ability to accept criticism and must be flexible."

THE DEPOT THEATRE, Box 414, Westport NY 12993. (518)962-4449. Associate Director: Keith Levenson. Play producer. Estab. 1979. Produces 3-5 plays/year; produces 2-3 musicals (1 new musical)/year. "Plays are performed in a renovated 19th century train depot with 136 seats and proscenium stage. Audience is regional/tourist from north of Albany to Montreal." Pays by commission.

How to Contact: Submit complete ms, score and tape of songs. SASE. Reports in 1-2 months.

Musical Theater: "We have no restrictions on the type of musical, though we prefer full-length. We are currently interested in cast sizes that do not exceed 13 people—preferably smaller! Our theater has no fly or wing space to speak of and designs tend to be limited to unit or 'conceptual' sets. Our 'orchestra' is limited to acoustic piano and synthesizers. We do not wish to see previously produced scripts unless there have been radical changes to the material or previous presentation was in workshop form. The purpose of the Depot Theatre's New American Musicals Project is to nurture the development of new musicals by emerging songwriters/composers. Our intent is to give the musical a full production so that the writers can see what they have and so the piece can have a life beyond our stage. We look for writers willing to listen to directors, work with them toward a common goal of the best production possible and be able to maintain a sense of humor and an understanding of our limited resources." Would consider original music for use in a play being developed.

Productions: *Winchell*, by Martin Charnin and Keith Levenson (Walter Winchell); *Willpower*, by Danny Troob and Jamie Donnelly (reverse Pygmalion theme, contemporary); and *Galileo*, by Jeanine Levenson, Alexa Junge and Keith Levenson.

Tips: "We enjoy working with people who view the process as a collaborative adventure, can be flexible, accept constructive criticism and keep smiling."

*STEVE DOBBINS PRODUCTIONS, 650 Geary St., San Francisco CA 94102. Administrative Director: Chuck Hilbert. Play producer. Estab. 1978. Produces 4 plays and 1 new musical/year. Plays performed for San Francisco Bay Area avante garde, racially mixed audiences. Pays 5% royalty.

How to Contact: Submit complete ms, score and tape of songs. SASE. Reports in 10 months.

Musical Theater: "We seek all types of material as long as the ideas are new. No formula scripts." Would consider original music for use in a play being developed.

Productions: *Doo Wop*, by Glover (blues); *Hoagy*, by Antony Nurden (Hoagy Carmichael); *Barbaras*, by Chuck Hilbert (Visigoth humor).

Tips: "Write to us explaining your idea."

EL TEATRO CAMPESINO, P.O. Box 1240, San Juan Bautista CA 95045. (408)623-2444. Theater company. Members are professionals and amateurs. Performs 2 concerts/year including 2 new works. Commissions 0-1 composer or new work/year. "Our audiences are varied—nontraditional and multicultural. We perform in our own theater as well as area theaters and other performing arts spaces (indoor and outdoor)." Pays $50-750 for outright purchase.

How to Contact: Query first. SASE. Reports in 1 month.
Musical Theater: "We are interested in cultural and multi-cultural music in all styles and lengths. We are especially interested in blends of cultural/contemporary and indigenous music."
Productions: *La Vizgen Del Tepeyac* (cultural); *The Rose of the Rancho* (Old California); and *Zoot-Suit* (1940s).

*THE EMERGING ARTISTS PROJECT INC., #3, 4646 N. Central Park, Chicago IL 60625. (312)463-9578. Artistic Director: Patrick Riviere. Play producer. Estab. 1990. Produces 6 plays and 2-3 new musicals/year. "We look for all types of musicals for mainstage and children's theater. We play to both urban and suburban audiences as well as touring to schools. We produce at numerous and varied venues in Chicago. Our primary space is located at North Pier Festival Market, with seating ranging from 25-100." Pays 5-25% per performance.
How to Contact: Query with synopsis, character breakdown and set description. SASE. Reports in 2-3 months.
Musical Theater: "We look for all types of musicals: adult theme and children's topics. Generally small cast (4-9). We work with emerging artists of all kinds, including up-and-coming young actors ages 17-35 and EAP Artistic Associates. Generally small cast and limited set/props; we gear our productions to touring and for smaller theaters. We are more interested in working with composers/writers who are interested in working in a collaborative environment—we rarely review or consider completed musicals by artists whose work we are unfamiliar with."
Productions: *The Baker's Daughter*, by Kevin Kosik and Sarah Montgomery (wacky '70s musical comedy); *Prince Watersplasher*, by Patrick Riviere (family fairy tale musical); and *'Tis the Season*, by various (holiday musical story series).
Tips: "Write about something important and meaningful to *you*! Write about something you are willing to invest a lot of your time, energy and resources towards."

THE EMPTY SPACE THEATRE, 3509 Fremont Ave. N., Seattle WA 98103. (206)547-7633. Artistic Director: Eddie Levi Lee. Play producer. Estab. 1970. Produces 5 plays and varying number of new musicals/year. "We have a subscription audience, mainly composed of professionals. We produce in our own theater." Pays by royalty.
How to Contact: Query with synopsis, character breakdown and set description. SASE. Reports in 4 months.
Musical Theater: "We want broadly comic, satirical or political pieces and all musical idioms, from classical to whatever is the current end of the musical spectrum. We have no limitations, though we rarely produce more than one large cast show per year. We don't want old-fashioned show biz yawners or yuppie angst. We regularly employ composers/sound designers."
Productions: *Smokey Joe's Cafe*, by Burke Walker (song revue).
Tips: "Avoid musical-comedy formulas."

GEOF ENGLISH, PRODUCER, Saddleback College, 28000 Marguerite Pkwy., Mission Viejo CA 92692. (714)582-4763. Performing Arts Director: Geofrey English. Play producer for musical theater. Produces 4 musicals/year. Community audience of mostly senior citizens. Pays by royalty and performance.
How to Contact: Submit complete ms, score and tape of songs. Does not return unsolicited material. Reports in 2-3 months.
Musical Theater: Looking for mainly family musicals. No limitations, open to options. It is important that music must be sent along with scripts. Best not to call. Just send materials.
Productions: More than 50 musicals produced since company formed in 1978. 1994 season includes *Camelot*, *Me And My Girl* and *The World Goes Round*.
Tips: "Submit materials in a timely manner—usually at least one year in advance."

*FERNDALE REPERTORY THEATRE, Box 892, Ferndale CA 95536. (707)725-4636. Artistic Director: Clinton Rebik. Play producer. Estab. 1972. Produces 6-8 plays and 1-2 musicals (1 new musical)/year. "Our audience is a community of 100,000; most with college education. Love comedies and dramas with uplifting ending." Performance space: 267 seats, proscenium arch with modified thrust, no fly space. Pays $250 for 8 performances.
How to Contact: Query first. SASE. Reports in 1-6 months, "depending on submission time."
Musical Theater: "Competition is open to all; comedies have best chance, although many dramas have been produced. No size limits, however, minimal technical support is available." Does not wish to see "heavy dramas."
Productions: *Dark Horse*, by Gary Blackwood (racial tension in 1880s); *Peach-Tree Two-Step*, by Janet Steiger-Carr (relationship of two sisters); and *Adventures of Bob*, by Peter Buckley and Roy Zimmerman (zany comedy).
Tips: "Always include a synopsis with your submission."

FOOLS COMPANY, INC., 358 W. 44th St., New York NY 10036. (212)307-6000. Artistic Director: Martin Russell. Play producer. Estab. 1970. Produces 4-6 plays/year; produces 1-2 musicals (1-2 new musicals)/year. "Audience is comprised of general public and teens, ages 16-20. Plays are performed at various Manhattan venues."
How to Contact: Query with synopsis, character breakdown and set description. SASE. Reports in 2-3 weeks.
Musical Theater: "We seek new and unusual, contemporary and experimental material. We would like small, easy-to-tour productions. Nothing classical, folkloric or previously produced." Would also consider original music for use in a play being developed.
Productions: *She Closed Her Eyes to the Sun*, by Jill Russell and Lewis Flinn (fantasies and realities of relationships); *Zen Puppies Unleashed* (company collective); and *Under the Bridge*, by Liek Saeffert (emigrating).
Tips: "Forget Broadway expectations."

THE FOOTHILL THEATRE COMPANY, P.O. Box 1812, Nevada City CA 95959. (916)265-9320. Artistic Director: Philip Charles Sneed. Play producer. Estab. 1977. Produces 6-10 plays and 1-2 musicals/year. Rural audience, with some urban visitors to the area. 250-seat historic proscenium house; built in 1865 (oldest in CA). "We haven't yet produced a new play, but will seriously consider it within the next 2 years; payment will be decided later." Payment negotiated.
How to Contact: Query with synopsis, character breakdown and set description. SASE. Reports in 6 months.
Musical Theater: "We're particularly interested in works which deal with the region's history or with issues relevant to the area today. We are also interested in one-act musicals and children's musicals. We have limited space backstage, especially in the wings. We also have very limited fly space. We're interested in original ideas, nothing derivative (except in an adaptation, of course). A good rock musical would be nice. Will consider original music for use in a play being developed, or for use in a pre-existing play. The use will depend upon the play: could be preshow, or underscoring, or scene change, or any combination."
Productions: *The Cherry Orchard*, by Chekov (comedy/drama); *Quilters*, by Barbara Damashek/Molly Newman; and *Hamlet*, by Shakespeare (tragedy).
Tips: "Know something about our region and its history."

THE WILL GEER THEATRICUM BOTANICUM, P.O. Box 1222, Topanga CA 90290. (310)455-2322. Artistic Director: Ellen Geer. Play producer. Produces 4 plays, 1 new musical/year. Plays are performed in "large outdoor amphitheater with 60′x 25′ wooden stage. Rustic setting." Pays per performance.
How to Contact: Query with synopsis, tape, character breakdown and set description. SASE. Submit scripts in September for prompt reply.
Musical Theater: Seeking social or biographical works, children's works, full length musicals with cast of up to 10 equity actors (the rest non-equity). Requires "low budget set and costumes. We emphasize paying performers." Would also consider original music for use in a play being developed. Does not wish to see "anything promoting avarice, greed, violence or apathy."

GEORGE STREET PLAYHOUSE, 9 Livingston Ave., New Brunswick NJ 08901. (908)846-2895. Associate Artistic Director: Wendy Liscow. Producing Director: Gregory Hurst. Produces 7 plays, including 1 new musical/year. "We are a 367-seat thrust theater working under a LORT C-contract with a 5,500 subscriber base." Fees vary. "Each situation is handled individually."
How to Contact: "Professional recommendation only." SASE. Reports in 4-6 months.
Musical Theater: Seeking musical adaptations. "We are interested in a variety of themes and formats. We aren't seeking to limit the things we read."
Productions: *Johnny Pye and the Fool Killer*, by Mark St. Germain and Randy Courts; *Jekyll and Hyde*, by Lee Thuna, Herman Sachs and Mel Mandel; and *Fields of Ambrosia*, by Joel Higgins and Martin Silvestri.

***GOLDEN FLEECE LTD.**, 204 W. 20th St., New York NY 10011. (212)691-6105. Producing Artistic Director: Lou Rodgers. Play producer. Estab. 1976. Produces 4 operas and 30 readings/year. Audience is "off-off Broadway, interested in new music and opera." Performance space holds 80 seats. Pays by an annual opera commission.
How to Contact: Query with synopsis, character breakdown and set description. SASE.
Musical Theater: "We produce one act chamber operas and musical theater works. We do readings of opera/musical theater works in progress. The works we produce are small scale productions, casts from 3-7, simple scenery, small musical ensemble. We are a composer's theater company, so all our works involve music."
Productions: *Last Chance Planet*, by Carman Moore; *Elevator*, by Memrie Innerasty/Owen Robertson; and *Desperate Waltz*, by John David Earnest/Mervyn Goldstein.

Tips: "Attend our performances if possible and see what we do."

GREAT AMERICAN CHILDREN'S THEATRE COMPANY, Dept. SM, 304 E. Florida, Milwaukee WI 53204. (414)276-4230. Managing Director: Annie Jurczyk. Producer: Teri Mitze. Play producer. Estab. 1976. Produces 1 or 2 plays/musicals/year. Has done new musicals in the past. Audience is school age children. Pays negotiable royalty.
How to Contact: Query with synopsis, character breakdown and set description. Does not return unsolicited material. Reports as quickly as possible, "depending on our workload."
Musical Theater: Children's musicals. Average cast size is 13. No adult productions. "We have used original music as background for our plays."
Productions: *Charlie & the Chocolate Factory,* by Roald Dahl (children's story); *Charlotte's Web,* by Joseph Robinette (children's story); and *Cinderella,* by Moses Goldberg (children's story).
Tips: "Persevere! Although we don't use a lot of musicals, we will consider one that is of excellent quality."

GREAT AMERICAN HISTORY THEATRE, 30 E. Tenth St., St. Paul MN 55101. (612)292-4323. Managing Director: Thomas Berger. Play producer. Estab. 1978. Produces 5-6 plays, 1 or 2 musicals (1 or 2 new musicals)/year. 597-seat thrust. Royalty varies.
How to Contact: Query first with synopsis, character breakdown and set description. SASE. Reports in 6-8 months.
Musical Theater: "Plays based on people, events, ideas in history. Preferably Midwestern or American history. However, must be *real* plays, we *do not* teach history. *No* pageants. No larger than cast of 10. Technical considerations must be simple. We like nonrealism."
Productions: *The Meeting,* by Jeff Stetson (Martin Luther King meets Malcolm X); *The Great Gatsby,* by F. Scott Fitzgerald (adapted by J. Carlisle) (the novel of love and murder); and *Days of Rondo,* by Greg Williams (a black neighborhood in St. Paul destroyed in the 1950s).

*GREAT AMERICAN MELODRAMA & VAUDEVILLE, P.O. Box 1026, Oceano CA 93445. (805)481-4880, ext. 32. Fax: (805)489-5539. Owner/producer: John Schlenker. Play producer. Estab. 1976. Produces 7 plays and 2-3 musicals/year. "Family entertainment—all ages." Performances held in a 260 seat theater, cabaret-style seating with bench seats surrounding theater. Payment negotiable.
How to Contact: Submit complete manuscript, score and tape of songs. SASE. "All plays are selected for the year July through September."
Musical Theater: "Everything from Gilbert & Sullivan, Cinderella to Western shoot-'em-up spoofs play extremely well here. Must be shows suitable for families. Victorian melodramas are our bread and butter, therefore, musical adaptations of period melodramas would be great! Cast size 10-12, usually 6 men and 4 women." Does not wish to see "realistic hardcore contemporary dramatic literature. People do not come to our theater looking for a slice of their daily lives. All plays and/or musicals must play in 75 minutes actual playing time, since they are followed with a 35 minute musical revue. High style action-packed shows work like gangbusters. A little adult humor is okay as long as it is done with taste and adults get it but children don't."
Productions: *The Imaginary Invalid,* by Moliere (French farce); *The Saga of Roarin' Gulch,* by Jack Canon (Western musical comedy spoof); and *Under the Gaslight,* by Augustin Daly (mid-Victorian social melodrama).

GREEN MOUNTAIN GUILD, Box 659, Pittsfield VT 05762. (802)746-8320. Managing Director: Marjorie O'Neill-Butler. Play producer. Estab. 1971. Produces 9 plays (5 musicals)/year. Produces plays for a summer theater audience in Killington, Vermont. Pays 5% royalty.
How to Contact: Submit complete ms, score and tape of songs. SASE. Reports in 3 months.
Musical Theater: "We are looking for musicals with a small cast, a good story line, well-developed characters, songs and music that come naturally out of the story and music that works with piano and drums only." No frivolous material. Prefers one-set shows.
Productions: *Yours Anne,* by Enid Fetterman/Michael Cohen; *Nunsense,* by Don Goggin; and *Godspell,* by S. Schwartz.

HIP POCKET THEATRE, 1627 Fairmount Ave., Ft. Worth TX 76104-4237. (817)927-2833. Producer: Diane Simons. Play producer. Produces 7 plays/year (including new musicals). Estab. 1977. "Our audience is an eclectic mix of Ft. Worth/Dallas area residents with varying levels of incomes and backgrounds. Payment varies according to type of script, reputation of playwright, etc."
How to Contact: Query with synopsis, character breakdown and set description; "please include tape if possible." SASE. Reports in 2 months.
Musical Theater: "We are not interested in cabaret revues, but rather in full-length pieces that can be for adults and/or children. We tend to produce more fanciful, whimsical musicals (something not likely to be found anywhere else), but would also consider political pieces and other subjects. Basically, we're open for anything fresh and well-written. We prefer no more than 15 in a cast, and a staging

adapted to an outdoor environmental thrust stage to be considered for summer season. Smaller cast shows are a requirement for the indoor, more intimate performance space."
Productions: *Huzzytown*, by Johnny Simons (premiere); *Saint Joan of the Stockyards*, by Bertolt Brecht, with original music by Bobby Griffith, and *Scarfish Vibrato*, by Johnny Simons (premiere); and *Everyman*, (anonymous author).
Tips: "Think creative, complex thoughts and musical visions that can be transformed into reality by creative, visionary musicians in theaters that rarely have the huge Broadway dollar."

THE HONOLULU IMPROVISATIONAL THEATRE CO., 3585 Pinao St., Honolulu HI 96822. (808)988-4859. Director: Rod Martin. Estab. 1989. Produces 3 plays and 3 musicals (3 new musicals)/year. Performs at community theaters and on public access TV. Pays by honorarium.
How to Contact: Submit complete ms, score and tape of songs. SASE. Reports in 7 weeks.
Musical Theater: "Prefer comedy and children's shows. A videotape of a production is helpful (VHS). A cassette tape should accompany musicals. We will consider original music for entrance/exit music."
Productions: *One More Time*, by Rod Martin (gospel musical); *Rhyme Time*, by Jane Smith-Martin (children's musical); and *Love Hurts but Murder Kills*, by Rod Martin (musical farce).
Tips: "Have professionally recorded instrumentals for the cast. Stage a reading of your work. We like to help beginners."

HORIZON THEATRE CO., P.O. Box 5376, Station E, Atlanta GA 31107. (404)523-1477. Co-Artistic Director: Lisa Adler. Play producer. Estab. 1983. Produces 3 plays and 1 musical/year. "Our audience is comprised mostly of young professionals looking for contemporary comedy with some social commentary. Our theater features a 160-200 seat facility with flexible stage." Pays 6-8% royalty.
How to Contact: Query with synopsis, character breakdown, set description and résumé. Does not return material. Reports in 1-2 years.
Musical Theater: "We prefer musicals that have a significant book and a lot of wit (particularly satire). Our casts are restricted to 10 actors. We prefer plays with equal number of male and female roles, or more female than male roles. We have a limited number of musicians available. No musical revues and no dinner theater fluff. One type of play we are currently seeking is a country musical with women's themes. We generally contract with a musician or sound designer to provide sound for each play we produce. If interested send résumé, synopsis, references, tape with music or sound design samples."
Productions: *Angry Housewives*, by A.M. Collins/Chad Henry; *A. . . . My Name Is Still Alice*, conceived by Julianne Boyd/Joan Micklin Silver; and *The Good Times Are Killing Me*, by Lynda Barry.
Tips: "Have patience and use subtle persistence. Work with other theater artists to get a good grasp of the form."

JEWISH REPERTORY THEATRE, 1395 Lexington Ave., New York NY 10128. (212)302-5200. Director: Ran Avni. Artistic Director: Edward M. Cohen. Play producer. Estab. 1974. Produces 4 plays and 1-2 new musicals/year. Pays 6% royalty.
How to Contact: Submit complete manuscript, score and tape of songs. SASE. Reports in 4 weeks.
Musical Theater: Seeking "musicals in English relating to the Jewish experience. No more than 8 characters. We do commission background scores for straight plays."
Productions: *The Special* (musical comedy); *Theda Bara and the Frontier Rabbi* (musical comedy); and *The Shop on Main Street* (musical drama).

*LA JOLLA PLAYHOUSE, Box 12039, La Jolla CA 92039. (619)550-1070. Fax: (619)550-1075. Literary Manager: Elissa Adams. Play producer. Estab. 1982. Produces 6-8 plays and 1 new musical/year. Audience is "adventurous, sophisticated, largely white." Performance space: 500 seat proscenium, 400 seat thrust. Pay is negotiable.
How to Contact: Submit through agent only. Does not return material. Reports in 4 months.
Musical Theater: "Rock & roll inspired. Cast size no larger than 15." Does not wish to see children's musicals.
Productions: *How to Succeed in Business*, by Frank Loesser (corporate satire); *Tommy*, by Pete Townsend/Des McAnuff (the Who's rock opera); and *The Good Person of Sezvan*, by David Hidalgo/Louie Perez (woman's struggle to be good in a corrupt world).

*LAGUNA PLAYHOUSE, 606 Laguna Canyon Rd., Laguna Beach CA 92651. (714)497-5900, ext. 206. Artistic Director: Andrew Barnicle. Play producer. Estab. 1920. Produces 7-10 plays/year; produces 2-3 musicals/year (3 new musicals in last 3 years). Audience is "middle to upper class suburban. 9,000 subscribers in resort town. Plays performed in 420 seat luxury theater."
How to Contact: Submit complete ms, score and tape of songs. SASE. Reports in 6 months.
Musical Theater: "Seek children's plays (we have an acclaimed youth theater), adult, aesthetic non-'dance' shows with small orchestra ('Tintypes', *1940's Radio Hour*), limited dance budget. Cast 15-20 maximum on large proscenium stage."

Productions: *1940's Radio Hour*, by Walton Jones; *Working*, by Terkel, Schwartz, et.al.; and *Oliver!*, by Bart (Dickens book).
Tips: "Allow at least one year advance on project."

THE LAMB'S THEATRE CO., 130 W. 44th St., New York NY 10036. (212)997-0210. Literary Manager: James Masters. Play producer. Estab. 1984. Produces 2-3 plays, 1 musical (1 new musical)/year. Plays are performed for "family-oriented audiences." Pays by royalty.
How to Contact: Query with synopsis, character breakdowns, dialogue or lyric sample. SASE. Reports in 3 months.
Musical Theater: "We are looking for full length musicals that are entertaining, but moving, and deal with serious issues as well as comic situations. No one-act plays. Large-cast epics are out. Both our spaces are intimate theaters, one a 160-seat black box space and one a 349-seat proscenium. Material with explicit sex and nudity and plays which require large amounts of obscene language are not appropriate for this theater. We require a small orchestra in a musical."
Productions: *Johnny Pye & The Foolkiller*, by R. Courts/M. St. Germain (original musical based on Stephen V. Benet short story); *The Gifts of the Magi*, by R. Courts/M. St. Germain (original musical based on O. Henry short stories).

LOS ANGELES DESIGNERS' THEATRE, P.O. Box 1883, Studio City CA 91614-0883. (818)769-9000, (213)650-9600. Fax: (818)985-9200. Artistic Director: Richard Niederberg. Play producer. Estab. 1970. Produces 20-25 plays, 8-10 new musicals/year. Plays are produced at several locations, primarily Studio City, California. Pay is negotiable.
How to Contact: Submit complete manuscript, score and tape of songs, character breakdown and set descriptions. Video tape submissions are also accepted. Does not return materials. Reports in 4+ months.
Musical Theater: "We seek out controversial material. Street language OK, nudity is fine, religious themes, social themes, political themes are encouraged. Our audience is very 'jaded' as it consists of TV, motion picture and music publisher executives who have 'seen it all.'" Does not wish to see bland, safe material. "We like first productions. In the cover letter state in great detail the proposed involvement of the songwriter, other than as a writer (i.e. director, actor, singer, publicist, designer, etc.). Also, state if there are any liens on the material or if anything has been promised."
Productions: *Rainbows' End* by Margaret Keifer (songwriters struggle/musical); *Hostages* (political musical) and *Love Song of Ned Wells* (poetry set to music; urban unrequited love story).
Tips: "Make it very 'commercial' and inexpensive to produce. Allow for non-traditional casting. Be prepared with ideas as to how to transform your work to film or videotaped entertainment."

*DON AND PAT MACPHERSON PRODUCTIONS, 461 Parkway, Gatlinburg TN 37738. (615)436-4039. Co-owners/producers: Don MacPherson and Pat MacPherson. Play producer. Estab. 1977. Produces 2 musicals/year. Plays are performed at Sweet Fanny Adams Theatre, Gatlinburg, Tennessee to tourist audience. Pays $100-200/week.
How to Contact: Query with synopsis, character breakdown and set description. SASE. Reports in 1 month.
Musical Theater: Produce musicals that are funny, fast—in fact, silly; musical farces. Theater is 1890 style so shows should fit that period. Have done many westerns. Cast size limited to 7 or 8 with 2 musicians. Stage very small. Use old-time backdrops forsets. Shows should be no longer than 90 minutes. Does not wish to see shows that would not fit 1890s style—unless it had a country theme.
Productions: *Phantom of the Opry*, by Don & Pat MacPherson/J. Lovensheimer (spoof of *Phantom of the Opera*); *Life & Times of Billy Kincaid*, by MacPherson/Lovensheimer (western); and *Not Quite Frankenstein*, by Don and Pat MacPherson.
Tips: "See a production at Sweet Fanny Adams."

MANHATTAN THEATRE CLUB, Dept. SM, 453 W. 16th St., New York NY 10011. (212)645-5590. Director of Musical Theater Program: Clifford Lee Johnson III. Associate Artistic Director: Michael Bush. Play producer. Estab. 1971. Produces 8 plays and sometimes 1 musical/year. Plays are performed at the Manhattan Theatre Club before varied audiences. Pays negotiated fee.
How to Contact: Query first. SASE. Reports in 6 months.
Musical Theater: "Original work."
Productions: *Groundhog*, by Elizabeth Swados; *1-2-3-4-5*, by Maury Yeston and Larry Gelbart; and *Putting It Together*, by Stephen Sondheim.

MILWAUKEE REPERTORY THEATER, Dept. SM, 108 E. Wells St., Milwaukee WI 53202. (414)224-1761. Cabaret Director: Fred Weiss. Play producer. Estab. 1954. Produces 17 plays and 5 cabaret shows/year. "The space is a 106 seat cabaret with a very small playing area (8×28)." Pay is negotiable.

How to Contact: Submit complete ms, score and tape of songs. SASE. Reports in 3-4 months.
Musical Theater: "Cast size must be limited to 4 singers/performers. Suitable for cabaret. Must appeal to a broad adult audience and should not run longer than 1 hour and 15 minutes. We also seek to explore a multi-cultural diversity of material."
Productions: *If These Shoes Could Talk*, by Kevin Ramsey and Lee Summers (tap dance); *The Road to the USO*, by Fred Weiss (USO shows); and *The Last Ride of the Bold Calhouns*, by Ed Morgan.

MIXED BLOOD THEATRE CO., 1501 S. Fourth St., Minneapolis MN 55454. (612)338-0937. Script Czar: David Kunz. Play producer. Estab. 1976. Produces 4-5 plays a year and perhaps 1 new musical every 2 years. "We have a 200-seat theater in a converted firehouse. The audience spans the socioeconomic spectrum." Pays 7-10% royalty.
How to Contact: Query first, then submit complete manuscript, score and tape of songs. SASE. Reports in 6 weeks.
Musical Theater: "We want full-length, non-children works with a message. Always query first. Never send unsolicited script or tape."
Productions: *Black Belts*, in house production (great African-American singers); and *A . . . My Name is Still Alice*.
Tips: "Always query first. Be professional. Surprise us."

MUSICAL THEATRE WORKS, INC., Dept. SM, 440 Lafayette St., New York NY 10003. (212)677-0040. Artistic Director: Anthony J. Stimac. Develops new musicals exclusively in stage readings and workshop productions. Estab. 1983. Fourteen productions have transferred to Broadway, off-Broadway and regional theater. Produces 3-4 workshop productions and 12-16 readings each season. Workshops and readings are held at 440 Lafayette St. in a flexible 80-seat rehearsal space. No payment for productions.
How to Contact: Submit complete script, cassette tape of songs and SASE. Reports in 2-4 months.
Musical Theater: "We are seeking musicals which have never been produced. Cast of 14 maximum. Full, but modest. Only completed drafts will be considered for development."
Productions: *Whatnot*, by Howard Crabtree and Mark Waldrop (won 1990 Richard Rodgers Award); *Love in Two Countries*, by Sheldon Harnick and Tom Shepard (operetta); and *Colette Collage*, by Tom Jones and Harvey Schmidt (on the life of French writer Colette).

MUSIC-THEATRE GROUP INC., 29 Bethune St., New York NY 10014. (212)924-3108. Director: Diane Wondisford. Producing Director: Lyn Austin. Music-theater production company. Produces 6 music-theater pieces/year. General works are performed "off-Broadway in New York City; year round in Stockbridge, MA and across the country."
How to Contact: Query with synopsis and tape of music. SASE. Reports in 3 months maximum.
Musical Theater: "We don't seek developed properties, but examples of people's work as an indication of their talent in the event that we might want to suggest them for a future collaboration. The music must be a driving element in the work. We generally work with not more than 10-12 in cast and a small band of 4-5."
Productions: *Cinderella/Cendrillon*, based on the opera by Jules Massenet; *The Garden of Earthly Delights*, by Martha Clarke; and *Juan Darien*, by Julie Taymor and Elliot Goldenthal.
Tips: "Don't try to imitate a formula or style—write from your own impulses."

NATIONAL MUSIC THEATER CONFERENCE, O'Neill Theater Center, #901, 234 W. 44th St., New York NY 10036. (212)382-2790. Artistic Director: Paulette Haupt. "The Conference develops new music theater works." Estab. 1978. Develops 3-4 musicals each August. 8-10 professional songwriters/musicians participate in each event. Participants include songwriters, composers, opera/musical theater and lyricists/librettists. "The O'Neill Theater Center is in Waterford, Connecticut. The audiences for the staged readings of works-in-progress are a combination of local residents, New York and regional theater professionals. Participants are selected by artistic director and selection panel of professionals." Pays a stipend, room and board, and all costs of the workshops are covered.
How to Contact: Query first. SASE. Response within 2-3 months. Entry fee $20.
Musical Theater: "The Conference is interested in all forms of music theater. Staged readings are presented with script in hand, minimal props, piano only. There are no cast limitations. We don't accept works which have been previously produced by a professional company."
Productions: *The Gig*, by Douglas J. Cohen; *Marco Polo*, by Tan Dun and Paul Griffiths; and *Time And Again*, by Jack Viertel and Walter Edgar Kennon.

THE NEW CONSERVATORY CHILDREN'S THEATRE COMPANY & SCHOOL, 25 Van Ness, Lower Lobby, San Francisco CA 94102. (415)861-4914. Executive Director: Ed Decker. Play producer. Estab. 1981. Produces 5 plays and 1 or 2 musicals (1 new musical)/year. Audience includes families and community groups; children ages 14-19. "Performance spaces are 50-150 seat theater, but we also tour some shows. Pays $25-35 per performance. If we commission, playwright receives a commission for the initial run and royalties thereafter; otherwise playwright just gets royalties."

How to Contact: Query with synopsis, character breakdown and set description. SASE. Reports in 3 months.

Musical Theater: "We seek innovative and preferably socially relevant musicals for children and families, with relatively small cast (stage is small), in which all roles can be played by children. We have a small stage, thus cannot accommodate plays casting more than 10 or 12 people, and prefer relatively simple set requirements. Children cast are in the 9-19 age range. We do not want mushy, cute material. Fantasy is fine, as is something like Sendak & King's *Really Rosie*, but nothing gooey. We are very interested in using original music for new or existing plays. Songwriters should submit a résumé and perhaps a tape to let us know what they do."

Productions: *Runaways*, by Elizabeth Swados; *Free to be a Family*, by Marlo Thomas; and *Don't Count Your Chickens*, by Carol Lynn Pearson.

Tips: "Be flexible, able to revise and open to suggestions!"

NEW TUNERS THEATRE, Theatre Building, 1225 Belmont, Chicago IL 60657. (312)929-7287. Associate Producer: Allan Chambers. Play producer. Estab. 1968. Produces 3 musicals (3 new musicals)/year. "We play to mixed urban and suburban audiences. We produce in three 148-seat theaters in the Theatre Building." Pays negotiable royalty.

How to Contact: Query with synopsis, character breakdown and music sample. SASE. Reports in 3 months.

Musical Theater: "We look at all types of musical theater, traditional as well as more innovative forms. Fifteen is the maximum cast size we can consider and less is decidedly better. We work with a younger (35 and under) company of actors."

Productions: *Steppers Ball*, by Phyllis Cartwright; *School Board Shuffle*, by various workshoppers (10-minute musicals); and *Hans Brinker & the Silver Skate*, by Jane Boyd, Phillip Seward and John Sparks (based on Mary Mapes Dodge classic novel).

Tips: "Write the musical that sings to you. Write the musical that you would be willing to invest your own money toward. Attend every musical that you can get a ticket to."

NEW YORK STATE THEATRE INSTITUTE, 155 River St., Troy NY 12180. (518)274-3200. Artistic Director: Patricia B. Snyder. Play producer. Produces approximately 5 plays (1 new musical)/year. Plays performed for student audiences grades K-12, family audiences and adult audiences. Theater seats 900 with full stage. Pay negotiable.

How to Contact: Submit complete ms and tape of songs. SASE. Reports in 3-4 months.

Musical Theater: Looking for "intelligent and well-written book with substance, a score that enhances and supplements the book and is musically well-crafted and theatrical. Length: up to 2 hours. Could be play with music, musical comedy, musical drama. Excellence and substance in material is essential. Cast could be up to 12; orchestra size up to 8."

Productions: *Pied Piper*, by Adrian Mitchell/Dominic Muldowney (musical adaptation of classic tale); *The Snow Queen*, by Adrian Mitchell/Richard Peaslee (musical adaptation of Andersen fairy tale).

Tips: "There is a great need for musicals that are well-written with intelligence and substance which are suitable for family audiences."

NEW YORK THEATRE WORKSHOP, 18th Floor, 220 W. 42 St., New York NY 10036. (212)302-7737. Artistic Director: James C. Nicola. Play producer. Produces 4 mainstage plays and approximately 50 readings/year. "Plays are performed in our theater on East Fourth St. Audiences include: subscription/single ticket buyers from New York area, theater professionals, and special interest groups." Pays by negotiable royalty.

How to Contact: Query with synopsis, character breakdown and set description. SASE. Reports in 5 months.

Musical Theater: "As with our nonmusicals, we seek musicals of intelligence and social consciousness that challenge our perceptions of the world and the events which shape our lives. We favor plays that possess a strong voice, distinctive and innovative use of language and visual imagery. Integration of text and music is particularly of interest. Musicals which require full orchestrations would generally be too big for us. We prefer 'musical theater pieces' rather than straightforward 'musicals' per-se. We often use original music for straight plays that we produce. This music may be employed as pre-show, post-show or interlude music. If the existing piece lends itself, music may also be incorporated within the play itself. Large casts (12 or more) are generally prohibitive and require soliciting of additional funds. Design elements for our productions are of the highest quality possible with our limited funds — approximately budgets of $10,000 are allotted for our productions."

Productions: *The Waves*, adapted from Virginia Woolf's novel, music and lyrics by David Bucknam and text and direction by Lisa Peterson; *My Children! My Africa*, by Athol Fugard; and *Mad Forest*, by Caryl Churchill.

Tips: "Submit a synopsis which captures the heart of your piece; inject your piece with a strong voice and intent and try to surprise and excite us."

NEXT ACT THEATRE, Dept. SM, Box 394, Milwaukee WI 53201. (414)278-7780. Fax: (414)278-5930. Producing Director: David Cecsarini. Estab. 1984. Produces 3 plays/year, of which 1 is a musical. Playwrights paid by royalty (5-8%). "Performances seat 200. We have 800 season subscribers and single ticket buyers of every age range and walk of life." Pays $30-50 per performance.
How to Contact: Submit complete ms, score and tape of songs with at least 1 professional letter of recommendation. SASE.
Musical Theater: "We produce Broadway and off-Broadway style material, preferring slightly controversial or cutting edge material (i.e., *March of the Falsettos*). We have never produced a work that has not been successful in some other theatrical center. We are very limited financially and rarely stage shows with more than 6 in the cast. Props, sets and costumes should be minimal. We have no interest in children's theater, mime, puppet shows, etc. We have never yet used original music for our plays. We may consider it, but there would be little if any money available for this purpose."
Productions: *Billy Bishop Goes to War*, by John Gray/Eric Peterson (World War I flying ace); *A . . . My Name is Alice*, by various writers (women's themes); and *Damn Tango*, by Helena Dynerman (European translation of 17 tangos with cast of 17 singer/dancers).

*NORTH CAROLINA BLACK REPERTORY COMPANY, 610 Coliseum Dr., Winston-Salem NC 27106. (919)723-2266. Executive/Artistic Director: Larry Leon Hamlin. Play producer. Estab. 1979. Produces 4 plays and 2 musicals (1 new musical)/year. "Musicals are produced primarily for a Black audience but should also appeal to the general public. Performance in a 540 seat proscenium theater." Pays by royalty, by outright purchase or per performance.
How to Contact: Query with synopsis, character breakdown and set description. Tape recording of songs should also be included. SASE. Reports in 4 months.
Musical Theatre: "Full length musicals are desired, even musicals for children. As well as being entertaining, musicals should support improving the quality of life for all humanity, offering solutions or alternatives to problems. The company prefers a cast of no larger than 15, but is not limited to that number." Will consider original music for a play in development or pre-existing play that would be used to set mood or enhance dramatic moments.
Productions: *Heroes*, by Larry Leon Hamlin (family); *The Time Is Now*, by Larenté (AIDS); and *Stop the Violence*, by J.W. Hall (youth).
Tips: "Constant communication is important. Keep the Artistic Director aware of your career progress."

NORTHSIDE THEATRE COMPANY OF SAN JOSE, 848 E. William St., San Jose CA 95116. (408)288-7820. Artistic Director: Richard T. Orlando. Play producer. Estab. 1979. Produces 5 plays, a touring show and an occasional musical/year. One premiere yearly. "Family-oriented plays are performed at the Olinder Theatre." Pays by royalty.
How to Contact: Query with synopsis, character breakdown and set description. SASE. Reports in 2 months.
Musical Theatre: "Classic family plays (with a twist or different concept)." Cast size: 6-15. Sets: Unit in concept with simple additions. Staging: proscenium with thrust. Small 90 seat theater fully equipped. "We are interested in new ideas and approaches. Production should have social relevance." Will consider using original music for already existing plays. "Example: the underscoring of a Shakespeare piece."
Productions: *A Christmas Carol*, by Charles Dickens (seasonal); *After the Rain*, by John Bowen (future civilization); and *Voices from the High School*, by Peter Dee (youth and their lives).
Tips: "Be aggressive, sell your idea and be able to work within the budget and limitations within which the artistic director is confined."

ODYSSEY THEATRE ENSEMBLE, Dept. SM, 2055 S. Sepulveda Blvd., Los Angeles CA 90025. (310)477-2055. Literary Manager: Jan Lewis. Play producer. Estab. 1969. Produces 9 plays, 1 musical and 1-2 new musicals/year. "Our audience is predominantly over 35, upper middle-class audience interested in eclectic brand of theater which is challenging and experimental." Pays by royalty (percentage to be negotiated).
How to Contact: Query with synopsis, character breakdown and set description. Query should include résumé(s) of artist(s) and tape of music. SASE. "Unsolicited material is not read or screened at all." Reports on query in 2 weeks; manuscript in 6 months.
Musical Theater: "We want nontraditional forms and provocative, unusual, challenging subject matter. We are not looking for Broadway-style musicals. Comedies should be highly stylized or highly farcical. Works should be full-length only and not requiring a complete orchestra (small band preferred.) Political material and satire are great for us. We're seeking interesting musical concepts and approaches. The more traditional Broadway-style musicals will generally not be done by the Odyssey. If we have a work in development that needs music, original music will often be used. In such a case, the writer and composer would work together during the development phase. In the case of a pre-existing play, the concept would originate with the director who would select the composer."

Productions: *McCarthy*, by Jeff Goldsmith (Senator Joe McCarthy); *Struggling Truths* (the Chinese invasion of Tibet); and *It's A Girl* (a cappella musical for 5 pregnant women).
Tips: "Stretch your work beyond the ordinary. Look for compelling themes or the enduring questions of human existence. If it's a comedy, go for broke, go all the way, be as inventive as you can be."

OLD GLOBE THEATRE, P.O. Box 2171, San Diego CA 92112. (619)231-1941. Literary Manager: Raul Moncado. Artistic Director: Jack O'Brien. Produces 12 or 13 plays/year, of which a varying number are musicals. "This is a regional theater with three spaces: 600-seat proscenium, 225-seat arena and large outdoor summer stage. We serve a national audience base of over 260,000."
How to Contact: Query with synopsis and letter of introduction, or submit through agent or professional affiliation. No unsolicited material please. SASE. Reports in 4-8 months.
Musical Theater: "We look for skill first, subject matter second. No prescribed limitations, though creators should appreciate the virtues of economy as well as the uses of extravagance. Musicals have been produced on all three of our stages."
Productions: *Pastorela '91*, by Raul Moncada (traditional Latin-American Christmas); *Lady Day at Emerson's Bar and Grill*, by Lanie Robertson (Billie Holiday); *Forever Plaid*, by Stuart Ross (50/60s male quartet).
Tips: "Fall in love with a great book and a great writer."

OMAHA MAGIC THEATRE, 1417 Farnam St., Omaha NE 68102. (402)346-1227. Artistic Director: Jo Ann Schmidman. Play producer. Estab. 1968. Produces 8 performance events with music/year. "Plays are produced in our Omaha facility and on tour throughout the nation. Our audience is a cross-section of the community." Pays standard royalty, outright purchase ($500-1,500), per performance $20-25.
How to Contact: Query with synopsis, character breakdown and set description. SASE. Reports in 6 months.
Musical Theater: "We want the most avant of the avant garde—plays that never get written, or if written are buried deep in a chest because the writer feels there are not production possibilities in this nation's theaters. Plays must push form and/or content to new dimensions. The clarity of the playwright's voice must be strong and fresh. We do not produce standard naturalistic or realistic musicals. At the Omaha Magic Theatre original music is considered as sound structure and for lyrics."
Productions: *Body Leaks*, by Megan Terry, Jo Ann Schmidman and Sora Kimberlain (self-censorship); *Sound Fields/Are We Here*, by Megan Terry, Jo Ann Schmidman and Sora Kimberlain (a new multi-dimensional performance event about acute listening); and *Belches on Couches*, by Megan Terry, Jo Ann Schmidman and Sora Kimberlain.

THE OPEN EYE: NEW STAGINGS, Dept. SM, 270 W. 89th St., New York NY 10024. (212)769-4143. Artistic Director: Amie Brockway. Play producer. Estab. 1972. Produces 9 one-acts, 3 full length or new stagings for youth; varying number of new musicals. "Plays are performed in a well-designed and pleasant theater seating 115 people." Pays on a fee basis.
How to Contact: "We deeply regret that we are forced to discontinue our policy of accepting unsolicited manuscripts. Until further notice, a manuscript will be accepted and read only if it is a play for multi-generational audiences and is: 1) Submitted by a recognized literary agent; 2) Requested or recommended by a staff or company member; or 3) Recommended by a professional colleague with whose work we are familiar. Playwrights may submit a one-page letter of inquiry including a very brief plot synopsis. Please enclose a self-addressed (but not stamped) envelope. We will reply only if we want you to submit the script."
Musical Theater: "The Open Eye: NEW STAGINGS draws on the creative power of the theater arts—music, dance, drama and comedy—to mount innovative productions of excellence that appeal to people of all cultures and ages. Our commitment to the city's youth, and those from surrounding suburban and rural regions, is seen in programs that help foster a strong sense of community and emphasize the power of diverse cultures. Through timely original works, we seek to bring people together, communicate our shared heritage, and provide a fresh perspective on universal human experience."
Productions: *The Odyssey*, adapted by Amie Brockway, music by Elliot Sokolov; *The Wise Men of Chelm*, by Sandra Fenichel Asher; and *Freedom is My Middle Name*, by Lee Hunkins.
Tips: "Come see our work before submitting."

How to Get the Most Out of Songwriter's Market (at the front of this book) contains comments and suggestions to help you understand and use the information in these listings.

PAPER MILL PLAYHOUSE, Brookside Dr., Milburn NJ 07041. (201)379-3636. Contact: Angelo Del Rossi. Executive producer. Equity theater producing 2 plays and 4 musicals/year. "Audience based on 42,000 subscribers; plays performed in 1,192-seat proscenium theater."
Musical Theater: "Paper Mill runs a Musical Theater Lab Project which develops 4-6 readings/ season, 3 of which went on to fully staged productions. The theater runs an open submission policy, and is especially interested in large scale shows."
Productions: *The Wizard of Oz, Sweeney Todd, Don't Dress for Dinner, Lost in Yonkers.*

PASTAGE (formerly Pennsylvania Stage Company), 837 Linden St., Allentown PA 18101. (215)434-6110. Artistic Director: Charles Richter. Play producer. Estab. 1979. Produces 7 plays (1 new musical)/ season "when feasible. We are a LORT D theater with a subscriber base of approximately 6,000 people. Plays are performed at the Pennsylvania Stage Company in the J.I. Rodale Theatre." Playwrights paid by 5% royalty (per Dramatist's Guild contract).
How to Contact: Query with synopsis, character breakdown, set description and a tape of the music. "Please do not send script first." SASE. Reports in 2 months.
Musical Theater: "We are interested in full-length musicals which reflect the social, historical and political fabric of America. We have no special requirements for format, structure or musical involvement. We ask that once submission of a musical has been requested, that it be bound, legibly typed and include SASE. Cast limit of 10, but we prefer cast limit of 8. One set or unit set. Ours is a 274 seat house, there is no fly area, and a 23-foot proscenium opening."
Productions: *Just So*, by Mark St. Germain (based on Rudyard Kipling's *Just So Stories*); *Smilin' Through*, by Ivan Menchell (British Music Hall circa WWII); *Song of Myself*, by Gayle Stahlhuth, Gregory Hurst and Arthur Harris.
Tips: "Avoid duplication of someone else's style just because it's been successful in the past. I see too many composers aping Sondheim's songwriting, for example, without nearly as much success. Despite all the commercial constraints, stick to your guns and write something original, unique."

PLAYHOUSE ON THE SQUARE, 51 S. Cooper, Memphis TN 38104. (901)725-0776. Executive Producer: Jackie Nichols. Play producer. Produces 12 plays (4 musicals)/year. Plays are produced in a 260-seat proscenium resident theater. Pays $500 for outright purchase.
How to Contact: Submit complete ms and score. Unsolicited submissions OK. SASE. Reports in 4 months.
Musical Theater: Seeking "any subject matter—adult and children's material. Small cast preferred. Stage is 26' deep by 43' wide with no fly system." Would also consider original music for use in a play being developed.
Productions: *Gypsy*, by Stein and Laurents; *The Spider Web*, by Agatha Christie; and *A Midsummer Night's Dream*, by William Shakespeare.

PLAYWRIGHTS HORIZONS, 416 W. 42nd St., New York NY 10036. (212)564-1235. Artistic Director: Don Scardino. Assistant Artistic Director: Nicholas Martin. Literary Manager: Tom Sanford. Musical Program Co-Ordinator: Dana Williams. Play producer. Estab. 1971. Produces about 6 plays and 2 new musicals/year. "A general New York City audience." Pays by fee/royalty.
How to Contact: Submit complete ms, score and tape of songs. SASE. Reports in 4-5 months.
Musical Theater: American writers. "No revivals or children's shows; otherwise we're flexible. We can't do a Broadway-size show. We generally develop work from scratch; we're open to proposals for shows, and ideas from bookwriters or songwriters or scripts in early stages of development."
Productions: *Once on This Island*, by Lynn Ahrens/Stephen Flaherty (musical comedy); *Avenue X*, by John Jiles/Ray Leslee (a cappella musical); and *Cather Country*, by Ed Dixon (based on Willa Cather short stories).

*PORTLAND REPERTORY THEATER, 815 NW 12th, Portland OR 97209. (503)224-2403. Fax: (503)224-0710. Literary Manager: Kit Koenig. Play producer. Estab. 1980. Produces 9 plays and/or musicals/ year. Mainstage: subscriber base ages 30-70; Stage II: new works, more experimental. Mainstage: 230 seat proscenium; Stage II: 160 seat thrust. Pays by royalty.
How to Contact: Query with synopsis, character breakdown and set description and first 10 pages of show; tape; or submit through agent. SASE. Reports in 2 months on synopsis; 6 months on script.
Musical Theater: "Comedy, thriller or drama with small casts, no more than two sets to run approximately 2 hours. Cast not to exceed 8; orchestra 3-4 pieces; no more than 2 sets. No puppet shows, mimes or children's shows."
Productions: *No Way to Treat a Lady* by Douglas Cohen (musical comedy about serial killer); *Monograms* by Susan Mach (life of poet Hazel Hall); and *Death and the Maiden* by Ariel Dorfman (victiom of political torture).

PUERTO RICAN TRAVELING THEATRE, Dept. SM, 141 W. 94th St., New York, NY 10025. (212)354-1293. Producer: Miriam Colon Valle. Play Producer. Estab. 1967. Produces 4 plays and 1 new musical/year. Primarily an Hispanic audience. Playwrights are paid by stipend.
How to Contact: Submit complete ms and tape of songs. SASE. Reports in 6 months.
Musical Theater: "Small cast musicals that will appeal to Hispanic audience. Musicals are bilingual; we work in Spanish and English. We need simple sets and props and a cast of about 8, no more. Musicals are generally performed outdoors and last for an hour to an hour and 15 minutes."
Productions: *Chinese Charades*, by Manuel Perralras, Sergio Garcia and Saul Spangenberg (domestic musical); *El Jardin*, by Carlos Morton, Sergio Garcia (Biblical musical); and *Lady with a View*, by Eduardo Ivan Lopez and Fernando Rivas (Statue of Liberty musical).
Tips: "Deal with some aspect of the contemporary Hispanic experience in this country."

THE REPERTORY THEATRE OF ST. LOUIS, P.O. Box 191730, St. Louis MO 63119. (314)968-7340. Associate Artistic Director: Susan Gregg. Play producer. Estab. 1966. Produces 9 plays and 1 or 2 musicals/year. "Conservative regional theater audience. We produce all our work at the Loretto Hilton Theatre." Pays by royalty.
How to Contact: Query with synopsis, character breakdown and set description. Does not return unsolicited material. Reports in 1 year.
Musical Theater: "We want plays with a small cast and simple setting. No children's shows or foul language. After a letter of inquiry we would prefer script and demo tape."
Productions: *1940's Radio Hour*, by Walt Jones; *Almost September*, by David Schechter; *The Merry Wives of Windsor, Texas*, by John Haber; and *Young Rube*, by John Pielmeier and Matthew Selman.

*RITES AND REASON THEATRE, (at Brown University), Box 1148, Providence RI 02912. (401)863-3558. Fax: (401)863-3559. Artistic Director: Elmo Terry-Morgan. Play producer. Estab. 1970. Produces 2 plays/year. Audience is "very diverse! All ages, races, ethnicities." Performance space: 150 seat black box. Offers "developmental contract fee with effort to get play produced in a commercial theater."
How to Contact: Query with synopsis, character breakdown and set description. SASE. Reports in 6 months.
Musical Theater: "Innovative musical approaches, live music that is organic to the play. Prefer African-American and other Black musical styles and themes. But seriously consider other ethnic and lifestyle themes. Cast size should not exceed 20. No limit on production qualities." Does not wish to see "fluff, plays without serious substance." Prefers writer/musician to be in residence for some period during the development process.
Productions: *Brer Rabbit*, by Loni Berry (Afro-American folktale); *Letters from a New England Negro*, by Sherley Ann Williams (one-woman show in Reconstruction South); and *Miss Morning*, by Elmo Terry-Morgan (Black Southern family drama).
Tips: "Only submit works that are serious in theme. Music and comedy are great devices to exploring important issues. Rites and Reason Theatre is an African-American cultural institution located on the Brown University campus that produces original works on themes that address the diverse cultural experiences of the world."

*ROCKWELL PRODUCTIONS, LTD., Suite 100, 300 W. State St., Media PA 19063. (610)891-0247. Artistic Director: Jesse Cline. Play producer. Estab. 1989. Produces 6 plays and 6 musicals/year. "We produce in a 680 seat newly restored 1927 movie house converted into a performing arts center." Pays negotiated royalty.
How to Contact: Submit complete manuscript, score and tape of songs. Does not return material.
Musical Theater: "We will consider all types of musical theater. Especially interested in pieces that require a trained vocalism. Cast size is not the primary determiner of production. Not interested in 'dance musicals.' "
Productions: *Evita, On the Twentieth Century* and *Carnival*.

SAN JOSE REPERTORY THEATRE, P.O. Box 2399, San Jose CA 95109. (408)291-2266. Fax: (408)995-0737. Artistic Director's Assistant: J.R. Orlando. Play producer. Estab. 1980. Produces 6 plays and 2 musicals/year. 500-seat, proscenium stage. Pays various royalty.
How to Contact: Query with synopsis, character breakdown and set description. Does not return material. Reports in 6-8 months.
Musical Theater: "We seek light-hearted, small-cast musicals for our Christmas and summer shows. Musical reviews are considered if they have an interesting format. Cast and musicians required should equal no more than 10."
Productions: *Cole!*, by Alan Strachan and Benny Green (Cole Porter review); *1940's Radio Hour*, by Walton Jones (Christmas show); and *Fire in the Rain*, by Holly Near (autobiographical).
Tips: "Send 5-10 pages of sample dialogue with your synopsis."

SEATTLE GROUP THEATRE, 305 Harrison St., Seattle WA 98109. (206)441-9480. Producing Director: Paul O'Connell. Artistic Director: Tim Bond. Estab. 1978. Produces 6 plays and 1 possible musical/year. 200 seat intimate theater; 10' ceiling limit; 35' wide modified thrust; 3 piece band.
How to Contact: Query with synopsis, sample pages of dialogue, a cassette of music and a SASE large enough to accommodate return of cassette. Address all submissions to Nancy Griffiths, Dramaturg/Literary Manager.
Musical Theater: "Multicultural themes; relevant social, cultural and political issues relevant to the contemporary world (race relations, cultural differences, war, poverty, women's issues, homosexuality, physically challenged, developmentally disabled). Address the issues that our mission focuses on." Past musicals include *A . . . My Name Is Alice*, *Rap Master Ronnie*, *Jacques Brel is Alive*, *Stealing*, *Voices of Christmas*. Cast size of 10 maximum.
Productions: *La Bete*, by David Hirson; *Unquestioned Integrity: The Hill/Thomas Hearings*, by Mame Hunt; and *To Be Young, Gifted & Black*, by Lorraine Hansberry, adapted by Robert Nemiroff.

SECOND STAGE THEATRE, P.O. Box 1807, Ansonia Station, New York NY 10023. (212)787-8302. Dramaturg/Literary Manager: Mr. Erin Sanders. Play producer. Estab. 1979. Produces 4 plays and 1 musical (1 new musical)/year. Plays are performed in a small, 108 seat off-Broadway House." Pays per performance.
How to Contact: Query with synopsis, character breakdown and set description. No unsolicited manuscripts. Does not return material. Reports in 4-6 months.
Musical Theater: "We are looking for innovative, unconventional musicals that deal with sociopolitical themes."
Productions: *In a Pig's Valise*, by Eric Overmyer and Kid Creole (spoof on 40's film noir); *A . . . My Name Is Still Alice*, by various (song/sketch revue); and *The Good Times Are Killing Me*, by Lynda Barry (a play with music).
Tips: "Submit through agent; have strong references; show a sample of the best material."

SHENANDOAH PLAYWRITES RETREAT (A PROJECT OF SHENAN ARTS, INC.), Rt. 5, Box 167-F, Staunton VA 24401. (703)248-1868. Director of Playwriting and Screenwriting Programs: Robert Graham Small. Play producer. Estab. 1976. Develops 12-15 plays/year. Pays fellowships.
How to Contact: Submit complete ms, score and tape of songs. SASE. Replies in 4 months.
Productions: *The Wall*, by Roger Waters (rock musical adaptation); *Gods Trombones*, by James Weldon Johnson (gospel musical adaptation); and *American Yarn*, by Robert Graham Small.
Tips: Submit materials January-March 1. Submit synopsis and demo tape to Paul Hildebrand for touring and full production."

STAGE ONE, 425 W. Market St., Louisville KY 40202. (502)589-5946. Producing Director: Moses Goldberg. Play producer. Estab. 1946. Produces 8-10 plays and 0-2 musicals (0-2 new musicals)/year. "Audience is mainly young people ages 5-18." Pays 3-6% royalty, $1,500-3,000 fee or $25-75 per performance.
How to Contact: Submit complete manuscript and score. SASE. Reports in 4 months.
Musical Theater: "We seek stageworthy and respectful dramatizations of the classic tales of childhood, both ancient and modern. Ideally, the plays are relevant to young people and their families, as well as related to school curriculum. Cast is rarely more than 12."
Productions: *Bridge to Terabitha*, by Paterson/Toland/Leibman (contemporary novel); *Little Red Riding Hood*, by Goldberg/Cornett (fairytale); and *Tale of Two Cities*, by Kesselmann.
Tips: "Stage One accepts unsolicited manuscripts that meet our artistic objectives. Please do not send plot summaries or reviews. Include author's résumé, if desired. In the case of musicals, a cassette tape is preferred. Cast size is not a factor, although, in practice, Stage One rarely employs casts of over 12. Scripts will be returned in approximately 3-4 months, if SASE is included. No materials can be returned without the inclusion of a SASE. Due to the volume of plays received, it is not possible to provide written evaluations."

TACOMA ACTORS GUILD, 6th Floor, 901 Broadway, Tacoma WA 98402. (206)272-3107. Fax: (206)272-3358. Artistic Director: Bruce K. Sevy or Company/Literary Manager: Nancy Hoadley. Play producer. Estab. 1978. Produces 6-7 plays and 1-2 musicals/year. "Payment is negotiable."
How to Contact: Query with synopsis, character breakdown and set description. SASE. Reports in 6-12 months.
Musical Theater: Side stream, mainstream, adaptions, standard, non-standard fare, revue, full-length, family, cutting edge. 10-12 cast/minimal set changes preferred. No extensive orchestration. No puppet, mime or children's pieces.
Productions: *Oil City Symphony*, by Craver/Monk/Hardwick/Murfitt (review); *A Chorus Line*, by Bennett/Kirkwood/Dante/Hamlisch (Broadway dancers); and *Pump Boys and Dinettes*, by Foley/Hardwick/Monk/Morgan/Schimmel/Wahn (C/W review).

TADA!, 120 West 28th St., New York NY 10001. (212)627-1732. Artistic Director: Janine Nina Trevens. Play producer. Estab. 1984. Produces 4 staged readings and 2-4 new musicals/year. "TADA! is a company producing works performed by children ages 6-17 for family audiences in New York City. Performances run approximately 30-45 performances. Pays 5% royalty.
How to Contact: Query with synopsis and character breakdown or submit complete ms, score and tape of songs. SASE. Reports in 2-3 months.
Musical Theater: "We do not produce plays as full productions. At this point, we do staged readings of plays. We produce original commissioned musicals written specifically for the company."
Productions: *B.O.T.C.H.*, by Daniel Feigelson and Jon Agee; and *Everything About Camp (Almost)*. Scenes by Michael Slade. Music and Lyrics by various artists including Robby Merkin, Jamie Bernstein, Faye Greenberg, David Lawrence, David Evans, James Beloff, Mary Ehlinger and others.
Tips: "When writing for children don't condescend. The subject matter should be appropriate but the music/treatment can still be complex and interesting."

THE TEN-MINUTE MUSICALS PROJECT, Box 461194, West Hollywood CA 90046. (213)656-8751. Producer: Michael Koppy. Play producer. Estab. 1987. All pieces are new musicals. Pays equal share of 6-7% royalty.
How to Contact: Submit complete manuscript, score and tape of songs. SASE. Reports in 3 months.
Musical Theater: Seeks complete short stage musicals of between 8 and 15 minutes in length. Maximum cast: 9. "No parodies—original music only."
Productions: *The Furnished Room*, by Saragail Katzman (the O. Henry story); *An Open Window*, by Enid Futterman and Sara Ackerman (the Saki story); and *Pulp's Big Favor*, by David Spencer and Bruce Peyton (an original detective mystery).
Tips: "Start with a *solid* story—either an adaptation or an original idea—but with a solid beginning, middle and end (probably with a plot twist at the climax)."

TENNESSEE REPERTORY THEATRE, 427 Chestnut St., Nashville TN 37203. (615)244-4878. Associate Artistic Director: Don Jones. Play producer. Estab. 1985. Produces 5-6 plays/year; produces 3-4 musicals (1-2 new musicals)/year. "A diverse audience of theatergoers including people from Nashville's music business. Performances in a 1,000-seat state-of-the-art proscenium stage."
How to Contact: Query with synopsis, character breakdown and set description, 10-page dialogue sample and cassette. If material is to be returned, send SASE. Reports in 6-8 months.
Musical Theater: "We are interested in all types of new musicals, with a leaning toward musicals that are indigenous or related to the Southern experience. We also prefer musicals with social merit. For our workshop productions there is minimal use of most elements because work on the piece is primary. For a mainstage production there are no particular limits. We budget accordingly."
Productions: *Some Sweet Day*, by D. Jones, M. Pirkle and L. Sikelu (overcoming racism to form a union); *Ain't Got Long to Stay Here*, by Barry Scott (Martin Luther King); and *A House Divided*, by M. Pirkle and Mike Reid (Civil War).
Tips: "You should submit your work with an open mind toward developing it to the fullest. Tennessee Rep can be integral to that."

*THEATRE EAST, 12655 Ventura Blvd., Los Angeles CA 91604. President/Artistic Director: Geoffrey Woodhall. Play producer. Estab. 1960. Produces 3-6 plays/year; "would like to consider new musicals." Very mixed audience, all ages and backgrounds. Los Angeles crowd. 99 seat equity-waiver theater, wide, deep stage, shallow stage right. Pay is negotiable.
How to Contact: Query with synopsis, character breakdown and set description. SASE. Reports in 3-6 months on material, 1 month on query.
Musical Theater: "Contemporary adult themes. New, different approach musically and thematically. 10 or less in cast is most preferable, simple set, no fly space, not a lot of wing space."
Productions: *One-Act Play Festival*, by various (adult contemporary themes); *Sold*, by Mel Green (adult contemporary monologues); and *Brushstrokes*, by Burt Nodella (dying artist reviewing his life).
Tips: "Be original, be daring, have a point of view."

*THEATRE THREE, INC., 2800 Routh St., Dallas TX 75201. (214)871-2933. Fax: (214)871-3139. Musical Director: Terry Dobson. Play producer. Estab. 1961. Produces 10-12 plays and 3-4 musicals (1 or 2 new musicals)/year. "Subscription audience of 4,500 enjoys adventurous, sophisticated musicals." Performance space is an "arena stage (modified). Seats 250 per performance. Quite an intimate space." Pays varying royalty.
How to Contact: Submit complete ms, score and tape of songs. SASE. Reports "depending on the workload."
Musical Theater: "Off the wall topics. We have, in the past, produced *Little Shop of Horrors*, *Angry Housewives*, *Sweeney Todd*, *Groucho*, *A Life in Revue*, *The Middle of Nowhere* (a Randy Newman revue) and *A . . . My Name Is Alice*. We prefer small cast shows, but have done shows with a cast as large as 15. Orchestrations can be problematic. We usually do keyboards and percussion or some variation.

Some shows can be a design problem . . . we cannot do 'spectacle.' Our audiences generally like good, intelligent musical properties. Very contemporary language is about the only thing that sometimes causes 'angst' among our subscribers. We appreciate honesty and forthrightness . . . and good material done in an original and creative manner."

Productions: *Always, Patsy Cline*, by Ted Swindley (the C&W musical legend); *Assassins*, by Stephen Sondheim (presidential assassins); and *BallGames*, by various (contemporary men's issues).

THEATRE WEST, 3333 Cahuenga Blvd. W., Los Angeles CA 90068. (213)851-4839. Contact: Writer's Workshop Moderator. Play producer. Estab. 1962. Produces 6 plays and 0-4 musicals, 0-4 new musicals/year. Audience is mainly young urban professionals—25 to 50. Plays are performed in a 180 seat proscenium theater. Pays $25/performance.
How to Contact: Query first. SASE. Reports in 2 months.
Musical Theater: "Sets are minimalistic. Writer must ask for membership in our company. Would consider original music for use as background or pre-show music."
Productions: *Sermon*, by James Dickey (women's sexuality); *Survival of the Heart*, by Dayton Callie (sitcom-relationships); *The Routine*, by David Abbott (magician's life).
Tips: "Theatre West is a dues-paying membership company. Only members can submit plays for production. So, consequently, you must seek membership in our workshop company."

THEATRE WEST VIRGINIA, Box 1205, Beckley WV 25802. (800)666-9142. Play producer. Estab. 1955. Produces 7-9 plays and 2-3 musicals/year. "Audience varies from main stream summer stock to educational tours to dinner theater." Pays 5% royalty or $25/performance.
How to Contact: Query with synopsis, character breakdown and set description; should include cassette tape. SASE. Reports in 2 months.
Musical Theater: "Theatre West Virginia is a year-round performing arts organization that presents a variety of productions including community performances such as dinner theater, *The Nutcracker* and statewide educational programs on primary, elementary and secondary levels. This is in addition to our summer, outdoor dramas of *Hatfields & McCoys* and *Honey in the Rock*, now in their 29th year." Anything suitable for secondary school tours and/or dinner theater type shows. No more than 7 in cast. Play should be able to be accompanied by piano/synthesizer.
Productions: *Thomas Jefferson Still Survives*, by Nancy Moss (historical); *Frogsong*, by Jean Battlo (literary/historical); *Guys & Dolls*, by Frank Loesser; *Grease*, by Jim Jacobs and Warren Casey.

THEATREVIRGINIA, 2800 Grove Ave., Richmond VA 23221-2466. (804)367-0840. Artistic Director: George Black. Play producer. Estab. 1955. Produces 5-9 plays (2-5 musicals)/year. "Plays are performed in a 500-seat LORT-C house for the Richmond-area community." Payment negotiable.
How to Contact: "Please submit synopsis, sample of dialogue and sample of music (on cassette) along with a self-addressed, stamped letter-size envelope. If material seems to be of interest to us, we will reply with a solicitation for a complete manuscript and cassette. Response time for synopses is 4 weeks; response time for scripts once solicited is 5 months."
Musical Theater: "We do not deal in one-acts or in children's material. We would like to see full length, adult musicals. There are no official limitations. We would be unlikely to use original music as incidental/underscoring for existing plays, but there is potential for adapting existing plays into musicals."
Productions: *West Memphis Mojo*, by Martin Jones; *Sweeney Todd*, by Stephen Sondheim; and *South Pacific*, by Rodgers and Hammerstein.
Tips: "Read plays. Study structure. Study character. Learn how to concisely articulate the nature of your work. A beginning musical playwright, wishing to work for our company should begin by writing a wonderful, theatrically viable piece of musical theater. Then he should send us the material requested in our listing, and wait patiently."

THEATREWORKS, 470 San Antonio Rd., Palo Alto CA 94306. (415)812-7550. Literary Manager: Jeannie Barroga. Play producer. Estab. 1970. Produces 7 plays and 5 musicals (2 new musicals)/year. Theatrically-educated suburban area bordering Stanford University 30 miles from San Francisco and San Jose—3 mainstages and 2 second stage performance spaces. Pays per contract.
How to Contact: Submit complete ms, score and tape of songs; synopses and character breakdowns helpful. SASE. Reports in 3-5 months.
Musical Theater: "We use original songs and music in many of our classics productions, for instance specially composed music was used in our production of the *The Tempest* for Ariel's song, the pageant song, the storm and the magic of the isles. We are looking both for full-scale large musicals and smaller chamber pieces. We also use original music and songs in non-musical plays. No ancient Roman, ancient Greek or biblical settings please!"
Productions: 1994 musical productions include: *Honor Song for Crazy Horse*, by Darrah Cloud/Kim Sherman (American Indian); *Almost September*, by David Schechter/Stephen Lutvak (Wind in the Willows re-enactment); and *Music of Stephen Schwartz*, by Stephen Schwartz (revue).

Tips: "Write a great musical. We wish there were more specific 'formula,' but that's about it. If it's really terrific, we're interested."

THEATREWORKS/USA, 890 Broadway, New York NY 10003. (212)677-5959. Literary Manager: Barbara Pasternack. Play producer. Produces 10-13 plays, most are musicals (3-4 new musicals)/year. Audience consists of children and families. Pays 6% royalty and aggregate of $1,500 commission-advance against future royalties.
How to Contact: Query with synopsis, character breakdown and sample scene and song. SASE. Reports in 6 months.
Musical Theater: "One hour long, 5-6 adult actors, highly portable, good musical theater structure; adaptations of children's literature, historical or biographical musicals, issues, fairy tales—all must have something to say. We demand a certain level of literary sophistication. No kiddy shows, no camp, no fractured fables, no shows written for school or camp groups to perform. Approach your material, not as a writer writing for kids, but as a writer addressing any universal audience. You have 1 hour to entertain, say something, make them care—don't preach, condescend. Don't forget an antagonist. Don't waste the audience's time. We always use original music—but most of the time a project team comes complete with a composer in tow."
Productions: *Columbus*, by Jonathan Bolt, music by Doug Cohen, lyrics by Thomas Toce; *Class Clown*, book by Thomas West, music by Kim Oles, lyrics by Alison Hubbard; and *Freaky Friday*, music by Mary Rodgers, book and lyrics by John Forster.
Tips: "Write a good show! Make sure the topic is something we can market! Come see our work to find out our style."

13TH STREET REPERTORY COMPANY, 50 W. 13th St., New York NY 10011. (212)675-6677. Dramaturg: Ken Terrell. Play producer. Estab. 1974. Produces 6 plays/year including 2 new musicals. Audience comes from New York and surrounding area. Children's theater performs at 50 W. 13th in NYC. "We do not pay. We are an off-off Broadway company and provide a stepping stone for writers, directors, actors."
How to Contact: Query with synopsis, character breakdown and set description. SASE. Reports in 2 months.
Musical Theater: Children's musicals and original musical shows. Small cast with limited musicians. Stagings are struck after each performance. Would consider original music for "pre-show music or incidental music."
Productions: *Journeys*, a collaborative effort about actors' work in New York City; *New York, Paris, Everywhere*, by Ken Terrell; and *The Smart Set*, by Enrico Garzilli.

TUACAHN CENTER FOR THE ARTS, (formerly Moorhead State University), Heritage Arts Foundation, 1030 S. Valley View Dr., St. George UT 84770. (218)236-4613. Managing Director: David Grapes. Play producer. Produces 16-20 plays and 5 musicals (1 new musical)/year. Educated, community/university audience. Pays $50-300/performance.
How to Contact: Submit complete ms, score and tape of songs. SASE. Reports in 6 months.
Musical Theater: "We look for outstanding works in all categories. Particular interest in scripts that deal with issues and topics of interest to LDS Church."
Productions: *Good News*, by DeSylva; *Grapes of Wrath*; and *Seekers of the Light*, by Zinober.

DON TURNER, 311 Nueces, Austin TX 78701. Fax: (512)472-7199. Literary Manager: Amparo Garcia. Play producer. Produces 8 plays and 2-3 musicals (1 new musical)/year. "Audience is mixed—we are a large university town so we attract a variety of people. Family oriented." 280 seat proscenium. "We follow Samuel French or other publisher's agreement."
How to Contact: Query with synopsis, character breakdown and set description. SASE. Reports in 3-6 months.
Musical Theater: "Musicals with widest appeal. We reserve the experimental genres to development/readings—musicals are biggest $ draw so we choose more established work. We appreciate all great writing; however, an original musical has a chance of production if it is a finalist in our new play awards."
Productions: *Nine*, by Authur Kopit/Maury Yeston (based on Fellini's *8½*); *Dancing at Lughnosa*, by Brian Friel (family portrait); and *Fiddler on the Roof*, by J. Stein, J. Buck and Sheldon Hamick.

*UNDERGROUND RAILWAY THEATER, 41 Foster, Arlington MA 02174. (617)643-6916. Play producer. Estab. 1976. Produces 1-2 plays and 1-2 new musicals/year. Performance space is a "200 seat modified thrust."
How to Contact: Submit tape of songs. Does not return material.
Musical Theater: "We are interested only in music. We hire our own writers." Cast size limited to 5-6 actor/singers. "No musicals, please and no texts (except song lyrics)."

Productions: *Washed Up Middle-aged Women*, by Debra Wise and Elaine Kenny; and *Creation of the World*, by Dennis Milhaud.
Tips: "Send only politically engaged texts, and only scenes. Will not read whole plays."

UNIVERSITY OF ALABAMA NEW PLAYWRIGHTS' PROGRAM, Box 870239, Tuscaloosa AL 35487-0239. (205)348-5283. Director/Dramaturg: Dr. Paul Castagno. Play producer. Estab. 1982. Produces 8-10 plays and 1 musical/year; 1 new musical every other year. Receives 2 musical submissions/month. University audience. Pays by arrangement. Stipend is competitive. Also expenses and travel.
How to Contact: Submit complete manuscript, score and tape of songs. SASE. Reports in 2 months.
Musical Theater: Any style or subject (but no children's or puppet plays). No limitations—just solid lyrics and melodic line. Drama with music, musical theater workshops, and chamber musicals. "We love to produce a small-scale musical."
Productions: *Gospel According to Esther*, by John Erlanger.
Tips: "Take your demos seriously. We really want to do something small scale, for actors, often without the greatest singing ability. Use fresh sounds not derivative of the latest fare. While not ironclad by any means, musicals with Southern themes might stand a better chance."

THE UNUSUAL CABARET, 14½ Mt. Desert St., Bar Harbor ME 04609. (207)288-3306. Play producer. Estab. 1990. Produces 4 plays and 4 new musicals/year. Educated adult audiences. 75 seat cabaret. "A casual, festive atmosphere." Pays by royalty (12% of Box).
How to Contact: Submit complete ms, score and tape of songs. SASE. Reports in 1 month.
Musical Theater: "We produce both musical and non-musical scripts—45 minutes to 1¼ hours in length. Stylistically or topically unique scripts are encouraged. We strive for as diverse a season as possible within our technical limitations. Our maximum cast size is 8, but cast sizes of 4 or fewer are necessary for some of our productions. Our technical capabilities are minimal. Audience participation and non-traditional staging are possible because of the cabaret setting. We encourage musical *plays* as well as more traditional musicals. Piano is usually the only instrument. We consider adaptations if the written material is being used in an original way in conjunciton with the music."
Productions: *Hamlet: the Anti-Musical*, by Mark Milbauer and David Becker; *The Alchemist*, by John Kaufmann/Mark Hollman; and *Time Traveler*, by Gina Kaufmann.
Tips: "Keep it accessible, fun and rich. With laughter we have their attention and with content we have their respect."

WALNUT STREET THEATRE COMPANY, 825 Walnut St., Philadelphia PA 19107. (215)574-3584. Literary Manager: Beverly Elliott. Play producer. Estab. 1982. Produces 8 plays and 2 musicals (1 new musical)/year. Plays produced on a mainstage with seating for 1,052 to a family audience; and in studio theaters with seating for 79-99 to adult audiences. Pays by royalty or outright purchase.
How to Contact: Query with synopsis, character breakdown, set description, and ten pages. SASE. Reports in 6 months.
Musical Theater: "Adult Musicals. Plays are for a subscription audience that comes to the theater to be entertained. We seek musicals with lyrical non-operatic scores and a solid book. We are looking for a small musical for springtime and one for a family audience at Christmas time. We would like to remain open on structure and subject matter and would expect a tape with the script. Cast size: around 20 equity members (10 for smaller musical); preferably one set with variations." Would consider original music for incidental music and/or underscore. This would be at each director's discretion.
Productions: *Jesus Christ Superstar*, by Rice/Lloyd-Webber; *Into the Woods*, by Sondheim; and *Another Kind of Hero*, by Steele/Alexander.
Tips: "Invest in sending the best quality musical tape that you can—don't leave us to imagine the orchestration and good singing."

WATERLOO COMMUNITY PLAYHOUSE, Box 433, Waterloo IA 50704. (319)235-0367. Managing Artistic Director: Charles Stilwill. Play producer. Estab. 1917. Produces 12 plays (1-2 musicals)/year. "Our audience prefers solid, wholesome entertainment, nothing risque or with strong language. We perform in Hope Martin Theatre, a 368-seat house." Pays $15-150/performance.
How to Contact: Submit complete manuscript, score and cassette tape of songs. SASE.
Musical Theater: "Casts may vary from as few as 6 people to 54. We are producing children's theater as well. We're *especially* interested in new adaptations of classic children stories."
Productions: *Bridge to Terabithia* (children's); *Guys & Dolls* (traditional); *A Christmas Carol* (holiday).
Tips: "Looking for new adaptations of classical children's stories or a good Christmas show."

WEST COAST ENSEMBLE, Box 38728, Los Angeles CA 90038. (213)871-8673. Artistic Director: Les Hanson. Play producer. Estab. 1982. Produces 6-9 plays and 1 new musical/year. "Our audience is a wide variety of Southern Californians. Plays will be produced in one of our two theaters on Hollywood Boulevard." Pays $35-50 per performance.

How to Contact: Submit complete manuscript, score and tape of songs. SASE. Reports in 6-8 months.
Musical Theater: "There are no limitations on subject matter or style. Cast size should be no more than 12 and sets should be simple. If music is required we would commission a composer, music would be used as a bridge between scenes or to underscore certain scenes in the play."
Productions: *Gorey Stories*, by Stephen Currens (review based on material of Edward Gorey) and *The Much Ado Musical*, by Tony Tanner (adaptation of Shakespeare).
Tips: "Submit work in good form and be patient. We look for musicals with a strong book and an engaging score with a variety of styles."

*WEST END PLAYHOUSE, #291, 18034 Ventura Blvd., Encino CA 91316. (818)996-0505. Artistic Director: Edmund Gaynes. Play producer. Estab. 1983. Produces 5 plays and 3 new musicals/year. Audience "covers a broad spectrum, from general public to heavy theater/film/TV industry crowds. Proscenium—83 seats, operating under A.E.A. 99-seat plan." Payment is negotiable.
How to Contact: Submit complete ms, score and tape of songs, if possible. SASE. Reports in 2 months.
Musical Theater: "Prefer small-cast musicals and revues. Full length preferred. Interested in children's shows also." Cast size: "Maximum 12; exceptional material with larger casts will be considered."
Productions: *Crazy Words, Crazy Tunes*, by Milt Larsen and Gene Casey (novelty songs of the '20s, '30s and '40s); *Starting Here, Starting Now*, by David Shire and Richard Maltby, Jr. (songs by Shire and Maltby); and *Broadway Sings Out!*, by Tay Malvani (Broadway songs of social significance).
Tips: "If you feel every word or note you have written is sacred and chiseled in stone, and are unwilling to work collaboratively with a professional director, don't bother to submit."

*WESTBETH THEATRE CENTER, 151 Bank St., New York NY 10014. (212)691-2272. Literary Manager: Steven Bloom. Play producer. Estab. 1978. Produces 1-2 musicals/year. Audience consists of New York theater professionals and Village neighborhood. "We have 5 performance spaces, including a music hall and cafe theater." Uses usual New York showcase contract.
How to Contact: Submit complete ms, score and tape of songs. SASE. Reports in 4-6 weeks.
Musical Theater: "Full length musicals, all Broadway styles. Small, ensemble casts the best." Does not wish to see "one character musicals, biographies and historical dramas. Musicals selected for development will undergo intense process. We look for strong collaborators."
Productions: *The Hunchback of Notre Dame*, by Hal Hackady/Tom Scully (book adaptation); *The Life*, by Cy Coleman (urban life); and *The Taffetas*, by Rick Lewis ('50s girl group revue).
Tips: "Be open to the collaborative effort. We are a professional theater company, competing in the competitive world of Broadway and off-Broadway, so the work we present must reach for the highest standard of excellence."

WILMA THEATER, 2030 Sansom St., Philadelphia PA 19103. (215)963-0249. Artistic Producing Directors: Jiri Zizka and Blanka Zizka. Play producer. Produces 4-5 plays (1-2 musicals)/year. Plays are performed for a "sophisticated, adventurous, off-beat and demanding audience," in a 100-seat theater. Pays 6-8% of gross income.
How to Contact: Submit synopsis, score and tape of songs. SASE. Reports in 2 months.
Musical Theater: Seeks "innovative staging, universal issues, political implications and inventive, witty approach to subject. We emphasize ensemble style, group choreography, actors and musicians overlapping, with new, inventive approach to staging. Do not exceed 4-5 musicians, cast of 12 (ideally under 8), or stage space of 30×20." Also interested in plays with music and songs.
Productions: *Marat/Sade* (basic questions of human existence); *Three Guys Naked from the Waist Down* (worship of success); and *Oedipus the King*, by Sophocles (with original music).
Tips: "Don't think what will sell. Find your own voice. Be original, tune to your ideas, characters and yourself."

*WINGS THEATRE CO., 154 Christopher St., New York NY 10014. (212)627-2960. Fax: (212)627-2961. Contact: Literary Director. Play producer. Estab. 1987. Produces 12-15 plays and 5 musicals/year. Performance space is a 74 seat O.O.B. proscenium, audience raked. Pays $100 for limited rights to produce against 3% of gross box office receipts.
How to Contact: Submit complete ms, score and tape of songs. SASE. Reports in 8-12 months.
Musical Theater: "Eclectic. Entertaining. Enlightening. This is an O.O.B. theater. Funds are limited." Does not wish to see "movies posing as plays. Television theater."
Productions: *Stars and Stripes*, by Bill Solly/Donald Ward (WWII musical); *Fangs, the Vampire Musical*, by Clint Jefferies (gay vampire musical thriller); and *Slasher, the Splatter Rock Musical*, by Hillyer/Wheeler/Paruolo/Calderwood (slasher movie satire).
Tips: "Be patient. We will return your script, but not until we can process it. We choose our scripts for next season once a year in the late Spring."

WOMEN'S PROJECT AND PRODUCTIONS, JULIA MILES, ARTISTIC DIRECTOR, 7 W. 63rd St., New York NY 10023. (212)873-3040. Literary Manager: Susan Bougetz. Estab. 1978. Produces 3 plays/year. Pays by outright purchase.
How to Contact: Submit synopsis, 10 sample pages of dialogue and sample tape. SASE. Reports in 3 months. "Adult audience. Plays by women only."
Musical Theater: "We usually prefer a small to medium cast of 3-6. We produce few musicals and produce *only* women playwrights."
Productions: *Ladies*, by Eve Ensler (homelessness); *O Pioneers!*, by Darrah Cloud (adapted) from Willa Cather's novel; and *Skirting the Issues* (musical cabaret).
Tips: "Resist sending early drafts of work."

WOOLLY MAMMOTH THEATRE CO., Dept. SM, 1401 Church St. NW, Washington DC 20005. (202)234-6130. Literary Manager: Jim Byrnes. Play producer. Estab. 1978. Produces 4 plays/year.
How to Contact: Submit letter of inquiry or full package (i.e., complete manuscript, score and tape of songs). SASE.
Musical Theater: "We do unusual works. We have done 1 musical, the *Rocky Horror Show* (very successful). 8-10 in cast. We do not wish to see one-acts. Be professional in presentation."
Productions: *Free Will and Wanton Lust*, *The Cockburn Rituals* and *Strindberg in Hollywood*.
Tips: "Just keep writing! Too many people expect to make it writing 1 or 2 plays."

Play Publishers

AMELIA MAGAZINE, 329 "E" St., Bakersfield CA 93304. (805)323-4064. Editor: Frederick A. Raborg, Jr. Play publisher. Estab. 1983. Publishes 1 play/year. General audience; one-act plays published in *Amelia Magazine*. Best play submitted is the winner of the annual Frank McClure One-Act Play Award.
How to Contact: Submit complete manuscript and score per contest rules by postmark deadline of May 15. SASE. Reports in 6-8 weeks. "We would consider publishing musical scores if submitted in clean, camera-ready copy — also single songs. Best bet is with single songs complete with clear, camera-ready scoresheets, for regular submissions. We use only first North American serial rights. All performance and recording rights remain with songwriter. Payment same as for poetry — $25 plus copies."
Tips: "Be polished, professional, and submit clear, clean copy."

ARAN PRESS, 1320 S. Third St., Louisville KY 40208. (502)636-0115. Editor/Publisher: Tom Eagan. Play publisher. Estab. 1983. Publishes 40-50 plays, 1-2 musicals and 1-2 new musicals/year. Professional, college/university, community, summer stock and dinner theater audience. Pays 50% production royalty or 10% book royalty.
How to Contact: Submit ms, score and tape of songs. SASE. Reports in 1-2 weeks.
Musical Theater: "The musical should include a small cast, simple set for professional, community, college, university, summer stock and dinner theater production."
Publications: *A Bee to Honey*, by Bruce Feld; *Puppy Love*, by Tom Eagan; and *O My Goodness!*, by Patricia Montley.

ART CRAFT PUBLISHING CO., Box 1058, Cedar Rapids IA 52406. (319)364-6311. Editor: C. Emmett McMullen. Play publisher. Estab. 1928. Publishes 10-15 plays/year. "We publish plays and musicals for the amateur market including middle, junior and smaller senior high schools and church groups."
How to Contact: Submit complete manuscript, score and tape of songs. SASE. Reports in 2 months.
Musical Theater: "Seeking material for high school productions. All writing within the scope of high school groups. No works with X-rated material or questionable taboos. Simplified staging and props. Currently seeking material with larger casts, preferably with more women than male roles."
Publications: *Robin Hood*, by Dan Neidermyer; *Rest Assured*, by Donald Payton; and *Murder At Coppersmith Inn*, by Dan Neidermyer.
Tips: "We are interested in working with new writers. Writers need to consider that many plays are presented in small — often not well-established stages."

BAKER'S PLAYS, 100 Chauncy St., Boston MA 02111. (617)482-1280. Editor: John B. Welch. Play publisher. Estab. 1845. Publishes 15-22 plays and 3-5 new musicals/year. Plays are used by children's theaters, junior and senior high schools, colleges and community theaters. Pays 50% royalty or 10% book royalty.
How to Contact: Submit complete manuscript, score and cassette tape of songs. SASE. Reports in 2-6 months.
Musical Theater: "Seeking musicals for teen production and children's theater production. We prefer large cast, contemporary musicals which are easy to stage and produce. Plot your shows strongly, keep your scenery and staging simple, your musical numbers and choreography easily explained and blocked out. Originality and style are up to the author. We want innovative and tuneful shows but no X-rated

material. We are very interested in the new writer and believe that, with revision and editorial help, he can achieve success in writing original musicals for the non-professional market." Would consider original music for use in a play being developed or in a pre-existing play.

Publications: *Dreadful Doings at the Cider Mill*, by Don A. Mueller; *Just Friends*, by Scanlan/Cangiano (high school friendships); and *Silent Bells*, by Jane O'Neill, Charles Apple (Christmas fable).

Tips: "As we publish musicals that can be produced by high school theater departments with high school talent, the writer should know if their play can be done on the high school stage. I recommend that the writer go to performances of original musicals whenever possible."

CONTEMPORARY DRAMA SERVICE, 885 Elkton Dr., Colorado Springs CO 80907. (719)594-4422. Executive Editor: Arthur Zapel. Assistant Editor: Rhonda Wray. Play publisher. Estab. 1979. Publishes 40-50 plays and 4-6 new musicals/year. "We publish for young children and teens in mainstream Christian churches and for teens and college level in the secular market. Our musicals are performed in churches, schools and colleges." Pays 10% royalty (for music books), 50% royalty for performance and "sometimes we pay royalty up to buy-out fee for minor works."

How to Contact: Submit complete ms, score and tape of songs. SASE. Reports in 6 weeks.

Musical Theater: "For churches we publish musical programs for children and teens to perform at Easter, Christmas or some special occasion. Our school musicals are for teens to perform as class plays or special entertainments. Cast size may vary from 5-25 depending on use. We prefer more parts for girls than boys. Music must be written in the vocal range of teens. Staging should be relatively simple but may vary as needed. We are not interested in elementary school material. Elementary level is OK for church music but not public school elementary. Music must have full piano accompaniment and be professionally scored for camera-ready publication."

Publications: *Where The Heart Is*, by Cynthia and Michael Marion (Christmas musical about the homeless); *Three Wishes* by Ted Sod/Suzanne Grant (musical about teenage pregnancy); and *Christmas Coming!*, by Jarl K. Juerson (Christmas musical for children).

Tips: "Familiarize yourself with the type of musicals we publish. Note general categories, then give us something that would fit, yet differs from what we've already published."

THE DRAMATIC PUBLISHING COMPANY, 311 Washington St., Woodstock IL 60098. (815)338-7170. Music Editor: Dana Wolworth. Play publisher. Publishes 35 plays (3-5 musicals)/year. Estab. 1885. Plays used by community theaters, high schools, colleges, stock and professional theaters, churches and camps.

How to Contact: Submit complete ms, score and tape of songs. SASE. Reports in 10-12 weeks.

Musical Theater: Seeking "children's musicals not over 1¼ hours, and adult musicals with 2 act format. No adaptations for which the rights to use the original work have not been cleared. If directed toward high school market, large casts with many female roles are preferred. For professional, stock and community theater small casts are better. Cost of producing a play is always a factor to consider in regard to costumes, scenery and special effects." Would also consider original music for use in a pre-existing play "if we or the composer hold the rights to the non-musical work."

Publications: *Dream on Royal St.*, by June and David Rogers/Alan Menken (based on *A Midsummer Night's Dream*); *Cotton Patch Gospel* by Harry Chapin/Tom Key/Russell Treyz (version of Matthew and John); *Treemonisha*, by Scott Joplin (opera – liberalism and education).

Tips: "Music should be 'tuneful.' Something one can go away humming."

ELDRIDGE PUBLISHING CO., INC., P.O. Box 1595, Venice FL 34284. (800)HI-STAGE. Editor: Nancy S. Vorhis. Play publisher. Estab. 1906. Publishes 40 plays and 2-3 musicals/year. Seeking "large cast musicals which appeal to students. We like variety and originality in the music, easy staging and costuming. We serve the school and church market, 6th grade through 12th; also Christmas and Easter musicals for churches." Would also consider original music for use in a play being developed; "music that could make an ordinary play extraordinary." Pays 50% royalty and 10% copy sales in school market.

How to Contact: Submit tape with manuscript if at all possible. Unsolicited submissions OK. SASE. Reports in 2 months.

Publications: *Phantom of the Soap Opera*, by Sodaro; *I am a Star!*, by Billie St. John and Wendell Jimerson (high schoolers vying for movie roles); *Magnolia*, by Sodaro and Francoeur (a *Gone with the Wind* takeoff).

Tips: "We're always looking for talented composers but not through individual songs. We're only interested in complete school or church musicals. Lead sheets, cassette tape and script are best way to submit. Let us see your work!"

ENCORE PERFORMANCE PUBLISHING, P.O. Box 692, Orem UT 84059. (801)225-0605. Editor: Michael C. Perry. Play publisher. Estab. 1979. Publishes 10-20 plays (including musicals)/year. "We are interested in plays which emphasize strong family values and play to all ages." Pays 50% royalty.

How to Contact: Query with synopsis, character breakdown and set description. SASE. Reports in 2-6 weeks on query, 1-2 months on submissions.

Musical Theater: Musicals of all types for all audiences. Can be original or adapted. "We tend to favor shows with at least an equal male/female cast." Do not wish to see works that can be termed offensive or vulgar. However, experimental theater forms are also of interest.

Publications: *One Magic Christmas*, by Fitzsimmons, Campbell and Silverstein (family); *Wonder Boy*, by Sidney Berger and Rob Landee (child/youth); and *State of Jefferson*, by Gerard Murphy.

Tips: "Always write with an audience in mind."

THE FREELANCE PRESS, Box 548, Dover MA 02030. (508)785-1260. Managing Editor: Narcissa Campion. Play publisher. Estab. 1979. Publishes 20 plays/year; 19 musicals (3 new musicals/year.) "Pieces are primarily for elementary to high school students; large casts (approximately 30); plays are produced by schools and children's theaters." Pays 10% of purchase price of script or score, 50% of collected royalty.

How to Contact: Query first. SASE. Reports in 6 months.

Musical Theater: "We publish previously produced musicals and plays for children in the primary grades through high school. Plays are for large casts (approximately 30 actors and speaking parts) and run between 45 minutes to 1 hour and 15 minutes. Subject matter should be contemporary issues (sibling rivalry, friendship, etc.) or adaptations of classic literature for children (*Alice in Wonderland*, *Treasure Island*, etc.). We do not accept any plays written for adults to perform for children."

Publications: *Monopoly*, by T. Dewey/Megan (3 high school students live out the board game); *No Zone*, by T. Dewey/Campion (environmental fantasy about effects of global warming); *The Pied Piper*, P. Houghton/Hutchins (adaptation of Browning poem).

Tips: "We enjoy receiving material that does not condescend to children. They are capable of understanding many current issues, playing complex characters, acting imaginative, handling unconventional material, and singing difficult music."

SAMUEL FRENCH, INC., 45 W. 25th St., New York NY 10010. (212)206-8990. Editor: Lawrence Harbison. Play publisher. Estab. 1830. Publishes 40-50 plays and 2-4 new musicals/year. Amateur and professional theaters. Pays 80% of amateur royalties; 90% of professional royalties.

How to Contact: Query first. SASE. Reports in minimum 10 weeks.

Musical Theater: "We publish primarily successful musicals from the NYC stage." Don't submit large-cast, big "Broadway" musicals which haven't been done on Broadway.

Publications: *Eating Raoul*, by Paul Bartel; *Hello Muddah Hello Faddah*, by Bernstein/Krause; and *Love and Shrimp*, by Judith Viorst.

HEUER PUBLISHING CO., Box 248, Cedar Rapids IA 52406. (319)364-6311. Publisher: C. Emmett McMullen. Musical play publisher. Estab. 1928. Publishes plays and musicals for the amateur market including middle schools, junior and senior high schools and church groups.

How to Contact: Submit complete ms, score and tape of songs. SASE. Reports in 2 months.

Musical Theater: "We prefer two or three act comedies or mystery-comedies with a large number of characters."

Publications: *Alibis*, by Peter Kennedy and *Aladdin*, by Dan Neidermyer.

LILLENAS DRAMA RESOURCES, P.O. Box 419527, Kansas City MO 64141. (816)931-1900. Editor/Consultant: Paul M. Miller. Play publisher. Estab. 1912. Publishes 10 collections (2 full-length) and 4 program collections, 3 musicals (3 new musicals)/year. "Our plays and musicals are performed by churches, Christian schools, and independent theater organizations that perform 'religious' plays." Pays 10% royalty.

How to Contact: Submit complete ms, score and tape of songs. SASE. Reports in 3 months.

Publications: *I'll Be Home For Christmas*, by Deborah Craig-Cleer.

Tips: "Remember that religious theater comes in all genres: do not become tied to a historically biblical approach; take truth and couch in terms that are understandable to contemporary audiences in and out of the church. Keep 'simplicity' as a key word in your writing; cast sizes, number of scenes/acts, costume and set requirements will affect the acceptance of your work by the publisher and the market."

MERIWETHER PUBLISHING, LTD. (CONTEMPORARY DRAMA SERVICE), 885 Elkton Dr., Colorado Springs CO 80907. (719)594-4422. Executive Editor: Arthur Zapel. Play publisher. Estab. 1968. Publishes 40 plays and 5-10 musicals (5 new musicals)/year. "We publish musicals for church school, elementary, middle grade and teens. We also publish musicals for high school secular use. Our musicals are performed in churches or high schools." Pays 10% royalty or by negotiated sale from royalties. "Sometimes we pay a royalty to a limited maximum."

How to Contact: Query with synopsis, character breakdown and set description or submit script with cassette tape of songs. SASE. Reports in 1 month.

Musical Theater: "We are always looking for good church/school musicals for children. We prefer a length of 15-20 minutes, though occasionally we will publish a 3-act musical adaptation of a classic with large casts and sets. We like informal styles, with a touch of humor, that allow many children and/or adults to participate. We like musicals that imitate Broadway shows or have some name appeal based on the Classics. Box office appeal is more critical than message—at least for teenage and adult level fare. Musical scripts with piano accompaniments only. We especially welcome short, simple musicals for elementary and teenage, church use during the holidays of Christmas and Easter. We would like to know of arrangers and copyists."

Publications: *Three Wishes*, by Ted Sod and Suzanne Grant; *Pinnochio*, by Larry Nestor and Miriam Schuman (children's story); and *Steamboat*, by Charles Boyd and Yvonne Boyd.

Tips: "Tell us clearly the intended market for the work and provide as much information as possible about its viability."

PIONEER DRAMA SERVICE, P.O. Box 4267, Englewood CO 80155. (303)779-4035. Play publisher. Estab. 1963. "Plays are performed by junior high and high school drama departments, church youth groups, college and university theaters, semi-professional and professional children's theaters, parks and recreation departments." Playwrights paid 50% royalty (10% sales).

How to Contact: Query first. SASE. Reports in 2 months.

Musical Theater: "We seek full length children's musicals, high school musicals and one act children's musicals to be performed by children, secondary school students, and/or adults. As always, we are seeking musicals easy to perform, simple sets, many female roles and very few solos. Must be appropriate for educational market. Developing a new area, we are actively seeking musicals to be produced by elementary schools—20 to 30 minutes in length, with 2 to 3 songs and large choruses. We are not interested in profanity, themes with exclusively adult interest, sex, drinking, smoking, etc. Several of our full-length plays are being converted to musicals. We edit them, decide where to insert music and then contact with someone to write the music and lyrics."

Publications: *You Ain't Nothin But A Werewolf*, by Tim Kelly/Bill Francoeur (spoof of '50s "B" horror films); *The Frog Prince*, by D.J. Leonard/David Reiser (tale by Bros. Grimm); and *Bedside Manor*, by Tim Kelly/G.V.Castle/M.C. Vigilant (hospital farce).

Tips: "Research and learn about the publisher and their market."

PLAYERS PRESS, INC., Box 1132, Studio City CA 91614. (818)789-4980. Associate Editor: Marjorie Clapper. Vice President: Robert W. Gordon. Play publisher. Estab. 1965. Publishes 10-20 plays and 1-3 new musicals/year. Plays are used primarily by general audience and children. Pays 10-50% royalty or 25-80% of performance.

How to Contact: Query first. SASE. Reports in 6 weeks to 12 months (1-10 days on query).

Musical Theater: "We will consider all submitted works. Presently musicals for adults and high schools are in demand. When cast size can be flexible (describe how it can be done in your work) it sells better."

Publications: *The Deerstalker*, by Terrence Mustoo (Sherlock Holmes-musical); *Foster*, by William-Alan Landes (Stephen Foster); and *Wild Imaginings*, by Michael Ficocelli (teen musical).

Tips: "We will consider all submitted musicals. Presently large cast, non-rock musicals that appeal to general audiences are in demand. When cast size is flexible please describe."

Play Producers and Publishers/'94-'95 Changes

The following markets appeared in the 1994 edition of *Songwriter's Market* but are absent from the 1995 edition. Most of these companies failed to respond to our request for an update of their listing for a variety of reasons. For example, they may have gone out of business or they may have requested deletion from the 1995 edition because they are backlogged with material. If we know the specific reason, it appears within parentheses.

Amas Musical Theatre Inc.
The Growing State Theatre
Invisible Theatre (not accepting submissions)

Magnificent Moorpark Melodrama and Vaudeville Co.
(unable to contact)
New Works Productions

(unable to contact)
South Western College
Warehouse Theatre

Fine Arts

For the aspiring composer it is vital to have his work performed for interested listeners. A resume of performances aids in identifying a composer within the concert music community. One excellent, exciting performance may lead to others by different groups or commissions for new works.

All of the groups listed in this section are interested in hearing new music. From chamber groups to symphony orchestras, they are open to new talent and feel their audiences are progressive and interested enough to support new music.

Bear in mind the financial and artistic concerns as you submit material. Many fine arts organizations are nonprofit, and may be understaffed. It could take a while for someone to get back to you, so it pays to be patient. Always follow submission instructions diligently. Be professional when you contact the music directors, and keep in mind the typical fine arts audience they are selecting music for. Chamber musicians and their audiences, for instance, are a good source for performance opportunities. Their repertoire is limited and most groups are enthusiastic about finding or commissioning new works. Furthermore, the chamber music audience is smaller and likewise enthusiastic enough to enjoy contemporary music.

Don't be disappointed if the payment offered by these groups is small or even non-existent. Most fine arts music organizations are struggling economically and can't pay large fees to even the most established composers. Inquire into other opportunities to submit your work; many of these groups also offer periodic competitions for new works. Also, most of these ensembles belong to a blanket organization representing that genre. See the Organizations and Contests and Awards sections for more information and possibilities.

*ADRIAN SYMPHONY ORCHESTRA, 110 S. Madison St., Adrian MI 49221. (517)264-3121. Music Director: David Katz. Symphony orchestra and chamber music ensemble. Estab. 1981. Members are professionals. Performs 21 concerts/year including 2-3 new works. Commissions 1 new composer or new work/year. 1,200 seat hall—"Rural city with remarkably active cultural life." $100-2,500 for outright purchase.
How to Contact: Submit complete score and tapes of piece(s). SASE. Reports in 6 months.
Music: Chamber ensemble to full orchestra. "Limited rehearsal time dictates difficulty of pieces selected." Does not wish to see "rock music or country—not at this time."
Performances: Michael Pratt's *Dancing on the Wall* (orchestral—some aleatoric); Sir Peter Maxwell Davies' *Orkney Wedding* (orchestral); and Gwyweth Walker's *Fanfare, Interlude, Finale* (orchestral).

THE AKRON CITY FAMILY MASS CHOIR, 429 Homestead St., Akron OH 44306. (216)773-8529. President: Walter E.L. Scrutchings. Vocal ensemble. Estab. 1984. Members are professionals. Performs 5-7 concerts/year; performs 30-35 new works/year. Commissions 10-15 composers or new works/year. Audience mostly interested in new original black gospel music. Performs in various venues. Composers paid 50% royalty.
How to Contact: Submit complete score and tapes of piece(s). Does not return material. Reports in 2 months.
Music: Seeks "traditional music for SATB black gospel; also light contemporary. No rap or non-spiritual themes."

Opera company provides opportunities for popular songwriters

Those attending an Opera Memphis performance these days may be treated to any one of a number of well-known "classical" opera performances, but they may also hear some blues, folk, bluegrass or country music as well. This is as it should be, says Michael Ching, who became artistic director of the regional opera two years ago.

Michael Ching

Since he took over, Opera Memphis has featured a surprising variety of work, including an opera taken from the first chapter of William Faulkner's *Light In August* and one based on the life of abolitionist John Brown. Still another, in development, features a bluesy score about a snapping turtle who lives on the Mississippi Delta.

It's clear one of Ching's goals has been to change how people think about opera. "People tend to think of opera as a certain repertoire of material written between 1800 and 1900 and it's not that. It's very much a living art form and there's so much creativity and energy in all kinds of music today, not just classical. It seems a shame to me not to tap into all the various kinds of music that are out there."

Ching wants to make opera more accessible and one way to do that is to look to the work of singer/songwriters. "I don't think opera can be for everyone unless the musical language used is one all are open to, and I think that is a goal of most songwriters."

A classically trained pianist and composer, Ching has performed all over the southeast and was associate artistic director of the Virginia Opera before coming to Opera Memphis. He is also a songwriter, and this has helped him appreciate the work that goes into popular music. "I have a great deal of respect for popular writers, because there's definitely a lot of craft involved. Music is a continuum. Just because someone writes R&B doesn't mean they can't work on a symphony. There may be some technical differences, but the craft is the same." Ching used his connections in popular music to find four Nashville songwriters to score the opera version of *Light In August*.

The company produces one new piece a year for its touring program, part of its educational outreach division, the National Center for the Development of American Opera. In the past Ching has commissioned works, but he is interested in hearing ideas from other songwriters.

"We usually suggest the subject and provide some direction, but the writer is given a lot of freedom. I'd like to see work from people who seem to have a burning desire to try something new and who have interesting material. Obviously, it takes a lot of work to do an opera and we don't expect a finished idea. We want to hear from people who have said, 'I've always thought this would make a good opera or a good musical show.' " To submit, he says, songwriters should send a three-song demo with lyric sheets.

"The main thing we look for is creativity—with a flair for language and the ability to stretch the songwriting form. Songwriters need to think of opera in a different way. Opera is storytelling and it's heavy in character. I think a good song is also heavy in character. The technical leap is really not all that great. Opera and certain kinds of popular music have at least one thing in common—they're very melodic."

Opera Memphis has not received many unsolicited submissions from aspiring composers, says Ching, mostly because putting together an opera is a major undertaking. "The kinds of writers who are interested in this type of opera are those who have either already reached a certain level in their careers and are looking for new challenges, or those whose work does not fit into the 'hit song' mold and who are also seeking challenges."

As with any full-scale production, songwriters interested in opera should consider performance limitations such as budget and cast size. For Opera Memphis, says Ching, choose subject matter that you'd want to take your family to see. The works produced for touring often go to schools and draw a very family-oriented audience.

When writing an opera or any musical stage piece, says Ching, "Think about the characters. You have to express what they think and feel, not just what you think and feel." Above all, he says, "Remember that if you write in a certain style, don't think you have to change that style to write opera."

—Robin Gee

Performances: R.W. Hinton's *I Can't Stop Praising God*; W. Scrutchings' *A Better Place*; and Rev. A. Wright's *Christ In Your Life*.

THE AMERICAN BOYCHOIR, Lambert Dr., Princeton NJ 08540. (609)924-5858. Music Director: James H. Litton. Professional boychoir. Estab. 1937. Members are highly skilled children. Performs 225 concerts/year, including 10-25 new works. Commissions 1-2 composers or new works/year. Performs community concerts, orchestral concerts, and for local concert associations, church concert series and other bookings. Pays for outright purchase.
How to Contact: Query first. SASE. Reports in 6 months.
Music: "Dramatic works for boys voices (age 10-14); 15 to 20 minutes short opera to be staged and performed throughout the US." Choral pieces, either in unison, SSA, SA or SSAA division; unaccompanied and with piano or organ; occasional chamber orchestra accompaniment. Pieces are usually sung by 26 to 50 boys. Composers must know boychoir sonority.
Performances: Daniel Gawthorp's *There Is Sweet Music Here*; Donald Fraser's *Missa Iona*; and Benjamin Bitten's *Children's Crusade*.

AMHERST SAXOPHONE QUARTET, 137 Eagle St., Williamsville NY 14221-5721. (716)632-2445. Director: Steve Rosenthal. Chamber music ensemble. Estab. 1978. Performs 80-100 concerts/year includ-

The asterisk before a listing indicates that the listing is new in this edition. New markets are often the most receptive to unsolicited submissions.

ing 10-20 new works. Commissions 1-2 composers or new works/year. "We are a touring ensemble." Payment varies.
How to Contact: Query first. SASE. Reports in 1 month.
Music: "Music for soprano, alto, tenor and baritone (low A) saxophone. We are interested in great music of many styles. Level of difficulty is commensurate with full-time touring ensembles."
Performances: Lukas Foss's *Saxophone Quartet* (classical); David Stock's *Sax Appeal* (New Age); and Chan Ka Nin's *Saxophone Quartet* (jazz).
Tips: "Professionally copied parts help! Write what you truly want to write."

ARCADY MUSIC SOCIETY, P.O. Box 780, Bar Harbor ME 04809. (207)288-3151. Artistic Director: Masanobu Ikemiga. Nonprofit presenter. Estab. 1980. Members are volunteers; performers are professionals. Performs 50 concerts/year including 1-5 new works. Commissions 0-1 new composer or new work/year. "Perform mainly in churches." Pays for outright purchase.
How to Contact: Query first. SASE.
Music: "Chamber music, from 5-15 minutes in length. No symphonic work. Not interested in popular songs."
Performances: Several études by Robert Dick (flute), Radvilovich (orchestral) and Mayazumi (piano concerto).

ASHEVILLE SYMPHONY ORCHESTRA, P.O. Box 2852, Asheville NC 28802. (704)254-7046. Music Director: Robert Hart Baker. Symphony orchestra, chamber ensemble, and youth orchestra. Performs 20 concerts/year, including 2 new works. Members are professionals. Commissions 1 composer or new work/year. Concerts performed in Thomas Wolfe Auditorium, which seats 2,400. Subscription audience size is approximately 1,900. Pays by outright purchase (up to $1,000 when commissioning) or via ASCAP or BMI.
How to Contact: Submit complete score and tape of pieces. SASE. Reports in 10 weeks.
Music: Seeks "classical, pops orchestrations, full modern orchestral works, concertos and chamber music. Winds in triplicate maximum; not too many extreme high ranges or exotic time signatures/ notation. Do not send unaccompanied choral works or songs for voice and piano only."
Performances: Douglas Ovens' *Play Us A Tune* (cycle for mezzo and orchestra); Howard Hanger's *For Barbara* (for jazz ensemble and orchestra); and Robert Hart Baker's *Fantasie* (arrangement of Chopin work for orchestra).

ASHLAND SYMPHONY ORCHESTRA, P.O. Box 13, Ashland OH 44805. (419)289-5115. General Manager: James E. Thomas. Symphony orchestra. Estab. 1970. Members are professionals and amateurs. Performs 5 concerts/year. "We usually perform in a hall which seats 729. For larger events there is another which seats 1,100. Audience comes from local university-oriented community and surrounding area."
How to Contact: Submit complete score. Does not return material. Reports in 6 months.
Music: "For full symphony orchestra, all styles with caution for extremely contemporary orchestration and arrangements."

*ATLANTA POPS ORCHESTRA, P.O. Box 723172, Atlanta GA 31139-0172. (404)435-1222. Musical Director/Conductor: Albert Coleman. Pops orchestra. Estab. 1945. Members are professionals. Performs 12 concerts/year.
How to Contact: Submit complete score and tape of piece(s). SASE. Reports in 2 weeks.
Performances: *Magic Bird of Fire*, by Vincent Montana, Jr.; *Manhattan Serenade*, by Louis Alter; and *It's Alright With Me*, by Nelson Riddle.

AUREUS QUARTET, 22 Lois Ave., Demarest NJ 07627-2220. (201)767-8704. Artistic Director: James J. Seiler. Vocal ensemble (a cappella). Estab. 1979. Members are professionals. Performs 40-50 concerts/year, including up to 10 new works. Pays for outright purchase.
How to Contact: Query first. SASE. Reports in 2 months.
Music: "We perform anything from pop to classic—mixed repertoire so anything goes. Some pieces can be scored for orchestras as we do pops concerts. Up to now, we've only worked with a quartet. Could be expanded if the right piece came along. Level of difficulty—no piece has ever been too hard." Does not wish to see electronic or sacred pieces. "Electronic pieces would be hard to program. Sacred pieces not performed much. Classical/jazz arrangements of old standards are great!"
Tips: "We perform for a very diverse audience—luscious, four part writing that can showcase well-trained voices is a must. Also, clever arrangements of old hits from '20s through '50s are sure bets. (Some pieces could take optional accompaniment.)"

BALTIMORE OPERA COMPANY, INC., 1202 Maryland Ave., Baltimore MD 21201. (410)625-1600. Artistic Administrator: James Harp. Opera company. Estab. 1950. Members are professionals. Performs 16 concerts/year. "The opera audience is becoming increasingly diverse. Our performances are given in the 3,000-seat Lyric Opera House." Pays by outright purchase.

How to Contact: Submit complete score and tapes of piece(s). SASE. Reports in 1-2 months.

Music: "Our General Director, Mr. Michael Harrison, is very much interested in presenting new works. These works would be anything from Grand Opera with a large cast to chamber works suitable for school and concert performances. We would be interested in perusing all music written for an operatic audience."

Performances: Donizetti's *Lucia di Lammermoor*; Verdi's *Macbeth*; and Puccini's *La Boheme*.

Tips: "Opera is the most expensive art form to produce. Given the current economic outlook, opera companies cannot be too avant garde in their selection of repertoire. The modern operatic composer must give evidence of a fertile and illuminating imagination, while also keeping in mind that opera companies have to sell tickets."

THE GARY BEARD CHORALE, 40 E. Parkway S., Memphis TN 38104. (901)458-1652. Fax: (901)458-0145. Director: Gary Beard. Vocal ensemble. Estab. 1987. Members are professionals and amateurs. Performs 25 concerts/year including 1-5 new works. "Audience consists of musically educated people with eclectic tastes, like variety in each concert. Concerts are performed in a church sanctuary, excellent acoustics, seats 1,200."

How to Contact: Submit complete score and tape of piece(s). Does not return material. Reports in 2 months.

Music: "Choral, with orchestrations if possible, no longer than 45 minutes, include vocal solos in composition, nothing overly 'avant.' Most performers read music, including atonal, yet compositions should have 'likeable' qualities to the average audience member's ear. Level of difficulty is open for interpretation. Must submit clean scores, orderly, be very well organized, utilize choral and solo on ensemble passages."

Performances: Poulenc's *Gloria* (concert setting of Gloria); various *Broadway Cabaret* (concert of Broadway music); and Barber's *Sure On This Shining Night* (art song).

Tips: "Be well organized, thorough, submit clean scores, not overly atonal compositions, supply English translations of foreign languages as well as transliterations."

BILLINGS SYMPHONY, Suite 530, Box 7055, 401 N. 31st St., Billings MT 59103. (406)252-3610. Fax: (406)252-3353. Music Director: Dr. Uri Barnea. Symphony orchestra, orchestra and chorale. Estab. 1950. Members are professionals and amateurs. Performs 10-12 concerts/year, including 5-8 new works. Traditional audience. Performs at Alberta Bair Theater (capacity 1,418).

How to Contact: Query first. SASE. Reports in 1-6 months.

Music: Any style. Traditional notation preferred.

Performances: John Rutter's *Gloria* (choral and orchestra); Leonard Bernstein's *Chichester Psalms* (choral and orchestra); and Morton Gould's *Symphonic Variations* (orchestral).

Tips: "Write what you feel (be honest) and sharpen your compositional and craftsmanship skills."

BIZARRE ARTE ENSEMBLE, 320 Milledge Terrace, Athens GA 30606-4940. (706)354-4445. Musical Director: David Boardman. Chamber music ensemble. Estab. 1975. Members are professionals. Performs 2-3 concerts/year including 4-6 new works. Commissions 1-2 composers or new works/year. Audience consists mainly of the university community. Pay varies for outright purchase, performance tape provided.

How to Contact: Submit complete score and tape of pieces (if available; not necessary.) SASE.

Music: "Ensemble consists of 4 percussionists. Addition of other instrumentalists/performers okay. Style left to discretion of composer. Serious pieces okay. Comic pieces okay. Experimental/improvisational pieces okay."

Performances: David Boardman's *Sferics* and *Sally's Wedding Piece* (percussion); and Robert Sheppard's *Without You* (percussion with vocal).

Tips: "Sense of humor a must."

THE BOSTON MUSICA VIVA, Suite 612, 295 Huntington Ave., Boston MA 02116-5713. Manager: Barbara Owens. Chamber music ensemble. Estab. 1969. Members are professionals. Performs 5-12 concerts/year, including 6-10 new works. Commissions 3-5 composers or new works/year. "We perform our subscription series in a hall that seats 300, and our audience comes from Boston, Cambridge and surrounding areas. Frequent tours have taken the ensemble across the U.S. and the world." Pays by commission.

How to Contact: Submit complete score and tapes of piece(s). Does not return unsolicited material. Reports in months.

Music: "We are looking for works for: flute, clarinet, percussion, piano, violin, viola and cello plus vocalist (or any combination thereof) made for no more than 10 performers. We're looking for exciting avant garde music. We don't particularly want to see anything on the pop side."

BRECKENRIDGE MUSIC INSTITUTE, P.O. Box 1254, Breckenridge CO 80424. (303)453-9142. Fax: (303)453-1423. Executive Director: Pamela G. Miller. Music Director: Gerhardt Zimmerman. Chamber orchestra. Estab. 1980. Members are professionals. Performs 25 concerts/year, including 2-3 new works. "We perform our main festival season in the Riverwalk Center, a performing arts amphitheater—we are in a resort area, so our audiences are a mix of local citizens and visitors." Chamber orchestra concerts: 800 people; chamber ensemble recitals: 125-250 people; choral/orchestra concert: 450 people. Payment varies.

• The Institute is part of the National Festival of Music at Breckenridge.

How to Contact: Query first. Does not return material. Usually reports in several months, but depends on the time of year the work is submitted.

Music: "Chamber music or music for chamber orchestra. We have in-residence string quartets, brass quintets, woodwind quintets and various trios and duos. Chamber: 5-20 minutes; orchestra: 10-25 minutes. 6-6-4-4-2 double winds, double brass, keyboard, percussion. Our performers are all professionals—no difficulty limitations. 3 rehearsals per performance. No 'pops'."

Performances: Tania French's *Passing Parade*; Carter's *Eight Etudes and a Fantas*; and Hanlon's *Lullaby of My Sorrows*.

BREMERTON SYMPHONY ASSOCIATION INC., 535B Sixth St., P.O. Box 996, Bremerton WA 98310. (206)373-1722. Association Manager: Ms.Pat Kidd. Symphony orchestra. Estab. 1942. Members are amateurs. Performs 7-8 concerts/year, including a varying number of new works. The audience is half seniors, half adult. 1,200-seat hall in Bremerton High School; excellent acoustics.

How to Contact: Submit complete score and tape of piece(s). SASE. Reports in 1 month. Full season is planned each spring.

Music: Submit works for full orchestra, chorus and soloists. "Should be good for competent community orchestras." Do not wish to see "pop" music charts.

Performances: Rick Vale's *Symphony #1 "Christmas"* (orchestra/chorus/soloists).

BREVARD SYMPHONY ORCHESTRA, INC., P.O. Box 361965, Melbourne FL 32936-1965. (407)242-2024. Chairman: Craig Suman. Symphony orchestra. Estab. 1954. Members are professionals and amateurs. Performs 15-20 concerts/year. "King Center for the Performing Arts, Melbourne, FL: 1,842 seats. Pay negotiable "(VERY limited funding)."

How to Contact: Submit complete score and tapes of piece(s). SASE. Reports in 2 months.

Music: "Submit orchestral works with and without soloists, full symphonic orchestration, 5-45 minutes in length, contemporary and popular styles as well as serious compositions. No nonorchestral materials. Our community is fairly conservative and inexperienced in contemporary music, so a subtle, gradual introduction would be appropriate."

Performances: 1994-95 season includes: Weber's *Der Freischutz Overature*; Hayden's Trumpet Concerto; and Brahm's *Symphony #1*.

Tips: "Remember the audience who we are trying to introduce and educate."

BRONX ARTS ENSEMBLE, % Golf House, Van Cortlandt Park, Bronx NY 10471. (718)601-7399. Artistic Director: William Scribner. Symphony orchestra and chamber music ensemble. Estab. 1972. Members are professionals. Performs 80 concerts/year. Commissions 1-2 new works/year. "Performs concerts at colleges and various historic sites in the Bronx; also in halls in Manhattan." Pays per performance.

How to Contact: Query first. Does not return unsolicited material.

Music: Seeks "primarily chamber music or orchestral. No pops or jazz."

Performances: William Mayer's *Good King Wenceslas*; Samuel Zyman's *Quintet for Winds, Strings & Piano*; and Soong Fu Yuan's *Two Little Fox*.

BUFFALO GUITAR QUARTET, 402 Bird Ave., Buffalo NY 14213. (716)883-8429. Fax: (716)673-3397. Executive Director: James Piorkoswki. Chamber music ensemble, classical guitar quartet. Estab. 1976. Members are professionals. Performs 35 concerts/year including 2 new works. Commissions 1 composer or new work/2 years. Pays for outright purchase.

How to Contact: Query first. SASE. Reports in 1 month.

Music: "Any style or length. 4 classical guitarists, high level of difficulty."

Performances: Leslie Bassett's *Narratives* (5 short movements); S. Funk Pearson's *Mummychogs (le Monde)* (prepared guitars); and Leo Brouwer's *Cuban Landscape with Rumba* (minimalist).

Tips: "Learn what the guitar does well, stay away from what it does poorly."

CANADIAN CHILDREN'S OPERA CHORUS, #215, 227 Front St. E., Toronto, Ontario M5A 1E8 **Canada.** (416)366-0467. Manager: Ann Hartford Marshall. Children's vocal ensemble. Estab. 1968. Members are amateurs. Performs 40 operas and concerts/year. Performs choral winter concert, spring opera production often at Harbourfront, Toronto. Pays for outright purchase; "CCOC applies to

Ontario Arts Council or the Canada Council for commission fees." Query first. SAE and IRC. Reports in 2 months.

Music: "Operas of approximately 1 hour in length representing quality composers. In addition, the portability of a production is important; minimal sets and accompaniment. CCOC prefers to engage Canadian composers whose standards are known to be high. Being a nonprofit organization with funding difficulties, we prefer piano accompaniments or just a few instruments."

Performances: John Greer's *The Snow Queen*; Poulenc's *Petites Voix*; and John Rutter's *Dancing Day*.

CANADIAN OPERA COMPANY, 227 Front St. E., Toronto, Ontario M5A 1E8 **Canada**. (416)363-6671. Scheduling Manager: Sandra J. Gavinchuk. Opera company. Estab. 1950. Members are professionals. 70 performances, including a minimum of 1 new work/year. "New works are done in the DuMaurier Theatre, which seats approximately 250." Pays by contract.

How to Contact: Submit complete score and tapes of piece(s). "Vocal works please." Reports in 3-5 weeks.

Music: Vocal works, operatic in nature. 12 singers maximum, 1½ hour in duration and 18 orchestral players. "Do not submit works which are not for voice. Ask for requirements for the Composers-In-Residence program."

Performances: Gary Kulesha's *Red Emma* (1994/95); Bartok's *Bluebeard's Castle* (1994-95); and Schöenberg's *Erwartung*.

Tips: "We have a Composers-In-Residence program which is open to Canadian composers or landed immigrants."

CANTATA ACADEMY, 2441 Pinecrest Dr., Ferndale MI 48220. (810)546-0420. Music Director: Frederick Bellinger. Vocal ensemble. Estab. 1961. Members are professionals. Performs 10-12 concerts/year including 5-6 new works. Commissions 1-2 composers or new works/year. "We perform in churches and small auditoriums throughout the Metro Detroit area for audiences of about 500 people." Pays $100-500 for outright purchase.

How to Contact: Submit complete score. SASE. Reports in 1-3 months.

Music: Four-part a cappella and keyboard accompanied works, two and three-part works for men's or women's voices. Some small instrumental ensemble accompaniments acceptable. Work must be suitable for forty voice choir. No works requiring orchestra or large ensemble accompaniment. No pop.

Performances: Charles S. Brown's *Five Spirituals* (concert spiritual); Kirke Mechem's *John Brown Cantata*; and Libby Larsen's *Ringeltanze* (Christmas choral with handbells & keyboard).

Tips: "Be patient. Would prefer to look at several different samples of work at one time."

CARSON CITY CHAMBER ORCHESTRA, P.O. Box 2001, Carson City NV 89702-2001 or 191 Heidi Circle, Carson City NV 89701-6532. (702)883-4154. Conductor: David C. Bugli. Amateur community orchestra. Estab. 1984. Members are amateurs. Performs 5 concerts, including 1 new work/year. "Most concerts are performed in the Carson City Community Center Auditorium, which seats 840. We have no provisions for paying composers at this time; however, we are working on plans for a joint commission for a future season. We will pay ⅓ of a set fee."

How to Contact: Submit complete score. Does not return material. Reports in 2 months.

Music: "We want classical, pop orchestrations, orchestrations of early music for modern orchestras, concertos for violin or piano, holiday music for chorus and orchestra (children's choirs and handbell ensemble available), music by women, music for brass choir. Most performers are amateurs, but there are a few professionals who perform with us. Available winds and percussion: 2 flutes and flute/piccolo, 2 oboes (E.H. double), 2 clarinets, 1 bass clarinet, 2 bassoons, 3 or 4 horns, 3 trumpets, 3 trombones, 1 tuba, timpani, and some percussion. Harp and piano. Strings: 8-10-3-5-2. Avoid rhythmic complexity (except in pops) and music that lacks melodic appeal. Composers should contact us first. Each concert has a different emphasis. Note: Associated choral group, Carson Chamber Singers, performs several times a year with the orchestra and independently."

Performances: David Bugli's *State of Metamorphosis, Variations on "My Dancing Day"*; Kenneth Lindner's *Sonata for Trumpet*; and Ronald R. Williams' *Noah: Suite After Andre Obey*. Premieres also include arrangements of Christmas and popular tunes.

Tips: "It is better to write several short movements well than to write long, unimaginative pieces, especially when starting out. Be willing to revise after submitting the work, even if it was premiered elsewhere."

Listings of companies in countries other than the U.S. have the name of the country in boldface type.

CASCADE SYMPHONY ORCHESTRA, 9630 214th Place SW, Edmonds WA 98020. (206)778-6934. Director/Conductor: Roupan Shakarian. Manager: Ed Aliverti. Symphony orchestra. Estab. 1962. Members are professionals and amateurs. Performs 4-5 concerts/year, including 2-3 new works. "Audience is knowledgeable with a variety of backgrounds and interests—excellent cross-section. Perform in a rather old auditorium seating 950."
How to Contact: Submit complete score and tape of pieces. SASE. Reports in 6 weeks.
Music: "Music should be suitable for symphony orchestra. Nothing over 20 minutes."
Performances: Paul Creston's *Dance Overture* (various dance rhythms); and Daniel Barry's *Sound Scapes* (premiere based on ostenatos).

CENTER FOR CONTEMPORARY OPERA, Box 1350, Gracie Station, New York NY 10028-0010. (212)308-6728. Director: Richard Marshall. Opera. Estab. 1982. Members are professionals. Performs 3 operas/year; all are modern works. 650-seat theater. Pays royalties.
How to Contact: Query first. SASE.
Music: "Looking for full-length operas. Limited orchestras and choruses. Orchestra—not over 25."
Performances: Britten's *The Prodigal Son* (opera); Beeson's *My Heart is in the Highlands* (stage premiere, opera); and Kelmanoff's *Insect Comedy* (premiere).
Tips: "Make work practical to perform. Have an excellent libretto. Have contacts to raise money."

CHEYENNE SYMPHONY ORCHESTRA, P.O. Box 851, Cheyenne WY 82003. (307)778-8561. CSO Music Director: Mark Russell Smith. Symphony orchestra. Estab. 1955. Members are professionals. Performs 6 concerts/year including sometimes 1 new work. "Orchestra performs for a conservative, mid-to-upper income audience at a 1,496 seat civic center." Pay negotiable.
How to Contact: Query first. Does not return material.
Performances: Bill Hill's *Seven Abstract Miniatures* (orchestral).

*THE CHICAGO STRING ENSEMBLE, 3524 W. Belmont Ave., Chicago IL 60618. (312)332-0567. Fax:(708)869-3925. General Manager: Mary Jo Deysach. Professional string orchestra. Estab. 1977. Members are professionals. Performs 20 concerts/year, including 2-3 new works. Commissions 2-3 new works/year. Audience is a Chicago and suburban cross section. Performance space: 3 large, acoustically favorable area churches. Composers are not paid.
How to Contact: Submit complete score. Does not return material. Reports in 6 months.
Music: "Open to any work for string orchestra, with or without a solo instrument. Additional instrumentation (e.g., harp, keyboard, percussion, a few winds) is possible but not encouraged. Must be possible to 6-6-4-4-2 or fewer strings."
Performances: Fengshi Yang's *Capriccio in July* (harp and strings); Ulysses Kay's *Dances for Strings* (6 movements for string orchestra); and Paul Seitz's *When Touched by Better Angels* (harp and strings).

CHORUS OF WESTERLY, 119 High St., Westerly RI 02891. (401)596-8663. Music Director: George Kent. Community chorus. Estab. 1959. Members are amateurs. Performs 4 works/year. Summer pops reaches audiences of 28,000. Pays for outright purchase.
How to Contact: Query first. SASE. Reports in 1 month.
Music: "We normally employ a full orchestra from Boston. Major works desired—although 'good' pops charts considered."
Performances: Adolphus Hailstork's *Psalm 72* (chorus/brass); Paul Patterson's *Mass of the Sea* (choral); and Peter Niedmann's *In The Ending of the Year* (chorus/orchestra Christmas).

*CIMARRON CIRCUIT OPERA COMPANY, P.O. Box 1085, Norman OK 73070. (405)364-8962. Music Director: Lisa Anderson. Opera company. Estab. 1975. Members are professionals. Performs 100 concerts/year including 1 or less new works. Commissions 1 or less new works/year. "CCOC performs for children across the state of Oklahoma and for a dedicated audience in central Oklahoma. We do not have a permanent location. As a touring company, we adapt to the performance space provided, ranging from a classroom to a full raised stage." Pay is negotiable.
How to Contact: Submit complete score and tape of piece(s). SASE. Reports in 6-12 weeks ("time may vary depending on time of year.")
Music: "We are seeking operas or operettas in English only. We would like to begin including new, American works in our repertoire. Children's operas should be no longer than 45 minutes and require no more than a synthesizer for accompaniment. Adult operas should be appropriate for families, and may require either full orchestration or synthesizer. CCOC is a professional company whose members have varying degrees of experience, so any difficulty level is appropriate. There should be a small to moderate number of principals. Children's work should have no more than 4 principals. Our slogan is 'Opera is a family thing to do.' If we cannot market a work to families, we do not want to see it."
Performances: Gian-Carlo Menotti's *Amahl and the Night Visitors* (Christmas theme); Seymour Barab's *La Pizza Con Funghi* (grand opera farce); and Malcolm Fox's *Sid the Serpent Who Wanted to Sing* (children's opera).

*CIVIC SYMPHONY ORCHESTRA OF BOSTON, P.O. Box 777, Boston MA 02102. Music Director: Max Hobart. Symphony orchestra. Estab. 1924. Members are professionals, amateurs and students. Performs 4 concerts/year including 2 new works. Performances held at Jordan Hall at NEC, 1025 seats; TSAI Center, Boston University, 650 seats. Pays negotiable amount per performance.
How to Contact: Submit complete score and tape of piece(s). SASE. Reports in 3 months.
Music: "Overtures, short opening works. Brassy fanfares. Unusual string pieces, solo winds or strings with orchestra. Looking for narrated works: adult or children's, especially Christmas stories or composers' life stories. Go easy on percussion."
Performances: Thomas Oboe Lee's *Jana* (world premiere); Augusta Thomas' *Ritual* (Boston premiere); and Bill Amrx's *Harp Concerto* (Boston premiere).

*COBB SYMPHONY ORCHESTRA, P.O. Box 452, Marietta GA 30061. Music Director: Steven Byess. Symphony orchestra. Estab. 1951. Members are professionals and amateurs. Performs 6-10 concerts/year including 1 new work. Metropolitan audience. 550-seat Jeannie T. Anderson Theater.
How to Contact: Query first. Does not return material. Reports in 1½-2 months.
Music: Overtures—folk based symphonic works with wide appeal. Jazz influences—general orchestration. Ten minutes to 20 minutes length. 70-90 performers. "Romantic"-sized orchestra, with respective orchestration. Not interested in popular or chamber (under 18-20 players) music.

COLORADO CHILDREN'S CHORALE, Suite 1020, 910 15th St., Denver CO 80202. (303)892-5600. Artistic Director: Duain Wolfe. Vocal ensemble and highly trained children's chorus. Estab. 1974. Members are professionals and amateurs. Performs 100-110 concerts/year, including 3-5 new works. Commissions 1-3 composers or new works/year. "Our audiences' ages range from 5-80. We give school performances and tour (national, international). We give subscription concerts and sing with orchestras (symphonic and chamber). Halls: schools to symphony halls to arenas to outdoor theaters." Pays $100-500 outright purchase (more for extended works).
How to Contact: Submit complete score and tapes of piece(s). Does not return unsolicited material. Reports in 2 months.
Music: "We want short pieces (3-5 minutes): novelty, folk arrangement, serious; longer works 5-20: serious; staged operas/musicals 30-45 minutes: piano accompaniment or small ensemble; or possible full orchestration if work is suitable for symphony concert. We are most interested in SA, SSA, SSAA. We look for a variety of difficulty ranges and encourage very challenging music for SSA-SSAA choruses (32 singers, unchanged voices). We don't want rock, charts without written accompaniments or texts that are inappropriate for children. We are accessible to all audiences. We like some of our repertoire to reflect a sense of humor, others to have a message. We're very interested in well crafted music that has a special mark of distinction."
Performances: Randall Thompson's *The Place of the Blest* (sacred, medieval text); Sherman and Sherman's *Tom Sawyer*; and Lee Hoiby's *The Nations Echo 'Round*.
Tips: "Submit score and tape with good cover letter, résumé and record of performance. Wait at least 3 weeks before a follow-up call or letter."

*COMMONWEALTH OPERA INC., 160 Main St., Northampton MA 01060. (413)586-5026. Artistic Director: Richard R. Rescia. Opera company. Estab. 1977. Members are professionals and amateurs. Performs 4 concerts/year. "We perform at the Academy of Music at Northampton in an 800-seat opera house. Depending on opera, audience could be family oriented or adult." Pays by royalty.
How to Contact: Query first. Does not return material.
Music: "We are open to all styles of opera. We have the limitations of a regional opera company with local chorus. Principals come from a wide area. We look only at opera scores."
Performances: Leoncavallo's *I Pagliacci* (opera); Mozart's *Don Giovanni* (opera); and Menotti's *Amahl and the Night Visitors* (opera).
Tips: "We're looking for opera that is accessible to the general public and performable by a standard opera orchestra."

COMMUNITY MUSIC PROJECT, 116 E. Third St., Jamestown NY 14701-5402. (716)664-2227. General Manager/Artistic Director: Philip Morris/Lee Spear. Vocal ensemble and community chorus. Estab. 1978. Members are both professionals and amateurs. Performs 12-15 concerts/year including 4-6 new works. "Performs in various venues: Civic Center (1,300-seat) and local churches (200-500 seat). Jamestown is a small city in western NY state with a moderately sophisticated audience."
How to Contact: Query first. SASE. Reports in 6 months.
Music: 3-10 minute choral work, SATB, in English, with or without accompaniment. "Emphasis on sensitive English language prosody."
Performances: Gerald M. Shapiro's *Prayer for the Great Family*; Lee Kesselman's *Buzzings*; and Stefania de Kenesseay's *Jumping Jacks*.

CONNECTICUT CHORAL ARTISTS/CONCORA, 90 Main St., New Britain CT 06051. (203)224-7500. Artistic Director: Richard Coffey. Professional concert choir. Estab. 1974. Members are professionals. Performs 10-15 concerts/year, including 2-3 new works. "Mixed audience in terms of age and background; performs in various halls and churches in the region." Payment "depends upon underwriting we can obtain for the project."
How to Contact: Call and obtain permission to submit. "No unsolicited submissions accepted." SASE. Reports in 6 months.
Music: Seeking "works for mixed chorus of 36 singers; unaccompanied or with keyboard and/or small instrumental ensemble; text sacred or secular/any language; prefers suites or cyclical works, total time not exceeding 15 minutes. Performance spaces and budgets prohibit large instrumental ensembles. Works suited for 750-seat halls are preferable. Substantial organ or piano parts acceptable. Scores should be very legible in every way."
Performances: Bernstein's *Missa Brevis* (1988 regional premiere; based upon his *The Lark*); Frank Martin's *Mass for Double Chorus* (regional premiere); Villa-Lobos' *Magdalena* (performed 1987 revival at Lincoln Center and recorded for CBS).
Tips: "Use conventional notation and be sure manuscript is legible in every way. Recognize and respect the vocal range of each vocal part. Work should have an identifiable *rhythmic* structure."

CYPRESS "POPS" ORCHESTRA, P.O. Box 2623, Cypress CA 90630-1323. (714)527-0964. Music Director: John E. Hall III. Symphony orchestra. Estab. 1989. Members are professionals. Performs 10-12 concerts/year including 15-20 new works. Commissions 2 composers or new works/year. Average family size 4—popular entertainment for all age levels. Pays by outright purchase $200-500.
How to Contact: Submit complete score and tapes of piece(s). SASE. Reports in 1-2 months.
Music: Strictly popular, light classical selections, 5-12 minute duration for full orchestra. Level of proficiency is very high. Contemporary films, TV themes/songs of 70s to present.
Performances: Friedman's *Gershwin Showcase* and *Salute to the Big Bands*.
Tips: "1990s composers need to be conscious of audiences listening capabilities. Should compose or arrange material in popular styled selections."

DENVER CHAMBER ORCHESTRA, #1360, 1616 Glenarm Place, Denver CO 80202. (303)825-4911. General Manager: Michael Miller. 35 piece chamber orchestra. Estab. 1968. Members are professionals. Performs 25 concerts/year, including 1 new work. Commissions 1 composer or new work/year. "Performs in a 500-seat auditorium in an arts complex and at Historic Trinity Church in Denver which seats 1,100. Usually pays the composer's air fare and room and board for the performance; sometimes an additional small stipend."
How to Contact: Query first. SASE. Reports in 2 months.
Music: Seeks "10-12 minute pieces orchestrated for 35-40 instruments. No pop, symphonic."
Performances: Edward Smaldone and Otto Luening's *Dialogue*; and Steven Heitzig's *Flower of the Earth: Homage to Georgia O'Keefe*.
Tips: "Submit a query, which we will submit to our music director."

DESERT CHORALE, P.O. Box 2813, Santa Fe NM 87504-2813. (505)988-2282. Fax: (505)988-7522. Music Director: Lawrence Bandfield. Vocal ensemble. Members are professionals. Performs 50 concerts/year including 2 new works. Commissions 1 new composer or new work/year. "Highly sophisticated, musically literate audiences. We sing most concerts in a 220-year-old adobe church which seats 250." Pays by royalty and/or additional commission.
How to Contact: Query first. Submit complete score and tape *after* query. Does not return unsolicited material. Reports in 8 months.
Music: "Challenging chamber choir works 6 to 20 minutes in length. Accompanied works are limited by space—normally no more than 5 or 6 players. No more than 24 singers, but they are all highly skilled musicians. No short church anthem-type pieces."
Performances: Dominick Argento's *al Toccata of Galuppi's* (mixed choir, stringtet, harpsichord); Lawrence Cave's *The Seasons of Meng-Hao-Jan* (unaccompanied mixed choir); and Steven Sametz's *O Llama de Amor Viva* (unaccompanied mixed choir).

DÚO CLÁSICO, 31-R Fayette St., Cambridge MA 02139-1111. (617)864-8524. Fax: (617)491-4696. Contact: David Witten. Chamber music ensemble. Estab. 1986. Members are professionals. Performs 8 concerts/year. Commissions 2 composers or new works/year. Performs in small recital halls.
How to Contact: Query first. SASE. Reports in 5 weeks.
Music: "We welcome scores for flute solo, piano solo or duo. Particular interest in Latin American composers."
Performances: Lee Brouwer's (Cuban) *La Región Más Transparente* (flute/piano duo); and Aaron Copland's (US) *Duo for Flute & Piano* (flute/piano duo).
Tips: "Extended techniques, or with tape, are fine!"

EAKEN PIANO TRIO, Dickinson College, Carlisle PA 17013-2896. (717)245-1433. Fax: (717)245-1899. Director: Nancy Baun. Chamber music ensemble. Estab. 1986. Members are professionals. Performs 25-30 concerts/year including 3-4 new works. Commissions 1 composer or new work/year. Audience is 50% college age, 50% age 40-60. Concerts are performed on standard concert stage.
How to Contact: Submit complete score and tape of piece(s). SASE. Reports in 6 weeks.
Music: "Romantic style – mood, energy are important elements. Piano trio (violin, cello, piano) only. Prefer standard notation. We encourage composers to visit with group prior to a commission to discuss mutual goals. Must be available for residencies."
Performances: George Shapiro's *Trio*; George Rochberg's *Trio*; and Rebecca Clarke's *Trio*, all for piano, cello and violin.
Tips: "Recognize that we, the performers, need to be moved by the work so we can move others. Kindly remind us by phone of your intentions – a call back doesn't mean we aren't interested, just busy!"

EASTERN NEW MEXICO UNIVERSITY, Station 16, Portales NM 88130. (505)562-2736. Director of Orchestral Activities: Robert Radmer. Symphony orchestra, small college-level orchestra with possible choral collaboration. Estab. 1934. Members are students (with some faculty). Performs 6 concerts/year. "Our audiences are members of a college community and small town. We perform in a beautiful, acoustically fine 240-seat hall with a pipe organ." Payment is negotiable.
How to Contact: Query first. SASE. Reports in 3 weeks.
Music: "Pieces should be 12-15 minutes; winds by 2, full brass. Work shouldn't be technically difficult. Organ, harpsicord, piano(s) are available. We are a small college orchestra; normal instrumentation is represented but technical level uneven throughout orchestra. We have faculty available to do special solo work. We like to see choral-orchestral combinations and writing at different technical levels within each family, i.e., 1st clarinet might be significantly more difficult than 2nd clarinet."
Performances: David Uber's *Gettysburg* (brass choir).
Tips: "I would like to see a choral/orchestral score in modern idiom for vocal solo(s), a chamber choir and large chorus used in concertino/ripieno fashion, with full brass and percussion, featuring first chair players."

EUROPEAN COMMUNITY CHAMBER ORCHESTRA, Fermain House, Dolphin St., Colyton EX13 6LU **United Kingdom**. Phone: (44)297 552272. General Manager: Ambrose Miller. Chamber orchestra. Members are professionals. Performs 70 concerts/year, including 3 new works. Commissions 1 composer or new work/year. Performs regular tours of Europe, Americas and Asia, including major venues. Pays per performance or for outright purchase, depending on work.
How to Contact: Query first. Does not return material. Reports in 2 months.
Music: Seeking compositions for strings, 2 oboes and 2 horns with a duration of about 10 minutes.
Performances: John McCabe's *Red Leaves* (strings, 2 oboes, 2 horns); Michael Nyman's *New Work*; and Alfred Schnitke's *Moz-art à la Haydn*.
Tips: "European Community Chamber Orchestra works without a conductor, so simplicity is paramount."

FINE ARTS STRINGS, 14507 Trading Post Dr., Sun City West AZ 85375. (602)584-6989. Musical Director & Conductor: Dr. Walter F. Moeck. String orchestra (27 members). Members are professionals and amateurs. Performs 4-6 concerts/year including 2 new works/year. "Concert Hall at the Scottsdale Jr. College. Other various halls in and around Phoenix and Scottsdale, Arizona."
How to Contact: Submit complete score and tape of piece(s). SASE. Reports in 6-8 weeks.
Music: "The 'Fine Arts' Orchestra is a string orchestra. We perform Mozart, Bach, Corelli and modern music for string orchestra. We have 27 performers in the orchestra. We perform rather difficult music. Example – Poulencs' *Organ Concerto*. We look for good musical substance for strings. Good rhythmic and melodic qualities."
Performances: Gillis' *Three Sketches*; Barber's *Adagio for Strings*; and Joio's *Choreography*.
Tips: "Compose to fit the instrument. Write in practical range and compose with melodic content and strong rhythmical figures."

FLORIDA SPACE COAST PHILHARMONIC, INC., P.O. Box 3344, Cocoa FL 32924 or 2150 Lake Dr., Cocoa FL 32926. (407)632-7445. General Manager: Alyce Christ. Artistic Director and Conductor: Maria Tunicka. Philharmonic orchestra and chamber music ensemble. Estab. 1986. Members are professionals. Performs 7-14 concerts/year. Concerts are performed for "average audience – they like familiar works and pops. Concert halls range from 600 to 2,000 seats." Pays 10% royalty (rental); outright purchase of $2,000; $50-600/performance; or by private arrangement.
How to Contact: Query first; submit complete score and tape of piece(s). SASE. Reports in 1-3 months. "Our conductor tours frequently thus we have to keep material until she has a chance to hear it."

Music: Seeks "pops and serious music for full symphony orchestra, but not an overly large orchestra with unusual instrumentation. We use about 60 musicians because of hall limitations. Works should be medium difficulty—not too easy and not too difficult—and not more than 10 minutes long." Does not wish to see avant-garde music.
Performances: Marta Ptaszynska's *Marimba Concerto* (marimba solo); Dr. Elaine Stone's *Christopher Columbus Suite for Symphony Orchestra* (world premiere).
Tips: "If we would commission a work it would be to feature the space theme in our area."

FONTANA CONCERT SOCIETY, 821 W. South St., Kalamazoo MI 49007. (616)382-0826. Artistic Director: Paul Nitsch. Chamber music ensemble presenter. Estab. 1980. Members are professionals. Performs 20 concerts/year including 1-3 new works. Commissions 1-2 composers or new works/year. Audience consists of well-educated people who expect to be challenged but like the traditional as well. Summer—180 seat hall; Fall/winter—various venues, from churches to libraries to 500-seat theaters.
How to Contact: Submit complete score and tapes of piece(s). SASE. Reports in 1 month.
Music: "Good chamber music—any combination of strings, winds, piano." No "pop" music, new age type. "We like to see enough interest for the composer to come for a premiere and talk to the audience."
Performances: Ramon Zupko's *Folksody* (piano trio-premiere); Sebastian Currier's *Vocalissimus* (soprano, 4 percussion, strings, winds, piano-premiere); and Mark Schultz's *Work for Horn & Piano*.
Tips: "Provide a résumé and clearly marked tape of a piece played by live performers."

THE GLORIAN DUO, 176 Logan Rd., New Canaan CT 06840. (203)966-7616. Contact: Wendy Kerner. Chamber music ensemble. Estab. 1986. Members are professionals. Performs 30 concerts/year including 3-5 new works. Commissions 1-2 new works/year. Pay varies. "We receive many works free of charge."
How to Contact: Submit complete score and tape of piece(s). Reports in 2-3 months.
Music: "We are particularly interested in flute and harp works that are openers, jazz-element work and other flute and harp or flute, harp and other instrument works. We are a duo—flute and harp but often work with other instruments—flute, harp and cello, 2 flutes and harp, flute, harp and voice, flute, harp and orchestra, etc."
Performances: David Diamond's *Concert Piece* (concert work—15 minutes); Vaclav Nelhybel's *Concertante*; and Yoon-Hee Kim-Hwang's *dharma-Dharma* (concert work based on Korean themes and Zen Buddhist poetry).
Tips: "Make the work interesting and compelling."

GREAT FALLS SYMPHONY ASSOCIATION, Box 1078, Great Falls MT 59403. (406)453-4102. Music Director and Conductor: Gordon J. Johnson. Symphony orchestra. Estab. 1959. Members are professionals and amateurs. Performs 9 concerts (2 youth concerts)/year, including 1-2 new works. Commissions 12 new works/year. "Our audience is conservative. Newer music is welcome; however, it might be more successful if it were programatic." Plays in Civic Center Auditorium seating 1,850. Negotiable payment.
How to Contact: Query first. SASE. Reports in 2 months.
Music: "Compositions should be for full orchestra. Should be composed idiomatically for instruments avoiding extended techniques. Duration 10-20 minutes. Avoid diverse instruments such as alto flute, saxophones, etc. Our orchestra carries 65 members, most of whom are talented amateurs. We have a resident string quartet and woodwind quintet that serve as principals. Would enjoy seeing a piece for quartet or quintet solo and orchestra. Send letter with clean score and tape (optional). We will reply within a few weeks."
Peformances: Bernstein's *Chichester Psalms* (choral and orchestra); Hodkinson's *Boogie, Tango and Grand Tarantella* (bass solo); and Stokes' *Native Dancer*.
Tips: "Music for orchestra and chorus is welcome. Cross cues will be helpful in places. Work should not require an undue amount of rehearsal time (remember that a concerto and symphony are probably on the program as well)."

GREELEY PHILHARMONIC ORCHESTRA, P.O. Box 1535, Greeley CO 80632. (303)353-1384. Secretary/Bookkeeper: Beverley Skinner. Symphony orchestra. Estab. 1911. Members are professionals and some amateurs. Performs 12 concerts/year. "We give 6 regular subscription concerts (mixed audience) and 2 nights of opera and 4 other special concerts. We have a wonderful 5-year-old hall seating 1,664."
How to Contact: Query first. SASE. Reports in 1 month.
Music: "We want high quality popular programming for pops, park and youth concerts; 5-15 minutes in length utilizing full orchestra. We don't want electric instruments. We like nostalgia, pops or light classical arrangement."
Performances: Peck's *Glory, The Grandeur* (orchestra with percussion ensemble) and *Thrill of the Orchestra* (children's concert); and Harbeson's *Remembering Gatsby* (orchestra).

HASTINGS SYMPHONY ORCHESTRA, Fuhr Hall, Ninth & Ash, Hastings NE 68901. (402)463-2402. Conductor/Music Director: Dr. James Johnson. Symphony orchestra. Estab. 1926. Members are professionals and amateurs. Performs 6-8 concerts/year, including 1 new work. "Audience consists of conservative residents of mid-Nebraska who haven't heard most of the classics." Concert Hall: Masonic Temple Auditorium (950). Pays commission or rental.
How to Contact: Submit complete score and tapes of piece(s). Does not return material. Reports in 2 months.
Music: "We are looking for all types of music within the range of an accomplished community orchestra. Write first and follow with a phone call."
Performances: Bernstein's *Candide Overture*; Richard Wilson's *Silhouette (1988)*; Menotti's *Double-bass Concerto (1983)*; and James Oliverio's *Pilgrimage Concerto for Brass and Orchestra* (1992).
Tips: "Think about the size, ability and budgetary limits. Confer with our music director about audience taste. Think of music with special ties to locality."

*HELENA SYMPHONY, P.O. Box 1073, Helena MT 59624. (406)442-1860. Music Director: Elizabeth Sellers. Symphony orchestra. Estab. 1955. Members are professionals and amateurs. Performs 12 concerts/year, including 1 new work. Commissions 1 new composer or work/year. Performance space is an 1,800 seat concert hall. Payment varies.
How to Contact: Query first. SASE. Reports in 3 months.
Music: "Imaginative, collaborative, not too atonal. We want to appeal to an audience of all ages. We don't have a huge string complement. Medium to difficult okay—at frontiers of professional ability we cannot do."
Performances: Eilzabeth Sellers' *Agincourt Concerto* (timpani/brass) and *Kirchen Concerto* (violin concerto); and Alan Houhaness' *Magnificat* (orchestra/chorale).
Tips: "Try to balance tension and repose in your works. New instrument combinations are appealing."

*HERSHEY SYMPHONY ORCHESTRA, Box 93, Hershey PA 17033. (800)533-3088. Music Director: Dr. Sandra Dackow. Symphony orchestra. Estab. 1969. Members are professionals and amateurs. Performs 7 concerts/year, including 3-4 new works. Performance space is a 1900 seat grand old movie theater. Payment varies.
How to Contact: Submit complete score and tape of piece(s). SASE. Reports in 3 months.
Music: "Symphonic works of various lengths and types which can be performed by a non-professional orchestra. We are flexible but like to involve all our players."
Performances: Paul W. Whear's *Decade Overture* (overture); Katherine Hoover's *Summer Night* (chamber orchestra); and Robert Ward's *Prairie Overture* (overture).
Tips: "Please lay out rehearsal numbers/letter and rests according to phrases and other logical musical divisions rather than in groups of 10 measures, etc., which is very unmusical and wastes time and causes a surprising number of problems. Also, please do not send a score written in concert pitch; use the usual transpositions so that the conductor sees what the players see; rehearsal is much more effective this way. Cross cue all important solos; this helps in rehearsal where instruments may be missing."

*HIGH DESERT SYMPHONY ASSOCIATION, 18422 Bear Valley Rd., Victorville CA 92392. (619)245-4271, ext. 387. Music Director: Dr. K.C. Manji. Symphony orchestra. Estab. 1967. Members are professionals and amateurs. Performs 6 concerts/year. 500 seat auditorium. Composers are not paid.
How to Contact: Submit complete score and tape of piece(s). SASE. Reports ASAP.
Music: "Any type of music but for a smaller orchestra. 2222 2200 T strings."

THE PAUL HILL CHORALE (AND) THE WASHINGTON SINGERS, 5630 Connecticut Ave. NW, Washington DC 20015. (202)364-4321. Music Director: Paul Hill. Vocal ensemble. Estab. 1967. Members are professionals and amateurs. Performs 8-10 concerts/year, including 4 new works. Commissions one new composer or work every 3-4 years. "Audience covers a wide range of ages and economic levels drawn from the greater Washington DC metropolitan area. Kennedy Center Concert Hall seats 2,700." Pays by outright purchase.
How to Contact: Submit complete score and tapes of pieces. SASE. Reports in 2 months.
Music: Seeks new works for: 1)large chorus with or without symphony orchestras; 2)chamber choir and small ensemble.
Performances: Gregg Smith's *Holy, Holy Holy*; Ned Rorem's *We Are the Music-Makers*; William Bolcom's *The Mask*; and David Maslanka's *Litany for Courage and the Seasons* (all choral).
Tips: "We are always looking for music that is high quality and accessible to Washington audiences."

*IRVING SYMPHONY ORCHESTRA, Suite 152, 4950 N. O'Connor, Irving TX 75062. Music Director: Hector Guzman. Symphony orchestra. Estab. 1963. Members are professionals. Performs 8 concerts/year, including 1 or 2 new works. Commissions 1 or 2 composers or new works/year. Audience is

"conservative, upper middle class couples 30 to 65 years on average. Excellent facilities: 720 seat auditorium." Pays per performance.
How to Contact: Submit complete score and tape of piece(s). Does not return material. Reports in 3-6 months.
Music: "Full orchestra, between 5 and 10 minutes. Overtures mainly, children's concerts, even pops. Orchestra size: 65-70. Nothing longer than 15 minutes."
Performances: M. Ruszynski's *Comic Overture* and Guevana Ochoa's *Danza Criella*.
Tips: "Submit good, lively works, with score and tape if possible."

*KEARNEY AREA SYMPHONY ORCHESTRA, University of Nebraska at Kearney, Kearney NE 68849. (308)234-8618. Director: Dr. Ron Crocker. University/community symphony. Estab. 1987. Members are amateurs. Performs 3 concerts/year including 1 new work. Audience consists of community members. Performance space seats 500.
How to Contact: Query first. SASE. Reports in 1 month.
Music: "Open to almost anything."
Performances: Ron Crocker's *Kaso Galka* (fun contemporary); Houkam's *Finding Athene* (orchestra with solo piano); and Vareese's *Ionisation* (percussion ensemble).
Tips: "Contact Dr. Crocker directly—he is open to all ideas and enjoys new things."

KENNETT SYMPHONY ORCHESTRA, Box 72, Kennett Square PA 19348. (215)444-6363. Music Director: Mary Woodmansee Green. Symphony orchestra. Estab. 1941. Members are professionals. Performs 6-7 concerts/year including 1-2 new works. "Performs at Kennett High School Auditorium (750), and in summer, Longwood Garden Open Air Theatre (2,000)."
How to Contact: Submit complete score and tape of piece(s). Does not return material.
Music: Work which can attract minority concert goers, children's concerts, narrated pieces and program music (no more than 20-30). Limited stage area and budget. "Nothing including extensive electronic instruments or huge percussion. No piano concertos (don't have concert instrument). We have 2-3 rehearsals for each concert—must work (with reset of concert rep) in that amount of time."
Performances: Ron Nelson's *Five Pieces After Paintings by Andrew Wyeth* (full orchestra program); Ann Wyeth McCoy's *In Memoriam* (piano transcription); and Peter Schickele's *The Chenoo Who Stayed to Dinner* (narrated children's fable).
Tips: "Have clean, easy-to-read parts, keep in mind unsophisticated audience."

KENTUCKY OPERA, 101 S. Eighth St. at Main, Louisville KY 40202. (502)584-4500. Opera. Estab. 1952. Members are professionals. Performs 22 times/year. Performs at Whitney Hall, The Kentucky Center for the Arts, seating is 2,400; Bomhard Theater, The Kentucky Center for the Arts, 620; Macauley Theater, 1,400. Pays by royalty, outright purchase or per performance.
How to Contact: Submit complete score and tapes of piece(s). SASE. Reports in 6 months.
Music: Seeks opera—1 to 3 acts with orchestrations. No limitations.
Performances: 4 performances/year. *La Boheme, H.M.S. Pinafore, The Phantom of the Opera* and *Rigoletto*.

KITCHENER-WATERLOO CHAMBER ORCHESTRA, Box 34015, Highland Hills P.O., Kitchener, Ontario N2N 3G2 **Canada**. (519)744-3828. Music Director: Graham Coles. Chamber Orchestra. Estab. 1985. Members are professionals and amateurs. Performs 6 concerts/year, including some new works. "We perform mainly baroque and classical repertoire, so that any contemporary works must not be too dissonant, long or far fetched." Pays per performance.
How to Contact: "It's best to query first so that we can outline what not to send. Include: complete CV—list of works, performances, sample reviews." Reports in 4 weeks.
Music: "Musical style must be accessible to our audience and players (3 rehearsals). Length should be under 20 minutes. Maximum orchestration 2/2/2/2 2/2/0/0 Timp/1 Percussion Harpsichord/organ String 5/5/3/3/1. We have limited rehearsal time, so keep technique close to that of Bach-Beethoven. We also play chamber ensemble works—octets, etc. We do not want choral or solo works."
Performances: John Weinzweig's *Divertimento I* (flute and strings); Peter Jona Korn's *4 Pieces for Strings* (string orch.); and Graham Coles *Variations on a Mozart Rondo* (string orch.).
Tips: "If you want a first-rate performance, keep the technical difficulties minimal."

KNOX-GALESBURG SYMPHONY, Box 31 Knox College, Galesburg IL 61401. (309)343-0112, ext. 208. Music Director: Bruce Polay. Symphony orchestra. Estab. 1951. Members are professionals and amateurs. Performs 7 concerts/year including 1 new work. Middle age audience; excellent, recently renovated historical theater. Pays by performance.
How to Contact: Submit complete score and tapes of piece(s). SASE. Reports in 3-6 weeks.
Music: Moderate difficulty 3222/4331/T piano, harpsichord, celesta and full strings. No country.
Performances: Polay's *Perspectives* for tape and orchestra and *Tranquil Cycle* for tenor and orchestra; Finko's *2nd Symphony*; and Sisson's *October Light*.

*L.A. JAZZ CHOIR, 5759 Wallis Ln., Woodland Hills CA 91367. (818)704-8657. Chairman, Repertoire Committee: Barbara Keating. Vocal ensemble. Estab. 1980. Members are professionals. Performs 15 concerts/year; performs 4 new works per year. Commissions 1 composer/year. Performs in large concert halls (Los Angeles Music Center, Hollywood Bowl), small club venues (At My Place, Birdland West) and convention functions. Audiences range from 18-60. Pays negotiable percentage or flat purchase fee.
How to Contact: Query first. SASE. Reports in 3 weeks.
Music: "We are looking for more fusion-type music, with specific instruments are represented by voices. We are also desirous of obtaining original popular music, both in ballad and uptempo form. A cappella or with rhythm section. 12 voices only, 6 male and 6 female. Level of difficulty must be of professional standard. Please do not submit '40s-style jazz standard or classical styles. If composer wishes, they can contact Barbara Keating for a sample packet including tapes and charts to see our scoring preference."
Performances: Milcho Leviev's *The Green House* (jazz cantata); and "Cole Porter Medley," arranged by Earl Brown (jazz medley).

LA STELLA FOUNDATION, 14323-64th Ave. W., Edmonds WA 98026. (206)743-5010. Managing Director: Thomas F. Chambers. Opera company. Estab. 1990. Members are professionals. Performs 1-2 concerts/year. Produces operatic performances exclusively for recordings, video and television markets. Payment individually negotiated.
How to Contact: Query first. SASE. Reports in 6 months.
Music: "Music must have strong melodic value (Puccini-ish) with good harmonic chord structures and regular solid rhythms. Smaller casts with no chorus parts and smaller orchestras will get first consideration. Do not submit contemporary 'a-tonal,' non-harmonic, non-melodic, rhythmically weird garbage!!! Looking for pieces with romantic flavor like Puccini and dramatic movement like Verdi, written to showcase heavy lyric voices (i.e. soprano, tenor, baritone)."
Performances: Mozart's *Bastien & Bastienne* and *Impresario* (contemporary libretto and script written in English); and Bizet's *Djamileh* (condensed version in English with new contemporary translation).
Tips: "We are looking for hit arias and duets which fit above listed criteria with emphasis on repertoire for heavy lyric tenor/soprano voices."

*LAKESIDE SUMMER SYMPHONY, 236 Walnut Ave., Lakeside OH 43440. (419)798-4461. Contact: G. Keith Addy. Conductor: Robert L. Cronquist. Symphony orchestra. Members are professionals. Performs 8 concerts/year. Perform "Chautauqua-type programs with an audience of all ages (2-102). Hoover Auditorium is a 3,000-seat auditorium."
How to Contact: Query first. SASE.
Music: Seeking "classical compositions for symphony composed of 50-55 musicians. The work needs to have substance and be a challenge to our symphony members. No modern jazz, popular music or hard rock."
Performances: Richard's Nanes' *Prelude, Canon & Fugue* (classical).

*LAMARCA SINGERS, 2655 W. 230th Place, Torrance CA 90505. (310)325-8708. Director: Priscilla LaMarca Kandel. Vocal ensemble. Estab. 1979. Members are professionals and amateurs. Performs 20 concerts/year including 3-10 new works. Commissions 2 new works/year. Performs at major hotels, conventions, community theaters, fund raising events, cable TV, community fairs and Disneyland.
How to Contact: Submit complete score and tapes of piece(s). SASE. Reports in 2 months.
Music: "Seeks 3-10 or 15 minute medleys; a variety of musical styles from Broadway—pop styles to humorous specialty songs. Top 40 dance music, Linda Ronstadt-style to Whitney Houston. Light rock and patriotic themes. Also interested in music for children. No heavy metal or anything not suitable for family audiences."
Tips: "Make sure the lyrics fit the accents of the music. Make sure there is continuity of the song's meaning throughout. Keep the beat about 120-140 bpm, and no lengthy instrumental interludes."

LEHIGH VALLEY CHAMBER ORCHESTRA, Box 20641, Lehigh Valley PA 18002-0641. (215)770-9666. Music Director: Donald Spieth. Symphony orchestra. Estab. 1979. Performs 25 concerts/year, including 2-3 new works. Members are professionals. Commissions 1-2 composers or new works/year. Typical orchestral audience, also youth concerts. Pays commission for first 2 performances, first right for recording.
How to Contact: Submit complete score and tape of piece(s). SASE. Reports in 4 months.
Music: "Classical orchestral; works for youth and pops concerts. Duration 10-15 minutes. Chamber orchestra 2222-2210 percussion, strings (76442). No limit on difficulty."
Performances: David Stock's *String Set* (4 dances for strings); John Scully's *Letters from Birmingham Jail* (soprano and orchestra).
Tips: "Send a sample type and score of a work(s) written for the requested medium."

LITHOPOLIS AREA FINE ARTS ASSOCIATION, 3825 Cedar Hill Rd., Canal Winchester OH 43110-9507. (614)837-8925. Series Director: Virginia E. Heffner. Performing Arts Series. Estab. 1973. Members are professionals and amateurs. Performs 5-6 concerts/year. "Our audience consists of couples and families 35-85 in age. Our hall is acoustically excellent and seats 400. It was designed as a lecture-recital hall in 1925." Composers "may apply for Ohio Arts Council Grant under the New Works category."
How to Contact: Query first. Does not return material. Reports in 3 weeks.
Music: "We prefer that a composer is also the performer and works in conjunction with another artist, so that they could be one of the performers on our series. Piece should be musically pleasant and not too dissonant. It should be scored for small vocal or instrumental ensemble. Dance ensembles have difficulty with 15' high 15' deep and 27' wide stage. We do not want avant-garde or obscene dance routines. No ballet (space problem). We're interested in something historical — national or Ohio emphasis would be nice. Small ensembles or solo format is fine."
Tips: "Call me to see what our series is consisting of that season."

LONG BEACH COMMUNITY BAND, 6422 Keynote St., Long Beach CA 90808. (714)527-0964. Music Director: John E. Hall III. Community band. Estab. 1947. Members are professionals and amateurs. Performs 15 concerts/year including 6-8 new works. Average age level of audiences: 40's-50's. Performs mostly in outdoor venues such as parks. Pays by outright purchase.
How to Contact: Query first. SASE. Reports in 1-2 months.
Music: 3-10 minute pieces for concert band of medium difficulty. Looking for arrangements of film and TV music, songs of '70s to present.
Performances: Dan Friedman's *Millenium* (concert band overture).
Tips: "Compose music that is easy for audiences' ears."

LYRIC OPERA OF CHICAGO, 20 N. Wacker Dr., Chicago IL 60606. (312)332-2244. Fax: (312)419-8345. Music Administrator: Philip Morehead. Opera company. Estab. 1953. Members are professionals. Performs 8 operas/year including 1 new work in some years. "Performances are held in a 3,563 seat house, for a sophisticated opera audience, predominantly 30+ years old." Pays by contract (to be negotiated) — royalty or fee.
How to Contact: Query first. Does not return unsolicited material. Reports in 2 months or longer.
Music: "Full-length opera suitable for a large house with full orchestra. No musical comedy or Broadway musical style. We rarely perform one-act operas. We are only interested in works by composers and librettists with extensive theatrical experience. We have few openings for new works, so candidates must be of the highest quality. Do not send score or other materials without a prior contact."
Performances: William Bolcom's *McTeague*; Carlysle Floyd's *Susannah*; and Serge Prokofief's *The Gambler* (all operas).
Tips: "Have extensive credentials. We are not the right place for a novice opera composer."

*JAMES MADISON UNIVERSITY POPS CONCERTS, SYMPHONY ORCHESTRA AND CHAMBER ORCHESTRA, School of Music, Harrisonburg VA 22807. (703)568-6197. Director of Orchestras: Dr. Robert McCashin. Symphony orchestra and chamber orchestra. Members are professionals and amateurs. Performs 8-10 concerts/year. Audience consists of "university student body, music students and citizens of Harrisonburg/Shenandoah Valley. Standard concert theater." Payment varies.
How to Contact: Query first, then submit complete score. SASE. Reporting time depends on time of year.
Music: "Full symphonic orchestrations. Pops style for one concert per year. Works for 2 youth concerts per year. Level of difficulty should not exceed that of a high caliber, primarily undergraduate level. We have some very fine solo caliber players in all the sections that can handle brief solo passages if any occur in a work."
Tips: "Make the works attractive in some musical way and make them approachable by a high caliber student ensemble — and keep them *affordable*!"

MEASURED BREATHS THEATRE COMPANY, #3R, 193 Spring St., New York NY 10012. (212)334-8402. Artistic Director: Robert Press. Nonprofit music-theater producing organization. Estab. 1989. Members are professionals. Performs 2 concerts/year. "Performances in small (less than 100 seats) halls in downtown Manhattan; strongly interested in highly theatrical/political vocal works for avant-garde audiences." Pays $500 for outright purchase.
How to Contact: Query first. SASE. Reports in 1 month.
Music: "Traditionally, we have produced revivals of baroque or modern vocal works. We are interested in soliciting for new works by theatrically adept composers. Typical orchestration should be 7 pieces or less. Would prefer full-length works." Chamber-size, full-length operas preferred. At most 10 performers. Difficult works encouraged.

Performances: Weill's *He Who Say Yes* (opera, German; 1930); Cavalieri's *The Representation of Body & Soul* (opera, Italian; 1600); and Handel's *Tamerlano* (opera, English; 1724). All works performed in English translation.

MIAMI CHAMBER SYMPHONY, 5690 N. Kendall Dr., Miami FL 33156. (305)858-3500. Music Director: Burton Dines. 33 player chamber orchestra. Estab. 1981. Members are professionals. Performs 5 concerts/year. Performs for a typical mature audience of local residents, most of whom attend concerts in large northern communities. Performances are held in a 600 seat hall at the U. of Miami. Best acoustics in South Florida. "We have no budget for new music. We will cooperate in obtaining grants for new music."
How to Contact: Query first. Submit complete score and tape of piece(s). Does not return material. Reports in 6 months.
Music: "We prefer highly accessible pieces of important artistic quality, especially Latin with nationalistic characteristics. Mostly works which a well known soloist is prepared to perform. Length from 5 to 20 mintutes. Chamber orchestra: 2222-2200-Timp. + 19 strings. We will add two more horns and trombones on occasion. The orchestra is very highly professional but we have, at the most, 7½ hours rehearsal. We are interested only in highly professional work of composers with some real background."
Performances: Jose Serebrier's *Winter* (violin and orchestra); Morton Gould's *Tap Dance Concerto* (tap dancer and orchestra); and Jorge Martinez's *Escenas Paraguayas* (nationalistic piece based on popular songs for Paraguyan Harp and Orchestra).
Tips: "Write an accessible work that a well-known artist will be prepared to perform or premiere with us."

*MID-AMERICA SINGERS AND CHILDREN'S CHOIRS, 109 Park Central Square, Springfield MO 65806. (417)863-7464. Managing Artistic Director: Charles Facer. Community chorus. Estab. 1967. Members are professionals and amateurs. Performs 4-5 concerts/year including 1 or 2 new works. Payment is negotiable.
How to Contact: Query first. SASE. Reports in 3-4 weeks.
Music: SATB or 2-part children's or a combination with piano or small instrument ensemble or a cappella in singable style. Variety of lengths. 50 adults, 36 children.
Performances: Mark Gresham's *Gloria Nova* (chorus, strings, piano); and Charles Facer's *O for a Thousand Tongues* (chorus, piano).
Tips: "Contact us first and then tailor work to group."

*MID-ATLANTIC CHAMBER ORCHESTRA, P.O. Box 53085, Washington DC 20009. (202)488-9320. Fax: (202)483-0473. Artistic Director: Yural Waldman. Chamber orchestra. Estab. 1986. Members are professionals. Performs 20 concerts/year including 3-4 new works. Commissions 2 composers or new works/year. "Concerts are performed for mid-and small-town audiences who think Copland is avant garde." Performances are conducted at colleges, high schools and civic theatres. Pays $500/ performance if composer performs, or flat fee for tour.
How to Contact: Query first. Does not return materials. Reports in 2 months.
Music: "Neoclassical, accessible, 8-15 minutes for small string orchestra, 5-4-3-2-1, plus other instruments already being used in the same program. No 12-tone scale or seriously minimalist works."
Performances: Susan Fallari's *Unobstructed Universe* (15-minute piece for Tibetan bowls and string orchestra); Stephanie de Kennessey's *Starry Night* (romantic strings); and Jeffrey Chappell's *Shadow Dance* (concerto for piano and jazz band).
Tips: "Compositions *must* be suitable for our audiences—intellectually sophisticated but with limited access to the arts because of geographic isolation."

MILWAUKEE YOUTH SYMPHONY ORCHESTRA, 929 N. Water St., Milwaukee WI 53202. (414)272-8540. Executive Director: Frances Richman. Youth orchestra. "We also have a Junior Wind Ensemble." Estab. 1956. Members are students. Performs 12-15 concerts/year, including 1-2 new works. "Our groups perform in Uihlein Hall at the Performing Arts Center in Milwaukee plus area sites. The audiences usually consist of parents, music teachers and other interested community members. We usually are reviewed in either the *Milwaukee Journal* or *Sentinel*."
How to Contact: Query first. Does not return material.
Performances: Ruggeri's *Symphonia for Strings*.
Tips: "Be sure you realize you are working with students and not professional musicians. The music needs to be technically on a level students can handle. Our students are 8-18 years of age, in 5 different orchestras."

THE MIRECOURT TRIO, 585 E. Second Ave. Apt. 9, Salt Lake City UT 84103-2920. (801)532-0469. Fax: (801)532-2533. Contact: Terry King. Chamber music ensemble; violin, cello, piano. Estab. 1973. Members are professionals. Performs 20 concerts/year, including 2-6 new works. Commissions 2-6

composers or new works/year. Concerts are performed for university, concert series, schools, societies and "general chamber music audiences of 100-1,500."
How to Contact: Query first. SASE. Reports in 6 months.
Music: Seeks "music of short to moderate duration (5-20 minutes) that entertains, yet is not derivative or clichéd. Orchestration should be basically piano, violin, cello, occasionally adding voice or instrument. We do not wish to see academic or experimental works."
Performances: Lou Harrison's *Trio*; Otto Leuning's *Fantasia No. 2*; and Henry Cowell's *Scenario*.
Tips: "Submit works that engage the audience or relate to them, that reward the players as well."

MISSOURI SYMPHONY SOCIETY, P.O. Box 1121, Columbia MO 65205. (314)875-0600. Artistic Director and Conductor: Hugo Vianello. Symphony orchestra, chamber music ensemble, youth orchestra and pops orchestra. Estab. 1970. Members are professionals. Performs 22 concerts/year. Commissions one composer or new work/year. "Our home base is a 1,200-seat renovated 1928 movie palace and vaudeville stage. Our home audience is well-educated, including professionals from Columbia's 5 hospitals and 3 institutions of higher education. Our touring program reaches a broad audience, including rural Missourians and prison inmates." Pays through ASCAP and BMI.
How to Contact: Query first. SASE.
Music: "We want good orchestral (chamber) music of any length — 2222/2200/timp/strings/piano. There are no limitations on difficulty."
Performances: Ibert's *Divertissement*; Copland's *Music for Movies*; Daniel's *Deep Forest Op. 34 #1*.

MOHAWK TRAIL CONCERTS, P.O. Box 75, Shelburne Falls MA 01370. (413)625-9511. Executive Director: John Bos. Artistic Director: Arnold Black. Chamber music presenter. Estab. 1970. Members are professionals. Performs approximately 10 concerts/year, including 2-3 new works. Conducts school performances. "Audience ranges from farmers to professors, children to elders. Concerts are performed in churches and town halls around rural Franklin County, Mass." Pays by performance.
How to Contact: Query first. Does not return unsolicited material. Reports in months.
Music: "We want chamber music, generally not longer than 30 minutes. We are open to a variety of styles and orchestrations for a maximum of 8 performers. We don't want pop, rock or theater music."
Performances: Michael Cohen's *Fantasia for Flute, Piano and Strings* (chamber); William Bolcom's *Nes Songs* (piano/voice duo); and Arnold Black's *Laments & Dances* (string quartet and guitar duo).
Tips: "We are looking for artistic excellence, a committment to quality performances of new music, and music that is accessible to a fairly conservative (musically) audience."

MOZART FESTIVAL ORCHESTRA, INC., 33 Greenwich Ave., New York NY 10014. (212)675-9127. Conductor: Baird Hastings. Symphony orchestra. Estab. 1960. Members are professionals. Performs 1-4 concerts/year, including 2 new works. Audience members are Greenwich Village professionals of all ages. Performances are held at the First Presbyterian Church, Fifth Ave. and 12th St., ("wonderful acoustics"). Pay varies.
How to Contact: Query first. SASE. Reports in 2 weeks.
Music: "We are an established chamber orchestra interested in *unusual* music of all periods, but not experimental. Orchestra size usually under 20 performers."

*NASHVILLE OPERA ASSOCIATION, 1900 Belmont Blvd., Nashville TN 37212. (615)292-5710. General Director: Kyle Ridout. Opera company. Estab. 1981. Members are professionals and amateurs. Performs 7 concerts/year. "Tennessee Performing Arts Center (Jackson Hall) has 2,400 seats and Tennessee Performing Arts Center (Polk Theatre) has 1,100 seats." Pays for outright purchase.
How to Contact: Submit complete score and tape of piece(s). SASE. Reports in 1 month.
Music: Seeks opera and music theater pieces, sometimes accept one-acts."
Performances: Verdi's *Rigoletto* (grand opera); Rossini's *The Barber of Seville* (grand opera); and Puccini's *Madama Butterfly* (grand opera).
Tips: "Be willing to work through the score. Be available for workshops, presentations."

*NATIONAL ASSOCIATION OF COMPOSERS/USA, NACUSA P.O. Box 49652, Los Angeles CA 90049. (310)541-8213. President: Marshall Bialosky. Chamber music ensemble and composers' service organization. Estab. 1932. Members are professionals. Performs 6 concerts/year — all new works. Receives 20-30 outside submissions/year. Usually performed at universities in Los Angeles and at a midtown church in New York City. Paid by ASCAP or BMI (NACUSA does not pay composers).
How to Contact: Submit complete score and tape of piece(s). SASE. Reports in a couple of weeks.
Music: Chamber music for five or fewer players; usually in the 5 to 20 minute range. "Level of difficulty is not a problem; number of performers is solely for financial reasons. We deal in serious, contemporary concert hall music. No 'popular' music."
Performances: Bruce Taub's *Sonata for Solo Viola*; Tom Flaherty's *Quartet for Viola, Cello, and Digital Synthesizer*; and Maria Newman's *Sonata for Bass Trombone and Piano*.

THE NEW YORK CONCERT SINGERS, Dept. SM, 401 E. 80th St., New York NY 10021. (212)879-4412. Music Director/Conductor: Judith Clurman. Chorus. Estab. 1988. Performs 4-5 concerts/year, including new works. Frequently commissions new composers. "Audience is mixture of young and old classical music 'lovers.' Chorus performs primarily at Menkin Concert Hall and Lincoln Center, NYC." Pays per performance.
How to Contact: Send score and tape with biographical data. SASE.
Music: Seeks music "for small professional ensemble, with or without solo parts, a cappella or small instrumental ensemble. Not for large orchestra and chorus (at this stage in the group's development). Looking for pieces ranging from 7-20 minutes."
Performances: William Bolcom's *Alleluia* (a cappella); Arvo Part's *Summa and Magnificent* (a cappella); and Milhaud's *Service Sacre* (chorus and ensemble).
Tips: "When choosing a piece for a program I study both the text and music. Both are equally important."

NORFOLK CHAMBER MUSIC FESTIVAL/YALE SUMMER SCHOOL OF MUSIC, 96 Wall St., New Haven CT 06520. (203)432-1966. Summer music festival. Estab. 1941. Members are international faculty/artists plus fellows who are young professionals. Performs 12 concerts, 14 recitals/year, including 3-6 new works. Commissions 1 composer or new work/year. "The 1,100-seat Music Shed (built in 1906 by architect Eric K. Rossiter) is lined with California redwood, with a peaked cathedral, which creates wonderful acoustics." Pays a commission fee (set fee). "Also offers a Composition Search and Residency for Summer 1995. The Norfolk Chamber Music Festival-Yale Summer School of Music seeks new chamber music works from American composers under the age of 30. The goal of this search is to identify promising young composers and to provide a visible and high quality venue for the premiere of their work. A maximum of two winning compositions will be selected. Winners will be invited to the Norfolk Chamber Music Festival for a week-long residency. Pieces will be rehearsed, coached, performed and professionally recorded on a Norfolk Chamber Music Festival series concert. Each composer selected will receive room and board during residency."
How to Contact: Submit complete score and tapes of piece(s). SASE. Reports in 1 month.
Music: "Chamber music of combinations, particularly for strings, woodwinds, brass and piano. There are 1-2 chamber orchestra concerts per season which include the students and feature the festival artists. Other than this, orchestra is not a featured medium, rather, chamber ensembles are the focus."

NORTH ARKANSAS SYMPHONY ORCHESTRA, P.O. Box 1243, Fayetteville AR 72702. (501)521-4166. Music Director: Carlton Woods. Symphony orchestra, chamber music ensemble, youth orchestra and community chorus. Estab. 1954. Members are professionals and amateurs. Performs 20 concerts/year, including 1-2 new works. "General audiences—performs in Walton Arts Center (capacity 1,200)." Pays $500 or more/performance.
How to Contact: Query first. SASE.
Music: Seeks "audience pleasers—rather short (10-15 minutes); and full orchestra pieces for subscription (classical) concerts. Orchestra is 60-70 members."
Performances: Mahler's *Symphony #1* and Beethoven's *9th Symphony*.

OPERA MEMPHIS, MSU South Campus #47, Memphis TN 38152. (901)678-2706. Fax: (901)678-3506. Artistic Director: Michael Ching. Opera company. Estab. 1965. Members are professionals. Performs 12 concerts/year including 1 new work. Commissions 1 composer or new work/year. Audience consists of older, wealthier patrons, along with many students and young professionals. Pay negotiable.
How to Contact: Query first. SASE. Reports in 1 year.
Music: Accessible practical pieces for educational or main stage programs. Educational pieces should not exceed 90 minutes or 4-6 performers. We encourage songwriters to contact us with proposals or work samples for theatrical works. We are very interested in crossover work.
Tips: "Spend many hours thinking about the synopsis (plot outline)."
Performances: David Olney's *Light in August* (folk opera); Sid Selvidge's *Riversongs* (one act opera); and John Baur's *The Vision of John Brown* (opera).

PERRY COUNTY COUNCIL OF THE ARTS, P.O. Box 354, Newport PA 17074. (717)567-7023. Executive Director: Carol O. Vracarich. Arts organization presenting various programs. Estab. 1978. Members are professionals and amateurs and anyone who pays membership dues. Performs 5-7 concerts/year.

Market conditions are constantly changing! If you're still using this book and it is 1996 or later, buy the newest edition of Songwriter's Market at your favorite bookstore or order directly from Writer's Digest Books.

"Performances are presented outdoors at a local state park or in a 500-seat high school auditorium. Outdoor area seats up to 5,000." Pays $50-2,000 per performance.

How to Contact: Submit complete tapes (or videocassette if available) and background info on composer/performer. Does not return unsolicited material.

Music: "We present a wide variety of programs, hence we are open to all types of music (folk, rock, classical, blues, jazz, ethnic). Most programs are 1-2 hours in length and must be suitable as family entertainment."

PICCOLO OPERA COMPANY, 24 Del Rio Blvd., Boca Raton FL 33432-4737. (800)282-3161. Executive Director: Marjorie Gordon. Opera company. Estab. 1962. Members are professionals. Commissions 1 composer or new work/year. Concerts are performed for a mixed audience of children and adults. Pays by royalty or outright purchase.

How to Contact: Submit complete score and tape of piece(s). Does not return material. Reports in 1 month.

Music: "Musical theater pieces, lasting about one hour, for adults to perform for adults and/or youngsters. Performers are mature singers with experience. The cast should have few performers (up to 10), no chorus or ballet, accompanied by piano or orchestra. Skeletal scenery. All in English."

Performances: *Cosi Fan Tutte* (opera); *The Telephone* (opera); and *The Old Maid & The Thief* (opera).

PRISM SAXOPHONE QUARTET, 257 Harvey St., Philadelphia PA 19144. (215)438-5282. Vice President, New Sounds Music Inc. Prism Quartet: Matthew Levy. Chamber music ensemble. Estab. 1984. Members are professionals. Performs 80 concerts/year including 15 new works. Commissions 7 composers or new works/year. "Performances are primarily held in concert halls for chamber music concert audiences." Pays royalty per performance from BMI or ASCAP or commission range from $100 to $5,000.

How to Contact: Submit complete score (with parts) and tape of piece(s). Does not return material.

Music: "Orchestration—sax quartet SATB or AATB. Lengths—5-60 minutes. Styles—contemporary, classical, jazz, crossover, ethnic, gospel, avant-garde. No limitations on level of difficulty. No more than 4 performers (SATB or AATB sax quartet). No arrangements or transcriptions. The prism quartet places special emphasis on crossover works which integrate a variety of musical styles."

Performances: Franch Amsallem's *The Farewell* (jazz); Bradford Ellis's *Tooka-Ood Zasch* (ethnic-world music); and Wm. Bolcom's *Concerto for Four Saxophones and Orchestra*.

QUEENS OPERA, P.O. Box 140066, Brooklyn NY 11214. (908)390-9472. General Director: Joe Messina. Opera company. Estab. 1961. Members are professionals. Performs 9 concerts/year, including 1 new work.

How to Contact: SASE. Reports in 1 month.

Music: "Operatic scores and songs, small orchestra."

Performances: Rossini's *Il Barbiere di Siviglia*; Verdi's *Il Trovatore*; and Owen's *Tom Sawyer*.

*QUINTESSENCE CHAMBER ENSEMBLE, P.O. Box 56642, Phoenix AZ 85079. (602)483-9430. Educational Director: Jill Marderness. Chamber music ensemble. Estab. 1980. Members are professionals. Performs 125 concerts/year including 6-10 new works. Commissions 2 composers/year. Audience consists of elementary school students to business people to senior citizens. Performances take place in school auditoriums, concert and recital halls and outdoor amphitheaters (average seating 1,000). Pays for outright purchase.

How to Contact: Query first. Does not return material. Reports in 3 months.

Music: "Classical, contemporary, pops, 5-15 minutes in length. Traditional wind quintet (flute, oboe, clarinet, bassoon, horn). No limitations on difficulty."

Performances: Peter Lieuwen's *Savannah* (contemporary wind quintet); Luciano Berio's *Opus Number Zoo* (light classical wind quintet); and selections from *Porgy and Bess* (pops).

*RENO CHAMBER ORCHESTRA, P.O. Box 547, Reno NV 89504. (702)348-9413. Fax: (702)348-0643. Music Director: Vahe Khochayan. Chamber orchestra. Estab. 1974. Members are professionals. Performs 7-8 concerts/year including 1 new work every other year. Students retirees largest segment 45-70. Nightingale concert hall, 615 seats with fine acoustics. Payment to be negotiated—depends if composer is also guest soloist.

How to Contact: Query first. Does not return material. Reports in 2 months.

Music: "Pieces of 10-15 minutes in length—can be longer if very accessible—for string orchestra or strings plus solo instrument, strings and winds. Preferably 35 players or less. Our professional orchestra can handle most anything." Not interested in stridently atonal compositions, pops, jazz.

Performances: James Winn's *Concerto in E Flat Minor* (piano concerto); Alan Hohraness's *Talin* (viola concerto); Wm. Kersten's *Earth & Paradise* (song cycle).

Tips: "Take advantage of our strong viola and cello sections."

RENO POPS ORCHESTRA, P.O. Box 9838, Reno NV 89507. (702)673-2276. Conductor, Musical Director: Joyce Williams. Symphony orchestra. Estab. 1983. Members are professionals and amateurs. Performs 6 concerts/year usually including 1 new work. Performances are held in 600-1,400 seat theaters and off site locations, i.e. schools, community centers for a mixed audience. Pay negotiable.
How to Contact: Query first. Does not return unsolicited material. Reports in 1 month.
Music: 15-20 minutes with strong rhythm, lyrical melodies of joyous, optimistic matter. Nothing for large orchestras.
Tips: "Write a playable piece that would work for college or community ensembles."

*RIDGEWOOD SYMPHONY ORCHESTRA, P.O. Box 176, Ridgewood NJ 07451. (201)612-0118. Fax: (201)445-2762. Music Director: Dr. Sandra Dackow. Symphony orchestra. Estab. 1939. Members are professionals and amateurs. Performs 6 concerts/year including 1 or 2 new works. Audience is "sophisticated." Performance space is 800-seat school auditorium. Payment varies.
How to Contact: Submit complete score and tape of piece(s). SASE. Reports in 3 months ("It depends on how busy we are.")
Music: "Symphonic works of various lengths and types which can be performed by a nonprofessional orchestra. We are flexible but would like to involve all of our players; very restrictive instrumentations do not suit our needs."
Performances: Raymond Helble's *Symphonic Variations* (large-scale variations – full orchestra); and Richard Lane's *Kaleidoscope Overture*.
Tips: "Please lay out rehearsal numbers/letters and rests according to phrases and other logical musical divisions rather than in groups of 10 measures, etc., which is very unmusical, wastes time and causes a surprising number of problems. Also, please *do not* send a score written in concert pitch; use the usual transpositions so that the conductor sees what the players see. Rehearsal is much more effective this way. Cross cue all important solos; this helps in rehearsal where instruments may be missing."

ST. LOUIS CHAMBER CHORUS, P.O. Box 11558, Clayton MO 63105. (314)458-4343. Music Director: Philip Barnes. Vocal ensemble, chamber music ensemble. Estab. 1956. Members are professionals and amateurs. Performs 5-6 concerts/year including 5 new works. Performances take place at various auditoria noted for their excellent acoustics – churches, synagogues, schools and university halls. Pays by arrangement.
How to Contact: Query first. SASE. Reports in 1 to 2 months.
Music: "Only *a cappella* writing; no contemporary 'popular' works; historical editions welcomed. No improvisatory works. Our programs are tailored for specific acoustics – composers should indicate their preference."
Performances: John Harbison's *Ave Maria* (motet); Henryu Gorecki's *Totus Tuus* (motet); Andrew Carter's *Ack Väarmeland* (folksong).
Tips: "Show awareness of the unique qualities of the voice."

SALT LAKE SYMPHONIC CHOIR, Box 45, Salt Lake City UT 84110. (801)466-8701. Manager: Richard M. Taggart. Professional touring choir. Estab. 1949. Members are professionals and amateurs. Performs 3-15 concerts/year, including 1-3 new works. Commissions 1-3 new works or composers/year. "We tour throughout U.S. and Canada for community concert series, colleges and universities." Pay is negotiable.
How to Contact: Query first. Does not return unsolicited material. Reports in 1-4 months.
Music: Seeking "4-8 part choral pieces for a 100-voice choir – from Bach to rock."

SASKATOON SYMPHONY ORCHESTRA, Box 1361, Saskatoon, Saskatchewan S7K 3N9 **Canada**. (306)665-6414. Fax: (306)652-3364. General Manager: Shirley Spafford. Symphony orchestra. Performs 20 full orchestra concerts/year, including 3-4 new works.
How to Contact: Query first. Does not return material.
Music: "We are a semi-professional orchestra with a full time core of ten artists-in-residence. Our season runs from September to April with classical concerts, pops series, chamber series, children's series and baroque series."
Performances: David Scott's *Nazca Lines* (symphonic); Alexander Brott's *Oracle* (reed trio); and Elizabeth Raum's *Concerto for Bass* (string quartet).

*SAULT STE. MARIE SYMPHONY ORCHESTRA, 3128 Lakeshore Dr., Sault Ste. Marie MI 49783. (906)635-2265. Music Director: Dr. John Wilkinson. Symphony orchestra. Estab. 1972. Members are professionals and amateurs. Performs 8-12 full orchestra concerts/year, including 1-2 new works. "Our audience is conservative. Our performance hall seats 964."
How to Contact: Query first. SASE.
Music: "We have traditional orchestra size 2222/4231/2, plus strings. String 88552. We want pieces of length (5-15 minutes) in approachable styles. We have 45-50 performers. Pieces should be of moderate difficulty (or less!). Engage the listener; make it playable."

Performances: Ridout-Quesnel's *Colas et Colinette* (light overture); S. Glick's *Elegy* (elegy); and J. Weinzweig's *The Red Ear of Corn* (ballet suite).

SEAWAY CHORALE AND ORCHESTRA, INC., 2450 Middlefield Rd., Trenton MI 48183. (313)676-2400. Conductor, Executive Director: David M. Ward. Auditioned chorus and orchestra. Estab. 1975. Members are professionals and amateurs. Performs 5 major concerts/year, including 4 new works/year. Commissions 0-2 composers or new works/year. "We perform in halls, some church settings and high school auditoriums—large stage with orchestra pit. Our audience is ecumenically, financially, racially, socially, musically, multi-generation and a cross section of our area." Pays by negotiation.
How to Contact: Submit score and tape of piece(s). SASE. Reports in 3 months.
Music: "We want 3-minute ballads for orchestra and chorus (for subscription concerts); sacred music, either accompanied or a cappella; Christmas music for chorus and orchestra. We have 3 performing groups: Voices of the Young—4th through 8th grades (40 members); Youth Sings—9th through 12th grades (a show choir, 24 members); Chorale—adults (70 members). Charismatic Christian music is not high on our priority list. Country music runs a close second. Our major concerts which draw large audiences utilize light selections such as show music, popular songs and music from movies. We present two concerts each year which we call Choral Masterpieces. These concerts include music from master composers of the past as well as contemporary. Our choral masterpieces concerts require Biblical or secular thoughts that are well-conceived musically."
Tips: "Don't settle for one musical avenue. Be as creatively prolific as possible. You may discover a lot about your own abilities and avoid redundancies as a result."

SINGERS FORUM, 39 W. 19th St., New York NY 10011. (212)366-0541. Fax: (212)366-0546. Administrator: Denise Galon. Vocal school and presenting organization. Estab. 1978. Members are professionals and amateurs. Performs more than 50 concerts/year, including 4 new works. Commissions 2 composers or new works/year. 75-seat performance space with varied audience. Pays through donations from patrons.
How to Contact: Query first. SASE. Reports in 2 months.
Music: "All popular music, art songs, full musicals, small operas with minimal orchestration. No rock. I'm always looking for works to fit our current voices, mainly new operas and musicals."
Performances: Maria Kildegaard's and Valerie Osterwalder's *Angels Part I* (new music); mixed *Women of a Certain Age Carrying On* (collection of women's music); mixed *Big Girls Don't Cry* (contemporary mixed cabaret).
Tips: "Think of the voice."

SINGING BOYS OF PENNSYLVANIA, P.O. Box 206, Wind Gap PA 18091. (610)759-6002. Director: K. Bernard Schade, Ed. D. Vocal ensemble. Estab. 1970. Members are professional children. Performs 120 concerts/year including 7-12 new works. Commissions 1-2 composers or new works/year. "We attract general audiences: family, senior citizens, churches, concert associations, university concert series and schools." Pays for outright purchase.
How to Contact: Query first. SASE. Reports in 3 months.
Music: "We want music for commercials, voices in the SSA or SSAA ranges, sacred works or arrangements of American folk music with accompaniment. Our range of voices are from G below middle C to A (13th above middle C). Reading ability of choir is good but works which require a lot of work with little possibility of more than one performance are of little value. We sing very few popular songs except for special events. We perform music by composers who are well-known and works by living composers who are writing in traditional choral forms. Works which have a full orchestral score are of interest. The orchestration should be fairly light, so as not to cover the voices. Works for Christmas have more value than some other, since we perform with orchestras on an annual basis."
Performances: Don Locklair's *The Columbus Madrigals* (opera).
Tips: "It must be appropriate music and words for children."

*SOLIDEO GLORIA CANTORUM, 3402 Woolworth Ave., Omaha NE 68105. (402)341-9381. Music Director: Almeda Berkey. Professional choir. Estab. 1988. Members are professionals. Performs 6-7 concerts/year. Commissions 1 new work/year. Performance space: "cathedral, symphony hall, smaller intimate recital halls as well." Payment is "dependent upon composition and composer."
How to Contact: Submit complete score and tape of piece(s). SASE. Reports in 1-2 months.
Music: "Generally a cappella compositions from very short to extended range (6-18 minutes) or multi-movements. Concerts are of a formal length (approx. 75 minutes) with 5 rehearsals. Difficulty must be balanced within program in order to adequately prepare in a limited rehearsal time. 28 singers. Not seeking orchestral pieces, due to limited budget."
Performances: Jackson Berkey's *Native American Ambiances* (3 movement a cappella flute reading); John Rutter's *Hymn to the Creator of Light* (8 minute a cappella, 2 choir); and Arvo Part's *Magnificat* (7 minute a cappella).

SUSQUEHANNA SYMPHONY ORCHESTRA, P.O. Box 485, Forest Hill MD 21050. (410)838-6465. Music Director: Sheldon Bair. Symphony orchestra. Estab. 1978. Members are amateurs. Performs 4 subscription concerts/year plus 2 outdoor concerts in June, including 2 new works. "We perform in 1 hall, 600 seats with fine acoustics. Our audience encompasses all ages."
How to Contact: Query first. SASE. Reports in 6+ months.
Music: "We desire works for large orchestra any length, in a 'conservative 20th century' style. Seek fine music for large orchestra. We are a community orchestra, so the music must be within our grasp. Violin I to 7th position by step only; Violin II—stay within 5th position; English horn and harp are OK. Full orchestra pieces preferred."
Performances: David Finko's *Moses*; Michael Horvit's *Concerto for Brass and Piano*; and Benjamin Lees' *Trumpet of the Swan*.

*THE SYMPHONY OF SOUTHEAST TEXAS, INC., Suite 101, 2626 Calder, Beaumont TX 77702-1925. (409)835-7100. Fax: (409)835-2631. Executive Director: Kathy Clark. Symphony orchestra. Estab. 1951. Members are professionals and amateurs. Performs 9 concerts/year including 1 new work. Audience is "fairly conservative upper and middle class. Mixture of cultures and races." Performance space is the Julie Rogers Theatre for the Performing Arts—concert hall with seating capacity of 1,650. Pays per performance; "amount depends on contract agreement."
How to Contact: Submit complete score and tape of piece(s). SASE. Reports in 6-8 months.
Music: "Style can range from very classical in style to light modern. Our audience tends to favor passionate, large orchestral works—tunes that can be remembered easily—some upbeat, lighter works. Pieces should be approximately 10-20 minutes in length. Vocal arrangements acceptable. Work should be capable of working up with only 4 rehearsals. Orchestra can fill maximum numbers in: flute—3 (one piccolo); clarinet—3 (one bass clarinet); oboe—3 (one English horn); bassoon—3 (one contra bassoon). General orchestrations: 12-10-8-8-6-3*-3*-2-4-3-3-1 timp + 3. No 'train wrecks' or 'hot dogs in space' pieces. Orchestra does not wish to 'verbalize,' sing, speak or clap in a piece."
Performances: Russell Peck's *The Glory and Grandeur* (contemporary); Dan Welcher's *Prairie Light* (modern tone poem type); and Li Wu Gee's *Spring Festival Overture* (traditional Chinese orchestration).
Tips: "We have a Meet the Composer Week program that runs in conjunction with a concert each spring. Always submit a tape—many people on our Meet the Composer panel are music lovers, not music readers."

*TE DEUM ORCHESTRA & SINGERS, 105 Victoria St., Dundas Ontario L9H 2C1 **Canada**. (905)628-4533. Artistic Director: Richard Birney-Smith. Chamber sized choir. Estab. 1968. Members are amateurs and professionals. Performs 6 concerts/year. Audience consists of "university students to pensioners; medium income and up; music lovers foremost; fairly knowledgeable."
How to Contact: Query first with tape. "We are a small staff, and overworked! A tape will get listened to most easily. Ask us for recent programs so that you understand our philosophy." SASE.
Music: "Chamber sized. Choral or organ. We play much baroque and accessible late 19th and 20th century works (Appalachian Spring). We have a good core string group, and an able choir. New works must be audience friendly. Rehearsal times are sometimes limited. As our name suggests, we program religious works carefully and consciously. We perform very few new works, but welcome tapes. Preference (and funding sources) is for Canadian composers. Our orchestra is accustomed to 'conventional' techniques, and accepted baroque practices. We tend to use 18 musicians or less. Our choir fluctuates between 25 and 30 voices. We own both harpsichord and portable organ. We perform according to the instrumentation and styles appropriate to the period and composer." Does not wish to see "pops material. Extreme avant-garde. Although we enjoy it, we don't program it."
Performances: Aaron Copland's *Appalachian Spring* (original small ensemble score); Clarence Watters' *Four Organ Versets on Adoro te Devote* (organ and voice alternating); and Bobby McFerrin's *23rd Psalm* (choral arrangement, presents the Trinity as feminine).
Tips: "Get to know us. Phone, fax, send tapes. We're friendly and supportive, but often too busy to reply to mail."

TORONTO MENDELSSOHN CHOIR, 60 Simcoe St., Toronto, Ontario M5J 2H5 **Canada**. Phone: (416)598-0422. Manager: Michael Ridout. Vocal ensemble. Members are professionals and amateurs. Performs 25 concerts/year including 1-3 new works. "Most performances take place in Roy Thomson Hall. The audience is reasonably sophisticated, musically knowledgeable but with moderately conservative tastes." Pays by commission and ASCAP/SOCAN.
How to Contact: Query first or submit complete score and tapes of pieces. SASE. Reports in 6 months.
Music: All works must suit a large choir (180 voices) and standard orchestral forces or with some other not-too-exotic accompaniment. Length should be restricted to no longer than ½ of a nocturnal concert. The choir sings at a very professional level and can sight-read almost anything. "Works

should fit naturally with the repertoire of a large choir which performs the standard choral orchestral repertoire."
Performances: Holman's *Jezebel* (world premiere); Orff's *Catulli Carmina*; and Lambert's *Rio Grande*.

*TOURING CONCERT OPERA CO. INC., 228 E. 80th, New York NY 10021. (212)988-2542. Director: Anne DeFigols. Opera company. Estab. 1971. Members are professionals. Performs 110 concerts/year including 2 new works. Pays per performance.
How to Contact: Query first. Does not return material. Reporting time varies.
Music: "Operas or similar with small casts."
Tips: "We are a touring company which travels all over the world. Therefore, operas with casts that are not large and simple but effective sets are the most practical."

TRIO OF THE AMERICAS, 16823 Liggett St., North Hills CA 91343. (818)766-6146. Fax: (818)892-1227. Director: Dr. Janice Foy. Chamber music ensemble. Estab. 1993. Members are professionals. Performs 4 concerts/year including 2 new works. "Focus of repertoire is music of the Americas. We perform on a concert stage; sometimes private residences or university halls."
How to Contact: Submit complete score and tape of piece(s). SASE. Reports in 1 month.
Music: "Contemporary chamber music, which could include the addition of voice and/or other instruments. 'Trio of the Americas' consists of clarinet, cello and piano. Preferable length is from 8-15 minutes. Try not to write for more than 5 performers. Could write for anything less than that, including duets and solos. Difficulty does not matter since the performers are among L.A.'s finest. Not interested in computer music. Very interested in the incorporation of jazz and the use of folk material. Prefer melodic/rhythmic interest in the music. All styles are acceptable. (No Steve Reich approaches please.)"
Performances: Hal Overton's *Sonata for Cello and Piano* (West Coast premiere) and Hindemith's *A Frog Went A-Courtin'*.
Tips: "Please be open to criticism/suggestions about your music and try to appeal to mixed audiences."

UNIVERSITY OF HOUSTON OPERA THEATRE, School of Music, Houston TX 77204-4893. (713)743-3162. Director of Opera: Buck Ross. Opera/music theater program. Members are professionals, amateurs and students. Performs 8-10 concerts/year, including 1 new work. Performs in a proscenium theater which seats 1,100. Pit seats approximately 40 players. Audience covers wide spectrum, from first time opera-goers to very sophisticated." Pays by royalty.
How to Contact: Submit complete score and tapes of piece(s). SASE. Reports in 3 months.
Music: "We seek music that is feasible for high graduate level student singers. Chamber orchestras are very useful. No more than 2½ hours. No children's operas."
Performances: Carlisle Floyd's *Bilby's Doll* (opera); Mary Carol Warwick's *Twins* (opera); Robert Nelson's *Tickets, Please* (opera); and Robert Nelson's *A Room With A View*.

*UNIVERSITY OF UTAH ORCHESTRAS, 204 DGH, Salt Lake City UT 84112. (801)581-6692. Fax: (801)581-5683. Music Director: Robert Debbaut. Symphony orchestra. Members are amateurs. Performs 9 concerts/year including 6-8 new works. Commissions 1 composer or new work/year. Pays per performance.
How to Contact: Submit complete score and tape of pieces(s). SASE. Replies only if interested.
Music: "Orchestral music for two very different orchestras. *Utah Philharmonia:* (3222/4231/T+3-5, Hp, Pf). This orchestra is 85% music majors, all of whom are students in either performance or education and who study with members of the Utah Symphony. This orchestra performs 6-7 concerts annually. Works of a moderate to advanced difficulty are considered. For this group, I am looking at a wide variety of musical styles. *University of Utah Symphony Orchestra:* (3333/4331/T+3-5, Hp, Pf). This group is mainly non-majors who do not study privately. I do perform new music with them, but that which is more accessible to advanced high school groups. I will never perform works using graph notation, or musical notations other than traditional. I will consider works with tape, aleatoric works or other experimental works, but not unless I can hear a performance tape of the work."
Performances: William Banfield's *Symphony No. 1*, (tonal jazz influences); Hunter Johnson's *Past the Evening Sun*, (tonal, modal); and William Bolcom's *Symphony No. 1* (tonal).
Tips: "I won't return a long distance phone call or write back unless I am interested in a work. Don't send scores and parts that are error-filled and illegible. Do not send tapes loaded with static. When you send materials, include a bio, include several ways one can reach you, send costs in a variety of settings (i.e., rates for academia, rates if admission is charged, etc.)."

VANCOUVER CHAMBER CHOIR, 1254 W. Seventh Ave., Vancouver, Britsh Columbia V6H 1B6 **Canada**. Artistic Director: Jon Washburn. Vocal ensemble. Members are professionals. Performs 40 concerts/year, including 5-8 new works/year. Commissions 3-4 composers or new works/year. Pays statutory SOCAN royalty.
How to Contact: Submit complete score and tapes of piece(s). Does not return material. Reports in 6 months.

Music: Seeks "choral works of all types for small chorus, with or without accompaniment and/or soloists. Concert music only. Choir made up of 20 singers. Large or unusual instrumental accompaniments are less likely to be appropriate. No pop music."

Performances: Have commissioned and/or premiered over 80 new works by Canadian, American and British composers, including Alice Parker's *That Sturdy Vine* (cantata for chorus, soloists and orchestra); R. Murray Schafer's *Magic Songs* (SATB a capella); and Jon Washburn's *A Stephen Foster Medley* (SSAATTBB/piano).

Tips: "We are looking for choral music that is performable yet innovative, and which has the potential to become 'standard repertoire.' Although we perform much new music, only a small portion of the many scores which are submitted can be utilized."

*VANCOUVER YOUTH SYMPHONY ORCHESTRA SOCIETY, #204, 3737 Oak St., Vancouver British Columbia V6H 2M4 **Canada.** Music Director: Arthur Polson. Youth orchestra. Estab. 1930. Members are amateurs. Performs 6-8 concerts/year. Perform in various venues from churches to major concert halls.

How to Contact: Query first. Does not return material.

Music: "The Senior Orchestra performs the standard symphony repertoire. Programs usually consist of an overture, a major symphony and perhaps a concerto or shorter work. The Christmas concert and tour programs are sometimes lighter works."

Performances: Glen Morley's *Coquihalla Legends* (tone poem); Fred Schiptzky's *Children's Suite* (string suite); and Benjamin Britten's *Men of Good Will.*

VENTUS MUSICUS, P.O. Box 141, Redlands CA 92373. (909)793-0513. Trumpet Player: Larry Johansen. Chamber music ensemble (organ/trumpet duo). Estab. 1978. Members are professionals. Performs 4-10 concerts/year including 1-4 new works (as available). Most performances done in churches.

How to Contact: Query first. SASE. Reports in 2 months.

Music: "Most organ/trumpet material is church oriented (hymns, chants, stained glass, etc.); this is useful, but not mandatory—we play for college and A.G.O. Groups as well as church recital series. We are open to pretty much anything, except improvised jazz. We are interested in the composer's ideas, not ours. Go for it! And we'll try it."

Performances: O.D. Hall's *Crown Him*; H. Genzmer's *Sonate*; E. Schmidt's *Rhapsodia Salre.*

Tips: "Unfortunately, we have no commission money, but we do play at conferences around the country, and we can offer some exposure."

*VEREINIGTE BÜHNEN/OPERNHAUS, Kaiser Josef Platz 10, A-8010 Graz **Austria.** Phone: 0316/826451. Operndramaturgie: Johannes Frankfurter, Bernd Krispin, Dr. Peter Stalder. Opera house. Members are professionals. Performs 8 operas/year, including 1 new work. "Operas are performed in our opera house with 1271 seats, and our studio 'Thalia' with 300 seats."

How to Contact: Submit complete score and tapes of pieces. SAE and IRC.

Music: "We would primarily like to find something for our studio, 'Thalia,' some kind of chamber opera for an orchestra of 20 members and between 1 and 6 singers. Any modern operas."

Performances: Roman Haubenstuck Ramati's *Amerika* (opera, 1992); and Gerd Kühr's *Stallerhof* (opera, 1993).

*VIRGINIA OPERA, P.O. Box 2580, Norfolk VA 23501. (804)627-9545. Fax:(804)622-0058. Artistic Administrator: Jerome Shannon. Opera company. Estab. 1974. Members are professionals. Performs 450 concerts/year. Concerts are performed for school children throughout Virginia, grades K-9 at the Harrison Opera House in Norfolk, and at public/private schools in Virginia. Pays for outright purchase or by royalty.

How to Contact: Submit complete score and tape of pieces. SASE. Reports in 3 months.

Music: "Audience accessible style approximately 45 minutes in length. Limit cast list to three vocal artists of any combination. Accompanied by piano and/or keyboard. Works are performed before school children of all ages. Pieces must be age appropriate both aurally and dramatically. Musical styles are encouraged to be diverse, contemporary as well as traditional. Works are produced and presented with sets, costumes, etc." Limitations: "Three vocal performers (any combination). One keyboardist. Medium to difficult acceptable, but prefer easy to medium. Seeking only pieces which are suitable for presentation as part of an opera education program for Virginia Opera's education and outreach department. Subject matter must meet strict guidelines relative to Learning Objectives, etc. Musical idiom must be representative of current trends in opera, musical theater. Extreme dissonance, row systems not applicable to this environment."

Tips: "Theatricality is very important. New works should stimulate interest in musical theater as a legitimate art form within school children with no prior exposure to live theatrical entertainment. Composer should be willing to create a product which will find success within the educational system."

*THE DALE WARLAND SINGERS, 120 N. Fourth St., Minneapolis MN 55401. (612)339-9707. Fax: (612)339-9826. Composer in Residence: Carol Barnett. Vocal ensemble. Estab. 1972. Members are professionals. Performs 50 concerts/year including 5 new works. Commissions 5 composers or new works/year. Audience is "diverse." Performance spaces vary, including concert halls, high school/college auditoriums and churches. Pays commission.
How to Contact: Submit complete score and tape of piece(s). SASE. Reports in 6-12 months.
Music: "A cappella or with small accompanying forces; texts primarily secular; works for concert choir or vocal jazz ensember (a 'cabaret' subgroup); 5-15 minutes in length (semi-extended)." Does not wish to see "show choir material or gospel."
Performances: Veljo Tormis's *Curse Upon Iron*; Frank Martin's *Mass*; and R. Murray Schafer's *Epitaph for Moonlight* (all serious concert music).
Tips: "Send a clean readable score and the best tape possible."

WARMINSTER SYMPHONY ORCHESTRA, 524 W. Pine St., Trevose PA 19053. (215)355-7421. Music Director/Principal Conductor: Gil Guglielmi, D.M.A. Community symphony orchestra. Estab. 1966. 12 "pros" and amateurs. Performs 4 concerts/year. "We *try* to commission one composer or new work every 2-3 years." Audience is blue collar and upper middle-class. The concert hall is a local junior high school with a seating capacity of 710. "We operate on a small budget. Composers are not paid, or paid very little (negotiable)."
How to Contact: Submit complete score. Does not return material.
Music: Romantic style. Length: 10 minutes to a full symphony. Orchestration: full orchestra with no sound effects, synthesizers, computers, etc. "We play from Mozart to Tschaikovsky. Performers: we have a maximum of about 60 players. Level of difficulty: medium advanced—one grade above a good high school orchestra. We rehearse 2 hours a week so that anything written should take about 20 minutes a week rehearsal time to allow rehearsal time for the remaining selections. Our musicians and our audiences are middle-of-the-road. The composer should write in *his* style and not try to contrive a piece for us. The orchestra has a full string section, 4 horns, 3 clarinets, 3 flutes, 2 bassons, 3 trumpets, 2 oboe, 1 English horn, 3 trombones, 1 tuba, 1 harp and a full percussion section."
Performances: Al Maene's *Perla Bella* (mini symphony); David Finko's *The Wailing Wall* (tone poem); and Daniel Nightengale's *Canticle*.
Tips: "Music should be very melodious and not too contemporary. No computers, synthesizer, etc."

WAUKEGAN SYMPHONY ORCHESTRA, 39 Jack Benny Dr., Waukegan IL 60087. (708)360-4742. Director: Dr. Richard Hynson. Symphony orchestra. Estab. 1972. Members are professionals and amateurs. Performs 5 concerts/year including 1-2 new works. "We have a middle-aged and older audience, basically conservative, small town, lower-middle income. We perform in a 1,800 seat house." Pays through BMI and ASCAP.
How to Contact: Query first. SASE. Reports in 3 months.
Music: "We want conservative music, especially regarding rhythmic complexities, 4-10 minutes in length, orchestrated for wind pairs, standard brass, strings, etc., up to 4 percussionists plus timpani. The number of performers basically limited to 75 member orchestra, difficulty level should be moderate to moderately difficult, more difficulty in winds and brass than strings. We don't want aleatoric 'chance' music, pointillistic—to a large extent non-melodic music. We are always looking for beautiful music that speaks to the heart as well as the mind, music with a discernable structure is more attractive."
Performances: Tomas Svoboda's *Symphony #6*; Ron Perera's *Outermost Home*; and John LaMontaine's *Marshes of Elyan*.
Tips: "Write beautiful, listenable music. Make the composition an exercise in understanding the orchestral medium, not an academic exercise in rehearsal problems."

WAYNE CHAMBER ORCHESTRA, 300 Pompton Rd., Wayne NJ 07470. (201)595-2694. Managing Director: Sheri Newberger. Chamber orchestra. Estab. 1986. Members are professionals. Performs 4 concerts/year including 1 new work. Regional audience from North Jersey area. Attractive and modern concert hall seating 960 patrons. Pays per performance.
How to Contact: Call first. SASE. Reports in 2 months.
Music: "We are looking for new American music for a 40-piece orchestra. Our only method of funding would be by grant so music may have to tie in with a theme. Although we have not yet performed new works, we hope to in the future."

The asterisk before a listing indicates that the listing is new in this edition. New markets are often the most receptive to unsolicited submissions.

Performances: Joan Tower's *Fanfare for the Uncommon Woman No. 1*; Zwilich's *Concerto to Grosso 1985*; and Creston's *Concerto for Marimbam, Op. 21*.

WHEATON SYMPHONY ORCHESTRA, 1600 E. Roosevelt, Wheaton IL 60187. (708)668-8585. Manager: Donald C. Mattison. Symphony orchestra. Estab. 1959. Members are professionals and amateurs. Performs 3 concerts/year including 1 new work.
How to Contact: Query first. SASE. Reports in 1 month.
Music: "This is a *good* amateur orchestra that wants pieces in a traditional idiom. Large scale works for orchestra. No avant garde, 12-tone or atonal material. Pieces should be 20 minutes or less and must be prepared in 3 rehearsals. Instrumentation is woodwinds in 3s, full brass 4-3-3-1, percussion."
Performances: Jerry Bilik's *Aspects of Man* (4-section suite); Walton's *Variations on a Theme of Hindeminth's*; and Augusta Read Thomas' *A Crystal Planet*.

WOMEN'S PHILHARMONIC, Suite 218, 330 Townsend St., San Francisco CA 94107. (415)543-2297. Philharmonic orchestra. Estab. 1980. Members are professionals. Performs 15 concerts/year; performs 6 new works/year. Commissions 3 composers or new works/year. "Audience median age is 39; urban professional. Performance space is downtown hall in prime retail district with 1,100 reserved seating." Pays by commission.
How to Contact: Query first. Does not return material. Reports in 6 months.
Music: Seeks symphonic/orchestral music with or without soloist by women composers, for performance and/or inclusion in National Women Composers Resource Center database."
Performances: Carolyn Yarnell's *L*; Chen Yi's *Symphony No. 2*; and Erica Muhl's *What Is The Sound of an Angel's Voice* . . . .

*WYOMING SYMPHONY ORCHESTRA, P.O. Box 667, Casper WY 82602. (307)266-1478. Fax: (307)266-4522. Manager: Dale Bohren. Symphony orchestra. Estab. 1920. Members are professionals and amateurs. Performs 8 concerts/year including 1 new work. Audience is "composed on multiple economic backgrounds, 600-1,200 in size. Performances are held in high school auditorium which seats 1,285." Payment varies according to arrangement.
How to Contact: Query first. SASE. Reporting time varies.
Music: "We are looking for music that bridges symphonic with other styles of music (i.e., jazz and symphonic, blues and symphonic, bluegrass, country or whatever styles one may be experimenting with). Classic oriented and modern classical also welcome. Our orchestra is a well-qualified semiprofessional orchestra of 75 members that has 5 rehearsals per concert. Choral and orchestral works are welcome. As usual, we are limited mostly by budget."
Performances: Don Grace's *Frozen Roses* (orchestral poem); and Del Hudson's *Ode to the Rockies* (symphonic piece).

Fine Arts/'94-'95 Changes

The following markets appeared in the 1994 edition of *Songwriter's Market* but are absent from the 1995 edition. Most of these companies failed to respond to our request for an update of their listing for a variety of reasons. For example, they may have gone out of business or they may have requested deletion from the 1995 edition because they are backlogged with material. If we know the specific reason, it appears within parentheses.

After Dinner Opera Co., Inc.
Capital University Conservatory of Music Opera/Musical Theatre
Chamber Music in Yellow Springs, Inc.
Concordia: A Chamber Symphony (unable to contact)
The Grinnell Orchestra
The Helios String Quartet (unable to contact)
Houston Youth Symphony

Ballet
I Cantori Di New York
Idaho State—Civic Symphony
Inter School Orchestras of New York
L.A. Solo Repertory Orchestra (requested deletion)
Livingston Symphony Orchestra
Longar Ebony Ensemble Ltd.
The Louisville Orchestra
Manitoba Chamber Orchestra

Opera On The Go
PFL Management (unable to contact)
Philadelphia College of Bible
Plymouth Music Series of Minnesota (requested deletion)
River City Brass Band (requested deletion)
The Williamsburg Symphonia
Youth Orchestra of Greater Fort Worth

Resources

Organizations

The vast majority of songwriter organizations are nonprofit groups with membership open to anyone interested in songwriting. Whether local, statewide or national in scope, such organizations can provide helpful information and much-needed encouragement to amateur and professional songwriters alike.

Songwriting organizations can provide you with an abundance of different opportunities. They're great places to meet collaborators, if you're searching for a co-writer but don't know where to find one. Songwriting organizations can provide excellent forums for having your work heard and critiqued in a constructive way by other songwriters and industry professionals, helping to improve your craft. They can help keep you abreast of the latest music industry news as it relates to songwriters, and can provide tips on publishers, artists and record companies looking for new material. And, perhaps most important, these organizations give you the opportunity to expand your network of friends and contacts in the music industry, which is vital to any songwriter seeking success in the music business.

Most organizations offer regular meetings of their general membership and occasional special events such as seminars and workshops to which music industry people are invited—to share their experiences and perhaps listen to and critique demo tapes. There are songwriting organizations all over the United States. If you can't find one within an easy distance from your home, you may want to consider joining one of the national groups. These groups, based in New York, Los Angeles and Nashville, welcome members from across the country and keep them involved and informed through newsletters and magazines, regular meetings and large yearly get-togethers. They are an excellent way for writers who feel "stranded" somewhere in the middle of the country to keep up contacts and get their music heard in the major music centers.

The type of organization you choose to join depends on what you want to get out of it. Local groups can give you the friendly, supportive encouragement you need to continue in your career. Larger, national organizations can give you access to music business executives and other songwriters across the country. In the following listings, organizations describe what they have to offer.

AMERICAN MUSIC CENTER, INC., Suite 1001, 30 W. 26th St., New York NY 10010-2011. (212)366-5260. Executive Director: Nancy Clarke. Estab. 1939. For composers and performers. Members are American composers, performers, critics, publishers and others interested in contemporary concert music and jazz. Offers circulating library of contemporary music scores and advice on opportunities for composers and new music performers; disseminates information on American music. Purpose is to encourage the recognition and performance of contemporary American music. Members receive professional monthly "Opportunity Updates," eligibility for group health insurance and the right to vote in AMC elections.

AMERICAN SOCIETY OF COMPOSERS, AUTHORS AND PUBLISHERS (ASCAP), 1 Lincoln Plaza, New York NY 10023. (212)621-6000. Contacts: Lisa K. Schmidt, Michael Kerker (Musical Theatre),

BMI provides valuable services for songwriters

Royalties are the main source of income for songwriters, and whenever a song is played either on the radio or in a live performance a writer is entitled to performance royalties. Performing rights organizations such as BMI, ASCAP and SESAC were created as nonprofit entities to help songwriters collect these royalties. They charge licensing fees to radio and TV stations, clubs and concert halls to ensure that songwriters are paid for the use of their material.

Jeff Cohen

Jeff Cohen, director of writer/publisher relations at BMI, sees the role of the performing rights organization as more than just an impersonal collector of royalties for its writers. "We emphasize personal relationships with our writers and publishers," he says. "BMI provides a forum to let writers know they're not out there alone. We can be a friend, but the bottom line is to collect licensing fees and distribute them as royalties to our writers and publishers."

How do songwriters become affiliated with a performing rights organization? "BMI has an open door policy," Cohen explains. "Call the office and we'll send you an application to fill out. Or you can stop by—we have offices in New York, Nashville, Los Angeles and London. It doesn't cost a thing. I think it's important for every writer to do his or her homework, get information from all three organizations (ASCAP, BMI and SESAC), talk to everyone, take the information and go where he's most comfortable."

Once you find the performing rights organization that's right for you, it's important to realize that they're there to help—not to do the work for you. "When you deal with BMI," says Cohen, "or any other performing rights organization, keep in mind that we can best help those who help themselves. A performing rights organization does not give record contracts; it does not give publishing deals. But when we see someone who's working really hard, of course we'll return his calls and try to answer questions no matter what."

BMI also offers workshops and writers' nights for songwriters. Cohen helped establish both the BMI Collaborator's Connection and the BMI Acoustic Roundup. "The Collaborator's Connection is a forum for writers to meet other writers; for artists, managers and publishers looking for songs. We have 10 writers per session, and we interview them à la David Letterman onstage, then we play one of their songs. Afterwards we have an hour of free food and all the writers get together to talk. If you like something you hear you can approach

GET YOUR WORK INTO THE RIGHT BUYERS' HANDS!

You work hard... and your hard work deserves to be seen by the right buyers. But with the constant changes in the industry, it's not always easy to know who those buyers are. That's why you'll want to keep up-to-date and on top with the most current edition of this indispensable market guide.

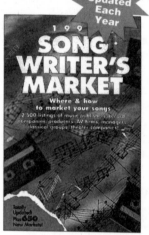

Keep ahead of the changes by ordering *1996 Songwriter's Market* today. You'll save the frustration of getting your songs returned in the mail, stamped MOVED: ADDRESS UNKNOWN. And of NOT submitting your work to new listings because you don't know they exist. All you have to do to order the upcoming 1996 edition is complete the attached order card and return it with your payment or credit card information. Order now and you'll get the 1996 edition at the 1995 price— just $21.99—no matter how much the regular price may increase! *1996 Songwriter's Market* will be published and ready for shipment in September 1995.

Keep on top of the changing industry and get a jump on selling your work with help from the *1996 Songwriter's Market*. Order today! You deserve it!

Turn over for more books to help you write and sell your songs ➡

More Great Books to Help You Sell Your Songs!

Creating Melodies
by Dick Weissman
You'll be singing all the way to the bank when you discover the secrets of creating memorable melodies—from love ballads to commercial jingles!
#10400/$18.95/144 pages

Hot off the press!
Hot Tips for Home Recording
by Hank Linderman
Discover the tricks to recording a tight, polished, professional demo! Musicians acquainted with recording technology will learn how to lay down basic tracks, add vocals, and mix to get exactly the sound they want.
#10415/$18.99/160 pages/available 10-94

Essential! Songwriter's Market Guide to Song and Demo Submission Formats
Get your foot in the door with knock-out query letters, slick demo presentation, and the best advice for dealing with every player in the industry! #10401/$19.95/160 pages

Making Money Making Music
by James Dearing
Cash-in on scores of ways to make a profitable living with your musical talent (no matter where you live). This guide covers performing as a solo or in a group, writing music for the radio, jingles and more! #10174/$18.95/180 pages/paperback

Fill out order card on reverse side and mail today!

the writer or the artist and set up a meeting." The workshop is free to all, and is held on the second Monday of every month at the Bitter End in New York City.

"We also have the BMI Acoustic Roundup, which consists of a group of songwriters getting together at a restaurant called the Cottonwood Cafe. We sit around onstage, talk about songwriting, talk about the songs, and play them acoustically. It's really laid back, very casual—and again, it's free for everyone. We wanted to provide a few nights where writers could know they have a place to go to meet other writers and people in the industry.

"At BMI, we're concerned with making sure that our affiliated writers get the best treatment. We place a high emphasis on relationships with writers, and accessibility. If you're going to call me, I'm going to answer your questions. Each of the offices is really accessible and each has events for songwriters. If you are affiliated with BMI, call us. We're there."

In conclusion, Cohen says, "I think songwriters should have confidence in their own ability, be persistent, have patience and not give up. Trust your instincts on that. If you truly believe in what you're writing, don't let anyone tell you what you can't do."

— *Cindy Laufenberg*

Ivan Alvarez (Latin Music) in New York office; or the following branch offices: Todd Brabec, Suite 300, 7920 Sunset Blvd., Los Angeles, CA 90046; Debra Cain, 2nd Floor, 3500 W. Hubbard St., Chicago, IL 60610; Connie Bradley, 2 Music Square W., Nashville, TN 37203, James Fisher, 52 Haymarket, London SW1Y 4RP **England**. Members are songwriters, composers, lyricists and music publishers. Applicants must "have at least one song copyrighted for associate membership; have at least one song commercially available as sheet music, available on rental, commercially recorded, or performed in media licensed by the Society (e.g., performed in a nightclub or radio station) for full membership. ASCAP is a membership-owned, performing right licensing organization that licenses its members' nondramatic musical compositions for public performance and distributes the fees collected from such licensing to its members based on a scientific random sample survey of performances." Primary value is "as a clearinghouse, giving users a practical and economical bulk licensing system and its members a vehicle through which the many thousands of users can be licensed and the members paid royalties for the use of their material. All monies collected are distributed after deducting only the Society's cost of doing business."
Tips: "The Society sponsors a series of writers' workshops in Los Angeles, Nashville and New York open to members and nonmembers. Grants to composers available to members and nonmembers."

*ARIZONA SONGWRITERS ASSOCIATION, Box 678, Phoenix AZ 85019. (602)973-1988. Membership Director: Gavan Wieser. Serves songwriters and musicians. "Membership is open to anyone wanting to learn the craft and business of songwriting. Our members are people of all ages (17-75 years) with interest in all kinds of music (country, rock, R&B, top 40, novelty, jingles). In addition to songwriters, members are studio owners, lyricists and working bands doing original material. We offer educational and promotional activities, and teach the business of songwriting from A-Z. Members have the chance to meet professionals and get first-hand advice and critiques on their songs on a monthly basis." Offers competitions, instruction, lectures, newsletter, performance opportunities, social outings and workshops. Open mike night on the second Wednesday of each month. "We offer a yearly seminar with panels and critique sessions made up of Los Angeles and Nashville professionals from all walks of the business. ASA gets invitations to co-sponsor song contests, perform at public events, do radio and TV spots and have special performance weeks featuring the best of our songwriter/performers. We're getting good press for our meetings and activities. Several members have had cuts from songs picked up at meetings. Local and national airplay received by several members." Applications accepted year round. Annual dues are $25 per year.

ARKANSAS SONGWRITERS, 6817 Gingerbread, Little Rock AR 72204. (501)569-8889. President: Peggy Vining. Estab. 1979. Serves songwriters, musicians and lovers of music. Any interested may join. To promote and encourage the art of songwriting. Offers competitions, instruction, lectures, newsletter, performance opportunities, social outings and workshops. Applications accepted year round. Membership fee is $15/year.

Tips: "We also contribute time, money and our energies to promoting our craft in other functions. Meetings are held on the first Tuesday of alternate months at 6:45 p.m."

*ARTS MIDWEST, Suite 310, 528 Hennepin Ave., Minneapolis MN 55403. (612)341-0755. Director of Funding Programs: Bobbi Morris. Estab. 1985. Serves composers, musicians, dancers, actors and visual artists. "Arts Midwest is a nonprofit arts organization which fosters and promotes the development of the arts in the Midwest. We are a resource for musicians, songwriters and other artists in the region which includes the states of Illinois, Indiana, Iowa, Michigan, Minnesota, North Dakota, Ohio, South Dakota and Wisconsin. Arts Midwest generates opportunities for artists and arts organizations, extending, enriching and complementing the programs and services of the member state arts agencies. Arts Midwest funding brings Midwest arts to Midwest audiences. Through funding programs like Meet The Composer/Midwest, Jazz Satellite Touring Fund, Performing Arts Touring Fund, and Dance on Tour, we encourage performing artists to travel to stages and community centers throughout the Midwest. Our Jazz Master Awards honor outstanding life-long achievements as performers, educators and preservers of the jazz tradition deserve greater recognition. We also publish a free quarterly newsletter, *Midwest Jazz*; *Applause!*, an annual catalog of Midwest performing artists; and *Insights on Jazz*, a series of five informative booklets for jazz artists, presenters, and educators." Applications are accepted throughout the year; however, "there are specific deadline periods for several of our funding programs, including the Performing Arts Touring Program, Meet the Composer, Visual Arts Fellowships, etc." Offers members competitions, lectures, performance opportunities, fellowships, workshops, touring programs and newsletter.

ATLANTIC CANADIAN COMPOSERS ASSOCIATION, 214 Jones St., Moncton, New Brunswick E1C 6K3 **Canada.** (506)388-4224. Member at Large: Richard Gibson. Estab. 1980. "Our membership consists of people who write 'serious' (as opposed to commercial, pop, jazz, industrial) music. An applicant must be resident in one of the four Atlantic Canadian provinces and must be able to demonstrate a fluency with a variety of genres of notated music. An applicant must be prepared to submit five completed scores." Offers performance opportunities. Applications accepted year round. Membership fee is 35 Canadian dollars.

*AUSTIN SONGWRITERS GROUP, P.O. Box 2578, Austin TX 78768. (512)442-TUNE. Fax: (512)288-0793. President: George Watson. Estab. 1986. Serves all ages and all levels, from just beginning to advanced. Perspective members should have an interest in the field of songwriting, whether it be for profit or hobby. The main purpose of this organization is "to educate members in the craft and business of songwriting; to provide resources for growth and advancement in the area of songwriting; and to provide opportunities for performance and contact with the music industry." The primary benefit of membership to a songwriter is "exposure to music industry professionals, which increases contacts and furthers the songwriter's education in both craft and business aspects." Offers competitions, instruction, lectures, library, newsletter, performance opportunities, evaluation services, workshops and "contact with music industry professionals through special guest speakers at meetings, plus our yearly 'Summer Songwriters Series,' which includes instruction, song evaluations, and song pitching direct to those pros currently seeking material for their artists, pub. co.'s, etc." Applications accepted year round. $35 membership fee/year.

Tips: "Our newsletter is top-quality—packed with helpful information on all aspects of songwriting—craft, business, recording and producing tips, and industry networking opportunities. (Members also receive and are included in the ASG Directory, which aids networking among the membership.)"

*THE BOSTON SONGWRITERS MARKET, P.O. Box 415, Brighton MA 02135. (617)499-6932. Executive Director: Elliott Jacobowitz. Estab. 1989. Serves songwriters. "Membership is very diverse. Members range in skill from professional to beginning level, and in age from late teens to mid-forties. Interests cover all styles and genres of music, songwriting as well as instrumental, and production and performance as well. We welcome anyone with a serious interest in songwriting or instrumental composition. We encourage professionals as well as non-professionals to join. The Boston Songwriters Workshop is a professional organization of songwriters and composers helping each other in the art, craft and business of songwriting and composition." Offers instruction, critique sessions, lectures, newsletter, performance opportunities and workshops. Applications accepted year round. $35 for Full Membership (includes free meetings and newsletter); $17.50 for Flyer Membership (includes newsletter and reduced guest fee for meetings). All memberships begin on January 1st, and are pro-rated throughout the year.

BROADCAST MUSIC, INC. (BMI), 320 W. 57th St., New York NY 10019. (212)586-2000; 8730 Sunset Blvd., Los Angeles CA 90069, (310)659-9109; and 10 Music Square E., Nashville TN 37203, (615)291-6700. President and CEO: Frances W. Preston. Senior Vice President, Performing Rights: Del R.

Bryant. Vice President, California: Rick Riccobono. Vice President, New York: Charlie Feldman. Vice President, Nashville: Roger Sovine. BMI is a performing rights organization representing over 140,000 songwriters, composers and music publishers in all genres of music, including pop, rock, country, R&B, rap, jazz, Latin, gospel and contemporary classical. "Applicants must have written a musical composition, alone or in collaboration with other writers, which is commercially published, recorded or otherwise likely to be performed." Purpose: BMI acts on behalf of its songwriters, composers and music publishers by insuring payment for performance of their works through the collection of licensing fees from radio stations, broadcast and cable TV stations, hotels, nightclubs, aerobics centers and other users of music. This income is distributed to the writers and publishers in the form of royalty payments, based on how the music is used. BMI also undertakes intensive lobbying efforts in Washington D.C. on behalf of its affiliates, seeking to protect their performing rights through the enactment of new legislation and enforcement of current copyright law. In addition, BMI helps aspiring songwriters develop their skills through various workshops, seminars and competitions it sponsors throughout the country. Applications accepted year round. There is no membership fee for songwriters; a one-time fee of $100 is required to affiliate a publishing company.

*BROADWAY ON SUNSET, Suite 9, 10800 Hesby, North Hollywood CA 91601. (818)508-9270. Fax: (818)508-1806. Executive Director: Kevin Kaufman. Estab. 1981. Sponsored by the Songwriters Guild of America as of 1992. Members are musical theater writers (composers, lyricists, librettists) at all skill levels. All styles of music and musicals accepted. Except for our Musical Theater Referral Service©, which draws from a national population, participants need to have access to the Los Angeles area to attend our programs. "We provide writers of new musicals with a structured development program that gives them a full understanding of the principles and standards of Broadway-level craft, and provides them with opportunities to test their material in front of an audience, in production at our theater, The Sunset Playhouse." Offers lectures, performance opportunities, evaluation services, workshops, instruction and musical theater referral service (free listing service for composers, lyricists and librettists looking for collaborators). Produces full productions of original musicals in their own theater, The Sunset Playhouse, located in the Duarte Center Theatre in Los Angeles County. Applications accepted year round. No membership fee per se; writers pay nominal fees to participate in classes and workshops.

CANADIAN ACADEMY OF RECORDING ARTS & SCIENCES (CARAS), 3rd Floor, 124 Merton St., Toronto, Ontario M4S 2Z2 **Canada**. (416)485-3135. Fax: (416)485-4978. Executive Director: Daisy C. Falle. Serves songwriters and musicians. Membership is open to all employees (including support staff) in broadcasting and record companies, as well as producers, personal managers, recording artists, recording engineers, arrangers, composers, music publishers, album designers, promoters, talent and booking agents, record retailers, rack jobbers, distributors, recording studios and other music industry related professions (on approval). Applicants must be affiliated with the Canadian recording industry. Offers newsletter, performance opportunities, Canadian artist record discount program, nomination and voting privileges for Juno Awards and discount tickets to Juno awards show. Also discount on trade magazines and complimentary Juno Awards CD. "CARAS strives to foster the development of the Canadian music and recording industries and to contribute toward higher artistic standards." Applications accepted year-round. Membership fee is $45/year. Applications accepted from individuals only, not from companies or organizations.

CANADIAN AMATEUR MUSICIANS/MUSICIENS AMATEURS DU CANADA (CAMMAC), #8224, 1751 Richardson, Montreal, Quebec H3K 1G6 **Canada**. (514)932-8755. Fax: (514)932-9811. Administrative Assistant: Veronica A. Leisse. Estab. 1953. Serves amateur musicians of all ages and skill levels. "CAMMAC is a nonprofit organization that provides opportunities for amateur musicians of all ages and levels to develop their skills in a supportive and non-competitive environment, and to enjoy making music together. We provide contact with musicians of varying levels and interests—the perfect testing ground for any number of styles and challenges. We also offer a variety of musical workshops, including singing, playing and improvisation at our summer camp at Lake McDonald (Arundel, Québec)." Offers performance opportunities, library, instruction, newsletter, workshops and summer camp (families and individuals). Applications accepted year-round. Membership fee is Adult: $35, Family: $50, Student and Senior: $20, Group $50 plus $2/member for library borrowing privileges.

*COMPOSERS GUILD, 40 N. 100 West, Box 586, Farmington UT 84025. (801)451-2275. Resident: Ruth Gatrell. Estab. 1963. Serves all ages, including children. Musical skill varies from beginners to professionals. An interest in composing is the only requirement. The purpose of this organization is to "help composers in every way possible through classes, workshops and symposiums, concerts, composition contests and association with others of similar interests." Offers competitions, instruction, lectures, newsletter, performance opportunities, evaluation services and workshops. Applications accepted year-round. Membership fee is $25/year. Associate memberships for child, spouse, parent, grandchild or grandparent of member: $15. "Holds four concerts/year. January: Composer's Spectacular featuring contest winners; June: Farmington Composers Concert in the Park; July: Americana, Patriotic and American Scene compositions; and December: New Sounds for Christmas. Annual Composition Contest: Deadline August 31. Fees: Less than 7 minutes: $5/members, $15/non-dues-paying; 7 minutes or more, including multi-movement works: $10/members, $20/non-members. Comments from judges given on all compositions. Return of materials if mailers and postage furnished. Categories: Arrangements, Children's, Choral, Instrumental, Jazz/New Age, Keyboard, Orchestra/Band, Popular, Vocal Solo and Young Composer (18 or under on Aug. 31). Age groups: 16-18, 13-15, 10-12, 7-9, 6 or under. Awards in each category: First prize $100, 2nd prize $50, 3rd prize: $25. Best of Contest in lieu of 1st prize: $500. Honorable Mention and Best of Age Group awards also given."

CONNECTICUT SONGWRITERS ASSOCIATION, Box 1292, Glastonbury CT 06033. (203)659-8992. Executive Director: Don Donegan. "We are an educational, nonprofit organization dedicated to improving the art and craft of original music. Founded in 1979 by Don Donegan, CSA has grown to become one of the best known songwriter's associations in the country. Membership in the CSA admits you to 16-24 seminars/workshops/song critique sessions per year at 5 locations throughout Connecticut. Out of state members may mail in songs for critique at our meetings. Noted professionals deal with all aspects of the craft and business of music including lyric writing, music theory, music technology, arrangement and production, legal and business aspects, performance techniques, song analysis and recording techniques. CSA also offers showcases and concerts which are open to the public and designed to give artists a venue for performing their original material for an attentive, listening audience. CSA benefits have helped United Cerebral Palsy, Muscular Dystrophy, group homes, Hospice, world hunger, libraries, nature centers, community centers and more. CSA shows encompass ballads to bluegrass and Bach to rock. Our monthly newsletter, *Connecticut Songsmith*, offers free classified advertising for members, and has been edited and published by Bill Pere since 1980. Annual dues are $40; senior citizen and full time students $20; organizations $80. Memberships are tax-deductible as business expenses or as charitable contributions to the extent allowed by law."

DALLAS SONGWRITERS ASSOCIATION, 7139 Azalea, Dallas TX 75230. (214)750-0916. President: Beverly Houston. Estab. 1988. Serves songwriters and lyricists of Dallas/Ft. Worth metroplex. Members are adults ages 18-65, Dallas/Ft. Worth area songwriters/lyricists who aspire to be professionals. Purpose is to provide songwriters an opportunity to meet other songwriters, share information, find co-writers and support each other through group discussions at monthly meetings; to provide songwriters an opportunity to have their songs heard and critiqued by peers and professionals by playing cassettes and providing an open mike at monthly meetings and by offering contests judged by publishers; to provide songwriters opportunities to meet other music business professionals by inviting guest speakers to monthly meetings and the Dallas Songwriters Seminar, which is held annually each April; and to provide songwriters opportunities to learn more about the craft of songwriting and the business of music by presenting mini-workshops at each monthly meeting. "We offer a chance for the songwriter to learn from peers and industry professionals and an opportunity to belong to a supportive group environment to encourage the individual to continue his/her songwriting endeavors." Offers competitions, field trips, instruction, lectures, newsletter, performance opportunities, social outings, workshops and seminars. "Our members are eligible to join the Southwest Community Credit Union and for discounts at several local music stores and seminars." Applications accepted year round. Membership fee is $35 US, $45 Foreign. When inquiring by phone, please leave complete mailing address and phone number where you can be reached day and night.

THE DRAMATISTS GUILD, INC., 234 W. 44th St., New York NY 10036. (212)398-9366. Executive Director: Andrew B. Farber. The Dramatists Guild is the professional association of playwrights, composers and lyricists, with more than 7,000 members across the country. All theater writers, whether produced or not, are eligible for Associate membership ($75/year); those who are engaged in a drama-related field but are not a playwright are eligible for Subscribing membership ($50/year); students enrolled in writing degree programs at colleges or universities are eligible for Student membership ($25/year); writers who have been produced on Broadway, Off-Broadway or on the main stage of a resident theater are eligible for Active membership ($125/year). The Guild offers its members the following activities and services: use of the Guild's contracts (including the Approved Production Contract for Broadway, the Off-Broadway contract, the LORT contract, the collaboration agreements for both musicals and drama, the 99 Seat Theatre Plan contract, the Small Theatre contract and the Underlying Agreements contract); advice on all theatrical contracts including Broadway, Off-Broadway, regional, showcase, Equity-waiver, dinner theater and collaboration contracts); a nationwide toll-free number for all members with business or contract questions or problems; advice and information on a wide spectrum of issues affecting writers; free and/or discounted ticket service; symposia led by experienced professionals in major cities nationwide; access to two health insurance programs and a group term life insurance plan; a reference library; a spacious and elegant meeting room which can accommodate up to 50 people for readings and auditions on a rental basis to members; and a Committee for Women. The Guild's publications are: *The Dramatists Guild Quarterly*, a journal containing articles on all aspects of the theater, an annual marketing directory with up-to-date information on agents, grants, producers, playwriting contests, conferences and workshops; and *The Dramatists Guild Newsletter*, issued 8 times a year, with announcements of all Guild activities and current information of interest to dramatists. Only subscribing members receive *The Dramatists Guild Quarterly*.

THE FOLK ALLIANCE, P.O. Box 5010, Chapel Hill NC 27514. (919)542-3957. Contact: Art Menius. Estab. 1989. Serves songwriters, musicians and folk music and dance organizations. Members are organizations and individuals involved in traditional and contemporary folk music and dance in the US and Canada. Members must be active in the field of folk music (singers/songwriters in any genre— blues, bluegrass, Celtic, Latino, old-time, etc.). The Folk Alliance serves members through education, advocacy, field development, professional development, networking and showcases. Offers newsletter, performance opportunities, social outings, workshops and "database of members, organizations, presenters, folk radio, etc." Applications accepted year round. Membership fee is $35/year/individual (voting); $75-350/year for organizational. "The Folk Alliance hosts its annual conference in late February at different locations in the US and Canada. 1995 site: Portland, OR; 1996: Washington, DC; 1997: Toronto, Ontario. We *do not* offer songwriting contests."

FORT BEND SONGWRITERS ASSOCIATION, P.O. Box 1273, Richmond TX 77406. (713)665-4676. Info line: 713-CONCERT (Access Code FBSA). Contact: Membership Director. Estab. 1991. Serves "any person, amateur or professional, interested in songwriting or music. Our members write pop, rock, country, rockabilly, gospel, R&B, children's music and musical plays." Open to all, regardless of geographic location or professional status. The FBSA provides its membership with help to perfect their songwriting crafts. The FBSA provides instruction for beginning writers and publishing and artist tips for the more accomplished writer. Offers competitions, field trips, instruction, lectures, newsletter, performance opportunities, workshops, mail-in critiques and collaboration opportunities. Applications accepted year-round. Membership fees are: Regular: $35; Renewals; $25; Family or Band: $45; Associate: $20; Business: $150; and Lifetime: $250. For more information send SASE.

GOSPEL MUSIC ASSOCIATION, 7 Music Circle N., Nashville TN 37203. (615)242-0303. Membership Coordinator: Mark Smeby. Estab. 1964. Serves songwriters, musicians and anyone directly involved in or who supports gospel music. Professional members include advertising agencies, musicians, agents/ managers, composers, retailers, music publishers, print and broadcast media, and other members of the recording industry. Associate members include supporters of gospel music and those whose involvement in the industry does not provide them with income. The primary purpose of the GMA is to promote the industry of gospel music, and provide professional development series for industry members. Offers library, newsletter, performance opportunities and workshops. Applications accepted year round. Membership fee is $50/year (professional) and $25/year (associate).

THE GUILD OF INTERNATIONAL SONGWRITERS & COMPOSERS, Sovereign House, 12 Trewartha Rd., Praa Sands, Penzance, Cornwall TR20 9ST **England**. Phone: (0736)762826. Fax: (0736)763328. Secretary: C.A. Jones. Serves songwriters, musicians, record companies, music publishers, etc. "Our members are amateur and professional songwriters and composers, musicians, publishers, independent record publishers, studio owners and producers. Membership is open to all persons throughout the world of any age and ability, from amateur to professional. The Guild gives advice and services relating to the music industry. A free magazine is available upon request with an SAE or 3 IRC's. We provide contact information for artists, record companies, music publishers, industry organizations; free copyright service; *Songwriting & Composing Magazine*; and many additional free services." Applications accepted year round. Annual dues are £20 in the U.K.; £25 in E.E.C. countries; £25 overseas. (Subscriptions in pounds sterling only).

*INDEPENDENT MUSIC ASSOCIATION, P.O. Box 609, Ringwood NJ 07456. (201)831-1317. Fax: (201)831-8762. President: Don Kulak. Estab. 1989. Serves independent record companies, distributors, musicians and songwriters. Members are those "serious about marketing their music." The purpose of this organization is to market and distribute independently produced music. "We provide contact with record labels looking for new material as well as information on forming a record label and distributing your own material." Offers instruction, newsletter, workshops, CD and cassette manufacturing discounts, trade show representation, the IMA syndicated radio program and how-to books on marketing and distribution. Applications accepted year round. Membership fee: $75/year.

INDEPENDENT MUSICIANS CO-OP, P.O. Box 571205, Murray UT 84157. (801)268-0174. President: Mark McLelland. Estab. 1992. "Our members range from young to old, from interested listener to accomplished songwriter/performer. Prospective members must be living in the United States, have a love for new music and be willing to help promote the independent music market. The IMC is a network sales organization dedicated to selling and promoting independent music product. Our members help to promote and sell member tapes and CDs to friends, family and associates. Our goal is to create a mid-level market for the independent artist/songwriter. Songwriters will have new chances at release, as our independent artists finally have a market to sell their product. We are creating a 'middle class' in the music industry. More releases will translate into more songwriters being paid. Call or write for free information." Offers performance opportunities, newsletter and product distribution. Applications accepted year-round. Membership fee: $40 1st year, $30/year renewal.

*INDIANAPOLIS SONGWRITERS, P.O. Box 44724, Indianapolis IN 46244-0724. (317)257-9200. Vice President: Liz Efroymson. Estab. 1983. Purpose is "to create an affiliation of serious-minded songwriters, promote the artistic value of the musical composition, the business of music and recognition for the songwriter and his craft." Sponsors quarterly newsletter, monthly meetings, periodic showcases and periodic seminars and workshops. "The monthly critiques are helpful for improving songwriting skills. The meetings offer opportunities to share information concerning publishing, demos, etc. In addition, it provides the opportunity for members to meet co-writers." Membership fee: $20/year.

*INTERNATIONAL BLUEGRASS MUSIC ASSOCIATION (IBMA), 207 E. Second St., Owensboro KY 42303. (502)684-9025. Executive Director: Dan Hays. Estab. 1985. Serves songwriters, musicians and professionals in bluegrass music. "IBMA is a trade association composed of people and organizations involved professionally and semi-professionally in the bluegrass music industry, including performers, agents, songwriters, music publishers, promoters, print and broadcast media, local associations, recording manufacturers and distributors. Voting members must be currently or formerly involved in the bluegrass industry as full or part-time professionals. A songwriter attempting to become professionally involved in our field would be eligible. We promote the bluegrass music industry and unity within it. IBMA publishes bimonthly *International Bluegrass*, holds an annual trade show/convention during September in Owensboro, represents our field outside the bluegrass music community, and compiles and disseminates databases of bluegrass related resources and organizations. The primary value in this organization for a songwriter is having current information about the bluegrass music field and contacts with other songwriters, publishers, musicians, and record companies." Offers social outings, workshops, liability insurance, rental car discounts, consultation and databases of record companies, radio stations, press, organizations and gigs. Applications accepted year round. Membership fee for a non-voting patron $20/year; for an individual voting professional $40/year; for an organizational voting professional $110/year.

INTERNATIONAL LEAGUE OF WOMEN COMPOSERS, Abilene Christian University, ACU Box 8274, Abilene TX 79699. (915)674-2044. Fax: (915)674-2232. Estab. 1975. Serves women composers of serious concert music. "Members are women composers and professional musicians, music libraries, institutions and organizations. Full composer membership is open to any woman composer whose seriousness of intent has been demonstrated in 1 or more of the following ways: (1) by any single degree in composition (if the degree is not recent, some evidence of recent activity should be offered); (2) by holding a current teaching position at the college level; (3) by having had a serious work published; (4) by having had a work performed at a recognized symposium or by professional musicans; or (5) by submitting 2 compositions to the Executive Board for review, exhibiting competence in scoring for chamber ensemble. Admission is governed neither by stylistic nor regional bias; however, primarily educational music is not considered sufficient. The ILWC is devoted to creating and expanding opportunties for, and documenting information about, women composers of serious music. This organization will help composers stay informed of various career/performance opportunties plus allow them to participate in projects spear-headed by ILWC." Offers competitions, journal and performance opportunities. Applications accepted year-round. Annual dues are $25 for individuals; $15 for students/senior citizens; $35 for institutions/organizations.

INTERNATIONAL SONGWRITERS ASSOCIATION LTD., 37b New Cavendish St., London WI **England**. (071)486 5353. Membership Department: Anna M. Sinden. Serves songwriters and music publishers. "The ISA headquarters is in Limerick City, Ireland, and from there it provides its members with assessment services, copyright services, legal and other advisory services and an investigations service, plus a magazine for one yearly fee. Our members are songwriters in more than 50 countries worldwide, of all ages. There are no qualifications, but applicants under 18 are not accepted. We provide information and assistance to professional or semi-professional songwriters. Our publication, *Songwriter*, which was founded in 1967, features detailed exclusive interviews with songwriters and music publishers, as well as directory information of value to writers." Offers competitions, instruction, library and newsletter. Applications accepted year round. Membership fee for European writers is £19.95; for non-European writers, US $30.

THE LAS VEGAS SONGWRITERS ASSOCIATION, P.O. Box 42683, Las Vegas NV 89116-0683. (702)459-9107. President: Betty Kay Miller. Estab. 1980. "We are an educational, nonprofit organization dedicated to improving the art and craft of the songwriter. We offer quarterly newsletters, monthly general information meetings, workshops three times a month and seminars held quarterly with professionals in the music business." Dues are $20 per year. Members must be at least 18 years of age.

THE LOS ANGELES SONGWRITERS SHOWCASE (LASS), Box 93759, Hollywood CA 90093. (213)467-7823. Fax: (213)467-0531. Showcase Hotline: (213)467-0533. Co-Directors: Len H. Chandler, Jr. and John Braheny. General Manager: Stephanie Perom. Membership Director: Josh Bernard. "The Los Angeles Songwriters Showcase (LASS) is a nonprofit service organization for songwriters, founded in 1971 and sponsored by Broadcast Music, Inc. (BMI). LASS also provides counseling and conducts classes and seminars. At our weekly Showcase, we feature Cassette Roulette™, in which a different publisher every week critiques songs submitted on cassette that night; and Pitch-A-Thon™, in which a different producer or record company executive every week screens songs for his/her current recording projects and/or acts for their labels. The Showcase takes place every Tuesday night in front of an audience of songwriters and the music industry guests; there is no prescreening necessary. LASS also produces an annual Songwriters Expo in October." General membership: $120/year. Professional membership: $150/year. Included in both "general" and "professional" membership benefits are: priorities to have tapes listened to first at Pitch-A-Thon™ sessions; discounts on numerous items such as blank tapes, books, demo production services, tapes of Songwriters Expo sessions and other seminars; discounts on admission to the weekly showcase; career counseling (in person or by phone) and a subscription to the LASS 'Songwriters Musepaper,' a magazine for songwriters (also available to non-members for $19 bulk rate/$29 first class).

LOUISIANA SONGWRITERS ASSOCIATION, P.O. Box 80425, Baton Rouge LA 70898-0425. (504)924-0804. President: Janice Calvert. Vice Presidents, Membership: Lea Ann Schroeder/Beverly Locker. Serves songwriters. "LSA has been organized to educate songwriters in all areas of their trade, and promote the art of songwriting in Louisiana. We are of course honored to have a growing number of songwriters from other states join LSA and fellowship with us. LSA membership is open to people interested in songwriting, regardless of age, musical ability, musical preference, ethnic background, etc. One of our goals is to work together as a group to establish a line of communication with industry professionals in order to develop a music center in our area of the country. LSA offers competitions, lectures, library, newsletter, directory, marketing, performance opportunities, workshops, discounts on various music related books and magazines, discounts on studio time, and we are developing a service manual that will contain information on music related topics, such as copyrighting, licensing, etc." General membership dues are $25/year.

LOUISVILLE AREA SONGWRITERS' COOPERATIVE, P.O. Box 16, Pewee Valley KY 40056. President: Paul M. Moffett. Estab. 1986. Serves songwriters and musicians of all ages, races and musical genres. "The Louisville Area Songwriters' Cooperative is a nonprofit corporation dedicated to the development and promotion of songwriting. Membership is open to any person in the Louisville area (and beyond) who is interested in songwriting. We offer a songwriter showcase 4 times/year, a series of tapes of songs by members of the cooperative, meetings, speakers, the LASC newsletter, a songwriting contest, referral for collaboration, promotion and song plugging to local, regional and national recording artists and occasional bookings for performing members." Applications accepted year round. Dues are $25/year.

MEMPHIS SONGWRITERS' ASSOCIATION, 1857 Capri St., Memphis TN 38117. (901)763-1957. President: Juanita Tullos. Estab. 1973. Serves songwriters, musicians and singers. Age limit: 18 years and up. No specific location requirement. Must be interested in music and have the desire to learn the basics of commercial songwriting. "We instruct potential songwriters on how to structure their songs and correctly use lyrics, commercially. We critique their material. We help them obtain copyrights and give them a chance to expose their material to the right people, such as publishers and A&R people. We hold monthly workshops, instructing members in the Commercial Music Techniques of songwriting. We have an annual Songwriters Showcase where their material is performed live for people in the publishing and recording professions and the general public. We have an annual Shindig, for bands and musicians and an annual seminar." Offers competitions, instruction, lectures, newsletter, performance opportunities and workshops. Applications accepted year-round. Annual dues: $25.
Tips: "Our association was founded in 1973. We have a charter, by laws and a board of directors (8). All directors are professionals in the music field. We are a nonprofit organization. No salaries are paid. Our directors donate their services to our association. We have a president, vice president, secretary, treasurer, music instructor and consultant, production manager, assistant production manager and executive director. Suggestions and feedback are welcome. Participation is welcomed by all who are interested."

MICHIGAN SONGWRITERS ASSOCIATION, 28935 Flanders Dr., Warren MI 48093. (313)771-8145. President: Terri Senecal. Estab. 1990. Serves songwriters, musicians, artists and beginners. "Members are from NY, IL, MI, OH, etc. with interests in country, pop, rock and gospel. The main purpose of

this organization is to educate songwriters, artists and musicians in the business of music." MSA offers performance opportunities, evaluation services, instruction, newsletter and workshops. Applications accepted year-round. Membership fee is $35/year, $50 for people who have cut a record!
Tips: "To be educated in this field is the most important thing in your career; without any knowledge you can bet you will be used."

MIDWESTERN SONGWRITERS ASSOCIATION, P.O. Box 282007, Columbus OH 43228. (614)274-2169. President: Al VanHoose. Estab. 1978. Serves songwriters. All interested songwriters are eligible—either amateur or professional residing in the midwestern region of US. Main purpose is the education of songwriters in the basics of their craft. Offers competitions, instruction, lectures, library, newsletter, weekly tip sheet, social outings and workshops. Applications accepted year-round. Membership fee is $20/year, pro-rated at $5 per calendar quarter (March, June, September, December).
Tips: "We do not refer songwriters to publishers or artists—we are strictly an educational organization."

MISSOURI SONGWRITERS ASSOCIATION, INC., 693 Green Forest Dr., Fenton MO 63026. (314)343-6661. President: John G. Nolan, Jr. Serves songwriters and musicians. No eligibility requirements. "The MSA (a non-profit organization founded in 1979) is a tremendously valuable resource for songwriting and music business information outside of the major music capitals. Only with the emphasis on education can the understanding of craft and the utilization of skill be fully realized and in turn become the foundation for the ultimate success of MSA members. Songwriters gain support from their fellow members when they join the MSA, and the organization provides 'strength in numbers' when approaching music industry professionals." As a means toward its goals the organization offers: (1) an extremely informative newsletter; (2) Annual Songwriting Contest; prizes include: CD and/or cassette release of winners, publishing contract, free musical merchandise and equipment, free recording studio time, plaque or certificate; (3) Annual St. Louis Original Music Celebration featuring live performances, recognition, showcase, radio simulcast, videotape for later broadcast and awards presentation; (4) seminars on such diverse topics as creativity, copyright law, brainstorming, publishing, recording the demo, craft and technique, songwriting business, collaborating, etc.; (5) workshops including song evaluation, establishing a relationship with publishers, hit song evaluations, the writer versus the writer/artist, the marriage of collaborators, the business side of songwriting, lyric craft, etc; (6) services such as collaborators referral, publisher contacts, consultation, recording discounts, musicians referral, library, etc. "The Missouri Songwriters Association belongs to its members and what a member puts into the organization is returned dynamically in terms of information, education, recognition, support, camaraderie, contacts, tips, confidence, career development, friendships and professional growth." Applications accepted year round. Tax deductible dues are $50/year.

*MUSICIANS CONTACT SERVICE, 7315 Sunset Blvd., Hollywood CA 90046. (213)851-2333. Estab. 1969. For musicians and bands seeking each other on the west coast."Provides 24-hour computerized call-in gig line of working bands needing players. Musicians and groups leave tapes, photos and résumés. Also for composers and lyricists seeking each other for collaboration."

NASHVILLE SONGWRITERS ASSOCIATION INTERNATIONAL (NSAI), 15 Music Square W., Nashville TN 37203. (615)256-3354. Executive Director: Pat Rogers. Purpose: a not-for-profit service organization for both aspiring and professional songwriters in all fields of music. Membership: Spans the United States and several foreign countries. Songwriters may apply in one of four annual categories: Active ($55—for songwriters who have at least one song contractually signed to a publisher affiliated with ASCAP, BMI or SESAC); Associate ($55—for songwriters who are not yet published or for anyone wishing to support songwriters); Student ($25—for full-time college students or for students of an accredited senior high school); Professional ($100—for songwriters who derive their primary source of income from songwriting or who are generally recognized as such by the professional songwriting community). Membership benefits: music industry information and advice, song evaluations by mail, quarterly newsletter, access to industry professionals through weekly Nashville workshop and several annual events, regional workshops, use of office facilities, discounts on books and blank audio cassettes, discounts on NSAI's three annual instructional/awards events. There are also "branch" workshops of NSAI. Workshops must meet certain standards and are accountable to NSAI. Interested coordinators may apply to NSAI.

NATIONAL ACADEMY OF SONGWRITERS (NAS), Suite 780, 6381 Hollywood Blvd., Hollywood CA 90028. (213)463-7178 or (800)826-7287. Executive Director: Dan Kirkpatrick. A nonprofit organization dedicated to the education and protection of songwriters. Estab. 1973. Offers group legal discount; toll free hotline; *SongTalk* newspaper with songwriter interviews, collaborators network and tipsheet; plus Los Angeles based *SongTalk* seminar series featuring top names in songwriting, song evaluation workshops, song screening sessions, open mics and more. "We offer services to all songwriter members from street-level to superstar: substantial discount on books and tapes, song evaluation through the mail, health insurance program and mail-in publisher pitches for members. Our services provide education in the craft and opportunities to market songs." Membership fees are $75 general; $125 professional; $200 gold.

*THE NATIONAL ASSOCIATION OF COMPOSERS/USA, Box 49652, Barrington Station, Los Angeles CA 90049. (310)541-8213. President: Marshall Bialosky. Estab. 1932. Serves songwriters, musicians and classical composers. "We are of most value to the concert hall composer. Members are serious music composers of all ages and from all parts of the country, who have a real interest in composing, performing, and listening to modern concert hall music. The main purpose of our organization is to perform, publish, broadcast and write news about composers of serious concert hall music – mostly chamber and solo pieces. Composers may achieve national notice of their work through our newsletter and concerts, and the fairly rare feeling of supporting a non-commercial music enterprise dedicated to raising the musical and social position of the serious composer." Offers competitions, lectures, performance opportunities, library and newsletter. Applications accepted year round. $15 membership fee; $35 for Los Angeles and New York chapter members.
Tips: "99% of the money earned in music is earned, or so it seems, by popular songwriters who might feel they owe the art of music something, and this is one way they might help support that art. It's a chance to foster fraternal solidarity with their less prosperous, but wonderfully interesting classical colleagues at a time when the very existence of serious art seems to be questioned by the general populace."

NETWORK OF LYRICISTS & SONGWRITERS, INC., P.O. Box 27501, Houston TX 77227-7501. (713)264-4330. President: John St. Wrba. Estab. 1991. "NLS is made up of every age group and every skill level. Members are interested in every genre of music including but not limited to country, pop, rock, gospel, alternative and children's. Members do not need to know how to read or write music or play a musical instrument. Some of our most active volunteers are simply music lovers. Our membership is open to anyone. The main purpose of the Network of Lyricists & Songwriters, Inc. is to educate and promote lyricists, songwriters and performers of original music. We are a nonprofit organization. We provide opportunities for songwriters to learn about all aspects of the music industry through our publication, *SONGNET* and through workshops and seminars. They also have plenty of opportunities to showcase their songs and themselves via performance showcases, open mikes, song contests and song pitch sessions. The regular yearly membership fee is $30. Senior citizens and students receive a discount of $10 off the regular fee. Cross memberships are strongly encouraged by offering members of any other arts-related organization a yearly fee of $20. Proof of membership is required. Bands and families may join for $40. We conduct an annual songwriting competition. The deadline for entry is November of each year."

*NEW DRAMATISTS, 424 W. 44th St., New York NY 10036. (212)757-6960. Service organization dedicated to the development of playwrights. "We sponsor a composer-librettist studio each year where 5 of our member writers work with 5 selected composers." For information about playwright membership, the studio and New Dramatists call (212)757-6960.

NEW ENGLAND SONGWRITERS/MUSICIANS ASSOCIATION, #11-312, 270 Lafayette Rd., Seabrook NH 03874. (800)448-3621. Director: Peter C. Knickles. "Our organization serves all ages and all types of music. We focus primarily on the business of songwriting and overall, the music business. We have done various co-promotions of seminars with BMI in the past and may continue to do so in the future. Membership is free. Call to be on our mailing list and receive our free quarterly newsletter."

*NEW JERSEY AND PENNSYLVANIA SONGWRITERS ASSOC., 226 E. Lawnside Ave., Westmont NJ 08108. (609)858-3849. President and Founder: Bruce M. Weissberg. Estab. 1985. Serves songwriters and musicians. Members are all ages 16-80, representing all types of music from Delaware, Philadelphia and North and South Jersey area. Must be serious about songwriting. Provides networking, information center and promotional center for workshops and guest speakers. "Primary value is that it enables musicians to network with other songwriters in the area." Offers lectures, library, newsletter, performance opportunities and workshops. Applications accepted year round. Membership fee is $30/year (single), $35/year (band). "Our group is always interested in new ideas, new interested guest speakers and a true professional type of atmosphere."

NORTH FLORIDA CHRISTIAN MUSIC WRITERS ASSOCIATION, P.O. Box 10394, Jacksonville FL 32247. (904)786-2372. President: Jackie Hand. Estab. 1974. "People from all walks of life who promote Christian music. Not just composers. Not just performers. But anyone who wants to share today's message in song with the world. No age limit. Anyone interested in promoting Christian music is invited to join. If you are talented in several areas you might be asked to conduct a training session or workshop. Your expertise is wanted and needed by our group. The group's purpose is to serve God by using our God given talents and abilities and to assist our fellow songwriter, getting their music in the best possible form to be ready for whatever door God chooses to open for them concerning their music. Members works are included in songbooks published by our organization – also biographies." Offers competitions, performance opportunities, field trips, instruction, newsletter, workshops and critique. Applications accepted year-round. Membership fee is $15/year. $20 for husband/wife team. Make checks payable to Jackie Hand.

Tips: "If you are serious about your craft, you need to fellowship with others who feel the same. A Christian songwriting organization is where you belong if you write Christian songs."

NORTHERN CALIFORNIA SONGWRITERS ASSOCIATION, Suite 211, 855 Oak Grove Ave., Menlo Park CA 94025. (415)327-8296. Fax: (415)327-0301, or (800)FORSONG (California and Nashville only). Executive Director: Ian Crombie. Serves songwriters and musicians. Estab. 1979. "Our 1,200 members are lyricists and composers from ages 16-80, from beginners to professional songwriters. No eligibility requirements. Our purpose is to provide the education and opportunities that will support our writers in creating and marketing outstanding songs. NCSA provides support and direction through local networking and input from Los Angeles and Nashville music industry leaders, as well as valuable marketing opportunities. Most songwriters need some form of collaboration, and by being a member they are exposed to other writers, ideas, critiquing, etc." Offers annual Northern California Songwriting Conference, "the largest event in northern California. This 2-day event held in September features 16 seminars, 50 screening sessions (over 1,200 songs listened to by industry profesionals) and a sunset concert with hit songwriters performing their songs." Also offers monthly visits from major publishers, songwriting classes, seminars conducted by hit songwriters ("we sell audio tapes of our seminars – list of tapes available on request"), a monthly newsletter, monthly performance opportunities and workshops. Applications accepted year round. Dues: $60/year; $30 extra for industry tipsheet (sent out on a quarterly basis).

Tips: "NCSA's functions draw local talent and nationally recognized names together. This is of a tremendous value to writers outside a major music center. We are developing a strong songwriting community in Northern California. We serve the San Jose, Monterey Bay, East Bay and San Francisco area and we have the support of some outstanding writers and publishers from both Los Angeles and Nashville. They provide us with invaluable direction and inspiration."

PACIFIC NORTHWEST SONGWRITERS ASSOCIATION, Box 98564, Seattle WA 98198. (206)824-1568. "We're a nonprofit association, and have served the songwriters of the Puget Sound area since 1977. Our focus is on professional songwriting for today's commercial markets. We hold monthly workshops and publish a quarterly newsletter. Our workshops are a great place to meet other writers, find collaborators, critique each other's songs and share news and encouragement. Our members get immediate contact with hundreds of the biggest national artists, producers, publishers and record companies. Members also get free legal advice from our staff attorney. All this for only $35 per year. We welcome new members. If you have any questions, just give us a call."

PITTSBURGH SONGWRITERS ASSOCIATION, 408 Greenside Ave., Canonsburg PA 15317. (412)745-9497. President: Frank J. DeGennaro. Estab. 1983. Serves songwriters. "Any age group is welcome. Current members are from mid-20s to mid-50s. All musical styles and interests are welcome. Country and pop predominate the current group; some instrumental, dance, rock and R&B also. Composers and lyricists in group. Our organization wants to serve as a source of quality material for publishers and other industry professionals. We assist members in developing their songs and getting their works published. Also, we provide a support group for area songwriters, network of contacts and collaboration opportunities. We offer field trips, instruction, lectures, library and social outings. Annual dues are $25. We have no initiation fee." Interested parties please contact membership coordinator: Roger Horne, 175 Melody Lane, Washington PA 15301.

PORTLAND MUSIC ASSOCIATION, P.O. Box 6723, Portland OR 97228. (503)223-9681. President: Peter Mott. Serves songwriters, musicians, booking agents and club owners. Members are all ages – amateur and professional musicians, music industry businesses, technical support, personnel, music lovers and songwriters. "Main purpose is in the development and advancement of music and related business opportunities within our metro area and to the international music industry." Benefits include networking opportunities, educational seminars, contests, new talent showcase, local music awards and Musicians' Ball. Offers songwriter contest, lectures, newsletters, performance opportunities, workshops and songwriter/musician referral. Annual dues are general $20; band $25; business $50; association $50; corporate $100.

PORTLAND SONGWRITERS ASSOCIATION, Suite 351, 11919 N. Jantzen Ave., Portland OR 97217. (503)657-6078. "The P.S.A. is a nonprofit organization dedicted to providing educational and networking opportunities for songwriters. All songwriters, lyricists, and musicians are welcome. The association offers monthly workshops, a Songwriters Showcase, weekly open mikes and seminars by industry pros for all members and non-members. Our goal is to provide you with the knowledge and contacts you will need to continue your growth as a songwriter and gain access to publishing, recording and related music markets. For more information please call us."

RECORDING INDUSTRY ASSOCIATION OF AMERICA, Suite 200, 1020 19th St., NW, Washington DC 20036. Chairman and CEO: Jason S. Berman. Estab. 1952. "The RIAA is a trade association whose member companies create, manufacture or distribute approximately 90 percent of all legitimate sound recordings produced and sold in the United States." Members include US-based manufacturers of sound recordings. RIAA has extensive programs on behalf of US-based sound recording industry in the areas of government relations, international trade and anti-piracy enforcement. The RIAA also coordinates industry market research and is the certifying body for gold and platinum records. Publications produced by the association include an annual sport/statistical overview and an industry newsletter.

RED RIVER SONGWRITERS ASSOCIATION, P.O. Box 412, Ft. Towson OK 74735. (405)326-9453. President: Dan Dee Beal. Estab. 1991. Members range from beginners to accomplished writers of all ages. Primarily country music. "The main purpose of this organization is to help songwriters get record cuts, obtain information and continually learn more about songwriting." Offers lectures, performance opportunities, library, evaluation services, instruction, newsletter and workshops. Applications accepted year round. Membership fee is $10/year; $2/month dues.

*RIVER VALLEY SONGWRITERS, Rt. 1 Box 51A, Dover AR 72837. (501)331-3453. President: Don Brooks. Estab. 1991. The main purpose is to promote lyrical and musical skills, to assist members in learning the craft and help members get in touch with publishers, artists and related people in industry. Offers competitions, performance opportunities, instruction and workshops. Applications accepted year round. "There are no structural dues. If monetary assistance is needed, we ask members for help. For beginning writers or writers who decide to 'get serious,' what can be learned at local organizations is invaluable."

ROCKY MOUNTAIN MUSIC ASSOCIATION, Suite 210, Union Station, 1701 Wynkoop, Denver CO 80222. (303)623-6910. Director of Membership: Andrea Ferguson. Estab. 1987. "We are open to all ages. Members are original musical performers and songwriters and range in skills from amateur to professional. Membership is open to anyone interested in the music industry. The only requirement is submiting an application with appropriate membership dues. The main purpose of the Rocky Mountain Music Assoc. is to encourage and support the development and performance of original music by providing educational programs broadening public appreciation, facilitating national access and exposure to regional talent and acting as central database for the regional community. The primary benefit of membership is to help in exposing talent and honing skills." Offers competitions, lectures, performance opportunities, evaluation services, newsletter and workshops. Applications accepted year round. Membership fee is $25 individual, $50 band, $100 business.

SAN FRANCISCO FOLK MUSIC CLUB, 885 Clayton, San Francisco CA 94117. (415)661-2217. Serves songwriters, musicians and anyone who enjoys folk music. "Our members range from age 2 to 80. The only requirement is that members enjoy, appreciate and be interested in sharing folk music. As a focal point for the San Francisco Bay Area folk music community, the SFFMC provides opportunities for people to get together to share folk music, and the newsletter *The Folknik* disseminates information. We publish 2 songs an issue (6 times a year) in our newsletter, our meetings provide an opportunity to share new songs, and at our camp-outs there are almost always songwriter workshops." Offers library, newsletter, informal performance opportunities, annual free folk festival, social outings and workshops. Applications accepted year round. Membership fee is $5/year.

SANTA BARBARA SONGWRITERS' GUILD, Box 22, Goleta CA 93116. (805)967-8864. President: Gary Heuer. Estab. 1981. "We are a nonprofit organization for aspiring songwriters, performers, those interested in the music industry, and anyone interested in original music. Our members are able to meet other songwriters, learn more about the craft of songwriting, get their songs heard and to network. The Guild sponsors monthly cassette tape presentations to L.A. publishers called Songsearches. We also sponsor workshops, classes and lectures on music, record production, song marketing, music composition and lyric writing." Membership is $35/year.

SESAC INC., 421 W. 54th St., New York NY 10019. (212)586-3450; 55 Music Square E., Nashville TN 37203. (615)320-0055 President and Chief Operating Officer: Vincent Candilora. Vice President: Dianne Petty, Nashville. Serves writers and publishers in all types of music who have their works performed by radio, television, nightclubs, cable TV, etc. Purpose of organization is to collect and distribute performance royalties to all active affiliates. "Prospective affiliates are requested to present a demo tape of their works which is reviewed by our Screening Committee." For possible affiliation, call Nashville or New York for appointment.

SOCIETY OF COMPOSERS, AUTHORS AND MUSIC PUBLISHERS OF CANADA (SOCAN), Head Office: 41 Valleybrook Dr., Don Mills, Ontario M3B 2S6 **Canada**. (416)445-8700. Fax: (416)445-7108. General Manager: Michael Rock. (415)445-8700. The purpose of the society is to collect music user license fees and distribute performance royalties to composers, lyricists, authors and music publishers. The SOCAN catalogue is licensed by ASCAP, BMI and SESAC in the United States.

SODRAC INC., Suite 420, 759, Victoria Square, Montreal, Quebec H2Y 2J7 **Canada**. (514)845-3268. Fax: (514)845-3401. Membership Department: Robert Hurtubise. Estab. 1985. Serves those with an interest in songwriting and music publishing no matter what their age or skill level is. "Members must have written or published at least one musical work that has been reproduced on an audio (CD, cassettte, LP) or audio-visual support (TV, video). The main purpose of this organization is to administer the reproduction rights of its members: authors/composers and publishers. The new member will benefit of a society working to secure his reproduction rights (mechanicals)." Applications accepted year-round. "There is no membership fee or annual dues. SODRAC retains a commission currently set at 10% for amounts collected in Canada and 5% for amounts collected abroad." SODRAC is the only Reproduction Rights Society in Canada where both songwriters and music publishers are represented, directly and equally.

SONGWRITERS ASSOCIATION OF WASHINGTON, Suite 632, 1377 K St. NW, Washington DC 20005. (301)654-8434. President: Jordan Musen. Estab. 1979. "S.A.W. is a nonprofit organization committed to providing its members with the means to improve their songwriting skills, learn more about the music business and gain exposure in the industry. S.A.W. sponsors various events to achieve this goal, such as workshops, song swaps, seminars, meetings, showcases and the Mid-Atlantic song contest. S.A.W. publishes *S.A.W. Notes*, a quarterly newsletter containing information on the music business, upcoming events around the country, and provides free classifieds to its members. For more information regarding membership write or call."

THE SONGWRITERS GUILD OF AMERICA, 1500 Harbor Blvd, Weehawken NJ 07087-6732. (201)867-7603. West Coast: Suite 317, 6430 Sunset Blvd., Hollywood CA 90028. (213)462-1108. Nashville: 1222 16th Ave. S., Nashville TN 37203. (615)329-1782. "The Songwriters Guild of America is the nation's largest, oldest, most respected and most experienced songwriters' association devoted exclusively to providing songwriters with the services, activities and protection they need to succeed in the business of music." President: George David Weiss. Executive Director: Lewis M. Bachman. National Projects Director: George Wurzbach. West Coast Regional Director: Aaron Meza. Nashville Regional Director: Kathy Hyland. "A full member must be a published songwriter. An associate member is any unpublished songwriter with a desire to learn more about the business and craft of songwriting. The third class of membership comprises estates of deceased writers. The Guild contract is conceded to be the best available in the industry, having the greatest number of built-in protections for the songwriter. The Guild's Royalty Collection Plan makes certain that prompt and accurate payments are made to writers. The ongoing Audit Program makes periodic checks of publishers' books. For the self-publisher, the Catalogue Administration Program (CAP) relieves a writer of the paperwork of publishing for a fee lower than the prevailing industry rates. The Copyright Renewal Service informs members a year in advance of a song's renewal date. Other services include workshops in New York and Los Angeles, free Ask-A-Pro rap sessions with industry pros, critique sessions, collaborator service and newsletters. In addition, the Guild reviews your songwriter contract on request (Guild or otherwise); fights to strengthen songwriters' rights and to increase writers' royalties by supporting legislation which directly affects copyright; offers a group medical and life insurance plan; issues news bulletins with essential information for songwriters; provides a songwriter collaboration service for younger writers; financially evaluates catalogues of copyrights in connection with possible sale and estate planning; operates an estates administration service; and maintains a nonprofit educational foundation (The Songwriters Guild Foundation)."

SONGWRITERS OF OKLAHOMA, 211 W. Waterloo Rd., Edmond OK 73034. (405)348-6534. President: Harvey Derrick. Estab. 1983. Serves songwriters and musicians, professional writers, amateur writers, college and university faculty, musicians, poets and others from labor force as well as retired individuals. Age range is from 18 to 90. "Must be interested in writing and composing and have a desire to help others in any way possible. We have members from coast to coast. We offer workshops, critique sessions, contests, civic benefits, education of members on copyright, contracts, publishers, demos, record companies, etc., as well as a sounding board of peers, education, camaraderie and sharing of knowledge." Offers competitions, field trips, instruction, lectures, library, newsletter, performance opportunities, social outings and workshops. Applications accepted year round. Membership fee is $15/year.

SONGWRITERS OF WISCONSIN, P.O. Box 874, Neenah WI 54957-0874. (414)725-1609. Director: Tony Ansems. Estab. 1983. Serves songwriters. "Membership is open to songwriters writing all styles of music. Residency in Wisconsin is recommended but not required. Members are encouraged to bring tapes and lyric sheets of their songs to the meetings, but it is not required. We are striving to improve the craft of songwriting in Wisconsin. Living in Wisconsin, a songwriter would be close to any of the workshops and showcases offered each month at different towns. The primary value of membership for a songwriter is in sharing ideas with other songwriters, being critiqued and helping other songwriters." Offers competitions, field trips, instruction, lectures, newsletter, performance opportunities, social outings, workshops and critique sessions. Applications accepted year round. $15 subscription fee for newsletter.

Tips: "Songwriters of Wisconsin now offers four critique meetings each month. For information call: Fox Valley chapter, Dana Erlandson (414)498-3412; Central Wisconsin chapter, Debra Abel (715)345-7146; Milwaukee chapter, Joe Warren (414)475-0314; La Crosse chapter, Jeff Cozy (608)781-4391."

*SOUTHERN SONGWRITERS GUILD, INC., P.O. Box 6817, Shreveport LA 71136-6817. (318)425-4515. Public Relations Officer: Tommy Cassel. Estab. 1983. Serves business owners, office and government workers, clergy, laborers, musicians, etc. No restrictions on geographic location, professional status, musical interest, etc. "Our main interest is to share knowledge with our membership, in order to create better quality material before presenting it to prospective users." The primary benefit of membership is education, an opportunity to meet prominent writers and entertainers as well as business promoters. Offers competitions, lectures, performance opportunities, evaluation services, instruction, newsletter, workshops and annual songwriter contest. Applications accepted year round. Membership $30/year.

SOUTHWEST VIRGINIA SONGWRITERS ASSOCIATION, P.O. Box 698, Salem VA 24153. (703)389-1525. President: Sidney V. Crosswhite. Estab. 1981. 80 members—all ages—all levels—mainly country and gospel and rock but other musical interests too. "Prospective members are subject to approval by SVSA Board of Directors. The purpose of SVSA is to increase, broaden and expand the knowledge of each member and to support, better and further the progress and success of each member in songwriting and related fields of endeavor." Offers performance opportunities, evaluation services, instruction, newsletter, workshops, monthly meetings, monthly newsletter. Application accepted year-round. Membership fee is $15 one time fee (initiation); $12/year—due in January.

*THE TENNESSEE SONGWRITERS ASSOCIATION, Box 2664, Hendersonville TN 37077. (615)824-4555 or (615)969-5967. Executive Director: Jim Sylvis. Serves songwriters. "Our membership is open to all ages and consists of both novice and experienced professional songwriters. The only requirement for membership is a serious interest in the craft and business of songwriting. Most of our members are local, but we also accept out-of-state memberships. Our main purpose and function is to educate and assist the songwriter, both in the art/craft of songwriting and in the business of songwriting. In addition to education, we also provide an opportunity for camaraderie, support and encouragement, as well a chance to meet co-writers. Our members often will play on each others' demo sessions. We also critique each others' material and offer suggestions for improvement, if needed. We offer the following to our members: 'Pro-Rap'—once a month a key person from the music industry addresses our membership on their field of specialty. They may be writers, publishers, producers and sometimes even the recording artists themselves. 'Pitch-A-Pro'—once a month we schedule a publisher, producer or artist who is currently looking for material, to come to our meeting and listen to songs pitched by our members. Annual Awards Dinner—honoring the most accomplished of our TSA membership during the past year. Tips—letting our members know who is recording and how to get their songs to the right people. Other activities—a TSA summer picnic, parties throughout the year, and opportunities to participate in music industry-related charitable events, such as the annual Christmas For Kids, which the TSA proudly supports." Applications accepted year round. Membership runs for one year from the date you join. Membership fee is $25/year.

*TEXAS MUSIC ASSOCIATION, Box 2664, Austin TX 78768. (512)441-7111. Estab. 1981. Local chapters in Austin, Dallas and San Antonio. Serves songwriters, musicians and music industry professionals. Voting members must have significant professional involvement in the music industry; non-voting (associate) membership is open to everyone who supports Texas music. The TMA is the principal trade association for the Texas music industry, offering educational and professional development programs, newsletters, awards programs and lobbying for the industry's interests. Networking with professionals working in other fields of the music business (such as publishers, managers, agents, publicists, studio personnel, etc.) Offers lectures, newsletter, workshops, group health insurance, credit union and discount long distance phone service. Applications accepted year-round. General membership (voting) $50/yr. Company membership (voting) $150/yr. (All full-time employees qualify for benefits.) Associate membership (nonvoting) $25/yr. "TMA members are also eligible for discounted registration fees at the annual South By Southwest Music and Media Conference in Austin. Songwriters can benefit from TMA membership by taking advantage of our many member services, our networking opportunities and our educational and professional development programs."

*TREASURE COAST SONGWRITERS ASSN (TCSA), P.O. Box 7066, Port St. Lucie FL 34985-7066. (407)879-4779. Fax: (407)879-1947. Co-Directors: Kriss Wagner and Judy Welden. Estab. 1993. A service organization for and about songwriters in conjunction with the National Academy of Songwriters, Los Angeles. Serves youth, 13-19, in "Youth in Songwriting" group; age range of other members, 20-85; varying levels of ability, from beginning writer to professional writers with substantial catalogs, publishing track records, radio airplay and releases. General Members—no requirement except desire to write and learn. Professional Members—at least 1 commercially released song, or a substantial marketable catalog, but no commercial releases. Gold Members—at least 1 song on RIAA-certified gold release. Offers competitions, lectures, performance opportunities, evaluation services, instruction, newsletter, workshops and local radio airplay through station-sponsored contests. Applications accepted year round. Membership fee is $45 general, $60 professional, $100 gold, $10 teen (13-19 years old only). Those with financial hardship can work as volunteers to entitle them to membership (except for Gold status.)

UTAH SONGWRITERS ASSOCIATION (USA), P.O. Box 71325, Salt Lake City UT 84107. (801)596-3058. Secretary/Treasurer: Marie Vosgerau. Estab. 1984. "Anyone who is interested in songwriting may join. Primarily we want to promote the craft of songwriting. USA is a support group for songwriters. We distribute information; teach workshops on how to write better songs; showcase members original material. Provides song analyses, contest opportunities; seminars with professional music business people. The newsletter, *The Melody Line*, gives valuable information on contests, publishers looking for material, tips, etc. Workshops and showcases build confidence. Annual seminar with publishers, etc." Offers a songwriting contest, performance opportunities, evaluation services, instruction, newsletter, workshops. Contribute talents and other items to worthy benefit causes. Applications accepted year-round. Membership fee is $25 per member/year or $30 for a family membership/year.
Tips: "The USA exchanges newsletters with many songwriting associations across the United States. We welcome any exchange of ideas with other songwriting associations."

VERMONT SONGWRITERS ASSOCIATION, RD 2 Box 277, Underhill VT 05489. (802)899-3787. President: Bobby Hackney. Estab. 1991. "Membership open to anyone desiring a career in songwriting, or anyone who seeks a supportive group to encourage co-writing, meeting other songwriters, or to continue their songwriting endeavors." Purpose is to give songwriters an opportunity to meet industry professionals at monthly meetings and seminars, to have their works critiqued by peers and to help learn more about the craft and the complete business of songwriting. Offers competitions, instruction, lectures, library, newsletter, performance opportunities and workshops. Applications accepted year-round. Membership fee is $30/year.
Tips: "We are a nonprofit association dedicated to creating opportunities for songwriters. Even though our office address in in Underhill, Vermont, our primary place of business is in Burlington, Vermont, where monthly meetings and seminars are held."

THE VIRGINIA ORGANIZATION OF COMPOSERS AND LYRICISTS, P.O. Box 34606, Richmond VA 23234. (804)733-5908. Vocal Coordinator: Cham Laughlin. Membership Director: Steve Roberts. Estab. 1986. Songwriters of all ages, all styles, all skill levels. "Applicants must have an interest in songwriting, recording or musical production of original material. The main purpose of this organization is educational—to teach songwriters about the business of songwriting, song structure and musical and lyrical composition. We offer a wealth of information from many sources—other songwriter groups, newsletters and publications. Offers competitions, lectures, performance opportunities, field trips, evaluation services (free), newsletter and a TV show featuring members. Applications accepted year round. Membership fee as of March 31, 1994—$20 annually.
Tips: "Networking is a very important part of this business—we offer our members a lot of information through our meetings and newsletter and the opportunity to network with us and others in the business. It takes a lot of time and a real commitment if you are going to make it work."

VOLUNTEER LAWYERS FOR THE ARTS, 6th Floor, 1 E. 53rd St., New York NY 10022. (212)319-2910. Estab. 1969. Serves songwriters, musicians and all performing, visual, literary and fine arts artists and groups. Offers legal assistance and representation to eligible individual artists and arts organizations who cannot afford private counsel. Also sells publications on arts-related issues. In addition, there are affiliates nationwide who assist local arts organizations and artists. Offers conferences, lectures, seminars and workshops. Call for information.
Tips: VLA now offers a monthly copyright seminar—"Copyright Basics," for songwriters and musicians as well as artists in other creative fields.

*WASHINGTON AREA MUSIC ASSOCIATION, 1690 36th St., NW, Washington DC 20007. (202)338-1134. Fax: (703)237-7923. President: Mike Schreibman. Estab. 1985. Serves songwriters, musicians and performers, managers, club owners and entertainment lawyers; "all those with an interest in the Washington music scene." The organization is designed to promote the Washington music scene and increase its visibility. Its primary value to members is its seminars and networking opportunities. Offers lectures, newsletter, performance opportunities and workshops. Applications accepted year round. Annual dues are $30.

WESTERN NORTH CAROLINA SONGWRITER'S ASSOC. INC., P.O. Box 72, Alexander NC 28701. (704)683-9105. President: Henry C. Tench. Estab. 1991. Serves songwriters and musicians. Comprised of persons 18 years or older who want to write lyrics, songs and musicians both professional and amateur. Members are welcome from all states who are trying to learn or better the craft of songwriting in general. "Endeavors to assist those interested in becoming great songwriters through a series of meetings, critiques, workshops and other educational means available. We are serious but still have fun. Association with other songwriters, locally as well as nationally. Serious songwriters need to study their craft as well as have them critiqued in a constructive way and make contacts from other parts of the country. We take this to be serious business on our part and will handle it in a professional manner." Offers competitions, field trips, instruction, lectures, library, newsletter, performance opportunities, social outings and workshops. Applications accepted year round. One time initiation fee of $20, then $24/year.

Tips: "Application must be approved by board. If you are serious about learning the craft of songwriting, come on and participate and support your local as well national songwriting organizations. We at WNCSA, Inc. will assist all who are sincere in their endeavor to excel in the songwriter's profession."

Workshops

Evaluation, suggestions, feedback and motivation—all are important to the aspiring songwriter. A songwriting organization may provide these, but to gain an idea of how your music stacks up in the larger world of music, alternatives are needed. Conferences and workshops provide a means for songwriters to have songs evaluated, hear suggestions for further improvement and receive feedback and motivation from industry experts in a broader context. They are also excellent places to make valuable industry contacts.

Usually these workshops take place in the music hubs: New York, Los Angeles and Nashville. In the past few years, major regional conferences have gained a lot of attention. Also, organizations exist that offer traveling workshops on just about every songwriting topic imaginable—from lyric writing and marketing strategy to contract negotiation. More small and mid-size cities with strong songwriter organizations are running their own workshops, drawing on resources from within their own group or bringing in professionals from the music centers.

A workshop exists to address every type of music. There are programs for songwriters, performers of all styles, musical playwrights and much more. Many also include instruction and suggestions on related business topics. The following list includes national and local workshops with a brief description of what each offers. Write or call any that interest you for further information.

APPEL FARM ARTS AND MUSIC FESTIVAL, Box 888, Elmer NJ 08318. (609)358-2472. Artistic Director: Sean Timmons. Estab. Festival: 1989; Series: 1970. "Our annual open air festival is the highlight of our year-round Performing Arts Series which was established to bring high quality arts programs to the people of South Jersey. Festival includes acoustic and folk music, blues, etc." Programs for songwriters and musicians include performance opportunities as part of Festival and Performing Arts Series. Programs for musical playwrights also include performance opportunities as part of Performing Arts Series. Festival is a one-day event held in June, and Performing Arts Series is held year-round. Both are held at the Appel Farm Arts and Music Center, a 176-acre farm in Southern New Jersey. Up to 20 songwriters/musicians participate in each event. Participants are songwriters, individual vocalists, bands, ensembles, vocal groups, composers, individual instrumentalists and dance/mime/ movement. Participants are selected by demo tape submissions. Applicants should send a press packet, demonstration tape and biographical information. Application materials accepted year round. Faculty opportunities are available as part of residential Summer Arts Program for children, July/August.

*ARCADY MUSIC FESTIVAL, P.O. Box 780, Bar Harbor ME 04609. (207)288-3151. Executive Director: Dr. Melba Wilson. Estab. 1980. Promotes classical chamber music, chamber orchestra concerts, master classes and a youth competition in Maine. Offers programs for performers. Workshops take place year round in several cities and towns in Eastern Maine. 30-50 professional, individual instrumentalists participate each year. Performers selected by invitation. "Sometimes we premiere new music by unknown songwriters in some of the concerts. They might be invited to work with our musicians."

ASPEN MUSIC FESTIVAL AND SCHOOL, P.O. Box AA, Aspen CO 81612. (303)925-3254. Fax: (303)925-3802. Estab. 1949. Promotes classical music by offering programs for composers. Offers several other music programs as well. Master classes in composition offered 3 times/week. School and Festival run June to August in Aspen CO. Participants are amateur and professional composers, individual instrumentalists and ensembles. Send for application. Charges $2,000 for full 9 weeks, $1,350 for one of two 4½ week sessions. Advanced Master Class in composition offered 1st half session only. Scholarship assistance is available.

BMI-LEHMAN ENGEL MUSICAL THEATRE WORKSHOP, 320 W. 57th St., New York NY 10019. (212)830-2515. Director of Musical Theatre: Norma Grossman. Estab. 1961. "BMI is a music licensing company, which collects royalties for affiliated writers. We have departments to help writers in jazz, concert, Latin, pop and musical theater writing." Offers programs "to musical theater composers and lyricists. The BMI-Lehman Engel Musical Theatre Workshops were formed in an effort to refresh and stimulate professional writers, as well as to encourage and develop new creative talent for the musical theater." Each workshop meets one afternoon a week for two hours at BMI, New York. Participants are professional songwriters, composers and playwrights. "BMI-Lehman Engel Musical Theatre Workshop Showcase presents the best of the workshop to producers, agents, record and publishing company execs, press, directors for possible option and production." Call for application. Tape and lyrics of 3 compositions required with application. "BMI nows sponsors a jazz composers workshop. For more information call Burt Korall at (212)586-2000."

BROADWAY TOMORROW PREVIEWS, % Broadway Tomorrow Musical Theatre, Suite 53, 191 Claremont Ave., New York NY 10027. Artistic Director: Elyse Curtis. Estab. 1983. Purpose is the enrichment of American theater by nurturing *new musicals*. Offers series in which composers living in New York City area present scores of their new musicals in concert. 2-3 composers/librettists/lyricists of same musical and 1 musical director/pianist participate. Participants are professional singers, composers and opera/musical theater writers. Submission by recommendation of past participants only. Submission is by audio cassette of music, script if completed, synopsis, cast breakdown, résumé, reviews, if any, acknowledgement postcard and SASE. Participants selected by screening of submissions. Programs are presented in fall and spring with possibility of full production of works presented in concert. No entry fee.

*CMJ MUSIC MARATHON, Suite 400, 11 Middle Neck Rd., Great Neck NY 11021-2301. (516)466-6000. Fax: (516)466-7159. Marketing Director: Ken Park. Estab. 1981. "A yearly conference focusing on new artist development in all genres of popular music. The conference is four exhilarating days of panel discussions, workshops, exhibits and live music showcases focusing on the new progressive music being played on college and alternative radio across the country. The conference is held in New York City and is attended by over 6,000 songwriters, musicians, radio programmers and music industry executives. You name it, they're there. CMJ Music Marathon Live! showcases feature over 350 bands/ performers and are held at over 35 clubs and venues throughout New York City. Showcase performers are chosen from demo tape auditions. Send for application. Deadline: July (domestic), June (international). Call or write for this year's dates and location."

*FIRST NIGHT, INC., Suite 927, Statler Office Building, 20 Park Plaza, Boston MA 02116. (617)542-1399. Fax: (617)426-9531. Estab. 1976. "First Night, the annual New Year's Eve celebration through the arts in Boston, is a festival which includes more than 275 performers and installations of the visual, performing, media and literary arts at over 70 indoor and outdoor locations on December 31. Proposals are accepted for all types of music including but not limited to folk, traditional, ethnic, new and classical. First Night issues a 'Call to Artists,' accepting proposals in all artistic disciplines. Proposals are reviewed by panelists in a peer review process. Artists whose proposals are accepted are paid fees by First Night, Inc. Anyone is eligible. Proposal deadline is March 1995." Event is held throughout the city of Boston, including "churches, historic halls, professional theaters, corporate halls, school gymnasiums, community theaters, etc." Over 1,000 mostly professional songwriters, bands, composers, individual vocalists and instrumentalists participate in each event. Participants are selected by proposal process. Send or call for guidelines and deadline. No entry fee.

FOLK ALLIANCE ANNUAL CONFERENCE, Box 5010, Chapel Hill NC 27514. (919)542-3997. Contact: Art Menius. Estab. 1989. Conference/workshop topics change each year. Conference takes place mid-February and lasts 4 days at a different location each year. 650 amateur and professional musicians participate. "Offers songwriter critique sessions." Artist showcase participants are songwriters, individual vocalists, bands, ensembles, vocal groups and individual instrumentalists. Participants are selected by demo tape submission. Applicants should write for application form. Closing date for application is May 31. Application fee $15 for members, $50 for non-members. Charges $75 on acceptance. Additional costs vary from year to year. For 1994 the cost was $135 in advance, which covers 3 meals, a dance, workshops and our showcase. Performers' housing is separate for the event, which is usually held in Convention hotel. 1995: Portland, OR; 1996: Washington DC; 1997: Toronto, Ontario.

*GUELPH SPRING FESTIVAL, Edward Johnson Music Foundation, P.O. Box 1718, Guelph, Ontario N1H 6Z9 **Canada**. (519)821-3210. Artistic Director: Simon Wynberg. Estab. 1968. "We are basically a 3-4 week festival of the performing arts, with an emphasis on professional performers. We strive to bring together the best international and Canadian talent, to promote emerging Canadian talent and new music. We promote opera, chamber music, choral music and some jazz. We regularly commission new works. In addition to concerts, the Edward Johnson Music Competition is for student musicians from Wellington County and Waterloo Region. A national vocal competition is held every 5 years for Canadian singers. Cash scholarships and awards are given." Festival lasts for 3-4 weeks in May. Participants are professional composers, vocalists, instrumentalists, bands, orchestras, choirs, ensembles, opera/musical theater writers and vocal groups. Participants are selected by the artistic director. Applicants should express interest by letter.

*INDEPENDENT LABEL FESTIVAL, 600 S. Michigan Ave., Chicago IL 60605. Executive Director: Leopoldo Lastre. Estab. 1993. An annual conference promoting all types of independent music. Offers programs for songwriters, composers and performers, such as seminars, workshops and showcases. Offers showcases year-round. "Workshops take place in the Fall, generally September or October in downtown Chicago (usually in or around Columbia College). Participants are professional songwriters, bands, composers, individual vocalists and instrumentalists, managers, promoters, and professionals in the music industry." Participants are selected by demo tape audition or invitation. Send demo and press kit. Closing date for application is September 1.

KERRVILLE FOLK FESTIVAL, Kerrville Festivals, Inc., P.O. Box 1466, Kerrville TX 78029. (210)257-3600. Founder/President: Rod Kennedy. Estab. 1972. Hosts 3-day songwriters school and new folk concert competition sponsored by the Kerrville Music Foundation. Programs held in late spring and late summer. Spring festival lasts 18 days and is held outdoors at Quiet Valley Ranch. Around 110 acts participate. Performers are professional instrumentalists, songwriters and bands. "Now hosting an annual 'house concert' seminar to encourage the establishment and promotion of monthly house concerts for traveling singers/songwriters to provide additional dates and income for touring." Participants selected by submitting demo tape, by invitation only. Send cassette, promotional material and list of upcoming appearances. "Songwriter schools are $100 and include breakfast, experienced professional instructors, camping on ranch and concerts. Rustic facilities—no electrical hookups. Food available at reasonable cost. Audition tapes accepted at P.O. Box 1466, Kerrville, TX 78029."

MUSIC BUSINESS SEMINARS, LTD., #11-312, 270 Lafayette Rd., Seabrook NH 03874. (800)448-3621. Contact: Peter C. Knickles. "Now in its eighth year MBS, Ltd., presents 'Doing Music & Nothing Else: The Music Business Weekend Seminar.' The program is a two-day long, classroom style, multi-media educational experience that is presented in 24 major cities each year. Seminar is for all ages, all styles of music, bands and soloists, who are pursuing a career in original music songwriting, recording and performing. Learn how to establish goals, attract a songwriting or recording contract, book profitable gigs, raise capital and much, much more. Aftercare opportunities include toll free counseling with the instructor, A&R Tip Sheet/Showcase program and free directories (A&R). Seminar is also available on 12 audio tapes with workbook. This is the only music seminar in US with a money back guarantee. Call for 2-year complimentary quarterly journal subscription and seminar brochure."

*MUSICAL THEATRE WORKS, INC., 440 Lafayette St., New York NY 10003. (212)677-0040. Literary Manager: Andrew Barrett. Estab. 1983. "We develop and produce new works for the musical theater: informal readings, staged readings and workshops of new musicals." Functions year-round. Participants are amateur and professional composers and songwriters and opera/musical theater writers. Participants are selected through a critique/evaluation of each musical by the Literary Manager and his staff. To contact, send complete script, cassette and SASE to the above address.

NATIONAL MUSIC THEATER CONFERENCE, 234 W. 44th St., New York NY 10036. (212)382-2790. Artistic Director: Paulette Haupt. Estab. 1978. Sponsored by the Eugene O'Neill Theater Center. 8-10 songwriters/musicians participate in each event. Participants are professional composers, opera/musical theater writers, lyricists, playwrights in collaboration with composers. "The Conference offers composers, lyricists and book writers the opportunity to develop new music theater works of all forms during a 2-4 week residency at the O'Neill Theater Center in Waterford, CT. Some works are given publicly staged readings; others are developed in private readings during the conference with artistic staff and dramaturgs. All works selected are developed over at least a 2-3 month period. A professional company of approximately 20 singer/actors provides the writers with daily musical and dramatic readings during the Conference period. Staged works are read with script in hand, with minimal lighting and no physical properties, to allow flexibility for day-to-day rewrites. The Conference is held in August of each year. Participants are selected by Artistic Director and a panel of theater professionals. Composers and writers selected receive room, board and a stipend." Send SASE for application after Sept. 15.

*NEW MUSIC SEMINAR, 632 Broadway, New York NY 10012. (212)473-4343. Fax: (212)353-3162. Vice President of Sales: Anita Daly. Estab. 1978. "NMS is a yearly seminar covering all forms of new music." Offers programs for songwriters and performers. Workshops take place during the summer. 1994 seminar was held at the New York Sheraton Hotel & Towers in New York City. Over 8,000 amateur and professional songwriters, composers, individual vocalists, bands and individual instrumentalists participate in each workshop. Participants are selected by registration. Send for application.

Registration up to the day of the seminar. Fee: $300/$380/$440, depending on time of registration.

*NORFOLK CHAMBER MUSIC FESTIVAL/YALE SUMMER SCHOOL, 96 Wall St., New Haven CT 06520. (203)432-1966. Director: Joan Panetti. Manager: Michael Geller. Estab. 1941. The Norfolk Festival/School offers training and performances, including a 2-week seminar in June specializing in a particular ensemble medium, followed by a 6-week intensive chamber music session. The Festival/School is geared towards the standard chamber music ensembles; string quartets, woodwind quintets, brass quintets and ensembles, including piano. Each student receives an Ellen Battell Stoeckel scholarship, which covers all costs except for administrative fees (covers room, board, faculty, music, etc.) Offered in summer only—mid-June through mid-August. 65-80 songwriters/musicians participate. Participants are young professionals, ensembles and individual instrumentalists and are selected by audition in person. Submit demonstration tape for consideration. Auditions are held in New Haven, CT and New York, NY—early to mid-March each year. Send for application or call (203)432-1966. Closing date for application is early to mid-February (some exceptions may apply). Application fee $35. 2-week session runs $280 and 6-week session runs approximately $600 (covers administrative fees). Students are housed in the town of Norfolk with host families in groups of 1 to 3/home. The festival takes place on the beautiful 70-acre Ellen Battell Stoeckel Estate which includes the 1,100-seat Music Shed, various barns and cabins for practice and coachings.

*ORFORD FESTIVAL, Orford Arts Centre, Box 280, Magog, Quebec J1X 3W8 **Canada**. (819)843-3981. Artistic Director: Agnès Grossman. Estab. 1951. "Each year, the Centre d'Arts Orford produces up to 30 concerts in the context of its Music Festival. It receives artists from all over the world in classical and chamber music." Offers master classes for young talented music students, young professional classical musicians and chamber music ensembles. Programs offered during summer only. Master classes last 7-8 weeks and take place at Orford Arts Centre during July and August. 250 students participate each year. Participants are selected by demo tape submissions. Send for application. Closing date for application is six months before festival. Scholarships for qualified students. Registration fees $45 (Canadian). Tuition fees $225 (Canadian)/week. Accommodations $250 (Canadian).

*PHILADELPHIA MUSIC CONFERENCE, P.O. Box 29363, Philadelphia PA 19125. (215)426-4109. Fax: (215)426-4138. Showcase Director: Adam McLaughlin. Estab. 1992. "The purpose of the PMC is to bring together rock, hip hop and acoustic music for 3 days of panels and four nights of showcases. Offers programs for songwriters, composers and performers. "We present 45 panels on topics of all facets of the music industry; 160 showcases at clubs around the city at night. Also offer a DJ cutting contest." Held annually; 1994 conference at the Penn Tower Hotel on the University of Pennsylvania campus in Philadelphia on November 3-6. 1,400 amateur and professional songwriters, composers, individual vocalists, bands, individual instrumentalists, attorneys, managers, agents, publishers, A&R, promotions, club owners, etc. participate each year. "As per showcase application, participants are selected by independent panel of press, radio and performing rights organizations." Send for application. Deadline: July 1. Fee: $15 showcase application fee. "The Philadelphia Music Conference is one of the fastest-growing and exciting events around. Our goal is not just to make the Philadelphia Music Conference one of the biggest in America, but to make it one of the best. We will continue to build upon our ideas and successes to keep this a dynamic event that is innovative, informative and fun."

SONGCRAFT SEMINARS, Suite 113, 441 E. 20th St., New York NY 10010-7515. (212)674-1143. Estab. 1986. Year-round classes for composers and lyricists conducted by teacher/consultant Sheila Davis, author of *The Craft of Lyric Writing, Successful Lyric Writing* and *The Songwriter's Idea Book*. The teaching method, grounded in fundamental principles, incorporates whole-brain writing techniques. The objective: To express your unique voice. All courses emphasize craftsmanship and teach principles that apply to every musical idiom—pop, theater, or cabaret. For details on starting dates, fees and location of classes, write or call for current listing.
Successful Lyric Writing: A 3-Saturday course. Three 6-hour classes on the fundamental principles of writing words for and to music. Required text: *Successful Lyric Writing.* Held 3 times a year at The New School. Limited to 12.
Beyond the Basics: An 8-week workshop open to all "grads" of the *Successful Lyric Writing* Basics Course. It features weekly assignments and in-depth criticism to help writers turn first drafts into "music-ready" lyrics. Held four times a year at The Songwriters Guild of America (SGA).
Song by Song by Sondheim: A one-day seminar focused on the elements of fine craftsmanship exemplified in the words and music of Stephen Sondheim, America's pre-eminent theater writer. Significant songs are played and analyzed from the standpoint of form, meter, rhyme, literary devices and thematic development. Attendees are helped to apply these elements to their own writing. Held twice a year at The New School.
Whole-Brain Creativity: A five-week workshop that puts you in touch with your thinking/writing style through an understanding of split-hemispheric specialization. While having fun doing exercises

to access each quadrant of the brain, you'll acquire new tools for increased creativity and successful songwriting.

The Lyricwriting Master Class: An 8-week intensive course/workshop that expands your usual ways of thinking and expressing ideas through the practice of figurative language. You'll learn to identify, define and use with competence the four master figures of speech—metaphor, synecdoche, metonymy and irony—and their many subtypes. And you'll acquire new skills in structuring your thoughts to make your songs more memorable and thus, more marketable. Held twice a year at the Songwriters Guild.

Successful Lyric Writing Consultation Course: This course, an outgrowth of the instructor's book, covers the same theory and assignments as The Basics Course. Participants receive critiques of their work by the book's author via 1-hour phone sessions.

THE SONGWRITERS GUILD FOUNDATION, Suite 1002, 6430 Sunset Blvd., Hollywood CA 90028. (213)462-1108. West Coast Director: B. Aaron Meza.

Ask-A-Pro/Song Critique: SGA members are given the opportunity to present their songs and receive constructive feedback from industry professionals. A great chance to meet industry people, make contacts, ask questions and get your song heard! Free to SGA members. Reservations required. Call for schedule. Members outside regional area send tape with lyric and SASE for tape return.

Jack Segal's Songshop: This very successful 9-week workshop focuses on working a song through to perfection, including title, idea, rewrites and pitching your songs. Please call for more information regarding this very informative workshop. Dates to be announced. Fee.

Broadway On Sunset: The only west coast musical theater program promoting craft, business and development of new shows. Whether you have completed a show or dreamed of writing one, this program will give you the tools you need to write a successful stage musical. For further information contact SGA or Broadway On Sunset at (818)508-9270. Fee.

Special Seminars and Workshops: Held through the year. Past workshops included Sheila Davis on lyrics, tax workshops for songwriters, MIDI workshops, etc. Call for schedule.

*SOUTHEASTERN MUSIC CENTER, P.O. Box 8348, Columbus GA 31907. (706)568-2465. Artistic Director: Dr. Ronald Wirt. Estab. 1983. Orchestral and chamber music experience for high school and college musicians. Offers lessons for piano, guitar and orchestral instruments, beginning music theory, repertoire, rehearsals and concerts of chamber and orchestral ensembles for performers. Concerto competition open to registered students. Prize is a performance with orchestra. Offers other programs summer only July 3-31 at Columbus College. 75 amateur student individual instrumentalists. Participants are selected by demo tape audition. Send for application. Deadline: May 1st. Fee: $25 application, $175 registration upon acceptance, $250 housing , $125 optional private lessons. Two concert halls, several rehearsal rooms and classrooms, MIDI lab.

*UNDERCURRENTS '95, P.O. Box 94040, Cleveland OH 44101-6040. (216)241-1902. Fax: (216)241-8288. Director: John Latimer. Estab. 1989. A yearly music industry expo featuring seminars, trade show, media center and showcases of rock, alternative, metal, folk, jazz and blues music. Offers programs for songwriters, composers, music industry professionals and performers. Dates for Undercurrents '95 are May 18-20. Participants are selected by demo tape, biography and 8×10 photo audition. Send for application. Deadline: February 15, 1995. Fee: $10.

*UTAH ARTS FESTIVAL, 4470 Arcadia Lane, Salt Lake City UT 84103. (801)322-2428. Fax: (801)363-8681. Administrative Coordinator: Michelle Hood. Estab. 1976. Covers "all musical styles, classical and contemporary. The event's purpose is to promote the best of Utah artists and performers and their contemporaries nationwide." Offers programs for composers and performers. "All performers performing at least 80% original work receive an additional stipend. UAC also commissions a symphonic piece each year from a Utah composer. All residents of Utah are eligible to submit representative past work for consideration of the annual Composer Commission. Commission award is $5,000. The commissioned piece is premiered by the Utah Symphony at the Utah Arts Festival." Workshops take place during the summer at Triad Center, Salt Lake City. 250 professional songwriters, bands, dancers and theater performers participate in each workshop. Participants are selected by submitting demo tape or by invitation. Write or call for application. Deadline: mid-February. No entry fee.

Contests and Awards

Songwriters should approach a contest, award or grant just as they would a music publisher or record company: with care, thorough research and professionalism. Treat your contest submission as you would any other; appropriate marketing techniques shouldn't be disregarded. Remember, you're still selling yourself and your work—and you always want both presented in the best light possible.

Participation in contests is a great way to gain exposure for your music. Winners receive cash prizes, musical merchandise, studio time and perhaps a recording deal. It can lead to performances of the work for musical theater and concert music composers. Even if you don't win, valuable contacts can be made. Some contests are judged by music publishers and other music industry professionals, so your music may reach the ears of important people. The bottom line is there is a chance that a beneficial relationship could result from entering.

Be sure to do proper research to ensure that you're not wasting your time and money on less-than-legitimate contests. We have confidence in the contests listed in this edition of *Songwriter's Market*. But, before entering any contest, be aware of several things. After obtaining the entry forms and contest rules, be sure you understand the contest stipulations before signing your name or sending an entrance fee. If a publishing contract is involved as a prize, don't give away your publishing rights. If you do, you're endangering possible future royalties from the song. This is clearly not in your best interest. In evaluating any contest, you must weigh what you will gain against what you will give up. Be particularly wary of exorbitant entry fees. And if you must give up any of your publishing rights or copyright, it's almost always a good idea to stay away.

Contests listed in this section encompass all types of music and all levels of competition. Read each listing carefully and contact the sponsoring organization if the contest interests you. Remember: When you receive the contest information, read the rules carefully and be sure you understand them before entering.

*AMERICAN GUILD OF ORGANISTS, #1260, 475 Riverside Dr., New York NY 10115. (212)870-2310. Fax: (212)870-2163. Estab. 1984. For composers. Two separate competitions: one in even numbered years, one odd.
Purpose: "To further the composition of works for the organ."
Requirements: "Entrant must be a citizen of the United States, Canada or Mexico." Deadline: late spring. Send for application. Samples are not required.
Awards: Holtkamp-AGO Award in organ composition: $2,000. AGO-ECS Publishing Award in choral competition: $2,000.

AMERICAN SONGWRITER LYRIC CONTEST, 121 17th Ave. S., Nashville TN 37203-2707. (615)244-6065. Fax: (615)244-4314. Editor: Vernell Hackett. Estab. 1987. For songwriters and composers. Award for each bimonthly issue of magazine, plus grand prize at year-end.
Purpose: To promote the art of songwriting and to allow readers the opportunity to be actively involved.
Requirements: Lyrics must be typed and check for $10 must be enclosed. Deadlines: February 1, April 1, June 1, August 1, October 1, December 1. Samples are not required.
Awards: A guitar, with different sponsors each year. Good for 3 months. Lyrics judged by 5-6 industry people—songwriters, publishers, journalists.

ARTISTS' FELLOWSHIPS, New York Foundation for the Arts, 14th Floor, 155 Avenue of Americas, New York NY 10013. (212)366-6900. Fax: (212)366-1778. Director, Artists' Programs and Services:

Penelope Dannenberg. For songwriters and composers. Annual award, but each category funded biennially. Estab. 1984.

Purpose: "Artists' Fellowships are $7,000 grants awarded by the New York Foundation for the Arts to individual originating artists living in New York State. The Foundation is committed to supporting artists from all over New York State at all stages of their professional careers. Fellows may use the grant according to their own needs; it should not be confused with project support."

Requirements: Must be 18 years of age or older; resident in New York State for 2 years prior to application; and cannot be enrolled in any graduate or undergraduate degree program. Deadline: October 1995. Samples of work are required with application. 1 or 2 original compositions on separate audiotapes and at least 2 copies of corresponding scores or fully harmonized lead sheets.

Awards: All Artists' Fellowships awards are for $7,000. Payment of $6,500 upon verification of NY State residency, and remainder upon completion of a mutually agreed upon public service activity. Nonrenewable. "Fellowships are awarded on the basis of the quality of work submitted and the evolving professional accomplishments of the applicant. Applications are reviewed by a panel of 5 composers representing the aesthetic, ethnic, sexual and geographic diversity within New York State. The panelists change each year and review all allowable material submitted."

CHRIS AUSTIN SONGWRITING CONTEST AT THE MERLE WATSON FESTIVAL, P.O. Box 1218555, Nashville TN 37212. (800)799-3838. Contest established in 1993, festival established in 1988. For songwriters. Annual award.

Purpose: "Open to individuals who consider themselves amateur songwriters."

Requirements: Categories: country, bluegrass, gospel, general. Each song must be on a separate cassette, labeled with category, song title, name of songwriter, phone. Each song must be accompanied by a typed lyric sheet. Deadline: March 18. Write for information and enclose SASE. 1st place winners in each category will perform winning song on the Cabin Main Stage at the Festival. Submissions will be judged by a panel of selected songwriters and music publishers from the Nashville music industry.

*BILLBOARD SONG CONTEST, P.O. Box 35346, Tulsa OK 74153-0346. (918)627-0351. Fax: (918)627-6681. Administrator: Kathy Purple. Estab. 1988. For songwriters. Annual contest.

Purpose: "To award cash, merchandise and press to the unknown but deserving songwriter."

Requirements: Entry form, audio cassette, lyrics and $15 fee. Deadline: Late summer. Send for application. Samples are not required.

Awards: $5,000: Grand prize; $1,000: 1st place (6 categories); 2nd place various types of musical instruments.

COLUMBIA ENTERTAINMENT COMPANY'S JACKIE WHITE MEMORIAL PLAYWRITING CONTEST, 309 Parkade Blvd., Columbia MO 65202. (314)874-5628. Chairperson, CEC Contest: Betsy Phillips. For musical playwrights. Annual award.

Purpose: "We are looking for top-notch scripts for theater school use, to challenge and expand the talents of our students, ages 10-15. We want good plays with large casts (20-30 characters) suitable for use with our theater school students. Full production of the winning script will be done by the students. A portion of travel expenses, room and board offered to winner for production of show."

Requirements: "Must be large cast plays, original story lines and cannot have been previously published. Please write for complete rules." Deadline for 1995: May 30. Send for application; then send scripts to address above. Full-length play, neatly typed. No name on title page, but name, address and name of play on a 3×5 index card. Cassette tape of musical numbers required. $10 entry fee. SASE for entry form."

Awards: $250 first prize and partial travel expenses to see play produced. Second place winner gets no prize money but receives production of the play by the theater school plus partial travel expenses. This is a one-time cash award, given after any revisions required are completed. "The judging committee is taken from members of Columbia Entertainment Company's Executive and Advisory boards. At least eight members, with at least three readings of all entries, and winning entries being read by entire committee. We are looking for plays that will work with our theater school students."

Tips: "Remember the play we are looking for will be performed by 10-15 year old students with normal talents—difficult vocal ranges, a lot of expert dancing and so forth will eliminate the play. We especially like plays that deal with current day problems and concerns. However, if the play is good enough, any suitable subject matter is fine. It should be fun for the audience to watch."

*DIVERSE VISIONS INTERDISCIPLINARY GRANTS PROGRAM, Intermedia Arts, 425 Ontario SE, Minneapolis MN 55414. (612)627-4444. Director of Artist Programs: Al Kosters. For artists working in all disciplines and genres. Annual award.

Purpose: "Intermedia Arts encourages artists to investigate diverse issues/concerns in their work while challenging traditional, conventional and widely accepted contemporary approaches when creating, producing and presenting that work. *Diverse Visions* is a regional grants program administered by Intermedia Arts which was developed to respond to those artists who attempt to explore new definitions of, or the boundaries between cultures, art disciplines and/or traditions in their work."

Requirements: Grants are available to artists working individually or collaboratively for personally-conceived productions. Only noncommercial projects over which the applicant has creative control and responsibility will be considered. Applicants must be a resident of Iowa, Kansas, Minnesota, Nebraska, North Dakota, South Dakota or Wisconsin, and must have physically resided in one of these states for at least 12 of the 24 months preceding the application deadline, and intend to remain a resident in that state during the grant period. Students who will be attending school full-time during the grant period are not eligible. Projects associated with degree programs will not be considered. Send for application. SASE required. Applications received by the deadline are reviewed by staff for eligibility and completeness. Late or incomplete applications will not be considered. To apply, all written materials must be typed. Do not reduce the size, staple or bind application materials. Do not submit additional pages and/or support materials that are not listed as required or optional. Place your name in the top right hand corner of each page of submitted material. Include application form, a one-page projected description, a current résumé and work samples. All applications must be submitted on appropriate grant form. Write *Diverse Visions* for more information.

Awards: 2 year period from date of award. "Extensions granted — but no additional money available."

Tips: "Submit quality work samples (of previous work) and be certain to respond with *all* that is required."

*FIRST BAR/INNER CITY CULTURAL CENTER'S COMPETITION FOR COMPOSERS & SONG-WRITERS, 1605 Ivar Ave., Hollywood CA 90028. (213)962-2102. Executive Director: C. Bernard Jackson. For songwriters, composers and musical playwrights. Annual award.

Purpose: "The primary purpose of the competition is to bring songwriters, composers and those who perform original music into contact with those in the music and entertainment industry who are in a position to hire them, and to bring to public prominence the role played by creators of original music."

Requirements: "One entry per participant, maximum length 7 minutes. Entry must be performed live, may not have been previously published. Deadline: June. Send for application. Samples are not required.

Awards: $1,000 (1st place), $500 (2nd place), $250 (3rd place). Additional prizes to be announced at time of competition. Criteria: 1. Originality 2. Overall presentation (performance) 3. Thematic development 4. Structural unity 5. Fullfillment of functional intent. Judges are recruited from the ranks of music industry professionals. Members of the audience cast ballots during a series of 3 elimination rounds to determine which entries proceed to the final round.

Tips: "Have a sponsor capable of providing the support necessary to gather resources needed to make an effective performance presentation (performers, transportation to competition site, rehearsal space, on-site accommodations, special equipment, etc.). This is done LIVE! Competition is open to all. There are NO categories or distinctions made based on genre (classical, jazz, country western, reggae, etc.). Lyrics or librettos may be in any language. There is no citizenship or U.S. residency requirement. Compositions designed to support other media (dance, film, etc.) must be presented in their original context. Keep in mind that the goal of the competition is to develop employment opportunities for gifted writers and to bring attention to the craft in all of its diversity. The competition is divided into 2 divisions: Adult (over 18) and youth (under 18). Youth division prizes normally consist of scholarship awards. ICCC has successfully conducted competitions resulting in professional employment and production for actors over the past 11 years as well as for playwrights and performers."

*HARVEY GAUL COMPOSITION CONTEST, The Pittsburgh New Music Ensemble, Inc., Duquesne University School of Music, Pittsburgh PA 15282. (412)261-0554. Conductor/Executive Director: David Stock/Eva Tumiel-Kozak. For composers. Biennial.

Purpose: Objective is to encourage composition of new music. Winning piece to be premiered by the PNME.

Requirements: "Must be citizen of the US. New works scored for 6 to 16 instruments drawn from the following: flute, oboe, 2 clarinets, bassoon, horn, trumpet, trombone, tuba, 2 violins, cello, bass, 2 percussion, piano, harp, electronic tape." Deadline: April 15. Send for application. Samples of work are required with application. "Real name must not appear on score — must be signed with a 'nom de plume'." Entry fee: $10.

Awards: Harvey Gaul Composition Contest: $1,500.

HENRICO THEATRE COMPANY ONE-ACT PLAYWRITING COMPETITION, Box 27032, Richmond VA 23273. (804)672-5100. Cultural Arts Coordinator: J. Larkin Brown. For musical playwrights. Annual award.

Purpose: Original one-act musicals for a community theater organization.

Requirements: "Only one-act plays or musicals will be considered. The manuscript should be a one-act original (not an adaptation), unpublished, and unproduced, free of royalty and copyright restrictions. Scripts with smaller casts and simpler sets may be given preference. Controversial themes should be avoided. Standard play script form should be used. All plays will be judged anonymous

therefore, there should be two title pages; the first must contain the play's title and the author's complete address and telephone number. The second title page must contain only the play's title. The playwright must submit two excellent quality copies. Receipt of all scripts will be acknowledged by mail. Scripts will be returned if SASE is included. No scripts will be returned until after the winner is announced. The HTC does not assume responsibility for loss, damage or return of scripts. All reasonable care will be taken." Deadline: September 1st. Send for application first.
Awards: 1st prize $250. 2nd prize $125. 3rd prize $125.

INTERMOUNTAIN SONGWRITING COMPETITION, Box 71325, Salt Lake City UT 84107. (801)596-3058. Estab. 1987. For songwriters and composers. Annual award by Utah Songwriters Association.
Requirements: Call (801)596-3058 for information or send SASE for entry forms. All amateur songwriters may enter. Deadline: January 31. One song per tape. Contest runs from October 15 to January 31 each year. Entry must be postmarked by January 31. Winners announced April 30. Entry fee: $10 for first song, $5 each additional song.
Awards: First place winner receives $500 cash, $100 for each category winner. Judging sheets returned to entrant.
Tips: "Submit a well-written song with a good vocal and instruments well in tune. Have the vocals out front and the words clear. Remember, this is a competition so make your song competitive by having a good recording. Type lyric sheets neatly and *please* have your lyrics match the words on your recording. We look for songs that say something important and have a good hook."

LEE KORF PLAYWRITING AWARD, Cerritos College, 11110 Alondra Blvd., Dept. of Theatre, Norwalk CA 90650. (310)860-2451, ext. 2638. Fax: (310)467-5005. Theatre Production: Gloria Manriquez. For musical playwrights and playwrights. Annual award.
Purpose: "We look for promising playwrights who have something exciting to say with a fresh innovative way of saying it."
Requirements: "Submit two firmly bound manuscripts with SASE for return." Deadline: January 1 postmark. Send for guidelines and application. Samples are not required.
Awards: Lee Korf Playwriting Award: $750 plus full scale production. Award is one time only. Award is nonrenewable. "Submissions are read by faculty. Recommended scripts are discussed by directors."
Tips: "Include any production history of submitted piece."

*THE KOSCIUSZKO FOUNDATION CHOPIN PIANO COMPETITION, 15 E. 65th St., New York NY 10021. (212)734-2130. Director: Monika Jasinski. For pianists only.
Purpose: "To encourage young pianists to further their studies and to perform the works of great Polish composers."
Requirements: Deadline: April 15. Send for application.
Awards: First prize: $2,500; second prize: $1,500; third prize: $1,000. "Scholarship monies may be awarded in the form of shared prizes." First prize is non-renewable. Other contestants may re-apply. Contestants judged on performance of the required repertoire.

L.A. DESIGNERS' THEATRE—MUSIC AWARDS, P.O. Box 1883, Studio City CA 91614-0883. (818)769-9000, (213)650-9600. Fax: (818)985-9200. Artistic Director: Richard Niederberg. For songwriters, composers, performing artists, musical playwrights and rights holders of music.
Purpose: To produce new musicals, operettas, opera-boufes and plays with music, as well as new dance pieces with new music scores.
Requirements: None—submit non-returnable cassette, tape, CD or other medium. Acceptance: continuous. Submit nonreturnable materials with cover letter. Samples of work required with application.
Awards: Music is commissioned for a particular project. Amounts are negotiable. Award/grant good upon receipt. Award is renewable. Applications judged by our artistic staff.
Tips: "Make the material 'classic, yet commercial' and easy to record/re-record/edit. Make sure rights are totally free of all 'strings,' 'understandings,' 'promises,' etc. ASCAP/BMI/SESAC registration is OK, as long as 'grand' or 'performing rights' are available."

MARIMOLIN COMPOSITION CONTEST, 475 Lake Dr., Princeton NJ 08540. (609)252-1262. For composers. Annual award.
Purpose: To encourage the creation of works for the combination of marimba and violin.
Requirements: Open to all composers. Deadline: July 1. Send for application. A completed new violin and marimba. 2 scores, or 1 score and parts. Winners announced by August 1.
Awards: "Up to 3 winners will be selected. A total of $600 will be awarded at the judges' discretion. Winning work(s) will be premiered during the following season."

MIMDAR NEW PLAY COMPETITION, One Curtain Up Alley, Buffalo NY 14202-1911. Dramaturg: Joyce Stilson. For musical playwrights. Annual award.

Purpose: Alleyway Theatre is dedicated to the development and production of new works. Winners of the competition will receive production and royalties.
Requirements: Unproduced full-length work not less than 90 minutes long with cast limit of 10 and unit or simple set, or unproduced one-act work less than 60 minutes long with cast limit of 6 and simple set; prefers work with unconventional setting that explores the boundaries of theatricality; limit of submission in each category; guidelines available, no entry form. $5 playwright entry fee, script, résumé, SASE optional. Cassette preferred, but not mandatory.
Awards: $400, production with royalty and travel and housing to attend rehearsals for full-length play or musical; $100 and production for one-act play or musical.
Tips: Entries may be of any style, but preference will be given to those scripts which take place in unconventional settings and explore the boundaries of theatricality. No more than ten performers is a definite, unchangeable requirement.

MIXED BLOOD VERSUS AMERICA PLAYWRITING CONTEST, 1501 S. Fourth St., Minneapolis MN 55454. (612)338-0937. Script Czar: Dave Kunz. For musical playwrights. Annual award. Estab. 1983.
Purpose: To encourage emerging musical playwrights.
Requirements: "Send previously unproduced play (musical), résumé, cover letter stipulating contest entry." Deadline March 15. Send SASE for copy of contest guidelines. Samples are not required.
Awards: Winner: $2,000 and full production of winning play/musical.
Tips: "Professionalism is always a plus. Surprise us. All subject matter accepted. Political satires and shows involving sports (baseball, golf etc.) always of interest."

MUSEUM IN THE COMMUNITY COMPOSER'S AWARD, Box 251, Scott Depot WV 25560. (304)562-0484. Contest Administrator: Trish Fisher. For composers. Biennial.
Purpose: The Composer's Competition is to promote the writing of new works for string quartet—two violins, viola and cello.
Requirements: Work must not have won any previous awards nor have been published, publicly performed or used commercially. Requires 3 copies of the original score, clearly legible and bound. Title to appear at the top of each composition, but the composer's name must not appear. Entry forms must be filled out and a SASE of the proper size enclosed for return of entry. Enclose $25 entry fee (non-refundable). Send for application.
Awards: Museum in the Community Composer's Award First place: $2,500. "Up to 3 honorable mentions will be awarded at the discretion of the judges." Jurors will be 3 nationally known musicologists. Winning composer will be awarded a cash prize and a premiere concert of the composition by the Montani String Quartet, the resident string quartet of the West Virginia Symphony. Transportation to the premiere from anywhere in the continental United States will be provided by the Museum.
Tips: "Read *and* follow rules listed in Prospectus. Neatness still counts!"

*NATIONAL YOUNG ARTIST COMPETITION, Midland-Odessa Symphony & Chorale, Inc., P.O. Box 60658, Midland TX 79701. (915)563-0921. For student musicians under 26 years (30 years for voice) who are not launched on a professional career under management. Annual competition the last Friday and Saturday of January.
Purpose: To encourage and promote young musicians' careers.
Requirements: Applicant must be a student musician under age 26 studying with music teacher. Send completed application forms, $25 entry fee and 5×7 glossy portrait-type photo (for publicity). Application deadline: December 1. Send for application. Samples are not required.
Awards: Lara Hoggard performance medallion. Up to $10,000 distributed among finalists and performing winners. Up to 3 winners perform with Midland-Odessa Symphony & Chorale, Inc., at regular classical subscription concerts. Contestants are judged by a panel of five judges.
Tips: Categories are for: piano, winds, strings, voice, guitar and percussion. Includes all categories but voice in secondary division. At least one of performing winners is from secondary division.

*NEW CELEBRITY COMPETITION, Box 57, Kamloops, British Columbia V2C 5K3 **Canada**. (604)372-5000. General Manager: Kathy Humphreys. Estab. 1980. For performing artists. Annual award.
Purpose: To assist and encourage the careers of Canadian instrumental music performance students.
Requirements: Canadian citizenship. Must be current student. Deadline: January 15th. Send for application. Samples of work are required with application. Audio tape—Specific requirements available upon request.
Awards: First prize: $1,000 cash and a solo performance with the Kamloops Symphony Orchestra. Second Prize: $500 cash. Panel of musicians will select finalists from tapes submitted. Panel of judges select winner from performance at competition finals. The Kamloops Symphony Society pays the co of travel to Kamloops for the finalists.

NEW FOLK CONCERTS FOR EMERGING SONGWRITERS, Box 1466, Kerrville TX 78029. (210) 3600. Attn: New Folk. For songwriters and composers. Annual award.

Purpose: "Our objective is to provide an opportunity for unknown songwriters to be heard and rewarded for excellence."

Requirements: Songwriter enters 2 previously unpublished songs on same side of cassette tape—$8 entry fee; no more than one tape may be entered; 6-8 minutes total for 2 songs. No written application necessary; no lyric sheets or press material needed. Deadline: April 15th. Call for detailed information.

Awards: New Folk Award Winner. 32 finalists invited to sing the 2 songs entered during The Kerrville Folk Festival. 6 writers are chosen as award winners. Each of the 6 receives a cash award of $150 and performs at a winner's concert during the Kerrville Folk Festival. Initial round of entries judged by the Festival Producer. 40 finalists judged by panel of 3 performer/songwriters.

Tips: "Make certain cassette is rewound and ready to play. Do not allow instrumental accompaniment to drown out lyric content. Don't enter without complete copy of the rules. Former winners include Lyle Lovett, Nanci Griffith, Hal Ketchum, John Gorka, David Wilcox, Lucinda Williams and Robert Earl Keen."

*OMAHA SYMPHONY GUILD NEW MUSIC COMPETITION, 310 Aquila Court, Omaha NE 68102. (402)342-3836. Contact: Chairman, New Music Competition. For composers with an annual award. Estab. 1976.

Purpose: "The objective of the competition is to promote new music scored for chamber orchestra."

Requirements: "Follow competition guidelines including orchestration and length of composition." Deadline: usually May 15. Send for application or call (402)342-3836. Each fall new guidelines and application forms are printed.

Awards: "Monetary award is $2,000. Winner has an optional premiere performance by the Omaha Symphony Chamber Orchestra. Applications are screened by Omaha Symphony music director. Finalists are judged by a national panel of judges."

Tips: "This is an annual competition and each year has a new Symphony Guild chairman; all requests for extra information sent to the Omaha Symphony office will be forwarded. Also, 1,700-1,800 application information brochures are sent to colleges, universities and music publications each Fall."

PLAYHOUSE ON THE SQUARE NEW PLAY COMPETITION, (formerly Mid-South Playwrights Contest), 51 S. Cooper, Memphis TN 38104. (901)725-0776. Executive Director: Jackie Nichols. For musical playwrights. Annual award. Estab. 1983.

Requirements: Send script, tape, SASE. "Playwrights from the South will be given preference." Open to full-length, unproduced plays. Musicals must be fully arranged for the piano when received. Deadline: April 1.

Awards: Grants may be renewed. Applications judged by 3 readers.

PULITZER PRIZE IN MUSIC, 702 Journalism, Columbia University, New York NY 10027. (212)854-3841. For composers and musical playwrights. Annual award.

Requirements: "The piece must have its American premiere between March 15 and March 1 of the one-year period in which it is submitted for consideration." Deadline: March 1. Samples of work are required with application and $20 entry fee. "Send tape and score."

Awards: "One award: $3,000. Applications are judged first by a nominating jury, then by the Pulitzer Prize Board."

V.O.C.A.L. SONGWRITER'S CONTEST, P.O. Box 34606, Richmond VA 23234. President: Gary Shaver (804)796-1444. Song Contest Director: Robert (Cham) Laughlin (804)733-5908. For songwriters and composers. Annual award with up to 12 categories.

Purpose: "To recognize good songs and lyrics as well as the writers of same."

Requirements: "Original songs/lyrics/compositions only." Postal deadline: March 31 of the contest year. Send for entry forms and information. Song entries must be on cassette tape. Lyric entries should be typed or neatly printed on white paper." Contest entries and inquiries should be sent to V.O.C.A.L. Song Contest, P.O. Box 2438, Petersburg VA 23804.

Awards: Prizes for first, second, third places overall, most appropriate production, and first, second nd third places in each category plus honorable mention. Prizes include: Cash, merchandise, T-shirts, tificates and more.

"Be sure to use a clean, fresh tape to record your entry. Listen to the entry to be sure it's not ed or too low in volume. A decent sounding tape stands a much better chance. The judges can le based on what they hear. Don't over produce your entry. That will take away from the Fill out the entry form completely and follow all rules of the contest. The contest begins nd entries must be postmarked no later than March 31 of that contest year. Mail your

SEMBLE—MUSICAL STAIRS, Box 38728, Los Angeles CA 90038. (213)871-8673. s Hanson. For composers and musical playwrights. Annual award.

PUBLIC DOMAIN REPORT, P.O. Box 3102, Margate NJ 08402. *Monthly guide to significant titles entering the public domain.*

RADIO AND RECORDS, 1930 Century Park W., Los Angeles CA 90067, *Weekly newspaper covering the radio and record industries.*

SINGER SONGWRITER, P.O. Box 257, Wynnewood PA 19096. *10 issues/year newsletter for songwriters.*

SONGCASTING, 15445 Ventura Blvd, Sherman Oaks CA 91403. *Monthly tip sheet providing 27 contacts and artists per month.*

SONGPUBLISHER, P.O. Box 409, East Meadow NY 11554-0409. *Monthly professional tip sheet.*

SONGWRITER'S MONTHLY, 332 Eastwood Ave., Feasterville PA 19053. *Monthly songwriters' magazine.*

WORDS AND MUSIC, 41 Valleybrook Dr., Don Mills, Ontario M3B 2S6 Canada. *Monthly songwriters' magazine.*

Books and Directories

ATTENTION: A&R, 2nd edition, by Teri Muench and Susan Pomerantz, Alfred Publishing Co. Inc., Box 10003, Van Nuys CA 91410-0003.

BEGINNING SONGWRITER'S ANSWER BOOK, by Paul Zollo, Writer's Digest Books, 1507 Dana Ave., Cincinnati OH 45207.

CMJ DIRECTORY, edited by Kathryn Krassner, Suite 400, 11 Middle Neck Road, Great Neck NY 11021-2301.

MUSIC DIRECTORY CANADA, 6th edition, edited by Shauna Kennedy, Norris-Whitney Communications Inc., #7, 23 Hannover Dr., St. Catherines, Ontario L2W 1A3 Canada.

MUSIC PUBLISHING: A SONGWRITER'S GUIDE, by Randy Poe, Writer's Digest Books, 1507 Dana Ave., Cincinnati OH 45027.

OFFICIAL COUNTRY MUSIC DIRECTORY, edited by Steve Tolin, Entertainment Media, P.O. Box 2772, Palm Springs CA 92263.

RECORDING INDUSTRY SOURCEBOOK, edited by Michael Fuchs, Ascona Group, Inc., Suite 300, 3301 Barham Blvd., Los Angeles CA 90068.

THE SONGWRITER'S DEMO MANUAL AND SUCCESS GUIDE, by George Williams, Music Business Books, Box 935-SM, Dayton NV 89403.

SONGWRITER'S GUIDE TO CHORDS AND PROGRESSIONS, by Joseph L. Lilore, Box 1272, Dept. WD, Clifton NJ 07012.

SONGWRITER'S GUIDE TO MELODIES, by Joseph R. Lilore, Lionhead Publishing, Box 1272, Dept. WD, Clifton NJ 07012.

THE SONGWRITER'S MARKET GUIDE TO SONG & DEMO SUBMISSION FORMATS, Writer's Digest Books, 1507 Dana Ave., Cincinnati OH 45207.

SUCCESSFUL SONGWRITING, by Carl E. Bolte, Jr., Holly Productions, 800 Greenway Terrace, Kansas City MO 64113.

TEXAS MUSIC INDUSTRY DIRECTORY, Texas Music Office, Office of the Governor, P.O. Box 13246, Austin TX 78711.

THE YELLOW PAGES OF ROCK, The Album Network, 120 N. Victory Blvd., Burbank CA 91502.

Glossary

A&R Director. Record company executive in charge of the Artists and Repertoire Department who is responsible for finding and developing new artists and matching songs with artists.

A/C. Adult contemporary music.

Advance. Money paid to the songwriter or recording artist before regular royalty payment begins. Sometimes called "up front" money, advances are deducted from royalties.

AOR. Album-Oriented Rock. A radio format which primarily plays selections from rock albums as opposed to hit singles.

Assignment. Transfer of rights of a song from writer to publisher.

Audiovisual. Refers to presentations which use audio backup for visual material.

Bed. Prerecorded music used as background material in commercials.

Beta. ½" videocassette format. The Beta System uses a smaller cassette than that used with the VHS system.

Booking agent. Person who solicits work and schedules performances for entertainers.

Business manager. Person who handles the financial aspects of artistic careers.

b/w. Backed with. Usually refers to the B-side of a single.

C&W. Country and western.

Catalog. The collected songs of one writer, or all songs handled by one publisher.

CD. Compact Disc (see below).

CHR. Comtemporary Hit Radio. Top 40 pop music.

Compact disc. A small disc (about 4.7 inches in diameter) holding digitally encoded music that is read by a laser beam in a CD player.

Co-publish. Two or more parties own publishing rights to the same song.

Copyright. The exclusive legal right giving the creator of a work the power to control the publishing, reproduction and selling of the work.

Crossover. A song that becomes popular in two or more musical categories (e.g., country and pop).

DAT. Digital Audio Tape. A professional and consumer audio cassette format for recording and playing back digitally-encoded material. DAT cassettes are approximately one-third smaller than conventional audio cassettes.

DCC. Digital Compact Cassette. A consumer audio cassette format for recording and playing back digitally-encoded tape. DCC tapes are the same size as analog cassettes.

Demo. A recording of a song submitted as a demonstration of writer's or artist's skills.

Distributor. Marketing agent responsible for getting records from manufacturers to retailers.

Donut. A jingle with singing at the beginning and end and instrumental background in the middle. Ad copy is recorded over the middle section.

EP. Extended play record or cassette containing more selections than a standard single, but fewer than a standard album.

Folio. A softcover collection of printed music prepared for sale.

Hip-hop. A dance oriented musical style derived from a combination of disco, rap and R&B.

Hit. A song or record that achieves top 40 status.

Hook. A memorable "catch" phrase or melody line which is repeated in a song.

House. Dance music created by DJ's remixing samples from other songs.

Indie. An independent record label, music publisher or producer.

ips. Inches per second; a speed designation for tape recording.

IRC. International reply coupon, necessary for the return of materials sent out of the country. Available at most post offices.

Jingle. Usually a short verse set to music designed as a commercial message.

Lead sheet. Written version (melody, chord symbols and lyric) of a song.

Leader. Plastic (non-recordable) tape at the beginning and between songs for ease in selection.

LP. Designation for long-playing record played at 33⅓ rpm.

Lyric sheet. A typed or written copy of a song's lyrics.

Master. Edited and mixed tape used in the production of records; a very high-quality recording; the best or original copy of a recording from which copies are made.

Maxi-single. The cassette equivalent of a 12″ single. Also called Maxi-cassettes or Maxi-plays. (See 12″ Single.)

MD. MiniDisc. A 2.5 inch disk for recording and playing back digitally-encoded music.

Mechanical right. The right to profit from the physical reproduction of a song.

Mechanical royalty. Money earned from record, tape and CD sales.

MIDI. Musical instrument digital interface. Universal standard interface which allows musical instruments to communicate with each other and computers.

MOR. Middle of the road. Easy-listening popular music.

Ms. Manuscript.

Needle-drop. Use of a prerecorded cut from a stock music house in an audiovisual soundtrack.

One-off. A deal between songwriter and publisher which includes only one song or project at a time. No future involvement is implicated. Many times a single song contract accompanies a one-off deal.

Performing rights. A specific right granted by US copyright law that protects a composition from being publicly performed without the owner's permission.

Performing rights organization. An organization that collects income from the public performance of songs written by its members and then proportionally distributes this income to the individual copyright holder based on the number of performances of each song.

Personal manager. A person who represents artists, in numerous and varying ways, to develop and enhance their careers. Personal managers may negotiate contracts, hire and dismiss other agencies and personnel relating to the artist's career, review possible material, help with artist promotions and perform many services.

Pitch. To attempt to sell a song by audition.

Playlist. List of songs that a radio station will play.

Points. A negotiable percentage paid to producers and artists for records sold.

Production company. Company that specializes in producing jingle packages for advertising agencies. May also refer to companies that specialize in audiovisual programs.

Professional manager. Member of a music publisher's staff who screens submitted material and tries to get the company's catalog of songs recorded.

Public domain. Any composition with an expired, lapsed or invalid copyright.

Purchase license. Fee paid for music used from a stock music library.

Query. A letter of inquiry to a potential song buyer soliciting his interest.

R&B. Rhythm and blues.

Rate. The percentage of royalty as specified by contract.

Release. Any record issued by a record company.

Residuals. In advertising or television, payments to singers and musicians for subsequent use of a performance.

Royalty. Percentage of money earned from the sale of records or use of a song.

RPM. Revolutions per minute. Refers to phonograph turntable speed.

SAE. Self-addressed envelope (with no postage attached).

SASE. Self-addressed stamped envelope.

Self-contained. A band or recording act that writes all their own material.

SFX. Sound effects.

Shop. To pitch songs to a number of companies or publishers.

Single. 45 rpm record with only one song per side. A 12″ single refers to a long version of one song on a 12″ disc, usually used for dance music.

Solicited. Songs or materials that have been requested.

Soundtrack. The audio, including music and narration, of a film, videotape or audiovisual program.

Split publishing. To divide publishing rights between two or more publishers.

Statutory royalty rate. The maximum payment for mechanical rights guaranteed by law that a record company may pay the songwriter and his publisher for each record or tape sold.

Subpublishing. Certain rights granted by a US publisher to a foreign publisher in exchange for promoting the US catalog in his territory.

Synchronization. Technique of timing a musical soundtrack to action on film or video.

Top 40. The first forty songs on the pop music charts at any given time. Also refers to a style of music which emulates that heard on the current top 40.

Track. Divisions of a recording tape (e.g., 24-track tape) that can be individually recorded in the studio, then mixed into a finished master.

Trades. Publications that cover the music industry.

12″ Single. A twelve inch record containing one or more remixes of a song, originally intended for dance club play.

Unsolicited. Songs or materials that were not requested and are not expected.

VHS. ½″ videocassette format. The VHS system uses a larger cassette than that used with the Beta system.

General Index

OTHER BOOKS TO HELP YOU MAKE
MONEY AND THE MOST OF
YOUR MUSIC TALENT

The Songwriter's Market Guide to Song & Demo Submission Formats, Editors of Songwriter's Market, 144 pages/$19.95
Creating Melodies: A Songwriter's Guide to Understanding, Writing and Polishing Melodies, by Dick Weissman 144 pages/$18.95
Hot Tips for the Home Recording Studio, by Hank Linderman, 160 pages/$18.99
Who Wrote That Song?, Dick Jacobs & Harriet Jacobs, 432 pages/$19.95, paperback
Beginning Songwriter's Answer Book, by Paul Zollo, 128 pages/$16.95, paperback
The Songwriter's Idea Book, by Sheila Davis, 240 pages/$17.95
88 Songwriting Wrongs & How to Right Them, by Pat & Pete Luboff, 160 pages/$17.95, paperback
The Songwriter's & Musician's Guide to Nashville, by Sherry Bond, 192 pages/$6.99, paperback
The Songwriter's Workshop, edited by Harvey Rachlin, 96 pages + 2 cassettes/$9.99, paperback
Singing for a Living, by Marta Woodhull, 160 pages/$9.50, paperback
Jingles: How to Write, Produce, & Sell Commercial Music, by Al Stone, 144 pages/$4.99, paperback
Music Publishing: A Songwriter's Guide, by Randy Poe, 144 pages/$18.95, paperback
Making Money Making Music (No Matter Where You Live), by James Dearing, 192 pages/$18.95, paperback
Networking in the Music Business, by Dan Kimpel, 128 pages/$17.95, paperback
Playing for Pay: How To Be A Working Musician, by James Gibson, 160 pages/$6.25, paperback
You Can Write Great Lyrics, by Pamela Phillips Oland, 192 pages/$3.99, paperback
Protecting Your Songs & Yourself, by Kent J. Klavens, 112 pages/$7.99, paperback
Gigging: The Musician's Underground Touring Directory, by Michael Dorf & Robert Appel, 224 pages/$1.99, paperback
The Craft of Lyric Writing, by Sheila Davis, 350 pages/$21.95, hardcover
Successful Lyric Writing: A Step-by-Step Course & Workbook, by Sheila Davis, 292 pages/$19.95, paperback
The Songwriter's Guide to Collaboration, by Walter Carter, 178 pages/$1.00, paperback
How to Pitch & Promote Your Songs, by Fred Koller, 144 pages/$2.99, paperback

A complete catalog of all Writer's Digest Books is available FREE by writing to the address shown below. To order books directly from the publisher, include $3.00 postage and handling for one book, $1.00 for each additional book. Ohio residents add 5½% sales tax. Allow 30 days for delivery.

Writer's Digest Books
1507 Dana Avenue
Cincinnati, Ohio 45207

Credit card orders call TOLL-FREE
1-800-289-0963

Prices subject to change without notice

Songwriter "Do's" and "Don'ts"

Do:

1. Read contracts carefully and have them reviewed by a music industry attorney.

2. Research before signing contracts with companies asking for payment in advance.

3. Ask companies for supporting material or samples of successful work.

4. Read song contest rules and procedures carefully.

5. Ask questions if you don't understand!